D0932462

VAX/VMS Internals and Data Structures

VERSION 5.2

VERSION 5.2

VAX/VMS Internals and Data Structures

Ruth E. Goldenberg and Lawrence J. Kenah

With the assistance of Denise E. Dumas

Digital Press

9 8 7 6 5 4 3 2

Order number EY-C171E-DP.

Printed in the United States of America by Hamilton Printing Company.

Design: David Ford
Copy editor: Alice Cheyer
Art editor: Carol Keller
Composition: Paul C. Anagnostopoulos and Alicia Quintano using z_ZTEX
Index: Rosemary Simpson and John Mann
PostScript output: Chiron, Inc.

Quotations from the following works appear as epigraphs in this book: Ray Cummings, *The Man Who Mastered Time*, copyright © 1957 by Gabrielle Cummings, reprinted by courtesy of Forrest J. Ackerman, 2495 Glendower Avenue, Hollywood, California 90027; Edgar A. Guest, "The Package of Seeds," *Collected Verse of Edgar A. Guest*, copyright 1934 by Contemporary Books, Chicago, Illinois 60601, reprinted by permission of Contemporary Books; excerpt from "The Hollow Men," in *Collected Poems 1909–1962* by T. S. Eliot, copyright 1936 by Harcourt Brace Jovanovich, Inc., copyright © 1964, 1963 by T. S. Eliot, reprinted by permission of Harcourt Brace Jovanovich and Faber and Faber Ltd.

PostScript is a trademark of Adobe Systems Incorporated; TEX is a trademark of the American Mathematical Society; CI, CMI, DDCMP, DDIF, DEC, DECnet, DECserver, DECwindows, Digital, Digital logo, DSSI, LSI-11, MASSBUS, MicroVAX, MicroVAX II, MSCP, NMI, PDP-11, Q22-bus, RSTS/E, RSX, RSX-11M, RT-11, SBI, TOPS-20, UDA, UNIBUS, VAX, VAX MACRO, VAX RMS, VAXBI, VAXcluster, VAXsim, VAXsimPLUS, VAXstation, VAXstation II/GPX, VMS, and XMI are trademarks of Digital Equipment Corporation.

Library of Congress Cataloging-in-Publication Data

Goldenberg, Ruth E.
    VAX/VMS internals and data structures: version 5.2
    Ruth E. Goldenberg, Lawrence J. Kenah,
    with the assistance of Denise E. Dumas.
p.   cm.   includes index.
ISBN 1-55558-059-9
    1. VMS (Computer operating system)   2. VAX computers
–Programming.   3. Data structures (Computer science)   I. Kenah,
Lawrence J., 1946–   II. Dumas, Denise E., 1956–   III. Title.
QA76.76.063G638   1991   005.4'449–dc20   90-23081   CIP

In memory of
Lillian Davis, my grandmother,
some of whose
strength and stubbornness
I was lucky to inherit.

R.E.G.

We would also like to dedicate
this book to **Dick Hustvedt**,
a very dear friend. His inspiration
created this book.
His example ensured its completion.
We learned more from him
than we can ever thank him for.

L.J.K. and R.E.G.

Preface

The main topic of this book is the kernel of the VAX/VMS Version 5.2 operating system: process management; memory management; the I/O subsystem; the mechanisms that transfer control to, from, and among these; and the system services that support and complement them.

In explaining the operation of a subsystem, this book emphasizes the data structures manipulated by that subsystem. Most VMS operations can be more easily understood once the contents of the various data structures are known. The book also provides a detailed description of the flow of some major routines and annotated excerpts from certain key routines.

The intended readers are system programmers and other users of VMS who wish to understand its components, mechanisms, and data structures. For system programmers, the book provides technical background helpful in activities such as writing privileged utilities and system services. Its detailed description of data structures should help system managers make better informed decisions when they configure systems for space- or time-critical applications. It should also help application designers appreciate the effects (in speed or in memory consumption) of different design and implementation decisions.

In addition, this book is intended as a case study of VMS for an advanced undergraduate or graduate course in operating systems.

It assumes that the reader is familiar with the VAX architecture, particularly its memory management, and with the VMS operating system, particularly its system services.

The book is divided into nine parts, each of which describes a different aspect of the operating system.

- Part 1 presents an overview of the operating system and reviews the concepts basic to its workings.
- Part 2 describes the mechanisms used to pass control between user programs and the operating system, and within the system itself.
- Part 3 describes the synchronization methods of VMS.
- Part 4 describes scheduling, time support, and process control.
- Part 5 discusses memory management, with emphasis on system data structures and their manipulation by paging and swapping routines. It also describes management of dynamic memory, such as nonpaged pool.
- Part 6 contains an overview of the I/O subsystem, paying particular attention to the I/O-related system services.
- Part 7 describes the life cycle of a process: its creation, the activation and termination of images within its context, and its deletion.

- Part 8 discusses the life of the system: its organization, initialization, error handling, powerfail recovery, and shutdown. It also explains symmetric multiprocessing support.
- Part 9 discusses the implementation of logical names and the internals of several miscellaneous system services.
- The appendixes include a summary of VMS data structures, a detailed layout of system and P1 virtual address spaces, information on the use of listing and map files, the conventions used in naming symbols, and information about lock and resource use by various VMS components.

This book does not include a discussion of VAXcluster systems.

There is no guarantee that any data structure or subroutine described here will remain the same from release to release. With each new version of the operating system, a privileged application program that relies on details contained in this book should be rebuilt and tested prior to production use.

The VMS document set supplies important background information for the topics discussed in this book. The following provide an especially important foundation: *VMS System Services Reference Manual*, *VMS Device Support Manual*, and the chapter in the *VMS Run-Time Library Routines Volume* that describes condition handling.

The *VAX Architecture Reference Manual, Second Edition* (Digital Press, 1991), edited by Richard Brunner, documents the VAX architecture in detail. *Computer Programming and Architecture: The VAX*, by Henry M. Levy and Richard H. Eckhouse, Jr. (Digital Press, 1988), contains an excellent description of the VAX architecture as well as a discussion of some of the design decisions made in various implementations. It also includes a bibliography of the literature dealing with operating system design. *VMS File System Internals* (Digital Press, 1990), by Kirby McCoy, provides an in-depth study of the internals of the file system.

CONVENTIONS

A number of conventions are used throughout the text and figures of this book.

The term *executive* refers to those parts of the operating system that are loaded into and execute from system space. The executive includes the system base image, SYS.EXE; loadable executive images; other loadable system images such as SCSLOA; and device drivers.

The terms *system* and *VMS system* describe the entire VMS software package, including privileged processes, utilities, and other support software as well as the executive itself. VMS consists of many different components, each a different file. One component is the system base image, SYS.EXE. Others are loadable executive images, device drivers, command language interpreters, and utility programs.

The source modules from which these components are built and their listings are divided into facilities. Each facility is a directory on a source or listing medium containing sources and command procedures to build one or more components. The facility [DRIVER], for example, contains sources for most of the device drivers. The facility [BOOTS] includes sources for the primary bootstrap program, VMB; the secondary bootstrap program, SYSBOOT; and the SYSGEN Utility. The facility [SYS] contains the sources that make up the base image and loadable executive images.

This book identifies a [SYS] facility source module only by its file name. It identifies a module from any other facility by facility directory name and file name. For example, [DRIVER]LPDRIVER refers to the source for the line printer device driver. Appendix B discusses how to locate a module in the VMS source listings.

In general, the component called INIT refers to a module of that name in the executive and not to the volume initialization utility. When the latter is referenced, it is clearly specified.

This book identifies a macro from SYS$LIBRARY:LIB.MLB by only its name, for instance, WFIKPCH. The macro library of all other macros is specified.

The unmodified terms *process control block* and *PCB* refer to the software data structure used by the scheduler. The data structure that contains a process's hardware context is always called the hardware PCB.

The term *inner access modes* means those access modes with more privilege. The term *outer access modes* means those with less privilege. Thus, the innermost access mode is kernel and the outermost mode is user.

SYSGEN parameters include both the dynamic parameters, which can be changed on the running system, and the static parameters, whose changes do not take effect until the next system boot. These parameters are referred to by their parameter names rather than by the global locations where their values are stored. Appendix C relates parameter names to their corresponding global locations.

The terms *byte index, word index, longword index,* and *quadword index* refer to methods of VAX operand access that use context-indexed addressing modes. That is, the index value is multiplied by 1, 2, 4, or 8 (for bytes, words, longwords, or quadwords, respectively) as part of operand evaluation, to calculate the effective address of the operand.

Except in the index, a subroutine is categorized as a routine or a procedure depending on its entry method. A routine is entered, or invoked, with a JSB instruction. A procedure is entered, or called, with a CALLG or CALLS.

Three conventions are observed for lists:

- In lists like this one, where no order or hierarchy exists, list elements are indicated by leading bullets (•). Sublists without hierarchy are indicated by dashes (—).

- Lists that indicate an ordered set of operations are numbered. Sublists that indicate an ordered set of operations are lettered.
- Numbered lists with the numbers enclosed in circles indicate a correspondence between the list elements and numbered items in a figure or example.

Several conventions are observed for figures. In all diagrams of memory, the lowest virtual address appears at the top of the page and addresses increase toward the bottom of the page. Thus, the direction of stack growth is depicted upward from the bottom of the page. In diagrams that display more detail, such as bytes within longwords, addresses increase from right to left. That is, the lowest addressed byte (or bit) in a longword is on the right-hand side of a figure and the most significant byte (or bit) is on the left-hand side.

Each field in a data structure layout is represented by a rectangle. In many figures, the rectangle contains the last part of the name of the field, excluding the structure name, data type designator, and leading underscore. A rectangle the full width of the diagram generally represents a longword regardless of its depth. A field smaller than a longword is represented in proportion to its size; for example, bytes and words are quarter- and half-width rectangles. A quadword is represented by a full-width rectangle with a short horizontal line segment midway down each side.

For example, Figure 8.1 shows the layout of a spinlock control block. The rectangle labeled SPINLOCK represents the byte SPL$B_SPINLOCK; the rectangle labeled OWN_CPU, the longword SPL$L_OWN_CPU; and the rectangle labeled ACQ_COUNT, the quadword SPL$Q_ACQ_COUNT.

In almost all data structures, the data structure's full-width rectangles represent longwords aligned on longword boundaries. In a few data structures, such as the logical name table header (LNMTH) shown in Figure 35.2 or the logical name translation block (LNMX) in Figure 35.4, a horizontal row of boxes represents fields whose sizes do not total a longword. Without this practice, most of the fields in this kind of structure would be split into two part-width rectangles in adjoining rows, because they are unaligned longwords.

A data structure field containing the address of another data structure in the same figure is represented by a bullet connected to an arrow pointing to the other structure. Where possible, the arrow points to the rightmost end of the field, that is, to bit 0. A field containing a value used as an index into that or another data structure is represented by an x connected to an arrow pointing to the indexed location.

Two conventions indicate elisions in a data structure layout. A specific amount of space is shown as a rectangle whose sides contain dots. Text within the rectangle indicates the amount of space it represents. Field SPL$L_OWN_PC_VEC in Figure 8.1, for example, represents 32 bytes.

An indeterminate amount of space, often unnamed, representing omitted and undescribed fields, is indicated by a rectangle whose sides are intersected by short parallel horizontal lines. For example, Figure 14.4, which identifies only the PCB fields related to memory management, contains four sets of omitted fields among the labeled fields.

Ruth E. Goldenberg
Lawrence J. Kenah
December 1990

Acknowledgments

VERSION 3.3 EDITION

Our first thanks must go to Joe Carchidi for suggesting that this book be written, and to Dick Hustvedt, for his help and enlightening conversations.

We would like to thank John Lucas for putting together the initial versions of Chapters 7, 11, 12, and 36 and Vik Muiznieks for writing the initial versions of Chapters 3, 21, and 24.

Appreciation goes to all those who reviewed the drafts for the VAX/VMS Version 2.2 and the VAX/VMS Version 3.3 editions of this book. We would particularly like to thank Kathy Morse for reviewing the V2.2 volume in its entirety and Wayne Cardoza for reviewing this entire V3.3 edition. Our special thanks go to Ruth Goldenberg for reviewing both in their entirety, and for her many corrections, comments, and suggestions. [The V2.2 book was published in 1981. Digital Press published the first edition of the present volume, for V3.3, in 1984.]

We owe a lot of thanks to our editing staff, especially to Jonathan Ostrowsky for his labors in preparing the V2.2 book, and Betty Steinfeld for her help and suggestions. Many thanks go to Jonathan Parsons for reviewing and editing the present edition, and for all his help, patience, and suggestions.

We would like to thank the Graphic Services department at Spitbrook, particularly Pat Walker for her help in paging and production of the V2.2 book and Paul King for his help in transforming innumerable slides and rough sketches into figures. Thanks go to Kathy Greenleaf and Jackie Markow for converting the files to our generic markup language.

Thanks go to Larry Bohn, Sue Gault, Bill Heffner, Kathleen Jensen, and Judy Jurgens for their support and interest in this project.

Finally, we would like to thank all those who originally designed and implemented the VAX/VMS operating system, and all those who have contributed to later releases.

Lawrence J. Kenah
Simon F. Bate
August 1983

VERSION 4.4 EDITION

First, I thank Larry Kenah for suggesting that I do this edition of the book, for providing such an excellent foundation to update, and for his astute review and responsive answers to my innumerable questions.

I was blessed with many dedicated reviewers, four of whom reviewed the

Acknowledgments

entire book: Dick Buttlar, Wayne Cardoza, Kathy Morse, and Rod Shepardson. Rod Shepardson, moreover, revised Chapter 24, Appendixes D and E and provided considerable update and enhancement to Chapter 21. Dick Buttlar also aided me in my struggles to format tables and tactfully suggested improvements to the book. Wayne Cardoza and Kathy Morse, who had critiqued earlier versions of the book, provided continuity, insight, and technical assistance and support.

A number of other people reviewed large portions of the book, significantly improving its quality: Stan Amway, Richard Bishop, George Claborn, Dan Doherty, Joy Dorman, Rod Gamache, and John Hallyburton. I also thank the many other reviewers and early readers who helped find errors and omissions.

Carl Rehbein helped update Chapters 3, 21, 24, and Appendixes C, D, and E.

Bob Kadlec, my manager, encouraged and supported me throughout this endeavor and intercepted many potential interrupts.

Joy Lanza edited the initial version of this edition and carefully, patiently shepherded the copy and artwork through its preliminary publication.

George Jakobsche acted as negotiator and facilitator and played an important part in catalyzing this edition of the book.

I thank all the people who produced this book. Alice Cheyer's meticulous editing corrected numerous errors that had escaped the rest of us. Carol Keller edited the artwork, polishing it and removing inconsistencies. Jonathan Weinert diligently orchestrated the entire production.

I would like to thank John Osborn and Mike Meehan of Digital Press for their strong support.

I am especially grateful to Chase Duffy of Digital Press for her comprehensive publishing experience and ready wit, which lightened the work.

My deepest thanks are to Jim Fraser, who wrote the final draft of several important sections, contributed much technical and editorial review, helped me through the gnarly bits, and, most important, supplied much gumption.

Finally, I, also, thank the original designers and implementers of VAX/VMS and the contributors to subsequent releases, those past and those to come.

Ruth E. Goldenberg
August 1987

VERSION 5.2 EDITION

I would especially like to acknowledge the work of Denise Dumas, the other major writer of this edition. She assembled Chapter 23, adding a considerable amount of new material. She researched and wrote Appendix H, a labor worthy of Hercules. She updated and enhanced Chapters 1, 6, 10, 13, 25, 26, 27, 28, 30, 31, 33, 36, and Appendixes C, F, and G. Denise's technical competence, unflagging energy, and hard work were critical to the successful completion of this book.

We were fortunate when, late in the project, Saro Saravanan joined us. Adding much new material, he assembled Chapters 3 and 22 and updated Chapters 11 and 24 and Appendix E. He also provided diligent assistance during the final production phase of the book, checking art edits and page proofs.

Two other people updated chapters in this edition. Rod Shepardson assembled Chapter 20 and updated and enhanced Chapter 21. He also reviewed most of the book. George Jakobsche updated and enhanced Chapter 19 and Appendixes A and B.

Joy Lanza was an important contributor to the creation of this book. She coordinated the production of the Update Xpress volumes on which this book is based and performed a variety of tasks from copy editing to preparing repro. She also created many of the figures in this book. Her persistence and extraordinary patience are much appreciated.

A number of people reviewed the book, contributing greatly to its quality: Stan Amway, Dick Buttlar, Wayne Cardoza, Jim Fraser, Mike Harvey, and Richie Holstein. Stan Amway was especially helpful in reviewing the memory management chapters. Dick Buttlar made many suggestions that improved the writing and advised us on VAX DOCUMENT. Wayne Cardoza caught many errors, could always be counted on to answer questions, and was our technical court of last resort. Jim Fraser wrote a great many key paragraphs and sentences, reviewed multiple drafts of many chapters, and was especially good at identifying areas needing more explanation. Mike Harvey provided many detailed explanations for omitted or unclear areas. A careful, thoughtful reviewer, Richie Holstein found errors that had escaped everyone else.

Other engineers reviewed substantial portions of the book, improving its quality: Richard Bishop, George Claborn, Stu Farnham, John Hallyburton, Forrest Kenney, and Ben Thomas. Bob Harris graciously allowed himself to be persuaded to review the index.

John Osborn, Director of Digital Press, initiated the program by which we published new and revised chapters of this book as Update Xpress volumes. His decision to fund the project made the book possible.

Chase Duffy of Digital Press astutely managed the production of the Update Xpress and the book. Her good humor, good advice, and great interpersonal skills kept the project going. Chase was ably supported by Beth French. Together they oversaw all aspects of the production and manufacture of the book.

David Ford created the book design for this and previous editions. For this edition, he designed an exceptionally elegant jacket that incorporates one of my favorite paintings.

I was delighted to work again with Alice Cheyer, who edited the Update Xpress and the book. With her lively intelligence and meticulous editing, she brought consistency to a collection of chapters written in different voices. I was also delighted to have Carol Keller as art editor again. She helped create and painstakingly incorporated visual conventions that improved the clarity of the art. She is responsible for the graceful appearance of the figures and the book pages.

Paul Anagnostopoulos wrote macros to convert our VAX DOCUMENT chapter files to TEX. His ingenuity, skill, and willingness to learn the book-making trade brought about the successful production of this unusually large book. Alicia Quintano ably assisted him.

Rosemary Simpson and John Mann created a totally new, exceptionally detailed index, one strengthened and enriched by their technical expertise.

Bob Kadlec, my previous manager, and Howard Hayakawa, my current manager, gave encouragement and support.

In addition to being one of the book's most helpful reviewers, Jim Fraser could always find a way to verbalize a complex idea with clarity and grace, to polish awkward writing, and to provide gumption when necessary.

Ruth E. Goldenberg
December 1990

Contents

Contents

Contents

Contents

VIII / Life of the System   821

Contents

Appendixes 1123

Contents

PART I / Introduction

1 System Overview

For the fashion of Minas Tirith was such that it was built on
seven levels, each delved into a hill, and about each was set a
wall, and in each wall was a gate.

J. R. R. Tolkien, *The Return of the King*

This chapter introduces the basic components of the VMS operating system.
Special attention is given to the features of the VAX architecture that are
utilized by the operating system or that exist solely to support an operating
system. In addition, some of the design goals that guided the implementation
of the VMS operating system are discussed.

1.1 PROCESS, JOB, AND IMAGE

The fundamental unit in the implementation of scheduling on the VMS
operating system, the entity that is selected for execution, is the process. If
a process creates subprocesses, the collection of the creator process, all the
subprocesses created by it, and all subprocesses created by its descendants
is called a job. The programs executed in the context of a process are called
images.

1.1.1 Process

A process is fully described by data structures that specify the hardware and
software context, and by a virtual address space description. This information is stored in several different places in the process and system address
space. The data structures that contain the various pieces of process context
are pictured in Figure 1.1.

1.1.1.1

Hardware Context. The hardware context consists of copies of the general-
purpose registers, the four per-process stack pointers, the program counter
(PC), the processor status longword (PSL), and the process-specific processor
registers, including the memory management registers and the asynchronous
system trap (AST) level register. The hardware context is stored in a data
structure called the hardware process control block (hardware PCB), which
is used primarily when a process is removed from or placed into execution.

Another part of process context that is related to hardware is four per-
process stacks, one for each of the four access modes. Code executing in
the context of a process uses the stack associated with the process's current
access mode.

1.1.1.2

Software Context. Software context consists of all the data required by
various parts of the operating system to control that portion of common

3

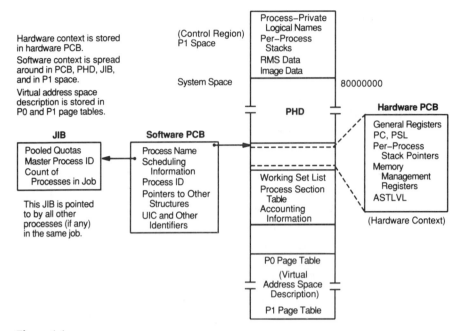

Figure 1.1
Data Structures That Describe Process Context

resources allocated to a given process. This context includes the process software priority, its current scheduling state, process privileges and "identifiers," quotas and limits, process page file assignments and reservations, and miscellaneous data, such as process name and process identification.

The information about a process that must be in memory at all times is stored in a data structure called the software process control block (PCB). This information includes the software priority of the process, its unique process identification (PID), and the particular scheduling state that the process is in at a given point in time. The software PCB also records some process quotas and limits. Other quotas and limits are recorded in the job information block (JIB).

The PCB incorporates another data structure called an access rights block (ARB), which lists the identifiers that the process holds. Identifiers are names that specify to what groups a process belongs for purposes of determining access to files and other protected objects. Identifiers are described briefly in Section 1.4.1.4.

The information about a process that does not have to be permanently resident (swappable process context) is contained in a data structure called the process header (PHD). This information is needed when the process is resident and consists mainly of information used by memory management when page faults occur. The swapper uses the data in the process header when it removes the process from memory (outswaps) or brings the process back into memory (inswaps). The hardware PCB, which contains the hardware context of a process, including its page tables, is a part of the process header. Some information in the process header is nonpageable and available to suitably privileged code whenever the process is resident. The process page tables, however, are pageable and only accessible from that process's context.

Other process-specific information is stored in the P1 portion of the process virtual address space (the control region). This includes exception dispatching information, Record Management Services (RMS) data tables, and information about the image that is currently executing. Information that is stored in P1 space is only accessible when the process is executing (is the current process), because P1 space is process-specific.

1.1.2   Image

The programs that execute in the context of a process are called images. Images usually reside in files that are produced by the linker. When the user initiates image execution (as part of process creation or through a Digital command language (DCL) command in an interactive or batch job), a component of the executive called the image activator sets up the process page tables to point to the appropriate sections of the image file. VMS uses the same paging mechanism that implements its virtual memory support to read image pages into memory as they are needed.

1.1.2.1   Virtual Address Space Description.

The virtual address space of a process is described by the process P0 and P1 page tables, stored in the high-address end of the process header. The process virtual address space is altered when an image is initially activated, during image execution through selected system services, and when an image terminates. The process page tables reside in system virtual address space and are in turn described by entries in the system page table. Unlike the other portions of the process header, the process page tables are themselves pageable, and they are faulted into the process working set only when they are needed.

1.1.2.1.1   *Control Region (P1 Space).*

Figure 1.2 shows the layout of P1 space. This figure was produced mainly from information contained in module SHELL, which contains a prototype of a P1 page table that is used whenever a process is created. A System Dump Analyzer (SDA) Utility listing of process page tables was used to determine the order and size of the portions of P1 space not defined in SHELL.

Some of the pieces of P1 space are created dynamically when the process is created. These include a P1 mapping of process header pages, a command language interpreter (CLI) if one is being used, a symbol table for that CLI, the process allocation region, and the process I/O segment. In addition, the

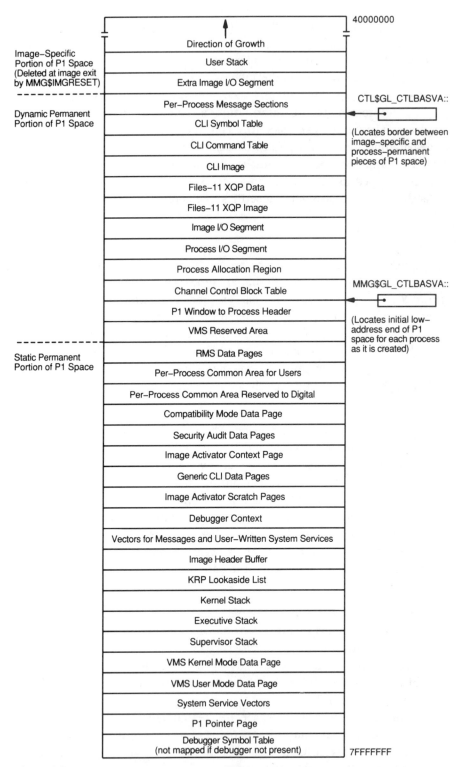

Figure 1.2
Layout of P1 Space

Files-11 Extended QIO Processor (XQP) and its data areas are mapped at process creation.

The two pieces of P1 space at the lowest virtual addresses (the user stack and any replacement image I/O segment) are created dynamically each time an image executes and are deleted as part of image rundown. Appendix F contains a description of the different pieces of P1 space, including their sizes and details such as memory management page protection and the name of the system component that maps a given portion.

1.1.2.1.2   *Program Region (P0 Space).* Figure 1.3 shows a typical layout of P0 space for both a native image (produced by the linker) and a compatibility mode image (produced by the RSX-11M task builder). This figure is much more conceptual than the previous illustration because the layout of P0 space depends upon the image being run.

By default, the first page of P0 space (0 to $1FF_{16}$) is not mapped (protection set to No Access). This no-access page allows easy detection of two common programming errors, using zero or a small number as the address of a data location or using such a small number as the destination of a control transfer. (A link-time request or system service call can alter the protection of virtual page zero. Note also that page zero is accessible to compatibility mode images.)

The main native image is placed into P0 space, starting at address 200_{16}. Any shareable images that are position-independent and shared (for example, LIBRTL) are placed at the end of the main image. The order in which these shareable images are placed into the image is determined during image activation.

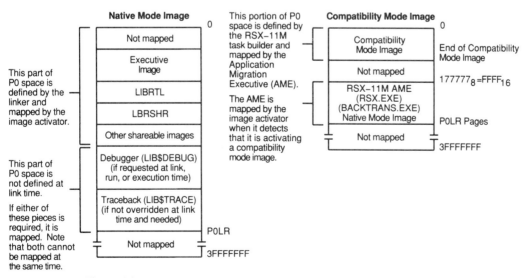

Figure 1.3
P0 Space Allocation

If the debugger or the traceback facility is required, these images are added at execution time (even if /DEBUG was selected at link time). This mapping is described in detail in Chapter 26.

1.1.3 Job

The collection of subprocesses that have a common root process is called a job. The concept of a job exists for the purpose of sharing resources. Some quotas and limits are shared among all processes in the same job. The current values of these quotas are contained in the JIB, which is shared by all processes in the same job. Figure 1.1 shows this structure.

1.2 VMS COMPONENTS

There are several names for different subsets of VMS. The terms *system* and *VMS system* describe the entire VMS software package, whose components include

- Utilities
- Program development tools
- System processes such as the job controller
- DCL interpreter
- RMS
- XQP
- The executive

The term *executive* refers to those components that reside in system space. During the development of VMS, it has grown to support different CPUs, more devices, and additional features. These have been generally supported by code with separate loadable images rather than by modules within one larger and larger image. Such loadable images include

- CPU-specific support such as the SYSLOA*xxx* modules
- System communication services support, SCSLOA
- VAXcluster connection and distributed lock management, CLUSTRLOA

The most recent stage in this evolution is a reorganization of the executive image, SYS.EXE. It has been divided into a base image and approximately 20 loadable executive images. SYS.EXE, the base image, contains transfer vectors to routines in the loadable executive images and storage for widely referenced system variables.

A loadable executive image consists of modules performing related functions and data and initialization code specific to those functions. The image PROCESS_MANAGEMENT.EXE, for example, includes the rescheduling interrupt service routine, process creation and deletion system services, and the subroutine for reporting scheduler events. To resolve references to routines in other executive images, PROCESS_MANAGEMENT.EXE links against the base image symbol table, SYS.STB.

As each executive image is loaded into system space, its associated transfer vectors in SYS.EXE are modified to contain the addresses of its routines. One image can dispatch into a routine in another image using a SYS.EXE transfer vector as bridge.

The address space of each loadable executive image is independent of that of the others. Each image is position-independent, linked to a base address of 0, and loaded into system space allocated for that purpose. This separation makes it possible for one image to be replaced by a newer version containing enhancements or source-level corrections with no impact on other executive images or the base image. Furthermore, there need be no impact on other images linked with SYS.STB. Such flexibility was a major goal of reorganizing the executive. For more information, see Chapter 29.

1.2.1 Functions Provided by VMS

VMS provides services at many levels so that user applications may execute easily and effectively. Its layered structure is pictured in Figure 1.4. In general, components in a given layer can make use of the facilities in all inner layers.

1.2.2 Operating System Kernel

The main topic of this book is the operating system kernel: the I/O subsystem, memory management, the scheduling subsystem, and the VMS system services that support and complement these components. The discussion of these three components and other miscellaneous parts of the operating system kernel focuses on the data structures that are manipulated by a given component. In describing what each major data structure represents and how that structure is altered by different sequences of events in the system, this chapter describes the detailed operations of each major piece of the kernel.

1.2.2.1 I/O Subsystem.
The I/O subsystem consists of device drivers and their associated data structures; device-independent routines within the executive; and several system services, the most important of which is the Queue I/O Request ($QIO) system service. All forms of I/O request made by outer layers of the system are transformed into $QIO requests. The I/O subsystem is described in detail from the point of view of adding a VMS device driver in the *VMS Device Support Manual*. Chapters 21 and 22 of this volume describe some aspects of the I/O subsystem that are not described in that manual.

1.2.2.2 Memory Management.
The main components of the memory management subsystem are the page fault handler, which implements VMS virtual memory support, and the working set swapper, which allows the system to utilize more fully the amount of physical memory that is available. The data structures used and manipulated by the page fault handler and swapper include

9

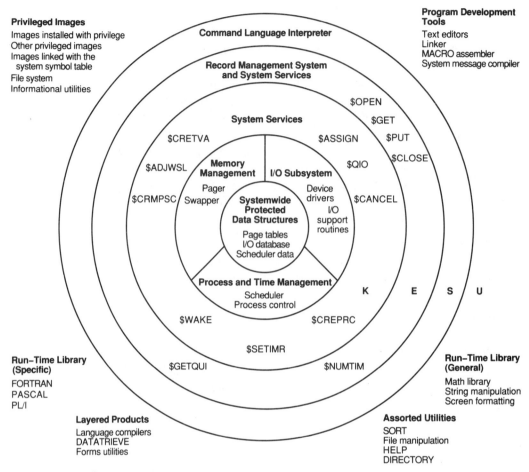

Privileged Images
Images installed with privilege
Other privileged images
Images linked with the
  system symbol table
File system
Informational utilities

**Program Development
Tools**
Text editors
Linker
MACRO assembler
System message compiler

**Run–Time Library
(Specific)**
FORTRAN
PASCAL
PL/I

**Run–Time Library
(General)**
Math library
String manipulation
Screen formatting

Layered Products
Language compilers
DATATRIEVE
Forms utilities

Assorted Utilities
SORT
File manipulation
HELP
DIRECTORY

Figure 1.4
Layered Design of the VMS Operating System

the page frame number (PFN) database and the page tables of each process. The PFN database describes each page of physical memory that is available for paging. A virtual address space description of each currently resident process is contained in its page tables. The system page table describes the system space portion of virtual address space.

System services enable a user (or the system on behalf of the user) to create or delete specific portions of virtual address space or to map a file into a specified virtual address range.

1.2.2.3 **Scheduling and Process Control.** The third major component of the kernel is the scheduling subsystem. It selects processes for execution and removes from execution processes that can no longer execute. It also handles clock servicing and includes timer-related system services. System services are available to allow a process to create or delete other processes. Other services provide one process the ability to obtain information about another and control its execution.

1.2.2.4   **Miscellaneous Services.** One area of the operating system kernel that is not pictured in Figure 1.4 involves the many miscellaneous services that are available in the operating system kernel. Some of these services for such tasks as logical name creation or string formatting are available to the user in the form of system services. Others, such as pool manipulation routines and certain synchronization techniques, are only used by the kernel and privileged utilities. Still others, such as the lock management system services, are used throughout the system—by users' programs, system services, RMS, the file system, and privileged utilities.

1.2.3   **Data Management**

VMS provides data management facilities at two levels. The record structure that exists within a file is interpreted by RMS, which exists in a layer just outside the kernel. RMS exists as a series of procedures located in system space, so it is in some ways just like the rest of the operating system kernel. Most of the procedures in RMS execute in executive access mode, providing a thin wall of protection between RMS and the kernel itself.

The placement of files on mass storage volumes is controlled by one of the disk or tape ancillary control processes (ACP) or by the Files-11 XQP. An ACP is implemented as a separate process because many of its operations must be serialized to avoid synchronous access conflicts. ACPs and the Files-11 XQP interact with the kernel both through the system service vector interface and by the use of utility routines not accessible to the general user.

The Files-11 XQP, introduced in VMS Version 4, controls the most commonly used on-disk structure. (The placement of files on a block-structured medium, such as a disk volume or a TU58, is referred to as on-disk structure.) The XQP is implemented as an extension to the $QIO system service and runs in process context. A process's XQP file operations are serialized with those of other processes and processors through lock management system services.

1.2.4   **User Interface**

The interface that is presented to the user (as distinct from the application programmer who is using system services and Run-Time Library procedures) is a command language interpreter. The DCL CLI is available on all VMS systems. The monitor console routine (MCR) CLI, the command language used with RSX-11M, is available as an optional software product. Some of the services performed by a CLI call RMS or the system services directly; others result in the execution of an external image. These images are generally no different from user-written applications because their only interface to the executive is through the system services and RMS calls.

1.2.4.1 **Images Installed with Privilege.** Some of the informational utilities and disk and tape volume manipulation utilities require that selected portions of protected data structures be read or written in a controlled fashion. Images that require privilege to perform their function can be installed (made known to the operating system) by the system manager so that they can perform their function in an ordinarily nonprivileged process environment. Images that fit this description include AUTHORIZE, LOGINOUT, MONITOR, SET, and SHOW. Appendix A lists those images that are installed with privilege in a typical VMS system.

1.2.4.2 **Other Privileged Images.** Other images that perform privileged functions are not installed with privilege because their functions are inherently sensitive and less controlled. These images could reveal security information or destroy the system if executed by naive or malicious users. They can only be executed by privileged users. Examples include SYSGEN, for loading device drivers; SDA, for examining the contents of memory; or the network control program, for network management. Other images that require privilege to execute but are not installed with privilege in a typical VMS system are listed in Appendix A.

1.2.4.3 **Images That Link with SYS$SYSTEM:SYS.STB.** Appendix A lists components that are linked with the system symbol table, SYS$SYSTEM:SYS.STB. These images access known locations through global cells in the system base image, SYS.EXE. The executive is divided into conceptual categories, each with its own version number. The version number of a category changes when an interface in that category changes. Each data cell or routine transfer vector in the system base image specifies the categories with which it is associated. For example, the MEMORY_MANAGEMENT category applies to all memory management data cells and routine transfer vectors, and the FILES_VOLUMES category applies to all RMS and file system related items. When a VMS release contains an incompatible change in a category, an image referencing a system data cell or routine transfer vector affected by the change must relink. For more information, see Chapter 29.

1.2.5 **Interface among Kernel Subsystems**

The connection among the three major subsystems pictured in Figure 1.4 is somewhat misleading because there is relatively little interaction between the three components. In addition, each of the three components has its own data structures for which it is responsible. When one of the other pieces of the system wishes to access such data structures, it does so through some controlled interface. Figure 1.5 shows the small amount of interaction that occurs between the three major subsystems in the operating system kernel.

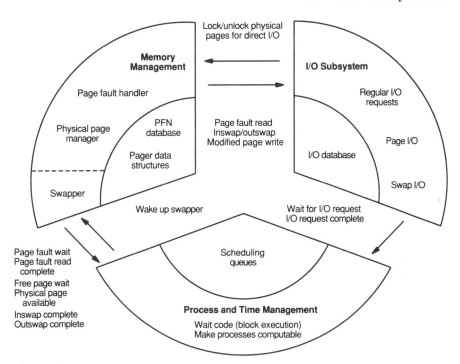

Figure 1.5
Interaction Between Components of VMS Kernel

1.2.5.1 **I/O Subsystem Requests.** The I/O subsystem makes a request to memory management to lock down specified pages for a direct I/O request. The page fault handler or swapper is notified directly when the I/O request that just completed was initiated by either one of them.

I/O requests can result in the requesting process's being placed in a wait state until the request completes. This change of state requires that the scheduling subsystem be notified. In addition, I/O completion can also cause a process to change its scheduling state. Again, the scheduler would be called.

1.2.5.2 **Memory Management Requests.** Both the page fault handler and swapper require input and output operations to fulfill their functions. The page fault handler and swapper use special entry points into the I/O subsystem rather than request the $QIO system service. These entry points queue prebuilt I/O packets directly to the driver, bypassing unnecessary protection checks and preventing an irrelevant attempt to lock pages associated with these direct I/O requests.

If a process incurs a page fault that results in a read from disk or if a process requires physical memory and none is available, the process is put into one of the memory management wait states by the scheduling subsystem. When the page read completes or physical memory becomes available, the process is made computable again.

1.2.5.3 **Scheduler Requests.** The scheduling subsystem interacts very little with the rest of the system. It plays a more passive role when cooperation with memory management or the I/O subsystem is required. One exception to this passive role is that the scheduling subsystem awakens the swapper when a process that is not currently memory-resident becomes computable.

1.3 **HARDWARE ASSISTANCE TO THE OPERATING SYSTEM KERNEL**

The method of implementing the services provided by VMS illustrates the close connection between the hardware design and the operating system. Many of the general features of the VAX architecture are used to advantage by the VMS operating system. Other features of the architecture exist entirely to support an operating system.

1.3.1 **VAX Architecture Features Utilized by VMS**

Several features of the VAX architecture that are available to all users are used for specific purposes by the operating system:

- The general-purpose calling mechanism is the primary path into the operating system from all outer layers of the system. Because all system services are procedures, invoked using the standard VAX procedure calling conventions, they are available to all native mode languages.
- The memory management protection scheme is used to protect code and data used by more privileged access modes from modification by less privileged modes. Read-only portions of the executive are protected in the same manner.
- Implicit protection is built into special instructions that can only be executed from kernel mode. Because only the executive (and suitably privileged process-based code) executes in kernel mode, such instructions as MTPR, LDPCTX, and HALT are protected from execution by nonprivileged users.
- The VAX architecture provides a small number of interlocked instructions to help synchronize simultaneous modifications of shared memory by more than one processor. A memory modification is not atomic (a single indivisible act), but is, in fact, a read followed by a write. When multiple processors modify the same memory at the same time, it is possible for each to read the same initial data but for one to overwrite the other's change. When all processors use interlocked instructions to modify the same memory, their modifications are atomic.

  VMS uses these instructions in its implementation of symmetric multiprocessing (SMP). The interlocked instructions provide atomic forms of queue manipulation, addition, and bit manipulation. With interlocked instructions, VMS implements spinlocks, structures that describe the state of a particular set of shared data and that enable a set of processors to serialize their access to the data. Chapter 8 provides more information on multiprocessor synchronization and spinlocks.

- The operating system uses interrupt priority level (IPL) for several purposes. IPL is elevated so that certain interrupts are blocked. For example, clock interrupts must be blocked while the system time (stored in a quadword) is checked because this checking takes more than one instruction. Clock interrupts are blocked to prevent the system time from being updated while it is being checked.
- IPL is also used as a synchronization tool. For example, any routine that accesses certain systemwide data structures, such as the scheduler database, must raise IPL to the level at which the data structures are synchronized. On a uniprocessor, this is sufficient to protect the data. On a multiprocessor, a routine must raise IPL and also acquire the spinlock associated with the data structure. The assignment of various hardware and software interrupts to specific IPL values establishes an order of importance to the hardware and software interrupt services that the VMS operating system performs.

Several other features of the VAX architecture are used by specific components of the operating system and are described in later chapters:

- The change mode instructions (CHME and CHMK), which increase the privilege of the access mode (see Figure 1.6). Note that most exceptions and all interrupts also result in changing mode to kernel. Section 1.3.5 presents an introduction to exceptions and interrupts.
- The inclusion of many protection checks and pending interrupt checks in the single instruction that is the common exception and interrupt exit path, REI.
- Software interrupts.
- Hardware context and the single instructions, SVPCTX and LDPCTX, that save and restore it.
- The use of ASTs to obtain and pass information.

1.3.2   VAX Instruction Set

While the VAX instruction set, data types, and addressing modes were designed to be somewhat compatible with the PDP-11, several features that were missing in the PDP-11 were added to the VAX architecture. True context indexing allows array elements to be addressed by element number, with the hardware accounting for the size (byte, word, longword, or quadword) of each element. Short literal addressing was added in recognition of the fact that the majority of literals appearing in a program are small numbers. Variable-length bit fields and character data types were added to serve the needs of several classes of users, including operating system designers.

The instruction set includes many instructions that are useful to any designer and occur often in the VMS executive. The queue instructions allow the construction of a doubly linked list as a common dynamic data structure. Character string instructions are useful when dealing with any data structure

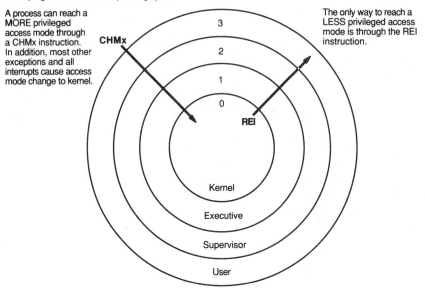

Access mode fields in the PSL are not directly accessible to the programmer or to the operating system.

A process can reach a MORE privileged access mode through a CHMx instruction. In addition, most other exceptions and all interrupts cause access mode change to kernel.

The only way to reach a LESS privileged access mode is through the REI instruction.

CHMx

REI

3
2
1
0

Kernel

Executive

Supervisor

User

The boundaries between the access modes are nearly identical to the layer boundaries pictured in Figure 1–4.
   Nearly all system services execute in kernel mode. RMS and some system services execute in executive mode.

Command language interpreters normally execute in supervisor mode.
Utilities, application programs, Run–Time Library procedures, and so on normally execute in user mode.
Privileged utilities sometimes execute in kernel or executive mode.

Figure 1.6
Methods for Altering Access Mode

that can be treated as an array of bytes. Bit field instructions allow efficient operations on flags and masks.

One of the most important features of the VAX architecture is the VAX Calling Standard. Any procedure that adheres to this standard can be called from any native language, an advantage for any large application that requires the use of the features of a wide range of languages. The VMS operating system adheres to this standard in its interfaces to the outside world through the system service interface, RMS entry points, and the Run-Time Library procedures. System services and RMS services are written as procedures that can be accessed by executing a CALLx instruction to absolute location SYS$*service* in the process P1 virtual address space. Run-Time Library procedures are mapped into a process's P0 space.

1.3.3 Implementation of VMS Kernel Routines

In Section 1.2.2, the VMS kernel was divided into three functional pieces plus the system service interface to the rest of the world. Alternatively, the operating system kernel can be partitioned according to the method used to gain access to each part. The three classes of routines within the kernel are procedure-based code, exception service routines, and interrupt

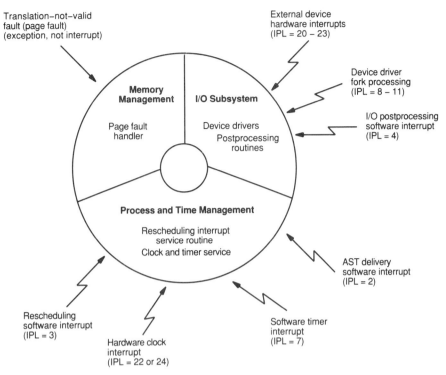

Figure 1.7
Paths into Components of VMS Kernel

service routines. Other systemwide functions, the working set swapping and modified page writing performed by the swapper, are implemented in a separate process that resides in system space. Figure 1.7 shows the various entry paths into the operating system kernel.

1.3.3.1 **Process Context and System Context.** The first section of this chapter discussed the pieces of the system that describe a process. Process context includes a complete address space description, quotas, privileges, scheduling data, and any other private data. Any portion of the system that executes in the context of a process has all these process attributes available.

A portion of the kernel, however, operates outside the context of a specific process. Most routines in this category are interrupt service routines, invoked in response to external events, regardless of the currently executing process. Portions of the initialization sequence also execute outside of process context. There are no process features, such as a kernel stack or a page fault handler, available when these routines are executing.

Because of the lack of a process, this system context or interrupt state can be characterized by the following limited context:

- All stack operations take place on the systemwide interrupt stack.

- The primary indication that the CPU is in this state is contained in the PSL. The PSL indicates that the interrupt stack is in use, the current access mode is kernel mode, and the IPL is higher than 2.
- The system control block (SCB), the data structure that controls the dispatching of interrupts and exceptions, can be thought of as the secondary structure that describes system context.
- Code that executes in system context can only refer to system virtual addresses. In particular, there is no P1 space available, so the systemwide interrupt stack must be located in system space.
- No page faults are allowed. The page fault handler generates a fatal bugcheck if a page fault occurs and the IPL is above IPL 2 or the processor is executing on the interrupt stack.
- No exceptions are allowed, other than subset instruction emulation exceptions. Exceptions such as page faults are associated with a process. The exception dispatcher generates a fatal bugcheck if an exception occurs above IPL 2 or while the processor is executing on the interrupt stack.
- ASTs, asynchronous events by which a process receives notification of external events, are not allowed. (The AST delivery interrupt is not requested when the processor is in system context and not granted until IPL drops below 2.)
- System services may not be requested from system context.

1.3.3.2   **Process Context Routines.** Procedure-based code (RMS services, Files-11 XQP, and system services) and exception service routines usually execute in the context of the current process (on the kernel stack when in kernel mode).

The system services are implemented as procedures and are available to all native mode languages. In addition, the fact that they are procedures means there is a call frame on the stack. Thus, a utility subroutine in a system service can signal an error simply by putting the error status into R0 and issuing a RET instruction. All superfluous information is cleaned off the stack by the RET instruction. The system service dispatchers, actually the dispatchers for the CHMK and CHME exceptions, are exception service routines.

System services must be called from process context. They are not available to system context code. One reason for requiring process context is that the various services assume that there is a process whose privileges can be checked and whose quotas can be charged as part of the normal operation of the service. Some system services reference locations in P1 space, a portion of address space only accessible from process context.

The page fault handler is the service routine for translation-not-valid exceptions. The page fault handler resolves a page fault in the context of the process that incurred the fault. Because page faults are associated with a process, the system cannot tolerate page faults incurred by interrupt service routines or other routines that execute in system context. The actual restriction imposed by the page fault handler is even more stringent. Page faults are not allowed above IPL 2. This restriction applies to process-based code executing at elevated IPL as well as to system context code.

1.3.3.3 **Interrupt Service Routines.** Most VMS interrupt service routines execute in system context on the systemwide interrupt stack.

- I/O requests are initiated through the $QIO system service, which can be requested directly by the user or by some intermediary, such as RMS or the Files-11 XQP, on the user's behalf. Once an I/O request has been placed into a device queue, it remains there until the driver is triggered, usually by an interrupt generated in the external device.

  Two classes of software interrupt support the I/O subsystem: fork level interrupts and the I/O postprocessing interrupt. Fork level interrupts enable a device driver to stall a driver code thread and resume it at a lower IPL, thus lowering IPL in a controlled fashion. The I/O postprocessing interrupt enters a software interrupt service routine for final processing of I/O requests.
- The timer functions in the operating system require both the interval timer interrupt service routine and a software interrupt service routine that actually dispatches individual timer requests.
- Another software interrupt performs rescheduling, by which one process is removed from execution and another selected and placed into execution.

1.3.3.4 **The Swapper Process.** Some VMS functions are best performed from process context. The swapper process performs the most significant of these. As the inswapper of all newly created processes, the swapper process cannot be created in the conventional way. Its code and process data structures are therefore built into the executive. During system initialization, its PCB is inserted into the scheduler database compute queues so that it can be the first process selected to execute.

Other characteristics of the swapper process include the following:

- Its process header is static and contains no working set list and no process section table. It does not support page faults. All code executed by the swapper must be locked into memory in some way. In fact, the swapper code is contained in a nonpageable section of a loadable executive image.
- The swapper executes entirely in kernel mode, thereby eliminating the need for stacks for the other three access modes.
- Its limited P1 space includes only the P1 pointer page, containing the location CTL$GL_PCB. Its kernel stack is located in system space.
- The swapper process temporarily maps P0 space to transform disjoint pages into a virtually contiguous I/O buffer, for example, to outswap a process working set.

Despite its limited context, the swapper process behaves in a normal fashion in every other way. It is selected for execution by the scheduling subsystem just like any other process in the system. It spends its idle time in the hibernate state until some component in the system recognizes a need for one of the swapper functions and awakens it.

Prior to Version 5.0, VMS included a null process with a context similar to that of the swapper process. All CPU time not used by any other process in the system was used executing the null process. In Version 5.0, a null PCB and PHD are defined as placeholders, but there is no null process to schedule for execution. SMP support necessitated a different form of idle loop.

1.3.3.5   **Special Subroutines.** There are several utility subroutines within the operating system related to scheduling and resource allocation that are called from both process context code, such as system services, and from software interrupt service routines. These subroutines are constrained to execute as though within system context. An example of such a routine is SCH$QAST, which is invoked to queue an AST to a process. It may be invoked from the I/O postprocessing and software timer interrupt service routines as well as from various system services.

1.3.4   **Memory Management and Access Modes**

The VAX address translation mechanism is summarized in Chapter 14 and described in more detail in the *VAX Architecture Reference Manual*. Two side effects are of special interest to VMS. When a page is not valid, a translation-not-valid exception is generated that transfers control to an exception service routine that takes the steps required to make the page valid. This exception transfers control from a hardware mechanism, address translation, to a software exception service routine, the page fault handler, and allows the operating system to gain control on address translation failures to implement its dynamic mapping of pages while a program is executing.

Before the VAX address translation mechanism checks the valid bit in the page table entry, it checks whether the requested access is allowable. The check is based on the current access mode in the PSL, a protection code that is defined for each virtual page, and the type of access (read, modify, or write). This protection check allows the operating system to make read-only portions of the executive write-inaccessible to any access mode, preventing corruption of operating system code. In addition, privileged data structures can be protected from even read access by nonprivileged users, preserving system integrity.

1.3.5   **Exceptions, Interrupts, and the REI Instruction**

The VAX exception and interrupt mechanisms are very important to VMS. The following sections compare the exception and interrupt mechanisms and briefly describe features of the mechanisms used by VMS.

1.3.5.1   **Comparison of Exceptions and Interrupts.** Interrupts occur asynchronously to the currently executing instruction stream. They are actually serviced between individual instructions and at well-defined points within the execution of a given instruction. Exceptions occur synchronously as a direct effect of the execution of the current instruction.

Both mechanisms pass control to service routines whose addresses are stored in the SCB. These routines perform exception-specific or interrupt-specific processing.

Exceptions are generally a part of the currently executing process. Their servicing is an extension of the instruction stream that is currently executing on behalf of that process. Interrupts are generally systemwide events that cannot rely on support of a process in their service routines.

Because interrupts are generally systemwide, the systemwide interrupt stack is usually used to store the PC and PSL of the process that was interrupted. Exceptions are usually serviced on the per-process kernel stack. Which stack to use is usually determined by control bits in the SCB entry for each exception or interrupt.

Interrupts cause a PC/PSL pair to be pushed onto the stack. Exceptions often cause exception-specific parameters to be stored in addition to a PC/PSL pair.

Interrupts cause the IPL to change. Most exceptions do not have an IPL change associated with them.

An interrupt can be blocked by elevating IPL to a value at or above the IPL associated with the interrupt. Exceptions, on the other hand, cannot be blocked. However, some exceptions can be disabled by clearing associated bits in the PSL.

When an interrupt or exception occurs, a new PSL is formed that specifies the new IPL, current access mode (usually kernel), and stack in use (interrupt or other). One difference between exceptions and interrupts, a difference that reflects the fact that interrupts are not related to the interrupted instruction stream, is that the previous access mode field in the new PSL is set to kernel for interrupts while the previous mode field for exceptions reflects the access mode in which the exception occurred. Chapter 2 describes the VAX architectural interrupt and exception mechanisms in more detail.

1.3.5.2   **Other Uses of Exceptions and Interrupts.** In addition to the translation-not-valid fault used by memory management software, the operating system also uses the CHMK and CHME exceptions as entry paths to the executive. System services that must execute in a more privileged access mode use either the CHMK or CHME instruction to increase access mode privilege (see Figure 1.6). The system handles most other exceptions by dispatching to user-defined condition handlers, as described in Chapter 5.

Hardware interrupts temporarily suspend code that is executing so that an interrupt-specific routine can service the interrupt. Each interrupt has a priority level, or IPL, associated with it. The CPU raises IPL when it grants the interrupt. High-level interrupt service routines thus prevent the recognition of low-level interrupts. Low-level interrupt service routines can be interrupted by subsequent high-level interrupts. Kernel mode routines can also block interrupts at certain levels by explicitly raising the IPL.

The VAX architecture also defines a set of software interrupt levels. VMS uses them for scheduling, I/O postprocessing, and to synchronize access to certain classes of data structures. Chapter 4 describes the software interrupt mechanism and its use.

Chapter 3 summarizes hardware interrupts and their service routines.

1.3.5.3   **The REI Instruction.** The REI instruction is the common exit path for interrupt and exception service routines. Many protection and privilege checks are incorporated into this instruction. Because most fields in the PSL are not accessible to the programmer, the REI instruction provides the only means for changing access mode to a less privileged mode (see Figure 1.6). It is also the only way to reach compatibility mode.

Although the IPL field of the PSL is accessible through the PR$_IPL processor register, execution of an REI instruction is a common way that IPL is lowered during normal execution. Because a change in IPL can alter the deliverability of pending interrupts, many hardware and software interrupts are delivered after an REI instruction is executed. Chapter 2 describes this instruction and its checks in detail.

1.3.6   **Process Structure**

The VAX architecture also defines a hardware PCB, which contains copies of all a process's general registers when the process is not active. When a process is selected for execution, the contents of this block are copied into the actual registers inside the processor with a single instruction, LDPCTX. The corresponding instruction that saves the contents of the general registers when the process is removed from execution is SVPCTX.

Chapter 12 contains a layout of the hardware PCB and detailed descriptions of the SVPCTX and LDPCTX instructions.

1.4   **OTHER SYSTEM CONCEPTS**

This chapter began by discussing the most important concepts in the VMS operating system: process and image. There are several other fundamental ideas that should be mentioned before beginning a detailed description of VMS internals.

1.4.1   **Resource Control**

VMS protects itself and other processes in the system from careless or malicious users, with hardware and software protection mechanisms, software privileges, and software quotas and limits.

1.4.1.1   **Hardware Protection.** The VAX memory management protection mechanism that is related to access mode prevents unauthorized users from modifying or even reading privileged data structures. Access mode protection also protects system and user code and other read-only data structures from modifications resulting from programming errors.

A more subtle but perhaps more important aspect of protection provided by the memory management architecture is that the process address space of one process (P0 space or P1 space) is not accessible to code running in the context of another process. When such accessibility is desired to share common routines or data, the operating system provides controlled access through global sections. System virtual address space is addressable by all processes, although page-by-page protection may deny read or write access to specific system virtual pages by certain access modes.

1.4.1.2   **Process Privileges.** Many operations that are performed by system services could destroy operating system code or data or corrupt existing files if performed carelessly. Other services allow a process to adversely affect other processes in the system. VMS requires that processes executing these potentially damaging operations be suitably privileged. Process privileges are assigned when a process is created, either by the creator or through the user's entry in the authorization file.

These privileges are described in the *Guide to Setting Up a VMS System* and in the *VMS System Services Reference Manual*. The privileges themselves are specific bits in a quadword that is stored in the process header. (The locations and manipulations of the several process privilege masks that the operating system maintains are discussed in Chapter 26.) When a VMS system service that requires privilege executes, it checks whether the associated bit in the process privilege mask is set.

1.4.1.3   **Quotas and Limits.** VMS also controls allocation of its systemwide resources, such as nonpaged dynamic memory and page file space, through the use of quotas and limits. Like privilege, these process attributes are assigned when the process is created. By restricting such items as the number of concurrent I/O requests or pending ASTs, VMS exercises control over the resource drain that a single process can exert on system resources, such as nonpaged dynamic memory. In general, a process cannot perform certain operations, such as queuing an AST, unless it has sufficient quota (nonzero PCB$W_ASTCNT in this case). The locations and values of the various quotas and limits are described in Chapter 25.

1.4.1.4   **User Access Control.** VMS uses a user identification code (UIC) for two different protection purposes. To perform some control operation (Suspend, Wake, Delete, and so on) on any other process, a process requires WORLD privilege. A process with GROUP privilege can affect only other processes with the same group number. A process with neither WORLD nor GROUP privilege can affect only other processes with the same UIC.

VMS also uses UIC as a basis for protection of various system objects, such as files, global sections, logical names, and mailboxes. The owner of a file, for example, specifies what access to the file she grants to herself, to other processes in the same group, and to other processes in the system.

VMS Version 4 introduced access control lists (ACLs), which provide more selective levels of sharing. An ACL lists individual users or groupings of users who are to be allowed or denied access to a system object. ACLs specify sharing on the basis of UIC, as well as other groupings, known as identifiers, that can be associated with a process. ACLs can be specified for files, directories, devices, global sections, queues, and shareable logical name tables.

1.4.2 Other System Primitives

Several other simple tools used by VMS are mentioned throughout this book and are described in Chapters 8, 19, and 35.

1.4.2.1

Synchronization. Any multiprogramming system must take measures to prevent simultaneous access to system data structures. The problem is further complicated by multiprocessing, where several CPUs have independent access to shared memory. The executive uses four synchronization techniques: elevated IPL, spinlocks, mutexes, and locks.

On a uniprocessor, elevating IPL is sufficient to synchronize access to systemwide data structures. By elevating IPL, the processor can block a subset of interrupts, allowing unrestricted and uncontested access to the data structures. The most common synchronization IPL used by VMS is IPL 8.

To extend the uniprocessor synchronization provided by IPL to a multiprocessing environment, VMS uses spinlocks. A spinlock describes the state of a particular set of shared data and enables a set of processors to serialize their access to the data. A resource synchronized by elevated IPL on a uniprocessor is synchronized by a combination of elevated IPL and spinlock on an SMP system.

A section of code that accesses shared data in a synchronized way first raises IPL and, in an SMP system, acquires a spinlock. When finished, the code lowers IPL and, in an SMP system, releases the spinlock. VMS provides macros to implement these IPL-raising/spinlock acquisition and IPL-lowering/spinlock release operations. The macros acquire and release spinlocks only on SMP systems; otherwise, they only elevate and restore IPL. For simplicity, this volume refers to this combined type of synchronization as acquiring and releasing spinlocks. That the macros merely alter IPL on a uniprocessor is implicit; that they also alter IPL on an SMP member often goes without saying.

The use of a spinlock to synchronize access to certain types of data structures is sometimes undesirable or even potentially harmful to system performance. For example, a process that has acquired a spinlock must execute at or above IPL 3, blocking process rescheduling on that CPU until it releases the spinlock. In addition, because page faults are not allowed above IPL 2, any pageable data structure cannot be synchronized with a spinlock.

Thus, the VMS executive requires a third synchronization tool to allow synchronized access to pageable data structures. This tool must also allow a process to be removed from execution while it maintains ownership of the structure in question. One synchronization tool that fulfills these requirements is called a mutual exclusion semaphore (mutex).

Synchronization, including the use of mutexes, is discussed in Chapter 8.

The VMS executive and other system components, such as the Files-11 XQP, RMS, and the job controller, use a fourth tool, the lock management system services, for more flexible sharing of resources among processes. These services provide a waiting mechanism for processes whose desired access to a resource is blocked. They also provide notification to a process whose use of a resource blocks another process. Most important, the lock management system services provide sharing of clusterwide resources. Chapter 10 describes the lock management system services.

1.4.2.2   **Dynamic Memory (Pool) Allocation.** The system maintains several dynamic memory areas from which blocks of memory can be allocated and deallocated. Nonpaged pool contains those systemwide structures that might be manipulated by (hardware or software) interrupt service routines or process context code executing above IPL 2. Paged pool contains systemwide structures that do not have to be kept memory-resident. The process allocation region and the kernel request packet (KRP) lookaside list, both in process P1 space, are used for pageable data structures that will not be shared by any other process. Dynamic memory allocation and deallocation are discussed in detail in Chapter 19.

1.4.2.3   **Logical Names.** The system uses logical names for many purposes, including a transparent way of implementing a device-independent I/O system. The use of logical names as a programming tool is discussed in the *VMS System Services Reference Manual*. The internal operations of the logical name system services, as well as the internal organization of the logical name tables, are described in Chapter 35.

1.5   **SYSTEM VIRTUAL ADDRESS SPACE**

The layout of system virtual address space is shown in Figure 1.8. Appendix F gives a more complete description of system space.

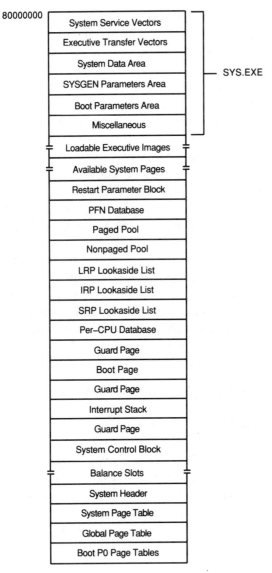

Figure 1.8
Layout of System Virtual Address Space

   This figure was produced by an SDA listing of the system page table and the contents of all global data areas in system space and from information in [BOOTS]SYSBOOT. The relations between the variable-size pieces of system space and their associated SYSGEN parameters are given in Appendix F.

PART II / Control Mechanisms

2 VAX Interrupts and Exceptions

By indirections find directions out.

Shakespeare, *Hamlet*, 2, i

This chapter describes the VAX architectural interrupt and exception mechanisms and the return from exception or interrupt (REI) instruction. It summarizes VMS use of the mechanisms.

2.1 OVERVIEW

During system operation, events occur that require the execution of software other than the current thread of execution. The processor responds to such events by altering the control flow from the current thread of execution. Some of these events are unrelated to the current thread and are asynchronous to it; these events are called interrupts. Other events, called exceptions, are triggered by the current thread and are synchronous to it.

The processor determines where to transfer control by examining the system control block (SCB). The SCB contains a longword vector for each interrupt and exception, specifying the address where control is to be transferred.

Most hardware interrupts are requested by signals from devices external to the processor when they need attention from the operating system. The hardware interrupt capability makes it unnecessary for the processor to poll the device to determine whether its state has changed. Some hardware interrupts are requested by signals from within processor components, such as the interval timer.

To permit arbitration among concurrent interrupt requests and their servicing, each interrupt request has an associated interrupt priority level (IPL). When an interrupt is granted, processor IPL is raised to that of the interrupt. When the processor IPL is at or above that of the interrupt request, the interrupt is blocked.

A software interrupt is an interrupt requested by kernel mode code rather than by an external device. The VAX architecture provides for 15 different software interrupts. The VMS executive is interrupt-driven and requests a particular software interrupt to cause the corresponding service routine to perform its designated function. That is, software interrupts are requested to schedule operating system functions, with the highest priority interrupt serviced first.

VAX microcode responds similarly to hardware and software interrupt requests. The microcode tests for pending interrupts between each instruction and at well-defined points during the evaluation and execution of more complicated instructions. The microcode determines the IPL of the highest outstanding interrupt request, whether it is requested by hardware or software. The microcode compares that IPL to the one at which the processor is running and takes one of two actions based on the comparison:

- If the processor is running at an IPL equal to or higher than that of the interrupt request, the interrupt request is deferred until processor IPL drops below the IPL level of the request.
- If the processor is running at a lower IPL than that of the interrupt request, the interrupt is granted.

To grant the interrupt, the microcode saves the processor state and dispatches through the SCB vector associated with the interrupt to its service routine.

An exception is the processor's response to an anomaly or error it encounters while executing an instruction, for example, a divisor of zero in a DIVL instruction. An exception occurs in direct response to a particular instruction sequence and would occur again if the instruction were repeated under the same circumstances. VAX microcode responds as it does to an interrupt, by saving the processor state and dispatching through the SCB vector associated with the exception to its service routine.

2.2   **SYSTEM CONTROL BLOCK**

The SCB may occupy multiple pages, depending on CPU type and adapter configuration. Its first page, however, is architecturally defined. Each exception and interrupt has a unique vector, identified by its offset from the beginning of the SCB. Each vector contains the address of a service routine for that exception or interrupt. Figure 2.1 shows the contents of a vector and meaning of the low-order two bits.

Operating system software initializes the SCB, and the VAX processor uses it to dispatch all interrupts and exceptions.

The SCB is page-aligned. A multiple-page SCB must be physically contiguous. Its starting physical address is stored in the system control block base register, PR$_SCBB. The processor calculates the address of a particular

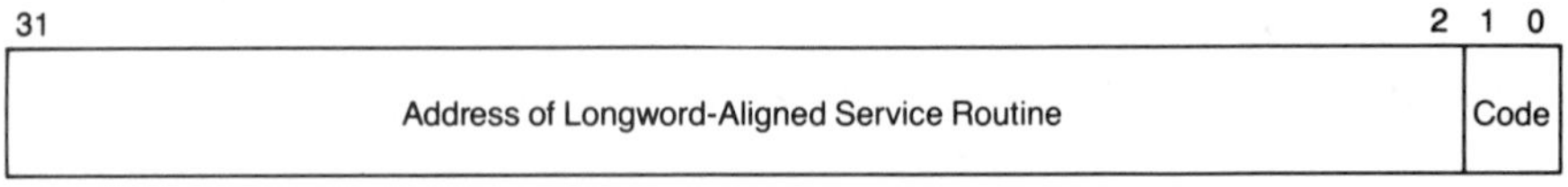

31	2	1	0
Address of Longword-Aligned Service Routine		Code	

Code	Meaning
00	Service the event on the kernel stack unless currently on the interrupt stack; in that case, use the interrupt stack.
01	Service the event on the interrupt stack; if the event is an exception, raise IPL to 31.
10	Service the event in the writable control store (WCS), passing bits <15:2> to the microcode; if the WCS does not exist or is not loaded, the operation is undefined.
11	The operation is undefined.

Figure 2.1
System Control Block Vector Format

vector using the contents of PR$_SCBB and the offset into the SCB of the vector. This design enables executive software to place the SCB in memory known to be good at system initialization. If the SCB were required to be at a fixed location, and that memory had uncorrectable errors, the system would be unable to run. VMS maps the SCB in system space and stores its starting virtual address in global location EXE$GL_SCB.

Once memory management is enabled, vectors must contain virtual addresses. Because there may be no current process at the time an interrupt occurs, all service routines must be in system space. Because the low-order two bits of the vector are not part of the service routine address, each service routine must begin on a longword boundary.

The low-order two bits of a vector specify the stack on which the interrupt or exception should be serviced. A value of 01 means that it should be serviced on the interrupt stack. If the vector contains the value 00, the processor will not switch to the interrupt stack; if, however, it was already running on the interrupt stack, it will continue to do so. A value of 01 in an exception vector also means that IPL should be raised to 31. VMS specifies that machine check and kernel-stack-not-valid exceptions be serviced on the interrupt stack at IPL 31.

On a CPU type that supports user-writable control store, a value of 10 means that the interrupt or exception should be serviced by microcode in user-writable control store. Most CPUs that do not support user-writable control store halt if an interrupt or exception occurs through a vector with 10 in the low-order two bits. A value of 11 in these bits has no defined meaning; most CPUs halt if they attempt to dispatch through a vector with these bits set.

Figure 2.2 shows the general organization of the first page of the SCB. It contains vectors for exceptions, software interrupts, CPU-specific error interrupts, and some hardware interrupts. The *VAX Architecture Reference Manual* contains the detailed SCB layout.

Table 5.1 lists the VAX exception vectors. The executive handles most exceptions in a uniform way. Some exceptions, however, result in special action. Chapter 5 describes VMS's handling of most exceptions and summarizes its responses to special exceptions.

Chapter 4 contains more details about the vectors used for software interrupts and describes their service routines.

The second half of the first page is reserved for adapter interrupts. As Figure 2.3 shows, it is divided among 16 possible adapters, each capable of interrupting at four possible IPL values from 20 to 23. The nature and type of the adapters vary on different VAX processors. Each adapter has an identifying number which, along with the IPL of the interrupt, selects a particular SCB vector. Chapter 22 describes adapter interrupts and their service routines. Chapter 3 summarizes other hardware interrupts and their service routines.

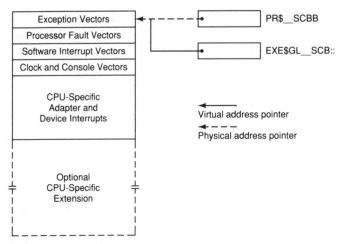

Figure 2.2
System Control Block Organization

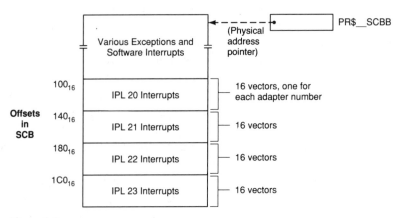

Figure 2.3
System Control Block Vectors for Adapter Interrupts

Beyond the first page, the size of the SCB varies with processor type and configuration. Appendix F contains further details of its sizing.

2.3 INTERRUPT REQUESTS

The VAX architecture provides 16 hardware IPLs, from IPL 31 down to IPL 16. The top eight levels are primarily for CPU-specific errors and power failure. The lower levels are primarily for external adapters and I/O devices.

There is no one-to-one correspondence between IPL and hardware interrupt vector. The SCB contains multiple vectors whose interrupts are at the same hardware IPL (see Figure 2.3). An external adapter or I/O device requests an interrupt at a particular hardware IPL. The SCB vector associated with the interrupt is typically determined by the combination of interrupt IPL and adapter or device (see the *VMS Device Support Manual*).

To block interrupts, kernel mode code can raise IPL to that of the highest interrupt to be blocked. The VAX architectural concept of an interrupt includes the idea that an interrupt request is expected to persist until serviced, or until the adapter or device withdraws the request. At appropriate times, a processor can sample outstanding interrupt requests.

The VAX architecture provides 15 vectors in the SCB for software interrupts at IPLs 1 through 15; there is a one-to-one correspondence between IPL and software interrupt vector. The architecture provides a means for kernel mode code and CPU console commands to request software interrupts.

Kernel mode code requests a software interrupt at a particular IPL by writing that IPL into the software interrupt request register, PR$_SIRR. VMS code generally uses the SOFTINT macro to write the PR$_SIRR. This macro expands into the following instruction:

```
MTPR    ipl,S^#PR$_SIRR
```

The following CPU console command can also write the PR$_SIRR:

```
>>>D/I 14 ipl            !for ipl, substitute a hexadecimal digit
```

Writing to PR$_SIRR causes the bit with the same number as the IPL to be set in another processor register, the software interrupt summary register (PR$_SISR). Figure 2.4 shows the layouts of these two registers. At any given time, PR$_SISR contains a bit set for each level at which a software interrupt has been requested but not yet granted. The VAX processor reads PR$_SISR to test for pending software interrupts. When the processor grants a software interrupt request, it clears the corresponding bit in PR$_SISR.

The VAX architecture provides both of these processor registers to simplify synchronization of access to PR$_SISR. If VMS were to modify the PR$_SISR directly, several instructions would be required to preserve already set bits in the register. VMS would have to raise IPL to block all interrupts, read PR$_

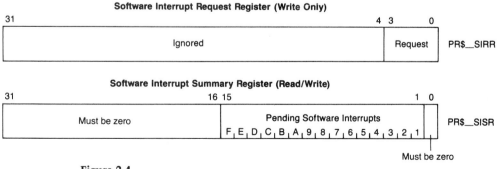

Figure 2.4
Formats of Software Interrupt Request Register and
Software Interrupt Summary Register

SISR, set the new bit, write PR$_SISR, and restore the previous IPL. (MTPR and MFPR are the only instructions that access these processor registers.) Instead, when kernel mode code (or CPU console command) writes PR$_SIRR, the processor modifies PR$_SISR with interrupts blocked.

2.4 INTERRUPT DISPATCHING

VAX initiate-exception-or-interrupt (IEI) microcode takes the following steps when an interrupt is requested and granted:

1. It examines the low-order bits of the SCB vector to determine on which stack the interrupt is to be serviced. VMS has specified that all hardware interrupts and most software interrupts be serviced on the interrupt stack.
2. VAX IEI microcode switches stacks, if necessary, and pushes the current program counter (PC) and processor status longword (PSL) onto the new stack. Saving the PC and PSL preserves state so that the interrupted thread of execution can continue after the interrupt is dismissed.
3. The microcode stores the address of the service routine in the PC and constructs a new PSL. Its IPL is that associated with the interrupt. Its compatibility mode, trace pending, first part done, decimal overflow enable, floating underflow enable, integer overflow enable, trace enable, and condition code bits are cleared. Its current mode is set to kernel, the mode in which the interrupt will be serviced. Its previous mode is expected to be irrelevant to the service routine and is set to kernel also. Its interrupt stack bit is set, if appropriate, to indicate that the processor is running on the interrupt stack.
4. When a software interrupt is dispatched, the microcode clears the bit in PR$_SISR corresponding to the IPL.

The interrupt service routine executes and eventually exits with an REI instruction that dismisses the interrupt. The REI instruction, described in Section 2.8, restores the PC and PSL, and the interrupted thread of execution (a process or lower priority interrupt service routine) continues where it was interrupted.

2.5 RESTRICTIONS IMPOSED ON INTERRUPT SERVICE ROUTINES

Most interrupt service routines execute in the limited system context described in Chapter 1. These routines execute at elevated IPL on the interrupt stack outside the context of a process.

Several restrictions are imposed on interrupt service routines by either the VAX architecture or VMS. Many of these result from the limitations of system context. The following list indicates some of the constraints placed on an interrupt service routine. The description of system context in Chapter 1 contains a more general list of these and other restrictions. Chapter 8 describes the synchronization rules applicable to an interrupt service routine.

- To reduce overhead, no context switch occurs with an interrupt. Therefore, the instructions executed and data referenced by an interrupt service routine must be in system address space. An interrupt service routine should not refer to per-process address space.
- An interrupt service routine should be short and do as little processing as possible at elevated IPL.
- An interrupt service routine must save any registers it uses. VMS saves some registers (usually R0 through R5) prior to calling a device driver interrupt service routine (see the *VMS Device Support Manual*).
- Prior to executing an REI instruction, an interrupt service routine must remove anything it pushed on the stack and restore all saved registers.
- An interrupt service routine should be conservative in its use of stack space. The interrupt stack is not very large on most VMS systems. Its size is determined by the SYSGEN parameter INTSTKPAGES, which has a default value of four pages.
- VMS does not allow any interrupt service routine (other than the IPL 2 interrupt service routine) to access pageable routines or data structures. The page fault exception service routine generates a fatal bugcheck if a page fault occurs while IPL is above 2.
- Although an interrupt service routine can raise IPL, it should not lower IPL below the level at which the original interrupt occurred.

2.6 EXCEPTION DISPATCHING

When an exception is detected, VAX IEI microcode takes the following steps:

1. It determines on which stack the exception is to be serviced. Which stack depends on the access mode in which the exception occurred, whether the CPU was previously executing on the interrupt stack, and what type of exception occurred.

   In general, VAX microcode uses the low two bits of the SCB vector to determine on which stack the exception is serviced. Table 2.1 summarizes the stack choices resulting from the architectural mechanisms and VMS SCB vector definitions. Its first column lists the exception name. The second column specifies the access mode in which the exception occurred. The third column specifies whether the interrupt stack is in use at the time of the exception. The fourth column shows the stack on which the exception is serviced.

   Machine check and kernel-stack-not-valid exceptions are serviced on the interrupt stack. A subset instruction emulation exception is serviced on the stack on which the exception occurred. Change mode exceptions are generally serviced on the stack of their target mode. VMS specifies that all other exceptions are to be serviced on the kernel stack, unless the processor is already running on the interrupt stack.

Table 2.1   Selection of Exception Stack

| | PSL AT TIME OF EXCEPTION | | |
| | | | |
Exception Name	*Previous Mode*	*Interrupt Stack*	*Resulting Stack*
Machine check	Any	0 or 1	ISP
Kernel stack not valid	K	0	ISP
Subset instruction emulation	Any	0 or 1	Same
CHMx	Any	0	xSP[1]
CHMx	K	1	Halt[2]
All others	U, S, E, K	0	KSP
All others	K	1	ISP

[1] The stack used is the destination of the CHMx instruction. Note, however, that a CHMx instruction issued from an inner access mode in an attempt to reach a less privileged (outer) access mode will not have the desired effect. The mode indicated by the instruction is minimized with the current access mode to determine the actual access mode that will be used. The exception is generated through the indicated SCB vector, but the final access mode is unchanged. In other words, as illustrated in Figure 1.6, the CHMx instruction can only reach equal or more privileged access modes.

[2] Execution of a CHMx instruction while the CPU is running on the interrupt stack is prohibited by the VAX architecture and results in a CPU halt.

The exception reporting mechanism assumes that the kernel stack is valid. The decision to use the kernel stack for most exceptions avoids the possibility of attempting to report an exception on, for example, the user stack, only to find that it is corrupted in some way (invalid or otherwise inaccessible), resulting in another exception. A kernel-stack-not-valid exception must be taken on the interrupt stack. The VMS service routine for this exception generates a fatal bugcheck.

If the interrupt stack is invalid, IEI microcode halts the processor.

2. The microcode switches stacks, if necessary, and pushes the PC and PSL onto the new stack. The exception PC that it pushes depends on the nature of the exception, that is, whether the exception is a fault, trap, or abort (see Table 5.1):

—For a fault, the processor pushes the PC of the faulting instruction onto the stack. When a fault is dismissed with an REI instruction, the faulting instruction executes again from the beginning.

—For a trap, the processor pushes the PC of the next instruction onto the destination stack. An instruction that causes a trap does not reexecute when the exception is dismissed with an REI instruction.

—For an abort, the processor pushes the PC of the aborted instruction onto the stack. An abort is not restartable. Exceptions that are aborts include kernel-stack-not-valid, some machine check codes, and some reserved operand exceptions.

3. The microcode loads the PC with the address of the service routine and constructs a new PSL. Its IPL is normally unchanged. If the vector contains 01 in the low-order two bits, the service routines run on the interrupt stack at IPL 31. Machine check and kernel-stack-not-valid exception vectors specify this value. The PSL compatibility mode, trace pending, first part done, decimal overflow enable, floating underflow enable, integer overflow enable, trace enable, and condition code bits are cleared. Its current mode is set to the mode in which the interrupt will be serviced. Its previous mode is set to the mode in which the exception occurred. Its interrupt stack bit is set, if appropriate, to indicate that the processor is running on the interrupt stack.

The exception service routine executes. It eventually exits by removing any exception-specific parameters from the stack and executing an REI instruction to dismiss the exception.

The REI instruction, described in Section 2.8, restores the PC and PSL, and the thread of execution that incurred the exception resumes.

2.7 COMPARISON OF EXCEPTIONS AND INTERRUPTS

The following list summarizes some of the distinctions between exceptions and interrupts.

- Interrupts occur asynchronously to the currently executing instruction stream. They are serviced between individual instructions or at well-defined points in the execution of a given instruction. Exceptions occur synchronously as a direct effect of execution of the current instruction.
- Interrupts are generally systemwide events that cannot rely on support of a process in their service routines. Exceptions are generally a part of the currently executing process. Their servicing is an extension of the instruction stream that is currently executing on behalf of that process.
- Because interrupts are generally systemwide, they are serviced on the systemwide interrupt stack. Exceptions are usually serviced on the per-process kernel stack.
- To save state at interrupt initiation, the processor records the PC and PSL on the stack. At exception initiation, the processor often records exception-specific parameters as well as the PC and PSL.
- Interrupts cause the IPL to change. Exceptions other than machine check and kernel-stack-not-valid do not cause IPL to change.
- An interrupt can be blocked by elevating IPL to a value at or above the IPL associated with the interrupt. Exceptions are not blocked by raising IPL. Some exceptions, however, can be disabled by clearing their enabling bits in the PSL.

- When an interrupt or exception occurs, the microcode constructs a new PSL. The previous mode field in the new PSL is set to kernel for an interrupt PSL, while the previous mode field for an exception PSL is set to the access mode in which the exception occurred. This difference between exceptions and interrupts reflects the fact that interrupts are not related to the interrupted instruction stream.

2.8 THE RETURN FROM EXCEPTION OR INTERRUPT INSTRUCTION

The REI instruction is the common exit path for interrupt and exception service routines. The VAX architecture limits the types of transitions from one access mode to another; the REI instruction is the only way to change access mode to a less privileged one (see Figure 1.6). This property of REI, and the VAX architecture constraint that an inner access mode will not be interrupted to deliver an asynchronous system trap (AST) to an outer mode, make REI the logical place to test whether an AST delivery interrupt should be requested.

The REI instruction is also the only way to reach compatibility mode.

Execution of an REI instruction is a common way for IPL to be lowered. Because a change in IPL can alter the deliverability of pending interrupts, hardware and software interrupts are often delivered after an REI instruction is executed.

Protection and privilege checks are incorporated into the REI instruction to prevent the system from entering illegal or inconsistent states. REI is not a privileged instruction, and these checks prevent, for example, an attempt to enter a more privileged access mode.

The REI microcode tests the following conditions to ensure that the saved PSL is well formed and that it is consistent with the current PSL. If any test fails, the microcode generates a reserved operand fault exception.

- If the saved PSL interrupt stack bit is nonzero, then the saved PSL IPL must be greater than 0. This test detects an illegal state in the saved PSL—being on the interrupt stack at IPL 0.
- If the saved PSL IPL is greater than 0, then its current mode must be kernel. This test prevents any mode other than kernel from raising IPL.
- The saved PSL previous mode must be no more privileged than its current mode. This test detects a previous illegal transition or stack corruption.
- The saved PSL must-be-zero bits must be 0. This test detects corruption of the stack.
- If the saved PSL compatibility mode bit is 1, the CPU must be one that implements compatibility mode, the saved PSL current mode must be user, and the saved PSL first part done, interrupt stack, floating underflow enable, decimal overflow enable, and integer overflow enable bits must all be 0. These tests restrict compatibility mode to user access mode and detect stack corruption and inconsistent state.

- The saved PSL current mode must be no more privileged than the current PSL current mode. This test prevents an attempt to REI to a more privileged mode.
- If the current PSL interrupt stack bit is 0, then the saved PSL interrupt stack bit must be 0. This test prevents an attempt to REI onto the interrupt stack.
- The saved PSL IPL must be no larger than the current PSL IPL. This test prevents an attempt to REI to a higher IPL. An interrupt service routine that lowers IPL below that of its interrupt breaks synchronization and risks a reserved operand fault when it executes an REI instruction.

After performing the previously listed tests, the REI microcode takes the following steps:

1. It pops the saved PC and PSL from the stack into temporary registers.
2. Depending on the current PSL interrupt stack bit and current mode, the microcode saves the contents of the SP register in the appropriate processor register (PR$_ISP, PR$_KSP, PR$_ESP, PR$_SSP, or PR$_USP). This step records the pointer into the current access mode's stack.

   A VAX processor is not required to implement the per-process stack pointer registers. One that does not implement them instead saves SP in the appropriate longword in the process's hardware process control block (PCB).
3. If the current PSL trace pending bit is set, the microcode sets the saved PSL trace pending bit. This step ensures a trace fault after the execution of the REI instruction.
4. The microcode copies the temporary registers to PC and PSL.
5. If the now-current PSL interrupt stack bit is 0, the microcode loads SP from the appropriate PR$_xSP register. This step restores the pointer into the now-current stack. (A VAX CPU type that does not implement these processor registers instead loads SP from the appropriate longword in the process's hardware PCB.)
6. If the now-current PSL interrupt stack bit is 0, the microcode compares the current mode to the contents of PR$_ASTLVL. If the current mode is less privileged, the microcode requests an IPL 2 interrupt.
7. The microcode reinitializes any instruction lookahead in the processor, flushing the instruction buffer. On some VAX CPUs, instruction execution is concurrent with the fetching and evaluation of subsequent instructions. The REI microcode clears any such CPU state. (The REI instruction is the only one guaranteed to do this clearing and is thus required between modifying the instruction stream and executing the modified instruction.)
8. Unless another interrupt occurs, execution resumes with the instruction being executed at the time of the interrupt or exception, at the interrupted instruction or the exception PC.

3 Hardware Interrupts

While I nodded, nearly napping, suddenly there came a tapping,
As of someone gently rapping, rapping at my chamber door.
Edgar Allan Poe, *The Raven*

The VMS operating system is often referred to as interrupt-driven and non-monolithic. Hardware interrupts notify VMS of such important events as power failure, device completion, device errors, device alerts, and work requests from one processor to another in a symmetric multiprocessing (SMP) system. In addition, the interval timer interrupt allows VMS to keep system time.

This chapter presents an overview of hardware interrupts, interrupt priority levels (IPLs), and interrupt dispatching in VMS.

3.1 OVERVIEW

As discussed in Chapter 2, many hardware interrupts are requested by signals from devices external to the processor when they need attention from the operating system. Hardware interrupts may be requested by devices, controllers, or other processors in an SMP system. In addition, the processor itself may request some hardware interrupts.

The VAX architecture provides 16 priority levels, 16 through 31, for hardware interrupts and 16 priority levels, 0 through 15, for software interrupts. When a hardware interrupt occurs, the interrupted processor raises its priority to the IPL associated with the hardware interrupt. Table 3.1 provides a summary of hardware interrupts and IPLs used by VMS. Software running in kernel mode may raise and lower the priority of the processor by using the MTPR instruction to load the register PR$_IPL. Thus, software has the ability to block hardware interrupts as necessary.

The response of the VAX processor to any interrupt request, hardware or software, is similar. If the processor priority permits the requested interrupt to be granted, the processor saves the current state and invokes the interrupt service routine for the interrupt through the interrupt vector in the system control block (SCB).

Interrupt vectors for software interrupts are architecturally defined at fixed offsets within the SCB. Interrupt vectors for certain hardware interrupts, such as the interval timer interrupt, the powerfail interrupt, and console interrupts, are also architecturally defined at fixed offsets within the SCB. SCB vectors for other hardware interrupts, such as device interrupts, are defined in a system-dependent manner, as discussed in Section 3.2.

The following sections provide brief descriptions of hardware interrupts on VAX systems. Chapter 4 discusses software interrupts.

3.1.1   **Urgent Conditions**

The VAX architecture provides for eight priority levels, 24 through 31, for urgent conditions such as power failure and CPU-specific bus and memory errors. IPL 30 is reserved for the powerfail interrupt. IPL 31 is reserved for those exceptions that must block all processing until the condition has been handled. IPL 31 is also used by device drivers to synchronize with powerfail recovery, as discussed in the *VMS Device Support Manual*.

3.1.1.1   **Powerfail Interrupt.**

The powerfail interrupt is requested by the CPU hardware when there is a drop in operating voltage. It is vectored through the SCB at offset $0C_{16}$, as defined by the VAX architecture, and serviced at IPL 30. EXE$POWERFAIL, in module POWERFAIL, is the VMS powerfail interrupt service routine. Chapter 33 discusses powerfail recovery in detail.

3.1.1.2   **System-Specific Errors.**

The VAX architecture reserves offsets 50_{16} through 60_{16} in the first page of the SCB for system-specific memory and bus errors.

Table 3.1   Hardware Interrupt Priority Levels and Their Use

Level	Name	Use
31	IPL$_POWER	Block all interrupts
	IPL$_EMB	Synchronize error logging
	IPL$_MÇHECK	Synchronize machine check processing
	IPL$_MEGA	Synchronize miscellaneous structures
30		Powerfail interrupt
30–24		CPU-specific error interrupts
24	IPL$_HWCLK	Interval timer interrupt [1]
22	IPL$_HWCLKLO	Interval timer interrupt [1]
23–20		Device interrupts
22 or 20	IPL$_IPINTR	Interprocessor interrupt [2]
20 or 22	IPL$_VIRTCONS	Console terminal interrupts [3]
19 or 21	IPL$_INVALIDATE	Synchronize translation buffer (TB) invalidation [4]
18–16		Unused

[1] The interval timer IPL is system-dependent.

[2] The interprocessor IPL is 22 on VAX 6000 series and VAXstation 35x0 systems and 20 on all others.

[3] IPL$_VIRTCONS has a value of 20. However, access to the virtual console database is synchronized at a system-dependent IPL. See Chapters 8 and 34.

[4] IPL$_INVALIDATE has a value of 19. However, synchronization of TB invalidation is done at a system-dependent IPL. See Chapters 8 and 34.

Common examples of such interrupts are corrected read data errors, vectored through SCB offset 54_{16} on some VAX systems, and system bus errors, vectored through SCB offset $5C_{16}$ on some VAX systems. Such interrupts are taken at the highest interrupt levels, IPLs 24 through 30.

The interrupt service routines for such interrupts typically raise IPL to 31 and log the error. These routines are usually in the [SYSLOA]MCHECK*xxx* modules, where *xxx* designates the CPU type. Appendix G lists CPU types and their corresponding suffixes. Chapter 32 provides more discussion on the handling and logging of system-specific errors.

3.1.2 Interval Timer Interrupt

The manner in which the CPU hardware requests the interval timer interrupt is implementation-dependent. Some VAX processors, such as the MicroVAX II, generate timer interrupts at constant 10-millisecond intervals. Other VAX processors have the ability to generate timer interrupts at specified intervals.

Interval timer interrupts are vectored to the service routine through offset $C0_{16}$ in the SCB, as defined by the VAX architecture. EXE$HWCLKINT, in module TIMESCHDL, is the interval timer interrupt service routine. The IPL of the interval timer interrupt is 24 on older VAX systems and 22 on the newer systems. Chapter 11 discusses the interval timer interrupt in detail.

3.1.3 Interprocessor Interrupt

On SMP systems, VMS uses the interprocessor interrupt mechanism to interrupt a specific processor for a specific task or to interrupt all processors or a subset of all processors to perform tasks as required. The interprocessor interrupt vector, priority level, and interrupt service routine vary on different VAX systems.

On all SMP systems other than VAXstation 35*x*0 CPUs, the interprocessor interrupt is vectored at SCB offset 80_{16}. On a VAXstation 35*x*0 CPU, the interprocessor interrupt is vectored through the upper half of the first page of the SCB just like any other adapter interrupt.

On all SMP systems other than VAX 6000 series and VAXstation 35*x*0 processors, the interprocessor interrupt vector in the SCB contains the address of SMP$INTSR1, in module [SYSLOA]SMPINT.

On VAX 6000 series and VAXstation 35*x*0 systems, the vector contains the address of SMP$IPINT_*xxx*, in module [SYSLOA]OPDRV*xxx*. After performing system-dependent actions, SMP$IPINT_*xxx* transfers to SMP$INTSR1. SMP$INTSR1 is in module [SYSLOA]SMPINT_60 for a VAXstation 35*x*0 system and in module [SYSLOA]SMPINT for all other systems.

The interprocessor interrupt priority level is IPL 20 on VAX 88*x*0 and VAX 83*x*0 systems, and IPL 22 on VAX 6000 series and VAXstation 35*x*0 systems. Chapter 34 discusses the use of interprocessor interrupts.

Table 3.2   Console Interrupts

Name	SCB Vector	IPL
Console storage receive [1]	$F0_{16}$	20 on the VAX-11/730, 23 on the VAX-11/750
Console storage transmit [1]	$F4_{16}$	20 on the VAX-11/730, 23 on the VAX-11/750
Console terminal receive	$F8_{16}$	20
Console terminal transmit	FC_{16}	20

[1] These interrupts are generated only on VAX-11/730 and VAX-11/750 processors.

3.1.4   Console Interrupts

On most VAX systems, the console block storage device and the console terminal are treated as a single entity with regard to interrupt processing. On VAX-11/750 and VAX-11/730 processors, the console block storage device is treated as distinct from the console terminal device.

Interrupts from the console are vectored through known offsets in the SCB. Table 3.2 shows the SCB vectors and IPLs of different console interrupts. Chapter 24 discusses console interrupts.

3.1.5   Unexpected Interrupts and Passive Releases

Architecturally defined SCB vectors are initialized during system initialization to point to appropriate VMS routines. Other vectors in the SCB are initialized to the VMS unexpected interrupt service routine, ERL$UN-EXP, in module ERRORLOG. ERL$UNEXP generates the nonfatal bugcheck UNXINTEXC and dismisses the interrupt.

When a CPU grants an interrupt request, and no device vector is returned by the device that generated the request, a condition known as passive release occurs. This can happen when the device determines, after it has requested an interrupt, that it no longer needs to interrupt the CPU. A passive release is treated as though a zero interrupt vector is returned by the device. Passive releases are vectored to the routine ERL$VEC_RETURN, in module ERRORLOG, which increments the global location IO$GL_SCB_INT0 to record the occurrence.

Passive releases on a UNIBUS that is adapted to a VAX system bus are vectored to UBA$INT0. UBA$INT0 is found in module [SYSLOA]INICOMBI for all VAX systems that use the VAX bus interconnect (VAXBI) bus for I/O; for all other systems it is found in [SYSLOA]ADPSUBxxx. UBA$INT0 increments the global location IO$GL_UBA_INT0 to record the passive release and dismisses the interrupt.

Before adapter initialization is done and the SYSGEN utility configures devices on the system, all the SCB vectors reserved for adapter and device interrupts are initialized to ERL$UNEXP. SCB vectors used for adapter and device interrupts are later reinitialized by the appropriate procedures. Thus, all unused SCB vectors on a system point to ERL$UNEXP, with the exception of unused SCB vectors for UNIBUS and Q22-bus device interrupts, which point to UBA$UNEXINT. UBA$UNEXINT, a base image transfer vector, actually jumps to the REI instruction in UBA$INT0 that dismisses the interrupt.

3.2 DEVICE INTERRUPTS

The VAX architecture provides eight priority levels, 16 through 23, for I/O device interrupts, although all VAX implementations use only levels 20 through 23. UNIBUS levels BR4 through BR7 correspond directly to IPLs 20 through 23.

When a VAX processor receives an interrupt request from an I/O device, it needs to determine which SCB vector corresponds to the interrupt. The manner in which each VAX processor does this is implementation-dependent, even though the principles used are common to all processors.

VAX systems are offered in a range of processor- and bus-specific configurations. This section provides a generic model of a VAX system and its interrupt handling as an aid to understanding the more specific descriptions in subsequent sections.

Figure 3.1 shows a generic model of a VAX system. The system bus connects the CPU, memory controllers, and I/O adapters. An adapter connects devices or another I/O bus to the system bus. Each slot on the system bus, potentially occupied by a CPU, memory controller, or adapter, is known as a nexus. Actually, the name for this varies from one VAX system type to another; for simplicity, this chapter uses the term *nexus*.

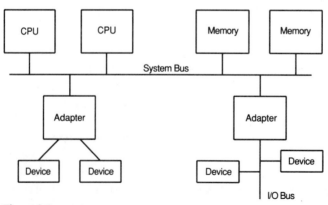

Figure 3.1
Generic Model of a VAX System

The VAX architecture specifies four interrupt vectors for each of 16 nexuses. Each vector corresponds to a different interrupt priority level; on current VAX system implementations, the levels are 20 through 23.

When an I/O adapter requests an interrupt, for example, in response to a device attention condition, the CPU microcode determines its nexus number. This nexus number, in conjunction with the IPL of the request (20, 21, 22, or 23), uniquely identifies an SCB vector through which the CPU dispatches the interrupt. The VAX architecture specifies that such vectors be located in the upper half of the first page of the SCB, as shown in Figure 2.3.

Typically, a new VAX CPU is designed with I/O adapters that support the bus structure and I/O architecture of a previous generation. This enables many of the peripherals of the previous generation to run on it, preserving the investment in them. A prime example of this is the support of PDP-11 UNIBUS peripherals on many VAX systems.

Such an adapter bridges the VAX CPU's main bus and an earlier bus, translating protocols and transmitting interrupt requests and grants. Support for the interrupt vectoring of the adapted bus usually requires an extension to the architecturally defined page of the SCB and an additional level of interrupt dispatching, either in the processor or in the operating system software. For instance, UNIBUS devices can interrupt at one of 128 possible vectors. Therefore, a UNIBUS adapter requires the capability to specify up to 128 vectors.

On some systems, such as the VAX-11/780 and VAX-11/785, UNIBUS interrupts are indirectly vectored through a UNIBUS adapter interrupt service routine (ISR). This means that the UNIBUS adapter transmits the UNIBUS device's interrupt request to the VAX CPU. When the CPU grants the interrupt, it dispatches through the SCB vector corresponding to the interrupt request level to a UNIBUS adapter ISR. The UNIBUS adapter ISR performs another level of dispatch based on the value of the UNIBUS device's interrupt vector.

On most other VAX implementations that support UNIBUS peripherals, UNIBUS interrupts are directly vectored. This means that CPU microcode uses the UNIBUS device vector directly as an offset into the appropriate page of the SCB to enter the device ISR. Direct vectoring requires that one page of the SCB be dedicated to each UNIBUS adapter on the system, because devices on its UNIBUS may generate any one of 128 possible vectors.

Another example is an adapter that supports the VAXBI bus. For instance, on a VAX 8800 system, up to four VAXBI buses can be connected to the VAX 8800 memory interconnect (NMI), the system bus. There are 16 slots on each VAXBI bus, and an adapter on any of these slots may generate an interrupt request. Every device on the system must have a unique interrupt vector in the SCB. This means that the interrupt vector in the VAX 8800 SCB must be unique with respect to the following:

- The number of the VAXBI bus (0, 1, 2, or 3)
- The node number (0 through 15) on that VAXBI bus of the adapter that requested the interrupt
- The IPL (20, 21, 22, or 23) of the interrupt

Therefore, one SCB page is reserved for each VAXBI bus on the system. In addition, each UNIBUS adapter on the system requires an additional page of the SCB.

Similarly, Q22-bus-based systems reserve the second page of the SCB for Q22-bus device vectors.

3.2.1 Adapter Initialization

VMS uses system-dependent system initialization procedures to determine the system configuration, build the data structures that represent it, and initialize the SCB vectors appropriately. These procedures typically test for the presence of adapters at all the nexuses on the system, as described later in this section.

There may be different numbers of nexuses on different systems. For example, on a VAX 8350 system, which uses the VAXBI as the system bus as well as the I/O bus, there are 16 nexuses. A VAX 8800 system, on the other hand, uses the NMI as the system bus and the VAXBI as the I/O bus. There are 16 nexuses for each VAXBI attached to the VAX 8800 system. MicroVAX 3400/3600/3900 series systems and the MicroVAX II system have exactly one nexus, nexus 0.

Nexuses are numbered starting at 0. A system with 16 nexuses has nexus numbers from 0 to 15. A system that has more than 16 nexuses implements a system-dependent numbering scheme. Subsequent sections describe the numbering schemes employed on different VAX systems.

The physical address layout of the VAX system determines the location of the node space for a given nexus number. The node space of a nexus is defined as that range of physical addresses through which the registers of an adapter that is seated on the nexus may be accessed. System initialization code loads the machine check vector in the SCB with the address of a special routine. It then tests the first longword in every nexus's node space. If a nonexistent memory machine check occurs, there is no adapter at the nexus being tested. If there is an adapter on the nexus, then the adapter type is returned, and the adapter is configured.

On some CPU types, VMB, the primary bootstrap program, determines the adapter configuration. On other CPU types, the configuration is determined at a later step of initialization. Chapters 30 and 31 give further information.

The result of this testing is stored in several arrays in nonpaged pool. Chapter 31 describes these arrays. During later stages of system initialization, this information is used when specific adapters are configured into the system.

3.2.2   VAX-11/730 Systems

On VAX-11/730 systems, the CPU, UNIBUS adapter, and memory controller are connected by the array bus. In addition to the array bus, communications between the CPU and the integrated disk controller (IDC) are performed over the accelerator bus, so named because the floating-point accelerator communicates over it. The IDC controls RL02 and R80 disks. A VAX-11/730 system is not expandable and does not have expansion slots.

The VAX-11/730 SCB is two pages long. The second page is used for directly vectored UNIBUS interrupts. Each vector in the second page corresponds to a UNIBUS vector in the range from 0 to $1FC_{16}$.

3.2.3   VAX-11/750 Systems

The VAX-11/750 SCB is two pages long or, if there is a second UNIBUS on the VAX-11/750 processor, three pages long. The second SCB page on VAX-11/750 processors is used for directly vectored UNIBUS device interrupts. Each SCB vector corresponds to a UNIBUS vector in the range from 0 to $1FC_{16}$. A third SCB page is used for directly vectored UNIBUS device interrupts on the second UNIBUS.

The backplane interconnect on VAX-11/750 systems, called the CPU-to-memory interconnect (CMI), connects the CPU, memory controllers, UNIBUS adapters, and MASSBUS adapters. Each connection to the CMI is identified by its slot number.

There are a total of 16 slots that can be used to connect adapters. The first ten of these are reserved for a memory controller, UNIBUS adapters, and MASSBUS adapters. These ten slots are called fixed slots because the mapping of controller/adapter to slot number is fixed. That is, a particular slot can have only a particular adapter placed in it. Table 3.3 lists these adapters.

The last six slots are reserved for adapters with configuration registers and are called floating slots. A CI750 port adapter or a DR750 would be connected to a floating slot.

Each slot is assigned four SCB vectors in the first SCB page, one for each IPL value from 20 to 23, as shown in Figure 2.3.

Table 3.3   Fixed Slots on VAX-11/750
Processors

Adapter Type	*Slot Number*
Memory controller	0
Up to three MASSBUS adapters	4 through 6
UNIBUS adapter	8
Second UNIBUS adapter	9

Table 3.4   Standard SBI Adapter Assignments on VAX-11/78x Systems

Interface Type	Nexus	Comments
	TR 0	Hold line for next cycle. TR 0 is the highest TR level and is not assigned to a device.
First memory controller	TR 1	
Second memory controller	TR 2	
First MA780 shared memory		If present, follows local memory controllers
Second MA780 shared memory		
First UNIBUS adapter	TR 3	Follows any MA780 controllers present
Second UNIBUS adapter	TR 4	
Third UNIBUS adapter	TR 5	
Fourth UNIBUS adapter	TR 6	
	TR 7	Reserved
First MASSBUS adapter	TR 8	
Second MASSBUS adapter	TR 9	
Third MASSBUS adapter	TR 10	
Fourth MASSBUS adapter	TR 11	
DR780 SBI interface	TR 12	
CI780	TR 14	
	TR 15	Reserved

3.2.4   VAX-11/780 and VAX-11/785 Systems

The SCB for VAX-11/780 and VAX-11/785 systems is one page. On these processors, the synchronous backplane interconnect (SBI) connects the CPU, memory controllers, DR780s, CI780s, UNIBUS adapters, and MASSBUS adapters. Each connection to the SBI is identified by its transfer request (TR) number.

The TR number determines SBI priority. TR numbers range from 0, the highest priority, to 15, the lowest priority. There is a limit of 15 connections to the SBI, as shown in Table 3.4. TR number 0 is used for a special purpose on the SBI and has no corresponding external adapter. The lowest priority level is reserved for the CPU and requires no actual TR signal line. The TR number defines the physical address space through which the device's registers are accessed and the vectors through which the device will interrupt. The SCB has four vectors for each possible TR, one vector each for IPLs 20, 21, 22, and 23. UNIBUS interrupts are indirectly vectored.

An adapter is not restricted to having a specific TR number. However, the relative priorities of the various adapters cannot change. That is, a system cannot have a MASSBUS adapter with a higher priority (lower TR number) than a UNIBUS adapter. For instance, if a system has two local memory controllers and an MA780 shared memory controller, the first UNIBUS adapter on that system could have TR number 4, with the MA780 having TR number 3, and the memory controllers having TR numbers 1 and 2.

3.2.5   **Q22-Bus-Based MicroVAX Systems**

The following systems fall into this category:

- MicroVAX II, VAXstation II, VAXstation II/GPX
- MicroVAX 3400, VAXstation 3400
- MicroVAX 3500, MicroVAX 3600, MicroVAX 3800, MicroVAX 3900
- VAXstation 3200, VAXstation 3500, MicroVAX 3800/GPX

Other MicroVAX systems that provide support for the Q22-bus are listed in subsequent sections.

The memory interconnect on these systems connects the CPU and memory modules. The CPU board contains an interface to the Q22-bus to which all I/O devices are connected. Interrupt requests from external I/O devices go directly to the CPU, which arbitrates interrupts. IPLs 20 through 23 correspond to Q22-bus interrupt request lines BIRQ4 through BIRQ7.

The SCB for these systems is two pages long. The second page is used for directly vectored Q22-bus device interrupts. Each vector in the second page corresponds to a Q22-bus vector in the range from 0 through $1FC_{16}$.

On these systems, there is exactly one nexus, numbered 0, that interfaces the CPU board to the Q22-bus.

An interrupt on these systems is arbitrated by comparing its IPL to the processor's IPL. However, when a Q22-bus interrupt is granted, processor IPL is raised to 23 by the microcode.

With VMS Version 5.0, multilevel interrupt dispatching is available on these systems. After the interrupt is granted by the processor at IPL 23, the VMS executive, with the help of additional code in the interrupt dispatch area of the channel request block (CRB) of the device controller, explicitly lowers IPL to the interrupting device's IPL. This, however, requires that the MicroVAX system be properly configured. See the *VMS Device Support Manual* for additional details on multilevel interrupt dispatching.

3.2.6   **MicroVAX 2000 Family Systems**

The MicroVAX 2000 family includes MicroVAX 2000, VAXstation 2000, and VAXstation 2000/GPX processors. A member of this family is sometimes known as a busless system because the CPU, memory, and all I/O adapters are on a single board.

There is exactly one nexus, 0, on this system, reserved for the CPU. All device and adapter registers are visible through the node space of the CPU.

An interrupt controller collects interrupts from all I/O devices and presents a single interrupt request to the CPU at IPL 20.

Table 3.5 MicroVAX 2000 Interrupt Vectors

SCB Vector	Interrupting Source
244_{16}	Video end-of-frame
248_{16}	Video controller secondary
250_{16}	Network controller primary
254_{16}	Network controller secondary
$2C0_{16}$	Serial line controller receiver done or silo full
$2C4_{16}$	Serial line controller transmitter done
$3F8_{16}$	SCSI controller
$3FC_{16}$	Disk controller

The SCB for this system is two pages long. Device interrupts are vectored through the second page of the SCB at one of eight possible device vectors, shown in Table 3.5.

3.2.7 MicroVAX 3100 Family Systems

The MicroVAX 3100 family includes the MicroVAX 3100, VAXstation 3100 (monochrome) models 30/40/38/48, and VAXstation 3100/GPX models 30/40/38/48. The memory interconnect on the MicroVAX 3100 connects the CPU and memory modules. The CPU board interfaces to one or two small computer system interface (SCSI) buses, each under the control of an NCR 5380 SCSI controller chip that supports asynchronous data transfers. Figure 3.2 shows a representative MicroVAX 3100 system configuration.

The SCB for this system is two pages long. The second page is used to vector device interrupts from all I/O devices.

3.2.8 VAXstation 3520 and 3540 Systems

The VAXstation 3520 system consists of two processors connected to a common backplane, the M-bus. The VAXstation 3540 system has four processors.

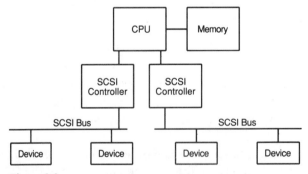

Figure 3.2
MicroVAX 3100 System Configuration

The processors access common memory on the M-bus. Each processor is interfaced to the bus through a cache that monitors the M-bus for other CPUs' memory references.

There are eight nexuses on the M-bus and a CPU module, a memory module, or an I/O adapter may be present on each nexus. Disk devices connect to a SCSI bus, which interfaces to the M-bus through an I/O adapter. An optional Q22-bus adapter module allows connection of additional peripherals, such as magnetic tape. Chapter 34 shows a sample VAX 3520 configuration.

The VAXstation 3520 and 3540 systems have a two-page SCB. I/O adapter interrupts are vectored through the upper half of the first page of the SCB. Interrupts from devices on the Q22-bus are vectored through the second page of the SCB.

3.2.9 VAX 6000 Series Systems

VAX 6000 series systems use a high-speed interconnect (XMI) as the backplane. There are 13 slots, or nodes, on the XMI, and each node can connect to a CPU module or memory module. I/O adapters may be connected only to slots 1 through 4 and 11 through 14. DWMBA adapters adapt the VAXBI bus to the XMI bus. The VAXBI bus connects I/O peripherals to the system. Chapter 34 shows a diagram of a VAX 6000 series system.

The first page of the SCB is the architecturally defined page. The nexus vectors in the upper half of this page are used for the I/O adapters on the XMI. Each VAXBI bus on the system gets an additional page of the SCB. Furthermore, if a UNIBUS adapter is present on the system, an additional page of SCB is allocated for vectoring UNIBUS device interrupts.

Nexus numbering of VAXBI-based adapters on VAX 6000 series systems is done according to the following formula:

nexus = (XMI slot number of DWMBA) * 16
+ (VAXBI node number of adapter)

Nexus numbering of XMI-based adapters is done according to the following formula:

nexus = (XMI slot number of adapter) * 16

3.2.10 VAX 8200 Family Systems

The VAX 8200 family consists of VAX 8200, VAX 8250, VAX 8300, VAX 8350, and VAXstation 8000 processors. The SCB for a member of the VAX 8200 family consists of the standard page defined by the VAX architecture, plus an additional page for each UNIBUS adapter present. UNIBUS interrupts are directly vectored. Note that the VAXstation 8000 does not support any UNIBUS options.

The VAX 8200 family uses the VAXBI as a system bus as well as the I/O bus. This means that the VAXBI allows CPU modules, memory modules, or I/O adapters to be connected to each of its 16 slots.

I/O adapters connect devices and controllers or other buses, such as the UNIBUS, to the VAXBI. Slots on the VAXBI are known as nodes, and nexus numbers in the VAX 8200 family are the same as the VAXBI node numbers of the adapters. Chapter 34 shows a diagram of a VAX 83x0 system.

Each node has four vectors in the first SCB page, one for each level at which it can request an interrupt. VAXBI interrupt levels 4 through 7 correspond to IPLs 20 through 23.

3.2.11 VAX 8600 and VAX 8650 Systems

VAX 8600 and VAX 8650 systems have a four-page SCB to support the theoretical maximum configuration of four SBI adapters (SBIAs), although only two are supported by VMS. On these systems, I/O adapters are connected to an SBI. Each SBI is connected through an SBIA to a bus called an adapter bus (A-bus). The A-bus connects the SBIAs to the memory subsystem. The supported I/O adapters are the UNIBUS, MASSBUS, and CI780 adapters supported on a VAX-11/78x system. Figure 3.3 shows a representative VAX 8600 system configuration.

Hardware interrupts for adapters on the first SBI are vectored through the first page of SCB. Interrupts for adapters on the second SBI use the second page of SCB. Interrupts generated by SBIA 0 are vectored through the first page of the SCB, and those generated by SBIA 1 are vectored through the second page of the SCB. A hardware interrupt vector is determined by the combination of interrupt level, TR number, and SBI number.

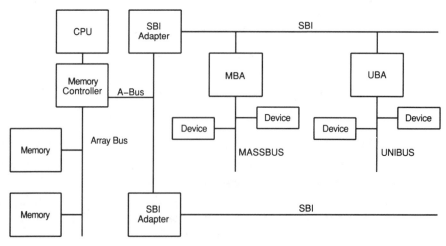

Figure 3.3
VAX 8600 System Configuration

UNIBUS interrupts are indirectly vectored, as they are on VAX-11/78x systems.

3.2.12 VAX 8800 Family Systems

The VAX 8800 family includes VAX 8500, VAX 8530, VAX 8550, VAX 8700, and VAX 8800 processors but not the VAX 88x0 family (see Section 3.2.13). A synchronous backplane interconnect bus, the NMI, connects CPUs, memory, and one or two I/O adapters called NMI-to-BI (NBI) adapters. The VAXBI is the VAX 8800 family I/O bus. Each NBI adapter can interface with up to two VAXBIs. Each VAXBI can have up to 15 adapters apart from the NBI. Chapter 34 shows a diagram of a VAX 8800 system.

A VAX 8800 family processor has a 32-page SCB. Memory and NBI interrupts vector through the architecturally defined page of the SCB. Interrupts from each of four possible VAXBIs vector through pages 28 through 31. Pages 1 through 27 are reserved for offsettable VAXBI nodes, nodes that are directly vectored, such as the UNIBUS adapter.

The nexus number of an adapter on such a system may be determined by the following formula:

nexus = (VAXBI number) * 16
            + (VAXBI node number of adapter)

where the VAXBI buses are numbered 0 and 1 or 2 and 3 on VAX 85x0 systems, from 0 through 3 on VAX 8700 and VAX 8800 systems, and from 0 through 5 on VAX 88x0 systems. For example, an adapter on node number 5 of VAXBI number 1 has a nexus number of 21.

3.2.13 VAX 88x0 Family Systems

The VAX 88x0 family includes VAX 8810, VAX 8820, VAX 8830, and VAX 8840 processors but not VAX 8800 CPUs. Most of the information in Section 3.2.12 applies to the VAX 88x0 family. However, the VAX 88x0 family reserves pages 1 through 25 for the offsettable VAXBI nodes, such as the UNIBUS adapter, and uses pages 26 through 31 for each of the six VAXBI buses supported.

4   Software Interrupts

And now I see with eye serene
The very pulse of the machine.

William Wordsworth, *She Was a Phantom of Delight*

Software interrupts are fundamental to the VMS operating system. Software interrupt service routines running at interrupt priority levels (IPLs) between 2 and 15 perform many of the most important system functions of VMS. These include dispatching fork processes (IPLs 6 and 8 to 11), servicing processes' time-dependent requests (IPL 7), I/O postprocessing (IPL 4), scheduling (IPL 3), and delivering ASTs (IPL 2). This chapter describes how software interrupts are requested and granted and how VMS uses them.

4.1   THE SOFTWARE INTERRUPT

The VMS executive requests a software interrupt to cause an interrupt service routine to execute and perform its designated function. It does this by writing to the software interrupt request register. When the interrupt request is granted, the VAX processor dispatches through the appropriate system control block (SCB) vector to an interrupt service routine. Chapter 2 describes the hardware mechanism of software interrupts.

VMS uses software interrupts to schedule operating system functions. Using software interrupts is more efficient than periodically checking to see whether these functions need to be done. IPLs are assigned to the different operating system functions, in part, as an indication of their relative importance.

VMS also uses specific IPLs and interrupt requests at those IPLs to synchronize access to shared data structures. Chapter 8 discusses synchronization through raising IPL.

VMS requests the software interrupt service routines for IPLs 3, 4, 6, 7, 8, and 11 from within a hardware interrupt service routine or another software interrupt service routine. Software interrupts at 12 and 14 are requested only through a CPU console command. The VAX architecture specifies that the IPL 2 software interrupt service routine be requested by REI microcode to deliver asynchronous system traps (ASTs). Although VMS provides for fork dispatching at IPLs 9 and 10, VMS itself makes little or no use of them. VMS Version 5 does not use software interrupts at IPLs 1, 5, 13, and 15.

The VAX architecture constrains software interrupt service routines by providing only one bit to indicate that a software interrupt has been requested at a particular IPL. The service routine is thus unable to determine how many requests for it were outstanding when the interrupt request was granted. As a result, either the software must supply some protocol for determining this number or it must be irrelevant to the execution of the service routine.

The scheduling interrupt service routine is an example of a routine that has one function to do, regardless of how many times that function has been requested. Other interrupt service routines use queues to keep track of their work. Each element in the queue represents a specific item of work for the interrupt service routine and an instance of the interrupt's having been requested.

An interrupt service routine that uses a queue generally performs all the work in the queue before dismissing the interrupt. It tries to remove an element from the queue with the REMQUE or REMQHI instruction. If an element was removed, the interrupt service routine processes that element and tries to remove another element from the queue. If the queue is empty and no item was removed from it, the interrupt service routine's work is complete and it then exits through an REI instruction. Such a software interrupt service routine reacts gracefully to a spurious interrupt, one granted when there is no work for it to do.

4.2 SOFTWARE INTERRUPT SERVICE ROUTINES

There is no central monitor routine in VMS that controls the sequence of operating system functions. Instead, any executive thread that identifies the need for a particular function performed within a software interrupt service routine can request the associated interrupt. Scheduling operating system functions as software interrupts eliminates any requirement for polling whether these functions need to be done. It also enables more important functions to interrupt less important ones.

Table 4.1 shows the software interrupt service routine functions and their associated IPLs. In some cases, the assigned IPL only indicates the relative importance of the interrupt, and the interrupt service routine runs primarily at a higher IPL for synchronization. The table also shows the more common symbolic names for the IPLs, defined by the macro $IPLDEF.

VMS interprets software interrupts, except the AST delivery and rescheduling interrupts, as systemwide events that are serviced independently of the context of a specific process. The rescheduling interrupt, discussed briefly in this chapter and in greater detail in Chapter 12, is taken on the kernel stack of the current process. The interrupt service routine immediately executes a SVPCTX instruction, saving the process's context and switching onto the interrupt stack. The AST delivery interrupt, discussed briefly at the end of this chapter and in greater detail in Chapter 7, is the only interrupt in use that is serviced in the context of a specific process. The interrupt service routines for unused software interrupts are serviced on the kernel stack. Each of these routines merely logs an error and dismisses the interrupt.

Table 4.1   Software Interrupt Levels Used by the Executive

IPL	IPL Names	Use	Stack
15		Unused	Kernel
14		XDELTA	Interrupt
13		Unused	Kernel
12		IPC intervention	Interrupt
11	IPL$_MAILBOX, IPL$_IOLOCK11	Fork dispatching	Interrupt
10	IPL$_IOLOCK10	Fork dispatching	Interrupt
9	IPL$_IOLOCK9	Fork dispatching	Interrupt
8	IPL$_SYNCH, IPL$_SCHED, IPL$_SCS, IPL$_TIMER, IPL$_MMG	Fork dispatching	Interrupt
7	IPL$_TIMERFORK	Software timer service routine	Interrupt
6	IPL$_QUEUEAST	Fork dispatching	Interrupt
5		Unused	Kernel
4	IPL$_IOPOST	I/O postprocessing	Interrupt
3	IPL$_RESCHED	Rescheduling	Kernel
2	IPL$_ASTDEL	AST delivery	Kernel
1		Unused	Kernel

The software interrupt service routines vary. Some perform the same functions every time they execute. The rescheduling interrupt service routine, for example, takes the current process out of execution, selects another one to run, and places it into execution. The functions of other software interrupt service routines are quite variable. The I/O postprocessing interrupt service routine has a specific function to perform but is data-driven by the I/O request packets (IRPs) in its work queue. A fork dispatching interrupt exists solely to dispatch to system routines running as fork processes. The routines that are dispatched vary as a result of system operation.

The software interrupts are described briefly in the following sections. Some are described at more length in subsequent chapters. The following sections are in order by interrupt level, except that the service routines for interrupts requested through console command are discussed last.

4.2.1   Fork Processing

Five software interrupts (IPLs 6 and 8 to 11) are used for dispatching to fork processes. Each of the interrupt service routines has its own work queue of fork blocks (FKBs).

When a fork dispatching interrupt is granted, the interrupt service routine saves the low general registers and removes from its queue the first fork block and dispatches to the fork process it describes.

The following sections describe fork process data structures and service routines in more detail.

4.2.1.1 **Fork Process Data Structures.** A fork block describes a routine to be called by a fork dispatching interrupt service routine and some context for that routine. The macro $FKBDEF defines symbolic names for the fields in a fork block. A minimal fork block, shown in Figure 4.1, includes the address, or saved program counter (PC), of the fork routine (FKB$L_FPC) and the contents of two registers. The first two longwords of a fork block link it into a queue. The fields FKB$W_SIZE and FKB$B_TYPE are the standard dynamic data structure header fields.

The field FKB$B_FIPL specifies in which fork block queue the fork block is inserted and at what IPL its routine will run. With VMS Version 5, this field has an alternative name and meaning: FKB$B_FLCK identifies the spinlock associated with the fork process. It is an index into a table of static spinlocks, pointed to by SMP$AR_SPNLKVEC, and also into a table of spinlock IPLs, at SMP$AL_IPLVEC. Because spinlock indexes are numbers 32 or larger, fork processing routines can test bit 5 in this fork block field to distinguish between its two uses: bit 5 is 0 in an IPL and 1 in a spinlock index. On a uniprocessor system, either use is permitted; on a symmetric multiprocessing (SMP) system, a fork block can only contain a spinlock index. Chapter 8 describes spinlocks in detail.

A fork block must be in nonpageable system space. Most often, it is part of a larger data structure, such as a unit control block or class driver request packet, which contains additional data. The combination of standard fork block fields, additional fork block data, and the routine that is to be executed is called a fork process.

Figure 4.2 shows the array of fork block queue listheads. The array is in the per-CPU database so that each CPU in an SMP system has its own fork block queues. (Chapter 34 contains more information on the per-CPU database.) The listheads of these queues are ordered in an array that includes a placeholder listhead for IPL 7. Since the IPL 7 interrupt is serviced by the software timer routine, there is no fork process dispatching at IPL 7.

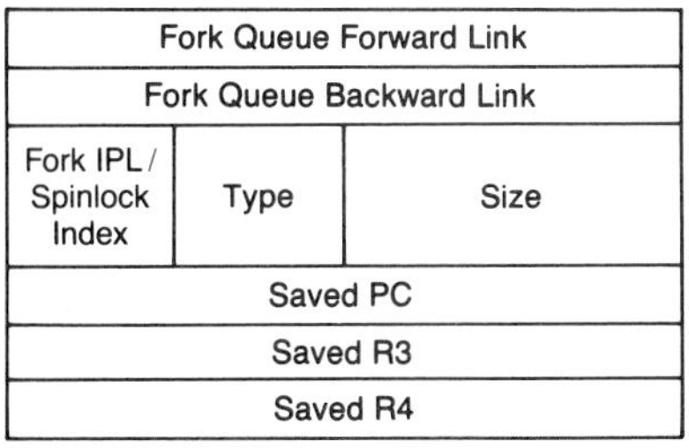

Fork Queue Forward Link		
Fork Queue Backward Link		
Fork IPL / Spinlock Index	Type	Size
Saved PC		
Saved R3		
Saved R4		

Figure 4.1
Layout of a Fork Block

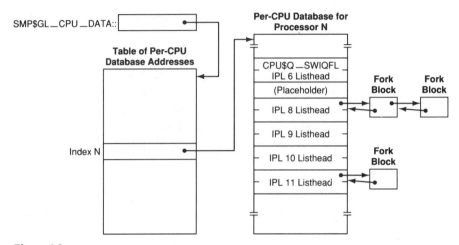

Figure 4.2
Fork Block Queues

However, having the placeholder listhead simplifies the fork process creation code.

4.2.1.2 **Reasons for Creating a Fork Process.** Fork processing exists, in part, so that device drivers do not have to execute at high IPLs for long periods of time, blocking other device interrupts. Device interrupt service routines run at device IPLs between 20 and 23. Often these routines perform lengthy processing that does not require execution at high IPL. Typically, a device interrupt service routine runs at a lower IPL as soon as possible. However, it may not simply lower IPL directly; that could interfere with the synchronization of code already running at the lower IPL. Instead, it creates a fork process that will run at the lower IPL when its turn comes.

A driver or any high-IPL thread of execution might also create a fork process at a lower IPL to access a system database synchronized at that lower IPL, for example, if the driver needed to queue an AST to a process. Another example is the routine that allocates nonpaged pool. It can be invoked from process context code and from interrupt threads of execution at IPLs up to 11. If the routine determines that pool must be expanded, but it is running on the interrupt stack or holding a higher ranking spinlock than MMG, it creates an IPL 6 fork process to perform the expansion. Chapter 19 gives information on pool allocation, and Chapter 34 discusses spinlocks.

4.2.1.3 **Creating a Fork Process.** To fork, a driver invokes routine EXE$IOFORK or EXE$FORK, in module FORKCNTRL, specifying the address of the fork block, the fork process context, and a return address. Fork process context consists of the fork block, the contents of R3 and R4, and the address of the routine the fork process is to execute (the fork PC). EXE$IOFORK clears a bit to disable an I/O timeout on the device and continues in the EXE$FORK routine.

EXE$FORK stores the specified fork process context in the fork block. It tests bit 5 in FKB$B_FLCK to determine whether the field contains a fork IPL or a spinlock index. To convert the spinlock index to an IPL, EXE$FORK uses it as a longword context index into the array at SMP$AL_IPLVEC. The specified entry contains the IPL associated with that spinlock. EXE$FORK inserts the fork block at the tail of the fork block queue for that IPL and requests a software interrupt at that IPL if the queue was empty.

EXE$FORK then transfers control to the return address its invoker specified, sometimes in its invoker but more often in the code that entered its invoker. This form of return is known as "returning to caller's caller." That form of return enables device driver code to appear as a sequential flow when in fact, for example, some of it executes as part of a device interrupt service routine and some of it executes as a fork process.

The instructions in EXE$FORK that perform these functions are listed in Example 4.1.

When IPL drops, the fork dispatching interrupt will be granted and serviced on the CPU on which it was requested. The fork process will execute on that CPU as well.

4.2.1.4 **Dispatching a Fork Process.** When a fork interrupt is granted, the VAX processor dispatches to its interrupt service routine. Each fork IPL has a unique interrupt service routine that performs setup for common fork dispatching code. The fork interrupt service routine saves R6 and R7. It stores the offset of the corresponding fork queue listhead in R6. It then branches to the common fork dispatching code. The interrupt service routines for IPLs 6 and

Example 4.1
EXE$FORK Routine Extract

```
EXE$FORK::                                  ;Create fork process
        MOVQ    R3,FKB$L_FR3(R5)            ;Save registers R3 and R4
        POPL    FKB$L_FPC(R5)              ;Get fork process PC
        MOVZBL  FKB$B_FLCK(R5),R4         ;Get fork lock/fork IPL
        BBC     #5,R4,5$                   ;Branch if direct IPL
        MOVL    G^SMP$AL_IPLVEC[R4],R4     ;Get fork IPL from spinlock
                                           ; database
5$:     FIND_CPU_DATA R3                    ;Get base of CPU data area
        MOVAQ   CPU$Q_SWIQFL-<6*8>(R3)[R4],R3
                                           ;Get address of fork queue
        INSQUE  (R5),@4(R3)                ;Insert fork block in fork queue
        BNEQ    10$                        ;If queue already populated,
                                           ; avoid extra interrupts
        SOFTINT R4                          ;Request software interrupt
10$:    RSB                                 ;And return
```

Example 4.2
Fork Dispatching Interrupt Service Routine Extract

```
        .ALIGN  LONG                        ;Entry point must be longword
                                            ; aligned
EXE$FRKIPL6DSP::                            ;Fork IPL 6 entry point
        PUSHQ   R6                          ;Save R6 and R7
        CLRL    R6                          ;Get offset to fork queue listhead
        BRB     EXE$FORKDSPTH               ;Branch to common code
          .

          .
        .ALIGN  LONG                        ;Entry point must be longword
                                            ; aligned
EXE$FRKIPL8DSP::                            ;Fork IPL 8 entry point
        PUSHQ   R6                          ;Save R6 and R7
        MOVZBL  #<2*8>,R6                   ;Get offset to fork queue listhead
;
; Drop through to common code
;
EXE$FORKDSPTH::                             ;Software interrupt fork dispatcher
        FIND_CPU_DATA R7,-                  ;Get base of per-CPU database
                ISTACK=YES                  ; from SP
        MOVAB   CPU$Q_SWIQFL(R7)[R6],R6 ;Get address of fork queue listhead
        PUSHL   R5                          ;Save R5 .
        PUSHL   R4                          ;Save R4  .
        PUSHL   R3                          ;Save R3    . PUSHLS are fastest!
        PUSHL   R2                          ;Save R2  .
        PUSHL   R1                          ;Save R1 .
        PUSHL   R0                          ;Save R0.
        BRB     80$                         ;Branch to body of dispatcher
;
; Dispatch a fork block that has no fork lock index, but rather just
; an IPL (an unmodified driver fork block perhaps).
;
10$:    JSB     @FKB$L_FPC(R5)              ;Dispatch fork
        BRB     80$                         ;Branch to get next fork block
;
; Dispatch fork process when queue is not yet empty
; Dispatch fork process with:
;       R0 through R2 = scratch registers
;       R3 and R4 = restored from fork block
;       R5 = address of fork block
20$:    MOVQ    FKB$L_FR3(R5),R3            ;Restore registers R3 and R4
        MOVZBL  FKB$B_FLCK(R5),R7           ;Get fork lock number/FIPL
        BBC     #5,R7,10$                   ;Branch if FIPL
        FORKLOCK LOCK=R7,-                  ;Acquire the spinlock
                PRESERVE=NO                 ;Don't preserve R0
        JSB     @FKB$L_FPC(R5)              ;Dispatch fork
        FORKUNLOCK LOCK=R7,-               ;Release the spinlock
                PRESERVE=NO                 ;Don't preserve R0
```

(continued)

Example 4.2 *(continued)*
Fork Dispatching Interrupt Service Routine Extract

```
80$:    REMQUE   @(R6),R5              ;Remove next entry from fork queue
        BNEQ     20$                  ;Branch if queue not yet empty
        BVS      90$                  ;If VS no entry removed
                                      ;Here when last entry dequeued
;
; Dispatch last entry in the queue
;
        MOVQ     FKB$L_FR3(R5),R3     ;Restore registers R3 and R4
        MOVZBL   FKB$B_FLCK(R5),R7    ;Get fork lock number
        BBC      #5,R7,100$           ;Branch if FIPL
        FORKLOCK LOCK=R7,-            ;Acquire the spinlock
                 PRESERVE=NO          ;Don't preserve R0
        JSB      @FKB$L_FPC(R5)       ;Dispatch fork
        FORKUNLOCK LOCK=R7,-          ;Release the spinlock
                 PRESERVE=NO          ;Don't preserve R0
90$:    MOVQ     (SP)+,R0             ;Restore registers
        MOVQ     (SP)+,R2             ;       .
        MOVQ     (SP)+,R4             ;       .
        MOVQ     (SP)+,R6             ;       .
        REI                          ;Dismiss interrupt
;
; Dispatch a fork block that has no fork lock index, but rather just
; an IPL (an unmodified driver fork block perhaps).
;
100$:   JSB      @FKB$L_FPC(R5)       ;Dispatch fork
        BRB      90$                  ;Exit
```

8 and the common fork dispatching code, EXE$FORKDSPTH, are listed in Example 4.2. These routines are in module FORKCNTRL.

EXE$FORKDSPTH loads R6 with the address of the fork block queue specified by the sum of R6 and the address of the per-CPU database for this processor. It saves R0 through R5 and removes the first fork block from the queue. It loads R3 and R4 from the fork block. If FKB$B_FLCK contains a spinlock index, EXE$FORKDSPTH acquires that spinlock before dispatching to the fork process. When the fork process returns, EXE$FORKDSPTH releases the spinlock. (It is very important that the fork process itself not release the spinlock before returning; if it does, EXE$FORKDSPTH's attempted release will cause the system to crash.) EXE$FORKDSPTH then removes the next fork block and processes it in the same manner as the first.

The removal and processing continue until the queue is empty, when the dispatcher restores the registers it saved and dismisses the interrupt with an REI instruction. Note that, to improve performance, EXE$FORKDSPTH detects removal of the last entry in the queue and avoids a subsequent fruitless REMQUE by dispatching the last entry in a separate code path.

Since a fork process routine runs on the interrupt stack at an IPL higher than 2, it must be in nonpageable system space; it must not incur page faults, execute change mode instructions, or incur any exceptions that are dispatched to user-defined condition handlers (see Chapter 5). While a fork process is executing, it may use R0 through R5 and, if saved and restored, the other general registers. A fork process may also use the interrupt stack. However, when a fork process returns control to the fork dispatcher, the stack must be in the same state as when the fork process was entered.

4.2.1.5   **Stalling a Fork Process.** A fork process may be stalled for various reasons and may have to wait. When a fork process waits, its context is saved by storing R3, R4, and the PC in the FKB. The FKB is then placed in a queue of FKBs. One example of such a wait is a fork process waiting in the fork dispatcher queue while the system is running at a higher IPL. Another example is a driver fork process that tries to allocate unavailable system resources, such as UNIBUS adapter map registers. The fork process is stalled until another fork process using the same adapter deallocates map registers. The routine called to deallocate map registers restores the context of the waiting fork process so that it can repeat its attempt to allocate map registers. (Note that all fork processes that may stall waiting for a particular resource must use the same fork IPL. On an SMP system, they must also use the same spinlock.)

VMS also implements a "fork and wait" wakeup mechanism so that a fork process can stall itself for a short while and be awakened automatically. To fork and wait, a fork process releases any spinlocks acquired as part of its execution and invokes the macro FORK_WAIT, which generates a call to EXE$FORK_WAIT, in module FORKCNTRL. EXE$FORK_WAIT saves the fork process's context in the fork block. Raising IPL to 31, it then acquires the MEGA spinlock, which serializes access to the systemwide fork and wait queue, and inserts the fork block at the tail of the queue. EXE$FORK_WAIT then releases the MEGA spinlock, restoring the IPL at entry, and returns to its "caller's caller," the return PC left on the stack by the fork process or its invoker.

The base image global EXE$AR_FORK_WAIT_QUEUE contains the address of the queue listhead, which is in the same loadable executive image that contains the module FORKCNTRL.

The fork and wait queue is serviced once every second by the routine EXE$TIMEOUT, in module TIMESCHDL. Thus, on average, the fork process waits for half a second. EXE$TIMEOUT and fork processes stalled in this way run on the primary processor of an SMP system. EXE$TIMEOUT acquires the MEGA spinlock to serialize its access to the fork and wait queue. It copies the queue listhead, initializes the listhead to represent an empty queue, and releases the MEGA spinlock. EXE$TIMEOUT removes each fork block in turn from its copy of the listhead and restores the fork process context. EXE$TIMEOUT tests FKB$B_FLCK and, if it contains a spinlock index, acquires that spinlock. EXE$TIMEOUT then dispatches to the fork process.

When the fork process returns, EXE$TIMEOUT releases the spinlock. When the copied listhead is empty, EXE$TIMEOUT is done servicing the queue and continues with other processing.

Part of the restoration of fork process context involves changing IPL from IPL$_TIMER to the IPL specified by FKB$B_FIPL/FLCK. Because lowering IPL would violate the interrupt nesting scheme, use of the fork and wait mechanism is limited to fork processes with fork IPLs at or above IPL$_TIMER.

The disk and tape class drivers use this mechanism after an unsuccessful attempt to allocate nonpaged pool, assuming that nonpaged pool will become available. When the fork process is reentered, it repeats its attempt to allocate nonpaged pool. In this example, the fork and wait mechanism is used in lieu of nonpaged pool availability reporting, the mechanism used by full processes (see Chapters 12 and 19).

The fork and wait mechanism is also used by the IPL 12 interrupt service routine when it recomputes quorum, following an unsuccessful attempt to send a message to the VAXcluster connection manager (see Section 4.2.7).

Chapter 11 contains further information about EXE$TIMEOUT.

4.2.1.6 **Use of Fork IPLs.** There are five different fork IPLs; three are used by most device drivers supplied as part of VMS:

- IPL 6 is used by the connect-to-interrupt driver and by drivers that support attention ASTs. Chapter 8 describes the reason for IPL 6 fork processing.
- IPL 11 is used by the mailbox driver and MA780 shared multiport memory mailbox driver. The mailbox driver runs at the highest fork IPL so that any driver fork process can write mailbox messages, primarily to the OPCOM process's mailbox.
- IPL 8 is the most commonly used driver fork IPL.

The following considerations affect the choice of fork IPL for any particular driver:

- Higher fork IPLs are serviced first.
- All device drivers on a Q22-bus or UNIBUS competing for resources such as map registers or data paths must use the same fork IPL. In particular, if any such VMS drivers exist, all DMA drivers servicing devices on that bus must use fork IPL 8. Moreover, with VMS Version 5, all such drivers on an SMP system must use a common spinlock, usually the IOLOCK8 spinlock.
- All SCS class and port drivers must use fork IPL 8 and, on an SMP system, the IOLOCK8 spinlock.
- A disk driver must use fork IPL 8 and, on an SMP system, the IOLOCK8 spinlock for clusterwide mount verification synchronization.
- A driver that accesses a systemwide database synchronized at IPL$_SYNCH can do so from fork level if its fork IPL is 8, the value of IPL$_

SYNCH. On an SMP system, there is a further requirement that the driver's spinlock be the same one that synchronizes the database of interest or that it be of lower rank so that the fork process can acquire the needed spinlock.

4.2.2 Software Timer

VMS includes both a hardware clock interrupt service routine and a software timer interrupt service routine. Together these routines service time-dependent requests. Chapter 11 describes these interrupt service routines in detail; this section summarizes some of their interaction.

The hardware interrupt service routine is EXE$HWCLKINT, in module TIMESCHDL. It runs every 10 milliseconds in response to a hardware interval timer interrupt, at IPL 22 or 24, depending on the CPU type. Some of its duties are to update the system time, perform CPU time accounting, check for quantum expiration of the current process, and check whether the first timer queue entry (TQE) has come due.

TQEs describe time-dependent requests usually made through the Schedule Wakeup ($SCHDWK) and Set Timer ($SETIMR) system services. The queue of TQEs is kept ordered by expiration time, with the most imminent first. Quantum-end processing and TQE servicing require lengthier execution than is appropriate at high IPL and require modification to the scheduler database, which is synchronized at IPL$_SCHED. For these reasons, if the current process has run out of quantum or if the first TQE has come due, EXE$HWCLKINT requests an IPL$_TIMERFORK (IPL 7) interrupt.

The IPL$_TIMERFORK interrupt service routine, EXE$SWTIMINT in module TIMESCHDL, checks whether the current process's quantum has expired. If so, EXE$SWTIMINT acquires the SCHED spinlock, raising IPL to IPL$_SCHED. It invokes the routine that performs quantum-end processing and then releases the SCHED spinlock, lowering IPL to IPL$_TIMERFORK.

EXE$SWTIMINT then checks whether it is running on the primary CPU of an SMP system (or the only CPU of a uniprocessor). If it is not, it dismisses the interrupt. Only the primary processor services the timer queue.

If this is the primary processor, EXE$SWTIMINT acquires the TIMER and HWCLK spinlocks to synchronize its access to the queue of TQEs and, in particular, the first TQE. It removes the first TQE if its expiration time is the same as or earlier than the current system time. It releases the two spinlocks, lowering IPL to IPL$_TIMER (IPL 8). EXE$SWTIMINT then processes the TQE.

It reacquires the two spinlocks and checks the TQE that is now first in the queue. EXE$SWTIMINT continues in this manner until it reaches a TQE that has not yet expired. It then releases the two spinlocks and executes an REI instruction, dismissing the interrupt and leaving unexpired TQEs in the queue.

4.2.3 I/O Postprocessing

When a device driver has completed an I/O request, it transfers to a routine that places the IRP associated with the request at the tail of the I/O post-processing queue. If the queue was empty, it requests a software interrupt at IPL$_IOPOST (IPL 4).

In earlier versions of VMS, there was one I/O postprocessing queue. In VMS Version 5, most IRPs are queued to one systemwide I/O postprocessing queue. The I/O postprocessing interrupt service routine, running on a uniprocessor or on the primary processor of an SMP system, services this queue. An IRP for a request completed in process context (that is, by a driver's preprocessing function decision table action routine) is typically queued to a postprocessing queue in the per-CPU database. Each CPU services its own per-CPU queue. See Chapters 22 and 34 for further details.

Example 4.3, a slightly simplified extract from routine IOC$REQCOM, in module IOSUBNPAG, shows the insertion of an IRP onto the systemwide queue.

The I/O postprocessing interrupt software routine, IOC$IOPOST in module IOCIOPOST, runs on each member of an SMP system. Running on the primary processor or on a uniprocessor, it removes each IRP in turn from the beginning of the systemwide queue and processes it. The details of the processing vary with the type of IRP. For example, IOC$IOPOST distinguishes between VMS buffered and direct I/O requests. When a direct I/O request completes, IOC$IOPOST unlocks the buffer pages from memory. When a buffered output request completes, IOC$IOPOST deallocates the buffer to

Example 4.3
IOC$REQCOM Routine Extract

```
IOC$REQCOM::
            .
            .

        $INSQTI (R3),G^IOC$GQ_POSTIQ     ;Insert IRP on IOPOST list
        BNEQ    49$                      ;Branch if queue is not empty
        FIND_CPU_DATA   R0               ;Get address of per-CPU data
        CMPL    G^SMP$GL_PRIMID,CPU$L_PHY_CPUID(R0)
                                         ;Are we the primary?
        BNEQ    46$                      ;Branch if not primary
        SOFTINT S^#IPL$_IOPOST           ;Request IOPOST interrupt
        BRB     49$                      ;Continue
; This is not the primary CPU on an SMP system, so request an
; interprocessor interrupt of the primary for it to request an
; IPL 4 interrupt.
46$:    IPINT_CPU IOPOST,G^SMP$GL_PRIMID ;Request interprocessor
                                         ; interrupt
49$:    .
            .
```

nonpaged pool and returns process byte count quota. Chapter 21 contains further information about I/O postprocessing.

IOC$IOPOST also performs I/O postprocessing of memory management requests, as described in Chapter 16.

IOC$IOPOST, running on a uniprocessor or any member of an SMP system, then services the per-CPU I/O postprocessing queue for that processor. After it processes all IRPs in the queue, it dismisses the interrupt with an REI instruction. Example 4.4, a slightly simplified extract from module IOCIOPOST, shows this sequence.

4.2.4 Rescheduling Interrupt

The executive requests a rescheduling interrupt at IPL 3 whenever a resident process that can preempt the current process becomes computable. (Although this statement is true for a uniprocessor system, it is a simplification of what happens on an SMP system. See Chapter 12 for further details.)

The IPL 3 interrupt service routine, SCH$RESCHED in module SCHED, removes the current process from execution. It begins execution at IPL 3 on the kernel stack of the current process. It immediately acquires the SCHED spinlock, raising IPL to IPL$_SCHED, and executes a SVPCTX instruction,

Example 4.4
IOC$IOPOST Interrupt Service Routine Extract

```
IOC$IOPOST::                               ;IOPOST interrupt
        MOVQ    R4,-(SP)                   ;Save
        MOVQ    R2,-(SP)                   ; normal
        MOVQ    R0,-(SP)                   ; registers (R0-R5)
IOPOST:
        FIND_CPU_DATA R1,ISTACK=YES        ;Get address of per-CPU database
        CMPL    CPU$L_PHY_CPUID(R1),G^SMP$GL_PRIMID
                                           ;Are we the primary?
        BNEQ    5$
        TSTL    G^IOC$GQ_POSTIQ            ;Is systemwide queue empty?
        BEQL    5$                         ;Branch if yes, service per-CPU
                                           ; queue
        $REMQHI G^IOC$GQ_POSTIQ,R5         ;Remove next packet
        BVC     60$                        ;Branch if got one
5$:     REMQUE  @CPU$L_PSFL(R1),R5         ;Remove next packet
        BVC     60$                        ;Branch if got one
        MOVQ    (SP)+,R0                   ;Restore
        MOVQ    (SP)+,R2                   ; registers
        MOVQ    (SP)+,R4                   ; and exit
        REI                                ; if queue empty
60$:    .                                  ;Postprocess this
                                           ; I/O request packet
        .
        BRW     IOPOST                     ;Get next I/O request packet
```

saving the context of the current process and switching to the interrupt stack.

The rescheduling interrupt service routine then selects the highest priority resident computable process and places it into execution. (On an SMP system, selecting the next process to execute is somewhat more complex.)

Many of the events that make a process computable occur as part of servicing software interrupts between IPL 4 and IPL$_SCHED. That the scheduler database is modified from these software interrupts implies the following:

- SCH$RESCHED must raise IPL to IPL$_SCHED and acquire the SCHED spinlock to block any other accesses to the scheduler database while it takes one process out of execution and selects another one to run.
- The IPL 3 interrupt may be requested a number of times before it is granted. The number of times the interrupt has been requested is irrelevant, since the interrupt service routine always has the same task to do.
- When the IPL 3 interrupt is granted, all events that might affect the choice of which process to run have been serviced. That is, the higher priority software interrupt service routines that affect the scheduler database have completed all their work. Thus, SCH$RESCHED can make the best possible choice at the time it blocks further alterations to the database.

Chapter 12 discusses the scheduler database, events that affect the scheduler database, the rescheduling interrupt, and the additional complexities of scheduling in an SMP system.

4.2.5 AST Delivery Interrupt

The AST delivery interrupt means that there is an AST for the current process to execute. This interrupt is unique: it is the only software interrupt requested by microcode and the only one that runs entirely in process context.

An AST is a mechanism for signaling an asynchronous event to a process. A designated AST routine runs in the context of the process at a specified access mode. Some ASTs are requested by the process, for example, as notification of I/O request completion. Some ASTs are queued to the process by VMS as part of normal system operations, such as automatic working set limit adjustment.

Chapter 7 describes the details of AST delivery.

4.2.6 XDELTA IPL 14 Interrupt Service Routine

XDELTA, the executive debugger, can optionally be made memory-resident at system initialization. If XDELTA is resident, the SCB vectors for breakpoint and T-bit exceptions contain addresses of service routines within XDELTA. XDELTA remains quiescent, transferring control to the usual exception service routines for breakpoint and T-bit exceptions, until a breakpoint (BPT) instruction in XDELTA's breakpoint table is executed. Initially, the only such breakpoint is at global location INI$BRK.

When such a breakpoint instruction is executed, XDELTA accepts command input from the CPU console terminal. These commands can include setting other breakpoints, setting single-step mode, and examining system space. Often programmers debugging kernel mode code, such as a device driver, insert a JSB instruction to INI$BRK in their code to activate XDELTA. The *VMS Delta/XDelta Utility Manual* provides further information about XDELTA (and DELTA) commands.

VMS provides the IPL 14 software interrupt service routine to enable a person to activate XDELTA at will by depositing a 14 in the software interrupt request register at the CPU console terminal. The interrupt service routine to activate XDELTA is INI$MASTERWAKE, in module SYSTEM_ROUTINES. The code of this interrupt service routine follows:

```
        .ALIGN  LONG
INI$MASTERWAKE:
        JSB     INI$BRK
        REI
```

However XDELTA is activated, it raises IPL and executes at IPL 31. Chapter 34 describes some of the complexities of XDELTA's operation in an SMP system.

When XDELTA is not resident, the instruction at INI$BRK is a NOP rather than a BPT. Thus, a system without XDELTA reacts gracefully to an XDELTA interrupt or a JSB to INI$BRK.

4.2.7   IPL 12 Interrupt Service Routine

The IPL 12 interrupt is similar to the XDELTA interrupt; it is only requested by a person depositing 12 into the software interrupt request register at the CPU console terminal. The IPL 12 interrupt service routine, EXE$IPCONTROL in module IPCONTROL, facilitates certain types of human intervention when the system might otherwise have to be crashed.

When the IPL 12 interrupt request is granted, the interrupt service routine temporarily disables SMP sanity and spinlock wait timeouts (see Chapter 34) so that operations below IPL 12 can be stalled on this CPU without adverse consequences. It then prompts on the console for human input with the following text: IPC>. (IPC is a shortened form of IPL C, where C_{16} is 12.) The IPL 12 interrupt service routine accepts the following commands:

Command	Meaning
C *ddcu:*	Cancel mount verification in progress
Q	Recalculate quorum for the VAXcluster
X	Activate XDELTA (if it is resident)
CTRL/Z	Return the system to normal operation

The C command is issued with a device specification to cancel mount verification on the specified disk or tape. Mount verification is a mechanism that enables the system to recover gracefully from certain kinds of transient device failures, by stalling I/O requests to a device while it is offline or inaccessible. If the device comes back on line, the system confirms that this is the same device as was previously mounted and resumes normal I/O processing on the volume. If SYSGEN parameter MVTIMEOUT seconds elapse before a disk comes back on line, mount verification times out and the system aborts I/O requests in progress to that disk. For a tape, the SYSGEN parameter TAPE_MVTIMEOUT specifies the length of the mount verification timeout period.

While a device is in a state of mount verification in progress, all users' I/O requests to it are stalled until the mount verification times out or the device comes back on line. An impatient user can type CTRL/C or CTRL/Y and STOP to abort the image and cancel its I/O requests. However, the user cannot cancel any I/O request the Files-11 XQP may have made on the user's behalf, and subsequent file system activity in the process will be blocked until mount verification times out or is canceled.

Therefore, if the device failure is known to be permanent, it may be appropriate to cancel mount verification before the mount verification timeout period has elapsed. In most cases, the DISMOUNT/ABORT command is the preferred way to cancel mount verification. (See the *VMS DCL Dictionary* for further information on this command.) However, if the state of the system prevents that command from being entered, the C command to the IPL 12 interrupt service routine may be used instead.

For additional information on mount verification, see the *Guide to Maintaining a VMS System*.

In response to a Q command, EXE$IPCONTROL requests the VAXcluster system connection manager to recalculate dynamic quorum based on the current cluster configuration. The Q command can be issued when a VAXcluster system hangs because of quorum loss, after a node crashes and fails to reboot. Running as an IPL 12 interrupt service routine, EXE$IPCONTROL cannot acquire the SCS spinlock to synchronize its access to the connection manager. The IPL associated with the SCS spinlock is IPL$_SCS, or IPL 8. EXE$IPCONTROL therefore creates an IPL 8 fork process whose fork lock is the SCS spinlock. See Section 4.2.1 for details about fork processing.

The fork process calls a connection manager routine to recompute quorum. If any error occurs, the fork process issues a fork and wait request (see

Section 4.2.1.5), retrying its call whenever it is reentered. Once the call to the routine is successful, the fork process exits.

In response to an X command, EXE$IPCONTROL invokes INI$BRK to activate XDELTA, as described in Section 4.2.6. Note, however, now that XDELTA can be activated through an IPL 14 interrupt, activation through the lower priority IPL 12 interrupt is less commonly used.

In response to CTRL/Z, EXE$IPCONTROL restores the previous state of the SMP sanity and spinlock wait timeouts and exits, dismissing the IPL 12 interrupt with an REI instruction.

5   Condition Handling

> "Would you tell me, please, which way I ought to go from here?"
> "That depends a good deal on where you want to get to," said
> the Cat.
>
> Lewis Carroll, *Alice's Adventures in Wonderland*

The VAX architecture defines a generalized uniform condition handling facility for two classes of conditions:

- Conditions detected and generated by the CPU, called exceptions
- Conditions detected and generated by software, called software conditions

The VMS operating system provides this facility for users and also uses the facility for its own purposes.

This chapter describes how VMS dispatches on exceptions and software conditions to user-specified procedures called condition handlers. It also briefly describes how VMS services exceptions that it handles itself.

5.1   OVERVIEW

An exception is the CPU's response to an anomaly or error it encounters while executing an instruction, for example, a divisor of zero in a DIVL instruction. In response, the CPU usually changes access mode to kernel. It pushes the exception program counter (PC), processor status longword (PSL), and any exception-specific parameters onto the stack on which the exception is to be serviced. It changes the flow of instruction execution to an exception service routine pointed to by an error-specific longword vector in the system control block (SCB). Chapter 2 describes the CPU exception mechanism in more detail.

The VAX architecture defines approximately 20 different exceptions, each with its own SCB vector. The VMS executive defines a unique exception service routine for each. VMS distinguishes two categories of exceptions:

- Those that the VMS executive always handles itself
- Those that may be handled by user-specified procedures

The VMS executive always handles

- Inner access mode exceptions indicating fatal software or hardware errors (for example, machine checks or bugchecks)
- Exceptions used in the course of normal system operations (for example, page faults and CHMK exceptions)

Section 5.4.1 summarizes their servicing.

VMS allows all other exceptions to be handled by a user-specified procedure called a condition handler. Section 5.4.2 summarizes their servicing. Section 5.3 describes how a process establishes condition handlers.

The other type of condition is a software condition, an error or anomaly detected by software, typically application software rather than operating system software, and treated like an exception. The software converts the error to a software condition by calling one of two Run-Time Library procedures. It calls LIB$SIGNAL when the image can continue; if the error is severe and the image should be aborted, it calls LIB$STOP. Each of these routines initiates the same condition handler search used for exceptions. Section 5.5 describes software conditions in more detail.

The primary differences between exceptions and software conditions are the mechanisms that generate them and the initial state of the stack that contains the condition parameters.

VMS treats exceptions and software conditions uniformly by using the same mechanisms to locate their condition handlers and pass information to them.

When a condition occurs, VMS searches for a condition handler. It calls any it finds with an argument list that includes a code describing the condition type, called a signal or signal name, and any condition-specific parameters. The argument list is known as a signal array.

A condition handler is established for a specific access mode. The search for a condition handler encompasses only those handlers that were established in the access mode at which the condition occurred.

The condition handler examines its arguments to decide which of three actions to take. The handler can fix the condition (continuing). If the handler cannot fix the condition, it can pass the condition on to the next handler in the calling hierarchy (resignaling) or it can alter the flow of control (unwinding the call stack). Section 5.8 describes these actions and the executive's response to them.

VMS establishes default condition handlers for each mode. If the search fails to locate any user-established condition handlers, or if all such condition handlers resignal, it invokes the appropriate default handler.

5.2 FEATURES OF THE CONDITION HANDLING FACILITY

The condition handling facility encompasses the declaration of a condition handler, the search for a condition handler, and the responses available to a condition handler. The condition handling facility provides that software conditions be directed to the same condition handlers as exceptions. Thus, application software can centralize its handling of errors, both hardware and software.

The *Introduction to VMS System Services* and the *VMS Run-Time Library Routines Volume* describe the declaration and coding of condition handlers.

The major goal of the condition handling facility is to provide an easy-to-use, general-purpose mechanism for handling errors. Application software and layered products can use this mechanism rather than inventing application-specific tools. Features of the condition handling facility in support of this goal include the following:

- The condition handling mechanism is available as part of the VAX architecture; space is reserved for a condition handler address in the first longword of each call frame.
- Condition handling can be an integral part of a procedure, a processwide facility, or both.

  Each procedure can establish its own condition handler. This enables condition handlers to be nested with the procedures that establish them. A nested inner handler can either service a detected exception or pass it along to some outer handler established by an earlier procedure.

  A condition handler is not called to service exceptions incurred by its own execution. Thus, a handler need not be written in a reentrant language and need not try to deal with its own errors. However, because a condition handler is itself a procedure, it can establish its own condition handler to field errors that it might cause.

- There is no cost to a procedure that does not establish a handler and minimal cost to one that does.

  Overhead is minimized by using only a single longword per procedure activation for storing the address of a handler. Establishing a handler can be as simple as executing a single MOVAx instruction. No time is spent looking for a condition handler until a condition actually occurs.

- As far as the user or application programmer is concerned, there is no difference in the handling of exceptions and software conditions.
- Some languages, such as BASIC and PL/I, specify signaling and error handling as part of the language. The general mechanism supports their needs.

  Because condition handling is part of a procedure, software written in a high-level language can establish a handler that examines its arguments to determine whether the signal was generated as a part of that language's support library. If so, the handler can attempt to fix the error in the manner defined by the language. If not, the handler can resignal the error.

5.3   ESTABLISHING A CONDITION HANDLER

There are two different methods for establishing a condition handler:

- One method uses the stack associated with each access mode. Each procedure call frame includes a longword that contains the address of the condition handler associated with that procedure.
- The other method uses software vectors in P1 space. Each access mode has its own software vectors. Vectored handlers do not possess the modular

properties associated with call frame handlers and are intended primarily for debuggers and performance monitors.

5.3.1 Establishing a Call Frame Condition Handler

A call frame handler is established by placing its address in the first longword of the currently active call frame. The following VAX MACRO instruction establishes a call frame condition handler:

```
MOVAB   new_handler,(FP)
```

The following VAX MACRO instruction removes a condition handler by clearing the first longword of the current call frame:

```
CLRL    (FP)
```

Because direct access to the call frame is usually not available from a high-level language, VMS provides the Run-Time Library procedures LIB$ESTABLISH to establish a handler and LIB$REVERT to remove one.

5.3.2 Establishing a Software-Vectored Condition Handler

There are three types of software-vectored condition handlers. They differ primarily in the order in which they are called during the search for a condition handler:

- First, the primary vector handler
- Second, the secondary vector handler
- Last, after all call frame condition handlers, the last chance handler

One of each of these handlers can be established for each access mode.

An array at CTL$AQ_EXCVEC, indexed by access mode, identifies the process's primary and secondary vector condition handlers. The first longword in each quadword contains zero or the address of a primary vector condition handler for that mode. The second longword contains zero or the address of a secondary vector condition handler. An array at CTL$AL_FINALEXC, also indexed by access mode, contains the addresses of the last chance condition handlers.

By default, VMS provides no primary or secondary vector handlers. It establishes the kernel, executive, and user mode last chance handlers described in Section 5.7.

An image requests the Set Exception Vector ($SETEXV) system service to establish or remove a software-vectored condition handler. The *VMS System Services Reference Manual* provides further information.

The system service has four arguments, all of which are optional:

- The VECTOR argument identifies the type of handler. If omitted or if the value is zero, the handler is the primary vector handler.
- The ADDRES argument contains the address of a handler. If omitted or if the address is zero, the existing handler is to be removed.

- The ACMODE argument specifies the access mode of the handler. If omitted, its default value is the mode from which the service was requested. If present, the less privileged of the requesting mode and ACMODE is used, preventing a process from declaring a handler for a more privileged mode.
- The PRVHND argument specifies the address of a longword to receive the address of the previously established handler.

The $SETEXV system service procedure, EXE$SETEXV in module SYS-SETEXV, runs in kernel mode. It determines the access mode of the handler and the type of handler to be established, and stores the address of the specified handler (or a longword containing zero) in the specified software vector.

User mode software-vectored condition handlers are automatically removed at image rundown, when the address space that contains them is being deleted. All others must be explicitly removed.

5.4   EXCEPTIONS

Table 5.1 lists the exceptions defined by the VAX architecture. VMS services most of them by preparing for the execution of a condition handler. Section 5.4.2 describes some of these preparations.

In addition, the VMS executive signals some errors it detects while running

Table 5.1   Exception Vectors in the System Control Block

Vector Offset	Exception Name	Extra Parameters	Type
4_{16}	Machine check [1]	0	Abort/Fault
8_{16}	Kernel stack not valid [1]	0	Abort
10_{16}	Reserved/privileged instruction [1]	0	Fault
14_{16}	Customer reserved instruction	0	Fault
18_{16}	Reserved operand	0	Abort/Fault
$1C_{16}$	Reserved addressing mode	0	Fault
20_{16}	Access violation	2	Fault
24_{16}	Translation not valid [1]	2	Fault
28_{16}	Trace pending	0	Fault
$2C_{16}$	BPT instruction	0	Fault
30_{16}	Compatibility mode	1	Abort/Fault
34_{16}	Arithmetic	1	Fault/Trap
40_{16}	CHMK [1]	1	Trap
44_{16}	CHME [1]	1	Trap
48_{16}	CHMS	1	Trap
$4C_{16}$	CHMU	1	Trap
$C8_{16}$	Subset instruction emulation [1]	10	Trap
CC_{16}	Suspended instruction emulation [1]	0	Trap

[1] These exceptions result in special action on the part of the operating system.

in inner access modes through the exception mechanism so that they can be dispatched to outer mode condition handlers.

Those exceptions that VMS services itself are discussed briefly in the next section.

5.4.1 **Exceptions Handled by the VMS Executive**

VMS itself services the CHME and CHMK exceptions to provide controlled paths into inner access mode code. These exception service routines, known as the change mode dispatchers, transfer control to Record Management Services (RMS) and system services, as described in Chapter 6.

VMS services several other exceptions for which only operating system action is appropriate.

The translation-not-valid exception means that a reference was made to a virtual address that is not currently mapped to physical memory. This exception is the entry path into the VMS paging facility. Its service routine, the page fault handler, is described in detail in Chapter 16.

A machine check exception is a processor-specific condition that may or may not be recoverable. A machine check is initially serviced on the interrupt stack at IPL 31. The exception service routine generates a fatal bugcheck in response to a nonrecoverable kernel or executive mode machine check. It reports a nonrecoverable machine check that occurred in supervisor or user mode through the normal exception dispatch method. Chapter 32 discusses the machine check exception service routine and the bugcheck mechanism.

A kernel-stack-not-valid exception indicates that the kernel stack was not valid when the processor tried to push information onto it during the initiation of an exception or interrupt. This exception is serviced on the interrupt stack at IPL 31. Its exception service routine generates a fatal KRNLSTAKNV bugcheck.

Not all types of VAX processors implement the entire VAX instruction set. For example, not all processors implement all types of floating-point operands, and not all processors implement all string and decimal instructions. VMS provides emulation for VAX instructions not implemented in CPU microcode.

VMS implements two different kinds of instruction emulation, using two different techniques. One, based on the reserved/privileged instruction exception, is available on all CPUs. On a CPU that requires floating-point instruction emulation, VMS alters the SCB vector for the reserved/privileged instruction vector to execute floating-point emulation code prior to the normal service routine for this exception. The floating-point emulation code checks the opcode of each instruction that incurs the exception, emulates those with appropriate opcodes, and passes all others on to the normal service routine.

The other technique is available only on certain VAX processor types. These CPUs assist in the emulation of unimplemented string and decimal instructions by providing two special VAX subset instruction emulation exceptions. These processors include the MicroVAX II, MicroVAX 3x00, and VAX 6000 series systems. When the microcode of such a processor encounters a string or decimal opcode not present in its instruction set, it evaluates the operands and pushes exception parameters onto the current stack describing the opcode and its operands. The processor sets the first part done bit in the PSL. It then dispatches through SCB vector $C8_{16}$ to the service routine VAX$EMULATE, in module [EMULAT]VAXEMULAT, without changing access mode.

While the emulation of the instruction is in progress, another exception, such as a page fault, can occur. After the page fault is satisfied and the exception dismissed, the emulated instruction is reexecuted. Finding the first part done bit set, the processor generates a "suspended" emulation exception through SCB vector CC_{16}. The second emulation vector dispatches back into the instruction emulation code at VAX$EMULATE_FPD, in module [EMULAT]VAXEMULAT.

For more details on these exceptions, see the *VAX Architecture Reference Manual*.

5.4.2 Exceptions Passed to a Condition Handler

Apart from the exceptions described in Section 5.4.1, VMS passes exceptions to condition handlers. The service routines for these exceptions are in module EXCEPTION. Each performs approximately the same actions in preparing for the execution of a condition handler. Table 5.2 lists the exceptions that VMS handles in this uniform way and the exception-specific information in their signal arrays.

Figure 5.1 shows the major steps in the flow from such an exception up to the routine that searches for a condition handler. The column headings in the figure describe the environment of each step, for example, its access mode and interrupt priority level (IPL). The numbers in the figure correspond to the steps in the following list.

Prior to the start of this flow, responding to the exception, the CPU has pushed onto the stack the exception PC, PSL, and any exception-specific parameters, and dispatched to the exception service routine.

①Each exception service routine pushes onto the stack a signal name, a status value of the form SS$_*signal-name.*

②Each pushes the total number of exception parameters (from the signal name to the saved PSL inclusive). The stack now contains the signal array (see Figure 5.2). It begins with the signal name and ends with the exception PC and PSL and may contain exception-specific arguments in between.

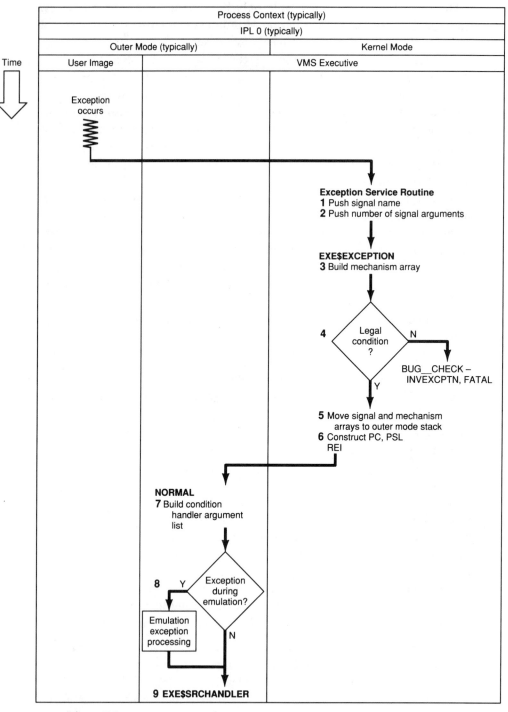

Figure 5.1
Flow from an Exception to EXE$SRCHANDLER

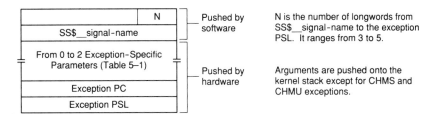

Figure 5.2
Signal Array Built by CPU and Exception Service
Routine

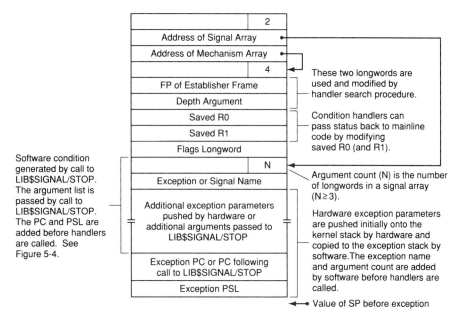

Figure 5.3
Signal and Mechanism Arrays

After an exception service routine has completed the signal array, it jumps to EXE$EXCEPTION, in module EXCEPTION.

③ EXE$EXCEPTION builds a second argument list, called a mechanism array, which serves the following purposes:

—It records the values of R0 and R1 at the time of the exception (the procedure calling standard prohibits their being saved in a procedure entry mask).

—It records the progress made in the search for a condition handler.

Figure 5.3 shows the layout of the mechanism array. Section 5.6 describes its use during the search for a condition handler.

④ EXE$EXCEPTION tests whether the exception should be dispatched to a condition handler (see Section 5.7.3.1). If not, EXE$EXCEPTION generates a fatal INVEXCPTN bugcheck.

⑤ Most exceptions that VMS passes on to a condition handler are initially serviced on the kernel stack. However, an exception must be signaled to the access mode in which it occurred. EXE$EXCEPTION checks that there is space on the stack of that mode, copies the signal and mechanism arrays to the target stack, and removes them from the stack on which the exception was serviced.

⑥ It constructs a PC/PSL pair and executes an REI instruction to transfer control to the local routine NORMAL in the access mode that incurred the exception.

⑦ NORMAL builds the condition handler argument list (see Figure 5.3), which contains the addresses of the signal and mechanism arrays.

⑧ NORMAL examines location EXE$GL_VAXEXCVEC. If it contains zero, NORMAL continues with the next step. Otherwise, NORMAL dispatches to the specified address. On a processor that provides assistance for instruction emulation, EXE$GL_VAXEXCVEC contains the address of routine VAX$MODIFY_EXCEPTION, in module [EMULAT]VAXHANDLR. This routine takes special action for an exception that occurs in the course of instruction emulation (see Section 5.4.3). For any other type of exception, it returns to NORMAL.

⑨ NORMAL then transfers control to EXE$SRCHANDLER, in module EXCEPTION, which locates any condition handlers that have been established for the access mode of the exception.

Section 5.6 describes the search for and dispatch to a condition handler.

5.4.3 Special Cases in Condition Dispatching

The sequence previously described omits some special cases that occur in the dispatching of several conditions. Most of these special cases involve the conditions listed in Table 5.2.

Several of these are detected by executive software rather than hardware. Rather than signal them through LIB$SIGNAL or LIB$STOP, the executive transfers control to condition-specific routines in module EXCEPTION, which build a signal array and dispatch to EXE$EXCEPTION or EXE$RE-FLECT, in module EXCEPTION. These conditions are typically detected in an inner mode but must be signaled to the mode associated with the condition. LIB$SIGNAL and LIB$STOP are unsuitable because they cannot perform the required access mode switch.

The following list summarizes the flow for such an error. Parts of it are congruent with the flow described in more detail in Section 5.4.2. At the start of this flow, an executive routine has detected an error and pushed onto the stack an exception PC, PSL, error-specific information, and the rest of the signal array.

Table 5.2   Exceptions Passed to a Condition Handler

Exception Type	Signal Name	Notes [1]	Signal Array Size	Extra Parameters in Signal Array
Access violation	SS$_ACCVIO	1, 3d	5	Reason mask, Faulting virtual address
Arithmetic	(See Table 5.3)	2	3	None [2]
AST delivery stack fault	SS$_ASTFLT	3c	7	SP value at fault, AST parameter, PC at AST interrupt, [3] PSL at AST interrupt, Address of AST procedure, PSL for AST procedure
Breakpoint	SS$_BREAK		3	None
Change mode to supervisor	SS$_CMODSUPR	4	4	Change mode operand
Change mode to user	SS$_CMODUSER	4	4	Change mode operand
Compatibility mode	SS$_COMPAT	4	4	Compatibility exception code
Debug signal	SS$_DEBUG	3e	3	None
Machine check	SS$_MCHECK		3	None [4]
Customer reserved instruction	SS$_OPCCUS		3	None
Reserved or privileged instruction	SS$_OPCDEC	5	3	None
Page fault read error	SS$_PAGRDERR	3b	5	Reason mask, Faulting virtual address
Reserved addressing mode	SS$_RADRMOD		3	None
Reserved operand	SS$_ROPRAND		3	None
System service failure	SS$_SSFAIL	3a	4	System service final status
Trace pending	SS$_TBIT		3	None

[1] These numbers refer to list items in Section 5.4.3.

[2] The arithmetic exception has no extra parameters, despite the fact that the CPU pushes an exception code onto the kernel stack. VMS converts this code into an exception-specific signal name (see Table 5.3) of the form 8 ∗ code + SS$_ARTRES.

[3] The AST delivery code exchanges the interrupt PC/PSL pair and the PC/PSL to which the AST would have been delivered.

[4] A machine check exception reported to a process does not have any extra parameters in the signal array. The machine check parameters have been examined, written to the error log, and discarded by the machine check exception service routine, as described in Chapter 32.

1. If the executive routine itself always runs in kernel mode, it jumps to EXE$EXCEPTION, which builds a mechanism array and continues with step 4. Otherwise, it jumps to EXE$REFLECT.
2. EXE$REFLECT builds a mechanism array. It checks whether it is running in kernel mode and, if so, continues with step 4.
3. Otherwise, EXE$REFLECT checks that there is space for the signal and mechanism arrays on the target stack using the Adjust Outer Mode Stack Pointer ($ADJSTK) system service. It merges with EXE$EXCEPTION, at step 5.
4. EXE$EXCEPTION tests whether the exception should be dispatched to a condition handler (see Section 5.7.3.1). If not, it generates a fatal IN-VEXCPTN bugcheck.
5. EXE$EXCEPTION moves the signal and mechanism arrays to the target stack.
6. It executes an REI instruction to transfer control to NORMAL, which builds the condition handler argument list.
7. NORMAL dispatches into VAX$MODIFY_EXCEPTION if the exception occurred during instruction emulation.
8. NORMAL transfers to EXE$SRCHANDLER to locate and dispatch to a condition handler.

The following list describes each of the special cases in Table 5.2. Its numbers correspond to the notes in that table.

1. User stack overflow is detected by the hardware as an access violation at the low-address end of P1 space. The access violation exception service routine tests whether the inaccessible virtual address is at the low end of P1 space. If it is, additional virtual address space is created below the stack and the exception dismissed. Thus, a user stack expands automatically and transparently. A condition handler is notified about such an exception only if the stack expansion is unsuccessful.
2. Ten types of arithmetic exceptions can occur. The CPU dispatches them all through the same SCB vector but uniquely identifies them through a code in the exception-specific parameters. The arithmetic exception service routine translates the code into a unique signal name. Table 5.3 lists these signal names and their codes.
3. The following conditions are detected by executive software:

    a. The system service failure (SS$_SSFAIL) condition is reported when a process has enabled signaling of system service failures through the Set System Service Failure Mode ($SETSFM) system service and a system or RMS service returns unsuccessfully with an error or severe error status. The change mode dispatchers detect such errors. They push information about the error onto the stack of the service

execution and transfer control to EXE$SSFAIL, in module EXCEP-
TION (see Chapter 6). EXE$SSFAIL completes the signal array and
jumps to EXE$REFLECT.

b. The page fault read error (SS$_PAGRDERR) condition is reported
   when a process incurs a page fault for a page on which a read error occurred during a previous fault for the same page. Information
   about the page fault that led to the condition is already on the
   stack. The translation-not-valid service routine transfers control to
   EXE$PAGRDERR, in module EXCEPTION. EXE$PAGRDERR completes the signal array and jumps to EXE$EXCEPTION.

c. The SS$_ASTFLT condition is reported when the asynchronous sys-
   tem trap (AST) delivery interrupt service routine detects an inaccessible stack while attempting to deliver an AST to a process. The AST
   delivery interrupt service routine pushes information about the error onto the kernel stack and transfers control to EXE$ASTFLT, in
   module EXCEPTION (see Chapter 7).

   EXE$ASTFLT completes the signal array. EXE$ASTFLT is entered
   with current and previous modes both kernel, since it runs as part
   of an interrupt service routine. The exception handling mechanism

Table 5.3 Signal Names for Arithmetic Exceptions

Exception Type	Code Pushed by CPU	Resulting Signal Name
TRAPS		
Integer overflow [1]	1	SS$_INTOVF
Integer divide by zero	2	SS$_INTDIV
Floating overflow [2]	3	SS$_FLTOVF
Floating/Decimal divide by zero [2]	4	SS$_FLTDIV
Floating underflow [2,3]	5	SS$_FLTUND
Decimal overflow [1]	6	SS$_DECOVF
Subscript range	7	SS$_SUBRNG
FAULTS		
Floating overflow	8	SS$_FLTOVF_F
Floating divide by zero	9	SS$_FLTDIV_F
Floating underflow	10	SS$_FLTUND_F

[1] Integer overflow enable and decimal overflow enable bits in the processor
status word (PSW) can be altered either directly or through the procedure
entry mask.

[2] The three floating-point traps can only occur on VAX-11/780 processors
earlier than microcode revision (rev) level 7.

[3] The floating underflow enable bit in the PSW can only be altered directly.
There is no corresponding bit in the procedure entry mask.

presumes that the previous mode is the mode of the exception. EXE$ASTFLT therefore executes an REI instruction with a PC and PSL constructed to transfer to EXE$EXCEPTION with the previous mode set to that of the AST.

d. Most access violations are exceptions detected by the CPU. In addition, however, the translation-not-valid exception service routine can signal an access violation. If it detects a process faulting a page in the process header of another process, then it transfers to EXE$ACVIO-LAT, in module EXCEPTION, the access violation exception service routine. Information about the error is already on the current stack. This is an unusual error, typically the result of a software failure in executive or kernel mode code.

e. The signal SS$_DEBUG is generated by either the Digital command language (DCL) or monitor console routine (MCR) command language interpreter (CLI) in response to a DEBUG command entered while an image exists in an interrupted state. The DEBUG command processor pushes the PC and PSL of the interrupted image, the signal name SS$_DEBUG, and the size of the signal array onto the supervisor stack and jumps to EXE$REFLECT.

A CLI uses this mechanism for the DEBUG signal, rather than simply calling LIB$SIGNAL, because the DEBUG command is processed by supervisor mode code but the condition has to be reported back to user mode.

4. The exception dispatching for the CHMS and CHMU exceptions and compatibility mode exceptions can be short-circuited by use of the Declare Change Mode or Compatibility Mode Handler ($DCLCMH) system service. The $DCLCMH system service enables a user to establish a per-process change-mode-to-supervisor, change-mode-to-user, or compatibility mode handler. This service stores the address of the handler in CTLGL_CMSUPR, CTLGL_CMUSER, or CTL$GL_COMPAT in the P1 pointer page.

The exception service routine for CHMS exceptions, EXE$CMOD-SUPR in module EXCEPTION, pushes the signal name onto the stack and determines in what mode the exception occurred. If it occurred in kernel or executive mode, EXE$CMODSUPR completes the signal array and jumps to EXE$REFLECT. If the exception occurred in user or supervisor mode but the process has declared no change-mode-to-supervisor handler, EXE$CMODSUPR also completes the signal array and jumps to EXE$REFLECT.

Otherwise, EXE$CMODSUPR removes the signal name from the stack and transfers control to the declared handler with the stack in the same state in which it was following the exception. That is, the change mode operand is at the top of the stack, followed by the exception PC and PSL.

The exception service routine for CHMU exceptions, EXE$CMOD-USER in module EXCEPTION, behaves similarly. For it to transfer to a declared change-mode-to-user handler, the exception must have occurred in user mode.

The DCL CLI requests the $DCLCMH service to establish a CHMS handler. Its handler is briefly described in Chapter 27. The job controller uses a CHMU handler for its processing of error messages. The Files-11 Extended QIO Processor (XQP), running in kernel mode, signals an error to its outermost procedure by executing a CHMU instruction from kernel mode.

The exception service routine for compatibility mode exceptions transfers control to the user-declared compatibility mode handler (if one was declared) with the user stack in the same state in which it was before the compatibility mode exception occurred. That is, no parameters are passed to the compatibility mode handler on the user stack. Instead, the service routine saves the compatibility mode code, exception PC and PSL, and contents of R0 through R6 in the first ten longwords of the compatibility mode context page, at location CTL$AL_CMCNTX.

5. The reserved instruction fault is generated whenever an unrecognized opcode is detected by the instruction decoder.

VMS uses this fault as a path into bugcheck processing. The reserved instruction exception service routine tests whether the reserved opcode is either $FEFF_{16}$ or $FDFF_{16}$. These two opcodes are reserved for the operating system to signal that it has detected a serious inconsistency in system behavior or data. If the opcode is one of these, the reserved instruction exception service routine jumps to the bugcheck routine, which is described in Chapter 32.

Another special case in exception dispatching is the handling of an exception in the middle of instruction emulation, itself an exception. When an exception occurs on a processor with subset instruction emulation, routine VAX$MODIFY_EXCEPTION (see Section 5.4.2) is invoked. If the exception occurred in the course of emulating an instruction, VAX$MODIFY_EXCEPTION transforms that exception into one incurred by the emulated instruction; it changes the exception PC to be that of the emulated instruction and rearranges the stack to remove any data pushed onto it during instruction emulation. It invokes EXE$EMULAT_REFLECT, in module EXCEPTION, to signal the exception as one incurred by the emulated instruction. Unlike EXE$REFLECT, EXE$EMULAT_REFLECT has no need to alter access mode; the dispatching that led to VAX$MODIFY_EXCEPTION has already restored the mode of the emulated instruction.

5.5 SOFTWARE CONDITIONS

One of the choices in the design of a modular procedure is the method for reporting exceptional conditions back to the caller. There are two common methods: returning a status in R0, and signaling the error by calling one of the Run-Time Library procedures LIB$SIGNAL or LIB$STOP.

There are two reasons why signaling may be preferable to returning status. In some procedures, such as the mathematics procedures in the Run-Time Library, R0 is already used for returning a function value and is unavailable for error return status. The procedure must therefore use the signaling mechanism to indicate exceptional conditions, such as an attempt to take the square root of a negative number.

A second common use of signaling occurs in an application using an indeterminate number of procedure calls to perform some action, such as a recursive procedure that parses a command line. In such a case, the use of a return status is often cumbersome and difficult to code. The signaling mechanism provides a graceful way not only to indicate that an error has occurred but also to return control (through the $UNWIND system service) to a known alternative return point in the calling hierarchy.

A procedure calls LIB$SIGNAL or LIB$STOP with the name of the condition to be signaled and whatever additional parameters are to be passed to a condition handler. LIB$STOP is an alternative entry point to LIB$SIGNAL. (This chapter refers to the combined procedures as LIB$SIGNAL/STOP.)

LIB$SIGNAL and LIB$STOP differ in whether normal execution may be resumed after the condition handler for the signaled error returns. Use of LIB$SIGNAL enables the image to continue if the condition handler returns the status SS$_CONTINUE. Use of LIB$STOP does not. The two entry points store different values in the stack flags longword, which is tested by the code to which a condition handler returns.

Before LIB$SIGNAL/STOP can initiate the search for a condition handler, it must transform the stack to one resembling an exception stack. LIB$SIGNAL/STOP constructs a signal array and removes the frame generated by the call to itself. If LIB$SIGNAL/STOP was entered with a CALLS instruction, it must also move the argument list onto the stack. It restores the saved argument pointer (AP) and frame pointer (FP). LIB$SIGNAL/STOP moves other information, such as the saved PC and processor status word (PSW) to a signal array it constructs on the stack. The signal array also incorporates any arguments from the call to LIB$SIGNAL/STOP. Figure 5.4 shows the transformed state of the stack following a call to LIB$SIGNAL/STOP.

LIB$SIGNAL/STOP next builds a mechanism array, saving R0 and R1 in it, and a condition handler argument list. After building the three argument lists, LIB$SIGNAL/STOP invokes the same condition handler search code as exception handling. It jumps to SYS$SRCHANDLER, a system service vector that contains a jump to EXE$SRCHANDLER. The indirection supplies the Run-Time Library with a constant address through which to dispatch to EXE$SRCHANDLER.

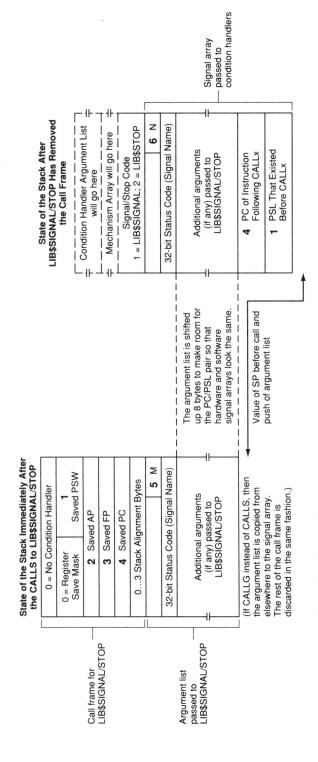

Figure 5.4
Transformation of Stack by LIB$SIGNAL/STOP

The search for condition handlers takes place on the stack of the caller of LIB$SIGNAL/STOP.

5.6 UNIFORM CONDITION DISPATCHING

Once information concerning the condition has been pushed onto the stack, there are few differences between exceptions and software conditions. The following sections discuss condition dispatching in general terms and explicitly mention EXE$EXCEPTION or LIB$SIGNAL/STOP only where their operations differ.

5.6.1 The Search for a Condition Handler

At this point in the dispatch sequence, the signal and mechanism arrays and the condition handler argument list have been set up on the stack of the access mode to which the condition will be reported. EXE$SRCHANDLER uses the mechanism array longword initially containing the FP of the establisher frame (see Figure 5.3) to record the extent of the search. The depth argument in the mechanism array not only provides useful information to a condition handler that unwinds but also enables EXE$SRCHANDLER to distinguish a call frame handler (non-negative depth) from a software-vectored condition handler (negative depth).

5.6.1.1 Primary and Secondary Exception Vectors. EXE$SRCHANDLER begins its search with the primary vector of the access mode in which the exception occurred. If the vector contains the address of a condition handler (any nonzero contents), EXE$SRCHANDLER sets the depth at -2 and calls the handler.

The primary handler (and any other condition handler) can return several status codes. One status code, SS$_RESIGNAL, known as a resignal, means that EXE$SRCHANDLER should continue its search for a condition handler. Resignaling and other condition handler responses are described in Section 5.8.

If the primary handler resignals or if none exists, EXE$SRCHANDLER performs the same step for the secondary vector handler, with the depth at -1. If the secondary handler resignals or there is none, EXE$SRCHANDLER next looks for call frame condition handlers.

5.6.1.2 Call Frame Condition Handlers. EXE$SRCHANDLER examines the contents of the current call frame. If the first longword in the current call frame is nonzero, EXE$SRCHANDLER calls that handler with the depth at 0. If the longword is zero or if that handler resignals, EXE$SRCHANDLER examines the next earlier call frame by using the saved frame pointer in the current call frame (see Figure 5.5). As it examines each earlier call frame, it increments

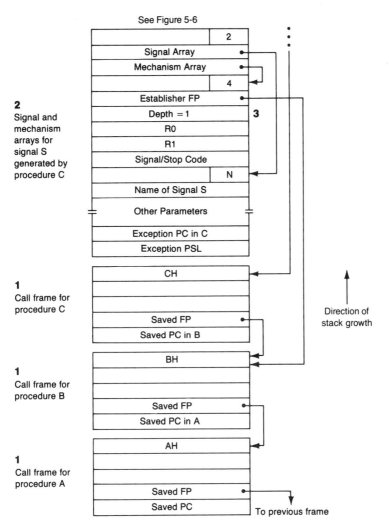

Figure 5.5
Order of Search for Condition Handler

the depth to record the number of frames examined and places that frame's address in the frame pointer of the mechanism array.

EXE$SRCHANDLER continues the search until one of the following occurs:

- A handler returns a status requesting the resumption of the thread of execution that incurred the exception.
- EXE$SRCHANDLER finds a saved frame pointer whose value is not within the bounds of that access mode's stack.

A saved frame pointer value may be out of range as a result of stack corruption. A saved frame pointer value of zero indicates the end of the call frame chain.

- EXE$SRCHANDLER reaches the end of the call frame chain.

A saved frame pointer that points outside the stack terminates the call frame chain. The end of an inner access mode call frame chain can also be indicated by either a change mode dispatcher call frame, described in Chapter 6, or an AST delivery call frame, described in Chapter 7. Either indicates that an access mode change occurred.

If a handler returns a status code with the low bit set, EXE$SRCHANDLER cleans off the stack, restores R0 and R1 from the mechanism array, and executes an REI instruction using the saved PC and PSL from the signal array. This resumes the thread of execution that incurred the exception. Note that EXE$SRCHANDLER passes control back with an REI instruction, even if the condition was caused by a call to LIB$SIGNAL/STOP. LIB$SIGNAL/STOP discarded the frame resulting from its call, so that the stack resembles an exception stack (see Figure 5.4).

5.6.1.3   **Last Chance Condition Handler.** If all handlers resignal or none is found, the search terminates at the end of the call frame chain. EXE$SRCHANDLER then calls the last chance handler with the depth at −3. (This handler is also called if any error occurs during the search for a condition handler.) The usual last chance handler is the catch-all condition handler established as part of image initiation. Section 5.7.2 describes this handler.

If the last chance handler returns or there is none, and the exception occurred in user or supervisor mode, EXE$SRCHANDLER calls the executive procedure EXE$EXCMSG (see Chapter 36). Its two input parameters are an ASCII string containing message text and the condition handler argument list. Following the call to EXE$EXCMSG, EXE$SRCHANDLER requests the Exit ($EXIT) system service with a status indicating either that no handler was found or that a bad stack was detected while searching for a condition handler.

If the exception occurred in executive or kernel mode, EXE$SRCHAN-DLER generates a FATALEXCPT bugcheck, nonfatal for executive mode or fatal for kernel mode.

5.6.2   **Multiple Active Signals**

An exception in a condition handler or in some procedure called by a condition handler results in a condition called multiple active signals. To avoid an infinite loop of exceptions, EXE$SRCHANDLER modifies its search algorithm so that when it services the second condition, it skips those frames it searched while servicing the first condition.

For this skipping to work correctly, call frames of condition handlers must be distinguishable from other call frames. VMS arranges this by calling all handlers from a known location, so that the saved PC of a condition handler call frame is unique.

5.6.2.1   **Common Call Site for Condition Handlers.** In order to dispatch to a handler, EXE$SRCHANDLER stores the address of the handler in R1 and transfers to the common call site with the following instruction:

```
JSB     @#SYS$CALL_HANDL
```

The code at SYS$CALL_HANDL simply calls the procedure whose address is stored in R1 and returns to its invoker with an RSB:

```
SYS$CALL_HANDL::
        CALLG   4(SP),(R1)
        RSB
```

When the CALLG instruction is executed, the address of the next instruction, SYS$CALL_HANDL + 4, is recorded in the call frame as the saved PC. Thus, the identifying characteristic of a condition handler call frame is the address SYS$CALL_HANDL + 4 as the saved PC. This signature is used not only by the search procedure, as described in the following section, but also by the Unwind Call Stack ($UNWIND) system service.

5.6.2.2   **Example of Multiple Active Signals.** The modified flow of control when the search procedure encounters a condition handler call frame can best be illustrated through an example. The example assumes that the primary and secondary condition handlers (if they exist) have already resignaled. The numbers in Figures 5.5 and 5.6 correspond to the following steps:

① Procedure A calls procedure B, which calls procedure C.
② Procedure C generates signal S.
③ Handler CH resignals. The depth argument is 1, and the establisher frame argument points to the call frame for procedure B, when BH is called. Figure 5.5 shows the stack at this point.
④ The call frame for handler BH is located later in time on the stack, at lower virtual addresses than the signal and mechanism arrays for signal S (see Figure 5.6). The saved frame pointer in the call frame for BH points to the frame for procedure C.
⑤ Handler BH now calls procedure X, which calls procedure Y.
⑥ Procedure Y generates signal T. The desired sequence of frames to be examined is frame Y, frame X, frame BH, and then frame A. Frames B and C are skipped because they were examined while servicing condition S.
⑦ EXE$SRCHANDLER proceeds in its normal fashion. The primary and secondary vectors are examined first (no skipping here). Then frames Y, X, and BH are examined, resulting in handlers YH, XH, and BHH being called in turn. Assume that all these handlers resignal. After handler BHH returns to EXE$SRCHANDLER with a status of SS$_RESIGNAL,

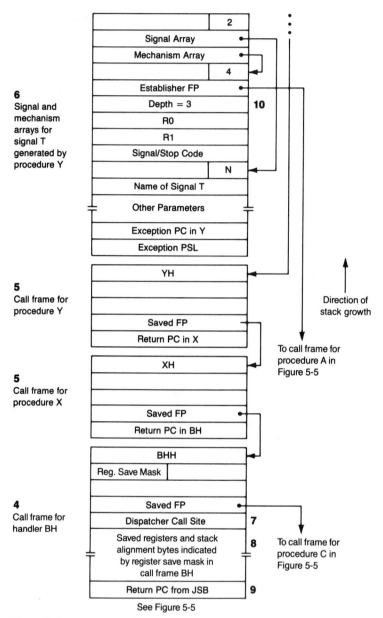

Figure 5.6
Modified Search with Multiple Active Signals

EXE$SRCHANDLER notes that frame BH is the frame of a condition handler, because its saved PC is SYS$CALL_HANDL + 4.

(8) The skipping is accomplished by locating the frame that established this handler. The address of that frame is located in the mechanism array for signal S.

To locate the mechanism array for signal S, EXE$SRCHANDLER cal-
culates the value of SP before the call to BH, using the register save mask
and stack alignment bits in the call frame.

⑨ One extra longword, the return PC from the JSB to SYS$CALL_HANDL,
must be skipped to locate the argument list (and thus the mechanism
array) for signal S.

⑩ The frame pointed to by the establisher frame pointer in the mechanism
array, which is the call frame for B, has already been searched. The next
frame examined by the search procedure is the call frame of A, which is
pointed to by the saved frame pointer in the call frame of B. The depths
that are passed to handlers as a result of the modified search are 0 for
YH, 1 for XH, 2 for BHH, and 3 for AH. Figure 5.6 shows the stack at the
point where handler AH has been located.

5.7 DEFAULT (VMS-SUPPLIED) CONDITION HANDLERS

The use of condition handlers is general and can be specified by the user.
However, some actions always occur as the result of default condition handlers that are established by the executive as a part of process creation or
image activation.

The discussions of process creation in Chapter 25 and image activation in
Chapter 26 point out exactly when and how each of the handlers described
in this section is established. The action of each of these handlers, once they
are invoked, is briefly described in the following sections.

5.7.1 Traceback Handler Established by Image Startup

When an image includes either the debugger or the traceback handler, another frame is put on the user stack before the image itself is called (see
Chapter 26). EXE$IMGSTA, in module SYSIMGSTA, the code that executes
before the image is called, stores the address of its own condition handler in
this frame so that it will be entered for any subsequent condition that is not
handled by an intervening condition handler.

This handler first checks whether the condition that occurred is SS$_
DEBUG. If so, it maps the debugger into P0 space (if not already mapped)
and passes control to it. The condition SS$_DEBUG is signaled by a CLI in
response to a DEBUG command. This feature allows an image that was not
linked or run with debugger support to be interrupted and have a debugger
invoked.

For all other conditions, if the severity level is warning, error, or severe
error, the handler maps the traceback facility above the end of defined P0
space and passes control to it. The traceback facility passes information
about the exception to SYS$OUTPUT and terminates the image.

If the severity level is other than the three listed, the traceback condition
handler resignals the condition, which usually means that the condition is
being passed on to the catch-all condition handler.

5.7.2   Catch-All Condition Handler

The address of this handler, EXE$CATCH_ALL, is placed in an initial call frame on the user stack and in the last chance vector for user mode by either EXE$PROCSTRT when the process is created or by a CLI before an image is called. This handler is always called if no other handlers exist or if all other handlers resignal. Because the address of the handler is duplicated in the last chance vector, it is also called in the event of an error in the search through the user stack.

The first step that EXE$CATCH_ALL takes is to call SYS$PUTMSG (see Chapter 36). If the handler was called through the last chance vector (the depth argument in the mechanism array is -3) or if the severity level of the condition name in the signal array indicates severe (condition-name ⟨2:0⟩ GEQU 4), then EXE$EXCMSG (see Chapter 36) is called to print a summary message, and the image is terminated; otherwise, the image is continued.

5.7.3   Handlers Used by Other Access Modes

In addition to the handlers that VMS supplies for user mode conditions, it sets up handlers for the other three access modes.

5.7.3.1   Exceptions in Kernel or Executive Mode.

When a kernel mode exception occurs, EXE$EXCEPTION makes special checks to determine whether it should dispatch the exception. It checks that

- The processor was running on the kernel stack
- IPL was at or below 2
- The P1 page containing the limits of the process's stacks is accessible (in fact, that the process has a typical P1 space)

If any of these is not true, the dispatcher generates a fatal INVEXCPTN bugcheck. Routines whose exceptions can cause this bugcheck include interrupt service routines, device drivers (except for their function decision table action routines), process-based code executing above IPL 2 (such as portions of various system services), and any code running in the context of the swapper process.

If all of these are true, then exception dispatching proceeds in its usual manner. If no primary, secondary, or call frame condition handlers service the exception, the dispatcher invokes the last chance condition handler.

The last chance exception vectors for both kernel and executive modes are initialized at process creation in module SHELL (see Chapter 25).

The kernel mode last chance handler, EXE$EXCPTN, in module SYSTEM_ROUTINES, generates a fatal SSRVEXCEPT bugcheck. Routines whose exceptions can result in this bugcheck include portions of many system services, many exception service routines, device driver function decision table action routines, and procedures that are entered through a user-written system service dispatcher or the Change to Kernel Mode ($CMKRNL) system service.

The executive mode last chance handler, EXE$EXCPTNE, in module SYSTEM_ROUTINES, generates a nonfatal SSRVEXCEPT bugcheck, causing an error to be logged, and exits the image from executive mode, causing the process to be deleted. Routines that execute in executive mode include RMS, parts of the executive, and procedures that are entered through either a user-written system service dispatcher or the Change to Executive Mode ($CMEXEC) system service. Note that if the SYSGEN parameter BUGCHECKFATAL is 1, a nonfatal SSRVEXCEPT bugcheck is treated as a fatal bugcheck and results in a crash.

Chapter 32 describes bugcheck processing in detail.

5.7.3.2 **Condition Handler Used by DCL or MCR.** The DCL and MCR CLIs establish nearly identical condition handlers at the beginning of their command loops to field conditions that occur in supervisor mode.

The LOGINOUT image activates a CLI (DCL or MCR) and calls it. The first step of the CLI is to establish a supervisor mode condition handler to handle its own internal errors. It establishes this handler as a call frame condition handler in the oldest call frame on the supervisor mode stack. The condition handler performs two tasks when it is called:

1. It cancels any exit handlers that have been established.
2. It resignals the error.

There are no other condition handlers. When the search ends, the image is exited in supervisor mode, resulting in process deletion.

5.8 **CONDITION HANDLER ACTION**

A condition handler first determines the nature of the condition by examining the signal name argument in the signal array (see Figure 5.2). It then decides what action to take:

- It can pass the condition along to another handler by resignaling.
- It can fix the condition and allow execution to continue at the point in the program that incurred the exception.
- It can also allow execution to resume at a previous place in the calling hierarchy by removing a number of call frames from the stack, a process called unwinding.

5.8.1 Resignal or Continue

If a condition handler cannot deal with the type of condition signaled, it returns the status SS$_RESIGNAL to inform EXE$SRCHANDLER that the search for a handler must continue. A condition handler, like any other procedure, returns a status in R0.

If, however, a condition handler can resolve the condition, it returns the status SS$_CONTINUE to EXE$SRCHANDLER. This status means that the thread of execution that incurred the condition can continue.

When EXE$SRCHANDLER receives the status SS$_CONTINUE, it first checks if this was a condition signaled through LIB$STOP. If so, normal execution cannot continue, and EXE$SRCHANDLER calls the last chance handler, if it has not already been called, and proceeds with the action described in Section 5.6.1.3.

If the condition was not signaled through LIB$STOP, EXE$SRCHANDLER removes the condition handler argument list and mechanism array from the stack, restoring R0 and R1 in the process. It then removes from the stack all of the signal array except the condition PC and PSL. Finally, it removes these by executing an REI instruction to dismiss the exception and to return to the thread of execution that incurred the condition.

Where control returns depends on what sort of condition occurred:

- If the condition was a fault type of exception (such as an access violation), control returns to the instruction that caused the exception.
- If the condition was a trap type of exception (such as integer overflow), control returns to the instruction following the instruction that caused the exception.
- If the condition was an abort type of exception, control returns to the instruction that caused the exception. Because an abort represents an instruction that could neither be completed nor rolled back, it would be ill-advised for a handler to continue from one.
- If the condition was a software condition, which is signaled by a call to LIB$SIGNAL, control returns to the instruction following the CALLx instruction.

5.8.2 Unwinding Call Frames from the Stack

A condition handler's third option is to alter the flow of control by requesting the $UNWIND system service. Through this service, the handler returns control to a previous level in the calling hierarchy by throwing away, or unwinding, a number of call frames.

The $UNWIND system service has two arguments, both of which are optional:

- The DEPADR argument specifies the number of frames to be removed from the call stack. If it is omitted, its default is for all the call frames to be unwound from the frame that incurred the condition up to and including the frame whose condition handler is executing.

- The NEWPC argument specifies the address to which control should be returned after the unwind is complete. If it is omitted, its default is for control to return to the PC saved in the call frame next outermost to the unwound ones.

The $UNWIND system service procedure, EXE$UNWIND in module SYS-UNWIND, runs in the mode from which it is called. It uses two local routines, STARTUNWIND and LOOPUNWIND. EXE$UNWIND does not actually remove frames from the stack. Rather, it replaces the saved PC in the specified number of frames so that STARTUNWIND or LOOPUNWIND will be entered when each unwound procedure executes a RET instruction. If the NEWPC argument was present, EXE$UNWIND replaces the saved PC in the call frame just earlier than the unwound ones (at higher addresses) with the specified value.

Figure 5.7 shows an example of the effects of the $UNWIND system service.

As each procedure executes a RET instruction, the registers saved in its call frame are restored and control is passed to LOOPUNWIND. If the current frame has an associated call frame condition handler, LOOPUNWIND signals it with the condition name SS$_UNWIND so that it can perform procedure-specific cleanup. When the condition handler returns, LOOPUN-WIND executes a RET instruction on behalf of the procedure to discard the current call frame. (If a handler called in this way requests the $UNWIND system service rather than returning, the $UNWIND system service returns the error status SS$_UNWINDING to indicate that an unwind is already in progress.)

This sequence continues until the specified number of call frames have been discarded. The technique of calling handlers as a part of the unwind sequence enables a handler that previously resignaled a condition to re-gain control and perform procedure-specific cleanup and also ensures correct restoration of registers saved within each call frame.

5.8.3   Example of Unwinding the Call Stack

Figure 5.7 illustrates an example of an unwind sequence. The example begins with the sequence pictured in Figure 5.5. Procedure A calls procedure B, which calls procedure C. Procedure C generates signal S. The primary and secondary handlers (if they exist) simply resignal. Handlers CH and BH also resignal.

Finally, handler AH is called. To unwind the call stack back to its estab-lisher frame, AH requests the $UNWIND system service with the DEPADR

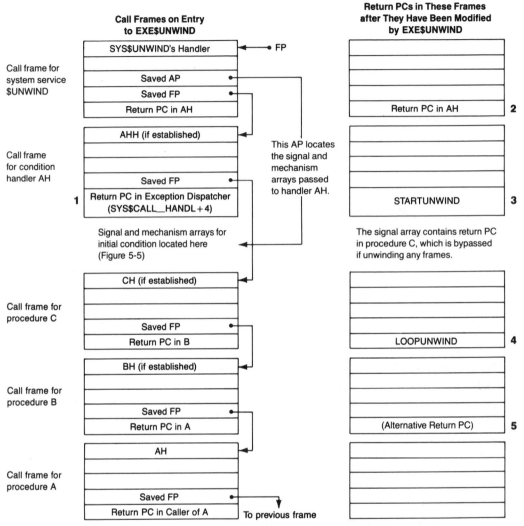

Figure 5.7
Call Frame Modification by EXE$UNWIND

argument equal to the value contained in the mechanism array, in this example, 2. After the call to $UNWIND, but before the frame modification occurs, the stack has the form pictured on the left-hand side of Figure 5.7.

EXE$UNWIND's frame modification proceeds as follows (the numbers in this list correspond to the numbers in Figure 5.7):

① EXE$UNWIND scans the stack for a condition handler call frame. Recall that a condition handler call frame is identified by a saved PC of SYS$CALL_HANDL + 4.

② EXE$UNWIND does not modify its own frame. Later, when it executes a RET instruction, control will return to handler AH.

③ The first frame EXE$UNWIND modifies is that of the first condition handler it encounters scanning the stack, the frame for AH. EXE$UN-WIND replaces its saved PC with the address of STARTUNWIND.

When handler AH later executes a RET instruction, control returns to STARTUNWIND rather than to SYS$CALL_HANDL and EXE$SRC-HANDLER. Consequently, control does not return to procedure C, which incurred the exception. Its return PC is stored in the mechanism array and could only be restored by an REI instruction.

④ EXE$UNWIND continues to modify the saved PC longword in successive frames on the call stack until the number of frames specified (or implied) in its DEPADR argument have been modified. In all frames except the first, it replaces the saved PC with the address of LOOPUNWIND.

⑤ If the NEWPC argument was present, the call frame in which it would be inserted is the next frame beyond the last frame specified (or implied) in the DEPADR argument. In this example, the value of the NEWPC argument would be stored in the call frame for procedure B.

Now that all the frames have been modified, the actual unwinding occurs. The sequence of steps is as follows:

1. EXE$UNWIND returns control to handler AH.
2. Handler AH does whatever else it needs to do to service the condition. When it is done, it executes a RET instruction, passing control to START-UNWIND.
3. STARTUNWIND first restores R0 and R1 from the mechanism array. It then performs the following three steps:
   a. If a handler is established for this frame, STARTUNWIND calls it with the signal name SS$_UNWIND.
   b. If either R0 or R1 is specified in the register save mask, STARTUN-WIND replaces the value of that register in the register save area of the call frame with the current contents of the register. Note that this is rather an unusual case. The procedure calling standard (see *Introduction to VMS System Routines*) specifies that R0 and R1 are to be used to return status codes and function values and that they should not appear in a procedure register save mask.
   c. STARTUNWIND returns control to the address specified by the saved PC longword of the current call frame by executing a RET instruction.
4. The RET executed in step 3c passes control to LOOPUNWIND, which repeats steps 3a through 3c.
5. The RET that discards the call frame for procedure B passes control back to the instruction in procedure A that follows the call to procedure B (assuming the NEWPC argument was omitted), where execution will resume.

In effect, STARTUNWIND and LOOPUNWIND simulate returns from

each nested procedure that is being unwound. These procedures never receive control again. However, the outermost procedure receives control as if all the nested procedures had returned normally.

5.8.4 Potential Infinite Loop

There is one possible problem that can occur with this implementation. The previous section pointed out that EXE$SRCHANDLER takes care (when multiple signals are active) not to search frames for the second condition that were examined on the first pass. If a condition handler generates an exception, it is not called in response to its own signal (unless it establishes itself to handle its own signals!).

However, EXE$UNWIND cannot perform such a check. It must call each condition handler that it encounters as it removes frames from the stack. Thus, a poorly written condition handler (one that generates an exception) could result in an infinite loop of exceptions if a handler higher up in the calling hierarchy unwinds the frame in which this poorly written handler is declared. This loop has no effect on the system beyond that of any compute-bound process but can ruin the process in which the handler executes.

5.8.5 Unwinding Multiple Active Signals

There is a slight change in EXE$UNWIND when multiple signals are active. While modifying saved PCs in call frames, EXE$UNWIND counts the number of frames that have been modified until the requested number has been reached. The only change that occurs with multiple active signals is that the loop stops counting while the skipped frames are being modified.

The example of multiple active signals pictured in Figures 5.5 and 5.6 can be used to illustrate the unwinding. Recall that procedure A called procedure B, which called procedure C, which signaled S. Handler CH resignaled. Handler BH called procedure X, which called procedure Y, which signaled T. Handlers YH, XH, and BHH all resignaled. Finally, handler AH was called for signal T with a depth of 3.

If AH requests the $UNWIND system service, the top of the stack is as pictured in Figure 5.8, with the continuations of this figure in Figure 5.6. Assume that the depth argument passed to $UNWIND is 3 (taken from the mechanism array and meaning unwind to the establisher of AH), and the alternative PC argument is not present.

The end result of the operation of EXE$UNWIND in this case is as follows:

1. EXE$UNWIND looks down the call stack until it locates a condition handler, which in this case is AH. The saved PC is modified to START-UNWIND.

2. The saved PC longwords in frames Y and X are altered to contain address LOOPUNWIND. Note that EXE$UNWIND has now altered three frames.

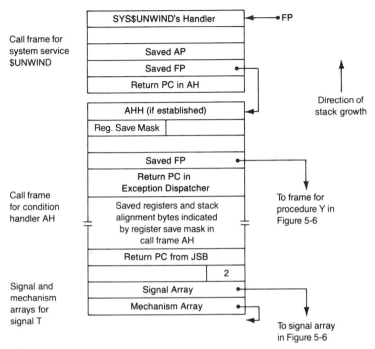

Figure 5.8
Modified Unwind with Multiple Active Signals

3. Because the next frame on the stack, BH, indicates a condition handler (saved PC of SYS$CALL_HANDL + 4), its associated mechanism array is located (by skipping saved registers, stack alignment bytes, and a saved PC from the JSB instruction). The saved PCs in all frames up to the frame pointed to by the mechanism array are modified (but not counted toward the number specified in the argument passed to the $UNWIND system service) to contain address LOOPUNWIND. This modification causes frames BH and C to get their saved PCs altered in the example.

4. The saved PC in the frame for procedure B is not altered, so that when the unwind takes place, control will return to the call site of procedure B in procedure A.

5.8.6   Correct Use of Default Depth in $UNWIND

A default depth argument of 0 to the $UNWIND system service specifies that the stack is to be unwound to the caller of the handler's establisher. In most cases, the caller of the handler's establisher is equivalent to the depth of the handler plus 1. However, because of an inherent ambiguity in counting the stack frames when multiple active signals are present, it is important that the default rather than an explicit depth be used when unwinding to the caller of the establisher.

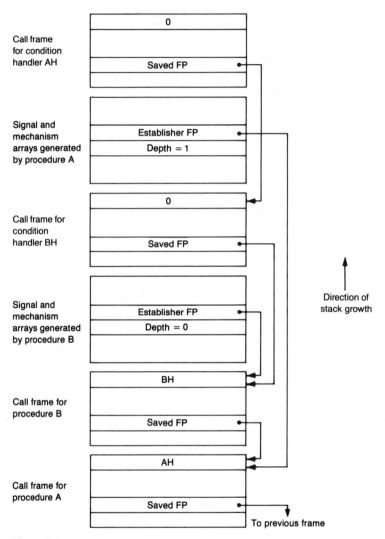

Figure 5.9
Nested Exception, Type 1

Consider the two following cases of nested conditions. In Figure 5.9, procedure A calls procedure B. A condition causes handler BH to be called. An exception within BH causes handler AH to be called (because frame B is skipped, as described in Section 5.6.2). The depth of the mechanism vector in AH's argument list is 1. For AH to unwind to its establisher, it must specify an explicit depth of 1 to the $UNWIND system service. EXE$UNWIND removes one frame, as specified by the count. EXE$UNWIND then notices that the next frame is a handler frame and therefore continues to remove stack frames until it finds the establisher of the handler. This discovery completes the unwind to frame A.

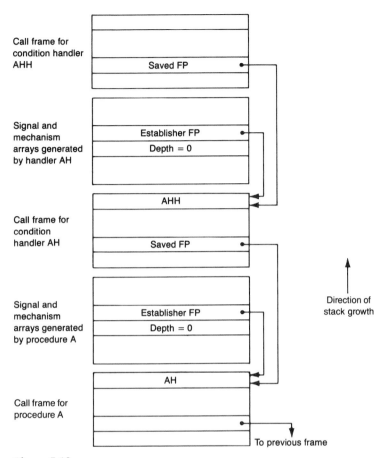

Figure 5.10
Nested Exception, Type 2

Now consider Figure 5.10, in which procedure A incurs an exception, resulting in the invoking of handler AH. Handler AH then causes an exception, causing its handler AHH to be invoked. The depth of AHH is 0. Suppose that AHH wishes to unwind to the caller of its establisher. The establisher of AHH is AH. Since AH is a handler, its caller is the condition dispatcher, *not* procedure A.

Compare Figure 5.10 with Figure 5.9 and consider what happens if AHH requests the $UNWIND system service with an explicit depth of 1 (its depth plus 1). The depth of 1 causes AHH's frame to be removed. EXE$UNWIND then notices that the next frame is a handler frame and therefore unwinds it back to its establisher (frame A). Note that once AHH's frame is removed, the stack is indistinguishable from the stack in Figure 5.9 (down to frame B). Thus, requesting $UNWIND with an explicit depth of 1 results in control being returned to procedure A, which is incorrect.

Therefore, for AHH to unwind to EXE$SRCHANDLER, the caller of its establisher, it must specify a default depth. When this is done, EXE$UN-WIND's behavior upon encountering a handler frame after the count has been exhausted is modified so that the stack is not unwound further, and control passes correctly back to the condition dispatcher.

Because of the inherent ambiguity of these two cases, it is important that handlers always use the default depth when unwinding to the caller of their establisher.

5.8.7 Unwinding ASTs

EXE$UNWIND must perform special processing to unwind out of ASTs. Simply removing the stack frames would ignore the presence of the AST and fail to dismiss the AST properly.

This situation is depicted in Figure 5.11. For handler XH to unwind to the caller of its establisher (procedure A), it must also unwind out of the AST.

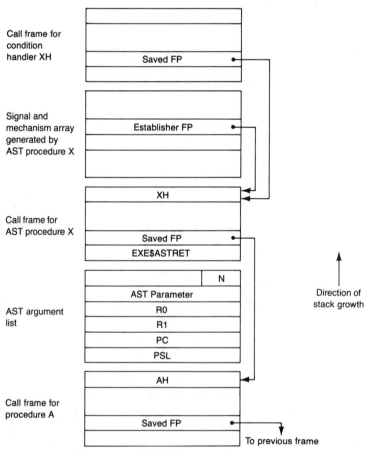

Figure 5.11
Exception During an AST

The problem is solved by having EXE$UNWIND recognize the return PC in an AST call frame, the address EXE$ASTRET. This PC in a call frame implies that the AST argument list immediately precedes the call frame on the stack; that is, the AST argument list is at higher virtual addresses. In this case, EXE$UNWIND stores the unwind PC (STARTUNWIND or LOOPUNWIND) not in the call frame but rather in the return PC of the AST argument list. EXE$UNWIND also stores the current R0 and R1 in the AST argument list so that they will propagate through the unwind process.

When the AST procedure returns during the actual unwinding of the stack, it returns to EXE$ASTRET, which dismisses the AST and executes an REI instruction, using the PC and PSL in the AST argument list. Control passes to STARTUNWIND or LOOPUNWIND because of the modified PC.

While it is technically possible to unwind out of an AST, this must be done with some caution. If the AST procedure has any sort of side effects, it is essential to have a condition handler declared by the AST procedure to clean up the side effects when the AST is unwound. (Note that issuing an I/O operation is a side effect of the highest order!) Cleaning up any procedures of the main line program from which an unwind was executed may be more difficult, because the asynchronous nature of ASTs means that unwinding could take place at any instant during the execution of a program.

6 System Service Dispatching

Between the idea
And the reality
Between the motion
And the act
Falls the Shadow.

T. S. Eliot, *The Hollow Men*

Many of the operations that the VMS operating system performs on behalf of the user are implemented as procedures called system services. Most of these procedures are contained in loadable executive images and reside in system space; others are contained in privileged shareable images. Application programs request system services directly. Components such as Record Management Services (RMS) request system services on behalf of the user. System services typically execute in kernel or executive access mode so that they can read or write data structures protected from access by less privileged access modes.

A system service is requested through a system service vector. The system service vector for an inner access mode system service contains either a CHMK or a CHME instruction whose operand identifies the system service. Executing a CHMK or a CHME causes an exception; the CHMK and CHME exception service routines are called change mode dispatchers. A change mode dispatcher transfers control to the actual procedure that implements the service.

This chapter describes how control is passed from a user program to the procedures that execute service-specific code.

6.1 SYSTEM SERVICE VECTORS

A process requests a particular system service by CALLing a procedure whose name has the form SYS$*service*. SYS$*service* is a system global symbol that is the address of a minimal procedure called a system service vector. The system service vector procedure executes in the mode of the caller and serves as a bridge between the caller and the actual procedure(s) that implement the service request. The actual procedure may be part of a loadable executive image and may execute in an inner access mode. The usual name of the procedure that performs the actual work of the system service is EXE$*service* or RMS$*service*.

6.1.1 Location of System Service Vectors

The address of a system service vector is constant for all versions of VMS so that existing user programs will not have to be relinked for a new version of

VMS. Prior to Version 3 of VMS, system service vectors were only defined in the lowest pages of system address space, beginning at location 80000000_{16}. In Version 3 and subsequent versions, each system service vector can be accessed through two different addresses, a system space address and a P1 space address. The physical pages containing the system service vectors are doubly mapped, both in system space and in the P1 space of each process. The P1 space definitions begin at $7FFEDE00_{16}$ and enable system services to be intercepted on a per-process basis. The linker, by default, resolves a system service vector global to its P1 space value using module SYS$P1_VECTOR in SYS$LIBRARY:STARLET.OLB.

VMS Version 5 reserves 16 pages of virtual address space for system service vectors. The system addresses of the vectors are defined in the base image SYS.EXE, from SYS$S0_VECTOR_BASE to SYS$S0_VECTOR_END. Currently, five pages of that area are occupied, to SYS$S0_VECTOR_LAST_USED.

6.1.2 Contents of System Service Vectors

Each system service vector consists of at least eight bytes of code and data. Many vectors consist solely of a global entry point named SYS$*service*, a register save mask, a single instruction that transfers control eventually to a service-specific procedure in the executive, and an instruction (usually a RET) that passes control back to the caller. Other vectors, called composite vectors, transfer control to multiple procedures.

Most of the system services execute in kernel mode; their system service vectors contain a CHMK instruction. A few system services and all RMS services contain a CHME instruction. Some services, such as the text formatting services, execute in the access mode of the caller and dispatch directly to the service-specific code in the executive with a JMP instruction. Following are the three sets of instructions found in simple system service vectors. Table 6.1 lists the VMS system services that use each of these three methods of initial dispatch.

Vectors for system services that change mode to kernel contain the following code:

```
SYS$service::                          ;Entry point for services that
                                       ; execute in kernel mode
        .WORD   entry-mask             ;Mask at EXE$service, OR'd with
                                       ; R2 and R4
        CHMK    I^#service-specific-code
        RET                            ;Return to caller
        .BLKB   1                      ;Spare byte to make vector
                                       ; eight bytes long
```

Vectors for system services that change mode to executive contain the following code:

107

```
SYS$service::                                   ;Entry point for services that
                                                ; execute in executive mode
        .WORD   entry-mask                      ;Mask at EXE$service, OR'd with
                                                ; R2 and R4
        CHME    I^#service-specific-code
        RET                                     ;Return to caller
        .BLKB   1                               ;Spare byte to make vector
                                                ; eight bytes long
```

Vectors for system services that do not change mode contain the following code:

```
SYS$service::                                   ;Entry point for services that
                                                ; execute in the access mode
                                                ; of the caller
        .WORD   entry-mask                      ;This mask is identical to the
                                                ; mask found at location
                                                ; EXE$service
        JMP     @#EXE$service + 2               ;Transfer control to
                                                ; first instruction after the
                                                ; entry mask at EXE$service
```

Some system services perform their requested function and always return immediately to their caller. Others, called asynchronous system services, initiate some system activity on behalf of the caller and return. To synchronize with completion of the initiated activity, the caller waits for an event flag associated with the system service request to be set. A synchronous service initiates the activity, just as its asynchronous counterpart does, but waits for completion of the activity before returning to its caller.

A synchronous system service is generally named for the asynchronous system service it requests. A trailing "W" in the name of the synchronous service distinguishes the two: $QIO and $QIOW, for example. RMS, however, does not use service names and additional system service vectors to distinguish between the synchronous and asynchronous forms of a service. For example, the RMS service $READ does not have a corresponding $READW form. Instead, the asynchronous or synchronous form of a particular RMS request is specified by the content of the file and record stream data structures.

The mechanism used by synchronous system services to test for and await completion varies. Most non-RMS services use composite system service vectors. RMS services use a special return mechanism.

A composite system service vector first dispatches to an asynchronous system service, which returns when the request is initiated. The code in the vector then branches to another system routine to wait for completion of the asynchronous request.

To guarantee completion of this type of synchronous system service request, the caller must specify both an event flag and a status block (I/O status block or lock status block). The asynchronous service procedure clears the event flag and status block associated with the request. The synchronous system service vector code uses a combination of event flag and status block to test for request completion, placing the process into event flag wait if the request is not complete.

This mechanism prevents a premature return to the synchronous service caller as the result of concurrent uses of the same event flag. (Note, however, that if the caller omits the optional status block, the mechanism reverts to being a simple wait for event flag.) The mechanism is requested explicitly as the Synchronize ($SYNCH) system service and implicitly as part of each synchronous system service. Section 6.3.5.3 gives more information on this mechanism.

Table 6.1 lists the synchronous system services.

The composite system service vector for the synchronous service Queue I/O Request and Wait ($QIOW) follows in a slightly simplified form. Note that its entry mask is the logical OR of the masks of all service procedures to which this composite vector dispatches.

```
SYS$QIOW::
        .WORD   ^M<R2,R3,R4,R5,R6,R7,R8,R9,R10,R11>
        CHMK    I^#QIO
        BLBC    R0,ERROR_QIOW           ;Don't wait if error
                                        ; queuing request
        PUSHL   QIO$_IOSB(AP)           ;Fetch IOSB address
                                        ; if specified
        BRW     QIO_ENQ_SYNCH           ;Branch to QIO_ENQ_SYNCH
                                        ; located in SYNCH system
                                        ; service
ERROR_QIOW:                             ;
        RET                             ;Return if error
```

In earlier versions of VMS, RMS services were implemented with composite vectors similar to the composite vectors previously described. For Version 5, RMS services and the Assign Channel ($ASSIGN) service use a different mechanism; the system service vector requests the asynchronous system service, but control does not return to the code in the vector. Instead, each service has a synchronization routine that conditionally stalls the process until its service request is complete. Section 6.3.5.2 describes this return mechanism in more detail.

6.1.3   Initialization of System Service Vectors

A loadable executive image containing system service procedures invokes the SYSTEM_SERVICE macro for each of them. This macro labels the system service procedure and creates a system service descriptor block that describes the system service: its vector, argument count, return path, synchronization method, access mode, and other characteristics.

At assembly time, each system service vector contains the instruction JMP @#EXE$LOAD_ERROR. EXE$LOAD_ERROR contains a HALT instruction. When a

Table 6.1 System Services and RMS Services That Use Each Form of System Service Vector

The following services execute initially in kernel mode.

$ADJSTK	$DASSGN	$GETPTI	$SETPRA
$ADJWSL	$DCLAST	$GETSECI	$SETPRI
$ALLOC	$DCLCMH	$GETSYI	$SETPRN
$ASCEFC	$DCLEXH	$GETTIM	$SETPRT
$ASSIGN[1]	$DELLNM	$HIBER	$SETPRV
$BRKTHRU	$DELMBX	$LCKPAG	$SETRWM
$CANCEL	$DELPRC	$LKWSET	$SETSFM
$CANEXH	$DELTVA	$MGBLSC	$SETSSF
$CANTIM	$DEQ	$MTACCESS	$SETSTK
$CANWAK	$DERLMB	$PROCESS_SCAN	$SETSWM
$CHKPRO	$DEVICE_SCAN	$PURGWS	$SIGPRC
$CLRAST	$DGBLSC	$QIO	$SNDERR
$CLREF	$DLCEFC	$READEF	$SUSPND
$CMKRNL	$ENQ	$RESCHED	$TRNLNM
$CNTREG	$ERAPAT	$RESUME	$ULKPAG
$CRELNM	$EXIT	$RUNDWN	$ULWSET
$CRELNT	$EXPREG	$SCHDWK	$UPDSEC
$CREMBX	$FORCEX	$SETAST	$WAITFR
$CREPRC	$GETCHN[2]	$SETEF	$WAKE
$CRETVA	$GETDEV[2]	$SETEXV	$WFLAND
$CRMPSC	$GETDVI	$SETIME	$WFLOR
$DACEFC	$GETJPI	$SETIMR	
$DALLOC	$GETLKI	$SETPFM	

The following system services execute initially in executive mode.

$ABORT_RU	$COMMIT_RU	$IDTOASC	$SETUAI[3]
$ADD_HOLDER[3]	$CREATE_RDB[3]	$IMGACT	$SNDACC[2]
$ADD_IDENT[3]	$DISMOU[3]	$MOD_HOLDER[3]	$SNDJBC
$ASCTOID	$FIND_HELD[3]	$MOD_IDENT[3]	$SNDOPR
$CHANGE_ACL[3]	$FIND_HOLDER[3]	$NUMTIM	$SNDSMB[2]
$CHANGE_CLASS[3]	$FINISH_RDB	$PREPARE_RU	$START_RU
$CHECK_ACCESS[3]	$GETQUI	$REM_HOLDER[3]	
$CMEXEC	$GETUAI[3]	$REM_IDENT[3]	

The following system services execute initially in the mode of the caller. Several of them change to a more privileged mode during their execution. Unless otherwise noted, each service can be called from any access mode.

$ASCTIM	$FAO	$IMGFIX	$REVOKID[5]
$BINTIM	$FAOL	$IMGSTA[4]	$TRNLOG[2]
$BRDCST[2]	$FORMAT_ACL[3]	$MOUNT[3,5]	$UNWIND
$CRELOG[2]	$GRANTID[5]	$PARSE_ACL[3]	
$DELLOG[2]	$FORMAT_CLASS[3]	$PARSE_CLASS[3]	
$EXCMSG[5]	$GETMSG[5]	$PUTMSG[4]	

(continued)

Table 6.1   System Services and RMS Services That Use Each Form of System Service Vector *(continued)*

The following RMS services execute in executive mode and transfer control to a synchronization routine before returning to the caller. All use the SYNCH$RMS_STALL routine except $WAIT, which uses SYNCH$RMS_WAIT.

$CLOSE	$EXTEND	$PARSE	$SPACE
$CONNECT	$FIND	$PUT	$TRUNCATE
$CREATE	$FLUSH	$READ	$UPDATE
$DELETE	$FREE	$RELEASE	$WAIT
$DISCONNECT	$GET	$REMOVE	$WRITE
$DISPLAY	$MODIFY	$RENAME	
$ENTER	$NXTVOL	$REWIND	
$ERASE	$OPEN	$SEARCH	

The following RMS services execute in executive mode. They do not require an RMS synchronization routine.

$FILESCAN	$SETDDIR	$SETDFPROT	$SSVEXC
$RMSRUNDWN			

The following synchronous system services use composite vectors. Unless otherwise noted, each service executes initially in kernel mode.

$BRKTHRUW	$GETDVIW	$GETQUIW [7]	$SNDJBCW [7]
$END_RU [7]	$GETJPIW	$GETSYIW	$SYNCH [6]
$ENQW	$GETLKIW	$QIOW	$UPDSECW

[1] This service executes a private synchronization routine.
[2] This service has been superseded.
[3] This service is implemented in a privileged shareable image.
[4] This system service can be called only from supervisor and user modes.
[5] This system service can be called only from executive and less privileged access modes.
[6] This service executes initially in the caller's mode.
[7] This service executes initially in executive mode.

loadable executive image containing a service is loaded, routine EXE$CONNECT_SERVICES, in module SYSTEM_SERVICE_LOADER, uses the system service descriptor block to associate the system service procedure with the appropriate system service vector, assign a CHMx operand, and initialize the vector. This process is summarized in Section 6.3.1 and detailed in Chapter 29.

Note that VMS Version 5 assigns change mode operands dynamically as system service procedures are loaded.

6.2   CHANGE MODE INSTRUCTIONS

There are four change mode instructions: CHMU, CHMS, CHME, and CHMK. Executing any of them generates an exception. Exception-processing VAX microcode alters the access mode and pushes the processor status longword

(PSL), the program counter (PC) of the next instruction, and the sign-extended change mode operand onto the stack indicated in the instruction. The actual access mode used is the innermost of the access mode indicated by the instruction and the current access mode contained in the PSL. The VAX microcode then dispatches through the system control block (SCB) vector for that CHMx instruction to its exception service routine.

CHME and CHMK instructions request VMS system services and RMS services. Their exception service routines are known as the change mode dispatchers.

CHMS and CHMU exceptions are treated much like other exceptions that VMS passes to a user-declared condition handler (see Chapter 5).

6.3 CHANGE MODE DISPATCHING IN THE VMS EXECUTIVE

Module SYSTEM_SERVICE_DISPATCHER contains the change mode dispatchers: EXE$CMODKRNL for CHMK exceptions and EXE$CMODEXEC for CHME exceptions. Each change mode dispatcher makes essential checks of the argument list and transfers control to the system service procedure indicated by the change mode operand. Like any other procedure, a system service procedure assumes there is a call frame on the stack and exits with a RET instruction. The dispatcher must therefore construct a call frame on the inner mode stack.

Building the call frame could be accomplished by using a CALLx instruction and a dispatch table of service entry points. However, the call frame is identical for each service. In addition, the registers that the service-specific procedure will modify have already been saved on the caller's mode stack, because the system service vector register save mask (at global location SYS$*service*) incorporates the register save mask at location EXE$*service*. So the dispatcher avoids the overhead of the general-purpose CALLx instruction and builds a minimal call frame "by hand."

The dispatcher achieves further speed improvement in this commonly executed code path by overlapping memory write operations (building the call frame) with register-to-register operations and instruction stream references.

Using the CHMx operand, the change mode dispatcher indexes into a table of system service procedure addresses. It transfers control to the procedure with a JMP instruction.

6.3.1 Change Mode Dispatcher Data Structures

Several data structures are internal to the change mode dispatcher. Two are dispatch tables: one, at CMOD$AR_KERNEL_DISPATCH_VECTOR, is for kernel mode system services; the other, at CMOD$AR_EXEC_DISPATCH_VECTOR, is for executive mode services. Each table contains a quadword entry for each system service declared in the table's access mode. The kernel mode dispatch table, for example, contains an entry for each loaded kernel

Exit Type Code	Argument Count	Argument List Size
Service Routine Address		

Figure 6.1
Change Mode Dispatch Table Entry

mode system service. Figure 6.1 shows the format of an individual dispatch table entry.

Each table entry has four fields, obtained from the system service descriptor block by EXE$CONNECT_SERVICES:

- The argument list size contains the size in bytes of the argument list required by this system service procedure, computed from the argument count in the system service descriptor block.
- The argument count contains the minimum number of arguments required for this service.
- The exit type field contains an index into the exit table, which begins at CMOD$AL_EXIT_TYPE. An entry in this table contains the address of a synchronization routine to be requested from the common return path.

  The CMOD$AL_EXIT_TYPE table entries are

  —0 (the default, indicating no synchronization routine)
  —SYNCH$RMS_STALL
  —SYNCH$RMS_WAIT
  —SYNCH$ASSIGN_EXIT

- The service routine address field contains the address of the entry point in the service-specific procedure to which the change mode dispatcher transfers control. Each service-specific procedure associated with a CHMx operand has a name of the form EXE$*service* or RMS$*service* and begins with a register save mask. The service routine address points to the first instruction beyond the register save mask and is therefore of the form EXE$*service* + 2 or RMS$*service* + 2.

EXE$CONNECT_SERVICES dynamically assigns a unique CHMx operand to each system service as the executive image containing the service is loaded. It maintains a count of loaded kernel mode and executive mode system services in CMOD$GW_CHMK_LIMIT and CMOD$GW_CHME_LIMIT. The maximum allowable CHMx value for VMS system services loaded in this manner is 255 for each mode. VMS reserves higher CHMx operands for its own system services in privileged shareable images and negative CHMx operands for customer-written system services. A change mode dispatcher compares the current CHMx operand to the value that is in CMOD$GW_CHMK_LIMIT or CMOD$GW_CHME_LIMIT to determine the dispatch method.

6.3.2 Operation of the Change Mode Dispatchers

The operations of the kernel and executive change mode dispatchers are almost identical. This section discusses their common points. Subsequent sections describe their differences.

The first instruction of each dispatcher pops the change mode operand from the stack into R0. Each dispatcher then builds the call frame on the stack with the following four instructions:

```
PUSHAB  SERVICE_EXIT        ;The next RET returns here
PUSHL   FP                  ;Address of the CALLx call frame
PUSHL   AP                  ;Address of the arguments
                            ; to the CALLx
CLRQ    -(SP)               ;No condition handler and
                            ; no registers to save
```

After the call frame is built, each dispatcher checks that the CHMx operand corresponds to a loaded system service. If not, it checks for services supplied in privileged shareable images, as described in Section 6.4. Otherwise, it uses the CHMx operand as an index into its dispatch table. From the dispatch table entry, it obtains the size of the service's argument list and the required argument count.

The dispatcher performs two checks on the argument list:

- It checks the read accessibility of the argument list with the PROBER instruction to verify that the argument list is accessible in the access mode of the caller.
- It compares the number of arguments actually passed (found in the first byte of the argument list) to the service-specific entry (from the dispatch table) to determine whether the required number of arguments for this service are present.

If the dispatcher detects an error, it places an error status into R0: either SS$_ACCVIO or SS$_INSFARG, depending on the error. The dispatcher then executes a RET instruction, which returns control through the saved PC in the call frame built by the dispatcher to the common exit path SERVICE_ EXIT. Section 6.3.5.1 describes the actions taken by SERVICE_EXIT when it is entered with a severe error.

If the argument list passes the checks, the dispatcher obtains the system service's exit type code from the service's dispatch table entry. The exit type code, if nonzero, identifies an additional synchronization routine to be executed at the completion of the common exit path, SERVICE_EXIT. The dispatcher overwrites the exception PC pushed onto the stack by the CHMx instruction with this address, thus altering the place to which control will return when SERVICE_EXIT executes an REI instruction. Section 6.3.5 discusses this mechanism in more detail.

The dispatcher finally transfers control to the system service procedure with a JMP instruction.

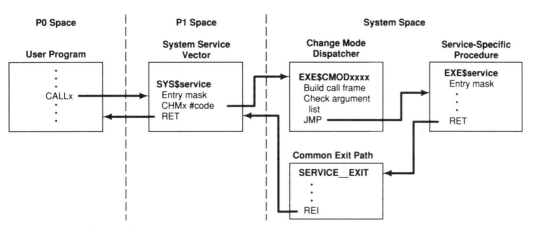

Figure 6.2
Control Flow of System Services That Change Mode

Figure 6.2 illustrates the control flow from the user program to the service-specific procedure. This flow is shown for both kernel and executive access modes.

6.3.3 Change-Mode-to-Kernel Dispatcher

The change-mode-to-kernel dispatcher, EXE$CMODKRNL, performs two steps that the change-mode-to-executive dispatcher does not. Before it transfers control to those services that execute in kernel mode, the change-mode-to-kernel dispatcher places the address of the process control block (PCB) for the current process (found at location CTL$GL_PCB) into R4.

Additionally, CHMK #0 is a special entry path into kernel mode for the undocumented $CLRAST service. If the CHMK operand was a zero, EXE$CMODKRNL transfers control to the routine CMOD$ASTEXIT, in module SYSTEM_SERVICE_DISPATCHER. Chapter 7 describes this routine in more detail.

6.3.4 Change-Mode-to-Executive Dispatcher

The change-mode-to-executive dispatcher, EXE$CMODEXEC, performs one step unique to executive mode. If the CHME operand was a zero, the executive dispatcher transfers control to the routine CMOD$SSVECX, in module SYSTEM_SERVICE_DISPATCHER. CMOD$SSVECX is entered with an error status. It transfers control to SERVICE_EXIT with the error so that a system service exception can be signaled or the error reported.

RMS synchronization code uses this mechanism when it detects a severe error. It requires a CHME instruction to return to executive mode, since RMS stalls in the mode of the caller.

Note that with VMS Version 5, RMS dispatching becomes a standard part of executive mode dispatching, with the exception of the return path.

6.3.5   **Return Paths for System Services**

When a service-specific procedure has completed its operation, it places a status in R0 and executes a RET instruction. In the case of an executive or kernel mode system service, the RET returns control to the address that the change mode dispatcher placed in the saved PC area of the call frame that it built, the common exit path SERVICE_EXIT, in module SYSTEM_SERVICE_DISPATCHER.

6.3.5.1   **Change Mode Dispatcher Common Exit Path.** SERVICE_EXIT is the common exit path for change mode dispatching. Its action depends on the status code returned in R0 by the system service procedure.

- If the status in R0 is a success or warning code, SERVICE_EXIT merely dismisses the CHMx exception by executing an REI instruction.

  —For most RMS services and $ASSIGN, the exception PC has been altered, so control transfers to the synchronization routine specified by its exit type code, in the mode of the caller.

  —For other system services, control returns to the instruction following the CHMx in the system service vector, in the mode of the caller. In most cases, this instruction is a RET, which returns control to the caller of the system service or RMS service.

    However, for synchronous system services, the system service vector contains code that conditionally stalls the process until its request is complete. Section 6.3.5.3 describes this synchronization method.

- If the status in R0 is an error code, SERVICE_EXIT checks whether the process owns any mutexes. In general, a system service procedure should release any mutexes that it has acquired before returning to SERVICE_EXIT. To minimize overhead, SERVICE_EXIT only performs the check for mutexes when a service returns an error or a severe error status.

  —If the process owns a mutex, SERVICE_EXIT tests whether the interrupt priority level (IPL) is 2. If so, the assumption is that one system service has acquired a mutex and then called another system service, which is returning an error status. In this case, SERVICE_EXIT merely executes an REI instruction to return control to the presumed original service.

  —If the process owns a mutex but is running at IPL 0, SERVICE_EXIT generates a fatal MTXCNTNONZ bugcheck.

  —If the process does not own a mutex, SERVICE_EXIT continues.

    Chapter 32 describes bugcheck processing, and Chapter 8 gives information on mutexes.

    If system service exceptions are disabled for the access mode in which the system service was requested, SERVICE_EXIT dismisses the CHMx exception by executing an REI instruction, as described previously.

Otherwise, the process has enabled system service exceptions for the access mode in which the service was requested. Since an exception routine must be entered at IPL 0, SERVICE_EXIT explicitly lowers IPL if the process is running in kernel mode. Executive mode services do not need a similar check because elevated IPL requires kernel mode operation. (Lowering IPL is unnecessary unless the process has enabled system service failure exceptions, because the REI instruction that dismisses the CHMK exception lowers the IPL.)

To signal the system service exception, SERVICE_EXIT transfers control to EXE$SSFAIL, in module EXCEPTION. It signals an exception of type SS$_SSFAIL to the caller.

Chapter 5 describes exception dispatching.

6.3.5.2 **Return Paths for RMS Services.** The dispatch table entry of most RMS services contains an exit type code identifying an additional synchronization routine to be executed at the completion of the common exit path, SERVICE_EXIT. The RMS synchronization routines, SYNCH$RMS_STALL and SYNCH$RMS_WAIT in module SYSTEM_SERVICE_EXIT, either return control immediately to the RMS service's caller or stall the process in an event flag wait state until some operation initiated by RMS on behalf of the caller has completed.

Figure 6.3 illustrates the control flow from the user program to the RMS service-specific procedure and to the synchronization routine.

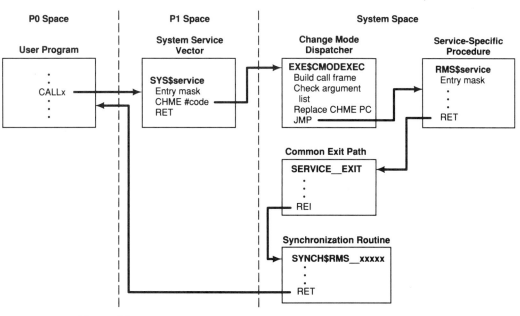

Figure 6.3
Control Flow of RMS Services

117

6.3.5.2.1 *RMS Synchronization.* An RMS service procedure might temporarily stall itself to wait either for the completion of a system service that RMS requested on behalf of the caller or for some internal RMS condition to be met. Though the RMS code thread is stalled, the process that requested the RMS service might be able to execute in the meantime. The process indicates its desire to execute even though the RMS operation is not complete by setting the asynchronous (ASY) bit in the file access block (FAB) or record access block (RAB). The RMS service procedure tests the ASY bit. If it is clear, the service procedure stores the status code RMS$_STALL in R0. It then returns to SERVICE_EXIT.

When SERVICE_EXIT REIs, it transfers control to a synchronization routine, either SYNCH$RMS_STALL, for most RMS services, or SYNCH$RMS_WAIT, for the $WAIT RMS service. Section 6.3.5.2.2 describes the routine SYNCH$RMS_WAIT.

SYNCH$RMS_STALL is entered with the following register contents:

Register	Contents
R0	Status RMS$_STALL
R3	Number of event flag to wait for (flags 27 to 31 are reserved for RMS)
R8	Address of FAB or RAB associated with stall

Executing in the caller's mode, SYNCH$RMS_STALL uses the status in R0 to decide whether a stall is required. If so, it places the process into an event flag wait state for the event flag specified in R3. Otherwise, for all status values except RMS$_STALL, the synchronization routine immediately returns to the caller.

The crucial point in this implementation is that the caller waits at the access mode associated with the original RMS service request and not in executive mode, thus allowing AST delivery to all access modes at least as privileged as that of the service request. In the usual case where an RMS service is requested from user mode, an AST of any access mode can be delivered while the process is waiting for the RMS operation to complete.

For example, when RMS requests the $QIO system service on behalf of its caller, it specifies an event flag from the range 27 through 31 to be set and an executive mode AST procedure to be executed when its I/O operation completes. If the process requested a synchronous operation, RMS returns to SERVICE_EXIT with the status RMS$_STALL in R0, the event flag number from the $QIO request in R3, and the address of the FAB or RAB in R8. SERVICE_EXIT REIs to SYNCH$RMS_STALL, which places the process into an event flag wait state.

When the I/O request completes, the associated event flag is set. RMS gains control first in the executive mode AST procedure associated with its $QIO request. If it determines that the $QIO request is complete, the AST

118

procedure sets final status in the data structure (FAB or RAB) associated with the operation. Otherwise, if the AST procedure determines that it requires further processing to complete the original request, it requests the next service.

Control returns from the RMS AST procedure to the synchronization routine. SYNCH$RMS_STALL, executing in the caller's access mode, checks whether the RAB or FAB status field is zero. If so, it again places the caller into an event flag wait state. In other words, a nonzero value in the status field of the FAB or RAB is the actual indication that the RMS operation is complete.

When the status field indicates successful completion or a warning, the synchronization routine executes a RET instruction, returning control to the instruction following the initial RMS service request. Otherwise, when the synchronization routine discovers an error or the status field indicates an error, it performs the error processing described in Section 6.3.5.2.3.

6.3.5.2.2 *SYNCH$RMS_WAIT.* SYNCH$RMS_WAIT is the synchronization routine for the $WAIT RMS service. It is entered from the REI in SERVICE_EXIT and so runs in the mode of the caller. This allows AST delivery to the caller's mode and inner modes while the process is waiting.

SYNCH$RMS_WAIT is entered with four arguments set up by the $WAIT service procedure:

Register	Contents
R0	Status RMS$_STALL
R3	Number of event flag to wait for (flags 27 to 31 are reserved for RMS)
R4	Action flag; if clear, stall on the RAB or FAB in R8. If set, wait for event flag in R3
R8	Address of FAB or RAB

If R0 contains the status RMS$_STALL, SYNCH$RMS_WAIT stalls process execution until an asynchronous RMS operation completes. The action flag in R4 determines the method used to decide whether the operation is complete. If the action flag is clear, the completion of the RMS operation is indicated by the status field in the RAB, so SYNCH$RMS_WAIT branches to SYNCH$RMS_STALL to stall in the normal manner. Otherwise, SYNCH$RMS_WAIT alone cannot determine completion of the operation. It requests the Wait for Single Event Flag ($WAITFR) system service, to wait for the event flag specified by the $WAIT service procedure. When the event flag is set, SYNCH$RMS_WAIT reexecutes the $WAIT service request to allow the $WAIT procedure to decide whether the operation is complete.

6.3.5.2.3 *RMS Error Detection.* An RMS synchronization routine reports errors via the system service dispatcher. The synchronization routine, running in the mode of the RMS service caller, executes the instruction CHME #SSVECX. In this manner, the routine changes the access mode to executive. In response to the operand SSVECX, a zero, the executive mode system service dispatcher transfers control to the routine CMOD$SSVECX without building the usual call frame. CMOD$SSVECX is an alternative entry point for SERVICE_EXIT. Running in executive mode, SERVICE_EXIT proceeds as described in Section 6.3.5.1.

6.3.5.3 **Return Path for Synchronous Services.** A synchronous system service vector requests an asynchronous service procedure and tests its return status for successful initiation of the request. If the asynchronous service procedure returns an error, that status is immediately returned to the requestor of the synchronous service. If the return status indicates success, the system service vector code branches to one of two synchronization routines. These routines are originally part of module EXCEPTION_INIT. During system initialization they are copied to the system service vector area. The routines differ only in minor detail and converge within the SYS$SYNCH composite system service vector.

Figure 6.4 illustrates the control flow from the user program, through the service-specific procedure, to the synchronization code.

SYS$SYNCH first tests whether a status block was specified by the requestor. For $GETLKIW and $ENQW, the lock status block serves this purpose; in all other cases, the I/O status block is used. If no status block was specified, SYS$SYNCH executes the instruction CHMK #WAITFR to place the process into an event flag wait state until the specified flag is set. When the flag is set, the process is taken out of its wait state, and SYS$SYNCH returns to the requestor of the synchronous service. If a status block was specified, SYS$SYNCH executes the following sequence:

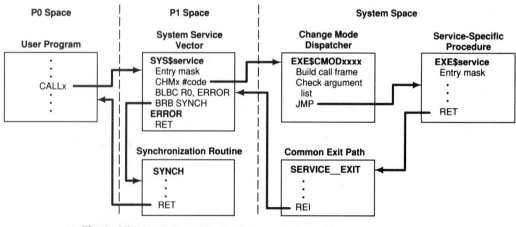

Figure 6.4
Control Flow of Synchronous Services

1. It tests the status word of the status block. A nonzero status indicates that the asynchronous service has completed, and SYS$SYNCH returns to the requestor of the synchronous service.
2. A zero status indicates the asynchronous service has not completed, and SYS$SYNCH executes the instruction CHMK #WAITFR to wait for the specified event flag.
3. When the event flag is set and the process is placed into execution, SYS$SYNCH tests the low word of the status block. If it is nonzero, SYS$SYNCH returns to the requestor of the synchronous service.
4. If the low word of the status block is zero, then the flag has been set spuriously, perhaps by another concurrent use. SYS$SYNCH clears the event flag by executing the instruction CHMK #CLREF and then proceeds with step 2.

A crucial point in this implementation is that the process waits at the access mode associated with the original synchronous system service request, thus allowing AST delivery to all access modes at least as privileged as that of the synchronous service request. In the usual case where a synchronous system service is requested from user mode, an AST of any access mode can be delivered while the process is waiting for the service to complete.

6.3.6 System Services That Do Not Change Mode

Some system services do not change to a more privileged access mode and instead execute in the mode from which they were requested. The system service vector for one of these "mode of caller" services contains a JMP instruction instead of a CHMx instruction and transfers control directly to the service procedure.

When the service-specific procedure has completed its operation, it places a status code in R0 and executes a RET instruction. In the case of a system service that does not change mode, the RET returns control to the caller of the service. (Because a mode of caller service does not change mode, the stack does not contain a call frame built by the change mode dispatcher.)

Table 6.1 lists the mode of caller VMS system services.

Figure 6.5 shows the control flow from the user program to the service procedure for those services that do not change mode.

6.4 DISPATCHING TO SYSTEM SERVICES IN PRIVILEGED SHAREABLE IMAGES

VMS does not require that all system services be part of a loadable executive image. A user may write system services as part of a privileged shareable image. Moreover, VMS supplies a number of system services in privileged shareable images. These include

- $MOUNT in SYS$SHARE:MOUNTSHR.EXE

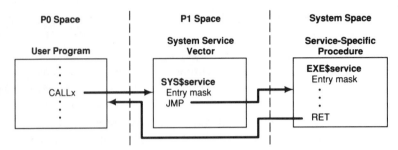

Figure 6.5
Control Flow of System Services That Do Not Change
Mode

- $DISMOU in SYS$SHARE:DISMNTSHR.EXE
- Services relating to system security in SYS$SHARE:SECURESHR.EXE

Implementing these less frequently used services as privileged shareable images means that they are resident only when explicitly requested and that they are mapped in process space.

The manual *Introduction to VMS System Services* describes the requirements for writing privileged shareable images. This section examines the manner in which control is passed to a system service that is part of a privileged shareable image.

EXE$CMODKRNL and EXE$CMODEXEC attempt to dispatch to a privileged shareable image whenever a CHMx instruction is executed with an operand whose value is outside the range of those for services in loadable executive images.

VMS system services in privileged shareable images have large positive change mode operands (for example, 16,527). The VAX architecture reserves negative change mode operands for customer use.

6.4.1 Per-Process System Service Dispatcher

For any CHMK or CHME exception, the change mode dispatcher performs some initial operations, such as building the call frame and, for kernel mode system services, storing the PCB address in R4. When it detects that the CHMx operand is outside the range from zero to the value in CMOD$GW_CHMx_ LIMIT, it tries to transfer control to a privileged shareable image dispatcher. The change mode dispatcher first checks a location in P1 space (CTL$GL_ USRCHMK or CTL$GL_USRCHME) to see whether a per-process dispatcher exists.

It interprets nonzero contents of this location as an address in the P1 space privileged vector list, built by the image activator. The privileged vector list contains a JSB instruction for each per-process system service dispatcher, invoking the dispatcher at its entry point within a privileged shareable image. Figure 6.6 shows the privileged vector list.

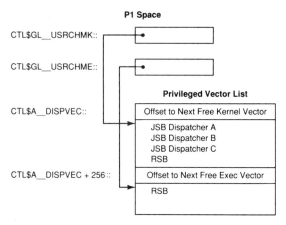

Figure 6.6
Privileged Vector List

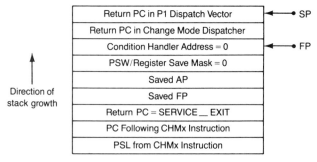

Figure 6.7
State of the Stack on Entry to a Per-Process Dispatcher

A per-process dispatcher is entered with the stack in the state shown in Figure 6.7. If the per-process dispatcher accepts the change mode operand, it requests a service-specific procedure that eventually returns to SERVICE_ EXIT by executing a RET instruction. If the per-process dispatcher rejects the operand, it hands control to the next per-process dispatcher in the privileged vector list by executing an RSB instruction. The privileged vector list ends with an RSB instruction, which returns control to the change mode dispatcher if all per-process dispatchers reject the code.

6.4.2   **Privileged Shareable Images**

In the P1 space privileged vector list, kernel mode and executive mode each have one half page (256 bytes) devoted to user-written system service dispatching. The first byte of each area is initialized during process creation to an RSB instruction. With the dispatch scheme described in the previous section, the RSB instruction initially prohibits per-process dispatching.

However, for an image linked with a privileged shareable image (linked with the /PROTECT and /SHAREABLE options and installed with the /PRO-TECTED and /SHARED options), the image activator replaces the RSB instruction with a JSB to the per-process dispatcher specified as a part of the privileged shareable image (see Figure 6.6). It maintains an RSB instruction after the last JSB instruction in the kernel and executive portions of the privileged vector list.

VMS allows multiple privileged shareable images to be linked with the same executable image. Each privileged image can contain multiple system service procedures. The example pictured in Figure 6.8 shows three privileged shareable images, each with a kernel mode dispatcher.

When the image activator, described in Chapter 26, encounters a reference to a privileged shareable image in the image it is activating, it checks that the privileged image is compatible with the running operating system. It maps the sections containing the user-written system services using information stored in a protected image section (a privileged library vector, defined by the macro $PLVDEF and pictured in Figure 6.9) to modify the privileged vector list. For example, if a privileged shareable image contained a change-mode-to-kernel dispatcher, the image activator would insert a JSB instruction in

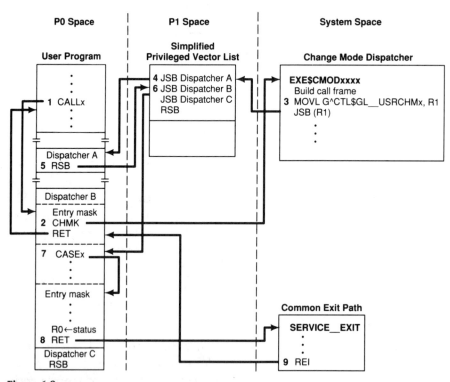

Figure 6.8
Dispatching to System Services in a Privileged
Shareable Image

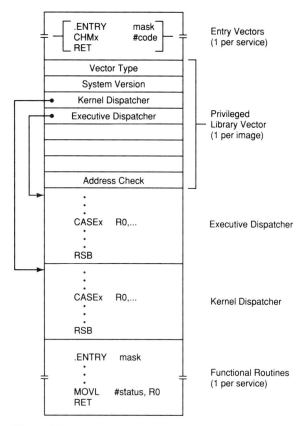

Figure 6.9
Structure of a Privileged Shareable Image

P1 space that transfers control to the dispatcher specified by the PLV$L_ KERNEL longword in the privileged library vector.

Once an image containing user-written system services is activated, execution proceeds normally until the process requests one of the services. Figure 6.8 shows an example of dispatching to a user-written system service. The numbers in the following list correspond to the numbers in the figure.

① A CALLx instruction transfers control to a user-written system service vector in P0 space.

② The CHMK or CHME instruction located there transfers control to the VMS change mode dispatcher.

③ Execution proceeds normally until an unsigned test of the change mode operand discovers that it exceeds the value found in CMOD$GW_CHMx_ LIMIT. The dispatcher tests the address in CTL$GL_USRCHMx. If it is nonzero, the dispatcher JSBs to that location.

④ The JSB instruction transfers control to the P1 privileged vector list, where another JSB instruction transfers control to the first dispatcher.

⑤ In this example, the first dispatcher rejects the change mode operand simply by executing an RSB back to the P1 privileged vector list.

⑥ The second JSB in the P1 privileged vector list is executed, transferring control to a second dispatcher.

⑦ In this example, the second dispatcher recognizes the change mode operand as valid and dispatches (probably with a CASEx instruction) to a service-specific procedure that is also a part of the second privileged shareable image.

⑧ When the service completes (successfully or unsuccessfully), it stores a final status into R0 and exits with a RET, which transfers control to SERVICE_EXIT.

⑨ A privileged shareable image system service return path merges at this point with the return paths described for other services.

If each dispatcher executed an RSB to reject the change mode operand, control eventually would reach the RSB instruction in the P1 privileged vector list. This RSB instruction transfers control back to the VMS change mode dispatcher, which checks next for a systemwide dispatcher.

6.4.3   Systemwide User-Written Dispatcher

If no per-process dispatcher exists or if the last per-process user-written dispatcher returns to the system service dispatcher with an RSB, the change mode dispatcher checks a location in system space (EXE$GL_USRCHMK or EXE$GL_USRCHME) for the existence of a systemwide user-written dispatcher. If none exists (contents are zero, its usual contents in a VMS system), or if this dispatcher transfers control back with an RSB, the change mode dispatcher returns the error status SS$_ILLSER to the system service requestor in R0.

This scheme assumes that privileged shareable image system services that complete successfully will exit with a RET back to SERVICE_EXIT, where an REI instruction will dismiss the CHMK or CHME exception.

Note that no standard method exists to add a systemwide user-written dispatcher to a system.

6.5   RELATED SYSTEM SERVICES

VMS provides five system services that are closely related to system service dispatching and the change mode instructions. Chapter 5 describes the Declare Change Mode or Compatibility Handler ($DCLCMH) system service. This section describes the Set System Service Failure Exception Mode ($SETSFM) system service, the change mode system services, and the Set System Service Filter ($SETSSF) system service.

6.5.1 **Set System Service Failure Exceptions System Service**

The $SETSFM system service either enables or disables the generation of exceptions when SERVICE_EXIT detects an error. The service itself simply sets (to enable) or clears (to disable) the bit in the process status longword (PCB$L_STS in the software PCB) for the access mode from which the system service was requested. By default the generation of an exception is disabled.

6.5.2 **Change Mode System Services**

The Change to Kernel Mode ($CMKRNL) and Change to Executive Mode ($CMEXEC) system services provide a simple path for privileged processes to execute code in kernel or executive mode. The services begin execution in the appropriate mode. They check for the necessary privilege (CMKRNL or CMEXEC) and then dispatch with a CALLG instruction to the procedure whose address is supplied as an argument to the service. (Note that if $CMKRNL is requested from executive mode, no privilege check is made.)

The procedure that executes in kernel or executive mode must store a return status code into R0. If not, the previous contents of R0 are used to determine whether an error occurred.

The service cleans the stack and REIs back to the instruction following the CHMx if the privileged procedure returned a success status. Otherwise it returns to SERVICE_EXIT with the error status for further processing.

6.5.3 **System Service Filtering**

Some applications (especially user-written CLIs) require that user mode programs have no direct access to system and RMS services. VMS provides the $SETSSF system service for this purpose.

Each VMS system service in a loadable executive image specifies an inhibit mask at assembly time as a parameter to the SYSTEM_SERVICE macro. The mask is stored in the system service descriptor block for the service. As a service is loaded, its inhibit mask is copied from its descriptor block into one of two tables, depending on the mode of the service.

CMOD$AB_KERNEL_INHIBIT_MASK and CMOD$AB_EXEC_INHIBIT_MASK contain the addresses of the kernel and executive mode tables. The tables are indexed by a change mode operand; for example, the kernel mode system service assigned change mode operand x stores its inhibit mask at offset x from the address in CMOD$AB_KERNEL_INHIBIT_MASK. The inhibit mask indicates whether the system service can be disabled by $SETSSF. If the service can be disabled by $SETSSF, the mask also indicates the system service filter groups for which the service is disabled. Group 0 specifies all services except $EXIT; group 1 specifies most services, with the exception of $EXIT and those services required for condition handling or image rundown. The *VMS System Services Reference Manual* lists the services that are not disabled by $SETSSF.

The byte at offset CTL$GB_SSFILTER in the per-process control region contains the system service filter mask for a particular process. Usually this mask contains the value zero. The $SETSSF service writes the mask value specified as its argument into this field.

The bit EXE$V_SSINHIBIT at global location EXE$GL_DEFFLAGS corresponds to the SYSGEN parameter SSINHIBIT, which, when set, enables system service filtering. If system initialization code discovers that the inhibit bit is set, it loads the SCB vectors for CHME and CHMK with the addresses of the alternative dispatchers EXE$CMODEXECX and EXE$CMODKRNLX, in module SYSTEM_SERVICE_DISPATCHER.

The processor dispatches to these alternative change mode dispatchers when CHME and CHMK exceptions occur. They branch to the standard change mode dispatchers for CHMx instructions executed in inner modes. However, for a CHMx instruction executed in user mode, the alternative dispatcher ANDs the value in CTL$GB_SSFILTER with the value in the appropriate system service filter table (CMOD$AB_EXEC_INHIBIT_MASK or CMOD$AB_KERNEL_INHIBIT_MASK) entry indexed by the CHMx operand. If the result of the AND is zero, the dispatcher branches to the standard change mode dispatcher. If the result of the AND is nonzero, the dispatcher returns the error status SS$_INHCHME or SS$_INHCHMK, depending on the mode of the system service.

If CTL$GB_SSFILTER is nonzero, the dispatcher also denies access to services in privileged shareable images. An attempt to request those services results in the error SS$_INHCHME or SS$_INHCHMK, depending on the mode of the service.

7 ASTs

What you want, what you're hanging around in the world
waiting for, is for something to occur to you.
Robert Frost

An asynchronous system trap (AST) is a mechanism that enables an asynchronous event to change the flow of control in a process. Specifically, as soon as possible after the asynchronous event occurs, a procedure or routine designated by either the process or the system executes in the context of the process.

A process may request an AST as notification that an asynchronous system service has completed. ASTs requested by the system result from operations such as I/O postprocessing, process suspension, and process deletion. These operations require that VMS executive code execute in the context of a specific process. ASTs fulfill this need.

To declare the asynchronous event, the executive queues an AST to the process. Once the AST has been queued, the process eventually becomes current. AST delivery, the actual dispatch into the AST procedure, occurs in the context of that process. This chapter discusses the queuing and delivery of ASTs and describes some examples of their use by VMS.

7.1 AST HARDWARE COMPONENTS

VAX hardware/microcode assists VMS in the queuing and delivery of ASTs. Three mechanisms contribute:

- The return from exception or interrupt (REI) instruction
- The PR$_ASTLVL processor register
- The interrupt priority level (IPL) 2 software interrupt

The first two features are discussed in this section. The software interrupt mechanism is discussed in Chapter 4. The IPL 2 interrupt service routine for AST delivery, SCH$ASTDEL, is discussed in Section 7.5.

7.1.1 REI Instruction

The REI instruction initiates the delivery of an AST to a process by requesting an IPL 2 interrupt if appropriate. (Note that a requested IPL 2 interrupt is not actually granted until IPL drops below 2.) The REI microcode performs the following tests to determine whether to request the interrupt:

1. The REI microcode checks whether process context is being restored. If the interrupt stack bit is set in the processor status longword (PSL) to be

129

restored, the REI microcode makes no further test and does not request an IPL 2 interrupt. AST delivery has no meaning outside of process context.

2. The REI microcode compares the value in PR$_ASTLVL to the access mode being restored. If the value in PR$_ASTLVL is less than or equal to the current mode field in the PSL to be restored (that is, if it represents a more or equally privileged access mode), the REI microcode requests a software interrupt at IPL 2. This test prevents a process running in an inner mode from being interrupted to deliver an AST to an outer mode.

The IPL of the AST interrupt is architecturally defined and cannot be changed by operating system software. Throughout the book, therefore, this IPL is referred to explicitly as 2 rather than symbolically as IPL$_ASTDEL.

7.1.2 ASTLVL Processor Register (PR$_ASTLVL)

The processor register PR$_ASTLVL is used in conjunction with the REI instruction to control IPL 2 software interrupts. This register is part of the hardware context of the process and has a save area in the process header (PHD) hardware process control block field PHD$B_ASTLVL. (Chapter 12 contains more information on the hardware PCB.) The LDPCTX instruction copies PHD$B_ASTLVL to PR$_ASTLVL when a process is placed into execution. The SVPCTX instruction does not store PR$_ASTLVL in PHD$B_ASTLVL, thus avoiding an often unnecessary memory reference. Therefore, any code that changes PR$_ASTLVL must also make the same change to PHD$B_ASTLVL.

PR$_ASTLVL normally contains the access mode of the first AST in the process's AST queue (see Section 7.2.1). Inner mode ASTs are more privileged than outer mode ASTs and are queued and delivered before them. Specifically, PR$_ASTLVL contains the mode of the first AST in the queue

- After an AST has been queued
- After an AST routine has completed and exited
- After ASTs at a given mode have been enabled or disabled by the Set AST Enable ($SETAST) system service
- After an AST routine has left AST level by requesting the Clear AST ($CLRAST) system service

While an AST routine is in progress, PR$_ASTLVL contains a value that is 1 greater than the current AST's mode. After an AST has been blocked (because an AST at that mode is active or delivery to that mode is disabled), PR$_ASTLVL contains a value that is 1 greater than the blocked AST's mode. In both cases, this helps prevent REI from requesting IPL 2 interrupts that cannot currently be processed.

If no AST is queued, PR$_ASTLVL contains a value of 4, chosen so that the REI test previously described will fail regardless of the access mode being restored by the REI instruction.

7.2   AST DATA STRUCTURES

The executive queues ASTs to a process as the corresponding events (I/O completion, timer expiration, etc.) occur. The AST queue is maintained as a queue of AST control blocks (ACBs) with the listhead in the process control block (PCB). Section 7.4 describes AST queues in more detail.

7.2.1   Process Control Block

The PCB contains several fields related to AST queuing and delivery (see Figure 7.1).

The fields PCB$L_ASTQFL and PCB$L_ASTQBL are the listhead for ACBs queued to the process. The list is a doubly linked queue.

The field PCB$W_ASTCNT specifies how many concurrent ASTs the process can request at the moment. It is initialized to the process's AST quota, typically from the user authorization file. When a process requests an asynchronous system service, requesting AST notification of completion, and when a process declares an AST by requesting the Declare AST ($DCLAST) system service, the system service confirms that PCB$W_AST-CNT is greater than zero and then decrements it, to charge the process AST quota.

It is the responsibility of the system service and of any code charging AST

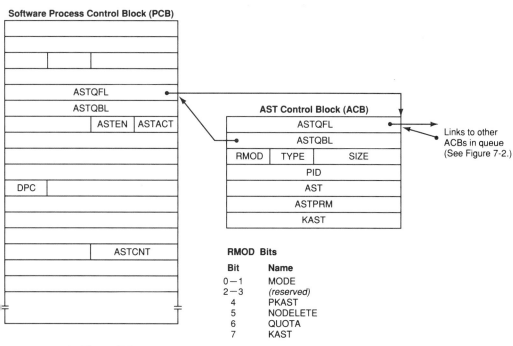

Figure 7.1
AST Control Block and AST-Related Fields in Software
PCB

quota to set the ACB$V_QUOTA bit in the ACB (see Section 7.2.2) as a flag that quota must be restored when this AST is delivered. When such an AST is delivered, the AST delivery interrupt service routine, SCH$ASTDEL, increments PCB$W_ASTCNT.

The process delete pending count, PCB$B_DPC, is incremented for every reason the process should not be deleted or suspended. It is incremented by the Files-11 Extended QIO Processor (XQP) to indicate that an XQP operation is in progress and that the process should not be deleted or suspended until the operation completes. Up through VMS Version 5.2, this is its only use. Section 7.8 discusses the use of this field and its significance to ASTs in more detail.

In both PCB$B_ASTEN and PCB$B_ASTACT, the low-order four bits contain AST-related information. One bit is used for each access mode, with bit 0 corresponding to kernel mode.

Each PCB$B_ASTEN bit, when set, indicates that AST delivery to that access mode is enabled. By default, all four bits are set. Section 7.6 describes how a process toggles one of these bits through the $SETAST system service.

Each PCB$B_ASTACT bit, when set, indicates that an AST is active at that access mode in the process. The AST delivery interrupt service routine sets the bit, and AST exit code clears it. The executive uses these bits to serialize ASTs for each access mode; that is, the executive will not interrupt an AST thread to deliver another AST to the same access mode. This serialization limits the number of concurrent threads of execution within a process and helps ensure that AST procedures are not entered recursively, thus simplifying synchronization among the different threads in an access mode. It is possible, though not usual, to reset a PCB$B_ASTACT bit using the $CLRAST system service (see Section 7.5.3).

7.2.2 AST Control Block

The ACB includes the following information:

- The process ID (PID) of the target process
- The AST procedure or routine address
- The access mode
- An optional argument to the AST procedure

The ACB is allocated from nonpaged pool, often as part of a larger structure associated with the requested asynchronous event. The ACB is actually included as the first section of several larger data structures. The I/O request packet (IRP), lock block (LKB), and timer queue entry (TQE), for example, are data structures whose first section is an ACB. (Compare the ACB format pictured in Figure 7.1 with the TQE format shown in Figure 11.1, the LKB format shown in Figure 10.4, or the IRP layout shown in Figure E.11.)

The macro $ACBDEF defines symbolic names for the fields in the ACB. ACB$L_ASTQFL and ACB$L_ASTQBL link the ACB into the AST queue in the PCB. The listhead of this queue is the pair of longwords PCB$L_ASTQFL and PCB$L_ASTQBL.

The field ACB$B_RMOD contains five bit fields:

- Bits ⟨0:1⟩ (ACB$V_MODE) contain the access mode in which the AST procedure is to execute.
- Bit ⟨4⟩ (ACB$V_PKAST), when set, indicates the presence of a "piggyback" special kernel mode AST (see Section 7.7.4).
- Bit ⟨5⟩ (ACB$V_NODELETE), when set, indicates that the ACB should not be deallocated after the AST is delivered.
- Bit ⟨6⟩ (ACB$V_QUOTA), when set, indicates that the process AST quota has been charged for this ACB.
- Bit ⟨7⟩ (ACB$V_KAST), when set, indicates the presence of a system-requested special kernel mode AST (see Section 7.7). If ACB$V_KAST is clear, this is a "normal" AST.

The field ACB$L_PID identifies which process is to receive the AST.

The fields ACB$L_AST and ACB$L_ASTPRM are the entry point of the designated AST procedure and its optional argument.

The field ACB$L_KAST contains the entry point of a system-requested special kernel mode AST routine if the ACB$V_PKAST or ACB$V_KAST bit of ACB$B_RMOD is set.

7.3   CREATING AN AST

ASTs can be created by three types of actions. The first is a process request for AST notification of the completion of an asynchronous system service, such as Queue I/O Request ($QIO) or Enqueue Lock Request ($ENQ). The arguments for these system services include an AST procedure address and an argument to be passed to the AST procedure. The system service charges the process AST quota.

The second is the system's queuing an AST to execute code in the context of the selected process. An ACB used in this situation is not deducted from the AST quota of the target process because of its involuntary nature; the ACB$V_QUOTA bit is clear to indicate this.

The system's ability to initiate the execution of code in a particular process context is crucial to VMS operations. Only the AST mechanism provides this capability. The executive employs this mechanism primarily to access the process's virtual address space.

In a virtual memory operating system such as VMS, resolving a per-process address outside of its process context is difficult at best. The process's pages, as well as page table pages, may not be resident; they may be in a page file, swap file, or in transition. Rather than attempt to locate the relevant page table page(s) and process page(s), VMS resolves the address in process context through the AST mechanism so that standard memory management mechanisms can be used.

Examples of the system's queuing an AST include the following:

- I/O postprocessing
- The Force Exit ($FORCEX) system service
- Expiration of CPU time quota
- Working set adjustment as part of the quantum-end event (see Chapter 12)
- The Get Job/Process Information ($GETJPI) system service

The third way to create an AST is an explicit declaration of an AST by a process through the $DCLAST system service. The $DCLAST system service procedure, EXE$DCLAST in module SYSASTCON, runs in kernel mode. It simply allocates an ACB, fills in the ACB information from its argument list, and invokes SCH$QAST to queue the ACB. The access mode in which the AST is to execute can be no more privileged than the mode from which $DCLAST was requested. The system service charges the process AST quota.

7.4   QUEUING AN AST TO A PROCESS

The routine SCH$QAST, in module ASTDEL, is invoked to queue an ACB to a process. It can be invoked from a thread of execution running at an IPL less than or equal to IPL$_SCHED and holding no spinlock of rank greater than SCHED.

SCH$QAST uses the ACB$V_KAST bit and ACB$V_MODE bits of the ACB$B_RMOD field to decide where in the process's AST queue to insert the ACB. The AST queue for a process is a doubly linked list with its head and tail at PCB fields PCB$L_ASTQFL and PCB$L_ASTQBL.

SCH$QAST maintains the queue as a first-in/first-out (FIFO) list for each access mode. ASTs of different access modes are placed into the queue in ascending access mode order, that is, kernel mode ASTs first and user mode ASTs last. Special kernel mode ASTs precede normal kernel mode ASTs. A piggyback special kernel mode AST is inserted in the AST queue according to the mode of the normal AST whose ACB it shares.

SCH$QAST performs the following steps:

1. SCH$QAST acquires the SCHED spinlock, raising IPL to IPL$_SCHED, to synchronize access to the scheduler database, the process's AST queue, and its PHD$B_ASTLVL.
2. If the process is nonexistent, SCH$QAST returns the error status SS$_NONEXPR. If bit ACB$V_NODELETE in ACB$B_RMOD is clear, its usual state, SCH$QAST deallocates the ACB before returning.
3. If the AST queue is empty (the contents of PCB$L_ASTQFL are equal to its address), then the ACB is inserted as the first element in the AST queue.
4. Otherwise, SCH$QAST scans the queue of ACBs. It inserts a normal ACB before the first ACB whose ACB$V_MODE bits indicate a less privileged access mode or, if it finds none, at the end of the queue. SCH$QAST

inserts a special kernel mode AST before the first normal ACB or, if it finds none, at the end of the queue. Figure 7.2 shows the organization of the AST queue.

5. SCH$QAST calculates ASTLVL as the mode of the first (innermost mode) ACB in the queue and stores it as follows:

—If the target process is currently executing on the same processor as SCH$QAST, SCH$QAST stores the new ASTLVL value in PHD$B_ASTLVL and in the processor register, PR$_ASTLVL. If the process is currently executing on a different member of a symmetric multiprocessing system, SCH$QAST stores the new value in PHD$B_ASTLVL and requests an interprocessor interrupt of the other CPU to update its PR$_ASTLVL register. Chapter 34 gives further details.

—If the process is memory-resident but is not currently executing, SCH$QAST stores the new value for ASTLVL in PHD$B_ASTLVL but not in the processor register.

—If a process is outswapped, PHD$B_ASTLVL cannot be updated because the PHD (including the hardware PCB) is not available. When the process becomes resident and computable at a later time, the swapper calculates and stores a value for PHD$B_ASTLVL, based on the first AST in the queue.

When setting ASTLVL, SCH$QAST does not check whether an AST is already active for this mode or whether ASTs at this mode are disabled. When either of these conditions is true, the next REI to drop IPL below 2 will cause an IPL 2 interrupt, and SCH$ASTDEL will dismiss it as undeliverable (blocked). This event is less frequent and thus less costly than having SCH$QAST make the checks each time it queues an AST.

6. Unless the process is currently executing, SCH$QAST invokes SCH$RSE, in module RSE, to report that an AST has been queued to the process. SCH$RSE makes the process computable if it is not current, already computable, or suspended in kernel mode.

7. SCH$QAST releases the SCHED spinlock, restoring the previous IPL, and returns to its invoker.

7.5   DELIVERING AN AST

AST delivery is initiated when the REI microcode determines from the destination access mode and the PR$_ASTLVL register that a pending AST is deliverable (see Sections 7.1 and 7.4) and requests a software interrupt at IPL 2. The amount of time before the AST is actually delivered depends upon the interrupt activity of the system. When IPL drops below 2, the AST delivery interrupt service routine will execute.

Note that a rescheduling interrupt at IPL 3 may be requested and granted prior to the granting of the IPL 2 AST delivery interrupt request. In this case, the REI microcode will have set the IPL 2 bit in the software interrupt

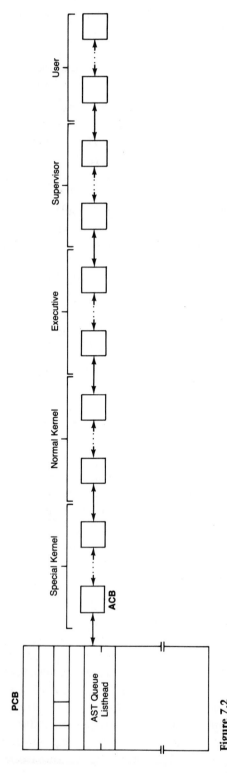

Figure 7.2
Organization of the AST Queue

136

service request (SISR) register PR$_SISR. Conceptually, the IPL 2 bit of the SISR is part of process context, but for reasons of optimization, both saving and restoring of process context ignore it. Thus, it is possible for a newly scheduled process to inherit an irrelevant IPL 2 bit in the SISR; an AST delivery interrupt is then granted in the context of a different process than was originally requested. The AST delivery interrupt service routine detects and ignores such spurious AST interrupts. The AST delivery interrupt in question will be requested again when the process for which it is intended is placed back into execution by the REI from the rescheduling interrupt.

7.5.1 AST Delivery Interrupt

The IPL 2 software interrupt is unique. It is the only one requested by microcode (REI) rather than by MTPR instructions in the executive, and the only one whose service routine runs entirely in process context. When the IPL 2 interrupt occurs, control is transferred to SCH$ASTDEL, in module ASTDEL, the address in the IPL 2 system control block (SCB) vector. The interrupt service routine's functions are to remove the first pending AST from the queue, determine that the interrupt request is not a spurious one, and dispatch to the specified AST routine at the specified access mode.

Figure 7.3 shows the major steps in SCH$ASTDEL's flow. The numbers in the figure correspond to the following steps. The column headings in the figure describe the environment of that step, for example, its access mode and IPL.

1. SCH$ASTDEL acquires the SCHED spinlock, raising IPL to IPL$_SCHED, to synchronize access to the process's AST queue.

② SCH$ASTDEL tries to remove the first ACB from the process AST queue. If the queue is empty, the IPL 2 interrupt must have been spurious. The routine sets ASTLVL to 4, releases the SCHED spinlock, and exits with an REI instruction.

③ Testing ACB$V_KAST in ACB$B_RMOD, SCH$ASTDEL determines if the ACB is a special kernel mode AST. It delivers a special kernel mode AST with the following steps:

   a. SCH$ASTDEL releases the SCHED spinlock, lowering IPL to 2.

   b. SCH$ASTDEL dispatches to the special kernel mode AST routine by executing an effective JSB instruction. (It pushes a return address onto the stack and executes a JMP instruction to minimize the number of branches taken on a common code path.)

   c. On return from the special kernel mode AST routine, SCH$ASTDEL returns to step 1 to check the AST queue again in case there is another pending AST, possibly queued by the special kernel mode AST routine. One common instance of this occurs in I/O postprocessing. The I/O postprocessing special kernel mode AST queues a normal AST to the process if AST notification of the I/O completion was requested.

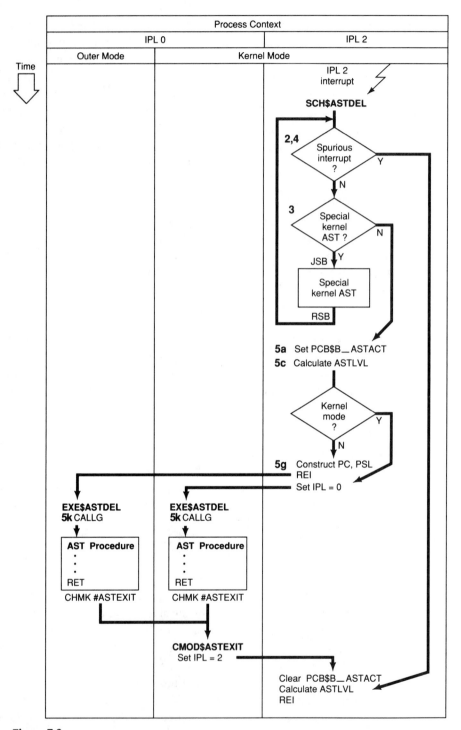

Figure 7.3
AST Delivery Flow

This is a frequent enough occurrence that checking the queue again is less costly than incurring the extra interrupt.

(4) If the AST removed from the queue is a normal AST, then SCH$ASTDEL checks that the mode of the AST is at least as privileged as the access mode being restored by the REI instruction that initiated AST delivery. It compares the mode in the saved PSL on the kernel stack to the mode of the AST. If the AST mode is less privileged, SCH$ASTDEL reinserts the ACB at the head of the queue, releases the SCHED spinlock, and dismisses the interrupt with an REI instruction. This test detects a spurious AST delivery interrupt.

Two other checks for spurious AST delivery interrupts are required. The first is that the appropriate PCB$B_ASTACT bit must be clear; this test prevents an AST from being interrupted by another AST at the same access mode. The second test is that the appropriate PCB$B_ASTEN bit must be set, indicating that AST delivery for that access mode is enabled. If either test fails, SCH$ASTDEL sets ASTLVL to the blocked access mode plus 1, requeues the ACB, releases the SCHED spinlock, and dismisses the interrupt.

A third test is required for a user mode AST: the low bit of CTL$GB_SOFT_AST_DISABLE must be clear, indicating no soft disabling of user mode ASTs. For further information, see Section 7.6.

(5) If the AST is deliverable, then SCH$ASTDEL performs the following operations before dispatching to the AST routine:

a. SCH$ASTDEL sets the bit corresponding to the AST access mode in PCB$B_ASTACT to indicate that there is an active AST at this mode and to block concurrent delivery of another AST.

b. If ACB$V_QUOTA is set in the ACB, SCH$ASTDEL returns process AST quota.

c. SCH$ASTDEL stores a new value of ASTLVL in PR$_ASTLVL and PHD$B_ASTLVL. The new value of ASTLVL is the access mode of the AST plus 1 (the next outer mode). The access mode is calculated in this manner to prevent another AST interrupt when SCH$ASTDEL switches to the access mode in which the AST procedure is executed.

d. Once modifications to the process's AST queue and ASTLVL are complete, SCH$ASTDEL releases the SCHED spinlock and lowers IPL to 2.

e. Delivery of an AST to kernel mode is simpler than to other modes because the process is already executing in kernel mode and on the appropriate stack. If the AST is for a mode other than kernel mode, SCH$ASTDEL obtains the stack pointer for that mode.

f. As described in the next section, SCH$ASTDEL builds an argument list on the stack of the AST's access mode.

g. If the AST is not for kernel mode, SCH$ASTDEL builds a program counter (PC) and PSL on the kernel stack. The stored PC is the address of EXE$ASTDEL, the AST dispatcher. The stored PSL contains the AST access mode in both its current mode and previous mode fields.

h. If a piggyback special kernel mode AST is associated with the current AST, the special kernel mode AST routine is dispatched through a JSB instruction. When the piggyback AST routine returns, SCH$ASTDEL continues with the next step.

i. SCH$ASTDEL tests the ACB$V_NODELETE bit. If the bit is set, processing continues with the next step; if the bit is clear, then SCH$ASTDEL deallocates the ACB to nonpaged pool.

j. The code that actually calls an AST procedure, EXE$ASTDEL, must execute in the access mode of the AST.

For access modes other than kernel mode, transfer of control to EXE$ASTDEL and change of access mode is accomplished through an REI instruction, the only way to reach a less privileged access mode. The PC and PSL used by the REI instruction are described in step 5g.

In order to deliver a kernel mode AST, SCH$ASTDEL merely drops IPL to 0 and falls through to EXE$ASTDEL.

k. EXE$ASTDEL executes a CALLG instruction, transferring control to the AST procedure, with the argument pointer (AP) pointing to the argument list. The use of a CALLx instruction to enter ASTs enables them to be written in any high-level language that supports the VAX Calling Standard. A CALLG instruction is used, rather than a CALLS, so that the argument list will remain on the stack after the AST procedure RETs.

7.5.2 Argument List

A normal AST procedure can be written in any language. By definition, a procedure begins with an entry mask, is passed an argument list, and returns control to its caller (in this case, the AST dispatcher) with a RET instruction.

Figure 7.4 shows the argument list with which an AST procedure is called. SCH$ASTDEL copies the AST parameter from the ACB where it was initially stored by a system service, such as $QIO, $ENQ, or $DCLAST. The AST parameter was originally an argument to the system service. The interpretation of the AST parameter depends on the AST procedure.

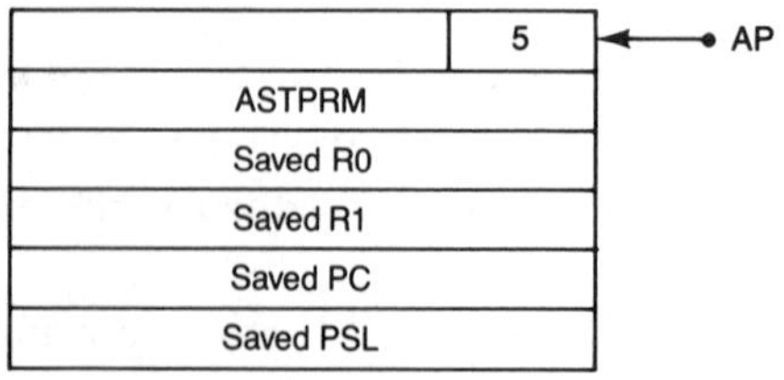

	5	◄────● AP
ASTPRM		
Saved R0		
Saved R1		
Saved PC		
Saved PSL		

Figure 7.4
Argument List Passed to AST by Dispatcher

SCH$ASTDEL saves the general registers R0 and R1 in the argument list. The AST procedure may not save them through its register save mask, because the VAX Calling Standard specifies that R0 and R1 be used to return status. The asynchronous nature of ASTs implies that the R0 and R1 contents are unpredictable and therefore must be preserved. The registers are saved and restored by the AST delivery mechanism.

The saved PC and PSL values are the register contents originally saved when the IPL 2 interrupt was granted. The values are normally the pair that was about to be used by the original REI instruction requesting the AST delivery.

7.5.3   AST Exit Path

When an AST procedure is done, its associated PCB$B_ASTACT bit must be cleared and ASTLVL must be recomputed. The AST procedure requests the $CLRAST system service to perform these steps, which can only be done from kernel mode. In most cases, the AST procedure indirectly requests $CLRAST by executing a RET instruction. Direct request of $CLRAST is discussed later in this section.

When the AST procedure executes the RET instruction, its call frame is removed from the stack and control returns to EXE$ASTRET in the access mode of the AST. The AST argument list remains on the stack. The following steps then occur:

1. EXE$ASTRET removes the argument count and the AST parameter from the stack, leaving R0, R1, PC, and PSL from the argument list.
2. EXE$ASTRET executes the instruction

   ```
   CHMK    #ASTEXIT
   ```

   This instruction requests the $CLRAST system service (ASTEXIT is a synonym for CLRAST).
3. The CHMK exception causes dispatch to the change-mode-to-kernel system service dispatcher, EXE$CMODKRNL, in module SYSTEM_SERVICE_DISPATCHER (see Chapter 6). EXE$CMODKRNL makes a special test for the system service code of zero (ASTEXIT = 0) to shorten the dispatching to the $CLRAST system service.
4. The $CLRAST system service procedure, CMOD$ASTEXIT in module SYSTEM_SERVICE_DISPATCHER, performs the following steps:

   a. It raises IPL to 2, to block AST delivery interrupts.
   b. It clears the appropriate PCB$B_ASTACT bit to indicate that no AST procedure is active at that mode.
   c. It invokes SCH$NEWLVL, in module ASTDEL, to recompute the ASTLVL value as the access mode of the first ACB in the queue.
   d. It executes an REI instruction to return to EXE$ASTRET.

5. EXE$ASTRET resumes at the previous access mode, the mode of the AST:

    a. It restores R0 and R1 from the stack.

    b. EXE$ASTRET executes another REI instruction to dismiss the interrupt. The REI instruction returns control to the access mode and location originally interrupted by AST delivery.

The REI instruction in the $CLRAST system service may cause another IPL 2 interrupt to occur, depending upon the ASTLVL value and the access mode transitions.

If another IPL 2 interrupt occurs at the REI instruction from the $CLRAST system service, the access mode stack of the first AST still contains the saved R0, R1, PC, and PSL. To prevent a stack from filling with these values as a result of recurring ASTs, SCH$ASTDEL checks whether an AST interrupt occurred at the instruction following the ASTEXIT system service. If so, SCH$ASTDEL checks further whether the current AST and the previous AST are for the same access mode. If they are, SCH$ASTDEL pops from the stack the newer copy of the saved values and reuses the original ones in the argument list it builds for the current AST.

If an AST procedure requests the $CLRAST system service directly rather than returning through EXE$ASTRET, the appropriate PCB$B_ASTACT bit is cleared and PR$_ASTLVL is set to the mode of the new first ACB in the queue. This has the effect that another AST can be delivered to the same mode; the current procedure is now an ordinary thread interruptible by ASTs. The frame built on the stack by the call to the former AST procedure remains on the stack. The former AST procedure is responsible for removing it. Furthermore, the former AST procedure is now responsible for any synchronization with another AST thread of execution.

The VAX BASIC Run-Time Library requests the $CLRAST system service from within CTRL/C attention AST procedures. VAX BASIC requires that user programs be notified of CTRL/C through an error signal rather than through the AST mechanism. The VAX BASIC Run-Time Library therefore dismisses the CTRL/C attention AST by requesting the $CLRAST system service and then signals the condition by calling LIB$SIGNAL (see Chapter 5).

Note that the $CLRAST system service is not supported by Digital, except for use within Digital software, and is not documented in the *VMS System Services Reference Manual*.

7.6   DISABLING AST DELIVERY

Through the $SETAST system service a process can enable or disable delivery of ASTs to the mode from which the process requests the system service. The $SETAST system service sets or clears the relevant PCB$B_ASTEN bit to enable or disable AST delivery to that mode. The system service enables synchronization between a normal thread of execution and an AST thread. The concept of AST reentrancy and ways of achieving it are described in the *Guide to Creating VMS Modular Procedures*.

The $SETAST system service procedure, EXE$SETAST in module SYS-ASTCON, runs in kernel mode. It determines the mode from which it was requested and tests the current setting of that PCB$B_ASTEN bit. It copies the ENBFLG argument value to the bit, setting or clearing it. It then invokes SCH$NEWLVL to compute a new value for ASTLVL, based on the current contents of the AST queue and the new state of the AST enable bit. EXE$ASTRET then returns either the status SS$_WASCLR or SS$_WASSET to reflect the original state of the AST enable bit.

VMS Version 5 adds an alternative way to disable delivery to user mode. User mode code sets the low bit in the P1 global location CTL$GB_SOFT_AST_DISABLE to communicate its intention to block user mode ASTs. The AST delivery interrupt service routine, SCH$ASTDEL, tests this bit whenever it is about to deliver a user mode AST.

If the bit is set, SCH$ASTDEL clears the user mode PCB$B_ASTEN bit to effect a conventional disable and requeues the ACB. SCH$ASTDEL also sets the low bit of CTL$GB_REENABLE_ASTS to notify the user mode thread that it must request the $SETAST system service to reenable AST delivery to user mode.

Requested to reenable delivery to user mode, EXE$SETAST clears both CTL$GB_REENABLE_ASTS and CTL$GB_SOFT_AST_DISABLE. Invoked to disable delivery to user mode, EXE$SETAST sets them both to 1.

If no user mode AST is delivered while CTL$GB_SOFT_AST_DISABLE is set, then PCB$B_ASTEN remains unchanged. The $SETAST system service requests to disable and reenable AST delivery are both saved. This mechanism enables fast disabling of user mode ASTs by DECwindows. Use of this mechanism is reserved to Digital and not supported except for use within Digital software.

7.7 SPECIAL KERNEL MODE ASTS

Special kernel mode ASTs differ from normal ASTs in several ways:

- A special kernel mode AST routine is dispatched at IPL 2 and executes at that level or higher. Synchronization is provided by the interrupt mechanism itself rather than requiring additional PCB$B_ASTACT and PCB$B_ASTEN bits. Only one special kernel mode AST can be active at any time because the AST delivery interrupt is blocked.

- Special kernel mode ASTs cannot be disabled through $SETAST. Delivery of a special kernel mode AST can only be blocked by raising IPL to 2 or above.

- All special kernel mode ASTs result from the operations of kernel mode code. That is, a user cannot directly request special kernel mode AST notification of an asynchronous event.

- A special kernel mode AST routine is invoked by a JSB instruction, which is a simpler and thus faster means of transferring control than a CALLG instruction.

  The arguments passed to a special kernel mode AST routine are the PCB address in R4 and the ACB address in R5. When the special kernel mode AST routine executes its RSB instruction, the stack must be in the same state as when the routine was entered. The routine may use R0 through R5 freely but must save R6 through R11 before use and restore them before exiting.

- A special kernel mode AST routine is responsible for the deallocation of the ACB to nonpaged pool. (For normal ASTs, this deallocation is done by the AST delivery routine.)

The next several sections briefly describe examples of the special kernel mode AST mechanism.

7.7.1   I/O Postprocessing in Process Context

Completing an I/O request requires the delivery of a special kernel mode AST to the process whose I/O completed. I/O postprocessing is described in more detail in Chapter 21. The I/O postprocessing interrupt service routine queues a former I/O request packet (IRP) as an ACB to the process whose I/O completed. The operations performed by the I/O completion AST routine are those that must execute in process context, particularly those that reference process virtual addresses. The special kernel mode AST routines BUFPOST and DIRPOST, in module IOCIOPOST, perform the following operations (DIRPOST is actually a subentry point of BUFPOST):

1. For buffered read I/O operations only, BUFPOST copies the data from the system buffer to the user buffer in process address space and deallocates the system buffer to nonpaged pool.

2. DIRPOST increments either PHD$L_DIOCNT or PHD$L_BIOCNT, the process's cumulative totals of completed direct I/O and buffered I/O requests.

3. If a user diagnostic buffer was associated with the I/O request, DIRPOST copies the diagnostic information from the system diagnostic buffer to the user's buffer and deallocates the system buffer.

4. DIRPOST decrements the channel control block field CCB$W_IOC, the number of I/O requests in progress on this channel. Channel control blocks are in P1 space.

5. If the I/O request specified an I/O status block (IOSB), the routine copies information from the IRP to the IOSB.

6. If a common event flag is associated with the I/O request, it is set. (Local event flags are set in IOC$IOPOST, as described in Chapter 21.)

7. If ACB$V_QUOTA was set in IRP$B_RMOD (the same offset as ACB$B_RMOD), AST notification of I/O completion was requested. The AST procedure address and the optional AST argument were originally stored in the IRP (now an ACB). DIRPOST invokes SCH$QAST to queue the former IRP as an ACB. This time the IRP/ACB represents a normal AST in the access mode at which the I/O request was made.

8. Otherwise, if ACB$V_QUOTA is clear, DIRPOST deallocates the IRP/ACB to nonpaged pool.

7.7.2 $GETJPI System Service

A process requests the $GETJPI system service to obtain information about itself or another process. If the request is for information in the virtual address space of another process on the same VAXcluster node, the $GETJPI system service queues an AST to the target process. Running in the context of the target process, $GETJPI's special kernel mode AST routine can easily examine per-process address space. Chapter 13 describes the $GETJPI system service in detail and discusses the additional steps necessary to obtain information from the virtual address space of a process running on another VAXcluster node.

The $GETJPI system service procedure, EXE$GETJPI in module SYS-GETJPI, performs the following steps:

1. It allocates and fills in an extended ACB to describe a special kernel mode AST and the desired items of information. The ACB includes a buffer to return the data.

2. The special kernel mode AST routine, executing in the context of the target process, moves the requested information into the buffer. It modifies the ACB so that it can be used to queue a second special kernel mode AST back to the requesting process.

3. The second special kernel mode AST routine copies data from the extended ACB buffer to buffers in the requesting process. It also sets the event flag associated with this request.

4. If the process has requested AST notification of request completion, the extended ACB is used for the third time. The special kernel mode AST routine uses it to cause delivery of a normal AST in the access mode from which the system service was requested.

   If the process has not requested AST notification, the extended ACB is deallocated to nonpaged pool.

7.7.3   Power Recovery ASTs

The implementation of power recovery ASTs relies on special kernel mode ASTs. A power recovery AST enables a process to receive notification that a power failure and successful restart have occurred. Chapter 33 describes this feature in more detail.

When a power recovery occurs, VMS queues a special kernel mode AST to each process that has requested power recovery AST notification. The special kernel mode AST routine copies the address of the user-requested AST procedure, which is stored in P1 space, to ACB$L_AST and requeues the ACB as a normal AST. The special kernel mode AST routine is required to access the process's P1 space.

7.7.4 Piggyback Special Kernel Mode ASTs

Piggyback special kernel mode ASTs (PKASTs) enable a special kernel mode AST to ride piggyback in the ACB$L_KAST field of a normal AST. The normal access mode determines the order of enqueuing and delivery. If delivery to that access mode is disabled or blocked, the piggyback special kernel mode AST cannot be delivered.

The AST delivery interrupt service routine JSBs to the piggyback special kernel mode AST routine just before calling the normal AST. When the special kernel mode AST returns, the normal AST is called.

There are several reasons for using piggyback special kernel mode ASTs:

- It is faster to deliver two ASTs together than to deliver two ASTs separately.
- There are times when delivering an AST requires some additional work in kernel mode in the context of the calling process. Piggyback special kernel mode ASTs facilitate this work.

  The $ENQ system service uses a piggyback special kernel mode AST to write to the caller's lock status block and lock value block. To copy the information from the lock database to the caller's process space, a piggyback special kernel mode AST is required.

  Piggyback special kernel mode ASTs are also used in terminal out-of-band ASTs (see Section 7.9.5.3).
- A piggyback special kernel mode AST can be used to queue other normal ASTs to a process. The $ENQ system service uses this feature to deliver both blocking and completion ASTs to a process through one ACB. Chapter 10 contains further information.

7.8 SYSTEM USE OF NORMAL ASTS

Several other executive features are implemented through normal ASTs. For example, the automatic working set limit adjustment that takes place at quantum end is implemented with a normal kernel mode AST. Chapter 12 discusses quantum-end activities, and Chapter 17 provides a detailed description of automatic working set limit adjustment.

CPU time limit expiration is implemented with potentially multiple ASTs. Beginning in user mode, the AST procedure requests the Exit ($EXIT) system service. If the process is not deleted, a supervisor mode time expiration AST is queued. This loop continues with higher access modes until the process is deleted.

The executive also uses the AST mechanism for the $FORCEX, Suspend Process ($SUSPND), and Delete Process ($DELPRC) system services. With VMS Version 5.2, these services can affect a process running on another VAXcluster node. If the target process is executing on the same VAXcluster node as the system service requestor, the system service queues an AST directly to the target process. Chapter 13 discusses the additional steps required to affect a process running on another VAXcluster node.

The $FORCEX system service, detailed in Chapter 13, queues a user mode AST that requests the $EXIT system service from the context of the target process.

The $SUSPND and $DELPRC system services queue an AST to the target process to implement suspension or deletion through code running in the context of the target process.

The $SUSPND system service queues either a supervisor or kernel mode AST to its target process, depending on the access mode of the suspension. A process suspended through a supervisor mode AST (the default) can execute kernel and executive mode ASTs. Supervisor mode suspension, new with VMS Version 5, is described in greater detail in Chapter 13. A process suspended through a kernel mode AST can become computable only when it is resumed through another process.

Process deletion and kernel mode suspension must take care to synchronize their actions with the activities of the Files-11 XQP.

The Files-11 XQP runs in process context as a kernel mode AST thread, taking out locks and making I/O requests in response to the process's file system requests. The XQP indicates that it is active by incrementing the PCB field PCB$B_DPC. When the XQP must wait for a lock to be granted or an I/O request to complete, it returns from the AST procedure so that the process can wait at the access mode in which the file system request originated.

Waiting in the outer mode allows delivery of ASTs to that mode and more privileged modes. While the XQP is executing or waiting, kernel mode suspension of the process would risk blocking other processes with interests in the same locks. Deletion of the process would risk relatively minor on-disk corruption, such as dangling directory entries and lost files.

Therefore, the kernel mode suspension and process deletion services queue normal kernel mode ASTs, which cannot be delivered until the XQP AST completes. Furthermore, these AST procedures check that PCB$B_DPC is zero before proceeding with actual process suspension or deletion.

If PCB$B_DPC is not zero, these AST procedures place the process into a wait. They clear bit 0 of PCB$B_ASTACT so that another kernel mode AST can be delivered, invoke SCH$NEWLVL to recompute ASTLVL, and place the process into the resource wait RSN$_ASTWAIT. The process waits in kernel mode at IPL 0. Thus, special and normal kernel mode ASTs can be delivered to it. The resource wait PC is an address within the AST procedure, so after the XQP AST completes, the suspend or delete AST procedure will be reentered to finish its job.

Some time later, queuing of an AST makes the process computable, and delivery of an XQP completion AST causes the XQP to be reentered. When the XQP is done, it decrements PCB$B_DPC and returns from its AST procedure. The suspend or delete AST procedure is reentered and can proceed, now that PCB$B_DPC is zero.

7.8.1 Process Suspension

The $SUSPND system service causes a target process to be placed into a suspended state. The system service procedure first checks the capability of the initiating process to affect the target process (see Chapter 13 for further details). It then checks whether a supervisor or kernel mode suspension is requested. Supervisor mode is the default. A kernel mode suspension request, specified in the optional FLAGS argument, must be made from executive or kernel mode.

The system service procedure then sets PCB$V_SUSPEN in the target process's PCB$L_STS and, for a supervisor mode suspension, PCB$V_SOFT-SUSP as well. It then queues either a kernel or supervisor mode AST to the target process so that the suspension and waiting will occur in that process's context. The wait mechanism in VMS requires that a process be placed into a wait from its own context.

When the kernel mode AST is delivered, the SUSPND AST procedure acquires the SCHED spinlock, raising IPL to IPL$_SCHED, and tests whether PCB$V_RESPEN in PCB$L_STS is set. The bit, when set, indicates that a Resume Process ($RESUME) system service has been requested for this process. If the bit is set, the SUSPND AST procedure clears both it and PCB$V_SUSPEN and RETs, leaving the process unsuspended.

If a $RESUME has not been requested for this process, SUSPND tests PCB$B_DPC to determine whether an XQP operation is in progress. If PCB$B_DPC is greater than zero, SUSPND places the process into a resource wait as previously described.

If PCB$B_DPC is zero, SUSPND places the process into a suspended wait state. The process waits in kernel mode at IPL 0. Its saved PC is an address within SUSPND, so when the process is later placed into execution, it again tests whether a $RESUME has been requested.

When the supervisor mode AST is delivered to a process undergoing supervisor mode suspension, the SUSPEND_SOFT AST procedure requests the $SUSPND system service. Running in kernel mode in the context of the target process, the $SUSPND system service procedure acquires the SCHED spinlock and tests whether PCB$V_RESPEN is set. If a $RESUME has not been requested for the process, the $SUSPND system service procedure cleans up the kernel stack and places the process into a suspended wait state. These actions can only be done from kernel mode.

The process waits in supervisor mode with the supervisor mode PCB$B_ ASTACT bit set. Its saved PC is an address within the SUSPEND_SOFT AST procedure, so when the process is placed back into execution, it again requests the $SUSPND system service to test whether a $RESUME has been requested. Waiting in this manner, the process can execute kernel and executive mode ASTs. For further details, see Chapter 13.

7.8.2 Process Deletion

The $DELPRC system service causes a target process to be deleted. After checking the capability of the initiating process to affect the target process (see Chapter 13), the system service procedure queues a normal kernel AST to the target process so that the deletion will occur in the context of that process. Chapter 28 provides a detailed explanation of process deletion. The use of the AST mechanism provides the following advantages:

- Queuing the AST makes the process computable, regardless of its wait state, unless the process is suspended. The $DELPRC system service ensures the deletion of a suspended process by requesting the $RESUME system service before queuing the AST.
- The process must be resident for the AST to be delivered. Therefore, special cases, such as the deletion of a process that is outswapped, simply do not exist.
- The DELETE AST procedure, running in process context, is able to request standard system services, such as Deassign Channel ($DASSGN), Deallocate Device ($DALLOC), and Delete Virtual Address Space ($DELTVA), to implement process deletion. These system services and the AST procedure reference per-process address space, and thus they must run in process context.

7.9 ATTENTION AND OUT-OF-BAND ASTS

Several VMS device drivers queue an AST to notify a process that a particular attention condition has occurred on a device. The terminal driver and mailbox driver use ASTs in this way. The terminal driver, for example, queues an attention AST to notify an interested process that CTRL/C or CTRL/Y has been typed on its terminal. The terminal driver can also queue an out-of-band AST as notification that a control character other than CTRL/C and CTRL/Y has been typed. The mailbox driver can queue an attention AST as notification that an unsolicited message has been put in a mailbox or that an attempt to read an empty mailbox is in progress.

The basic sequence for both attention ASTs and out-of-band ASTs follows:

1. A process assigns a channel and requests the $QIO system service, specifying that it should receive AST notification of an attention condition on that device.
2. The device driver builds a data structure to describe the attention AST request, inserts it on a list connected to the device UCB, and completes the I/O request.
3. If the attention condition occurs, the device interrupt service routine delivers the attention AST by queuing an AST to the process.

The major distinction between the attention AST and the out-of-band AST mechanisms is that out-of-band ASTs automatically repeat, whereas attention ASTs must be "rearmed." That is, a process must repeat its $QIO request for each attention notification.

Attention ASTs are described in the following sections, and out-of-band ASTs are described in Section 7.9.5.

7.9.1 Set Attention AST Mechanism

To establish an attention AST for a particular device whose driver supports this feature, the user requests the $QIO system service with the I/O function IO$_SETMODE or, for some devices, IO$_SETCHAR. The kind of attention AST requested is indicated by a function modifier.

The relevant function decision table (FDT) action routine for such a driver invokes COM$SETATTNAST, in module COMDRVSUB, which performs the following actions:

1. If the user AST procedure address (the $QIO P1 parameter) is zero, the request is interpreted as a flush attention AST list request (see Section 7.9.3).
2. Otherwise, COM$SETATTNAST allocates an expanded ACB from nonpaged pool and charges it against the process AST quota, PCB$W_AST-CNT. The expanded ACB will be used both as a fork block (FKB) and as an ACB and is referred to as a FKB/ACB.
3. COM$SETATTNAST copies information into the FKB/ACB, such as the AST procedure address, AST argument, channel number, and PID.
4. It acquires the device lock, raising IPL to UCB$B_DIPL, to synchronize access to the attention AST list. It then inserts the FKB/ACB into a singly linked, last-in/first-out (LIFO) list of FKB/ACBs connected to the UCB of the associated device.

   The location of the FKB/ACB listhead is device-specific; some UCBs have multiple listheads—one for each attention condition the driver supports. The FDT action routine passes the address of the listhead in a register to COM$SETATTNAST.
5. COM$SETATTNAST then releases the device lock, restoring the previous IPL, and returns to the FDT action routine.

7.9.2   **Delivery of Attention ASTs**

When the driver (typically the device interrupt service routine) determines that the attention condition has occurred, it invokes COM$DELATTNAST with the address of the FKB/ACB listhead.

A driver uses an alternative entry point, COM$DELATTNASTP, to specify that only ASTs requested by a particular process be delivered.

COM$DELATTNAST is entered at device IPL with the device lock held to synchronize access to the attention AST list. The queuing of ASTs must occur at IPL$_SCHED with the SCHED spinlock held to synchronize access to the scheduler database (see Chapter 8). Specifically, IPL must not be lowered to IPL$_SCHED. To accomplish correct synchronization and not block activities at IPL 7 and IPL 8, COM$DELATTNAST creates an IPL$_QUEUEAST (6) fork process to queue each AST.

The following steps summarize the delivery of attention ASTs:

1. COM$DELATTNAST scans each FKB/ACB in the list. In the case of entry through COM$DELATTNASTP, the routine compares the PID in the FKB/ACB to the requested PID. If they are not equal, the routine leaves the data structure in the queue and goes on to the next entry. If the PIDs match, the routine performs the actions described in the next step.

2. The routine removes the FKB/ACB from its list and dispatches to EXE$FORK, specifying the address of a fork process to be stored in FKB$L_FPC of the FKB/ACB. EXE$FORK records the fork process address, queues the fork block to the fork IPL 6 listhead, and requests an interrupt at that IPL.

3. When IPL drops below 6, the fork interrupt is granted. The IPL 6 fork dispatcher removes the FKB/ACB from the IPL 6 fork block queue and dispatches to COM$DELATTNAST's fork process.

4. At IPL 6, COM$DELATTNAST's fork process reformats the fork control block into an ACB, describing the AST procedure and the access mode of the original attention AST request.

5. The fork process invokes SCH$QAST, which acquires the SCHED spinlock and then queues the ACB to the process that requested the attention AST.

7.9.3   **Flushing an Attention AST List**

The list of attention ASTs is flushed as the result of an explicit user request, a Cancel I/O ($CANCEL), or a $DASSGN system service request for the associated device.

A user explicitly requests that the attention AST list be flushed by requesting a $QIO set attention AST with an AST routine address of zero (see Section 7.9.1). When COM$SETATTNAST is invoked with an AST procedure address of zero, it branches to COM$FLUSHATTNS.

COM$FLUSHATTNS is entered with the PID and channel number of the attention ASTs to be deleted. COM$FLUSHATTNS performs the following operations:

1. It acquires the device lock, raising IPL to UCB$B_DIPL of the device.
2. It scans the FKB/ACB list looking for any FKB/ACBs with a PID and channel number that match those of the requested flush operation.
3. If the PIDs and channel numbers match, COM$FLUSHATTNS removes the FKB/ACB from the attention AST list.
4. COM$FLUSHATTNS releases the device lock, restoring the IPL at which it was entered.
5. COM$FLUSHATTNS increments the process AST quota and deallocates the FKB/ACB to nonpaged pool.
6. COM$FLUSHATTNS continues processing until it has scanned the entire attention AST list. It then releases the device lock and returns to its invoker.

7.9.4 Examples in the VMS Executive

Users frequently request attention ASTs for terminals and mailboxes. Brief descriptions follow of the terminal driver's and mailbox driver's support of attention ASTs.

7.9.4.1 Terminal Driver and CTRL/C–CTRL/Y Notification.

A process requests CTRL/C notification or CTRL/Y notification by requesting the $QIO system service, specifying IO$_SETMODE (or IO$_SETCHAR) with the function modifier IO$M_CTRLCAST or IO$M_CTRLYAST. When an interactive user spawns a new process, that new process may also request CTRL/C and CTRL/Y attention ASTs. If the user types CTRL/C or CTRL/Y, the AST should be delivered only to the process currently associated with the terminal rather than to every process in the job. As the user spawns new subprocesses and attaches to already created processes, DCL tells the terminal driver the PID of the process currently associated with the terminal. When CTRL/C is typed, the terminal driver invokes COM$DELATTNASTP to deliver only the ASTs that were requested by the process associated with the terminal.

If no CTRL/C attention AST has been requested, then the CTRL/C is interpreted as a CTRL/Y, and the terminal driver searches the CTRL/Y AST list instead. If a CTRL/Y is typed, only the CTRL/Y attention AST list is searched.

Because the FKB/ACB data structures are not reused, CTRL/C and CTRL/Y attention ASTs must be reenabled each time they are delivered to a process.

The CTRL/Y attention AST list is flushed by a $DASSGN request. The CTRL/C attention AST list is flushed by $CANCEL as well as by $DASSGN. Both lists can be flushed by an explicit user request.

7.9.4.2   **Mailbox Driver.** A process requests mailbox attention ASTs by requesting the $QIO system service with the function code IO$_SETMODE or IO$_SETCHAR. The possible function modifiers are IO$M_READATTN and IO$M_WRTATTN. IO$M_WRTATTN requests notification of an unsolicited message written to that mailbox. An unsolicited message is one written to a mailbox that has no outstanding read request. IO$M_READATTN requests notification when any process requests a read from that mailbox and there is no message in it.

Attention ASTs of each type may be declared by multiple processes for the same mailbox. When a condition corresponding to an attention AST occurs, all ASTs of the appropriate type are delivered. Only the first process to make a corresponding I/O request will be able to complete the transfer of data signaled by the attention ASTs.

Read and write attention ASTs must be reenabled after delivery because the entire attention AST list is delivered and removed after each occurrence of the specified condition.

7.9.5   **Out-of-Band ASTs**

The terminal driver uses a newer form of AST mechanism to notify a process that an out-of-band character has been received from its terminal. Out-of-band characters are control characters, the ASCII codes 00 to 20_{16}. (Although CTRL/C and CTRL/Y are in this range, the terminal driver provides the attention AST mechanism described previously to notify a process of their receipt for compatibility with earlier versions of VMS.) Out-of-band ASTs are similar to attention ASTs in that the terminal driver forks down to IPL$_QUEUEAST to queue an ACB to the process.

The most significant difference between the attention AST mechanism and the out-of-band AST mechanism is that out-of-band ASTs are repeating; that is, once declared, out-of-band ASTs are delivered to the process for the life of the process or until the $CANCEL system service is requested to flush the AST list. Another difference is that the out-of-band AST mechanism employs a piggyback special kernel mode AST routine.

7.9.5.1   **The Terminal AST Block.** The terminal driver builds a data structure called a terminal AST block (TAST) to describe an out-of-band AST request. Figure 7.5 illustrates the TAST.

The TAST can be in two lists at once because of its structure. Through TAST$L_FLINK, the TAST is always queued to the terminal UCB in a singly linked list. Through the first two longwords of the TAST, it can be inserted into a fork queue or a process's ACB queue. The terminal driver sets the bit TAST$V_BUSY in TAST$B_CTRL when the TAST is in use as a fork block or ACB. The TAST includes space for fork process context (that is, a fork PC, fork R3, and fork R4) and the AST information (address of the AST procedure and its argument, PID, and RMOD fields).

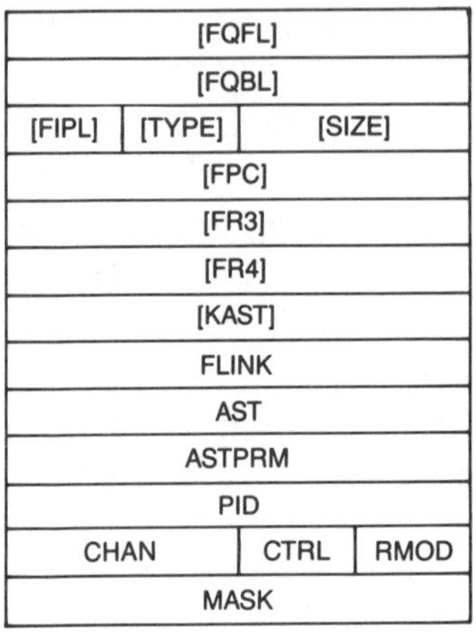

[FQFL]			
[FQBL]			
[FIPL]	[TYPE]	[SIZE]	
[FPC]			
[FR3]			
[FR4]			
[KAST]			
FLINK			
AST			
ASTPRM			
PID			
CHAN		CTRL	RMOD
MASK			

Figure 7.5
Terminal AST Block

7.9.5.2 **Set Out-of-Band AST Mechanism.** A process requests out-of-band notification by requesting the $QIO system service, specifying IO$_SETMODE (or IO$_SETCHAR) with the function modifier IO$M_OUTBAND.

The terminal driver's FDT action routine invokes COM$SETCTRLAST, in module COMDRVSUB, which performs the following steps:

1. If the user AST procedure address ($QIO P1 parameter) is zero or the character mask ($QIO P2 parameter) is zero, COM$SETCTRLAST interprets the request as a flush out-of-band AST list request (see Section 7.9.5.4).
2. Otherwise, COM$SETCTRLAST allocates a TAST from nonpaged pool.
3. It then acquires the device lock, raising IPL to UCB$B_DIPL, to synchronize access to the TAST list.
4. COM$SETCTRLAST next scans the list of out-of-band TASTs, searching for one with the same characteristics as the QIO request. The following items are checked:

   —The PID. Out-of-band ASTs can be requested for the same terminal device from a process and its subprocesses (which will have different PIDs).
   —The channel number

5. If COM$SETCTRLAST finds a TAST with the same characteristics that is not in use, it modifies the existing TAST by replacing the AST address and the control mask. It then invokes COM$DRVDEALMEM, in module COMDRVSUB, to create an IPL 8 fork process to deallocate the just-allocated TAST. This unusual sequence is required because COM$SET-CTRLAST must hold the device lock while scanning the TAST list. During that time, it cannot allocate pool, synchronization to which is controlled at a lower IPL.

If the TAST is in use (perhaps queued as an ACB to the process),
COM$SETCTRLAST marks it as "lost" and removes it from the list.
COM$SETCTRLAST charges the process AST quota and initializes the
just-allocated TAST to describe the request. It copies information from
the IRP (the AST procedure address, channel number, and PID) and the
$QIO character mask into the TAST. It inserts the TAST in the queue
position of the lost TAST.

6. If it does not find a similar TAST, it initializes the just-allocated TAST
   and charges the process AST quota. It places the TAST at the tail of the
   list.

7. COM$SETCTRLAST ORs the $QIO character mask into the terminal's
   out-of-band AST summary mask, the field UCB$L_TL_OUTBAND. This
   mask represents all the control characters for which the terminal driver
   must deliver an out-of-band AST. It then releases the device lock, restoring the previous IPL.

7.9.5.3   **Delivery of Out-of-Band ASTs.** When a control key is typed at a terminal, the
terminal driver checks whether that control character is represented in the
terminal's out-of-band AST summary mask. If the bit in the summary mask
is set, an out-of-band AST has been requested for that control character. The
terminal driver interrupt service routine invokes COM$DELCTRLAST, in
module COMDRVSUB, to deliver the out-of-band AST. The terminal driver
uses an alternative entry point, COM$DELCTRLASTP, to specify that only
ASTs requested by a particular process be delivered.

The following steps summarize the delivery of out-of-band ASTs:

1. COM$DELCTRLAST is entered at device IPL with the device lock held
   to synchronize access to the TAST list. It scans the list of TASTs for one
   whose character mask contains the character typed at the terminal.

   When it finds one with a matching character mask, it checks the busy
   bit to see whether the control block is already in use. In the case of entry
   through COM$DELCTRLASTP, the routine also compares the PID in
   the TAST to the requested PID. If they are not equal, the routine goes
   on to the next TAST in the queue.

   If TAST$V_BUSY is set, COM$DELCTRLAST skips that TAST. If
   TAST$V_BUSY is clear, COM$DELCTRLAST sets it, marking the TAST
   in use, and records in TAST$L_ASTPRM the control character that was
   received.

2. The synchronization considerations described for COM$DELATTNAST
   apply to COM$DELCTRLAST as well. It creates an IPL 6 fork process,
   using the TAST as an FKB, to queue each AST. The TAST also remains
   linked to the terminal UCB list of TASTs. Figure 7.6 shows the TAST in
   the terminal UCB's TAST list and in the fork block queue.

3. When IPL drops below 6, the fork interrupt is granted. The IPL 6 fork

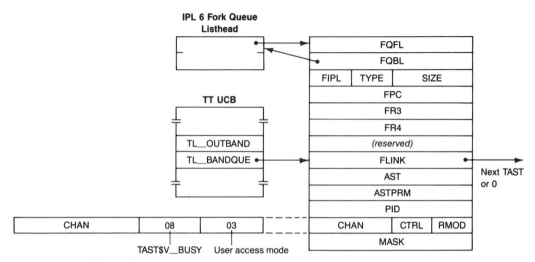

Figure 7.6
TAST Used as a Fork Block

dispatcher removes the TAST from the IPL 6 fork block queue and dispatches to COM$DELCTRLAST's fork process.

4. At IPL 6, COM$DELCTRLAST's fork process reformats the FKB into an ACB describing the AST procedure and the access mode of the original out-of-band AST request. The no-delete and piggyback special kernel mode AST flags are set in the ACB, and the special kernel mode AST field is loaded with the address of COM$DELCTRLAST's piggyback special kernel mode AST.

5. The fork process invokes SCH$QAST, which acquires the SCHED spinlock and then queues the ACB to the process that requested the attention AST. Figure 7.7 shows the TAST in use as an ACB.

6. When the process receives the AST, the piggyback special kernel mode AST routine is executed first. The piggyback special kernel mode AST performs two functions:

   a. It clears TAST$V_BUSY.

   b. If the TAST is marked as "lost," the piggyback special kernel mode AST routine deallocates it and returns AST quota to the process. A TAST is "lost" when COM$FLUSHCTRLS is unable to deallocate it because its busy bit is set (see Section 7.9.5.4). Once the AST has been delivered, the TAST is no longer needed.

7.9.5.4 **Flushing an Out-of-Band AST List.** The list of out-of-band ASTs is flushed as the result of an explicit user request, a $CANCEL, or a $DASSGN request for the associated device.

A user explicitly requests that the out-of-band AST list be flushed by requesting a $QIO set out-of-band AST with an AST routine address of zero

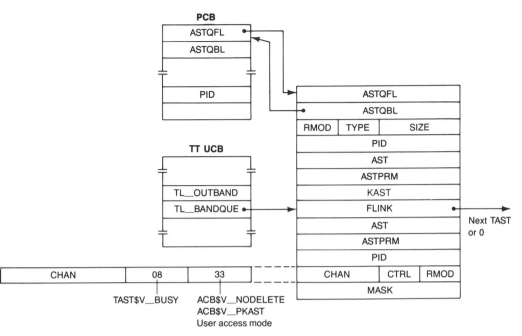

Figure 7.7
TAST Used as an ACB

or a character mask of zero (see Section 7.9.5.2). When COM$SETCTRLAST receives such a request, it branches to COM$FLUSHCTRLS.

COM$FLUSHCTRLS is entered with the PID and channel number of the attention ASTs to be deleted. COM$FLUSHCTRLS performs the following operations:

1. It acquires the device lock, raising IPL to UCB$B_DIPL of the device.
2. It scans the out-of-band AST list and compares the PID and channel number in the TAST with those of the requested flush operation. As it scans the list, it builds a new out-of-band AST summary mask. If COM$FLUSHCTRLS finds a TAST that does not match, COM$FLUSH-CTRLS ORs its control characters into the summary mask being built and goes on to the next TAST.
3. If the PIDs and channel numbers match, COM$FLUSHCTRLS removes the TAST from the list. It checks TAST$V_BUSY to see whether the TAST is in use as a FKB or ACB. If TAST$V_BUSY is set, the "lost" bit is set so that the TAST will be deallocated once its AST is delivered.
4. If the TAST is not busy, COM$FLUSHCTRLS returns the process AST quota and deallocates the TAST to nonpaged pool.
5. COM$FLUSHCTRLS continues processing until it has scanned the entire list. It then replaces the old summary mask with the one just built.
6. COM$FLUSHCTRLS releases the device lock, restoring the IPL at which it was entered.

PART III / Synchronization

8 Synchronization Techniques

"Time," said George, "why I can give you a definition of time.
It's what keeps everything from happening at once."
Ray Cummings, *The Man Who Mastered Time*

In an operating system that allows interrupts, the interrupting code must coordinate, or synchronize, with the code being interrupted to ensure correct behavior. Similarly, when an operating system runs on two or more processors sharing the same memory, code running on one processor must synchronize with code running on the others.

VMS uses a combination of the following VAX hardware mechanisms and software techniques to synchronize the actions of code threads that might otherwise interfere with each other:

- Atomic memory accesses
- Uninterruptible instructions
- Interlocked memory accesses
- Interrupt priority level (IPL)
- Spinlocks (new with VMS Version 5) to synchronize access to shared data by multiple processors
- Queues
- Mutual exclusion semaphores (mutexes)
- Lock management system services
- Event flags

8.1 OVERVIEW

Synchronization is a term commonly used to refer to the simultaneous occurrence of two or more events. In a computer context, however, the word is used to refer to the coordination of events. The coordination may still be as specific as the simultaneous occurrence of events; this use of the term occurs most often in descriptions of hardware mechanisms. In descriptions of software, *synchronization* usually refers to the coordination of events in such a way that only one event happens at a time. This specialized kind of synchronization is known as serialization. Serialized events are assigned an order and processed one at a time in that order. While a serialized event is being processed, no other event in the series is allowed to disrupt it.

Atomicity and mutual exclusion are frequently described as different types of serialization, although the two concepts overlap. *Atomicity* often refers to the serialization of a small number of actions, such as those occurring during the execution of a single instruction or a small number of instructions.

Mutual exclusion is usually applied to the serialization of larger groups of instructions.

Algorithms requiring synchronization take many forms and arise in many contexts. Most of them reduce to solving a small number of fundamental problems, for example, the requirement that a thread of execution change multiple storage locations as an atomic operation. When the first location is changed but the last is not, the storage is temporarily inconsistent. If another thread of execution can access the locations at that moment, that change is not synchronized and system disruption can occur.

Another closely related synchronization problem is the requirement that a thread of execution read a storage location and, depending on its value, write a new value into the location. If another thread with the same intent toward that location can intervene after the read and before the write, then the change to that location is not atomic and system disruption can occur. Specifically, the change made by one of the threads can overlay the change made by the other.

8.1.1 Synchronization at the Hardware Level

VAX hardware provides several mechanisms to assist with synchronization, including atomic memory accesses, uninterruptible instructions, IPL, and interlocked memory accesses.

8.1.1.1 Atomic Memory Accesses.

VAX hardware is required to read or write the following memory operands atomically, in a single memory operation:

- Byte operand
- Aligned word operand
- Aligned longword operand
- Bit field contained in one byte
- Aligned longword address used in a displacement deferred mode or autoincrement deferred mode operand specifier

VAX hardware is not required to implement any other operands atomically. An unaligned word, for example, containing a byte on either side of a longword boundary, may require two separate commands to be read or written. Reading and writing quadword data, whether aligned or not, may require multiple commands.

A piece of data accessed nonatomically by multiple processors can become corrupted. Written nonatomically, it can become any bytewise combination of all the data concurrently being written to it. The value read from it can be any bytewise combination of the original value and the new values concurrently being written to it. This type of corruption is known as data incoherency and word-tearing.

Operands that are either read atomically or written atomically are not necessarily modified atomically (read and written in the same instruction).

For example, although the CPU executes INCB X as a single instruction, it performs the memory read and write necessary to carry out the instruction as independent accesses. If another thread of execution is running concurrently, it may issue a command to the memory controller that reads or writes location X between the INCB's read and write.

8.1.1.2 **Uninterruptible Instructions.** Whether an instruction's memory references are atomic depends on whether the CPU permits interrupts during its execution, and whether more than one thread can execute concurrently. When only one thread can execute at a time (as in a system with only one CPU and no intelligent I/O controllers), memory references can be atomic if interrupts are prevented.

The VAX architecture allows interrupts in one category of instructions, called first part done or FPD instructions. FPD instructions can be interrupted at well-defined points during the course of their execution; sufficient status is saved in general registers to permit instruction restart at the point of interruption.

The VAX architecture specifies that all other instructions are to be uninterruptible in the following sense. If an instruction is interrupted, the microcode must restore the software-visible state of the CPU to what it was at the start of the instruction; when the interrupt is dismissed, the instruction can restart from the beginning. This guarantee of restartability for non-FPD instructions means that their execution is effectively uninterrupted.

For example, the absolute queue instructions INSQUE and REMQUE each make several memory references in manipulating a queue. The CPU allows no interrupts during the execution of these instructions. Thus, the insertion or removal of an element at the head or tail of an absolute queue is synchronized when only one processor can access it.

8.1.1.3 **Interrupt Priority Level.** On a system with only one CPU (a uniprocessor), VMS synchronizes access to its data structures by requiring all threads that access a shared data structure to run at the highest IPL at which any thread that accesses it can interrupt. IPL is a processor-specific mechanism; when more than one processor accesses the same memory, raising IPL on one processor has no effect on the others. Section 8.2 describes the use of IPL.

8.1.1.4 **Interlocked Memory Accesses.** Many simple operations that must make atomic memory accesses cannot do so with a single uninterruptible instruction. For example, a sequence of code that scans a queue to determine where to insert a new element is vulnerable to interrupts. While it follows queue elements' forward links and examines a field in each element, an interrupt could occur whose service routine changes the makeup of the queue. When the service routine dismisses the interrupt, the code scanning the queue could have a stale forward link that no longer points to a valid queue element.

On a uniprocessor, such a sequence can be protected by executing it at the highest IPL at which any thread that accesses the queue can interrupt. On a multiprocessor, this technique fails. The memory controller provides a mechanism called a memory interlock, which does provide synchronization in this situation. A memory interlock enables a processor to make an atomic modification to a location in memory shared by multiple processors.

Both CPUs and intelligent I/O controllers can make interlocked references to memory. When a CPU executes an instruction that interlocks memory, it first issues an interlock-read command to the memory controller. The memory controller sets an internal flag and responds with the requested data. While the flag is set, the memory controller stalls any subsequent interlock-read commands for that same aligned longword from other processors, although it continues to process ordinary reads and writes. When the CPU executing the interlocked instruction issues a write-unlock command, the memory controller writes the modified data back and clears its internal flag. The memory interlock persists for the duration of only one instruction. That is, execution of an interlocked instruction includes paired interlock-read and write-unlock memory controller commands.

Synchronizing data with memory interlocks requires that all accessors of that data use them. In other words, the memory references of an interlocked instruction can be atomic only with respect to other interlocked memory references.

The granularity of the interlock is VAX-implementation-dependent. For example, on some processors, while an interlocked access to a location is in progress, no interlocked access to any other location in memory is allowed. The VAX architecture guarantees only aligned longword granularity.

The VAX architecture provides seven instructions that interlock memory. The *VAX Architecture Reference Manual* describes their operation in detail. They are

- ADAWI—Add aligned word, interlocked
- BBCCI—Branch on bit clear and clear, interlocked
- BBSSI—Branch on bit set and set, interlocked
- INSQHI—Insert entry into queue at head, interlocked
- INSQTI—Insert entry into queue at tail, interlocked
- REMQHI—Remove entry from queue at head, interlocked
- REMQTI—Remove entry from queue at tail, interlocked

An interlocked queue instruction does its interlocking in two stages. In the first stage, the processor issues an interlock-read command to read the forward link. It then makes a bit test and issues a write-unlock command, setting and checking the low-order bit of the forward link. (Self-relative queue elements are constrained to be quadword-aligned; the low-order three address bits are thus available for other uses.) If the low-order bit was clear, the processor continues with the second stage of the instruction.

During execution, the queue itself is interlocked by the low-order bit in the forward link, but only the queue is interlocked; the rest of the memory that would otherwise be interlocked is free. The use of this "secondary interlock" reduces memory interlock contention.

If the low-order bit of the forward link was already set, the processor sets the C condition code bit and completes instruction execution without performing any queue manipulations. The code containing the interlocked queue instruction is expected to test the C bit and, if it is set, try to execute the instruction again. After a number of failures, the queue is presumed corrupt.

Typically, the VMS executive performs interlocked queue manipulations through macro invocation. Each of the interlocked queue instructions has a corresponding macro: $INSQHI, $INSQTI, $REMQHI, and $REMQTI. A sample invocation of $INSQTI and its generated code follows:

```
;the macro invocation
        $INSQTI (R3),G^IOC$GQ_POSTIQ     ;Insert packet on queue
;its generated code
        CLRL    R0
30000$: INSQTI  (R3),G^IOC$GQ_POSTIQ
        BCC     30001$
        AOBLSS  #900000,R0,30000$
        BUG_CHECK BADQHDR,FATAL
30001$:
```

Interlocked queues can be shared between a CPU and an intelligent I/O controller:

• The DR32 is a general-purpose, intelligent data port that connects a VAX internal memory bus to a bus accessible to foreign devices. An application program accesses the DR32 through command and response queues in VAX memory. Synchronizing access to the queues requires that both the DR32 and the application program interlock the memory: the application program uses interlocked queue instructions; the DR32 issues the equivalent memory controller commands.

• The CI adapter (for example, CI780) is a microcoded intelligent controller that connects a VAX to a CI bus and communicates with its counterparts on other nodes. The CI port driver communicates with the CI adapter through command and response queues. Both the CI adapter and the port driver must make interlocked queue references, as previously described.

8.1.2 **Synchronization at the Software Level**

VMS uses the synchronization primitives provided by the hardware as the basis for several different synchronization techniques. The following sections summarize techniques used by the executive and application software.

Table 8.1   Characteristics of Executive Synchronization Methods

Characteristic	IPL	Spinlocks	Mutexes	Locks
VAXcluster-wide	No	No	No	Yes
SMP systemwide	No	Yes	Yes	Yes
Available to outer modes	No	No	No	Yes
Usable from process context	Yes	Yes	Yes	Yes
Usable from system context	Yes	Yes	Yes [1]	No
Kinds of sharing	Exclusive	Exclusive	Multiple readers or one writer	Varied modes
Creation	n/a	Most fixed; some dynamic	Most fixed; some dynamic [2]	Dynamic

[1] Mutexes are used almost entirely for process context synchronization. The I/O database mutex is the only one currently locked by system threads.

[2] Most mutexes are fixed. There are several data structures, however, with a field containing a mutex to synchronize access to other fields in the data structure. These mutexes are created dynamically with the data structures that contain them.

8.1.2.1   Executive Synchronization Techniques. Table 8.1 contrasts the synchronization techniques most commonly used by the VMS executive.

8.1.2.1.1   *Spinlocks.* When running on a uniprocessor, VMS synchronizes access to system data structures using IPL. However, VMS cannot use IPL to control access to data structures in memory shared by the multiple CPUs of a symmetric multiprocessing (SMP) system. To extend to an SMP environment the uniprocessor synchronization provided by IPL, VMS Version 5 introduces a mechanism called a spinlock.

In Version 5, a thread of execution not only raises IPL to block interrupts on the same processor but also acquires a spinlock to block concurrent accesses by other processors. Section 8.3 describes spinlocks in detail.

Each VMS Version 4 systemwide absolute queue is now a per-processor absolute queue, a systemwide interlocked queue, or a systemwide absolute queue protected by a spinlock.

Some shared system data was accessed in previous versions by a single noninterruptible instruction. In VMS Version 5, such accesses have been converted to an interlocked instruction or are made under the protection of a spinlock.

8.1.2.1.2   *Mutexes.* Accesses to shared system data structures by multiple processes from IPLs below 3 can be synchronized by mutexes. Section 8.5 describes mutexes.

8.1.2.1.3   *Lock Management System Services.* The lock management system services (Enqueue Lock Request, $ENQ, and Dequeue Lock Request, $DEQ) provide synchronization tools that can be requested from all access modes. Furthermore, lock management is the fundamental VAXcluster-wide synchronization primitive. Lock management system services are used, for example, by Record Management Services (RMS), the file system, the job controller, the device allocation routines, and the Mount Utility to provide clusterwide synchronization. (See Appendix H for a description of some of these uses.) The lock management system services are described in the *VMS System Services Reference Manual;* Chapter 10 in this book describes their internal workings.

Another important synchronization issue for VMS involves disk storage. Data structures on a shared disk (for example, files and records within files and the actual disk structure) are protected by lock management system services. This form of synchronization serves whether the disk is accessed by multiple processes on a single system or by multiple processes on multiple nodes of a VAXcluster system.

8.1.2.2   **Application Synchronization Techniques.** A process-private data structure accessed from both asynchronous system trap (AST) and non-AST threads of execution must be protected against concurrent access. Access to the data structure can be synchronized by blocking AST delivery, either by raising IPL to 2 or by requesting the Set AST Enable ($SETAST) system service. The concept of AST reentrancy and ways of achieving it are described in the *Guide to Creating VMS Modular Procedures*.

The design of a multiprocess application that runs on an SMP system must take into account the possibility that multiple processes may run on different CPUs and access shared data concurrently. User processes that share global sections can execute interlocked instructions to synchronize their accesses to data in the global sections. They can also use the lock management system services for synchronization.

New with VMS Version 5, the parallel processing Run-Time Library procedures provide support for a number of different synchronization techniques suitable for user access mode applications. These techniques include

- Mutual exclusion implemented through an application-created semaphore or spinlock
- Event synchronization, by which one or more processes can wait for the occurrence of a user-defined event that is triggered by another process
- Barrier synchronization, by which multiple processes wait until a specified number of them have all reached a designated point in their execution

The *VMS RTL Parallel Processing (PPL$) Manual* describes these procedures and their use.

VMS provides more basic event synchronization through event flags. Event flags are local to a process or shared among a group of cooperating processes running on a uniprocessor or an SMP system. An event flag can represent the completion of an asynchronous system or RMS service. A shared, or common, event flag can represent any event detectable and agreed upon by the cooperating processes. Chapter 9 describes the implementation of event flags, and Chapter 6 details their use in asynchronous services.

8.2 ELEVATED IPL

Raising IPL on a processor blocks all interrupts on that processor at the specified IPL value and all lower values of IPL. The traditional VMS method of synchronizing access to system data has been to raise IPL to a high enough level to block all interrupts whose service routines touch that data. For example, access to the variable-length nonpaged pool list is synchronized at IPL 11, the IPL of the highest interrupt thread from which nonpaged pool allocation is permitted. At IPL 11, all fork process interrupts are blocked, but higher priority software and hardware interrupts can still be granted.

The IPL, stored in the processor status longword (PSL) register bits ⟨20:16⟩, is altered by writing the desired IPL value to the processor register PR$_IPL with the MTPR instruction. This change in IPL has traditionally been made by invoking the SETIPL or DSBINT macro. Their macro definitions, somewhat simplified, follow:

```
.MACRO  SETIPL  IPL = #31
        MTPR    IPL,S^#PR$_IPL
.ENDM   SETIPL
.MACRO  DSBINT  IPL = #31, DST = -(SP)
        MFPR    S^#PR$_IPL,DST
        MTPR    IPL,S^#PR$_IPL
.ENDM   DSBINT
```

The SETIPL macro changes IPL to the specified value. If no argument is present, IPL is elevated to 31. This macro is used when the IPL will later be explicitly lowered with another SETIPL or simply as a result of executing an REI instruction. That is, the value of the saved IPL is not important to the routine that is using the SETIPL macro.

The DSBINT macro first saves the current IPL before elevating IPL to the specified value. If no alternative destination is specified, the old IPL is saved on the stack. The default IPL value is 31. This macro is usually used when a later sequence of code must restore the IPL to the saved value with the ENBINT macro. ENBINT, the counterpart to the DSBINT macro, restores the IPL to the value found in the designated source argument.

The successful use of IPL as a synchronization tool requires that IPL be raised (not lowered) to the appropriate synchronization level. Lowering IPL defeats any attempt at synchronization. Moreover, a thread of execution entered as the result of an interrupt cannot lower IPL below its entry IPL without risking a reserved operand fault. If it lowered IPL and then tried to REI, restoring a PSL with a higher IPL, the REI microcode would generate a reserved operand fault. (However, a thread of execution may raise and then lower its IPL as long as it does not lower IPL below that of its entry.)

Suppose a thread of execution modifying more than one location in a shared database raises IPL to x to block interrupts from other accessors of the database. The first thread of execution is interrupted, after partly making its modifications, by a second thread running in response to a higher priority interrupt. The shared database is now in an inconsistent state. If the second thread were to lower IPL to x in a mistaken attempt to synchronize access to the database, it could receive incorrect data or corrupt the database.

Integrity of the database would, however, be maintained if the second thread of execution were to reschedule itself to run as the result of an interrupt at or below x and access the database from the rescheduled thread. Forking is the primary way in which an interrupt thread of execution reschedules itself to run at a lower IPL. Chapter 4 describes forking in more detail.

The sections immediately following briefly describe the synchronization use of various IPLs. Note, however, that most of the SETIPL, DSBINT, and ENBINT macro invocations in the executive have been replaced by invocations to macros that acquire and release spinlocks. Each of the IPLs traditionally used for synchronizing access to shared data now has one or more spinlocks associated with it. On a uniprocessor system, the act of acquiring a spinlock is transparently reduced to raising IPL to that of the spinlock. Section 8.3.6 describes the use of each spinlock. From the perspective of a uniprocessor system, those sections can be interpreted as describing the synchronization use of the spinlocks' IPLs.

The macro $IPLDEF defines symbolic names for IPL values.

8.2.1 IPL$_POWER

Routines in the executive raise IPL to IPL$_POWER, or 31, to block all interrupts, including power failure, an IPL 30 interrupt. IPL is raised to this level only for a short period of time once the system has been initialized. IPL$_EMB and IPL$_MCHECK are synonyms for IPL$_POWER; they are two different names for the same spinlock.

- Device drivers raise IPL to 31 to prevent a powerfail interrupt from occurring, just before they invoke IOC$WFI*xx*CH.
- The entire bootstrap sequence operates at IPL 31 to put the system into a known state before allowing interrupts to occur.
- As described in Section 8.3.6.19, error log buffer allocation and deallocation occur at this IPL.
- As described in Section 8.3.6.18, machine check exception and parts of the CPU-specific error interrupt service routines execute at IPL 31.
- XDELTA, the executive debugger, runs at IPL 31.

8.2.2   IPL$_HWCLK and IPL$_HWCLKLO

When IPL is raised to IPL$_HWCLK, or 24, interval timer interrupts are blocked. On newer VAX processors, the interval timer interrupts at IPL$_HWCLKLO, or 22; on older ones, it interrupts at IPL 24. Chapter 11 identifies the interval timer IPL associated with each processor type. Section 8.3.6.16 describes the use of the associated spinlock.

8.2.3   Device IPLs

A device driver raises IPL to the level at which its associated device interrupts. Raising IPL prevents the device from interrupting while its device registers are being read or written.

8.2.4   Fork IPLs

The executive uses fork IPLs to synchronize access to unit control blocks (UCBs). UCBs are accessed by device drivers and by process-based code, such as the Queue I/O ($QIO) and Cancel I/O on Channel ($CANCEL) system services.

A device driver also uses its associated fork IPL as a synchronization level when accessing data structures that control shared resources, such as multi-unit controllers, data path registers, or map registers. For this synchronization to work properly, all devices sharing a given resource must use the same fork IPL.

Fork processing, the technique whereby a device driver lowers IPL below device interrupt level in a manner consistent with the interrupt nesting scheme, also uses the serialization technique described in Section 8.4.

8.2.5   IPL$_SYNCH

IPL$_SYNCH is the IPL at which the software timer routine executes. This routine services timer queue entries (TQEs) and handles quantum expiration. (The software timer interrupt is requested and granted at IPL 7, but the interrupt service routine raises IPL and runs primarily at IPL$_SYNCH. See Chapter 11 for further details.)

IPL$_SYNCH is the level to which IPL must be raised for any routine to access several systemwide data structures, for example, the scheduler database. By raising IPL to IPL$_SYNCH, all other interrupt service routines on that processor that might access the same systemwide data structure are blocked from execution until IPL is lowered.

IPL$_SYNCH is also the IPL at which most driver fork processing occurs. While the processor is executing at IPL$_SYNCH, certain systemwide events, such as scheduling and I/O postprocessing, are blocked. However, other more important operations, such as hardware interrupt servicing, can continue.

The following are synonyms of IPL$_SYNCH with the same numeric value: IPL$_MMG, IPL$_SCHED, IPL$_FILSYS, IPL$_TIMER, and IPL$_JIB. (Note that this is a change in the meaning of IPL$_SCHED, whose value was 3 in versions of VMS prior to Version 5.) Each of these synonyms corresponds to a spinlock. IPL$_SCS and IPL$_IOLOCK8 are also synonyms of IPL$_SYNCH; they are two different names for the same spinlock.

In early versions of VMS, the value of IPL$_SYNCH was 7. In VMS Version 4, its value was changed to 8 to enable three executive components to run at the same IPL: the distributed lock manager, system communication services (SCS), and the CI port driver.

On a VAXcluster system, the lock manager must communicate cluster-wide with its counterparts on other nodes to perform locking. The lock managers communicate using the message services of SCS. SCS is also used heavily by class and port drivers and runs at the same IPL they do, IPL$_SCS, or 8. The SCS port drivers must run at IPL 8 because some of them need to synchronize access to shared resources and data structures such as buffer and response descriptor tables and with mount verification activity.

In addition to having to communicate with SCS at IPL$_SCS, the lock manager also requires access to the scheduler database, which is synchronized at IPL$_SYNCH. To simplify the interactions among the lock manager, SCS, and other threads of execution modifying the scheduler database, IPL$_SYNCH and IPL$_SCS were made the same value by changing the value of IPL$_SYNCH.

8.2.6   **IPL$_QUEUEAST**

When IPL$_SYNCH had a value of 7, device drivers and other high IPL threads of execution that needed to access data such as the scheduler database forked to IPL 6 so that they could raise IPL to IPL$_SYNCH.

The terminal driver, for example, might notify a requesting process of unsolicited input or a CTRL/Y through an AST (see Chapter 7). Queuing an AST to a process requires scheduler database modifications, which must be made at IPL$_SYNCH. The IPL 7 interrupt could not have been used to achieve the same result because it is reserved for software timer interrupts. Thus, this synchronization technique used the first free IPL below 7, the IPL 6 software interrupt. IPL 6 was named IPL$_QUEUEAST, since its primary use as a fork IPL was AST enqueuing.

As a result of changing IPL$_SYNCH to 8, IPL$_QUEUEAST forking is generally unnecessary for serializing access to databases synchronized at IPL$_SYNCH. Fork processes running at IPL 8 can remain at 8; device interrupt service routines and fork processes running at IPLs above 8 can fork to 8. However, many instances of IPL$_QUEUEAST fork processing remain in

VMS, unchanged from earlier versions. Executing these operations at IPL$_QUEUEAST, rather than at IPL 8, results in placing a somewhat higher priority on IPL 8 fork processing, which is typically I/O processing.

8.2.7 IPL$_RESCHED

IPL$_RESCHED (3) is the IPL of the rescheduling interrupt, whose service routine removes the current process from execution and selects another process to execute. Kernel mode code running in process context raises IPL to IPL$_RESCHED to block this interrupt. For example, the System Generation (SYSGEN) utility raises to this IPL while performing a WRITE ACTIVE command or while accessing the processor's per-CPU data area.

There are only two IPLs used for synchronization that do not have an associated spinlock. One is IPL$_RESCHED; the other is IPL 2.

8.2.8 IPL 2

IPL 2 is used to block AST interrupts within a process. When system service procedures raise IPL to 2, they are blocking the delivery of all ASTs, but often particularly the kernel AST that causes process deletion. In other words, if a process is executing at IPL 2 or above, it cannot be deleted or suspended. As a result of a change in VMS Version 4, it is also possible to block process deletion and suspension by disabling AST delivery to kernel mode.

Raising IPL to 2 is used in several places to prevent process deletion between the time that some system resource (such as system dynamic memory) is allocated and the time that ownership of that resource is recorded (such as the insertion of a data structure into a list). For example, the $QIO system service executes at IPL 2 from the time that an I/O request packet is allocated from nonpaged dynamic memory until that packet is queued to a UCB or placed into the I/O postprocessing queue.

IPL 2 has another significance: it is the highest IPL at which page faults are permitted. If a page fault occurs above IPL 2, the page fault exception service routine generates the fatal bugcheck PGFIPLHI. If there is any possibility that a page fault can occur, because either the code executing or the data being referenced is pageable, that code cannot execute above IPL 2. The converse of this constraint is that any code that executes above IPL 2, and all data referenced by such code, must be locked into memory in some way. Appendix B shows some of the techniques that the VMS executive uses to dynamically lock code or data into memory referenced from IPLs above 2.

8.3 SPINLOCKS

A spinlock is acquired by a processor to synchronize access to data shared by members of an SMP system. The most basic form of spinlock is a bit that describes the state of a particular set of shared data; the bit is set to indicate that a processor is accessing the data. Interlocked instructions are used to test and set the bit or clear it. A spinlock enables a set of processors to serialize their access to shared data.

A processor needing access to some shared data tests and sets the spinlock associated with that data with a BBSSI instruction. If the bit was clear, the processor is allowed access to the data. This is known as locking or acquiring the spinlock. If the bit was already set, the processor must wait, because another processor is accessing the data.

The waiting processor essentially spins in a tight loop, executing repeated bit test instructions to test the state of the spinlock. This is known as a busy wait. It is from this spinning that the term *spinlock* derives. The busy wait ends when the processor accessing the data clears the bit with a BBCCI instruction to indicate that it is done. Clearing the bit is known as unlocking or releasing the spinlock.

A resource synchronized through elevated IPL on a uniprocessor is synchronized through a combination of spinlock and elevated IPL on an SMP system. A thread of execution running on one processor acquires a spinlock to serialize access to the data with threads of execution running on other processors. Before acquiring the spinlock, the thread of execution raises IPL to block accesses by other threads of execution running on the same processor. The IPL value is determined by the spinlock being locked.

The concept of spinlock adds a dimension to the concept of raising IPL and extends its effect across all processors in the SMP system. Acquiring a spinlock, however, is different from causing IPL to be raised on all SMP members to block all threads running at lower IPL. Instead, only those threads of execution that try to acquire a spinlock owned by another processor are blocked. This provides more parallelism than simply extending an IPL raise would. Furthermore, since some IPLs, such as IPL$_SYNCH, are now represented by multiple spinlocks, the granularity of locking is finer, allowing for even more parallelism.

To adapt more easily from IPL-based synchronization to the needs of symmetric multiprocessing, the implementation of spinlocks permits nested acquisitions of a spinlock. For example, many routines that manipulate the scheduler database raised IPL to IPL$_SYNCH in earlier versions of VMS. If one routine already at IPL$_SYNCH invoked another routine that raised IPL to IPL$_SYNCH to access the same database, no harm was done. Under VMS Version 5, this sequence results in multiple concurrent, or nested, acquisitions of the SCHED spinlock by the same processor.

A bit used as a spinlock is actually part of a larger data structure called a spinlock control block. Some spinlock control blocks are defined in the VMS executive; these are called static spinlocks. Others, created during system operation, are called dynamic. Section 8.3.1 describes the spinlock control block; Section 8.3.3, static spinlocks; and Section 8.3.4, dynamic spinlocks.

To acquire or release a spinlock, kernel mode code invokes one of several macros, identifying the spinlock in a macro argument. The macros generate code that tests that multiprocessing has been enabled and dispatches to executive routines that perform the actual spinlock operations.

The executive routines are invoked through base image transfer vectors (see Chapter 29). There are actually three different versions of these routines, conditionally assembled from one source module and built into three loadable executive images:

- Module SPINLOCKS, in SYSTEM_SYNCHRONIZATION_MIN.EXE, is the default version on an SMP system. It is optimized for performance and is referred to as the minimum or streamlined version.
- Module SPINLOCKS_MON, in SYSTEM_SYNCHRONIZATION.EXE, is the full-checking version that monitors spinlock activity. It is designed to facilitate troubleshooting of synchronization problems.
- Module SPINLOCKS_UNI, in SYSTEM_SYNCHRONIZATION_UNI.EXE, runs on a uniprocessor, a processor that is not a member of an SMP system.

The SYSGEN parameter MULTIPROCESSING dictates which of these is loaded at system initialization. Its possible values are

- 0—Load the uniprocessor image.
- 1—Load the full-checking multiprocessing version if the CPU type is capable of symmetric multiprocessing and if there are two or more CPUs present or the CPU type is capable of adding CPUs dynamically after bootstrap; otherwise, load the uniprocessing version.
- 2—Always load the full-checking version, regardless of CPU configuration.
- 3—Load the streamlined multiprocessing version if the CPU type is capable of symmetric multiprocessing and if there are two or more CPUs present or the CPU type is capable of adding CPUs dynamically after bootstrap; otherwise, load the uniprocessing version.

The default value for this parameter is 3.

Section 8.3.8 describes the streamlined versions of the spinlock routines. Section 8.3.9 describes the full-checking versions, which implement a more complex form of spinlock than the streamlined ones do. The routines in the uniprocessor version are mostly null routines, each consisting of an RSB instruction, and are not described here. They enable code requiring synchronization to invoke the same macros and routines regardless of the CPU configuration.

8.3.1 Spinlock Control Block

Figure 8.1 shows the layout of a spinlock control block. The macro $SPLDEF defines symbolic names for its fields.

The low bit of field SPL$B_SPINLOCK has two meanings: one for the streamlined spinlock routines, and one for the full-checking routines. The former use the basic form of spinlock; the low bit of SPL$B_SPINLOCK is the actual spinlock. For the full-checking routines, this bit merely serializes

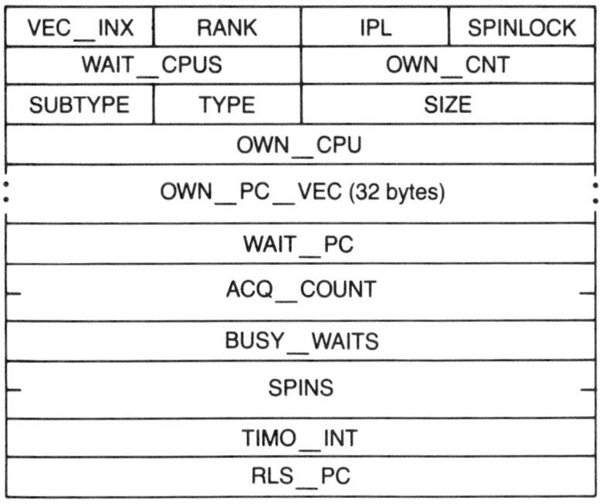

VEC__INX	RANK	IPL	SPINLOCK
WAIT__CPUS		OWN__CNT	
SUBTYPE	TYPE	SIZE	
OWN__CPU			
OWN__PC__VEC (32 bytes)			
WAIT__PC			
ACQ__COUNT			
BUSY__WAITS			
SPINS			
TIMO__INT			
RLS__PC			

Figure 8.1
Layout of a Spinlock Control Block

access to the spinlock control block; the fields SPL$W_OWN_CNT and SPL$L_OWN_CPU are the actual lock (see Section 8.3.9).

SPL$B_IPL specifies the IPL associated with the spinlock, the value to which IPL is raised when a processor acquires the spinlock.

SPL$B_RANK defines the rank of the spinlock. Spinlock rank is stored in an inverted form. Its possible values range from 0 to 31, with 0 being the highest rank. That is, rank increases from 31 to 30 to 29, and so on. This chapter uses the inverted form in its descriptions. Each static spinlock has a unique rank; all dynamic spinlocks have the same rank, which is 31. A thread of execution that acquires multiple static spinlocks must acquire them in increasing rank (see Section 8.3.5).

SPL$W_OWN_CNT records how many concurrent and nested times a processor has locked the spinlock. This field is initialized to −1 to indicate that a spinlock is unowned. With an owner count biased by −1, the acquire code can more easily distinguish increments that cause a transition between unowned and owned from those that do not. When a processor first acquires a spinlock, the value is incremented to 0. If a thread of execution invokes another routine that acquires the same spinlock, the owner count is incremented to 1.

SPL$W_SIZE and SPL$B_TYPE contain the spinlock control block's size and type. SPL$B_SUBTYPE indicates the type of spinlock: static spinlock, fork spinlock, or device spinlock. These types are described further in the sections that follow.

SPL$L_OWN_CPU contains the address of the per-CPU database of the processor that has acquired the spinlock. The address is recorded when a processor acquires the spinlock. The field is cleared when a processor releases its last nested acquisition of the lock.

SPL$L_TIMO_INT is the maximum amount of time a processor can wait for the spinlock. After this interval has elapsed, the attempted spinlock acquisition times out. During system initialization, the timeout value is initialized to one of two values: if the spinlock IPL is less than or equal to 8, the value of the SYSGEN parameter SMP_LNGSPINWAIT is used; otherwise, the value of the SYSGEN parameter SMP_SPINWAIT is used. There are two different values because the MMG and SCHED spinlocks are occasionally held longer than would be reasonable for spinlocks at higher IPLs.

The spinlock control block fields that follow are used only by the full-checking version of the spinlock routines.

SPL$W_WAIT_CPUS contains the number of processors waiting to acquire the spinlock.

The eight longwords beginning at SPL$L_OWN_PC_VEC form a ring buffer that records the most recent program counters (PCs) from which an owner CPU acquired and released the spinlock. SPL$B_VEC_INX contains the index of the next entry to be written in the ring buffer.

SPL$L_WAIT_PC contains the address of the most recent busy wait for the spinlock.

SPL$Q_ACQ_COUNT is the cumulative number of successful acquisitions of the spinlock. SPL$L_BUSY_WAITS is the cumulative number of failed acquisitions. SPL$Q_SPINS is the cumulative number of spins.

SPL$L_RLS_PC is the most recent return PC of a thread of execution that releases all nested acquisitions at once.

8.3.2 Spinlock-Related Per-CPU Database Fields

In an SMP system, all processors map to the same system space. Each processor, however, has a piece of system space for its own use. The space contains, for example, the processor's interrupt stack and fork queues. VMS executive code invokes the FIND_CPU_DATA macro to determine the address of the processor's space as a function of the location of its interrupt stack.

Each processor's private area is called its per-CPU data area. Chapter 34 contains more information on the organization and use of the per-CPU data area. The macro $CPUDEF defines symbolic names for the fields in the per-CPU database, a part of the per-CPU data area.

There are several fields in the per-CPU database whose use is related to spinlocks:

- CPU$L_PHY_CPUID—Processor physical ID number
- CPU$L_RANK_VEC—Summary of spinlocks that are currently held by the processor
- CPU$L_IPL_VEC—Summary of IPLs at which spinlocks are currently held
- CPU$L_IPL_ARRAY—Count of spinlocks currently held at each IPL

When a processor acquires a spinlock, the processor's physical ID is recorded in the spinlock control block. When a processor tries to acquire a spinlock that is already owned, the physical ID in the spinlock control block is compared with that of the processor; if the IDs are the same, the processor's nested acquisition succeeds.

The other three per-CPU database fields previously listed are used only by the full-checking spinlock routines.

Each bit, excluding bit 31, set in the per-CPU database field CPU$L_RANK_VEC corresponds to a static spinlock held by the processor; its bit position identifies the spinlock rank. As a processor acquires and releases a spinlock, the bit corresponding to the spinlock's rank is set and cleared. Since each spinlock has a unique rank, the number of bits set in the longword are the number of different spinlocks held by the processor. Bit 31 is not used in this way because the rank 31 is for dynamic spinlocks, more than one of which can be held concurrently.

Each bit set in the field CPU$L_IPL_VEC corresponds to an IPL at which the processor holds one or more spinlocks. The IPL representation is inverted. When a processor acquires a spinlock, the IPL of the spinlock is subtracted from 31. The bit in CPU$L_IPL_VEC corresponding to that number is set. The field thus represents the current set of (inverted) spinlock IPLs active on the processor.

The inverted number is also used as an index into the 32-longword array at CPU$L_IPL_ARRAY. It counts the number of different spinlocks held at each IPL. There is no one-to-one mapping of spinlock to IPL: each IPL does not have a unique spinlock associated with it; some IPLs have more than one associated spinlock.

8.3.3 Static Spinlocks

All static spinlock control blocks are defined in module LDAT, which also contains a table listing their addresses. The base image global SMP$AR_SPNLKVEC contains the address of the table, and SMP$GW_SPNLKCNT contains the number of spinlocks in the table. Figure 8.2 shows this table and several representative spinlocks.

A static spinlock is identified by the position of its address in the table. This is known as its index, and is the longword postindex offset of its address in the table. The macro $SPLCODDEF defines symbolic names for these indexes; for example, SPL$C_SCHED is the index of the SCHED spinlock. The lowest index used is 32. Table entries with lower indexes are empty. Having index values of 32 or greater makes it possible to distinguish a spinlock index from an IPL value by testing whether bit 5 is set. Section 8.3.7 describes why making this distinction is necessary.

Table 8.2 lists the static spinlocks with a brief description of what each synchronizes and its associated IPL. The spinlocks are listed in order by rank, with lower ranking spinlocks first. Section 8.3.6 describes their use in somewhat more detail.

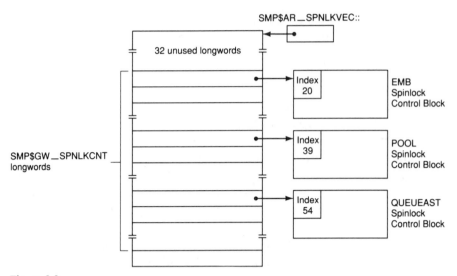

Figure 8.2
Static Spinlock Table

A static spinlock that synchronizes fork processing is called a fork spin-lock, often shortened to fork lock. A device UCB and any other type of fork block (FKB) identify the driver's fork lock, and indirectly its fork IPL, by specifying the spinlock index in the field named UCB$B_FLCK or FKB$B_FLCK. Some static spinlocks are never used as fork locks; their associated IPLs are not in the fork IPL range. Some static spinlocks are only used as fork locks, for example, the IOLOCK8 spinlock, and some are sometimes used as fork locks, for example, the MAILBOX spinlock.

The SPL$B_SUBTYPE field of a spinlock used only as a fork lock contains the value SPL$C_SPL_FORKLOCK; all other static spinlocks are identified simply as spinlocks, with the value SPL$C_SPL_SPINLOCK. The main distinction between fork locks and other static spinlocks is that fork locks are typically acquired and released through different macros. Kernel mode code acquires and releases a static spinlock by invoking the LOCK and UNLOCK macros; the FORKLOCK and FORKUNLOCK macros are used for fork locks. Section 8.3.7 describes these macros.

Another table with information about static spinlocks is the spinlock IPL table, at base image global symbol SMP$AL_IPLVEC. The table is indexed by static spinlock index and contains the IPL corresponding to that spinlock. This table is referenced in the code generated by the FORKLOCK macro (see Section 8.3.7) and by the routine EXE$FORK (see Chapter 4).

8.3.4 Dynamic Spinlocks

A dynamic spinlock is not listed in the spinlock table and has no index. A dynamic spinlock control block is allocated from nonpaged pool and is

Table 8.2 Static Spinlocks

Name	IPL	Synchronizes
QUEUEAST	6	IPL 6 fork processing
FILSYS	8	File system data structures such as file control blocks
IOLOCK8/SCS [1]	8	IPL 8 fork processing; SCS-related code
PR_LK8	8	Primary processor's IPL 8 processing
TIMER	8	Timer queue entries
JIB	8	Job information block fields JIB$L_BYTCNT and JIB$L_BYTLM
MMG	8	Memory management data structures
SCHED	8	Scheduler database
IOLOCK9	9	IPL 9 fork processing
PR_LK9	9	Primary processor's IPL 9 processing
IOLOCK10	10	IPL 10 fork processing
PR_LK10	10	Primary processor's IPL 10 processing
IOLOCK11	11	IPL 11 fork processing
PR_LK11	11	Primary processor's IPL 11 processing
MAILBOX	11	Writing mailbox messages
POOL	11	Nonpaged pool lists and related data
PERFMON	15	Performance monitoring
INVALIDATE	19 or 21 [2]	Translation buffer invalidation
VIRTCONS	20 or 22 [3]	Virtual console database
HWCLK	22 or 24 [4]	Hardware clock database
MEGA	31	Miscellaneous data structures such as the fork and wait queue
MCHECK/EMB [1]	31	Machine check serialization; error log buffers

[1] These two names are synonyms for the same spinlock.

[2] The IPL associated with this spinlock is determined at system initialization and is 1 less than the IPL of the system's interprocessor interrupt. On VAX 88x0 and VAX 83x0 systems, its value is 19. On VAX 6000 series systems, its value is 21.

[3] The IPL associated with this spinlock is determined at system initialization as the IPL of the interprocessor interrupt: for VAX 6000 series systems, its value is 22; for other SMP systems, its value is 20.

[4] The IPL associated with this spinlock is determined at system initialization as the IPL of the interval timer.

identified by its address. Currently, the only type of dynamic spinlock VMS uses is a device spinlock, usually called a device lock. The SPL$B_SUBTYPE field of a device lock's spinlock control block contains the value SPL$C_SPL_DEVICELOCK.

All dynamic spinlocks have the same rank, 31. However, the field SPL$B_RANK in a dynamic spinlock control block is initialized to −1 for quick identification in the routines that acquire and release spinlocks.

As SYSGEN identifies the I/O configuration and builds the I/O database, it creates device locks. SYSGEN invokes the routine SMP$ALLOC_SPL to create a device lock and SMP$INIT_SPL to initialize it. (Both routines are in the module SPINLOCKS.)

There is one device lock for each unique device controller. SYSGEN stores its address in the controller's channel request block field CRB$L_DLCK and in the field UCB$L_DLCK for each unit on that controller.

A device driver acquires and releases the device lock by invoking the DEVICELOCK and DEVICEUNLOCK macros (see Section 8.3.7). The device lock synchronizes access to the controller's registers and to fields in the UCB that describe the controller's state.

8.3.5   Rules for Acquiring and Releasing Spinlocks

For synchronization with spinlocks to be successful, threads of execution that use spinlocks must follow certain rules.

A thread of execution that acquires a spinlock to serialize access to some shared data is guaranteed exclusive access to the data while it holds the spinlock. Thus, all its modifications to the data can be considered atomic from the point of view of another thread trying to acquire the same spinlock to access the same data. To ensure this degree of atomicity, the implementation of spinlocks does not include breaking spinlock deadlocks. Rather, deadlocks are prevented by requiring threads of execution that use spinlocks to acquire spinlocks in a particular order.

The rank values of static spinlocks were carefully selected to reflect VMS code paths and interdependencies among the shared data structures protected by spinlocks. A thread of execution that acquires multiple spinlocks must acquire them in order by increasing rank. This rule is designed to prevent a deadlock such as the following: one processor has acquired spinlock A and is busy waiting to acquire spinlock B to complete its task; a second processor has acquired spinlock B and is busy waiting to acquire spinlock A to complete its task.

All device locks share the same rank, 31, which is lower than that of any static spinlock. However, a processor holding a static spinlock may acquire a device lock; the rule previously listed does not apply to acquisition of a device lock. The assumption is that the shared resource protected by a device lock is not dependent on the resources protected by the static spinlocks. Furthermore, each device lock is assumed to be independent of others, and a processor is permitted to hold more than one device lock at a time. All code acquiring multiple device locks concurrently must be written to prevent deadlocks; all threads must acquire such device locks in the same order.

A thread of execution about to acquire a spinlock must be running at an IPL less than or equal to that of the spinlock. This is analogous to the principle of raising IPL to synchronize on a uniprocessor system. This rule prevents the following type of synchronization failure:

1. Thread A, running at IPL x, acquires a spinlock and begins to manipulate the database it protects.
2. An interrupt at IPL $x + 1$ is requested and granted on the same processor, and thread B begins execution, interrupting thread A.
3. To access the same database, thread B tries to acquire its spinlock. Because threads A and B are running on the same processor, the nested acquisition is successful, and thread B begins to manipulate the database left in an inconsistent state by the interruption to thread A.

A thread of execution that has acquired a spinlock may raise IPL but must not lower it below the value associated with the spinlock. Lowering IPL could lead to the synchronization failure just described.

8.3.6   Use of Static Spinlocks

The sections that follow describe the use of each of the static spinlocks.

8.3.6.1   Use of the QUEUEAST Spinlock.

The QUEUEAST spinlock synchronizes fork processing at IPL 6. The need for IPL 6 fork processing is largely historical, based on constraints from VMS Version 3 and earlier versions, as described in Section 8.2.6.

8.3.6.2   Use of the FILSYS Spinlock.

The file system database consists of data structures that describe the mount state of a volume and the condition of open files on the volume. The FILSYS spinlock synchronizes access to pieces of the file system database that are accessed by routines external to the file system. (As described in Appendix H, lock management system services synchronize access to much of the file system database.)

For example, each open file is described by one or more window control blocks (WCBs). A WCB contains retrieval pointers that map the virtual blocks of a file to logical blocks on a device. As part of processing an I/O request to a file, IOC$MAPVBLK, in module IOSUBRAMS, uses WCB contents to convert virtual block numbers to their equivalent logical block numbers. IOC$MAPVBLK and the file system routines that alter WCBs synchronize their access to WCBs by acquiring the FILSYS spinlock.

8.3.6.3   Use of the IOLOCK8 and SCS Spinlocks.

A driver can specify one of the IOLOCKx spinlocks as its fork lock. A device UCB, which is also used as a fork block, contains the fork spinlock index in the field UCB$B_FLCK. The fork lock synchronizes access to data structures modified by the fork process, in particular its UCB.

To synchronize access to UCB fields manipulated at fork level, an executive routine or the driver fork process itself acquires the spinlock specified in UCB$B_FLCK.

IOLOCK8 is the fork lock most commonly used by device driver fork processes. It is used by all standard drivers that compete for shared adapter resources, like UNIBUS map registers. On a VAXcluster system that supports remote I/O, the MSCP server uses the IOLOCK8 spinlock.

IOLOCK8 and SCS are actually two names for the same spinlock.

System communication services (SCS) routines and lock manager routines coordinate access to VAXcluster and lock management data structures using the SCS spinlock. An SCS routine that executes as a fork process uses the SCS spinlock as its fork lock. The $ENQ and $DEQ system services acquire the SCS spinlock before altering the lock database.

8.3.6.4 **Use of the PR_LK8 Spinlock.** The PR_LK8 spinlock is a fork lock intended for use only by the primary processor. Currently, it is not used.

8.3.6.5 **Use of the TIMER Spinlock.** The software timer interrupt service routine, running on the primary processor in an SMP system, acquires the TIMER and HWCLK spinlocks while it tests whether the first entry in the time-ordered queue of TQEs has expired.

The routines that insert and remove TQEs from the timer queue acquire the TIMER spinlock if they have to manipulate TQEs other than the first in the list. The $SETIME system service acquires the TIMER spinlock when it resets the time-of-year clock and reorders the timer queue as a result of recalibrating pending TQEs with delta times. Chapter 11 provides more information on these two interrupt service routines and the timer queue.

8.3.6.6 **Use of the JIB Spinlock.** The JIB spinlock synchronizes access to the job information block (JIB) fields JIB$L_BYTCNT and JIB$L_BYTLM. The process context routines EXE$DEBIT_BYTCNT and EXE$CREDIT_BYTCNT and their alternative entry points acquire this spinlock to debit and credit the job's available byte count. The intent of the spinlock is to block other processes in the same job from simultaneously accessing these fields. Because there is only one systemwide JIB spinlock, however, all other processes in the system are blocked from accessing these fields in their own JIBs. This implementation, however, has the virtue of simplicity, and such accesses are believed to be sufficiently infrequent so as to present no performance issue.

8.3.6.7 **Use of the MMG Spinlock.** The MMG spinlock synchronizes access to the memory management database. This includes the page frame number database, section tables, page and swap file bitmaps, list of available system page table entries, and working set lists.

Its main users are the page fault exception service routine, swapper, memory management system services, and routines that lock and unlock direct I/O buffer pages into memory.

8.3.6.8 **Use of the SCHED Spinlock.** The SCHED spinlock synchronizes access to the scheduler database, the set of software process control blocks and their state queues, and mutex data structures. It also synchronizes access to a process's AST data: the queue of pending AST control blocks, the PCB$B_ ASTEN and PCB$B_ASTACT bits, and the process's ASTLVL.

8.3.6.9 **Use of the IOLOCK*n* Fork Spinlocks.** The spinlocks IOLOCK9, IOLOCK10, and IOLOCK11 are fork locks intended for use on any processor. Their use is similar to that of IOLOCK8, although they are not as commonly used.

8.3.6.10 **Use of the PR_LK*n* Fork Spinlocks.** The spinlocks PR_LK9, PR_LK10, and PR_LK11 are fork locks intended for use only by the primary processor. Currently, they have only one application: they are used in the logical console interface on a VAX 83x0 system. This interface provides console support for the secondary processor. VMS, running on the primary processor, emulates a console terminal, passing characters to and from the console subsystem of the secondary processor. This interface is used only for console mode communication; in particular, it is used to send commands to the secondary processor's console subsystem to boot the processor and to restart it after powerfail recovery.

The processor console subsystem is sensitive to interrupt latency. To avoid contention, the primary processor-specific fork locks were used rather than the ordinary fork locks.

8.3.6.11 **Use of the MAILBOX Spinlock.** The MAILBOX spinlock synchronizes access to mailboxes. It is the fork lock for the mailbox driver and the MA780 shared memory mailbox driver. The mailbox driver's internal routines EXE$WRT-MAILBOX and EXE$SNDEVMSG, invoked to write messages to a mailbox without going through the $QIO system service, acquire this spinlock to synchronize access to the mailbox.

8.3.6.12 **Use of the POOL Spinlock.** The POOL spinlock synchronizes access to the nonpaged variable-length list. Its main users are routines such as EXE$ALO-NONPAGED and EXE$DEANONPAGED, in module MEMORYALC. It also synchronizes access to the performance monitoring statistics kept on nonpaged variable-length pool allocation failures. Note that the nonpaged lookaside lists are accessed with interlocked queue instructions and thus do not need the protection of a spinlock.

The code that implements the DCL SHOW MEMORY command acquires the POOL spinlock while it scans the list to collect information for its display. The Monitor Utility acquires the POOL spinlock while it gathers information on pool use.

8.3.6.13 **Use of the PERFMON Spinlock.** The PERFMON spinlock synchronizes access to the I/O performance database. Its main users are routines such as PMS$START_REQ, in module IOPERFORM. It also synchronizes access to the system global PMS$GL_IOPFMSEQ, the counter from which the $QIO system service and the mass storage control protocol (MSCP) server assign I/O request sequence numbers.

8.3.6.14 **Use of the INVALIDATE Spinlock.** To invalidate a cached system space address translation, a member of an SMP system acquires the INVALIDATE spinlock. The spinlock prevents more than one processor at a time from initiating the sequence required for all SMP members to invalidate the entry in their translation buffers (see Chapter 34).

8.3.6.15 **Use of the VIRTCONS Spinlock.** On existing SMP systems, there is only one console terminal, which is controlled by the primary processor. The primary processor provides an interface for secondary processors' program mode console I/O. This interface is called a virtual console.

The VIRTCONS spinlock ensures that only one secondary processor at a time performs I/O through virtual console support to the physical console (see Chapter 34).

8.3.6.16 **Use of the HWCLK Spinlock.** The HWCLK spinlock synchronizes access to the hardware clock database, which consists of

- EXE$GQ_SYSTIME—System time quadword
- EXE$GL_ABSTIM_TICS—System tick counter
- EXE$GQ_1ST_TIME—Expiration time of the first TQE

The interval timer interrupt service routine, when running on the primary processor of an SMP system, acquires the HWCLK spinlock to update the system time quadword and tick counter, and to test whether the first TQE has expired. If it has, the interrupt service routine requests an IPL 7 interrupt for the software timer.

The software timer interrupt service routine, running on the primary processor in an SMP system, acquires the TIMER and HWCLK spinlocks while it tests whether the first TQE has expired.

The routines that insert and remove TQEs from the timer queue acquire the HWCLK spinlock if they have to manipulate the first TQE in the list. Chapter 11 gives more information on these two interrupt service routines and the timer queue.

Any code that needs to read the system time acquires this spinlock. Generally, this is done indirectly through the macro READ_SYSTIME, which generates the following code with *destination* supplied by the macro invoker:

```
        .EXTERNAL EXE$GQ_SYSTIME
        LOCK    LOCKNAME=HWCLK,-
                SAVIPL=-(SP)
        MOVQ    G^EXE$GQ_SYSTIME,destination
        UNLOCK  LOCKNAME=HWCLK,-
                NEWIPL=(SP)+
```

8.3.6.17 **Use of the MEGA Spinlock.** The MEGA spinlock has two uses: to synchro-nize access to the fork and wait queue, used by fork processes to stall them-selves for approximately half a second (see Chapter 4), and to synchronize the entry of processors into the benign state (see Chapter 34).

8.3.6.18 **Use of the MCHECK Spinlock.** The machine check exception service rou-tines for CPUs that can be members of an SMP system acquire the MCHECK spinlock as needed. For example, the spinlock serializes access to VAXBI registers or memory controller registers. Other CPU-specific error interrupt service routines acquire the spinlock for similar reasons.

8.3.6.19 **Use of the EMB Spinlock.** The EMB spinlock synchronizes access to the error log allocation buffers (see Chapter 32). The routines that reserve and release pieces of error log allocation buffer for error messages acquire the EMB spinlock.

The ERRFMT process locks the EMB spinlock when it is altering data structures that describe the state of the error log allocation buffer. As Chap-ter 32 describes, ERRFMT copies an error log allocation buffer in several stages. It examines the error log buffer status flags and message counts with the spinlock held. If it can copy the buffer, it sets a flag in the buffer to inhibit further allocations in it and then releases the spinlock. At IPL 0, ERRFMT copies the error log allocation buffer to its P0 space and formats and writes the messages to the error log file.

This spinlock also synchronizes access to a buffer pool used by SMP code. A fork block is allocated from the buffer pool to create a thread of execution that runs on the primary SMP processor.

8.3.7 **Macros for Acquiring and Releasing Spinlocks**

There are three sets of macros for acquiring and releasing spinlocks:

- LOCK and UNLOCK for static spinlocks
- FORKLOCK and FORKUNLOCK for static spinlocks used to synchronize fork processing
- DEVICELOCK and DEVICEUNLOCK for dynamic spinlocks

These macros hide the details of the actual synchronization method used; they facilitate writing code that can synchronize properly whether it exe-cutes on a uniprocessor or a member of an SMP system.

Each of these macros has a number of arguments, only a few of which are described here. The *VMS Device Support Manual* describes the use of these macros and their arguments in more detail.

These macros differ primarily in the way their arguments identify the spinlock of interest:

- An argument to LOCK and UNLOCK specifies the symbolic index of a static spinlock.
- In a typical use of FORKLOCK or FORKUNLOCK, R5 contains the address of a UCB in which the field UCB$B_FLCK has a static spinlock index.
- In a typical use of DEVICELOCK or DEVICEUNLOCK, R5 contains the address of a UCB in which the field UCB$L_DLCK has the address of the device lock.

The lock macros generate the following approximate sequence:

1. Optionally (determined by macro argument SAVIPL), save the current IPL.
2. If SMP is not enabled, set IPL as requested and branch around the rest of the instructions. The low bit of system global SMP$GL_FLAGS is set when SMP is enabled.
3. Optionally (determined by macro argument PRESERVE), save R0.
4. Store the static spinlock index or the address of a dynamic spinlock in R0.
5. Execute a JSB instruction to SMP$ACQUIRE in the case of a static spinlock, or to SMP$ACQUIREL or SMP$ACQNOIPL in the case of a dynamic spinlock.
6. If R0 was saved, restore it.

A sample invocation of LOCK with its generated code follows:

```
;the macro invocation
;locks spinlock with index SPL$C_MMG
        LOCK    LOCKNAME=MMG,-            ;Lock MMG database
                PRESERVE=NO              ;Don't preserve R0
;its generated code, slightly simplified
        BLBC    G^SMP$GL_FLAGS,30002$
        MOVZBL  S^#SPL$C_MMG,R0
        JSB     G^SMP$ACQUIRE
        BRB     30003$
30002$:
        MTPR    S^#IPL$_MMG,S^#PR$_IPL
30003$:
```

A sample invocation of FORKLOCK with its generated code follows:

```
;the macro invocation
;locks spinlock whose index is in UCB$B_FLCK
        FORKLOCK -
                UCB$B_FLCK(R5),-         ;Lock fork access
                SAVIPL=-(SP)             ;Save current IPL
```

```
;its generated code, slightly simplified
        MFPR    S^#PR$_IPL,-(SP)
        PUSHL   R0
        MOVZBL  UCB$B_FLCK(R5),R0
        BLBC    G^SMP$GL_FLAGS,30002$
        JSB     G^SMP$ACQUIRE
        BRB     30003$
30002$:
        MTPR    G^SMP$AL_IPLVEC[R0],S^#PR$_IPL
30003$:
        POPL    R0
```

A different invocation of FORKLOCK with its generated code follows. This invocation specifies that the field UCB$B_FLCK may contain a fork IPL rather than a spinlock index. The generated code tests bit 5 of UCB$B_FLCK to see which it really is: a number less than 32 is an IPL; a number higher than that is a spinlock index. If the number is an IPL, the generated code sets IPL to that value. If the number is a spinlock index, the generated code tests whether multiprocessing is enabled. If it is, the code invokes SMP$ACQUIRE; otherwise, it uses the spinlock index into an array containing the IPL associated with each static spinlock.

```
;the macro invocation
;specifies that UCB$B_FLCK has a fork IPL
        FORKLOCK -
                FIPL=YES
;its generated code, slightly simplified
        PUSHL   R0
        MOVZBL  B^FKB$B_FLCK(R5),R0
        BBC     #5,R0,30001$
        BLBC    G^SMP$GL_FLAGS,30002$
        JSB     G^SMP$ACQUIRE
        BRB     30003$
30001$:
        MTPR    R0,S^#PR$_IPL
        BRB     30003$
30002$:
        MTPR    G^SMP$AL_IPLVEC[R0],S^#PR$_IPL
30003$:
        POPL    R0
```

A sample invocation of DEVICELOCK with its generated code follows:

```
;the macro invocation
;locks spinlock whose address is in UCB$L_DLCK
        DEVICELOCK -
                LOCKADDR=UCB$L_DLCK(R5),- ;Lock device interrupts
                CONDITION=NOSETIPL        ;Don't alter IPL
;its generated code, slightly simplified
        BLBC    G^SMP$GL_FLAGS,30006$
        PUSHL   R0
        MOVL    UCB$L_DLCK(R5),R0
        JSB     G^SMP$ACQNOIPL
```

```
30004$:
30005$:
        POPL    R0
30006$:
```

The unlock macros generate the following approximate code sequence:

1. If SMP is not enabled, go to step 6.
2. Optionally (determined by macro argument PRESERVE), save R0.
3. Store the static spinlock index or the address of a dynamic spinlock in R0.
4. If the macro argument CONDITION=RESTORE is present, execute a JSB instruction to SMP$RESTORE to relinquish one acquisition of a static spinlock or to SMP$RESTOREL for a dynamic spinlock.

   If the macro argument is not present, execute a JSB instruction to SMP$RELEASE to relinquish all nested acquisitions of a static spinlock or to SMP$RELEASEL for a dynamic spinlock.
5. If R0 was saved, restore it.
6. Optionally (determined by macro argument NEWIPL), set IPL to the value requested.

A sample invocation of the UNLOCK macro with its generated code follows:

```
;the macro invocation
        UNLOCK LOCKNAME=INVALIDATE,-
               PRESERVE=NO,-              ;Don't save R0
               NEWIPL=(SP)+              ;Restore IPL from stack
;its generated code, slightly simplified
        BLBC    G^SMP$GL_FLAGS,30033$
        MOVZBL  S^#SPL$C_INVALIDATE,R0
        JSB     G^SMP$RELEASE
30033$:
        MTPR    (SP)+,S^#PR$_IPL
```

A sample invocation of FORKUNLOCK with its generated code follows:

```
;the macro invocation
        FORKUNLOCK -
               UCB$B_FLCK(R5),-          ;Release fork access
               NEWIPL=(SP)+              ;Restore IPL from stack
;its generated code, slightly simplified
        BLBC    G^SMP$GL_FLAGS,30004$
        PUSHL   R0
        MOVZBL  UCB$B_FLCK(R5),R0
        JSB     G^SMP$RELEASE
        POPL    R0
30004$:
        MTPR    (SP)+,S^#PR$_IPL
```

A sample invocation of DEVICEUNLOCK with its generated code follows. This example results in dispatch to SMP$RESTOREL rather than to SMP$RELEASEL.

```
;the macro invocation
        DEVICEUNLOCK -
                LOCKADDR=UCB$L_DLCK(R5),-
                                    ;Release device interrupts
                NEWIPL=(SP)+,-      ;Restore IPL
                CONDITION=RESTORE   ;Conditionally release spinlock
;its generated code, slightly simplified
        BLBC    G^SMP$GL_FLAGS,30007$
        PUSHL   R0
        MOVL    UCB$L_DLCK(R5),R0
        JSB     G^SMP$RESTOREL
        POPL    R0
30007$:
        MTPR    (SP)+,S^#PR$_IPL
```

8.3.8 Streamlined Spinlock Routines

As described in Section 8.3, there are three versions of the spinlock routines, conditionally assembled from one source. This section describes the streamlined versions of the spinlock routines, in module SPINLOCKS. Section 8.3.9 describes the full-checking versions of these routines.

The spinlock routines run in kernel mode, at IPL 3 and above. They include

- SMP$ACQUIRE—Acquire a static spinlock
- SMP$ACQUIREL—Acquire a dynamic spinlock
- SMP$ACQNOIPL—Acquire a dynamic spinlock without altering IPL
- SMP$RESTORE—Relinquish one acquisition of a static spinlock
- SMP$RESTOREL—Relinquish one acquisition of a dynamic spinlock
- SMP$RELEASE—Relinquish all nested acquisitions of a static spinlock
- SMP$RELEASEL—Relinquish all nested acquisitions of a dynamic spinlock

The spinlock lock macros dispatch to SMP$ACQUIRE or one of its alternative entry points, SMP$ACQNOIPL or SMP$ACQUIREL. Following is a description of their actions, with some details of SMP operations omitted for simplicity:

1. At entry to SMP$ACQUIRE, R0 contains the index of a static spinlock. Indexing into the static spinlock table, SMP$ACQUIRE obtains the address of the spinlock and stores it in R0. (Entry points SMP$ACQUIREL and SMP$ACQNOIPL are entered with the address of a dynamic spinlock already in R0.)

2. The routine raises IPL to that of the spinlock, SPL$B_IPL. (Entry point SMP$ACQNOIPL is entered with an IPL that is known to be correct and thus not to be altered.)

189

3. SMP$ACQUIRE obtains the physical ID of the processor from its per-CPU database.

4. It executes a BBSSI instruction, testing whether the spinlock bit is set and setting it.

5. If the bit was clear, this processor now owns the spinlock. SMP$AC-QUIRE stores the address of the processor's per-CPU database in SPL$L_OWN_CPU, increments SPL$W_OWN_CNT, and returns to its invoker.

6. If the bit was set, the spinlock has already been acquired, possibly by the processor trying to acquire it now. SMP$ACQUIRE compares the address of the processor's per-CPU database with that stored in SPL$L_OWN_CPU. If the two are equal, this attempted lock is a nested acquisition. SMP$ACQUIRE increments SPL$W_OWN_CNT and returns to its invoker.

7. If the two addresses are not equal, another processor has acquired the spinlock and this processor must wait for it to be released.

   SMP$ACQUIRE increments the field CPU$B_BUSYWAIT in the per-CPU database as a flag to the interval timer interrupt service routine. When this field is nonzero, the interrupt service routine does not charge the tick against process quantum. Chapter 11 gives further details.

   SMP$ACQUIRE invokes the SPINWAIT macro, whose generated code is described in the following paragraphs, through step 11. Executing the generated code, SMP$ACQUIRE loops, testing the spinlock bit with a BLBC instruction rather than with an interlocked instruction. When the bit becomes clear, SMP$ACQUIRE repeats its attempt to acquire it with an interlocked BBSSI instruction. If the attempt is successful, SMP$AC-QUIRE takes the actions in step 5.

   One distinction between the two forms of bit test is that an interlocked instruction must fetch data with an interlock operation. On a system with write-through cache, this means fetching the operand from memory. A noninterlocked instruction can fetch its operands from cache if they are present and valid in the cache. Thus, the noninterlocked bit test instruction BLBC usually accesses the spinlock bit stored in the processor's cache. On a system capable of SMP processing, the processor hardware monitors writes to memory and invalidates any cached locations that have been overwritten. A processor that performs these functions is said to have cache coherency. When the owning processor releases the spinlock, the stale value in the cache of the spinning processor is invalidated; the next BLBC instruction on the spinning processor tests the updated value.

   Use of a noninterlocked bit test instruction reduces memory bus traffic while the waiting processor is spinning. If the granularity of the memory interlock is larger than a spinlock or if there are multiple processors trying to acquire the same spinlock, use of the noninterlocked bit test also reduces memory interlock contention.

8. The waiting processor does more than execute repeated BLBC instructions. If the IPL at which it spins is higher than that of an interprocessor interrupt, the processor cannot receive interrupts requesting that it perform various SMP functions (see Chapter 34). Under such circumstances, SMP$ACQUIRE must make explicit tests for these requests and perform them as necessary.

9. Also, while SMP$ACQUIRE is spinning, it performs a countdown and times out the attempted acquisition if its wait time exceeds the spinlock timeout value stored in SPL$L_TIMO_INT. At the end of the interval, SMP$ACQUIRE tests whether the spinlock's current owner is the same as the processor that owned it at the beginning of the interval.

10. If the owners are not the same, the original owner released the spinlock and some other processor acquired it before this one was able to. SMP$ACQUIRE then repeats the countdown, attempting to acquire the spinlock.

11. If the owners are the same, something is interfering with the proper operation of the owning processor. SMP$ACQUIRE invokes SMP$TIMEOUT, in module SMPROUT. If it is possible that a recoverable condition led to the timeout, SMP$TIMEOUT returns, and SMP$ACQUIRE repeats the countdown. If it is not possible, SMP$TIMEOUT generates the fatal bugcheck CPUSPINWAIT.

The spinlock unlock macro invocations that request a restore (relinquish one acquisition of a spinlock) dispatch to SMP$RESTORE or to its alternative entry point SMP$RESTOREL. Those that request a release (relinquish all nested acquisitions) dispatch to SMP$RELEASE or to SMP$RELEASEL. If SMP$RESTORE relinquishes the only acquisition of a spinlock, it branches to SMP$RELEASE.

These routines run in kernel mode, at IPL 3 and above. Following is a description of their typical actions. These routines do not alter IPL; they run at the IPL at which they are entered.

1. At entry to SMP$RESTORE, R0 contains the index of a static spinlock. Indexing into the static spinlock table, SMP$RESTORE obtains the address of the spinlock and stores it in R0. (Entry point SMP$RESTOREL is entered with the address of a dynamic spinlock already in R0.)

2. SMP$RESTORE decrements the spinlock owner count. If the count is zero or positive, indicating that the spinlock is still owned, the routine returns to its invoker.

3. If the spinlock is now free, SMP$RESTORE's path joins that of SMP$RELEASE, at step 6, below.

4. At entry to SMP$RELEASE, R0 contains the index of a static spinlock. Indexing into the static spinlock table, SMP$RELEASE obtains the address of the spinlock and stores it in R0. (Entry point SMP$RELEASEL is entered with the address of a dynamic spinlock in R0.)

5. The routine sets the spinlock owner count to −1.

6. It clears SPL$L_OWN_CPU and executes a BBCCI instruction to clear the low bit of SPL$B_SPINLOCK. If the low bit was already clear, the routine generates the fatal bugcheck SPLRELERR on the presumption that a serious failure has occurred.

7. Otherwise, the routine returns to its invoker.

8.3.9   **Full-Checking Spinlock Routines**

The full-checking version of the spinlock routines are in module SPIN-LOCKS_MON. This module includes the same entry points as the stream-lined version. The entry points are invoked from the same lock and unlock macros.

Following is a description of the full-checking version of the acquire routines, with some details of SMP operations omitted for simplicity:

1. When SMP$ACQUIRE is entered, R0 contains the index of a static spinlock. Indexing into the static spinlock table, SMP$ACQUIRE obtains the address of the spinlock and stores it in R0. (Entry points SMP$ACQUIREL and SMP$ACQNOIPL are entered with the address of a dynamic spinlock already in R0.)

2. The routine tests whether the IPL at entry is higher than that of the spinlock, indicating a synchronization failure. If it is, the routine generates the fatal bugcheck SPLIPLHIGH. (The routine continues when the entry IPL is too high if the spinlock is a device lock; this exception exists for MicroVAX systems, in which the interrupt arbitration IPL and bus grant IPL differ.) If it is not, SMP$ACQUIRE sets the IPL to that of the spinlock. (Entry point SMP$ACQNOIPL is entered with an IPL already known to be correct.)

3. SMP$ACQUIRE obtains the physical ID of the processor from its per-CPU database.

4. It tests whether the target spinlock is a device lock. If it is, SMP$ACQUIRE skips the next step; a processor may acquire multiple device locks, and the spinlock acquisition rule does not apply.

5. If the target lock is not a device lock, SMP$ACQUIRE tests whether the attempted lock would violate the spinlock acquisition rule (see Section 8.3.5). It executes an FFS instruction on CPU$L_RANK_VEC to determine if the processor already holds a higher ranking spinlock. (Recall that spinlock ranks are inverted, with zero being the highest rank.) If the processor holds a higher ranking spinlock, the routine generates the fatal bugcheck SPLACQERR.

6. SMP$ACQUIRE raises IPL to 31 and executes a BBSSI instruction to test and set the low bit of SPL$B_SPINLOCK. If the bit is already set, some other processor has exclusive access to the spinlock control block and this processor must wait. SMP$ACQUIRE restores the previous IPL and

spinwaits, as described in Section 8.3.8, retesting the bit with a BLBC instruction.

When the bit becomes clear, the routine raises IPL to 31 and repeats its attempt to acquire exclusive access to the spinlock control block. The processor runs at IPL 31 to block all interrupts while it has exclusive access to the spinlock control block. This avoids potential delays and deadlocks that could occur if another processor, the owner of the spinlock, were unable to release it while the processor with exclusive access to the control block was executing some interrupt service routine.

7. When the processor obtains exclusive access to the spinlock control block, SMP$ACQUIRE examines the spinlock owner count and, if necessary, owner CPU, to determine whether this processor may acquire the spinlock.

8. If some other processor owns the spinlock, SMP$ACQUIRE takes the following steps:

    a. It increments the field CPU$B_BUSYWAIT in the per-CPU database as a flag to the interval timer interrupt service routine. When this field is nonzero, the interrupt service routine does not charge the tick against process quantum (see Chapter 11).

    b. It increments SPL$W_WAIT_CPUS, the number of processors waiting for the spinlock, and SPL$L_BUSY_WAITS, the cumulative number of acquisitions that had to wait. The quotient of SPL$Q_SPINS, the number of cumulative spins by all processors waiting for the spinlock during its current use, and SPL$L_BUSY_WAITS is the basis of the Monitor Utility statistic "spins per failed acquisition."

    c. It clears the low bit of SPL$B_SPINLOCK to release its exclusive access to the spinlock control block and lowers IPL to the larger of the invoker's IPL and IPL$_RESCHED. This prevents any rescheduling during the spinwait.

    d. It zeros two registers to serve as its own spin counter.

    e. It then spins, incrementing the spin counter each time and testing the spinlock owner count to see whether the spinlock has been released. While it spins, it performs a countdown and tests whether it must perform SMP functions, as described in Section 8.3.8.

    f. When the owner count indicates no owner, SMP$ACQUIRE raises IPL to 31 and executes a BBSSI instruction to acquire exclusive access to the spinlock control block, as described in step 6.

    g. When SMP$ACQUIRE has exclusive access to the spinlock control block, it adds its spin count to the total in SPL$Q_SPINS. It decrements SPL$W_WAIT_CPUS to indicate one less processor waiting for the spinlock. It decrements CPU$B_BUSYWAIT.

    h. Reentering the main flow at step 7, SMP$ACQUIRE repeats its attempt to acquire the spinlock.

9. If the spinlock is already owned by this processor, SMP$ACQUIRE increments the owner count. It continues with step 11.

10. If the owner count is −1, indicating no owners, SMP$ACQUIRE increments the count and stores the address of the processor's per-CPU database in SPL$L_OWN_CPU. It sets the bit corresponding to the spinlock's rank in the per-CPU database field CPU$L_RANK_VEC.

    It inverts the IPL of the spinlock and sets the corresponding bit in CPU$L_IPL_VEC. It increments the corresponding longword in CPU$L_IPL_ARRAY.

11. At each successful acquisition, it saves the invoking thread's return PC at the next position in the spinlock ring buffer at SPL$L_OWN_PC_VEC and updates the pointer to the next entry. It increments SPL$Q_ACQ_COUNT to indicate one more successful acquisition.

12. It executes a BBCCI instruction to release its exclusive access to the spinlock control block, lowers IPL to that associated with the spinlock, and returns to its invoker with the spinlock held.

Following is a description of the full-checking version of the restore/release routines, with some details of SMP operations omitted for simplicity. These routines do not alter IPL; they run at the IPL at which they are entered.

1. At entry to SMP$RESTORE, R0 contains the index of a static spinlock. Indexing into the static spinlock table, SMP$RESTORE obtains the address of the spinlock and stores it in R0. (Entry point SMP$RESTOREL is entered with the address of a dynamic spinlock in R0.)

2. SMP$RESTORE compares the IPL at entry to the spinlock IPL. If the IPL is lower than that of the spinlock, the routine generates the fatal bugcheck SPLIPLLOW. (The routine continues when the entry IPL is too low if the spinlock is a device lock; this exception exists for MicroVAX systems, in which the interrupt arbitration IPL and bus grant IPL differ.)

3. SMP$RESTORE gets the physical ID of the processor from its per-CPU database.

4. It executes a BBSSI instruction to obtain exclusive access to the spinlock control block, spinwaiting (see Section 8.3.8) until the block is available.

5. It checks whether the spinlock is indeed owned by this processor. If not, the routine generates the fatal bugcheck SPLRSTERR.

6. It decrements the spinlock owner count. If the count is zero or positive, indicating that the spinlock is owned, the routine saves the invoking thread's return PC at the next position in the spinlock ring buffer at SPL$L_OWN_PC_VEC and updates the pointer to the next entry.

    It executes a BBCCI instruction to release its exclusive access to the spinlock control block and returns to its invoker.

7. If the owner count is −1, indicating that the spinlock is now free, SMP$RESTORE's path joins that of SMP$RELEASE, at step 12, below.

8. At entry to SMP$RELEASE, R0 contains the index of a static spinlock. Indexing into the static spinlock table, SMP$RELEASE obtains the address of the spinlock and stores it in R0. (Entry point SMP$RELEASEL is entered with the address of a dynamic spinlock already in R0.)

9. SMP$RELEASE makes the check against entry IPL (described in step 2) and, if it is too low, generates the fatal bugcheck SPLIPLLOW.

10. It tests that the processor is indeed the spinlock owner and, if it is not, generates the fatal bugcheck SPLRELERR.

11. It sets the spinlock owner count to −1 and records the invoking thread's return PC in SPL$L_RLS_PC as the most recent thread to relinquish all nested acquisitions of the spinlock.

12. It inverts the IPL associated with the spinlock and decrements the corresponding longword in CPU$L_IPL_ARRAY, to indicate one less spinlock held at that IPL. If the count becomes zero, SMP$RELEASE clears the corresponding bit in CPU$L_IPL_VEC.

13. It clears the bit corresponding to the spinlock's rank in CPU$L_RANK_VEC.

14. It clears the spinlock owner field.

15. It saves the invoking thread's return PC at the next position in the spinlock ring buffer at SPL$L_OWN_PC_VEC and updates the pointer to the next entry.

16. It executes a `BBCCI` instruction to release its exclusive access to the spinlock control block and returns to its invoker.

8.4   **SERIALIZED ACCESS**

VMS uses a combination of software interrupts and queues to cause several requests for the same data structure or procedure to be serialized. An important example of this serialization is the use of fork processes by device drivers and other parts of the executive.

Fork processing is the technique that allows a device driver to lower IPL in a manner consistent with the interrupt nesting scheme defined by the VAX architecture. When a device driver receives control in response to a device interrupt, it performs whatever steps are necessary to service the interrupt at device IPL. For example, any device registers whose contents would be destroyed by another interrupt must be read before dismissing the device interrupt.

Usually, some processing can be deferred. For direct memory access (DMA) devices, an interrupt signifies either completion of the operation or an error. The code that distinguishes these two cases and performs error processing is usually lengthy. If it executed at device IPL for extended periods of time, it would reduce response to high-priority interrupts.

To delay further processing until IPL drops below the fork IPL associated with this driver, the device driver interrupt service code invokes an executive routine, EXE$FORK, in module FORKCNTRL. EXE$FORK saves some minimal context in a fork block, shown in Figure 4.1. It saves two general registers and the address in the driver where control should return when IPL drops.

EXE$FORK examines the field FKB$B_FLCK in the fork block. The other name for this field is FKB$B_FIPL. This field contains either a fork IPL, in the range 6 to 11, or a static spinlock index. EXE$FORK tests bit 5 in the field to distinguish the two. If bit 5 is clear, EXE$FORK uses the fork IPL to select the corresponding CPU-specific fork queue. If bit 5 is set, EXE$FORK indexes the spinlock IPL table, at location SMP$AL_IPLVEC, to obtain the IPL value associated with that spinlock. EXE$FORK inserts the fork block at the end of the fork queue for that IPL and requests a software interrupt at that IPL if the queue was empty.

A thread of execution that creates a fork process can use any appropriate static spinlock as its fork lock. The only requirement is that the spinlock IPL be one at which fork processing is performed: 6, 8, 9, 10, or 11.

Chapter 4 describes fork processing in further detail.

8.5   MUTUAL EXCLUSION SEMAPHORES (MUTEXES)

The synchronization techniques described so far all execute at elevated IPL, thus blocking certain operations, such as a rescheduling request. However, in some situations requiring synchronization, elevated IPL is an unacceptable technique. One reason elevated IPL might be unacceptable is that the processor would have to remain at an elevated IPL for an indeterminately long time because of the structure of the data. For example, associating to a common event block cluster requires a search of the list of common event blocks (CEBs) for the specified CEB. This might be a lengthy operation on a system with many CEBs.

Furthermore, elevated IPL is unacceptable for synchronizing access to pageable data. VMS bugchecks if a page fault occurs at an IPL above 2. Thus, a pageable data structure cannot be protected by elevating IPL.

One synchronization mechanism that does not require elevated IPL is a mutual exclusion semaphore, or mutex. VMS uses mutexes for synchronizing kernel mode accesses to certain shared data structures. A mutex is essentially a counter that controls read or write access to a given data structure or database. VMS allows either multiple readers or one writer of a data structure or database synchronized through mutex acquisition. Typically, the threads of execution whose accesses are synchronized through a mutex are process context threads.

Access to a mutex itself must be gained at elevated IPL with the SCHED spinlock held. However, once a mutex is acquired, elevated IPL is not required to access the database represented by the mutex.

Table 8.3   List of Data Structures Protected by Mutexes

Data Structure	*Global Name of Mutex*
Shared logical name data structures	LNM$AL_MUTEX
I/O database	IOC$GL_MUTEX [1]
Common event block list	EXE$GL_CEBMTX
Paged dynamic memory list	EXE$GL_PGDYNMTX
Global section descriptor list	EXE$GL_GSDMTX
Shared memory global section descriptor table	EXE$GL_SHMGSMTX
Shared memory mailbox descriptor table	EXE$GL_SHMMBMTX
Not currently used	EXE$GL_ENQMTX
Line printer unit control block	UCB$L_LP_MUTEX [2]
Not currently used	EXE$GL_ACLMTX
System intruder lists	CIA$GL_MUTEX
Object rights block access control list	ORB$L_ACL_MUTEX [3]
System service database	CHANGE_MODE_MUTEX [4]
Terminal fallback database	TFF$L_VEC_MUTEX [5]
Loadable executive image data structures	EXE$GL_BASIMGMTX

[1] This mutex is used by the Assign Channel and Allocate Device system services when searching through the linked list of device data blocks and UCBs for a device. It is also used when UCBs are added or deleted, for example, during the creation of mailboxes and network devices.

[2] This mutex does not have a fixed address. As a field in a line printer UCB, its location depends on that of the UCB.

[3] This mutex does not have a fixed address. As a field in an object rights block (ORB), its location depends on that of the ORB.

[4] This mutex is local to the EXCEPTION.EXE loadable executive image and does not have a fixed address.

[5] This mutex does not have a fixed address. As a field in the fallback driver, its location depends on that of the driver.

Table 8.3 lists the executive data structures protected by mutexes and the names of the corresponding mutexes. (The "CPU mutex," used in SMP code, is discussed in Chapter 34.)

A mutex is a data structure consisting of a single longword. Figure 8.3 shows its layout. The macro $MTXDEF defines symbolic names for its fields. Its low-order word, field MTX$W_OWNCNT, contains the number of processes accessing the data, that is, the number of processes that have locked the mutex. The owner count value is initialized to −1 to indicate no owners. Thus, a mutex with a zero in the low-order word has one owner. Biasing the owner count by −1 simplifies the code that tests for the transition between unowned and owned. The high-order word of a mutex, field MTX$W_STS, contains status flags. The only flag currently implemented, MTX$V_WRT, is set to indicate that a write is either in progress or pending for this mutex.

The process control block (PCB) field PCB$W_MTXCNT contains the

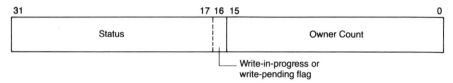

Figure 8.3
Layout of a Mutex

number of mutexes a process currently owns. This field is initialized to zero and incremented each time a process acquires a mutex.

8.5.1 Locking a Mutex for Read Access

When a process needs read access to a data structure protected by a mutex, it invokes routine SCH$LOCKR, in module MUTEX, with the address of the mutex. SCH$LOCKR takes the following steps:

1. It acquires the SCHED spinlock, raising IPL to IPL$_SCHED.
2. It tests whether the mutex's write flag is set. If so, no further readers are allowed to acquire the mutex. SCH$LOCKR transparently stalls the process (see Section 8.5.3) until the mutex is available.
3. If the write flag is clear and thus no write operation is in progress or pending, SCH$LOCKR grants the process read ownership of the mutex—it increments the mutex's owner count and increments the count of mutexes owned by this process.
4. If this mutex is the first that the process currently has locked and if the process is not a real-time process, its current and base priorities are saved in the PCB fields PCB$B_PRISAV and PCB$B_PRIBSAV and then both are elevated to 16. The process receives a priority boost to minimize the time during which it holds the mutex and blocks other processes that require the mutex. The check on the number of owned mutexes prevents a process that gains ownership of two or more mutexes from receiving a permanent priority elevation to 16.
5. SCH$LOCKR releases the SCHED spinlock and returns control to its invoker with IPL at 2.

The process is expected to remain at IPL 2 or above while it owns the mutex to prevent its own deletion or suspension. Neither the Delete Process ($DELPRC) system service nor the Suspend Process ($SUSPND) system service checks whether the target process owns any mutexes. If the process deletion or suspension were to succeed, the locked mutex would no longer be lockable and thus the locked data structure would be inaccessible.

8.5.2 Locking a Mutex for Write Access

When a process needs write access to a data structure that is protected by

a mutex, it invokes routine SCH$LOCKW, in module MUTEX, with the
address of the mutex. SCH$LOCKW takes the following steps:

1. It acquires the SCHED spinlock, raising IPL to IPL$_SCHED.
2. It tests and sets the mutex's write flag.
3. If the flag was set, no further readers or writers are allowed to acquire the
   mutex. SCH$LOCKW transparently stalls the process (see Section 8.5.3)
   until the mutex is available.
4. If the write flag was clear, SCH$LOCKW tests whether there are any
   current owners of the mutex. If there are, it transparently stalls the
   process.
5. If the write flag was clear and there were no owners of the mutex,
   SCH$LOCKW grants the process write ownership of the mutex: it in-
   crements MTX$W_OWNCNT and PCB$W_MTXCNT, and it may alter
   the process's software priority, as previously described. It releases the
   SCHED spinlock and returns to its invoker at IPL 2.

When SCH$LOCKW stalls the process, the mutex write flag is set so that
future requests for read access will also be denied. This prevents a stream of
read accesses from continuously locking the mutex. When the last current
owner of the mutex releases it, the write flag is cleared. At that point, the
highest priority process waiting for the mutex gets first access to it, whether
the process is requesting a read or a write access.

If a reader acquires the mutex, other previously waiting would-be readers
whose priority is greater than that of the highest priority would-be writer
can also acquire read access, as a result of standard scheduling operations.
The higher priority would-be readers execute first, and their read accesses are
granted. If readers still own the mutex when the would-be writer executes,
its attempted write access is blocked again.

An alternative entry point, SCH$LOCKWNOWAIT, returns control to
the invoker with R0⟨0⟩ cleared to indicate failure if the requested mutex
is already owned.

8.5.3   Mutex Wait State

SCH$LOCKR and SCH$LOCKW transparently stall a process when its requested mutex acquisition cannot be granted. They save the process context
and place the process into the miscellaneous wait state (MWAIT). They store
the address of the mutex being requested in the software PCB field PCB$L_
EFWM. Because the process is not waiting for an event flag, the field is
available for this purpose. They transfer control to the routine that selects a
new process to place into execution and that releases the SCHED spinlock.
Chapter 12 describes miscellaneous waits and rescheduling in more detail.

The saved PC of such a process is an address within either SCH$LOCKR or
SCH$LOCKW, depending on whether its intended access is a read or write.
Its saved PSL has kernel mode and IPL 2. When the mutex becomes available,

the process becomes computable again. When the saved process context is loaded, the process reattempts its mutex acquisition.

8.5.4 Unlocking a Mutex

A process releases a mutex by invoking routine SCH$UNLOCK, in module MUTEX, with the address of the mutex to be released. SCH$UNLOCK takes the following steps:

1. It acquires the SCHED spinlock, raising IPL to IPL$_SCHED.
2. It decrements the process's PCB$W_MTXCNT. If this process does not own any more mutexes, SCH$UNLOCK restores the saved base and current priorities from PCB$B_PRIBSAV and PCB$B_PRISAV.

   If there is a computable resident process with a higher priority than this process's restored priority, a rescheduling interrupt is requested. This situation is known as delayed preemption of the current process.
3. SCH$UNLOCK also decrements MTX$W_OWNCNT. If the mutex owner count is greater than −1, there are other outstanding owners of this mutex; SCH$UNLOCK simply releases the SCHED spinlock, restoring the IPL at entry, and returns to its invoker.
4. If the mutex count is decremented to −1, the mutex is now unowned. SCH$UNLOCK executes a BBCCI instruction to test and clear its write flag. If the bit was clear, SCH$UNLOCK releases the SCHED spinlock, restoring the IPL at entry, and returns to its invoker.
5. If the bit was set, there may be processes waiting to acquire this mutex. (A waiting or owning writer would have set this bit, blocking any new potential readers and any writers.) SCH$UNLOCK scans the miscellaneous resource wait queue to locate any process whose PCB$L_EFWM field contains the address of the unlocked mutex.

   For each such process, SCH$UNLOCK reports the availability of the mutex by invoking a scheduler routine to make the process computable. If the priority of any of these processes is greater than or equal to the priority of the current process, a rescheduling interrupt is requested. SCH$UNLOCK then releases the SCHED spinlock, restoring the IPL at entry, and returns to its invoker.

8.5.5 Accessing a Mutex from System Context

Although mutexes were originally designed for use from process context, VMS Version 5 adds the capability for a system thread of execution to acquire a mutex. This enables a system thread to synchronize its access with those of full processes to a database protected by a mutex. In general, this capability is limited to nonpageable databases, since VMS bugchecks in response to page faults occurring above IPL 2. Currently, the capability is only used by fork processes to acquire the I/O database mutex.

The I/O database mutex basically synchronizes the lists of I/O data structures, for example, the linked list of UCBs associated with a particular device. A device driver that clones new device units from template devices must insert new units into the UCB list and remove units being deleted. Although these insertions and deletions can usually be done from process context, in some cases they must be done from fork process context. For example, when the disk class driver fork process receives a message from an MSCP server that a new disk unit has come on line, it must clone a UCB and add it to the list.

Routines have been added to module MUTEX to serve this need:

- SCH$LOCKWEXEC—Acquire write ownership of a mutex from a system thread
- SCH$LOCKREXEC—Acquire read ownership of a mutex from a system thread
- SCH$UNLOCKEXEC—Release a mutex from a system thread

The main difference between SCH$LOCKWEXEC and SCH$LOCKREXEC and their process context counterparts is that they return a failure status if the mutex is unavailable. There is no mechanism that transparently stalls a fork process and awakens it when the mutex becomes available. If a fork process receives a failure status, it must wait itself by using the fork and wait mechanism described in Chapter 4.

These routines acquire the SCHED spinlock, which is held at IPL$_SCHED. This mechanism is therefore restricted to threads of execution that run at IPL 8 or below and that hold no higher ranking spinlock.

9 Event Flags

I claim not to have controlled events, but confess plainly that
events have controlled me.

Abraham Lincoln, Letter to A. G. Hodges, April 4, 1864

Event flags are status bits maintained by the VMS operating system for general programming use. Each event flag can be either set or clear, and its status can be tested.

System services read, set, and clear event flags. A process can specify that an event flag be set at the completion of an operation such as an I/O request. When the process can proceed no further until the request is complete, the process can call a system service to wait for the event flag to be set.

This chapter describes the implementation of event flags and the services that support them.

9.1 EVENT FLAGS

An event flag can be used within a single process for synchronization with the completion of certain system services, such as I/O, lock, information, and timer requests. Each of these services includes an argument identifying the event flag associated with the request. When a process requests such a system service, that event flag is cleared. It is subsequently set when the request has been completed as a signal to the process that the operation is complete. Event flags can also be used as application-specific synchronization tools.

Event flags can be local to one process or shared among processes in the same user identification code (UIC) group. Shared event flags are called common event flags. Processes sharing common event flags must be running on a single VAXcluster member; that is, common event flags are not visible clusterwide.

VMS also supports common event flags in MA780 multiport memory shared among multiple VAX-11/78x processors. A process can use these flags to synchronize with other processes in the same group running on any of the processors connected to the shared memory. The use of such flags is discussed in *Introduction to VMS System Services*. Details on the implementation of MA780 common event flags are beyond the scope of this book.

Each process has available to it 64 local (process-specific) event flags, in two clusters of 32 flags each, and can access 64 common event flags at once, in two clusters of 32 flags each. Before a process can refer to the flags in a particular common event flag cluster, it must explicitly associate with the cluster (see Section 9.1.2), specifying which numbers it will use to refer to the flags.

VMS assigns no inherent meaning to any particular event flag, although certain flags are reserved for particular uses (see Section 9.1.1). A process defines the meaning of a flag by the way it uses the flag. For example, when a process requests the Queue I/O Request ($QIO) system service, specifying event flag 10 as the EFN argument, the process can subsequently wait for completion of that I/O request by waiting for event flag 10 to be set. After the process's wait is satisfied, the meaning of event flag 10 is undefined.

If the process concurrently uses event flag 10 in two different ways, the meaning of its being set is ambiguous. VMS provides the Run-Time Library procedures LIB$GET_EF and LIB$FREE_EF (see *VMS RTL Library (LIB$) Manual*) to help prevent inadvertent concurrent use of the same flags.

The services that include an event flag argument are

- Breakthrough [and Wait] ($BRKTHRU[W])
- Enqueue Lock Request [and Wait] ($ENQ[W])
- Get Device/Volume Information [and Wait] ($GETDVI[W])
- Get Job/Process Information [and Wait] ($GETJPI[W])
- Get Lock Information [and Wait] ($GETLKI[W])
- Get Queue Information [and Wait] ($GETQUI[W])
- Get Systemwide Information [and Wait] ($GETSYI[W])
- Queue I/O Request [and Wait] ($QIO[W])
- Send to Job Controller [and Wait] ($SNDJBC[W])
- Set Timer ($SETIMR)
- Synchronize ($SYNCH)
- Update Section File on Disk [and Wait] ($UPDSEC[W])

9.1.1   Local Event Flags

The 64 local event flags are contained in each process's process control block (PCB), at offsets PCB$L_EFCS and PCB$L_EFCU (see Figure 9.1). All local event flags are initialized to zero during process creation.

Local event flags 0 to 31 make up cluster 0 and are located in longword PCB$L_EFCS. Bit 0 in PCB$L_EFCS corresponds to event flag 0, bit 1 to event flag 1, and so on. Local event flags 32 to 63 make up cluster 1 and are located in longword PCB$L_EFCU. Bit 0 in PCB$L_EFCU corresponds to event flag 32, bit 1 to event flag 33, and so on.

Event flag 0 is the default event flag. Whenever a process requests a system service with an event flag number argument, but does not specify a particular flag, event flag 0 is used. Consequently, it is more likely than others to be used incorrectly for multiple concurrent requests.

Event flag numbers 24 through 31 are reserved for system use; this means they can be set and cleared at any time by VMS executive software and should not be used by application software.

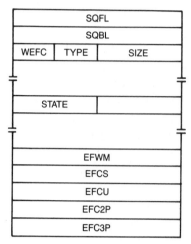

Figure 9.1
Software PCB Fields That Support Event Flags

9.1.2 Common Event Flags

A process creates a common event flag cluster dynamically, by requesting the Associate Common Event Flag Cluster ($ASCEFC) system service (see Section 9.3). Each common event flag cluster is described by a nonpaged pool data structure called a common event block (CEB), shown in Figure 9.2.

The process specifies whether it will access the flags in that cluster using event flag numbers 64 through 95 (cluster 2) or 96 through 127 (cluster 3). If the flags are associated as cluster 2, the field PCB$L_EFC2P contains the address of their CEB. Otherwise, PCB$L_EFC3P contains its address.

CEB$L_CEBFL and CEB$L_CEBBL link each CEB into a systemwide list whose listhead is SCH$GQ_CEBHD (see Figure 9.3). The system global SCH$GW_CEBCNT contains the number of CEBs in the list. The mutex EXE$GL_CEBMTX synchronizes access to the CEB list. Chapter 8 describes the use of mutexes.

A particular common event flag cluster is identified by its name, CEB$T_EFCNAM, and UIC group, CEB$W_GRP. There cannot be more than one cluster with the same name and group.

Two bits are defined in the status byte, CEB$B_STS:

- CEB$V_PERM, when set, indicates that the cluster is a permanent one rather than a temporary one.
- CEB$V_NOQUOTA, when set, indicates that no quota was charged for the creation of the cluster.

Creation of a temporary cluster is charged against a job's timer queue entry (TQE) quota. Creation of a permanent cluster uses no quota but requires the privilege PRMCEB. A temporary cluster exists only as long as a process is associated to it, while a permanent cluster must be explicitly deleted.

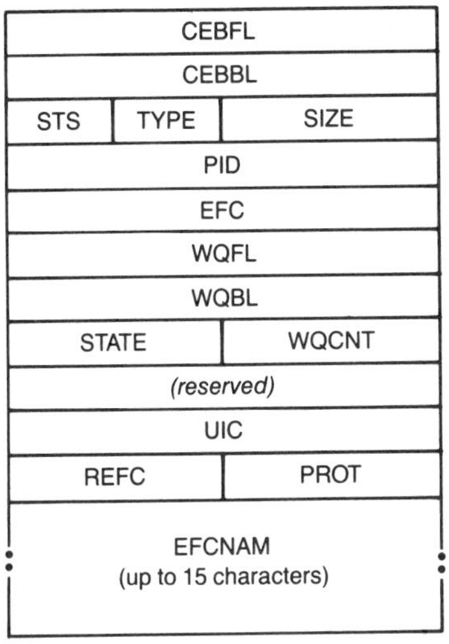

CEBFL
CEBBL
STS
TYPE
SIZE
PID
EFC
WQFL
WQBL
STATE
WQCNT
(reserved)
UIC
REFC
PROT
EFCNAM
(up to 15 characters)

Figure 9.2
Layout of Common Event Block

CEB
CEB
SCH$GQ__CEBHD::
PCB
PCB
WQFL
WQBL
WQCNT = 0
WQFL
WQBL
WQCNT = 2
EFC2P=
Address of
CEB ALPHA
EFC3P=
Address of
CEB ALPHA
EFCNAM = BETA
EFCNAM = ALPHA

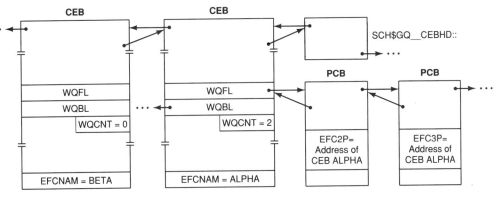

Figure 9.3
Common Event Flag Wait Queues

CEB$L_PID contains the internal process ID (IPID) of the master process in the job tree of the process that created the cluster.

The field CEB$L_EFC contains the 32 event flags. These are all initialized to zero when the cluster is created.

The fields CEB$L_WQFL and CEB$L_WQBL, CEB$B_WQCNT, and CEB$W_STATE form a wait queue (see Chapter 12) for processes waiting for flags in that cluster.

CEB$L_UIC contains the UIC of the creating process.

CEB$W_PROT contains the value 0 if other processes in the same UIC group are permitted access; otherwise, the value 1 prevents access by processes with a different UIC.

CEB$W_REFC contains the number of processes that are currently associated to the cluster.

9.2   **PCB FIELDS RELATED TO EVENT FLAGS**

Figure 9.1 shows the PCB fields related to the use of event flags.

Previous sections described the meaning of the fields PCBL_EFCS, PCBL_EFCU, PCB$L_EFC2P, and PCB$L_EFC3P.

The other fields are significant for a process in an event flag wait. PCB$B_WEFC contains the number of the cluster containing the flags for which a process waits. PCB$L_EFWM contains a mask that is the one's complement of the flags in the cluster for which the process is waiting. The PCB$L_STS bit PCB$V_WALL, when set, indicates that the process is waiting for all those flags to be set.

These fields are loaded only when a process initiates an event flag wait. Consequently, for a process in a state other than event flag wait, they may be stale. Furthermore, the field PCB$L_EFWM has an additional use: it identifies the resource waited for by a process in a miscellaneous wait state.

9.3   **ASSOCIATING TO A COMMON EVENT FLAG CLUSTER**

A process invokes the $ASCEFC system service to create a named common event flag cluster if it does not already exist and to access its flags. The process specifies the name of the cluster and implicitly, through its PCB$L_UIC field, the UIC group of the cluster.

The $ASCEFC system service procedure, EXE$ASCEFC in module SYS-ASCEFC, runs in kernel mode. It takes the following steps:

1. EXE$ASCEFC confirms that the event flag number is within cluster 2 or 3, returning the error status SS$_ILLEFC if it is not.
2. It locks the CEB mutex for write access.
3. It searches the CEB list for a cluster with the same name and group.
4. If one exists, EXE$ASCEFC checks whether the process can access it. If the process's UIC matches that of the CEB owner or if the CEB protection code allows group access, the process is allowed to associate to the cluster.

   If the process is allowed access, EXE$ASCEFC continues with step 7. Otherwise, EXE$ASCEFC unlocks the mutex and returns the error status SS$_NOPRIV to its caller.
5. If the common event flag cluster does not already exist, the process is requesting its creation.

   —If the process requests a permanent cluster, it must have the privilege PRMCEB. If it does not have the privilege, EXE$ASCEFC unlocks the mutex and returns the error status SS$_NOPRIV.
   —If the process is not requesting a permanent cluster, EXE$ASCEFC charges it against the job's TQE quota. If the process has insufficient quota, EXE$ASCEFC unlocks the mutex and returns the error status SS$_EXQUOTA.

6. EXE$ASCEFC invokes EXE$ALLOCCEB, in module MEMORYALC, to allocate a CEB from nonpaged pool and initializes the CEB. EXE$ASCEFC sets the bit CEB$V_PERM in CEB$B_STS if the cluster is a permanent one. It increments SCH$GW_CEBCNT, the number of CEBs, and links the new CEB into the list.

7. Whether or not the cluster existed previously, EXE$ASCEFC associates the process and the cluster by incrementing the cluster's reference count, CEB$W_REFC, and by storing the address of the CEB in either PCB$L_EFC2P or PCB$L_EFC3P.

   EXE$ASCEFC first saves the old contents of PCB$L_EFC2P or PCB$L_EFC3P. If they are not zero, the process has been using those event flag numbers to associate with another cluster. EXE$ASCEFC severs the connection between the process and the other cluster by taking the steps described in Section 9.4.

8. EXE$ASCEFC unlocks the mutex and returns to its caller.

9.4 DISSOCIATING FROM A COMMON EVENT FLAG CLUSTER

A process dissociates itself from a common event flag cluster explicitly by requesting the Dissociate Common Event Flag Cluster ($DACEFC) system service with an event flag number within that cluster. Implicitly, the service is requested on behalf of the process when it associates a new event flag cluster using a cluster number already in use.

The $DACEFC system service procedure, EXE$DACEFC in module SYS-ASCEFC, runs in kernel mode. It takes the following steps:

1. EXE$DACEFC confirms that the event flag number is within cluster 2 or 3, returning the error status SS$_ILLEFC if it is not.
2. It locks the CEB mutex for write.
3. It confirms that the process has an associated cluster corresponding to the flag number. If not, it unlocks the mutex and returns.
4. It locates the CEB using the pointer to the cluster in the PCB and clears the pointer.
5. It decrements CEB$W_REFC in the associated cluster. If there are other processes associated to the cluster or if the cluster is a permanent one, it unlocks the mutex and returns.
6. Otherwise (the cluster is temporary and has no processes still associated with it), EXE$DACEFC deletes it by taking the following steps:

   a. If CEB$V_NOQUOTA is clear, EXE$DACEFC returns quota to the job against which it was originally charged.
   b. EXE$DACEFC removes the CEB from the CEB list, deallocates it to nonpaged pool, and decrements SCH$GW_CEBCNT.
   c. EXE$DACEFC unlocks the mutex and returns.

During image rundown, a process is automatically dissociated from any common event flag clusters to which it had associated.

9.5   **DELETING AN EVENT FLAG CLUSTER**

To delete a permanent event flag cluster, a process requests the Delete Common Event Flag Cluster ($DLCEFC) system service with the name of the cluster to be deleted.

A cluster cannot be deleted if processes are still associated with it. In such a case, the $DLCEFC service transforms the permanent cluster to a temporary one so that it will be deleted when the last process associated with the cluster requests the $DACEFC service.

The $DLCEFC system service procedure, EXE$DLCEFC in module SYS-ASCEFC, runs in kernel mode. It takes the following steps:

1. EXE$DLCEFC locks the CEB mutex for write.
2. It scans the CEB list for a cluster of the specified name and a group code matching that of the process. If it fails to find one, it unlocks the mutex and simply returns.
3. If it finds one, it tests whether the process is allowed to delete the CEB. If the process's UIC is not that of the CEB and if the CEB protection does not allow a group member to delete it, EXE$DLCEFC returns the error status SS$_NOPRIV.

   If the process does not have the privilege PRMCEB, EXE$DLCEFC also returns the error status SS$_NOPRIV.
4. Unless the process is deleting a temporary CEB, EXE$DLCEFC clears CEB$V_PERM and sets CEB$V_NOQUOTA. This effectively changes the cluster to a temporary one for which no quota need be returned. The cluster's deletion is deferred until all processes have dissociated from it.
5. EXE$DLCEFC increments CEB$W_REFC and transfers to code within EXE$DACEFC, described in step 5 in Section 9.4. (The increment balances a decrement in EXE$DACEFC.)

9.6   **WAITING FOR AN EVENT FLAG**

A process can be placed into an event flag wait state to wait for the setting of one or more flags. When a process waits for more than one flag, all the flags must be in the same cluster. A process waits for event flags by performing any of the following actions:

- Requesting one of the three event flag wait system services directly:
  —Wait for Single Event Flag ($WAITFR)
  —Wait for Logical OR of Event Flags ($WFLOR)
  —Wait for Logical AND of Event Flags ($WFLAND)

- Requesting the $SYNCH system service, which combines $WAITFR and a status block test to wait for service completion (thus minimizing problems caused by multiple concurrent uses of the same flag)
- Requesting the synchronous version of the services listed in Section 9.1, each of which incorporates $SYNCH
- Requesting Record Management Services (RMS) as a synchronous operation, which results in requesting $WAITFR

The distinction between $WFLOR and $WFLAND lies in how many of the flags must be set for the wait condition to be satisfied. If any of the flags in the mask is set when $WFLOR is requested, the process is not placed into a wait state. Instead, the service immediately returns to its caller.

Each of the flags specified in the $WFLAND system service argument must have been set for the wait to be satisfied. However, the flags need not be set simultaneously.

However the wait-for system service is requested, it examines the current state of the event flag or flags. If the event flag wait condition is satisfied, it returns control to the process. Otherwise, it places the process into a wait state until the flag or flags are set. The wait-for system services are described in the following paragraphs. The $SYNCH system service and synchronous RMS completions are described in Chapter 6.

The wait-for system service procedures, EXE$WAITFR, EXE$WFLOR, and EXE$WFLAND, are in module SYSWAIT and run in kernel mode. The three procedures converge to a common routine, EXE$WAIT, also in module SYSWAIT.

EXE$WAIT is entered with a mask identifying the flags to be waited for, the number of a flag in that cluster, and a wait-all flag that is set if the entry is from $WFLAND.

EXE$WAIT takes the following steps:

1. EXE$WAIT raises IPL to 2 to block delivery of a kernel mode AST procedure that might request another wait-for service.
2. It checks that the event flag number is legal, returning the error status SS$_ILLEFC if the number is out of range.
3. It determines which cluster contains that event flag and records the cluster number in PCB$B_WEFC.
4. If the cluster number is 2 or 3, indicating a common event flag cluster, EXE$WAIT first checks that there is an associated cluster and returns the error status SS$_UNASCEFC if there is none.

   If there is an associated cluster, it gets the CEB address from either PCB$L_EFC2P or PCB$L_EFC3P, depending on the cluster number.
5. It acquires the SCHED spinlock, raising IPL to IPL$_SCHED, to block concurrent access to the event flags by SCH$POSTEF (see Section 9.7) and to synchronize access to the scheduler database.

6. It tests whether the event flag wait condition is satisfied by the current state of the flags.

7. If the wait condition is satisfied, EXE$WAIT releases the spinlock and returns to the caller of the system service. As an optimization, EXE$WAIT removes the change mode dispatcher call frame from the stack and returns directly to the instruction following the CHMK that initiated it (see Chapter 6).

8. If the event flag wait condition is unsatisfied, EXE$WAIT checks whether the wait is wait-all. If so, it sets the PCB$V_WALL bit in PCB$L_STS.

9. EXE$WAIT stores a mask representing the flags to be waited for in PCB$L_EFWM:

   —If the process requested $WFLOR, the PCB$L_EFWM mask contains the one's complement of the input mask passed to the system service.
   —If the process requested $WAITFR, the PCB$L_EFWM mask contains a 1 in every bit except the bit number corresponding to the specified flag. (The $WAITFR mask is thus a special case of a wait for any one of a group of flags to be set.)
   —If the process requested $WFLAND, the system service clears any bits in the input mask corresponding to currently set flags, complements it, and then stores it in PCB$L_EFWM.

10. EXE$WAIT jumps to SCH$WAIT, in module RSE, to place the process into either a local or common event flag wait state, depending on the cluster number.

   There are two systemwide local event flag wait states (LEF and LEFO) and two corresponding wait queue listheads (SCH$GQ_LEFWQ and SCH$GQ_LEFOWQ). Only one common event flag wait state exists for both resident and outswapped processes. However, there is a separate common event flag wait queue listhead (see Figure 9.2) in each common event flag cluster. Each has the same overall structure as any other wait queue listhead (see Figure 9.3). Both resident and outswapped processes waiting for flags in a common event flag cluster are queued to the same CEB wait queue. Having one queue in each CEB makes it easier to locate processes whose wait is satisfied by the setting of a flag in that cluster.

The saved program counter (PC) in the waiting process's hardware PCB is the address of the CHMK instruction that initiated the system service, typically one in a system service vector. If the process becomes computable because its event flag wait has been satisfied and is placed into execution, it may reexecute the event flag wait system service, which will complete with EXE$WAIT's step 7. If the process becomes computable as the result of asynchronous system trap (AST) enqueuing, at the completion of the AST it will reexecute the service and be placed back into a wait. Chapter 12 gives additional information.

While this technique permits ASTs to be delivered to a process waiting for event flags to be set, it constrains the ways in which event flags can be used: flags for which a process is waiting should not be cleared by other threads of execution. The result of clearing an event flag might be that a process becomes computable as the result of the flag's having been set but reenters the event flag wait state indefinitely when it reexecutes the event flag wait service and finds the flag no longer set. This could happen, for example, if process A waited for a common event flag set and then cleared by process B.

This constraint applies to all wait-for services but has particular significance for the $WFLAND system service. The $WFLAND system service generates a wait mask based on the input mask flags that are not already set at the time the service is requested. However, each time the process is placed back into execution as a result of AST delivery, the process reexecutes the $WFLAND service and, each time, the event flag wait mask is built anew. No record is kept that some of the flags have been set and should not be waited for again if the service is reexecuted.

9.7 SETTING AN EVENT FLAG

A process sets an event flag directly by calling the Set Event Flag ($SETEF) system service. A process can use this service at AST level to communicate with its mainline code. It can also use this service to set common event flags to communicate with other processes.

The VMS executive sets event flags in response to I/O completion, timer expiration, the granting of a lock request, and completion of any of the system services listed in Section 9.1.

The $SETEF system service and any other executive code that sets an event flag invokes the routine SCH$POSTEF, in module POSTEF. SCH$POSTEF performs the actual event flag setting and checks whether a process's event flag wait is satisfied. Its arguments are the number of the flag to be set, the IPID of the process in whose context that flag number is defined, and a priority increment class number (see Chapter 12).

SCH$POSTEF runs in kernel mode. It takes the following steps:

1. It first acquires the SCHED spinlock, raising IPL to IPL$_SCHED, to block concurrent access to the flags from a wait-for service and to synchronize access to the scheduler database.
2. It then confirms that the specified process still exists. If not, it releases the spinlock and returns the error status SS$_NONEXPR to its invoker.
3. It checks that the event flag number is legal, returning the error status SS$_ILLEFC if the number is out of range.
4. It then determines what kind of event flag is being set. For a common event flag, it continues with step 8.
5. If a local event flag is being set, SCH$POSTEF sets it and checks whether this flag satisfies a wait request for this process. In the case of a $WFLOR wait, this flag merely has to match one of the flags being waited for. For

a $WFLAND wait, all the flags in the mask must be set to satisfy the process's wait request.

6. If the process's wait is satisfied, SCH$POSTEF reports an event-flag-setting event for the process by invoking routine SCH$RSE, in module RSE. (Note that SCH$POSTEF examines PCB event-flag-related fields to decide if a wait is satisfied but ignores the process's scheduling state. Thus, SCH$POSTEF's event report may be based on stale values in these fields. SCH$RSE confirms that the process is in an event flag wait state prior to acting on the event report.)

7. Whether or not a wait was satisfied, SCH$POSTEF then unlocks the SCHED spinlock and returns with the success status SS$_WASSET or SS$_WASCLR, depending on the initial state of the flag. This completes its processing for a local event flag.

8. If a common event flag is being set, SCH$POSTEF first checks that there is an associated common event flag cluster, returning the error SS$_UNASCEFC if there is none.

9. It gets the CEB address, using the contents of either PCB$L_EFC2P or PCB$L_EFC3P, depending on the flag number. SCH$POSTEF must scan the list of PCBs in the CEB wait queue to determine which, if any, of the processes waiting for flags in this cluster has its wait request satisfied. SCH$POSTEF reports an event-flag-setting event for each such process.

10. SCH$POSTEF releases the SCHED spinlock, restoring the previous IPL.

SCH$RSE ignores an event-flag-setting event reported for a process not in an event flag wait state and simply returns. When an event-flag-setting event is reported for a process in an event flag wait state, SCH$RSE changes its state to computable resident (COM) or computable outswap (COMO) and, if appropriate, applies a priority boost, using the priority increment class number passed through from SCH$POSTEF. SCH$RSE may request a rescheduling interrupt on behalf of the process or awaken the swapper process. Chapter 12 gives more details.

If the process is resident, SCH$RSE adds 4 to the saved PC in the hardware PCB so that the process does not reexecute the event flag wait service.

9.8   READING AND CLEARING EVENT FLAGS

The Read Event Flag ($READEF) system service is informational. It has no effect on the computability of any process. The $READEF system service procedure, EXE$READEF in module SYSEVTSRV, runs in kernel mode. It determines which cluster to read from its EFN argument. It copies the flags from either the PCB or the CEB that contains them to the location specified by its caller. It returns the success status SS$_WASSET if any flag was set; otherwise, it returns SS$_WASCLR, which is equal to SS$_NORMAL.

The Clear Event Flag ($CLREF) system service simply clears the event flag specified by its EFN argument. The $CLREF system service procedure,

EXE$CLREF in module SYSEVTSRV, runs in kernel mode. It locates the cluster that contains the specified flag and executes a BBCCI instruction to clear the flag. It returns the success status SS$_WASCLR or SS$_WASSET, depending on the initial state of the flag. It has no immediate effect on the scheduling state of any process.

INTERPROCESS SYNCHRONIZATION THROUGH COMMON EVENT FLAGS

The use of common event flags is one method of interprocess synchronization. One process can reach a critical point in its execution and wait for a common event flag. Another process can enable this process to continue its execution by setting the flag.

A common event flag can also be used as a semaphore to gain access to a resource shared among processes. One such application is outlined here. It first requires creation of a common event flag cluster with all its flags set. Each flag can be used as an individual lock. Each cooperating process must associate to the common event flag cluster.

Before any process uses the resource represented by a particular event flag, it must execute the following sequence, which uses event flag number 65 as an example:

```
5$:     $CLREF_S EFN=#65              ;Clear the  event flag
        CMPL    R0,#SS$_WASSET        ;Was its previous state = 1?
        BEQL    10$                   ;Branch if yes
        $WAITFR_S EFN=#65             ;Else wait for flag
        BRB     5$
10$:                                  ;Proceed to access resource
        .
        .
        .
        $SETEF_S   EFN=#65            ;Set the event flag
```

Clearing an event flag is an interlocked operation implemented by the VMS software (except for MA780 shared memory common event flags). Only one process at a time can clear the flag and cause the transition in its state from set to clear. That process then "owns" the flag and its associated resource. Any other process that clears the flag receives a was-clear status and must wait for the flag to be set.

The process that owns the flag can then access the resource without synchronization problems. When the process's accesses to the resource are complete, the process sets the flag, relinquishing ownership of the flag and resource. The processes that were waiting for the flag are made computable and repeat their attempts to cause the event flag transition from set to clear.

10 Lock Management

'Tis in my memory lock'd,
And you yourself shall keep the key of it.
Shakespeare, *Hamlet*, 1, iii

VMS lock management system services enable cooperating processes to synchronize their access to shared memory, files, and other entities. Using these services, a process assigns a name to an entity and requests a lock on the name. In response to the first request to lock any given name, VMS creates a data structure called a resource block, commonly referred to as a resource. VMS lock management system services do not maintain any linkage between that structure and any actual VMS entity. Processes requiring synchronized access to an entity must explicitly cooperate by locking the resource name representing that entity.

A lock is characterized by the extent to which it allows shared access with other locks on the same resource. Locks that permit mutual shared access are termed compatible. Processes holding compatible locks on a resource have concurrent access to it and, if they behave consistently, to the entity it represents. A process requesting an incompatible lock is denied access. Optionally, such a process can be placed into a wait state until blocking locks are released and the resource becomes available.

This chapter discusses first the lock management data structures and then the operations of the lock management system services:

- Enqueue Lock Request [and Wait] ($ENQ[W])
- Dequeue Lock Request ($DEQ)
- Get Lock Information [and Wait] ($GETLKI[W])

The last section in this chapter describes deadlock detection.

The treatment in this chapter assumes that the reader is familiar with the description of the VMS lock management system services found in the *VMS System Services Reference Manual*. This chapter briefly discusses VAXcluster distributed lock management, the details of which are beyond the scope of this book.

10.1 LOCK MANAGEMENT DATA STRUCTURES

The lock database consists of the following kinds of structures:

- Resource blocks (RSBs), which represent the entities for which locks have been requested
- One resource hash table, which locates the RSBs
- Lock blocks (LKBs), which describe locks requested by processes

• One lock ID table, which locates the LKBs

10.1.1   Resource Blocks

A new RSB is allocated from nonpaged pool whenever a process requests the $ENQ system service specifying a resource name not already in use. A resource can be created for any desired use but is generally used to represent an actual VMS entity, such as a file or global section. Because the representation is arbitrary, VMS lock management cannot maintain any linkage between the resource and the entity it represents. The VMS operating system provides tools that cooperating processes can use to synchronize access to the resource. If the processes honor the relation of the resource to the entity it represents, access to that entity is synchronized as well.

Resources can be hierarchical. For example, a resource can be defined to represent a particular file, with subresources for particular records in the file. The file resource is a parent resource to the resources representing records in the file. A record subresource may be a parent resource to additional subresources that represent fields in the record. The combination of a resource and all its subresources is called a resource tree. The top-level resource in the tree, the one with no parent, is called the root resource. The root resource list, whose listhead is the global symbol LCK$GL_RRSFL, links the root resources known by the local system. Subresources are linked to these root RSBs.

The maximum depth of a resource tree is, by default, 32. The depth value is related to the SYSGEN parameters INTSTKPAGES and DLCKEXTRASTK (see Section 10.3.2.2).

A resource is uniquely identified by the following combination:

• Resource name string of 1 to 31 characters
• User identification code (UIC) group number (or zero if the resource is systemwide)
• Access mode
• Address of parent RSB, if any

Therefore, two resources with identical resource name strings are completely different if their UIC groups, access modes, and parents are not also identical.

Figure 10.1 shows the layout of an RSB. RSB$T_RESNAM and RSB$B_RSNLEN contain the resource name string and its length. Together with RSBW_GROUP, RSBB_RMOD, and RSB$L_PARENT, these fields uniquely identify a particular resource.

RSB$B_DEPTH indicates the position of the resource in a resource tree; a root resource has a depth of zero. The depth of a subresource is set to 1 more than its parent's RSB$B_DEPTH. Root resources are linked to form a queue through their RSB$L_RRSFL and RSB$L_RRSBL fields. All subresources of the root resource are linked to form a queue through the fields RSB$L_SRSFL and RSB$L_SRSBL. Each subresource contains the address of its root RSB in

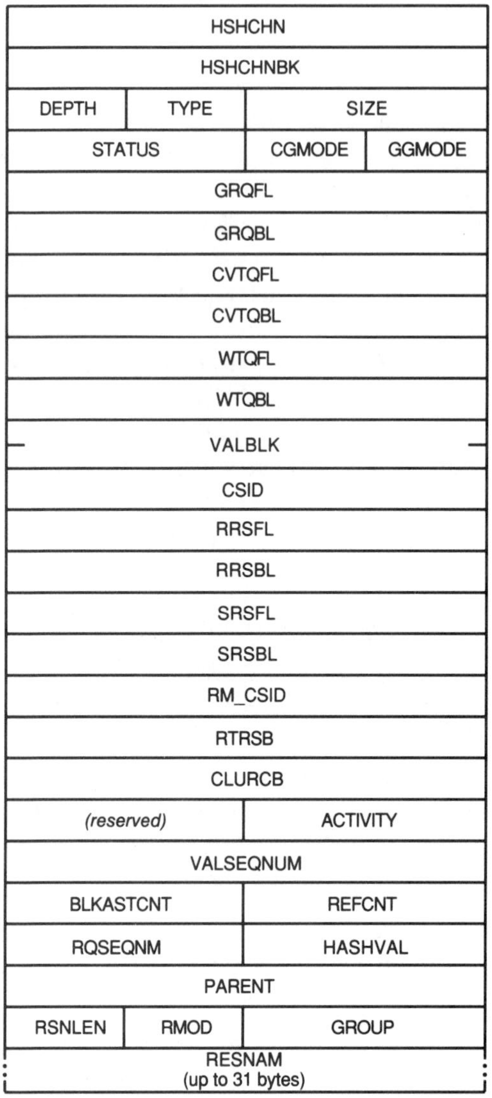

HSHCHN			
HSHCHNBK			
DEPTH	TYPE	SIZE	
STATUS		CGMODE	GGMODE
GRQFL			
GRQBL			
CVTQFL			
CVTQBL			
WTQFL			
WTQBL			
VALBLK			
CSID			
RRSFL			
RRSBL			
SRSFL			
SRSBL			
RM_CSID			
RTRSB			
CLURCB			
(reserved)		ACTIVITY	
VALSEQNUM			
BLKASTCNT		REFCNT	
RQSEQNM		HASHVAL	
PARENT			
RSNLEN	RMOD	GROUP	
RESNAM (up to 31 bytes)			

Figure 10.1
Layout of a Resource Block

RSB$L_RTRSB; a root resource contains its own address. Figure 10.2 shows this linkage of root and subresources. RSB$W_ACTIVITY tracks the local node's use of the resource; a root resource with a low value is more likely to be remastered (see Section 10.1.6).

If the resource has a parent resource, its access mode is taken from the parent. Otherwise, the access mode is specified by the $ENQ system service argument ACMODE. The argument is maximized with the mode from which the service was requested, which is the default if the argument is omitted. The resource's access mode defines the name space in which the resource

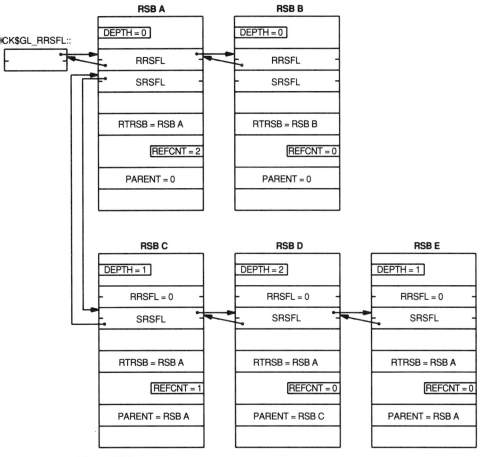

Figure 10.2
Root Resources and Subresources

exists. It specifies the least privileged mode from which locks can be queued to the resource and from which information about the locks can be obtained. In a parent RSB, RSB$W_REFCNT counts the number of its immediate subresources.

An RSB contains listheads for the granted, conversion, and wait queues of LKBs associated with the resource. The listhead for the granted LKB queue is the fields RSB$L_GRQFL and RSB$L_GRQBL. The listhead for the conversion queue is the fields RSB$L_CVTQFL and RSB$L_CVTQBL. The listhead for the wait queue is the fields RSB$L_WTQFL and RSB$L_WTQBL. Section 10.1.3 describes the significance of these queues.

An RSB also contains 16 bytes that form the value block for the resource at the field RSB$Q_VALBLK. RSB$L_VALSEQNUM contains the sequence number associated with the contents of the value block.

Other RSB fields are described in later sections of this chapter.

10.1.2 Resource Hash Table

The resource hash table locates all the RSBs in use. The combination of the resource name string and its length, resource access mode, UIC group number, and parent RSB hash value is hashed and the result stored in RSB$W_HASHVAL. The hashing algorithm is similar to the algorithm used for hashing logical names, described in Chapter 35. The contents of RSB$W_HASHVAL index a particular entry in the resource hash table. More than one resource name can hash to the same value. Each longword entry in the hash table is either zero or a pointer to a list of RSBs with that hash value. If a longword entry in the resource hash table contains a zero, there is no RSB with that hash value.

Because the RSBs are maintained in a list that is doubly linked but not circular (the resource hash table itself contains no backward pointers), the list of RSBs is termed a chain. The first two longwords in each RSB contain the forward and backward pointers for the resource hash chain. The last block in each chain has a zero forward pointer.

The resource hash table is allocated from nonpaged pool. The global location LCK$GL_HASHTBL contains its address. The number of longword entries in the resource hash table is determined by the SYSGEN parameter RESHASHTBL. Note that the parameter does not limit the number of RSBs that can be created. However, the combination of a small hash table and many RSBs can result in longer hash chains than might be desirable.

Figure 10.3 shows the structure of the resource hash table and its relation to hash chains.

10.1.3 Lock Blocks

An LKB is allocated from nonpaged pool when a process requests the $ENQ system service. The LKB is assigned a unique lock ID used to identify the lock in subsequent lock conversion or dequeue requests. The LKB is owned only by the creator process. When a process dequeues a lock, the LKB is deallocated. When a process is deleted, all its locks are dequeued. Figure 10.4 shows the layout of a lock block.

The lock is characterized by its lock mode—one of six degrees of shareability. Table 10.1 lists the lock modes and the other granted lock modes with which each lock is compatible. A lock granted at one mode can later be converted to another mode. LKB$B_RQMODE specifies the requested lock mode of the lock, and LKB$B_GRMODE, the granted lock mode.

A lock can be granted, converting, or waiting, depending on the lock modes of other locks on the resource. A new lock is granted and its LKB placed on the RSB granted queue if its lock mode is compatible with those of locks already granted on the resource and if the conversion and wait queues are empty. Otherwise, it is placed at the end of the wait queue. A subsequent attempt to convert a granted lock to a more restrictive lock mode can result

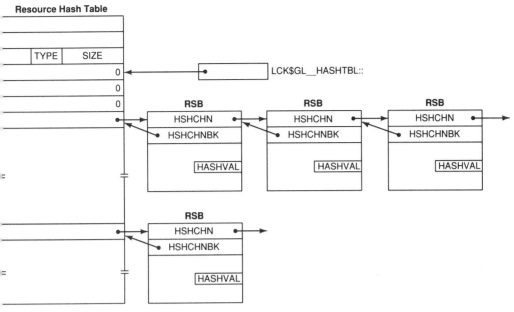

Figure 10.3
Resource Hash Table and Hash Chains

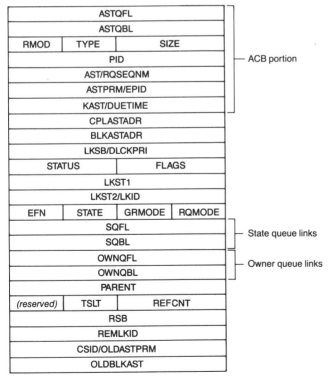

Figure 10.4
Layout of a Lock Block

Table 10.1   Compatibility of Lock Modes

Mode of Requested Lock[1]	Mode of Currently Granted Locks					
	NL	CR	CW	PR	PW	EX
NL	Yes	Yes	Yes	Yes	Yes	Yes
CR	Yes	Yes	Yes	Yes	Yes	No
CW	Yes	Yes	Yes	No	No	No
PR	Yes	Yes	No	Yes	No	No
PW	Yes	Yes	No	No	No	No
EX	Yes	No	No	No	No	No

[1] NL, null lock; CR, concurrent read; CW, concurrent write; PR, protected read; PW, protected write; EX, exclusive lock.

in the insertion of its LKB at the end of the conversion queue. Conversion requests have precedence over all waiting requests and all new lock requests. Waiting requests have precedence over all new lock requests.

LKB$B_STATE specifies the current lock condition, for example, granted, waiting, or in a conversion queue. LKB$L_SQFL and LKB$L_SQBL link the LKB into the appropriate state queue in its RSB. Typically, a lock in the conversion or wait queue is also queued to the lock timeout queue through the fields LKB$L_ASTQFL and LKB$L_ASTQBL. If the lock request is not granted within a certain amount of time, a deadlock search is triggered (see Section 10.3.1).

A lock with a parent lock and resource is termed a sublock. An LKB describing a sublock contains the address of the parent LKB in field LKB$L_PARENT; the parent LKB has no corresponding pointer to the sublock. The RSB associated with the sublock points to the parent resource through the field RSB$L_PARENT; the parent resource has no corresponding pointer to the subresource. These relations are shown in Figure 10.5. LKB$W_REFCNT specifies how many sublocks have that LKB as their parent.

The first part of an LKB is an asynchronous system trap (AST) control block (ACB). When a lock request is granted, the LKB/ACB can be queued to the process's PCB through the fields LKB$L_ASTQFL and LKB$L_ASTQBL. Queued as an ACB, it describes a special kernel mode AST, a blocking AST, or a completion AST (see Section 10.2.4). LKB$L_PID contains the internal process ID of the process that requested the lock.

LKB$B_RMOD specifies the access mode at which completion and blocking ASTs for this lock are delivered. The access mode from which the $ENQ system service is requested, rather than an $ENQ service argument, determines the value of LKB$B_RMOD. This field also specifies the least privileged access mode from which the lock can be converted or dequeued. If a

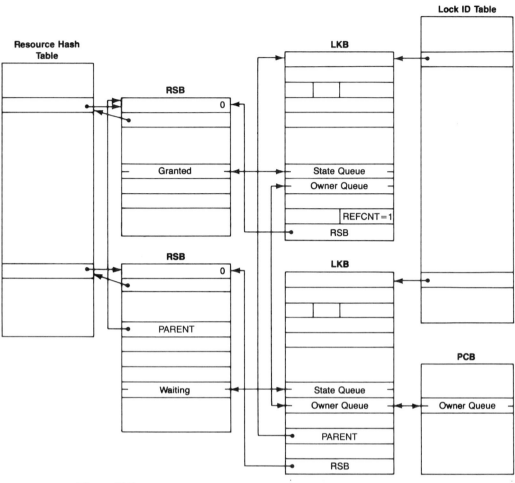

Figure 10.5
Relations Between Locks and Sublocks

lock has a parent, the lock's access mode must not be more privileged than that of its parent.

LKB$L_EPID contains the extended process ID (see Chapter 25). LKB$L_CPLASTADR and LKB$L_BLKASTADR contain the addresses of the completion and blocking AST procedures requested by the process. LKB$L_LKSB contains the address of the process's lock status block. LKB$L_LKST1 contains the condition value to be copied to the lock status block. The second longword of lock status, LKB$L_LKID, contains the lock ID itself.

Other LKB fields are described in later sections of this chapter.

10.1.4   Lock ID Table

The lock ID table locates all LKBs. A lock ID consists of an index into the lock ID table and a sequence number identifying this particular use of that index. When a lock index is in use, its entry in the lock ID table contains the address of the associated LKB.

The entry for an unused index has two pieces of information. The high-order word contains the updated sequence number for that index. The low-order word contains the index of the next unused entry in the lock ID table. The unused entries in the lock ID table are thus linked together, with the listhead at global location LCK$GL_NXTID. When a new lock is requested, its index is taken from LCK$GL_NXTID, which is updated to point to the next unused entry.

A lock to be dequeued is identified by its lock ID. The lock ID locates the corresponding lock ID table entry. The table entry has the address of the LKB to be deallocated. After the LKB is deallocated, the lock ID of the dequeued lock is stored in LCK$GL_NXTID.

Because it is possible that an erroneous value can be passed as a lock ID to a lock management system service, the system services validate the lock ID. They compare the caller's process identification (PID) and access mode with the PID and access mode stored in the LKB. The PIDs must match and the caller's access mode must be at least as privileged as that of the lock. If the comparison fails, the service exits with the error status SS$_IVLOCKID.

The global symbol LCK$GL_IDTBL points to the lock ID table, whose structure is shown in Figure 10.6. The SYSGEN parameters LOCKIDTBL and LOCKIDTBL_MAX control the size of the lock ID table. The global location LCK$GL_MAXID contains the index to the last entry in the lock ID table. The lock ID table entry at that location always contains a zero.

During system initialization, a table of LOCKIDTBL longwords is allocated from nonpaged pool. If more locks are requested than can fit in the table, the $ENQ system service builds a new table, which is LOCKIDTBL entries longer than the old one. It copies the old table's entries to the new table, initializes the additional entries in the new table, and deallocates the old table. LOCKIDTBL_MAX specifies the maximum size of the table and thus the maximum number of locks.

10.1.5 Relations in the Lock Database

There are three ways in which the lock database can be accessed:

- As described in Section 10.1.2, the RSB for a given resource name can be located through the resource hash table. All locks associated with the resource can be located through the RSB state queue heads.
- As described in Section 10.1.4, the LKB for a given lock ID can be located through the lock ID table. The resource address field in the LKB points to the resource associated with the lock.
- All locks owned by a specific process can be located through the process lock queue.

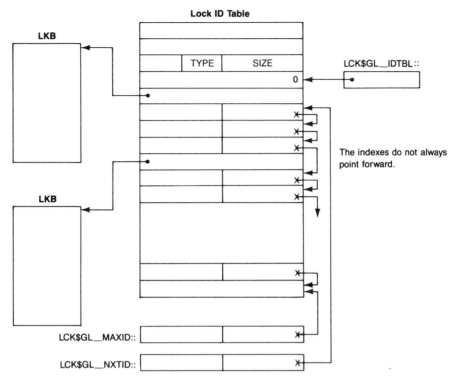

Figure 10.6
Structure of the Lock ID Table

Each process has a lock queue, a doubly linked list of all the locks it has requested. The listhead is in the PCB at the fields PCB$L_LOCKQFL and PCB$L_LOCKQBL. An LKB is linked into this list through the fields LKB$L_OWNQFL and LKB$L_OWNQBL. That is, PCB$L_LOCKQFL points not to the beginning of the first LKB in the queue but to field LKB$L_OWNQFL in that LKB. All granted locks are first, followed by converting and waiting locks. The locks are ordered this way to facilitate deadlock detection (see Section 10.3.2.2).

10.1.6   VAXcluster Lock Database

All resource names are clusterwide in scope, and processes running on any node can cooperate in sharing resources. Lock management is the fundamental VAXcluster synchronization primitive. Lock management system services are used by VMS facilities and user applications to provide clusterwide synchronization. Appendix H describes the manner in which some VMS facilities use locks.

Lock management data structures, RSBs and LKBs, are distributed among

223

the nodes of a VAXcluster system. This section provides an overview of how the lock management database is organized.

A resource tree, consisting of a resource and all its subresources, is "mastered" on one node at a time. The master node keeps track of all locks taken out on that resource tree and performs the actual locking. A resource is initially mastered on the first node to define that resource. When the $ENQ system service is requested for a root resource name that is not currently in use, a master RSB is created on the requesting node.

There is also an RSB on each node other than the master with a lock on the resource. The RSB on a node not mastering the resource contains the cluster system ID (CSID) of the mastering node in the field RSB$L_CSID. The RSB on the mastering node contains zero in that field to indicate that it is the master RSB. The CSID field is also zero on a system that is not a VAXcluster member.

When the node mastering a resource tree receives a lock request from another VAXcluster node, it compares its own use of the tree, from the field RSB$W_ACTIVITY, with that of the requesting node. If the requesting node would be a more efficient resource master, that is, if its RSB$W_ACTIVITY value is lower than the local value, the current master node directs an exchange that transfers mastership of the lock to the other node. This procedure is called remastering. During remastering, all other access to the resource is denied; requests stall until remastering is complete.

A distributed directory is maintained to enable VAXcluster members to track the existence of root resources and their associated master nodes. The directory is composed of directory entry RSBs distributed among the VAXcluster members. A directory entry RSB has the RSB$V_DIRENTRY bit set in the RSB$W_STATUS field and the CSID of the resource's master node in the RSB$L_CSID field. The VAXcluster member maintaining a directory entry for a particular resource is termed its directory node. If the directory node is also the resource's master node, the RSB$L_CSID field contains a zero, and one RSB serves both functions; if not, there are RSBs on both the directory and master nodes. Thus, there can potentially be an RSB on the directory node, an RSB on the master node, and one RSB on each node with a lock on the resource.

An individual member serves as the directory node for a subset of the root resources. Its relative participation in directory activity is based on the value of its SYSGEN parameter LOCKDIRWT. All members maintain an identical list of CSIDs called the directory vector by exchanging LOCKDIRWT values during VAXcluster state transitions. A member's LOCKDIRWT value determines the number of contiguous slots in the directory vector that are filled with its CSID. The address of the directory vector is stored in global location LCK$GL_DIRVEC.

To determine the directory node for a particular root resource, the RSB field RSB$W_HASHVAL is hashed and the resulting value is used as an index into the directory vector. Since all members have an identical copy of the list, they perform the directory determination with identical results.

In a VAXcluster system, there are three types of LKB. Under some circumstances, a process's lock is represented by two LKBs on two different nodes.

- A local copy is an LKB for a lock on one node whose resource is mastered on that same node. This LKB is the only one representing the process's lock. This is similar to the nonclustered case.
- A process copy is an LKB for a lock on one node whose resource is mastered on another node. The process copy describes the process's interest in the resource. The other node has the master copy of the lock. The field LKB$L_REMLKID in the process copy identifies the lock ID of the master copy. (Lock IDs are specific to a single node.) RSB$L_CSID identifies the master node.
- A master copy is an LKB that exists on a node mastering a resource but that represents the lock of a process on a different node. The field LKB$L_REMLKID in the master copy identifies the lock ID of the process copy. The field LKB$L_CSID in the master copy identifies the node of the process copy. A process copy and a master copy are always paired.

The three types of LKB can be distinguished based on the setting of the bit LKB$V_MSTCPY in LKB$W_FLAGS and the contents of RSB$L_CSID in the associated resource's RSB:

- Local copy—LKB$V_MSTCPY is zero and RSB$L_CSID is zero.
- Process copy—LKB$V_MSTCPY is zero and RSB$L_CSID is nonzero.
- Master copy—LKB$V_MSTCPY is nonzero and RSB$L_CSID is zero.

10.2 LOCK MANAGEMENT SYSTEM SERVICES

The $ENQ system service attempts to grant a requested new lock or lock conversion immediately. If the new lock or conversion cannot be granted, the LKB is placed on the RSB's wait or conversion queue. The $DEQ system service dequeues or cancels a lock from a resource and then searches the resource's state queues for locks to grant that are compatible with the currently granted locks. The $GETLKI system service returns information about a specified lock or locks.

The following sections describe the operations of the $ENQ[W], $DEQ, and $GETLKI[W] system services on a single node. VAXcluster operation is mentioned, but the details are beyond the scope of this book.

10.2.1 The $ENQ[W] System Service

The $ENQ system service procedure, EXE$ENQ in module SYSENQDEQ, runs in kernel mode. EXE$ENQ first validates the event flag and lock mode arguments and tests accessibility of the lock status block. If any of these tests fails, EXE$ENQ returns to its requestor with an error status. If the tests succeed, EXE$ENQ tests whether LCK$V_CONVERT is set in the FLAGS argument to determine whether this is a new lock request or conversion of an existing lock. Section 10.2.2 describes lock conversions.

When a new lock is requested, EXE$ENQ allocates an LKB and RSB from nonpaged pool and initializes them. EXE$ENQ allocates the RSB on the assumption that the resource is being defined for the first time. EXE$ENQ then raises IPL to IPL$_SCS and acquires the system communication services (SCS) spinlock to synchronize access to the lock database. All error paths release the SCS spinlock and lower IPL before exiting.

If the requestor specified the PARID argument, EXE$ENQ verifies that the parent lock ID is valid, that the access mode of the $ENQ requestor is not more privileged than that of the parent lock, and that the parent lock's PID matches that of the current process. If any of these tests fails, EXE$ENQ returns the error status SS$_IVLOCKID to its requestor. If the tests complete successfully but the parent lock request has not been granted, EXE$ENQ returns the error status SS$_PARNOTGRANT. If the parent lock request has been granted, EXE$ENQ increments the reference count in the parent's lock and stores the parent lock's address in the new lock's LKB$L_PARENT field.

If the requestor requested a UIC-specific resource, EXE$ENQ stores the process's UIC group in the RSB. Otherwise, if the requestor requested a systemwide resource name by specifying the FLAGS argument bit LCKV_SYSTEM, EXEENQ checks that the process either has the SYSLCK privilege or requested the $ENQ system service from kernel or executive mode. If neither condition is true, EXE$ENQ returns the error status SS$_NOSYSLCK to its requestor.

EXE$ENQ charges the lock against the job quota JIB$W_ENQCNT unless the request specified the FLAGS argument bit LCK$V_NOQUOTA, which requires that the request was made from executive or kernel mode. (Use of this flag is reserved to Digital.) If the job exceeds its ENQLM quota, EXE$ENQ returns the error status SS$_EXENQLM. Otherwise, EXE$ENQ allocates a lock ID, expanding the lock ID table if necessary, and stores the address of the LKB in the table entry for that lock ID.

Next, EXE$ENQ determines whether the resource already exists on this node. It computes the resource hash value, indexes into the resource hash table, and searches the resource hash chain for the named RSB. The resource specified by the lock request must match an RSB with the same hash value in the following fields:

- Parent RSB address
- UIC group number (or zero for systemwide resource names)
- Access mode
- Resource name string

If the RSB for the named resource is not found, the new RSB is added to the end of the hash chain. EXE$ENQ initializes the rest of the RSB fields, including the three lock queue headers, the value block and sequence number, and the reference count.

If the resource has no parent, EXE$ENQ inserts it onto the tail of the systemwide list of root resources whose listhead is LCK$GL_RRSFL. The RSB's own address is stored in its root resource field, RSB$L_RTRSB.

If the resource has a parent, the new resource inherits its CSID from the parent resource. The parent RSB's reference count is incremented. Resource depth is initialized to 1 more than the parent resource depth. If maximum lock depth is exceeded, EXE$ENQ deallocates the RSB and LKB and returns the error status SS$_EXDEPTH. The new resource also inherits the parent's root resource, RSB$L_RTRSB. It is inserted onto the subresource queue of its parent.

If the resource is new and mastered locally, no further checks are necessary; the new lock is granted immediately (see Section 10.2.4).

If the RSB for the named resource is found, the new RSB is superfluous and is deallocated. If the resource is mastered locally, the new lock is granted immediately when the conversion and wait queues are empty and the request mode in the LKB is compatible with the currently granted locks (see Section 10.2.4). EXE$ENQ returns the success code SS$_SYNCH to its requestor if the FLAGS argument bit LCK$V_SYNCSTS is set. The event flag and completion AST are omitted in this case. Otherwise, EXE$ENQ returns the status SS$_NORMAL and proceeds to set the event flag and deliver the completion AST as requested by the user.

If the lock cannot be granted immediately, the FLAGS argument bit LCK$V_NOQUEUE determines EXE$ENQ's action. If LCK$V_NOQUEUE is set, EXE$ENQ deallocates the LKB and returns the failure status SS$_NOT-QUEUED to its requestor. If LCK$V_NOQUEUE is clear, EXE$ENQ sets the lock state to LKB$K_WAITING and places the LKB at the end of the wait queue in the RSB. The wait queue is maintained in first-in/first-out (FIFO) order. If the waiting LKB is not a master copy LKB, it is also queued onto PCB$L_LOCKQFL in the PCB of the requesting (current) process. If the LKB is not a process copy and has not disabled deadlock wait (LCK$V_NO-DLCKWT is clear), and if deadlock wait is enabled on the system (LCK$GL_WAITTIME nonzero), then a due time is computed and the LKB is inserted on the timeout queue. See Section 10.3.1 for more information on deadlock searches initiated by timeout.

The asynchronous form of the system service ($ENQ) returns to its requestor. The requestor can either wait for the lock to be granted or continue processing. The synchronous form of the system service ($ENQW) waits both for the event flag associated with the request to be set and for status to be returned in the Lock Status Block (LKSB). Chapter 6 provides more information concerning synchronous and asynchronous system services.

To speed checks for compatibility with the currently granted locks, each RSB contains a single field indicating the highest granted lock mode of all locks in both the granted and conversion queues for that resource. This field is termed the group grant mode. Note that locks on the conversion queue retain their original grant mode while waiting for their conversion requests to complete. It is the original grant mode of these locks that is used in calculating the group grant mode, not their request mode.

The value of the group grant mode is stored in the RSB at the field RSB$B_GGMODE. Because this value is calculated when a lock is granted and maintained in the RSB, compatibility checking involves only one compare operation. Note that in a VAXcluster system, the group grant mode is maintained only in the master RSB.

10.2.2 Lock Conversions

When a process requests the $ENQ system service, the value of the LCK$V_CONVERT bit in the FLAGS argument differentiates between a new lock request and a lock conversion. When LCK$V_CONVERT is set, EXE$ENQ performs a lock conversion. EXE$ENQ obtains the lock ID of the lock to be converted from the LOCKID argument and uses the LKMODE argument as the request mode.

Four lock modes affect EXE$ENQ's actions:

- The current mode of the converting lock, called its grant mode and stored in LKB$B_GRMODE.
- The converting lock's desired new value, called its request mode and stored in LKB$B_RQMODE when the lock is on the conversion or wait queue.
- The most restrictive grant mode found in a lock on the resource's conversion or granted queues, called the group grant mode and stored in RSB$B_GGMODE.
- The blocking condition to compare against when locks are removed from the granted queue, called the conversion grant mode and stored in RSB$B_CGMODE.

The conversion grant mode prevents a lock from blocking its own conversion and determines when an attempt to grant queued lock conversions is worthwhile. Most of the time, the conversion grant mode contains the same value as the group grant mode. The conversion grant mode differs from the group grant mode when both of the following are true:

- The grant mode of the lock at the head of the conversion queue is the most restrictive lock mode for the resource.
- No other locks are granted at that same lock mode.

In this case, the resource's conversion grant mode summarizes only the grant modes of locks on the granted queue. It contains a less restrictive lock mode than the group grant mode does, because group grant mode includes the grant modes of locks on the conversion queue.

EXE$ENQ begins by removing the lock specified by LOCKID from the granted queue. If no locks remain on the granted or conversion queue, the converting lock is granted immediately and EXE$ENQ attempts to grant any waiting locks after clearing the group and conversion grant modes. Section 10.2.4 describes the grant procedure.

When additional locks exist on the conversion or grant queue, the conversion grant mode and the lock's grant mode are compared:

- If they are not equal, the compatibility of the converting lock's request mode and the resource's group grant mode determines whether the lock is granted or placed on the tail of the conversion queue. Because the converting lock was not the most restrictive lock on the granted queue, its conversion has no effect on locks in the conversion or wait queue. EXE$ENQ will not attempt to grant any locks except the converting lock.
- If the lock's grant mode matches the resource's conversion grant mode, the converting lock was granted in the most restrictive lock mode present on the granted queue. The resource's group and conversion grant modes must be recalculated without including the grant mode of the converting lock, to prevent it from blocking its own conversion.

  If the recalculated grant value proves compatible with the lock's request mode, the value is stored in the group grant and conversion grant fields and the lock conversion is granted. Since the change in this lock's status may be significant for other locks on the conversion or wait queue, EXE$ENQ attempts to grant locks first from the conversion queue, then from the wait queue, until it reaches a lock that it cannot grant.

In either case, if the lock's request mode is incompatible, EXE$ENQ tests the LCK$V_NOQUEUE bit. If LCK$V_NOQUEUE is set, EXE$ENQ inserts the lock back onto the granted queue and returns the status SS$_NOTQUEUED to the user. Otherwise, EXE$ENQ clears the lock state and places the lock at the tail of the conversion queue, which is maintained as a FIFO queue. The group grant mode is not altered, but the conversion grant field is set to the recalculated value if the lock is first in the conversion queue. EXE$ENQ also moves the LKB to the end of the PCB queue. The PCB queue has granted locks first, followed by waiting and converting locks. If the LKB is not a process copy, if the conversion request did not disable deadlock wait, and if deadlock wait is enabled on the system (LCK$GL_WAITTIME nonzero), then a due time is computed and the LKB is inserted on the timeout queue. Section 10.3.1 gives more information on deadlock searches initiated by timeouts.

Locks on the conversion or wait queue are granted later, by EXE$DEQ when blocking locks are removed from the granted or conversion queue, and by EXE$ENQ when blocking locks are converted to less restrictive lock modes.

10.2.3 The $DEQ System Service

A process requests the $DEQ system service to dequeue locks or sublocks that are granted or to cancel ungranted lock requests. The $DEQ system service procedure, EXE$DEQ in module SYSENQDEQ, runs in kernel mode. EXE$DEQ examines the LOCKID argument and the FLAGS argument bit LCK$V_DEQALL to determine whether a specific lock or a number of locks are to be dequeued.

- If the FLAGS argument has the LCK$V_DEQALL bit set, then the process is requesting the dequeuing of multiple locks. The locks to be dequeued are determined by the $DEQ access mode argument ACMODE and by the LOCKID argument. The ACMODE argument is maximized with the access mode from which the $DEQ system service was requested. If omitted, it defaults to the access mode from which the system service was requested.

  —If the LOCKID argument is specified, EXE$DEQ dequeues all sublocks of that lock whose access modes are not more privileged than the dequeue access mode.

  Note that if LOCKID is specified with LCK$V_DEQALL, sublocks of that lock are dequeued, but the lock itself is not dequeued.

  —Otherwise, if the LOCKID argument is zero, EXE$DEQ checks every lock held by the process and dequeues each one whose lock access mode is not more privileged than the dequeue access mode.

- If the FLAGS argument has the LCK$V_DEQALL bit clear, then the process is requesting that one lock be dequeued or canceled. In this case, EXE$DEQ uses the LOCKID argument to locate the LKB and the FLAGS argument bit LCK$V_CANCEL to determine the operation.

To dequeue each individual lock, EXE$DEQ acquires the SCS spinlock and raises IPL to IPL$_SCS. It verifies that the access mode of the $DEQ requestor is not less privileged than that of the lock (LKB$B_RMOD) and that the lock PID matches that of the current process. If either of these tests fail, EXE$DEQ returns the error status SS$_IVLOCKID to its requestor. Once the lock is verified, EXE$DEQ checks whether the lock has sublocks. Before a lock is deleted, its sublocks must be dequeued. Unless the LCK$V_DEQALL flag is set, EXE$DEQ returns the error status SS$_SUBLOCKS.

All error paths release the SCS spinlock and lower IPL to IPL 2 before exiting. When dequeuing multiple locks, EXE$DEQ releases and reacquires the spinlock between individual lock requests.

EXE$DEQ removes the LKB from whichever resource queue it is found on.

- If the lock is dequeued from the granted queue, EXE$DEQ checks whether the LKB is the only lock on the resource. If so, EXE$DEQ removes the

RSB from its resource hash chain and deallocates it. If other locks remain, EXE$DEQ recomputes the resource's group grant mode and conversion grant mode and attempts to grant locks on the conversion and wait queues.

- If the lock is dequeued from the conversion queue, it might have blocked other lock requests. If it was at the head of the queue, or if its grant mode is equal to the resource's conversion grant mode, EXE$DEQ recomputes the resource's group grant mode and conversion grant mode. EXE$DEQ attempts to grant locks beginning with the new first lock in the conversion queue. It repeats this with the conversion and wait queues until it reaches a lock whose lock mode is incompatible with the resource group grant mode.

- If the lock is dequeued from the head of the wait queue and the conversion queue is empty, EXE$DEQ tries to grant the first lock in the wait queue. If it succeeds, EXE$DEQ continues with the next lock in the wait queue. It repeats this until it reaches a lock whose lock mode is incompatible with the resource group grant mode.

If the lock being dequeued was a sublock, EXE$DEQ decrements its parent lock's reference count. It releases the lock ID and removes the LKB from the process's PCB lock queue.

If the lock was waiting or in the conversion queue, EXE$DEQ sets the event flag associated with the lock request and queues the LKB as an ACB to the process to return final lock status. The LKB is deallocated when the AST is delivered.

If the lock was granted, its LKB may still be queued as an ACB. If the ACB was merely to deliver a blocking AST, EXE$DEQ removes the LKB/ACB from the ACB queue and deallocates the LKB. Otherwise, the LKB/ACB will be deallocated when the AST is delivered. Whenever the LKB is deallocated, the lock quota is returned to the process.

10.2.4 Granting a Lock

The routine LCK$GRANT_LOCK, in module SYSENQDEQ, is invoked to grant a lock request. LCK$GRANT_LOCK is invoked under three different sets of circumstances:

- EXE$ENQ receives a request for a lock on a new resource or a resource with locks whose modes are compatible. The lock request can be granted immediately, synchronously with the original system service call.

- EXE$ENQ converts a lock on a resource to a less restrictive lock mode. Another lock that was blocked can now be granted, asynchronously to its original lock request.

- EXE$DEQ dequeues or cancels a lock on a resource. A lock that was blocked can now be granted, asynchronously to its original lock request.

LCK$GRANT_LOCK takes the following steps in granting a lock:

1. If the mode of the lock being granted is more restrictive than the existing group grant mode, LCK$GRANT_LOCK copies the mode of the lock being granted to the group grant mode field and the conversion grant mode field.
2. It places the LKB on the granted queue, changing its state to granted. LCK$GRANT_LOCK writes the requested lock mode in LKB$B_GR-MODE.
3. If the lock is being granted asynchronously, it might be on the timeout queue. If so, LCK$GRANT_LOCK removes it.
4. After processing the AST delivery requirements described below, LCK$GRANT_LOCK invokes SCH$POSTEF to set the event flag associated with the lock request (LKB$B_EFN). If the process was waiting for this event flag to be set, the process scheduling priority and state may be altered. Chapter 9 discusses event flags, and Chapter 12 gives information about process scheduling.

LCK$GRANT_LOCK makes a series of tests to determine whether an AST should be queued to the process whose lock request it granted. There are three possible requirements for an AST:

- A special kernel mode AST
- A user-requested blocking AST
- A user-requested completion AST

The three are independent of each other. Thus, it is possible that no AST will be requested or as many as three ASTs will be required.

LCK$GRANT_LOCK must queue a blocking AST to the process if it requested one and if the newly granted lock is blocking another lock. No blocking AST is necessary if none was requested or if the lock is not blocking another lock.

If the process requested a completion AST, LCK$GRANT_LOCK queues one unless the lock request was granted synchronously and the FLAGS argument bit LCK$V_SYNCSTS was set.

The special kernel mode AST must be queued if the lock request completed asynchronously. The special kernel mode AST routine writes the status to the process's lock status block and possibly a value to the lock value block. Even if the lock request completed synchronously, the special kernel mode AST routine is necessary to perform cleanup if a completion or blocking AST is to be queued.

An ACB can describe one normal AST procedure or one special kernel mode AST routine. An ACB can also describe a special kernel mode AST routine piggybacked on a normal AST procedure. Chapter 7 gives a detailed description of ASTs. If an AST is required, LCK$GRANT_LOCK invokes SCH$QAST to queue an ACB to the process. The LKB is used as the ACB.

LCK$GRANT_LOCK chooses one of the following:

- It does not queue an ACB if the lock request is synchronous and neither a blocking nor a completion AST is required.
- It queues an ACB specifying a special kernel mode AST if the lock request is asynchronous and neither a blocking nor a completion AST is required.
- It queues an ACB specifying a piggyback special kernel mode AST if either or both a blocking and a completion AST are required.

Because the ACB can contain the address of only one AST procedure, special treatment is required when both completion and blocking ASTs must be delivered. When the lock is granted, LCK$GRANT_LOCK writes the address of the completion AST procedure (stored at the field LKB$L_CPLASTADR) in the field LKB$L_AST. It then queues the LKB as an ACB.

Just before entering the completion AST procedure, the AST delivery service routine dispatches to the piggyback special kernel mode AST routine. This routine writes the address of the blocking AST (stored at the field LKB$L_BLKASTADR) in LKB$L_AST. It then requeues the LKB as an ACB. When the piggyback special kernel mode AST routine exits, the completion AST procedure executes. When the completion AST procedure exits, the blocking AST is delivered.

10.2.5   System-Owned Locks

Some locks, called system-owned locks, are not associated with any process. A system-owned lock, its resource, and thus its value block remain in existence when no process has any interest in the resource. A system-owned lock has zero in its LKB$L_PID field and is not queued to any PCB lock queue. The scope of its resource name may be systemwide or qualified by UIC group. Note the distinction between a system-owned lock and a resource that is defined systemwide.

A system-owned lock may only be requested from kernel or executive mode. The special $ENQ system service FLAGS argument LCK$V_CVTSYS indicates that the lock should be granted as a system-owned lock or converted from a process-owned lock to a system-owned lock.

Although the service request must be made from kernel or executive mode, the access mode of the resource is determined by the $ENQ system service argument ACMODE, as it would be for any resource. One additional restriction applies—if a lock is system-owned, its parent lock (if any) must also be system-owned. A process-owned lock may have a system-owned lock as its parent, but a system-owned lock must not be a sublock of a process-owned lock.

The only possible state of a system-owned lock is granted. That is, a lock in a wait or conversion queue cannot be system-owned. This restriction exists partly because delivery of a completion AST or special kernel mode AST requires a process context. Furthermore, locks in the wait and conversion queues are examined during deadlock detection on the assumption that each lock is owned by a process.

When the FLAGS argument bit LCK$V_CVTSYS is set in a new lock request, EXE$ENQ sets the LCK$V_SYNCSTS and LCK$V_NOQUEUE flags as well. When LCK$V_NOQUEUE is set, EXE$ENQ returns the error status SS$_NOTQUEUED if it cannot grant the lock immediately. If it can grant the lock immediately and LCK$V_SYNCSTS is set, it does not queue a completion AST or set an event flag.

By specifying the FLAGS argument bit LCK$V_CVTSYS with LCK$V_CONVERT, a process can request the conversion of a process-owned lock to a system-owned lock or a system-owned lock to a less restrictive lock mode.

A process can request conversion of a system-owned lock to a more restrictive mode, but the request can succeed only if the conversion can complete immediately. Otherwise, the system-owned lock is converted to a process-owned lock, the lock remains granted at its original lock mode, and EXE$ENQ returns the error status SS$_BADPARAM.

A mechanism is defined for delivery of a blocking AST for a system-owned lock. The field LKB$L_BLKASTADR in a system-owned lock contains the address of a blocking AST routine in system space. Instead of queuing a blocking AST to a process, the lock management services dispatch to that routine at IPL$_SCS holding the SCS spinlock.

Certain VMS components, such as the Files-11 Extended QIO Processor (XQP), use system-owned locks. The XQP synchronizes access to the individual entries in its I/O buffer cache through system-owned locks. The XQP, running in the context of each process in the system, maintains a systemwide cache of blocks read from the on-disk file structure. A process's XQP requests a lock on a buffer cache entry only while it is reading or writing that entry in the cache. The cache entry exists, however, even when no process is accessing it. The lock management data structures representing the cache entry must also continue to exist.

The use of system-owned locks is reserved to Digital. Any other use is strongly discouraged by Digital and completely unsupported.

10.2.6   The $GETLKI[W] System Service

The $GETLKI[W] system service enables a process to obtain information about one or more locks that it is allowed to interrogate. The process may only obtain information about locks on resources with access modes equal to or less privileged than the access mode at which the $GETLKI request is issued. For example, a process running in user mode cannot obtain information about locks taken out on executive mode resources. The field RSB$B_RMOD defines the resource access mode.

The process can be further limited to a subset of the resource name space by its lack of privilege. Without any privilege, a process can interrogate only locks on resources with the same UIC group number as its own. With WORLD privilege, a process can interrogate locks on resources of any UIC group. Obtaining information about the locks of systemwide resources requires either that the process have SYSLCK privilege or that it make the $GETLKI request from kernel or executive mode.

The $GETLKI system service procedure, EXE$GETLKI in module SYS-GETLKI, runs in kernel mode. The system service is called with a LOCKID argument that either identifies a particular lock or specifies a wildcard operation. First, EXE$GETLKI locates the LKB associated with the specified lock ID and verifies that the process can interrogate it. If the process specified a wildcard operation, EXE$GETLKI locates the first LKB that the process can interrogate. EXE$GETLKI begins with lock index 1 and scans the lock ID table. On each successive call, it returns information about one lock, maintaining the lock index context for the next call.

EXE$GETLKI is called with the address of an item list that includes, for each specified item, which kind of lock information is to be returned, the size and address of the buffer to receive the information, and a location to receive the size of the information returned. EXE$GETLKI checks each item in the item list for correctness: its item code must be valid; its buffer descriptor and buffer must be writable in the access mode of $GETLKI's caller. In general, it then copies the requested information, either from the LKB or its RSB, to the buffer and records the size of the returned information in the specified location.

Certain types of information are not obtainable through simply copying data structure fields, for example, a list of all locks blocking the specified lock. EXE$GETLKI contains special routines for such information.

When EXE$GETLKI has either processed all items in the item list or found one that is incorrect or that has an inaccessible buffer, it is done. It sets the event flag associated with the request and queues a completion AST if one was requested and if the system service completed without error. EXE$GETLKI then returns to its requestor with completion status in R0.

10.3   HANDLING DEADLOCKS

A deadlock occurs when several locks are waiting for each other in a circular fashion. VMS resolves deadlocks by choosing a participant in the deadlock cycle and refusing that participant's lock request. The participant chosen to break the deadlock is termed the victim. The victim's lock or conversion request fails and the error status SS$_DEADLOCK is returned in the victim's lock status block.

None of the victim's already granted locks are affected, even when they are part of the deadlock. Resolution of the deadlock is the responsibility of the victim.

There are three phases of deadlock handling:

1. A deadlock is suspected.
2. A deadlock search proves that a deadlock actually exists.
3. A victim is chosen.

These three phases are described in subsequent sections. The descriptions are limited to handling of deadlocks within one system that is not a VAXcluster member. VAXcluster deadlock handling is beyond the scope of this book.

10.3.1   Initiating a Deadlock Search

Because deadlock detection is time-consuming, it is not desirable to search for deadlocks every time a lock or conversion request is blocked. Instead, the VMS software searches for a deadlock only when a lock request has been waiting for a resource for a specified amount of time. The SYSGEN parameter DEADLOCK_WAIT specifies how many seconds a blocked lock request must have been waiting before a deadlock search is initiated.

A way of restricting a particular lock's participation in deadlock searches is provided through the special $ENQ FLAGS arguments LCK$V_NODLCK-WT and LCK$V_NODLCKBLK. The LCK$V_NODLCKWT flag in a lock or conversion request inhibits the deadlock search mechanism on a per-lock basis. Locks requested in this manner cannot initiate conversion deadlock searches because they never time out. They are disregarded in multiple resource deadlock searches initiated for other locks. Incorrect use of this flag may cause genuine deadlocks to be ignored, however. For more information, see the *VMS System Services Reference Manual*.

When a lock request specifies a blocking AST procedure that dequeues the blocking lock or converts it to a less restrictive mode, that lock request may also specify the LCK$V_NODLCKBLK flag. This exempts the LKB from multiple resource deadlock searches, on the assumption that the potential deadlock condition will be resolved by the blocking AST procedure. Again, incorrect use of this flag may cause genuine deadlocks to be ignored. For more information, see the *VMS System Services Reference Manual*.

When an LKB requested without the flag LCK$V_NODLCKWT is placed into a conversion or wait queue, EXE$ENQ also places the LKB on the lock timeout queue. The lock timeout queue listhead is at global location LCK$GL_TIMOUTQ. The AST queue fields in the LKB link it into the lock timeout queue. Figure 10.7 shows LKBs on the timeout queue.

When an LKB is placed on the timeout queue, the time at which the lock request will time out is computed and stored in LKB$L_DUETIME. (LKB$L_DUETIME is actually a double use of the special kernel mode AST routine address field, LKB$L_KAST.) The due time is the sum of DEADLOCK_WAIT, stored in LCK$GL_WAITTIME, and the current system time in seconds (EXE$GL_ABSTIM).

Once every second, the routine EXE$TIMEOUT, in module TIMESCHDL, executes. EXE$TIMEOUT has various functions (see Chapter 11). One of

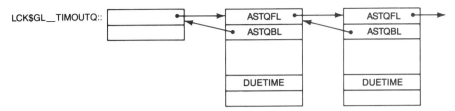

Figure 10.7
Lock Timeout Queue Ordered by LKB$L_DUETIME

them is to check whether the first entry in the lock timeout queue has
timed out by comparing its LKB$L_DUETIME to the contents of EXE$GL_
ABSTIM. Because the queue is time-ordered, checking the due time of the
first entry is sufficient to determine whether a deadlock search is necessary.
If the first entry has not timed out, no other entry could have. If the first
entry has timed out, EXE$TIMEOUT initiates a deadlock search by invoking
the routine LCK$SEARCHDLCK, in module DEADLOCK.

10.3.2 Deadlock Detection

There are two forms of deadlock, each requiring a different detection method.
A conversion deadlock is easily detected, because it is restricted to locks for
a single resource. A multiple resource deadlock is harder to detect, requiring
a more complex search.

10.3.2.1 Conversion Deadlocks.

A conversion deadlock can occur when there are at
least two LKBs in an RSB's conversion queue for a resource. If the request
mode of one lock in the queue is incompatible with the grant mode of
another lock in the queue, a deadlock exists.

For example, assume there are two protected read (PR) mode locks on
a resource. The process with one PR mode lock requests a conversion to
EX mode. Because PR mode is incompatible with EX mode, the conversion
request must wait. While the first conversion request is waiting, the process
with the second PR mode lock also requests a conversion to EX mode. The
first lock cannot be granted because its request mode (EX) is incompatible
with the second lock's grant mode (PR). The second conversion request
cannot be granted because it is waiting behind the first.

The search for a conversion deadlock begins with the first LKB on the
lock timeout queue. The LKB's state queue backward link points to the
previous LKB in the conversion queue. The grant mode of the previous lock is
compared with the request mode of the lock that timed out. If the modes are
compatible, the next previous lock in the conversion queue is examined. The
test is repeated until an incompatible lock is found or the beginning of the
queue is reached. The flags LCK$V_NODLCKWT and LCK$V_NODLCKBLK
are ignored.

If a lock with an incompatible grant mode is found, a deadlock exists. A victim LKB is selected (see Section 10.3.3). If the beginning of the queue is reached, a conversion deadlock does not exist, and a search for a multiple resource deadlock is initiated.

10.3.2.2   **Multiple Resource Deadlocks.**   A multiple resource deadlock occurs when a circular list of processes are each waiting for one another on two or more resources.

For example, assume process A locks resource 1 and process B locks resource 2. Process A then requests a lock on resource 2 that is incompatible with B's lock on resource 2, and thus process A must wait. Note that at this point, a circular list does not exist. When process B then requests a lock on resource 1 that is incompatible with A's lock on resource 1, it must wait. A multiple resource deadlock now exists. Processes A and B are both waiting for each other to release different resources. These steps are shown in Figure 10.8. In the figure, locks that are blocking a resource (incompatible with waiting locks) are shown beneath the RSB; locks that are waiting for a resource are shown above the RSB.

This type of deadlock normally involves two or more resources, unless one process locks the same resource twice. (Usually a process does not lock the same resource twice. However, if the process is multithreaded, double locking can occur. Double locking can result in a multiple resource deadlock.)

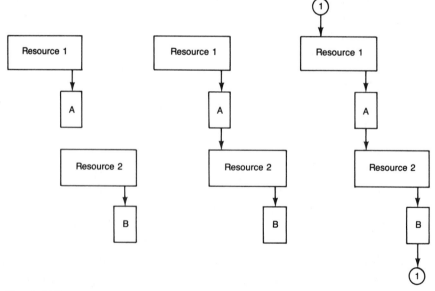

Figure 10.8
Example of a Deadlock Occurring

Saved R2
Saved R3
Saved R4 (PCB + PCB$L__LOCKQFL)
Saved R5
Saved R6 (Address of LKB)
Return Address

Figure 10.9
Stack Frame Built for LCK$SRCH_RESDLCK

To verify that a multiple resource deadlock exists, LCK$SEARCHDLCK uses a recursive algorithm. Its approach is based upon the following:

- A waiting lock is blocked by locks owned by other processes.
- Any of the other processes might themselves have waiting locks.
- Those waiting locks are blocked by locks owned by other blocking processes.

LCK$SEARCHDLCK starts with the lock that timed out on the lock time-out queue. It saves the extended process ID (EPID) of the owner process of the lock that timed out and invokes the multiple resource deadlock routine (LCK$SRCH_RESDLCK). If it finds a lock with the same owner EPID blocking a resource, a deadlock exists.

Each time LCK$SRCH_RESDLCK is invoked, a stack frame is pushed onto the stack. Each stack frame contains information on the current position in the search. Figure 10.9 shows the contents of the stack frame.

The recursive nature of the deadlock search algorithm limits the maximum depth of the resource tree as a function of the SYSGEN parameters INTSTKPAGES and DLCKEXTRASTK. INTSTKPAGES is the size of the interrupt stack, and DLCKEXTRASTK is the amount of interrupt stack space in bytes that should not be used for deadlock searches. The difference between them is the amount of stack available for LCK$SRCH_RESDLCK's stack frames.

Each invocation of LCK$SRCH_RESDLCK specifies the address of a waiting LKB. The resource associated with the LKB is located and the resource state queues are searched for LKBs whose granted or requested lock mode is incompatible with that of the waiting LKB. If an incompatible LKB is found, that lock is considered to be blocking the waiting LKB unless it has the LCK$V_NODLCKBLK bit set in the LKB flags word.

When a blocking lock is found, its EPID is compared to that of the lock that initiated the deadlock search:

- If they are the same, the list is proved to be circular and a deadlock exists. A victim lock is chosen (see Section 10.3.3), and deadlock detection returns control to EXE$TIMEOUT.

- If the EPID of the blocking lock is not the same as the saved EPID and the search bitmap does not indicate that this process has been visited already, the PCB lock queue of the process owning the blocking lock is searched. If an LKB is found in a convert or wait state with the LCK$V_NODLCKWT bit clear, another invocation of LCK$SRCH_RESDLCK is made, specifying that LKB's address.

Each time LCK$SRCH_RESDLCK is invoked, it searches the state queues associated with the specified LKB to see if it is waiting for a resource.

When all the state queues for a given resource have been searched and no blocking lock has been found for that LKB, the routine removes the stack frame and returns control to its invoker. If the invoker itself was LCK$SRCH_RESDLCK, the previous search for blocked locks on the resource can now be resumed.

A process bitmap is maintained to reduce the number of repeated searches for blocking locks on a particular process. Each time a new blocking PCB is located, a bit corresponding to that process is set. If the bit for the PCB is set already, the search for locks blocking that process is terminated, because its locks have been searched already.

10.3.2.3 **Unsuspected Deadlocks.** Note that the use of the process bitmap speeds the location of the suspected deadlock but prevents the accidental detection of unsuspected deadlocks. An unsuspected deadlock is one that exists within the lock management database, but that has not been detected so far, because none of its locks have timed out on the lock timeout queue. This behavior is accepted for the following reasons:

- The lock manager design assumes that individual locking protocols are designed so that deadlocks are rare.
- Finding a process a second time in a deadlock search does not necessarily indicate that an unsuspected deadlock exists.
- The occurrence of unsuspected deadlocks should be rarer still.
- Any deadlock search that does not find a deadlock is a waste of processor time.
- The unsuspected deadlock will become a suspected deadlock when one of its own locks times out on the lock timeout queue and a deadlock search is initiated on its behalf.

Figure 10.10 shows two deadlocks. In the figure, locks that are blocking a resource (incompatible with waiting locks) are shown beneath the RSB; locks that are waiting for a resource are shown above the RSB. One deadlock is suspected and a search is in progress for it. The heavy arrows in the figure show the path of that deadlock cycle. The other is unsuspected. This figure is an extension of the deadlock cycle shown in Figure 10.8.

In this case, the deadlock search was initiated as a search for the locks

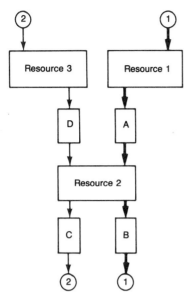

Figure 10.10
Suspected and Unsuspected Deadlocks

blocking process A. Because process C's lock is the first one found granted for resource 2, it is the first lock that is investigated for participation in the deadlock cycle. Process C is waiting for resource 3. The bit corresponding to process C is set in the process bitmap. The context of the search is saved on the stack, and LCK$SRCH_RESDLCK is invoked to search for processes blocking process C's lock.

Process D has a blocking lock on resource 3. Process D is also waiting for resource 2. The bit corresponding to process D is set in the process bitmap. The context of the search is saved on the stack and LCK$SRCH_RESDLCK is invoked to search for processes blocking process D's lock. Process C has a blocking lock on resource 2. This situation is a deadlock. However, because the bit corresponding to process C was set in the process bitmap, the deadlock search for process C is abandoned. One by one, the stack frames are removed and the search whose context was saved continues. Eventually the deadlock search continues with locks blocking resource 2, and the deadlock cycle of processes A and B is discovered.

Eventually one of the locks requested by processes C and D will time out, and a deadlock search will be initiated.

10.3.2.4 **Example of a Search for a Multiple Resource Deadlock.** Figure 10.11 shows a series of locks that result in a deadlock. In the figure, locks that are blocking a resource (incompatible with waiting locks) are shown beneath the RSB; locks that are waiting for a resource are shown above the RSB. The heavy arrows in the figure show the path of the deadlock cycle.

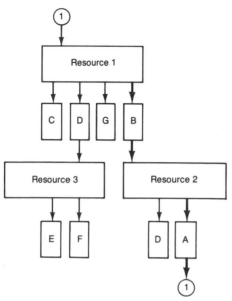

Figure 10.11
Example of a Multiple Resource Deadlock

Assume that the lock owned by process A timed out. Process A is waiting for a lock on resource 1. The deadlock search routine saves process A's EPID and invokes LCK$SRCH_RESDLCK, passing the address of process A's LKB.

The first incompatible lock on resource 1 is owned by process C. Process C has no other waiting locks, so LCK$SRCH_RESDLCK moves on to the next incompatible lock. This lock is owned by process D. When LCK$SRCH_RESDLCK follows the PCB queue for process D, it finds that this process is waiting for a lock on resource 3.

LCK$SRCH_RESDLCK invokes itself, passing the address of the LKB owned by process D. The new invocation of LCK$SRCH_RESDLCK pushes a stack frame detailing the position of the search on resource 1, and LCK$SRCH_RESDLCK starts to search for locks on resource 3 that are incompatible with process D's lock. Resource 3 has two incompatible locks, owned by processes E and F. Neither of these processes is waiting for a lock, so the search on resource 3 terminates. The contents of the stack frame are restored and LCK$SRCH_RESDLCK returns to its previous invocation. The search for processes blocking process A resumes.

The next incompatible lock found on resource 1 is owned by process G. Process G has no waiting locks, so the search continues with process B. The PCB queue for process B shows that it is waiting for a lock on resource 2.

Again, LCK$SRCH_RESDLCK invokes itself, passing the address of the LKB owned by process B. The new invocation of LCK$SRCH_RESDLCK pushes a new stack frame onto the stack, and LCK$SRCH_RESDLCK finds that process D owns a lock that is incompatible with the lock owned by process B. However, because locks owned by process D have been searched already (the bit for process D is set in the process bitmap), the search moves on to the next process.

The next incompatible lock is owned by process A. Because the EPID of process A matches the EPID that was saved initially, the list is proved to be circular and a deadlock exists. Now a victim must be chosen.

10.3.3   **Victim Selection**

Because conversion deadlocks involve only two processes, the victim selection routine simply chooses the process with the lower deadlock priority, stored in the PCB at the field PCB$L_DLCKPRI.

For a multiple resource deadlock, the victim selection routine is only slightly more complicated. The frames that were pushed onto the stack in each recursion into the deadlock location routine are searched for the lowest deadlock priority. Each time a lower deadlock priority value is found, the priority and the owner process are noted. If a deadlock priority of zero is found, that process is immediately chosen as the victim. When all frames have been searched or a deadlock priority of zero is found, the stack pointer is restored and the process with the lowest deadlock priority is chosen as the victim.

Note that the current VMS implementation initializes the deadlock priority of all new processes to zero. Thus, it is not possible to determine which process will be chosen as the victim. With the current implementation, victim selection depends primarily on timing.

PART IV / Scheduling and Time Support

11 Time Support

Love, all alike, no season knows, nor clime,
Nor hours, days, months, which are the rags of time.

John Donne, *The Sun Rising*

Support for activities that require either the date and time or the measurement of an interval of time is implemented in both the VAX hardware and the VMS operating system.

11.1 OVERVIEW

A hardware component called the interval timer interrupts at regular intervals. VMS uses this timer to keep time and to service time-dependent requests. VMS keeps two different times, the current date and time (the system time) and the time elapsed since the system was bootstrapped (the system uptime).

On most VAX systems, a processor register (PRxxx$_TODR) or a time-of-year clock or, in some cases, both help VMS maintain the system time across system bootstraps, power failures, and shutdowns. Battery backup is usually provided to this component, generically referred to as the time-of-year clock, so that it can maintain the time while the CPU has no power. Note that the time-of-year clock is a longword value and can only represent the time within a year.

VMS maintains the system time in the cell EXE$GQ_SYSTIME in increments of 100 nanoseconds from a known base time. Upon bootstrapping, VMS determines the initial value of this cell as follows:

- When a system is bootstrapped for the first time, VMS requests the current date and time from the operator and initializes the time-of-year clock. VMS also records the date and time on disk whenever the system time is initialized or changed.
- When rebooting, VMS uses the following strategy to initialize EXE$GQ_SYSTIME.

  —VMS validates the time-of-year clock by comparing its contents with the recorded value on disk.

  —If the time-of-year clock appears valid, the initial value of EXE$GQ_SYSTIME is determined from the recorded value and the time-of-year clock, as explained in Section 11.3.1.

  —If the time-of-year clock is more than one day *behind* the recorded value, the time-of-year clock is invalid. VMS either asks the operator for the new system time or, if human intervention is not desired, resets the time-of-year clock to the recorded value plus 10 milliseconds.

- A node joining a VAXcluster obtains the initial date and time from a node that has already joined the cluster.

Once initialized, EXE$GQ_SYSTIME is incremented for every interval timer interrupt. Typically, the timer interrupts at 10-millisecond intervals and EXE$GQ_SYSTIME is incremented by 100,000, which is the number of 100-nanosecond intervals in 10 milliseconds. This is done by the interval timer interrupt service routine, EXE$HWCLKINT. On a symmetric multiprocessing (SMP) system, only the primary CPU is responsible for updating EXE$GQ_SYSTIME.

The system manager may change the system date and time using the SET TIME DCL command or the Set Time ($SETIME) system service. The Get Time ($GETTIM) system service enables users to read the current date and time. VMS provides two system services, Schedule Wakeup ($SCHDWK) and Set Timer ($SETIMR), to support users' time-dependent requests. In addition, there are several other services, described briefly in Chapter 36, that convert the date and time between ASCII and binary formats.

In addition to updating the system time, the interval timer interrupt service routine also requests a software timer interrupt when the current process's quantum has expired or when the most imminent timer request on the system is due. The software timer interrupt service routine is responsible for initiating quantum-end processing and managing the timer queue to deliver timer requests.

11.2 HARDWARE CLOCKS

The two hardware clocks, the interval timer and the time-of-year clock, are updated regularly by timing circuitry. Initialization, calibration, and interpretation of the clocks are performed by VMS routines during system initialization and normal operations.

The processor registers that implement these components are summarized in Table 11.1, along with the memory locations that record the various software time values.

The implementations of the interval timer and time-of-year clock vary on the different VAX CPUs.

11.2.1 Interval Timer

All VAX CPUs implement an interval timer that can interrupt at 10-millisecond intervals. The minimum implementation is the processor register PR$_ICCS, containing a single bit, Interrupt Enable (IE) which, when set, causes interrupts every 10 milliseconds. The MicroVAX II implements the minimum interval timer.

Table 11.1   VMS Hardware Clocks and Software Timers

Name	Use	Units	Frequency	Updated by
PRxxx$_ICR [1]	Interval count	1 μs	1 μs	CPU hardware
PRxxx$_NICR [1]	Next interval count	1 μs	–	EXE$INIPROCREG [2]
PR$_ICCS	Interval timer control/status	–	10 ms	EXE$HWCLKINT, EXE$INIPROCREG
PRxxx$_TODR [1]	Time-of-year clock	10 ms	10 ms	CPU hardware, EXE$INIT_TODR, EXE$SETIME [3]
EXE$GQ_SYSTIME	System date and time	100 ns	10 ms	EXE$HWCLKINT, EXE$SETIME, EXE$RESTART
EXE$GL_ABSTIM	System uptime	1 s	1 s	System initialization, EXE$TIMEOUT
EXE$GL_ABSTIM_TICS	System uptime	10 ms	10 ms	EXE$HWCLKINT
EXE$GL_TODR	Time-of-year base value	10 ms	–	EXE$SETIME
EXE$GQ_TODCBASE	Time-of-year base value (in system time form)	100 ns	–	EXE$SETIME

[1] This is a CPU-specific register that does not exist on all processors.

[2] PRxxx$_NICR is written only at system initialization and after powerfail recovery.

[3] PRxxx$_TODR is actually modified through the CPU-specific routine EXE$WRITE_TODR.

Other VAX processors have two additional processor registers to control the interval timer, PRxxx$_ICR and PRxxx$_NICR. The additional processor registers are defined by the CPU-specific macros $PRxxxDEF, where xxx is the CPU designation. Appendix G lists the CPU designations and their corresponding CPU types.

A description of the full interval timer implementation follows. It applies to all the VAX processors listed in Table 11.2 except the MicroVAX II.

The full implementation of the interval timer is the set of three processor registers. The clock ticks at 1-microsecond intervals with an accuracy of at least 0.01 percent, an error of less than 9 seconds per day. The frequency at which the interval timer causes an interrupt is determined by the value in the processor register PRxxx$_NICR.

The three interval timer registers (see Table 11.1) are used as follows:

• The interval timer control/status register (PR$_ICCS) controls the interrupt status of the interval timer. This register contains several bits, notably the IE and INT bits. During system initialization, VMS sets the IE bit to cause interval timer interrupts. The INT bit is set by the hardware when it generates an interrupt, and the interval timer interrupt service routine clears it to acknowledge that the interrupt was serviced (see Section 11.7).

Table 11.2   Implementations of the Time-of-Year Clock on VAX CPUs

Processor	PRxxx$_TODR	Console Clock	Watch Chip	Battery Backup
MicroVAX II	–	–	Y	Y
VAX 3000 series	Y	–	Y	Y
VAX-11/730	Y	–	–	Y[1]
VAX-11/750	Y	–	–	Y
VAX-11/78x	Y	–	–	Y
VAX 82x0/83x0	Y	–	Y	Y[2]
VAX 85x0/8700/88x0	–	Y[3]	–	Y
VAX 6000 series	Y	–	–	Y

[1] Certain VAX-11/730 configurations have battery backup for the time-of-year processor register.

[2] The watch chip has battery backup; the time-of-year processor register does not.

[3] VMS must communicate with the console subsystem to read the time-of-year clock.

- The next interval count register (PRxxx$_NICR) defines how often the interval timer will cause a hardware interrupt. At system initialization, this processor register is initialized with a value of -10000. This value specifies an interval timer interrupt period of 10 milliseconds (10,000 microseconds). PRxxx$_ICR is initialized from PRxxx$_NICR.
- Every microsecond the hardware increments the interval count register (PRxxx$_ICR). Thus, it counts from the PRxxx$_NICR value toward zero. When PRxxx$_ICR becomes zero, the register overflows, with the following results:

  a. The hardware copies the contents of PRxxx$_NICR into PRxxx$_ICR to define the next interval.

  b. The hardware sets the INT bit in PR$_ICCS to indicate the overflow condition. The setting of this bit causes an interval timer interrupt.

  The interrupt priority level (IPL) at which the hardware interrupt occurs is either 22 or 24, depending on the processor type. Earlier VAX CPU models, namely, the VAX-11/730, VAX-11/750, VAX-11/780 and the VAX 86x0 processors, use IPL 24. The VAX architecture now defines 22 as the IPL associated with the interval timer, and that value is used by all other processors.

Because the interval timer implementation varies, the interval timer register or registers are initialized by the routine EXE$INIPROCREG, in module [SYSLOA]ERRSUBxxx, image SYSLOAxxx.EXE, the CPU-specific code loaded during system initialization.

11.2.2   **Time-of-Year Clock**

A time-of-year clock is a hardware clock updated by hardware timing circuitry to maintain the date and time across system reboots and power failures. On most VAX CPUs, the time-of-year clock is powered by a battery when there is no power to the system so that the clock keeps correct time. At system initialization, the operating system uses the time-of-year clock and the system global locations EXE$GQ_TODCBASE and EXE$GL_TODR to determine the date and time (see Section 11.3.1). If there is no time-of-year clock or if its battery lacks power, VMS cannot determine the correct date and time without human intervention.

On many VAX CPUs, the time-of-year clock is implemented as a processor register, PRxxx_TODR. The register is an unsigned 32-bit counter, the least significant bit of which represents a resolution of 10 milliseconds.

The time kept by the time-of-year clock includes no year. Instead, the time is kept relative to 00:00:00.00 hours on January 1 of the year in which the clock was initialized. The value 10000000_{16} represents this base time. The time-of-year clock is initialized to that number rather than zero to facilitate detection of loss of power to the clock, which causes a reset to zero.

This scheme allows the time-of-year clock to represent, in 10-millisecond intervals, up to about 466 days: from January 1 of the base year to about April 11 of the next year. Once the time-of-year clock is initialized relative to a base year and the system time crosses from December into January of the ensuing year, the time-of-year clock must be reset, before April 11 of that year, to be relative to January 1 of the new year.

EXE$SETIME, the system service routine for the $SETIME system service, automatically resets a time-of-year clock that represents a value greater than the number of 10-millisecond intervals in the base year. This system service is invoked whenever the DCL command SET TIME is issued. This system service is also invoked through a special entry point during system initialization, as discussed in Section 11.4.

The implementation of the time-of-year clock varies on different VAX CPUs. Table 11.2 summarizes implementations of the time-of-year clock on the various VAX CPUs.

Access to the time-of-year clock is through CPU-specific routines in the image SYSLOAxxx. Thus, the actual implementation of the time-of-year clock is transparent to the rest of VMS.

The SYSLOAxxx routines for accessing the time-of-year clock are

- EXE$INIT_TODR, in module [SYSLOA]INIADPxxx, which uses the clock to initialize the system time
- EXE$READ_TODR, EXE$READ_LOCAL_TODR, and EXE$READP_LOCAL_TODR, in module [SYSLOA]ERRSUBxxx, which read the clock
- EXE$WRITE_TODR and EXE$WRITEP_LOCAL_TODR, in module [SYSLOA]ERRSUBxxx, which write the clock

EXE$READ_TODR and EXE$WRITE_TODR are generally the routines used to access the time-of-year clock. These routines may be invoked from any processor in an SMP system. However, when invoked from a secondary processor on an SMP system, these routines require the services of the primary to access the clock. Chapter 34 describes the interprocessor dialogue employed for this purpose.

EXE$READP_LOCAL_TODR and EXE$WRITEP_LOCAL_TODR are primary-only routines that access the physical clock register.

EXE$READ_LOCAL_TODR is a routine employed by EXE$POWERFAIL, in module POWERFAIL, to read the clock in the fastest way possible. EXE$POWERFAIL invokes this routine only from the primary processor. Thus, EXE$READ_LOCAL_TODR does not require any multiprocessing synchronization.

On systems with no time-of-year processor register, EXE$READ_LOCAL_TODR and EXE$READ_TODR simulate one, using EXE$GL_TODR and the elapsed time since the time was last set, which is the difference between EXE$GQ_SYSTIME and EXE$GQ_TODCBASE.

11.3 TIMEKEEPING IN VMS

During system initialization, VMS determines the date and time from the time-of-year clock and the system global locations EXE$GQ_TODCBASE and EXE$GL_TODR. During normal system operation, VMS uses the interval timer interrupts to keep time. Global location EXE$GQ_SYSTIME contains the system date and time. Global locations EXE$GL_ABSTIM and EXE$GL_ABSTIM_TICS contain the system uptime, the former in units of seconds and the latter in 10-millisecond intervals. Table 11.1 summarizes these global locations.

11.3.1 Initializing the Date and Time

The contents of EXE$GQ_TODCBASE and EXE$GL_TODR are maintained both in memory and on disk in the base image file, SYS.EXE. The record on disk is nonvolatile and survives across system bootstraps. Both represent the same time in different formats. EXE$GQ_TODCBASE represents the time of last adjustment in standard 64-bit time, the same format as EXE$GQ_SYSTIME. EXE$GL_TODR represents the time of last adjustment in the same 32-bit format as the time-of-year clock. Whenever these cells are adjusted on the system, they are written back to disk as well.

Recording up-to-date values of these variables ensures that

- VMS can determine the current year from EXE$GQ_TODCBASE. A 32-bit time-of-year clock can represent only date and time within year, but not year.
- VMS can use the recorded value of EXE$GL_TODR as a validity test for the time-of-year clock.

- The date and time are as recent as possible for a system that is without battery backup for the time-of-year clock and is to boot unattended.

During system initialization, SYSINIT invokes the routine EXE$INIT_TODR, in module [SYSLOA]INIADPxxx, to validate the time of year and to initialize EXE$GQ_SYSTIME from either the time-of-year clock and system global locations or from a date and time entered by the operator. For a node joining a VAXcluster system, SYSINIT obtains the date and time from a node that has already joined and invokes EXE$SETIME_INT, described in Section 11.4, to set the date and time. When a new VAXcluster system is being formed, the time from one system is sent to all other nodes, each of which invokes EXE$SETIME_INT. After the system disk is mounted, SYSINIT invokes the $SETIME service to record new values for the time-of-year global locations in the base image on disk.

The basic algorithm in EXE$INIT_TODR is similar for all VAX CPUs, although there are some CPU-specific variants:

1. EXE$INIT_TODR examines the SYSGEN parameter SETTIME.
2. If SETTIME is 0, EXE$INIT_TODR reads the time-of-year clock and compares its contents with those of EXE$GL_TODR. If EXE$GL_TODR is more than one day ahead of the time-of-year clock, the time of year is presumed invalid. This test detects a clock that has lost power. It also detects cases where the clock has overflowed or is otherwise desynchronized with the SYS.EXE base image being bootstrapped.

   If the time-of-year clock is within a day of EXE$GL_TODR, then its contents and those of EXE$GL_TODR and EXE$GQ_TODCBASE are used to reset the system time.
3. If SETTIME is 1, or if the time-of-year clock is invalid, EXE$INIT_TODR examines the SYSGEN parameter TIMEPROMPTWAIT to determine how to reset the time of year:

   a. A TIMEPROMPTWAIT value of zero means that the routine is to reset the time without human intervention. EXE$INIT_TODR computes a new value for the time of year, based on the contents of EXE$GL_TODR plus 10 milliseconds.

   b. A nonzero TIMEPROMPTWAIT value causes the routine to prompt for the date and time on the console terminal and wait until the operator enters valid data. If TIMEPROMPTWAIT is negative, the system will not proceed unless the operator enters the date and time. If TIMEPROMPTWAIT is positive, its value represents an upper limit on the amount of time EXE$INIT_TODR waits for the operator to enter a new date and time. If that time elapses without the input of valid data, EXE$INIT_TODR proceeds as if TIMEPROMPTWAIT were zero.

4. EXE$INIT_TODR calls EXE$SETIME_INT, an internal entry point for

the system service $SETIME, to initialize the system time and update EXE$GQ_TODCBASE and EXE$GL_TODR. The base image on disk cannot be modified until the system disk is mounted.

11.3.2 Maintaining the Date and Time

The system time, EXE$GQ_SYSTIME, is the number of 100-nanosecond intervals since 00:00 hours, November 17, 1858, the base time for the Smithsonian Institution astronomical calendar. EXE$GQ_SYSTIME is updated every 10 milliseconds by the interval timer interrupt service routine (see Section 11.7). EXE$GQ_SYSTIME is the reference for nearly all user-requested time-dependent software activities in the system. For example, the $GETTIM system service simply writes this quadword value into a user-defined buffer.

EXE$GL_ABSTIM, incremented by the routine EXE$TIMEOUT (see Section 11.8.2), contains the number of 1-second intervals that have elapsed since the system was bootstrapped. EXE$GL_ABSTIM is the reference time for a number of VMS operations. In particular, it is used to check periodically for I/O device, I/O controller, mount verification, and lock request timeouts.

EXE$GL_ABSTIM_TICS contains the number of interval timer ticks that have elapsed since the system was bootstrapped. It is defined as zero at assembly time and incremented by the interval timer interrupt service routine (see Section 11.7). EXE$GL_ABSTIM_TICS is the reference time for the VMS scheduling subsystem. Its contents are recorded in the field PCB$L_WAITIME whenever a process is placed into a wait state and in the field PCB$L_ONQTIME when a process incurs quantum end. A comparison between PCB$L_WAITIME and EXE$GL_ABSTIM_TICS enables outswap scheduling code to determine if the process can be considered to be in a long wait, and a comparison between PCB$L_ONQTIME and EXE$GL_ABSTIM_TICS to determine if the process is dormant (see Chapter 18).

EXE$GQ_SYSTIME is adjusted at powerfail recovery by routine EXE$RESTART, in module POWERFAIL (see Chapter 33), and through the system service $SETIME. EXE$GL_ABSTIM and EXE$GL_ABSTIM_TICS are never adjusted.

11.4 SET TIME SYSTEM SERVICE

The $SETIME system service allows a system manager or operator to change the system time while the operating system is running. This may be necessary because of a power failure longer than the battery backup time of the time-of-year clock or changes between standard and daylight saving time, for example. The new system time is passed as the optional single argument of the system service.

The $SETIME system service is also called directly at a special entry point, EXE$SETIME_INT. This entry point is used during system initialization to compute the system time from the contents of the time-of-year clock and system variables. The difference between the two entry points is that EXE$SETIME_INT is called at a point in SYSINIT before the system disk is mounted, and hence must disable recording the values of EXE$GL_TODR and EXE$GQ_TODCBASE in the base image.

The system service procedure EXE$SETIME, in module SYSSETIME, runs in kernel mode. It first validates the request. If the requesting process does not have the privileges OPER and LOG_IO, EXE$SETIME returns the error SS$_NOPRIV. If the input quadword cannot be read, the procedure returns the error SS$_ACCVIO.

The procedure diverges into the two paths described in the following sections, based on the presence or absence of the new time argument.

11.4.1   **$SETIME System Time Recalibration Requests**

If no time argument, or an argument of zero, is passed to the system service, this is considered a request to recalibrate EXE$GQ_SYSTIME from the time-of-year clock, EXE$GL_TODR, and EXE$GQ_TODCBASE. Sometimes recalibration is done during normal operation, because on some VAX systems the time-of-year clock is more accurate than the interval clock.

EXE$SETIME performs the following actions:

1. It calls the scheduler routine SCH$REQUIRE_CAPABILITY, in module SCHED, to ensure that EXE$SETIME is running on the primary processor in a multiprocessing system.

2. EXE$SETIME invokes routine EXE$READP_LOCAL_TODR, in module [SYSLOA]ERRSUBxxx, to read the time-of-year clock, whose contents are referenced in the following items and equations as TOY_CLOCK.

3. It compares the TOY_CLOCK to EXE$GL_TODR. If the latter represents a time more than one day later, the TOY_CLOCK is not valid and EXE$SETIME returns the error status SS$_IVTIME.

4. It computes the new system time, EXE$GQ_SYSTIME, using the following equation:

$$\text{EXE\$GQ\_SYSTIME} = \text{EXE\$GQ\_TODCBASE} \\ + ((\text{TOY\_CLOCK} - \text{EXE\$GL\_TODR}) * 100000)$$

EXE$GQ_SYSTIME and EXE$GQ_TODCBASE contain quadword system times in units of 100 nanoseconds. TOY_CLOCK and EXE$GL_TODR contain longword time-of-year times in units of 10 milliseconds. The multiplier of 100,000 represents the number of 100-nanosecond intervals in 10 milliseconds.

5. It corrects the values in TOY_CLOCK, EXE$GL_TODR, and EXE$GQ_TODCBASE if TOY_CLOCK represents a value larger than one year. This prevents the time-of-year clock from overflowing its limit.

6. EXE$SETIME adjusts the expiration time of each entry in the timer queue that specifies a relative (or delta) time by the difference between the previous system time and the new system time. This modification preserves the correct relative time across the modification to the system time. EXE$SETIME does not adjust an entry containing an absolute time; this ensures that the event will occur at the time specified by the user. Section 11.5 describes the form and use of timer queue entries.

7. EXE$SETIME writes the pages of the base image in memory that contain EXE$GQ_TODCBASE and EXE$GL_TODR back to the base image file if the procedure was entered at EXE$SETIME.

11.4.2 $SETIME Time-of-Year Readjustment Requests

If a nonzero time value is given as an argument to $SETIME, EXE$SETIME performs the following operations:

1. It converts the input argument, specified in system time units of 100 nanoseconds, into time-of-year units, the number of 10-millisecond intervals after 00:00 hours on January 1 of the base year.

2. EXE$SETIME calls the scheduler routine SCH$REQUIRE_CAPABILITY, in module SCHED, to ensure that it is running on the primary processor in a multiprocessing system.

3. It writes the specified time, converted to 32-bit time-of-year format, into the time-of-year clock and EXE$GL_TODR.

4. It writes the specified time into EXE$GQ_TODCBASE and EXE$GQ_SYSTIME.

5. Finally, it updates the timer queue and, if the procedure was entered at EXE$SETIME, writes the new values for the time-of-year clock base to the base image file. Steps 6 and 7 in Section 11.4.1 give details.

11.5 TIMER QUEUE AND TIMER QUEUE ENTRIES

VMS describes each timer request with a data structure called a timer queue entry (TQE). It maintains an absolute queue of TQEs, ordered by their expiration times, at the system global location EXE$GL_TQFL. The TIMER spinlock synchronizes access to the timer queue.

Timer requests in VMS may be characterized according to the following attributes:

- What action VMS takes to satisfy the request, for example, setting an event flag or waking up a process
- Whether the request is a recurring one, to be repeated at specified intervals
- How the expiration time is determined

A user can specify that a request come due at a particular absolute time or at a time relative to the time of the request. With VMS Version 5, the user has the choice of specifying a due time in terms of a process's accumulated CPU time.

TQEs are generally allocated from nonpaged dynamic memory and inserted into the timer queue as a result of $SETIMR and $SCHDWK system service requests (see Section 11.6). The allocation of TQEs is governed by the pooled job quota JIB$W_TQCNT.

The format of a TQE is shown in Figure 11.1. The link fields TQE$L_TQFL and TQE$L_TQBL, the TQE$W_SIZE field, and the TQE$B_TYPE field are characteristic of system data structures allocated from dynamic memory.

The TQE$B_RQTYPE field describes the timer request. Its two low-order bits define the type of timer request: process timer request, periodic system routine request, or process wake request. Bit TQE$V_REPEAT is set if the request is a repeating request rather than a one-time request. Bit TQE$V_ABSOLUTE is set if the timer event was requested at a particular absolute time rather than at a relative interval from the current time. Bit TQE$V_CHK_CPUTIM is set if the timer event was requested based on the CPU time accumulated by the target process. Figure 11.1 summarizes the bits in TQE$B_RQTYPE.

The interpretation of the next three longword fields depends upon the type of timer request. For system routine requests, these fields contain the PC, R3, and R4 register values to be loaded before control is passed to the routine. For process requests, these fields define the process ID of the process to which to report the event, the address of an asynchronous system trap (AST) procedure to execute (if requested), and an optional AST parameter.

For both process and system routine requests, the field TQE$Q_TIME is the quadword system time at which a particular timer event is to occur. TQE$Q_DELTA is the absolute value of the repeat interval time for repeating requests.

Several fields are meaningful only for process requests. The access mode of the requesting process is stored in TQE$B_RMOD. Bit ACB$V_QUOTA

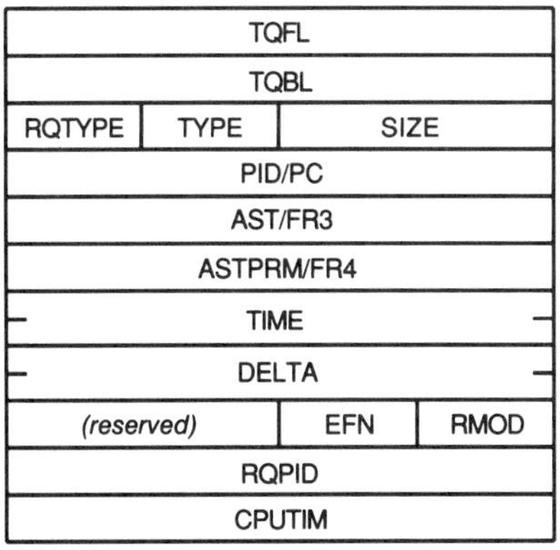

| TQFL |
| TQBL |
| RQTYPE | TYPE | SIZE |
| PID/PC |
| AST/FR3 |
| ASTPRM/FR4 |
| TIME |
| DELTA |
| (reserved) | EFN | RMOD |
| RQPID |
| CPUTIM |

RQTYPE Bits

Bit	Value	Meaning
0–1	0	Process timer request
	1	System subroutine request
	2	Scheduled wake request
2	0	One–time request
	1	Repeat request (not allowed for process timer requests)
3	0	Relative time request
	1	Absolute time request
4	1	Timer is based on CPU time accumulated
5		(reserved)
6	1	AST is associated with timer event
7		(reserved)

Figure 11.1
Layout of a Timer Queue Entry

of TQE$B_RMOD is set if an AST is to be delivered when the timer event occurs. The event flag to be set when the timer event occurs is stored in TQE$B_EFN. TQE$L_RQPID contains the process ID of the process that made the initial timer request, since the requesting process is not necessarily the same as the target process whose ID is stored in TQE$L_PID.

For a request based on accumulated CPU time, TQE$L_CPUTIM contains the amount of CPU time, in CPU time units, that the process should accumulate for the timer event to occur.

11.6 TIMER SYSTEM SERVICES

Two system services are used to request time-dependent services, $SCHDWK and $SETIMR, both in module SYSSCHEVT. Two complementary services, Cancel Wakeup ($CANWAK) and Cancel Timer Request ($CANTIM), both in module SYSCANEVT, cancel time-dependent requests.

11.6.1 $SETIMR System Service

The $SETIMR system service creates TQEs for nonrecurring process timer requests. Its system service procedure, EXE$SETIMR, runs in kernel mode, performing the following steps:

1. The event flag specified as an argument to the system service is cleared in preparation for a subsequent setting at expiration time.
2. If a fifth nonzero argument is present, this timer request is based on the CPU time accumulated by this process; EXE$SETIMR sets the TQE$V_CHK_CPUTIM bit in the TQE that it builds for this request.
3. EXE$SETIMR checks the request to ascertain that

   —The time location is accessible to the requesting process
   —The requesting process does not exceed its PCB$W_ASTCNT if an AST is to be associated with this timer request

4. EXE$SETIMR decrements JIB$W_TQCNT to charge the allocation of the TQE. If the job runs out of the pooled resource JIB$W_TQCNT, then EXE$SETIMR puts the process into a miscellaneous wait state with its PCB$L_EFWM field containing the address of the JIB, and bit JIB$V_TQCNT_WAITERS set in JIB$B_FLAGS. When JIB$W_TQCNT is restored, this process will resume at the next step.
5. EXE$SETIMR allocates a TQE from nonpaged pool and initializes it from the system service arguments of time, request type, and process ID.
6. If the time argument is negative, indicating that it is a relative time, then EXE$SETIMR calculates the absolute expiration time of the request by adding the absolute value of this argument to the current system time, EXE$GQ_SYSTIME. Bit TQE$V_ABSOLUTE is cleared for this element if this was a relative time request; otherwise, the bit is set.

7. EXE$SETIMR stores the access mode from which the system service was requested in the TQE$B_RMOD field. If AST notification was requested, then EXE$SETIMR decrements the process PCB$W_ASTCNT to indicate the future AST delivery and sets bit ACB$V_QUOTA of TQE$B_RMOD to indicate the AST accounting.

8. EXE$SETIMR copies the AST parameter, which is used as request identification, and event flag number, both arguments for the $SETIMR request, to the TQE.

9. If bit TQE$V_CHK_CPUTIM is set in the TQE, the time argument represents the amount of CPU time the process must accumulate for the timer event to occur. EXE$SETIMR estimates the earliest absolute time at which this could happen and stores it in the TQE$Q_TIME field.

   It also calculates the total number of CPU time increments the process must accumulate for this and stores it in TQE$L_CPUTIM. When the TQE expires, EXE$SWTIMINT, in module TIMESCHDL, compares this value with either PHD$L_CPUTIM or PCB$L_CPUTIM, depending on whether the process is resident, to determine if the timer event is indeed due (see Section 11.8.1). If it is not, EXE$SWTIMINT reestimates the expiration time of the TQE and requeues it.

10. EXE$SETIMR invokes EXE$INSTIMQ, in module EXSUBROUT, to insert the TQE into the right place in the timer queue and then returns.

11.6.2 $CANTIM System Service

The $CANTIM system service removes one or more TQEs before expiration. Two arguments, the request identification parameter and the access mode, control the actions taken by this service. EXE$CANTIM, the system service procedure, invokes EXE$RMVTIMQ, in module EXSUBROUT, to remove and deallocate each TQE on the timer queue that meets all of the following criteria:

- The current process's ID is the same as TQE$L_PID.
- The access mode from which the service was requested is at least as privileged as the access mode stored in the TQE. This ensures that no request can be deleted for an access mode more privileged than that of the requestor.
- The request identification parameter argument is the same as that stored in the TQE. If the argument value is zero, then all TQEs meeting the first two criteria are removed.

11.6.3 $SCHDWK System Service

The logic for managing scheduled wakeup requests is similar to that of $SETIMR requests. Two differences are the ability to specify repeating scheduled wakeup requests and the ability to schedule wakeup requests for another process. The $SCHDWK system service procedure, EXE$SCHDWK in module SYSSCHEVT, runs in kernel mode. It performs the following actions:

1. EXE$SCHDWK invokes EXE$NAMPID, in module SYSPCNTRL, to locate the PCB of the process to be awakened.

   EXE$NAMPID determines whether the input arguments specify a target process on this VAXcluster node or on another node. In the former case, EXE$NAMPID confirms the existence of the target process and the ability of the current process to delete it. (Chapter 13 describes the possible relations between the two processes and the privileges required in each case.) If the process is identified as one on another VAXcluster node, EXE$NAMPID cannot make those checks; it can only confirm that the VAXcluster node identification is valid.

   If further action is possible, EXE$NAMPID returns at IPL$_SCHED with the SCHED spinlock held; otherwise it returns at IPL 0. In either case, it returns an appropriate status.

2. If EXE$NAMPID returns the status SS$_REMOTE_PROC, indicating that the process may exist on another VAXcluster node, EXE$SCHDWK validates the time arguments and transfers control to a clusterwide process service (CWPS) routine in module SYSPCNTRL. The routine transmits the wake request to the appropriate VAXcluster node and places the requesting process into a wait state. A cooperating CWPS routine on the other node performs the request and transmits status back to this node. Through mechanisms described in Chapter 13, control returns to a CWPS routine running in the context of the $SCHDWK requestor. This routine exits from the $SCHDWK system service, returning the status transmitted from the other node.

3. If EXE$NAMPID returns any other error status, EXE$SCHDWK simply exits, returning the error status to its requestor.

4. If EXE$NAMPID returns a status indicating that the target process exists on this node and that the requesting process may affect it, EXE$SCHDWK continues.

5. It tests the repeat time argument to determine whether the request is a one-time or repeating scheduled wakeup.

6. If it is a repeating request, EXE$SCHDWK converts the requested repeat time into system time format. If the repeat time is less than 10 milliseconds, it is increased to that value (the resolution of the interval timer interrupt).

7. It allocates a TQE from nonpaged pool and initializes its repeat time, request time, and target process ID fields.

8. If the initial scheduled wakeup time was expressed as a relative time, then EXE$SCHDWK clears bit TQE$V_ABSOLUTE and calculates the expiration time as the sum of the absolute value of the initial delta time

and the current system time. If the initial scheduled wakeup time was expressed as an absolute time, it sets bit TQE$V_ABSOLUTE.

9. It decrements the PCB$W_ASTCNT quota of the requesting process to account for the allocation of the TQE.
10. It invokes EXE$INSTIMQ, in module EXSUBROUT, to insert the TQE into the ordered timer queue according to its expiration time.

When the expiration time is reached, the target process is awakened (see Section 11.8.3). Deallocation of the TQE occurs after delivery of a one-time scheduled wakeup request or as a result of a $CANWAK system service call.

11.6.4 $CANWAK System Service

The $CANWAK system service cancels all one-time and repeat scheduled wakeup requests for a target process. EXE$CANWAK, the system service procedure, first tests that the requesting process has the ability to affect the target process. It then deallocates each canceled TQE to nonpaged pool and, if the initial requesting process still exists, returns its PCB$W_ASTCNT quota to indicate the deallocation.

11.7 INTERVAL TIMER INTERRUPT SERVICE ROUTINE

The interval timer interrupt service routine, EXE$HWCLKINT in module TIMESCHDL, services the hardware interrupt signaled by the interval timer every 10 milliseconds.

On some CPUs, this is an IPL 24 interrupt; on others, it is an IPL 22 interrupt (see Section 11.2.1). The interval timer interrupt service routine has the following major functions:

- Updating the system time
- Process and CPU accounting
- Implementing the sanity timer in a multiprocessing configuration
- Checking whether the most imminent TQE is due

In a multiprocessing configuration, the interval timer interrupt is taken by all processors, and all of them execute EXE$HWCLKINT. However, only the primary CPU is responsible for updating the system time and checking the timer queue.

EXE$HWCLKINT performs the following actions:

1. EXE$HWCLKINT resets the PR$_ICCS register to indicate the servicing of the interrupt and the reenabling of the interval timer.
2. In an SMP system, EXE$HWCLKINT performs the operations necessary to implement this processor's part of the sanity timer mechanism, as described in Chapter 34.
3. Running on a uniprocessor or on the primary processor of an SMP system, EXE$HWCLKINT does the following:

Table 11.3 Per-CPU Statistics Counters

Index	*Meaning*
0	Kernel mode on kernel stack, no spinlock busy wait is active
1	Executive mode
2	Supervisor mode
3	User mode
4	Kernel mode on interrupt stack
5	Compatibility mode
6	Kernel mode on kernel or interrupt stack, spinlock busy wait is active

---

 a. It acquires the HWCLK spinlock in a multiprocessing environment.

 b. It updates the system time quadword, EXE$GQ_SYSTIME, by adding to it the value in EXE$GL_TICKLENGTH.

  EXE$GL_TICKLENGTH is used to maintain the system time relative to an external time standard. Normally, EXE$GL_TICKLENGTH is initialized to the value in EXE$GL_SYSTICK, the VMS representation of 10 milliseconds. However, in some circumstances, privileged VMS applications may adjust EXE$GL_TICKLENGTH, thus speeding up or slowing down the VMS clock until it is synchronized with the reference time. Varying the tick length guarantees a monotonically increasing system time and avoids the pitfalls of other means of changing the system time.

  Use of the cells EXE$GL_SYSTICK and EXE$GL_TICKLENGTH is reserved to Digital and not supported except for use within Digital software.

 c. It increments EXE$GL_ABSTIM_TICS.

 d. It compares the updated system time with the quadword EXE$GQ_1ST_TIME, which is the time of expiration of the most imminent timer queue entry. If this entry is due, then EXE$HWCLKINT requests an IPL$_TIMERFORK software interrupt.

 e. It releases the HWCLK spinlock in a multiprocessing environment.

4. EXE$HWCLKINT then updates time statistics fields maintained as an array in the per-CPU database at CPU$L_KERNEL. (Chapter 34 describes the per-CPU database.) The meaning of each counter within this array of seven longwords is explained in Table 11.3.

5. EXE$HWCLKINT determines whether this interval timer tick should be charged to a process:

 —If CPU$B_BUSYWAIT is nonzero, indicating that the processor was in a spinwait trying to acquire a spinlock, the tick is not charged.

—If the processor was running on the interrupt stack at the time of the interrupt, the tick is not charged.

If neither of those is true, EXE$HWCLKINT increments the process's accumulated CPU time, PHD$L_CPUTIM, and its quantum, PHD$W_QUANT. If the quantum, initialized to a negative value, reaches zero, EXE$HWCLKINT requests an IPL$_TIMERFORK software interrupt to initiate quantum-end processing for this process.

11.8   SOFTWARE TIMER INTERRUPT SERVICE ROUTINE

The software timer interrupt service routine, EXE$SWTIMINT in module TIMESCHDL, is entered through the IPL$_TIMERFORK (IPL 7) software interrupt. Note that IPL$_TIMERFORK is the IPL at which this software interrupt is taken, but the interrupt service routine performs its functions at IPL$_TIMER (IPL 8). The software timer interrupt is requested by the interval timer interrupt service routine either because the current process has reached quantum end or the first TQE must be serviced.

EXE$SWTIMINT examines CPU$L_CURPCB in the processor's per-CPU database to get the current process's PCB and locates the process's header. EXE$SWTIMINT then tests PHD$W_QUANT to determine whether the current process on this processor has reached quantum end. This field is initialized to the negative value of the SYSGEN parameter QUANTUM and incremented by the interval timer interrupt service routine. A zero or positive quantum value indicates quantum expiration. If the process has reached quantum end, EXE$SWTIMINT obtains the SCHED spinlock and invokes routine SCH$QEND, in module RSE, to perform quantum-end processing (see Chapter 12).

Running on a uniprocessor or on the primary CPU in a multiprocessing system, EXE$SWTIMINT checks whether the system time, EXE$GQ_SYSTIME, is greater than or equal to the expiration time of the first entry in the timer queue. If it is, then the timer event is due. On an SMP system, this multiple-instruction comparison with the system time must be performed while holding the TIMER and HWCLK spinlocks to synchronize with the interval timer interrupt service routine. On a uniprocessor, IPL is raised to the level of the interval timer interrupt.

If the timer request is due, then EXE$SWTIMINT removes the first TQE from the timer queue, releases the HWCLK and TIMER spinlocks, lowering IPL to IPL$_TIMER, and performs one of three sequences of code depending upon the type of timer request. The following sections describe these sequences.

11.8.1   Process Timer Requests

If the TQE is a process timer request, created by a $SETIMR system service call, then EXE$SWTIMINT performs the following operations:

1. If bit TQE$V_CHK_CPUTIM is set to indicate that the timer request is in terms of CPU time accumulated by the process, then EXE$SWTIMINT takes the following steps:

   a. If the requesting process is not in the system any more, it simply deallocates the TQE.

   b. Otherwise, it obtains the CPU time from PHD$L_CPUTIM if the requesting process is resident and from PCB$L_CPUTIM if it is not. (The swapper copies PHD$L_CPUTIM to PCB$L_CPUTIM when it outswaps a process.) EXE$SWTIMINT compares the process's CPU time to TQE$L_CPUTIM to see if the timer request has expired.

   If the timer has expired, EXE$SWTIMINT proceeds as if this were a normal TQE expiration. Otherwise, it converts the number of remaining CPU time increments to system time format. It adds that value to the expiration time, making a new estimate of when the process might have accumulated enough CPU time. EXE$SWTIMINT then reinserts the TQE in the queue.

2. Holding the SCHED spinlock, it sets the event flag associated with this timer request by invoking SCH$POSTEF with the contents of the TQE$L_PID and TQE$B_EFN fields. A software priority boost of 3 may be applied to the process (see Chapter 12).

3. If the target process is no longer in the system or the event flag number is illegal, EXE$SWTIMINT simply deallocates the TQE.

4. It increments the process's JIB$W_TQCNT quota, using an interlocked instruction, to indicate the pending deallocation of the TQE.

   EXE$SWTIMINT tests JIB$B_FLAGS to determine if any processes in the same job are waiting for TQE quota. For each such process, it invokes SCH$CHSE, in module RSE, to make the process computable.

5. If ACB$V_QUOTA in TQE$B_RMOD is set, the user requested AST notification. EXE$SWTIMINT copies the TQE$B_RMOD field to TQE$B_RQTYPE to reformat the TQE into an AST control block (ACB). EXE$SWTIMINT invokes SCH$QAST to queue the ACB to the process (see Chapter 7).

When the processing of this TQE has been completed, EXE$SWTIMINT checks whether the next TQE is due.

Note that process timer requests are strictly one-time requests. Any repetition of timer requests must be implemented by the requesting process. A process can request $SETIMR events only on its own behalf.

11.8.2 Periodic System Routine Requests

The second type of TQE, a system routine request, is a system-initiated time-dependent request to execute a specified system routine. EXE$SWTIMINT handles this type of TQE by performing the following actions:

1. It loads R3 and R4 from the TQE$L_FR3 and TQE$L_FR4 fields. R5 points to the beginning of the TQE.
2. It executes a JSB instruction using the TQE$L_FPC field, which points to the system routine to be invoked.

EXE$SWTIMINT assumes that on return from the system routine, R5 points to a TQE. It tests the TQE$V_REPEAT bit for this TQE. If the bit is set, it reinserts the TQE into the timer queue, having computed a new expiration time from TQE$Q_DELTA. EXE$SWTIMINT then checks the timer queue for further TQEs to service.

Note that even if the TQE is not reinserted in the queue, EXE$SWTIMINT does not deallocate the TQE. This type of TQE can be defined in a static nonpaged portion of system space or within a device driver data structure.

One example of this type of request, a repeating system subroutine request, is the once-per-second execution of the routine EXE$TIMEOUT, in module TIMESCHDL. The TQE for EXE$TIMEOUT is permanently defined in the same module, and the timer queue is initialized at bootstrap time with this TQE as the first entry in the queue. EXE$TIMEOUT performs the following:

1. Holding the SCHED spinlock, it invokes the routine SCH$SWPWAKE to awaken the swapper process, if appropriate (see Chapter 18).
2. EXE$TIMEOUT increments the EXE$GL_ABSTIM field to indicate the passing of 1 second of system uptime.
3. It invokes the routine ERL$WAKE, in module ERRORLOG, to awaken the ERRFMT process, if appropriate (see Chapter 32).
4. EXE$TIMEOUT invokes ECC$REENABLE, a routine in SYSLOAxxx. ECC$REENABLE scans the memory controllers to log any unreported corrected read data (CRD) errors and possibly to reenable CRD interrupts.
5. EXE$TIMEOUT scans the I/O database for devices that have exceeded their timeout intervals. Holding the appropriate fork lock and device lock, it invokes the driver for each such device at its timeout entry point.

   This scan also invokes the driver's timeout routine for terminal timed reads that have expired.
6. EXE$TIMEOUT scans the list of channel (controller) request blocks (CRBs) on the list IOC$GL_CRBTMOUT for any that have timed out. The CRB timeout mechanism enables a driver to be entered periodically for controller-related functions. The driver stores the address of a timeout routine in the field CRB$L_TOUTROUT and an expiration time in CRB$L_DUETIME and invokes IOC$THREADCRB, in module IOSUBNPAG, to thread its CRB on the list. EXE$TIMEOUT compares the expiration time with EXE$GL_ABSTIM and, if the CRB due time has arrived, invokes the timeout routine holding the appropriate fork lock.

   The system communication services (SCS) class and port drivers employ this mechanism. The disk class driver, for example, must send its server periodic messages to inform the server that the host system is running. The disk class driver timeout routine also checks that the server has made progress on the oldest outstanding request.

7. If a process is running the Monitor Utility to display disk and disk queue length information, EXE$TIMEOUT scans the I/O database to collect information about disk queue lengths.

8. Next, EXE$TIMEOUT scans the fork and wait queue. Chapter 4 describes this queue and its use by fork processes.

9. The first entry on the lock manager timeout queue is checked to see if it has expired. If it has, a deadlock search is initiated by invoking LCK$SEARCHDLCK, in module DEADLOCK (see Chapter 10).

10. EXE$TIMEOUT invokes SCH$ONE_SEC, in module RSE. Its primary task is to invoke SCH$PIX_SCAN, also in module RSE. SCH$PIX_SCAN gives selected computable resident (COM) and computable outswapped (COMO) processes a priority boost, as described in Chapter 12.

11. Invoking SCH$RAVAIL, EXE$TIMEOUT declares several system resources available: RSN$_NPDYNMEM, RSN$_PGDYNMEM, RSN$_MAILBOX, and RSN$_ASTWAIT. This is necessary because, in certain rare cases, these resources are not declared available when they should be.

Another example of a repeating system timer routine is one the terminal driver uses to implement its modem polling. The controller initialization routine in the terminal driver loads the expiration time field in a TQE in the terminal driver with the current system time, sets the repeat bit, and loads the repeat interval with the SYSGEN parameter TTY_SCANDELTA. When the timer routine expires, it polls each modem looking for state changes.

11.8.3 Scheduled Wakeup Requests

The third type of TQE is a request for a scheduled wakeup ($SCHDWK) of a hibernating process. This type of request may be either one-time or repeating and may be requested by a process other than the target process.

EXE$SWTIMINT performs the following operations for a scheduled wake-up TQE:

1. EXE$SWTIMINT invokes SCH$WAKE, in module RSE, to awaken the target process, which is identified by TQE$L_PID. If the target process is no longer in the system, it deallocates the TQE to nonpaged dynamic memory. Otherwise, if the requesting process (TQE$L_RQPID) still exists, EXE$SWTIMINT increments its PCB$W_ASTCNT quota.

2. If the request is a one-time request, indicated by a zero TQE$V_REPEAT bit in the TQE$B_RQTYPE field, then EXE$SWTIMINT performs the cleanup described in step 1.

3. If the request is a repeating type, then EXE$SWTIMINT adds the repeat interval, TQE$Q_DELTA, to the request's expiration time, TQE$Q_

TIME, computing its new expiration time. Based on this value, it reinserts the TQE in the appropriate position in the timer queue, by invoking EXE$INSTIMQ, in module EXSUBROUT.

EXE$SWTIMINT then checks to see whether the next TQE is due.

12   Scheduling

It is equally bad when one speeds on the guest unwilling to
go, and when he holds back one who is hastening. Rather one
should befriend the guest who is there, but speed him when
he wishes.

Homer, *The Odyssey*

Only one process can run on a processor at once. Scheduling is the mechanism that selects a process to run.

The characteristics most significant to the scheduling of a process are

- Process priority, which determines the execution precedence of processes
- Scheduling state, which defines the readiness of a process to be scheduled
  for execution, its computability or lack thereof
- Processor capability or affinity requirements (new with VMS Version 5),
  which constrain the set of processors of a symmetric multiprocessing (SMP)
  system on which a process can execute

Running on a particular processor, the scheduler identifies and selects for
execution the highest priority process that can execute on that processor and
places it into execution. A process currently executing enters a wait state
when it makes a direct or indirect request for a system operation that cannot
complete immediately. A waiting process becomes computable as the result
of system events, such as the setting of an event flag or the queuing of an
AST, and may preempt a current process.

This chapter first describes the data structures related to scheduling and
the significance of process priority, scheduling state, capabilities, and affinity. It then describes the dynamics of their interactions—how changes in
one characteristic can affect the others and the mechanisms by which the
characteristics change. Finally, it describes the rescheduling interrupt service
routine in detail.

12.1   SCHEDULING DATA STRUCTURES

Most of the system data structures relevant to scheduling are described in
this section.

The fundamental data structure is the software process control block
(PCB). It specifies the scheduling state, process priority, and capability and
affinity requirements of a process and records many other process characteristics. Section 12.1.1 describes fields in the PCB relevant to scheduling.

One PCB, the null PCB, is defined statically as a placeholder. In earlier
versions of VMS, the null PCB described a process called the null process.
This process no longer exists, but there is still a need for a placeholder PCB

so that each system pointer to a PCB can point to a valid PCB, even if there is no associated process.

Section 12.1.2 describes the process state queues, the queues in which PCBs of processes in the same scheduling states are linked.

As part of support for SMP, VMS Version 5 adds a data structure called the per-CPU database. The per-CPU database records processor-specific information. Each CPU has its own per-CPU database. Section 12.1.3 describes the fields in this structure relevant to scheduling.

Each CPU is identified by an ID, a number from 0 to 31. The system mask SCH$GL_IDLE_CPUS has a bit corresponding to each CPU. When set, the bit indicates that the CPU is idle and has no current process. The bit is cleared as a signal to indicate that the CPU should repeat its attempt to select a process to execute.

Several other systemwide data structures related to process priority are described in Section 12.2.

The set of PCBs, process state queues, and related data structures is known as the scheduler database. The SCHED spinlock synchronizes access to it. Chapter 8 describes the implementation and use of spinlocks. The SCHED spinlock does not synchronize access to all PCB or per-CPU database fields, just those related to scheduling.

12.1.1 PCB Fields Related to Scheduling

When a process is created, a PCB is allocated for it from nonpaged pool. A process continues to use the same PCB until the process is deleted and its PCB deallocated.

Figure 12.1 illustrates the fields of the PCB that are particularly important to scheduling. Others are shown in other chapters, in particular, in Chapters 7, 8, and 9.

The scheduling state of a process is specified by its PCB$W_STATE field. All processes in the system are in either the current (CUR) state, a wait state, computable resident (COM) state, or computable outswapped (COMO) state. Table 12.1 lists the scheduling states; Section 12.3 summarizes them and the transitions among them.

The PCBs of processes in most scheduling states are queued together with those of other processes in the same state so that they can be located more easily by scheduling routines. The scheduling state queue link fields, PCB$L_SQFL and PCB$L_SQBL, link a PCB into a process scheduling state queue (hereafter referred to as a process state queue). The various process state queues are described in Section 12.1.2.

The data structure that contains the hardware context of the process is called the hardware PCB. Its physical address is stored in the software PCB field PCB$L_PHYPCB. Section 12.6.1 describes the hardware PCB.

PCB$L_STS, the process status longword, contains various flags describing

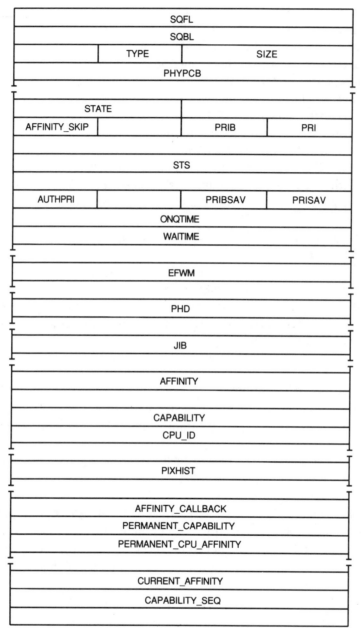

Figure 12.1
Process Control Block Fields Used in Scheduling

the status of the process. The bit PCB$V_RES is of particular significance to scheduling. When set, it indicates that the process is in memory rather than outswapped. Table 25.2 describes the flags in the process status longword.

Several PCB fields are related to process priority. Section 12.2 describes these fields.

When a process is in an event flag wait (see Section 12.3.3.1) or miscellaneous wait (MWAIT) state (see Section 12.3.3.3), PCB$L_EFWM identifies the flags or resource for which the process waits.

PCB$L_PHD contains the address of the process header (PHD). The PHD contains the hardware PCB and the field PHD$W_QUANT, the amount of quantum remaining to the process.

PCB$L_JIB contains the address of the job information block (JIB). The PCBs of all processes in a job tree share the JIB, which contains information common to all processes in the job, notably pooled quotas.

PCB$L_CPU_ID contains the processor ID of the CPU on which the process is currently executing or has last executed.

PCB$L_WAITIME contains the system absolute time in interval timer ticks at which a process was most recently placed into a wait state.

PCB$L_ONQTIME records the system absolute time in interval timer ticks at which a process most recently reached quantum end.

PCB$L_PIXHIST is described in Section 12.5.6.

The other PCB fields shown in Figure 12.1 are described in Section 12.4.

12.1.2   Process State Queues

PCBs of processes in the same scheduling state are linked together in doubly linked queues. There are queues for computable processes and for processes in different wait states. The listheads for all these queues are defined in the module SYSTEM_DATA_CELLS. Each CPU has a pointer to the PCB of its current (CUR) process in the per-CPU database.

There are 32 queues for COM processes, one for each possible process priority. The quadword listheads of these queues are defined as an array whose starting address is global location SCH$AQ_COMH. A process is inserted into the queue corresponding to the internal value of its current process priority (see Section 12.2). There is a similar array of 32 quadword listheads for the COMO state at global location SCH$AQ_COMOH.

The condition (empty or not) of each computable queue is summarized by a bit. If the queue contains one or more PCBs, the bit is set; if the queue is empty, the bit is clear. The 32 bits describing the COM queues are in the longword at global location SCH$GL_COMQS; the COMO queues are summarized in the longword SCH$GL_COMOQS. Bit 0 in each longword corresponds to the process priority 31 queue, bit 1 to priority 30, and so forth. (Section 12.2 explains the inverted order.) These summary longwords facilitate selection of the next process to execute and selection of the next process to be inswapped. Figure 12.2 shows the computable queues and their summary longwords.

Figure 12.3 shows the array of scheduler wait queue headers. Each header is a listhead for processes in one of the wait states. The first two longwords are the links to the PCBs in this queue. The field WQH$W_WQSTATE contains

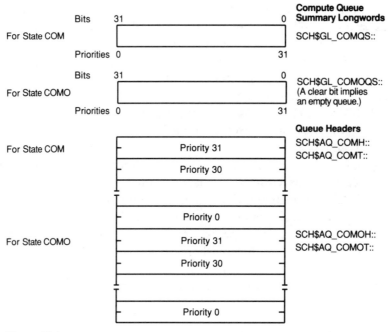

Figure 12.2
Computable (Executable) State Queues

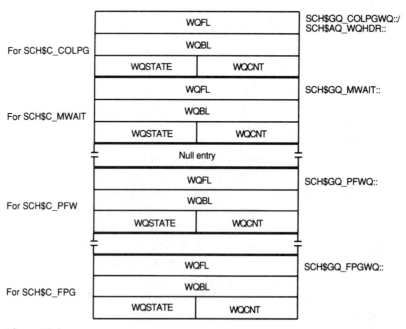

Figure 12.3
Array of Wait Queue Headers

the numerical value corresponding to the scheduling state (see Table 12.1). All PCBs in a process state queue have PCB$W_STATE values identical to the state value of the wait queue header. The field WQH$W_WQCNT contains the number of PCBs currently in this state and queue.

The wait queue headers for all wait states except common event flag (CEF) wait are defined within this array ordered by increasing state number, with the collided page wait state first. Each wait queue header except CEF has its own global pointer. A scheduling routine can access a particular wait queue by specifying its global name or using its state number as an index into the wait queue header array. The global location SCH$AQ_WQHDR is the address of the beginning of the array and corresponds to index number 1. (There is no state whose numeric value is 0.) Note that there is no actual header with an index value of 3, or CEF, although space is reserved.

A process waiting for one or more common event flags is queued to a wait queue in the common event block (CEB) defining the common event flag cluster with which the process is associated. A CEB includes three longwords that correspond to a wait queue header. The entire format of the CEB is shown in Chapter 9. Having a wait queue in each CEB makes it easier to determine which CEF processes are computable when a common event flag is set. The wait queue in the CEB contains both resident and outswapped processes.

12.1.3 Per-CPU Database Fields Related to Scheduling

The per-CPU database records processor-specific information such as the address of the PCB of the process current on that processor, the address of the processor's interrupt stack, and the processor's fork queues. Chapter 34 contains further information, including a detailed description of the per-CPU database. Figure 12.4 illustrates the fields of the per-CPU database that are related to scheduling.

CPU$L_CURPCB contains the PCB address of the process currently executing on this processor. CPU$B_CUR_PRI contains the process's current priority. If the processor is idle, CPU$L_CURPCB contains the address of the null PCB, and CPU$B_CUR_PRI contains −1.

CPU$L_PHY_CPUID contains the ID of the processor, a number from 0 to 31. CPU$L_CPUID_MASK is a mask of all zeros with one bit set corresponding to the CPU ID.

CPU$L_CAPABILITY is a bit mask with bits set to represent the capabilities of this processor. The low bit, when set, means that this CPU is the primary processor. The macro $CPBDEF defines symbolic values for the bits in this field. CPU$W_HARDAFF is the number of processes that have explicit affinity for this CPU. Section 12.4 describes the meaning and use of these two fields.

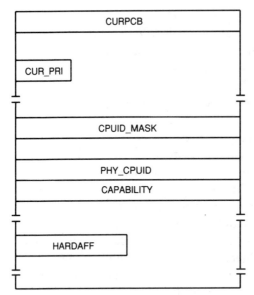

Figure 12.4
Per-CPU Database Fields Used in Scheduling

12.2 PROCESS PRIORITY

Two different mechanisms whose names contain the term *priority* are associated with each process. Interrupt priority level (IPL) applies to process-based and system-based code alike. IPL governs the hardware precedence of interrupts, as described in Chapter 2.

Process priority determines the precedence of a process for execution and memory residence. Throughout this book, the term *priority* used without qualification refers to process priority.

Process priorities have two different representations, an external one for presentation to the user and an internal one for use by most scheduling code. External process priorities take on values from 0 to 31; 0 is the lowest priority, and 31 the highest. This representation matches the tendency of most users to associate higher values with higher priorities.

The range of 32 priorities is divided in half. The high-priority half, 16 to 31, is assigned to real-time processes; the low-priority half, 0 to 15, is assigned to normal processes. The scheduling of a process is significantly affected by its type (normal or real-time) and its assigned priority level.

Internal process priorities are stored in an inverted order. For example, 0, the lowest external priority, is stored internally as 31; external priority 31 is stored internally as 0. Subtracting one priority form from 31 converts it to the other form.

Inverting the values facilitates selection of the next process to execute and the next process to be inswapped; these functions use the find first set (FFS) instruction, which begins its search for a set bit at bit position 0. (In other data structures, external priority is used instead, for convenience of the code referencing them.) As a result of this inversion, priority promotions or boosts are implemented through subtract or decrement instructions.

System utilities, such as the System Dump Analyzer (SDA), MONITOR, and the code that implements the Digital command language (DCL) command SHOW SYSTEM, convert internal priorities to external ones for display. The Get Job Process Information ($GETJPI) system service returns an external priority when a process priority is requested.

All discussions in this book use external priority representation unless otherwise noted. This convention should be taken into account when relating descriptions in this book to the actual routines in the listings, where internal priorities predominate.

Several fields of the PCB describe process priority. The values in these fields are in internal priority representation. The field PCB$B_PRI defines the current process priority, which is used to make scheduling decisions. PCB$B_PRIB defines the base priority of the process, from which the current priority is calculated. For normal or time-sharing processes, these priority values are sometimes different, while real-time processes always have identical current and base priority values.

When a process is first created, its base priority is initialized from an argument to the Create Process ($CREPRC) system service. Subsequently, if the process executes the LOGINOUT.EXE image, it may reset the base priority using the value from the user's record in the system authorization file.

A process with the ALTPRI privilege can raise and lower its current and base priorities without constraint, using the Set Priority ($SETPRI) system service or the DCL command SET PROCESS/PRIORITY. Chapter 13 describes the operation of the $SETPRI system service. The field PCB$B_AUTHPRI contains the base priority authorized at the time the process was created. A process without the ALTPRI privilege may raise and lower its priorities only between 0 and the contents of PCB$B_AUTHPRI.

System mechanisms that adjust priority dynamically are described in Section 12.2.3.

The fields PCB$B_PRIBSAV and PCB$B_PRISAV record the base and current priority values at the time a process first locks a mutex, before it receives a temporary elevation into the real-time range. When the process unlocks the mutex, its priority values are restored from these fields.

SCH$AL_PREEMPT_MASK is a 32-longword array of constants, with one longword for each priority. The array is indexed by internal priority; the longword at SCH$AL_PREEMPT_MASK corresponds to internal priority 0. The longword for a priority represents the priorities that it can preempt. Each bit in the longword represents a priority, with bit 0 representing *external* priority 0. The bits are organized that way because they are masked against the data in SCH$GL_ACTIVE_PRIORITY, described later in this section.

When a resident process becomes computable, scheduling code must decide whether the process should preempt one currently executing. In earlier versions of VMS, the test for preemption was a simple comparison of priorities. In VMS Version 5.2, the test, while more complex, minimizes unnecessary rescheduling and improves overall system performance. Scheduling code indexes the preemption array using the priority of the newly computable process. The selected mask indicates which priorities the process can preempt. The values in the masks implement two preemption rules and thus simplify the decision code:

- A real-time process can preempt any process of lower priority.
- A normal process at external priority n can preempt a process at priority $n - 3$.

Preventing preemption by a newly computable process only one or two priority levels higher than a current process helps to minimize movement of a process from one processor to another on an SMP system. If no other scheduling events intervene, such a newly computable process will be favored at quantum end of the current process.

The VMS Version 5.2 change in preemption policy may require system management changes on systems that have classes of users with different base priorities. In previous versions of VMS, defining the base priority for one class of processes (say, batch jobs) to be 3, and the base priority for another class (say, interactive users) to be 4, created an environment in which the processes of the higher priority were assured maximum responsiveness. To achieve the same effect in VMS Version 5.2, the base priorities for the two classes must differ by 3.

The per-CPU database field CPU$B_CUR_PRI contains the internal form of the current priority of the process current on that CPU. If the CPU is idle and has no current process, the field contains -1.

The priorities of the processes current on each member of an SMP system are described by two system data structures, defined in SYSTEM_DATA_CELLS:

- SCH$AL_CPU_PRIORITY is a 32-longword array, with one longword for each priority. The array is indexed by internal priority; the longword at SCH$AL_CPU_PRIORITY corresponds to internal priority 0. Each bit in a longword represents one SMP member, with bit 0, for example, corresponding to CPU ID 0. Bit m set in longword n means that the process current on CPU ID m is at internal priority n.
- SCH$GL_ACTIVE_PRIORITY, summarizing SCH$AL_CPU_PRIORITY, has a bit for each priority. When set, a particular bit indicates that one or more SMP members have a current process at that priority. Bit 0, for example, corresponds to external priority 0. The longword is indexed by

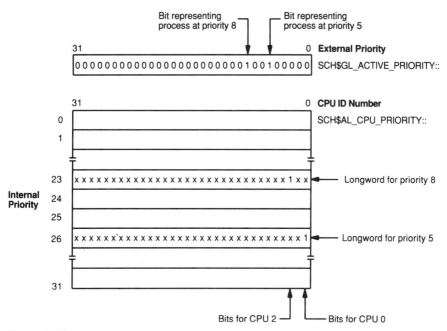

Figure 12.5
SMP Priority Summary Data Structures

external priority so that scheduling code can execute an FFS instruction to locate the lowest priority current process.

Figure 12.5 shows how these data structures might look for an SMP system of two members with CPU IDs 0 and 2. CPU 0 is executing a process at external priority 5, and CPU 2 a process at external priority 8. For simplicity, most of the bits are omitted.

12.2.1   Real-Time Priority Range

Processes with priority levels 16 through 31 are considered real-time processes. There are two scheduling characteristics that distinguish real-time processes from normal processes:

- The current priority of a real-time process does not change over time unless there is a direct program or operator request to change it. No dynamic priority adjustment (see Section 12.2.3) is applied by the VMS executive.
- A real-time process executes until it is preempted by a higher priority process or it enters a wait state (see Section 12.3.3). A real-time process is not susceptible to quantum end (see Section 12.5.2); it is not removed from execution because some interval of execution time has expired.

Taken in isolation, the real-time range of VMS priorities provides a scheduling environment like traditional real-time systems: preemptive, priority-driven scheduling without a time slice or quantum.

12.2.2 Normal Priority Range

Most user processes are normal processes. All system processes except the swapper and the Files-11 Extended QIO Processor (XQP) cache server process are normal processes.

The current priority of a normal process varies over time, while its base priority remains constant unless there is a direct program or operator request to change it. This behavior is the result of dynamic priority adjustment applied by the VMS system to favor I/O-bound processes and processes performing terminal I/O over those performing other types of I/O and compute-bound processes. The mechanism of priority adjustment is discussed in the following section.

Normal processes run in a time-sharing environment that allocates time slices (or quanta) to processes in turn. A normal process executes until one of the following events occurs:

- It is preempted by a higher priority computable process. In VMS Version 5.2, for one normal process to preempt another, the priority of the preempting process must be at least 3 more than that of the preempted process. (In VMS Versions 5.0 and 5.1, a higher priority process can preempt a lower priority one.)
- It enters a resource or event wait state.
- It has used its current quantum, and there is another computable process at the same or higher priority.

Processes with identical current priorities are scheduled on a round-robin basis. That is, apart from the affinity and capability constraints described in Section 12.4, each process at a given priority level executes in turn before any other process at that level executes again.

Most normal processes experience round-robin scheduling because, by default, the user authorization file defines the base priority for users as the value of SYSGEN parameter DEFPRI. Its usual value is 4.

12.2.3 Dynamic Priority Adjustment

Normal processes do not generally execute at a single priority level. Rather, the priority of a normal process changes over time in a range of zero to six priority levels above the base process priority. Two mechanisms provide this priority adjustment:

- As a condition for which the process has been waiting is satisfied or a needed resource becomes available, its current priority may be recomputed as its base plus a boost or priority increment to improve the scheduling response for the process (see Section 12.5.5.1).

- Each time the process executes without further system events (see Section 12.5.5), the current priority is moved toward the base priority (or demoted) by one priority level (see Section 12.6.4).

Over time, compute-bound process priorities tend to remain at their base priority levels, while I/O-bound processes tend to have average current priorities somewhat higher than their base priorities.

An example of priority adjustment that occurs over time for several processes is described in Section 12.5.5.1 and illustrated in Figure 12.9.

A normal process occasionally has its priority boosted by the pixscan mechanism, described in Section 12.5.6.

Temporary priority adjustment can also occur as a result of locking a mutex and through action by the $GETJPI system service, which is described in Chapter 13.

12.3   SCHEDULING STATES

This section describes the various scheduling states and some of the transitions among them. Figure 12.6 shows the common transitions but omits a few of the less frequent ones.

Symbolic names for scheduling states, which are defined by the macro $STATEDEF, have the form SCH$C_*mnemonic* (for example, SCH$C_COM). Table 12.1 lists the scheduling state names and the corresponding PCB$W_STATE values.

Certain wait conditions are represented by two different scheduling states: one resident and one outswapped. A process waiting for a local event flag is in the LEF or the LEFO state, depending on its residence. Other scheduling states, such as CEF, include both resident and outswapped processes. The PCB$V_RES bit in PCB$L_STS always specifies whether the process is resident or outswapped, regardless of its scheduling state.

12.3.1   Current State

A process in the CUR state is currently being executed. Its PCB address is recorded in its processor's per-CPU database at CPU$L_CURPCB.

A CUR process makes a transition to the COM state when it is preempted by a higher priority process. A CUR process of normal priority also makes this transition when it reaches quantum end and there is another computable process of higher or equal priority. A CUR process can make a transition to any of the resident wait states by directly or indirectly requesting a system operation that cannot complete immediately.

Direct requests like $HIBER and $SUSPND place the process in the voluntary wait states HIB and SUSP. Direct requests like $QIOW, $SYNCH, and $WAITFR place the process in the voluntary wait states LEF or CEF.

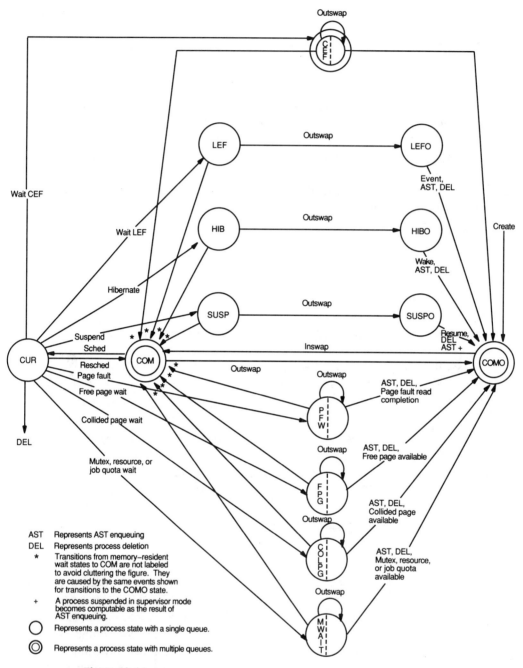

Figure 12.6
State Transitions

Table 12.1 Scheduling States

State Name	Mnemonic	Value
Collided page wait	COLPG	1
Miscellaneous wait	MWAIT	2
Mutex wait		
Resource wait		
Job quota wait		
Common event flag wait	CEF	3
Page fault wait	PFW	4
Local event flag wait (resident)	LEF	5
Local event flag wait (outswapped)	LEFO	6
Hibernate wait (resident)	HIB	7
Hibernate wait (outswapped)	HIBO	8
Suspend wait (resident)	SUSP	9
Suspend wait (outswapped)	SUSPO	10
Free page wait	FPG	11
Computable (resident)	COM	12
Computable (outswapped)	COMO	13
Currently executing process	CUR	14

Indirect wait requests occur as a result of paging or contention for system resources. A process does not request PFW, FPG, COLPG, or MWAIT transitions. Rather, the transitions to these wait states occur because direct service requests to the system cannot be completed or satisfied at the moment.

Deletion of a process can only occur while it is CUR. The process's address space and PHD are accessible only while it is current. Furthermore, process deletion in the context of the process being deleted enables the use of system services, such as Deassign I/O Channel ($DASSGN) and Delete Virtual Address Space ($DELTVA). Chapter 28 describes process deletion in detail.

12.3.2 **Computable States**

A process in the COM state is not waiting for events or resources, other than acquiring control of the CPU for execution. A COM process enters the CUR state after having been selected as the next process to run by SCH$SCHED (see Section 12.6.4).

A COM process enters the COMO state when it is outswapped.

A process in the COMO state is waiting for the swapper process to bring it into memory. As a COM process, it can then be scheduled for execution. Processes are created in the COMO state.

A COM process selected for execution can enter the RWCAP miscellaneous wait state if its capability and affinity requirements have no match on any active member of an SMP system. Section 12.4 describes capability and affinity requirements. (Note that this particular transition is omitted from Figure 12.6.)

12.3.3   Wait States

A process that is not current or computable is waiting for the availability of a system resource or the occurrence of an event. The process is in one of several distinct wait states. The wait state reflects the particular condition that must be satisfied for the process to become computable again.

A process in a wait state makes the transition to COM or COMO through a system event such as the availability of a requested resource or the satisfaction of a wait condition. For most process wait states, the queuing of an asynchronous system trap (AST) makes a process computable even if the wait condition is not satisfied.

12.3.3.1   Voluntary Wait States.

Several scheduling states are associated with event flag waits: LEF, LEFO, and CEF. A process enters the LEF or CEF state as a result of requesting the $WAITFR, $WFLOR, $WFLAND, and $SYNCH system services directly or indirectly (for example, with a $QIOW or $ENQW system service call, issued either by the process or on its behalf by some system component such as Record Management Services (RMS)). A process enters the LEF state when it waits for local event flags or the CEF state when it waits for flags in a common event flag cluster.

An LEF process enters the LEFO state when it is outswapped. The transition from the LEF, LEFO, or CEF states to the computable (COM or COMO) states can occur as a result of an event flag's being set that satisfies the wait condition, AST queuing, or process deletion (a special case of AST queuing). Chapter 9 describes event flag waits in more detail.

There are separate resident and outswapped states and queues for hibernating and suspended processes. The $HIBER and $SUSPND system services cause processes to enter the HIB and SUSP wait states. Outswapping a HIB or SUSP process causes it to enter the HIBO or SUSPO state.

A process makes the transition from the HIB or HIBO state to COM or COMO as a result of execution of a $WAKE or $SCHDWK system service, AST queuing, or process deletion.

In VMS Version 5, the SUSP and SUSPO states are categorized by the access mode of the suspension. A process in supervisor mode suspension, the default, is made computable by the queuing of an AST. (The nature of its wait, however, enables only executive and kernel mode ASTs to be delivered.) A process in kernel mode suspension is not made computable by the enqueuing of an AST. Prior to VMS Version 5, the only form of suspension was kernel mode. A process in either type of suspension is made computable when another process requests the $RESUME system service for the suspended process. Chapter 7 contains further information on ASTs, and

Chapter 13 further information on the implementation of the $SUSPND and
$HIBER system services.

Process deletion, implemented with a kernel mode AST, makes any process that is being deleted computable, even one in the SUSP or SUSPO state,
because the target process is resumed before the AST is queued.

12.3.3.2   **Memory Management Wait States.** Three process wait states are associated
with memory management. For each there is a single queue that includes
resident and outswapped processes. Memory management wait states are
discussed in more detail in Chapter 16.

A process enters the page fault (PFW) wait state when code running in
its context refers to a page that is not in physical memory. While the page
read is in progress, the process is placed into the PFW state. Completion of
the page read, AST queuing, or process deletion can cause a PFW process to
become COM or COMO, depending upon its PCB$V_RES bit value when
the satisfying condition occurs.

A process enters the free page (FPG) wait state when it requests a physical
page to be added to its working set but there are no free pages to be allocated
from the free page list. This state is essentially a resource wait that ends
when the supply of free pages is replenished through modified page writing,
working set trimming, process outswapping, or virtual address space deletion. When a physical page becomes available, all FPG processes are made
COM or COMO.

A process enters the collided page (COLPG) wait state when more than one
process causes page faults on the same shared page at the same time. The
initial faulting process enters the PFW state, while the second and succeeding
processes enter the COLPG state. All COLPG processes are made COM or
COMO when the read operation completes.

A PFW process can also enter the COLPG state following an AST:

1. The process faults a page, private or shared, and is placed into PFW state.
2. An AST is queued and delivered to the process.
3. After the AST procedure completes, an REI instruction returns control
   to the instruction that caused the initial page fault. The instruction
   reexecutes.
4. If the page is still not valid, it is in transition from its backing store, and
   the process is placed into COLPG.

12.3.3.3   **Miscellaneous Wait State.** A process in the MWAIT state waits for the
availability of a depleted system resource or job quota or a locked mutex.
The contents of the field PCB$L_EFWM identify the entity for which the
process waits:

• A small positive integer identifies a system resource.

- The system virtual address of the process's JIB specifies that the process is waiting for a job quota.
- The system virtual address of a mutex specifies that the process is waiting for that mutex.

There is a single MWAIT queue for resident and outswapped processes.

12.3.3.3.1   *System Resource Miscellaneous Waits.* A process may enter a resource wait if a resource it needs is not available. Common examples are the depletion of nonpaged pool or an already full mailbox. The process becomes computable when an executive routine declares the resource available. AST enqueuing makes the process computable, temporarily at least (see Section 12.5.1.4).

Table 12.2 lists the resources associated with the MWAIT state. Their symbolic values are defined by the $RSNDEF macro. System utilities such as SDA, MONITOR, and the DCL command SHOW SYSTEM display the state of a process in a resource wait using one of the mnemonic names in this table.

The system global SCH$GL_RESMASK summarizes the system resources for which processes in the MWAIT state are currently waiting. For example, bit 3 corresponds to RSN$_NPDYNMEM. When set, it indicates that one or more PCBs are in the MWAIT queue waiting for nonpaged pool to become available.

RWAST is a general-purpose resource used primarily when the wait is expected to be satisfied by the queuing or delivery of an AST to the process.

Table 12.2   Types of Resource MWAIT State

Resource Wait Name	Mnemonic	Symbolic Name	Number
AST wait (wait for AST)	RWAST	RSN$_ASTWAIT	1
Mailbox full	RWMBX	RSN$_MAILBOX	2
Nonpaged dynamic memory	RWNPG	RSN$_NPDYNMEM	3
Page file full [1]	RWPFF	RSN$_PGFILE	4
Paged dynamic memory	RWPAG	RSN$_PGDYNMEM	5
Breakthrough [1]	RWBRK	RSN$_BRKTHRU	6
Image activation lock [1]	RWIMG	RSN$_IACLOCK	7
Job pooled quota [1]	RWQUO	RSN$_JQUOTA	8
Lock identifier [1]	RWLCK	RSN$_LOCKID	9
Swap file space [1]	RWSWP	RSN$_SWPFILE	10
Modified page list empty	RWMPE	RSN$_MPLEMPTY	11
Modified page writer busy	RWMPB	RSN$_MPWBUSY	12
Distributed lock manager wait	RWSCS	RSN$_SCS	13
Cluster transition	RWCLU	RSN$_CLUSTRAN	14
CPU capability	RWCAP	RSN$_CPUCAP	15
Cluster server process	RWCSV	RSN$_CLUSRV	16

[1] This resource wait is not currently used.

There is no concrete resource corresponding to the name RSN$_ASTWAIT. The Queue I/O Request ($QIO) system service can place a process into this resource wait when the process is not allowed to issue another buffered or direct I/O request until one completes. Another use of RSN$_ASTWAIT is to wait for all the I/O requests on a channel to complete after the process has requested the $DASSGN system service. A process about to be suspended or deleted waits for the RSN$_ASTWAIT resource until all its Files-11 XQP activity completes (see Chapter 7).

A process is placed into RWMBX wait when it has resource wait mode enabled and tries to write to a mailbox that is full or has insufficient buffer space.

A process is placed into RWNPG wait when it is unsuccessful in allocating nonpaged pool. With the expandability of nonpaged pool, this wait is relatively rare.

A process is placed into RWPAG wait when it is unsuccessful in allocating paged pool.

A process in RWMPE wait is waiting for the modified page writer to signal that it has flushed the modified page list. With VMS Version 5.2, the only process placed into this wait is one running the OPCCRASH image, which forces a flush of the modified page list prior to stopping the system.

A process that faults a modified page out of its working set is placed into RWMPB wait when either of the following is true:

- The modified page list contains more pages than the SYSGEN parameter MPW_WAITLIMIT.
- The modified page list contains more pages than the SYSGEN parameter MPW_LOWAITLIMIT and the modified page writer is active, writing modified pages.

Generally, this resource wait occurs on a system whose modified page list has grown faster than it could be written. A process in such a wait becomes computable when enough modified pages have been written so that there are MPW_LOWAITLIMIT or fewer pages left on the list.

The lock manager uses RWSCS to stall execution of a process on a VAX-cluster node when the lock manager must wait for a response from a remote system that has information about a particular lock resource.

A process that issues any lock requests on any node of a VAXcluster in transition (that is, while a node is being added or removed) is placed into RWCLU wait until the VAXcluster membership stabilizes.

A computable process that requires one or more CPU capabilities that cannot all be satisfied by a single active member of the SMP system is placed into RWCAP wait (see Section 12.4).

There is a maximum number of outstanding transfer requests from one VAXcluster node to a remote node's cluster server process. When this limit has been reached and a process requests a service that would initiate another such transfer, the process is placed into RWCSV wait until transfer requests complete.

The Set Resource Wait Mode ($SETRWM) system service can cause a subsequent system service to return an error status, rather than placing the process in the MWAIT state. The $SETRWM system service sets the PCB$V_SSRWAIT bit in PCB$L_STS. Disabling resource wait affects many directly requested operations (such as I/O requests or timer requests) but has no effect on allocation requests by the system on behalf of the user. Although a process can respond to a depleted resource error from a system service call or an RMS request, it has no means of reacting to a similar error in case of an unexpected event such as a page fault. For example, when the page fault service routine is unable to allocate an I/O request packet for a page read, it places the process into an MWAIT wait regardless of the value of PCB$V_SSRWAIT.

12.3.3.3.2 *Mutex Miscellaneous Waits.* A system routine that accesses data structures protected by a mutex places a process in the MWAIT state if the requested mutex ownership cannot be granted. Thus, the mutex wait state indicates a locked resource and not necessarily a depleted one. When the mutex is unlocked, each process waiting to lock that mutex is made COM or COMO to repeat its attempt to lock the mutex. AST queuing makes a mutex-waiting process computable only temporarily; the IPL in its stored processor status longword (PSL) is 2, blocking the AST delivery interrupt.

Chapter 8 lists the names of mutexes whose addresses may be stored in PCB$L_EFWM and describes the mutex lock and unlock routines. System utilities such as SDA, MONITOR, and the DCL command SHOW SYSTEM display the state of a process that is waiting for a mutex as MUTEX.

12.3.3.3.3 *Job Quota Miscellaneous Waits.* VMS Version 5 adds another type of miscellaneous wait, a wait for a depleted job quota. Currently, there are two job quotas for which a process may have to wait:

- Buffered I/O byte count quota—used in a large number of ways, including I/O requests buffered in nonpaged pool, temporary mailboxes, and window control blocks
- Timer queue entry (TQE) quota—used for timer requests and common event flag cluster creation

When a job has one or more processes in such a wait, the field JIB$B_FLAGS has a bit set to indicate each job quota for which processes in that job are waiting. Bit 0, when set, means that one or more processes are waiting for JIB$L_BYTCNT. Bit 1, when set, means that one or more processes are waiting for TQE quota.

When another process in the job returns one of these quotas, the corresponding bit is checked to see if there is any waiting process. If there is, the waiting process is made computable to repeat its attempt to charge against the job quota.

A process in a job quota wait has the address of its JIB in PCB$L_EFWM. System utilities such as SDA, MONITOR, and the DCL command SHOW SYSTEM display the state of a process that is waiting for a jobwide resource as MUTEX.

12.4 CAPABILITIES AND AFFINITY

A capability represents a CPU attribute that a given process requires in order to execute. Generally a capability is a hardware feature. In an SMP system, a process's requirement for a particular capability may limit its execution to a subset of the available processors. For example, a process might require the capability CPB$V_PRIMARY and thus only be able to execute on the primary processor.

Affinity is the requirement that a process execute on a specific processor of an SMP system. VMS provides for both explicit and implicit affinity. A process must explicitly request explicit affinity and must explicitly dismiss it. Explicit affinity might allow processes to be segregated by CPU. In contrast, a process acquires implicit affinity for a processor when there are advantages to its continuing execution on that processor. For example, a process that executed on a CPU with a large physical memory cache might have data still cached if it were placed back into execution on that CPU.

VMS Version 5.2 contains data structures and code to implement capabilities and implicit and explicit affinity at an executive level. It makes limited use of them currently and contains no user-level interface to either mechanism. However, because their implementation is closely related to scheduling, this chapter describes the relevant data structures and code where appropriate.

Each processor's per-CPU database field CPU$L_CAPABILITY describes its set of capabilities. When a new CPU joins the SMP system, its capability mask is copied from the system default one, SCH$GL_DEFAULT_CPU_CAP, currently defined as 0. The 32-longword array SCH$AL_CPU_CAP, indexed by CPU ID, collects that information for all CPUs, simplifying a search for a CPU with a set of particular capabilities. In VMS Version 5.2, the only capability in use is that of being primary, which is set at system initialization in the primary processor's CPU$L_CAPABILITY field and entered in the SCH$AL_CPU_CAP array.

The routines SCH$ADD_CPU_CAP and SCH$REMOVE_CPU_CAP, both in module SCHED, provide for dynamic changes to CPU capabilities. The contents of SCH$GL_CAPABILITY_SEQUENCE indicate to which generation the data in SCH$AL_CPU_CAP belong; whenever the data changes by the addition or removal of a CPU capability, SCH$GL_CAPABILITY_

SEQUENCE is incremented. Keeping track of the generation enables processes with capability constraints to detect changes in the set of processors available to meet those constraints.

Fields in each process's PCB describe its current and permanent capability requirements and affinity.

PCB$L_CAPABILITY and PCB$L_PERMANENT_CAPABILITY are the current and permanent capability requirements. When a process is created, the permanent capability mask is copied from the system default one, SCH$GL_DEFAULT_PROCESS_CAP, currently defined as 0. The routines SCH$REQUIRE_CAPABILITY and SCH$RELEASE_CAPABILITY, both in module SCHED, provide for dynamic changes to process requirements. These routines initialize the target process's PCB$L_CURRENT_AFFINITY as a mask with bits set to represent the CPUs that satisfy the capability requirements. These are the CPUs on which the process can execute. The routines also copy the current value of SCH$GL_CAPABILITY_SEQUENCE to PCB$L_CAPABILITY_SEQ for future use as a validity check on the current affinity mask.

Two of the process capability mask bits represent affinity:

- CPB$V_IMPLICIT_AFFINITY, when set, means that the process has acquired implicit affinity for a particular CPU.
- CPB$V_EXPLICIT_AFFINITY, when set, means that the process has acquired explicit affinity for a particular CPU.

SCH$REQUIRE_CAPABILITY can be invoked to request that a particular process acquire current or permanent explicit affinity for a particular CPU. The routine stores a new value with only one bit set in the affected process's PCB$L_CURRENT_AFFINITY and stores the CPU ID of the processor in PCB$L_AFFINITY. If the request was for permanent affinity, it also stores the CPU ID in PCB$L_PERMANENT_CPU_AFFINITY and sets the capability bit in PCB$L_PERMANENT_CAPABILITY. The processor's CPU$W_HARDAFF is incremented as a count of processes that have explicit affinity for it.

Following are examples of executive routines that employ capabilities and explicit affinity:

- The Set Time ($SETIME) system service must run on the primary processor when it reads and writes the time-of-year clock. It invokes SCH$REQUIRE_CAPABILITY to require the current capability of primary processor.
- The interval timer interrupt service routine runs on each SMP member but performs system timekeeping functions only on the primary processor. It tests the low bit of the current processor's per-CPU database field CPU$L_CAPABILITY to determine whether it is running on the primary.

- When SMP$SHUTDOWN_CPU, in module SMPROUT, is invoked to shut down a particular CPU, it establishes explicit affinity for that CPU to cause itself to be rescheduled on that CPU if it is not already running on it.

The routine SCH$ACQUIRE_AFFINITY can be invoked to request that a target process acquire implicit affinity for a particular CPU. The routine stores a new value for PCB$L_CURRENT_AFFINITY with only one bit set and the CPU ID in PCB$L_AFFINITY. It sets CPB$V_IMPLICIT_AFFINITY in the target process's PCB$L_CAPABILITY. When a process with implicit affinity is selected for execution, if its affinity is not for the current CPU, the scheduler returns the process to the compute queue and attempts to select another process to run. A successful alternative process is one whose priority is high enough so that it could not be preempted by the process with implicit affinity.

Potentially, the process can be skipped for execution in this manner repeatedly up to the number in PCB$B_AFFINITY_SKIP, which is decremented at each failed attempt. PCB$B_AFFINITY_SKIP is initialized from the SYSGEN parameter AFFINITY_SKIP, whose default value is 2. When PCB$B_AFFINITY_SKIP reaches 0 or whenever the scheduler cannot find an alternative process that can execute on this CPU, it breaks implicit affinity. That is, a process's having implicit affinity for one CPU is not a compelling reason to leave another CPU idle. If PCB$L_AFFINITY_CALLBACK is nonzero, the scheduler calls the specified procedure to perform any processor-specific cleanup associated with breaking affinity. The procedure is called with the SCHED spinlock held, at IPL$_SCHED, and with two arguments, the address of the PCB and the ID of the CPU. Currently, no use is made of implicit affinity.

At image rundown, the capability mask is restored from the permanent capability mask and the affinity from the permanent affinity. Explicit affinity counts in the per-CPU database are adjusted. If any change is required in capabilities or affinity, the image rundown routine requests an IPL 3 interrupt for the scheduler to determine where the process should run.

At deletion of a process with explicit affinity, the CPU$W_HARDAFF field of its associated processor is decremented.

12.5 SCHEDULING DYNAMICS

In general, on a VMS system in equilibrium, the available processors execute the highest priority COM processes. A number of events can alter this equilibrium and require that the scheduler reschedule: that is, take a current process out of execution, saving its context; select another process to run; and load its context, placing it into execution.

The principal events that require rescheduling are

- A current process goes into a wait state.

- A current process reaches the end of its quantum, and there is another COM process of equal or higher priority.
- A current process changes its priority, and there is a higher priority COM process.
- There is no longer a match between the capabilities required by a current process and the processor on which it is executing.
- A system event alters the scheduling state of a noncurrent process to COM, and its priority permits it to preempt a current process.

Figures 12.7, 12.8, and 12.12 show the relations among the routines involved in these events. The sections that follow describe the events and the routines that handle them. Section 12.6 describes the rescheduling interrupt.

12.5.1 Placing a Current Process into a Wait State

When a process directly or indirectly requests a system operation for which it must wait, the process is placed into a wait state. The actions to place a process into a wait state are centralized in the routine SCH$WAIT, in module RSE.

The routines that invoke SCH$WAIT include

- EXE$WAITFR, EXE$WFLOR, and EXE$WFLAND, in module SYSWAIT, to place a process into an LEF or CEF wait (see Chapter 9)
- EXE$HIBER, in module SYSPCNTRL, to place a process into a HIB wait (see Chapter 13)
- EXE$SUSPND and SUSPND, in module SYSPCNTRL, to place a process into a SUSP wait (see Chapter 13)
- EXE$JIB_WAIT, in module MUTEX, to place a process into an MWAIT for JIB byte count quota
- SCH$LOCKR and SCH$LOCKW, in module MUTEX, to place a process into an MWAIT for a mutex (see Chapter 8)
- SCH$RWAIT, in module MUTEX, to place a process into an MWAIT for a system resource

Figure 12.7 shows the invokers of SCH$WAIT.

SCH$WAIT is entered in process context at IPL$_SCHED and with the SCHED spinlock held. Register arguments specify the addresses of the software PCB of the current process and the wait queue into which the process is to be inserted.

Depending on which subentry point of SCH$WAIT is invoked, some or all of the following operations are performed:

1. SCH$WAIT assumes it has been entered from a system service. It removes the call frame from the kernel stack and establishes the program counter (PC) at which the process will wait, as described in the following section.

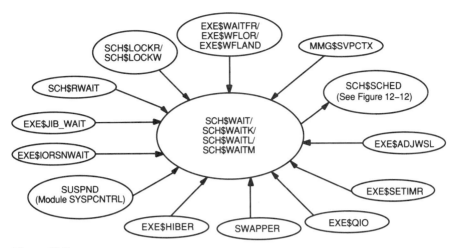

Figure 12.7
Paths Leading to a Process Wait

2. At subentry point SCH$WAITK, it changes the process state to that in the WQH$W_WQSTATE field of the specified wait queue header, inserts the PCB into the wait queue, and increments WQH$W_WQCNT to show the addition of a process to the queue.

3. At subentry point SCH$WAITL, it executes a SVPCTX instruction to remove the current process from execution.

4. At subentry point SCH$WAITM, it charges the SYSGEN parameter IOTA against the process quantum, as described in Section 12.5.2. It also adjusts PHD$L_TIMREF by the value of IOTA. PHD$L_TIMREF and the process quantum must be adjusted together for automatic working set limit adjustment to be responsive (see Chapter 17).

5. SCH$WAIT copies the contents of the system global EXE$GL_ABSTIM_TICS, the system time in interval timer ticks, to PCB$L_WAITIME, to record the time at which the process began its wait. If the process remains in a wait state for long, it becomes a candidate for working set shrinkage and possibly outswapping (see Chapter 18).

6. It tests PR$_ASTLVL and the process's saved PSL to determine whether a deliverable AST has been queued to the process but not yet delivered. This test prevents an AST event that should take the process out of its wait from being ignored. If a deliverable AST has been queued, SCH$WAIT reports an AST queuing event to SCH$RSE (see Section 12.5.5), which changes the process state to COM.

7. SCH$WAIT then branches to SCH$SCHED (see Section 12.6.4), the second half of the rescheduling interrupt service routine, to select a new process to run.

One of the responsibilities of the routines that invoke SCH$WAIT and its subentry points is to ensure that a process can reenter the appropriate wait state, if necessary, after the process is placed back into execution as the result of AST delivery. (Recall that AST enqueuing makes a process in most wait states computable.) These routines therefore establish a carefully chosen PC and PSL at which the process is to wait. The PC and PSL control what thread of execution will run, and its access mode and IPL. Its access mode affects AST delivery: only ASTs equally or more privileged can be delivered. If the access mode is kernel, then the wait IPL is also significant: an IPL of 2 blocks AST delivery interrupts. Several different techniques are used, depending on the particular wait state being entered.

12.5.1.1 **Context for CEF, HIB, or LEF Wait States.** When a process enters a CEF, HIB, or LEF wait state, the system service establishes the system service CHMK exception PSL as the wait PSL. Consequently, the process waits in the access mode in which the system service was issued.

For the wait PC, the code subtracts 4 from the CHMK exception PC so that it is the address of the CHMx instruction in the system service vector. Chapter 6 contains more information about system service vectors and change mode exceptions.

If an AST is delivered to a process in such a wait state, when the AST exits, the AST delivery interrupt service routine's REI uses the wait PC and PSL. The system service executes again, typically placing the process back into the wait state.

12.5.1.2 **Context for Memory Management Wait States.** Only the page fault exception service routine (see Chapter 16) places processes into the three wait states associated with memory management. This routine uses the page fault exception PC and PSL as the wait PC and PSL. Because the PSL reflects the access mode in which the page fault occurred, ASTs can be delivered for that and all inner access modes. The exception PC does not need to be changed; a page fault exception pushes the PC of the faulting instruction onto the exception stack.

After an AST executes in such a process, the process executes the faulting instruction again. If the reason for the fault has been removed (a free page became available or the page read completed) while the AST was being delivered or was executing, the process simply continues with its execution. If the situation that caused the process to wait still exists, the process reincurs the page fault and is placed back into a memory management wait state. (Note that a process that was initially in a PFW state would be placed into a COLPG state by such a sequence of events.)

12.5.1.3 **Context for a SUSP Wait.** A process is suspended as the result of executing an AST. In VMS Version 5, the access mode of the AST can be supervisor or kernel mode, depending on which form of suspend is requested. The default is supervisor mode. While a process is suspended in kernel mode, the wait PC is an address in the kernel AST that caused the process to enter the suspend state. The saved PSL indicates kernel mode and IPL 0. ASTs can be queued to a process suspended in kernel mode but not delivered. That is, when an AST is queued to a kernel mode suspended process, the AST event is ignored.

While a process is suspended in supervisor mode, the saved PC is an address in the supervisor mode AST. AST enqueuing makes the process computable. When the process is placed into execution, a kernel or executive mode AST can be executed, but a user or supervisor mode AST cannot: the AST control block remains queued, and the interrupt is dismissed. In either case, an REI instruction is executed, which causes control to return to the wait PC. It repeats the test that suspended the process. If the process has not been resumed, it is suspended again.

12.5.1.4   **Context for an MWAIT Wait.** When a process is placed into a wait for a mutex, its saved PC is either SCH$LOCKR or SCH$LOCKW, depending on whether it is attempting to lock the mutex for read or write access. Its saved PSL indicates kernel mode and IPL 2, making it impossible for a process in an MWAIT state waiting for a mutex to receive ASTs.

A process can also be placed into an MWAIT state while waiting for an arbitrary system resource. In this case, the invoker of routine SCH$RWAIT, in module MUTEX, determines the wait PC and PSL.

A process with resource wait mode enabled can be placed into an MWAIT state while waiting for a job quota, either byte count or TQE quota. The routines that invoke EXE$JIB_WAIT determine the wait PC and PSL.

In the case of byte count, the routine EXE$DEBIT_BYTCNT, in module EXSUBROUT, checks whether the job has sufficient byte count quota for a particular request. If it does not, EXE$DEBIT_BYTCNT places the process into a wait with kernel access mode and IPL equal to that at entry to EXE$DEBIT_BYTCNT. Typically, this routine and its subentry points are invoked from device driver preprocessing routines at IPL 2, and thus the process is waited at IPL 2. The wait PC is an address within EXE$DEBIT_BYTCNT that repeats the test.

In the case of TQE quota, the process is placed into a wait similar to that for HIB, LEF, and CEF—its wait PC is the address of the CHMK in the system service vector and its PSL is the change mode exception PSL, so that the process waits in the access mode from which it requested the service.

12.5.2   **Quantum Expiration**

The SYSGEN parameter QUANTUM defines the size of the time slice for the round-robin scheduling of normal processes. The quantum also determines, for most process states, the minimum amount of time a process remains in memory after an inswap operation, but it is not an absolute guarantee of memory residence. The swapper's use of the initial quantum flag in selecting an outswap candidate is described in Chapter 18. The value of QUANTUM is the number of 10-millisecond intervals (interval timer ticks) in the quantum. The default QUANTUM value of 20, therefore, produces a scheduling interval of 200 milliseconds.

A process's quantum is expressed as a negative number of timer ticks. After each 10-millisecond interval, the interval timer interrupt service routine increments the PHD$W_QUANT field in the current process's PHD. When this value becomes zero or positive, the interrupt service routine requests a software timer interrupt. The software timer interrupt service routine signals a quantum-end event by invoking the subroutine SCH$QEND, in module RSE.

An additional deduction from quantum is governed by the special SYSGEN parameter IOTA. Its default value is 2, representing two 10-millisecond ticks. This value is deducted from PHD$W_QUANT each time a process enters a wait state. This mechanism ensures that all processes experience quantum-end events with some regularity. Processes that are compute-bound experience quantum end as a result of using a certain amount of CPU time. Processes that are I/O-bound experience quantum end as a result of performing a reasonable number of I/O requests.

The routine SCH$QEND is executed whenever a current process reaches quantum end. It runs on the same CPU as the process, but it executes in system context, as part of the software timer interrupt service routine. Its minimum actions are to reset the field PHD$W_QUANT to the full quantum value; clear the initial quantum flag, PCB$V_INQUAN in the field PCB$L_STS; and record EXE$GL_ABSTIM_TICS in PCB$L_ONQTIME. It performs those actions for both real-time and normal processes.

For a normal process, SCH$QEND takes the following additional steps:

1. SCH$QEND updates PCB$L_PIXHIST, the pixscan history summary longword (see Section 12.5.6), by shifting it left one bit.
2. SCH$QEND tests whether a CPU time limit has been imposed and, if so, compares the process's limit field, PHD$L_CPULIM, against its accumulated CPU time, PHD$L_CPUTIM, to determine whether that limit has been reached. If the CPU limit has been reached, each access mode has an interval of time to clean up or run down before the image exits and the process is deleted. The size of the warning interval for each access mode is defined by the SYSGEN parameter EXTRACPU, which has a default value of 10 seconds.
3. SCH$QEND checks whether automatic working set limit adjustment is enabled and appropriate for this process. If both are true, the size of the process working set list may be expanded or contracted. Chapter 17 describes automatic working set limit adjustment.

4. If there is an inswap candidate (if SCH$GL_COMOQS is nonzero, indicating at least one nonempty COMO state queue), SCH$QEND sets the current priority of the process to its base priority. It changes, as appropriate, CPUB_CUR_PRI, SCHAL_CPU_PRIORITY, and SCH$GL_ACTIVE_PRIORITY.

   Furthermore, it invokes SCH$SWPWAKE, in module RSE, to awaken the swapper. As a computable, resident, real-time process of software priority 16, the swapper is likely to be the next process scheduled.

5. SCH$QEND checks whether there is a COM process of equal or higher priority. If there is none, this process will continue to execute. If its current priority is not equal to its base priority, SCH$QEND decrements its current priority, making the appropriate changes to CPUB_CUR_PRI, SCHAL_CPU_PRIORITY, and SCH$GL_ACTIVE_PRIORITY. This decrement is equivalent to the one made every time a process is placed into execution. SCH$QEND then returns to the software timer interrupt service routine.

   This behavior is new with VMS Version 5.2. It saves unnecessary SVPCTX and LDPCTX instructions (and the associated translation buffer flush) when this process continues to be the best candidate to execute. Earlier versions of VMS simply requested a rescheduling interrupt.

6. If there is a COM process of equal or higher priority, SCH$QEND requests an IPL 3 rescheduling interrupt and returns. When the interrupt is granted, the current process will be taken out of execution and another selected to execute.

Figure 12.12 includes SCH$QEND as a requestor of a rescheduling interrupt.

12.5.3   **Changing the Priority of a Current Process**

Several routines change the priority of a current process:

- SCH$QEND, when a normal process reaches quantum end and there is a COMO process
- SCH$QEND, when a normal process not yet at its base priority will continue to execute (see Section 12.5.2 for a description of quantum-end processing)
- EXE$SETPRI, in module SYSSETPRI, when a process requests the $SETPRI system service (see Chapter 13)
- SCH$LOCKR and SCH$LOCKW, in module MUTEX, when a normal process locks a mutex and gets a temporary alteration to priority 16
- SCH$UNLOCK, in module MUTEX, when a normal process unlocks a mutex and has its priority restored (see Chapter 8 for information on locking and unlocking mutexes)
- EXE$GETJPI, in module SYSGETJPI, when the target process's original priority is restored after a boost (see Chapter 36)

- EXE$RESCHED, in module SYSPARPRC, when a process requests the Reschedule ($RESCHED) system service to lower its priority to its base and request a rescheduling interrupt (see Chapter 13)

The actions to change the priority of a current process are centralized in the routine SCH$CHANGE_CUR_PRIORITY, in module RSE. All the routines in the previous list except the first invoke SCH$CHANGE_CUR_PRIORITY. Figure 12.12 shows its invokers.

SCH$CHANGE_CUR_PRIORITY is entered at IPL$_SCHED and with the SCHED spinlock held. It can run in system context, invoked from SCH$QEND; in the context of the process whose priority is changing; or in the context of a process requesting a $SETPRI service on behalf of another process.

Register arguments specify the address of the software PCB of the target process, the one whose priority is to be changed; the address of the per-CPU database of its CPU; and the new priority.

SCH$CHANGE_CUR_PRIORITY takes the following steps:

1. It clears the bit corresponding to the CPU's ID in the longword corresponding to the priority in the array at SCH$AL_CPU_PRIORITY.
2. If there are no other processes at this priority current on any CPU, it clears the bit corresponding to that priority in SCH$GL_ACTIVE_PRIORITY.
3. It copies the new priority to PCB$B_PRI and CPU$B_CUR_PRI.
4. It sets the bit corresponding to the CPU's ID in the longword corresponding to the priority in the array at SCH$AL_CPU_PRIORITY.
5. It sets the bit corresponding to the process's new priority in SCH$GL_ACTIVE_PRIORITY.
6. It executes an FFS instruction to locate the least significant set bit in the longword SCH$GL_COMQS. The located bit position indicates the highest priority nonempty computable resident state queue.
7. It compares the changed priority of the target process with that of the highest priority COM process. If the changed priority is higher or equal, SCH$CHANGE_CUR_PRIORITY returns.
8. Otherwise, it requests a rescheduling interrupt on the CPU on which the target process is current.

    —If SCH$CHANGE_CUR_PRIORITY and the target process are executing on the same CPU, this is simply an IPL 3 software interrupt request.
    —If the CPUs are different, SCH$CHANGE_CUR_PRIORITY requests an interprocessor interrupt on the other CPU so that the IPL 3 interrupt can be requested there. Chapter 34 describes interprocessor interrupts.

Clearly, this priority comparison can result in rescheduling when the priority of a current process is lowered. Moreover, under some circumstances, it could also result in rescheduling even when the priority of a current process is raised a small amount. Because preemption of a current process by a newly computable process requires a priority difference of 3, a normal computable process might continue to execute despite the existence of a slightly higher priority process that had just become computable. Under these circumstances, if the current process were to raise its priority to a value less than that of the newly computable process, the current process would be rescheduled.

12.5.4   **Capability Mismatch**

This section describes how a mismatch in capability requirements occurs between a current process and the processor on which it is executing and how the mismatch is handled.

There are several routines that can affect process capability and affinity requirements and CPU capabilities so as to produce a mismatch.

SCH$ACQUIRE_AFFINITY, in module SCHED, can be called to request that a current process acquire implicit affinity for a processor other than the one on which it is executing. If the process already has implicit affinity or has explicit affinity for a different CPU, the routine returns an error status. Otherwise, it performs the following steps:

1. SCH$ACQUIRE_AFFINITY initializes PCB$B_AFFINITY_SKIP and sets CPB$V_IMPLICIT_AFFINITY in PCB$L_CAPABILITY. It stores the address of the routine to be called if implicit affinity is broken.
2. It stores the intended CPU ID in PCB$L_AFFINITY and tests whether the process is current.
3. If so, it compares PCB$L_AFFINITY to PCB$L_CPU_ID. If the two are different, SCH$ACQUIRE_AFFINITY requests a rescheduling interrupt. If the process is current on a different CPU than the one on which SCH$ACQUIRE_AFFINITY is executing, the routine requests an interprocessor interrupt so that the rescheduling interrupt is requested on the right CPU.

SCH$REMOVE_CPU_CAP, in module SCHED, is called to remove a capability from one or all CPUs. It takes the following steps, looping through them if all CPUs are to be affected:

1. It increments SCH$GL_CAPABILITY_SEQUENCE to indicate a change in the capabilities of the active members of the SMP system.
2. It clears the bit corresponding to the capability in the target CPU's per-CPU database field CPU$L_CAPABILITY and its longword in the SCH$AL_CPU_CAP array.
3. It gets the address of the process current on that CPU from CPU$L_CURPCB and examines its capability mask.

4. If this capability is not required by the process current on the target CPU, the routine returns.
5. Otherwise, it requests a rescheduling interrupt, through an interprocessor interrupt if necessary.

SCH$REQUIRE_CAPABILITY, in module SCHED, is called for a particular process to acquire a new capability. It takes the following steps:

1. It acquires the SCHED spinlock, raising IPL to IPL$_SCHED.
2. It sets the capability in the target process's PCB$L_CAPABILITY.
3. If a different explicit affinity is being requested than was previously set, the routine decrements CPU$W_HARDAFF of the current CPU and increments it for the new CPU. It stores the new CPU ID in PCB$L_AFFINITY.
4. If this is a request to alter permanent capabilities, the routine also changes PCB$L_PERMANENT_CAPABILITY.
5. It invokes SCH$CALCULATE_AFFINITY to get the new current affinity mask.
6. It then checks whether the process is current.
7. If so, it compares PCB$L_CURRENT_AFFINITY to PCB$L_CPU_ID. If the two are different, the routine requests a rescheduling interrupt, through an interprocessor interrupt if necessary.
8. It releases the SCHED spinlock.

EXE$RUNDWN, in module SYSRUNDWN, implements the Image Rundown ($RUNDWN) system service. It takes the following steps to reset the process's current capabilities:

1. It acquires the SCHED spinlock, raising IPL to IPL$_SCHED.
2. It compares the current process's PCB$L_CAPABILITY with PCB$L_PERMANENT_CAPABILITY and PCB$L_AFFINITY with PCB$L_PERMANENT_CPU_AFFINITY. If neither has changed, this part of rundown is complete. EXE$RUNDWN releases the SCHED spinlock and continues with other processing.
3. If there is an affinity change, then the routine decrements CPU$W_HARDAFF for the CPU to which the process currently has explicit affinity, if any. It increments it for the CPU to which the process has permanent affinity, if any.
4. It resets the capabilities and clears PCB$L_CURRENT_AFFINITY and PCB$L_CAPABILITY_SEQ. It then requests a rescheduling interrupt so that the rescheduling interrupt service routine will determine where the process should continue execution.
5. It releases the SCHED spinlock, restoring the previous IPL and permitting the rescheduling interrupt to be granted.

12.5.5   **Event Reporting**

This section describes how a process makes a transition to a COM state and how it preempts a current process.

A system event potentially changes the scheduling state of a process, making it computable, memory-resident, or outswapped. Examples of system events include the setting of an event flag for which a process is waiting, AST queuing, and page fault I/O completion. An executive routine aware of a system event that may take a process out of a wait state reports it on behalf of the affected process.

Holding the SCHED spinlock and running at IPL$_SCHED, such a routine invokes the RPTEVT macro, which generates the following code:

```
JSB     SCH$RSE
.BYTE   EVT$_event_name
```

The byte event value identifies the event being reported. The address of the event value is pushed onto the stack by the JSB instruction.

SCH$RSE is responsible for making many of the process state transitions shown in Figure 12.6. Figure 12.8 shows the invokers of SCH$RSE and its entry points SCH$CHSE and SCH$CHSEP.

SCH$RSE is passed the address of the PCB of the affected process and a priority increment class in registers. If the event makes the process computable, the process may receive a priority boost, depending on the priority class, its current priority, and its base priority.

SCH$RSE and routines it invokes, all in module RSE, perform the following operations:

1. SCH$RSE obtains the byte event value, which is pointed to by the return PC on the stack, and increments the return PC to point to the next instruction.
2. It checks an internal table to determine whether the event is significant for the process, based on its current state.

   Each event has a bit mask defining which states this event can affect. The current state of the process is obtained from the PCB$W_STATE field.

   —A wake event is only significant for processes that are hibernating (HIB or HIBO states).

   —An outswap event is only significant for the four states (COM, HIB, LEF, and SUSP) where a wait queue change is required.

   —The queuing of an AST is significant to all process states except kernel mode SUSP and SUSPO, COM, COMO, and CUR, and results in a transition to COM or COMO.

3. If the event is not significant for the current process state, SCH$RSE ignores the event and simply executes an RSB instruction.

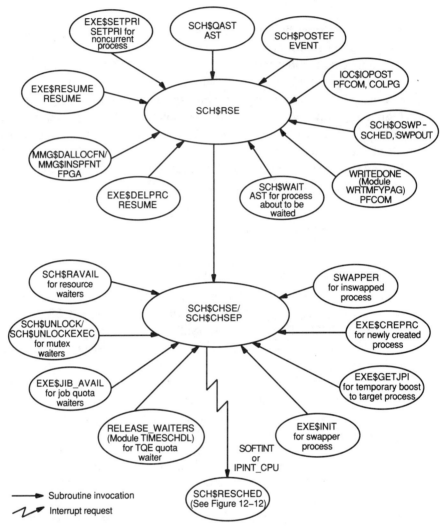

Figure 12.8
Paths to Event Reporting

4. For an outswap event producing an LEF to LEFO, HIB to HIBO, or SUSP to SUSPO transition, SCH$RSE simply removes the PCB of the process from the resident wait queue and inserts it in the corresponding outswapped wait queue. It adjusts the corresponding wait queue header count fields and PCB$W_STATE. It then executes an RSB instruction to return.

5. For an outswap event producing a COM to COMO transition, SCH$RSE removes the PCB from the COM priority queue corresponding to PCB$B_PRI and then inserts it into the corresponding COMO priority queue. It changes PCB$W_STATE. It clears the SCH$GL_COMQS compute queue summary longword bit corresponding to PCB$B_PRI if that COM queue

is now empty and unconditionally sets the corresponding SCH$GL_
COMOQS bit. It then executes an RSB instruction to return.

6. For transitions from the LEF or resident CEF state to the COM state,
   SCH$RSE adds 4 to the saved PC in the hardware PCB so that it points
   past the CHMx instruction. This modification to the PC value allows the
   process to begin execution immediately following the system service
   request rather than re-requesting a wait-for system service for a flag that
   is already set. The check for CEF residence is necessary because the saved
   PC of a nonresident process is usually not accessible. (The saved PC is
   stored in the hardware PCB in the PHD, which may be outswapped if the
   process is not resident.) It then executes an RSB instruction to return.

7. For any transition that makes a process computable, SCH$RSE removes
   the process from its wait queue and decrements the wait queue header
   count.

8. It subtracts PCB$L_WAITIME from the current time in interval timer
   ticks and adds the result to PCB$L_ONQTIME to subtract out from it
   the effect of the time spent waiting.

9. It performs whatever priority adjustment is appropriate (see
   Section 12.5.5.1).

10. If the now computable process is outswapped at present, SCH$RSE
    changes its state to COMO, inserts the process into the COMO queue
    corresponding to its priority, and unconditionally sets the SCH$GL_
    COMOQS summary bit corresponding to the selected priority queue. It
    awakens the swapper and returns. Later, after the process is inswapped,
    it will become eligible for execution.

11. If the now computable process is resident, SCH$RSE changes its state
    to COM, inserts the process into the COM queue corresponding to its
    priority, and unconditionally sets the SCH$GL_COMQS summary bit
    corresponding to the selected priority queue.

    It compares the process's current affinity mask with the mask of idle
    CPUs. If there are potential CPUs on which the process can execute,
    SCH$RSE clears SCH$GL_IDLE_CPUS as a signal to each of them to try
    to reschedule (see Section 12.6.4). If it appears that there are no potential
    CPUs, SCH$RSE checks that the process's PCB$L_CAPABILITY_SEQ is
    current, recalculating current affinity if it is not. If there are still no idle
    candidate CPUs and the process's priority is not high enough for it to
    preempt any active process, SCH$RSE simply executes an RSB instruction
    to return.

    If the process's priority permits it to preempt some active processes,
    SCH$RSE searches for a candidate to preempt on a CPU whose capabili-
    ties fit. If it finds one, it requests either an interprocessor interrupt or an
    IPL 3 interrupt, depending on where the process to be preempted is exe-
    cuting. When the interprocessor interrupt is granted, its service routine
    will request an IPL 3 interrupt to cause rescheduling.

Scheduling

On a uniprocessor system, the issue is simpler: if there is a current process, can it be preempted by the newly computable process? The preemption test is based upon the SCH$AL_PREEMPT_MASK array, described in Section 12.2. If there is no current process or if it can be preempted by the newly computable one, SCH$RSE requests an IPL 3 software interrupt.

SCH$RSE then executes an RSB instruction to return.

12.5.5.1 **System Events and Associated Priority Boosts.** System routines that report events to SCH$RSE not only describe the event and the process to which it applies but also specify one of five classes of priority increments or boosts that may be applied to the base priority of the process. Table 12.3 lists the events, priority class, and potential amount of priority increment applied to the process. The table does not show AST queuing, because system routines queuing ASTs to a process can select any of the priority increment classes to be associated with the queuing of an AST.

The actual software priority of the process is determined by the following steps:

1. The priority boost for the event class (see Table 12.3) is added to the base priority of the process (PCB$B_PRIB).
2. If the process has a current priority higher than the result of step 1, the current priority is retained (as occurs in Figure 12.9, event 13).
3. If the higher priority of steps 1 and 2 is more than 15, then the base priority of the process is used. (Note that this test accomplishes two checks at the same time. First, all real-time processes fit this criterion, with the result that real-time processes do not have their priorities adjusted in response to system events. Second, priority boosts cannot move a normal process into the real-time priority range.)

A side effect of step 3 is that real-time processes always execute at their base priorities. Further, note that normal processes with base priorities from 10 to 15 do not always receive priority increments as events occur. As the base priority of a normal process is moved closer to 15, the process spends a greater amount of time at its base priority. Priority 14 and 15 processes experience no priority boosts. Thus, this strategy benefits those processes that most need it—I/O-bound and interactive processes with base priorities of 4 through 9. Processes with elevated base priorities do not require this assistance as they are always at these levels.

An example of priority adjustment that occurs over time for several processes is given in Figure 12.9. The following notes relate to the event numbers along the time axis of the figure:

①Process C becomes computable. Process A is preempted.
②C hibernates. A executes again, one priority level lower.

302

Table 12.3 System Events and Associated Priority Boosts

Event	Priority Class[1]	Priority Boost
Page fault read complete	0 (PRI$_NULL)	0
Inswap	0	0
Outswap	0	0
Collided page available	0	0
Quantum end	0	0[2]
$GETxxI completion[3]	0	0
$SNDJBC completion[3]	0	0
Direct I/O completion[3]	1 (PRI$_IOCOM)	2
Nonterminal buffered I/O completion[3]	1	2
Update section write completion[3]	1	2
Set priority	1	2
Event flag set through $SETEF	1	2
Modified write of deleted page complete	1	2
Resource available	2 (PRI$_RESAVL)	3
Mutex available	2	3
Job quota returned	2	3
Free page available	2	3
Resource lock granted[3]	2	3
Wake a process	2	3
Resume a process	2	3
Resume a process for deletion	2	3
Timer request expiration[3]	2 (PRI$_TIMER)	3
Terminal output completion[3]	3 (PRI$_TOCOM)	4
Terminal input completion[3]	4 (PRI$_TICOM)	6
Process creation	4	6

[1] Routines that report system events pass an increment class to the scheduler. The scheduler uses this class as a byte index into a table of values (local symbol B_PINC in module RSE) to compute the actual boost.

[2] When a normal process reaches quantum end, its priority is lowered to its base if there is a COMO process. Otherwise, the process's priority is decremented.

[3] This priority boost is part of reporting that the event flag associated with the request has been set. An AST may be queued to the process as well, with the same boost specified. The process priority is affected only if the process is in a wait.

③ A experiences quantum end. Because there is a computable outswapped process (which is B), A is rescheduled at its base priority.

④ The swapper process now executes to inswap B, and B is scheduled for execution.

⑤ B is preempted by C.

⑥ B executes again, one priority level lower.

⑦ B requests an I/O operation to a device other than a terminal. A executes at its base priority.

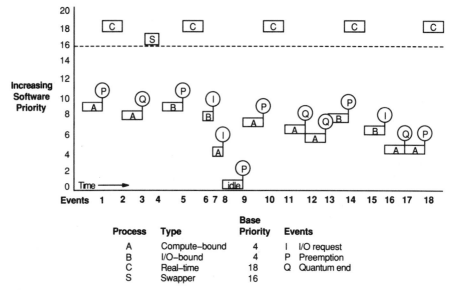

Process	Type	Base Priority	Events	
A	Compute–bound	4	I	I/O request
B	I/O–bound	4	P	Preemption
C	Real–time	18	Q	Quantum end
S	Swapper	16		

Figure 12.9
Priorities and Priority Adjustments

⑧ A requests a terminal output operation and waits for its completion. There is no process that can be scheduled. The idle loop (see Section 12.6.4) executes.

⑨ A executes following I/O completion at its base priority + 3. (The applied boost was 4, and A's priority was subsequently decremented when it was rescheduled.)

⑩ A is preempted by C.

⑪ A executes again, one priority level lower.

⑫ A experiences quantum end and is rescheduled at one priority level lower. A's priority is not lowered to its base because there is no computable outswapped process.

⑬ B's output completes. A priority boost of 2 is not applied to B's base priority because the result would be less than B's current priority. Although B's priority is higher than that of A, it is not high enough to preempt A, which continues to execute until quantum end. B then executes.

⑭ B is preempted by C.

⑮ B executes again, one priority level lower.

⑯ B requests an I/O operation. A executes again, one priority level lower. (A has reached its base priority.)

⑰ A experiences quantum end, and because there are no other computable processes of equal or higher priority, A continues to execute at the same priority (its base priority).

⑱ A is preempted by C.

12.5.6   **PIXSCAN Priority Boosts**

The pixscan mechanism gives occasional priority boosts to normal priority COM and COMO processes. The SYSGEN parameter PIXSCAN specifies the maximum number of processes that can receive this boost each second. The priority boost prevents a high-priority, compute-intensive job from continuously blocking lower priority processes and causing potential deadlocks. A deadlock might occur, for example, if a low-priority process acquired a volume lock on a critical disk but could not receive enough CPU time to complete its use of the lock and release it.

The mechanism is implemented in the routine SCH$PIXSCAN, in module RSE, invoked once a second from EXE$TIMEOUT (see Chapter 11).

SCH$PIXSCAN takes the following steps:

1. It first tests whether SGN$GW_PIXSCAN, the SYSGEN parameter, is 0. A zero value disables this mechanism, and SCH$PIXSCAN simply returns to its invoker. Its default value is 1.
2. A nonzero value in SGN$GW_PIXSCAN is the maximum number of processes that may be boosted. SCH$PIXSCAN acquires the SCHED spinlock. No IPL change is necessary because it is already executing at IPL 8.
3. SCH$PIXSCAN determines whether there are any processes eligible for boost, that is, COM and COMO processes with external priorities 0 through 15. If there are none, it releases the SCHED spinlock and returns.
4. If there are eligible processes, it determines the priority of the highest priority normal process that is CUR, COM, or COMO. This is the value to which selected processes will be boosted.
5. SCH$PIXSCAN uses the low bit of EXE$GL_ABSTIM as a "coin" to determine whether to begin scanning each priority level's compute queues with the COM or COMO queue. In an outer loop, it scans the COM and COMO queues, starting with the (external) priority 0. SCH$PIXSCAN stops when one of the following occurs:

    —It reaches the queues with the same priority as the boost value computed in step 4.
    —It has boosted the maximum number of processes.
    —It reaches a process that has reached quantum end within a time interval less than the SYSGEN parameter DORMANTWAIT.

    Examining the processes in a particular nonempty compute queue, SCH$PIXSCAN performs the following steps for each process:

    a. It compares PCB$L_ONQTIME plus the SYSGEN parameter DORMANTWAIT, expressed in 10-millisecond units, to the current absolute time, EXE$GL_ABSTIM_TICS. If the latter is less, the process is not dormant and has not been waiting for the CPU long enough to get a boost. By implication, no other process in that or any higher priority queue is likely to be dormant. The default value of DORMANTWAIT is 2 seconds.

    b. If the process is dormant, SCH$PIXSCAN sets the low-order bit in its pixscan history longword, PCB$L_PIXHIST. This longword is shifted left at each quantum end to record whether the process had a pixscan boost during its past executions. The pixscan history of a process is significant for quantum-end automatic working set limit reductions, as described in Chapter 17. It invokes SCH$CHSEP, in module RSE, to boost the process's priority.

    6. SCH$PIXSCAN releases the SCHED spinlock and returns.

12.6 RESCHEDULING INTERRUPT

The IPL 3 interrupt service routine schedules processes for execution. The function of this interrupt service routine is to remove the currently executing process by storing the contents of the process-private processor (hardware) registers and to replace the register contents with those of the highest priority computable resident process. This operation, known as context switching, is accompanied by modifications to the process state, current priority, and state queue of the affected processes.

The VAX architecture was designed to assist the software in performing critical, commonly performed operations. The mechanism of replacing the hardware context of the current process with the context of a different process is an example of hardware assistance to the operating system. The switching of hardware context is performed by two special-purpose instructions, SVPCTX and LDPCTX, which save and load the hardware context of a process.

12.6.1 Hardware Context

The definition of a process from the viewpoint of the hardware is known as the hardware context. This collection of data is the set of processor registers whose contents are unique to the process. These include the following:

- General registers: R0 through R11, AP, FP, SP, and PC
- Per-process stack pointers for kernel, executive, supervisor, and user mode stacks (some VAX CPUs implement these stack pointers only as locations in the hardware PCB)
- PSL
- AST level processor register, PR$_ASTLVL
- Memory-mapping registers for the program and control regions: P0BR, P0LR, P1BR, and P1LR

The current values for most registers forming the hardware context of the current process are maintained only in the registers themselves. When a

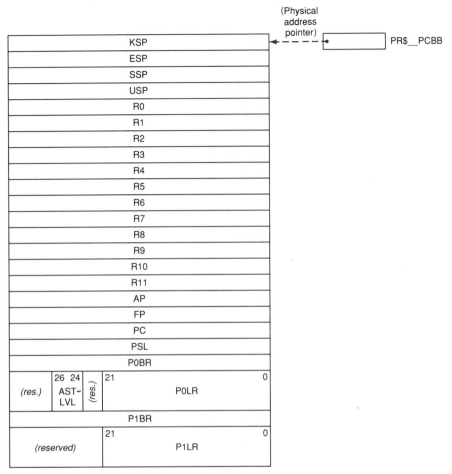

Figure 12.10
Layout of the Hardware Process Control Block

process is not executing, its hardware context is contained in the hardware PCB.

The hardware PCB (see Figures 12.10 and 12.11) is a part of the fixed portion of the PHD for each process. It is resident in memory whenever the corresponding process is. The VMS executive normally accesses a PHD through offsets from its starting virtual address.

However, during context switches, the CPU microcode must access the hardware PCB directly without address translation; it uses the value in the PCB base register (PR$_PCBB), the physical address of the hardware PCB for the currently executing process. SCH$SCHED is responsible for initializing PR$_PCBB. When it selects a process for execution, it copies the value in PCB$L_PHYPCB. The swapper initializes PCB$L_PHYPCB when it swaps a process into memory.

Figure 12.11 illustrates access to the hardware PCB.

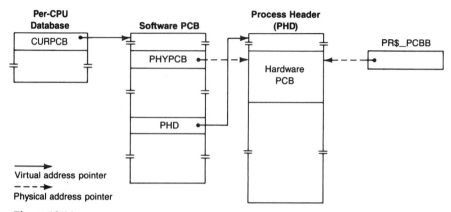

Figure 12.11
Access to the Hardware Process Control Block

12.6.2   **SVPCTX Instruction**

The save process context instruction, SVPCTX, performs several operations, assuming a special set of initial and final conditions. It assumes the following initial conditions:

- The current access mode is kernel.
- The PC and PSL to be saved for the process are on the current stack. If the SVPCTX instruction that executes is the one in the rescheduling interrupt service routine, the PC and PSL are on the kernel stack as a result of the IPL 3 software interrupt. If the SVPCTX instruction that executes is one in a routine that places a process into a wait, the PC and PSL have been chosen to place the process back into the wait, if necessary, after it is reexecuted.
- The register PR$_PCBB contains the physical address of the hardware PCB for the current process.
- The current values of ASTLVL, P0BR, P0LR, P1BR, and P1LR are already stored in the hardware PCB.

When the SVPCTX instruction is executed, VAX CPU microcode performs the following operations:

1. It stores the per-process stack pointers for the four access mode stacks in the hardware PCB, unless this is a processor type that implements only the hardware PCB forms of them.
2. It copies the general registers (R0 through R11, AP, and FP) to the hardware PCB.
3. It pops the PC and PSL from the current stack into the hardware PCB.

Finally, the SVPCTX instruction microcode saves the current stack pointer (SP) in the kernel stack field of the hardware PCB and switches to the interrupt stack (by setting the PSL$V_IS bit and copying the PR$_ISP register contents into the SP register). Switching to the systemwide interrupt stack is essential because there is no current process once the instruction completes.

The ASTLVL, P0BR, P0LR, P1BR, and P1LR fields of the hardware PCB are not changed. It is the responsibility of the various system components that alter these fields always to update both the hardware PCB fields and the per-process processor registers. ASTLVL is unusual in that it is altered as a result of normal system operation when the process is not current. In that case, only the hardware PCB field is altered. The processor register is not altered because the process does not own that register when it is not the current process.

The memory-mapping fields do not change frequently compared to the frequency of context switching. The overhead of storing these fields in the hardware PCB is incurred only when the field values change.

The SVPCTX instruction occurs in several locations in the executive:

- SCH$RESCHED, the rescheduling interrupt service routine, executes this instruction to remove the current (and still computable) process from execution.
- SCH$WAIT, in module RSE, executes this instruction to place the current process into a wait state.
- MMG$SVPCTX, in module PAGEFAULT, executes a SVPCTX instruction to place a process into one of the memory management wait states (PFW, FPG, COLPG).
- At the end of process deletion, the process being deleted is removed from execution with a SVPCTX instruction.
- SCH$CUR_TO_COM, in module RSE, saves the context of a process current on a CPU about to be shut down.

12.6.3 LDPCTX Instruction

The load process context instruction, LDPCTX, performs the operations required in establishing the hardware context of the process. The instruction assumes the following initial conditions:

- The processor is in kernel mode on the interrupt stack.
- The register PR$_PCBB contains the physical address of the hardware PCB for the process that is to become current.

When the LDPCTX instruction is executed, VAX CPU microcode performs the following operations:

1. Per-process translation buffer entries are invalidated. A translation buffer caches virtual page numbers and the numbers of the physical pages to which they are mapped, thus speeding up address translation. All the per-process translation buffer entries belong to the previous process. They are invalidated to prevent mistranslation of virtual addresses and to protect the data of the previous process.

2. It loads the per-process stack pointers (KSP, ESP, SSP, and USP) from the hardware PCB, unless this is a processor type that implements only the hardware PCB forms of them.

3. It loads the general registers (R0 through R11, AP, and FP) into the corresponding processor registers.

4. It checks the legality of the memory-mapping registers' values saved in the hardware PCB (P0BR, P0LR, P1BR, and P1LR) and then loads the values into the registers. Until they are loaded, the values in the registers belong to the previous process.

5. It loads the PR$_ASTLVL register.

6. It saves the contents of the current stack pointer register (SP) in the interrupt stack pointer register (ISP).

7. It clears the PSL$V_IS bit to indicate the switch to the kernel stack.

8. It copies the saved kernel stack pointer register (KSP) to SP.

9. Finally, it pushes the saved PC and PSL onto the kernel stack. The next instruction is expected to be an REI instruction. The REI microcode pops the two longwords. It validates the PSL against the rules described in Chapter 2 and loads the PC and PSL registers.

The only occurrence of a LDPCTX instruction in the VMS executive is the one shown in Example 12.1, the rescheduling interrupt service routine.

12.6.4 Rescheduling Interrupt Service Routine

The IPL 3 interrupt service routine contains two parts:

- SCH$RESCHED, which preserves the hardware context of the currently executing process and removes it from execution
- SCH$SCHED, which selects the next process to be scheduled for execution

As shown in Figure 12.12, SCH$RESCHED is requested as an IPL 3 software interrupt by several different routines:

- SCH$RSE and SCH$CHSE/SCH$CHSEP, when a resident process becomes computable whose priority allows it to preempt the current process
- SCH$QEND, when a current process reaches quantum end, it is a normal process, and there is a COM process of equal or higher priority
- SCH$CHANGE_CUR_PRIORITY, when a current process changes its priority and there is a COM process whose priority is higher
- SCH$ACQUIRE_AFFINITY, when a current process acquires implicit affinity for a processor other than the one on which it is executing
- SCH$REMOVE_CPU_CAP, when a current process is executing on a CPU that just lost a capability required by the process
- SCH$REQUIRE_CAPABILITY, when a current process requires a capability not present on the CPU on which it is executing
- EXE$RUNDWN, when a process's just-restored permanently required capabilities do not match those of the CPU on which it is executing

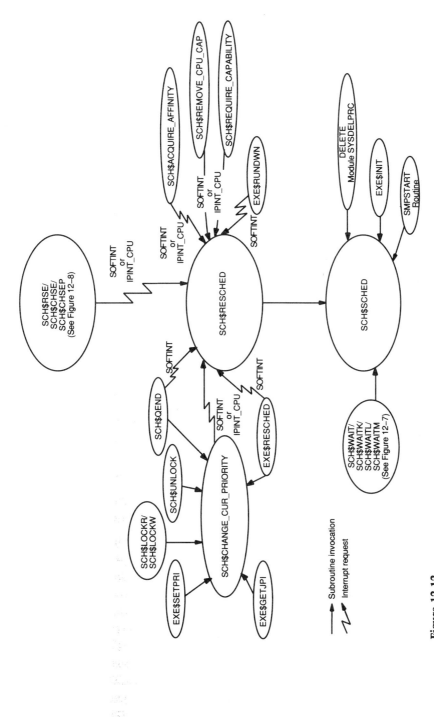

Figure 12.12
Paths to Rescheduling

Note that sometimes an IPL 3 interrupt can be directly requested on the appropriate CPU. Other times, an interprocessor interrupt must be requested first so that the IPL 3 interrupt can be requested on the appropriate CPU by the interprocessor interrupt service routine.

Under some circumstances, there may not be a current process to be saved by SCH$RESCHED. In these cases, executive routines transfer control directly to SCH$SCHED for process selection.

As shown in Figure 12.12, the routines that transfer directly to SCH$SCHED include the following:

- SCH$WAIT and its subentry points, when a current process has been placed into a wait state
- DELETE, in module SYSDELPRC, when a current process has been deleted
- EXE$INIT, in module INIT, leaving system context during system initialization, to schedule the first process on the primary processor (or only processor)
- STRVA, in module [SYSLOA]SMPSTART_*xxx*, the routine that performs secondary processor initialization, leaving system context on a secondary processor, to schedule its first process

SCH$RESCHED performs the following steps. (The numbers in the following list correspond to numbers in Example 12.1, a slightly simplified and rearranged version of the code.)

①SCH$RESCHED first acquires the SCHED spinlock, raising IPL to IPL$_ SCHED to block concurrent access to and modification of the scheduler database.

②It then executes a SVPCTX instruction to save the hardware context of the current process in its hardware PCB. The register PR$_PCBB contains the physical address of the current process's hardware PCB. The detailed operation of the SVPCTX instruction is described in Section 12.6.2.

③It gets the address of the current process's software PCB and its current priority from the per-CPU database.

④It clears the bit corresponding to the CPU's ID in the longword corresponding to the priority in the array at SCH$AL_CPU_PRIORITY.

⑤If there are no other processes at this priority current on any CPU, it clears the bit corresponding to that priority in SCH$GL_ACTIVE_PRIORITY.

⑥It sets the bit corresponding to the process's priority in the compute queue summary longword, SCH$GL_COMQS.

⑦It changes the state of the process from CUR to COM by updating the PCB$W_STATE field.

⑧It inserts the software PCB at the tail of the COM queue corresponding to the process's current priority.

⑨It clears SCH$GL_IDLE_CPUS to signal any idle CPU that it should attempt to reschedule. The scheduler idle loop is described later in this section.

⑩ SCH$RESCHED branches into SCH$SCHED, skipping its beginning instructions. SCH$SCHED is entered directly from code that places the current process into a wait. Under these circumstances, SCH$SCHED must acquire the SCHED spinlock and update priority summary data structures to reflect the fact that the current process has been taken out of execution.

At this point, there is no current process, and SCH$SCHED searches for the next process to execute. It performs the following operations. (The numbers in the following list correspond to numbers in Example 12.1.)

⑪ It executes an FFS instruction to locate the least significant set bit in the longword SCH$GL_COMQS. The located bit position indicates the highest priority nonempty computable resident state queue.

⑫ If there is no computable resident process, SCH$SCHED branches to SCH$IDLE, which is described later in this section.

⑬ It uses the bit number as an index into the COM listheads to get the address of the listhead of the selected computable resident queue.

⑭ It removes the first PCB in the selected queue.

Note that the search for the highest priority computable resident process and the removal of its PCB from the COM queue are achieved in four instructions. The efficiency of this operation is attributable to the instruction set and the design of the scheduler database for the computable states.

⑮ If the removed PCB was the only one in the queue, SCH$SCHED clears the corresponding SCH$GL_COMQS bit to indicate that the queue is empty.

⑯ SCH$SCHED tests whether the process's required capabilities, including explicit affinity, match those of the CPU. If they do not match, it tests further to see if the capabilities can be met by any active SMP member. If they cannot, it places the process into a RWCAP MWAIT state and selects another process to run. If the process has implicit affinity for a different CPU, SCH$SCHED tries to honor it but may not (see Section 12.4).

⑰ If the capabilities match, SCH$SCHED stores the address of the new current process PCB in the per-CPU database.

⑱ SCH$SCHED changes the state of the process to current by storing the value SCH$C_CUR into the PCB$W_STATE field.

⑲ It stores the CPU's ID in PCB$L_CPU_ID.

⑳ It examines the current process priority and potentially modifies it. If the process is a real-time process or a normal process already at its base priority, then the process is scheduled at its current or base priority (they are the same). If the current process is a normal process above its base priority, then a decrease of one software priority level is performed before scheduling. Thus, priority demotions always occur before execution, and a process executes at the priority of the queue to which it will be returned (and not at the priority of the queue from which it was removed).

㉑ It copies the process's current priority to the per-CPU database.

㉒ It clears the bit corresponding to this CPU in SCH$GL_IDLE_CPUS to indicate that the CPU is not idle.

㉓ It sets the bit corresponding to the CPU's ID in the longword corresponding to the priority in the array at SCH$AL_CPU_PRIORITY.

㉔ It sets the bit corresponding to the process's current priority in SCH$GL_ACTIVE_PRIORITY.

㉕ It copies the physical address of the hardware PCB for the scheduled process from PCB$L_PHYPCB to the PR$_PCBB register.

㉖ It executes a LDPCTX instruction (see Section 12.6.3).

㉗ It releases the SCHED spinlock.

㉘ It executes an REI instruction to pass control to the scheduled process. This transfer of control is possible because the LDPCTX instruction left the PC and PSL of the scheduled process on the kernel stack. Execution of the REI instruction has the following additional effects:

—The interrupt priority level is dropped from IPL$_SCHED.

—The access mode is typically changed from kernel to a less privileged one.

—If ASTs are queued to the PCB, they are likely to be delivered at this time, depending on their access mode and the access mode at which the process is reentered (see Chapter 7).

㉙ SCH$SCHED makes consistency checks to ensure that the COM queue selected contains at least one data structure and that the data structure is actually a PCB. Failure of these tests results in a QUEUEMPTY fatal bugcheck.

If SCH$SCHED found no computable process to execute, it executes code known as the idle loop. SCH$IDLE performs the following operations. (The numbers in the following list correspond to numbers in Example 12.1.)

㉚ SCH$IDLE sets the bit corresponding to the CPU in SCH$GL_IDLE_CPUS to indicate that the CPU is idle.

㉛ It stores the address of the null PCB and a priority value of −1 in the CPU's per-CPU database.

㉜ Having made those changes, it can release the SCHED spinlock, lowering IPL to IPL$_RESCHED (3), the IPL of the rescheduling interrupt. This IPL permits software interrupts on this processor that can alter the scheduler database.

㉝ SCH$IDLE loops, testing whether its bit in SCH$GL_IDLE_CPUS is clear.

The bit is cleared as a signal that there is a resident computable process available. The time during which the routine loops is counted as null time, which the Monitor Utility displays as "Idle Time."

㉞ When this CPU's idle bit is cleared, SCH$IDLE sets bit CPU$V_SCHED in its per-CPU database to indicate that it is still idle and trying to acquire the SCHED spinlock. If an interval timer interrupt occurs while this bit is set, the interval timer interrupt service routine accounts for the CPU time as null time rather than as busy wait (MPSYNCH) time.

㉟ SCH$IDLE tries to acquire the SCHED spinlock.

㊱ Once successful, it clears CPU$V_SCHED and branches back into SCH$SCHED to repeat the attempt to select a process to execute. If another idle processor has already scheduled the computable process, this CPU may reexecute the idle loop.

Example 12.1
Rescheduling Interrupt Service Routine

```
        DECLARE_PSECT EXEC$NONPAGED_CODE ;Nonpaged exec
        .SBTTL  SCH$RESCHED RESCHEDULING  INTERRUPT HANDLER
;++
; SCH$RESCHED    - RESCHEDULING INTERRUPT HANDLER
; This routine is entered via the IPL 3 rescheduling interrupt.
; The vector for this interrupt is coded to cause execution
; on the kernel stack.
;
; ENVIRONMENT:
;       IPL = 3  Mode = kernel  IS = 0
; INPUT:
;       00(SP) = PC at reschedule interrupt
;       04(SP) = PSL at interrupt
; --
        .ALIGN  LONG
        .ENABL  LSB
        UNIVERSAL_SYMBOL SCH$RESCHED
;SCH$RESCHED::                           ;Reschedule interrupt handler
        LOCK    LOCKNAME=SCHED,-         ;Lock sched database    ①
                LOCKIPL=#IPL$_SCHED      ;Raise to SCHED IPL
        SVPCTX                           ;Save context of process ②
        FIND_CPU_DATA R3,ISTACK=YES      ;Get this CPU's per-CPU database
                                         ; (We can assume we're on
                                         ; interrupt stack)
        MOVL    CPU$L_CURPCB(R3),R1      ;Get address of current PCB ③
        MOVZBL  CPU$B_CUR_PRI(R3),R0     ;Current priority
        BICL    CPU$L_CPUID_MASK(R3),-   ;Get mask for current CPU ID
                W^SCH$AL_CPU_PRIORITY[R0]
                                         ;Clear CPU bit  ④
        BNEQ    5$                       ;Anyone else at this priority?
        SUBL3   R0,#31,R2                ;Get priority in external format
```

(continued)

Scheduling

Example 12.1 _(continued)_
Rescheduling Interrupt Service Routine

```
          BBCC    R2,-                         ;No one else  (5)
                  G^SCH$GL_ACTIVE_PRIORITY,5$
5$:       BBSS    R0,L^SCH$GL_COMQS,10$        ;Mark queue nonempty (6)
10$:      MOVW    #SCH$C_COM,PCB$W_STATE(R1)
                                               ;Set state to res compute  (7)
          MOVAQ   SCH$AQ_COMT[R0],R2           ;R2 = address of queue header
                                               ; back link
          INSQUE  (R1),@(R2)+                  ;Insert at tail of queue  (8)
          CLRL    G^SCH$GL_IDLE_CPUS           ;Tell everyone else (9)
          BRW     30$                          ;Skip acquiring spinlock again (10)
;+
; SCH$SCHED  -  SCHEDULE NEW PROCESS FOR EXECUTION
; This routine selects the highest priority executable process
; and places it in execution.
; -
          .ALIGN  LONG
          UNIVERSAL_SYMBOL SCH$SCHED
;SCH$SCHED::                                   ;Schedule for execution
          FIND_CPU_DATA R3,ISTACK=YES          ;Get base of per-CPU data
                                               ; (We can assume int. stack here)
          LOCK    LOCKNAME=SCHED,-             ;Lock sched database
                  LOCKIPL=#IPL$_SCHED          ;Raise to SCHED IPL
          MOVZBL  CPU$B_CUR_PRI(R3),R0         ;Get previous CPU priority
          BICL    CPU$L_CPUID_MASK(R3),-       ;Get mask for current CPU ID
                  W^SCH$AL_CPU_PRIORITY[R0]
                                               ;Clear CPU bit
          BNEQ    30$                          ;Anyone else at this priority?
          SUBL3   R0,#31,R2                    ;Get priority in external format
          BBCC    R2,-                         ;No one else
                  G^SCH$GL_ACTIVE_PRIORITY,30$
30$:      CLRL    R7                           ;Clear implicit affinity state
          FFS     #0,#32,L^SCH$GL_COMQS,R0
                                               ;Find first full state (11)
          BEQL    SCH$IDLE                     ;No executable process? (12)
35$:      MOVAQ   SCH$AQ_COMH[R0],R2           ;Compute queue head address  (13)
          REMQUE  @(R2)+,R4                    ;Get head of queue (14)
          BVS     QEMPTY                       ;Br if queue was empty (BUGCHECK)
          BNEQ    40$                          ;Queue not empty
          BBCC    R0,L^SCH$GL_COMQS,40$        ;Set queue empty (15)
40$:      CMPB    #DYN$C_PCB,PCB$B_TYPE(R4)
                                               ;Must be a process control block
          BNEQ    QEMPTY                       ;Otherwise fatal error
          BICL3   CPU$L_CAPABILITY(R3),-       ;Do the CPU and process match? (16)
                  PCB$L_CAPABILITY(R4),R1
          BNEQ    200$                         ;No
45$:      MOVL    R4,CPU$L_CURPCB(R3)          ;Note current PCB location (17)
          MOVW    #SCH$C_CUR,PCB$W_STATE(R4)
                                               ;Set state to current (18)
```

(continued)

316

Example 12.1 *(continued)*
Rescheduling Interrupt Service Routine

```
MOVL    CPU$L_PHY_CPUID(R3),PCB$L_CPU_ID(R4)
                                ;Save CPU ID in PCB (19)
        CMPB    R0,PCB$B_PRIB(R4)       ;Check for base priority=current
                                ; - should never be greater (20)
        BGEQ    50$             ;Yes, don't float priority
        INCB    R0              ;Move toward base priority
        MOVB    R0,PCB$B_PRI(R4)        ;Reflect priority change in PCB
50$:    MOVB    R0,CPU$B_CUR_PRI(R3)    ;Set global priority (21)
        MOVL    CPU$L_CPUID_MASK(R3),R2 ;Get CPU mask
        BICL2   R2,G^SCH$GL_IDLE_CPUS   ;Show this CPU as not idle (22)
        BISL    R2,W^SCH$AL_CPU_PRIORITY[R0]
                                ;Set CPU bit (23)
        SUBL3   R0,#31,R2       ;Get priority in external format
        BBSS    R2,G^SCH$GL_ACTIVE_PRIORITY,51$
                                ;Priority now active (24)
51$:    MTPR    PCB$L_PHYPCB(R4),#PR$_PCBB
                                ;Set PCB base phys addr (25)
        LDPCTX                  ;Restore context (26)
        UNLOCK  LOCKNAME=SCHED          ;Unlock SCHED database -
                                ; no IPL change (27)
        REI                     ;Normal return (28)
QEMPTY: BUG_CHECK QUEUEMPTY,FATAL       ;Scheduling queue empty (29)
;
; Make assorted checks to determine the type of capability mismatch
;
200$:   .
        .
SCH$IDLE:                       ;No active, executable process
        BISL2   CPU$L_CPUID_MASK(R3),-  ;Show this CPU as idle (30)
                G^SCH$GL_IDLE_CPUS
        MOVL    G^SCH$AR_NULLPCB,CPU$L_CURPCB(R3)
                                ;Note null PCB as default
        MNEGB   #1,CPU$B_CUR_PRI(R3)    ;Set priority to -1
                                ; to signal idle (31)
        UNLOCK  LOCKNAME=SCHED,-        ;Unlock sched database (32)
                NEWIPL=#IPL$_RESCHED    ;Drop IPL to rescheduling level
        MOVL    CPU$L_PHY_CPUID(R3),R1  ;Get our CPU ID
61$:    BBS     R1,G^SCH$GL_IDLE_CPUS,61$
                                ;Loop until we aren't idle (33)
65$:    BISB    #CPU$M_SCHED,CPU$B_FLAGS(R3)
                                ;Indicate idle vying for SCHED (34)
        LOCK    LOCKNAME=SCHED,-        ;Lock sched database (35)
                LOCKIPL=#IPL$_SCHED     ;Raise to SCHED IPL
        BICB    #CPU$M_SCHED,CPU$B_FLAGS(R3)
                                ;Indicate no longer vying
                                ; for SCHED (36)
        BRW     30$             ;Go try for process
```

317

13 Process Control and Communication

I was alone and unable to communicate with anyone. I did
not know the names of anything. I did not even know things
had names. Then one day, after she had tried a number of
approaches, my teacher held my hand under the water pump
on our farm. As the cool water ran over my hand and arm, she
spelled the word water in my other hand. She spelled it over and
over, and suddenly I knew there was a name for things and that
I would never be completely alone again.

Helen Keller

VMS provides a number of services that allow one process to control the execution of another. It also provides a variety of mechanisms by which processes can obtain information about each other and communicate with one another.

VMS process control system services enable a process to affect its own scheduling state or that of another process, either on the local system or on a remote VAXcluster node. These services also enable a process to alter some of its own characteristics (such as name or priority). The process information system services allow a process to obtain detailed information about other processes, both on the local system and on other VAXcluster nodes. This chapter describes the implementation of the process control and process information system services.

Communication mechanisms available to VMS processes include event flags, mailboxes, the lock management system services (lock manager), global shared data sections, and shared files. Other chapters describe the implementation of these mechanisms. This chapter briefly discusses the manner in which a process might use these mechanisms to communicate with another process.

Table 13.1 summarizes the system services related to process control and process information.

13.1 REQUIREMENTS FOR AFFECTING ANOTHER PROCESS

Before a process can obtain information on another process or alter it in any way, it must have a means of uniquely identifying the process within a VAXcluster system. In addition, it must have appropriate privileges or user identification code (UIC) based access to the process.

Process identification and privilege checking are centralized in the routine

318

Table 13.1 Summary of Process System Services

Service Name	Scope of Processes Affected	Privileges Checked
Hibernate ($HIBER)	Issuing process [1]	None
Wake Process from Hibernation ($WAKE)	Same VAXcluster	GROUP or WORLD
Schedule Wakeup ($SCHDWK)	Same VAXcluster	GROUP or WORLD
Cancel Wakeup ($CANWAK)	Same VAXcluster	GROUP or WORLD
Suspend Process ($SUSPND)	Same VAXcluster	GROUP or WORLD
Resume Process ($RESUME)	Same VAXcluster	GROUP or WORLD
Exit ($EXIT)	Issuing process	None
Force Exit ($FORCEX)	Same VAXcluster	GROUP or WORLD
Create Process ($CREPRC)	Same node	DETACH for different user identification codes (UICs)
Delete Process ($DELPRC)	Same VAXcluster	GROUP or WORLD
Set AST Enable ($SETAST)	Issuing process	Access mode check
Set Power Recovery AST ($SETPRA)	Issuing process	Access mode check
Set Priority ($SETPRI)	Same VAXcluster	ALTPRI and either GROUP or WORLD
Set Process Name ($SETPRN)	Issuing process	None
Set Resource Wait Mode ($SETRWM)	Issuing process [2]	None
Set System Service Failure Exception Mode ($SETSFM)	Issuing process [2]	Access mode check
Set Process Swap Mode ($SETSWM)	Issuing process [2]	PSWAPM
Reschedule Process ($RESCHED)	Issuing process	None
Get Job/Process Information ($GETJPI)	Same VAXcluster	GROUP or WORLD
Process Scan ($PROCESS_SCAN)	Same VAXcluster	GROUP or WORLD

[1] As part of the $CREPRC system service, a process can specify that the process being created hibernate before a specified image executes.

[2] Through the $CREPRC system service, a process can be created with this characteristic.

EXE$NAMPID, in module SYSPCNTRL. Process control and process information system services that can affect processes other than their requestor all invoke EXE$NAMPID; thus they all identify processes and check privileges in the same manner.

Before VMS Version 5.2, the scope of the process control and process information system services was restricted to the local node; the scope has become VAXcluster-wide with the addition of clusterwide process service (CWPS) routines. These routines provide a transparent mechanism by which a process can affect a target process on another VAXcluster member. Section 13.1.3 contains more information on CWPS routines.

13.1.1 Identifying the Target Process

Process control and process information system services have arguments that specify the target process by process name and process ID (PID). The process requesting the service specifies one or the other of these arguments, or neither one to default to itself.

Process name is always implicitly qualified by UIC group. That is, a process can identify by name only processes within the same UIC group as itself. With VMS Version 5.2, the PRCNAM argument can identify a process on another VAXcluster node. It can include up to six characters for the node name, followed by a double colon.

Two forms of PID identify a process: an internally visible PID, called an IPID, and an externally visible PID, called an EPID. The IPID, stored in PCB$L_PID, uniquely identifies a process on a single node. The low word of the IPID is the index of the process control block (PCB) in the local PCB vector. The EPID, an extension of the IPID, uniquely identifies a process in a VAXcluster system by including a VAXcluster node identifier. It is stored in PCB$L_EPID. Chapter 25 describes the layout and creation of the IPID and EPID.

Because the IPID is only relevant to kernel mode code on the local node, most system utilities, such as SHOW SYSTEM and the Monitor Utility, display EPIDs. An EPID is passed as a system service argument to identify a process by its PID.

A legitimate EPID never has its high-order bit set; the Get Job/Process Information ($GETJPI) and Process Scan ($PROCESS_SCAN) system services can thus use a negative value in an EPID field as a wildcard indicator.

13.1.2 Locating the Process and Checking Privileges

Regardless of how the target of a process control or process information service is specified, VMS must determine whether the process exists within the VAXcluster system and whether the requesting process has the ability to affect the target. These two checks are centralized in EXE$NAMPID.

EXE$NAMPID's argument list includes the EPID of the target process and the process name from the process control system service's PRCNAM argument. When neither argument is specified, the most common case, the requesting process is also the target process. EXE$NAMPID is optimized for this case. When both arguments are present, EXE$NAMPID uses the EPID to identify the target.

EXE$NAMPID performs the following:

1. It determines whether the requesting process is also the target process. If so, privilege checks are unnecessary. EXE$NAMPID obtains the SCHED

spinlock, raising interrupt priority level (IPL) to IPL$_SCHED, and returns successfully to the system service with the IPID, the PCB address, and optionally the EPID. It returns at IPL$_SCHED, holding the SCHED spinlock.

2. Otherwise, when the requesting process is not the target, EXE$NAMPID attempts to locate the target process using the EPID or, if the EPID is not specified, the process name.

   If the EPID or process name indicates a valid local process, EXE$NAMPID proceeds to step 3.

   If the target process is not valid locally, the EPID or the process name must designate a legitimate remote VAXcluster node. Only the remote node can determine if the target process is valid.

   —If the EPID or process name indicates that the target process is on a valid VAXcluster node, EXE$NAMPID returns the error status SS$_REMOTE_PROC. Section 13.1.3 describes the steps taken to locate a target process on a remote node.

   —If the EPID specifies an unknown VAXcluster node, EXE$NAMPID returns the error status SS$_NONEXPR (nonexistent process), which becomes the system service's return status.

   —If the process name specifies an unknown VAXcluster node, EXE$NAMPID returns the error status SS$_NOSUCHNODE (nonexistent node).

   —If the process name uses an incorrect format for the node name, EXE$NAMPID attempts to interpret it as a logical name and returns the error status SS$_IVLOGNAM.

3. For a local target process, EXE$NAMPID invokes EXE$CHECK_PCB_PRIV, in module SYSPCNTRL, to determine whether the requesting process has the ability to examine or modify its target.

   EXE$CHECK_PCB_PRIV makes the following tests, proceeding until one is successful or until there are no more:

   a. If the requesting and target processes are in the same job tree, that is, share a job information block (JIB), EXE$CHECK_PCB_PRIV returns successfully.

   b. If the requesting process and the target process have the same UIC, EXE$CHECK_PCB_PRIV returns successfully.

   c. If the requesting process has WORLD privilege, EXE$CHECK_PCB_PRIV returns successfully.

   d. If the requesting process and the target process are members of the same UIC group and the requesting process has GROUP privilege, EXE$CHECK_PCB_PRIV returns successfully.

4. If any test is successful, EXE$NAMPID returns control to the system service at IPL$_SCHED, holding the SCHED spinlock. It returns the

address of the target process PCB in R4. Note that this return alters the contents of R4, which formerly contained the PCB address of the requesting process.

If all these tests fail, EXE$NAMPID returns the error SS$_NOPRIV, which becomes the system service's return status.

13.1.3 Servicing a Request for a Remote Process

An EPID identifies the VAXcluster node on which a process might exist and the PCB vector slot on that node that contains the process's PCB. Validating an EPID occurs in two parts; any node in the VAXcluster system can confirm that the node identifier is legitimate, but only the node thus identified can access the PCB vector slot.

EXE$NAMPID is invoked by a process control or process information system service to locate its target process. If EXE$NAMPID does not locate the target process on the local node, it invokes a CWPS routine to verify that the node identified by the EPID or PRCNAM argument exists within the VAXcluster system. Executive code running on the identified node must subsequently confirm the existence of the target process.

If the CWPS routine successfully identifies the remote VAXcluster node, it returns the error status SS$_REMOTE_PROC. In response to this status, the system service procedure routes the request to CWPS. CWPS allocates and initializes a structure to describe the service request and the requesting process and transmits it to the remote node using system communication services (SCS). If the system service is a synchronous one, such as $SUSPND, the process enters the RSN$_CLUSRV resource wait state until a response is received from the remote node. For a system service such as $GETJPI[W], the status SS$_NORMAL is returned to the caller for the asynchronous form or to a synchronization routine for the synchronous form.

On the remote node, a CWPS dispatch routine executing in system context receives the service request. It allocates a composite structure to describe the request locally. It then queues a kernel mode asynchronous system trap (AST) to the CLUSTER_SERVER process, determining the address of the AST routine from the function to be performed; for instance, a process control function causes the CLUSTER_SERVER process to execute CWPS$SRCV_PCNTRL_AST, in module [SYSLOA]CWPS_SERVICE_RECV.

For a typical process control function, the CLUSTER_SERVER process initializes a structure that mimics the PCB of the requesting process and invokes EXE$NAMPID. Thus, EXE$NAMPID performs privilege and access checks, which require a PCB, regardless of whether a request is remote or local. If EXE$NAMPID detects an error, the CWPS routine returns the error status to the requesting process on the original node. Otherwise, it requests the system service on behalf of the requesting process. The system service returns status and information to the CWPS routine, which transmits that information to a CWPS receiver on the initiating node. This routine returns the status and data to the original requestor of the system service. (In the case of an asynchronous service like $GETJPI, the standard kernel mode AST is delivered at service completion.)

Figure 13.1 shows this sequence of events, slightly simplified, for an asynchronous process control system service such as $GETJPI.

13.2 PROCESS INFORMATION SYSTEM SERVICES

The process information system services, $GETJPI and $PROCESS_SCAN, return selected information about a process or group of processes within a VAXcluster system.

The $PROCESS_SCAN system service, introduced in VMS Version 5.2, functions as an adjunct to the $GETJPI system service. It creates and maintains a search context that filters the information returned by $GETJPI. In the traditional form of $GETJPI wildcard processing, an image requests the $GETJPI service from a loop, obtaining information about the next sequential process with each request. The image tests the returned information to decide whether the process is really of interest; for instance, an image looking for all processes belonging to a particular user name obtains the user name field through the $GETJPI service and compares each returned user name with its desired user name.

The $PROCESS_SCAN service simplifies this path; an image requests the service $PROCESS_SCAN to record its search criteria in a context block, then passes that context block address on subsequent $GETJPI requests. When the $GETJPI system service procedure is passed a context block address, it invokes process scan subroutines for the actual processing. Its requestor only receives information on processes matching the search criteria and is no longer required to filter the data itself.

13.2.1 Data Structures Related to the $PROCESS_SCAN System Service

The $PROCESS_SCAN system service uses fields in the process header (PHD), context blocks, $GETJPI buffer areas, and CWPS structures to service requests.

An image can request the $PROCESS_SCAN service multiple times with different search criteria to create multiple context blocks. For instance, to search a VAXcluster system, the image could either create one context block matching all cluster nodes, or create a separate context block for each node and conduct the remote scans in parallel. The PHD contains a listhead for a process's context blocks at offset PHD$Q_PSCANCTX_QUEUE. At PHD$W_PSCANCTX_SEQNUM, the PHD contains a sequence number that matches the value in the PSCANCTX$W_SEQNUM field of valid context blocks.

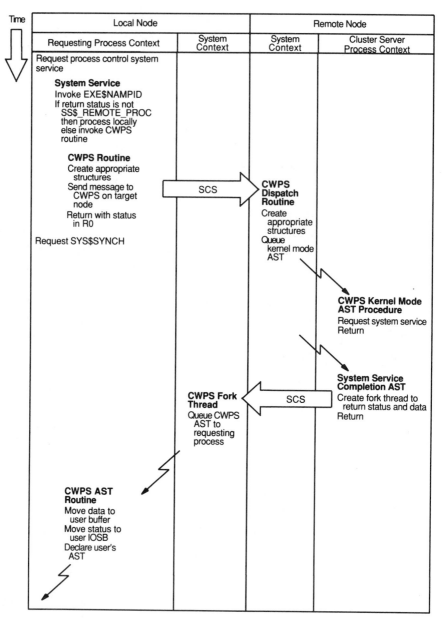

Figure 13.1
CWPS Remote Request Processing

The context block, pictured in Figure 13.2, is the primary data structure created and maintained by the $PROCESS_SCAN service. The $PSCAN-CTXDEF macro defines its header; the size of the structure varies. The item list and data areas follow the header. They contain copies of the $PROCESS_SCAN items comprising the process filter and the associated comparison data. PSCANCTX$W_ITMLSTOFF and PSCANCTX$W_BUFFEROFF contain the offsets from the PSCANCTX structure to these areas. The $PROCESS_SCAN service allocates the PSCANCTX structure from the process allocation region.

If a search involves VAXcluster nodes other than the local node, the context block includes a cluster system ID (CSID) area. This area contains the CSID of each node where the search is to be conducted. PSCANCTX$W_CSIDOFF contains the offset to this area. PSCANCTX$L_CUR_CSID stores the CSID of the node currently being scanned, with zero indicating the local node. The context block fields PSCANCTX$L_CUR_IPID, PSCAN$L_CUR_EPID, and PSCANCTX$L_NEXT_IPID track local PCB vector scans (see Section 13.2.3).

Only one $GETJPI request at a time can use a particular context block to reference other VAXcluster nodes. PSCANCTX$V_BUSY in PSCANCTX$L_FLAGS locks the context block; Section 13.2.3 describes its use.

When a remote node is scanned, the offset PSCANCTX$L_CWPSSRV contains the address of a structure whose symbolic offsets are defined by the $CWPSSRV macro. Allocated from nonpaged pool, this variable-sized structure contains information to be passed to the remote node by CWPS.

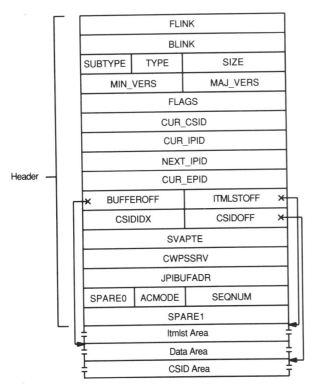

Figure 13.2
$PROCESS_SCAN Context Block (PSCANCTX)

325

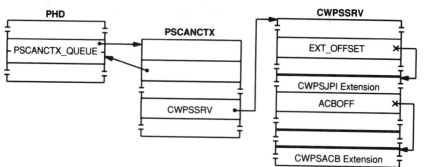

Figure 13.3
Structure Linkage

CWPSSRV$L_EXT_OFFSET contains the index to a CWPSSRV extension created for a $GETJPI request, defined by the $CWPSJPI macro. Figure 13.3 shows this linkage.

To execute more efficiently on a wildcard request in a VAXcluster system, an image can request that the $PROCESS_SCAN and $GETJPI services bundle information about several target processes rather than return the information one process at a time. If the image requests this $GETJPI buffering, the $PROCESS_SCAN service allocates a buffer from the process allocation region and stores its address in PSCANCTX$L_JPIBUFADR. This variable-sized structure, whose header offsets are defined by the $PSCANBUFDEF macro, contains a copy of the requested $GETJPI item codes followed by the area where returned data is stored.

13.2.2 The $PROCESS_SCAN System Service

The $PROCESS_SCAN system service procedure EXE$PROCESS_SCAN, in module PROCESS_SCAN, executes in kernel mode. The service includes additional routines in modules PROCESS_SCAN_ITMLST and PROCESS_SCAN_CHECK.

The service has two arguments: PIDCTX and ITMLST.

- PIDCTX is a longword in which the service returns the address of the context block. The program passes the returned PIDCTX to the $GETJPI service as the PID argument.
- ITMLST is the address of an item list composed of one or more entries. Each entry contains the coded value of a selection criterion for $PROCESS_SCAN, either the value or the address of the item, and flags controlling the manner in which the $PROCESS_SCAN and $GETJPI services use the item.

EXE$PROCESS_SCAN performs the following:

1. It verifies that the PIDCTX argument was supplied and that it specifies a location writable from the access mode of the requestor, returning the error status SS$_INVSRQ or SS$_ACCVIO as appropriate.

2. If EXE$PROCESS_SCAN discovers that the PIDCTX argument contains the address of a previous context block, it removes the context block from the process's queue of active context blocks and deallocates the block and any data structures linked to it. (Otherwise, context blocks are deallocated at image exit.)

3. If no ITMLST argument is specified, EXE$PROCESS_SCAN merely returns a success status to its caller, accomplishing no useful work. Otherwise, EXE$PROCESS_SCAN checks each item in the item list for the following conditions:

   —The requested item code is recognized.
   —The length of the buffer is appropriate for the item code.
   —The buffer descriptor and the buffer contents are readable.
   —The flags specified for a particular item code are appropriate.

   In addition, the item list must be well formed; for example, the last item cannot specify the flag PSCAN$V_OR.

4. Some item codes apply to processes; others, like PSCAN$_NODE_CSID and PSCAN$_HW_NAME, apply to VAXcluster nodes. If the node is part of a VAXcluster system and a specified item code indicates a node context, EXE$PROCESS_SCAN invokes a CWPS routine to create a list of the current VAXcluster nodes and their characteristics. From this, it eliminates nodes that do not meet the search criteria and constructs a table of the remaining CSIDs. Only processes on these nodes are scanned.

5. EXE$PROCESS_SCAN allocates a longword-aligned piece of memory from the process allocation region for the context block. The structure size is the sum of the sizes of the fixed header, the item list entries that apply to processes, their associated data for comparison, and the CSID area (see Figure 13.2). If a $GETJPI buffer was requested, its size is included in the allocation as well.

6. It increments the process scan sequence number in the PHD, copies that value to the context block, and inserts the new context block onto the PHD queue.

7. It initializes the context block, including the offset to the item list (PSCANCTX$W_ITMLSTOFF), the offset to the data area (PSCAN-CTX$W_BUFFEROFF), the CSID table and the offset to the table (PSCANCTX$W_CSIDIDX), the item list and data areas, the address of the $GETJPI buffer (PSCANCTX$L_JPIBUFADR), and the flags.

8. Finally, it negates the address of the context block. This indicates a wildcard context, yet also locates the context block and differentiates the context from the traditional $GETJPI wildcard indicator, −1 in the high word of the PID. EXE$PROCESS_SCAN returns this value to its caller in the PIDCTX location.

The $GETJPI service can now be requested to use the context created by $PROCESS_SCAN.

13.2.3   **The $GETJPI System Service**

The $GETJPI[W] system service provides selected information about a specified process: the process requesting the $GETJPI service (the default), a process explicitly identified by EPID, or the next process located in a wildcard scan. The service can obtain information from the PCB, JIB, PHD, and control region.

$GETJPI arguments include the following:

- The EFN argument: the number of an event flag to be set when the request is complete. If none is specified, event flag 0 is used.
- The PID argument: the EPID of one process from which to collect information, a traditional $GETJPI wildcard indicator, or a context block from $PROCESS_SCAN.
- The PRCNAM argument: the node and process name of the target process, used if the process ID is not specified.
- The ITMLST argument: the address of an item list. The item list can contain multiple entries, each of which includes a code indicating the information to be returned, the size and address of a buffer to hold the information, and a location to contain the actual size of the returned information. The item list terminates with a longword of zero.
- The IOSB argument: the address of an I/O status block where $GETJPI records final status information.
- The ASTADR and ASTPRM arguments: the address and parameter of an AST procedure to be called when the request completes.

The $GETJPI system service procedure, EXE$GETJPI in module SYS-GETJPI, executes in kernel mode. It performs the following operations:

1. EXE$GETJPI allocates ten longwords of stack space as a storage area for local context items, such as the PCB address and a set of control flags.
2. EXE$GETJPI tests the first item list entry. Like all item list entries, it must be readable from the access mode of the requestor. The first item list entry is the only legal location for the item code JPI$_GETJPI_CONTROL_FLAGS, introduced in VMS Version 5.2. This item code allows the caller to limit EXE$GETJPI's behavior with outswapped processes, to restrict AST delivery, and to obtain information on processes that are suspended or marked for deletion. EXE$GETJPI copies the control flags, if specified, to its local context area.
3. It checks the PID argument; a value of zero indicates the current process, a positive value indicates an EPID, and a negative value indicates a wildcard specification.

   —For zero or a possible EPID, EXE$GETJPI continues at step 6.
   —For a negative value, EXE$GETJPI invokes the process scan routine EXE$PSCAN_LOCKCTX, in module PROCESS_SCAN, which negates

the argument and compares it to the context blocks on PHD$Q_
PSCANCTX_QUEUE.

If no matching context block is found, EXE$GETJPI attempts to
process the argument as a traditional $GETJPI wildcard. It obtains the
next EPID (see Section 13.2.6) and continues at step 6.

If a matching context block exists, EXE$PSCAN_LOCKCTX sets
PSCANCTX$V_BUSY in it to lock the context. Only one $GETJPI
request at a time can use a context block to reference other VAXcluster nodes. PSCANCTX$V_BUSY in PSCANCTX$L_FLAGS locks the
context block; if the bit is set when the process attempts to acquire
the context block, it enters the RSN$_ASTWAIT resource wait state
until the context block is available. When the request referencing the
context block completes, the process is reentered with an AST routine
that clears PSCANCTX$V_BUSY. On return from the AST routine,
the process reexecutes the test of the busy bit, acquires the context
block, and continues from this point.

4. EXE$GETJPI invokes the process scan routine EXE$PSCAN_NEXT_PID
   to obtain the next EPID and update the context block.

5. EXE$PSCAN_NEXT_PID, in module PROCESS_SCAN, tries to find a
   local process that matches the search criteria in the context block and
   that the $GETJPI requestor can access. To scan the local node, it steps
   through the PCB vector one process at a time. It updates the process
   index (PIX) with each iteration, and the next request using the same
   context begins where the previous scan left off. The context block fields
   PSCANCTX$L_CUR_IPID, PSCAN$L_CUR_EPID, and PSCANCTX$L_
   NEXT_IPID track this local scan.

   When EXE$PSCAN_NEXT_PID finds a process matching the search
   criteria, it returns the EPID of the matching process to EXE$GETJPI and
   EXE$GETJPI continues at step 6.

   If it does not find a local process, EXE$PSCAN_NEXT_PID returns
   the CSID of the next node to search and the error status SS$_REMOTE_
   PROC. EXE$GETJPI passes control to CWPS$GETJPI_PSCAN, which
   continues the $GETJPI processing (see Section 13.2.4).

   If it does not find a local process and the context block contains no
   more CSIDs to search, EXE$PSCAN_NEXT_PID returns the error status
   SS$_NOMOREPROC, which becomes the $GETJPI status return.

6. EXE$GETJPI invokes EXE$NAMPID to obtain the target PCB address and
   check privileges. As described in Section 13.1.2, EXE$NAMPID deter-
   mines whether the current process has the ability to obtain information
   about the target.

   If the target is not on the local node, EXE$NAMPID returns the er-
   ror SS$_REMOTE_PROC. EXE$GETJPI passes control to CWPS$GETJPI,
   which continues the $GETJPI processing (see Section 13.2.4).

If the target process is on the local node, EXE$GETJPI continues with the steps that follow. These steps apply only to a target process on the local node.

7. EXE$GETJPI checks for write access to the I/O status block (IOSB) and clears the IOSB, if one was specified.

8. It clears the specified event flag or event flag 0.

9. If AST notification was requested, EXE$GETJPI checks that the process has sufficient AST quota. If so, it charges for the AST; otherwise it returns the error status SS$_EXASTLM.

10. EXE$GETJPI checks each item for the following conditions:

    —The buffer descriptor must be readable and the buffer writable.
    —The requested item must be a recognized one.

11. If these conditions are met, then the requested item can be retrieved. All data about the current process and PCB and JIB data about another process can be obtained directly without entering the context of the target process. (The PCB and JIB are nonpaged pool data structures allocated for the life of the process and job.) In addition, data from the PHD of another process can be obtained directly if the PHD is resident (if the PCB$V_PHDRES bit in PCB$L_STS is set). EXE$GETJPI moves all such information to the user-defined buffers for each corresponding item.

12. If no information remains to be gathered, then EXE$GETJPI returns to the caller after performing the following actions:

    —Setting the specified event flag
    —Queuing AST notification, if it was requested
    —Writing status to an IOSB, if one was supplied

13. Information in the target process's control region can only be retrieved by executing in the context of the target process. Information stored in the target process's process header may not be available if the process is outswapped. To collect information from the control region or from an outswapped process header, EXE$GETJPI queues a special kernel mode AST to the target process, enabling EXE$GETJPI code to execute in the target context.

    VMS Version 5.2 allows the $GETJPI requestor to control this behavior through two $GETJPI control flags, JPI$V_NO_TARGET_INSWAP and JPI$V_NO_TARGET_AST.

    —If the caller specifies JPI$V_NO_TARGET_INSWAP, EXE$GETJPI does not queue an AST to the target unless it is resident. Thus, EXE$GETJPI is unable to obtain any information about an outswapped process, but it can obtain information from the PHD and from the control region of a resident process.
    —If the caller specifies JPI$V_NO_TARGET_AST, EXE$GETJPI never

queues an AST to the target process. Thus, it returns data from a resident PHD but never from the control region.

Depending on the control flags, EXE$GETJPI allocates nonpaged pool for an extended AST control block (ACB) and an information buffer. It charges the pool against the process's JIB$L_BYTCNT quota. EXE$GET-JPI initializes the normal ACB fields, then stores descriptors of all the information that must be retrieved while executing in the context of the other process into the extension. It creates a buffer to receive the retrieved information for transmission to the requesting process.

14. EXE$GETJPI checks the status and state of the target process. If the target process is in any of the following states, information from it cannot be obtained:

—It no longer exists.
—Deletion or suspension is pending.
—The process state is suspended (SUSP), suspended outswapped (SUSPO), or miscellaneous wait (MWAIT) (see Chapter 12).

If the process is in any of these states, EXE$GETJPI deallocates the non-paged pool and restores the quota charged. If the process no longer exists, EXE$GETJPI returns the error status SS$_NONEXPR to its requestor. For the other conditions, EXE$GETJPI's behavior is based on the $GETJPI control flag JPI$V_IGNORE_TARGET_STATUS. If the flag is specified, EXE$GETJPI returns the status SS$_NORMAL to its requestor; otherwise it returns the error status SS$_SUSPENDED. Even in this case, at step 11 EXE$GETJPI has already moved data from the PCB, JIB, and possibly the PHD into user-defined buffers.

Note that the completion mechanisms are all triggered if any error condition occurs. That is, the event flag is set, a user-requested AST is queued, and an IOSB is written with the failure status.

15. EXE$GETJPI queues the ACB to the target process with a priority increment class of PRI$_TICOM. However, if the target process is computable (COM) or computable outswapped (COMO), queuing the AST does not result in a priority boost. (See Chapter 12 for information on event reporting.) In that case, EXE$GETJPI boosts the target process's priority enough to make it equal to the priority of the requesting process (unless the requesting process is a real-time process or its priority is lower than that of the target process). The target priority boost ensures that even a low-priority target process will eventually return an answer to the requestor.

16. The asynchronous form of the system service returns to the requestor. The requestor can either wait for the information to be returned or continue processing. The synchronous form of the system service waits for the event flag associated with the request to be set and status to be

returned. See Chapter 6 for more information concerning synchronous and asynchronous system services.

13.2.4 Remote $GETJPI Support

The CWPS routines CWPS$GETJPI and CWPS$GETJPI_PSCAN, in module CWPS_GETJPI, dispatch $GETJPI requests to other VAXcluster nodes and return status and item list information to the original requestor. EXE$GETJPI passes control to CWPS$GETJPI when no context block is associated with the request, merely an EPID or process name identifying a remote VAXcluster node. It passes control to the alternative entry point CWPS$GETJPI_PSCAN when a context block exists.

CWPS$GETJPI does the same argument list validation as EXE$GETJPI: checking the IOSB for write access and clearing it, clearing the specified event flag, checking and charging AST quota, and validating the item list.

If these checks succeed, CWPS$GETJPI allocates sufficient nonpaged pool to describe the $GETJPI request. It creates a variable-sized data structure with space for the context block, item list, return buffer, and an ACB. The $CWPSSRV macro defines the symbolic offsets for the fields in the structure header. The $CWPSJPI macro defines symbolic offsets for the fields in an extension for $GETJPI requests.

CWPS$GETJPI initializes this structure and stores its address in the context block at offset PSCANCTX$L_CWPSSRV. It invokes a CWPS subroutine to transmit the request to the appropriate remote node using SCS.

On the remote node, a CWPS dispatch routine executing in system context receives the service request. It allocates a structure to describe the request, including the context block. It then queues a kernel mode AST to the CLUSTER_SERVER process, determining the address of the AST procedure from the function to be performed; in this case, CWPS$SRCV_GETJPI_AST in module CWPS_SERVICE_RECV.

CWPS$SRCV_GETJPI_AST, executing in the context of the CLUSTER_SERVER process, builds a structure that mimics the PCB of the requesting process. If it did not receive a context block, it merely requests the $GETJPI system service on behalf of the original requestor. Otherwise, it inserts the context block onto the PHD queue in the CLUSTER_SERVER process and invokes the process scan routines EXE$PSCAN_LOCKCTX and EXE$PSCAN_NEXT_PID as EXE$GETJPI does. These locate the EPID of the next process matching the search context. CWPS$SRCV_GETJPI_AST then requests the $GETJPI service with the explicit EPID of a local process, specifying a completion AST procedure. EXE$GETJPI follows the steps described in Section 13.2.3 for a local process.

When the $GETJPI request completes, the completion AST procedure passes control to another CWPS routine to return status and data to the originating node using SCS.

When the response arrives from the remote node, a cleanup routine tests the status returned from the remote node. On a successful return, it copies the returned data to the $GETJPI requestor's buffer area after suitable accessibility checks, updates the context block, and clears the busy flag. It sets the event flag, queues the user-requested AST, and returns the status in the IOSB.

13.2.5   **$GETJPI Special Kernel Mode ASTs**

To obtain information about a target process on the local node, EXE$GETJPI must sometimes queue a special kernel mode AST to the target. From either the context of the requesting process (if the requestor is local) or the context of the CLUSTER_SERVER process, EXE$GETJPI queues this AST when the required information resides in an outswapped PHD or in the control region of the target process.

The special kernel mode AST routine executes in the context of the target process to access the information. Once the AST has obtained the information, it queues another special kernel mode AST to the requesting process or the CLUSTER_SERVER process to pass the information back to the service requestor.

A summary of the operations performed by these two special kernel mode AST routines follows:

1. The first special kernel mode AST routine runs when the target process is placed into execution. It examines the extended ACB to determine the information that was requested and stores that information in the associated system buffer. It reformats the extended ACB to deliver a second special kernel mode AST, this time to the requesting process or the CLUSTER_SERVER process. It queues the extended ACB to the requesting process if it still exists and is not marked for deletion. (The CLUSTER_SERVER process cannot be deleted or suspended.) Otherwise, it deallocates the nonpaged pool and returns.

2. The second kernel mode AST routine executes in the context of the requesting process or CLUSTER_SERVER process. If the PHD image counter has changed since the service was requested, then the requesting image has been run down. In this case, the AST routine deallocates the block of nonpaged pool, restores the JIB$L_BYTCNT quota, and returns.

3. If the image counter in the PHD agrees with the image counter in the extended ACB, the special kernel mode AST routine copies the retrieved data from the system buffer into the user-defined buffers.

   Note that the asynchronous nature of this aspect of the system service requires that the IOSB and all data buffers be probed again for write accessibility. This check ensures that the original requestor of $GET-JPI has not altered the IOSB and data buffer protection in the interval between the call to $GETJPI and the delivery of the return special kernel mode AST.

4. The event flag is set and the IOSB is written if it was specified.

5. If a completion AST was requested, the extended ACB is used for the third time to queue an AST to the requesting process in the access mode of the caller. Otherwise, the ACB is deallocated to nonpaged pool.

The CLUSTER_SERVER process always specifies CWPS$SRCV_ GETJPI_SRV_AST as its completion AST procedure when requesting the $GETJPI system service. Therefore, for a remote request, the ACB is always reused.

13.2.6 Traditional Wildcard Support in $GETJPI

In addition to the wildcard search available through the $PROCESS_SCAN system service, VMS preserves the traditional $GETJPI wildcard behavior. The $GETJPI system service provides the ability to obtain information about all processes on the local node. An image requests this feature by passing −1 as the PID argument to the $GETJPI system service. An internal routine in EXE$GETJPI searches the PCB vector for the first slot containing a valid PCB and passes information back to the caller about the associated process.

EXE$GETJPI alters the process index field of the requestor's PID argument to contain the process index of the target process. When the $GETJPI service is requested again, the negative sequence number (in the high-order word of the process ID) indicates that a wildcard operation is in progress, and the positive process index indicates the offset in the PCB vector where the search should continue.

Chapter 25 provides more information on the PCB vector. Note that the user image will not work correctly if it alters the value of the PID argument between $GETJPI requests.

The image continues to request the $GETJPI service until a status code of SS$_NOMOREPROC is returned, indicating that the PCB vector search routine has reached the end of the PCB vector. *VMS System Services Reference Manual* and *VMS Version 5.2 New Features Manual* contain sample programs using $GETJPI wildcards.

13.3 SYSTEM SERVICES AFFECTING PROCESS COMPUTABILITY

The controlling process in a multiprocess application typically creates other processes to perform designated work. When these processes have completed their work, the controlling process may delete them or place them into some wait state in anticipation of additional work. Chapter 25 describes the detailed operation of process creation. Process deletion is described in Chapter 28.

Hibernation and suspension are the two different ways in which a process can temporarily stall execution. The system services Hibernate ($HIBER) and

Suspend Process ($SUSPND) implement hibernation and suspension. The associated services Wake Process ($WAKE), Schedule Wakeup ($SCHDWK), and Resume Process ($RESUME) cause execution to recommence.

13.3.1 Hibernate/Wake

A process requests the $HIBER service to place itself into hibernation; it cannot put another process into the HIB state. The $HIBER system service procedure is EXE$HIBER, in module SYSPCNTRL. It performs the following:

1. EXE$HIBER acquires the SCHED spinlock, raising IPL to IPL$_SCHED.
2. It uses an interlocked instruction to test the state of the wake pending flag, PCB$V_WAKEPEN in PCB$L_STS, and to clear the flag.
3. If the flag was set, a wake request preceded the hibernate call. EXE$HIBER merely releases the spinlock and returns to its requestor at IPL 0.
4. Otherwise, if the flag was clear, EXE$HIBER jumps to SCH$WAIT to place the process into the hibernate wait state.

As Chapter 12 describes, SCH$WAIT alters the saved program counter (PC) to contain the address of the CHMK instruction in the system service vector. Thus, if the process receives an AST while hibernating, it reexecutes EXE$HIBER upon completion of the AST routine. Since EXE$HIBER tests the wake pending flag, a hibernating process is easily awakened if an AST procedure requests the $WAKE service.

$HIBER's complementary services are $WAKE and $SCHDWK, which remove a process from hibernation. To awaken itself, a process can request $WAKE from an AST procedure or schedule a wake through $SCHDWK. Another process with the ability to affect the hibernating process, as determined by EXE$NAMPID, can request $WAKE or $SCHDWK on the process's behalf.

The $WAKE system service procedure, EXE$WAKE in module SYS-PCNTRL, runs in kernel mode. It invokes EXE$NAMPID, described in Section 13.1.2. For a local process, EXE$WAKE invokes SCH$WAKE in module RSE. SCH$WAKE sets the wake pending flag, PCB$V_WAKEPEN, and reports the awakening event to the scheduler routine SCH$RSE, specifying the priority boost class PRI$_RESAVL for the awakening process. SCH$RSE removes the process from the HIB or HIBO queue and places it in the COM or COMO queue corresponding to its updated priority.

The next time the process is scheduled at non-AST level, EXE$HIBER reexecutes because of the altered PC. Since SCH$WAKE set the wake pending flag, EXE$HIBER clears the flag and returns immediately. Note that if a process is awakened from any state other than HIB or HIBO, the net result is to leave the wake pending flag set with no other change in the process scheduling state.

If the process is remote, EXE$WAKE branches to CWPS$PCNTRL, in module SYSPCNTRL. Section 13.1.3 summarizes the result.

Chapter 12 provides further details on SCH$RSE, priority boosts, and process state queues, and Chapter 11 describes the $SCHDWK system service.

13.3.2 Suspend/Resume

Because one process can suspend other processes within the VAXcluster system, the implementation of process suspension is more complicated than that of hibernation. The VMS scheduling philosophy illustrated in Figure 12.6 assumes that processes enter various wait states from the state of being the current process and in no other way. This assumption requires that the process being suspended (the target) become the current process on some CPU, possibly replacing the requestor of the $SUSPND system service.

To accommodate this scheduling constraint, a process is suspended as the result of executing a kernel or supervisor mode AST. AST execution ensures that the process is first made current before being placed into the SUSP scheduling state.

Prior to VMS Version 5, process suspension always occurred in kernel mode. Only the $RESUME system service could make the suspended process computable; no ASTs could be delivered to the suspended process. In VMS Version 5, suspension can occur in supervisor or kernel mode. Executive and kernel mode ASTs can be delivered to a process suspended in supervisor mode; non-AST execution recommences after the process is the target of a $RESUME system service request. A process suspended in kernel mode maintains the pre-Version 5 behavior. ASTs cannot be delivered and the process only becomes computable following a $RESUME system service request.

13.3.2.1 Process Suspension.

Process suspension occurs in two parts, both in module SYSPCNTRL: the $SUSPND system service procedure, EXE$SUSPND, and a supervisor or kernel mode AST procedure, depending on the suspension request. The default is supervisor mode.

13.3.2.1.1 *EXE$SUSPND.*

EXE$SUSPND executes in kernel mode in the context of the requesting process. It performs the following:

1. EXE$SUSPND checks for the presence of its FLAGS argument. If the low bit of the FLAGS argument is clear or the argument is not specified, the request is for supervisor suspension, also called soft suspension.
2. Otherwise, the request is for kernel mode suspension, also called hard suspension. EXE$SUSPND checks that its caller was in kernel or executive mode; otherwise, it returns the error status SS$_NOPRIV.
3. EXE$SUSPND invokes EXE$NAMPID to identify the target process and perform access checking.

4. If the target process is not local, EXE$NAMPID returns the error status SS$_REMOTE_PROC. EXE$SUSPND passes the request to a CWPS routine for transmission to a remote VAXcluster node. If the local process has appropriate access to the remote target process, a CWPS routine on the remote node eventually executes the $SUSPND request from the context of the CLUSTER_SERVER process. It transmits status to a CWPS receiver on the requesting node, which reenters the context of the requesting process via an AST to return the status to the user image.

5. Otherwise, if the target process is local, EXE$NAMPID returns holding the SCHED spinlock. EXE$SUSPND continues with the steps that follow. (Exit paths from EXE$SUSPND must release this spinlock and lower IPL to 0.)

6. EXE$SUSPND checks the delete pending bit PCB$V_DELPEN, in PCB$L_STS, in the PCB of the target process. If the process is marked for deletion, EXE$SUSPND returns the error status SS$_NONEXPR.

7. EXE$SUSPND checks the bit PCB$V_NOSUSPEND in PCB$L_STS. If EXE$SUSPND cannot safely suspend the process, it returns the error status SS$_NOSUSPEND.

8. It tests and sets PCB$V_SUSPEN, the suspend pending bit in PCB$L_STS. If suspension is pending, EXE$SUSPND tests the bit PCB$V_SOFTSUSP. If the pending suspension is supervisor mode, PCB$V_SOFTSUSP is set; otherwise, a kernel mode suspension is pending.

    If a kernel mode suspension is pending, EXE$SUSPND returns with the status SS$_NORMAL.

    Otherwise, if a supervisor mode suspension is pending or no suspension is pending, EXE$SUSPND's actions depend on the mode of the new suspension request:

    —If the new suspension request is for kernel mode, EXE$SUSPND queues the kernel mode AST (the second part of suspension) to the target process (possibly itself).

    —If the new suspension request is for supervisor mode, EXE$SUSPND determines whether it is executing within the context of its supervisor mode AST procedure. If not, it marks the process for soft suspension by setting PCB$V_SOFTSUSP. It then queues a supervisor mode AST to the target process. Otherwise, if EXE$SUSPND is executing within its supervisor mode AST context, it performs as described in Section 13.3.2.1.3.

Through the normal scheduling selection process, the target process eventually executes the kernel or supervisor mode AST procedure.

13.3.2.1.2 *The Kernel Mode AST Procedure.* The kernel mode AST procedure SUSPND, in module SYSPCNTRL, executes in the context of the target process. SUSPND obtains the current PCB address and acquires the SCHED spinlock.

It then tests the bit PCB$V_SOFTSUSP in PCB$L_STS. A set bit indicates supervisor mode suspension. Since kernel mode suspension preempts supervisor mode suspension, SUSPND clears PCB$V_SOFTSUSP and sets PCB$V_PREEMPTED.

SUSPND checks and clears the resume pending flag PCB$V_RESPEN, in PCB$L_STS. This check prevents the deadlock that might otherwise occur if the associated call to the $RESUME system service preceded the execution of the AST procedure. If the resume pending flag is set, the AST procedure simply releases the SCHED spinlock, lowers IPL to 0, clears the suspend pending bit, and returns. The process continues execution.

If the resume pending flag is clear, the kernel mode AST procedure checks whether there is a Files-11 Extended QIO Processor (XQP) operation in progress. Chapter 7 discusses this check and the action taken if an operation is in progress.

If no Files-11 operation is in progress, the kernel mode AST procedure places the process into the SUSP wait state. Its saved PC is an address in the AST procedure and the saved processor status longword (PSL) indicates kernel mode and IPL 0. ASTs can be queued to a process suspended in kernel mode but they cannot be delivered. When an AST is queued to a process suspended in kernel mode, SCH$RSE ignores the AST event. Only the $RESUME system service can cause a process suspended in kernel mode to continue with execution. At that time, the process reexecutes the check of the resume pending flag, which would be set, causing the process to return successfully from the AST.

13.3.2.1.3 *The Supervisor Mode AST Procedure.* The supervisor mode AST procedure, SUSPEND_SOFT in module SYSPCNTRL, executes in the context of the target process. Its only action is to request the $SUSPND system service, thus reentering EXE$SUSPND.

When EXE$SUSPND is reentered, it determines that it is executing within the context of its supervisor mode AST procedure. It tests the bit PCB$V_PREEMPTED in PCB$L_STS. If it is set, the supervisor mode suspension was preempted by a kernel mode suspension. If PCB$V_SOFTSUSP is clear as well, EXE$SUSPND clears PCB$V_SUSPEN and PCB$V_PREEMPTED and returns successfully to the caller.

If the supervisor mode suspension was not preempted by a kernel mode suspension, PCB$V_PREEMPTED is clear. If PCB$V_RESPEN is also clear, indicating that the process has not been resumed, EXE$SUSPND suspends the process.

While a process is suspended in supervisor mode, its saved PC contains the address of the CHMK instruction in the SYS$SUSPND system service vector. Its saved PSL indicates supervisor mode. The process's supervisor mode AST active bit is set, blocking delivery of another supervisor mode AST. The enqueuing of an AST makes the process computable. When the process is placed into execution, a kernel or executive mode AST can be executed, but a user or supervisor mode AST cannot; the AST control block is queued and the interrupt is dismissed.

In either case, an REI instruction is executed, which causes the $SUSPND system service to be reexecuted. EXE$SUSPND repeats the test that suspended the process. If PCB$V_RESPEN is not set, the process is once more suspended.

13.3.2.2   **Operation of the $RESUME System Service.** The $RESUME system service is very simple. It invokes EXE$NAMPID and, for an accessible process on the local system, sets the resume pending flag PCB$V_RESPEN in the target process PCB. It then reports a resume event, invoking SCH$RSE. As with all other system events, this report may result in a rescheduling interrupt request, a request to wake the swapper process, or nothing at all.

If the target process is not local, the $RESUME request is passed to a CWPS routine for transmission to a remote VAXcluster node. If the local process has appropriate access to the remote target process, a CWPS routine on the remote node eventually executes the $RESUME request from the context of the CLUSTER_SERVER process. It transmits status to a CWPS receiver on the requesting node, which reenters the context of the requesting process via an AST to return the status to the user image.

13.3.3   **Exit and Forced Exit**

The Exit ($EXIT) system service terminates the currently executing image. If the process is executing a single image without a command language interpreter, image exit usually results in process deletion. A detailed discussion of the $EXIT system service is given in Chapter 26.

The Force Exit ($FORCEX) system service enables one process to force a target process to request the $EXIT system service. The system service procedure EXE$FORCEX, in module SYSFORCEX, locates the process through EXE$NAMPID.

If the target process is not local, EXE$NAMPID returns the error status SS$_REMOTE_PROC. EXE$FORCEX passes the request to a CWPS routine for transmission to a remote VAXcluster node. If the local process has appropriate access to the remote target process, a CWPS routine on the remote node eventually executes the $FORCEX request in the context of the CLUSTER_SERVER process, performing the steps described in the following paragraphs. The remote CWPS routine transmits status to a CWPS receiver on the requesting node, which reenters the context of the requesting process via an AST to return the status to the user image.

For a local process, EXE$FORCEX simply sets the force exit pending flag, PCB$V_FORCPEN in PCB$L_STS, and queues a user mode AST to the target process. This AST procedure, executing in user mode, requests the $EXIT system service after clearing the AST active flag by executing the following instruction:

```
CHMK    #ASTEXIT
```

Chapter 7 provides more information on this instruction. The call to $EXIT executes in the context of the target process. Execution proceeds as if the target process had called the system service itself.

13.4 MISCELLANEOUS PROCESS ATTRIBUTE CHANGES

Several system services allow a process to alter its characteristics, such as its response to resource allocation failures, its priority, and its process name. Some of these changes (such as priority elevation or swap disabling) require privilege. The Set Priority ($SETPRI) system service is the only service described in this section that a process can issue for a target other than itself.

13.4.1 Set Priority

The $SETPRI system service allows a process to alter its own priority or the priority of other processes within the VAXcluster system, limited by the privilege checks in EXE$NAMPID (see Section 13.1.2). A process with the ALTPRI privilege can change priority to any value between 0 and 31. A process without this privilege is restricted to the range between zero and the authorized base priority of its target process (PCB$B_AUTHPRI) or the current base priority of its target process (PCB$B_PRIB), whichever is higher.

The system service procedure EXE$SETPRI, in module SYSSETPRI, runs in kernel mode. It locates the target process via EXE$NAMPID.

If the target process is not local, EXE$NAMPID returns the error status SS$_REMOTE_PROC. EXE$SETPRI passes the request to a CWPS routine for transmission to a remote VAXcluster node. If the local process has appropriate access to the remote target process, a CWPS routine on the remote node eventually executes the $SETPRI request in the context of the CLUSTER_SERVER process, performing the steps described in the following paragraphs. The remote CWPS routine transmits status to a CWPS receiver on the requesting node, which reenters the context of the requesting process via an AST to return the status to the user image.

For a local process, EXE$SETPRI changes the base priority in the PCB at offsets PCB$B_PRIBSAV and PCB$B_PRIB and the saved base priority at offset PCB$B_PRISAV. (For a target process at elevated priority with a mutex locked, EXE$SETPRI only alters PCB$B_PRIBSAV and PCB$B_PRISAV.) Chapter 12 provides further information on these PCB fields.

If the target process is current, EXE$SETPRI invokes SCH$CHANGE_CUR_PRIORITY, in module RSE, to alter its current priority, stored in offset PCB$B_PRI. Chapter 12 describes SCH$CHANGE_CUR_PRIORITY.

EXE$SETPRI reports a set-priority system event for the target process by invoking SCH$RSE with a priority boost class of PRI$_IOCOM. If the target process is COM or COMO, SCH$RSE removes it from its current COM or COMO queue and places it into the COM or COMO queue corresponding to its new current priority. SCH$RSE clears and sets, as appropriate, the bits in SCH$GL_COMQS or SCH$GL_COMOQS. SCH$RSE requests a rescheduling interrupt if the target process is resident and can preempt a current process. If the target process is outswapped, SCH$RSE attempts to awaken the swapper process.

Chapter 12 provides further details.

13.4.2   Reschedule Current Process

The Reschedule Current Process ($RESCHED) system service was introduced in VMS Version 5.0. $RESCHED provides run-time support for the parallel processing features of VAX FORTRAN and VAX C. It enables the currently executing process to request a reschedule, allowing other processes at the same base priority to run.

The $RESCHED system service procedure, EXE$RESCHED in module SYSPARPRC, runs in kernel mode. It takes the following steps:

1. It acquires the SCHED spinlock, raising IPL to IPL$_SCHED.
2. It records the system absolute time in interval timer ticks in PCB$L_ONQTIME.
3. It invokes SCH$CHANGE_CUR_PRIORITY, described in Chapter 12, to lower the process's priority to its base.
4. It requests a rescheduling interrupt.
5. It releases the SCHED spinlock, restoring the previous IPL (thus enabling the rescheduling interrupt to be granted).
6. It returns a success status to its caller.

Use of this undocumented system service is reserved to Digital. Any other use is completely unsupported.

13.4.3   Set Process Name

The Set Process Name ($SETPRN) system service allows a process to change or eliminate its own process name. The new name cannot contain more than 15 characters. If no other process in the same group has the same name, EXE$SETPRN, in module SYSPCNTRL, places the new name into the PCB at offset PCB$T_LNAME. Note that this service allows more flexibility in establishing a process name than is available from the usual channels, such as the authorization file, $JOB card, or Digital command language (DCL) command SET PROCESS /NAME, because there are no restrictions imposed by the service on characters that can make up the process name.

13.4.4 Process Mode Services

The PCB contains a status longword (not to be confused with the hardware entity, the PSL) that records the current software status of the process. The longword is PCB$L_STS. Table 13.2 lists each of the flags in the longword and the direct or indirect ways to set or clear these flags. Each of these flags has a symbolic name of the form PCB$V_*name*, where *name* is one of those listed in the table.

The module SYSSETMOD contains three miscellaneous system services whose only action is to set or clear a bit in PCB$L_STS. These are the Set Resource Wait Mode ($SETRWM), Set System Service Failure Exception Mode ($SETSFM), and Set Swap Mode ($SETSWM) system services. To disable swapping, a process must possess the PSWAPM privilege. The other two services require no privilege.

Several system services (such as $DELPRC, $FORCEX, $RESUME, and $SUSPND) set or clear bits in PCB$L_STS as an indication that the service's primary operation has been initiated.

The Set AST Enable ($SETAST) system service sets or clears (enables or disables) delivery of ASTs to a given access mode. The offset PCB$B_ASTEN contains the AST enable flags (see Chapter 7).

13.5 INTERPROCESS COMMUNICATION

In applications involving more than one process, the processes commonly share data or transfer information from one process to another. VMS provides various mechanisms that accomplish this information exchange. These mechanisms vary in the amount of information that can be transmitted, transparency of the transmission, and amount of synchronization provided by the VMS operating system.

This section discusses event flags, lock management system services, mailboxes, logical names, and global sections. In addition to these, VMS provides file sharing and DECnet task-to-task communication. The *Guide to VMS File Applications* describes use of the former and the *VMS Networking Manual* the latter.

13.5.1 Event Flags

Common event flags can be treated as a method for several processes to share single bits of information. However, the typical use of common event flags is as a synchronization tool for other, more complicated, communication techniques.

Common event flags can be shared by processes in the same UIC group executing on processors accessing common memory, that is, processors participating in a symmetric multiprocessing (SMP) system or processors sharing MA780 memory. However, event flags cannot be shared by processes

Table 13.2   Meanings of Flags in PCB$L_STS

Flag Name	Meaning if Set	Set by	Cleared by
RES	Process is resident	Swapper	Swapper
DELPEN	Process deletion is pending	$DELPRC	
FORCPEN	Forced exit is pending	$FORCEX	Image rundown, Process rundown
INQUAN	Process is in initial quantum after inswap	Swapper	SCH$QEND
PSWAPM	Process swapping is disabled	$SETSWM, $CREPRC	$SETSWM
RESPEN	Resume is pending (skip suspend)	$RESUME	Suspend AST
SSFEXC	Enable system service exceptions for kernel mode	$SETSFM	$SETSFM, Process rundown
SSFEXCE	Enable system service exceptions for executive mode	$SETSFM	$SETSFM, Process rundown
SSFEXCS	Enable system service exceptions for supervisor mode	$SETSFM	$SETSFM, Process rundown
SSFEXCU	Enable system service exceptions for user mode	$SETSFM, $CREPRC	$SETSFM, Image rundown
SSRWAIT	Disable resource wait mode	$SETRWM, $CREPRC	$SETRWM
SUSPEN	Suspend is pending	$SUSPND	Suspend AST
WAKEPEN	Wake is pending (skip hibernate)	$WAKE, $SCHDWK	$HIBER
WALL	Wait for all event flags in mask	$WFLAND	Next $WFLOR or $WAITFR
BATCH	Process is a batch job	$CREPRC	
NOACNT	No accounting records for this process	$CREPRC	
NOSUSPEND	Do not suspend this process	CWPS, Audit Server	Audit Server
ASTPEN	AST is pending (not used)		
PHDRES	Process header is resident	Swapper	Swapper
HIBER	Hibernate after initial image activation	$CREPRC	
LOGIN	Log in without reading the authorization file	$CREPRC	
NETWRK	Process is a network job	$CREPRC	
PWRAST	Process has declared a power recovery AST	$SETPRA	Queuing of recovery AST, Image rundown, Process rundown
NODELET	Do not delete this process	CWPS, NETACP	NETACP
DISAWS	Disable automatic working set adjustment on this process	SET WORK /NOADJUST, $CREPRC	SET WORK /ADJUST

(continued)

Table 13.2   Meanings of Flags in PCB$L_STS *(continued)*

Flag Name	Meaning if Set	Set by	Cleared by
INTER	Process is interactive job	$CREPRC	
RECOVER	(Reserved)		
SECAUDIT	Perform mandatory process auditing	LOGINOUT, $CREPRC	LOGINOUT
HARDAFF	(Reserved)		
ERDACT	Exec mode rundown active	Process rundown	Process rundown
SOFTSUSP	Process is in soft suspend	$SUSPND	$SUSPND
PREEMPTED	Hard suspend has preempted soft	$SUSPND	$SUSPND

on different VAXcluster nodes. Chapter 9 contains more information on the implementation of common event flags.

13.5.2   Lock Management System Services

The lock management system services (also known as the lock manager) enable a process to name an arbitrary resource and share it VAXcluster-wide. A process can request locks on the named resource in a variety of lock modes to control the manner in which the process shares the resource with other processes. In each lock request, the process can declare a blocking AST procedure, which is invoked by the lock manager if the process's granted lock blocks another request for the resource. The process can also specify the lock manager behavior when access to a resource cannot be immediately granted: either that it wait until the resource is available, or return immediately with notification of the failure.

Each resource includes a 16-byte area available to store process data. The lock manager synchronizes access to this area, allowing cooperating processes to read and write the area using lock value blocks.

Chapter 10 describes the implementation of the lock management system services. Appendix A provides examples of VMS modules that use lock management system services to coordinate access to system resources.

13.5.3   Mailboxes

Mailboxes are software-implemented I/O devices that can be read and written through Record Management Services (RMS) requests or the Queue I/O Request ($QIO) system service on the local node. Although process-specific or systemwide parameters may control the amount of data that can be written to a mailbox in one operation, there is no limit to the total amount of information that can be passed through a mailbox with a series of reads and writes.

Typically, one process reads messages written to a mailbox by one or more other processes. In the simple method of synchronizing mailbox I/O, the receiving process initiates its read of the mailbox and waits until the read completes. The read completes when another process writes to the mailbox. Since the receiving process cannot do anything else while waiting for data, this technique is restrictive.

In most applications, the receiving process performs other tasks in addition to servicing the mailbox. Putting such a process into a wait state for the mailbox prevents it from servicing any of its other tasks. In these applications, the receiving process could read the mailbox asynchronously with AST notification. However, even in this case, the process must have an I/O request outstanding at all times to receive notification that the mailbox contains a message.

For some applications, this may not be acceptable. Thus, VMS provides a special $QIO request function code, set attention AST, which requests AST notification that a message has been written to the mailbox. This technique allows a process to continue its mainline processing and to handle mailbox requests from other processes only when such work is needed, without having an I/O request outstanding at all times.

Chapter 23 discusses the implementation of mailboxes and Chapter 7 describes attention ASTs.

13.5.4   Logical Names

VMS makes extensive use of logical names to provide device independence in the I/O system. However, logical names can be used for many other purposes as well. Specifically, one process can pass information to another process by creating a logical name in a shared logical name table and storing information in the equivalence string. The receiving process simply translates the name to retrieve the data.

Although an error return (SS$_NOTRAN) from the Translate Logical Name ($TRNLNM) system service provides a form of synchronization, a well-behaved process generally synchronizes communication via logical name translation by using event flags or an equivalent method. An exception to this rule occurs when a process creates a subprocess or detached process and passes data to the new process in the equivalence strings for SYS$INPUT, SYS$OUTPUT, or SYS$ERROR. Chapter 35 provides details on the implementation of logical names.

13.5.5   Global Sections

Global sections provide the fastest method for one process to pass information to another process. Because the processes map the data area into their address space, no movement of data takes place; the data is shared. The sharing, however, is not transparent. Each process must map the global section and the participating processes must agree upon a synchronization technique to coordinate the reading and writing of the global section and provide notification of new data. It can be implemented with event flags, lock management system services, or some similar mechanism.

A global section implemented on a multiprocessor system or in MA780 shared memory can be simultaneously accessed by multiple processes. Synchronization in such an environment requires use of interlocked instructions or a protocol based on event flags or locks. Chapter 8 briefly describes synchronization of shared memory.

Chapter 15 describes the implementation of global sections.

PART V / Memory Management

14 Memory Management Overview and Data Structures

> ... but there's one great advantage in it, that one's memory
> works both ways.
>
> Lewis Carroll, *Through the Looking Glass*

This chapter provides an overview of VMS memory management and describes data structures used by the memory management subsystem. Virtual memory support for the VMS operating system is implemented partly by the VAX processor and partly by the VMS executive.

The four chapters that follow this one describe different aspects of VMS memory management in more detail:

- Chapter 15 describes system services that an image requests to alter the process's virtual address space.
- Chapter 16 discusses the translation-not-valid (page fault) fault handler, the exception service routine that responds to page faults and brings virtual pages into memory.
- Chapter 17 describes the working set list and the mechanisms that alter, shrink, and expand it.
- Chapter 18 examines the swapper process, a system process that manages physical memory by writing modified pages, shrinking process working sets, and swapping processes.

14.1 OVERVIEW OF MEMORY MANAGEMENT

Physical memory is the real memory supplied by the hardware. A virtual memory environment supports software that has memory requirements greater than the available physical memory. An individual process can require more memory than is available, or the total requirements of multiple processes can exceed available memory. A virtual memory system simulates real memory by transparently moving the contents of memory to and from block-addressable mass storage.

A VAX processor and the VMS executive cooperate to support virtual memory. In normal operation, the system interprets all instruction and operand addresses as virtual addresses (addresses in virtual memory). A VAX processor translates virtual addresses to physical addresses (addresses in physical memory) as the instructions are being executed. This execution time translation capability allows the VMS executive to execute any particular image in whichever physical memory is available. It also allows VMS and a VAX processor in combination to implement memory protection.

The term *memory management* describes not only virtual memory support but also the ways in which VMS exploits this capability. Memory management is fundamentally concerned with the following issues:

- Movement of code and data between mass storage and physical memory as required to simulate a virtual memory larger than the physical one
- Support of memory areas in which individual processes can run without interference from others, areas in which system code can be shared but not modified by its users, and common memory for shared code and data
- Arbitration among competing uses of physical memory to optimize system operation and equitable memory allocation

14.1.1   **Virtual Memory**

Support for virtual memory enables a process to execute an image that only partly resides in physical memory. Only the portion of virtual address space actually in use occupies physical memory. This enables the execution of images larger than the available physical memory. It also makes it possible for parts of different processes' images and address spaces to be resident simultaneously. Virtual memory is implemented in such a way that each process can access only its own address space; each process is thereby protected against references from other processes. Address references in an image built for a virtual memory system are independent of the physical memory in which the image actually executes.

A physical address is one that can be transmitted by the processor over the system bus, typically to a memory controller. Physical memory, also known as physical address space, is the set of all physical addresses that identify unique memory locations and I/O adapter registers.

During normal operations, an instruction accesses memory using the 32-bit virtual address of a particular byte. A VAX processor translates the virtual address to a physical address using information provided by the operating system.

The set of all possible 32-bit virtual addresses is called virtual memory, or virtual address space. The low half of the address space (addresses between 0 and $7FFFFFFF_{16}$) is called per-process space. This space is further divided into two equal pieces called P0 space (addresses between 0 and $3FFFFFFF_{16}$) and P1 space (addresses between 40000000_{16} and $7FFFFFFF_{16}$). One process at a time executes on a VAX processor. (On a symmetric multiprocessing (SMP) system, one process at a time executes on each VAX processor.) As a process is placed into execution, its per-process address space is mapped; that is, its virtual addresses are associated with physical addresses.

The high half of the virtual address space is called system space. The lower half of system space (the addresses between 80000000_{16} and $BFFFFFFF_{16}$) is called S0 space; the upper half is undefined and reserved to Digital. Thus the terms *system space* and *S0 space* are used synonymously.

Virtual address space is divided into pages. Each page is a group of 512 contiguous bytes starting on a 512-byte address boundary. The first page starts at address 0, the second at address 200_{16} (or 512_{10}), the third at address 400_{16} (or 1024_{10}), and so on. The virtual page is the unit of address translation; the physical location of a particular virtual page is generally independent of those of its adjacent virtual pages. The virtual page is also the unit of memory access checking. Each virtual page has a protection code specifying from which access modes it can be read and written.

When a VAX processor is initialized, memory management is disabled. All addresses generated by the CPU are physical addresses that do not require translation. Once memory management is enabled, or turned on, an instruction can no longer access memory using a physical address. The processor treats all instruction-generated addresses as virtual and translates them to physical addresses using data structures called page tables, which record the association of virtual to physical pages. (A physical page is the same size as a virtual page, 512 bytes.) Once having enabled memory management, VMS does not disable it.

While memory management is enabled, translation of system space addresses must always be possible. Per-process addresses, however, only have meaning in the context of a process. If there is no current process, it is not meaningful to access or translate P0 and P1 virtual addresses.

A page table is associated with each region of virtual address space. The processor translates system space addresses with the system page table. Each process has its own P0 and P1 page tables.

A page table does not map the full virtual address space possible; instead, it maps only the part of its region that has been created. P0 space starts at location 0 and expands toward increasing addresses; P1 space starts at location $7FFFFFFF_{16}$ and expands toward decreasing addresses; and S0 space begins at 80000000_{16} and expands toward increasing addresses.

In a page table, each page table entry (PTE) associates one page of virtual address space with its physical location, either in memory or on a mass storage medium. (This description is slightly simplified; Sections 14.2 and 14.3.3 contain more details.)

A PTE contains a bit called the valid bit, which, when set, means that the virtual page is in a particular page of physical memory; in that case, the PTE also contains all but the low nine bits of the physical page's address. This part of a physical address is called the page frame number. When a reference is made to a virtual address whose PTE valid bit is set, the processor uses the page frame number to transform the virtual address into a physical address. This transformation is called virtual address translation. Section 14.2 contains more information on the VAX address translation algorithm.

When a reference is made to a virtual address whose PTE valid bit is clear, the processor cannot perform address translation and instead generates a translation-not-valid exception, also known as a page fault. The page fault exception service routine, called the page fault handler, runs in the context of the process that incurred the page fault. It examines the PTE to determine the physical location of the invalid page. If the invalid page is in physical memory, the page fault handler simply updates the PTE. Otherwise, it obtains an available page of physical memory and initiates I/O to read the virtual page into it. When this occurs, the process is said to be faulting the page in.

When the I/O completes, the page fault handler sets the PTE valid bit and dismisses the exception. With the virtual page now valid, control returns to the instruction whose previous execution triggered the page fault. Reading a virtual page into memory in response to an attempted access is called demand paging.

VMS limits the number of pages of physical memory a process can use at the same time. When this limit has been reached and the process incurs a page fault, the page fault handler selects one of the process's virtual pages to remove from physical memory. When this occurs, the process is said to be faulting the page out. Removing one virtual page from a process to make room for another is called replacement paging.

The mass storage location from which a virtual page is read is called its backing store. A common example of backing store is a block in an image file. If the virtual page is guaranteed not to change (that is, it contains pure code or read-only data), the page fault handler need not write the page to mass storage when it is faulted out (thus saving the I/O) and can reread it from the image file as often as required. Thus, the backing store file remains the image file. If, however, the virtual page is writable data of which each process gets its own copy, the page is faulted in once from the image and later faulted out to page file backing store, from which any subsequent faults will be satisfied.

Chapter 16 describes in detail how the page fault handler deals with various types of page fault.

14.1.1.1   **VMS Address Space.** VMS uses the three regions of address space differently:

- The VMS executive occupies system space, along with systemwide data structures.
- P1 space contains the process stacks and permanent process control information maintained by the VMS executive. It also contains address space used on the process's behalf by inner access mode components such as Record Management Services (RMS), the file system, and a command language interpreter.
- P0 space maps whatever images the user activates.

Chapter 1, which contains layouts of P1 and system space, describes these uses in more detail. Appendix F describes the layout of each address space in more detail.

Different areas of virtual address space have different protections. The protection codes on most system space data pages prohibit access from all but kernel and executive mode. System space pages occupied by executive code allow read access from user mode. Certain parts of P1 space are protected against access from outer access modes. The protection on P0 space pages usually allows read access from user mode and sometimes write access as well.

Virtual address space is created (and recreated) at different times during system operation. System space is formed once and always mapped. Per-process address space is created for each process and mapped only when that process is current.

During system initialization, SYSBOOT calculates system space requirements and allocates physical memory for the system page table. SYSBOOT and other initialization routines load the executive images into system space, form the dynamic memory pools, and initialize the other regions of system space. Chapters 30 and 31 describe the formation and initialization of system space in detail. Once initialization is complete, the maximum size of system space is fixed, although individual system page table entries can be altered to create, delete, or modify particular pages of system space.

When a process is created, its P1 space is created in several stages, as described in Chapters 25 and 27. The global cell CTL$GL_CTLBASVA contains the address that is the boundary between the permanent and temporary portions of P1 space. The regions of P1 space below this address, namely, the user stack and a possible replacement image I/O section, are recreated by the image activator when it activates an executable image. P1 space can expand toward lower addresses during image execution as a result of system services requested explicitly by the image or implicitly on its behalf.

P0 space and the nonpermanent part of P1 space are deleted at image rundown and recreated with each new image run. The image activator creates address space for the image and every shareable image that it references. During image execution, it creates additional address space as necessary to activate images requested through the Run-Time Library procedure LIB$FIND_IMAGE_SYMBOL. P0 and P1 space can also change during image execution as a result of system services requested explicitly by an image or implicitly on its behalf.

As the image activator processes images, it creates process sections for the image sections it encounters. (A process section can also be created dynamically in response to a system service request.) A process section is a group of contiguous virtual pages with the same characteristics, such as writability and shareability.

Each per-process address region is architecturally limited to one gigabyte. Each per-process address space may be further constrained by the SYSGEN parameter VIRTUALPAGECNT, the page file quota available to the process, and some additional factors, as described in Chapter 15.

Chapter 26 describes the image activator and the memory management system services it requests to map the sections of an image. Chapter 15 describes those system services.

14.1.1.2   **Virtual Address Space Data Structures.** The major data structures that describe virtual address space are

- System page table (SPT)
- Per-process page tables (P0PT and P1PT)
- Process section table (PST)
- System section table (better known as the global section table)

The SPT is contained in contiguous physical pages, generally at the high-address end of physical memory. Section 14.5.1 describes it in further detail.

When the VMS executive creates a process, it allocates a data structure called a process header (PHD) to record memory management data about the process. A process's page tables are contained in its PHD. Section 14.3.3 describes process page tables in further detail.

The PHD also contains the PST, which has one process section table entry (PSTE) to describe each process section created in that process's address space. A PSTE contains information necessary to resolve a page fault for a page in the section. The PTE for an invalid page that is part of a process section contains a pointer to the section's PSTE. Section 14.3.5 contains more information on the PST.

Sections 14.5.2 and 14.6.2 discuss systemwide structures that are analogous to the process-specific PHD and PST: the system header and its section table, containing descriptions of system space sections and global sections.

14.1.2   **Physical Memory**

Physical memory is divided into 512-byte pages. Each page has an identifying number called a page frame number (PFN). A PFN is simply the portion of the physical address that specifies the physical page, namely all but the low-order nine bits. Generally, physical memory page numbers start at 0 and increase toward higher numbers. The size of physical address space varies with VAX processor type. Generally, the low half of the physical address space is used for memory locations and the high half for I/O adapters. The maximum amount of memory addressable on any VAX processor is limited by the layout of the PTE: on processors supported by VMS Version 5.2, it has space for a 21-bit PFN. Thus, the maximum physical address space is 2^{21} pages, or one gigabyte.

Some pages of physical memory are allocated permanently, for example, the pages that contain the SPT or the system base image. More typically,

VMS allocates a physical page of memory for a particular need, such as a virtual page in a process's address space, and deallocates the page when it is no longer needed.

14.1.2.1   **Physical Memory Data Structures.** A database called the PFN database, described in Section 14.4, records significant information about each physical page, such as whether it is currently in use and for what purpose.

The pages of physical memory allocated to a process are called its working set. A structure within the PHD called the working set list represents just those pages in a compact form. (In contrast, PTEs describing valid pages are scattered among those describing invalid pages in a per-process page table.) The working set list is briefly described in Section 14.3.4 and in more detail in Chapter 17. A working set list within the system header describes pageable system pages that are valid (see Section 14.5.2).

Physical pages available for allocation are linked together into a list called the free page list. A page is allocated from the front of the list and generally deallocated to the back of the list. At allocation a physical page is associated with a virtual page: the PFN of the physical page is placed in the PTE corresponding to the virtual page, and the virtual page is read into the physical page. The physical page retains its virtual contents until it is allocated for a new use. Even when the physical page is removed from a process's working set and the valid bit in the virtual page's PTE is cleared, the PTE still contains the physical page's PFN. Until the physical page is reused, it is possible to resolve a fault for the virtual page by removing the physical page from the free page list and setting the PTE valid bit again. A page fault resolved in this manner without the need for mass storage I/O is sometimes called a soft page fault.

When a physical page that has been modified is removed from a process's working set, the page is inserted at the back of another list, called the modified page list. The modified page list differs from the free page list in that a physical page on the modified page list cannot be reused until its contents are written to backing store, for example, a page file or the section file to which the virtual page belongs. Once the swapper has written the contents of the modified page to backing store, the swapper moves the page to the back of the free page list. (Acting in this capacity, the swapper is referred to as the modified page writer.)

While a physical page is on either the modified or free page list, a page fault for its virtual page can be resolved without I/O. Thus these lists act as systemwide caches of recently used virtual pages.

14.1.2.2   **Sharing Physical Memory.** Because system space addresses are mapped by the system page table, the physical memory occupied by system pages is shared by all processes. In addition, to enable process pages to share physical memory, VMS can map multiple processes' PTEs to the same physical pages. For example, multiple processes using the same command language interpreter can share the read-only pages of the image. (However, each process needs a private copy of its writable data pages.) Sharing physical pages makes more efficient use of memory and reduces the number of page faults that require mass storage I/O.

VMS implements the sharing of physical memory by multiple processes through a mechanism called a global section. All the pages of a global section have the same attributes. A global section resembles a process section and is dealt with similarly by the page fault handler.

There are several data structures associated with global sections:

- Global section table
- Global section descriptors
- Global page table

The global section table (GST) is analogous to a process section table and contains a global section table entry (GSTE) for each global section. Like a PSTE, a GSTE has information necessary to resolve a page fault for a page in the section. Section 14.6.2 contains more details.

A global section descriptor (GSD) identifies a particular global section by name and associates the name with a GSTE. A global section descriptor contains information used to determine whether a particular process is allowed to access the global section. Section 14.6.1 describes this data structure.

The global page table (GPT), described in Section 14.6.3, contains global PTEs that serve as templates for the process PTEs that map global pages.

When multiple processes are mapped to a global section, all processes can potentially benefit from each other's page faults. When process A incurs a page fault for a global page not in its working set, if the page is not valid, it is read in from its backing store. After the page fault completes, the global page table entry (GPTE) is modified to show that the global page is valid. If process B then incurs a page fault for that page, the page fault handler copies the information from the GPTE to B's PTE and resolves the fault without the need for I/O.

14.1.2.3   **Managing Physical Memory.** Physical memory is used in the following ways:

- Permanently, by pages occupied by the resident executive (system base image and the nonpageable sections of loadable executive images) and its systemwide nonpageable data structures (for example, the per-CPU interrupt stacks and nonpaged pool)
- Dynamically, by pages on the free and modified page lists
- Dynamically, by pages in processes' working sets
- Dynamically, by pages in the system working set (pageable sections of loadable executive images and pageable system data)

The VMS executive must apportion physical memory among these uses based on

- SYSGEN parameters that specify various minimum and maximum limits, such as the sizes of the free and modified page lists and the systemwide maximum process working set size
- Process quotas and limits that specify process-specific minimum and maximum working set sizes
- Statistics and measurements that describe the current environment, such as the size of the free page list and the rate at which a particular process has been page faulting recently

14.1.3   **Memory Management Mechanisms**

This section provides an overview of the mechanisms by which VMS manages physical and virtual memory.

VMS memory management mechanisms are best introduced from a historical perspective. Historically, VMS has had two basic mechanisms to control its allocation of physical memory to processes: paging and swapping. Several auxiliary mechanisms, such as automatic working set limit adjustment and swapper trimming, supplement these fundamental ones.

14.1.3.1   **Original Design.** An important goal of the initial release of the VMS operating system was to provide an environment for a variety of applications, including real-time, batch, and time-sharing, on a family of VAX processors with a wide range of performance and capacity. The memory management subsystem was designed to adjust to the changing demands of time-sharing loads and to meet the more predictable performance required by real-time processes.

The major problems common to virtual memory systems that concerned the original designers were the following:

- The negative effect that one heavily paging process has on the performance of others
- The high cost of starting a process that has to fault all its pages into memory
- The high I/O load imposed by paging

VMS support of virtual memory was designed to address these problems. With some modifications, the original design remains intact in the current release.

The VMS designers chose to implement process-local page replacement instead of global replacement. A process pages against itself, for the most part, rather than against other processes. This minimizes the risk of page fault thrashing among processes and also makes possible more predictable performance for a real-time process.

A process is created with a working set quota that limits its maximum use of physical memory. The default and maximum sizes of each process's working set are specified at process creation. As the process executes and faults pages, they are read into memory from backing store and placed into the process's working set. When the process's working set reaches its maximum size, a subsequent page fault must be a replacement page fault, requiring that a page first be removed from the working set. In this manner, the process pages against itself. (Note, however, that a heavily paging process that causes the contents of the free and modified page lists to turn over rapidly can indirectly affect other processes.)

Unlike some virtual memory architectures, the VAX does not include a reference bit in each page table entry by means of which less recently referenced pages can be identified. Instead, VMS uses the order of working set list entries to determine length of residence. The working set list, which describes the pages in the process's working set, is a ring buffer with a pointer to the entry most recently added to the working set. In general, the page most likely to be removed from the working set is the one following the most recently added, that is, the oldest.

Although this working set replacement algorithm is simple to implement and has low CPU overhead, its selection of a page to be removed is not optimal and may cause more page faults. For those reasons, the original algorithm has been enhanced. Chapter 17 describes the current algorithm.

To minimize the performance impact of this algorithm, VMS caches pages removed from a working set so that they can be faulted back into it without the need for mass storage I/O; the executive inserts a page removed from a working set at the tail of the free page list or the modified page list, depending on whether the page had been modified. When a process needs a physical page of memory, for example, to fault a nonresident page, the executive allocates the physical page at the head of the free page list. Thus an unmodified page is cached for a length of time proportional to the size of the free page list and the frequency with which pages are allocated from it. When the modified page list grows beyond a certain size or the free page list shrinks below a certain size, the executive writes modified pages to their backing store, typically a page file, and then inserts them at the tail of the free page list. A modified page is thus cached while it is on both the modified and free page lists.

Because a page faulted into the working set becomes the newest page and is thus less likely to be removed, the page list caches considerably improve the performance of the working set list replacement algorithm, bringing it close to that possible with a least-recently-used algorithm but with less overhead. (Note that a heavily paging process can affect others indirectly by causing the page lists to turn over more rapidly, thus reducing their effectiveness as caches for the other processes.)

VMS provides services by which a process can exercise some control over its working set list: it can lock and unlock selected pages into its working set and purge its working set of pages in a specified address range. At image exit, VMS deletes P0 space and the nonpermanent part of P1 space, thereby removing these pages from the working set. Before a process executes a new image, VMS purges the working set of no longer needed pages, such as command language interpreter code and data.

VMS was designed to manage memory by both paging and swapping. Paging occurs in response to process page fault exceptions and results in moving virtual pages into and out of physical memory. Swapping, which occurs in response to events detected by the executive, results in moving whole working sets into and out of physical memory. Swapping all of a process's working set minimizes the time to start up the process and the number of I/O operations to remove its pages from memory and to read them back in. Swapping makes it possible for more processes to coexist even when their working sets cannot all fit into memory at once.

Processes in certain long-lasting wait states are more likely to be out-swapped than computable processes. When an outswapped process becomes computable, it is eventually inswapped. Chapter 18 describes the relation between process scheduling states and the swapper's selection of inswap and outswap candidates. A privileged process can prevent itself from being swapped.

To reduce the I/O overhead of paging, VMS reads and writes multiple pages at a time. A page fault cluster size is defined for each pageable entity, for example, an image section or a process page table. When a page is faulted, VMS tries to read a cluster's worth of pages. It writes modified pages in clusters also, to reduce I/O overhead. A SYSGEN parameter specifies the number of modified pages written to a page file at once. Within this larger cluster, the modified page writer groups related virtual pages so that they can be faulted back in as a cluster. Chapter 16 describes both types of clustering.

Simply deferring the writing of modified pages reduces I/O overhead to some extent: some pages are deleted before they are written; some pages are faulted in from the modified page list and modified again before they are written.

In VMS Version 1, the following parameters controlled the memory management subsystem:

- The minimum sizes of the free and modified page lists
- The maximum size the modified page list could grow before the system began to write its pages to a page file
- The maximum number of concurrently resident processes
- For each process, a default and maximum working set size

As processes were created, used free pages, and faulted pages, the free page list would shrink and the modified page list would grow. If the free page list shrunk too low, the swapper would write modified pages and, if necessary, outswap a process. If the modified page list grew too large, the swapper would write modified pages. Occasionally, the swapper would have to write the entire modified page list, or flush it, in order to force specific pages out of memory. A process could alter its working set size from its default to its maximum through a system service to use that many more pages. Its working set size would be reset to its default at image exit.

14.1.3.2   **Auxiliary Mechanisms.** VMS Version 2 added a mechanism called automatic working set limit adjustment, by which a process's working set size was altered in response to its page fault rate. The working set of a heavily faulting process grew so as to reduce its page fault rate. The working set of a process that incurred very few page faults was shrunk. With expansion considered the more significant part of the mechanism, it was triggered at quantum end, based on the idea that a process that could not execute even for a quantum did not need its working set limit adjusted. Chapter 17 describes automatic working set limit adjustment.

VMS Version 2 also employed an enhancement to the VAX architecture that made it possible to test whether a page had been referenced recently enough so that its page table entry was in the translation buffer cache.

In VMS Version 3, the mechanism was enhanced to permit a heavily faulting process to grow beyond its normal maximum working set if the free page list was sufficiently large. An alternative mechanism for reclaiming physical pages was added, called swapper trimming. The basic idea was that when the swapper process detected that the free page list had shrunk too low, it could reclaim memory from the working sets of processes expanded in times of plenty. If more memory was needed, it could either outswap a process or shrink a process working set as low as the SYSGEN parameter SWPOUTPGCNT. This added considerable flexibility to the original design; by altering this and several other parameters, a system manager could tune the system to favor swapping over paging, or vice versa.

VMS Version 4 refined swapper trimming, correcting a failure to reclaim memory from a low-priority compute-bound process whose working set had expanded when the system was lightly loaded. As a result of the pixscan mechanism (see Chapter 12), the refinement was not always effective.

In VMS Version 5 there were several changes to the modified page writer, the most significant being that it no longer flushed the modified page list to force specific pages out of memory. Instead, it could be requested to search the list for selected pages and write them, leaving the rest of the pages as cache.

14.1.3.3   **Comparison of Paging and Swapping.** VMS uses both paging and swapping to make efficient use of available physical memory. The page fault handler

---

Table 14.1   Comparison of Paging and Swapping

DIFFERENCES

Paging	*Swapping*
The page fault handler moves pages in and out of process working sets.	The swapper moves entire processes in and out of physical memory.
The page fault handler is an exception service routine that executes in the context of the process incurring the page fault.	The swapper is a separate process that is awakened from its hibernating state by components that detect a need for swapper activity.
The unit of paging is the page, although the page fault handler attempts to read more than one page with a single disk read.	The unit of swapping is the process or, actually, the pages of the process currently in its working set.
Page read requests for process pages are queued to the driver according to the base priority of the process incurring the page fault. [1]	Swapper I/O requests are queued according to the value of the SYSGEN parameter SWP_PRIO. Modified page write requests are queued according to the SYSGEN parameter MPW_PRIO. [1]
Paging supports images with very large address spaces.	Swapping supports a large number of concurrently active processes.

SIMILARITIES

The page fault handler and swapper work from a common database. The most important structures used for both paging and swapping are the process page tables, the working set list, and the PFN database.

The page fault handler and swapper do conventional I/O. There are only slight differences in detail between pager and swapper I/O on the one hand and normal Queue I/O requests on the other.

Both components attempt to maximize the number of blocks read or written with a given I/O request. The page fault handler accomplishes this with read clustering. The swapper attempts to inswap or outswap the entire working set in one (or a small number of) I/O request(s). The modified page writer writes clusters of pages.

---

[1] This consideration has meaning primarily for older, conventional mass storage device drivers. The priority at which an I/O request is queued to the disk class driver is largely irrelevant because the driver handles most requests immediately by queuing them to the device, which is likely to reorder them based on considerations such as disk head position.

executes in the context of the process that incurs a page fault. It supports programs with virtual address spaces larger than physical memory. The swapper enables a system to support more active processes than can fit into physical memory at one time. The swapper's responsibilities are more global and systemwide than those of the page fault hander. Table 14.1 compares the page fault handler and the swapper.

14.2   **VAX ADDRESS TRANSLATION AND ACCESS CHECKING**

As mentioned in Section 14.1.1, virtual to physical address translation is supported by three page tables. Each of these page tables is described by processor registers that specify the table's location and size:

- PR\$_SBR and PR\$_SLR, the system base and length registers
- PR\$_P0BR and PR\$_P0LR, the P0 base and length registers
- PR\$_P1BR and PR\$_P1LR, the P1 base and length registers

The registers that describe the SPT are loaded during system initialization, before memory management is enabled. PR\$_SBR contains the physical address of the SPT. The SPT provides the basis for all virtual addresses; thus, to access PTEs within the SPT, the VAX processor must use physical addresses.

The registers that describe per-process page tables are loaded from the process's hardware process control block when the LDPCTX instruction is executed. In contrast to the SPT, which is physically located, per-process page tables are located in system virtual address space. PR\$_P0BR and PR\$_P1BR contain the base virtual addresses of the P0PT and the P1PT.

As shown in Figure 14.1, a virtual address has three parts. The high-order two bits identify the address space and select a page table:

- The value 00_2 selects the P0 page table. Another way of expressing this fact is that P0 space addresses range between 0 and $3FFFFFFF_{16}$.
- The value 01_2 selects the P1 page table. P1 space addresses range between 40000000_{16} and $7FFFFFFF_{16}$.
- The value 10_2 selects the SPT. System space addresses range between 80000000_{16} and $BFFFFFFF_{16}$.
- The value 11_2 is undefined and, when used in an address, causes an access violation exception. Addresses between $C0000000_{16}$ and $FFFFFFFF_{16}$ are undefined.

The low-order nine bits identify a particular byte within a page. Bits $\langle 29:9 \rangle$ are called the virtual page number. A virtual page number is used as a longword context index into a page table to select the PTE that contains information about the location of that virtual page.

Figure 14.2 shows the VAX architectural definition of a valid PTE. Bit $\langle 31 \rangle$ in the PTE is set to indicate that the virtual page is valid and that the processor can use bits $\langle 20:0 \rangle$ as a PFN. Bit $\langle 26 \rangle$, when set, indicates that the

Figure 14.1
Parts of a Virtual Address

Figure 14.2
Valid Page Table Entry

page has been modified. Bit ⟨25⟩ is reserved and must be zero. Bits ⟨24:21⟩ are reserved for software; they are explained further in Section 14.3.3.

Bits ⟨30:27⟩ of the PTE are the protection code for the virtual page. When a reference is made to a virtual address, whether or not the page is valid, the processor tests the access mode and intended type of access against the protection code in the PTE to determine whether the access is legal. This enables the legality of an intended access to an invalid page to be checked without having to fault the page into memory.

Table 14.2 lists the symbolic and numeric forms of possible protection codes.

If the protection on the page prohibits the access, the processor generates an exception called an access violation. The exception-specific parameters it pushes onto the stack include an identification of the virtual address to which access was attempted. (Although the address pushed is typically the faulting virtual address, the VAX architecture requires only that the processor push a virtual address within the same page as the faulting virtual address.) The exception parameter information is the same for all memory management exceptions and is shown in Figure 16.1.

In translating a system virtual address, the processor takes the following steps:

1. It selects the SPT, based on the high-order bits of the address, and gets its base address from PR$_SBR.
2. It compares the virtual page number to the contents of PR$_SLR. If the page number is greater, an attempt is being made to reference an address past the end of defined system space. The processor generates a type of access violation known as a length violation.
3. If the virtual page number is less than or equal to the contents of PR$_SLR, the processor computes the physical address of the PTE by multiplying the page number by 4 (the number of bytes in a longword) and adding it to the base address of the page table.
4. It fetches the PTE.

   —If the valid bit is set, the processor merges the PFN in the PTE with the low nine bits of the virtual address to form the physical address.

   —If the valid bit is clear, the processor generates a page fault. The VMS page fault exception service routine, the page fault handler, locates

Table 14.2 Memory Access Protection Codes in Page Table Entries

Protection[1]	Symbol	Binary Value	Protection Mask Hexadecimal
No access allowed	PRT$C_NA	0000	00000000
Reserved	PRT$C_RESERVED	0001	08000000
Kernel write (kernel read)	PRT$C_KW	0010	10000000
Kernel read (no write)	PRT$C_KR	0011	18000000
User write (user read)	PRT$C_UW	0100	20000000
Executive write (executive read)	PRT$C_EW	0101	28000000
Executive read, kernel write	PRT$C_ERKW	0110	30000000
Executive read (no write)	PRT$C_ER	0111	38000000
Supervisor write (supervisor read)	PRT$C_SW	1000	40000000
Supervisor read, executive write	PRT$C_SREW	1001	48000000
Supervisor read, kernel write	PRT$C_SRKW	1010	50000000
Supervisor read (no write)	PRT$C_SR	1011	58000000
User read, supervisor write	PRT$C_URSW	1100	60000000
User read, executive write	PRT$C_UREW	1101	68000000
User read, kernel write	PRT$C_URKW	1110	70000000
User read (no write)	PRT$C_UR	1111	78000000

Note that the following rules govern memory access protection:
- If a given access mode has write access to a specific page, then that access mode also has read access to that page.
- If a given access mode can read a specific page, then all more privileged access modes can read the same page.
- If a given access mode can write a specific page, then all more privileged access modes can write the same page.

---

[1] Access that is implied (rather than explicitly a part of the symbolic protection name) is included in parentheses.

the virtual page, reads it into memory, and changes the PTE. Subsequently, the instruction that triggered the page fault can be reexecuted successfully. Chapter 16 describes the page fault handler's operations.

Figure 14.3 shows a simplified form of these steps.

Translating a per-process virtual address requires additional steps. The processor must first calculate the system virtual address of the per-process PTE. Then, using steps analogous to those used for system virtual address translation, the processor translates the process virtual address to a physical address.

That process page tables are themselves accessed via system virtual addresses rather than physical addresses means that they can be paged. Thus the translation of a process virtual address can conceivably incur two page faults, one for the appropriate page table page and one for the process page itself.

The *VAX Architecture Reference Manual* contains further details of the architecturally defined address translation mechanism.

As a performance optimization, a VAX processor includes a cache called a translation buffer, which records virtual address translations. Each translation buffer entry associates a virtual address with its PTE contents. Only the contents of valid PTEs are cached. An attempted translation that results in a page fault is not cached; however, once the page is read in from backing store, the faulting instruction is reexecuted and the now-valid PTE is cached.

When the LDPCTX instruction is executed to load a new process's context, the per-process translation buffer entries for the previous process are invalidated. Whenever the executive changes a valid PTE, it must write to the translation buffer invalidate single processor register, PR$_TBIS, to invalidate any possible cached entry. Running on a symmetric multiprocessing (SMP) system, the executive must ensure that whenever any processor modifies a valid SPTE, all processors invalidate any possible corresponding cached entry. Chapter 34 describes this operation in detail.

14.3   PROCESS DATA STRUCTURES

Memory management information about the process is maintained in the software process control block (PCB) and in the PHD. These are described in the sections that follow.

14.3.1   Software Process Control Block

The software PCB is allocated from nonpaged pool at process creation and remains resident for the life of the process, whether the process is resident or outswapped. When a process is outswapped, the PCB remains as the representation of the existence of that process and must contain all information that the swapper requires to inswap the process. Figure 14.4 shows the PCB fields related to memory management.

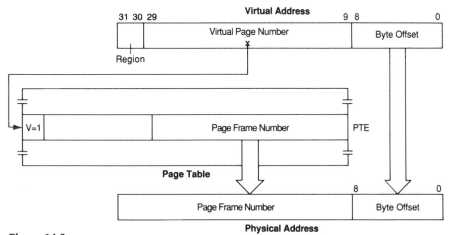

Figure 14.3
VAX Address Translation

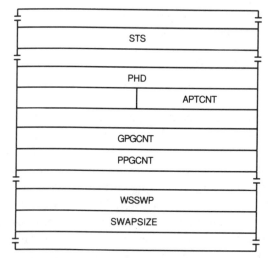

Figure 14.4
PCB Fields Related to Memory Management

PCB$L_STS contains several relevant status bits:

- PCB$V_RES, when set, means that the process (that is, its PHD and its working set) is resident in memory.
- PCB$V_PSWAPM, when set, means that the process has disabled outswapping of itself.
- PCB$V_PHDRES, when set, means that the process's PHD is resident. (When a process is outswapped, its header may remain in memory.)
- PCB$V_DISAWS, when set, means that the process has disabled automatic working set limit adjustment.

PCB$L_PHD contains the address of the PHD, if PCB$V_PHDRES in PCB$L_STS is set.

PCB$W_APTCNT only has meaning for an outswapped process; the swapper records in it the number of active and valid pages in the PHD.

PCB$L_GPGCNT contains the number of global pages in the process's working set, and PCB$L_PPGCNT, the number of process-private pages. The sum of these two fields is the number of physically resident pages, the size of the process's working set.

When a process is newly created, PCB$L_WSSWP is cleared to signal the swapper that the process's initial pages come from the shell. The field has a different use later in the life of the process: when a process is outswapped, PCB$L_WSSWP contains its mass storage location. If the process has been outswapped in one extent, PCB$L_WSSWP contains a systemwide page file index (see Section 14.8.2) identifying the swap file and the starting virtual block number. The high bit of PCB$L_SWAPSIZE is set to indicate such a process; the low 31 bits of PCB$L_SWAPSIZE contain its outswapped size in blocks. If the process is outswapped in more than one extent, PCB$L_WSSWP contains the address of a page/swap file mapping window block (PFLMAP), a data structure that lists the locations and sizes of the extents. Chapter 18 describes the PFLMAP and process swapping.

14.3.2   **Process Header**

The most important process-specific memory management data structures are contained in the PHD:

- The P0 and P1 page tables are the largest contributors to the size of the PHD and contain the complete description of the per-process virtual address space currently in use by the process, including both valid and invalid pages.
- The working set list describes the subset of PTEs that are currently valid.
- The process section table contains entries that associate the process sections created in the process's address space with the corresponding sections in the files where the pages originate.
- Because the sizes of the pieces of the PHD vary from system to system, there must be some method of determining where each piece is located. Pointers or indexes in the fixed portion of the PHD serve this purpose. Process accounting information, some of which is used by the page fault handler or by the swapper, is also located in this area. The hardware PCB, the area in which the register context of the process is saved, is also in the fixed part of the PHD.
- Several arrays contain information about the pages in the PHD itself. The swapper uses this information when it outswaps the PHD.

Figure 14.5 shows these parts of the PHD. The smaller figure to the right shows the relative sizes of the portions of the PHD on a typical system. Figure E.15 shows the detailed layout of the PHD. Specific fields in the PHD are described, where appropriate, in this chapter and the memory management chapters that follow.

The PHD has several unusual characteristics that distinguish it from other data structures:

- The PHD is swappable.

    When a process is outswapped, its PHD can be outswapped as well. When later inswapped, the PHD is likely to be placed in a different balance slot at a different system space address. (Section 14.7.1 describes balance slots.) Consequently, accesses to the PHD that use its system space address must be synchronized against swapper interference. Accesses from a current process can be made with the SCHED spinlock held to block any rescheduling and possible swapping of the process. Holding the MMG spinlock is an alternative way to block swapping.

- The PHD is referenced using both system space addresses and P1 space addresses.

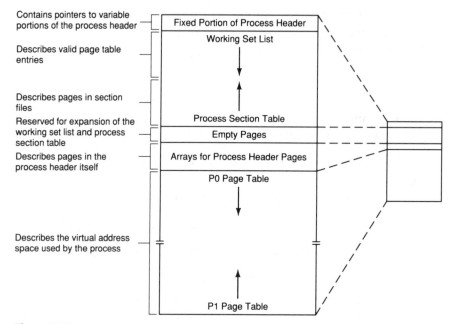

Contains pointers to variable portions of the process header — Fixed Portion of Process Header

Working Set List

Describes valid page table entries —

Describes pages in section files —

Process Section Table

Reserved for expansion of the working set list and process section table — Empty Pages

Describes pages in the process header itself — Arrays for Process Header Pages

P0 Page Table

Describes the virtual address space used by the process —

P1 Page Table

Figure 14.5
Discrete Portions of the Process Header

The PHD is located in system space partly so that the swapper can access it. Furthermore, VAX address translation requires that per-process page tables be in system space.

The PHD, excluding the per-process page tables, is also mapped in P1 space and accessed through global pointer CTL$GL_PHD. This P1 window to the PHD is at a fixed virtual address range and remains the same across outswaps and inswaps. The exact location of the window varies with system version; its size varies with several SYSGEN parameters. Most executive code that runs in process context accesses the PHD through the P1 window and thus avoids the need for blocking possible movement of the PHD to a different balance slot. Chapter 18 contains more information on double mapping of the PHD.

- The PHD has both pageable and nonpageable parts. The per-process page tables are pageable; the rest of the PHD is not pageable.

The memory-resident portion of the PHD is described by the process's working set list, and its nonpageable portion is locked into the working set list. PHD pages are the only pages with system virtual addresses that are part of a process working set.

An attempt by one process to fault a page in another process's PHD is viewed as an error. The page fault handler simulates an access violation for any such attempted fault.

- The PHD has four variable-length pieces: the two per-process page tables, the working set list, and the PST. The maximum sizes of these pieces are fixed by SYSGEN parameters, but their actual sizes vary in response to process needs.

However, the balance slots in which PHDs reside are of fixed size to enable VMS memory management routines to associate easily the address of a process PTE with the process, as described in Section 14.7.3.

The per-process page tables are at a fixed place (for a given set of SYSGEN parameters) at the high-address portion of the PHD. The P0 page table grows toward increasing addresses and the P1 page table toward decreasing addresses. The system virtual addresses of the page tables must remain stable while the process is resident or has I/O in progress. Every resident page has a back pointer to the address of the PTE that maps it in the PFN database for that page. Any outstanding I/O request refers to its buffer using the system virtual address of the buffer's PTEs.

The dynamic growth area of the PHD must accommodate the growth of both the PST and the working set list. Expansion in either of these can result in moving the PST to higher addresses in the PHD. Section 14.3.5 describes PST/working set list expansion.

The sections that follow describe the memory management structures in the PHD.

14.3.3   Process Page Tables

The VAX architecture specifies that per-process page tables be virtually based, unlike the system page table, which is physically based. As a result, the pages of a process page table need only be virtually contiguous, not necessarily physically contiguous. A process page table can therefore grow as required to reflect expansion of the address space it maps; VMS merely maps additional page table pages into the virtual addresses contiguous to the end of the page table. Because the dynamic growth of a process page table can easily accommodate the dynamic expansion of a process's virtual address space, the size of a process's page tables can be adjusted to suit its needs. VMS does not need to allocate maximum-size process page tables for all processes. Furthermore, per-process page tables can themselves be paged.

Figure 14.6 shows the per-process page tables in the PHD and the fields in the fixed portion of the PHD that locate the P0 and P1 page tables.

The P0 page table contains PTEs for all pages currently defined in P0 space (P0PTEs). The starting virtual address of the P0 page table is stored in offset PHD$L_P0BR and copied to the P0 base register (PR$_P0BR) by LDPCTX when the process is placed in execution. The number of pages in P0 space is stored in offset PHD$L_P0LR and copied to the P0 length register (PR$_P0LR).

PHD$L_FREP0VA contains the process virtual address corresponding to the first unmapped page in P0 space. The P0 page table maps process addresses from 0 to 1 less than the contents of PHD$L_FREP0VA. In other

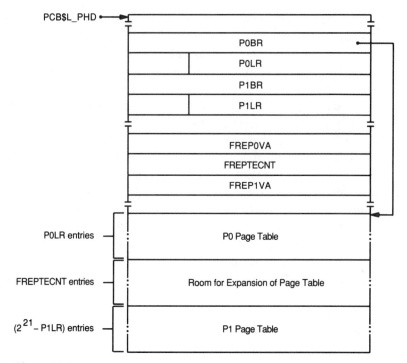

Figure 14.6
Process Page Tables

words, the contents of PHD$L_FREP0VA are the product of 200_{16} and the number of P0PTEs.

In a similar manner, the P1 page table contains PTEs for the pages in P1 space (P1PTEs). Its base address and length are stored in fields PHD$L_P1BR and PHD$L_P1LR. The LDPCTX instruction copies these fields to the processor registers PR$_P1BR and PR$_P1LR. Like P1 space itself, the P1 page table grows toward smaller addresses. To simplify VAX address translation, the base address of the P1 page table is the virtual address of the P1PTE that would map virtual address 40000000_{16}. This allows a P1 virtual page number to be used as an index into the P1 page table. PHD$L_P1LR contains the number of P1PTEs between virtual page 0 and the first defined (that is, lowest) page of P1 space.

The virtual address corresponding to the first unmapped page in P1 space is stored at offset PHD$L_FREP1VA. The P1 page table maps addresses from the contents of PHD$L_FREP1VA plus 200_{16} to $7FFFFFFF_{16}$. In other words, the contents of PHD$L_FREP1VA are 40000000_{16} minus 200_{16}, plus the product of 200_{16} and the contents of PHD$L_P1LR.

The processor registers that describe the page tables are not stored by the SVPCTX instruction. These registers change relatively rarely (for example, as a result of address space creation or deletion). Instead, VMS explicitly records such changes in the hardware PCB whenever it changes the processor registers. This strategy saves the memory writes that would otherwise be required every time the process context is saved.

The SYSGEN parameter VIRTUALPAGECNT is the upper limit on the maximum combined number of PTEs in the P0 and P1 page tables. Chapter 15 describes additional limits to the growth of virtual address space. The number of PTEs available for the expansion of either P0 space or P1 space is stored in offset PHD$L_FREPTECNT. This number is the SYSGEN parameter VIRTUALPAGECNT minus the current sizes of the P0 and P1 page tables.

Figure 14.7 shows the various forms of valid and invalid PTE that can appear in a process page table. Notice that the valid bit, protection code bits, and owner access mode bits have the same meaning in all forms of PTE. Section 14.2 describes the valid and protection code bits and the use of the PFN. The owner access mode bits record the access mode that owns that page. The VMS executive allows a process to modify the characteristics of a virtual page or delete it from an access mode equal to or more privileged than the page's owner access mode.

A PTE for an invalid page contains either the location of the page or a pointer to further information about the page. The page fault handler uses the type bits, bits ⟨26⟩ and ⟨22⟩, in the invalid PTE to distinguish the different forms of invalid PTE. These are described in the sections that follow. Chapter 16 describes the processing of page faults for various types of invalid PTEs.

One form of invalid PTE not pictured in Figure 14.7 is a null page, a longword of zero. A PTE with a zero protection code disallows any access to the page by any mode. This form of PTE describes an unmapped page of address space.

14.3.3.1 **PTE Containing a Process Section Table Index.** The PTE of each page in a process section contains the index of the PSTE describing that section. The PSTE has information about the location of the file mapped into the process address space and the virtual block in the file containing each section page.

The PSTE also contains control bits that are copied to the PTE of each page in the section:

- Bit ⟨18⟩ is set to indicate the page is writable.
- Bit ⟨17⟩ is set to indicate the page is demand zero.
- Bit ⟨16⟩ is set to indicate the page is copy-on-reference.

Section 14.3.5 describes the PST organization and layout of the PSTE.

14.3.3.2 **PTE Containing a Page File Virtual Block Number.** A process can page in up to four different page files. This behavior is new with VMS Version 5; in earlier versions, a process was assigned to one page file at process creation

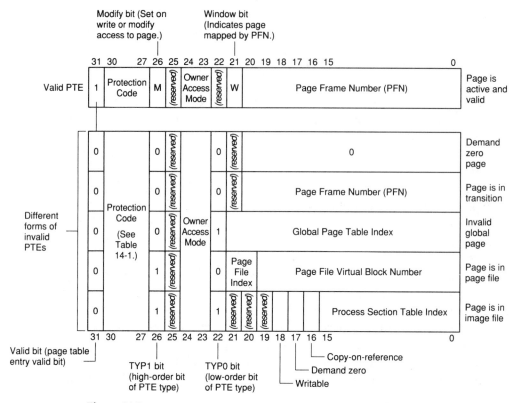

Figure 14.7
Different Forms of Page Table Entry

and could page only in that file. Each process has a four-byte array in its PHD, beginning at offset PHD$B_PRCPGFL, that identifies the page files it can use. Each byte can contain a different systemwide page file index, an index into the page-and-swap-file-vector. Section 14.8.2 contains more information on the page-and-swap-file vector, and Chapter 16 discusses the assignment of a process to a page file.

When a virtual page has been faulted out to a page file, its PTE contains the virtual block number of the page within the page file and a two-bit number in bits ⟨21:20⟩ indicating the page file in which the page is located. The two-bit number, referred to as a process-local page file index, indexes the PHD array at PHD$B_PRCPGFL. With this extra level of indirection, there are 20 bits available for the virtual block number.

A process has a current page file in which pages have been reserved for its use as backing store. PHD$B_PRCPAGFIL contains the process-local index of the process's current page file. (Note, PHD$B_PRCPGFL and PHD$B_PRCPAGFIL are different PHD fields.) PHD$B_PAGFIL contains the corresponding systemwide index into the page-and-swap-file vector.

The longword PHD$L_PAGFIL, of which PHD$B_PAGFIL is the high-order byte, is a template for a virtual page that requires a page file backing store address. When such a page is first faulted, the template is copied to the PFN BAK array element (see Section 14.4.2) for the physical page. Bits ⟨21:20⟩ of the template contain the same value as PHD$B_PRCPAGFIL. Bits ⟨19:0⟩ are zero. A BAK array element containing such a template backing store address indicates that a block in the specified page file has been reserved for the virtual page but not yet allocated.

14.3.3.3   **PTE Containing a Global Page Table Index.** The PTE of an invalid process page mapped to a global page contains an index into the global page table, where an associated global PTE contains the information used to locate the page. Section 14.6.4 describes the contents of global PTEs.

14.3.3.4   **PTE of a Page in Transition.** When a physical page is removed from a process working set, it is not discarded but put on the free or modified page list. The invalid virtual page, still associated with the physical page, is called a transition page. Its PTE contains a PFN, but the valid bit is clear. The two type bits are also clear. Retaining the connection to a physical page enables VMS to fault the virtual page back into the working set with minimal overhead until the physical page is reallocated for another use.

Another type of transition page is a virtual page in transit between mass storage and physical memory. When a process faults a page not in memory, the page fault handler allocates a physical page and requests an I/O operation to read the virtual page from its backing store. While the I/O request is in progress, the virtual page has a transition PTE.

A transition page is described further by its physical page's entries in the PFN database (see Section 14.4). In particular, the PFN STATE array (see Section 14.4.3) identifies the state of the page and distinguishes among the different types of transition page.

14.3.3.5   **PTE of a Demand Zero Page.** One form of transition PTE has a zero in the PFN field. This zero indicates a special form of page called a demand-allocate, zero-fill page, or demand zero page for short. When a page fault occurs for such a page, the page fault handler allocates a physical page, fills the page with zeros, inserts the PFN into the PTE, sets the valid bit, and dismisses the exception.

14.3.4   **Working Set List**

Another memory management data structure located in the PHD is the working set list. The working set list describes the subset of a process's pages that are currently valid. Pages described in a process's working set list are P0, P1, or PHD pages. Its capacity to describe pages is the upper limit on the number of physical pages the process can occupy.

The page fault handler and swapper use the working set list to determine which virtual page to discard (to mark invalid) when it is necessary to remove a physical page from the process. The swapper also uses the working set list to determine which virtual pages need to be written to the swap file when the process is outswapped.

Chapter 17 describes the organization and use of the working set list and the layout of a working set list entry (WSLE).

14.3.5 Process Section Table

The process section table is another memory management data structure located in the PHD. It contains PSTEs. A PSTE describes the association between a contiguous portion of virtual address space and a contiguous portion of a file. Both these portions are known as sections and consist of pages with identical characteristics, for example, protection, owner access mode, writability, and file location. Much of virtual address space management is done in units of sections.

When an image is activated (see Chapter 26), the file containing the image is opened and a process section is created for each process-private image section. Although each image section is mapped separately, the image file is opened only once, and the image's sections page using the same assigned channel and window control block.

A process section is also created when

- A process opens a file and requests the Create and Map Section ($CRMPSC) system service to map the file or some part of it into its address space
- A shareable image is activated that is not shared (that is, one that has not been installed with the /SHARE qualifier through the Install Utility)
- A shared image is activated that has a copy-on-reference section

PSTEs enable the memory management subsystem to keep track of process pages in different sections, potentially in different files on different mass storage devices.

Figure 14.8 shows the location of the PST within the PHD. PHD$L_PST-BASOFF contains the byte offset from the beginning of the PHD to the high-address end of the PST.

Each PSTE within the table is 32 bytes long and is located through a negative longword context index from the base of the PST. The first PSTE has an index of -8, the second -10_{16}. Successive PSTEs are at lower addresses. Since all references to a PSTE are relative to PHD$L_PSTBASOFF, the PST can be moved within the PHD without requiring changes in process PTEs that contain process section table indexes.

The following operations compute the address of a particular PSTE:

1. Add the contents of PHD$L_PSTBASOFF to the address of the PHD. The result is the address of the base of the PST.

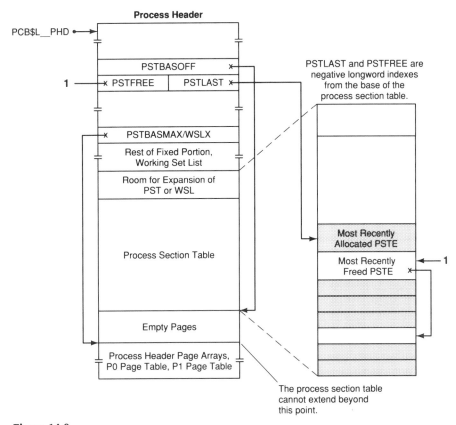

Figure 14.8
Process Section Table

2. Multiply the negative process section table longword context index by 4.
3. Add the (negative) result to the address of the PST.

A PST is organized into a variable number of linked lists of PSTEs. Figure 14.8 shows a typical PST with free and allocated PSTEs; the allocated PSTEs are shaded. The negative index in PHD$W_PSTLAST is the largest index of any entry ever allocated and is thus a "high-water mark."

All the process sections that page from the same section file using the same assigned channel are linked together. The entries are linked together through the backward and forward link index fields of each entry.

When a section is deleted, the PSTE that mapped the section is placed on the list of free entries so that it can be reused. The negative index PHD$W_ PSTFREE points to the most recent addition to the free list. If no entry has been deleted, PHD$W_PSTFREE contains zero. The first longword in a PSTE on the free list contains the negative index to the previous element on the free list. When a section is created, the PSTE allocation routine first checks the free list. If there is no free PSTE, a new one is created from the expansion region between the working set list and the PST, and PHD$W_PSTLAST is modified.

VMS attempts to keep the working set list and PST virtually adjacent, partly to simplify and shorten manipulation of the PHD during outswap and inswap and partly to minimize the chances of wasting physical memory for partial pages of both. When VMS must expand the working set list into the area already occupied by the PST or expand the PST into the area already occupied by the working set list, it allocates space from the existing empty page area (see Figure 14.8). Then, it moves the entire PST into the allocated space at higher addresses and stores the new base address in PHD$L_PSTBASOFF.

The longword at PHD$L_PSTBASMAX/PHD$L_WSLX specifies the maximum size of the PST. This longword points to the high-address end of the empty page area. It contains a longword context index from the beginning of the PHD.

Room is reserved in the PHD for the maximum PST and working set list, specified by the SYSGEN parameters PROCSECTCNT and WSMAX. It is possible for the PST to grow larger than PROCSECTCNT specifies, at the expense of the working set list.

Figure 14.9 shows the format of a process/global section table entry. (Section 14.6.2 describes global section table entries.) Note that the field names within a section table entry are defined by the STARLET.MLB macro $SECDEF and begin with SEC$.

The first longword in the PSTE has two names: in a PSTE, SEC$L_CCB contains the address of the channel control block (CCB) on which the section file has been opened; in a GSTE, SEC$L_GSD contains the address of the global section descriptor for that section.

SEC$W_SEXFL and SEC$W_SEXBL contain negative indexes from the base of the section table to the previous and next section table entry. These link an entry in use into a list of others that page using the same CCB. They also link all free entries together.

The low-order 22 bits of SEC$L_VPXPFC contain the starting virtual page number at which the section's pages are mapped in the address space.

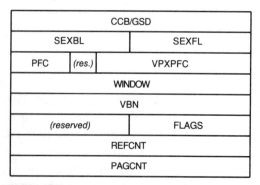

Figure 14.9
Layout of Process/Global Section Table Entry

SEC$B_PFC is the number of section pages that the page fault handler will attempt to read in together when a page fault occurs.

SEC$L_WINDOW is the address of the window control block (WCB) that describes the locations of the section file on a mass storage volume. The WCB points to the unit control block (UCB) for the volume.

SEC$L_VBN specifies the starting virtual, or file-relative, block number (VBN) of the section file at which the pages in this section begin.

SEC$W_FLAGS contains flag bits that describe the section.

SEC$L_REFCNT contains the number of PTEs that refer to the section.

SEC$L_PAGCNT contains the number of pages in the section.

For a process-private section, SEC$L_REFCNT and SEC$L_PAGCNT are typically equal. For a global section, SEC$L_REFCNT is typically some multiple of SEC$L_PAGCNT, depending on how many processes have mapped the global section. Note, however, that if a process maps only a portion of a global section, the reference count reflects only those pages that it has mapped. For either type of section, SEC$L_REFCNT is decreased if a process deletes pages in its address space that map the section.

The following steps locate a virtual page in a section file through information in the PSTE:

1. Subtract the section's starting virtual page number from the virtual page number of the faulting page to get the page offset into the section.
2. Add the contents of SEC$L_VBN to the page offset computed in step 1 to get the VBN of the virtual page within the file.
3. Use the mapping information in the WCB to transform the VBN to a logical block number on a mass storage volume.

14.3.6   Process Header Page Arrays

When a PHD is outswapped, some information about each PHD page is stored in the PHD page array portion of the outswapped PHD. Figure 14.10 shows this area. Two of the arrays, the BAK and WSLX arrays, save information about each PHD page in the working set, copied either from the PFN database (see Section 14.4) or from the SPTE that maps that PHD page.

While a PHD is resident, the backing store location of each of its valid or transition pages is stored in the PFN database; the backing store location of a PHD page in a page file is stored in the SPTE that maps the PHD page. For a valid page in a resident PHD, the PFN database stores information about the location of the page's entry in the process's working set list. When the PHD is outswapped, both the physical pages and the balance set slot it occupied are released for other uses. The PHD BAK array records the backing store information for each PHD page, which would otherwise be lost.

The PHD WSLX array records the location in the working set list of each PHD page. Without this information, locating the PHD pages in the working set list at inswap would require searching the working set list. (The virtual

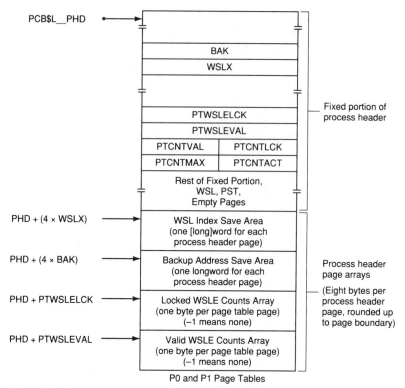

Figure 14.10
Process Header Page Arrays

address information in each PHD page's WSLE will have to be recalculated when the PHD is inswapped into a different balance slot.)

The other two arrays, locked WSLE count and valid WSLE count, contain a reference count for each page table page. These four arrays are described in greater detail in Chapter 18.

14.4   PFN DATABASE

The memory management data structures include information about the available pages of physical memory. The fact that this information must be accessible while the page is in use means that it cannot be stored in the page itself. In addition, the caching strategy for the free and modified lists requires physical page information to be accessible, even when pages are not currently active and valid. The PFN database records this information.

The PFN database consists of eight arrays (see Figure 14.11). Each array contains a specific item of information about physical pages of memory. Information about a specific page of physical memory is in the same element of each array. Table 14.3 lists each kind of information in the PFN database, including the global name of the pointer to the beginning of each array.

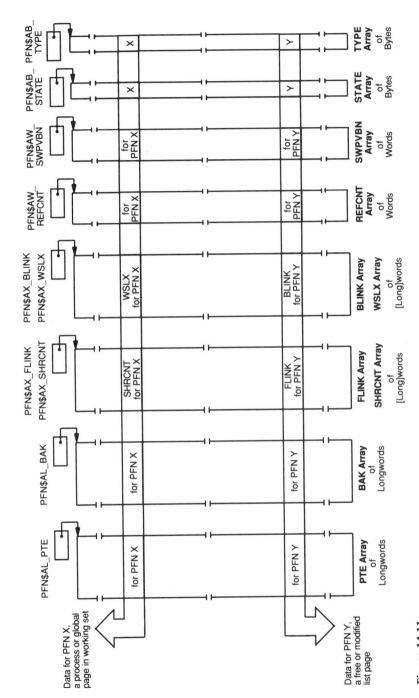

Figure 14.11
PFN Database Arrays

379

Table 14.3 PFN Database Arrays

Array Element Contents	Name of Pointer to Array	Size of Element	Comments
System virtual address of PTE	PFN$AL_PTE	Longword	
Backing store address	PFN$AL_BAK	Longword	Figure 14.12
Physical page state	PFN$AB_STATE	Byte	Figure 14.13
Page type	PFN$AB_TYPE	Byte	Figure 14.14
Forward link	PFN$AX_FLINK	[Long]word [1]	Figure 14.15; Overlays the SHRCNT array
Backward link	PFN$AX_BLINK	[Long]word [1]	Figure 14.15; Overlays the WSLX array
Reference count	PFN$AW_REFCNT	Word	
Global share count	PFN$AX_SHRCNT	[Long]word [1]	Overlays the FLINK array
Working set list index	PFN$AX_WSLX	[Long]word [1]	Overlays the BLINK array
Swap file virtual block number	PFN$AW_SWPVBN	Word	

[1] The size of this array element is a function of the amount of physical memory on the system (see Section 14.4.5).

Most of the information in the PFN database relates to the current virtual use of a physical page. For a physical page that is not mapped by any virtual page the only meaningful information is that in the FLINK and BLINK arrays.

The PFN itself is the index to each array in the PFN database; that is, information about a particular page is located by indexing each PFN array with the PFN of that page. The global location MMG$GL_MINPFN contains the lowest valid subscript into the PFN database. It is currently initialized to zero, and thus the PFN arrays are zero-based.

During system initialization, the highest physical pages of memory are allocated for permanent uses, such as the system base image, nonpaged pool, and SPT. To save physical memory, VMS does not include such pages in the PFN database because their virtual state will never change since they do not page. The global location MMG$GL_MAXPFN contains the highest valid subscript in the PFN database. That is, it contains not the highest PFN on the system but rather the PFN of the highest physical page for which there are corresponding PFN data array elements, the highest PFN that can be used for paging.

VMS maintains a small list of allocatable physical pages that have no PFN database. In circumstances such as extending nonpaged pool or loading a nonpageable section of a loadable executive image, the executive attempts allocation from this list first. If the list is empty, VMS simply allocates a page from the free page list. The global cell MMG$GL_FREE_NO_PFN_DB_ LIST contains the PFN of the first page on the list. The first longword of each page contains the PFN of the next page on the list. The end of the list is a pointer of zero.

At system initialization, an SPTE is reserved for temporarily mapping one of these PFNs to access its forward pointer. To allocate such a page, the routine MMG$ALLOCPFN_NO_DB, in module ALLOCPFN, maps the first physical page on the list using the reserved SPTE, invalidates the corresponding translation buffer entry, and copies the page's forward pointer to MMG$GL_FREE_NO_PFN_DB_LIST.

The sections that follow describe the arrays that make up the PFN database.

14.4.1 PTE Array

Each PFN PTE array element contains the system virtual address of the PTE that maps that physical page. If no virtual page is mapped to a physical page, its PTE array element contains the value 0. A PFN PTE array element for a global page contains the virtual address of the global PTE.

When assigning a physical page to a new use, the executive examines its PTE array element to determine whether the page is a transition page and still pointed to by a PTE associated with its previous use. If the array element value is nonzero, the executive must take steps to sever the connection between the physical page and its previous use.

14.4.2 BAK Array

A PFN BAK array element contains the backing store location for the virtual page occupying a physical page. When a physical page is assigned to another use, the PTE, if any, that currently maps the page must be updated. VMS replaces information about the location of the virtual page in memory (the PFN of the physical page that contains it) with information about its location in mass storage copied from the BAK array element. Figure 14.12 shows the possible contents of a PFN BAK array element.

14.4.3 PFN STATE Array

A PFN STATE array element, shown in Figure 14.13, indicates the state of a physical page. As shown in the figure, the low three bits contain the page location code, indicating, for example, whether the page is on the free list or valid in a working set.

Several codes require further explanation:

- Release pending means that the virtual page has been removed from a working set but still has a nonzero reference count. When the reference

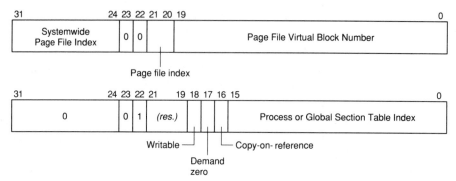

Figure 14.12
Possible Contents of PFN BAK Array Element

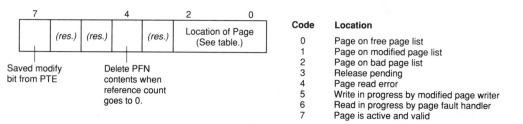

Code	Location
0	Page on free page list
1	Page on modified page list
2	Page on bad page list
3	Release pending
4	Page read error
5	Write in progress by modified page writer
6	Read in progress by page fault handler
7	Page is active and valid

Figure 14.13
Contents of PFN STATE Array Element

count is decremented to zero at I/O completion, the physical page will be placed on the free or modified list.

• Page read error means that a nonrecoverable I/O error occurred during an attempt to read the virtual page from its backing store into the physical page. During postprocessing of the I/O request, when the error is noted, this code is stored in the PFN STATE array element. Consequently, when the page is later refaulted, the page fault handler will signal a page read error exception.

• Write in progress means that the modified page writer has initiated I/O to write the page to its backing store.

• Read in progress means that the page fault handler has initiated I/O to read the page from its backing store.

Bit 4 in a PFN STATE array element is the delete bit. When the reference count of a physical page whose delete bit is set becomes zero, all ties with its virtual page (PFN PTE array contents) are severed. The physical page is then put at the front of the free page list, where it will be reused before pages that are still associated with virtual pages.

Bit 7 in a PFN STATE array element is the modify bit. It determines whether a physical page is put on the free page list or the modified page list when the page's reference count reaches zero. The modify bit is set under a number of circumstances:

- If a virtual page was modified while it was valid, the modify bit in its PTE is set. When a virtual page is removed from a working set, the modify bit in its PTE is logically ORed into the saved modify bit in the PFN STATE array element for the physical page. The modify bit must be recorded in the PFN STATE array element because that bit in an invalid PTE has another use as the TYP1 bit.

- When a page is used as a direct I/O read buffer, the executive routine that locks down pages, MMG$IOLOCK, in module IOLOCK, sets the modify bit in its PTE. When the page is removed from the process's working set, the OR operation described in the previous item sets the modify bit in the PFN STATE array element.

- When a copy-on-reference page is faulted into a working set, the executive sets the modify bit in the PFN STATE array element of the physical page. Thus, even if the virtual page is not modified while it is valid, when the page is removed from the working set, the physical page is inserted into the modified list. This ensures that it will be written to page file backing store, from where it will be read on a subsequent page fault.

- When a demand zero page is faulted into a process's working set, the modify bit in the PFN STATE array element is set.

14.4.4   PFN TYPE Array

A PFN TYPE array element specifies the type of virtual page that occupies the corresponding physical page, for example, whether it is a process or system page or page table page. Figure 14.14 shows the contents of the PFN TYPE array element. The page fault handler, swapper, and other parts of the executive take action dependent on page type. In addition to type information, the PFN TYPE array element has three status bits.

The bad page bit is set when a nonrecoverable error, such as a read data substitute machine check, occurs trying to access the page in memory. The page will be put onto the bad page list when it is deallocated.

The collided page bit is set when a page fault occurs for a virtual page that is already being read in from its backing store address (one whose corresponding PFN STATE array element shows it as read in progress). This can happen, for example, if multiple processes fault a shared page. It can also happen if a process in a page fault wait is interrupted for asynchronous system trap (AST) delivery and then reexecutes the instruction that triggered

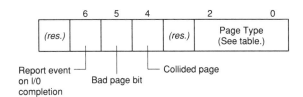

Code	Type
0	Process page
1	System page
2	Global read-only page
3	Global read/write page
4	Process page table page
5	Global page table page

Figure 14.14
Contents of PFN TYPE Array Element

the page fault. When I/O completes for a page with this TYPE bit set, I/O postprocessing code clears the bit and reports the system event collided page available for all processes in the collided page wait state. Chapter 12 describes system events. Collided pages are discussed briefly in Chapter 16.

The report event bit is set when an attempt is made to delete a virtual page that cannot be deleted immediately, for example, because the modified page writer is writing the page to its backing store. The executive places the process into a page fault wait. When the modified page writer's I/O completes, it reports a page fault completion system event. When the process is placed back into execution, the page deletion proceeds.

14.4.5   **PFN FLINK and BLINK Arrays**

A physical page that is not mapped by a valid virtual page is in one of three lists: the free, modified, or bad page list. The heads of these lists are in an array of longwords that begins at global location PFN$AL_HEAD. The list tails are in the array PFN$AL_TAIL. Each array has three elements: the first for the free page list, the second for the modified page list, and the third for the bad page list.

The three page lists must all be doubly linked lists because an arbitrary page is often removed from the middle of the list. The links cannot exist in the pages themselves because the contents of each page must be preserved. The PFN forward link (FLINK) and backward link (BLINK) arrays implement the links for each page. The PFN FLINK array element contains the PFN of the successor page, and the PFN BLINK array element, that of the predecessor page.

A zero in one of the link fields indicates the end of the list, rather than being a pointer to physical page 0. This is one reason why physical page 0 cannot be used in any dynamic function. Another reason is that the representation of invalid demand zero PTEs assumes that a PFN of zero can never appear in an invalid PTE (see Figure 14.7). However, it can be used by a system virtual page that is always resident. Physical page 0 usually contains the restart parameter block (see Chapter 30).

The amount of memory present on a particular system determines the size of the maximum PFN. On certain VAX processor types, enough memory can be connected to the system that the maximum PFN cannot be expressed in 16 bits. On such a system, the PFN FLINK and BLINK arrays are longword arrays rather than word arrays. During system initialization, VMS determines how much memory is to be described by the PFN database. Appendix F describes how this number is calculated. If there are 32 or more megabytes to be described in the PFN database, the PFN FLINK and BLINK arrays must contain longword elements. The global location MMG$GW_BIGPFN contains 0 if the element size is a word; otherwise, it contains 1.

Any code that accesses these arrays (and the arrays that overlay them)

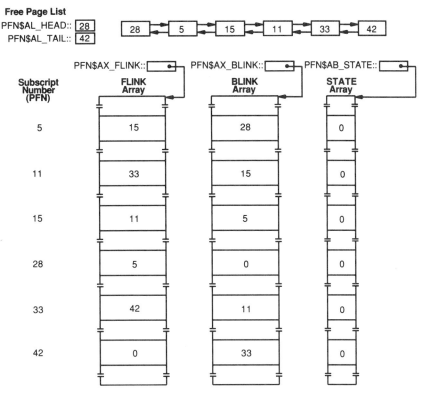

Figure 14.15
Example of Free Page List Showing Linkage Method

must use an instruction appropriate to the element size. Two techniques are employed: one, which adds no overhead, for critical code paths and one for less frequently used code paths. References to these arrays made within critical code paths in the nonpaged executive are assembled to be word context instructions. If the PFN database describes 32 or more megabytes, system initialization code alters these references to longword context instructions. Code in less frequently used code paths that depends on the size of a PFN tests the contents of MMG$GW_BIGPFN and executes the appropriate instruction.

Figure 14.15 shows an example of pages on the free list, along with their corresponding PFN FLINK and BLINK array elements. The PFN STATE array element for each of these pages contains zero, indicating that the physical page is on the free page list.

14.4.6   PFN REFCNT Array

A PFN reference count (REFCNT) array element counts the number of reasons a physical page should not be placed on the free or modified page list. One reason for incrementing the reference count is that a page is in a process working set. Another reason is that a page is part of a direct I/O buffer with I/O in progress.

I/O completion and working set replacement use the same routine to decrement the reference count. If the reference count goes to zero, the physical page is released to the free or modified page list, depending on the saved modify bit in its PFN STATE array element. Manipulations of the reference count are illustrated in Chapter 16.

14.4.7 PFN SHRCNT Array

A second form of reference count is kept for global pages. A PFN share count (SHRCNT) array element counts the number of process PTEs that are mapped to a particular global page. When the share count for a particular page goes from 0 to 1, the PFN REFCNT array element is incremented. Further additions to the share count do not affect the reference count.

As the global page is removed from the working set of each process mapped to the page, the share count is decremented. When the share count reaches zero, the PFN REFCNT array element for the page is also decremented.

When a physical page has a nonzero share count, it cannot be on one of the page lists; therefore, the forward and backward links are not needed. The PFN SHRCNT array overlays the PFN FLINK array. (PFN$AX_FLINK and PFN$AX_SHRCNT are the same location in system space.) Thus, the size of elements in the SHRCNT array can be a word or a longword, depending on the size of a PFN FLINK array element.

Process and global page table pages also use the PFN SHRCNT array. In either of these cases, the array element counts the number of PTEs in the page table page that contain a PFN, that is, the number of PTEs mapping valid or transition pages. When this count goes from zero to nonzero, the page table page is dynamically locked into a working set: a process page table page into a process working set, and a global page table page into the system working set.

14.4.8 PFN WSLX Array

A PFN working set list index (WSLX) array element for a valid page contains a longword context index from the beginning of the process (or system) header to the WSLE for that page. The WSLX element is used, for example, during the deallocation of a page of memory. If the virtual page is valid, the WSLE that describes it must be altered. Without the PFN WSLX array, it would be necessary to search the working set list to locate the WSLE.

Because a physical page in a working set is not on one of the page lists, the PFN FLINK and BLINK array elements are not needed. The PFN WSLX array overlays the PFN BLINK array. (PFN$AX_BLINK and PFN$AX_WSLX are the same location in system space.) The size of elements in the PFN

WSLX array is either a word or longword, depending on the size of a PFN BLINK array element. The PFN WSLX array is not used for global pages.

14.4.9   PFN SWPVBN Array

The swap virtual block number (SWPVBN) array supports the outswap of a process with I/O in progress. When outswap occurs, the virtual block number in the swap file where the locked down page would go is recorded in the PFN SWPVBN array element for that virtual page. The modified page writer checks this array element and, if it is nonzero, diverts a modified page from its normal backing store address to the designated block in the swap file.

14.5   SYSTEM MEMORY MANAGEMENT DATA STRUCTURES

There are several systemwide memory management data structures analogous to process data structures.

14.5.1   System Page Table

During system initialization, SYSBOOT allocates contiguous physical pages for the SPT from the high-address end of physical memory. The SPT maps itself, so that the operating system can alter SPTEs when necessary. (Recall that once memory management is enabled, all addresses are translated.) The global cell MMG$GL_SPTBASE contains the system virtual address of the system page table. MMG$GL_SPTLEN contains the number of SPTEs in it.

The SPT is not merely a system analog to process page tables: it is the basis of any virtual address translation and is accessed during the translations of per-process address space, as described in Section 14.2.

For the most part, SPTEs can take on the same forms as valid and invalid process PTEs. Figure 14.7 shows these forms. The one exception is that an invalid SPTE cannot have the global page table index form.

14.5.2   System Header and PCB

The VMS executive maintains two data structures for itself that parallel process structures: the system PCB and system header. Using these, the page fault handler can treat page faults of system pages almost identically to page faults for process pages.

The system PCB, whose address is in MMG$AR_SYSPCB, contains a base priority used for I/O requests for page faults of system space pages and global pages. It also has a pointer to the system header, parallel to the PHD pointer in any process PCB.

The system header, shown in Figure 14.16, contains a working set list and a section table. The working set list governs page replacement for pageable system pages (other than those within the balance slots). Pageable system pages come from pageable sections in loadable executive images, paged pool,

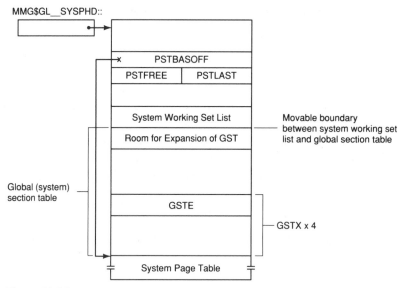

Figure 14.16
System Header Containing the System Working Set
List and the Global Section Table

and the global page table. These are all paged in the system working set list. Its size is determined by the SYSGEN parameter SYSMWCNT. Unlike other working set lists, the system working set list does not expand or contract in response to system page fault rate. Once the system working set fills, replacement paging is required.

The backing store for pageable writable executive data and page file global sections is within page files. Like a PHD, the system header contains a four-byte array at PHD$B_PRCPGFL with systemwide indexes of the page files that have been assigned. PHD$B_PRCPAGFIL contains the process-local index of the current page file, and PHD$B_PAGFIL contains the systemwide index of the current page file.

The section table in the system header contains entries for sections in files that contain pageable system pages and for global sections. The SYSGEN parameter GBLSECTIONS specifies the number of entries in the section table.

14.6 DATA STRUCTURES FOR GLOBAL PAGES

The treatment of global pages is somewhat different from that for process-private pages; VMS must keep additional systemwide data to describe global pages and sections. The sections that follow describe these data structures.

14.6.1 Global Section Descriptor

All global sections are created by the Create and Map Section ($CRMPSC) system service, requested directly from a user image or indirectly through the Install Utility. When the service creates a global section, it allocates a GSD, a paged pool data structure, to describe the section. Figure 14.17 shows the layout of a GSD. A GSD associates the global section name to its GSTE. The information in the GSD is only used when some process attempts to map to or delete the section. The page fault handler does not use this data structure.

GSD$L_GSDFL and GSD$L_GSDBL link the GSD into one of several GSD lists maintained by the system. All system global sections are linked into one list, whose listhead is formed by global cells EXE$GL_GSDSYSFL and EXE$GL_GSDSYSBL. Group global sections (independent of group number) are linked into the other list, at EXE$GL_GSDGRPFL and EXE$GL_GSDGRPBL. When a request is made to delete a global section to which processes are still mapped, its GSD is removed from its current list and inserted into a list of delete-pending GSDs, the listhead of which is at EXE$GL_GSDDELFL and EXE$GL_GSDDELBL. The mutex EXE$GL_GSDMTX (see Chapter 8) serializes access to all three lists.

GSD$W_SIZE and GSD$B_TYPE are the standard dynamic data structure fields.

GSD$B_HASH contains a hashed representation of the global section name. Comparing hash values rather than section names speeds up a search for a global section with a particular name.

GSD$L_PCBUIC is the user identification code (UIC) from the software PCB of the creating process. GSD$L_FILUIC is the UIC of the owner of the section file.

GSD$W_PROT contains the protection specified by the global section creator.

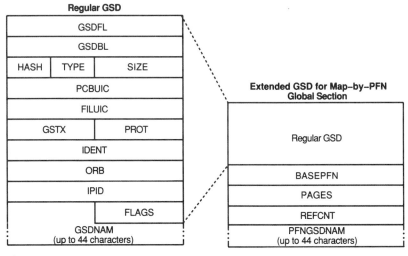

Figure 14.17
Layout of Global Section Descriptor

GSD$W_GSTX contains the global section table index for the section's GSTE.

GSD$L_IDENT contains the version identification of the global section. The value is specified by the $CRMPSC system service requestor. The Install Utility copies it from the image header of the image being installed.

GSD$L_ORB contains the address of the associated object rights block (ORB). In the case of a section that maps a file, the global section shares the ORB associated with the open file.

When a process requests that a global section be deleted, its internal process ID is copied to GSD$L_IPID. If the global section is writable, when all its modified pages have been written, the modified page writer queues an AST to that process to perform the cleanup and deletion of the global section.

GSD$T_GSDNAM contains a counted ASCII string that is the section's name.

A global section created with the PFN map option of the $CRMPSC system service has no associated GSTE; its pages are not paged. Such a section has an extended GSD, as shown in Figure 14.17. In the extended GSD, GSD$L_BASEPFN contains the starting PFN of the section. GSD$L_PAGES specifies its size in pages. GSD$L_REFCNT specifies how many PTEs map to this section. GSD$T_PFNGSDNAM, rather than GSD$T_GSDNAM, contains the section name.

14.6.2 Global Section Table Entries

The section table in the system header serves a second purpose. When a global section is created, a section table entry that describes the global section file is allocated from the section table in the system header. Because of this use, the system header's section table is usually called the global section table (GST).

The format of a GSTE is nearly identical to the format of a PSTE. Figure 14.9 illustrates both kinds of section table entry.

GSTEs are accessed in a similar way to PSTEs, with a negative longword context index from the bottom of the GST (see Section 14.3.5). The global section table index (GSTX) in the GSD is such an index, associating a GSD with a GSTE.

14.6.3 Global Page Table

Like the other page tables, the GPT describes the state of the pages it maps. Unlike the other page tables, the GPT is not accessed by the VAX processor during address translation; it is only accessed by VMS memory management routines.

As shown in Figure 14.18, VMS creates the GPT as an extension to the SPT. This extension is virtually, but not physically, contiguous to the SPT. This

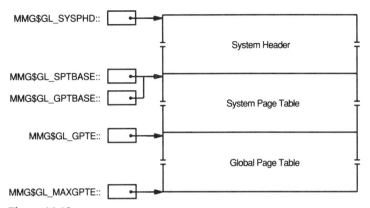

Figure 14.18
Location of Global Page Table at Virtual End of
System Page Table

extension is invisible to the VAX processor; the processor register PR$_SLR records only the number of SPTEs. VMS uses the same base address for the GPT as for the SPT, though this address is stored separately in MMG$GL_GPTBASE.

VMS locates specific GPTEs in the GPT in a manner analogous to the way the VAX processor locates a PTE. Recall that in address translation, the VAX processor uses a virtual page number as a longword context index from the base address of the page table. In place of a virtual page number, VMS uses a global page table index (GPTX) as a longword context index from the contents of MMG$GL_GPTBASE. The first GPTX is 1 greater than the largest system virtual page number.

When a process maps a portion of its address space to a global section, its process PTEs that map the section are initialized to the GPTX form of PTE (see Figure 14.7). The process PTE that maps the first global section page contains the GPTX of the first page in the global section. Each successive process PTE contains the next higher GPTX, so that each PTE effectively points to the GPTE that maps that particular page in the global section.

The relation between process and global GPTEs is shown in Figure 14.19. In the picture, the SPT maps M pages, and the global section is mapped by the first N GPTEs.

When a process first accesses an invalid global section page, it incurs a page fault. Determining that the invalid page is a global page, the page fault handler indexes the GPT with the GPTX to locate the GPTE that describes the global page.

The juxtaposition of the SPT and GPT is of benefit to other parts of the VMS memory management subsystem. For example, the GST contains entries for both system space sections and global sections; both types can use the low-order 22 bits of SEC$L_VPXPFC to contain the index into the page table that maps the section's pages.

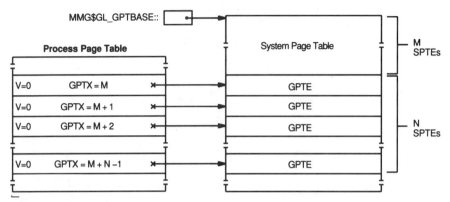

Figure 14.19
Relation Between Process PTEs and Global PTEs

14.6.4 Global Page Table Entries

Each page in a global section is described by a GPTE. GPTEs are restricted to the following forms of PTE. The first three are illustrated in Figure 14.7; the others are illustrated in Figure 14.20.

- The GPTE can be valid, indicating that the global page is in at least one process working set.
- The GPTE can indicate a demand zero page.
- The GPTE can indicate a page in some transition state. The corresponding PFN STATE array element identifies the transition state.
- For a global page in a global section file, the GPTE contains a global section table index.
- The GPTE can indicate a demand zero page in a global page-file section.
- The GPTE can indicate a global page-file section page that has been created and is in use.

When a global page is faulted in, the bits shown in Figure 14.20 labeled Global Bit and Global Write Bit are incorporated into the PFN TYPE array element for the physical page and the entry corresponding to the page in the working set lists of processes that have mapped to it.

14.6.5 Relations among Global Section Data Structures

Figure 14.21 shows the relations among the GSD, GSTE, and GPTEs for a given section. There are several relations among these three structures:

- The central shaded structure is the GSTE (see Figure 14.9 for its layout) within the GST. The first longword in the GSTE points to the GSD.
- The virtual page number field (which contains J in Figure 14.21) contains the GPTX of the first GPTE that maps this section.
- The GSD contains a GSTX that locates the GSTE.

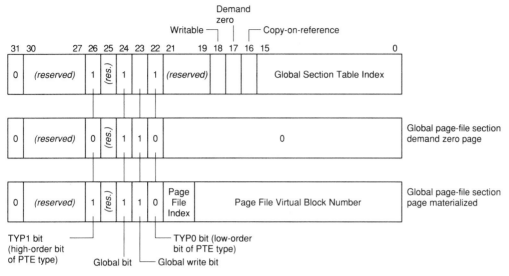

Figure 14.20
Section Table Index Forms of GPTE

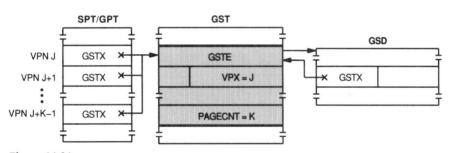

Figure 14.21
Relations among Global Section Data Structures

- The original form of each GPTE contains the same GSTX found in the GSD. When any given GPTE is either valid or in transition, the GSTX is stored in the corresponding PFN BAK array element. Note that a GPTE for a global page-file section contains a page file backing store address.

The allocation and initialization of global section data structures are described along with the $CRMPSC and Map Global Section ($MGBLSC) system services in Chapter 15.

14.7   SWAPPING DATA STRUCTURES

The following three data structures are used primarily by the swapper but also indirectly by the page fault handler:

- Balance slots
- PHD reference count array

- Process index array

The SYSGEN parameter BALSETCNT specifies the number of elements in each array.

14.7.1   Balance Slots

A balance slot is a piece of system virtual address space reserved for a PHD. The number of balance slots, the SYSGEN parameter BALSETCNT, defines the maximum number of concurrently resident processes.

When the system is initialized, an amount of system virtual address space equal to the size of a PHD times BALSETCNT is allocated. The location of the beginning of the balance slots is stored in global location SWP$GL_BALBASE. The size of a PHD in pages is stored in global location SWP$GL_BSLOTSZ. Figure 14.22 shows this area. Appendix F describes the calculations performed by SYSGEN to determine the size of the PHD.

14.7.2   Balance Slot Arrays

As shown in Figure 14.23, the system maintains two word arrays describing each process with a PHD stored in a balance slot. Both of the word arrays are indexed by the balance slot number occupied by the resident process. The balance slot number is stored in the fixed portion of the PHD at offset PHD$W_PHVINDEX. Entries in the first array contain the number of references to each PHD. Entries in the second array contain an index into a longword array that points to the PCB for each PHD.

The global location PHV$GL_REFCBAS contains the starting address of the reference count array. Each of its elements counts the number of reasons why the corresponding PHD cannot be removed from memory. Specifically,

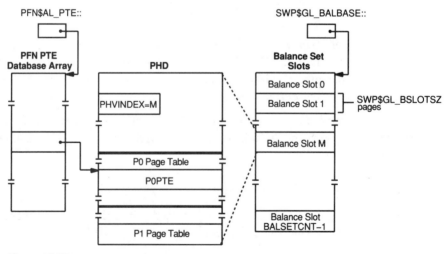

Figure 14.22
Balance Slots Containing Process Headers

PHV$GL__REFCBAS::   PHV$GL__PIXBAS::

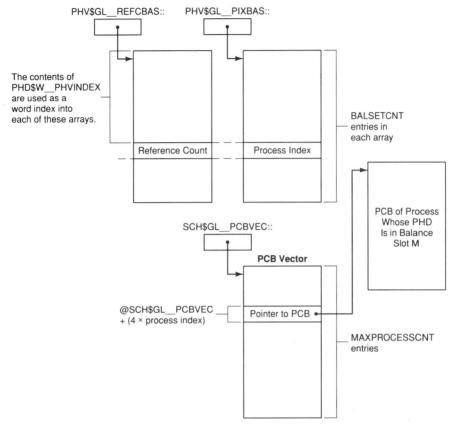

The contents of
PHD$W__PHVINDEX
are used as a
word index into
each of these arrays.

Reference Count   Process Index

BALSETCNT
entries in
each array

PCB of Process
Whose PHD
Is in Balance
Slot M

SCH$GL__PCBVEC::

PCB Vector

@SCH$GL__PCBVEC
+ (4 × process index)

Pointer to PCB

MAXPROCESSCNT
entries

Figure 14.23
Process Header Vector Arrays

an array element counts the number of page table pages that contain either
valid or transition PTEs. A value of -1 in a reference count array element
means that the corresponding balance slot is not in use.

The global location PHV$GL_PIXBAS contains the starting address of the
process index array. Each of its elements contains an index into the longword
array, based at the global pointer SCH$GL_PCBVEC. An element in the
longword PCB vector contains the address of the PCB of the process with
that process index. Figure 14.23 illustrates how the address of a PHD is
transformed into the address of the PCB for that process, using the entry in
the process index array.

A zero in the process index array entry means that the corresponding
balance slot is not in use. A -1 in a process index array entry means that
the process whose PHD used that balance slot has been deleted and its PHD
can be deleted to reclaim physical memory as well as the balance slot.

If the PHD address is known, the balance slot index can be calculated
(as described in the next section). By using this as a word index into the

process index array, the longword index into the PCB vector is found. The array element in the PCB vector is the address of the PCB, whose PCB$L_PHD entry points back to the balance slot. Chapter 25 contains a more detailed description of the PCB vector and its use by the Create Process system service.

14.7.3 Comment on Equal-Size Balance Slots

The choice of equal-size balance slots, at first sight seemingly inefficient, has some subtle benefits to portions of the memory management subsystem. There are several instances, most notably within the modified page writer, when it is necessary to obtain a PHD address from a physical page's PFN. With fixed-size balance slots, this operation is straightforward.

As shown in Figure 14.22, a PFN PTE array element points to a PTE somewhere in the balance slot area. Subtracting the contents of SWP$GL_BALBASE from the PFN PTE array element contents and dividing the result by the size of a balance slot (the size of a PHD) in bytes produces the balance slot index. If this index is multiplied by the size of the PHD in bytes and added to the contents of SWP$GL_BALBASE, the final result is the address of the PHD containing the PTE that maps the physical page in question.

Furthermore, as described in the previous section, the balance slot index can locate the process index and its PCB address.

14.8 DATA STRUCTURES THAT DESCRIBE THE PAGE AND SWAP FILES

Page and swap files are used by the memory management subsystem to save physical page contents or process working sets. Page files are used to save the contents of modified pages that are not in physical memory. Both the swap and page files are used to save the working sets of processes that are not in the balance set.

14.8.1 Page File Control Blocks

Each page and swap file in use is described by a data structure called a page file control block (PFL). A page or swap file can be placed in use either automatically during system initialization or manually through SYSGEN commands. In either case, code in module [BOOTS]INITPGFIL allocates a PFL from nonpaged pool and initializes it.

Initializing the PFL includes the following operations:

1. The file is opened and a special window control block (WCB) is built to describe all the file's extents. The special WCB, called a cathedral window, ensures that the memory management subsystem does not have to take a window turn (see Chapter 21), which could lead to a system deadlock.

2. The address of the WCB is stored in the PFL.

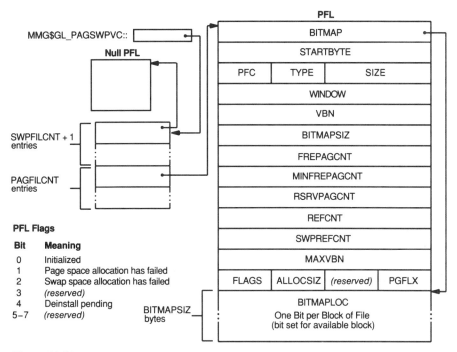

Figure 14.24
Page and Swap File Database

3. A bitmap is allocated from nonpaged pool and initialized to all 1's. Each
bit in the map represents one block of swap or page file. A set bit indicates
the availability of the corresponding block.

Figure 14.24 shows the layout of a PFL. PFL$L_BITMAP is the address
of the start of the bitmap that describes the state of the blocks in the file.
PFL$L_BITMAPSIZ is the length of the bitmap in bytes. PFL$L_STARTBYTE
is the address of the bitmap byte at which the next scan for free blocks should
begin.

PFL$W_SIZE and PFL$B_TYPE are the standard dynamic data structure
fields.

PFL$B_PFC is the number of blocks to cluster together on a page read.

PFL$L_WINDOW is the address of the WCB that describes the mapping
extents of the file so that file-relative, or virtual, block numbers can be
converted to volume-relative, or logical, block numbers.

Generally, PFL$L_VBN contains the value 0; in the case of a primary page
file in use as a crash dump file, it contains the value 1, to reserve the first
block of the page file for a dump header block. Chapter 32 discusses using
the primary page file as a dump file.

PFL$L_VBN has an additional use for a page file larger than $FFFFF_{16}$ blocks.
When installing such a file, SYSGEN divides it into segments of $FFFFF_{16}$
blocks. It initializes a PFL for each segment, plus one for the last partial

397

segment. PFL$L_VBN indicates the starting virtual block number of each segment. A block in a segment is represented by the combination of page file index and a block number relative to the start of the segment. The block number is thus small enough to fit into the page file virtual block number portion of a page file backing store PTE. To calculate the actual backing store address, the contents of the associated PFL$L_VBN are added to the page file virtual block number.

When installing a swap file larger than $FFFFFF_{16}$ blocks, SYSGEN similarly divides it into segments of $FFFFFF_{16}$ blocks.

Note that the PFL contains a WCB field, virtual block number field, and page fault cluster factor field at the same relative offsets as they are in a section table entry. Because all fields are present and at the same offsets, page file and section file I/O requests can be processed by common code, independent of the data structure that describes the file being read or written.

PFL$L_FREPAGCNT is the number of blocks, less 1, that can be allocated.

PFL$L_MINFREPAGCNT is the "low-water mark" for the file and represents the smallest number of blocks free during the use of the file.

PFL$L_RSRVPAGCNT is the number of blocks that can be reserved without overcommitting the page file.

PFL$L_REFCNT contains the number of processes using the file for paging or swapping. PFL$L_SWPREFCNT contains the number using it only for swapping.

PFL$L_MAXVBN is the mask applied to a PTE with a page file backing store address. For a swap file, it contains the value $FFFFFF_{16}$; for a page file, the value $FFFFF_{16}$.

PFL$B_PGFLX is the systemwide index number of the page-and-swap-file vector entry that contains the address of the PFL.

PFL$B_ALLOCSIZ is the current allocation request size in the file, the number of contiguous blocks the modified page writer or the swapper tries to allocate. It is initialized to the value of the SYSGEN parameter MPW_WRTCLUSTER and adjusted dynamically with available space in the file.

PFL$B_FLAGS contains bits describing the state of the file.

At offset PFL$L_BITMAPLOC the bitmap begins. It has one bit for each block in the file. A value of 0 means the block is in use; a value of 1 means the block is free.

Chapter 16 describes the use of page files; and Chapter 18 the use of swap files.

14.8.2 Page-and-Swap-File Vector

Pointers to the PFLs are stored in a nonpaged pool array called the page-and-swap-file vector. The number of longword pointers in this array is the maximum number of page and swap files that can be in use on the system (the sum of SYSGEN parameters SWPFILCNT and PAGFILCNT) plus 1. A page or swap file is identified by an index number indicating the position of its PFL address in this array. This is called a systemwide index to distinguish it from a two-bit process-local page file index (see Section 14.3.3.2). The page-and-swap-file vector can contain up to 128 pointers.

During system initialization, the routine EXE$INIT in module INIT (see Chapter 31), allocates and initializes the page-and-swap-file vector, which is a standard dynamic data structure. It stores the address of the beginning of the actual data in global location MMG$GL_PAGSWPVC. Figure 14.24 shows the use of the page-and-swap-file vector data area to point to PFLs.

EXE$INIT initializes each pointer with the address of the null page file control block, the contents of MMG$AR_NULLPFL. For the most part, this address serves as a zero value, indicating that no page or swap file with this index is in use. The null PFL, however, is also used to describe the shell process.

The shell process, a module in the system image, is accessed as page file index zero. It is the prototype for creating a new process. The information in the null PFL may be used during process creation to read a copy of the shell process into memory.

The SYSINIT process (see Chapter 31) places in use the primary page file, SYS$SPECIFIC:[SYSEXE]PAGEFILE.SYS, if it exists. (Any page file installed at a later stage of system initialization or operation is not considered a primary page file, even if it is the first page file installed.) SYSINIT builds a PFL and places its address in the page-and-swap-file vector. The primary page file has a systemwide index value equal to 1 more than the SYSGEN parameter SWPFILCNT.

SYSINIT also installs SYS$SPECIFIC:[SYSEXE]SWAPFILE.SYS, if it exists, as the primary swap file. (A swap file installed at a later state is not a primary swap file, even if it is the first one.) The first swap file that is installed has index 1. If there is no swap file, index 1 points to the null PFL. If the value of the SYSGEN parameter SWPFILCNT is zero, index 1 points to the primary page file.

If there are no swap files, all swap operations are performed to page files. Although the system can run this way, it is desirable that there be at least one swap file. For example, after several large processes are outswapped into a page file, the page file may be sufficiently full that modified page writer clustering is hindered.

Any additional page and swap files are placed in use by SYSGEN in response to the commands INSTALL/PAGEFILE and INSTALL/SWAPFILE. Installing page files other than the primary one on different disks allows for balancing the paging load. A system with alternative swap files can support a greater number of processes or processes with larger working sets.

With VMS Version 5.2, it is possible to deinstall page and swap files, that is, to remove an inactive file from use. After a privileged user issues the SYSGEN command DEINSTALL to initiate the removal of a page or swap file, no new allocations are made from it. However, the actual removal from use is deferred until the file is inactive and PFL$L_REFCNT has gone to zero.

14.9   SWAPPER AND MODIFIED PAGE WRITER PAGE TABLE ARRAYS

The VMS I/O subsystem enables an image to make a direct I/O request (direct memory access transfer) to a virtually contiguous buffer. There is no requirement that pages in a buffer be physically contiguous, only virtually contiguous. This capability is called scatter-read/gather-write or, more simply, scatter/gather.

14.9.1   Direct I/O and Scatter/Gather

A combination of VAX hardware and VMS I/O subsystem software supports I/O to physically noncontiguous pages. The manner in which this is supported varies with processor type and I/O adapter type. For example, on a VAX processor with a UNIBUS or MASSBUS adapter, the device driver maps the memory buffer to I/O bus space. The result of this mapping is a set of contiguous addresses in the I/O bus space. Certain I/O adapters, such as CI adapters, read the relevant PTEs to determine the physical location of the buffer pages. On some processors, such as a MicroVAX I, there is no adapter hardware to support bus mapping. The device driver must transform the request into multiple transfers to or from physically contiguous memory.

Regardless of the manner of the support, a direct I/O request results in locking the buffer pages into memory. The I/O locking mechanism brings each page into the working set of the requesting process, makes it valid, and increments that page's reference count (in the PFN REFCNT array element) to reflect the pending read or write. The buffer is generally described in the I/O request packet (IRP) through three fields:

- IRP$L_SVAPTE contains the system virtual address of the first PTE that maps the buffer.
- IRP$W_BOFF and IRP$L_BCNT are used to calculate how many PTEs are required to map the buffer.

A driver processes this I/O request in a manner suitable to the processor and I/O adapter. For example, it may allocate adapter mapping registers and load them with the PFNs found in the PTEs or it may simply pass the system virtual address of the first PTE to an I/O adapter.

14.9.2   Swapper I/O

The swapper is presented with a more difficult problem. It must write a collection of pages to disk that are not even virtually contiguous. It solves this problem elegantly.

When the system is initialized, an array of WSMAX longwords is allocated from nonpaged pool for use as the swapper's I/O table. The starting address of this array is stored in global pointer SWP$GL_MAP. (The address is also stored in the saved P0 base register in the swapper's PHD so the pages mapped by this array are effectively the swapper's P0 space. This use is discussed in Chapter 25.)

When the swapper scans the working set list of the process being out-swapped, it copies the PFNs in every valid PTE to successive entries in its I/O table. The swapper places the address of the base of the table into the field IRP$L_SVAPTE before the IRP is passed to the driver. (The swapper can exercise this control because it builds a portion of its own IRP.) The I/O table looks just like any other page table to the hardware/software combination that implements scatter/gather I/O.

What the swapper has succeeded in doing is making pages that were not virtually contiguous into pages that are virtually contiguous in the P0 space of the swapper, the process that is actually performing the I/O. At the same time that each PTE is being processed, any special actions based on the type of page are also taken care of. The whole operation of outswap and the complementary steps taken when the process is swapped back into memory are discussed in Chapter 18.

The swapper map supports only one use at a time. When an inswap or outswap operation is in progress, the swap-in-progress flag (SCH$V_SIP), in location SCH$GB_SIP, is set to indicate its use.

14.9.3   Modified Page Writer PTE Array

The modified page writer, in its attempt to write many pages to backing store with a single write request (so-called modified page write clustering), is faced with a problem similar to that of the swapper. The modified page writer must build a table of PTEs just as the swapper does. Unlike the swapper, which can perform only one swap operation at a time, with VMS Version 5 the modified page writer can perform concurrent multiple modified page writes. The SYSGEN parameter MPW_IOLIMIT specifies its maximum number of concurrent I/O operations.

When the modified page writer is building an I/O request, it can encounter three different types of page:

- Pages that are bound for a swap file (SWPVBN nonzero) are written individually.
- Pages that are bound for a section file are not necessarily virtually contiguous; these pages will be written as a group only if they are virtually contiguous.
- Pages on the modified page list that are to be written to a particular page file may not only be noncontiguous within one process address space but

may also belong to several processes. It is these pages that the modified page writer must cluster so they appear virtually contiguous.

During system initialization, the modified page writer's initialization routine, MPW$INIT in module WRTMFYPAG, allocates nonpaged pool to build I/O maps. It allocates MPW_IOLIMIT number of structures and links them into a lookaside list. Each structure is large enough for an IRP and two arrays, each of MPW_WRTCLUSTER elements. One is a longword array, and the other a word array.

The longword array will be filled with PTEs containing PFNs in a manner analogous to the way in which the swapper map is used. The word array contains an index into the PHD vector for each page in the map. In this way, each page that is put into the map and written to its backing store location is related to the PHD containing the PTE that maps this page. The operation of the modified page writer, including its clustered writes to a page file, is discussed in detail in Chapter 16.

15 Memory Management System Services

A place for everything and everything in its place.

Isabella Mary Beeton, *The Book of Household Management*

This chapter describes those system services that affect a process's virtual address space and several others:

- Create Virtual Address Space ($CRETVA), by which a process creates demand zero pages in P0 or P1 space
- Expand Region ($EXPREG), by which a process creates demand zero pages at the high end of P0 space or the low end of P1 space
- Create and Map Section ($CRMPSC), by which a process creates a process-private or global section that maps the blocks of a file to a portion of process address space
- Map Global Section ($MGBLSC), by which a process maps to an existing global section
- Delete Virtual Address Space ($DELTVA), by which a process deletes P0 or P1 pages
- Contract Region ($CNTREG), by which the upper end of P0 space or the lower end of P1 space is deleted
- Delete Global Section ($DGBLSC), by which a global section is marked for deletion when no more processes are mapped to it
- Set Process Swap Mode ($SETSWM), by which process swapping can be enabled or disabled
- Set Protection on Pages ($SETPRT), by which the protection on a page of virtual address space can be changed

Chapter 17 describes the system services that control a process's working set list. Chapter 16 describes the Update Section File on Disk ($UPDSEC) system service, by which the contents of all modified pages in a section are written to their backing store.

15.1 COMMON CHARACTERISTICS OF MEMORY MANAGEMENT SYSTEM SERVICES

A process's ability to use the services described in this chapter may be limited by access mode, process quotas, limits, privileges, and SYSGEN parameters.

The page table entry (PTE) associated with each page of virtual address space contains an owner field (see Figure 14.7). The owner field specifies

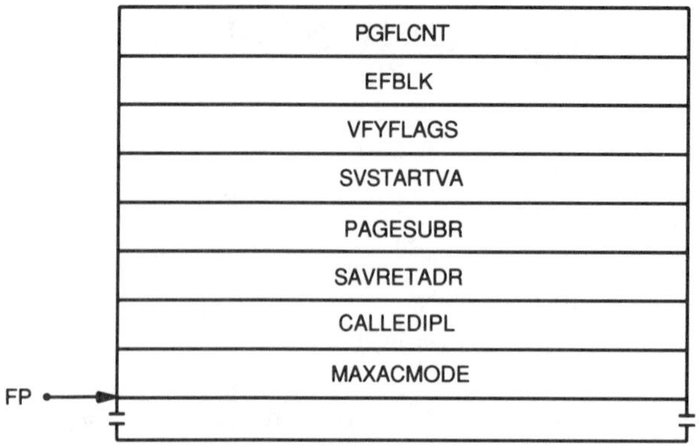

PGFLCNT
EFBLK
VFYFLAGS
SVSTARTVA
PAGESUBR
SAVRETADR
CALLEDIPL
MAXACMODE

FP →

Figure 15.1
Layout of Stack Scratch Space

which access mode owns the page. The memory management system service checks the owner field to determine whether the requestor of the service is at least as privileged as the owner of the page and thus able to manipulate the page in the desired fashion.

In general, a process is only permitted to affect per-process address space with these services.

Almost all the memory management system services accept a desired virtual address range as an input argument. Many of the services can partly succeed, that is, affect only a portion of the specified address range. A system service indicates partial success by returning an error status and the address range for which the operation completed in the optional RETADR argument.

Many of the memory management system services have a common sequence. First, each creates scratch space on the stack to record information about the service request. The macro $MMGDEF defines symbolic offsets into this scratch space, which is pointed to by the frame pointer (FP) register while the system service procedure is executing. Figure 15.1 shows its layout. Some fields are used by only a few system services; others are common to all.

MMG$L_MAXACMODE contains flag bits and the access mode associated with the operation, the less privileged of the mode from which the service was requested and the mode specified in the ACMODE argument. Bit MMG$V_CHGPAGFIL in this longword, when set, means page file quota should be charged for the operation. Bit MMG$V_NO_OVERMAP, when set, means that address space to be created may not overlap existing address space. Bit MMG$V_NOWAIT_IPL0, when set, means that a memory management routine should return with an error status rather than waiting at interrupt priority level (IPL) 0 for I/O completion. Bit MMG$V_DELGBLDON, when set, means that global pages in the range have already been purged.

MMG$L_CALLEDIPL records the IPL from which the service was requested, typically 0.

MMG$L_SAVRETADR contains the value of the optional service RETADR argument, the address of a two-longword array to receive the starting and ending virtual addresses affected by the service.

MMG$L_PAGESUBR contains the address of the executive routine that performs the requested service on a single page.

MMG$L_SVSTARTVA saves the starting virtual address specified by the user.

MMG$L_VFYFLAGS contains the section flags passed as an argument to a service such as $CRMPSC and verified by the service.

MMG$L_EFBLK contains the number of the end-of-file block for a section file.

MMG$L_PGFLCNT contains the amount of page file quota that has been reserved against the job's quota for this request.

After creating and initializing the stack scratch space, such a memory management system service takes the following steps:

1. It raises IPL to 2 to block the delivery of an asynchronous system trap (AST). In addition to blocking process deletion, this prevents the execution of AST code that could cause unexpected changes to the page tables, working set list, and other process data structures.
2. If appropriate, it checks page ownership to ensure that a less privileged access mode is not attempting to alter the properties of pages owned by a more privileged access mode.
3. It invokes the routine MMG$CREDEL, in module SYSCREDEL, passing it the address of a per-page service-specific routine to accomplish the desired action of the system service. MMG$CREDEL performs general page processing and invokes the per-page routine for each page in the desired range.
4. It returns the address range actually affected through MMG$CREDEL's actions in the optional RETADR argument.
5. It restores the entry IPL and returns to its invoker.

In some cases, step 3 in that sequence is replaced by the single invocation of a routine that affects all pages in the desired range.

MMG$CREDEL takes the following steps:

1. It tests the starting and ending addresses and, if either is in system space, returns the error status SS$_NOPRIV.
2. It initializes MMG$L_PAGESUBR and MMG$L_SVSTARTVA in the scratch space and stores in general registers information such as process control block (PCB) address, process header (PHD) address, page count, starting virtual address, and ending virtual address.
3. MMG$CREDEL invokes the per-page routine. Unless the routine returns an error status, MMG$CREDEL continues to invoke it, once per page.

4. When an error occurs or there are no more pages, MMG$CREDEL returns to its invoker with a status code and the address of the last affected page in registers.

15.2 PER-PROCESS VIRTUAL ADDRESS SPACE CREATION

Among the most basic memory management services are those that create per-process virtual address space: $CRETVA, $EXPREG, $CRMPSC, and $MGBLSC. The image activator requests these services during image activation, as described in Chapter 26. An image can request these services directly to alter the process address space.

Each per-process address space is described by a page table, with a PTE for each page of address space. As described in Chapter 14, both page tables are part of the PHD. Each is described by two processor registers: a base address register, PR$_PxBR, and a length register, PR$_PxLR, where x is 0 or 1, depending on the per-process space.

Four longwords in the hardware PCB save the contents of the process's four mapping registers when the process is not current. The PHD also contains two longwords PHD$L_FREPxVA, each of which contains the address just beyond the space mapped by the corresponding page table. Figure 14.6 shows the process page tables and the registers and fields that describe them.

Creating address space typically requires expanding the appropriate page table and modifying the length register and PHD fields that delimit it. It always requires initializing PTEs. In the case of address space associated with a process-private section file, it also involves allocating and initializing a process section table entry.

There are several limits on the amount of per-process virtual address space that can be created.

The SYSGEN parameter VIRTUALPAGECNT controls the total number of page table entries (P0PTEs plus P1PTEs) that any process can have. The division of these pages between P0 space and P1 space is arbitrary and process-specific; VIRTUALPAGECNT limits only their sum.

The size of a process working set can also constrain the size of that process's address space. When a process tries to expand its address space, the executive checks whether there is enough room in the dynamic working set list for the fluid working set (PHD$L_WSFLUID, initialized from the SYSGEN parameter MINWSCNT), plus the worst-case number of page table pages required to map it, to allow the process to perform useful work. If this check succeeds, the virtual address space creation can proceed. Otherwise, if the process's working set list is smaller than its quota, the working set list is expanded. If the working set list is full and cannot be expanded (see Chapter 17), the virtual address creation fails with the error status SS$_INSFWSL.

A third constraint on the total size of the process address space is the page file quota. Each demand zero page and copy-on-reference section page is charged against the job's page file quota, JIB$L_PGFLCNT.

A fourth constraint on address space with page file backing store is based on the number of page files to which the process has been assigned. The form of invalid PTE that describes a page in a page file has space for a two-bit process-local page file index and a 20-bit virtual block number. Thus, for each page file to which the process has been assigned, it can create a theoretical maximum of 2^{20} pages of pageable address space that requires page file backing store (for example, demand zero or copy-on-reference sections). The current theoretical maximum is stored in PHD$L_PPGFLVA and decremented by each page of such address space the process creates. Each time a process is assigned or deassigned to a page file, the cell is increased or decreased by 2^{20}. The cell is decremented for each demand zero or copy-on-reference page the process creates and incremented when each such page is deleted.

15.3 DEMAND ZERO VIRTUAL ADDRESS SPACE CREATION

The simplest form of address space creation is the creation of a series of demand zero pages through the $CRETVA and $EXPREG system services.

For the $EXPREG system service, the demand zero pages are created at the end of the designated per-process address space. For the $CRETVA system service, the pages are created in the specified address range. If any pages already exist in the requested range, they must be deleted first. On the other hand, if the requested range begins beyond the end of the region, the space between them must also be created.

These two system services can partly succeed. That is, a number of pages smaller than the number originally requested may be created. After several pages have already been successfully created, the service can run into one of the limits to address space creation.

15.3.1 $CRETVA System Service

The $CRETVA system service procedure, EXE$CRETVA in module SYSCRE-DEL, runs in kernel mode. It has an alternative entry point, MMG$CRETVA, called from code already in kernel mode, such as image activator routines and EXE$PROCSTRT in module PROCSTRT. The alternative entry point has additional arguments that enable the caller to specify what the protection of the new address space is and whether the new space may overlap existing space.

EXE$CRETVA takes the following steps:

1. It creates and initializes the stack scratch space.
2. It constructs template PTE contents for the new pages.

   The template PTE indicates a demand zero page, with owner access mode the less privileged of the requesting access mode and the ACMODE argument. In the case of a normal system service request, the PTE has a protection granting write access to the owner mode. In the case of entry through MMG$CRETVA, the protection is specified by the caller.

3. It raises IPL to 2 to block AST delivery.

4. It tests the starting and ending addresses and, if either is a system space address, returns the error status SS$_NOPRIV.

5. It checks whether the specified address range overlaps any existing space. If there is overlap, EXE$CRETVA continues with step 8.

6. Typically, there is no overlap; the process is requesting the creation of address space just beyond the end of what has already been defined. As an optimization for this common case, EXE$CRETVA invokes MMG$TRY_ALL, in module SYSCREDEL, to test further whether the entire space can be created. MMG$TRY_ALL tests whether there are enough free PTEs, enough room in the dynamic working set list, enough page file quota, and enough PHD$L_PPGFLVA capacity. If all tests pass, it adjusts PR$_PxLR, its copy in the PHD, PHD$L_FREPTCNT, and PHD$L_FREPxVA; charges against page file quota and PHD$L_PPGFLVA; and returns a status indicating its findings.

    If the entire address space cannot be created, EXE$CRETVA proceeds with step 8.

7. If none of the limits to growth of the process's virtual address space has been reached, EXE$CRETVA invokes MMG$FAST_CREATE, in module SYSCREDEL.

    MMG$FAST_CREATE determines in which region space is being created and with which starting PTE. It loops, initializing four PTEs in each iteration. Creating the address space in this manner is significantly faster than creating it one page at a time.

    EXE$CRETVA continues with step 9.

8. If any of the limits to virtual address space growth described in the previous section prevent creation of the entire space, EXE$CRETVA creates it one page at a time, stopping when the limit is reached. Page-by-page creation is also necessary if the specified address space overlaps already existing space, since the existing pages must first be deleted. In either of these cases, EXE$CRETVA invokes MMG$CREDEL, specifying MMG$CREPAG, in module SYSCREDEL, as the per-page service-specific routine.

9. EXE$CRETVA returns any unused page file quota, records peak page file usage and virtual size statistics, and stores return information in the optional RETADR argument.

10. It restores the IPL at entry and returns to its requestor.

MMG$CREPAG is the per-page service-specific routine for the $CRETVA and $EXPREG system services. It is invoked with an argument specifying the PTE contents for the new page. It takes the following steps:

1. It tests whether the page to be created is beyond the limit of its defined address space and, if not, continues with step 3.
2. If the page is outside its address space, MMG$CREPAG tests whether there are enough free PTEs and enough room in the dynamic working set list to expand the region to add all the desired pages. If there is, it adjusts PR$_PxLR, its copy in the PHD, PHD$L_FREPxVA, and PHD$L_FREPTCNT.

   MMG$CREPAG must deal with the possibility that the requested page may not be adjacent to the current end of the region and that the intervening pages also have to be created.

   —If there are insufficient PTEs to allow expansion up to the requested starting virtual address, MMG$CREPAG returns the error status SS$_VASFULL to its invoker.
   —If there are insufficient PTEs to allow the full expansion, but the region can be expanded at least to the first requested page, the routine adjusts the items previously listed to show expansion of as many pages as there are PTEs left.
   —If there is insufficient room in the dynamic working set list for expansion up to the first requested page, the routine returns the error status SS$_INSFWSL.
   —If there is insufficient room in the dynamic working set list for the full expansion but enough for at least the first requested page, the routine adjusts the listed items to show expansion through the first requested page.
   —If both tests pass, it adjusts the listed items to include the total expansion. The tests and this step will not be repeated in subsequent invocations of MMG$CREPAG.

3. It tests whether the page to be created already exists. If it does and the service requestor specified no address overmap, MMG$CREPAG returns the status SS$_VA_IN_USE to its invoker, which returns it as the system service status. (The image activator specifies the NO_OVERMAP flag when it requests the $CRETVA system service.)
4. If the page already exists but overmap is allowed, MMG$CREPAG invokes MMG$DELPAG, described in Section 15.5.2, to delete the virtual page.
5. If page file quota does not need to be charged, MMG$CREPAG continues with step 6. Otherwise, it must charge the pages against MMG$L_PGFLCNT and PHD$L_PPGFLVA.

   If no more reserved quota is left, MMG$CREPAG tries to reserve more quota from the process's job page file quota.

   If PHD$L_PPGFLVA would be exceeded, MMG$CREPAG tries to assign the process to another page file.

   If either charge cannot be made, MMG$CREPAG adjusts PR$_PxVA, its copy in the PHD, PHD$L_FREPxVA, and PHD$L_FREPTCNT to show expansion up to but not including the page that could not be created for lack of page file quota or PHD$L_PPGFLVA. MMG$CREPAG returns the error status SS$_EXQUOTA.

6. It stores the requested value into the PTE.

7. It returns to its invoker.

15.3.2 $EXPREG System Service

The $EXPREG system service is very similar to the $CRETVA system service. Its system service procedure, EXE$EXPREG in module SYSCREDEL, runs in kernel mode. Depending on the region that is to be expanded, EXE$EXPREG uses either PHD$L_FREP0VA or PHD$L_FREP1VA as one end of the address range. It adds its PAGCNT argument to that address to form the other end of the address region.

It forms template PTE contents for the new page as EXE$CRETVA does.

As an optimization, EXE$EXPREG first checks whether the entire address space can be created. If so, EXE$EXPREG creates it all at once rather than page by page, invoking the routine MMG$FAST_CREATE. Otherwise, it invokes the routine MMG$CREDEL, specifying MMG$CREPAG as the per-page service-specific routine. Section 15.3.1 describes these routines.

15.3.3 Automatic User Stack Expansion

A special form of P1 space expansion occurs when a request for user stack space exceeds the remaining size of the user stack. Such a request can be reported by the VAX processor as an access violation exception or by software.

Several software routines detect the need to expand the user stack:

- The AST delivery interrupt service routine (see Chapter 7), when it is unable to build the AST argument list on the user stack
- The Adjust Stack ($ADJSTK) system service
- The exception dispatching routine, EXE$EXCEPTION in module EXCEPTION, when it is unable to copy the signal and mechanism arrays onto the user stack (see Chapter 5)

These routines invoke EXE$EXPANDSTK, in module EXCEPTION, to try to expand the user stack. EXE$EXPANDSTK is also invoked by the access violation exception service routine, EXE$ACVIOLAT in module EXCEPTION, for an access violation that occurred in user mode. EXE$EXPANDSTK checks that a length violation rather than a protection violation occurred and that the inaccessible address is in P1 space. If so, EXE$EXPANDSTK requests the $CRETVA system service to expand P1 space from its current low-address end to the specified inaccessible address. For the usual case, one in which a program requires more user stack space than requested at link time, the expansion typically occurs one page at a time.

Because this automatic expansion cannot be disabled on a process-specific or systemwide basis, a runaway program that uses stack space without returning it is not aborted immediately. Instead, the program runs until it reaches one of the limits to growth of virtual address space previously described.

Another side effect of automatic expansion occurs when a program makes a possibly incorrect reference to an arbitrary P1 address lower than the top of the user stack. Rather than exiting with some error status, the program will probably continue to execute (after the creation of many demand zero pages).

If the stack expansion fails for any reason, the process is notified in a way that depends on the invoker of EXE$EXPANDSTK:

- The $ADJSTK system service can fail with several of the error codes returned by $CRETVA.
- An attempt to deliver an AST to a process with insufficient user stack space results in an AST delivery stack fault condition being reported to the process.
- If the user stack cannot be expanded in response to a P1 space length violation, then an access violation fault is reported to the process.
- If there is not enough user stack to report an exception, EXE$EXCEPTION first tries to reset the user stack pointer to the high-address end of the stack. If that fails, EXE$EXCEPTION requests the $CRETVA system service in an attempt to recreate the address space. If that fails, EXE$EXCEPTION bypasses the normal condition handler search and reports the exception directly to the last chance handler. Typically, this handler aborts the currently executing image. Chapter 5 contains more details.

15.4 PROCESS-PRIVATE AND GLOBAL SECTIONS

The $CRMPSC system service is an alternative method of creating address space, one that enables a process to associate a portion of its address space with a specified portion of a file. The section may be specific to a process (called a process-private section or sometimes simply a process section) or it may be a global section, shared among several processes.

The $CRMPSC system service also provides special options. For example, a process with PFNMAP privilege can map virtual address space to specific physical addresses. Typically, a process uses this capability to access a physical page in I/O space in order to communicate with a particular I/O device.

The $CRMPSC service also enables the creation of global page-file sections, demand zero global sections whose pages are backed by a page file.

The $MGBLSC system service is another way to create address space, one that enables a process to map a portion of its address space to an already existing global section.

The image activator (see Chapter 26) requests these two services to map portions of process address space to sections in image files and to previously installed global sections.

15.4.1 $CRMPSC System Service

The $CRMPSC system service creates a process-private or global section and maps it into process address space. The particular actions it takes are determined by the options or flags with which the service is requested. The *VMS System Services Reference Manual* describes the system service arguments and shows which flags can be used together.

15.4.1.1 Process-Private Section Creation.

The $CRMPSC system service procedure, EXE$CRMPSC in module SYSCRMPSC, runs in kernel mode. When requested to map a process-private section, it takes the following steps:

1. It creates and initializes the stack scratch space.
2. It invokes MMG$VFYSECFLG, in module SYSDGBLSC, to test the compatibility of the FLAGS arguments with each other and with the process's privileges, and then confirms that the CHAN argument was supplied. (The requestor must have already opened the section file on the specified channel.) If the flags are incompatible or the argument is absent, it returns the error status SS$_IVSECFLG to its requestor.
3. It confirms that the specified channel has been assigned; that its associated device is directory-structured, files-oriented, and random access; and that a file is open on the channel. In case of error, it returns a suitable error status to its requestor.
4. It checks whether the associated window control block (WCB) maps the entire file. (When the image activator opens a file, it does so specifying that all extents of the file should be mapped. However, an image may open a file itself and then request the $CRMPSC system service; in that case, the WCB might not contain a complete description of the file.)

   The memory management subsystem cannot take a window turn (see Chapter 21) on pages within a section. It therefore requires that the WCB describe all the extents of the mapped file. If the WCB does not, EXE$CRMPSC queues an I/O request to remap the file with a cathedral WCB, one that does describe all the file extents.

   Because the WCB occupies nonpaged pool, its extension is charged against the job's buffered I/O byte count quota (JIB$L_BYTCNT). Because the quota charge persists until the section is deleted, this charge is also made against the job's JIB$L_BYTLM, which limits the maximum charge against JIB$L_BYTCNT. When a job has insufficient JIB$L_BYTCNT for a request, VMS checks that the request is not larger than JIB$L_BYTLM before placing the process in resource wait. Charging the WCB extension against JIB$L_BYTLM prevents placing the process into what might otherwise be a never-ending resource wait.

5. If the section to be mapped is a copy-on-reference section, EXE$CRMPSC sets bit MMG$V_CHGPAGFIL in MMG$L_MAXACMODE as a signal that the section must be charged against the job's page file quota and PHD$L_PPGFLVA.

6. It raises IPL to 2 to block AST delivery.

7. It invokes MMG$DALCSTXSCN, in module PHDUTL, to check the process section table for any sections to be deallocated. A section table entry cannot always be deallocated synchronously on request. For example, if direct I/O is in progress to pages in the section, those pages cannot be deleted and hence the section cannot be. After the I/O completes, the next invocation of MMG$DALCSTXSCN results in deallocation of the section table entry. Section 15.4.3 describes this routine.

8. Unless the section is copy-on-reference and demand zero, EXE$CRMPSC allocates a process section table entry (PSTE, pictured in Figure 14.9) and initializes it. A demand zero section does not need a PSTE; its page faults require no I/O from a section file.

   When the process section is being created as a part of image activation, as described in Chapter 26, the original source for much of the data stored in the PSTE is an image section descriptor contained in the image file.

   a. EXE$CRMPSC copies the section flags to SEC$W_FLAGS.

   b. It stores in SEC$L_WINDOW the address of the WCB from the channel control block (CCB) or from the PSTE to which the CCB points. Recall that if multiple sections are mapped from the same file, there is one PSTE for each section but only one CCB and one WCB.

   c. It checks that the file has been opened in a manner consistent with the section flags: if the section is writable but not copy-on-reference, the file must have been opened for write access. If the file was opened for write access, then EXE$CRMPSC sets the writable flag in SEC$W_FLAGS.

   d. It copies the VBN argument to SEC$L_VBN. If the VBN argument is 0, its default, EXE$CRMPSC replaces it with 1.

   e. It copies the PAGCNT argument, if present, to SEC$L_PAGCNT, after checking that the file contains at least that many blocks between SEC$L_VBN and its end of file. If the argument is absent, EXE$CRMPSC initializes the page count to the difference between the end-of-file block and SEC$L_VBN.

   f. If this is the first section mapped on this file, EXE$CRMPSC stores the section index in CCB$L_WIND and in the PSTE forward and backward links. If this is not the first section, EXE$CRMPSC inserts the PSTE into the chain of other PSTEs paging on that channel.

g. It initializes SEC$L_REFCNT to 1 and sets the section table entry flag SEC$V_INPROG to ensure that the section is not inadvertently deleted before its PTEs are initialized. If the system service cannot complete, it may place the process into a wait state at IPL 0. If the process were deleted at that point, the Delete Process ($DELPRC) system service would be able to detect such a section by the set SEC$V_INPROG flag and decrement the biased reference count.

h. It initializes the section page fault cluster, SEC$B_PFC, as the minimum of the PFC argument and 127.

9. EXE$CRMPSC forms a template PTE for the section's pages (see Figure 14.7). The PTE has both type bits set; the section table index in the low 16 bits (or zero for a copy-on-reference demand zero section); and the WRT, CRF, and DZRO bits copied from the section flags. EXE$CRMPSC calculates the protection code based on MMG$L_MAXACMODE, the writable flag in SEC$W_FLAGS, and the input section flags specifying the mode allowed to write the section pages.

10. If the expand-region flag was specified in the FLAGS system service argument, EXE$CRMPSC calculates the starting and ending section address based on the page count and the contents of PHD$L_FREPxVA. The IN-ADR argument identifies in which per-process region the section is to be created.

   If the flag is absent, the starting and ending addresses are determined by the INADR argument.

11. EXE$CRMPSC determines whether the new address space overmaps existing space.

   —If the space does not already exist and can all be created, EXE$CRMPSC invokes MMG$FAST_CREATE, in module SYSCREDEL, to initialize the section's PTEs. It then increases the section's reference count by the number of pages just mapped.

   —If the space to be created overmaps existing space or cannot all be created, EXE$CRMPSC invokes MMG$CREDEL, described in Section 15.1, specifying MMG$MAPSECPAG as the per-page routine.

12. EXE$CRMPSC calculates the starting virtual page number of the section and stores it in the low bytes of SEC$L_VPXPFC.

13. It decrements SEC$L_REFCNT to remove the extra reference, unnecessary now that the reference count reflects the mapped PTEs, and clears the SEC$V_INPROG flag.

14. EXE$CRMPSC returns any unused page file quota, records peak page file use and virtual size statistics, and stores return information in the optional RETADR argument.

15. It restores the IPL at entry and returns to its requestor.

MMG$MAPSECPAG, in module SYSCRMPSC, is the per-page service-specific routine for $CRMPSC. It is invoked with a number of arguments, including the PTE contents for the new page, number of pages in the section, number of pages to be mapped, and address of the section table entry.

For a process section, it takes the following steps:

1. Within initialization code, executed only once, MMG$MAPSECPAG sets the NO_OVERMAP flag in MMG$L_MAXACMODE if it is set in MMG$L_VFYFLAGS. It minimizes the requested number of pages to be mapped with the number of pages in the section. It replaces its own address in MMG$L_PAGESUBR so as to bypass the initialization code the next time it is entered.

2. MMG$MAPSECPAG invokes MMG$CREPAG, described in Section 15.3.1, which stores the template PTE contents into the next PTE and charges against job page file quota and PHD$L_PPGFLVA.

3. MMG$MAPSECPAG increments the reference count in the section table entry to reflect that one more PTE maps a page in that section.

4. It returns to its invoker, MMG$CREDEL, which continues to invoke it until there are no more pages to be mapped or until one of the limits to growth is reached.

15.4.1.2   **PFN-Mapped Process Section.** The $CRMPSC system service enables a process with PFNMAP privilege to map a portion of its virtual address space to a specific range of physical addresses. Although the primary purpose of this feature is to map process address space to I/O addresses, it is also used to map specific physical memory pages. When such a section is larger than one page, it maps physically contiguous pages.

When a process section mapped by a page frame number (PFN) is created, the effect is to add a series of valid PTEs to the process page table. The PFN fields in these PTEs contain the requested physical page numbers. The window bit is set in each PTE to indicate that the virtual page is PFN-mapped. These pages do not count against the process working set. They cannot be paged, swapped, or locked in the process working set. Moreover, no record is maintained in the PFN database that such pages are PFN-mapped.

Requested to create a PFN-mapped section, EXE$CRMPSC takes the following steps:

1. It invokes MMG$VFYSECFLG to test the compatibility of the section flags.

2. It raises IPL to 2 to block AST delivery.

3. It confirms that the process has PFNMAP privilege, returning the error status SS$_NOPRIV if not.

4. It invokes MMG$DALCSTXSCN, described in Section 15.4.3, to deallocate any process section whose reference count has gone to zero.

5. EXE$CRMPSC forms a template PTE for pages in the section. The PTE has the valid and window bits set. EXE$CRMPSC calculates its protection code based on MMG$L_MAXACMODE, the writable flag in SEC$W_FLAGS, and the flags in the FLAGS argument specifying the mode allowed to write the section pages. The PFN in the first PTE is specified by the VBN argument (named for its more typical use).

6. If the expand-region flag was specified in the FLAGS system service argument, EXE$CRMPSC calculates the starting and ending section address based on the page count and contents of PHD$L_FREPxVA. The INADR argument identifies in which per-process region the section is to be created.

   If the flag is absent, the starting and ending addresses are determined by the INADR argument.

7. EXE$CRMPSC invokes MMG$CREDEL, described in Section 15.1, specifying MMG$MAPSECPAG as the per-page routine.

8. EXE$CRMPSC records peak virtual size statistics and stores return information in the optional RETADR argument.

9. It restores the IPL at entry and returns to its requestor.

Invoked to create a PFN-mapped section page, MMG$MAPSECPAG takes the following steps:

1. Within initialization code, executed only once, MMG$MAPSECPAG sets the NO_OVERMAP flag in MMG$L_MAXACMODE if it is set in MMG$L_VFYFLAGS. It minimizes the number of pages requested in the PAGCNT argument with the number of pages in the address range specified by the INADR argument. It replaces its own address in MMG$L_PAGESUBR so as to bypass the initialization code the next time it is entered.

2. MMG$MAPSECPAG invokes MMG$CREPAG, described in Section 15.3.1. MMG$CREPAG stores the template PTE contents into the next PTE. For a window page (or a page in shared MA780 multiport memory), MMG$CREPAG acquires the MMG spinlock, locks the page table page that maps the newly created page into the process's working set list, and releases the spinlock.

3. MMG$MAPSECPAG calculates the contents of the next PTE by adding 1 to the PFN in the current PTE.

4. It returns to its invoker, MMG$CREDEL, which continues to invoke it until there are no more pages to be mapped or until one of the limits to growth is reached.

15.4.1.3 Global Section Creation.

The $CRMPSC system service enables a process to create a global section or, if the section already exists, to map to it. The Install Utility requests the $CRMPSC system service to create one or more global sections when an image is installed with the /SHARE qualifier.

The global section to be created can be a group global section to be shared by processes in the same user identification code (UIC) group, or a systemwide global section. Creation of the latter requires the SYSGBL privilege. The global section can be a temporary one that is deleted as soon as no process is mapped to it or a permanent one that must be explicitly deleted through the $DGBLSC system service. Creation of the latter requires the PRMGBL privilege.

The creation of a global section in local memory is similar to the creation of a process section except that additional data structures are involved. Chapter 14 shows the layouts of these data structures and describes them and their interrelations in more detail.

- A global section descriptor (GSD; see Figure 14.17), which enables subsequent $MGBLSC system service requests to determine whether the named section exists and to locate its global section table entry (GSTE).
- A GSTE (see Figure 14.9), analogous to the PSTE but part of the system header rather than of a PHD.
- Global page table entries (GPTEs), each of which describes the state of one global page in the section. GPTEs are not used by VAX memory management microcode but by the page fault handler when a process incurs a page fault for a global page.

When a process maps to a global section, its PTEs that describe the specified address range are initialized with global page table indexes (GPTXs; see Figure 14.21).

Like a process-private section, a global section can consist of specific pages of memory or I/O address space. Creation of a global PFN-mapped section requires the PFNMAP privilege. The only data structure necessary to describe a global PFN-mapped section is a special form of GSD (see Figure 14.17). There are no GPTEs nor is there a GSTE. When a process maps to such a section, its PTEs are initialized with the valid and window bits set and PFNs based on GSD$L_BASEPFN.

Another type of global section is a demand zero section whose pages are backed in a page file. This type of section is called a global page-file section. Record Management Services (RMS) uses this type of section to implement global buffers on a file. The SYSGEN parameter GBLPAGFIL specifies the maximum number of page file blocks that can be put to this use.

Another type of global section is a resident section, all of whose virtual pages are in physical memory. This type of section can only be created during system initialization, before the initiation of normal system operations. Its only current use is to create resident global sections from the read-only sections of the file system image, F11BXQP.EXE, when the SYSGEN parameter ACP_XQP_RES is 1. Creation of a resident section is reserved to Digital; any other use is unsupported.

Requested to create or map a global section, EXE$CRMPSC takes the following steps:

1. As described in Section 15.4.1.1, it initializes stack scratch space and tests the compatibility of the FLAGS arguments. It examines the specified flags to determine what type of global section is to be created and what further checks are required.

   —If a PFN-mapped section or global page-file section is to be created, the CHAN argument should not be present.

   —If a disk-file section is to be created, the CHAN argument must be present, the file must have been opened, and the WCB must map the entire file. If the section already exists, the CHAN argument need not be present.

   —If the section is to be copy-on-reference, EXE$CRMPSC sets MMG$V_CHGPAGFIL in MMG$L_MAXACMODE.

2. It locks the GSD mutex for write access, raising IPL to 2 as a side effect. The GSD mutex synchronizes access to both the systemwide and group GSD lists.

3. It invokes MMG$GSDSCN, in module SYSDGBLSC, to find the GSD, if any, that corresponds to the GSDNAM argument.

   MMG$GSDSCN scans the group or systemwide GSD list, depending on which kind of section was requested, examining each GSD to see if it is the requested one. If scanning the group list, it first compares the process's UIC group code with the high word of GSD$L_PCBUIC. It then compares the global section names. Because a character string comparison is relatively lengthy, the routine first confirms that one is necessary by requiring that the hash values and the character string lengths be the same for the target section name and the one in the candidate GSD. If they are not the same, the global section names cannot be.

   If the names match, MMG$GSDSCN checks the match control information specified in the IDENT argument against the GSD$L_IDENT. If there is a version incompatibility, MMG$GSDSCN continues to scan the list until it reaches the end or finds a match. Multiple versions of a global section with different version identifications and match control information can be installed. If a newer one were installed last and had match control specifying upward compatibility (match less or equal), it could be used with executables linked against it or earlier versions. If it had match control specifying no upward compatibility (match equal), an executable linked against an earlier version would not match; EXE$CRMPSC would continue to scan the list and find the earlier one.

4. If MMG$GSDSCN locates a matching GSD, EXE$CRMPSC is being requested to map to an existing section. It transfers control to EXE$M-GBLSC, at step 6 in the description in Section 15.4.2.

5. If no match is found, EXE$CRMPSC is being requested to create a new section. It first checks whether the process has the required privileges for the requested section type. If not, EXE$CRMPSC unlocks the GSD mutex and returns the error status SS$_NOPRIV.

6. It allocates paged pool for a GSD. If pool is unavailable, it unlocks the GSD mutex and returns the error status SS$_GSDFULL.

7. It begins to initialize the GSD, copying the section name to GSD$T_GSDNAM, storing the hash value in GSD$B_HASH, and clearing GSD$L_IPID.

8. If the section is PFN-mapped, EXE$CRMPSC clears GSD fields irrelevant to this type of section and copies the VBN argument to GSD$L_BASEPFN, the section name to GSD$T_PFNGSDNAM, and the page count to GSD$L_PAGES.

9. If the section is to map a disk file, EXE$CRMPSC stores the address of the object rights block (ORB) associated with the open file in GSD$L_ORB.

   If the section is a PFN-mapped or global page-file section, EXE$CRMPSC allocates an ORB from paged pool and initializes it, copying PCB$L_UIC to ORB$L_OWNER and the PROT argument to ORB$W_PROT. If pool for the ORB is unavailable, it unlocks the GSD mutex and returns the error status SS$_GSDFULL.

10. EXE$CRMPSC copies PCB$L_UIC to GSD$L_PCBUIC and initializes GSD$W_FLAGS from the section flags and access mode. It initializes GSD$L_IDENT from the IDENT argument.

11. If the section is PFN-mapped, EXE$CRMPSC continues with step 22.

12. Otherwise, it allocates a GSTE from the system header. If none is available, it deallocates the ORB and GSD, unlocks the mutex, and returns the error status SS$_SECTBLFUL.

13. EXE$CRMPSC takes most of the same steps to initialize a GSTE as it does a PSTE for a process section (see steps 8a through 8h in Section 15.4.1.1). One additional step required for a global section is making the WCB a "shared" one if it is not already. This chiefly involves returning the byte count quota charged for it to the appropriate job, setting the bit WCB$V_SHRWCB in WCB$B_ACCESS, and incrementing WCB$W_REFCNT to indicate one more reason the file should not be closed.

14. It stores the GSTE index in GSD$W_GSTX and the PROT argument in GSD$W_PROT.

15. If the section is a disk-file section rather than a global page-file section, EXE$CRMPSC copies the file owner to GSD$L_FILUIC.

16. If the section is a global page-file section, EXE$CRMPSC subtracts its page count from MMG$GL_GBLPAGFIL, the number of blocks of page file that can be used for this purpose, which is initialized from the SYSGEN parameter GBLPAGFIL. It must also charge the section's pages against PHD$L_PPGFLVA in the system header.

If mapping this section would exceed the allowed global page file count or if it would exceed PHD$L_PPGFLVA and another page file cannot be assigned, EXE$CRMPSC deallocates the GSD, ORB, and GSTE, unlocks the mutex, and returns the error status SS$_EXGBLPAGFIL.

17. It allocates a set of contiguous GPTEs, one for each global page plus two additional GPTEs, one at the beginning of the set and one at the end. The two additional GPTEs are cleared and serve as "stoppers," limits to modified page write clustering (see Chapter 16 and Figure 14.18).

    If there are insufficient GPTEs, EXE$CRMPSC deallocates the data structures it built, restores the page file charges, unlocks the mutex, and returns the error status SS$_GPTFULL.

18. It calculates the virtual page number of the second GPTE (skipping the stopper GPTE) and stores that in SEC$L_VPXPFC.

19. It forms template PTE contents for the GPTEs. Figure 14.20 shows the layout of the section table index forms of GPTE.

20. EXE$CRMPSC then loops, initializing GPTEs. Its loop includes the following steps:

    a. It faults the page of global page table that contains the GPTE, if it is not valid.

    b. It acquires the MMG spinlock, raising IPL to IPL$_MMG.

    c. It confirms that the page table page is still valid. If not, it releases the MMG spinlock and returns to step a.

    d. It increments the PFN SHRCNT array element corresponding to the physical page in which the global page table page resides.

    e. If the SHRCNT makes the transition from 0 to 1 (this is the first sharer), EXE$CRMPSC locks it into the system working set list; increments the system header field PHD$W_PTCNTACT, the number of active page table pages; and increments the reference count for the system header.

    f. If this is a resident section, it allocates a physical page from the free list and stores its PFN into the GPTE along with the valid bit. EXE$CRMPSC intializes the PFN database to describe the page as active and global, with a reference count of 1, and a section backing store.

    g. It releases the MMG spinlock, restoring an IPL of 2.

21. If this is a resident section, EXE$CRMPSC reads it into the allocated physical memory, using the swapper's interface to the Queue I/O Request ($QIO) system service.

22. It inserts the GSD at the front of the group or systemwide list.

23. The global section has been created. EXE$CRMPSC transfers control to EXE$MGBLSC to map it into the process's virtual address space as an existing section. It transfers control to EXE$MGBLSC at step 10 in the description in Section 15.4.2.

15.4.2 $MGBLSC System Service

The $MGBLSC system service can be considered a special case of the $CRMPSC system service, where the global section already exists. This service maps a range of process addresses to the named global section. It usually has no effect on the global database other than to include the latest mapping in various reference counts.

When a process maps to a global section backed by a file rather than a PFN-mapped section, each of its process PTEs in the designated range is initialized with a GPTX (see Figures 14.7 and 14.19). A GPTX is a pointer to the GPTE that records the current state of the global page.

The $MGBLSC system service procedure, EXE$MGBLSC in module SYS-CRMPSC, runs in kernel mode. It takes the following steps:

1. It invokes MMG$VFYSECFLG, in module SYSDGBLSC, to test the compatibility of the section flags with each other. If the flags are incompatible, it returns the error status SS$_IVSECFLG to its requestor.
2. It initializes stack scratch space.
3. It locks the GSD mutex for write access to synchronize access to the GSD lists, raising IPL to 2.
4. It invokes MMG$DALCSTXSCN1, in module PHDUTL, described in Section 15.4.3, to check the global (system) section table for any sections to be deleted.
5. It invokes MMG$GSDSCN to scan the GSD list for the specified global section. Section 15.4.1.3 describes MMG$GSDSCN's actions.
6. If the global section is mapped to a file, EXE$MGBLSC calculates the address of its GSTE from GSD$W_GSTX and the contents of PHD$L_PSTBASOFF in the system header.
7. If the section is copy-on-reference, it sets MMG$V_CHGPAGFIL in MMG$L_MAXACMODE so that the section pages will be charged against the page file quota and PHD$L_PPGFLVA.
8. It compares the section access mode with the mode bits in MMG$L_MAXACMODE to determine if the system service requestor is allowed to map the section. If not, EXE$MGBLSC unlocks the GSD mutex and returns the error status SS$_NOPRIV to its requestor.
9. If the section is not PFN-mapped, it increments SEC$L_REFCNT so that the section cannot inadvertently be deleted before its pages are mapped into the process's address space.

    If the section is PFN-mapped, EXE$MGBLSC increments GSD$L_REFCNT to prevent section deletion. (Recall that a PFN-mapped global section has no associated GSTE.)
10. With the section locked against deletion, EXE$MGBLSC can safely unlock the GSD mutex.
11. If the expand-region flag was specified in the FLAGS system service argument, EXE$MGBLSC calculates the starting and ending section addresses

based on the section page count (GSD$L_PAGES for a PFN-mapped section or SEC$L_PAGES for all others) and contents of PHD$L_FREPxVA. The INADR argument identifies in which per-process region the section is to be created.

12. EXE$MGBLSC forms a template PTE for pages in the section. If the section is PFN-mapped, the PTE has the valid and window bits set, and the PFN in the first PTE is specified by GSD$L_BASEPFN. If the section is backed by a section file, the PTE has the type 0 bit set and the type 1 bit clear to indicate a global page, and the first PTE has the GPTX from SEC$L_VPXPFC.

EXE$MGBLSC calculates a PTE protection code based on MMG$L_MAXACMODE, the writable flag in SEC$W_FLAGS, and the input section flags specifying the mode allowed to write the section pages.

13. It then tests whether the process has the necessary access (read, write, or execute) to the section based on the process's access rights list and the ORB associated with the section.

If the process does not have the desired access, EXE$MGBLSC decrements the appropriate reference count, based on the section type; invokes security auditing code, which may record the unsuccessful access; and returns an error status to its requestor.

If the process is allowed access, EXE$MGBLSC also invokes security auditing code, which checks whether a successful access should be audited and, if so, builds a message to be logged before the service exits.

14. EXE$MGBLSC determines whether the address space into which the section will be mapped overmaps existing space.

—If the space does not exist, the number of pages in the section is equal to the number of pages to be mapped, and all pages can be created, EXE$MGBLSC increases the section's reference count by the number of pages to be mapped. It initializes all the process's PTEs. In the case of a resident global section, it copies the PFNs from the GPTEs into process PTEs; for a nonresident section, it inserts GPTXs into the process PTEs.

When mapping a resident global section, it must also lock each process page table page that maps the section into the process working set list.

—If the space to be created overmaps existing space or if it cannot all be created, then EXE$MGBLSC invokes the routine MMG$CRE-DEL (see Section 15.1), specifying that MMG$MAPSECPAG (see Section 15.4.1.1) is to be the per-page routine.

15. EXE$MGBLSC returns any unused page file quota, records peak page file use and virtual size statistics, and stores return information in the optional RETADR argument.

16. It decrements the section reference count to remove the extra reference, unnecessary now that the reference count reflects the mapped PTEs.

17. It invokes MMG$DELGBLWCB to close open files associated with temporary global sections whose reference counts have gone to zero and to delete the WCB. Section 15.4.3 describes this routine in more detail.

18. It invokes a security audit routine, which may log successful access to the section.

19. It restores the IPL at entry and returns to its requestor.

15.4.3 $DGBLSC System Service

The operation of the $DGBLSC system service is more complex than that of global section creation because the section must be reduced from one of many states to nonexistence. In addition, global writable pages must be written to their backing store before a global section can be fully deleted. To avoid stalling the process requesting the service until all associated I/O completes, the final steps in the deletion of a global section are often deferred to a time after the system service request and return.

The actual section deletion cannot occur until the reference count in the GSTE, the count of process PTEs mapped to the section, goes to zero. Although the reference count can be zero when the $DGBLSC service is requested, more commonly global section deletion occurs as a side effect of virtual address deletion, which itself might occur as a result of image exit or process deletion.

The $DGBLSC system service procedure, EXE$DGBLSC in module SYS-DGBLSC, runs in kernel mode. It takes the following steps:

1. It confirms that the process has PRMGBL privilege and, if the section to be deleted is a system global section, SYSGBL privilege. If the process lacks a necessary privilege, EXE$DGBLSC returns the error status SS$_NOPRIV.

2. It invokes MMG$VFYSECFLG to test the compatibility of the specified section flags.

3. It locks the GSD mutex for write access, raising IPL to 2.

4. It invokes MMG$GSDSCN, described in Section 15.4.1.3, to locate the GSD for the specified global section. If the section does not exist, it unlocks the mutex and returns the error status SS$_NOSUCHSEC to its requestor.

5. If the global section is a PFN-mapped section, EXE$DGBLSC confirms that the process has PFNMAP privilege, unlocking the mutex and returning the error status SS$_NOPRIV if not. A PFN-mapped section is described solely by a GSD; there are no GSTE, no GPTEs, and no section reference count. The section can be deleted immediately. EXE$DGBLSC deallocates the ORB and GSD to paged pool. It continues with step 7.

6. If the global section is mapped to a file, EXE$DGBLSC removes the GSD from its current list and inserts it on the delete pending list, at global location EXE$GL_GSDDELFL. It clears the global section's permanent flag, SEC$V_PERM in GSD$W_FLAGS and, if there is an associated GSTE, in SEC$W_FLAGS as well. This step changes the section to a temporary global section that can be deleted when its reference count becomes zero.

   If the reference count in the GSTE is zero, the section can be deleted now; EXE$DGBLSC sets PHD$V_DALCSTX in the system header PHD$W_FLAGS as a signal for MMG$DALCSTXSCN.

7. It invokes MMG$DALCSTXSCN, described later in this section, in case this section or any other can be deleted now.
8. It unlocks the GSD mutex.
9. It invokes MMG$DELGBLWCB, described later in this section.
10. It restores the IPL at entry and returns to its requestor.

MMG$DALCSTXSCN, in module PHDUTL, is invoked to locate and deal with deletable section table entries, in both the global section and process section tables. Section deletion cannot occur until the section reference count goes to zero, generally as the result of virtual address space deletion or modified page writing. A scan for deletable GSTEs is initiated from the $MGBLSC and $DGBLSC system services, and from the $CRMPSC system service when it is creating a global section.

MMG$DALCSTXSCN is entered at IPL 2 in kernel mode, with the address of a PHD whose section table should be scanned. In the case of deleted global sections, it is entered with the address of the system header and with the GSD mutex locked.

At alternative entry point MMG$DALCSTXSCN1, the routine first gets the address of the system header and then merges with MMG$DALC-STXSCN.

MMG$DALCSTXSCN takes the following steps:

1. It tests and clears PHD$V_DALCSTX, returning immediately if the bit was already clear.
2. It scans the list of section table entries, returning when it reaches the end of the list. It examines each entry's reference count, skipping to the next one if the count is nonzero.
3. If the reference count is zero, MMG$DALCSTXSCN tests whether the section is permanent and, if so, continues with step 2.
4. Otherwise, it tests whether the section is a global section. If it is, it invokes MMG$DELGBLSEC to delete it and then continues with step 2.
5. For a process-private section, MMG$DALCSTXSCN checks whether this section is the only one still mapped from its section file.

   —If so, it restores the address of the WCB to CCB$L_WIND and inserts the section table entry on the free list.

—If there are other sections still mapped, it removes this one from the chain, inserts it on the free list, and, if necessary, adjusts CCB$L_WIND to point to a section table entry other than the one being deleted.

In either case, it continues with step 2.

MMG$DELGBLSEC, in module SYSDGBLSC, is invoked to delete a temporary global section whose reference count has gone to zero, that is, one with no pages mapped by any process.

1. It removes the GSD from the group or systemwide list and inserts it onto the delete pending list so that no more processes can map to it.
2. It gets the starting GPTX and number of pages from the GSTE.
3. It acquires the MMG spinlock, raising IPL to IPL$_MMG.
4. It scans the section's GPTEs. If it reaches the last GPTE, rather than reaching one of the end conditions in the following list, it continues with step 7.

   —If it finds a transition page on the free list, it invokes MMG$DELPFN-LST, in module ALLOCPFN, to delete the page's virtual contents. The PFN is moved from its current position on the free list to the head of the list, so that it can be reallocated before pages whose contents might still be useful. Its PFN database entries are reinitialized. The reference count for the global page table page that contains the GPTE is decremented. When an entire page of GPTEs is freed, the global page table page can be unlocked from the system working set. MMG$DEL-GBLSEC continues its scan of the section's GPTEs.

   —If it finds a global page-file section page on the modified list, it clears the saved modify bit in the PFN STATE array element and invokes MMG$DELPFNLST as described. It continues its scan of the section's GPTEs.

   —If it finds a transition page on the modified page list that is not part of a global page-file section, the page must be written to its backing store before the section is deleted, and MMG$DELGBLSEC goes to step 5.

   —If it finds a transition page that is not on the free or modified page list, the page is being read in from its backing store. That I/O must complete before the section is deleted, and MMG$DELGBLSEC goes to step 6.

5. It requests the modified page writer to perform a selective purge of the modified page list to write this section's global pages to their backing store and release them. Chapter 16 describes the modified page writer.
6. It releases the MMG spinlock, restoring IPL to 2, stores the process ID of the current process in GSD$L_IPID as the target of an eventual cleanup AST, sets PHD$V_DALCSTX in the system header, and returns.
7. If MMG$DELGBLSEC has scanned all the GPTEs for the section and

found none for whose I/O it must wait, it scans the GPTEs again, this time to decrement the global page table page reference count and to release page file backing store.

—If it finds a global page in a page file, it deallocates that block of page file, decrements the global page table page reference count, and clears the GPTE.

—If it finds a demand zero global page, it simply decrements the global page table reference count and clears the GPTE.

8. It releases the MMG spinlock, setting IPL to 2.
9. It deallocates the GPTEs.
10. If there is a file open on the section, it decrements the reference count in the WCB. If the count is now zero, it inserts the WCB on a queue of delete pending WCBs.
11. If this was a global page-file section, it adds its page count back to MMG$GL_GBLPAGFIL and to PHD$L_PPGFLVA in the system header.
12. It removes the GSD from the delete pending list and deallocates it to paged pool, along with the ORB, unless the ORB is still in use for an open section file.
13. It inserts the GSTE onto the free list.
14. It allocates nonpaged pool, forms it into an AST control block, queues a normal kernel AST to the current process, and returns to its invoker. The specified AST procedure is GSD_CLEAN_AST.

GSD_CLEAN_AST executes as a normal kernel AST procedure in the context of the process that requested the system service that triggered MMG$DELGBLSEC, possibly but not necessarily the process that requested global section deletion. Its enqueuing can be requested from MMG$DEL-GBLSEC or the modified page writer. Its enqueuing can also be requested by the routines that decrease section reference count, MMG$SUBSECREF and MMG$DECSECREF in module PHDUTL, when a temporary global section's reference count goes to zero. It takes the following steps:

1. It tests whether the process is being deleted or already has this procedure active. If either is true, it returns.
2. It requests the Clear AST ($CLRAST) system service so that a subsequent kernel AST can be delivered.
3. If PHD$V_DALCSTX in the system header is set, it locks the GSD mutex; invokes MMG$DALCSTXSCN, previously described; and unlocks the mutex.
4. It invokes MMG$DELGBLWCB, described later in this section, to close the section file.
5. It returns.

MMG$DELGBLWCB, in module SYSDGBLSC, is invoked to close an open file associated with a temporary global section whose reference count has gone to zero and to delete the WCB. It takes the following steps:

1. It makes several consistency checks, returning immediately if it is executing within a process that owns any mutexes, has kernel mode AST delivery disabled, or has an active kernel mode AST. Its subsequent processing requires delivery of a kernel mode AST and IPL 0 execution.
2. It removes a WCB from the delete pending list, returning if there is none.
3. It finds an available channel control block and stores in it the address of the unit control block on which the file represented by the WCB is open and an indication that the channel has been assigned in kernel mode.
4. It lowers IPL to 0 and requests the Deassign Channel ($DASSGN) system service, the actions of which result in closing the file.
5. It raises IPL back to 2 and continues with step 2.

15.5   VIRTUAL ADDRESS SPACE DELETION

Page deletion is generally more complicated than page creation. Creation involves taking the process from one known state (the address space does not yet exist) to another known state (for example, the PTEs contain demand zero PTEs). Page deletion must deal with initial conditions that include all possible states of a virtual page.

Page creation may first require that the specified pages be deleted to put the process page tables into their known state. Thus, page deletion is often an integral part of page creation.

A process deletes part of its address space by requesting the $DELTVA system service.

15.5.1   Page Deletion and Process Waits

A page that has I/O in progress cannot be deleted until the I/O completes. A process trying to delete such a private page is placed into a page fault wait state (with a request that a system event be reported when I/O completes) until the page read or write completes. Deleting a page in the write-in-progress transition state has the same effect. A page in the read-in-progress transition state is faulted, with the immediate result that the process is placed into the collided page wait state.

Special action must be taken for a global page with I/O in progress because there is no way to determine if the process deleting the page is also responsible for the I/O. Hence, if the process has any direct I/O in progress, the process is placed into a resource wait for the resource RSN$_ASTWAIT until its direct I/O completes.

15.5.2 $DELTVA System Service

The $DELTVA system service procedure, EXE$DELTVA in module SYSCRE-DEL, runs in kernel mode. EXE$DELTVA takes the following steps:

1. It creates and initializes the stack scratch space and raises IPL to 2.
2. It invokes MMG$CREDEL, specifying MMG$DELPAG as the per-page service-specific routine.
3. It restores the IPL at entry.
4. It records peak page file use and virtual size statistics, and stores return information in the optional RETADR argument.
5. It returns to its requestor.

When a virtual page is deleted, MMG$DELPAG (and routines it invokes) must return all process and system resources associated with the page. These can include the following:

- A physical page of memory for a valid or transition page
- A page file virtual block for a page whose backing store address indicates an already allocated block
- A working set list entry for a page in a process working set list
- Page file quota for a page with a page file backing store address and the charge against PHD$L_PPGFLVA, even if the page has not yet been allocated a block in a page file

Deleting a process-private section page results in decrementing the reference count in the PSTE (see Figure 14.9). If the reference count goes to zero, the PSTE itself can be released.

In addition, a valid or modified page with a section file backing store address rather than a page file backing store address must have its latest contents written back to the section file. (The contents of a page with a page file backing store address are unimportant after the virtual page is deleted and do not have to be saved before the physical page is reused.)

Deleting a physical page means that the PFN PTE array element is cleared, destroying all ties between the physical page and any process virtual address. In addition, the page is placed at the head of the free page list, so that it can be reallocated before other pages whose contents might still be useful.

MMG$DELPAG is the per-page service-specific routine for the $DELTVA and $CNTREG system services. It is invoked with an argument specifying the address to be deleted. It takes the following steps:

1. It saves the IPL at entry and acquires the MMG spinlock, raising IPL to IPL$_MMG.
2. It examines the PTE that maps the page to be deleted.
3. If the PTE contains zero, the page has already been deleted, and the routine MMG$DELPAG returns to its invoker after releasing the MMG spinlock and restoring the previous IPL.
4. It confirms that the access mode passed in MMG$L_MAXACMODE is at least as privileged as that of the page owner. If not, it returns the error status SS$_PAGOWNVIO to its invoker after releasing the MMG spinlock and restoring the previous IPL.

5. Otherwise, it examines the PTE type bits to determine whether the page is in a page file, an invalid process section page, a transition page, a valid page, or a section file global page.

6. If the page is in a page file, MMG$DELPAG deallocates the occupied block of page file, restores job page file quota and PHD$L_PPGFLVA, clears the PTE, and releases the MMG spinlock. If this is the last page of the address region, MMG$DELPAG removes null pages from the end of the region. It returns to its invoker.

7. If the page is from a demand zero process section, MMG$DELPAG releases the MMG spinlock, lowers IPL, touches the page to fault it into the working set, and continues with step 1. Faulting it into the working set first ensures that an untouched demand zero page backed by a section file will be written back to it as all zeros. Handling it in this way minimizes the need for complex code to handle a relatively rare case.

8. If the page is an invalid page from any other type of process section, MMG$DELPAG decrements the section reference count. If the page is copy-on-reference, MMG$DELPAG increments the job page file quota and PHD$L_PPGFLVA. It clears the PTE and releases the MMG spinlock. If this is the last page of the address region, MMG$DELPAG removes null pages from the end of the region. It returns to its invoker.

9. If the page is a demand zero page (created by the $CRETVA or $EXPREG system service), MMG$DELPAG restores job page file quota and PHD$L_PPGFLVA, clears the PTE, and releases the MMG spinlock. If this is the last page of the address region, MMG$DELPAG removes null pages from the end of the region. It returns to its invoker.

10. If the page is any other type of transition page, MMG$DELPAG examines the PFN STATE array entry to see where the page is.

   —If the page is on the free list, MMG$DELPAG invokes MMG$DELPFNLST, in module ALLOCPFN, to delete the page's virtual contents. The PFN is moved from its current position on the free list to the head of the list. Its PFN database entries are reinitialized. The PFN SHRCNT array entry for the page table page that maps it is decremented. If the count goes to zero, the page table page is released from the working set list.

   —If the page is on the modify list and has page file backing store, MMG$DELPAG clears the saved modify bit in the PFN STATE array entry so that the page, when deleted, will be placed on the free list, and invokes MMG$DELPFNLST, as just described.

   —If the page state is read in progress or release pending, MMG$DELPAG releases the MMG spinlock, lowers IPL, touches the page to fault it into the working set, and continues with step 1.

   —If the page state is active or there was an I/O error reading the page in from mass storage, MMG$DELPAG continues with the next step.

11. If the page is valid, MMG$DELPAG examines its PFN TYPE array element to determine its type.

—If the page is a resident global section page, it decrements the section reference count and the PHD$L_PTWSLELCK array byte, which counts the number of reasons the page table page that maps the section page is locked in the working set list. It clears the PTE and, if it is the last page of the region, removes null pages from the end of the region before releasing the MMG spinlock and returning to its invoker.

—If the page is a PFN-mapped section page, it invokes the INVALIDATE_TB macro to invalidate any corresponding translation buffer entry. It tests whether the process has direct I/O in progress. If not, it decrements the corresponding PHD$L_PTWSLELCK array byte and clears the PTE. If it is the last page of the region, MMG$DELPAG removes null pages from the end of the region before releasing the MMG spinlock and returning to its invoker.

If the process has direct I/O in progress, its I/O must complete before this page can be deleted. When there is direct I/O in progress to a typical process page, its PFN REFCNT array element is incremented. Thus a value larger than 1 indicates I/O in progress. A PFN-mapped page may have other processes mapped to it, some of which could be doing I/O to it, so its REFCNT value is not precise enough to determine whether the page is in use as an I/O buffer for this process. Furthermore, a page mapped by PFN may be one without any PFN database to examine.

If bit MMG$V_NOWAIT_IPL0 in MMG$L_MAXACMODE is set (as it would be if the page were being deleted as a side effect of creating a process section that overmapped the page), the process cannot wait at IPL 0 for the I/O to complete, and MMG$DELPAG returns the error status SS$_ABORT to its invoker. Otherwise, it releases the MMG spinlock and places the process into a resource wait for resource RSN$_ASTWAIT (effectively, wait for an I/O completion) at IPL 0. When the process is placed back into execution, MMG$DELPAG raises IPL to 2 and resumes at step 1.

—If the page is permanently locked into the working set, MMG$DELPAG releases the MMG spinlock and returns a success code. Such a page cannot be deleted until the process is deleted or outswapped.

—If the process has locked the page into its working set, MMG$DELPAG releases the MMG spinlock; invokes MMG$LCKULKPAG, in module SYSLKWSET (described in Chapter 17) to unlock the page; and then resumes at step 1.

—If the PFN REFCNT array element for this (process-private) page is larger than 1, the page is in use as an I/O buffer. MMG$DELPAG tests against MMG$V_NOWAIT_IPL0 as described and either returns an error status or places the process into a wait until the I/O completes.

—If the page has been modified but it has page file backing store, MMG$DELPAG sets the PFN$V_DELCON bit in the PFN STATE array element so its contents will be deleted when it is inserted on the free list; invokes INVALIDATE_TB to clear the valid and modify bits in the PTE; removes the page from the working set list; and decrements its PFN REFCNT array element.

If the reference count is greater than zero, the page has I/O in progress, and MMG$DELPAG must wait for I/O completion as previously described.

If the reference count is zero, MMG$DELPAG deallocates the associated physical page, as a result of which the PTE once again contains a backing store format, and then resumes with step 1, deleting the page as an invalid unmodified page-file section page.

—If the page has been modified and is backed by a section file rather than a page file, it has to be written to its backing store before it can be deleted. MMG$DELPAG uses a routine within the $UPDSEC system service to write the page to its backing store, in addition to setting the PFN$V_WRTINPROG bit for the page and taking the actions described in the previous step.

12. If the process page is an invalid global page, MMG$DELPAG examines its GPTE to determine the page type and validity of the master page.

—If the master page is a demand zero page or a page in a global page-file section, MMG$DELPAG decrements the global section reference count and clears the process PTE. If the process page is the last page of the region, MMG$DELPAG removes null pages from the end of the region before releasing the MMG spinlock and returning to its invoker.

—If the global page is in transition being faulted from its backing store, MMG$DELPAG tests and sets MMG$V_DELGBLDON in MMG$L_MAXACMODE. If the bit was already set, it continues with the next step. Otherwise, MMG$DELPAG must free the process's working set list entry associated with the global page. It invokes a routine within the Purge Working Set ($PURGWS) system service to remove that page and any other global pages in the address range being deleted from the working set list and to change the PFN database accordingly. It then resumes with step 1.

—If the global page is valid or in transition, has I/O in progress, and the process has outstanding direct I/O, the direct I/O may be to the global page that the process is trying to delete. MMG$DELPAG therefore places the process into a resource wait, as previously described, until the I/O completes. It then resumes with step 1.

If the process has no outstanding direct I/O, MMG$DELPAG continues with the next step.

—If the global page is valid with no I/O in progress, invalid and in a section file, or a transition page with no I/O in progress, MMG$DELPAG examines the PFN BAK array element to determine the type of section. If the section is demand zero, it continues with the next step. If the section is copy-on-reference, it first increments the job page file quota and PHD$L_PPGFLVA. For any type of section that is not demand zero, MMG$DELPAG decrements the global section reference count, clears the process PTE, releases the MMG spinlock, and returns.

—If the global page is invalid and a page from a demand zero writable section, MMG$DELPAG allocates a physical page, initializes its PFN database array entries, inserts it onto the modified list, and then clears the process PTE, releases the MMG spinlock, and returns. These steps ensure that an untouched demand zero page backed by a global section file will be written back to it as all zeros. This requirement is similar to that for a demand zero page in a writable process section. However, MMG$DELPAG takes these steps rather than fault the page in first as it does a process-private page, for better performance in a more common case.

15.5.3 $CNTREG System Service

The $CNTREG system service procedure, EXE$CNTREG in module SYS-CREDEL, runs in kernel mode. The $CNTREG system service is a special case of the $DELTVA system service. EXE$CNTREG simply converts the requested number of pages into a P0 or P1 page range and merges with EXE$DELTVA at step 2 in the description in Section 15.5.2.

15.6 $SETSWM SYSTEM SERVICE

A process with PSWAPM privilege can lock and unlock itself into the balance set by requesting the $SETSWM system service. A process locked into the balance set cannot be outswapped.

The $SETSWM system service procedure, EXE$SETSWM in module SYS-SETMOD, runs in kernel mode. EXE$SETSWM checks that the process has privilege and simply sets (or clears) the PCB$V_PSWAPM bit in PCB$L_STS, the status longword in the software PCB.

When the swapper is searching for suitable outswap candidates, a process whose PCB$V_PSWAPM bit is set is passed over.

15.7 $SETPRT SYSTEM SERVICE

A process can alter the protection of a set of pages in its address space by requesting the $SETPRT system service.

The $SETPRT system service procedure, EXE$SETPRT in module SYS-SETPRT, runs in kernel mode. It takes the following steps:

1. It performs several consistency checks on the desired protection. For example, if the desired protection is specified as no access, EXE$SETPRT changes it to kernel read so that the page can be faulted and can be deleted later in the life of the process.
2. EXE$SETPRT invokes MMG$CREDEL, specifying MMG$SETPRTPAG as the per-page service-specific routine.

MMG$SETPRTPAG, in module SYSSETPRT, takes the following steps:

1. It gets the address of the PTE that maps the specified virtual address and faults the page table page into the process's working set list. It acquires the MMG spinlock.
2. It compares the requestor access mode with that of the page owner. If the access mode is insufficiently privileged, it releases the MMG spinlock and returns the error status SS$_PAGOWNVIO, which is passed back to the $SETPRT requestor.
3. Otherwise, it gets the type of the virtual page.
4. If the page is a transition page or is a demand zero page that is to become read-only, MMG$SETPRTPAG releases the MMG spinlock, lowers IPL, touches the page to make it valid, and continues at step 1.
5. If the page is a demand zero page and will remain writable or is a page file page, MMG$SETPRTPAG continues with step 9.
6. If the page is a process-private section page and the protection change is not from read-only to writable, MMG$SETPRTPAG continues with step 9.

   If the protection change would make the page writable, MMG$SET-PRTPAG must change the page to be a copy-on-reference page: it charges the page against the process's job page file quota and PHD$L_PPGFLVA, decrements the section reference count, and changes the page's backing store to a page file. It continues with step 9, also setting the copy-on-reference bit in the PTE. An inability to charge the page against quota or PHD$L_PPGFLVA results in an error return.
7. If the page is valid, MMG$SETPRTPAG checks that it is not a PFN-mapped page and that it is a process page. If either is false, it returns the error status SS$_NOPRIV.

   If the page is a valid process page and the protection change does not make it writable or if the page already has page file backing store, MMG$SETPRTPAG continues with step 9. Otherwise, it decrements the section reference count and changes the PFN BAK array for the physical page to a page file backing store form. It completes changing the page to a copy-on-reference page, as in step 6.

8. If the page is a global section page, MMG$SETPRTPAG determines the page type from the global PTE. If it contains anything but a global section index for a copy-on-reference page, MMG$SETPRTPAG returns the error status SS$_NOPRIV. Otherwise, it continues.

9. It invokes the INVALIDATE_TB macro, described in Chapter 34, to invalidate any cached translation buffer entry for the page and change its protection.

10. It releases the MMG spinlock, restoring the previous IPL of 2, and returns to its invoker.

In general, the operation of this service is straightforward. However, its actions have one interesting side effect. If a section page for a read-only section has its protection set to writable, the copy-on-reference bit is set. This set bit forces the page to have its backing store address changed to the page file when the page is faulted, preventing a later attempt to write the modified section pages back to a file to which the process may be denied write access.

The VMS debugger uses this service to implement its watchpoint facility. The page containing the data element in question is set to no-write access for user mode. When the program being debugged attempts to access the page, an access violation occurs, which is fielded by the debugger's condition handler. This handler performs the following actions:

1. Checks whether the inaccessible address is the one being watched and reports the modification if it is

2. Sets the page protection to PRT$C_UW to allow the modification

3. Sets the TBIT in the processor status longword to give the debugger control after the instruction completes

4. Dismisses the exception

When the instruction completes, the debugger's TBIT handler gains control, sets the page protection back to no-write access for user mode, and allows the program to continue execution.

16 Paging Dynamics

I consider that a man's brain originally is like a little empty
attic, and you have to stock it with such furniture as you
choose. . . . Now, the skillful workman is very careful indeed as
to what he takes into his brain-attic. He will have nothing but
the tools which may help him in doing his work, but of these
he has a large assortment, and all in the most perfect order. It
is a mistake to think that that little room has elastic walls
and can distend to any extent. Depend upon it, there comes a
time when for every addition of knowledge you forget something that you knew before. It is of highest importance, therefore, not to have useless facts elbowing out the useful ones.

Sir Arthur Conan Doyle, *A Study in Scarlet*

This chapter's subject is paging dynamics, the movement of pages of code
and data between memory and mass storage. Specifically, it describes the
transitions a page makes as it is faulted into and out of a working set list,
and as it moves between its backing store and memory.

This chapter also discusses the allocation and use of page files and the
operation of the Update Section File on Disk ($UPDSEC) system service.

16.1 OVERVIEW

A typical virtual page, 512 bytes of virtual address space, begins life as
a block of an image file on a mass storage medium. A process initiates
execution of the image by requesting the Image Activate ($IMGACT) system
service, better known as the image activator. The image activator, described
in detail in Chapter 26, maps the image into the process's address space,
using the memory management system services described in Chapter 15.
The image activator initializes data structures such as process section table
entries (PSTEs) and page table entries (PTEs) to associate blocks of the image
file with the process pages they are to occupy. Chapter 14 explains the
various memory management data structures and the VAX processor's steps
in translating virtual addresses.

When a reference is made to an address that is not valid (one whose PTE
valid bit is clear), the VAX processor generates a page fault. When an image
begins to execute, none of its pages have been read into memory from the
image file, and all of its PTEs have been initialized to be invalid. When it
first references one of its pages, a page fault exception results. As with most
exceptions, the processor changes access mode to kernel and switches to
the kernel stack, unless it was already executing on the kernel stack. (It
is possible, but illegal and fatal, for a thread of execution running on the

interrupt stack to incur a page fault.) It dispatches to the translation-not-valid exception service routine, also known as the page fault handler.

The page fault handler examines the memory management data structures to determine which mass storage block contains the virtual page that triggered the fault, allocates a physical page of memory from the free page list, stores its page frame number (PFN) in the PTE, finds an available entry in the process's working set list, and requests an I/O operation to read that block into the allocated page. It places the process into a page fault wait state. When the I/O completes, the page fault handler updates the PTE so that its valid bit is set and makes the process computable.

When the process is placed into execution, it reexecutes the instruction that incurred the page fault. This time, with the PTE valid bit set, the processor translates the virtual address to a physical address and execution continues.

The virtual page remains valid and in the working set until one of the following occurs:

- Room is required for another page.
- The virtual page is deleted.
- The Purge Working Set ($PURGWS) system service removes it.
- Swapper trimming removes it (see Chapter 18).
- Working set limit adjustment removes it.

Removed from the working set list, the page is inserted on the modified page list, if it has been modified; otherwise, it is inserted on the free page list. Sometime later, the swapper, in response to insufficient free pages or an excess of modified pages, writes modified pages to their backing store, typically a page file. It then inserts them on the free page list. (Acting in this capacity, the swapper is called the modified page writer.) While the page is on the free or modified page list, it is essentially cached; the page fault handler can resolve a fault for it by simply updating the memory management data structures and placing the page back in the process's working set list.

This chapter shows how the page fault handler manipulates the various memory management data structures in response to faults for different types of pages. It presents page fault handler action in terms of modifications to data structures and state transitions rather than as a flowchart or series of decisions. It also describes the transitions that a virtual page makes when it is removed from a working set list.

16.2   INITIAL PAGE FAULT HANDLING

The VMS page fault handler is MMG$PAGEFAULT, in module PAGEFAULT. Figure 16.1 shows the state of the stack when it is entered.

Its first step is to check the interrupt priority level (IPL) at which the page fault occurred. If the IPL is higher than 2, MMG$PAGEFAULT generates the

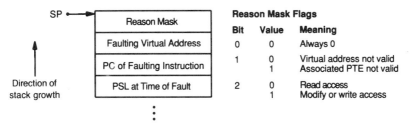

	Reason Mask Flags		
	Bit	Value	Meaning
	0	0	Always 0
	1	0	Virtual address not valid
		1	Associated PTE not valid
	2	0	Read access
		1	Modify or write access

Figure 16.1
State of the Stack Following a Translation-Not-Valid
Fault

fatal bugcheck PGFIPLHI. Page faults above IPL 2 are not allowed for the following reasons:

- Code executes at an elevated IPL to perform a series of synchronized instructions. If a page fault occurs, the faulting process might be removed from execution, allowing another process to execute the same routine or access the same protected data structure. The alternative, looping in process context at elevated IPL until the page fault I/O completes, would reduce system performance and responsiveness. Moreover, any loop at IPL 4 or above would block the I/O postprocessing necessary for page fault resolution. On a uniprocessor system, a loop above IPL 2 blocks the swapper from running and would result in a deadlock if the free page list were empty and the page fault required allocation of a physical page of memory.
- When the system is executing at an IPL higher than 2, it is often on the interrupt stack, running in system context. MMG$PAGEFAULT and routines it invokes perform operations that require process context.

Next, MMG$PAGEFAULT acquires the MMG spinlock, raising IPL to IPL$_MMG, to serialize access to the memory management database.

If the faulting virtual address is in system space, MMG$PAGEFAULT checks that the address is not within another process's process header (PHD). Unlike other system pages, PHD pages belong to the associated process; pageable PHD pages are part of its working set. A process is therefore not allowed to fault a page in another process's PHD. When MMG$PAGEFAULT detects this type of fault, it transforms the page fault into an access violation.

It is possible, however, for a process to fault a page in its own PHD and immediately be context-switched. If the process is outswapped and inswapped before its next execution, the swapper may have moved its PHD to a different balance set slot. At inswap, the swapper sets the bit PHD$V_NOACCVIO in PHD$W_FLAGS to signal this possibility.

If the PHD does occupy a different balance set slot when the process resumes execution in MMG$PAGEFAULT, the faulting virtual address on its kernel stack is now an address in the balance set slots but not in the process's own PHD. For this reason, MMG$PAGEFAULT makes a further

check before simulating an access violation: it tests and clears PHD$V_
NOACCVIO in PHD$W_FLAGS.

If the bit was set, MMG$PAGEFAULT dismisses the page fault, and the
faulting instruction reexecutes with the PHD$V_NOACCVIO bit clear. If
the instruction again faults a page in another balance set slot, MMG$PAGE-
FAULT releases the MMG spinlock and simulates an access violation, using
the page fault exception parameters as access violation parameters.

If the faulting virtual address is not within another process's PHD,
MMG$PAGEFAULT continues. It locates the PTE that maps the page con-
taining the faulting virtual address by performing the same operations as the
VAX address translation hardware/microcode:

1. The upper two bits of the virtual address (VA⟨31:30⟩) select which page
   table to use.
2. The virtual address field (VA⟨29:9⟩) is a longword context index into the
   page table. The low-order bits specify byte offset in the page and are
   ignored.

Before examining the PTE, MMG$PAGEFAULT determines whether the
system PTE (SPTE) for the page table page containing the PTE is itself valid.
This check avoids the necessity of making the page fault handler recursive.
Note that MMG$PAGEFAULT checks the valid bit in the SPTE for the page
table page rather than the page table valid bit in the exception parameter.
Between the time of the page fault and the time of the check, the SPTE could
have been altered, invalidating the exception parameter.

If the SPTE for the page containing the PTE is invalid, MMG$PAGEFAULT
transforms the page fault into a fault for the page table page. Once the
page table page is faulted in and its SPTE made valid, MMG$PAGEFAULT
will execute an REI instruction to dismiss the page fault exception. The
instruction that caused the original fault will reexecute and refault, and this
time MMG$PAGEFAULT will fault in the process page.

MMG$PAGEFAULT invokes MMG$FREWSLE, in module PAGEFAULT,
to find room in the working set list for a new page, possibly by removing a
page from it. Chapter 17 describes MMG$FREWSLE in detail. MMG$PAGE-
FAULT then takes different actions, depending on the nature of the invalid
PTE. See Figure 14.7 for the different forms of invalid PTE.

The next sections describe some of the major paths through MMG$PAGE-
FAULT. Extraordinary conditions, such as read and write errors, are only
mentioned in passing.

16.3 PAGE FAULTS FOR PROCESS-PRIVATE PAGES

This section describes page faults for process-private pages. Section 16.4 describes the paths through MMG$PAGEFAULT for global pages. Section 16.5
describes the path for system pages.

There are four cases of process-private page faults:

- Two cases involve a page that is originally faulted from a section file. The two cases are distinguished by whether or not the section is copy-on-reference.
- A third case is a fault for a page in a private section of demand zero pages.
- A fourth case is a fault for a page in a page file, which began as a copy-on-reference page or a demand zero page.

16.3.1   Page Located in a Section File

A page that initially resides in a private section file can be characterized by whether it is copy-on-reference. A PTE for either type of page contains a process section table index (PSTX). Figure 14.7 shows this and the other forms of invalid PTE.

16.3.1.1   Private Page That Is Not Copy-on-Reference. The PTE of a page that is not copy-on-reference initially contains a PSTX with the copy-on-reference bit (PTE⟨16⟩) clear. The transitions that such a page can make are illustrated in Figure 16.2. The numbers in the figure are keyed to the following explanations of each of the transitions. For simplicity, clustered reads and writes are ignored in the discussion that follows. Section 16.7 discusses aspects of paging I/O, including read/write clustering.

①As described in Section 16.2, MMG$PAGEFAULT first locates the PTE that maps the faulting page and ensures the validity of the page table page containing it. MMG$PAGEFAULT invokes three other routines, all in module PAGEFAULT, to perform some of the related updates to memory management data structures:

   a. MMG$ININEWPFN allocates a physical page from the head of the free page list. It stores the address of the PTE in that page's PFN PTE array element and a type code of process page in its PFN TYPE array element.

   b. MMG$INCPTREF updates the data structures describing the page table page that maps the faulted page. It increments the PFN SHRCNT array element of the page table page to indicate that it maps one more valid page. If this is the first valid page mapped by the page table page (that is, if the SHRCNT makes the transition from 0 to 1), MMG$INCPTREF locks the working set list entry (WSLE) for the page table page into the process's working set list. It also increments PHD$W_PTCNTACT, the number of active page table pages for the process, and the PHD's entry in the array at PHV$GL_REFCBAS, the number of reasons the PHD should remain in memory.

   c. MMG$MAKEWSLE updates the data structures related to the working set list. It initializes the WSLE with the virtual address and page type of the page being faulted and sets its valid bit. It increments the PHD$L_PTWSLEVAL array element corresponding to the page table

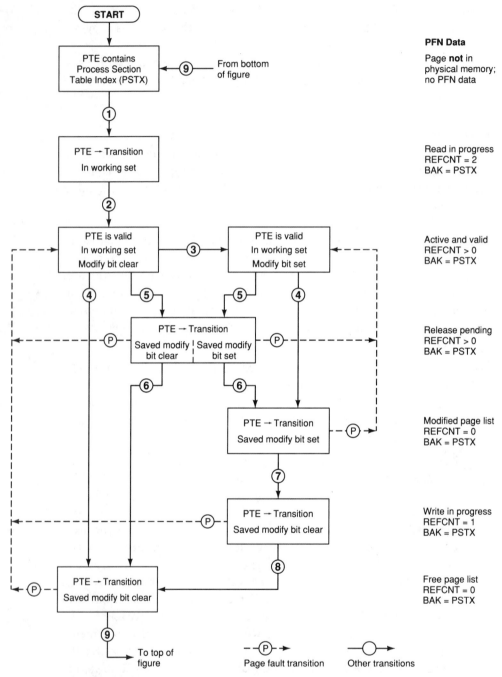

Figure 16.2
Page Transitions for Private Section Page That Is Not
Copy-on-Reference

page to indicate one more valid entry in the process's working set list mapped by the page table page. If the count makes the transition from 0 to 1, MMG$MAKEWSLE also increments PHD$W_PTCNTVAL, the number of page table pages that map valid WSLEs. It increments the field PCB$L_PPGCNT to indicate one more process-private page in the working set. It stores the index of the WSLE just set up in the PFN working set list index (WSLX) array element for the physical page and also increments its PFN REFCNT array element to indicate that the page is in a working set list.

MMG$PAGEFAULT itself increments the PFN REFCNT array, bringing the count to 2, to indicate the I/O request about to be queued for this page. It copies the original PTE contents to the PFN BAK array element for the page and initializes the PTE to have a protection code, owner field, the allocated PFN, and type bits indicating a transition page. It initializes the PFN STATE array element for the page to read in progress.

MMG$PAGEFAULT builds an I/O request packet (see Section 16.7) that describes the read to be done. From the PSTX in the original PTE contents, MMG$PAGEFAULT locates the corresponding PSTE in the PHD. From information in the PSTE, it can calculate which virtual block in the file contains the virtual page. It queues the request to the driver for the device containing the page.

It releases the MMG spinlock and acquires the SCHED spinlock. Before placing the process into a page fault wait state, MMG$PAGEFAULT tests whether the faulted page is still invalid. On a symmetric multiprocessing (SMP) system where MMG$PAGEFAULT is running on a secondary processor, concurrent processing of the I/O request may have already made the page valid. If the page is valid, MMG$PAGEFAULT releases the SCHED spinlock, cleans up the stack, and executes an REI instruction to dismiss the exception. If the page is still invalid, MMG$PAGEFAULT removes everything from the stack except the page fault program counter (PC) and processor status longword (PSL). It inserts the process's PCB into the page fault wait queue, executes a SVPCTX instruction to save the process's context, and then transfers control to the scheduler.

②Because most of the work was done in response to the initial fault, there is little left to do when the page read completes. Page read completion occurs as part of I/O postprocessing (see Chapter 21) and runs in system context. Holding the MMG spinlock, routine PAGIO, in module IOCIO-POST, decrements the PFN REFCNT array element. In the usual case, the reference count remains greater than zero. In that case, PAGIO changes the PFN STATE array element to active and sets the valid bit in the process PTE.

It is, however, possible for PAGIO to decrement the reference count to zero. This can happen if the page was removed from the working set list, for example, through swapper trimming, automatic working set limit adjustment, or the $PURGWS system service, before the page read completes. The page would have been put in the release pending state with a reference count of 1. If PAGIO decrements the reference count to zero, then instead of setting the valid bit, it inserts the page on the free page list.

PAGIO reports the scheduling event page fault completion for the process so that it becomes computable. Chapter 12 explains how scheduling events are reported. The next time the process is selected for execution, it reexecutes the instruction that caused the page fault, this time with the page valid.

③ One transition that a valid page can undergo and still remain valid occurs when the page is modified as a result of instruction execution. The VAX processor sets the modify bit in the PTE. The change is not noted at this time in the PFN database.

④ A valid page becomes invalid when it is removed from the working set list as a result of any of the conditions described in Section 16.1. Most of those result in the invocation of MMG$FREWSLE or its alternative entry point, MMG$FREWSLX, both in module PAGEFAULT. Chapter 17 describes them in detail. Of most relevance to this chapter are the changes to memory management data structures when a non-copy-on-reference page is removed from the process working set list:

a. The modify bit in the PTE is saved. The valid, modify, TYP0, and TYP1 bits in the PTE are all cleared. The PFN field is unchanged.

b. The translation buffer is invalidated to remove the cached but now obsolete contents of the PTE.

c. The saved modify bit from the PTE is logically ORed into the PFN STATE array element, saving its value.

d. If the page has been modified and its assigned page file backing store, if any, contains an obsolete copy, that storage is deallocated and the PFN BAK array element is cleared of its block number. The process-local page file index remains intact.

e. The PFN REFCNT array element is decremented. If the reference count goes to zero, the page is put on the free or modified page list, according to the setting of the saved modify bit in the PFN STATE array element. Since the PFN BLINK array overlays the PFN WSLX array, inserting the page into the free or modified page list supplants the PFN WSLX array contents. The new location of the page is inserted into the PFN STATE array.

f. The WSLE is made available (that is, zeroed). The PHD$L_PTWSLE-VAL array element for the page table page mapping this page is decremented. If the count makes the transition to zero, the page table page is now "dead," that is, it maps no valid pages, and PHD$W_

PTCNTVAL is also decremented. Chapter 17 contains further information on dead page table pages. PCB$L_PPGCNT is decremented to indicate one less private page.

⑤ If the reference count (decremented in step 4e) does not go to zero, there is outstanding I/O for this page. MMG$FREWSLX changes the PFN STATE array element value to release pending. It updates the modify bit in the PFN STATE array to record the ultimate destination for the page (the free or modified page list).

⑥ When direct I/O for the page completes, the I/O completion routine invokes MMG$UNLOCK, in module IOLOCK. It acquires the MMG spinlock and invokes MMG$DECPTREF, in module PAGEFAULT, to update the data structures describing the page table page that maps the page.

MMG$DECPTREF decrements the PFN SHRCNT array element for the page table page to indicate that it maps one less valid page. If this is the last valid or transition page mapped by the page table page (that is, if the SHRCNT makes the transition from 1 to 0), MMG$DECPTREF locates the WSLE for the page table page and unlocks it from the process's working set list. It also decrements PHD$W_PTCNTACT, the number of active page table pages for the process, and the PHD's entry in the array at PHV$GL_REFCBAS, the number of reasons the PHD should remain in memory. If that count goes to zero, MMG$DECPTREF awakens the swapper process to outswap the PHD.

MMG$UNLOCK decrements the page's PFN REFCNT array element. If it goes to zero, MMG$UNLOCK places the page on either the free or the modified page list, based on the setting of the saved modify bit, and changes the PFN STATE array element. It releases the MMG spinlock and returns.

⑦ If the page was placed on the modified page list, the next stages in its processing are performed by the modified page writer and described in this step and step 8. If the page was placed on the free page list, the next stages in its processing are described in step 9.

The modified page writer eventually initiates a write of this physical page to the backing store address in the PFN BAK array. A writable page that is not copy-on-reference is written back to the file where it originated. The modified page writer then removes the page from the modified page list.

It sets the PFN STATE array element for the page to write in progress and clears the saved modify bit. The REFCNT of 1 reflects the outstanding I/O operation.

Note that a section containing writable private pages that are not copy-on-reference cannot be produced by the linker. Such a section must be created with the Create and Map Section ($CRMPSC) system service.

⑧ When the modified page write completes, the page's PFN REFCNT array element is decremented to zero. Because the saved modify bit is clear, the page is placed on the free page list.

(9) A page placed on the free page list normally remains attached to the process for some time; that is, the PTE contains its PFN, and the PFN PTE array contains the address of the process PTE.

When the physical page is allocated for another purpose, several steps must be taken to break the ties between the process virtual page and the physical page that is about to be reused. The routine MMG$DELCONPFN, in module ALLOCPFN, performs these steps:

a. It locates the PTE from the contents of the PFN PTE array element.
b. The process PTE must be altered to reflect the backing store address of the page. For a non-copy-on-reference page, it changes the PTE to contain a PSTX, the same contents it had before the initial page fault. It leaves the protection and owner fields the same.
c. It invokes MMG$DECPTREF, described in step 6.
d. It clears the PFN array elements for the physical page before reallocating it. In particular, it clears the PFN PTE array element, the only connection from the PFN database to the process page table.

16.3.1.2 **Page Faults Out of Transition States.** Figure 16.2 also shows some of the transitions that a page makes when a page fault occurs while the physical page is in the transition state. While the changes back to the active state are straightforward, there are details about each fault that should be mentioned. (Most of the following transitions are represented in the figure by a P within a circle.)

- MMG$PAGEFAULT resolves a page fault from the free page list by first removing the page from the list. It invokes MMG$MAKEWSLE, described in step 1c of Section 16.3.1.1, to update the memory management data structures to reflect the fact that the page is in the working set list (the PHD$L_PTWSLEVAL array, possibly PHD$W_PTCNTVAL, the PFN WSLX and REFCNT array elements, and PCB$L_PPGCNT).

  MMG$PAGEFAULT changes the PFN STATE array element for the page to active and sets the valid bit in the PTE. (Recall that a transition PTE retains the PFN of the physical page in which the virtual page resides.) It releases the MMG spinlock, cleans up the stack, and executes an REI instruction to return control to the faulting instruction.

- A page fault from the modified page list is resolved in exactly the same way. The figure shows that the page was previously modified but never written to its backing store by returning the page to its modified state.

  In fact, the modify bit in the PTE is not set by MMG$PAGEFAULT. Rather, the saved modify bit in the PFN STATE array records the fact that the page is modified but has not been backed up.

- A page fault from the release pending state is similar, except that the page does not have to be removed from a page list. MMG$PAGEFAULT changes the PFN STATE array element for the page to active, sets the valid bit in the PTE, and increments the PFN REFCNT array element.

  Artistic license is taken in the figure to differentiate physical pages that were modified from pages that were not. Again, the only difference between the two pages is the setting of the saved modify bit in the PFN STATE array, not the setting of the modify bit in the PTE.

- A transition that deserves special comment is a page fault that occurs while the modified page writer is writing the page to its backing store. The saved modify bit is cleared before the write begins so that the page will be placed on the free page list when the write completes. Although the page has not yet been completely backed up, it is assumed that the write will complete successfully. A page fault for the page can thus put it into the active but unmodified state. The only difficulty occurs in the event of a write error. The modified page writer's I/O completion routine, WRITEDONE in module WRTMFYPAG, detects this state of affairs and turns the saved modify bit back on.

- A page fault for a page being read in response to a previous page fault results in placing the process into a collided page wait state (see Section 16.10.3).

16.3.1.3 **Copy-on-Reference Page.** The more common type of writable process-private page is a copy-on-reference page. Figure 16.3 illustrates the transitions that such a page makes from its initial page fault until it is written to some backing store. The numbers in the figure are keyed to the following explanations of the transitions.

Many of the transitions that occur here are the same as the case just described. This section notes each transition but elaborates only those areas that are different.

①The initial value in the PTE (START 1 in Figure 16.3) is a PSTX; the copy-on-reference bit (PTE⟨16⟩) is set. The writable bit (PTE⟨18⟩) is usually set. When a page fault occurs, MMG$PAGEFAULT performs the actions described in step 1 in Section 16.3.1.1. It also takes two additional steps:

  a. First, it updates the PFN STATE array element to the value read in progress, with the saved modify bit set. The page's backing store will be a page file, not the image file; the image page must not be modified, yet each of the potentially many copies of the page may be modified. Setting the saved modify bit guarantees that an initial copy of the page will be written to the page file when it is first paged out, whether or not it has been modified.

  b. Second, it assigns the page a backing store (namely, the process's current page file), decrements the reserved block count, and copies PHD$L_PAGFIL to the PFN BAK array element. (Section 16.6 provides

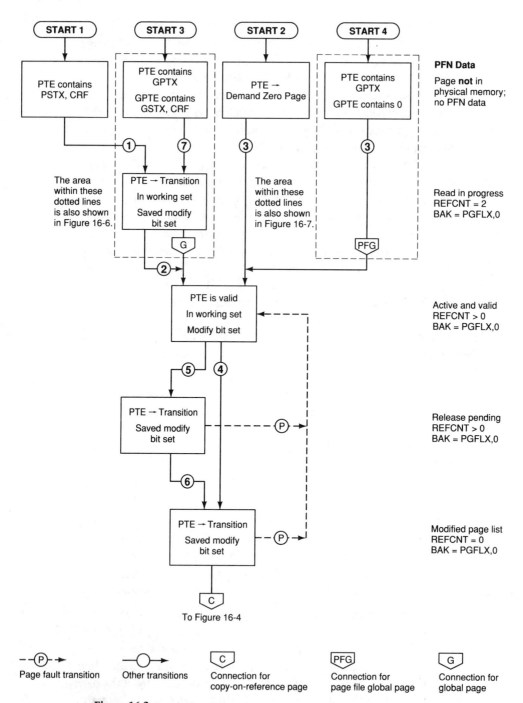

Figure 16.3
Page Transitions for Private and Global
Copy-on-Reference Pages and for Demand Zero Pages

further details on page file assignment, reservation, and allocation.) At this time, all ties to the original section file have been broken. When the modified page writer first writes this page to its backing store (as it certainly will because the saved modify bit was just set), it will allocate an actual block in the page file.

(2) After the read completes, the I/O postprocessing routine PAGIO, in module IOCIOPOST, updates the page PFN STATE array element value to active and sets the PTE valid bit. It also subtracts the number of pages read from the PSTE's reference count to show that many fewer PTEs mapping pages from that section file.

(3) This transition is described in Section 16.3.2.

(4) When the copy-on-reference page is removed from the process working set and its REFCNT goes to zero, the page is placed on the modified page list.

(5) If the REFCNT did not go to zero when the page was removed from the process working set, the physical page is placed into the release pending state until the I/O completes.

(6) At that time, the page is placed on the modified page list.

(7) This transition is described as transition 3 in Section 16.4.3.

A page fault from either the release pending state or from the modified page list puts the page back into the active (but effectively modified) state. That is, the saved modify bit in the PFN STATE array element remains set, causing the page to be put back on the modified page list when it is removed from the working set again.

When the modified page writer writes the page to its backing store in a page file, the page makes a transition from the modified page list. Figure 16.4, the diagram for faults from the page file, shows this transition. The connection between Figure 16.3 and Figure 16.4 is indicated by path C in the two figures.

16.3.2   Demand Zero Page

A demand zero page is created by the Create Virtual Address ($CRETVA) and Expand Region ($EXPREG) system services. These services can be requested explicitly by an image or implicitly by the system on behalf of the process, for example, as part of image activation.

When MMG$PAGEFAULT detects a page fault for a demand zero page, it takes the following steps. (These steps all take place beginning at the path labeled START 2 in Figure 16.3.)

1. It invokes MMG$ININEWPFN, MMG$INCPTREF, and MMG$MAKE-WSLE, described in step 1 of Section 16.3.1.1, to allocate a physical page and update the relevant memory management data structures.

2. MMG$PAGEFAULT initializes the PTE with the PFN of the allocated

page, a protection allowing kernel mode write, an owner of kernel mode, and the valid and modify bits set.

3. It assigns the page a backing store (namely, the process's current page file), decrements the reserved block count, and copies PHD$L_PAGFIL to the PFN BAK array element. Allocation of an actual block in the page file is done later by the modified page writer.

4. It zeros the page by executing a MOVC5 instruction with a zero-length source string and a null fill character.

5. It invalidates the translation buffer to remove the cached PTE contents and replaces owner and protection in the PTE with the original ones.

6. Finally, MMG$PAGEFAULT releases the MMG spinlock, cleans up the stack, and dismisses the fault by executing an REI instruction, returning to the instruction that incurred the page fault.

16.3.3 Global Copy-on-Reference and Page-File Section Pages

There are two types of pages that undergo the same set of state transitions as private copy-on-reference section and demand zero pages. These are global copy-on-reference pages and global page-file section pages. The details of global page fault resolution are discussed in Section 16.4.

Suffice it to say here that a global copy-on-reference page is initially faulted from a global file but is subsequently indistinguishable from other process-private pages. A global page-file section page is initially faulted as a demand zero page and from then on is indistinguishable from other global writable pages, except that its backing store is in a page file.

These transitions are shown in the paths labeled START 3 and START 4 in Figure 16.3.

16.3.4 Page Located in a Page File

The transitions that a page faulted from the page file goes through (see Figure 16.4) are the same as the transitions described for pages that are not copy-on-reference (see Figure 16.2). The only difference in the PFN data between the two figures is that the PFN BAK array element in Figure 16.4 indicates that the page belongs in a page file, while the PFN BAK array element in Figure 16.2 contains a PSTX.

The other difference between the two figures is the entry point into the transition diagram. A page can start out in a section file (PTE contains PSTX) but a page can never start out in a page file. The entry into Figure 16.4 is from path C in Figure 16.3, from one of four initial states that eventually result in the physical page contents' being written to the page file.

16.4 PAGE FAULTS FOR GLOBAL PAGES

The transitions of a global page table entry (GPTE) and its associated PFN

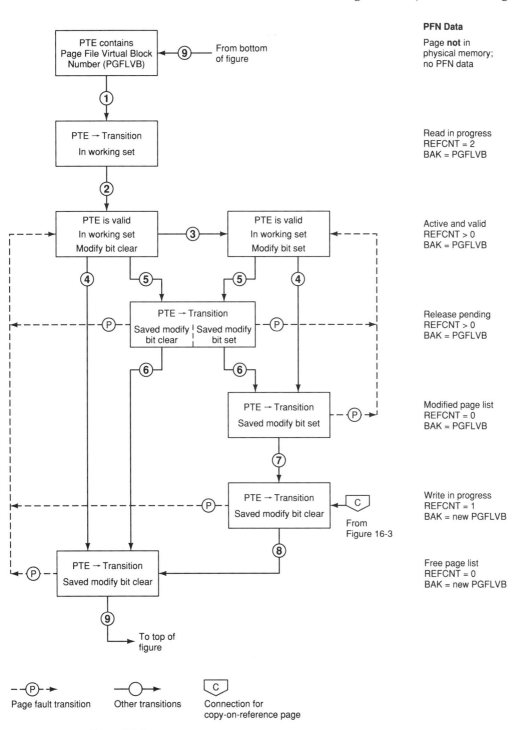

Figure 16.4
Transitions for a Page Located in a Page File

database entries can be described in much the same way as those for process-private pages. A major difference, however, is the presence of both a GPTE and potentially multiple process PTEs referring to the same page. This section assumes much of the detail shown earlier in Figure 16.2 and focuses on an example in which two processes map to the same global page.

16.4.1 Global Read-Only Page

Figure 16.5 illustrates the transitions that occur for a global read-only page (in an already created section) that is mapped by two processes. The numbers in the figure are keyed to the explanations of the transitions that follow. The figure assumes the page to be read-only. The implications of a read/write global page are described in Section 16.4.2.

When the global section is initially created, as described in Chapter 15, the data structures described in Chapter 14 are initialized. The GPTE for the page represented in the figure contains a global section table index (GSTX), which locates the global section table entry (GSTE) containing information about the global file.

① When process A maps to the section, the process PTE contains a global page table index (GPTX), effectively a pointer to the GPTE.

② When process B maps to the section, its PTE contains exactly the same GPTX as found in process A's PTE.

③ Process B happens to fault this global page first. Several things happen:

    a. MMG$PAGEFAULT, noting that process B's PTE contains a GPTX, indexes the global page table with it to get the GPTE.

    b. The GPTE contains a GSTX, indicating that the global page resides on mass storage. In order to initiate the read of a global section page, MMG$PAGEFAULT performs many of the same steps as for a process-private section page (see step 1 of Section 16.3.1.1).

    c. MMG$PAGEFAULT invokes MMG$ININEWPFN to allocate a physical page and MMG$INCPTREF to update the data structures describing the global page table page that maps the page. (The PHD in this case is the system header.) The address of the GPTE is stored in the PFN PTE array element, rather than the address of a process PTE, and a type code of global page is stored in the PFN TYPE array element.

    d. MMG$MAKEWSLE updates the data structures related to process B's working set list, initializing the WSLE. WSLX information is not kept for a global page. Instead, MMG$MAKEWSLE increments the PFN SHRCNT array element for the page and, because the count makes the transition from 0 to 1, the PFN REFCNT array element as well.

        It invokes MMG$INCPTREF, which processes B's process page table that maps the global page and increments the PHD$L_PTWSLEVAL array element corresponding to that page table page. It increments

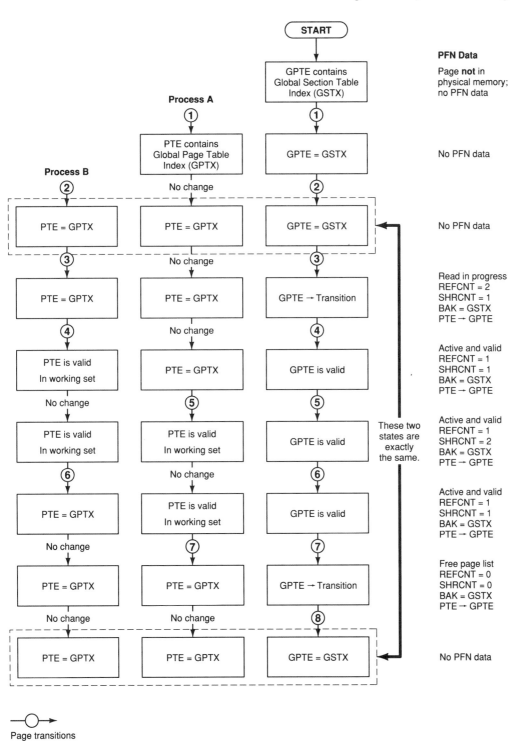

Figure 16.5
Page Transitions Made by a Global Page Mapped by
Two Processes

PCB$L_GPGCNT to indicate that process B has one more valid global page.

  e. MMG$PAGEFAULT sets the PFN STATE array element for the page to read in progress.

  f. It stores the GSTX in the PFN BAK array element.

  g. While the read is in progress, the GPTE contains a transition PTE but process B's PTE still contains the GPTX.

  h. The PFN REFCNT array element indicates two references: one for the read in progress and one because the page is in process B's working set (the PFN SHRCNT array element is nonzero).

④ After the read completes, the I/O postprocessing routine PAGIO, in module IOCIOPOST, takes the following steps:

  a. It acquires the MMG spinlock.

  b. It decrements the PFN REFCNT array element. (The REFCNT and SHRCNT are both 1 at this point.)

  c. It changes the PFN STATE array element for the page to active.

  d. It sets the valid bit in the GPTE to record the fact that this page is in a process working set.

  e. The process PTE, located through its address stored in the I/O request packet, is set up to contain the low-order 21 bits from the GPTE, with the valid bit set and the window and modify bits cleared.

  f. PAGIO reports the scheduling event page fault completion for process B so that it becomes computable.

  g. It releases the MMG spinlock.

⑤ When process A faults the same global page, MMG$PAGEFAULT's initial action is the same as it was in step 3, because the PTE is a GPTX. Now, however, MMG$PAGEFAULT finds a valid GPTE. Resolution of this page fault is simple.

Through MMG$MAKEWSLE and MMG$INCPTREF, whose actions are described in more detail in step 3d, MMG$PAGEFAULT initializes the WSLE for process A, increments its PCB$L_GPGCNT, increments the PFN SHRCNT array element to 2, and locks process A's page table page that maps the global page.

MMG$PAGEFAULT copies the low-order 21 bits of the GPTE to process A's PTE, sets the valid bit, and clears the window and modify bits. It releases the MMG spinlock, cleans up the stack, and executes an REI instruction to dismiss the fault.

⑥ When MMG$FREWSLE removes the global page from process B's working set, it restores process B's PTE to its previous state (and not some transition form). Because the PFN PTE array element contains the address of the GPTE, MMG$FREWSLE must recalculate the GPTX. The calculation is straightforward. It subtracts the contents of MMG$GL_ GPTBASE from the PFN PTE array element's contents, divides the result by 4 (to create a longword index), and stores the quotient in process B's PTE as a GPTX.

It invokes MMG$DECPTREF, described in step 6 of Section 16.3.1.1.

MMG$FREWSLE decrements the PFN SHRCNT array element for the page of memory. Because the SHRCNT is still positive, the GPTE remains valid.

MMG$FREWSLE updates the data structures related to process B's working set list, clearing the WSLE, decrementing the PHD$L_PTWSLE-VAL array element for the process page table page that mapped the page and, if appropriate, PHD$W_PTCNTVAL. It decrements process B's PCB$L_GPGCNT.

⑦ When MMG$FREWSLE removes the global page from process A's working set, it restores the process PTE as described in step 6.

It decrements the PFN SHRCNT array element, this time to zero. It therefore clears the valid and modify bits in the GPTE, to turn it into a transition PTE and decrements the PFN REFCNT array element. In the case of a global read-only page with a REFCNT of zero, such as this one, the page is placed on the free page list and the PFN STATE array element set to the free page list. The other PFN array elements are unchanged.

⑧ When the physical page is reused, the ties must be broken between the physical page and, in this case, the GPTE. (None of the processes mapped to this page are affected in any way by this step.)

The contents of the PFN BAK array element, a GSTX, are inserted into the GPTE, located by the contents of the PFN PTE array element. MMG$DECPTREF, described in step 6 of Section 16.3.1.1, is invoked to update the global page table page that contains the GPTE. The PFN PTE array element is then cleared, breaking the connection between the physical page and the global page table.

These steps put the process and global page tables back to the state they were in following step 2 (although it is pictured here as a different state to simplify the figure.)

16.4.2 Global Read/Write Page

The transitions that occur for a global writable page are the same as those for a process-private page that is not copy-on-reference. The only difference between such transitions and those illustrated in Figure 16.2 is that the GPTE, not the process PTE, is affected by the transitions of the physical page.

The process PTE for a global page contains a GPTX up to the time that the page is made valid. Only then is a PFN inserted into the process PTE. As soon as the page is removed from the process working set, the GPTX is restored to the process PTE. All ties to the PFN database are made through

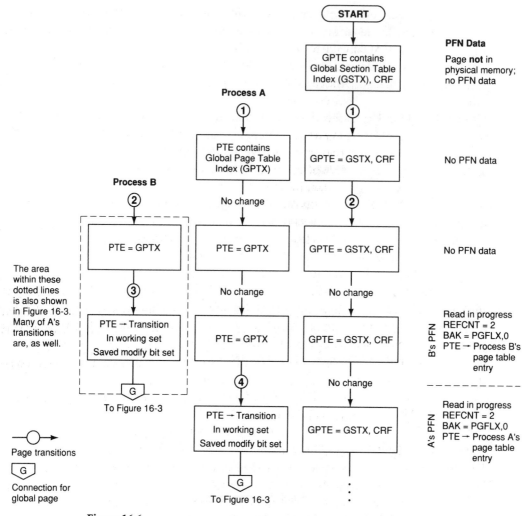

Figure 16.6
Page Transitions for a Global Copy-on-Reference Page

the GPTE, which retains the PFN while the physical page is in the various transition states.

16.4.3   Global Copy-on-Reference Page

The global pages thus far described are all shared pages. A global copy-on-reference page, however, is shared only in its initial state. As soon as the fault occurs, the page is treated exactly like a process-private page.

Figure 16.6 illustrates the transitions for a global copy-on-reference page. The numbers in the figure are keyed to the explanations of the transitions that follow.

①The initial conditions are identical to those in Figure 16.5. After the section is created, each of its GPTEs contains a GSTX. In this case, the copy-on-reference bit is set in each GPTE.

②Process A maps the page; the GPTX is stored in its PTE.

Process B maps the page; the same GPTX is stored in its PTE. Up to this point, nothing is different from Figure 16.5.

③When process B faults the page, MMG$PAGEFAULT locates the GPTE from the GPTX and notes that the page is located in a global section file and is copy-on-reference. MMG$PAGEFAULT, in concert with the routines described in step 1 of Section 16.3.1.1, allocates a page from the free page list and makes the following modifications to the involved memory management data structures:

a. The GPTE is not altered and retains its GSTX contents.

b. Process B's PTE is set to a transition PTE containing the PFN of the allocated page.

c. The PFN SHRCNT array element for the page table page containing process B's PTE is incremented. If the count was zero, the page table page is locked in process B's working set list, PHD$W_PTCNTACT is incremented, and the PHD's entry in the array at PHV$GL_REFCBAS is incremented.

d. The PFN TYPE array element for the physical page is set to process page.

e. An entry in process B's working set list is initialized to describe the faulted page.

f. The PFN WSLX array element is set to the index of the WSLE.

g. The PHD$L_PTWSLEVAL array element corresponding to the page table page that maps the faulted page is incremented. If the count was zero, PHD$W_PTCNTVAL is incremented.

h. PCB$L_PPGCNT is incremented.

i. The PFN REFCNT array element is incremented twice, once for the page's membership in the working set and once for the I/O in progress.

j. The PFN STATE array element is set to read in progress and modify.

k. A backing store is assigned to the page, typically a reserved page from the process's current page file. The contents of PHD$L_PAGFIL are stored in the PFN BAK array element.

Note that all ties between process B and the global section are broken. The page is now treated exactly like a private copy-on-reference page. The two boxes for process B within the dotted lines in Figure 16.6 are also pictured within dotted lines in Figure 16.3.

MMG$PAGEFAULT initiates a read of the faulted page.

④When process A faults the same page, exactly the same steps are taken, this time with a totally different physical page.

Thus, both process A and process B get exactly the same initial copy of

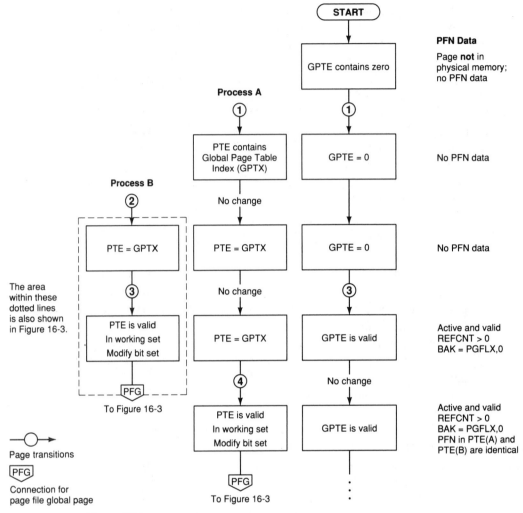

Figure 16.7
Page Transitions for a Global Page-File Section Page

the global page from the global file but, from that point on, each process has its own private copy of the page to modify.

16.4.4   Global Page-File Section Page

A global page-file section provides a means for processes to share global pages without the need of a backing store file. By its nature, such a global page has no initial contents and is thus initialized as a demand zero page.

Figure 16.7 illustrates the transitions that occur for a global page-file section page. The numbers in the figure are keyed to the explanations of the transitions that follow.

①The initial conditions are identical to those in Figure 16.5. The section is created; each of its GPTEs contains a zero in the PFN field.

②Process A maps the page; the GPTX is stored in its PTE. Process B maps the page; the same GPTX is stored in its PTE.

③When process B faults this page, MMG$PAGEFAULT locates the GPTE from the GPTX and notes that the page is demand zero. MMG$PAGE-FAULT, in concert with the routines described in step 1 of Section 16.3.1.1, allocates a page from the free page list and makes the following modifications to the involved memory management data structures:

    a. The PFN SHRCNT array element for the global page table page containing the GPTE is incremented. If the count was zero, the page table page is locked in the system working set list, the system header PHD$W_PTCNTACT is incremented, and the system header's entry in the array at PHV$GL_REFCBAS is incremented.

    b. The PFN TYPE array element for the allocated page is set to global page.

    c. An entry in process B's working set list is initialized to describe the faulted page.

    d. The PFN WSLX array element is set to the index of the WSLE.

    e. The PFN SHRCNT array element for the page table page containing process B's PTE is incremented. If the count was zero, the page table page is locked in process B's working set list, PHD$W_PTCNTACT is incremented, and the PHD's entry in the array at PHV$GL_REFCBAS is incremented.

    f. The PFN PTE array element for the allocated page points to the GPTE.

    g. The PHD$L_PTWSLEVAL array element corresponding to the page table page that maps the faulted page is incremented. If the count was zero, PHD$W_PTCNTVAL is incremented.

    h. PCB$L_GPGCNT is incremented.

    i. The PFN SHRCNT and REFCNT array elements for the allocated page are incremented.

    j. The PFN STATE array element is set to active.

    k. A backing store is assigned to the page, a reserved page from the current page file in use for system working set list paging. The contents of field PHD$L_PAGFIL in the system header are stored in the PFN BAK array element.

    l. The process PTE is initialized with the PFN of the allocated page, a protection allowing kernel mode writes, an owner of kernel mode, and the valid and modify bits set.

    m. The page is zeroed.

    n. The cached PTE is invalidated in the translation buffer, and the correct owner mode and protection code are inserted into the PTE. The PTE modify bit is left set.

    o. The contents of the process PTE are copied to the GPTE.

④ When process A faults the same page, MMG$PAGEFAULT locates the GPTE from the GPTX and finds that the GPTE is valid. The valid GPTE is copied to process A's PTE.

Transitions for a global page-file section page are the same as those for a page located in a page file (see Figure 16.4). However, for a global page-file section page, the GPTE, not the process PTE, is affected by the transitions that the physical page makes. Once the global page is removed from a process's working set, the process PTE reverts to the GPTX form.

16.5 PAGE FAULTS FOR SYSTEM PAGES

Four kinds of pageable system space pages occur in the system working set list:

- Read-only pages from image sections in loadable executive images
- Read/write pages from image sections in loadable executive images
- Paged pool pages
- Global page table pages

This section summarizes how their page faults are handled.

In theory, the base image, SYS.EXE, can contain pageable code and data. However, in VMS Version 5.2, it has no pageable sections; the only pageable sections in system space are from loadable executive images. When a loadable executive image is mapped, a section table entry in the system section table (which also serves as the global section table) is initialized to describe each pageable section in the image. Each SPTE that maps a page in a pageable section has both type bits set to indicate the process section index form of invalid PTE and contains the index of the section's entry in the system section table.

If the section is writable, each of its SPTEs also has the copy-on-reference and writable bits set. Chapter 29 describes the mapping of loadable executive images in detail.

The SPTEs that map both paged pool and the global page table have the demand zero page form of invalid PTE.

16.5.1 System Page That Is Not Copy-on-Reference

The transitions for a read-only system section page resemble those described in Section 16.3.1.1 and shown in Figure 16.2. This section notes only the transitions that differ from those for a private page that is not copy-on-reference.

1. MMG$PAGEFAULT locates an entry in the system working set list for the faulted page. It allocates a page from the free list. There is no need to update data structures describing the page table page that contains the

SPTE. The SPT does not page; its page table pages are always valid. The page type stored in the PFN TYPE array element is system page. The system header does not have a PHD$L_PTWSLEVAL array, nor is there any need to record the number of page table pages with valid WSLEs; the system working set list is not outswapped.

MMG$PAGEFAULT copies the original SPTE contents to the PFN BAK array element. It locates the system section table entry just as it would a PSTX and calculates the virtual block number of the faulted page.

2. After the I/O completes, PAGIO, the I/O postprocessing routine, reports a page fault completion scheduling event for the process that faulted the page.

3. The system working set is not subject to purging, swapper trimming, or working set limit adjustment. A page is removed from the system working set list when space is required for another page. Also, unloading of a loadable executive image may result in deletion of pages.

On an SMP system, when a page is removed from the system working set list, the cached SPTE contents must be flushed from the translation buffers of all members of the system. Chapter 34 describes how the processors cooperate to perform the invalidation.

16.5.2 System Page That Is Copy-on-Reference

The transitions for a copy-on-reference system section page resemble those described in Section 16.3.1.3 and shown in Figure 16.3.

One difference worth noting is that space is reserved in one or more page files for backing writable system pages. Field PHD$L_PAGFIL in the system header is a template backing store value for writable system pages.

The page type stored in the PFN TYPE array element is system page.

16.5.3 Demand Zero System Page

The transitions for a demand zero system page resemble those described in Section 16.3.2 and shown in the path labeled START 2 in Figure 16.3.

One difference worth noting is that the page type stored in the PFN TYPE array element is either global page table page or, for paged pool, system page.

After the page is zeroed, its SPTE entry is flushed from the translation buffer, and each active member of an SMP system must invalidate its entry. The correct owner and protection are stored in the SPTE.

16.6 USE OF PAGE FILES

During system initialization and operation, one or more page files are placed into use. When a process is created, it is assigned to a page file, and space in that page file is reserved for it. When a process faults a copy-on-reference or demand zero page, the page is charged against the reserved space. Assignment to a particular block in the page file is deferred until the modified page writer actually prepares to write the page. During the lifetime of the process, it can be assigned concurrently to as many as four page files.

This section describes the data structures and mechanisms related to process page file use.

16.6.1   Related Data Structures

A nonpaged pool data structure called a page file control block (PFL) describes each page file in use. Chapter 14 depicts the PFL (see Figure 14.24) and describes its fields. Those with particular importance to this discussion are PFL$L_FREPAGCNT, the number of blocks that can be allocated, and PFL$L_RSRVPAGCNT, the number of blocks that can be reserved without overcommitting the file. Both fields are initialized to the number of total blocks in the file available for use.

PFL$L_FREPAGCNT is the actual number of blocks free in the page file. This field is not decremented until the modified page writer actually assigns a particular block to a particular page. It is incremented whenever a page file page is released, either because its virtual page is being deleted or its contents are known to be obsolete. (That is, when a page previously assigned a block in a page file is placed on the modified page list, its backing store copy can no longer be regarded as good.)

In contrast, PFL$L_RSRVPAGCNT is charged when page file blocks are reserved for a process's use. Reserved space is only a logical claim on the page file; actual allocation of blocks is not made until the modified page writer is about to write a cluster of pages to the file. The executive computes the ratio of reservable block count to total size for each page file to select the most lightly loaded one, when reserving space for a newly created process or one that has used its current reservation. PFL$L_RSRVPAGCNT can, in fact, become negative if the number of pages assigned backing store in the file exceeds the physical size of the file. On most systems, however, only a small percentage of reserved blocks are written; thus, an overcommitment is viewed as benign. (The display for the Digital command language SHOW MEMORY/FILES command shows the overcommitment as a negative number.)

A number of PHD fields describe the process's connection to page files.

Beginning at PHD$B_PRCPGFL, there is a four-byte array representing the page files to which the process has been assigned. The array is indexed by a two-bit process-local page file number. The elements of this array are initialized to zero to indicate no assignment. When a process is assigned to a page file, that file's index (see Figure 14.24) is stored in the next available element of PHD$B_PRCPGFL.

The low four bits of PHD$B_PGFLCNT contain the number of page files to which the process has been assigned, that is, the number of valid elements in the four-byte array. Each of the high four bits, when set, means that the corresponding page file has a pending deassign.

PHD$B_PAGFIL contains the systemwide index of the page file in which the process has reserved blocks. It is part of the longword field PHD$L_PAGFIL, which contains the corresponding process-local page file index in bits $\langle 21:20 \rangle$ and zero in the low-order bits. This field serves as template backing store for the construction of a PTE with a page file backing store address. PHD$B_PRCPAGFIL contains the process-local index associated with that page file.

PHD$W_PRCPGFLOPAGES contains the total reserved blocks in the current page file, including blocks already allocated by the modified page writer. PHD$W_PRCPGFLPAGES contains the reserved blocks not yet allocated in the current page file.

Beginning at PHD$L_PRCPGFLREFS, there is a four-longword array indexed by the two-bit process-local page file index. Each of its elements represents the number of process PTEs currently associated with that page file. The elements count downward from 100000_{16}, 1 larger than the maximum page file block number that can be accommodated in a PTE, $FFFFF_{16}$. (Counting downward simplifies the test for whether the number has reached its maximum.) The difference between 100000_{16} and an array element's contents represents the total number of blocks in the page file referenced by that process's PTEs. The array element for the current page file is updated only when the currently reserved pages have been used. Thus for the current page file, the difference between PHD$W_PRCPGFLOPAGES and PHD$W_PRCPGFLPAGES represents additional referenced blocks.

16.6.2   Assignment and Deassignment to a Page File

When a process is created, MMG$ASNPRCPGFLP, in module PAGEFILE, is invoked to assign to it the page file estimated to have the most available space, the one with the largest ratio of reservable blocks to total blocks. The routine stores the systemwide index of that page file in PHD$B_PAGFIL and in the byte at PHD$B_PRCPGFL. It stores a process-local index of 0 in PHD$B_PRCPAGFIL.

MMG$RSRVPRCPGFL2, in module PAGEFILE, is invoked to reserve a number of blocks in the page file for the process's use. The number is stored in PHD$W_PRCPGFLOPAGES and PHD$W_PRCPGFLPAGES and subtracted from PFL$L_RSRVPAGCNT in the page file block.

Whenever the process faults a page that requires page file backing store, MMG$PAGEFAULT decrements PHD$W_PRCPGFLPAGES and copies PHD$L_PAGFIL to the PFN BAK array element for the page. When no more reserved pages remain (when PHD$W_PRCPGFLPAGES becomes zero), MMG$PAGEFAULT invokes MMG$SWITCH_PRCPGFL, in module PAGEFAULT, to reserve more page file space for the process.

MMG$SWITCH_PRCPGFL subtracts PHD$W_PRCPGFLOPAGES from the PHD$L_PRCPGFLREFS element corresponding to the current page file, generating the fatal bugcheck BADPRCPGFLC if the result is negative.

MMG$SWITCH_PRCPGFL invokes MMG$ASNPRCPAGFL to select the best page file for a new reservation. Unless the process has already been assigned to four page files, the best page file is the one estimated to have the most available space; it may be the same one the process was just using. If the process has been assigned to four page files, the new reservation must come from one of them. If the process has not been assigned space in the chosen page file, MMG$ASNPRCPAGFL stores its systemwide page file index in the next available slot in the array at PHD$B_PRCPGFL and increments PHD$B_PGFLCNT to point to the next slot. It initializes PHD$L_PAGFIL and PHD$B_PRCPAGFIL.

MMG$SWITCH_PRCPGFL invokes MMG$RSRVPRCPGFL2 to reserve the SYSGEN parameter RSRVPAGCNT number of blocks in that page file. The default value of this parameter is 2,048. MMG$RSRVPRCPGFL2 subtracts that many blocks from PFL$L_RSRVPAGCNT of the chosen page file and adds it to PHD$W_PRCPGFLPAGES and PHD$W_PRCPGFLOPAGES.

Section 16.8.6 describes the allocation of actual pages in the page file.

When a process page backed by a page file is deleted, MMG$DALCPRC-PGFL, in module PAGEFILE, is invoked to deallocate the page file block, if any, and returns the reservation. It increments the appropriate PHD$L_PRCPGFLREFS longword; if, as a result, there are no more references to that page file, the routine deassigns the process from the page file.

When a process is deleted, it is deassigned from any remaining page file assignments.

16.7 INPUT AND OUTPUT THAT SUPPORT PAGING

There is little special-purpose code in the I/O subsystem to support page and swap I/O. MMG$PAGEFAULT and the swapper each build their own I/O request packets (IRPs) but queue these packets to a device driver in the normal fashion. These are the only differences:

- There are special Queue I/O Request ($QIO) entry points for page and swap I/O in module SYSQIOREQ. These entry points bypass many of the usual $QIO checks to minimize overhead. An IRP describing a page or swap request is distinguished from other IRPs by a flag in the IRP status word.
- These flags are detected by the I/O postprocessing routine, which dispatches to special completion paths for page read and other types of memory management I/O.

To make reading and writing as efficient as possible, MMG$PAGEFAULT implements a feature called clustering. It checks to see whether pages adjacent to the virtual page that it is reading are located in the same file in adjacent virtual blocks. If so, it requests a multiple-block read, and a cluster

Table 16.1   Summary of I/O Requests Issued by Memory Management—Part I

Type of I/O Request	Priority IRP$B_PRI	Process ID IRP$L_PID	Priority Boost at Completion
Process page read	Base priority of faulting process	PID of faulting process	0
System page read	Base priority from system PCB—16	PID of faulting process	0
Modified page write	MPW_PRIO [1]	PID of swapper [2]	None [3]
$UPDSEC page write	Base priority of caller	PID of caller	2
Swapper I/O	SWP_PRIO [1]	PID of swapper	None [3]

[1] This is a SYSGEN parameter.

[2] The modified page writer is a subroutine of the swapper process.

[3] The swapper is a real-time process and is therefore not subject to priority boosts.

of pages is brought into the working set at one time. One N-block request has less CPU and I/O overhead than N one-block requests.

The modified page writer and the $UPDSEC system service also cluster their write operations, both to make their writes as efficient as possible and to allow subsequent clustered reads for the pages that are being written.

Tables 16.1 and 16.2 summarize the I/O requests issued by memory management components. The first table lists the type of paging or swapping I/O, the priority of each such request, the relevant process identification, and information about the priority boost the process receives at I/O completion. For more information on priority classes and boosts, see Chapter 12.

Table 16.2 lists more information about each type of I/O request, summarizing the unusual uses to which the memory management components put several fields in the IRP. These fields are not required for their more typical uses and can thus be used for storing other information needed by these components.

The columns SVAPTE, AST, and ASTPRM describe the contents of the IRP fields for each type of I/O operation requested by the memory management subsystem. The SVAPTE column identifies the type of PTE whose address is in that field. For certain types of request, the ASTPRM field contains the address of a special kernel asynchronous system trap (KAST) routine. The column WCB Source specifies from which memory management data structure the address of the window control block (WCB) is obtained. (This address is stored in the field IRP$L_WIND.) The last column indicates the limit to which VMS clusters the object of each type of I/O request.

16.7.1   Page Read Clustering

When MMG$PAGEFAULT determines that a read is required to satisfy a page fault, it allocates an IRP and fills it with parameters that describe the

463

Table 16.2 Summary of I/O Requests Issued by Memory Management—Part II

Type of I/O Request	SVAPTE	AST	ASTPRM	WCB Source	Cluster Factor
PROCESS PAGE READ					
Page in section file	PxPTE	0	0/PSTX[1]	PSTE	pfc/PFCDEFAULT[2]
Page in page file	PxPTE	0	0	PFL	PFCDEFAULT[3]
Page table page	SPTE	0	0	PFL[4]	PAGTBLPFC[3]
SYSTEM PAGE READ					
System page[5]	SPTE	0	0	SSTE	SYSPFC[3]
Paged pool page	SPTE	0	0	PFL	PFCDEFAULT[3]
Global page	GPTE	Slave PTE address	0	GSTE	pfc/PFCDEFAULT[2]
Global CRF page	PxPTE	Master PTE contents	GSTX	GSTE	pfc/PFCDEFAULT[2]
Global page table page	SPTE	0	0	PFL[4]	1
MODIFIED PAGE WRITE					
To page file	MPW map	0	MPW KAST, WRITEDONE	PFL	MPW_WRTCLUSTER[3]
To private section file	MPW map	0	MPW KAST, WRITEDONE	PSTE	MPW_WRTCLUSTER[3]
To global section file	MPW map	0	MPW KAST, WRITEDONE	GSTE	MPW_WRTCLUSTER[3]
To swap file (nonzero SWPVBN)	MPW map	0	MPW KAST, WRITEDONE	PFL	1
$UPDSEC WRITE					
Private section	PxPTE	AST address	AST argument	PSTE	MPW_WRTCLUSTER[3]
Global section	GPTE	AST address	AST argument	GSTE	MPW_WRTCLUSTER[3]
SWAPPER I/O					
Swapper I/O	Swapper map	0	Swapper KAST, IODONE	PFL	n/a

[1] If the page is copy-on-reference, IRP$L_ASTPRM contains the PSTX.

[2] For a private or global section, at link time or when the cluster is mapped, a cluster factor (pfc) may be explicitly declared. If unspecified, the SYSGEN parameter PFCDEFAULT is used.

[3] This is a SYSGEN parameter.

[4] Process page and global page tables originate as demand zero pages whose backing store is a page file.

[5] Pageable executive routines originate in loadable executive images, described by section table entries in the system header.

read. Table 16.2 lists those fields that it uses for special purposes. It attempts to identify a cluster of pages to be read at once. The manner in which this cluster is formed depends on the initial state of the faulting PTE.

16.7.1.1   **Terminating Condition for Clustered Reads.** Beginning with the PTE of the faulting page, MMG$PAGEFAULT scans adjacent PTEs in the direction of higher virtual addresses, checking for adjacent virtual pages that have the same backing store location. It continues until it reaches the desired cluster size or until it reaches one of the following other terminating conditions:

- It encounters a type of PTE different from that of the original faulting PTE (see Section 16.7.1.2).
- The page table page containing the next PTE is itself not valid. (Satisfying this fault first, to make a larger cluster, would offset the benefits gained by clustering.)
- No more WSLEs are available. (Each page in the cluster must be added to the working set.)
- No physical page is available.

If MMG$PAGEFAULT has not clustered any pages after scanning the adjacent PTEs toward higher virtual addresses, it scans toward lower virtual addresses with the same terminating conditions. The scan is made initially toward higher virtual addresses because programs typically execute sequentially toward higher virtual addresses and these pages are more likely to be needed soon. If that scan fails, MMG$PAGEFAULT scans for pages at lower virtual addresses on the assumption that pages at lower virtual addresses but near the faulting page are likely to be needed soon.

16.7.1.2   **Matching Conditions During the Page Table Scan.** The match criterion for adjacent PTEs depends on the form of the initial PTE:

- If the original PTE contains a PSTX, successive PTEs must contain exactly the same PSTX.
- If the original PTE contains a page file virtual block number, successive PTEs must contain PTEs with successively increasing (or decreasing) virtual block numbers.
- If the original PTE contains a GPTX, successive PTEs must contain successively increasing (or decreasing) indexes. In addition, the GPTEs must all contain exactly the same GSTX.

16.7.1.3   **Maximum Cluster Size for Page Read.** The maximum number of pages that can make up a cluster is a function of the type of page being read:

- Global page table pages are not clustered.
- The cluster factor for process page table pages is taken from PHD$B_
  PGTBPFC. The default value of this field is the special SYSGEN parameter
  PAGTBLPFC.

    The default value for this parameter is 2. This value is chosen to avoid
    an artificial end to building a cluster when the page table page also had to
    be faulted. Decreasing this value may defeat clustered reads. Increasing it
    is likely to have a negligible effect on most systems.
- The cluster factor for pages read from a page file is taken from the PFL$B_
  PFC field of the page file control block (see Figure 14.24). The usual contents of this field are zero. In that case, the cluster factor is taken from the
  process's PHD$B_DFPFC. The default value of this field is the SYSGEN
  parameter PFCDEFAULT.
- The cluster factor for pages read from a private or global section file is taken
  from the SEC$B_PFC field of the process or global section table entry (see
  Figure 14.9). This field usually contains zero, in which case the default
  page fault cluster is used. (Just as for clustered reads from the page file,
  this default is taken from PHD$B_DFPFC.)

    There are two methods by which the cluster factor of a process or global
    section can be controlled. At link time, the page fault cluster factor in an
    image section descriptor can be set to nonzero through the linker cluster
    option and its PFC argument:

```
CLUSTER = cluster-name, [base-address] ,pfc ,file-spec [, ...]
```

Second, the page fault cluster factor for a section mapped through the
$CRMPSC system service can be specified in the optional PFC argument.

16.7.2   Page Read Completion

The I/O postprocessing routine, IOC$IOPOST in module IOCIOPOST, de-
tects page read completion, using the flag IRP$V_PAGIO in the IRP status
word.

Page read completion is not reported to the faulting process in the normal
fashion with a special KAST because none of the postprocessing has to be
performed in the context of the faulting process. Holding the MMG spinlock,
the routine PAGIO performs the postprocessing needed. It then makes the
process computable.

When a page read completes successfully, PAGIO performs the following
steps for each page:

1. The PFN REFCNT array element is decremented, indicating that the read
   in progress has completed.
2. The page STATE is set to active.
3. The valid bit in the PTE is set.

4. If the page is a global page, the valid bit set in step 3 was in the GPTE. In this case, the process (slave) PTE must also be altered: PAGIO inserts the PFN into it and sets the valid bit.

After tending to the individual pages, PAGIO reports the scheduling event page fault completion for the process so that it is made computable. The priority increment value is 0; that is, there is no boost to the process's scheduling priority. If any of the pages just read were collided pages, it also empties the collided page wait queue. That is, it makes all processes in that state computable. Collided pages are discussed in Section 16.10.3.

16.8   MODIFIED PAGE WRITING

Once a second, the executive checks whether any of the swapper's tasks need to be performed and wakes it if necessary; one such task is writing pages from the modified page list to mass storage. The modified page writer, MMG$WRTMFYPAG, in module WRTMFYPAG, is a subroutine of the swapper process. Within its main loop, the swapper invokes MMG$WRT-MFYPAG to write modified pages to their backing store locations. It forms a cluster of pages that have the same backing store and requests a write I/O operation.

At completion of the write I/O request, its KAST routine is entered to place the pages on the free page list and, if appropriate, to initiate the writing of more modified pages.

16.8.1   Requesting the Modified Page Writer

During system operation, other executive routines request the writing of pages in the modified page list by invoking the routine MMG$PURGEMPL, in module WRTMFYPAG, with arguments identifying the requested operation and its scope. The possible operations are writing pages to shrink the modified list to a target size (called a MAINTAIN request), writing pages within a virtual address range (an SVAPTE request), and writing all pages backed by section files (an OPCCRASH request).

Modified page writing is requested in a number of circumstances:

- When the modified page list has exceeded its high limit, defined by the SYSGEN parameter MPW_HILIMIT (MAINTAIN)
- When the free page list is below its low limit and can be replenished by writing modified pages (MAINTAIN)
- When particular modified pages must be written to their backing store (SVAPTE)
- When the OPCCRASH image, running during system shutdown, must write all pages in the list that are backed by section files to their backing store (OPCCRASH)

In earlier versions of VMS, the modified page list was sometimes emptied, or flushed, during normal operations. In VMS Version 5.2, the flushing has been replaced by selective purging, that is, writing all modified pages whose PTEs fall within a specified system virtual address range (the SVAPTE request).

Selective purging is requested under the following circumstances:

- When a process body has been outswapped but its PHD, whose slot is needed, cannot be outswapped because some of its PTEs map transition pages on the modified page list (see Chapter 18)
- When a writable global section with transition pages still on the modified page list is deleted (see Chapter 15)
- When a process needs to reuse a WSLE that describes a page table page that is now inactive but still maps transition pages on the modified page list (a dead page table page, described in Chapter 17)

The modified page writer may be requested multiple times before it is actually invoked by the swapper. MMG$PURGEMPL therefore records information about the request. It stores the requested command with the highest rank in MPW$GB_STATE; from low to high, the ordering is MAINTAIN, SVAPTE, and OPCCRASH.

For a MAINTAIN request, it typically compares the target modified page list size with the value of the SYSGEN parameter MPW_LOLIMIT and uses the larger as a target size. (If a previous MAINTAIN request has been made, MMG$PURGEMPL uses the lesser of its target size and the current target size.) It records the target size in SCH$GL_MFYLOLIM and SCH$GL_MFYLIM.

For an SVAPTE request, it also records the highest addressed PTE of interest in MPW$GL_SVAPTEHIGH and the lowest in MPW$GL_SVAPTELOW. If there are multiple outstanding SVAPTE requests, the count of such requests is stored in MPW$GB_REQCNT, and the low and high SVAPTE addresses of each request are stored in elements of a 32-quadword array beginning at MPW$GQ_SVAPTE. MPW$GL_SVAPTEHIGH and MPW$GL_SVAPTELOW record the highest and lowest addresses of any PTE in any of the requests. When the modified page writer scans the list for a page that meets any of the SVAPTE requests, it can easily reject one whose PTE address is outside that range without having to compare its PTE address to all the ranges. These cells facilitate easy rejection of any pages on the modified page list.

For an OPCCRASH request, it stores 80000000_{16} in MPW$GL_SVAPTELOW and $BFFFFFFF_{16}$ in MPW$GL_SVAPTEHIGH so that all pages on the modified page list will match the PTE address range.

Once modified page writing to shrink the list (MAINTAIN) is initiated, the modified page writer continues writing modified pages until the size of the list is at or below the contents of SCH$GL_MFYLOLIM. Chapter 18 describes the calculation of the target modified page list size for the different circumstances in which the swapper initiates modified page writing.

When an SVAPTE or OPCCRASH request initiates modified page writing to purge or flush the list, both the lower and upper limits for the modified page list are set to zero. For an SVAPTE request, the modified page writer scans the entire list and writes all pages whose PTE addresses fall within the specified range. For an OPCCRASH request, the modified page writer scans the entire list and writes all pages not backed by a page file.

Before the modified page writer exits, it restores its two limits to the values contained in the SYSGEN parameters MPW_HILIMIT and MPW_LOLIMIT.

16.8.2 **Operation of the Modified Page Writer**

The swapper invokes the modified page writer to initiate the writing of modified pages. The modified page writer forms a cluster and queues an I/O request. When the I/O request completes, the modified page writer's KAST routine is entered. After performing necessary processing on the pages that have been written, it checks whether more modified pages must be written and, if so, forms another cluster. At the completion of that request, the KAST routine may queue yet another request. To prevent the modified page writer from being incorrectly reentered by the swapper, it tests and sets the SCH$V_MPW bit in SCH$GB_SIP as a signal that modified page writing is in progress.

In earlier versions of VMS, the modified page writer was single-streamed and could only write one cluster of pages at a time. In VMS Version 5, it can initiate up to SYSGEN parameter MPW_IOLIMIT concurrent I/O requests. The default value of MPW_IOLIMIT is 4. As described in Chapter 14, during system initialization MPW_IOLIMIT nonpaged pool data structures are allocated. Each contains an IRP and two arrays that describe the pages in the cluster. These structures are queued to a listhead at MPW$GL_IRPFL and MPW$GL_IRPBL. Figure 16.8 shows this data structure, known as a modified page writer I/O request packet (MPW IRP).

MMG$WRTMFYPAG proceeds in the following fashion:

1. It compares the number of pages on the modified page list to SCH$GL_MFYLIM. If there are fewer pages on the list, it simply exits.
2. It sets bit SCH$V_MPW in SCH$GB_SIP to indicate that modified page writing is active. If the bit was already set, MMG$WRTMFYPAG exits.
3. Otherwise, it proceeds, first acquiring the MMG spinlock.
4. It zeros cells used to keep track of its progress.
5. It invokes MMG$PURGEMPL, specifying the default command MAINTAIN to shrink the list to MPW_LOWAITLIMIT pages.

   —If a previous SVAPTE request has been made, MMG$PURGEMPL returns immediately.

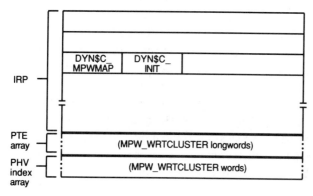

Figure 16.8
Modified Page Writer IRP

—If no previous SVAPTE or other MAINTAIN requests have been made, MMG$PURGEMPL changes MPW$GB_STATE to MAINTAIN and stores the lesser of MPW_LOWAITLIMIT and SCH$GL_MFYLOSV in SCH$GL_MFYLIM and SCH$GL_MFYLOLIM.

—If a previous MAINTAIN request has been made, MMG$PURGE-MPL stores the lesser of the previous and current requested limits in SCH$GL_MFYLIM and SCH$GL_MFYLOLIM.

6. MMG$WRTMFYPAG removes an MPW IRP from the list. If none is available, it exits.

7. Otherwise, it scans the modified page list, starting at the first page, to find a page to be the beginning of a cluster. Its actions depend on the type of request it is performing (the value of MPW$GB_STATE):

—If performing a MAINTAIN request, it accepts the page.

—If performing an SVAPTE request, it tests whether the PTE address of the page falls within any of the requested ranges. If not, it goes on to the next page in the list.

—If performing an OPCCRASH request, it tests whether the page's backing store is something other than a page file. If not, it goes on to the next page in the list.

8. It determines the type of the first page in the cluster by examining the PTE whose address is in its PFN PTE array element.

9. Based on the page type, it gets the address of the relevant PHD, either that of a process or the system.

10. It examines the PFN BAK array element to determine the type of backing store: page file, section file, or swap file virtual block (see Section 16.8.5).

11. Unless the backing store is a swap file block, MMG$WRTMFYPAG tries to form a cluster of pages, as described in Section 16.8.5. It scans adjacent PTEs (first toward lower virtual addresses and then toward higher virtual addresses), looking for transition PTEs that map pages on the modified

page list, until either the desired cluster size is reached or until one of the other terminating conditions described in Section 16.8.4 is reached.

This scan begins first toward smaller virtual addresses for the same reason that the page read cluster routine begins toward larger addresses. If the program is more likely to reference higher addresses, the modified page writer does not want to initiate a write operation, only to have the page immediately faulted and likely modified again. The modified page writer chooses to write first those pages with a smaller likelihood of being referenced in the near future.

12. When it can no longer cluster, it records the PTEs and their associated PHD vector indexes in the MPW IRP.

13. If the cluster is one of page file pages, MMG$WRTMFYPAG updates the PFN BAK array element for each page to show the actual block allocated.

14. It removes each page from the modified page list, decrementing SCH$GL_MFYCNT to show one less modified page.

15. It changes the PFN STATE array element for each of the pages to a value indicating write in progress, also clearing the saved modify bit. It increments the PFN REFCNT array element for each page to reflect the I/O in progress. If the page is a page table page, MMG$WRTMFYPAG also increments the PHV$GL_REFCBAS array element corresponding to the PHD.

16. It releases the MMG spinlock, fills in the MPW IRP, and queues it to the backing store driver.

17. It reacquires the MMG spinlock and goes to step 6 to try to form another cluster of pages to write.

When a modified page write request completes, MMG$WRTMFYPAG's KAST routine is entered. Section 16.8.3 describes this routine.

16.8.3 Modified Page Write Completion

The modified page writer's KAST routine, WRITEDONE in module WRT-MFYPAG, takes the following steps:

1. It acquires the MMG spinlock, raising IPL to IPL$_MMG.

2. It deallocates the MPW IRP to its own lookaside list.

3. It examines each page in the cluster.

4. If the page is a page table page, it decrements the PHV$GL_REFCBAS array element corresponding to that PHD.

5. If the page's backing store was a swap file block, WRITEDONE clears the PFN SWPVBN array element.

6. It decrements the PFN REFCNT array element for the page. If the count goes to zero, it places the page on the free page list.

7. If the RPTEVT bit in the PFN TYPE array element is set, WRITEDONE reports an I/O completion scheduling event for the process that owns the

page. This bit is set when deletion of the page has been stalled while it is being written to its backing store.

8. It releases the MMG spinlock, restoring the previous IPL, and then reacquires it. This lets any waiting SMP member acquire the spinlock and also lets any pending software interrupts between IPL 3 and 8 be serviced.

9. It attempts to form another MPW cluster, rejoining the flow described in the previous section at step 6.

16.8.4 Modified Page Write Clustering

The modified page writer scans the page table, attempting to form a cluster. The terminating conditions for its scan include the following:

- The page table page is not valid, implying that there are no transition pages in this page table page. The special check is made to avoid an unnecessary page fault.
- The PTE does not indicate a transition format.
- The PTE indicates a page in transition, but the physical page is not on the modified page list.
- The physical page number is greater than the contents of global location MMG$GL_MAXPFN. This check avoids pages in shared memory, which have no PFN data associated with them.
- The PFN SWPVBN array element must be zero. Pages with nonzero PFN SWPVBN array elements are treated in a special way by the modified page writer.
- If the contents of the PFN BAK array indicate that the backing store location for the page is a private or global file, the section index must be the same for all pages in the cluster.
- If the PFN BAK array element indicates that the pages are to be written to a page file, the contents of the virtual block number field are ignored. However, all pages must contain the same page file index in their PFN BAK array elements.

16.8.5 Backing Store for Modified Pages

The modified page writer attempts to cluster when writing modified pages to their backing store addresses. It encounters three different clustering situations for the three possible backing store locations.

A nonzero PFN SWPVBN array element indicates that the process has been outswapped and this page remained behind, probably as the result of an outstanding read request. The modified page writer issues a write of a single page to the designated block in the swap file. It does not attempt to cluster because virtually contiguous pages in an I/O buffer are unlikely to be adjacent in the outswapped process body. The process body is outswapped with pages ordered as they appear in the working set list, not in virtual address order.

A description of how the PFN SWPVBN array element is loaded is found in Chapter 18, where the entire outswap operation is discussed.

If the backing store address is in a section file, the modified page writer creates a cluster up to the value of the SYSGEN parameter MPW_WRTCLUS-TER. Any of the terminating conditions listed in the previous section can limit the size of the cluster.

If the backing store address is in a page file, adjacent pages bound for the same page file are also written at the same time. The modified page writer attempts to allocate a number of blocks in the page file equal to MPW_WRTCLUSTER. The desired cluster factor is reduced to the number of blocks actually allocated. Section 16.8.6 describes allocation of space within the page file.

The actual cluster created for a write to the page file consists of several smaller clusters, each one representing a series of virtually contiguous pages (see Figure 16.9):

1. The modified page writer creates a cluster of virtually contiguous pages, all bound for the same page file.
2. If the desired cluster size has not yet been reached, the modified page list is searched until another physical page bound for the same page file is found.
3. Pages virtually contiguous to this page form the second minicluster that is added to the eventual cluster to be written to the page file.
4. The modified page writer continues in this manner until either the cluster size is reached or no more pages on the modified page list have the designated page file as their backing store address. The modified page writer is building a large cluster that consists of a series of smaller clusters. The large cluster terminates only when the desired size is reached or when the modified page list contains no more pages bound to the page file in question. Each smaller cluster can terminate on any of the conditions listed in the previous section, or on the two terminating conditions for the large cluster.

16.8.6   **Page File Space Allocation**

Before the modified page writer searches for more pages to form a cluster, it must determine the maximum size of the write cluster. To do this, it determines the number of contiguous blocks that can be allocated in the page file associated with the current page.

The modified page writer invokes MMG$ALLOCPAGFIL1, in module PAGEFILE, to allocate a cluster of blocks in that page file. The number of blocks it tries to allocate is stored in the page file control block at the offset PFL$B_ALLOCSIZ and is usually equal to MPW_WRTCLUSTER. If that many blocks are not available, MMG$WRTMFYPAG reduces the PFL$B_ALLOCSIZ size by 16 blocks, if it can, and invokes MMG$ALLOCPAGFIL1 again to search for contiguous blocks starting back at the beginning of the page file.

The allocation size is raised sometime later when space frees up in the page file. When the page file deallocation routine determines that it has freed a large enough cluster, it increases the allocation size by 8, to a maximum of MPW_WRTCLUSTER.

When the allocation size for the page file is less than or equal to 16, the modified page writer invokes a special-case allocation routine, MMG$AL-LOCPAGFIL2, in module PAGEFILE. This special-case allocation routine searches for and allocates the first available cluster of blocks, starting from the beginning of the page file. The routine can allocate between 1 and 16 contiguous blocks. If the first available cluster of blocks is not in the first quarter of the page file, MMG$ALLOCPAGFIL2 issues the following message on the console terminal:

```
%SYSTEM-W-PAGEFRAG, Pagefile badly fragmented, system continuing
```

If the first available cluster is found in the last quarter of the page file, MMG$ALLOCPAGFIL2 issues the following message on the terminal:

```
%SYSTEM-W-PAGECRIT, Pagefile space critical, system trying to continue
```

Each of these messages is issued only once during a boot of the system, even if more than one page file becomes full. The first message is issued when one page file becomes fragmented or full; the second, when the same or a different page file becomes fragmented or full. These messages on the console terminal may be a good indication that the system requires an(other) alternative page file. However, because of the nature of the checks, it is possible for the system to run out of page file space without any message having been displayed.

If the modified page writer is unable to allocate any blocks in a particular page file, it skips any pages with backing store in that page file.

16.8.7 Example of Modified Page Write to a Page File

Figure 16.9 illustrates a sample cluster for writing to a page file. The modified page list, pictured in the upper right-hand corner of the figure, is shown as a sequential array to simplify the figure.

1. The first page on the modified page list is PFN A. By scanning backwards through the process's page table, first PFN F and then PFN H are located. The PTE preceding the one that contains PFN H is also a transition PTE, but the page is on the free page list. This page terminates the backward search.
2. The modified page writer's map begins with PFN H, PFN F, and PFN A. The search now goes in the forward direction, with each page bound for

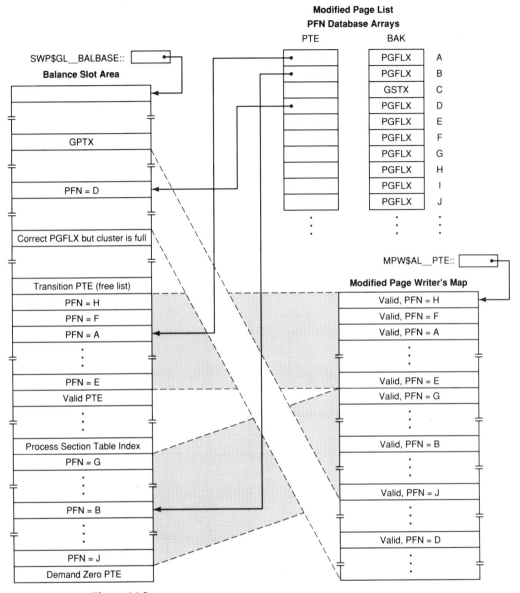

Figure 16.9
Example of Clustered Write to a Page File

the page file added to the map up to and including PFN E. The next PTE is valid, so the first minicluster is terminated.

3. The next page on the modified page list, PFN B, leads to the addition of a second cluster to the map. This cluster begins with PFN G and ends with PFN J. The backward search was terminated with a PTE containing a section table index. The forward search terminated with a demand zero PTE.

Note that this second cluster consists of pages belonging to a different process than that of the first cluster. The difference is reflected in the process header vector index array, which contains a word element for each PTE in the map (see Figure 16.8).

4. The next page on the modified page list is PFN C. This page belongs in a global section file and is skipped over during the current write attempt.

5. PFN D leads to a third cluster that was terminated in the backward direction with a PTE that contains a GPTX. The search in the forward direction terminated when the desired cluster size was reached, even though the next PTE was bound to the same page file. The cluster size is either MPW_WRTCLUSTER or the number of adjacent blocks available in the page file, whichever is smaller. In any case, this cluster will be written with a single write request.

6. Note that reaching the desired cluster size resulted in leaving some pages on the modified page list bound for the same page file, such as PFN I.

16.9 $UPDSEC SYSTEM SERVICE

The $UPDSEC[W] system service enables a process to write a specified range of pages in a process or global section to their backing store in a controlled fashion, without waiting for the modified page writer to do the backup. This system service is especially useful for frequently accessed pages that may never be written by the modified page writer, because they are always being faulted from the modified page list back into the working set before they are backed up.

This system service is a cross between modified page writing and a normal write request. As for any I/O request, the requestor can request completion notification with an event flag and I/O status block or an AST. The number of pages written is specified by the address range that is passed as an input parameter to the service. The cluster factor is the minimum of MPW_WRTCLUSTER and the number of pages in the input range. The direction of search for modified pages is determined by the order in which the address range is specified to the service.

The system service procedure EXE$UPDSEC, in module SYSUPDSEC, runs in kernel mode. It first clears the event flag associated with the I/O request, charges process direct I/O quota, and allocates nonpaged pool to serve as an extended I/O packet. The pool is used to queue one or more modified page write I/O requests and to keep track of how much of the section the service has processed.

EXE$UPDSEC then invokes MMG$CREDEL, in module SYSCREDEL, specifying MMG$UPDSECPAG, in module SYSUPDSEC, as the per-page service-specific routine. (Chapter 15 describes the actions of MMG$CREDEL and its use of per-page service-specific routines.) Other routines that take part in performing this service are MMG$UPDSECQWT, MMG$PTEPFNMFY, MMG$WRTPGSBAK, and MMG$UPDSECAST, all in SYSUPDSEC.

MMG$UPDSECPAG invokes MMG$UPDSECQWT to form the first cluster and initialize and queue the IRP to the driver for the backing store driver.

MMG$UPDSECQWT takes the following steps:

1. It touches the next page table page that maps pages in the specified range to fault it into the working set list.
2. It acquires the MMG spinlock, raising IPL to IPL$_MMG.
3. It scans in the specified direction of the range for the first candidate page: one whose owner access mode is not more privileged than that of the service requestor; that is a valid or transition page (or a valid or transition global page); that is writable but not copy-on-reference; and that has been modified.
4. Having found one candidate page, it scans in the specified direction for adjacent pages that have similar characteristics; in particular, the backing store for the pages must be the same. The adjacent pages do not necessarily have to have been modified but they do all have to be valid or transition, that is, resident.

   In the case of process pages, it forms a cluster from the first modified page through the last modified page in the MPW_WRTCLUSTER adjacent pages.

   In the case of global pages, determining which pages have been modified is not feasible. The system service runs in the context of one process and can scan its PTEs for set modify bits. However, to determine whether a particular page has been modified requires looking at the PFN database and the PTEs of all processes mapped to this global page. (The GPTE is not used in address translation and thus the state of its modify bit is not meaningful.) Because there are no back pointers for valid global pages, this information is unavailable. Therefore, all pages in a global section are written to their backing store location, regardless of whether the pages have been modified.

   By setting the low bit of the FLAGS parameter, the requestor can indicate that it is the only process whose modifed pages should be written. In that case, the process's PTEs and the PFN database are used to select candidate pages for backing up. Only pages modified by this process can be the beginning and end pages of a cluster.
5. Having formed a cluster, MMG$WRTPGSBAK modifies the PFN database for the pages in it. It increments the PFN REFCNT array element for each page. If the page is on the free or modified page list, it removes it from the list and changes its PFN STATE array element to write in progress and clears the saved modify bit. If the page was valid, it also clears the modify bit in the PTE.

6. It initializes an IRP, releases the MMG spinlock, and queues the I/O request to the backing store driver.

When the write completes, the process that requested the $UPDSEC system service receives a KAST. The AST routine MMG$UPDSECAST first checks whether all the pages requested by the system service call have been written or whether another write is required. To perform the check, it invokes MMG$UPDSECQWT, which forms another cluster and queues another write request if necessary. If all requested pages have been written, MMG$UPDSECAST enters the normal I/O completion path involving event flags, I/O status blocks, and user-requested ASTs, thus notifying the process.

16.10 PAGING AND SCHEDULING

Page fault handling can influence the scheduling state of processes in several different ways. If a read is required to satisfy a page fault, the faulting process is placed into a page fault wait state. If a resource such as physical memory is not available, the process is placed into an appropriate wait state. There are several other wait states that a process may be placed into as a result of a page fault. Chapter 12 describes process scheduling, wait states, priority increment classes, resource waits, and the reporting of scheduler events.

16.10.1 Page Fault Wait State

The most obvious wait state is page fault wait, in which a process is placed when a read is required to resolve a page fault. The I/O postprocessing routine, PAGIO, in module IOCIOPOST, detects that a page read has completed and reports the scheduling event page fault completion for the process. As a result, the process is removed from the page fault wait state and made computable. No priority boost is associated with page fault read completion.

16.10.2 Free Page Wait State

If there is not enough physical memory available to satisfy a page fault, the faulting process is placed in a free page wait state. Whenever a page is deallocated and the free page list was formerly empty, routine MMG$DAL-LOCPFN, in module ALLOCPFN, checks for processes in this state. It reports the scheduling event free page available so that each process in the free page wait state is made computable.

MMG$DALLOCPFN makes no scheduling decision about which process will get the page. There is no first-in/first-out approach to the free page wait state; rather, all processes waiting for the page are made computable. The next process to execute will be the highest priority resident computable process.

16.10.3   **Collided Page Wait State**

It is possible for a page fault to occur for a page that is already being read from its backing store. Such a page is referred to as a collided page. The collided bit is set in the PFN TYPE array element, and the process is placed into the collided page (COLPG) wait state.

One way that this can occur is when a process in a page fault wait state is made computable by AST enqueuing. When the AST procedure completes execution and returns, the process reexecutes the instruction that triggered the page fault. If the page is still invalid, that is, if it is still being read, the process is placed into a COLPG wait.

One of the details that the page read completion routine checks is the collided bit in the TYPE array element for the page. If the collided bit is set, it reports the scheduling event collided page available for each process in that wait state. It does not check whether a process is waiting for the collided page that was faulted in.

This lack of check has two advantages:

- There is no special code to determine which process executes first. All processes are made computable, and the normal scheduling algorithm selects the process that executes next.
- The probability of a collided page is small. The probability of two different collided pages is even smaller. If a process waiting for another collided page is selected for execution, that process will incur a page fault and be placed back into the collided wait state. Nothing unusual occurs, and the operating system avoids a lot of special-case code to handle a situation that rarely, if ever, occurs.

16.10.4   **Resource Wait States**

There are two types of resource wait associated with memory management. A process waiting for one of these resources is placed in the miscellaneous wait state (see Chapter 12) until the resource is available.

Earlier versions of VMS also could place a process into a wait for resource RSN$_SWPFILE (RWSWP). When a process was unable to increase its swap file allocation to accommodate a larger working set, it was placed into this resource wait until space became available in the swap file. The timing and form of swap file allocation have changed in VMS Version 5, and this resource wait is no longer used.

16.10.4.1   **Resource Wait for RSN$_MPWBUSY (RWMPB).** A process that faults a modified page out of its working set is placed into this resource wait when either of the following is true:

- The modified page list contains more pages than the SYSGEN parameter MPW_WAITLIMIT.
- The modified page list contains more pages than the SYSGEN parameter MPW_LOWAITLIMIT and the modified page writer is active, writing modified pages.

The modified page writer declares the availability of the resource RSN$_MPWBUSY when it writes enough modified pages so that the list has MPW_LOWAITLIMIT or fewer pages on it.

16.10.4.2 **Resource Wait for RSN$_MPLEMPTY (RWMPE).** A process in RWMPE is waiting for the modified page writer to signal that it has flushed the modified page list. With VMS Version 5.2, the only process placed into this wait is one running the OPCCRASH image, which forces a flush of the modified page list prior to stopping the system.

In earlier versions of VMS, pages on the modified page list were written in order, and this resource wait was more widely used to force certain modified pages to be written. These uses have been replaced by more selective writing of the modified page list.

17 Working Set List Dynamics

"Then you keep moving round, I suppose?" said Alice.
"Exactly so," said the Hatter: "as the things get used up."
"But what happens when you come to the beginning again?"
Alice ventured to ask.
"Suppose we change the subject," the March Hare interrupted,
yawning. "I'm getting tired of this. I vote the young lady
tell us a story."

Lewis Carroll, *Alice's Adventures in Wonderland*

The pages of physical memory in use by a process are called its working set. A data structure within the process header (PHD) called the working set list describes just those pages in a compact form.

This chapter describes the composition of the working set list, the ways in which it shrinks and expands to describe a varying number of pages, and the system services by which a process affects its working set and working set list.

17.1 OVERVIEW

The term *working set* refers to the virtual pages of a process that are currently valid and in physical memory. A valid page is one whose page table entry (PTE) valid bit is set.

As a process executes an image, it faults image code and data pages into its working set. Chapter 16 describes the page fault mechanism in detail. Execution of asynchronous system trap (AST) procedures, condition handlers, and system services that touch pageable process space can cause additional faults into the working set. The working set continues to grow as the process faults pages until the process occupies as much physical memory as it is allowed. Each subsequent page fault requires that a page be removed from the working set.

The VMS executive maintains a list of working set pages for each process, called the working set list. The list facilitates

- Selecting a page to remove from the working set when a process needs to fault in a page but already occupies all the physical memory it is currently allowed, or when the process's working set is being shrunk
- Determining which pages to write when a process is outswapped
- Determining which pages to read when a process is inswapped

Section 17.2 describes the structure and makeup of the working set list. Section 17.3 gives a detailed description of replacement paging, that is, removing one virtual page from the working set to make room for another.

The size of the working set list and the number of its entries constrain a process's use of physical memory. The working set list size varies over the process's lifetime. It can be affected by the system authorization file entry for an interactive user, SYSGEN parameters, availability of physical memory, and the recent paging history of the process. Section 17.4 describes these effects, and Section 17.2.3 discusses the capacity of the working set list.

By requesting the following system services, a process can affect its own working set and working set list:

- Adjust Working Set Limit ($ADJWSL)
- Lock Pages in Working Set ($LKWSET)
- Lock Pages in Memory ($LCKPAG)
- Unlock Pages from Working Set ($ULWSET)
- Unlock Pages from Memory ($ULKPAG)
- Purge Working Set ($PURGWS)

These services are described in later sections of this chapter.

Section 17.9 explains the means by which a process can prevent the removal of a particular page from its working set.

Chapter 14 describes the system working set list. This chapter is primarily concerned with the process working set list, although much of it is equally applicable to the system working set list.

17.2 THE WORKING SET LIST

A process working set includes the process's P0 and P1 space pages and the system space pages that contain its PHD. The working set also includes global pages in use by the process. Each of these pages is described by a working set list entry (WSLE). Because the data structure containing the WSLEs, the working set list, is part of the PHD, the working set list is self-describing, containing WSLEs that describe the working set list itself as well as the other PHD pages.

Certain other types of page are valid for the entire time the process maps them and never appear in the working set list. These include pages mapped by page frame number (PFN), P1 space system service vector pages, pages in a resident global section (namely, those of the Files-11 Extended QIO Processor, XQP), and pages in MA780 shared memory sections.

17.2.1 The WSLE

The format of a valid WSLE is shown in Figure 17.1. Note that the upper 23 bits are the same as the upper 23 bits of a virtual address. This format allows the WSLE to be passed as a virtual address to several utility routines that ignore the byte offset bits (WSLE control bits). Table 17.1 shows the meanings of the WSLE control bits.

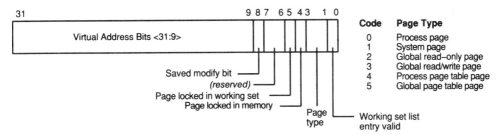

Figure 17.1
Format of Working Set List Entry

Table 17.1   WSLE Control Bits

Field Name	Meaning
VALID	When set, this bit indicates that the WSLE is in use.
PAGTYP	This field (a duplicate of the contents of the PFN TYPE array element) identifies the page type and specifies the action required when the page is removed from the working set.
PFNLOCK	When set, this bit indicates that the page has been locked into physical memory with the $LCKPAG system service.
WSLOCK	When set, this bit indicates one of the following types of page locked into the working set: • Permanently locked page • Page locked with the $LKWSET system service • Per-process page table page that maps one or more valid or transition pages
MODIFY	This bit, used when the process is outswapped, records the logical OR of the modify bit in the PTE and the saved modify bit in the PFN STATE array.

17.2.2   Regions of the Working Set List

The working set list is divided into three regions: one containing entries for pages that are permanently locked; one containing entries for pages locked after process creation, chiefly by user request; and one containing dynamic entries. These regions are described in more detail later in this section.

Figure 17.2 shows the fields in the fixed portion of the PHD that describe the working set list. Many of them locate the different regions of the working set list through a longword context index to a particular WSLE. For example, the following steps compute the address of the beginning of the working set list from the longword context in PHD$L_WSLIST:

1. Multiply the contents of PHD$L_WSLIST by 4.
2. Add the result to the address of the PHD.

Three of the fields shown, PHD$L_DFWSCNT, PHD$L_WSQUOTA, and PHD$L_WSEXTENT, do not locate region boundaries but instead represent

483

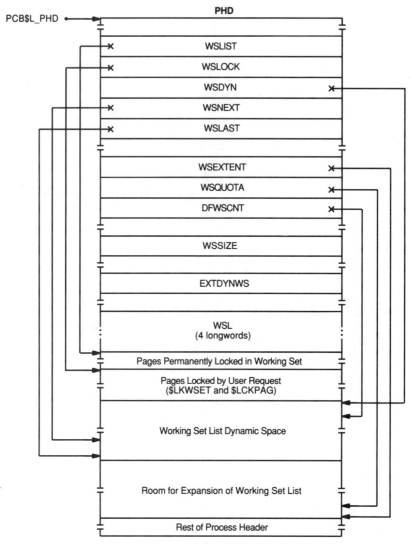

Figure 17.2
Working Set List

a number of WSLEs. These fields nonetheless contain longword context indexes, providing easier comparison with fields that do locate boundaries.

The following steps convert such a field into the number it represents:

1. Subtract the contents of PHD$L_WSLIST from it.
2. Add 1 to the result.

This chapter refers to the converted contents of such a field using its field name without the PHD$L_ prefix, for example, WSQUOTA.

Two of the fields shown, PHD$L_WSSIZE and PHD$L_EXTDYNWS, represent a number of WSLEs.

The permanently locked region of the working set list describes pages that are forever a part of the process working set. Pages whose WSLEs are in this region cannot be unlocked and are not candidates for working set replacement. They include the following:

- Kernel stack pages
- P1 pointer page
- P1 page table page that maps the kernel stack and the P1 pointer page
- P1 page table pages that map the P1 window to the PHD
- PHD pages that are not page table pages—the fixed portion, the PHD page arrays, the maximum process section table, and enough pages for a working set list that contains the SYSGEN parameter PQL_DWSDEFAULT number of entries

The value in PHD$L_WSLIST is a longword context index to the first WSLE in this region. Its value, calculated during process creation, is the same for all processes running on a particular VMS version. Because WSLIST is a pointer to the beginning of the working set list, its value is simply a function of the size of the fixed PHD that precedes it.

The offset PHD$L_WSL is at a lower address in the PHD than the WSLE identified by PHD$L_WSLIST. There is space for four WSLEs between them. This space is available to describe kernel stack expansion pages, which, once created, must be represented in this region of the working set list. The SYSINIT process, for example, requires a considerably larger kernel stack than other processes. Expanding its kernel stack is an alternative to increasing the memory requirements for every process.

When the kernel stack is expanded, it grows by four pages. The value 4 is subtracted from PHD$L_WSLIST so that it indexes the first newly created WSLE. Kernel stack expansion is the only way this region of the working set list can grow; its size and contents are otherwise fixed at process creation.

The second region contains WSLEs for pages that are locked by user request, specifically through the $LKWSET and $LCKPAG system services. Pages whose WSLEs are in this region are not candidates for working set replacement. Any per-process page table page that maps a PFN-mapped section or an MA780 shared memory section is also locked in this region of the working set list, as are PHD expansion pages resulting from working set list growth.

PHD$L_WSLOCK contains the longword context index to the first WSLE in this region. PHD$L_WSDYN points to the WSLE immediately following the last WSLE in this region. To lock a page in the working set list, the executive swaps its WSLE with that pointed to by PHD$L_WSDYN and increments PHD$L_WSDYN. Consequently, the user-locked region is increased by one WSLE and the dynamic region decreased by one.

The two locked regions of the working set list are completely filled with valid WSLEs. Rather than keep a count of locked pages, the executive can simply calculate the difference between the contents of PHD$L_WSDYN and PHD$L_WSLIST.

The dynamic region of the working set list describes per-process and global pages that have not been locked in the working set list and per-process page table pages. Per-process and global pages are candidates for working set replacement. A page table page that maps valid or transition pages is locked into this region of the working set list (through the WSLOCK bit in the WSLE) and is not a candidate for working set replacement while still locked. Page table pages locked in this manner remain in the dynamic region, although locked, for a number of reasons. They are considered dynamic because they are unlocked as the result of the release of the dynamic entries and transition pages. Also, leaving them in the dynamic region results in less CPU overhead than switching them in and out of the locked region.

The dynamic region is treated as a ring buffer for page replacement. It begins at the entry identified by the contents of PHD$L_WSDYN. PHD$L_WSLAST contains the longword context index for the last WSLE; its contents identify the end of the dynamic region. The entry most recently inserted into the working set list is pointed to by PHD$L_WSNEXT. This marks the point in the ring buffer at which page replacement typically occurs. The page replacement algorithm, explained in detail in Section 17.3.1, is a modified first-in/first-out (FIFO) scheme.

The dynamic region of the working set list is not necessarily dense; there may be empty entries between those specified by PHD$L_WSDYN and PHD$L_WSLAST.

17.2.3 Size of the Working Set List

Three critical parameters govern the dynamics of the working set list: size, limit, and capacity.

The process's working set size is the number of WSLEs currently in use. There is no single field that contains this value; instead, it is the sum of two separately maintained counts, PCB$L_PPGCNT and PCB$L_GPGCNT.

The maximum number of WSLEs the process is allowed to use is known as its working set limit. It is maintained in a field that is somewhat confusingly called PHD$L_WSSIZE. Despite its name, it contains the working set limit, not the size (which is the sum of the two fields previously noted).

The maximum number of WSLEs that the current working set can potentially contain (PHD$L_WSLAST minus PHD$L_WSLIST, plus 1) is referred to in this chapter as the working set list capacity. When the capacity increases, the working set list data structure itself consumes more physical memory.

Figure 17.3 contrasts these three values.

Table 17.2 shows process-specific and systemwide working set list parameters, quotas, and limits.

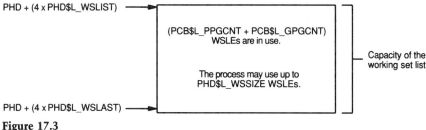

Figure 17.3
Working Set List Parameters

During system initialization, enough virtual address space is reserved in each PHD for the maximum-sized working set list, one with SYSGEN parameter WSMAX entries.

Each process is created with its initial working set limit and working set list capacity set to the same value, the process's default working set limit, DFWSCNT (assuming that DFWSCNT is less than or equal to WSMAX). VMS thus initially allocates physical memory for only a relatively small working set list.

When a process runs an image, it begins faulting pages; the working set size increases, growing toward the working set limit. Once it reaches the limit, subsequent page faults require the removal of pages from the working set. With the working set limit, VMS governs the amount of physical memory a process may use.

The process can increase the working set limit by issuing the Digital command language (DCL) command SET WORKING_SET or requesting the $ADJWSL system service. The executive can increase a process's working set limit through automatic working set limit adjustment. These mechanisms are discussed in Section 17.4.

Whenever the working set limit would exceed the working set list capacity, the capacity must grow as well to accommodate the new limit. As described in Chapter 14, the working set list capacity is dynamic; it grows toward the process section table (PST). When the working set list must expand into the area already occupied by the PST, the PST is moved to higher addresses. However, there is not always room in the PHD to accommodate the expanded working set list. The total space available for both the working set list and the PST is determined by the two SYSGEN parameters WSMAX and PROCSECTCNT. The PST is allowed to grow beyond PROCSECTCNT entries, leaving less working set list area available. In that case, the working set list capacity can grow no further, and the process must make do with the memory it has already.

Furthermore, because the working set list contains WSLEs for all the PHD pages in physical memory, its size and the size of the PHD are interrelated. As the working set grows, the working set list in the PHD grows, and more

Table 17.2   Working Set Lists: Limits and Quotas

Description	Location or Name	Comments
Index of first WSLE	PHD$L_WSLIST	Contains 69_{16}, unless kernel stack has been expanded
Working set limit	PHD$L_WSSIZE	Set by LOGINOUT; Altered by $ADJWSL; Altered by automatic working set limit adjustment, image exit, swapper trimming
Index of first locked WSLE	PHD$L_WSLOCK	The same for all processes in a given system
Index of first dynamic WSLE	PHD$L_WSDYN	Altered by $LKWSET, $LCKPAG, $ULWSET, and $ULKPAG
Index of most recently inserted WSLE	PHD$L_WSNEXT	Updated each time an entry is added to or released from working set
Index of last WSLE	PHD$L_WSLAST	May be altered by $ADJWSL, page fault handler, image exit, or automatic working set limit adjustment
Default working set limit	PHD$L_DFWSCNT	Set by LOGINOUT; Altered by command SET WORKING_SET/LIMIT
Normal maximum working set limit	PHD$L_WSQUOTA	Set by LOGINOUT; Altered by command SET WORKING_SET/QUOTA
Extended maximum working set limit	PHD$L_WSEXTENT	Set by LOGINOUT; Altered by command SET WORKING_SET/EXTENT
Upper limit to normal maximum working set limit	PHD$L_WSAUTH	Set by LOGINOUT; Cannot be altered
Upper limit to extended maximum working set limit	PHD$L_WSAUTHEXT	Set by LOGINOUT; Cannot be altered
Minimum number of dynamic WSLEs for pages accessed in one instruction	PHD$L_WSFLUID	Set by SHELL to the value of MINWSCNT
Number of dynamic WSLEs not counting PHD$L_WSFLUID process pages and a reasonable number of page table pages	PHD$L_EXTDYNWS	Updated each time size of dynamic working set region is changed
Working set size	PCB$L_PPGCNT +PCB$L_GPGCNT	Updated each time a page is added to or removed from the working set
Authorized default working set limit	UAF$L_DFWSCNT	Copied to PHD$L_DFWSCNT
Authorized normal maximum working set limit	UAF$L_WSQUOTA	Copied to PHD$L_WSAUTH and PHD$L_WSQUOTA

(continued)

Table 17.2 Working Set Lists: Limits and Quotas *(continued)*

Description	Location or Name	Comments
Authorized extended maximum working set limit	UAF$L_WSEXTENT	Copied to PHD$L_WSEXTENT and PHD$L_WSAUTHEXT
Systemwide minimum number of fluid working set pages	MINWSCNT	SYSGEN parameter
Systemwide maximum working set limit	WSMAX	SYSGEN parameter
System working set limit	SYSMWCNT	SYSGEN parameter
Default value for working set limit default (used by $CREPRC)	PQL_DWSDEFAULT	SYSGEN parameter
Minimum value for working set limit default (used by $CREPRC)	PQL_MWSDEFAULT	SYSGEN parameter
Default value for normal maximum working set limit (used by $CREPRC)	PQL_DWSQUOTA	SYSGEN parameter
Minimum value for normal maximum working set limit (used by $CREPRC)	PQL_MWSQUOTA	SYSGEN parameter
Default value for extended maximum working set limit (used by $CREPRC)	PQL_DWSEXTENT	SYSGEN parameter
Minimum value for extended maximum working set limit (used by $CREPRC)	PQL_MWSEXTENT	SYSGEN parameter

WSLEs are required to describe the PHD pages in memory. The size of the PHD (excluding the page table pages) is constrained to be no larger in pages than half of the process's working set quota. This constraint preserves a reasonable number of WSLEs for non-PHD pages. A process with a large value for working set extent and a relatively small value for working set quota may have the expansion of its working set limited by this constraint.

The process's working set size decreases as the result of deleting virtual address space (explicitly or, for example, at image exit), requesting the $PURGWS system service, and as an effect of having the working set limit decreased below the working set size.

The working set limit is a count of WSLEs, not the boundary of a working set region. When it is reduced, the working set list simply becomes more sparsely populated with valid WSLEs and more heavily populated with invalid WSLEs.

An image with a good understanding of its paging behavior can voluntarily reduce its working set limit by requesting the $ADJWSL system service. VMS has several mechanisms for decreasing the working set limit. Automatic working set limit adjustment can reduce the limit (see Section 17.4.3). The swapper process can initiate a reduction of working set limit with a mechanism known as swapper trimming. Chapter 18 describes the conditions that trigger this mechanism and the criteria by which processes are selected. The process working set limit is also reset at image exit to its default value, DFWSCNT (see Chapter 26).

Reducing the working set list capacity can also occur at image exit: if possible, VMS resets PHD$L_WSLAST by moving it toward lower addresses past any invalid WSLEs. It continues until it reaches a valid WSLE or until the working set list capacity is just equal to the working set limit. Additionally, when VMS is scanning the working set list to find an entry for a page being faulted, it may move PHD$L_WSLAST in the same way, compressing invalid entries at the high-address end of the working set list. VMS must strike a balance between spending too much overhead compressing empty entries so that PHD$L_WSLAST is precise and spending too much overhead searching for a valid replacement WSLE when the working set list is sparse (see Section 17.3.1).

VMS guarantees a minimum size for the dynamic region of the working set list. One of its concerns is the successful execution of an instruction that references a large but reasonable number of pages. All the pages referenced in a non-first-part-done instruction must be valid for the instruction to complete execution. If the dynamic region of the working set is too small, an infinite page fault loop could occur during the attempted execution of one instruction. An instruction could begin to execute, incur a page fault, restart, incur a different page fault, replace the first faulted page in the working set list, restart, reincur the first page fault, and so on, unable to complete execution.

During system initialization, the SYSGEN parameters that affect minimum working set sizes are adjusted to allow for at least this minimum. That is, SYSBOOT ensures that the values of PQL_MWSDEFAULT and PQL_DWSDEFAULT are at least large enough to accommodate the sum of the following:

- The SYSGEN parameter MINWSCNT, the minimum number of fluid pages in the working set
- The worst-case number of page table pages to map MINWSCNT pages, namely MINWSCNT
- The maximum process header, not counting page table pages
- The kernel stack pages
- The P1 pointer page

• The minimum number of page tables to map the P1 space defined by the SHELL module

Subsequently, the executive checks that the dynamic working set list has enough space whenever it adjusts the working set limit or locks pages into the working set list. For a typical process and address space, the executive checks that the number of dynamic WSLEs is at least twice MINWSCNT. In this check, it ignores any working set list extension above WSQUOTA, since any extension above quota is subject to swapper trimming. To facilitate the check, the executive maintains the field PHD$L_EXTDYNWS, which effectively contains the number of WSLEs in the dynamic region of the working set list beyond the minimum number required. The calculation of PHD$L_EXTDYNWS is based upon a working set no bigger than WSQUOTA.

For example, when a process tries to lock a page into its working set list, the executive checks that PHD$L_EXTDYNWS has a value of at least 2, one entry for the page and another for its page table page.

The manner in which a process is created determines how values for WSQUOTA and WSEXTENT are defined. They are defined and potentially redefined several times during different steps of process creation. In the case of the typical interactive process, the values come from its authorization file record. See Chapters 25 and 27 for further information.

17.3   WORKING SET REPLACEMENT

When a process references an invalid virtual page, the page fault handler must take whatever steps are necessary to make the page valid. It must also create a WSLE for the page. If there is no room in the working set list for another entry, one must be removed. The page fault handler uses the dynamic region of the working set list to decide which virtual page to discard.

The dynamic region of the working set list can contain unused WSLEs. When the working set limit is reduced, the working set list capacity is usually left intact, resulting in a sparse working set list. This makes adding a page to the working set slightly more complex. That a WSLE is empty does not necessarily mean the process can make use of it; the size of the working set must be less than the working set limit. If the process is already at its limit, a nonempty WSLE must be found whose virtual page can be removed from the working set to make room for the new page.

The VMS executive uses a modified FIFO scheme for its working set list replacement algorithm. The entry most likely to have been in the working set list for the longest time, the one following that pointed to by PHD$L_WSNEXT, is the one first considered for replacement.

17.3.1   Scan of the Working Set List

When the page fault handler needs an empty WSLE, it invokes routine

MMG$FREWSLE, in module PAGEFAULT. The following steps summarize its flow. Subsequent sections describe more details of particular aspects of its flow.

MMG$FREWSLE scans the working set list. It begins by checking whether the WSLE whose index is in PHD$L_WSNEXT is empty. If not, it starts with the next WSLE.

1. If the WSLE is empty (contents are zero), MMG$FREWSLE checks if the entry can be used (see Section 17.3.2). If it can be used, it is selected.
2. If the WSLE is not empty (its contents are nonzero) but is an active page table page (one that maps valid pages), the WSLE cannot be used.
3. If the WSLE is not empty but is a page table page that maps no valid pages, it may be usable. MMG$FREWSLE takes the steps described in Section 17.3.3 to determine whether the page table page can be released and its WSLE reused.
4. If the WSLE is not empty, but its virtual page has been recently enough accessed that it appears in the translation buffer, the WSLE is skipped (see Section 17.3.4).
5. If the WSLE is selected for reuse and is not empty, MMG$FREWSLE takes the actions described in Section 17.3.5.
6. If the WSLE is not selected, the index is incremented, and the steps in this list are repeated until a WSLE that can be used is found. If the index exceeds the end of the list, it is reset to the beginning of the dynamic working set list.

Once a WSLE is selected for reuse, PHD$L_WSNEXT is updated to contain its longword context index.

17.3.2 Using an Empty Entry in the Working Set List

If an empty WSLE is found, checks are made to see if a page can be added to the working set. If there are fewer pages in the working set than WSQUOTA, a new physical page can be added to the working set. It may also be possible to add physical pages to the working set above WSQUOTA (up to WSEXTENT), depending on the size of the free page list.

The following checks are required for an empty WSLE to be usable:

1. If the working set size (PCB$L_PPGCNT plus PCB$L_GPGCNT) equals the working set limit, the empty WSLE cannot be used, and a page in the working set must be replaced.
2. If the working set size has not reached its limit, the size is compared to WSQUOTA. If the size is less than WSQUOTA, a new page is allowed in the working set. The empty WSLE is used.
3. If the working set has WSQUOTA or more pages, the number of pages on the free page list is compared to the SYSGEN parameter GROWLIM.

If there are more than GROWLIM pages on the free page list, a new page is allowed in the working set. The empty WSLE is used.

Note that to extend the working set size above WSQUOTA, the working set limit must have been extended above WSQUOTA. For the working set limit to be extended above WSQUOTA, the free page list must contain more than the SYSGEN parameter BORROWLIM pages. For more information on working set limits, BORROWLIM, and automatic working set limit adjustment, see Section 17.4.

If an empty but unusable WSLE is found at the end of the working set list, the working set list capacity is reduced; PHD$L_WSLAST is reset to point to the last unavailable (nonzero) WSLE in the working set list.

17.3.3   Releasing a Dead Page Table Page

MMG$FREWSLE invokes SCANDEADPT, in module PAGEFAULT, to determine whether a WSLE describing a page table page can be reused to describe a page being faulted into the working set list. There are several possible outcomes:

- The WSLE describes a page table page that maps valid pages and is therefore not reusable.
- The WSLE describes a page table page that maps transition pages and can be released from its current use for reuse after the ties beween the transition pages and the page table page are severed, that is, after no virtual pages mapped by the page table page are cached in the free or modified page list.
- The WSLE describes such a reusable page table page, but the working set list contains enough dynamic entries that this one need not be released now. An attempt is made to leave a page table page in the working set list to keep its virtual pages cached on page lists, in case the process refaults them.

SCANDEADPT first determines whether the process has any dead page table pages. A dead page table page is one that maps no valid pages. It may, however, map pages on the free or modified page list. SCANDEADPT checks this by comparing PHD$W_PTCNTVAL, the number of page table pages with valid WSLEs, to PHD$W_PTCNTACT, the number of active page table pages. If PHD$W_PTCNTACT is larger than PHD$W_PTCNTVAL, the difference between them is the number of dead page table pages. If there are none, SCANDEADPT returns immediately. MMG$FREWSLE skips this WSLE and continues its scan of the working set list.

If there are any dead page table pages, SCANDEADPT checks how full the working set list is. It checks whether the dynamic region of the working set list has at least twice MINWSCNT entries, not counting those that describe dead page table pages or page table pages that map pages locked in memory or in the working set list. If so, it has sufficient dynamic entries; the dead page table page scan is postponed, and SCANDEADPT returns. MMG$FREWSLE skips this WSLE and continues its scan of the working set list.

SCANDEADPT checks whether this page is a dead page table page by testing its element in the PHD$L_PTWSLEVAL array. If the element is nonzero, the page table page maps pages in the working set list and cannot be released. SCANDEADPT returns, and MMG$FREWSLE goes on to the next WSLE.

Having determined that the WSLE describes a dead page table page, SCAN-DEADPT must scan each PTE within the page table page to determine whether any are transition PTEs. If the page table page contains transition PTEs for pages on the free page list, SCANDEADPT must modify the PFN database for those pages before the WSLE can be reused. If the page table page contains transition PTEs for pages on the modified page list, those pages must be written to their backing store before the page table page can be released from the working set list.

SCANDEADPT reinserts such pages at the beginning of the modified page list and requests a selective purge of the modified page list so that those pages will be written. SCANDEADPT returns to the invoker of MMG$FREWSLE. The process is placed into a resource wait for RSN$_MPWBUSY until the modified page list is selectively purged. Chapter 16 describes the selective purge mechanism; Chapter 18 the resource wait.

17.3.4 Skipping WSLEs

The working set replacement routine is not strictly FIFO. It uses the special SYSGEN parameter TBSKIPWSL to permit recently referenced pages to remain in the working set. This allows the operating system to modify its strict FIFO page replacement algorithm with some frequency of use information maintained by the hardware on most types of VAX processor.

The modified algorithm works in the following manner. Before a valid WSLE is reused, a check is made to see if the virtual page described by that WSLE is in the translation buffer (TB). If the PTE for that page is cached in the TB, the search for an available WSLE starts again with the next WSLE. If the PTE for that page is not cached in the TB, the WSLE is selected for reuse.

After TBSKIPWSL WSLEs have been skipped in this manner, the translation buffer checks are abandoned and the next valid WSLE is simply reused. If the value of TBSKIPWSL is set to zero, the mechanism is disabled and no entries are checked in the translation buffer. The default value of TBSKIP-WSL is 8.

17.3.5 Reusing WSLEs

The virtual page that the WSLE represents must be removed before the WSLE can be reused. Typically, the virtual page is valid and must be made invalid.

This section confines itself to a description of valid WSLEs that map process and global pages. For such pages, MMG$FREWSLE takes the following steps:

1. If the page has been modified, MMG$FREWSLE tests how full the modified page list is.

    —If it has fewer pages on it than the SYSGEN parameter MPW_WAIT-LIMIT, or if modified page writing is in progress and the list has fewer pages than the SYSGEN parameter MPW_LOWAITLIMIT, MMG$FRE-WSLE proceeds with step 2.

    —Otherwise, MMG$FREWSLE, to avoid deadlocks, checks that the process does not hold any mutexes, that the process is not the swapper, and that at least one page file has been installed. If any is false, MMG$FREWSLE proceeds with step 2.

    If all are true, it returns a status to the page fault handler indicating that the process should be placed into the resource wait RSN$_MPWBUSY until the modified page list has dropped below MPW_LOWAITLIMIT pages.

2. At alternative entry point MMG$FREWSLX, the routine saves the modify bit from the associated PTE in the PFN STATE array element. It clears the valid and modify bits in the PTE and invalidates any cached copy of the PTE in the translation buffer.

3. If the page has been modified and has assigned page file backing store, MMG$FREWSLX releases its backing store, which has a now-obsolete copy of the page. The PFN BAK array element is reset to a process-local page file index and a block number of zero.

4. If the page is a global page, MMG$FREWSLX changes the PTE to the global page table index form. It invokes MMG$DECPTREF, in module PAGEFAULT, to update the data structures describing the process page table page that maps the page.

    MMG$DECPTREF decrements the PFN SHRCNT array element for the page table page to indicate that it maps one less valid page. If this is the last valid or transition page mapped by the page table page (that is, if the SHRCNT makes the transition from 1 to 0), MMG$DECPTREF locates the WSLE for the page table page and clears its WSL$V_WSLOCK bit. It also decrements PHD$W_PTCNTACT, the number of active page table pages for the process, and the PHD's entry in the array at PHV$GL_REFCBAS, the number of reasons the PHD should remain in memory.

    MMG$FREWSLX decrements the PFN SHRCNT array element for the global page to indicate one less process is mapping it. If the count is still nonzero, MMG$FREWSLX proceeds with step 6. If the count goes to zero, it clears the valid and modify bits in the GPTE.

5. For a page that is a process page or a global page with a zero SHRCNT, MMG$FREWSLX decrements the PFN REFCNT array element for the page to indicate one less reference to it. If the reference count goes to

zero, MMG$FREWSLX inserts the page at the end of the free or modified page list, depending on the state of its saved modify bit. If the reference count is nonzero, indicating possible direct or paging I/O in progress, it examines the PFN STATE array element and, if the page is not active, changes its state to release pending.

6. MMG$FREWSLX invokes MMG$DELWSLEX, in module PAGEFAULT.

MMG$DELWSLEX decrements the appropriate element in the PHD$L_PTWSLEVAL array to indicate the page table page that mapped this page maps one less valid page. If that count goes to zero, it also decrements PHD$L_PTCNTVAL to indicate one less page table page mapping valid pages. It decrements either PCB$L_PPGCNT or PCB$L_GPGCNT, depending on page type. It clears the WSLE and returns.

17.4 WORKING SET LIMIT ADJUSTMENT

A process's working set limit (see Table 17.2) varies over its lifetime as a result of events such as image execution and exit, dynamic working set limit adjustment, and swapper trimming.

The working set limit can be altered with the $ADJWSL system service. A process can request the service implicitly, through the DCL command SET WORKING_SET, or explicitly. The service can also be requested automatically on behalf of the process, for example, as part of the quantum-end routine.

Directly requested, the system service can alter the working set limit up to WSEXTENT. The service is indirectly requested by automatic working set limit adjustment. Through this means, the maximum size to which the working set limit can grow is WSQUOTA, unless there are sufficient pages on the free page list (more than the SYSGEN parameter BORROWLIM). In that case, automatic working set limit adjustment can enlarge the limit up to WSEXTENT.

Once the working set limit is increased, if there are more than the SYSGEN parameter GROWLIM pages on the free page list, the executive allows the process to use the extended limit by adding more pages to its working set without removing already valid entries. Adding pages to a process's working set decreases the probability that the process will incur a page fault.

Section 17.4.3 describes the automatic mechanism for working set limit adjustment.

17.4.1 $ADJWSL System Service

The $ADJWSL system service is requested to alter the process's working set limit. Its procedure, EXE$ADJWSL, in module SYSADJWSL, runs in kernel mode, at interrupt priority level (IPL) 2 and above. There are two different paths in the procedure, one to increase the limit and the other to reduce it.

To increase the limit, EXE$ADJWSL first checks and possibly reduces the size of the increase. The new limit must be less than or equal to the SYSGEN parameter WSMAX, less than or equal to the process's extended maximum working set limit, and within the system's physical memory capacity.

If the new working set limit is within the current capacity of the working set list, EXE$ADJWSL computes a new value for PHD$L_EXTDYNWS and returns. Otherwise, EXE$ADJWSL first invokes MMG$ALCPHD, in module PHDUTL, to increase the working set list capacity.

MMG$ALCPHD tests whether there is a gap between the high-address end of the working set list and the low-address end of the PST that is large enough for the working set list expansion. If not, it tries to compress enough unused entries from the low-address end of the PST to accommodate the expansion. If that also fails, MMG$ALCPHD tries to shift the PST to higher addresses by moving it to as yet unused pages of the PHD. As previously described, the PHD cannot be expanded in this manner if the number of pages in the nonpageable part of the current PHD is half the size of the process's WSQUOTA. If the PHD cannot be expanded, the error status SS$_SECTBFUL is returned to EXE$ADJWSL.

If expanded working set list pages are created, they must be locked into the working set list. It is possible that locking all the expansion pages at once would leave insufficient extra dynamic entries in the existing working set list. However, if the working set list were partially expanded, the number of dynamic entries would increase, allowing more expansion pages to be locked. Thus, expanding the working set limit may require multiple iterations.

EXE$ADJWSL changes PHD$L_WSNEXT to point to the first of the newly added WSLEs and initializes them. It adds the number of new WSLEs to both PHD$L_WSLAST and PHD$L_WSSIZE. It recalculates PHD$L_EXTDYNWS and returns to its requestor.

To decrease the limit, EXE$ADJWSL first acquires the MMG spinlock, raising IPL to IPL$_MMG, to block swapper trimming and possible quantum-end and working set adjustment. It invokes MMG$SHRINKWS, in module SYSADJWSL.

MMG$SHRINKWS checks and possibly reduces the size of the decrease. The new limit must allow for at least the SYSGEN parameter MINWSCNT WSLEs in the dynamic portion of the working set list. In addition, PHD$L_EXTDYNWS cannot be reduced below zero.

MMG$SHRINKWS modifies the working set limit. If the process's working set size is already less than or equal to the new limit, it simply returns to EXE$ADJWSL. Otherwise, MMG$SHRINKWS repeatedly invokes MMG$FREWSLE (see Section 17.3.1), in module PAGEFAULT, for each page to be removed from the process's working set. The reduced list can be sparse, that is, can contain unused and unusable WSLEs; the working set capacity is not necessarily decreased with the working set limit. Control returns to EXE$ADJWSL.

EXE$ADJWSL releases the spinlock, recalculates PHD$L_EXTDYNWS, and returns.

17.4.2 SET WORKING_SET Command

The DCL command SET WORKING_SET enables the user to alter the default working set limit (DFWSCNT), the normal maximum working set limit (WSQUOTA), or the extended maximum working set limit (WSEXTENT). None of them can be set to a value larger than the authorized extended maximum working set limit (WSAUTHEXT).

Altering the normal maximum working set limit affects the maximum working set limit when physical memory is not plentiful. It changes the upper limit for future $ADJWSL system service requests. Altering the default limit affects the working set list reset operation performed by the routine MMG$IMGRESET, in module PHDUTL, which is invoked at image exit.

With the /[NO]ADJUST qualifier to this command, a user can also disable or reenable automatic working set limit adjustment. Use of that qualifier sets or clears the process control block (PCB) status longword bit PCB$V_DISAWS.

17.4.3 Automatic Working Set Limit Adjustment

In addition to adjusting working set limit through an explicit $ADJWSL request or as a side effect of image exit, VMS also provides automatic working set limit adjustment to keep a process's page fault rate within limits set by one of several SYSGEN parameters. Note that no such adjustment takes place for real-time processes or for a process that has disabled automatic working set limit adjustment through the DCL command SET WORKING_SET/NOADJUST. New with VMS Version 5 is the provision that the executive can also use automatic working set limit adjustment to reclaim an extension to the working set of a low-priority process.

Table 17.3 shows the parameters that control automatic working set limit adjustment. All the SYSGEN parameters listed in this table are dynamic and can be altered without rebooting the system.

The automatic working set limit adjustment takes place as part of the quantum-end routine (see Chapter 12).

The quantum-end routine, SCH$QEND in module RSE, adjusts the working set limit in several steps:

1. SCH$QEND makes the following checks. If any of these conditions is true, it performs no adjustment.

   —If the WSINC parameter is set to zero, the adjustment is disabled on a systemwide basis.

   —If the user has entered the DCL command SET WORKING_SET/NO-ADJUST, PCB$V_DISAWS is set and automatic working set limit adjustment for the process has been disabled.

Table 17.3   Process and System Parameters Used by Automatic Working Set Limit Adjustment

Description	Location or Name	Comments
Total amount of CPU time charged to this process	PHD$L_CPUTIM	Updated by interval timer interrupt service routine
Amount of CPU time at last adjustment check	PHD$L_TIMREF	Updated by quantum-end routine when adjustment check is made; Altered when process is placed into a wait
Total number of page faults for this process	PHD$L_PAGEFLTS	Updated each time this process incurs a page fault
Number of page faults at last adjustment check	PHD$L_PFLREF	Updated by quantum-end routine when adjustment check is made
Most recent page fault rate for this process	PHD$L_PFLTRATE	Recorded at each adjustment check; Compared to PFRATH, PFRATL
Process automatic working set limit adjustment flag	PCB$V_DISAWS in PCB$L_STS	When set, disables adjustment for process
Amount of CPU time process must accumulate before page fault rate check is made	AWSTIME [1]	
Lower limit page fault rate	PFRATL [1]	When 0, disables adjustment based on page fault rate for entire system
Amount by which to decrease working set limit	WSDEC [1]	Also, amount to reclaim from low-priority process with extended working set
Lower bound for decreasing working set list size	AWSMIN [1]	Do not adjust if PCB$W_PPGCNT is less than or equal to this
Upper limit page fault rate	PFRATH [1]	
Amount by which to increase working set limit	WSINC [1]	When 0, disables adjustment for entire system
Free page list size that allows growth of working set	GROWLIM [1]	Do not add new page to working set if @SCH$GL_FREECNT is less than or equal to this value
Free page list size that allows extension of working set limit	BORROWLIM [1]	Do not extend working set limit beyond WSQUOTA if @SCH$GL_FREECNT is less than or equal to this value; When −1, disables working set limit extension for entire system

[1] This value is a SYSGEN parameter.

—If PHD$V_NO_WS_CHNG is set, the executive has temporarily blocked changes to the working set list of this process.

2. If the process has not been executing long enough since the last adjustment (if the difference between PHD$L_CPUTIM, the accumulated CPU

time, and PHD$L_TIMREF, the time of the last adjustment attempt, is less than the SYSGEN parameter AWSTIME), no adjustment based on page fault rate is done. SCH$QEND proceeds with step 5.

If the process has accumulated enough CPU time, the reference time is updated (PHD$L_CPUTIM is copied to PHD$L_TIMREF), and the rate checks are made.

Between adjustment checks, PHD$L_TIMREF is also altered when the process is placed in a wait. As described in Chapter 12, when a process goes into a wait, the SYSGEN parameter IOTA is charged against its quantum. To balance the quantum charge, IOTA is subtracted from PHD$L_TIMREF, so that the last check for adjustment appears to have taken place longer ago than it really did and AWSTIME is more quickly reached. This subtraction helps ensure the expansion of the working set limit of a process that is faulting heavily. Without it, a process that undergoes many page fault waits could reach quantum end without having accumulated AWSTIME worth of CPU time and thus not be considered for automatic working set limit adjustment.

3. SCH$QEND calculates the current page fault rate. The philosophy for automatic working set limit adjustment is based on two premises. If the page fault rate is low enough, the system can reclaim physical memory from the process, by reducing its working set limit, without harming the process by causing it to fault heavily. If the page fault rate is too high, the process can benefit from a larger working set limit because it will incur fewer faults without degrading the system.

4. If the current page fault rate is too high (greater than or equal to PFRATH), SCH$QEND checks whether the working set limit should be increased.

   —If the working set size is less than 75 percent of the working set limit, the working set limit is not expanded.

   —If the working set limit is below WSQUOTA, it is expanded by WSINC.

   —If the working set limit is greater than or equal to WSQUOTA, the number of pages on the free page list is compared to the SYSGEN parameter BORROWLIM. If there are more than BORROWLIM pages on the free page list, the working set limit is increased by WSINC. If there are fewer than BORROWLIM pages on the free page list, the working set limit is not increased. The working set limit can only be expanded up to WSEXTENT. Setting BORROWLIM to −1 disables working set limit expansion above WSQUOTA for the entire system.

   Once the working set limit has been expanded, newly faulted pages may be added to the working set. The page fault handler adds pages to the working set above WSQUOTA only when there are more than the SYSGEN parameter GROWLIM pages on the free page list (see Section 17.4). SCH$QEND proceeds with step 6.

5. If WSDEC is zero, shrinking the working set by automatic working set

limit adjustment is disabled and no adjustment occurs. If WSDEC is nonzero, two types of decrease to the working set limit are possible. First, if the current page fault rate is low enough (less than PFRATL), the working set limit is shrunk by WSDEC. However, if the contents of PCB$L_PPGCNT are less than or equal to AWSMIN, no adjustment takes place. This decision is based on the assumption that many of the pages in the working set are global pages and therefore the system will not benefit (and the process may suffer) if the working set limit is decreased.

Note that PFRATL is zero by default. This default value effectively disables this method of working set limit reduction in favor of swapper working set trimming. The rationale for this change is explained at the end of this list.

Alternatively, even if a meaningful interval has not elapsed for computing a page fault rate, the process's working set limit will be shrunk, whatever its page fault rate and whatever the value of PFRATL, if all the following are true:

—The process has had a pixscan priority boost in its last 32 execution quantums (PCB$L_PIXHIST is nonzero). Chapter 12 describes the pixscan mechanism.
—The free page list contains fewer than GROWLIM pages.
—The process's working set limit is larger than WSQUOTA.

Its working set limit will be decreased by the smaller of WSDEC and the amount by which its working set limit exceeds WSQUOTA. This mechanism reclaims working set growth beyond WSQUOTA, which is regarded as temporary growth to be permitted only when sufficient memory is available.

6. The actual working set limit adjustment is accomplished by a kernel mode AST that requests the $ADJWSL system service. The AST parameter passed to this AST is the amount of previously determined increase or decrease. This step is required because the system service must be called from process context (at IPL 0) and SCH$QEND is executing in system context in response to the IPL$_TIMERFORK software timer interrupt.

Three other pieces of the executive affect the size of a process's working set: the page fault handler, the swapper, and the image reset routine, MMG$IMGRESET, in module PHDUTL. As described previously, the page fault handler can add a page to a process's working set when it is already above WSQUOTA only if the size of the free page list is greater than GROWLIM. In an effort to acquire needed physical memory, the swapper reduces the working sets of processes in the balance set before actually removing processes from the balance set. This working set reduction is known as swapper trimming or working set shrinking. Process selection is performed by a table-driven, prioritized scheme (see Chapter 18). The working set limit is reset to its default value, DFWSCNT, when image exit processing invokes MMG$IMGRESET.

Two problems are inherent in using the quantum-end scheme of automatic working set limit adjustment: processes that are compute-intensive will reach quantum end many times, and images that have been written to be efficient with respect to page faults (and incur a low page fault rate) will qualify for working set limit reduction, because their page fault rate is lower than PFRATL. In both these cases, working set limit reduction is not desirable. In contrast, swapper trimming selects processes starting with those that are less likely to need large working sets.

In what can be seen as an evolutionary change to the operating system, working set limit reduction based on page fault rate at quantum end was disabled by default in Version 3.1 of the VMS software by setting the default value of PFRATL to zero. Swapper trimming and the image exit reset became the primary methods used to reduce working set limit.

VMS Version 5 also uses automatic working set adjustment at quantum end to reclaim extensions from the working sets of low-priority processes.

17.5 $LKWSET SYSTEM SERVICE

A process requests the $LKWSET system service to lock a virtual page into its process working set and thus prevent page faults from occurring on references to the page. Locking a page into the working set guarantees that when the process is current, the locked page is always valid. This service has obvious benefit for time-critical applications and other situations in which a program must access code or data without incurring a page fault.

The $LKWSET system service is also requested by process-based kernel mode routines that execute at IPLs above 2, to ensure the validity of code and data pages. VMS prohibits page faults at IPLs above 2; if one occurs, the page fault handler generates the fatal bugcheck PGFIPLHI.

Pages locked into a process working set do not necessarily remain resident in physical memory when the process is not current; the entire working set might be outswapped. To guarantee residency of the pages, a process must request either the $LCKPAG system service or both the $LKWSET and the Set Swap Mode ($SETSWM) system services.

The $LKWSET system service procedure, EXE$LKWSET in module SYS-LKWSET, executes in kernel mode. It takes the following steps:

1. It creates and initializes scratch space on the stack and raises IPL to 2.
2. It sets the bit PHD$V_NO_WS_CHNG in PHD$W_FLAGS to block swapper trimming of the working set and automatic working set limit adjustment (see Section 17.9).
3. If necessary and possible, it increases the working set limit to have sufficient extra dynamic entries to accommodate the pages to be locked and a page table page for each such page.

If the process has disabled working set limit adjustment, or if its working set limit is already larger than its quota, no increase is possible. As a result, MMG$LCKULKPAG may be able to lock only a limited number of pages.

4. EXE$LKWSET invokes MMG$CREDEL, in module SYSCREDEL, specifying MMG$LCKULKPAG, in module SYSLKWSET, as the per-page service-specific routine. Chapter 15 describes the memory management stack scratch space, the actions of MMG$CREDEL, and its invocation of the specified service-specific routine.

5. When MMG$CREDEL returns, EXE$LKWSET clears PHD$V_NO_WS_CHNG.

6. It restores the previous IPL and returns to its requestor with the status from MMG$CREDEL.

To lock a page into the working set, MMG$LCKULKPAG takes the following steps:

1. It tests whether the page is readable from the system service requestor's access mode. If the page is inaccessible, it returns the error status SS$_ACCVIO, which becomes the status returned by the system service.

2. It acquires the MMG spinlock, raising IPL to IPL$_MMG.

3. MMG$LCKULKPAG examines the PTE that maps the page. If the page is not valid, it releases the MMG spinlock, faults the page, and continues with step 2.

4. It compares the page owner access mode with the mode of the system service requestor. If the page is owned by a more privileged mode, the requestor is not allowed to alter its state, and MMG$LCKULKPAG releases the MMG spinlock and returns the error status SS$_PAGOWNVIO.

5. It tests whether the WINDOW bit is set in the PTE and, if so, immediately returns the success status SS$_WASSET. A virtual page whose PTE's WINDOW bit is set is always valid and is not described by a WSLE, so no further action is appropriate.

6. MMG$LCKULKPAG examines the PFN TYPE array element for the page to determine if the page type is process or read-only global. If neither, it releases the MMG spinlock and returns the error status SS$_NOPRIV; a process is not permitted to lock any other type of page into its working set. In particular, it may not lock global writable pages because when a process is outswapped, the swapper must be able to remove global writable pages from the working set. The removal avoids any ambiguity at inswap concerning the location of the most recent copy of a global writable page.

7. MMG$LCKULKPAG gets the working set list index (WSLX) for a process page from its PFN WSLX array element. WSLX information is not kept for a global page; instead, MMG$LCKULKPAG must scan the process's working set list to locate the entry for the page. In the case of a resident

global section, MMG$LCKULKPAG returns immediately with the success status SS$_WASSET; pages from a resident global section are already permanently resident and valid.

8. MMG$LCKULKPAG examines the WSLE. If the page is already locked in the working set, the routine releases the MMG spinlock and returns the success status SS$_WASSET.

9. Otherwise, it checks that PHD$L_EXTDYNWS is at least 2 (to allow for the page table page as well as the page being locked). This ensures that the process will have enough dynamic WSLEs after the page is locked into its working set. If not, it releases the MMG spinlock and returns the error status SS$_LKWSETFUL.

10. It sets the WSL$V_WSLOCK bit in the WSLE of the newly locked page.

11. It must reorganize the working set list, pictured in Figure 17.2, so that the locked page is in the user-locked region of the working set list, following the PHD$L_WSLOCK pointer. MMG$LCKULKPAG accomplishes this reorganization by exchanging the newly locked WSLE with the entry pointed to by PHD$L_WSDYN and incrementing PHD$L_WSDYN to point to the next entry in the list. If PHD$L_WSDYN pointed to a valid WSLE, it exchanges the PFN WSLX array elements for the two valid pages; otherwise, it updates the PFN WSLX array element for the newly locked page.

12. MMG$LCKULKPAG increments the PHD$L_PTWSLELCK array element corresponding to the page table page mapping the locked page. If the count was zero, it also increments PHD$W_PTCNTLCK, the number of page table pages mapping locked WSLEs.

13. It checks that PHD$L_WSNEXT is still pointing into the dynamic part of the working set list (and not at the former PHD$L_WSDYN, which is now in the user-locked region), moving it if necessary to point to the same WSLE as PHD$L_WSLAST.

14. It recalculates PHD$L_EXTDYNWS.

15. It releases the MMG spinlock and returns to MMG$CREDEL.

17.6   **$LCKPAG SYSTEM SERVICE**

The $LCKPAG system service procedure, EXE$LCKPAG in module SYSLK-WSET, is similar to that of the $LKWSET system service. However, the $LCKPAG service guarantees permanent residency for the specified virtual address range, in addition to performing an implicit working set lock of those pages. Because this operation permanently allocates a system resource, physical memory, it requires the privilege PSWAPM.

Executing in kernel mode, EXE$LCKPAG tests whether the process has the privilege PSWAPM and, if not, returns the error status SS$_NOPRIV. It raises IPL to 2, sets the PHD$V_NO_WS_CHNG flag, and increases the working set limit as necessary and possible. It invokes MMG$CREDEL, specifying

MMG$LCKULKPAG as the per-page service-specific routine. MMG$LCK-ULKPAG is invoked with a flag that specifies the page is to be locked in memory rather than in the working set.

Although the results of invoking the two lock services are similar, the following differences exist:

- The WSLE of a page locked in memory has the WSL$V_PFNLOCK bit set, rather than the WSL$V_WSLOCK bit.
- A PHD mapping a page locked in memory must be locked in memory itself to ensure residency of the page table page mapping the locked page.
- A global writable page can be locked in memory, although it cannot be explicitly locked in the working set.

17.7 $ULWSET AND $ULKPAG SYSTEM SERVICES

These system services unlock pages from either the working set or physical memory. The two system service procedures are EXE$ULWSET and EXE$ULKPAG, both in SYSLKWSET. Both, executing in kernel mode, invoke MMG$CREDEL with MMG$LCKULKPAG as the per-page service-specific routine. Both execute at IPL 0; working set trimming and adjustment do not interfere with unlocking pages.

MMG$LCKULKPAG is invoked with one flag that specifies the operation is an unlock and a second flag that specifies whether the page is to be unlocked from the working set or from memory. It takes the following steps to unlock each page:

1. Its first steps are identical to steps 1 through 7 described for MMG$LCK-ULKPAG in Section 17.5.
2. MMG$LCKULKPAG examines the WSLE. If the page is not locked in the working set, the routine releases the MMG spinlock and returns the success status SS$_WASCLR.
3. Otherwise, depending on the operation requested, it clears the appropriate WSLE bit (WSL$V_WSLOCK or WSL$V_PFNLOCK).
4. If one of the lock bits is still set, it goes on to step 6. Otherwise, it decrements PHD$L_WSDYN and swaps the WSLE of the page being unlocked with the one pointed to by PHD$L_WSDYN, thus making the unlocked WSLE the first one in the dynamic region. If PHD$L_WSDYN pointed to a valid WSLE, it exchanges the PFN WSLX array elements for the two valid pages; otherwise, it updates the PFN WSLX array element for the newly unlocked page. MMG$LCKULKPAG decrements the PHD$L_PTWSLELCK array element corresponding to the page table page mapping the locked page. If the count goes to zero, it also decrements PHD$W_PTCNTLCK, the number of page table pages mapping locked WSLEs.
5. It recalculates PHD$L_EXTDYNWS.
6. It releases the MMG spinlock and returns to MMG$CREDEL.

17.8 $PURGWS SYSTEM SERVICE

A process requests the $PURGWS system service to remove all virtual pages in a specified address range from its working set. A process might request this service if a certain set of routines or data were no longer required. By voluntarily removing entries from the working set, a process can exercise some control over the working set list replacement algorithm, increasing the chances for frequently used pages to remain in the working set.

The VMS executive uses this service as part of the image startup sequence (see Chapter 26) to ensure that a program starts its execution without unnecessary pages such as command language interpreter command processing routines in its working set.

The $PURGWS system service procedure, EXE$PURGWS in module SYS-PURGWS, runs in kernel mode. It takes the following steps:

1. It creates and initializes the stack scratch space and raises IPL to 2.
2. It invokes MMG$CREDEL, specifying MMG$PURGWSPAG, in module SYSPURGWS, as the per-page service-specific routine.
3. EXE$PURGWS returns the status from MMG$CREDEL to its requestor.

MMG$PURGWSPAG immediately invokes MMG$PURGWSSCN, in module SYSPURGWS, which takes the following steps:

1. It acquires the MMG spinlock, raising IPL to IPL$_MMG.
2. It scans the dynamic region of the working set list, examining each WSLE.

    —If the WSLE is not valid, is locked in the working set, or is that of a page table page, or if the address of the associated virtual page does not fall within the boundaries specified by the system service requestor, MMG$PURGWSSCN goes on to the next entry.
    —Otherwise, MMG$PURGWSSCN invokes MMG$FREWSLX, described in Section 17.3.5, to take whatever steps are necessary to release the WSLE and change the state of the page.

3. When MMG$PURGWSSCN reaches the end of the dynamic region, it releases the MMG spinlock, restoring the entry IPL, and returns.

17.9   KEEPING A PAGE IN THE WORKING SET LIST

Occasionally a page must be faulted into the working set list and remain there. The issue may be one of improved or more predictable performance for an application. However, code executing in kernel mode has a different concern. Because a page fault from IPL 3 or above results in a PGFIPLHI fatal bugcheck, a code thread executing at elevated IPL must ensure the residency of all code and data pages it accesses. This section describes issues related to the residency of pages in the process working set lists and then to the system working set list. Its focus is on pages that are not page table pages.

A number of things can lead to replacement paging and the removal of pages from a process's working set list:

- Execution in the process's context of a code thread of any access mode that incurs page faults, whether mainline code, procedure in a shareable image, inner access mode service (Record Management Services, system, or command language interpreter callback), AST thread, or condition handler
- Execution of a code thread that directly locks an invalid page into memory or the working set list or indirectly locks buffer pages by requesting direct I/O operations
- Quantum-end automatic working set limit adjustment of a current process
- Swapper trimming of a noncurrent process

For a process to fault a page into its working set list and have it remain there, it must either ensure that the page is not a candidate for replacement paging or prevent all the items previously listed that lead to replacement paging.

The most straightforward measure, available to any access mode, is to lock the page with the $LKWSET system service. As a result, the page's WSLE is placed in the user-locked region of the working set list and is not a candidate for replacement paging. The page remains in the working set list regardless of the process's scheduling state and throughout any outswap and inswap. The only page type for which this mechanism fails is a global writable page. VMS prohibits locking global writable pages into the working set list to avoid ambiguity at inswap concerning the location of the most recent version of the page. To ensure the residency of a global writable page, a process must lock the page into memory.

Locking many pages into the working set list is not always possible. To minimize page faults once the desired pages are in the working set, a process can do the following:

- Prevent swapper trimming by entering the DCL command SET WORK-ING_SET/QUOTA=*authquota* and /EXTENT=*authquota*, where *authquota* is the authorized normal maximum working set limit. This prevents first-level swapper trimming by ensuring that the working set limit is not above the authorized maximum limit.
- Disable automatic working set limit adjustment and second-level swapper trimming by entering the DCL command SET WORKING_SET/NO-ADJUST.
- Execute a constrained sequence of already resident code that touches already resident data. This is likely to require blocking AST delivery, causing no exceptions, signaling no conditions, and calling no procedures outside the address space already resident.

For kernel mode code, typically, the issue is one of preventing any page fault during elevated IPL execution rather than one of performance. Kernel mode code, whether running as part of an image or as part of the executive, may be able to request the $LKWSET system service but is unable to alter the process's working set quotas and limits through the DCL command. Other measures available to it include

- "Poor man's lockdown" for pages in a process working set list and continued execution at elevated IPL to block AST delivery and remain current
- The LOCK_SYSTEM_PAGES and UNLOCK_SYSTEM_PAGES macros for system working set list pages

"Poor man's lockdown" is an instruction that both faults one or more pages into the working set and raises IPL, for example:

```
        ASSUME NEWIPL - . LE 511      ;Check that instruction and target
                                      ; IPL are on the same or
                                      ; adjacent pages
        MTPR    NEWIPL,#PR$_IPL       ;Raise IPL to level in NEWIPL
        .
        .
; Code to be faulted into the working set
        .
        .
NEWIPL: .LONG 8
```

For the instruction to execute, the page or pages containing the instruction and NEWIPL must both be resident. The processor generates page faults if the instruction and pages it references are not resident, and VMS must page them in before the instruction can successfully execute. At the completion of the instruction, IPL is raised, after which no further page faulting is possible. Running at IPL 3 or above blocks the delivery of an AST that might cause unexpected instruction execution and potential page faults. It also blocks the delivery of the automatic working set limit adjustment AST and the rescheduling interrupt, thus also preventing swapper trimming.

This technique is not acceptable for system working set list pages, such as paged pool and pageable code or data in loadable executive images. The technique assumes that the only thread of execution that could run (and thus trigger replacement paging) is the one that has just executed the instruction sequence. This is not necessarily true; on a symmetric multiprocessing system, system working set list replacement paging could be triggered by code executing on any of the other processors. For kernel mode code that needs to fault pages into the system working set list and have them remain there, VMS provides the macros previously listed. Use of these macros is described in detail in the *VMS Device Support Manual*.

The LOCK_SYSTEM_PAGES macro generates code that invokes the routine MMG$LOCK_SYSTEM_PAGES, in module LOCK_SYSTEM_PAGES. For each page to be locked, it takes the following steps:

1. It faults the page.
2. It acquires the MMG spinlock.
3. It tests whether the page is still valid, and if not, it releases the spinlock and returns to step 1.
4. It increments the PFN SHRCNT array element for the physical page, gets the WSLX from the PFN WSLX array element, and sets the WSL$V_ WSLOCK bit in the WSLE in the system working set list.
5. It releases the MMG spinlock.

The routine returns to its invoker through a co-routine call. When the invoker no longer requires the residency of the pages, it invokes the macro UNLOCK_SYSTEM_PAGES. The code generated by the macro executes a co-routine return to the routine, which clears the WSL$V_WSLOCK bit and decrements the PFN SHRCNT array element for each page.

One other option available to kernel mode code involves the PHD$V_ NO_WS_CHNG bit. The general sequence is to raise IPL to 2, set the bit, and fault the page or pages into the working set list. Setting this bit blocks swapper trimming and automatic working set limit adjustment. The code must execute a constrained instruction sequence to ensure the continued residency of the page, since the working set list is still subject to replacement paging. The memory management subsystem and other parts of the VMS executive employ this option, setting the bit for relatively brief periods of time. Use of this bit is reserved to Digital; any other use is unsupported.

18   The Swapper

A time to cast away stones and a time to gather stones together . . .
Ecclesiastes 3:5

The amount of physical memory present on the system is not a hard limit to
the number of processes in the system. The VMS operating system effectively
extends physical memory by keeping a subset of active processes resident at
once. It maximizes the number of such processes by limiting the number
of pages that each process has in memory at any given time. Processes not
resident in memory reside on mass storage in swap files; that is, they are
outswapped.

The swapper process is the systemwide physical memory manager. Its
responsibilities include maintaining an adequate supply of physical memory
and ensuring that the highest priority computable processes are resident in
memory.

18.1   SWAPPER OVERVIEW

This section reviews some basic swapper concepts.

18.1.1   Swapper Responsibilities

The swapper has several main responsibilities. The first is to ensure that the
currently resident processes are the highest priority computable processes in
the system. When a nonresident process becomes computable, the swapper
must bring it back into memory if its priority and the available memory
allow.

The swapper maintains the number of pages on the free page list above
the threshold established by the SYSGEN parameter FREELIM. The free page
list is depleted by requests for physical pages for resolving page faults and
inswapping computable processes. The swapper performs four operations to
keep the free page list above FREELIM. These are described in more detail
in subsequent sections of this chapter.

1. The swapper deletes process headers (PHDs) of already deleted processes.
   It outswaps any PHDs of previously outswapped process bodies that are
   eligible for outswap.
2. It invokes the modified page writer subroutine to write modified pages.
3. It shrinks the working sets of one or more resident processes.
4. If necessary, the swapper selects an eligible process for outswap and
   removes that process from memory. The table that determines outswap
   selection also determines the order in which processes are selected for
   working set reduction.

The swapper stops reclaiming pages for the free page list when its size exceeds the SYSGEN parameter FREEGOAL.

The swapper ensures that there are fewer pages on the modified page list than the threshold established by the SYSGEN parameter MPW_HILIMIT. When the modified page list grows above this limit, the modified page writer writes pages to their backing store and moves them to the free page list.

18.1.2   System Events That Trigger Swapper Activity

The swapper spends its idle time hibernating. Those executive components that detect a need for swapper activity wake the swapper by invoking routine SCH$SWPWAKE, in module RSE. In addition, SCH$SWPWAKE is invoked once a second from system timer code. SCH$SWPWAKE performs a series of checks to determine whether there is a real need for the swapper to run. If so, it awakens the swapper. If not, it simply returns. Performing these checks in SCH$SWPWAKE, rather than in the swapper process itself, avoids the overhead of two needless context switches.

Table 18.1 lists the system events that trigger a possible need for swapper activity, the module containing the routine that detects each need, and the action the swapper takes in response.

The swapper can be awakened in another, more indirect way: clearing the cell that contains the modified page list high limit so that a subsequent test for whether the list size exceeds its high limit will fail. The routine MMG$PURGEMPL, in module WRTMFYPAG, uses this method. This routine, invoked to request the writing of modified pages, is described in Chapter 16.

18.1.3   Swapper Implementation

The swapper is implemented as a separate process with a priority of 16, the lowest real-time priority. It is selected for execution like any other process in the system.

The swapper executes entirely in kernel mode. All swapper code resides in system space. The swapper uses its P0 space only to swap processes. It has a small amount of P1 space as of VMS Version 5, namely a P1 pointer page. The major reason for this change was to eliminate a number of special-case checks in the executive for swapper process context.

The swapper serves as a convenient process context for several system functions. In particular, during system initialization it performs those initialization tasks that require process context and must be performed prior to the creation of any other process, for example, initializing paged pool and creating the SYSINIT process. Chapter 31 describes these functions of the swapper.

Table 18.1   Events That May Cause the Swapper to Be Awakened

System Event	Routine Name (Module)	Swapper Action
Process that is out-swapped becomes computable	SCH$CHSE (RSE)	The swapper attempts to make this process resident.
Quantum end	SCH$QEND (RSE)	The swapper may be able to perform an outswap previously blocked by initial quantum flag setting or process priority.
Modified page list exceeds upper limit	MMG$DALLOCPFN, MMG$INSPFNH/T (ALLOCPFN)	The swapper writes modified pages.
Free page list drops below low limit	MMG$REMPFN (ALLOCPFN)	The swapper increases the free page count, taking the steps summarized in Section 18.1.1.
Balance slot of deleted process becomes available	DELETE (SYSDELPRC)	The swapper can delete the PHD and may be able to perform a previously blocked inswap.
PHD reference count goes to zero	MMG$DECPHDREF (PAGEFAULT)	The swapper can outswap a PHD to join the previously outswapped process body.
Powerfail recovery	EXE$RESTART (POWERFAIL)	The swapper queues a power recovery AST to any process that requested one.
System timer subroutine executes once a second	EXE$TIMEOUT (TIMESCHDL)	The swapper is awakened if there is any work for it.

18.2   SWAPPER'S USE OF MEMORY MANAGEMENT DATA STRUCTURES

Chapter 14 describes the memory management data structures used by both the page fault handler and the swapper. The discussion here reviews those structures and adds descriptions of the structures used exclusively by the swapper.

18.2.1   Process Header

Most of the information used by the swapper in managing the details of inswapping or outswapping is contained in the PHD of the process to be swapped. The process page tables contain a complete description of the address space for a given process.

The working set list describes those page table entries (PTEs) that are valid. This list is crucial for the swapper because only the working set is written to the process's swap space when the process is outswapped. In a similar fashion, when a process is inswapped, the working set list in the process's PHD describes the process pages in the swap file.

18.2.1.1   **Working Set List.** The working set list describes the portion of a process virtual address space that must be written to the swap file or otherwise dealt with when the process is outswapped; the working set list is trimmed to a maximum of WSQUOTA pages before outswap. A page in the process working set can be in one of the following three states:

- The page is valid.
- The page is currently being read into memory. The swapper treats page reads like any other I/O in progress when swapping a process.
- The process PTE contains a global page table index (GPTX), and the indexed global page table entry (GPTE) indicates a transition state. The swapper handles global pages in a special manner when outswapping a process.

The swapper's scan of the process working set list at outswap is discussed in Section 18.5.

18.2.1.2   **Process Page Tables.** The working set list does not supply the swapper with all the information necessary to outswap a process. Other information about a virtual page is contained in its PTE or in one of the page frame number (PFN) array elements associated with the physical page. Each working set list entry (WSLE) effectively points to a PTE that contains a PFN. When outswapping, the swapper copies the PTE to the swapper's I/O map (see Section 18.2.2). It then inserts the contents of the PFN BAK array element for this physical page in the PTE, disassociating it from the physical memory that its virtual page occupied.

18.2.1.3   **Process Header Page Arrays.** PHD pages are also part of the process working set. These pages reside in system space; their system page table entries (SPTEs) map the balance set slot in which the PHD resides. As part of outswapping, the swapper disassociates the PHD pages from their SPTEs so that it can reuse the balance set slot. Thus, unlike process pages, PHD pages' PTEs are not available to hold these pages' backing store addresses while they are outswapped.

Instead, when a process is outswapped, the contents of the PFN BAK array element for each PHD page currently in the working set is stored in the corresponding array element in the PHD page BAK array (see Figure 14.10). When the process is inswapped, the PHD page arrays can be scanned and the BAK contents copied from the array back into the PFN BAK array elements for the physical pages that contain the PHD.

The swapper also records where each PHD page fits into the working set list. It stores the PFN WSLX array element in the corresponding PHD page

WSLX array element. The use of this array while the PHD is being rebuilt following inswap prevents a prohibitively long search of the working set list for each PHD page.

18.2.2 Swapper I/O Data Structures

Like the page fault handler, the swapper uses the conventional VMS I/O subsystem. It allocates its own I/O request packet and fills in some of the fields that will be interpreted in a special manner by the I/O postprocessing routine. After these fields have been filled in, it jumps to one of the swapper I/O entry points in module SYSQIOREQ (EXE$BLDPKTSWPR or EXE$BLD-PKTSWPW) that fills in an appropriate function code and queues the packet to the appropriate disk driver. Tables 16.1 and 16.2 show how the I/O request packet is used by the swapper for its I/O activities.

The swapper uses a private I/O map that allows it to read or write a process working set, a collection of virtually noncontiguous pages, in one or more I/O requests. The swapper I/O map is an array of WSMAX longwords whose address is stored in the global cell SWP$GL_MAP. It can describe one outswap or one inswap operation at a time.

Certain swapper operations complete asynchronously. The swapper maintains two bits in the cell SCH$GB_SIP as signals of ongoing operation: when set, SCH$V_SIP means that an inswap or outswap is in progress and described by the swapper I/O map; when set, SCH$V_MPW means that modified page writes are in progress.

At outswap, the PFN of each page to be written to a swap file is stored in an array element of the swapper I/O map. The address of this array is passed to the I/O system as the system virtual address of the PTE that maps the first page of the I/O buffer. At inswap, the swapper allocates physical pages of memory for the process working set and records their PFNs in the I/O map. The swap image is read into these pages. As the swapper rebuilds the process's working set list and page tables, it copies the PFN from each entry of its I/O map to the appropriate system or process PTE.

18.2.3 Swap File Data Structures

The system maintains a page file control block for each page and swap file in the system. Figure 14.24 shows the layout of this data structure and describes its fields. Both page and swap files can be used for swapping.

During system initialization, the SYSINIT process opens the primary swap file SYS$SPECIFIC:[SYSEXE]SWAPFILE.SYS, if it exists, and initializes its page file control block. When any additional swap file is installed (with the SYSGEN command INSTALL), SYSGEN initializes its page file control block.

In earlier versions of VMS, when a process was created, space for its working set was assigned in the first swap file with enough free space. When the process's working set grew too large for the swap space, a replacement swap slot was allocated. VMS required that there be a swap slot large enough to outswap the process at its current size, up to the maximum of its authorized quota. When the working set limit was adjusted at image reset, a smaller swap slot was allocated. Each swap slot consisted of virtually contiguous blocks within a single swap file.

In VMS Version 5, swap space allocation has changed considerably, reflecting the fact that processes are outswapped relatively infrequently and that they are typically outswapped with shrunken working sets. Now swap space is not assigned until a process has been selected for outswap, subsequent to any swapper trimming. VMS attempts to allocate virtually contiguous space in a single swap or page file. If that fails, however, it allocates multiple extents in a number of swap and page files.

This approach requires less dedicated swap file space than in earlier versions of VMS and results in less fragmentation in swap and page files. The overhead of allocating and deallocating seldom-used swap space has been eliminated.

Two fields in the process control block (PCB) of an outswapped process record information about its swap space: PCB$L_WSSWP, its location, and PCB$L_SWAPSIZE, its size. These two fields must be adjacent.

The value in PCB$L_WSSWP has several interpretations:

- When a process is first created, its PCB$L_WSSWP is zeroed to indicate to the swapper that this process requires an inswap from the shell.
- A positive value indicates that the swap space consists of a single extent. The upper byte is a longword index into the page-and-swap-file vector (see Figure 14.24). The indexed element of the array contains the address of the page file control block that describes the process's swap file. The other three bytes specify the starting virtual block number of the swap space.
- A negative value is the system virtual address of a new nonpaged pool data structure, called a page file map (PFLMAP). Whenever the swap space consists of more than one extent, the swapper allocates a PFLMAP with one pointer for each extent.

Figure 18.1 shows the layout of a PFLMAP. PFLMAP$L_PAGECNT is the total number of pages described in all the PFLMAP's pointers. PFLMAP$W_SIZE and PFLMAP$B_TYPE are the standard dynamic data structure fields. The size of a PFLMAP depends on the number of pointers it contains. Its maximum size is 512 bytes. PFLMAP$B_ACTPTRS is the number of pointers in the structure. The pointers begin at offset PFLMAP$Q_PTR.

Each pointer is a quadword. Its first longword contains a swap file index and starting virtual block number, just like the contents of PCB$L_WSSWP for a single-extent swap space. The second longword contains the number of blocks in the extent. Bit 31 is set in the second longword of the last pointer to flag it as the end.

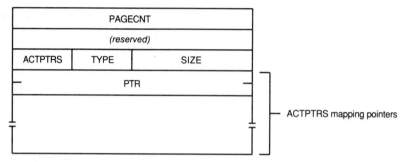

Figure 18.1
Page File Map Data Structure

In the case of a single-extent swap space, PCB$L_SWAPSIZE contains the size of the slot, with bit 31 set to indicate it is the only pointer. Thus, the executive can treat the quadword beginning at PCB$L_WSSWP as a pointer with the same form as one in a PFLMAP.

Figure 18.2 shows the relations among the data structures involved in swap file use and also the structure of a single-extent swap space. The upper byte of PCB$L_WSSWP indexes the page-and-swap-file vector array element that contains the address of the page file control block for that swap file. The page file control block field PFL$L_WINDOW contains the address of the window control block (WCB) describing the location on a mass storage medium of the swap file. The field WCB$L_ORGUCB contains the address of the unit control block for that device.

Within the swap file, the process's slot begins at the virtual block whose number is in the low three bytes of PCB$L_WSSWP. It must contain room for the PHD and the process body (the P0 and P1 pages belonging to the process). The total size of the swap space, contained in PCB$L_SWAPSIZE, is the same as the process's working set size, the sum of PCB$L_PPGCNT and PCB$L_GPGCNT. The field PCB$W_APTCNT contains the size of the first part of the space, which is reserved for the PHD. This field has no meaning for a resident process; the swapper calculates its value by scanning the working set list of a process about to be outswapped.

18.3   SWAPPER MAIN LOOP

The swapper does not determine why it was awakened. Every time it is awakened, it tends to all the tasks for which it is responsible. The main loop of the swapper consists of the following steps:

1. It invokes local routine BALANCE, which tests the size of the free page list.

   —If there are sufficient free pages, BALANCE transfers to local routine OUTSWAP to clean up any deleted PHDs.

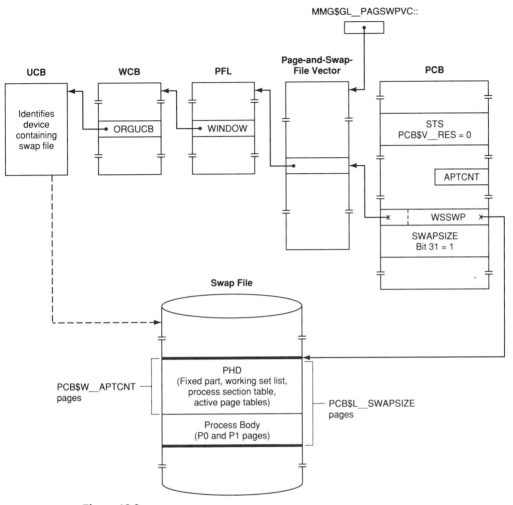

Figure 18.2
Swap File Database

> —If there are insufficient free pages and the size of the modified page list is large enough, BALANCE requests the writing of modified pages to make up the deficit; otherwise, it transfers to OUTSWAP.

Section 18.3.1 describes BALANCE in more detail.

2. The swapper invokes the modified page writer routine, MMG$WRTMFY-PAG, in module WRTMFYPAG, which initiates modified page writing in response to any pending requests. For example, if the size of the modified page list exceeds its current upper limit, modified pages are written until the size of the list falls below the SYSGEN parameter MPW_LOWAITLIMIT. Chapter 16 describes the initiation of modified page writing.

3. It invokes local routine SWAPSCHED to identify the highest priority

computable outswapped process. If there is none, SWAPSCHED returns. Otherwise, it calculates the size of the process's working set and tests whether there are enough free pages to accommodate it.

—If there are enough pages, SWAPSCHED transfers to local routine IN-SWAP to initiate the inswap.

—If there are not enough pages, SWAPSCHED enters the OUTSWAP routine to make up the free page deficit.

Section 18.3.2 discusses SWAPSCHED in more detail.

4. Because the swapper is a system process that executes fairly frequently, it is a convenient vehicle for testing whether a powerfail recovery has occurred and, if so, notifying all processes that have requested power recovery asynchronous system trap (AST) notification through the Set Powerfail Recovery AST ($SETPRA) system service. This delivery mechanism is described in Chapter 33.

5. Finally, the swapper puts itself into the hibernate state, after checking its wake pending flag. If any thread of execution, including the swapper itself in one of its main routines, has requested swapper activity since the swapper began execution, the hibernate is skipped and the swapper goes back to step 1.

18.3.1 The BALANCE Routine

BALANCE takes the following steps:

1. BALANCE acquires the MMG and SCHED spinlocks, raising IPL to IPL$_MMG.

2. It compares the size of the free page list to its low limit, the SYSGEN parameter FREELIM. If modified page writing is in progress, BALANCE includes the number of pages being written in the size of the free page list. If the number is larger than FREELIM, BALANCE goes on to step 5.

3. If the number is smaller than FREELIM, the free page list must be replenished to a target size of SYSGEN parameter FREEGOAL pages. The swapper tries to free enough pages to make up the difference. BALANCE tests whether modified page writing is already in progress. If so, it continues with step 6. If not, it tests whether the modified page list contains as many pages as the SYSGEN parameter MPW_THRESH. If the threshold has been reached, BALANCE further tests that the difference between the list's current size and its low limit (the SYSGEN parameter MPW_LOLIMIT) is large enough to satisfy the deficit. That is, the modified page list must contain enough pages to pass both tests before the swapper can replenish the free page list from it. If the modified page list is not large enough, BALANCE goes to step 6.

4. If the modified page list is large enough, it invokes MMG$PURGEMPL, in routine WRTMFYPAG, to request that enough pages be written from

the modified page list to make up the free page deficit. (Chapter 16 describes MMG$PURGEMPL and the modified page writer.) BALANCE releases the spinlocks and returns.

5. If there are no PHDs belonging to deleted processes from which to reclaim memory, BALANCE releases the spinlocks and returns.

6. Otherwise, it tests and sets SCH$V_SIP. If the swapper already has an I/O operation in progress, BALANCE releases the spinlocks and returns. If not, it transfers to routine OUTSWAP, with the frame pointer (FP) register and SWP$GB_ISWPRI set to zero. Section 18.3.3 discusses OUTSWAP and the meaning of its arguments.

18.3.2   **The SWAPSCHED Routine and Selection of Inswap Process**

SWAPSCHED takes the following steps:

1. It acquires the MMG and SCHED spinlocks.

2. It tests and sets bit SCH$V_SIP in SCH$GB_SIP. If the bit was already set, indicating that the swapper map is in use, SWAPSCHED releases the spinlocks and returns.

   Otherwise, it selects a process in the computable outswap (COMO) state, if one exists, to inswap. Later paragraphs in this section describe its selection. If there is no process in the COMO state, SWAPSCHED clears SCH$V_SIP, releases the spinlocks, and returns.

3. If a COMO process exists and there are enough pages for its working set, SWAPSCHED transfers to INSWAP to read the process into memory, as described in Section 18.6.

4. If a COMO process exists but there are insufficient pages for its working set, SWAPSCHED attempts an optimization aimed at minimizing swapping on systems with more compute-bound processes than can fit into available memory. It makes two checks. One is whether the process's priority is no higher than the SYSGEN parameter DEFPRI, the default process priority. The other is whether less time than the SYSGEN parameter SWPRATE (a time interval with a default value of 5 seconds) has elapsed since the last inswap of a process with a priority as low as DEFPRI. If both are true, SWAPSCHED abandons the inswap.

   Otherwise, it sets SWP$GB_ISWPRI to the priority of the inswap process and FP to the complement of the free page deficit and enters OUTSWAP to reclaim enough memory for the inswap.

The VMS scheduling subsystem maintains 32 quadword listheads for COMO processes, one for each software priority (see Figure 12.2). These queues are identical to the 32 queues maintained for the computable resident (COM) processes. The steps taken by the swapper to decide which process to inswap parallel the steps taken by the rescheduling interrupt service routine (see Chapter 12) to select the next process for execution. This

The Swapper

Example 18.1
Parallels Between Inswap Selection and Execution Selection

```
Swapper's Inswap Selection                    Scheduler's Execution Selection

                                              SCH$IDLE:
                                                BISL2   CPU$L_CPUID_MASK(R3),-
                                                        G^SCH$GL_IDLE_CPUS
                                                MOVL    G^SCH$AR_NULLPCB,-
                                                        CPU$L_CURPCB(R3)
                                                MNEGB   #1,CPU$B_CUR_PRI(R3)
                                                UNLOCK  LOCKNAME=SCHED,-
                                                        NEWIPL=#IPL$_RESCHED
                                              61$:
                                                BBS     R1,G^SCH$GL_IDLE_CPUS,61$
                                                LOCK    LOCKNAME=SCHED,-
                                                        LOCKIPL=#IPL$_SYNCH
                                                BRW     30$

SWAPSCHED:                                    SCH$SCHED::
    LOCK    LOCKNAME=MMG                        FIND_CPU_DATA R3,ISTACK=YES
    LOCK    LOCKNAME=SCHED          (1)         LOCK    LOCKNAME=SCHED
    BBSS    S^#SCH$V_SIP,W^SCH$GB_SIP,5$      30$:
    FFS     #0,#32,W^SCH$GL_COMOQS,R2  (2)      FFS     #0,#32,G^SCH$GL_COMQS,R0
    BNEQ    10$                                 BEQL    SCH$IDLE
    BBCC    S^#SCH$V_SIP,W^SCH$GB_SIP,5$
5$:
    UNLOCK  LOCKNAME=MMG
    UNLOCK  LOCKNAME=SCHED,-
            NEWIPL=#0
    RSB
10$:
    PUSHR   #^M<R6,R7,R8,R9,R10,R11,AP,FP>
    MOVAQ   G^SCH$AQ_COMOH[R2],R3   (3)         MOVAQ   G^SCH$AQ_COMH[R0],R2
    MOVL    (R3),R4                 (4)         REMQUE  @(R2)+,R4
    CMPB    #DYN$C_PCB,PCB$B_TYPE(R4)           BVS     QEMPTY
    BNEQ    QEMPTY
    .
    .

        State Change from COMO to COM    State Change from  COM to CUR

SCH$CHSEP::
    REMQUE  (R4),R1                 (5)         REMQUE  @(R2)+,R4
                                                BVS     QEMPTY
    BNEQ    10$                                 BNEQ    40$
    MOVZWL  PCB$W_STATE(R4),R1
    BBC     R1,EXESTATE,10$
    MOVZBL  PCB$B_PRI(R4),R1
    BLBC    PCB$W_STATE(R4),5$
    ADDL    #32,R1
5$:
    BBCC    R1,G^SCH$GL_COMQS,10$   (6)         BBCC    R0,G^SCH$GL_COMQS,40$
```

(continued)

520

Example 18.1 *(continued)*
Parallels Between Inswap Selection and Execution Selection

```
10$:
    MOVB    R0,PCB$B_PRI(R4)
    MOVL    #SCH$C_COM,R1
                                              40$:
         .                                        CMPB    #DYN$C_PCB,PCB$B_TYPE(R4)
         .                                        BNEQ    QEMPTY
         .
30$:
    BBSS    R0,G^SCH$GL_COMQS,35$
35$:
    MOVW    R1,PCB$W_STATE(R4)           (7)      MOVW    #SCH$C_CUR,PCB$W_STATE(R4)
    MOVAQ   G^SCH$AQ_COMT[R0],R2
40$:
    INSQUE  (R4),@(R2)+                  (8)      MOVL    R4,CPU$L_CURPCB(R3)
    RSB
```

parallel is shown in Example 18.1, which contains code extracts from the modules SWAPPER, SCHED, and RSE.

The first half of the example shows the swapper's selection of the next inswap process and the nearly identical instructions in the rescheduling interrupt service routine, often called the scheduler. The numbers in the example correspond to the numbered steps in the following list:

(1) The SCHED spinlock is acquired to synchronize access to the scheduler database.

(2) The highest priority nonempty (COMO/COM) queue is selected.

(3) The address of its forward pointer is loaded into a register.

(4) The address of the selected PCB is loaded into R4.

At this point, SWAPSCHED has found a process to inswap. As previously described, it tests whether the free page list is large enough. If so, the inswap proceeds. If not, SWAPSCHED enters the OUTSWAP routine to reclaim memory.

After enough pages are available, the swapper takes the steps necessary to bring the selected process into memory.

The scheduler, on the other hand, continues execution. The REMQUE instruction shown in the example for the scheduler is duplicated for ease of comparison.

Some time later, the inswap operation completes. The swapper rebuilds the working set list and process page tables. The parallel resumes when the swapper invokes routine SCH$CHSEP, in module RSE, to change the state of the newly inswapped process to computable.

(5) The selected PCB is removed from its former state (COMO/COM).

(6) If the removal of the PCB emptied the queue, the associated priority bit in the summary longword is cleared. Note that SCH$CHSEP has biased

R1 so that it points to SCH$GL_COMOQS, the summary longword for the COMO state.

⑦ The STATE field in the PCB is loaded with the new state (COM/CUR) of the process.

⑧ Finally, the address of the PCB is stored appropriately: the PCB for the inswapped process is inserted into a COM queue; the address of the current process's PCB is stored in the processor's per-CPU database.

At this point, the parallel ends. The newly inswapped process will be scheduled when the processor (or a member of a symmetric multiprocessing system) is available and the process is the highest priority computable process able to execute.

18.3.3   The OUTSWAP Routine

The swapper executes the OUTSWAP routine to perform one or more tasks related to memory reclamation. OUTSWAP is entered with the MMG and SCHED spinlocks held. It has two arguments. The first is the contents of FP, the desired function:

- A value of zero means OUTSWAP is to free deleted PHDs and, if possible, outswap a PHD to join its outswapped process body.
- A positive value is the size of the free page deficit that OUTSWAP must make up without outswapping a process.
- A value of 80000000_{16} means OUTSWAP must free a balance set slot, either by outswapping a PHD or, less immediately, by outswapping a process body.
- Any other negative value is the complement of the free page deficit that OUTSWAP is to make up any way possible.

The second is SWP$GB_ISWPRI, which contains zero or the priority of the inswap candidate. SCH$OSWPSCHED, invoked by OUTSWAP, compares this priority to that of certain processes to determine if they are suitable candidates for shrinking or outswapping; when zero is supplied, all those processes are considered candidates. An internal priority of zero represents the highest priority. Section 18.4 provides details on the selection of shrink and outswap candidates.

OUTSWAP takes the following steps:

1. It first attempts to reclaim memory by releasing the PHD of a previously deleted process or by outswapping the PHD of a previously outswapped process. It scans the PHD reference count array for a suitable header.

2. If OUTSWAP finds a PHD with a zero reference count, it tests the corresponding PHV$GL_PIXBAS array element.

   —If it contains −1, the process has been deleted and the swapper can release its PHD slot. OUTSWAP scans the SPTEs that map the slot, releases any valid pages to the free page list, and deallocates any page file backing store associated with any invalid pages. When done, it clears the PHV$GL_PIXBAS array element and changes the PHD reference count array element to −1. It returns to the beginning of the swapper's main loop.

—If the corresponding PHV$GL_PIXBAS array element contains a positive value, the process has been outswapped and OUTSWAP can outswap its PHD, as described in Section 18.5.3.

3. If the PHD has a nonzero reference count and belongs to an outswapped process, OUTSWAP takes the steps described in Section 18.5.3.1 to attempt to sever all the connections between the PHD and memory so it can be outswapped.

4. If the reference count is still nonzero, requiring that modified pages be written, OUTSWAP returns to step 2, to scan for another PHD.

5. If OUTSWAP scans all the balance set slots without finding a PHD to release or outswap, it tests the FP argument.

—If the argument is positive or zero, OUTSWAP returns to BALANCE, the only routine that invokes it with either of these values.

—If the argument is negative, OUTSWAP continues with the next step.

6. OUTSWAP invokes SCH$OSWPSCHED, in module OSWPSCHED, to shrink working sets and possibly select a process to outswap. Section 18.4 describes these operations.

Whenever SCH$OSWPSCHED shrinks a process working set, it checks whether the free page deficit has been made up. If the deficit has not yet been made up, it makes checks similar to those previously described to determine whether writing the modified page list is appropriate and whether it would satisfy the deficit. If it would, SCH$OSWPSCHED invokes MMG$PURGEMPL, in routine WRTMFYPAG, to request that enough modified pages be written to make up the free page deficit.

7. If SCH$OSWPSCHED returns with an identified outswap candidate, OUTSWAP takes the steps described in Section 18.5 to outswap it. After outswapping the process and attempting to outswap its PHD, OUTSWAP returns to the beginning of the swapper's main loop.

If SCH$OSWPSCHED returns without an identified outswap candidate, OUTSWAP simply returns to its invoker.

18.4 SELECTION OF SHRINK AND OUTSWAP PROCESSES

When the swapper needs physical memory or a balance set slot, it invokes the routine SCH$OSWPSCHED, in module OSWPSCHED. It specifies either how many pages of memory it needs or that it needs a balance set slot. SCH$OSWPSCHED can shrink the working sets of selected processes, select a process to be outswapped, or perform both operations. SCH$OSWP-SCHED performs two levels of shrinking: in first-level trimming, it shrinks an extended working set back to the normal maximum working set limit (WSQUOTA); in second-level trimming, it attempts to shrink a working set to the SYSGEN parameter SWPOUTPGCNT. Before performing any second-level trimming, it shrinks all working sets that have been extended. Note that with VMS Version 5, SCH$OSWPSCHED stops trimming after reclaiming the requested number of pages.

SCH$OSWPSCHED scans the scheduler database looking for processes to be shrunk or outswapped. Whenever it gains free pages from shrinking a process working set, it checks whether there are enough pages on the free and modified page lists to satisfy the swapper's need. If enough pages are available, SCH$OSWPSCHED returns. It also returns if it finds a process to be outswapped.

The search for a candidate process is table-driven. The following sections describe first the table and then information about the multiple passes through the table.

18.4.1 The OSWPSCHED Table

The OSWPSCHED table is divided into sections, each specifying one or more resident process scheduling states and a set of conditions associated with each state. Table 18.2 lists the individual entries and sections in the OSWPSCHED table. States in the same section are considered equivalent. Selection of shrink and outswap candidates depends on the factors named in the column heads of Table 18.2.

SCH$OSWPSCHED scans the scheduling queues in the order shown in the State column. It checks whether any process in that state queue satisfies the conditions in the second through sixth columns. If a process satisfies those conditions, it is a candidate for shrinking and possibly for swapping. When SCH$OSWPSCHED finds such a process, its subsequent action depends on the flags described in the last column.

The conditions in the table entries discriminate among processes, based on their likelihood of becoming computable in a short while and the effects of shrinking or swapping them. When the system needs to reclaim physical memory, process working sets extended in times of plentiful memory are shrunk first. In general, the intent is to prevent the outswap of a process that is about to become computable when the only reason for the swap is to bring a computable process of equal priority into memory. Overall system performance may be improved by shrinking processes rather than swapping them. However, a process in some states may be affected less by being swapped than by having its working set reduced.

Descriptions of the various conditions and flags follow:

- I/O—A table entry in this column can specify No direct, Direct, No buffered, Buffered, and n/a.

Table 18.2 Selection of Shrink and Outswap Candidates

State	I/O	Priority	Initial Quantum	Long Wait	Dormant	Flags
SUSP	No buffered	n/a	n/a	n/a	n/a	Swap (SWAPASAP)
SUSP	Buffered	n/a	n/a	n/a	n/a	Second (SWPOGOAL)
COM	n/a	n/a	n/a	n/a	Yes	First only (LVL1_TRIM)
HIB	n/a	n/a	n/a	Yes	n/a	Second
LEF	No direct	n/a	n/a	Yes	n/a	Second
CEF	No direct	n/a	n/a	n/a	n/a	Second
HIB	n/a	n/a	n/a	No	n/a	Second
LEF	No direct	n/a	n/a	No	n/a	Second
FPG	n/a	Yes	n/a	n/a	n/a	n/a
COLPG	n/a	Yes	n/a	n/a	n/a	n/a
MWAIT	n/a	n/a	n/a	n/a	n/a	n/a
CEF	Direct	Yes	Yes	n/a	n/a	n/a
LEF	Direct	Yes	Yes	n/a	n/a	n/a
PFW	n/a	Yes	Yes	n/a	n/a	n/a
COM	n/a	Yes [1]	Yes	n/a	No	n/a

[1] This constraint is not present in the table; however, it is present in the algorithm and thus shown here.

When a process that is in a local event flag (LEF) or common event flag (CEF) scheduling state has an outstanding direct I/O request, there is a high probability that the process is waiting for the direct I/O to complete. If so, the process will soon become computable and thus be a less desirable shrink or outswap candidate. SCH$OSWPSCHED therefore distinguishes between processes with and without outstanding I/O requests.

With VMS Version 5, a suspended process, by default, can receive kernel and executive ASTs. To prevent such a process from being outswapped and then becoming computable again as the result of buffered I/O completion, the table distinguishes between suspended processes with and without outstanding buffered I/O requests.

In this column, n/a means that the existence of either type of outstanding I/O request is irrelevant. No test is made for either.

- Priority—A table entry in this column can specify Yes or n/a.

Yes in this column means that SCH$OSWPSCHED compares the priorities of the inswap process with that of any process that may be shrunk or outswapped. A process that is computable or likely to be computable soon is not considered a candidate, unless its priority is less than or equal to that of the potential inswap process, stored in global location SWP$GB_ISWPRI. (The swapper zeros SWP$GB_ISWPRI before invoking SCH$OSWPSCHED to make up a free page list deficit.)

In this column, n/a means no test is made.

- Initial Quantum—A table entry in this column can specify Yes or n/a.

Yes in this column means that SCH$OSWPSCHED rejects a process that is in its initial memory residency quantum. A process likely to become computable soon is not considered a candidate for second-level trimming or outswapping if it is within its initial memory residency quantum. If SWP$GB_ISWPRI is less than or equal to 15, the constraint is ignored. The intent is to leave the process in memory long enough to do useful work, after the system has expended the overhead of inswapping it. This reduces the possibility of swap thrashing, a condition in which the system spends more time swapping in and out than in process execution.

In this column, n/a means that SCH$OSWPSCHED does not test if the process is in its initial quantum.

- Long Wait—A table entry in this column can specify Yes, No, or n/a.

Either Yes or No in this column means that SCH$OSWPSCHED determines whether a process has been waiting in an LEF or hibernate (HIB) state longer than the SYSGEN parameter LONGWAIT. Yes means that for a process to be a candidate, it must be in a long wait. A process that has been waiting a long time is likely to wait longer still; one that has been waiting a short time is more likely to become computable soon. For example, a process waiting for terminal input longer than a LONGWAIT interval is likely to remain in LEF longer still.

No in this column means that the process must not have been waiting a long time; n/a means that SCH$OSWPSCHED does not test for this condition.

- Dormant—A table entry in this column can specify Yes, No, or n/a.

Either Yes or No in this column means that SCH$OSWPSCHED determines whether a computable process is dormant, that is, one whose priority is less than or equal to the SYSGEN parameter DEFPRI and that has been on a COM or COMO queue for longer than the SYSGEN parameter DORMANTWAIT. Yes in this column means that the process must be dormant to be a candidate. A dormant process is considered a very good candidate to be shrunk. An example of such a process is a compute-bound process with a priority too low to get CPU time. This condition was added to expedite the shrinking and outswap of a process such as a low-priority batch job. While the process runs at night on a lightly loaded system, its working set is expanded and it can acquire extensive physical memory, but once interactive users log in, the process cannot get CPU time.

No in this column means the process must not be dormant to be a candidate; n/a means that SCH$OSWPSCHED does not test for this condition.

This older mechanism for dealing with dormant processes persists in case the system manager has disabled the newer, preferred mechanism, the combination of PIXSCAN priority boost and quantum-end working set trimming. Chapter 17 contains information on quantum-end trimming, and Chapter 12 describes the PIXSCAN mechanism.

- Flags—Three flags direct SCH$OSWPSCHED to take specific action on a particular pass through the table. In this column, n/a means no specific action is indicated.

The LVL1_TRIM flag, shown in the table as First Only, means that the working set of a process selected by this entry should only be trimmed to WSQUOTA. Such a process is ignored in the second pass of the table.

The SWAPASAP flag, shown in the table as Swap, indicates that SCH$O-SWPSCHED should outswap a process selected by this entry after reducing its working set to WSQUOTA. When the outswapped process becomes computable again, it will not have to waste compute time rebuilding its working set.

The SWPOGOAL flag, shown in the table as Second, indicates that SCH$OSWPSCHED must try to shrink the working set size of a process selected by that table entry to SWPOUTPGCNT. Shrinking the working set of such a process may reclaim enough memory that the process need not be outswapped.

In addition to conditions imposed by the table entries, there are several implicit constraints on the suitability of a particular process to be shrunk or outswapped. A process cannot be outswapped if it has locked itself into the balance set. The working set of a process that has disabled automatic working set adjustment cannot be shrunk. The working set of a real-time process cannot be shrunk below WSQUOTA. If the executive has temporarily blocked changes to the working set list and PTEs of a process (by setting the bit PHD$V_NO_WS_CHNG in PHD$W_FLAGS), the process's working set cannot be shrunk or outswapped. A process that is already outswapped cannot be shrunk or outswapped.

18.4.2 Passes Through the OSWPSCHED Table

SCH$OSWPSCHED makes two passes through the table. On its first pass, it potentially traverses all sections of the table, performing first-level trimming of any candidate processes. If it has been entered with a request to outswap a process to free a balance set slot, the first candidate process that is shrunk and that has not locked itself into the balance set is also selected as an outswap candidate.

If SCH$OSWPSCHED has been entered to satisfy a free page deficit, it reclaims memory from working sets that had been extended until it reaches the end of the table, reclaims enough free pages to satisfy the deficit, or finds a process to be outswapped. A suitable outswap candidate is one that meets the scheduling state and conditions of a table entry that includes the SWAPASAP flag and that has not locked itself into the balance set.

If SCH$OSWPSCHED reaches the end of the table without satisfying the deficit or locating an outswap candidate, it scans the table again, starting at the beginning. If it has been entered to satisfy a free page deficit, it performs second-level trimming. If it has been entered to free a balance set slot, it selects for outswap with no trimming the first candidate process that has not locked itself into the balance set.

In second-level swapper trimming, SCH$OSWPSCHED can scan each section of the table twice. First, if the entry contains the SWPOGOAL flag, SCH$OSWPSCHED shrinks the working set of a process selected by this entry (unless the process has disabled automatic working set adjustment). The working set is reduced, if possible, to the SYSGEN parameter SWPOUTPG-CNT. If the deficit is not satisfied, SCH$OSWPSCHED continues scanning through processes selected by the table section. When it gets to the end of the section, it restarts at the beginning of the section, looking for a process to outswap. When SCH$OSWPSCHED gets to the end of the section for the second time, it goes to the next section. The pass ends when the deficit is satisfied or a process is found to outswap. If outswapping a process does not satisfy the deficit, eventually the swapper will reexecute the OUTSWAP and SCH$OSWPSCHED routines.

The swapper maintains a failure counter that records the number of times it has failed to locate a candidate to shrink or swap. This count is maintained across invocations of SCH$OSWPSCHED. It is intended to loosen the constraints in situations where the normal conditions have failed to produce candidates. When this count reaches a value equal to SWPFAIL, the swapper ignores certain constraints when selecting a process to shrink or outswap: it ignores the initial quantum condition for all processes and the priority constraint for all processes except COM ones. The counter is reset each time an outswap candidate is successfully located.

When the swapper scans a series of processes in a particular scheduling queue, the scan begins with the least recently queued entry (at the tail of the queue). This starting point ensures that the longer a process has been in a wait queue, the more chance it has of being shrunk or swapped. (A process is inserted into a wait queue at the front of the list, unlike most queues.)

18.5 OUTSWAP OPERATION

Outswap is described before inswap because it is easier to explain inswap in terms of what the swapper puts into the swap file. The swapper does not remove processes from the balance set indiscriminately. In practice, the swapper tries hard not to swap. It tries to satisfy the deficit first by shrinking working sets, deleting or outswapping PHDs, and writing modified pages. If those fail to free enough pages, if SCH$OSWPSCHED encounters a process that meets the constraints of a table entry with the SWAPASAP flag, or if the system needs a balance set slot (PHD slot), the swapper outswaps a process.

18.5.1 Selection of Outswap Candidate

As described in Section 18.4, the outswap selection is driven by an ordered table of scheduling states and associated conditions. The swapper selects a process less likely to benefit from remaining in memory. Once a candidate is selected, the swapper prepares the working set of that process for outswap.

18.5.2 Outswap of the Process Body

The swapper outswaps the process body (P0 and P1 pages) separately from the PHD. There are two reasons for doing this:

- Fields in the PHD (most notably WSLEs and process PTEs) are modified as the working set list is processed.
- The PHD may not be swappable at the same time as the body because of outstanding I/O, pages on the modified page list, or some other reason.

18.5.2.1 Scanning the Working Set List.
To prepare the process body for outswap, the swapper scans the working set list. It must examine each page in the working set list to determine if any special action is required. The swapper looks at a combination of the page type (found in the WSLE as well as the PFN TYPE array) and the valid bit. Table 18.3 lists all combinations of page type and valid bit setting that the swapper encounters and the action that it takes for each. Several combinations are discussed further in the following sections. (One type of page not discussed further is a page locked into memory, one whose WSLE PFNLOCK bit is set. The swapper ignores such pages; they remain in memory, and no action is required.)

The basic step that the swapper takes as it scans the working set list is to add a description of each swappable page to the swapper I/O map. As a result, the virtually noncontiguous pages in the process's working set appear virtually contiguous to the I/O system (see Figures 18.4 and 18.7) in the swapper's P0 address space. For each page, the swapper performs the following steps:

1. Locates the PTE from the virtual page number in the WSLE
2. Determines any special action, based on page validity and page type
3. Copies the PFN from the PTE to the swapper map
4. Records the modify bit (logical OR of PTE modify bit and PFN STATE array element saved modify bit) in the WSLE

Table 18.3   Scan of Working Set List of Outswap Process

Page Type WSLE⟨3:1⟩	Page Validity PTE	Action of Swapper for This Page
Process page	Transition	(STATE = Read in Progress) Treat as page with I/O in progress. Special action may be taken at inswap or by the modified page writer. (STATE = Read Error) Drop from working set. No other transition states are possible for a page in the working set.
Process page	Valid	Outswap page. If there is outstanding I/O and the page is modified, store in its PFN SWPVBN array element the swap file address where the updated page contents should be written when the I/O completes.
System page		It is impossible for a system page to be in a process working set. The swapper generates an error.
Global read-only	Transition	If the process PTE still contains a PFN, this page is an active transition page. Outswap the page. If the process PTE contains a GPTX, then the global page table must contain a transition PTE. The page is dropped from the process working set.
Global read-only	Valid	If SHRCNT = 1, then outswap. If SHRCNT > 1, drop from working set. It is highly likely that a process can fault such a page later without I/O. This check avoids multiple copies of the same page in the swap file.
Global read/write		Drop from working set. At inswap, it would be difficult to determine whether the page in memory is more up-to-date than the swap file copy.
Page table page		Not part of the process body. However, while the swapper is scanning the process body, the virtual address field in the working set list is modified to reflect the offset from the beginning of the PHD because page table pages will probably be located at different virtual addresses following inswap.

5. Sets the Delete Contents bit in the PFN STATE array element. This bit causes the page to be placed at the head of the free page list when its reference count goes to zero (normally, when the swap write completes).

Note that the swapper does not explicitly restore each PTE to the contents of its PFN BAK array element. The contents will be replaced when the page is released (after the swap write completes and all other references to the page are eliminated).

18.5.2.2   **Pages with Direct I/O in Progress.** If, in the swapper's scan of the working set list, it encounters a modified page with outstanding I/O, it stores in the page's PFN SWPVBN array element the location in the swap file where that page belongs. The page will be swapped along with the rest of the process body to reserve a place for it in the swap file.

If the I/O operation is a read (or if it is a write and some other action has caused the page to be modified), the physical page will be placed on the modified page list when the I/O completes. The modified page writer takes special action for a modified page with nonzero contents in its PFN SWP-VBN array element. That is, it writes the page to the designated block in the swap file rather than to its normal backing store address.

If the I/O operation is a write (from memory to mass storage) and the page was not otherwise modified, the contents currently being written to the swap file are good. The page will be placed on the free list when the I/O operation completes.

18.5.2.3   **Global Pages.** Global pages are also given special treatment at outswap. If the global page is writable, it is dropped from the process working set before the process is outswapped. The task of determining whether the contents that are swapped are up-to-date when the process is brought back into memory is more complicated than simply refaulting the page (often without I/O) when the process is swapped back into memory.

A global read-only page is only swapped if its global share count (PFN SHRCNT array element) is 1. In all other cases, the page is dropped from the working set and must be refaulted (most likely without I/O) after the process is inswapped. (Global pages that are explicitly or implicitly locked into the process working set are not dropped from the working set.) Global transition pages are also dropped from the process working set.

18.5.2.4   **Example of Process Body Outswap.** Figures 18.3 through 18.5 show some of the special cases the swapper encounters while it is scanning the process working set list. The key information about each page is a combination of the PTE validity and the page type. The order of the scan is defined by the order of the working set list. Figure 18.3 shows the process working set, the process page tables, and the associated PFN database entries before the swapper begins its working set scan. Figure 18.4 shows the modified working set and the swapper map after the working set list scan but before the I/O request is initiated. Figure 18.5 shows the state of the PTEs after the swap write has completed and the physical pages have been released.

    1. WSLE 1 is a global read-only page. The VPN field of the WSLE locates the PTE. The PFN field of the PTE locates the PFN data associated with

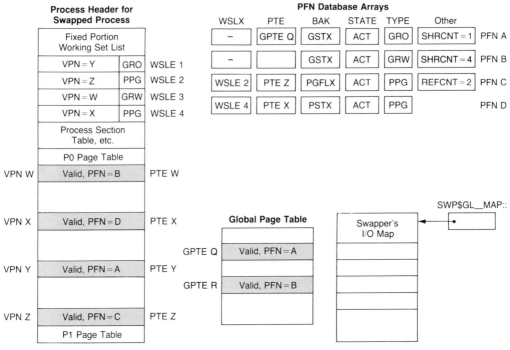

Figure 18.3
Example Working Set List before Outswap Scan

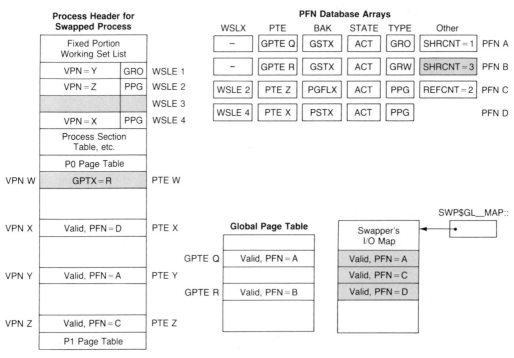

Figure 18.4
Example Working Set List after Outswap Scan

this physical page. In particular, the PFN SHRCNT array element for this page is 1. (This process is the only process that currently has this page in its working set.) The swapper writes this page out as part of the swap image for this process. Thus, PFN A is the first page in the swapper's I/O map (see Figure 18.4).

When the swapper's write completes, the page will be deleted; that is, the PTE array element will be cleared and the page will be placed at the head of the free page list (see Figure 18.5).

2. WSLE 2 is a process page that also has I/O in progress (a REFCNT of 2). This page will be swapped; its PFN is shown in the swapper map.

If the page was previously modified (if either the PTE modify bit or saved modify bit in the PFN STATE array element is set), the address in the swap file where the page belongs is stored in the PFN SWPVBN array element. Nonzero contents in the PFN SWPVBN array element cause the page to be placed on the modified page list when it is released. If the process is still outswapped when the modified page writer writes this page, the page will be written to the block reserved for it in the swap file.

The page is marked for deletion. That is, when the REFCNT for the page reaches zero (because of completion of both the outstanding I/O and

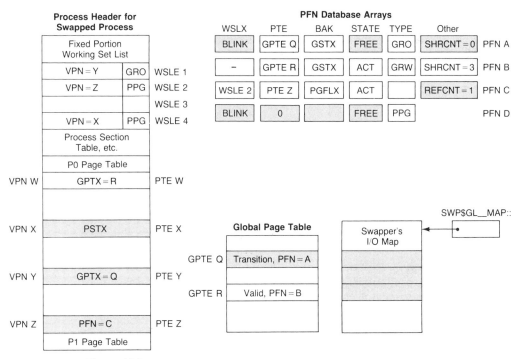

Figure 18.5
Changes after Swapper's Write Completes

the swapper's write), the page is placed at the head of the free page list and its PTE array element cleared.

3. WSLE 3 is a global read/write page. The page is dropped from the process working set (see Figure 18.4); the process PTE contents are replaced with the GPTX of GPTE R, and the PFN SHRCNT array element for PFN B is decremented. Notice that PFN B is not included in the swapper map, which contains a list of the physical pages that will be written to the swap file.

4. WSLE 4, the last WSLE in this example, is an ordinary process page. The page is added to the swapper map (PFN D) and it is marked for deletion. The deletion will actually occur after the swapper's write operation completes.

18.5.3   Outswap of the Process Header

The PHD is not outswapped until after the process body has been successfully written to the swap file. Before the PHD can be outswapped, all ties between physical pages and the process page tables must be severed, including not only those pages that were in the process working set and written to the swap file but also those pages that are in some transition state, notably pages on the free and modified page lists.

18.5.3.1   Partial Outswap.

After the process body has been outswapped, the PHD becomes eligible for outswap. In fact, the header of an outswapped process is one of the first things that the swapper looks for in an attempt to add pages to the free page list.

The indication that the PHD cannot be outswapped yet is found in the PHD vector reference count array (see Figure 14.23). This array counts the number of reasons (transition pages, active page table pages, and so on) that prevent the PHD from being outswapped.

Because the outswap of the header need not immediately follow the body outswap (a situation referred to as a partial outswap), it is possible that a PHD will not be swapped in the time between the outswap and subsequent inswap of its process body. In the corresponding partial inswap, the swapper need not allocate a balance set slot and bring the PHD into memory because it is already resident.

If the swapper locates a PHD with a nonzero reference count belonging to an outswapped process, it takes whatever actions are required to remove the ties that bind the PHD to physical memory. The first such step is to eliminate any transition PTE whose physical page is on the free page list.

It locates a transition PTE by scanning the free page list for a page whose PFN PTE array element contents lie within the P0 or P1 page tables of the PHD being examined. It starts its scan at the back of the list with the most recently queued entries, on the assumption that the transition pages are more frequently in the back half of the list. Whenever it finds such a page, it resets the process PTE to the contents of its PFN BAK array element. The swapper clears the PFN REFCNT and PTE array elements and moves the page from its current location to the head of the free page list.

Because the free page list is only one of several transition states, the scan of the free page list may not free the PHD for removal. Pages may be in some other transition state. Transition states that represent some form of I/O in progress (release pending, read in progress, write in progress) are left alone because there is nothing that the swapper can do until the I/O completes. After the free page list is scanned, if the process still has transition pages, the swapper invokes MMG$PURGEMPL to request that all modified pages be written that are mapped by page tables in the PHD or that are in the PHD itself. A modified page written to its backing store is released to the free page list. After the pages are selectively purged from modified page list, the swapper scans the free list again.

If the swapper succeeds in releasing a PHD with the previously described free page list scan, it can take the steps described in the next section to outswap the PHD.

18.5.3.2   **Outswap of the Process Header.** Once the reference count for the PHD reaches zero, it can be outswapped and the balance slot freed. The outswap of the PHD is entirely analogous to the outswap of a process body. That is, all the header pages in the working set list are scanned and put into the swapper's I/O map to form a virtually contiguous block for the I/O subsystem.

There are several differences between the outswap of a PHD and a process body. When a process body is outswapped, the header that maps that body is still resident. When the swapper's write completes and each physical page is being deleted, the contents of the PFN BAK array element for each page are put back into the process PTE.

PHD pages are mapped by SPTEs for that balance set slot. The SPTEs are not available to hold the PFN BAK array contents because they will be used by the next occupant of this balance set slot. Instead, the PHD page BAK array (see Section 18.2.1.3) serves this purpose. As the PHD is processed for outswap, the contents of the PFN BAK array for each active header page are stored in the corresponding PHD page BAK array element.

At the same time, the location of each header page within the working set list is stored in the WSLX array. This array prevents a prohibitively long search to rebuild the PHD when the process is swapped back into memory.

Once the header is successfully outswapped, PCB$V_PHDRES in PCB$L_STS, the header-resident bit, is cleared and the balance slot is available for further use.

18.6   **INSWAP OPERATION**

The inswap is exactly the opposite of the outswap operation. The swapper brings the PHD, including active page tables and the process body, back into physical memory. It then uses the contents of the working set list to rebuild the process page tables, an operation that primarily involves updating each valid PTE to reflect the new PFN used by that PTE. At the same time that each page is being processed, the swapper can resolve any special cases that existed when the process was outswapped.

18.6.1   **Selection of an Inswap Candidate**

As described in Section 18.3.2, the swapper selects a process for inswap, much as the scheduler selects a candidate for execution. The following processes may be potential candidates for inswap:

- Newly created processes
- Processes in some outswapped wait state that were just made computable
- Processes that were outswapped while in the computable state

The highest priority COMO process is the one selected for inswap.

18.6.2   **Preparation for Inswap**

The swapper must ensure that there is a balance set slot for the PHD and allocate physical memory for the working set.

If the PHD is resident, the number of header pages (PCB$W_APTCNT) is subtracted from the size of the outswap image in the swap file; even though the PHD is not in the swap file, space has been reserved for it there. Thus, whether the header is resident determines the total number of blocks that must be read from the swap file and the virtual block number where the read should begin.

If the PHD has been outswapped, the swapper scans the PHD reference count array for a balance set slot with a negative reference count. If it fails to find one, it transfers control to the routine OUTSWAP, specifying that a process should be outswapped to free a balance set slot. (Section 18.3.3 summarizes OUTSWAP's actions.) If it does find one, it increments the PHD reference count to zero, stores the low word of the process's ID in the corresponding PHV$GL_PIXBAS array, and stores the address of the slot in PCB$L_PHD.

It then allocates as many physical pages from the free page list as are required to accommodate the process working set. If it cannot allocate enough pages from the free page list, it transfers control to OUTSWAP, specifying the number of free pages to be reclaimed. If enough free pages are available, it updates the PFN database arrays for each page and builds a PTE to insert in the swapper I/O map.

18.6.3   **Inswap of the Process Header**

If the PHD was outswapped, it must be brought back into memory before the process body can be reconstructed. The swapper must adjust those process parameters that are tied to a specific balance set slot (that is, specific system virtual or physical addresses) to reflect the PHD's new location. These include the following:

- Each SPTE that maps a PHD page must be initialized with the appropriate PFN.
- The virtual addresses of the P0 and P1 page tables must be calculated and loaded into their locations in the hardware PCB.
- The physical address of the hardware PCB must be calculated and loaded into the software PCB field PCB$L_PHYPCB.
- Finally, the P1 PTEs that double-map the PHD pages that are not page table pages must be initialized with the PFNs that contain the corresponding pages.

18.6.3.1   **Rebuilding the Process Header.** When a PHD is read from the swap image into a new balance slot, the SPTEs that map each balance slot page must be loaded with the PFNs from the swapper map that contain each header page. In addition, the PFN database must be set up for each of these physical pages. The swapper does all this work in a simple loop that it executes for each header page.

The simplicity (and speed) of the loop results from the use of the two PHD page arrays in the PHD. These arrays enable the PFN BAK and WSLX array elements to be loaded from the information copied to the two header arrays when the process was outswapped. To access these arrays, the swapper temporarily maps the PHD into its P0 space using the swapper I/O map.

18.6.3.2   **P1 Window to the Process Header.** In any resident process, all the PHD pages except process page tables are double-mapped into the process's P1 space. This P1 mapping provides invariant addresses for the nonpageable part of the PHD. The system space mapping is subject to change with outswap and inswap: if the header is outswapped, it is likely to be inswapped into a different balance set slot. No routine can safely store a system address of a PHD or any part of a PHD in a register, unless it blocks swapping, because the address could change between the register initialization and its use.

The executive observes the following conventions with respect to PHD references:

- Any process context reference to the PHD should use the P1 address where possible (CTL$GL_PHD contains the P1 address of the PHD).
- Any reference to the system space header must execute at an IPL high enough to block rescheduling and thus swapping.

- A reference to a process page table must be made through the system space address because the page table pages are not doubly mapped. Because a process page table must be accessed with swapping blocked, at an IPL too high to permit page faults, the executive must first examine the SPTE that maps the page table to determine the validity of the page table page.

There are two implications for the operating system:

- These physical pages are not kept track of through reference counts. However, all these header pages are a permanent part of the process working set.
- The P1 page table page that maps these pages must also be a permanent member of the process working set.

18.6.4 Rebuilding the Process Body

The PHD must be in a known state before the process body can be restored to the state it was in before the process was outswapped. If the PHD was never outswapped, very little need be done; otherwise, it is first inswapped and restored, as previously described.

18.6.4.1 Rebuilding the Working Set List and Process Page Tables. Rebuilding the process body involves a scan of both the swapper map and the process working set list. Recall that at outswap, the processing of each page was determined by a combination of page type and validity. On inswap, the key to the processing of each page is the contents of the PTE located by the virtual address field in the WSLE. An approximation of swapper activity for each page is as follows:

1. The PTE is located from the virtual address in the WSLE.
2. In the usual case, the original contents of the PTE are put into the PFN BAK array element, and the PFN from the swapper map is loaded into the now valid PTE.
3. If, for some reason, a copy of the page already exists in memory, that page is put into the process working set. The duplicate page from the swapper map is released to the front of the free page list.

If the virtual address field represents a system space address, the WSLE describes a page in the PHD. The swapper must calculate the new system virtual address corresponding to that page and modify the WSLE.

Table 18.4 details the different cases the swapper can encounter when rebuilding the process page tables. At inswap time, the swapper uses the contents of the PTE to determine what action to take for each particular page.

18.6.4.2 Pages with I/O in Progress When Outswap Occurred. Pages that had I/O in progress when the process was outswapped were written to the swap file

Table 18.4 Rebuilding the Working Set List and the Process Page Tables

Type of Page Table Entry	*Action of Swapper for This Page*
PTE is valid.	Page is locked into memory and was never outswapped. No action is required.
PTE indicates a transition page (probably because of outstanding I/O when process was outswapped).	Fault transition page into process working set. Release duplicate page that was just inswapped.
PTE contains a GPTX. (Page must be global read-only because global read/write pages were dropped from the working set at outswap time.)	Swapper action is based on the contents of the GPTE: • If the GPTE is valid, copy the PFN in the GPTE to the process PTE and release the duplicate page. • If the GPTE indicates a transition page, make the GPTE valid, add that physical page to the process working set, and release the duplicate page. • If the GPTE indicates a GSTX, then keep the page just inswapped and make that the master page in the GPTE as well as the slave page in the process PTE.
PTE contains a page file index or a process section table index.	These are the usual contents for a page that did not have outstanding I/O or other page references when the process was outswapped. The PFN in the swapper map is inserted into the process page table. The PFN arrays are initialized for that page.

anyway to reserve space. If the page was previously unmodified, it would be put onto the free page list when both the swap write and the outstanding write operation completed. If the page was previously modified, it would be put onto the modified page list when both the swap write and the outstanding write operation completed (because the contents of the SWPVBN array were nonzero).

In either case, it is possible for the process to be swapped back in before one of these physical pages was reused. The swapper uses the physical page that is already contained in the process PTE (as a transition page) and releases the duplicate physical page from the swapper map to the front of the free page list.

In the case of a page on the free page list, this decision is simply one of convenience. In the case of a page on the modified page list, the contents of the page in the swap image are out-of-date, and the swapper has no choice but to use the physical page that is already in memory.

18.6.4.3 **Resolution of Global Read-Only Pages.** The only possible global page that could be in the swap file is a global read-only page that had a share count of 1 when the process was outswapped (or a page that was explicitly locked). All other global pages were dropped from the process working set before the process was outswapped.

There are two cases that the swapper can find when rebuilding the process page tables. At inswap, the process PTE for a global read-only page always contains a GPTX. The swapper's treatment of the page is determined by the contents of the GPTE indexed by the GPTX:

- If no other process has mapped the global page, the GPTE contains a GSTX. The swapper stores the PFN from the swapper map in both the process PTE and the GPTE.
- If some other process referenced the global page while this process was outswapped, the GPTE can indicate a valid or a transition page. In either case, the swapper releases the duplicate page to the free page list and stores the PFN from the GPTE in the process PTE. If the page is in transition, the swapper makes it valid.

18.6.4.4 **Example of an Inswap Operation.** Figures 18.6 through 18.8 show an inswap operation that illustrates some of the special cases that the swapper encounters when inswapping a process body. Note that this example is not related to the outswap example shown in Figures 18.3 to 18.5.

Figure 18.6 shows the state of the PHD after the process has been selected to be inswapped. Figure 18.7 shows that four physical pages have been allocated to contain the four working set pages that the example describes. Figure 18.8 shows the rebuilt process page tables and the PFN database changes that result from rebuilding the working set and process page tables.

1. WSLE 1 locates virtual page number X. This PTE contains a GPTX. The referenced GPTE (GPTE T) contains a GSTX, indicating that the GPTE is not valid.

   PFN D is put into the process page table. It is also added to the global page database by making the GPTE valid (see Figure 18.8), putting PFN D into the GPTE, and updating the PFN data for physical page D to reflect its new state.

2. WSLE 2 is a process page mapped by PTE W (see Figure 18.7). This PTE contains a process section table index. The PTE is updated to contain PFN C, and the PSTX is stored in the BAK array element for that page (see Figure 18.7). Other PFN array elements are updated accordingly.

3. WSLE 3, which locates PTE Y, is exactly like the first, as far as the process data is concerned. However, the GPTE (GPTE S) is valid, indicating that another copy of this page already exists. (This could occur only if another process faulted the page while this process was outswapped.)

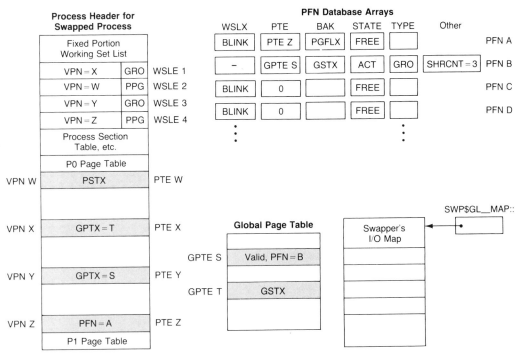

Figure 18.6
Working Set List and Swapper Map before Physical
Page Allocation

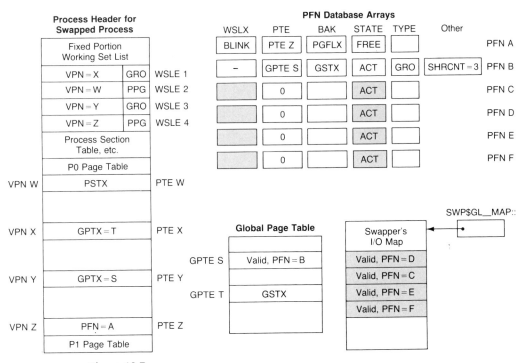

Figure 18.7
Working Set List and Swapper Map after Physical
Page Allocation

541

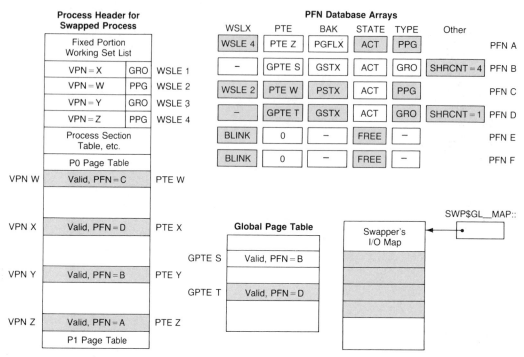

Figure 18.8
Working Set List and Rebuilt Page Tables

The duplicate page (PFN E) is released to the front of the free page list. The process PTE is altered to contain the physical page that already exists (PFN B) and the share count for that page is incremented (from 3 to 4).

4. WSLE 4 resembles the second. However, the process PTE indicates a transition page. (This implies that the header in this example was never outswapped.)

The action taken here is similar to step 3, where a duplicate global page was discovered. The page just read (PFN F) is released to the head of the free list. The transition page (PFN A) is faulted back into the process working set by removing the page from the free list, setting its state to active, and turning the valid bit in the PTE back on.

18.6.4.5 **Final Processing of the Inswap Operation.** After the working set list has been scanned and the process page tables rebuilt, the process is ready to have its state changed from COMO to COM. Several other scheduling actions must be completed before the scheduler is notified:

1. A new value of ASTLVL is calculated and stored in the hardware PCB in the PHD. (ASTs may have been queued to the process while it was

outswapped. The hardware PCB, which contains a copy of the ASTLVL register, was not available while the header was not resident.)

2. The resident bit and the initial quantum bit are set in PCB$L_STS.
3. The process's swap space is deallocated.
4. A new quantum interval is loaded into the PHD.
5. Finally, SCH$CHSEP is invoked to make the process computable.

19 Pool Management

In this bright little package, now isn't it odd?
You've a dime's worth of something known only to God!

Edgar Albert Guest, *The Package of Seeds*

The VMS operating system creates and uses many data structures in the course of its work. It creates some of them at system initialization; it creates others when they are needed and destroys them when their useful life is finished. VMS maintains several areas of virtual address memory, called pools, in which it allocates and deallocates data structures. Each such area has different characteristics. This chapter describes these memory areas, their uses, and their allocation and deallocation algorithms.

19.1 DYNAMIC DATA STRUCTURES AND THEIR STORAGE AREAS

Almost all the VMS data structures created after system initialization are volatile, allocated on demand and deallocated when no longer needed. These data structures have similar headers (see Section 19.1.4). Their memory requirements vary in a number of ways:

- Pageability—Data structures accessed by code running at interrupt priority level (IPL) 2 or below can be pageable; data structures accessed at higher IPLs cannot.
- Virtual location—Some data structures are local to one process, mapped in its per-process address space; others must be mapped in system space, accessible to multiple processes and to system context code.
- Protection—Many dynamic data structures are created and modified only by kernel mode code, but some data structures are accessed by outer modes.

19.1.1 Storage Areas for Dynamic Data Structures

VMS provides different storage areas to meet the memory requirements of dynamic data structures. There are several pools of storage for variable-length allocation: a nonpageable system space pool, a pageable system space pool, and a pageable per-process space pool. On systems with MA780 multiport memory, there is an additional pool of nonpageable shared memory.

In addition, VMS provides lookaside lists of preformed, fixed-length packets; these enable faster allocation and deallocation of the most frequently used sizes and types of storage. Throughout this chapter, *packet* refers to a preformed, fixed-length allocation, and *block* refers to a variable-length allocation. The storage areas are summarized in Table 19.1 and are described in more detail in later sections of this chapter.

Table 19.1   Comparison of Different Pool Areas

System Space

NONPAGED POOL

Protection	ERKW
Synchronization technique	Spinlock
Type of list	Variable-length
Allocation	Multiple of 16 bytes
Minimum request size	1 byte
Characteristics	Nonpageable, expandable

LARGE REQUEST PACKET (LRP) LOOKASIDE LIST

Protection	ERKW
Synchronization technique	Interlocked queue
Type of list	Fixed-length packets
Allocation	@IOC$GL_LRPSIZE [1]
Minimum request size	@IOC$GL_LRPMIN [1]
Characteristics	Nonpageable, expandable

INTERMEDIATE REQUEST PACKET (IRP) LOOKASIDE LIST

Protection	ERKW
Synchronization technique	Interlocked queue
Type of list	Fixed-length packets
Allocation	176 bytes
Minimum request size	1+@IOC$GL_SRPSIZE [1]
Characteristics	Nonpageable, expandable

SMALL REQUEST PACKET (SRP) LOOKASIDE LIST

Protection	ERKW
Synchronization technique	Interlocked queue
Type of list	Fixed-length packets
Allocation	@IOC$GL_SRPSIZE [1]
Minimum request size	1 byte
Characteristics	Nonpageable, expandable

PAGED POOL

Protection	ERKW
Synchronization technique	Mutex
Type of list	Variable-length
Allocation	Multiple of 16 bytes
Minimum request size	1 byte
Characteristics	Pageable

Per-Process Space

PROCESS ALLOCATION REGION

Protection	UREW
Synchronization technique	Access mode and IPL

(continued)

Table 19.1   Comparison of Different Pool Areas *(continued)*

Per-Process Space

PROCESS ALLOCATION REGION

Type of list	Variable-length
Allocation	Multiple of 16 bytes
Minimum request size	1 byte
Characteristics	Pageable, expandable into P0 space

KERNEL REQUEST PACKET (KRP) LOOKASIDE LIST

Protection	URKW
Synchronization technique	Access mode and INSQUE/REMQUE
Type of list	Fixed-length packets
Allocation	CTL$C_KRP_SIZE
Minimum request size	KRP$C_KRP_SIZE
Characteristics	Pageable

---

[1] The @ symbol precedes the address of a location containing the specified value.

19.1.2   Variable-Length Blocks

Pools that permit allocation of variable-length blocks have a common structure. Each pool has a listhead containing the address of the first unused block in the pool. The first two longwords of each unused block describe the block. As illustrated in Figure 19.1, the first longword in a block contains the address of the next unused block in the list. The second longword contains the size in bytes of the unused block. Each successive unused block is found at a higher address. Thus, the unused blocks in each pool area form a singly linked, memory-ordered list. Table 19.2 summarizes the listheads and other related locations.

Each variable-length pool has its own set of allocation and deallocation routines. Each of the allocation routines for the variable-length pools rounds the requested size up to the next multiple of 16 bytes to impose a granularity on both the allocated and unused areas. Because all the pool areas are initially page-aligned, this rounding causes every structure allocated from the pool areas to be at least octaword-aligned.

The various allocation and deallocation routines invoke the lower level routines EXE$ALLOCATE and EXE$DEALLOCATE, which support the structure common to the variable-length lists. Each routine has two arguments: the address of the pool listhead and the size of the data structure to be allocated or deallocated. These general-purpose routines are also used for several other pools, including symbol table space of the Digital command

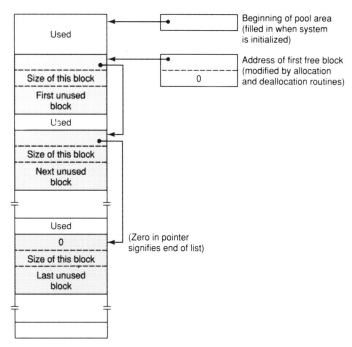

Figure 19.1
Layout of Unused Areas in Variable-Length Pools

language (DCL) interpreter, the process space pool of the network ancillary control process (NETACP), and the global page table.

All the allocation and deallocation routines described in this chapter are in module MEMORYALC.

19.1.2.1   **Variable-Length Block Allocation.** When the allocation routine EXE$ALLO-CATE is invoked, it searches from the beginning of the list until it encounters an unused block large enough to satisfy the request. If the fit is exact, the allocation routine simply adjusts the previous pointer to point to the next free block. If the fit is not exact, it subtracts the allocated size from the original size of the block, puts the new size into the remainder of the block, and adjusts the previous pointer to point to the remainder of the block. That is, if the fit is not exact, the low-address end of the block is allocated, and the high-address end is placed back on the list. The two possible allocation situations (exact and inexact fit) are illustrated in Figure 19.2.

19.1.2.2   **Variable-Length Block Allocation Examples.** The first part of Figure 19.2 (Initial Condition) shows a section of paged pool; MMG$GL_PAGEDYN,

Table 19.2   Pool Listheads and Selected Data Cells

Location	Contents	*Static or Dynamic*[1]
	NONPAGED POOL	
EXE$GL_NONPAGED[2]+4	Address of first free block	Dynamic
EXE$GL_NONPAGED[2]+8	Size of zero (for dummy listhead) to speed allocation	Static
MMG$GL_NPAGEDYN[3]	Address of beginning of nonpaged pool area	Static
MMG$GL_NPAGNEXT[3]	Address of beginning of pool expansion area	Dynamic
	LRP LOOKASIDE LIST	
IOC$GQ_LRPIQ[4]	Displacement to first free block	Dynamic
IOC$GQ_LRPIQ[4]+4	Displacement to last free block	Dynamic
IOC$GL_LRPSPLIT[4]	Address of beginning of LRP area	Static
MMG$GL_LRPNEXT[3]	Address of beginning of LRP expansion area	Dynamic
	IRP LOOKASIDE LIST	
IOC$GQ_IRPIQ[4]	Displacement to first free block	Dynamic
IOC$GQ_IRPIQ[4]+4	Displacement to last free block	Dynamic
EXE$GL_SPLITADR[2]	Address of beginning of IRP area	Static
MMG$GL_IRPNEXT[3]	Address of beginning of IRP expansion area	Dynamic
	SRP LOOKASIDE LIST	
IOC$GQ_SRPIQ[4]	Displacement to first free block	Dynamic
IOC$GQ_SRPIQ[4]+4	Displacement to last free block	Dynamic
IOC$GL_SRPSPLIT[4]	Address of beginning of SRP area	Static
MMG$GL_SRPNEXT[3]	Address of beginning of SRP expansion area	Dynamic
	PAGED POOL	
EXE$GL_PAGED[2]	Address of first free block	Dynamic
EXE$GL_PAGED[2]+4	Size of zero (for dummy listhead) to speed allocation	Static
MMG$GL_PAGEDYN[3]	Address of beginning of paged pool area	Static
	PROCESS QUOTA BLOCK (PQB) LOOKASIDE LIST	
EXE$GL_PQBIQ[2]	Displacement to first free block	Dynamic
EXE$GL_PQBIQ[2]+4	Displacement to last free block	Dynamic
	PROCESS ALLOCATION REGION	
CTL$GQ_ALLOCREG[5]	Address of first free block	Dynamic
CTL$GQ_ALLOCREG[5]+4	Size of zero (for dummy listhead) to speed allocation	Static

(continued)

Table 19.2   Pool Listheads and Selected Data Cells *(continued)*

Location	Contents	Static or Dynamic [1]
	PROCESS ALLOCATION REGION	
CTL$GQ_P0ALLOC [5]	Address of first free block	Dynamic
CTL$GQ_P0ALLOC [5]+4	Size of zero (for dummy listhead) to speed allocation	Static
	KRP LOOKASIDE LIST	
CTL$GL_KRPFL [5]	Address of first free block	Dynamic
CTL$GL_KRPBL [5]	Address of last free block	Dynamic
CTL$GL_KRP [5]	Address of beginning of KRP area	Static

[1] Static locations are loaded at initialization time, and their contents do not change during the life of the system. The contents of dynamic locations change as pool is allocated, deallocated, and expanded.

[2] The module SYSTEM_DATA_CELLS (part of the base image, SYS.EXE) defines these symbols.

[3] The module SYSPARAM (part of the base image, SYS.EXE) defines these symbols.

[4] For improved performance, these symbols are defined as global cells in module MEMORYALC, part of a loadable executive image, rather than as universal symbols vectored through the base image. Routines in other loadable executive images refer to them as offsets from the contents of the universal location EXE$AR_SYSTEM_PRIMITIVES_DATA. For more information on loadable executive images, the base image, and vectored universal symbols, see Chapter 29.

[5] The module SHELL defines these P1 space symbols.

which points to the beginning of paged pool; and EXE$GL_PAGED, which points to the first available block of paged pool. In this example, allocated blocks of memory are identified only by the total number of bytes in use, with no indication of the number and size of the individual data structures within each block.

The second part of Figure 19.2 (80 Bytes Allocated) shows the structure of paged pool after the allocation of an 80-byte block. Note that the discrete portions of 96 bytes and 48 bytes in use and the 80 bytes that were allocated are now combined to show a 224-byte block of paged pool in use.

The third part of Figure 19.2 (48 Bytes Allocated) shows an alternative scenario, the structure of paged pool after the allocation of a 48-byte block. The 48 bytes were taken from the low-address end of the first unused block large enough to contain it. Because this allocation was not an exact fit, an unused 32-byte block remains.

19.1.2.3   **Variable-Length Block Deallocation.** When a block is deallocated, it must be inserted into the list according to its address. EXE$DEALLOCATE follows

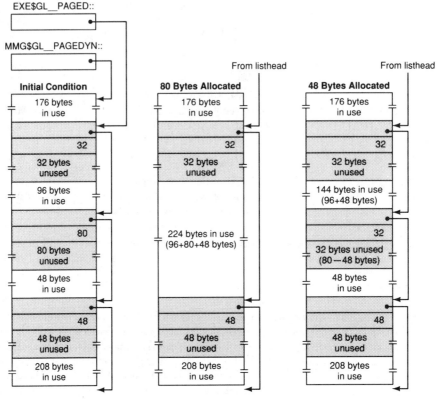

Figure 19.2
Examples of Variable-Length Block Allocation

the unused area pointers until it encounters a block whose address is larger than the address of the block to be deallocated. If the deallocated block is adjacent to another unused block, the two blocks are merged into a single unused area.

This merging, or agglomeration, can occur at the end of the preceding unused block or at the beginning of the following block (or both). Because merging occurs automatically as a part of deallocation, there is no need for any externally triggered routine to consolidate pool fragmentation.

19.1.2.4 **Variable-Length Block Deallocation Examples.** Figure 19.3 shows three sample deallocations, two of which illustrate merging. The first part of the figure (Initial Condition) shows an area of paged pool containing logical name blocks for three logical names: ADAM, GREGORY, and ROSAMUND. These three logical name blocks are bracketed by two unused portions of paged pool, one 64 bytes long, the other 176 bytes long.

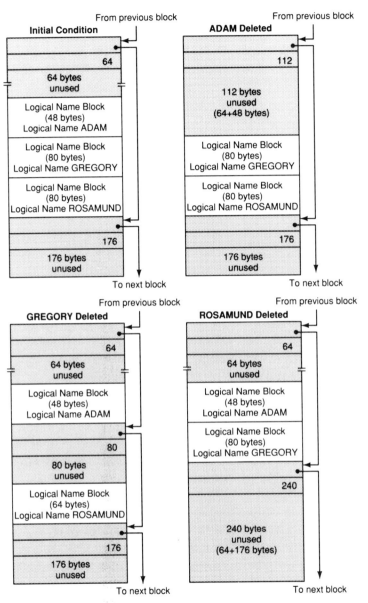

Figure 19.3
Examples of Variable-Length Block Deallocation

The second part of Figure 19.3 (ADAM Deleted) shows the result of deleting the logical name ADAM. Because the logical name block was adjacent to the high-address end of an unused block, the blocks are merged. The size of the deallocated block is simply added to the size of the unused block. No pointers need to be adjusted.

The structure shown in the third part of Figure 19.3 (GREGORY Deleted) shows an alternative scenario, the result of deleting the logical name GREGORY. The pointer in the unused block of 64 bytes is altered to point to the deallocated block; a new pointer and size longword are created within the deallocated block.

The fourth part of Figure 19.3 (ROSAMUND Deleted) shows the result of deleting the logical name ROSAMUND. In this case, the deallocated block is adjacent to the low-address end of an unused block, so the blocks are merged. The pointer to the next unused block that was previously in the adjacent block is moved to the beginning of the newly deallocated block. The following longword is loaded with the size of the merged block (240 bytes).

19.1.3 Fixed-Length Packets

Fixed-length lists, also known as lookaside lists, consist of fixed-length packets available for allocation. With VMS Version 5, each (with the exception of the KRP lookaside list) is a doubly linked, self-relative queue with a listhead containing the displacements to the first and last unused blocks in the list. Figure 19.4 (Initial Condition) shows the form of a fixed-length list. Table 19.2 summarizes the listheads and other related locations.

Fixed-length lists expedite the allocation and deallocation of the most commonly used sizes and types of storage. In contrast to variable-length allocation, fixed-length allocation is very simple. There is no overhead searching for a sufficiently large block of free memory to accommodate a specific request. Instead, a REMQHI instruction allocates a packet from the front of the appropriate list (see Figure 19.4, Packet Removed from Head). An INSQTI instruction deallocates a packet to the back of a list (see Figure 19.4, Packet Inserted at Tail).

Interlocked queue instructions synchronize concurrent access to system space lookaside lists on symmetrical multiprocessor (SMP) systems. Chapter 8 contains further information on interlocked queue instructions.

A KRP lookaside list exists in each process's P1 space and is accessed only from the owning process's context. The list is a doubly linked, absolute queue, whose listhead contains the addresses of the first and last blocks in the list. REMQUE and INSQUE instructions remove and insert KRPs in the lookaside list, and provide sufficient synchronization in this context. Section 19.5 describes the use of KRPs.

19.1.4 Dynamic Data Structures

Almost all dynamic data structures have a common header format, shown in Figure 19.5. The header includes two structure-describing fields: the number of bytes allocated for the data structure in the word at offset 8 and the type code in a byte at offset 10.

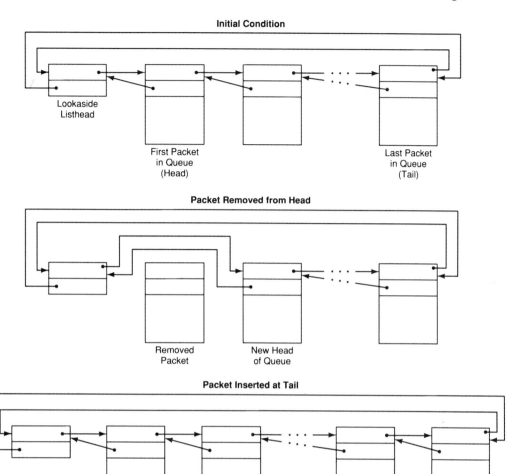

Note: Pointers are absolute or self-relative, depending on the type of queue.

Figure 19.4
Fixed-Length Packet Allocation and Deallocation

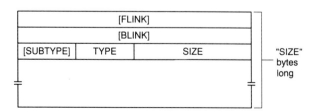

Figure 19.5
Format of Dynamic Data Structures

The third longword of a data structure contains the size, type, and (optional) subtype fields, leaving the first two longwords available to link the data structure into a list or queue.

The type field enables VMS to distinguish different data structures and to confirm that a piece of dynamic storage contains the expected data structure type. Data structures with a type code value equal to or larger than 96 also have a one-byte subtype code at offset 11. The macro $DYNDEF defines the possible values for the type and subtype fields. The high-order bit's being set in the type field indicates that a structure is allocated from MA780 multiport memory.

When a dynamic data structure is deallocated to the variable-length list, the size field specifies how much storage is being returned.

The System Dump Analyzer (SDA) Utility uses the type and size fields to produce a formatted display of a dynamic data structure and to determine the portions of variable-length pool that are in use.

19.2 NONPAGED POOL REGIONS

Nonpaged dynamic memory contains data structures and code used by the portions of VMS that run in system context, such as interrupt service routines and device drivers. For these parts of the operating system, only system space is accessible. Furthermore, they execute at IPLs above 2, where page faults are not permitted.

Nonpaged dynamic memory, more commonly known as nonpaged pool, also contains data structures that are shared by several processes and that may be accessed above IPL 2.

The protection on nonpaged pool is ERKW, allowing it to be read from executive and kernel modes but written only from kernel mode.

Nonpaged pool is the most heavily used of the storage areas. It consists of a variable-length list and three fixed-length lookaside lists. The three lookaside lists are the large request packet (LRP), intermediate request packet (IRP), and small request packet (SRP) lists. These lists provide for the most frequently allocated nonpaged pool data structures. Nonpaged pool is sometimes allocated explicitly from a lookaside list and sometimes implicitly, as the result of general nonpaged pool allocation. Section 19.2.2 discusses allocation in detail.

Early versions of VMS had only one lookaside list, whose primary use was for I/O request packets; it was called the I/O request packet lookaside list. Many other types of packets use the IRP lookaside list today, and the *I* has come to stand for *intermediate*. Nevertheless, I/O request packets are still among the most performance-critical and frequent users of this list, and although the intermediate packet size varies from VMS version to version, it is always at least the size of an I/O request packet.

19.2.1   **Nonpaged Pool Initialization**

SYSGEN parameters determine the sizes of the nonpaged pool lists. Non-paged pool is potentially expandable during normal system operation. Two SYSGEN parameters specify the initial size and the maximum size of each of the four nonpaged pool regions.

SYSGEN parameters NPAGEDYN and NPAGEVIR control the size in bytes of the variable-length region of nonpaged pool. Both are rounded down to an integral number of pages. During system initialization, SYSBOOT allocates sufficient contiguous system page table entries (SPTEs) for the maximum size of the region, NPAGEVIR. It then allocates physical pages of memory for the initial size of the region, NPAGEDYN, and maps them using the first portion of the allocated SPTEs. To minimize overhead, the initial allocations of physical pages of memory come from pages whose state is not described by the page frame number (PFN) database. The remaining SPTEs remain invalid. Later pool expansions also come from such pages, as long as any are available. Chapter 14 describes page table entries.

SYSBOOT allocates SPTEs and physical pages of memory for the lookaside lists in the same manner as for the variable-length list. It allocates nonpaged system space following the variable-length list for each lookaside list. Table 19.3 lists the SYSGEN parameters relevant to each lookaside list. Figure 19.6 shows the four regions of nonpaged pool. In each of the three lookaside lists, the elements in the initial allocation are formed and inserted into a list with the INSQTI instruction, resulting in a doubly linked list of fixed-size elements.

During system operation, a failure to allocate from a nonpaged pool region results in an attempt to expand it. Section 19.2.4 describes pool expansion. The deallocation merge strategy described in Section 19.2.3 requires that the four nonpaged pool regions occupy progressively higher virtual memory addresses. That is, all the blocks on the variable-length list must have addresses that are less than all LRP addresses; all LRPs must have addresses that are less than all IRP addresses; and so on. It is because of this restriction that

Table 19.3   SYSGEN Parameters Controlling Lookaside List Sizes

List Type	Size of Packet	Initial Count	Maximum Count
SRP	SRPSIZE	SRPCOUNT	SRPCOUNTV
IRP	176	IRPCOUNT	IRPCOUNTV
LRP	LRPSIZE+140 [1]	LRPCOUNT	LRPCOUNTV

[1] The actual packet size is the sum of LRPSIZE and 140, rounded up to a multiple of 16.

Pool Management

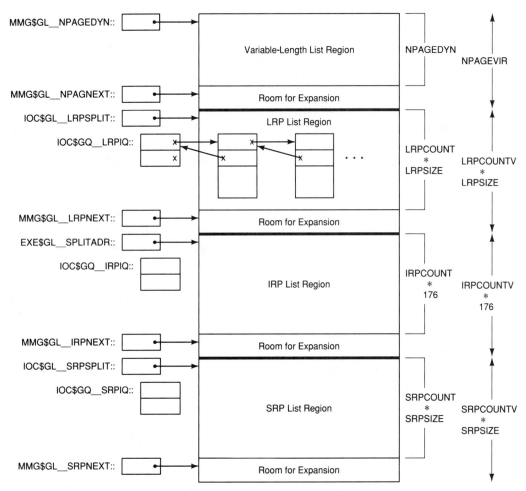

Figure 19.6
Nonpaged Pool Regions

the maximum number of SPTEs are allocated contiguously for each region, even if some of them are initially unused.

The cell IOC$GL_SRPSIZE contains the size of the elements in the SRP list. The SYSGEN parameter SRPSIZE determines this value. SYSBOOT rounds SRPSIZE up to a multiple of 16.

The symbol IRP$C_LENGTH, rounded up to the next multiple of 16, determines the size of an IRP list element. In VMS Version 5.2, an IRP is 176 bytes.

The cell IOC$GL_LRPSIZE contains the size of the elements in the LRP list. SYSBOOT computes IOC$GL_LRPSIZE by adding CXB$C_OVERHEAD (140 in VMS Version 5.2) to the SYSGEN parameter LRPSIZE and rounding up the sum to a multiple of 16. The parameter LRPSIZE is intended to be the DECnet buffer size, exclusive of a 140-byte internal buffer header. (Note that the output of SHOW MEMORY displays the inclusive packet size.)

19.2.2   Nonpaged Pool Allocation

A number of routines in module MEMORYALC allocate nonpaged pool. Some of these routines, such as EXE$ALLOCPCB or EXE$ALLOCTQE, allocate pool for a particular type of data structure, filling in its size and type. Some routines, intended for use only within process context, conditionally place the process into a resource wait (see Chapter 12) for resource RSN$_NPDYNMEM if pool is unavailable. All these routines invoke EXE$ALONONPAGED, the general nonpaged pool allocation routine.

In several instances, VMS routines explicitly allocate request packets from a lookaside list. For example, when the Queue I/O Request ($QIO) system service needs an IRP, it executes a REMQHI instruction. Several other system routines allocate IRPs this way. Only if the lookaside list is empty (indicated by the V-bit set in the processor status word (PSW) following the REMQHI) is the general nonpaged pool allocation routine invoked.

Similarly, the Enqueue Lock Request ($ENQ) system service allocates pool for a lock block by removing an SRP from the lookaside list. The SYSGEN parameter SRPSIZE is constrained to be at least the size of a lock block. It allocates pool for a resource block by removing an IRP from the lookaside list.

Because allocation from and deallocation to a lookaside list are so much faster than the equivalent operations involving the variable-length list, EXE$ALONONPAGED performs special checks to determine whether the requested block can be allocated from one of the lookaside lists. These checks compare the request size to the lists' upper and lower limits. Figure 19.7 shows the size ranges for the lookaside lists. The ranges are defined so that the majority of requests can be satisfied from one of the lookaside lists.

Requests that must be allocated from the variable-length list are either

- Larger than an LRP, or
- Larger than an IRP but smaller than the SYSGEN parameter LRPMIN

The symbolic names in Figure 19.7 are defined as follows:

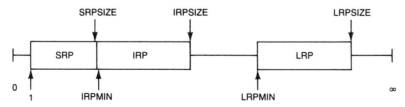

Figure 19.7
Lookaside List Allocation Ranges

Symbol	Meaning
SRPSIZE	IOC$GL_SRPSIZE, the SYSGEN parameter SRPSIZE rounded up to a multiple of 16
IRPMIN	IOC$GL_IRPMIN, the sum of IOC$GL_SRPSIZE plus 1
IRPSIZE	IRP$C_LENGTH rounded up to a multiple of 16, the constant 176 in VMS Version 5.2
LRPMIN	IOC$GL_LRPMIN, the SYSGEN parameter LRPMIN
LRPSIZE	IOC$GL_LRPSIZE, the sum of SYSGEN parameter LRPSIZE plus 140 in VMS Version 5.2

EXE$ALONONPAGED allocates nonpaged pool by the following steps:

1. It compares the requested size to the ranges just described to determine which, if any, lookaside list it can use.
2. If none of the lookaside lists is appropriate, it branches to EXE$ALONPAGVAR to allocate the pool from the variable-length list.
3. If one of the lookaside lists is appropriate and the list is not empty, the routine removes the first packet from the list and returns its address to the caller.
4. If one of the lookaside lists is appropriate but is empty, EXE$ALONONPAGED attempts to expand the list (see Section 19.2.4) and, if it succeeds, retries the allocation. If the lookaside list cannot be extended, it branches to EXE$ALONPAGVAR to allocate the pool from the variable-length list.

EXE$ALONPAGVAR, an alternative entry point to EXE$ALONONPAGED, allocates pool only from the variable-length list. It is invoked directly whenever multiple pieces of pool are allocated as a single larger piece but deallocated in a piecemeal fashion. EXE$ALONPAGVAR performs the following steps:

1. It rounds the allocation size up to a multiple of 16.
2. It acquires the POOL spinlock, raising IPL to IPL$_POOL.
3. It invokes the lower level routine EXE$ALLOCATE, described in Section 19.1.2.
4. It releases the POOL spinlock, restoring the previous IPL. If EXE$ALLOCATE succeeded, EXE$ALONPAGVAR returns the size and address of the allocated block. If the allocation failed, EXE$ALONPAGVAR attempts to expand the list (see Section 19.2.4). If the expansion succeeds, EXE$ALONPAGVAR repeats the allocation attempt. If the expansion fails, it returns the error status SS$_INSFMEM to its invoker.

19.2.3   Nonpaged Pool Deallocation

A consumer of nonpaged pool invokes EXE$DEANONPAGED to deallocate nonpaged pool back to any of the four regions. Figure 19.6 shows the four regions and the cells that identify their boundaries.

EXE$DEANONPAGED determines to which region the packet or block of pool is being returned, not by its size but by its address, taking the following steps:

1. It compares the address of the block being deallocated to the contents of global location IOC$GL_SRPSPLIT. If the address is greater or equal, the block came from the SRP list.
2. If the block's address is less than the contents of IOC$GL_SRPSPLIT, EXE$DEANONPAGED compares it to the contents of EXE$GL_SPLIT-ADR. If the address is greater or equal, the block came from the IRP list.
3. If the block's address is less than the contents of EXE$GL_SPLITADR, EXE$DEANONPAGED compares it to the contents of IOC$GL_LRP-SPLIT. If the address is greater or equal, the block came from the LRP list.
4. If the block's address is less than the contents of IOC$GL_LRPSPLIT, the block came from the variable-length list.

EXE$DEANONPAGED returns a packet to one of the lookaside lists with an INSQTI instruction, as described in Section 19.1.3. By allocating packets from one end of the list and deallocating them to the other end, VMS maintains a transaction history as long as the list itself.

If the block was allocated from the variable-length list, EXE$DEANON-PAGED acquires the POOL spinlock, raising IPL to IPL$_POOL; invokes EXE$DEALLOCATE, the lower level routine described in Section 19.1.2; and then releases the POOL spinlock, restoring the previous IPL.

When any variable-length block is returned or when a lookaside packet is returned to an empty list, EXE$DEANONPAGED must declare that nonpaged pool is available. It acquires the SCHED spinlock, raising IPL to IPL$_SCHED; invokes SCH$RAVAIL to declare the availability of nonpaged pool for any process that might be waiting for resource RSN$_NPDYNMEM; and releases the SCHED spinlock, restoring the previous IPL. The consequences of this declaration are discussed briefly in Section 19.2.5 and at greater length in Chapter 12.

Deallocating a block back to a list based on the address of the block has an important implication. Lookaside list corruption results if a nonpaged pool consumer deallocates part of a lookaside list packet. That is, VMS treats all lookaside packets as indivisible. A partial packet deallocated to a lookaside list is eventually allocated as a whole packet, resulting in double use of the same memory. The entry point EXE$ALONPAGVAR should be used for allocating nonpaged pool that may be deallocated in a piecemeal way. EXE$ALONPAGVAR always allocates from the variable-length list.

19.2.4   **Nonpaged Pool Expansion**

Dynamic nonpaged pool expansion creates additional nonpaged pool as it is needed. At system initialization, SYSBOOT allocates enough system space for the maximum size of each nonpaged pool region, but it only allocates enough physical memory for the initial size of each region. When an attempt to allocate nonpaged pool fails, the pool can be expanded by allocating more physical memory for it and altering the system page table (SPT) accordingly.

If EXE$ALONONPAGED or EXE$ALONPAGVAR fails to allocate nonpaged pool from any of the four regions, it attempts to expand the failing region by invoking the routine EXE$EXTENDPOOL with an argument indicating which list is to be expanded.

EXE$EXTENDPOOL acquires the MMG spinlock, raising IPL to IPL$_MMG to synchronize access to the PFN database. It then attempts to allocate eight pages of physical memory if expanding one of the lookaside lists, or 63 pages if expanding the variable-length list. First, it checks whether the physical pages can be allocated without reducing the number of physical pages available to the system below the minimum required. Pool expansion must leave sufficient fluid pages to accommodate the sum of the maximum swap image (for VMS Version 5, the lesser of WSMAX and 64K– 1 pages), the modified list low limit, and the free page list low limit. This check may result in fewer pages being allocated for the expansion.

If the memory sufficiency check fails, the routine attempts to broadcast a message to the operator's console and logs an expansion failure event (see Section 19.6).

For each allocated page, EXE$EXTENDPOOL places its PFN in the next invalid SPTE for that list and sets the valid bit. If the region is a lookaside list, the new virtual page and any fragment from the previous virtual page are formatted into packets of the appropriate size and placed on the list. EXE$EXTENDPOOL records the size and address of any fragment left from the last new page. If the region is the variable-length list, it invokes EXE$DEANONPGDSIZ to add the new virtual pages to the list. EXE$EXTENDPOOL then releases the MMG spinlock, restoring the previous IPL.

If EXE$EXTENDPOOL is able to expand the failing region, it reports that resource RSN$_NPDYNMEM is available for any waiting processes.

For proper synchronization of system databases, the resource availability report and the allocation of physical memory must not be done from a thread of execution running on a CPU that owns a spinlock of rank higher than MMG. (The SCHED spinlock is the only IPL$_SYNCH spinlock with a rank higher than MMG.) EXE$EXTENDPOOL examines the processor status longword (PSL) to determine at what IPL the system is running. If EXE$EXTENDPOOL was entered from an interrupt service routine running above IPL$_SYNCH or is running on a CPU that owns the SCHED spinlock, EXE$EXTENDPOOL creates an IPL$_QUEUEAST fork process to expand the lists at some later time and returns an allocation failure status to its caller.

Nonpaged pool expansion provides a degree of automatic system tuning. The penalty for setting an inadequate initial allocation size is the increased overhead in allocating requests that cause expansion. As an additional minor physical penalty, unnecessary PFN database entries are built for those physical pages that are subsequently added to nonpaged pool as a result of expansion. (Original nonpaged pool pages need no PFN database entries.) The cost is about 4 percent of the size of the page per added page.

The penalty for a maximum allocation that is too large is one longword (for the SPTE) for each unused page. If the maximum size of a lookaside list is too small, system performance may be adversely affected when the system is prevented from using the lookaside mechanism for pool requests. If the maximum size of the variable-length region is too small, processes may be placed into a resource wait state, waiting for nonpaged pool to become available.

Nonpaged pool expands, but it does not contract. No mechanism returns PFNs from the nonpaged pool to the free page list. The nonpaged pool regions return to their original sizes only at the next bootstrap, assuming that the SYSGEN parameters that control their sizes have not changed.

19.2.5 Nonpaged Pool Synchronization

The POOL spinlock serializes access to the nonpaged pool variable-length list. Acquiring the POOL spinlock raises IPL to IPL$_POOL. The allocation and deallocation routines for the nonpaged pool variable-length list acquire and release the POOL spinlock.

Device drivers running at fork level frequently allocate dynamic storage. The POOL spinlock ranks higher than the IOLOCK11 and MAILBOX spinlocks. This allows a CPU executing a driver fork process to acquire the POOL spinlock while owning the MAILBOX or any of the IOLOCKx spinlocks. However, a CPU executing at device IPL may not acquire the POOL spinlock, because device IPL is higher than IPL$_POOL.

Each nonpaged pool allocation routine that runs in process context (for example, EXE$ALLOCCEB) invokes EXE$ALONONPAGED without acquiring the SCHED spinlock. If this attempt to allocate pool is successful, the routine has avoided the overhead of spinlock acquisition and release.

If EXE$ALONONPAGED fails to allocate the pool, the routine acquires the SCHED spinlock, raising IPL to IPL$_SCHED and synchronizing access to the scheduler database, and invokes EXE$ALONONPAGED again. If the second allocation attempt fails, the routine tests PCB$V_SSRWAIT in PCB$L_STS. If it is set, the routine invokes a scheduling routine to place the process into a resource wait state, waiting for RSN$_NPDYNMEM. The scheduling routine releases the SCHED spinlock and restores the previous IPL. The SCHED spinlock is held throughout this sequence to block deallocation of pool and the accompanying report of resource availability between the time of the second allocation failure and the time the process is actually placed into a wait state.

The spinlock acquisition scheme requires that spinlocks be acquired in increasing rank. This rule dictates that nonpaged pool be deallocated from a thread of execution owning spinlocks ranked no higher than SCHED. The interrupt nesting scheme requires that IPL never be lowered below the IPL value at which the current interrupt occurred. This rule dictates that nonpaged pool be deallocated from a thread of execution running as the result of an interrupt no higher than IPL$_SYNCH.

Note the asymmetry in allocating and deallocating nonpaged pool. Although threads of execution owning spinlocks ranked as high as MAILBOX can allocate nonpaged pool, they must not own any spinlocks ranked higher than SCHED when they deallocate nonpaged pool. Although code running at IPL levels up to IPL$_POOL can allocate nonpaged pool, code running as a result of an interrupt above IPL$_SYNCH must not deallocate nonpaged pool.

Processes might be waiting for nonpaged pool, since it is a systemwide resource. When EXE$DEANONPAGED reports the availability of nonpaged pool, any waiting processes are made computable. These modifications to the scheduler database take place while the CPU owns the SCHED spinlock and runs at IPL$_SCHED.

Code executing as the result of an interrupt at IPL$_SYNCH or above deallocates nonpaged pool through routine COM$DRVDEALMEM, in module COMDRVSUB. If COM$DRVDEALMEM is invoked from below IPL$_SYNCH, it merely deallocates the pool by jumping to EXE$DEANONPAGED. If, however, COM$DRVDEALMEM is invoked from IPL$_SYNCH or above, it transforms the block that is to be deallocated into a fork block (see Figure 4.1) and requests an IPL$_QUEUEAST software interrupt. (Note that the block to be deallocated must be at least 24 bytes, large enough for a fork block. If it is not, COM$DRVDEALMEM generates a nonfatal bugcheck and returns to its invoker. The block of pool space is lost.)

The code that executes as the IPL$_QUEUEAST fork process (the saved program counter in the fork block) simply executes a JMP to EXE$DEANON-PAGED to deallocate the block. Because EXE$DEANONPAGED is entered at IPL$_QUEUEAST, the synchronized access to the scheduler's database is preserved. This technique is similar to the one used by device drivers that need to interact with the scheduler by declaring asynchronous system traps (ASTs). The attention AST mechanism is described briefly in Chapter 8 and in greater detail in Chapter 7.

By convention, process context code that allocates a nonpaged pool data structure executes at IPL 2 or above as long as the data structure's existence is recorded solely in a temporary process location, such as in a register or on the stack. Running at IPL 2 blocks AST delivery and prevents the possible loss of the pool if the process were to be deleted.

19.2.6   **Uses of Nonpaged Pool**

Nonpaged pool serves many purposes. This section describes typical uses of the nonpaged pool lists. Note, however, that nondefault choices for SYSGEN parameters LRPSIZE, LRPMIN, and SRPSIZE may result in different use.

The variable-length list is used for allocating nonpaged pool that does not fit the allocation constraints of the lookaside lists. Typically, device drivers and the larger unit control blocks describing I/O device units are allocated from the variable-length list. Also, process control blocks, which contain process-related information that must remain resident, are allocated from the variable-length list.

Nonpaged pool is allocated during early stages of system initialization. SYSBOOT loads several images into nonpaged variable-length pool. These include the system disk driver, terminal driver, and CPU-dependent routines. The detailed use of nonpaged pool by the initialization routines is described in Chapter 31.

The LRP lookaside list is typically used by DECnet for receiving messages from other nodes. On a system connected to a CI bus, CI datagrams (CIDGs), used to provide best-effort message service among the nodes on the CI, may be allocated from the LRP lookaside list. On a system with a relatively large value for LRPSIZE, many loaded images, such as device drivers, may be allocated from the LRP lookaside list rather than from the variable-length list.

The IRP lookaside list is typically used for the following data structures:

- I/O and class driver request packets, which describe a particular I/O request
- Job information blocks, which contain the quotas and limits shared by processes in a job
- Resource blocks, used by the lock management system services
- Unit control blocks, which describe the state of an I/O device unit
- Larger buffered I/O buffers
- On a system with a CI bus, CI sequenced messages used to provide highly reliable communication among the nodes on the CI
- Channel (controller) request blocks, which describe the state of a device controller

The SRP lookaside list is typically used for the following data structures:

- Lock and small resource blocks, used by the lock management system services
- Window control blocks, which contain the location of a file's extents
- Timer queue entries, which describe time-dependent requests such as Schedule Wakeup ($SCHDWK) system service requests
- Smaller buffered I/O buffers
- Interrupt dispatch blocks, which describe the state of a device controller

- Object rights blocks (ORBs), which describe the rights that a process must have in order to access the object (such as a device) with which the ORB is associated

19.3   PAGED POOL

Paged dynamic memory contains data structures that are used by multiple processes but that are not required to be permanently memory-resident. Its protection is ERKW, allowing it to be read from executive and kernel modes but written only from kernel mode.

During system initialization, SYSBOOT reserves system space for paged pool, placing its starting address in MMG$GL_PAGEDYN. The SYSGEN parameter PAGEDYN specifies the size of this area in bytes. Paged pool is created as a set of demand zero pages. The loadable executive image EXEC_ INIT places the address of the beginning of the paged pool area in EXE$GL_ PAGED. System initialization code running in the context of the swapper process initializes the pool as one data structure encompassing the entire pool. That initialization incurs a page fault and thus requires process context.

Process context kernel mode code invokes the routine EXE$ALOPAGED to allocate paged pool and EXE$DEAPAGED to deallocate paged pool. These routines, both in module MEMORYALC, invoke the lower level variable-length allocation and deallocation routines described in Section 19.1.2.

If an allocation request cannot be satisfied, EXE$ALOPAGED returns to its invoker with a failure status. The invoker may return an error, for example, SS$_INSFMEM, to the user program, or the invoker may place the process into a resource wait state, waiting for resource RSN$_PGDYNMEM.

Whenever paged pool is deallocated, EXE$DEAPAGED invokes SCH$R-AVAIL, in module MUTEX, to declare the availability of paged pool for any waiting process. Chapter 12 describes process resource waits.

Paged pool requires little system overhead: one SPTE per page of pool. Because paged pool is created as demand zero SPTEs (see Chapter 14), it expands on demand through page faults.

Because this area is pageable, code that accesses it must run at IPL 2 or below while accessing it. Elevated IPL, therefore, cannot be used for synchronizing access to the paged pool list or to any data structures allocated from it. The EXE$GL_PGDYNMTX mutex serializes access to the paged pool list. Both EXE$ALOPAGED and EXE$DEAPAGED lock this mutex for write access.

By convention, process context code that allocates a paged pool data structure executes at IPL 2 as long as the data structure's existence is recorded solely in a temporary process location, such as in a register or on the stack. Running at IPL 2 blocks AST delivery and prevents the possible loss of the pool if the process were to be deleted.

The following data structures are located in the paged pool area:

- The shareable logical name tables and logical name blocks
- The Files-11 Extended QIO Processor (XQP) I/O buffer cache, which is used for data such as file headers, index file bit map blocks, directory data file blocks, and quota file data blocks
- Global section descriptors, which are used when a global section is mapped or unmapped
- Mounted volume list entries, which associate a mounted volume name with its corresponding logical name and unit control block address
- Access control list elements, which specify what access to an object is allowed for different classes of users
- ORBs that are accessed at IPL 2 and below
- Data structures required by the Install Utility to describe known images

  Any image that is installed has a known file entry created to describe it. Some frequently accessed known images also have their image headers permanently resident in paged pool. These data structures are described in more detail in Chapter 26.

- Process quota blocks (PQBs), which are temporarily used during process creation to store the quotas and limits of the new process

  PQBs, initially allocated from paged pool, are not deallocated back to the paged pool list. Instead, they are queued to a lookaside list whose listhead is at global label EXE$GL_PQBIQ. Starting with VMS Version 5, this is a self-relative queue. Process creation code attempts to allocate a PQB by removing an element from this queue, as a faster alternative to general paged pool allocation.

19.4   PROCESS ALLOCATION REGION

The process allocation region contains variable-length data structures that are used only by a single process and are not required to be permanently memory-resident. (Process allocation region pages are pageable.) Its protection is set to UREW, allowing executive and kernel modes to write it and any access mode to read it.

The process allocation region consists of a P1 space variable-length pool and may include a P0 space variable-length pool as well. The P0 space allocation pool is useful only for image-specific data structures that do not need to survive image exit. The P1 space pool can be used for both image-specific data structures and data structures that must survive the rundown of an image, such as logical name tables.

During process startup, EXE$PROCSTRT reserves P1 address space for the process allocation region. The SYSGEN parameter CTLPAGES specifies the number of pages in the P1 pool. Free space in the P1 process allocation region is maintained in a singly linked, memory-ordered list (see Section 19.1.2). EXE$PROCSTRT initializes the pool and its listhead, CTL$GQ_

ALLOCREG. There is no global pointer that locates the beginning of the process allocation region.

Executive or kernel mode code running in process context invokes EXE$ALOP1PROC, EXE$ALOP1IMAG, or EXE$ALOP0IMAG to allocate space from the process allocation region, and EXE$DEAP1 to deallocate a data structure to the region. These routines are in module MEMORYALC. When the data structure must be allocated from the P1 pool, EXE$ALOP1-PROC is used. When the data structure is image-specific, EXE$ALOP1IMAG or EXE$ALOP0IMAG is used.

EXE$ALOP1IMAG and EXE$ALOP0IMAG differ in which region they first attempt the allocation. EXE$ALOP1IMAG tries the P1 region first, while EXE$ALOP0IMAG tries the P0 region first. If EXE$ALOP1IMAG finds that there is insufficient space, or EXE$ALOP0IMAG finds that allocation in the P0 region is disallowed, each attempts to allocate from the other region. Neither routine can allocate from P1 space if the P1 process allocation region reaches a threshold of use specified by the SYSGEN parameter CTLIMGLIM. The current image's being linked with the NOP0BUFS option prevents allocation from P0 space. If the allocation fails, these routines return the SS$_INSFMEM error status.

The CTLIMGLIM limit does not apply to EXE$ALOP1PROC. It may allocate space until the P1 allocation region is exhausted. The arithmetic difference between CTLPAGES and CTLIMGLIM guarantees a minimum number of pages exclusively for EXE$ALOP1PROC. EXE$ALOP1PROC only allocates space from the P1 region. If an allocation fails, it returns the error status SS$_INSFMEM.

Free space in the P0 process allocation region is maintained in a singly linked, memory-ordered list, as described in Section 19.1.2. SHELL initializes the listhead, CTL$GQ_P0ALLOC, to zero. The image rundown routine deletes P0 space and zeros the listhead.

If not prevented by the presence of the NOP0BUFS linker option, EXE$ALOP1IMAG and EXE$ALOP0IMAG create and expand the P0 process allocation region by invoking the routine MMG$EXPREG, in module SYS-CREDEL. This routine functions much like the Expand Program/Control Region ($EXPREG) system service. EXE$ALOP1IMAG and EXE$ALOP0IMAG expand the P0 region as needed to satisfy allocation requests, but always by at least 16 pages. Each time one of these routines expands the P0 region, it invokes EXE$DEALLOCATE to link the new space into the free list.

The current image and other VMS routines may also expand the P0 virtual address space for their own purposes. Depending on the sequence of these expansions, multiple P0 allocation region expansions can result in a noncontiguous P0 allocation region. Note that this contrasts with the paged, nonpaged, and P1 allocation pools, which are always contiguous.

EXE$ALOP1PROC, EXE$ALOP1IMAG, and EXE$ALOP0IMAG each store

the address of the appropriate listhead in a register and invoke EXE$ALLO-CATE to perform the variable-length allocation described in Section 19.1.2.1. EXE$DEAP1 determines whether the block being deallocated is from the P0 or P1 space pool and invokes EXE$DEALLOCATE with the address of the appropriate listhead.

No special synchronization mechanism is currently used for either the process allocation region or the process logical names found there. However, the allocation routines change to kernel mode and execute at IPL 2, effectively blocking any other mainline or AST code from executing and perhaps attempting a simultaneous allocation from the process allocation region.

The following data structures are located in the process allocation region:

- The process-private logical name tables and logical name blocks
- Data structures, called image control blocks, built by the image activator to describe what images have been activated in the process
- Rights database identifier blocks, containing Record Management Services context (internal file and stream identifiers) for the rights database file
- A context block in which the Breakthrough ($BRKTHRU) system service maintains status information as the service asynchronously broadcasts messages to the terminals specified by the user
- Process scan context blocks, used by the Process Scan ($PROCESS_SCAN) system service, described in Chapter 13

There is enough room in the process allocation region for privileged application software to allocate process-specific data structures of reasonable size.

19.5 KRP LOOKASIDE LIST

The KRP lookaside list is a P1 space list for process-private kernel mode data structures that are not required to be permanently memory-resident. The protection on this storage area is URKW, allowing it to be read from any mode but modified only from kernel mode.

Address space for this list is defined at assembly time of the SHELL module, which defines the fixed part of P1 space. Two global symbols, CTL$C_KRP_COUNT and CTL$C_KRP_SIZE, control the number of KRP packets created and the size of each packet. Routine EXE$PROCSTRT, in module PROCSTRT, initializes the list, forming packets and inserting them in the list at CTL$GL_KRPFL and CTL$GL_KRPBL.

A KRP is used as pageable storage, local to a kernel mode subroutine. KRPs should be used only for temporary storage that is deallocated before the subroutine returns. The most common use of KRPs is to store an equivalence name returned from a logical name translation.

Allocation and deallocation to this list is through INSQUE and REMQUE instructions. Both allocation and deallocation are always done from the front of the list. There is no need for synchronization other than that provided by the queue instructions. Because KRPs are used only for storage local to the execution of a procedure, a failure to allocate a KRP is very unexpected and indicates a serious error rather than a temporary resource shortage. Kernel mode code that is unsuccessful at allocating from this list thus generates the fatal bugcheck KRPEMPTY.

19.6   **COLLECTING POOL ALLOCATION STATISTICS**

VMS requires adequate pool space to operate properly. Inadequate pool space can contribute to poor system performance and, in extreme cases, can cause the system to become totally unresponsive. VMS Version 5 adds a feedback mechanism to the AUTOGEN facility. Based on data gathered by various VMS components, this mechanism can adjust SYSGEN parameter values to a given system's workload.

The pool allocation and expansion routines described in this chapter store pool allocation and failure statistics in data cells. (An allocation request that results in a pool expansion is not classified as a failure; pool expansion is assumed to be a routine event.) From these statistics, AUTOGEN's feedback mechanism can calculate new values for the SYSGEN parameters that control the system paged and nonpaged pool sizes.

The statistics measure the appropriateness of the various pool sizes. From the statistical point of view, a lookaside list allocation fails when the list is empty and cannot be expanded. Although space may be allocated from the variable-length pool to satisfy the request, the allocation is nonetheless classified as a failure because the lookaside list parameters (initial or maximum size) are inadequate. Data cells contain the number of expansion failures for each of the three lookaside lists.

A variable-length list (paged or nonpaged) allocation fails when no sufficiently large free block is found and, in the case of the nonpaged pool, the list cannot be expanded.

An epoch is the 10-second period starting at a variable-length pool allocation failure. The routine that detects the allocation failure keeps a total of the number of bytes that fail to be allocated during an epoch. At the end of an epoch, the routine converts that to a whole number of pages and adds it to the appropriate data cell. It collects four categories of statistics for paged pool and variable-length nonpaged pool:

- Total number of allocation attempts
- Number of allocation failures
- Number of epochs during which allocation attempts failed
- Total number of pages that could not be allocated

Table 19.4 lists the data collected and the routines responsible for updating the data cells. The program AGEN$FEEDBACK.EXE (part of the MANAGE

Table 19.4   Pool Allocation Statistics

Statistic	*Location*	*Maintained By*
NONPAGED POOL LOOKASIDE AND VARIABLE-LENGTH LISTS		
Total number of expansion failures	PMS$GL_NPAGDYNEXPF	EXTENDPAGE
NONPAGED POOL LOOKASIDE LISTS		
Number of expansion failures: one count for each of the three lists	PMS$GL_XRPFAIL [1]	EXE$ALONONPAGED
VARIABLE-LENGTH NONPAGED POOL LIST		
Number of allocation attempts	PMS$GL_NPAGDYNREQ	EXE$ALONPAGVAR
Number of allocation failures	PMS$GL_NPAGDYNREQF	EXTEND_FAIL
Number of allocation failure epochs	PMS$GL_NPAGDYNF	EXTEND_FAIL
Total number of pages that failed to be allocated	PMS$GL_NPAGDYNFPAGES	EXTEND_FAIL
PAGED POOL		
Number of allocation attempts	PMS$GL_PAGDYNREQ	EXE$ALOPAGED
Number of allocation failures	PMS$GL_PAGDYNREQF	EXE$ALOPAGED
Number of allocation failure epochs	PMS$GL_PAGDYNF	EXE$ALOPAGED
Total number of pages that failed to be allocated	PMS$GL_PAGDYNFPAGES	EXE$ALOPAGED

[1] This symbol is the address of an array of three longwords.

facility) reads these data cells during the SAVPARAMS phase of AUTO-GEN.COM. See the *Guide to Setting Up a VMS System* for a description of AUTOGEN's operational phases and instructions for running it.

19.7   DETECTING POOL CORRUPTION

VMS Version 5 implements a mechanism to help troubleshoot pool corruption problems. Certain pool misuses lead to more obscure problems if left unchecked. This mechanism can detect pool misuses such as

- Continued use of a piece of pool after it is deallocated
- Use of uninitialized fields in a piece of allocated pool
- Use of a piece of pool that was not allocated

The mechanism applies to the variable-length pools (paged pool, nonpaged pool, and process allocation region) and to the lookaside lists (SRP, IRP, and LRP). It involves

Table 19.5 POOLCHECK Parameter FLAGS Bits

Bit	Meaning
0	Variable-length pools; fill with FREE pattern on deallocation. If bit 1 is also set, check for FREE pattern and fill with ALLO pattern on allocation.
1	Pool checking "master switch".
2	SRP; save caller's address and fill with FREE pattern on deallocation. If bit 1 is also set, check for FREE pattern and fill with ALLO pattern on allocation.
3	IRP; same as bit 2.
4	LRP; same as bit 2.
5, 6	Unused.
7	Process allocation region; fill and check as controlled by bits 0 and 1.

- Filling deallocated pool with a unique pattern, called the FREE or "poison" pattern
- Checking that the poison pattern is intact in pool being allocated and generating the fatal bugcheck POOLCHECK if the pattern is not intact
- Filling allocated pool with a second pattern, called the ALLO pattern

This section describes the POOLCHECK SYSGEN parameter, which controls the mechanism. It explains the mechanism's workings and lists some limits to its ability to detect corruption. Note that use of the POOLCHECK parameter is reserved to Digital. Any other use is completely unsupported.

19.7.1 POOLCHECK Parameter

The dynamic SYSGEN parameter POOLCHECK consists of four eight-bit fields, one of which must be zero (see Table 19.5 and Figure 19.8). The bits in the FLAGS byte enable and disable pool filling and checking and specify which pools are affected. The rest of this section describes the individual bits. The FREE and ALLO bytes specify the patterns written into pool when the space is deallocated and allocated.

Bits in the FLAGS byte put the mechanism into one of three states:

- Do not fill or check blocks
- Fill blocks only upon deallocation
- Fill blocks upon deallocation; check and fill blocks upon allocation

Bits 0, 2, 3, 4, and 7 enable the filling of blocks during deallocation. Bit 0 enables the filling, with the FREE pattern, of blocks deallocated to the

31	24	23	16	15	8	7	0
ALLO		FREE		Must be zero		FLAGS	

Figure 19.8
POOLCHECK Parameter

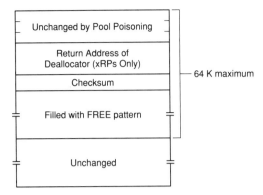

Figure 19.9
Format of Poisoned Pool Space

paged and variable-length nonpaged pools. Bits 2, 3, and 4 enable the filling of deallocated SRP, IRP, and LRP lookaside packets. Bits 0 and 7 together enable the filling of blocks deallocated to the process allocation region.

When set in combination with the other bits, bit 1 enables the checking and filling of blocks during allocation. If set with bit 0, it enables the checking and filling of blocks allocated from the paged and variable-length nonpaged pool with the ALLO pattern. If set with bits 2, 3, or 4, it enables the checking and filling of allocated SRP, IRP, or LRP packets. If set with bit 7, it enables the checking and filling of blocks allocated from the process allocation region.

19.7.2   **Pool Poisoning**

The routine POISON_PACKET, in module MEMORYALC, fills pool space with a predictable pattern under several circumstances:

- Space deallocated by EXE$DEANONPAGED, EXE$DEANONPGSIZ, or EXE$DEALLOCATE is filled.
- The entire result of merging a deallocated variable-length block with free blocks above or below it is filled.
- Space returned to a variable-length pool by EXE$ALLOCATE as a result of an inexact fit is filled.
- Space added to variable-length nonpaged pool as a result of pool expansion is filled.

If enabled by the previously described bits, POISON_PACKET fills pool space. The first five longwords form a header. The remainder of the space receives the FREE pattern. Figure 19.9 shows the format of poisoned pool space.

The header is as follows:

- The first three longwords are unchanged by the pool filling mechanism. They contain the forward pointer to the next free block; the size of the block, if it is a variable-length block; and the original size, type, and subtype fields.

- The fourth longword of lookaside packets contains the return address of the caller to the deallocation routine. It remains unchanged in variable-length pool pieces.

- The fifth longword contains a checksum, which is the sum (ignoring any carry) of the following:

  —FREE pattern byte
  —Block address
  —Contents of the third longword
  —Contents of the fourth longword
  —Contents of the longword beginning at EXE$GQ_BOOTTIME + 1

Under certain circumstances and for certain VAX processors, it is possible for the contents of memory to be preserved from one bootstrap of the operating system to the next. The last longword used in calculating the checksum enables the checking routine to differentiate between stale poisoned pool and pool space poisoned during this bootstrap of the operating system.

19.7.3   Pool Checking

The routine CHECK_PACKET, in module MEMORYALC, checks pool space. It is invoked by

- EXE$ALLOCATE, when allocating variable-length pool space from paged pool, nonpaged pool, or the process allocation region
- EXE$ALONONPAGED, when allocating an SRP, IRP, or LRP lookaside packet

CHECK_PACKET calculates the expected checksum using the same algorithm described in Section 19.7.2. If the expected checksum does not match the checksum found in the fifth longword, CHECK_PACKET assumes that the block is unpoisoned and makes no further checks. (Since POOLCHECK is a dynamic SYSGEN parameter, it is possible that pool poisoning was disabled for a time, resulting in unpoisoned blocks being put on the free list. Alternatively, the block may have been poisoned during a previous bootstrap of the operating system.)

If the checksum matches, CHECK_PACKET examines the remainder of the block for the FREE pattern. If the FREE pattern is not intact, it generates the fatal bugcheck POOLCHECK. If the FREE pattern is intact, CHECK_PACKET fills the entire block (including the first five longwords) with the ALLO pattern.

19.7.4   Constraints on the Pool-Checking Mechanism

Some circumstances can circumvent the pool-checking mechanism:

- Allocation and deallocation of lookaside list packets by any routine directly via REMQHI and INSQTI instructions bypass the filling and checking performed by the previously described routines.

- Any corruption of pool space that corrupts the third, fourth, or fifth (checksum) longword effectively disables checking for that block.

- Checking occurs only at allocation time. Corruption that occurs after a block is allocated is not detected.

- When a block being deallocated to variable-length pool is merged with a free block above or below it, the entire resulting free block is filled. This masks any corruption that may have previously occurred in an adjacent free block.

- When a lookaside list is expanded, the checksum longword of each added packet is zeroed to prevent checking until after the packet is allocated.

- The mechanism fills and checks a maximum of 65,516 bytes (64K bytes, less the five-longword header).

Disabling and reenabling pool poisoning with the same FREE pattern can lead to false POOLCHECK bugchecks. If EXE$DEALLOCATE concatenates a variable-length block to the bottom of a poisoned free block while pool poisoning is disabled, only the top part of the resulting free block contains the FREE pattern. If pool checking is subsequently enabled with the same FREE pattern and this free block is allocated, CHECK_PACKET interprets it as being corrupt.

Certain system initialization routines reside in pool space and deallocate the space they occupy before they exit. To prevent these routines from being overwritten with the FREE pattern, no checking or poisoning is done during the early stages of system initialization (while BOOSTATE$V_STARTUP is set in EXE$GL_STATE). See Chapter 31 for more information on system initialization.

Potentially useful values for the FREE and ALLO patterns cause an access violation when a longword filled with either pattern is interpreted as an address. For example, any pattern containing 1's in the two high-order bits results in an address beyond the end of system space. Additional suggestions for using pool checking and for analyzing POOLCHECK bugchecks are given in the *VMS Device Support Manual*.

PART VI / Input/Output

20 Overview of the I/O Subsystem

Many small make a great.

Geoffrey Chaucer, *Canterbury Tales*

The VMS I/O subsystem consists of device drivers and their associated data structures; device-independent routines within the executive; and several system services, the most important of which is the Queue I/O Request ($QIO) system service, which handles the eventual requests issued by all outer layers of the system. This chapter provides an overview of the I/O subsystem. Subsequent chapters provide more detail of its operation. The I/O subsystem is described in detail from the point of view of adding a device driver to a VMS operating system in the *VMS Device Support Manual*.

The I/O subsystem has two major functions: to provide an interface that is device-independent for images that perform I/O-related operations, and to provide device-dependent support for hardware devices. Four major components of the I/O subsystem are the I/O database, I/O system services, device drivers, and ancillary control processes (ACPs).

20.1 HARDWARE OVERVIEW

This section discusses a sample I/O hardware configuration, pictured in Figure 20.1, and introduces the terms used to describe such components. VAX I/O configurations vary in complexity. The book *Computer Programming and Architecture: The VAX* discusses them, and the I/O configurations of specific VAX processors are described in the *VMS Device Support Manual*.

The major components of an I/O hardware configuration are

- CPU. There may be more than one CPU in some configurations.
- Main memory. If there are multiple CPUs, main memory is shared by all of them.
- System bus. This is the electrical connection between the CPU(s), memory, and the I/O bus adapters. The address space of this bus is the physical address space of the processor.
- I/O bus adapters. An I/O bus adapter connects an I/O bus to the system bus and thus allows communication among the I/O bus, the CPU(s), and memory. Some of the adapter's resources may need to be shared, such as map registers for translating I/O bus addresses into system bus addresses.
- I/O bus. The I/O bus connects the various device controllers and the I/O bus adapter. Common VAX I/O buses are the UNIBUS, the MASSBUS, and the VAXBI.
- I/O device controllers and device units. A device controller contains the logic necessary to connect to the I/O bus and to control the specific device

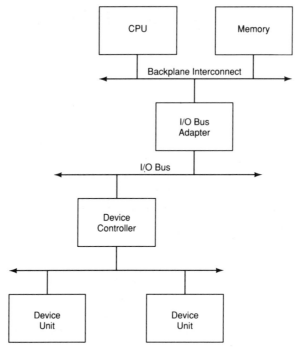

Figure 20.1
A Sample I/O Hardware Configuration

units. A device unit is the individual hardware component, such as a line printer or a tape drive.

In the case of single-unit devices, the distinction between device controller and device unit may be artificial. In the case of some multiunit devices, such as a terminal controller, it may be possible to treat each unit as if it had a separate controller. In the case of multiunit devices such as tape or disk drives, an individual unit may contain some control logic dedicated to the unit, while the device controller contains control logic shared by the various units.

20.2   I/O DATABASE

Because a device driver and the VMS executive cooperate to process an I/O request, they must have a common and current source of information about the request. This is the I/O database, which consists of three parts:

- Data structures that describe every I/O bus adapter, device type, device unit, device controller, and logical path from a process to a device
- Request packets, which define individual requests for I/O activity
- Driver tables, which allow the system to load drivers, validate device functions, and invoke drivers at their entry points (see Section 20.3.1)

Illustrations of I/O database structures and detailed descriptions of their fields appear in the *VMS Device Support Manual*. Figure 20.2 illustrates some of the relations among VMS I/O routines, the I/O database, and a device driver.

20.2.1   Data Structures

I/O database data structures describe I/O hardware components and synchronize access to them. VMS creates these data structures either at system startup or when a driver is loaded into the system. Except where noted, these data structures are located in nonpaged pool.

The I/O database is unit-oriented. The item of interest to the process that requests the I/O operation is the device unit involved in the operation. In most cases, the device controller, I/O bus adapter, and so on, are significant to the process only because they are used to communicate between the CPU and the device unit.

VMS creates a unit control block (UCB) for each device unit attached to the system. A UCB defines the characteristics and current state of an individual device unit, and is the focal point for controlling access to it. In addition, the UCB contains the listhead for the queue of pending request packets for the unit.

When a driver is stalled or interrupted, the UCB keeps the context of the driver in a set of fields collectively known as a fork block. Chapter 4 provides more detail about fork blocks and fork routines.

VMS creates an object rights block (ORB) for each device unit when the

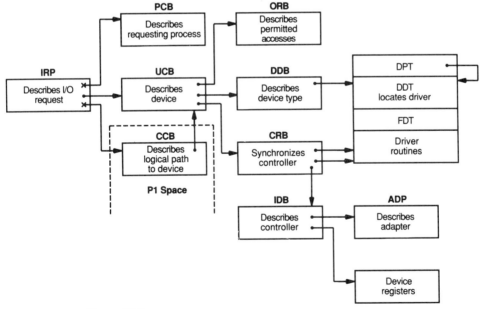

Figure 20.2
The I/O Database

associated UCB is created. An ORB describes the rights that a process must have to access the object with which the ORB is associated. UCBs are not the only entities in VMS that have an associated ORB. Thus, ORBs are not unique to the I/O database but form a part of it.

A device data block (DDB) contains information common to all devices of the same type that are connected to a particular controller. It records the generic device name concatenated with the controller designator (for example, LPA) and the name and location of the associated device driver. In addition, the DDB contains a pointer to the first UCB for the device units attached to the controller. The DDB is not used directly for controlling access to either the device controller or the associated device units. IOC$GL_ DEVLIST is the listhead for the DDB list. From this, any part of the I/O database can be found.

VMS creates a two-part data structure to describe each device controller. The first part, the channel request block (CRB), is of variable length depending on the number of interrupt vectors associated with the controller. The second part, the interrupt dispatch block (IDB), is of variable length depending on the number of units connected to the controller.

The CRB defines the current state of a given controller and lists the devices waiting for the controller's data channel. It also contains the code that dispatches a device interrupt to the interrupt service routine for that unit's driver. Chapter 3 gives more information on device interrupts. The CRB is the focal point for controlling access to the device controller.

The IDB lists the device units associated with a controller and points to the UCB of the device unit that the controller is currently serving. The driver's interrupt service routine uses the IDB to dispatch an interrupt to the appropriate fork process. In addition, an IDB points to the device registers and the controller's I/O bus adapter control block.

An adapter control block (ADP) defines the characteristics and current state of an I/O bus adapter, such as the VAX UNIBUS and MASSBUS adapters and the MicroVAX Q22-bus interface. An ADP contains the queues and allocation bitmaps necessary to allocate adapter resources. VMS provides routines that drivers can invoke to allocate these resources.

A channel control block (CCB) describes the logical path between a process and the UCB of a specific device unit. Unlike the data structures mentioned earlier, CCBs are not located in nonpaged system space but in the P1 space of each process (see Chapter 21).

VMS creates several additional data structures for a file-structured device (see Section 20.5.1).

20.2.2 Request Packets

The I/O database includes a set of request packets. There are two types of request packets, I/O request packets (IRPs) and class driver request packets

(CDRPs). An IRP describes an I/O request that has been processed by the $QIO system service. These are the request packets most commonly handled by device drivers.

When a process requests I/O activity via the $QIO system service, VMS constructs an IRP that describes the I/O request in a standard format. The packet contains fields into which system and driver I/O preprocessing routines can write information. For instance, the device-dependent arguments specified in the $QIO system service call are placed in the packet. The packet also includes buffer addresses, a pointer to the UCB for the target device, and the I/O function codes.

A CDRP describes a request to be handled by a system communication services (SCS) port driver. Such requests are generated by the disk class driver and the VAXcluster connection manager, for example. To economize on system overhead encountered by the disk and tape class drivers, all IRPs have space for a suitable CDRP appended to them, for use by the class drivers. Various portions of VMS rely on the fact that each IRP has this extra space appended to it, although the space may not always be used to contain a CDRP.

20.2.3   **Synchronizing Access to the I/O Database**

Four methods are used to synchronize access to the I/O database: mutexes, interrupt priority level (IPL), spinlocks, and the lock management system services. Chapter 8 discusses the use of IPL, spinlocks, and mutexes for synchronization. Chapter 10 discusses resources, locks, and the lock management system services. The *VMS Device Support Manual* explains the use of IPL and spinlocks for synchronization from the perspective of device drivers.

The I/O database mutex, IOC$GL_MUTEX, synchronizes access to the I/O database. This mutex does not synchronize access to any of the hardware components of the I/O subsystem. Its major purpose is to synchronize the addition or deletion of data structures with searches of the I/O database.

The spinlocks of most interest to the I/O subsystem are fork locks and device locks. Fork locks synchronize fork processing. A device lock synchronizes access to the device controller data structures and thus to the controller.

IPL synchronization of the I/O database normally occurs as part of spinlock acquisition and release. Less frequently, IPL is used to synchronize access in a context where coordination with other processors is irrelevant. For example, a driver fork process raises IPL to IPL$_POWER (31) to block powerfail interrupts on the local processor just before initiating device activity.

If the system is a VAXcluster member, lock management system services synchronize access to the UCBs for devices that are cluster-available (DEV$V_CLU set in UCB$L_DEVCHAR2). Each such device is described by a resource name that is the string SYS$ concatenated with the allocation class device name. Appendix H gives more information on specific locks.

Spinlocks and resource locks are quite different in nature and should not be confused. In Part VI the terms *spinlock, fork lock,* and *device lock* are used to refer to the various types of spinlocks. The locks provided by the lock management system services are referred to as resource locks.

20.3 DEVICE DRIVERS

A device driver controls I/O operations on an I/O device by performing the following functions:

- Defining the I/O device for the rest of the operating system
- Preparing a device unit or its controller for operation at system startup, during connection of the device via SYSGEN, and during recovery from a power failure
- Performing device-dependent I/O preprocessing
- Translating requests for I/O operations into device-specific commands
- Activating a device unit
- Responding to hardware interrupts generated by a device unit
- Responding to device timeout conditions
- Responding to requests to cancel I/O on a device unit
- Reporting device errors to an error logging program
- Returning status from a device unit to the process that requested the I/O operation

Normally, a device driver image consists of the routines and tables discussed in the following sections.

20.3.1 Driver Tables

Three driver tables—driver prologue table, driver dispatch table, and function decision table—are included in every driver.

The driver prologue table (DPT) defines the identity and size of the driver to the system routine that loads the driver into memory and creates the associated database. With the information provided in the DPT, the driver-loading procedure can both load and reload the driver and perform the required I/O database initialization.

The driver dispatch table (DDT) lists the addresses of the entry points of standard routines within the driver and records the size of the diagnostic and error log buffers for drivers that perform error logging.

The function decision table (FDT) lists all valid I/O function codes for the device and associates valid codes with the addresses of I/O preprocessing routines called FDT routines. Figure 20.3 illustrates the layout of a function decision table. The FDT consists of a series of 64-bit masks, each of whose bits corresponds to an I/O function code. For example, bit 33 in a mask corresponds to I/O function code 33.

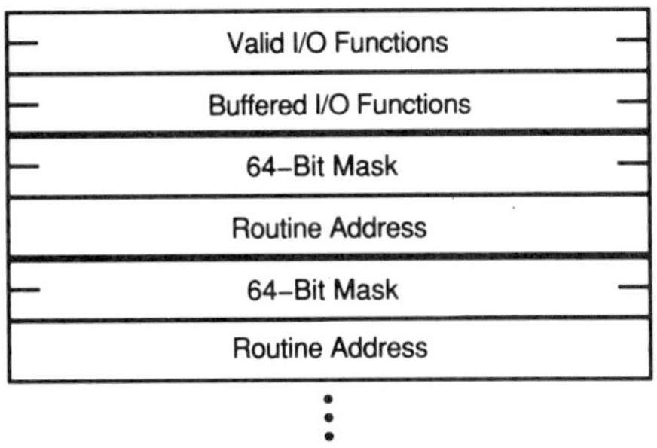

—	Valid I/O Functions	—
—	Buffered I/O Functions	—
—	64–Bit Mask	—
	Routine Address	
—	64–Bit Mask	—
	Routine Address	

⋮

Figure 20.3
Layout of a Function Decision Table

The first two entries consist of just a mask. Bits set in the first mask indicate which functions are legal for the associated devices. Bits set in the second mask indicate which functions are buffered I/O operations. Subsequent entries consist of both a mask and the address of an FDT routine. Bits set in this mask indicate which functions are processed by that FDT routine.

Some FDT routines are contained within device driver images. Others, used by multiple drivers, are contained in loadable executive images. FDT routines are discussed in Chapter 21 and in more detail in the *VMS Device Support Manual*.

20.3.2 Driver Routines

In addition to any FDT routines it may contain, a device driver generally contains controller and unit initialization routines, a start I/O routine, an interrupt service routine, and a cancel I/O routine. A summary of these routines follows; more information is available in the *VMS Device Support Manual*.

The unit and controller initialization routines prepare a device or controller for operation when the driver-loading procedure loads the driver into memory and when VMS recovers from a power failure.

The start I/O routine performs additional device-dependent tasks such as translating the I/O function code into a device-specific command, storing the details of the request in the device's UCB, and if necessary, obtaining access to controller and adapter resources. Whenever the start I/O routine must wait for these resources to become available, VMS stalls the routine, reactivating it when the resources become available.

The start I/O routine ultimately activates the device by loading the device's registers. At this stage, the start I/O routine invokes a VMS macro that stalls the routine until the device completes the I/O operation and requests an interrupt. The start I/O routine remains stalled until the driver's interrupt service routine handles the interrupt.

When a device requests an interrupt, its driver's interrupt service routine determines whether the interrupt is expected or unexpected and takes appropriate action. If the interrupt is expected, the interrupt service routine reactivates the driver's start I/O routine. Generally the start I/O routine performs device-dependent I/O postprocessing and transfers control to VMS for device-independent I/O postprocessing.

The timeout handling routine retries the I/O operation and performs other error handling when a device fails to complete an operation within a reasonable period of time. Chapter 11 discusses timeout handling in more detail.

The cancel I/O routine handles requests to cancel I/O on a unit. It is invoked when an image requests the Cancel I/O on Channel ($CANCEL) system service for the unit, and when the reference count for the unit goes to zero. Chapter 21 discusses cancel I/O routines in more detail.

20.4 I/O SYSTEM SERVICES

VMS provides system services to allow images to request I/O operations and to obtain information about the I/O subsystem. The I/O system services provide direct access to the device. An image can take advantage of specific characteristics of a given device, not just the generic device characteristics supported by Record Management Services (RMS). Subsequent chapters discuss the various I/O system services in more detail.

20.5 ANCILLARY CONTROL PROCESSES

An ACP is a separate process that assists device drivers in processing I/O requests. ACPs perform device-independent functions, such as opening files and establishing a network link. Direct ACP involvement in processing an I/O request is the exception rather than the rule for most ACPs. For example, reads and writes to a file do not usually require ACP intervention. Chapter 21 provides more details of this example in its discussion of I/O postprocessing.

VMS provides the following ACPs:

- F11AACP—Files-11 structure level 1 ACP
- MTAAACP—Magnetic tape ACP
- NETACP—DECnet-VAX ACP
- REMACP—Remote terminal ACP

In VMS Version 4, the Files-11 structure level 2 ACP, F11BACP, was converted to the Extended QIO Processor (XQP), F11BXQP. Unlike an ACP, the XQP runs in the context of the process making the I/O request. For purposes of this part of the book, there is no essential difference between ACPs and the XQP. Any reference to ACPs is equally applicable to the XQP unless stated otherwise.

20.5.1 ACP Data Structures

While not all the ACPs provided by VMS deal with true files, all use a set of data structures that are based on the needs of the file system ACPs. These

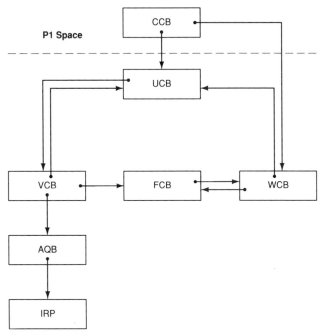

Figure 20.4
File System Data Structures

data structures are sufficiently general to make their use by the non–file system ACPs straightforward. Figure 20.4 illustrates the relations among the file system data structures common to all ACPs.

The ACP creates a volume control block (VCB) when the volume is mounted. In the case of DECnet, the volume is the network as a whole.

VMS creates an ACP queue block (AQB) as part of the creation of the process in which the ACP runs. The AQB contains the queue of IRPs that the ACP is to process. (For the XQP, there is also a per-process queue of IRPs. The XQP uses both queues, depending on the nature of the operation.) A given AQB may be associated with more than one VCB.

The ACP creates a file control block (FCB) for each file open on the volume or each logical link open on the network. In the case of a file, the FCB contains the listhead for the queue of window control blocks (WCB) for the file. One WCB for each channel is associated with the file or logical link.

A WCB describes the virtual-to-logical correspondence for the blocks in a file and the access characteristics of the user. The CCB points to the WCB for the file open on the channel. The WCB contains a base virtual block number and a variable number of map entries. The map entries are a subset of the file retrieval information for the file. An extent is a virtually contiguous series of blocks that are also logically contiguous on the disk. Each map entry represents one extent and consists of an extent size and a starting logical block number. As a result, the entire file does not have to reside in one logically contiguous set of logical blocks.

20.6   VMS I/O ROUTINES

VMS supplies routines that perform various functions common to device drivers. Among these routines are FDT routines and routines to manage adapter resources such as map registers. These routines enable common functions to be performed in a consistent fashion and relieve the device driver writer of the need to master the details of these functions. The *VMS Device Support Manual* contains descriptions of many of these routines. Subsequent chapters describe some of them in more detail.

21   I/O System Services

Delay not Caesar! Read it instantly!
Shakespeare, *Julius Caesar*, 3, i

Here is a letter, read it at your leisure.
Shakespeare, *Merchant of Venice*, 5, i

An image performs I/O operations on a device by requesting I/O system services. The I/O system services also are requested on behalf of a process by system components, for example, Record Management Services (RMS) and file processors, such as Files-11 Extended QIO Processor (XQP) or ancillary control processes (ACPs). This chapter describes the basic I/O system services and the device-independent portions of the flow of an I/O request. Chapter 22 describes the device-dependent portion of that flow.

21.1   OVERVIEW

The basic I/O system services are

- Allocate Device ($ALLOC), by which an image reserves a particular device for exclusive use
- Deallocate Device ($DALLOC), by which an image relinquishes such a device
- Assign I/O Channel ($ASSIGN), by which an image creates a logical link to a device
- Deassign I/O Channel ($DASSGN), by which an image deletes the logical link
- Queue I/O Request [and Wait] ($QIO[W]), by which an image requests an I/O operation on a particular logical link to a device
- Cancel I/O on Channel ($CANCEL), by which an image cancels outstanding I/O requests on a particular logical link to a device

VMS provides other I/O system services in addition to those discussed in this chapter. See the *Introduction to VMS System Services* for a discussion of all the I/O system services.

All the system service routines discussed in this chapter that have a device name argument accept a logical name instead of a device name. Each routine uses the same criteria to process the device name argument. See the *Introduction to VMS System Services* for a discussion of these criteria. Logical names and logical name translation are discussed in Chapter 35.

A typical service sequence for an image is the following:

1. If appropriate, it requests the $ALLOC system service.

2. It requests the $ASSIGN system service.

3. Either it requests the $QIO system service followed by an event flag wait system service (for example, Wait for Single Event Flag, $WAITFR, or Synchronize, $SYNCH) or it requests the $QIOW system service. This step is repeated for each I/O operation.

4. Upon completion of its I/O operations, the image requests the $DASSGN system service (which can instead be requested implicitly as part of image rundown or process deletion).

5. If necessary, it requests the $DALLOC system service (which can also be requested implicitly as part of image rundown or process deletion).

An I/O request is processed in a number of steps and threads of execution. A typical sequence is shown in Figure 21.1; the numbers in the figure correspond to those in the following list:

①The image requests the $QIO[W] system service.

②EXE$QIO, the $QIO system service procedure, runs in process context. It validates its device-independent arguments and builds a data structure, called an I/O request packet (IRP), that describes the I/O request.

③It invokes one or more function decision table (FDT) action routines specific to the device and I/O function. The FDT action routines, also running in process context, complete argument validation and any necessary I/O request preprocessing. An FDT routine may allocate a nonpaged pool buffer for use by the driver, and it may lock user buffer pages into memory so that they can be accessed by a direct memory access (DMA) device.

④The last FDT action routine invokes an executive routine to pass the IRP to the device driver and to return control to the user.

⑤The device driver's start I/O routine, which executes in system context, initiates the device activity corresponding to the I/O request and then waits for the device interrupt that signals completion of the activity.

⑥The device interrupt service routine (ISR), which executes at device interrupt priority level (IPL), copies device status and then forks to dismiss the interrupt and reenter the start I/O routine at a lower IPL.

⑦Reentered as a fork process, the start I/O routine verifies that the request has been satisfied, copies status to the IRP, and queues the IRP for postprocessing.

⑧The I/O postprocessing interrupt service routine, running in system context, performs some postprocessing functions, for example, unlock buffer pages, restore charged quota, and set the event flag associated with the I/O request. It queues a special kernel mode asynchronous system trap (AST) to the process whose I/O completed.

⑨Running in process context, the special kernel mode AST routine can copy I/O status to the image's I/O status block (IOSB) and copy input

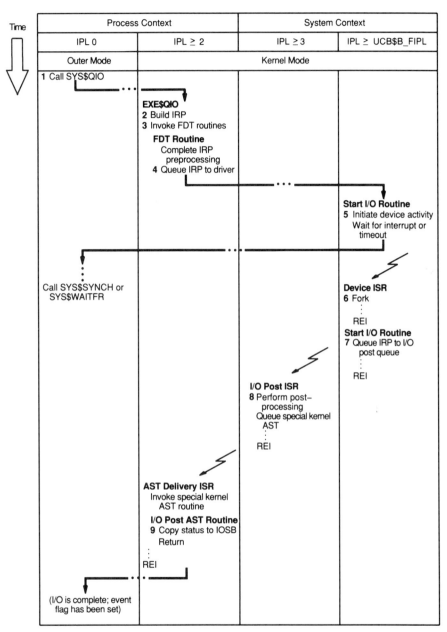

Figure 21.1
Flow of an I/O Request

589

data from a nonpaged pool buffer to a user buffer. If the user requested AST notification of the I/O completion, the special kernel mode AST routine queues a normal AST.

21.2 DEVICE DRIVERS AND FORK LOCKS

Prior to VMS Version 5, VMS and device drivers used IPL alone to synchronize access to the unit control block (UCB). To run on a VMS Version 5 symmetric multiprocessing (SMP) system, a driver must synchronize access to its UCB with a type of spinlock called a fork lock. While all drivers provided with VMS Version 5 have been modified to use fork locks, VMS must work with drivers that use either style of synchronization.

VMS distinguishes the two styles by the contents of UCB$B_FIPL, the same offset as UCB$B_FLCK. If the driver uses fork locks, this location contains the spinlock index for the fork lock, which is a value with bit 5 set. If the driver uses IPL alone, this location contains the fork IPL, which is a value with bit 5 clear. Thus, the two styles can be distinguished by the state of bit 5 in UCB$B_FIPL.

21.3 DEVICE CATEGORIES

Several I/O system services use the following categories to classify devices. A device may be in more than one category. The two categories that are mutually exclusive are local and remote.

- Local devices. These are devices attached directly to the system, pseudo devices, and cluster-available devices.
- Pseudo devices. These are local devices that do not correspond to a physical device. One example of a pseudo device is the mailbox device, described in Chapter 23.
- Template devices. These are pseudo devices that have bit UCB$V_TEMPLATE in UCB$W_STS set. All cluster-available devices and most other local devices are not template devices. Template devices are discussed in more detail in Section 21.5.2.2.2.
- Network devices. These are pseudo devices used by network software to represent logical links. A network device has bit DEV$V_NET in UCB$L_DEVCHAR set.
- Cluster-available devices. These are devices that are served via the mass storage control protocol (MSCP) server and devices that are attached to device servers such as an HSC-50. Cluster-available devices have bit DEV$V_CLU in UCB$L_DEVCHAR2 set.

   Access to cluster-available devices is coordinated across the VAXcluster system by means of resource locks. A cluster-available device has the same name on each VAXcluster node on which it appears. The device name is prefixed with SYS$_ to form the resource name. Resource locks are described in Chapter 10.

- Remote devices. These are devices accessed via DECnet-VAX, specifically those whose device specification includes a DECnet node name, indicated by the presence of :: in the device specification.

21.4   ALLOCATING AND DEALLOCATING DEVICES

An I/O device is characterized as shareable or not, based on whether multiple independent processes are allowed to use it concurrently. A device is nonshareable, for example, if its I/O is inherently sequential and concurrent requests from independent processes would read and write indeterminate data. Before a process can request I/O of a nonshareable device, the device must be allocated for the process's exclusive use.

A device allocated to a process can nonetheless be used by another process under the following two conditions:

- The other process is a subprocess of the first. This condition provides, for example, flexible access to an interactive terminal among a user's process and its spawned subprocesses.
- The other process has the SHARE privilege. For example, the print symbiont uses the SHARE privilege to access a disk mounted privately when the owner queues files on the disk for printing.

In either set of circumstances, the processes sharing the device are responsible for arbitrating their accesses to it.

There are two forms of device allocation: explicit, requested by the process through the $ALLOC system service, and implicit, performed as necessary on behalf of the process by the $ASSIGN system service. In either form, the process ID (PID) of the process that allocated the device is stored in the UCB device owner field, UCB$L_PID.

Explicit allocation differs from implicit allocation in several ways:

- An implicitly allocated device is transparently deallocated when its last channel is deassigned; an explicitly allocated device must be explicitly deallocated.
- A process can request explicit allocation of a generic device type or a specific device unit.
- In the case of explicit allocation, the device allocated bit, DEV$V_ALL in UCB$L_DEVCHAR, is set and the device reference count, UCB$W_REFC, is incremented twice, once by $ALLOC and once by $ASSIGN. In the case of implicit device allocation, the device allocated bit is clear and the device reference count is incremented only once, by $ASSIGN.

A process requests the $ALLOC system service to allocate a device explicitly. The device can be released only through the $DALLOC system service, requested by the process directly or by code running on its behalf at image rundown or process deletion.

The $ASSIGN system service, described in Section 21.5.2, performs implicit allocation of a device that has not been explicitly allocated, provided the device is not shareable.

21.4.1 Allocate Device System Service

The $ALLOC system service has five arguments, of which only the DEVNAM argument is required:

- The DEVNAM argument identifies the device to be allocated.
- The PHYBUF argument specifies where the $ALLOC system service should return the name of the device.
- The PHYLEN argument specifies where it should return the length of the device name.
- The ACMODE argument identifies the access mode to be associated with the device. It is maximized with the mode of the caller. Once allocated, the device can only be deallocated from the same or a more privileged mode.
- The FLAGS argument contains only one flag, the low bit. When set, the low bit indicates that any device of a particular type can be allocated, not just a specific device.

The $ALLOC system service procedure, EXE$ALLOC in module SYS-DEVALC, will not allocate the device if any one of the following conditions is true:

- The device is already allocated by another process (UCB$L_PID is nonzero and does not match PCB$L_PID).
- The device reference count is nonzero.
- A volume is mounted on the device.
- The device is spooled (DEV$V_SPL in UCB$L_DEVCHAR is set), and the process does not have the ALLSPOOL privilege.
- The requesting process does not have access rights to allocate the device, based on the device owner's user identification code (UIC) and protection (fields UCB$L_UIC and UCB$W_PROT) and its access control list.
- The device is not available (DEV$V_AVL in UCB$L_DEVCHAR is clear) or not online (UCB$V_ONLINE in UCB$L_STS is clear).
- The device is a template device.
- The device is cluster-available and a conflicting resource lock exists.

EXE$ALLOC runs in kernel mode. It takes the following steps to allocate a device:

1. It locks the I/O database mutex for write access.
2. It verifies that the DEVNAM argument's string descriptor is read-accessible.
3. If the FLAGS argument is specified, EXE$ALLOC verifies that it is read-accessible and does not have undefined bits set.
4. It invokes IOC$SEARCH, in module IOSUBPAGD, to locate a suitable device.

—If the FLAGS argument is not specified or is 0, EXE$ALLOC requests a
search for the exact device specified by the DEVNAM argument.

—If the FLAGS argument is 1, EXE$ALLOC requests a search for the first
available device having the type specified by the DEVNAM argument.

IOC$SEARCH invokes IOC$TRANDEVNAM, in module IOSUB-
PAGD, to translate the DEVNAM argument. It then searches the I/O
database for either the specific device or one of the particular type.
IOC$SEARCH and routines it invokes verify the suitability of the de-
vice and its accessibility to this process.

If the appropriate device is found, IOC$SEARCH checks that the pro-
cess has access to the device. If the device is cluster-available, it invokes
IOC$LOCK_DEV, in module IOSUBPAGD. IOC$LOCK_DEV requests
the Enqueue Lock Request ($ENQ) system service to queue an exclusive
mode resource lock on the device. IOC$LOCK_DEV stores the lock ID
in UCB$L_LOCKID.

5. EXE$ALLOC returns the translated device name if the PHYBUF argument
is specified, the descriptor is readable, and the buffer is writable. If the
PHYLEN argument is also specified and is write-accessible, EXE$ALLOC
also returns the length of the device name.

6. It allocates the device:

   a. It sets the device allocated bit, DEV$V_ALL in UCB$L_DEVCHAR.

   b. It maximizes the ACMODE argument with the access mode of its requestor and stores the result in UCB$B_AMOD.

   c. It increments the device reference count, UCB$W_REFCNT.

   d. It copies the process ID, PCB$L_PID, to the UCB device owner field,
   UCB$L_PID.

7. It jumps to IOC$UNLOCK, in module IOSUBPAGD, to unlock the I/O
database mutex and to return to the requestor with the success status
SS$_NORMAL.

21.4.2 Deallocate Device System Service

An image can deallocate a single device or all devices allocated to the process
by requesting the $DALLOC system service. The $DALLOC system service
is also requested by the Rundown ($RUNDWN) system service during image
rundown to deallocate all user-mode devices and during process deletion to
deallocate all devices still allocated to the process. The $RUNDWN system
service is discussed in Chapter 26. Process deletion is discussed in Chapter 28.

The $DALLOC system service has two optional arguments:

• The DEVNAM argument specifies the device to be deallocated. If the DEVNAM
argument is specified, it must translate to a physical device name. If the
DEVNAM argument is not specified, all devices allocated by the process from

access modes equal to or less privileged than that specified by the DEVNAM argument are deallocated.

- The ACMODE argument specifies the access mode on behalf of which the deallocation is to be performed. It is maximized with the mode of the caller.

The $DALLOC system service procedure, EXE$DALLOC in module SYS-DEVALC, runs in kernel mode. It performs the following steps:

1. It maximizes the ACMODE argument with the access mode of its requestor.
2. It locks the I/O database mutex for write access.
3. It determines if the DEVNAM argument is present.

   —If the argument is present, it invokes IOC$SEARCHDEV, in module IOSUBPAGD, to locate the specified device.

   —If the argument is absent, it invokes IOC$SCAN_IODB, in module IOSUBNPAG, to find the first UCB in the I/O database.

4. In either case, EXE$DALLOC makes the following checks before deallocating the device.

   —The UCB$L_PID field must match the PCB$L_PID field of the process requesting the $DALLOC system service.

   —The access mode in UCB$B_AMOD must be greater than or equal to the access mode computed in step 1.

   —The device must have been explicitly allocated.

   —The device must not be mounted (DEV$V_MNT in UCB$L_DEV-CHAR must be clear), unless the device is a terminal (DEV$V_TRM in UCB$L_DEVCHAR is set). DECnet remote terminals are marked as mounted but need not be interlocked against deallocation.

5. It deallocates the device by invoking IOC$DALLOC_DEV, in module IOSUBPAGD, which takes the following steps:

   a. It clears the device allocated bit.
   b. If the device is shareable, it clears the device owner field.
   c. It decrements the device reference count.
   d. If the reference count is now zero, IOC$DALLOC_DEV clears the owner field in the UCB and invokes IOC$LAST_CHAN, which performs last channel processing (see Section 21.5.4).
   e. If the device is cluster-available, IOC$DALLOC_DEV invokes IOC$UNLOCK_DEV, in module IOSUBPAGD, to deal with the resource lock on the device. IOC$UNLOCK_DEV tests UCB$L_LOCK-ID to determine whether there is a resource lock, and the device reference count to determine whether there are still channels assigned to the device.

      If there is no resource lock or if the device is still allocated, the routine returns.

If there is a resource lock and channels are still assigned to the device, the routine requests the $ENQ system service to convert the resource lock to concurrent read mode.

If there is a resource lock and no channel still assigned, the routine requests the Dequeue Lock Request ($DEQ) system service to dequeue the resource lock.

6. If the DEVNAM argument was present, EXE$DALLOC is done. It jumps to IOC$UNLOCK to unlock the I/O database mutex and to return to its requestor with the success status SS$_NORMAL.

Otherwise, EXE$DALLOC goes to step 3 to get the next UCB in the I/O database. When no more UCBs are found, EXE$DALLOC is done and exits as described.

21.5   **ASSIGNING AND DEASSIGNING CHANNELS**

The software mechanism that links a process to a device is called a channel. To perform I/O on a device, an image first creates a channel to it by requesting the $ASSIGN system service. The image then identifies the device to the $QIO system service through its channel number. When the image is done with the device, it requests the $DASSGN system service to break the link between the process and the device.

21.5.1   **Channel Control Block**

A channel is described by a process-specific data structure called a channel control block (CCB). A process's CCBs are contained in a table located in its P1 space (see Figure 1.2 and Table F.6). The global location CTL$GL_CCBBASE contains the address of the table's high-address end. The table is accessed using negative byte displacements. That is, a particular CCB is identified by its displacement from the contents of CTL$GL_CCBBASE. The number of CCBs in the table is determined by the SYSGEN parameter CHANNELCNT. Figure 21.2 shows the layout of a CCB.

The field CCB$B_AMOD contains 0 if the channel is unassigned. Otherwise, it contains the access mode from which the channel was assigned, biased by 1. For example, the value 1 indicates that the channel was assigned

UCB		
WIND		
IOC	AMOD	STS
DIRP		

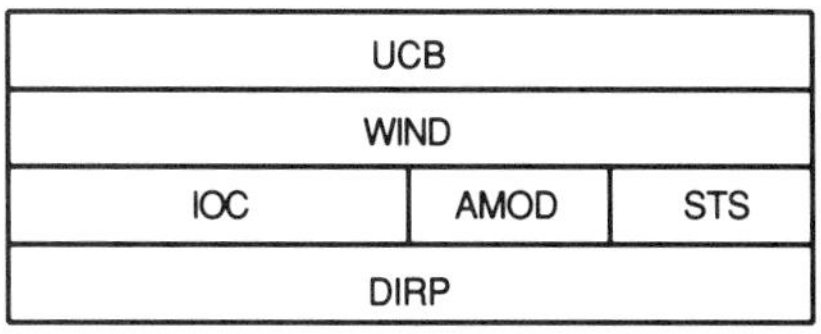

Figure 21.2
Layout of Channel Control Block

from kernel mode. A $QIO system service request on a particular channel must be made from an access mode at least as privileged as the mode from which the channel was assigned.

CCB$L_UCB contains the address of the UCB of the device to which the channel is assigned.

Any comparison of CCB$B_AMOD with an access mode value must be a signed comparison. The Files-11 Extended QIO Processor (XQP) prevents deassignment of its channel when the channel is inactive by storing −1 in CCB$B_AMOD. Prior to using the channel, the XQP transforms the CCB into a normal kernel mode channel to the device of the XQP's choice.

If a file has been opened on the channel, CCB$L_WIND contains the address of its window control block (WCB). If the file is associated with a process section, CCB$L_WIND contains the process section index. CCB$L_WIND contains an unnamed flag in the low bit that is set to indicate either an access (open) request in progress or a deaccess (close) request waiting for all other outstanding I/O requests to be completed.

- If there is an access request pending, CCB$L_WIND contains a 1.
- If there is a deaccess request pending, CCB$L_WIND contains the WCB address or process section index ORed with 1. CCB$L_DIRP contains the address of the IRP that describes the deaccess request. Since WCB addresses and process section indexes are always even, system routines can recover these values by masking out the low bit of CCB$L_WIND.

CCB$B_STS contains several status bits.

The field CCB$W_IOC indicates how many I/O requests are outstanding on the channel.

21.5.2 Assign I/O Channel System Service

The $ASSIGN system service has four arguments; the first two are required and the last two are optional:

- The DEVNAM argument is the name of the device to which to assign the channel.
- The CHAN argument is the address of the word in which to return the assigned channel number.
- The ACMODE argument, indicating the access mode to be associated with the channel, is maximized with the mode of the requestor.
- The MBXNAM argument is the name of the mailbox to be associated with the channel. An image associates a mailbox with a nonshareable device to receive status information, such as the arrival of unsolicited input from a terminal. The device driver for the device either uses or ignores this associated mailbox.

The $ASSIGN system service procedure, EXE$ASSIGN in module SYSAS-SIGN, runs in kernel mode. There are two major paths through EXE$AS-SIGN. The first path handles assignment to a local device. The second handles assignment to a remote device. Both have the same initial steps. They then diverge and do not rejoin.

21.5.2.1   **Common Initial Steps.**   EXE$ASSIGN performs the following steps for both local and remote device assignment:

1. It verifies that the CHAN argument is write-accessible.
2. If the MBXNAM argument was specified, EXE$ASSIGN verifies that it is read-accessible.
3. It verifies that the DEVNAM argument is read-accessible.
4. It verifies that the ACMODE argument is read-accessible and maximizes the argument with the access mode of its requestor.
5. It invokes IOC$FFCHAN, in module IOSUBPAGD, to find a free CCB.

   IOC$FFCHAN begins its search for a free CCB at the high-address end of the CCB table. It examines offset CCB$B_AMOD to determine whether the CCB is free. If the CCB is in use, IOC$FFCHAN examines the next CCB, repeating its test. This sequence continues until IOC$FFCHAN locates a free CCB or reaches the end of the table.

   If IOC$FFCHAN locates a CCB, it returns the address of the free CCB and a positive offset into the CCB table. This offset is the channel number returned from the system service request.

   If no free CCB is located, IOC$FFCHAN returns the error status SS$_NOIOCHN.

6. EXE$ASSIGN locks the I/O database mutex for write access.
7. If MBXNAM was specified, EXE$ASSIGN invokes IOC$SEARCHDEV to get the address of the specified mailbox UCB. The device must be a mailbox device (DEV$V_MBX in UCB$L_DEVCHAR is set) but not a network device.
8. It invokes IOC$SEARCH to locate the device specified in the DEVNAM argument. If the device name is a logical name, IOC$SEARCH invokes IOC$TRANDEVNAM to perform logical name translation.

   If IOC$TRANDEVNAM returns a success status, IOC$SEARCH then scans the I/O database for a device with the resulting equivalence name.

   —If IOC$SEARCH locates the device, it returns the address of the device's UCB. EXE$ASSIGN then takes the steps discussed in Section 21.5.2.2.

   —If IOC$SEARCH does not locate the device, EXE$ASSIGN jumps to IOC$UNLOCK to unlock the I/O database mutex and to return to the caller with the error status from IOC$SEARCH.

9. If the device name contains a node delimiter (::), IOC$TRANDEVNAM

returns the error status SS$_NONLOCAL, and EXE$ASSIGN takes the steps described in Section 21.5.2.3 for remote device assignment.

10. If IOC$TRANDEVNAM returns any other error status, EXE$ASSIGN jumps to IOC$UNLOCK to unlock the I/O database mutex and to return to the caller with that error status.

21.5.2.2   **Local Device Assignment.**   EXE$ASSIGN first checks for several special kinds of device:

1. If the UCB is a redirected UCB (DEV$V_RED in UCB$L_DEVCHAR2 is set), EXE$ASSIGN replaces the original UCB address with the address of the logical UCB by using the value in field UCB$L_TT_LOGUCB of the original UCB. This mechanism associates the assigned channel with the virtual terminal rather than with the physical. (The physical terminal may be a pseudo device such as a LAT terminal.) Only terminal UCBs can be redirected.

2. If the device is set spooled, EXE$ASSIGN goes directly to local device final processing, described in Section 21.5.2.2.4.

3. If the device is a shadow set member (bit DEV$V_SSM in DEV$L_DEV-CHAR2 is set), EXE$ASSIGN performs associated mailbox processing, described in Section 21.5.2.2.3.

EXE$ASSIGN then determines whether the device is a template device. If it is, EXE$ASSIGN clones the UCB to create a new device, as described in Section 21.5.2.2.2.

21.5.2.2.1   *Nontemplate Device Processing.* Before assigning a channel to a local non-template device, EXE$ASSIGN confirms the following:

- If the device is allocated (UCB$L_PID is nonzero) and nonshareable, one of the following two conditions must be true:

  —The requesting process must be the owner of the device or a descendant of the owner process.

  —The requesting process must have the SHARE privilege, and the volume protection and owner UIC must allow access.

- If the device is not allocated, the volume protection and owner UIC must allow access.

If the requestor is allowed to assign a channel to the device, EXE$ASSIGN handles the associated mailbox, if any, and performs final processing (see Section 21.5.2.2.4).

If the requestor is not allowed to assign the channel, EXE$ASSIGN jumps to IOC$UNLOCK to unlock the I/O database mutex and to return to the requestor with an error status.

21.5.2.2.2   *Template Device Processing.* If the device is a template device, EXE$ASSIGN creates a new UCB, called the cloned UCB, by copying the template UCB, and assigns the channel to the cloned UCB as follows:

1. If the template device is a network device, it verifies that the process has NETMBX privilege.

2. EXE$ASSIGN invokes IOC$CHKUCBQUOTA, in module UCBCREDEL, to verify that the process has as much BYTLM quota as the sum of the size of the template UCB plus 256 additional bytes to satisfy process deletion needs.

   IOC$CHKUCBQUOTA invokes EXE$DEBIT_BYTCNT_BYTLIM_NW, in module EXSUBROUT, to check and charge the quota. Both the byte count quota (JIB$L_BYTCNT) and limit (JIB$L_BYTLIM) are charged. Since the amount charged by IOC$CHKUCBQUOTA will not be restored until the UCB is deleted, the process has effectively had its byte limit reduced by the amount of the charge. EXE$DEBIT_BYTCNT_BYTLIM_NW decrements the byte limit as well to reflect this fact.

3. EXE$ASSIGN invokes IOC$CLONE_UCB, in module UCBCREDEL, to create the cloned UCB and an object rights block (ORB).

   IOC$CLONE_UCB copies the template UCB and then makes several modifications to the cloned UCB. The following are of particular interest:

   —It sets the reference count to 1.
   —It marks the unit online.
   —It clears the template bit.
   —It stores the size of the UCB in UCB$W_CHARGE.
   —It gives the UCB a unique unit number between 1 and 9999.
   —It links the UCB into the UCB chain of the related device data block (DDB).

4. EXE$ASSIGN stores the current process's UIC in the ORB owner field (ORB$L_OWNER). At this point, the owner field of the cloned UCB is still clear.

5. It sets UCB$V_DELETEUCB in UCB$L_STS to mark the cloned UCB for deletion when its reference count goes to 0.

6. If the template UCB is a mailbox, it sets the mailbox delete bit (UCB$V_DELMBX in UCB$W_DEVSTS). This is done because special steps are required to delete a mailbox UCB.

7. It clears the device reference count. This is done because the device reference count will be incremented later and IOC$CLONE_UCB sets it to 1. If the reference count were not cleared here, it would never go to 0.

8. EXE$ASSIGN invokes IOC$DEBIT_UCB, in module UCBCREDEL, to record the master PID charged for the UCB (JIB$L_MPID) into the charge PID field (UCB$L_CPID).

In earlier versions of VMS, IOC$DEBIT_UCB decremented the job information block (JIB) byte count quota and byte limit fields. In VMS Version 5, this function has been moved to EXE$DEBIT_BYTCNT_BYTLIM_NW, which now charges the quotas while holding the JIB spinlock.

9. EXE$ASSIGN invokes the driver at the entry point specified by DDT$L_CLONEUCB, passing it the addresses of the template and cloned UCBs. The driver can perform any additional checks necessary. If the driver returns any error status, the process of cloning the UCB is undone and the $ASSIGN completes with failure.

The driver's cloned UCB routine runs in the context of the process that requested the $ASSIGN system service. It executes at IPL 2 because the I/O database mutex is owned by the process.

10. If the device is not shareable, EXE$ASSIGN copies the process's PID to UCB$L_PID, implicitly allocating it.

11. It takes the steps described in Section 21.5.2.2.3.

21.5.2.2.3 *Associated Mailbox Processing.* If an associated mailbox was requested, EXE$ASSIGN stores the address of the associated mailbox UCB in the UCB$L_AMB field of the UCB to which the channel is being assigned. It increments the reference count in the associated mailbox UCB and sets CCB$V_AMB for later storage in CCB$B_STS to indicate that there is an associated mailbox.

No association is made if either of the following is true:

- The device is a file-oriented device (DEV$V_FOD in UCB$L_DEVCHAR is set) or the device is shareable. In either case, the request for an associated mailbox is simply ignored.
- The device already has an associated mailbox (UCB$L_AMB is nonzero), and the MBXNAM argument specifies a different mailbox. In this case, EXE$ASSIGN unlocks the I/O database and returns the failure status SS$_DEVACTIVE.

Upon completing any steps required for the associated mailbox, EXE$ASSIGN proceeds to final processing (see Section 21.5.2.2.4).

21.5.2.2.4 *Local Device Final Processing.* At this point, EXE$ASSIGN has found a free channel, verified the existence of the device (creating the UCB in the case of a template device), and verified that the process has access to the device. It completes the assignment of an I/O channel to a local device in the following steps:

1. If appropriate, it invokes IOC$LOCK_DEV, described in Section 21.4.1, to queue a concurrent read mode resource lock on it. The following conditions must all be met for EXE$ASSIGN to take this action:

—The device reference count is 0.

—The system is an active member of a VAXcluster system.

—The device is cluster-available.

2. If the device is not shareable and not currently owned, EXE$ASSIGN implicitly allocates the device to the current process by storing the current process's PID (PCB$L_PID) in UCB$L_PID.

3. It copies the device's UCB address to CCB$L_UCB.

4. It increments the device reference count.

5. It stores the access mode biased by 1 in CCB$B_AMOD.

6. It sets CCB$B_STS appropriately. The only bit that may be set as a result of this step is CCB$V_AMB.

7. EXE$ASSIGN writes the channel number, the offset into the CCB table, in the word specified by the CHAN argument.

8. It jumps to IOC$UNLOCK to unlock the I/O database mutex and to return the success status SS$_NORMAL to its requestor.

21.5.2.3 **Assigning a Channel to a Remote Device.** If the device is a remote device, EXE$ASSIGN performs the first step in transparent network communication, converting the transparent network communication into the related nontransparent network communication. This section assumes familiarity with transparent and nontransparent network communication, described in the *VMS Networking Manual*.

The initiation of nontransparent network communication involves requesting the $ASSIGN system service again. Since this second request could take some time to complete, EXE$ASSIGN returns to the mode of its caller so that any waits take place in that mode rather than in kernel mode.

EXE$ASSIGN returns to the mode of its caller in the following manner:

1. It enters the remote path when IOC$TRANDEVNAM returns the failure status SS$_NONLOCAL (see Section 21.5.2.1). EXE$ASSIGN converts SS$_NONLOCAL to a success status and jumps to IOC$UNLOCK to unlock the I/O database mutex and to return the now-modified SS$_NONLOCAL status.

2. IOC$UNLOCK exits with a RET instruction, returning control to SERVICE_EXIT, in module SYSTEM_SERVICE_DISPATCHER, as described in Chapter 6. Since the status returned in R0 is a success status, SERVICE_EXIT takes the success path and executes an REI instruction. Normally, this would return control to the instruction after the CHMK instruction in the system service vector. However, as noted in Chapter 6, the system service dispatcher modified the exception program counter (PC) pushed by the CHMK instruction to be the address of SYNCH$ASSIGN_EXIT, in module SYSTEM_SERVICE_EXIT. Thus, control passes to SYNCH$ASSIGN_EXIT.

3. SYNCH$ASSIGN_EXIT executes in the mode from which the original $ASSIGN system service request was made. If the return status contained in R0 is not SS$_NONLOCAL modified to be a success status, SYNCH$ASSIGN_EXIT executes a RET instruction, returning control to the requestor of the $ASSIGN system service.

4. If the return status is SS$_NONLOCAL, SYNCH$ASSIGN_EXIT transfers control to EXE$NETWORK_ASSIGN, in module SYSASSIGN.

5. Since EXE$NETWORK_ASSIGN runs in the mode from which the $ASSIGN system service was requested, its waits are in that mode, allowing ASTs to be delivered to that and more privileged access modes. In previous versions of VMS, the work done by EXE$NETWORK_ASSIGN was done entirely in kernel mode. This resulted in blocking delivery of all ASTs except special kernel ASTs during any waits.

EXE$NETWORK_ASSIGN initiates nontransparent network communication by taking the following steps:

1. It establishes a condition handler in case system service failure exception mode has been enabled. This condition handler will resignal any conditions other than SS$_NOLOGNAM, which occurs normally in logical name translation and should not be passed back to the requestor of the $ASSIGN system service.

2. It allocates a buffer on the stack for use as the data area for logical name translation and initializes this area to request the equivalence name and its attributes.

3. It requests the Translate Logical Name ($TRNLNM) system service to translate the DEVNAM argument. This repetition of the logical name translation done at the beginning of EXE$ASSIGN is necessary because the result of the earlier translation was not saved.

   The result of this step should be a network connect block suitable for use in an outbound connection request operation. EXE$ASSIGN makes no attempt to ensure that the result of this step is in the proper format. If it is not, an error will be returned when the connection is attempted in the next step.

4. EXE$NETWORK_ASSIGN requests the $ASSIGN system service with the following items in the argument list:

   —The DEVNAM argument is the network device name, _NET.

   —The CHAN argument is a stack location that temporarily holds the assigned channel number.

   —The ACMODE argument is the ACMODE argument of the original $ASSIGN request, maximized with the access mode of the requestor.

   —The MBXNAM argument is the same argument passed in the original $ASSIGN system service request.

Since NET0 is a template device, the unit to which the channel is assigned is a new unit, created as described in Section 21.5.2.2.2.

5. It requests the $QIOW system service to establish a connection to the remote device:

   —The FUNC argument is IO$_ACCESS ORed with IO$M_ACCESS.
   —The event flag is EXE$C_SYSEFN.
   —The CHAN argument is the one to which the device was assigned in the previous step.
   —The network connect block is the one obtained in step 3.

6. If the $QIO completes successfully, EXE$NETWORK_ASSIGN records the channel number from step 4 in the word specified by the CHAN argument of the original $ASSIGN system service request. It then returns the success status SS$_REMOTE to its requestor.

7. If the $QIO fails, EXE$NETWORK_ASSIGN requests the $DASSGN system service to deassign the channel. It then returns the failure status from the $QIO system service to its requestor.

21.5.3   Deassign I/O Channel System Service

The $DASSGN system service deassigns a previously assigned I/O channel and clears the linkage and control information in the corresponding CCB, freeing the CCB for reuse. Any outstanding I/O request on the device is terminated in the process. $DASSGN has only one argument, the CHAN argument, which specifies the channel to be deassigned.

The $DASSGN system service procedure, EXE$DASSGN in module SYS-DASSGN, runs in kernel mode. It takes the following steps:

1. It invokes IOC$VERIFYCHAN, in module IOSUBPAGD, which performs the following steps:

   a. It verifies that the channel is legal.
   b. It verifies that the channel was assigned from an access mode no more privileged than the access mode from which it is to be deassigned. CCB$B_AMOD must be greater than the processor status longword (PSL) previous mode field.
   c. It returns the address and the index of the CCB for the channel.

2. EXE$DASSGN calls EXE$CANCELN with a reason code of CAN$C_DASSGN (channel is being deassigned) to cancel all outstanding I/O on the channel. EXE$CANCELN is an entry point in the $CANCEL system service, discussed in Section 21.9.

3. It invokes IOC$VERIFYCHAN again in case the cancel I/O operation triggered a kernel mode AST routine that requested the $DASSGN system service again. This second call to $DASSGN could have completely deassigned the channel.

4. If a file is open on the channel (CCB$L_WIND is nonzero), EXE$DASSGN requests the $QIOW system service to close the file. It specifies a function code of IO$_DEACCESS and event flag number 30. Event flag 30 is used to avoid conflict with the use of event flag 31 by $CANCEL.

   A network logical link appears to be a file; the $QIOW system service dissolves the link.

5. EXE$DASSGN examines CCB$W_IOC to determine whether there is I/O outstanding on the channel. If there is, EXE$DASSGN must wait for its completion AST before proceeding further. EXE$DASSGN acquires the SCHED spinlock and tests whether the process has a pending kernel mode AST whose delivery has been blocked by EXE$DASSGN's execution at IPL 2 and above.

   —If there is a pending kernel mode AST, EXE$DASSGN releases the spinlock and executes an REI instruction that lowers IPL to 0 and transfers control to step 3.

   —If there is not, EXE$DASSGN invokes SCH$RWAIT, in module MUTEX, to place the process into a resource wait. SCH$RWAIT releases the SCHED spinlock and waits the process at IPL 0 and at a PC corresponding to step 3.

   Chapter 7 discusses ASTs in more detail, and Chapter 12 wait states.

6. It locks the I/O database mutex for write access.

7. It clears CCB$B_AMOD.

8. If there is an associated mailbox (CCB$V_AMB in CCB$B_STS is set), EXE$DASSGN dissociates the mailbox by taking the following steps:

   a. It clears UCB$L_AMB in the device UCB.

   b. It decrements the reference count in the mailbox UCB.

   c. If the mailbox reference count is now 0, it invokes IOC$LAST_CHAN_AMBX, in module IOSUBNPAG, to perform last channel processing for an associated mailbox (see Section 21.5.4).

9. It decrements the reference count in the device UCB.

10. If the device reference count is now 0, indicating that the device was not explicitly allocated, EXE$DASSGN takes the following steps:

    a. It clears the device owner field, deallocating the device.

    b. If the device is cluster-available, it invokes IOC$UNLOCK_DEV to remove the resource lock on the device (see Section 21.4.2).

    c. It invokes IOC$LAST_CHAN to perform last channel processing.

11. If the device reference count is 1 and the device has been explicitly allocated, EXE$DASSGN invokes IOC$LAST_CHAN to perform last channel processing.

12. It invokes IOC$UNLOCK to unlock the I/O database mutex and returns the success status SS$_NORMAL to its requestor.

21.5.4   **Last Channel Processing**

Last channel processing is performed when the last channel to a device is deassigned:

- When the device reference count goes to 0, and the device was not explicitly allocated
- When the device reference count goes to 1, and the device was explicitly allocated

There are two entry points to last channel processing: IOC$LAST_CHAN and IOC$LAST_CHAN_AMBX. The latter routine is invoked when the device is an associated mailbox, the former routine in all other cases. They differ only in their initial steps:

- IOC$LAST_CHAN is invoked with the channel number and the address of the UCB of the device assigned to the channel. It saves the reason code CAN$C_DASSGN for later use.
- IOC$LAST_CHAN_AMBX is invoked with the address of the mailbox UCB, not the UCB of the device assigned to the channel. (The channel is not assigned to the mailbox and is not needed by the mailbox driver. The current IRP is also not needed by the mailbox driver.) It saves the reason code CAN$C_AMBXDGN for later use.

At this point, IOC$LAST_CHAN and IOC$LAST_CHAN_AMBX converge in the following steps:

1. If the UCB specifies primary affinity and the process does not already require primary affinity, the routine invokes SCH$REQUIRE_CAPABILITY, in module SCHED, to acquire affinity for the primary. This is done to handle those cases where the device registers should be accessed only from the primary processor in an SMP system. Chapter 12 discusses processor affinity.
2. If the driver uses fork locks, IOC$LAST_CHAN acquires the fork lock, raising IPL to the associated fork IPL. Otherwise, it simply raises IPL to fork IPL. This step synchronizes access to the UCB.
3. It invokes the device driver's cancel I/O routine, passing the reason code saved previously.
4. If the driver uses a fork lock, IOC$LAST_CHAN releases it without changing IPL.
5. It lowers IPL to 2, leaving it there to prevent process deletion.
6. If primary affinity was acquired, the routine releases it.
7. If the device is explicitly allocated, the routine returns to its invoker.
8. If the device is a terminal or mailbox, the routine clears DEV$V_OPR in UCB$L_DEVCHAR, disabling the device as an operator terminal.
9. If UCB$V_DELETEUCB in UCB$L_STS is set, the routine takes the following two steps:

a. It invokes IOC$CREDIT_UCB, in module UCBCREDEL, to return the quota charged against the byte count and byte limit.

b. It invokes IOC$DELETE_UCB, in module UCBCREDEL, to delete the UCB and the associated ORB.

10. The routine returns to its invoker.

21.6 QUEUING AN I/O REQUEST

The $QIO[W] system service performs device-independent preprocessing and, via FDT routines, device-dependent preprocessing. It then queues an I/O request to the driver for the device associated with a channel. Any additional work to be done is performed by the device driver's start I/O routine.

The $QIO system service has the following arguments:

- The EFN argument is the number of the event flag to be associated with the I/O request. Since this argument is passed by value, omitting it is the same as specifying event flag 0.
- The CHAN argument is the number of the I/O channel. This is the same as the CHAN argument returned by the $ASSIGN system service.
- The FUNC argument identifies what operation is to be performed by the device driver. It is divided into two portions, the function code proper and function modifiers. Throughout the chapter, the term *function code* means just the function code proper; the term FUNC means the entire argument.
- The IOSB argument is the address of the IOSB, a quadword to receive final status of the I/O operation. See the *VMS System Services Reference Manual* for a detailed description of the format of the IOSB.
- The ASTADR argument is the address of an AST procedure to be executed in the mode of the requestor when the I/O operation completes.
- The ASTPRM argument is the parameter to be passed to the AST procedure.
- There are six optional device- and function-specific parameters, P1 through P6.

The CHAN and FUNC arguments must be specified. All others are optional and, if not specified, default to a value of zero.

21.6.1 Device-Independent Preprocessing

The $QIO[W] system service procedure, EXE$QIO in module SYSQIOREQ, executes in kernel mode.

To perform device-independent preprocessing, EXE$QIO validates and processes all its arguments except for P1 through P6. It takes the following steps:

1. It clears the specified event flag so that the process will be placed into a wait state until the I/O operation completes, should the caller invoke either the $SYNCH system service or one of the event flag wait system services to wait for the I/O operation to complete.

2. It verifies that the channel number is valid and has been assigned from
an access mode no more privileged than the mode of the $QIO requestor
by performing the following checks:

—The channel number is greater than zero and less than or equal to
the contents of CTL$GW_CHINDX. CTL$GW_CHINDX contains the
number of the highest assigned channel. Note that not all the channels
whose numbers are less than the contents of CTL$GW_CHINDX are
necessarily currently assigned. They could have been deassigned since
the channel whose number is stored in CTL$GW_CHINDX was last
assigned.

—The access mode of the caller (specified by the previous mode field,
PSL$V_PRVMOD, of the current PSL) is less than the access mode
specified by the CCB access mode field. This ensures that the channel
is used only from access modes at least as privileged as the access mode
from which the channel was assigned.

3. If an access or deaccess request is pending on the channel (low bit in
CCB$L_WIND is set), the process is placed in an AST wait state, to wait
for the access or deaccess to complete. When the AST wait is satisfied,
EXE$QIO will restart at the beginning.

4. It extracts the function code from the FUNC argument.

5. If the device is spooled and the function code specifies a virtual I/O
function, EXE$QIO substitutes the intermediate device UCB for the UCB
specified in the CCB. The intermediate device UCB address is stored in
UCB$L_AMB of the UCB specified by the CCB. Virtual I/O to a spooled
device is assumed to be I/O that should be spooled. I/O done by the
software implementing spooling, for example, the print symbiont, would
be logical or physical I/O.

6. Under some circumstances, EXE$QIO must verify the process's access
to the device. If the device is file-oriented, then a file processor (ACP
or Files-11 XQP) has been or will be involved in checking the process's
access to the device when it opens a file. If the device is neither file-
oriented nor shareable, the process's access has already been checked as
part of implicit or explicit device allocation.

However, when a process requests a read or write operation from a
shareable, non-file-oriented device (for example, a real-time device or
one mounted foreign), EXE$QIO checks whether the access is allowed. It
invokes either EXE$CHKRDACCES or EXE$CHKWRTACCES, in module EXSUBROUT. If the process has the needed access, the routine sets
the appropriate bit (CCB$V_RDCHKDON or CCB$V_WRTCHKDON) in
CCB$B_STS.

Note that EXE$QIO contains two lists of functions, one for reads
and one for writes. While the interpretation of function codes is almost
entirely up to the device driver, EXE$QIO does know that the "correct"

interpretation of certain codes is a read or a write operation and performs access checking based on this interpretation.

In step 16, EXE$QIO performs additional access checks based on whether the I/O function is physical, logical, or virtual.

7. EXE$QIO verifies that the function code is a legal function by checking the legal function mask in the FDT (see Chapter 20).

8. If the device is offline, EXE$QIO checks that the function code is either IO$_DEACCESS or IO$_ACPCONTROL. If it is not, EXE$QIO returns the error status SS$_DEVOFFLINE.

9. If the IOSB argument is nonzero, EXE$QIO verifies that the IOSB can be written by the requesting mode and then clears it.

10. EXE$QIO uses the buffered I/O function mask in the FDT to determine whether the function code specifies a direct or buffered operation.

11. It raises IPL to 2 to prevent process deletion. This step is necessary for two reasons:

—EXE$QIO will allocate an IRP. The fact that this IRP is allocated to this process will not be reflected in any data structure until much later. If the process were to be deleted before this allocation were recorded, the IRP would be lost.

—In steps 12 and 14, EXE$QIO indicates that this process has outstanding I/O. If process deletion were begun after these steps, but before the request was actually queued, the process would become deadlocked, trying to run down nonexistent I/O.

12. It determines whether the process has sufficient I/O quota (direct or buffered, depending upon the previous determination) and, if so, charges against it.

If quota is insufficient, EXE$QIO invokes EXE$SNGLQUOTA, in module EXSUBROUT, to place the process in an AST wait if the process has resource wait mode enabled.

13. It allocates an IRP from nonpaged pool (see Chapter 19).

14. It increments the outstanding I/O count in the CCB.

15. It initializes the IRP. Most of this initialization is straightforward, for example, storing the EFN argument in IRP$B_EFN. There are some steps that deserve special comment:

—If the ASTADR argument is nonzero, EXE$QIO charges the process AST quota for an AST control block (ACB). It also sets ACB$V_QUOTA in IRP$B_RMOD to indicate that the process has been charged for the ACB.

—If the function code specifies a buffered I/O operation, EXE$QIO sets IRP$V_BUFIO in IRP$W_STS. Otherwise, it clears the bit.

—EXE$QIO clears the fields that describe the buffer, IRPL_SVAPTE, IRPW_BOFF, and IRP$L_BCNT, the transfer parameters.

—If CCB$L_WIND is nonzero, the channel is associated with either a file or a process section. If the channel is associated with a file, CCB$L_WIND contains the system space address of a WCB, a negative number. EXE$QIO stores the address of this WCB in IRP$L_WIND.

If the channel is associated with a process section, CCB$L_WIND contains the process section index, a positive number. EXE$QIO uses this value to index the process section table (PST) and obtain the address of the WCB associated with the process section. (See Chapter 14 for details on the PST.) EXE$QIO stores the address of this WCB in IRP$L_WIND.

—If the function code is a virtual read or write to a non-file-oriented device, EXE$QIO converts the function code into the corresponding logical function code. It stores the converted function code in IRP$W_FUNC and uses the converted function code for all further checking it performs. EXE$QIO stores the function modifiers specified in the FUNC argument in IRP$W_FUNC without change.

16. If the device is not spooled, shareable, or file-oriented, EXE$QIO does not perform any additional privilege checks. Otherwise, it verifies that the process has the necessary privilege to access the device based on whether the I/O function is physical, logical, or virtual.

17. If the request specifies a diagnostic buffer, EXE$QIO allocates the buffer and stores its address in IRP$L_DIAGBUF.

The device-independent preprocessing is complete. EXE$QIO invokes FDT routines to perform device-dependent preprocessing.

21.6.2   FDT Routines

The primary purpose of FDT routines is to validate and process the device-dependent $QIO parameters, P1 to P6. A device driver can include custom FDT routines or use some of the general-purpose routines that are part of the VMS executive. Regardless of the location of FDT routines, they are logically device-dependent extensions of the $QIO[W] system service.

EXE$QIO searches the FDT entries looking for a mask that specifies the function code. When such a mask is found, EXE$QIO invokes the associated FDT routine. If the FDT routine returns control to EXEQIO, EXEQIO continues its search. Successive FDT routines are invoked until an FDT routine invokes one of the routines that terminates FDT processing. These routines are described in the next section.

Note that no FDT entry marks the end of the FDT. It is possible for the search of the FDT to continue past the end of the FDT. Such an occurrence would be an error and would cause unpredictable results.

FDT routines execute in the context of the process that requested the $QIO system service. Therefore, they have access to data in the process's P0 and P1 address space. FDT routines communicate information about the I/O request to the driver through IRP fields. FDT routines may also modify I/O database structures associated with the device assigned to the channel.

FDT routines for direct I/O (I/O done directly between a user buffer and the device) ensure that each buffer page is locked into memory by incrementing its reference count in the page frame number (PFN) database (see Chapter 14).

In the case of direct I/O, these routines initialize the transfer parameters to describe the buffer as follows:

- IRP$L_SVAPTE contains the system virtual address of the first page table entry that maps the buffer.
- IRP$W_BOFF contains the buffer's offset in bytes from the beginning of that page.
- IRP$L_BCNT is the number of bytes to be transferred.

FDT routines for buffered I/O operations must allocate a buffer from non-paged pool that will be used by the driver for the actual transfer. If the operation is a buffered write, the FDT routine copies data that is being written to this buffer.

The use of system space buffers permits the device driver to access the data in the buffer from system context.

In the case of buffered I/O, these routines initialize the transfer parameters to describe the buffer as follows:

- IRP$L_SVAPTE is the address of the nonpaged pool buffer, which begins with a 12-byte header, shown in Figure 21.3 (see Section 21.7.3.1).
- IRP$W_BOFF is the amount charged against the process's job byte count quota.
- IRP$L_BCNT is the number of bytes to be transferred.

Transfers that may take a long time to complete (such as a terminal read or write) are often implemented as buffered I/O operations, whereas transfers that should complete quickly (such as a disk read or write) are implemented as direct I/O operations. Direct I/O requires locking process pages and page tables into memory, thus tying up the process header, or balance slot, for the duration of the I/O request. Chapter 18 contains more information on the complexity of swapping a process with direct I/O in progress.

21.6.3 I/O Completion

It is important to distinguish between completion of the $QIO[W] system service request, which signals either that the I/O is underway or that the service was requested incorrectly, and the completion of the I/O request.

Passing a status in R0, EXE$QIO returns through the change mode dispatcher to the access mode from which it was requested. If the status is not a success, control returns to the image at a point following its service request. If the status is a success and the image requested the asynchronous form ($QIO) of the service, control returns to the image, which later will request the $SYNCH or an event flag wait service to await I/O completion. If the status is a success and the image requested the synchronous form ($QIOW), the executive places the process into an event flag wait until the I/O completes. Chapter 6 has more information on how a synchronous system service waits a process.

Some I/O requests complete simultaneously with EXE$QIO. EXE$QIO or an FDT routine it invokes can abort or complete an I/O request. More typically, however, an FDT routine must pass a request on to a device driver for device operation and further processing. When the I/O request needs no further device operation or driver processing, it is placed on the I/O postprocessing queue. When IOC$IOPOST processes the request, it sets the associated event flag, ending the process's event flag wait.

This section describes the various ways in which requests complete.

21.6.3.1   **$QIO Completion by EXE$QIO.** The only case in which EXE$QIO itself completes the I/O request are error conditions.

As discussed previously, EXE$QIO makes certain checks before it allocates an IRP; for example, the CHAN argument must specify a usable channel. If EXE$QIO detects an error before allocating an IRP, it takes the following steps:

1. It invokes SCH$POSTEF, in module POSTEF, to set the event flag specified by the EFN argument.
2. It returns an error status in R0 to the requestor.

If EXE$QIO detects an error after it has allocated an IRP, it aborts the I/O, as described in Section 21.6.3.2.

21.6.3.2   **Aborting an I/O Request.** If EXE$QIO (after it has allocated an IRP) or an FDT routine detects a device-independent error (for example, insufficient privilege), it loads the final status of the system service in R0 and invokes EXE$ABORTIO, in module SYSQIOREQ, to abort the I/O. EXE$ABORTIO takes the following steps:

1. If the driver uses a fork lock, EXE$ABORTIO acquires it, raising IPL to fork IPL at the same time. Otherwise, it simply raises IPL to fork IPL.
2. It clears IRP$L_IOSB, the address of the IOSB, so that no status is written to it.
3. It clears ACB$V_QUOTA in IRP$B_RMOD and increments the process's AST quota if the bit was set. This prevents a user-specified AST procedure from being called.

611

4. It inserts the IRP in the current CPU's per-CPU I/O postprocessing queue and requests an IPL$_IOPOST interrupt (see Section 21.7). During post-processing, any quotas charged will be restored and buffers deallocated or unlocked, if necessary.

Use of the per-CPU I/O postprocessing queue ensures that I/O post-processing occurs before the system service completes. If, instead, the systemwide I/O postprocessing queue were used and the process were not current on the primary, it is possible that the process would run before the I/O postprocessing occurred. See Chapter 34 for details on the two types of I/O postprocessing queues.

5. If the driver uses a fork lock, EXE$ABORTIO releases it.
6. It lowers IPL to 0 and returns to the system service requestor.

The effect of these steps is to finish the system service request without performing any I/O operation.

21.6.3.3   **Completing the I/O Request in the FDT Routine.** Some I/O requests can be completed by an FDT routine without the need for driver processing and device operation. There are two circumstances under which this can occur:

- If the FDT routine detects a device-specific error, for example, a buffer not properly aligned
- If the FDT routine can perform all requested operations, for example, an IO$_SENSEMODE operation that returns only fields in the UCB

The FDT routine takes essentially the same action in both cases; the difference is the status it returns.

The FDT routine invokes either EXE$FINISHIO or EXE$FINISHIOC, both in module SYSQIOREQ. These are alternative entry points to the same routine.

1. EXE$FINISHIOC clears R1 and then continues like EXE$FINISHIO.
2. EXE$FINISHIO increments the operation count in the UCB.
3. It stores R0 and R1 in IRP$L_MEDIA and IRP$L_MEDIA + 4. R0 on entry to both routines contains the first longword to be stored in the IOSB. R1 on entry to EXE$FINISHIO contains the second longword to be stored in the IOSB.
4. If the driver uses a fork lock, EXE$FINISHIO acquires it, raising IPL to fork IPL at the same time. Otherwise, it simply raises IPL to fork IPL.
5. It loads the success status SS$_NORMAL in R0 as the final status of the $QIO[W] system service. Note that the final status of the I/O operation, now in the low-order word of IRP$L_MEDIA, may be a failure status.
6. It inserts the IRP in the current CPU's per-CPU I/O postprocessing queue and requests an IPL$_IOPOST interrupt.
7. If the driver uses a fork lock, EXE$FINISHIO releases it.
8. It lowers IPL to 0 and returns to the system service requestor.

21.6.3.4   **Queuing the Request to the Driver.** Most I/O requests require driver processing and device action. An FDT routine passes the IRP to the driver by transferring to either EXE$QIODRVPKT or EXE$ALTQUEPKT, both in module SYSQIOREQ.

EXE$QIODRVPKT is used more commonly. It enters the driver only if the device unit is currently idle. If the device unit is busy, EXE$QIODRVPKT queues the request to the unit so that the driver will process it when the unit becomes available.

EXE$ALTQUEPKT enters the driver without regard for the device unit's activity status.

21.7   I/O POSTPROCESSING

VMS performs I/O postprocessing after an I/O operation has been completed by the associated driver. The I/O postprocessing routine IOC$IOPOST, in module IOCIOPOST, is the interrupt service routine for the IPL$_IOPOST software interrupt. It implements the device-independent steps necessary to complete an I/O request.

Some I/O postprocessing operations, for example, unlocking buffer pages and deallocating buffers, are performed by IOC$IOPOST. Other operations, such as writing the IOSB, are performed by its special kernel mode AST routine, discussed in Section 21.7.3.

There is one systemwide I/O postprocessing queue and one per-CPU I/O postprocessing queue for each CPU. IOC$IOPOST always removes entries from the per-CPU queue for the current CPU. It removes entries from the systemwide queue only when it is running on the primary. When running on the primary, it checks the systemwide queue and then, when the systemwide queue is empty, the per-CPU queue. For simplicity, the following discussion treats these queues as if they were one. Chapter 34 describes the need for both types of queue.

IOC$IOPOST removes the first IRP in the I/O postprocessing queue. It takes one of two paths, depending upon the value in IRP$L_PID. If the value in IRP$L_PID is negative, IOC$IOPOST performs system I/O completion. If the value in IRP$L_PID is positive, IOC$IOPOST performs normal I/O completion. These two paths are described in the following sections.

21.7.1   System I/O Completion

A negative value in IRP$L_PID is the system space address of the system completion routine to be invoked when the I/O completes. IOC$IOPOST invokes this routine with a JSB instruction. When it returns, IOC$IOPOST removes the next IRP from the queue and processes it.

Various components use system completion routines to perform specialized I/O postprocessing. For example, the VAXcluster connection manager uses them for the I/O to the quorum disk. The connection manager, which runs as a fork process, creates the IRP and inserts it into the driver's request queue. Although the driver does not do anything unusual to process the request, IOC$IOPOST cannot perform its usual process-related I/O completion tasks. Instead, the specified system completion routine returns data and status to the connection manager and deallocates the IRP.

21.7.2 Normal I/O Completion

A positive value in IRP$L_PID is the process ID of the I/O requestor. IOC$IO-POST determines the type of I/O operation by testing IRP$V_BUFIO in IRP$W_STS. If the bit is set, the I/O operation is buffered; otherwise, it is direct. IOC$IOPOST performs action appropriate to the type of I/O operation and then queues a special kernel mode AST to the requestor. The AST routine will perform the completion that must be done in the context of the requestor.

21.7.2.1 Buffered I/O Completion.
Buffered I/O involves a transfer to or from a system space buffer in nonpaged pool. IOC$IOPOST takes the following initial steps in the case of buffered I/O:

1. It increments PCB$W_BIOCNT, the number of concurrent buffered I/O requests allowed.
2. If IRP$V_FILACP in IRP$W_STS is set, IOC$IOPOST also increments PCB$W_DIOCNT, the number of concurrent direct I/O requests allowed. This bit is set if the original I/O request involved an ACP that also requested direct I/O.
3. It invokes EXE$CREDIT_BYTCNT, in module EXSUBROUT, to restore the byte count quota that was charged for the system buffer. Note that IRP$W_BOFF does not contain a buffer offset in this case; it contains a byte count. The FDT routine that allocated the system buffer stored the size of the buffer in IRP$W_BOFF and charged the JIB for the buffer.
4. IOC$IOPOST stores the address of the special kernel mode AST routine in the IRP at offset ACB$L_KAST. The IRP will also be used as an ACB. ACB$L_KAST and IRP$L_WIND are the same offset. At this point, the WCB address is no longer needed and that location can be reused safely.

   The special kernel mode AST routine, in module IOCIOPOST, has two entry points: BUFPOST, for buffered read completion, and DIRPOST, for all others. The first case differs from the others in that data must be copied from the system buffer to the process buffer before the process is informed that the I/O is complete. In the case of a buffered write, there is no need to copy data between the process buffer and the system buffer. It was copied earlier from the process buffer to the system buffer by an FDT routine. In the case of direct I/O, there is no system buffer.

It is possible that there was no need for a system buffer; an I/O request with no transfer of data is usually performed as a buffered I/O request. If a buffer was needed, its address is in IRP$L_SVAPTE.

— If IRP$L_SVAPTE is nonzero and IRP$V_FUNC in IRP$W_STS is set, the I/O function is a read requiring a buffer. In this case, IOC$IOPOST stores the address of BUFPOST in ACB$L_KAST.

— Otherwise, IOC$IOPOST stores the address of DIRPOST in ACB$L_KAST. If IRP$L_SVAPTE is nonzero, IOC$IOPOST deallocates the buffer.

5. It performs the steps described in Section 21.7.2.3.

21.7.2.2   **Direct I/O Completion.** Direct I/O requests involve the transfer of data directly to or from the process buffer, which can be paged. Since paging must not occur during the processing of the I/O request, the pages are locked in memory by one of the FDT routines invoked by EXE$QIO.

IOC$IOPOST takes the following initial steps for direct I/O (other than paging and swapping I/O, discussed in Chapters 16 and 18):

1. It performs the steps necessary to handle segmented transfers, if needed, as described in Section 21.8.
2. It determines the number of pages the direct I/O buffer occupies from IRP$W_BOFF and IRP$W_BCNT. IRP$L_SVAPTE contains the address of the first page table entry that maps the buffer. It unlocks the pages by invoking MMG$UNLOCK, in module IOLOCK, which decrements the pages' associated reference counts in the PFN database (see Chapter 14). This step may result in the pages being placed on the free or modified page list.
3. An IRP by itself can only describe one direct I/O buffer. If a direct I/O request has more than one buffer, an FDT routine allocates one or more IRP extensions (IRPEs) to describe them. Each IRPE can describe two buffers. An IRP with an extension IRPE has bit IRP$V_EXTEND set in IRP$W_STS and the address of the IRPE in IRP$L_EXTEND. Similarly, each IRPE can point to another IRPE.

    IOC$IOPOST tests whether IRPEs are present and unlocks whatever additional buffers are described.
4. It increments PCB$W_DIOCNT, the number of concurrent allowed direct I/O requests.
5. It stores the address of DIRPOST in ACB$L_KAST.
6. It performs the steps described in Section 21.7.2.3.

21.7.2.3   **Final Steps in IOC$IOPOST.** IOC$IOPOST performs the same final steps for each buffered and direct I/O request:

1. If appropriate, it invokes SCH$POSTEF to set the specified event flag for the process whose I/O just completed.
2. It queues a postprocessing special kernel mode AST to the process.

Whether IOC$IOPOST or its AST routine sets the event flag is determined by the type of flag: if the flag is local, IOC$IOPOST sets it; otherwise, the AST routine sets it.

A potential synchronization problem could occur if a process whose event flag wait is satisfied executes before the postprocessing AST routine copies possible buffered input to a process buffer and records status in the I/O status block. This race condition could occur in two sets of circumstances:

• Multiple processes are waiting for a common event flag associated with an I/O request and one of them executes before the process that requested the I/O could execute the postprocessing AST routine. IOC$IOPOST avoids this race condition by not setting a common event flag itself; instead, its AST routine does.
• IOC$IOPOST and the newly computable process execute on different processors and the process begins to execute before the AST routine is queued. IOC$IOPOST avoids this race condition by acquiring the SCHED spinlock before setting the flag and not releasing it until the AST is queued.

By setting the event flag before queuing the AST, IOC$IOPOST is able to optimize the execution of the image if the process is in a local event flag wait state (LEF) that is satisfied by setting the event flag. If the process is in LEF, the saved PC in the process's hardware process control block (PCB) points to the CHMK instruction in the system service vector for event flag wait system service. When the process is placed back into execution, it will reexecute the event flag wait system service.

SCH$POSTEF invokes SCH$RSE if setting the event flag satisfies the wait. SCH$RSE modifies the saved PC in the hardware PCB to point to the instruction after the CHMK, since the system service does not need to be reexecuted. Chapter 9 gives more information on event flag waits; Chapter 12 on SCH$RSE.

If SCH$POSTEF were invoked after SCH$QAST, the process would be in the computable state, COM. Thus, SCH$RSE would not modify the saved PC and the event flag wait system service would be reexecuted unnecessarily.

If the process is current (possibly on another member of an SMP system), IOC$IOPOST invokes SCH$QAST before it invokes SCH$POSTEF. This ensures that the special kernel mode AST routine runs before the event flag is set and thus before the image runs again. The optimization noted earlier has to be sacrificed to prevent this race condition.

IOC$IOPOST sets ACB$V_KAST in IRP$B_RMOD to indicate that this is a special kernel mode AST and invokes SCH$QAST, in module ASTDEL, to queue the AST to the process identified by the IRP$L_PID field. The IRP is used as the ACB for SCH$QAST, as described in Chapter 7. Except for ACBL_KAST, IOCIOPOST does not change any fields in the IRP/ACB.

IOC$IOPOST attempts to remove another IRP from the I/O postprocessing queue. If it is successful, it processes that IRP. Otherwise, it executes an REI instruction to exit the interrupt service routine.

21.7.3   I/O Completion Special Kernel Mode AST Routine

The I/O completion special kernel mode AST routine has two entry points: BUFPOST and DIRPOST. BUFPOST performs certain steps unique to buffered read completion and then falls into DIRPOST.

21.7.3.1   Buffered Read Completion. BUFPOST copies data from system buffers allocated by an FDT routine to user buffers in per-process address space. BUFPOST processes three types of system buffer, identified by IRP$W_STS bits:

- Simple buffer—IRP$V_COMPLEX clear
- Complex buffer—IRP$V_COMPLEX set and IRP$V_CHAINED clear
- Chained complex buffer—IRP$V_COMPLEX and IRP$V_CHAINED set

When a simple buffer is associated with an I/O request, IRP$L_SVAPTE contains its address and IRP$L_BCNT contains the number of bytes of data in the buffer. Figure 21.3 shows the layout of a simple buffer.

The first longword of the buffer points to the data, beyond the header. The second longword contains the address of the user buffer. The next word contains the size of the simple I/O buffer. The next byte contains the type, typically DYN$C_BUFIO. The next byte is spare. The rest of the buffer contains the data.

BUFPOST invokes routine MOVBUF, in module IOCIOPOST, to move the data. MOVBUF takes the following steps:

1. It verifies that the user buffer is still write-accessible to the access mode in IRP$B_RMOD.

    If it is not write-accessible, MOVBUF modifies the final status in IRP$L_IOST1 to be SS$_ACCVIO.

2. Otherwise, MOVBUF moves the data from the system buffer to the user buffer.

3. It deallocates the system buffer to nonpaged pool.

4. It returns to its invoker.

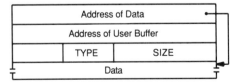

Figure 21.3
Layout of a Simple Buffer

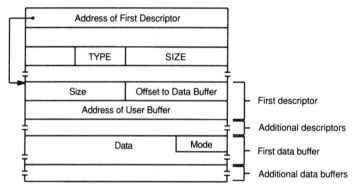

Figure 21.4
Layout of a Complex Buffer

If the I/O request is a mailbox read (IRP$V_MBXIO in IRP$W_STS is set), BUFPOST invokes SCH$RAVAIL, in module MUTEX, to declare the mailbox resource available in case a process is waiting for this resource. Resources are discussed in Chapter 12.

When a complex buffer is associated with an I/O request, IRP$L_SVAPTE contains its address and IRP$L_BCNT contains the number of decriptors in the packet.

The layout of a complex buffer is shown in Figure 21.4. The first longword points to the first descriptor. The second longword is ignored by BUFPOST. The third longword contains the size and type. There may be space between the third longword and the first descriptor. The rest of the buffer consists of descriptors and the associated data buffers.

Each descriptor has the same format. The offset field contains the offset from the start of the descriptor to the data buffer in the packet. The size field contains the number of bytes in the data buffer; the size may be zero. The user buffer address is the address of the per-process space user buffer. The first byte in the data buffer is the access mode associated with the user buffer.

One common instance of the complex buffer is the ACP I/O buffer (AIB) used by the file system ACPs and Files-11 XQP. In the AIB, the third long-word is followed by an access rights block (ARB) copied from the requestor's PCB. The descriptors apply to input data as well as output data. In the case of input data, the size field in the descriptor is set to zero before the IRP is completed by the file system. The file system may also reduce the count of descriptors in IRP$L_BCNT; this is done when the last descriptors are for input data. Since the size contained in the third longword of the buffer reflects the entire buffer, no space is lost when the buffer is deallocated to nonpaged pool.

BUFPOST processes the buffer in the following steps:

1. It gets the address of the first descriptor.

2. It verifies that the user buffer is still write-accessible. (If the size field is zero, BUFPOST goes to step 5 without verifying the accessibility of the user buffer.)

3. If the user buffer is write-accessible, BUFPOST transfers the data from the data buffer to the user buffer.

4. If the user buffer is not write-accessible, BUFPOST modifies the final status in IRP$L_IOST1 to be SS$_ACCVIO and goes to step 6.

5. If there are more descriptors, BUFPOST gets the address of the next descriptor and then goes to step 2.

6. It deallocates the buffer to nonpaged pool.

When a chained complex buffer is associated with an I/O request, IRP$L_SVAPTE contains the address of the first chained complex buffer and IRP$L_BCNT contains the size of the user buffer.

Chained complex buffers are used by some of the communications drivers. They provide a mechanism for one logical buffer to be split into several segments that are not combined until they are transferred to the user buffer.

The layout of a chained complex buffer is shown in Figure 21.5. The first longword contains the address of the data area. The second longword contains the address of the user buffer; this field is valid only in the first descriptor in the chain. CXB$W_SIZE contains the size of the chained complex buffer. CXB$B_TYPE contains the type, DYN$C_CXB. CXB$W_LENGTH contains the size of the data area. CXB$L_LINK contains the address of the next chained complex buffer in the chain; zero indicates the end of the chain.

BUFPOST processes the chained complex buffers in the following manner:

1. It verifies that the user buffer is write-accessible to the access mode in IRP$B_RMOD.

2. If the user buffer is not write-accessible, BUFPOST modifies the final status in IRP$L_IOST1 to be SS$_ACCVIO. It then goes to step 6.

3. If the user buffer is write-accessible, BUFPOST sets CXB$L_LENGTH

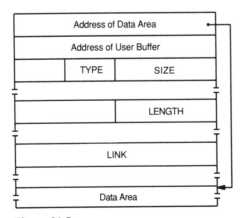

Figure 21.5
Layout of a Chained Complex Buffer

to be the smaller of the amount of space left in the user buffer and the original contents of CXB$L_LENGTH.

4. It moves that amount of data from the data area to the user buffer and reduces the amount of space left in the user buffer by the amount transferred.

5. If there is space left in the user buffer, BUFPOST moves to the next buffer. If there is a next buffer, BUFPOST goes to step 3.

6. BUFPOST deallocates all the buffers to nonpaged pool.

21.7.3.2   **Common Completion.** DIRPOST performs the completion common to buffered and direct I/O requests:

1. It increments either PHD$L_DIOCNT or PHD$L_BIOCNT, the process's cumulative totals of completed direct I/O and buffered I/O requests.

2. If a user's diagnostic buffer was associated with the I/O request, DIRPOST invokes routine MOVBUF to copy the diagnostic information from the system diagnostic buffer to the user's diagnostic buffer. DIRPOST then deallocates the system diagnostic buffer. The system diagnostic buffer has the same format as a simple buffered I/O buffer.

3. It decrements the CCB count of I/O requests in progress on this channel.

4. If this was the last I/O for the channel and there is a deaccess request for the channel pending, DIRPOST queues that deaccess request to the ACP by invoking IOC$WAKACP, in module IOCIOPOST.

5. If the I/O request specified an IOSB, DIRPOST copies the quadword at IRP$L_IOST1 to the IOSB.

6. If a common event flag is associated with the I/O request, DIRPOST invokes SCH$POSTEF to set the flag.

7. If any IRPEs were used, it deallocates them.

8. If ACB$V_QUOTA is set in IRP$B_RMOD, then the user requested AST notification of I/O completion. The AST procedure address and the optional AST argument were originally stored in the IRP (now used as an ACB). DIRPOST invokes SCH$QAST to queue the IRP as an ACB, this time for a normal AST in the access mode at which the I/O request was made.

9. Otherwise, if ACB$V_QUOTA is clear, DIRPOST deallocates the IRP-/ACB to nonpaged pool.

10. It returns to its invoker, SCH$ASTDEL in module ASTDEL.

21.8   **SEGMENTED VIRTUAL AND LOGICAL I/O**

Under certain circumstances, the I/O subsystem must break I/O transfer requests involving a block-addressable mass storage device into segments and pass the request to the device driver segment by segment. This section describes the means by which such requests are segmented and successive segments are passed on to a device driver.

A file is stored on such a device in a series of blocks. There are three ways of referring to the blocks: file-relative (virtual), volume-relative (logical), and absolute (physical). An image performing I/O to a file describes its request in terms of the starting virtual block number (VBN) and the number of bytes to be transferred. The I/O subsystem must convert the VBN into its corresponding logical block number (LBN) for the device driver. For some devices, the LBN must be converted into the corresponding physical block number.

A logically contiguous series of blocks in a file is called an extent. An extent is described by its starting LBN and the number of blocks in it. Most files are made up of multiple extents; a physically contiguous file has only one extent. Each file has an on-disk data structure called a file header that lists the extents that make up the file. When a file is opened, information about its extents is copied from the file header into the WCB. If the image's I/O request crosses a file extent boundary, the I/O subsystem must break the request into segments, each of which fits within one extent.

Certain mass storage devices and their associated drivers cannot handle transfers greater than 64K bytes at one time. In this case the I/O subsystem must break the transfers into segments no greater than 64K. Note that the request may already have been segmented to fit within file extents, which may be greater than 64K bytes.

21.8.1   Segmentation by FDT Routines

Usually, a mass storage device driver specifies the following FDT routines: ACP$READBLK for reads and ACP$WRITEBLK for writes, both in module SYSACPFDT. These routines store the total byte count of the request in the original byte count field of the IRP, IRP$L_OBCNT, and clear the accumulated byte count field of the IRP, IRP$L_ABCNT.

21.8.1.1   Segmenting Virtual I/O. If the transfer is a virtual I/O transfer, these routines then invoke IOC$MAPVBLK, in module IOSUBRAMS, to perform the actual conversion from VBNs to LBNs. IOC$MAPVBLK (see Section 21.8.2) returns the number of bytes not mapped.

If the number of bytes mapped is zero, the FDT routines store the starting VBN in IRP$L_SEGVBN, the number of bytes not mapped (in this case, the total number of bytes requested) in IRP$L_BCNT, and then invoke EXE$QIOACPPKT, in module SYSQIOREQ, to send the IRP to the ACP.

When the file system processes this IRP, it detects that the WCB does not map the requested virtual range and performs a window turn. It reads the file header to obtain the mapping information necessary for the transfer in question and stores the information in the WCB, replacing other mapping information already contained there. The file system performs the equivalent steps that IOC$MAPVBLK performs and then queues the IRP to the driver. Note that the number of bytes mapped at this point is nonzero.

If the number of bytes mapped is nonzero, each FDT routine takes the following steps:

1. It computes the number of bytes mapped by subtracting the number of bytes not mapped from IRP$L_OBCNT and stores this number in IRP$L_BCNT.
2. It stores the starting LBN in IRP$L_MEDIA.
3. It stores the starting VBN in IRP$L_SEGVBN.
4. It converts the I/O function to the equivalent physical I/O function.
5. It takes the steps discussed in Section 21.8.1.2.

21.8.1.2   **Segmenting Logical and Physical I/O.** If the function is not a physical I/O function, the FDT routines convert it to the equivalent physical I/O function. The FDT routines then take the steps necessary to handle transfers greater than 64K bytes, as discussed in Section 21.8.3. Note that these steps are not required for all disk devices.

The routines then queue the IRP to the driver. The driver performs the transfer without regard for whether the entire range is to be transferred. IOC$IOPOST will check whether the entire range has been transferred when the driver completes the I/O request and will take the necessary action, as described in Section 21.8.4.

21.8.2   **IOC$MAPVBLK**

IOC$MAPVBLK uses the information passed (via registers and the IRP) to convert the VBNs to LBNs. The goal is to convert the starting VBN to the related LBN. The gating factor is the information stored in the WCB (the address of the WCB is obtained from CCB$L_WIND) that was created by the file system when the file was opened.

If the WCB contains enough mapping information to convert the entire virtual range of the transfer into corresponding LBNs on the volume, then the virtual I/O transfer will be handled directly by the driver and IOC$IOPOST, even if the transfer consists of several logically noncontiguous pieces. If the WCB does not contain enough information to completely map the virtual range of the transfer, the intervention of the file system will be required at some time to complete the transfer. This intervention is known as a window turn.

Because a deadlock situation could occur if a file mapped by the memory management subsystem requires a window turn, the memory management subsystem must avoid window turns. To do this, each file mapped by the memory management subsystem must have all its mapping information in the WCB. A special, large variation of the WCB is used, called a cathedral window (see Chapter 20).

IOC$MAPVBLK can encounter five possible cases:

- The virtual range is logically contiguous and the WCB contains the needed mapping information. In this case, all that IOC$MAPVBLK needs to do is convert the starting VBN into the related LBN. The driver can transfer the data without further conversion of VBNs into LBNs.
- The WCB contains mapping information for the beginning of the virtual range, but more than two map entries are required to map the range. In this case, IOC$MAPVBLK converts the starting VBN into the related LBN. The driver can transfer the start of the virtual range but will need further conversion of VBNs into LBNs to transfer the rest of the range.

   IOC$MAPVBLK uses only the map entry that maps the starting VBN and the next map entry, if that map entry is logically contiguous with its predecessor. Since the block count field in the map entry is a word in size, it is possible that a logically contiguous range will require more than one map entry to cover the entire logical range.
- The WCB contains mapping information for the beginning of the virtual range but not for the entire virtual range. In this case, IOC$MAPVBLK converts the starting VBN into the related LBN. The driver can transfer the start of the virtual range but will need further conversion of VBNs into LBNs to transfer the rest of the range.

   In this case, the virtual range may be logically contiguous, but not enough mapping information is contained in the WCB to verify this. A window turn will be needed later.
- The virtual range is not logically contiguous, but the WCB does contain mapping information for the beginning of the virtual range. IOC$MAPV-BLK handles this case in the same way it handles the previous case. ·

   The driver can transfer the start of the virtual range but will need further conversion of VBNs into LBNs to transfer the rest of the range. The WCB may or may not contain the needed information. If it does not, a window turn will be needed. Whether a window turn will be needed later is irrelevant at this point.
- The mapping information that maps the first virtual block in the range to its logical counterpart is not in the WCB. A window turn is needed before any data can be transferred.

In all five cases, IOC$MAPVBLK returns the number of bytes not mapped, which is zero in the fifth case. If the number of bytes mapped is nonzero, IOC$MAPVBLK also returns the starting LBN.

21.8.3   Segmenting Transfers Greater Than 64K Bytes

VMS supports I/O transfers greater than 64K bytes for mass storage devices, even though a device and its driver may only support transfers up to 64K bytes. This is done by breaking the transfer into segments no larger than the maximum transfer size supported by the driver. The UCB$L_MAXBCNT field contains the largest transfer size supported by the driver. If it is zero, it is assumed to be 65,024 (64K bytes minus 512).

If the IRP$L_BCNT field is greater than the maximum transfer size specified by UCB$L_MAXBCNT, the FDT routines set IRP$L_BCNT to the maximum transfer size accepted by the driver. Otherwise, they do not modify IRP$L_BCNT. Remember that the FDT routines store the requested size in IRP$L_OBCNT, as noted in Section 21.8.1.

As a result, the first transfer will be the size specified by UCB$L_MAXB-CNT. The remainder will be transferred as a result of the steps taken by IOC$IOPOST, as described in Section 21.8.4.

21.8.4 IOC$IOPOST Processing of Segmented Transfers

Whenever IOC$IOPOST encounters an IRP for a direct I/O data transfer request, it determines if another segment must be transferred by comparing the original byte count to the number of bytes transferred thus far. If the difference is not zero, another segment must be transferred. If the two numbers agree, the request is completed exactly like other direct I/O requests.

If the two numbers do not agree, IOC$IOPOST prepares the IRP for the transfer of the next segment by taking the following steps:

1. If the transfer is a virtual I/O transfer, IOC$IOPOST invokes IOC$MAPV-BLK.

   The same five cases exist here as when IOC$MAPVBLK is invoked by the FDT routines. IOC$IOPOST takes the equivalent steps in each case for the transfer that starts at the VBN in IRP$L_SEGVBN. If there is a total mapping failure of the remaining transfer, IOC$IOPOST invokes IOC$QTOACP to pass the IRP to the ACP. Otherwise, IOC$IOPOST continues.

2. It places the lesser of the remaining byte count and the maximum transfer size accepted by the driver in IRP$L_BCNT.

3. It updates the starting VBN in IRP$L_SEGVBN by the number of blocks transferred in the last transfer.

4. It invokes EXE$INSIOQC, in module SYSQIOREQ, to queue the IRP to the driver.

Thus, in a fashion transparent to the requestor, the original request is segmented to satisfy the limitations of the WCB or the maximum transfer size permitted by the device.

21.9 CANCEL I/O ON CHANNEL SYSTEM SERVICE

The $CANCEL system service cancels pending I/O requests on a specified channel. These include queued I/O requests as well as the request in progress. The $CANCEL system service may be requested by an image. It is also requested by the $DASSGN system service, which is requested during image and process rundown. The $CANCEL system service has only the CHAN argument, which specifies the I/O channel on which I/O is to be canceled.

The $CANCEL system service procedure, EXE$CANCEL in module SYS-CANCEL, executes in kernel mode. Kernel mode code can request a second form of the $CANCEL system service by calling the system service procedure directly at an alternative entry point, EXE$CANCELN. This form of the system service has two arguments:

- The CHAN argument
- The optional CODE argument, the reason for the cancellation

EXE$CANCELN determines if the CODE argument is present. If it is present, the procedure saves it for later use. Otherwise, the procedure saves a reason code of CAN$C_CANCEL. EXE$CANCEL, on the other hand, always saves a reason code of CAN$C_CANCEL. Once the reason code has been saved, EXE$CANCEL and EXE$CANCELN converge.

1. EXE$CANCEL invokes IOC$VERIFYCHAN, as discussed in Section 21.5.3, to verify the channel.
2. If the driver specifies primary affinity and the process has not already acquired primary affinity, EXE$CANCEL calls SCH$REQUIRE_CAPABILITY to acquire primary affinity. Chapter 12 gives details on processor affinity.
3. It raises IPL to 2 to block process deletion.
4. It page faults the CCB into memory and raises IPL to UCB$B_FIPL, effectively locking the CCB into memory. If the driver uses a fork lock, EXE$CANCEL also acquires the fork lock.
5. It searches the IRPs queued to the UCB (starting at UCB$L_IOQFL), looking for those that meet the following criteria:

   —The requesting process ID (PCB$L_PID) matches the process ID in IRP$L_PID.
   —The channel number in IRP$W_CHAN matches the requested channel.
   —The request is not a virtual request (IRP$V_VIRTUAL in IRP$W_STS is clear). In general, I/O cannot be canceled on disk or tape devices. Drivers for these devices ensure that IRP$V_VIRTUAL is set on all requests that cannot be canceled.

   For each IRP that satisfies these criteria, EXE$CANCEL takes the following steps and then resumes the search:

   a. It removes the IRP from the queue.
   b. It clears the buffered read bit (IRP$V_FUNC in IRP$W_STS) for buffered I/O functions. Since this I/O operation has not been started, there is no data to be transferred to the user's buffers.
   c. It places the error status SS$_CANCEL in the low-order word of

IRP$L_MEDIA and clears the high-order word. This is the final status of the I/O operation.

   d. It inserts the IRP at the tail of the systemwide I/O postprocessing queue and requests an IPL$_IOPOST interrupt (see Section 21.7).

6. After scanning the IRP queue, EXE$CANCEL invokes the driver cancel I/O routine, whose address is stored in the driver dispatch table. The driver is passed the cancel reason saved at the start of EXE$CANCEL or EXE$CANCELN. The driver should perform any actions appropriate to canceling I/O.

   Some driver cancel I/O routines execute a RET instruction if an error occurs. In such a case, control does not return to EXE$CANCEL but to its requestor.

7. EXE$CANCEL tests the device type to determine whether canceling its active request is appropriate. If the device is a disk, it is likely that the request will complete quickly enough that canceling it is unnecessary. If canceling the active request is not appropriate, EXE$CANCEL exits, as described in step 8. Otherwise, EXE$CANCEL continues with step 9.

8. If a fork lock was acquired, EXE$CANCEL releases it. If primary affinity was acquired, EXE$CANCEL relinquishes it. EXE$CANCEL lowers IPL to 0 and returns the success status SS$_NORMAL to its requestor.

9. If there is no outstanding I/O (CCB$W_IOC is zero) and there is no file activity (CCB$L_WIND is zero), EXE$CANCEL exits, as described in step 8. (If there is file activity, then CCB$L_WIND contains the address of the WCB associated with the channel or a process section index. At this point, the distinction is not significant.)

10. If the device is not mounted or is mounted foreign, EXE$CANCEL exits, as described in step 8.

11. If there is a process section associated with the channel, EXE$CANCEL exits, as described in step 8.

12. At this point, EXE$CANCEL has determined that there is a file open on this channel. If WCB$V_NOTFCP in WCB$B_ACCESS is set, EXE$CANCEL exits, as described in step 8.

   The WCB$V_NOTFCP bit identifies a WCB created by special routines that run only during system startup. These routines open files before the Files-11 XQP is available. When these files are opened again after the XQP is available, new WCBs are created. The original WCBs are not destroyed and are not used by the XQP.

13. At this point, EXE$CANCEL has determined that there is a user file open on the channel. It attempts to allocate an IRP to request an IO$_ACPCONTROL function. If it cannot allocate an IRP, it does one of two things:

   —If the process does not have resource wait mode enabled, EXE$CANCEL exits, as described in step 8, with a status indicating the reason that EXE$CANCEL could not allocate an IRP.

—Otherwise, EXE$CANCEL invokes SCH$RWAIT to place the process into an RSN$_NPDYNMEM wait. If the fork lock was acquired, it is released prior to invoking SCH$RWAIT. If primary affinity was acquired, it is relinquished prior to invoking SCH$RWAIT. When the wait completes, EXE$CANCEL returns to step 2.

14. It initializes the IRP as follows:
    a. The process ID of the requestor is set to the value in PCB$L_PID.
    b. The AST procedure address and parameter are cleared (no user AST).
    c. The WCB address is set to the value in CCB$L_WIND.
    d. The UCB address is stored in IRP$L_UCB.
    e. The function code is set to IO$_ACPCONTROL.
    f. The event flag is set to EXE$C_SYSEFN.
    g. The priority is set to the process's base priority.
    h. The IOSB address is set to zero.
    i. The channel number is stored in IRP$W_CHAN.
    j. The I/O is marked as buffered I/O with no buffer.
    k. The access rights block address is set to the value in PCB$L_ARB.

    This ACP control function is special by virtue of there being no I/O buffer. It is ignored by disk ACPs and the Files-11 XQP. It is recognized by the magnetic tape ACP as a special I/O abort function (equivalent to invoking the driver's cancel I/O routine) that causes the ACP to abort the mounting of a multivolume tape file.

15. EXE$CANCEL charges the user's buffered I/O quota, PCB$W_BIOCNT, for an I/O request.
16. If the fork lock was acquired, it is released.
17. If primary affinity was acquired, it is relinquished.
18. EXE$CANCEL invokes EXE$QIOACPPKT to queue the packet to the file system. EXE$QIOACPPKT will execute a RET instruction, returning control to the requestor of the system service.

22   I/O Device Drivers and Interrupt Service Routines

"Open the pod-bay doors, HAL."
Arthur C. Clarke, *2001: A Space Odyssey*

Once a user's I/O request is preprocessed and validated by the Queue I/O Request ($QIO) system service and the device driver's function decision table (FDT) action routine, the VMS executive invokes the driver's start I/O routine so that the driver may actually perform the requested function. Chapter 21 describes the validation of the I/O request. This chapter discusses how VMS and a driver's start I/O routine cooperate to perform the user-requested function and relay the status of the I/O operation, as well as any necessary data, back to the user.

In addition, various interrupt dispatching schemes employed by different types of adapters on VAX systems, as well as the connect-to-interrupt mechanism, are briefly described.

22.1   DEVICE DRIVER MODELS IN VMS

The two categories of device driver models in VMS systems are the traditional wait-for-interrupt model and the port/class driver model.

The former includes drivers for most devices that are not block-structured as well as drivers for older block-structured devices that do not conform to the Digital Storage Architecture. Examples of such device drivers are LPDRIVER, for the UNIBUS line printer controller, and DRDRIVER, for MASSBUS RMxx disks.

The port/class model includes device drivers for most modern block-structured devices and those for different types of terminal devices. Note, however, that a number of differences exist between the port/class model as applied to block-structured devices and the port/class model as applied to terminal drivers in VMS. Chapter 24 briefly discusses both types of drivers.

This chapter discusses the traditional wait-for-interrupt model of device drivers. In particular, the following issues are addressed:

- How VMS invokes a driver's start I/O routine
- How the start I/O routine initiates a transfer and waits for an interrupt from the device
- How VMS dispatches an interrupt from the device to the interrupt service routine (ISR) of the driver
- How the ISR resumes the start I/O routine

- How the start I/O routine resumes processing at a lower interrupt priority level (IPL)
- How the start I/O routine requests I/O completion processing
- How VMS initiates I/O postprocessing

22.2   EXITING THE FDT ROUTINE

As described in Chapter 21, an image requests an I/O operation on a device through the $QIO system service. Its system service procedure, EXE$QIO in module SYSQIOREQ, validates the device-independent parameters of the request, builds an I/O request packet (IRP) describing it, and invokes one or more FDT action routines.

The FDT routines validate the function-dependent parameters of the request and set up any necessary I/O buffers. Some FDT routines may complete an I/O request without device action or fork processing by entering EXE$FINISHIO or EXE$FINISHIOC, in module SYSQIOREQ. An FDT routine may abort the I/O request by entering EXE$ABORTIO, in module SYSQIOREQ.

If the I/O operation is requested on a file-structured device, and either a file system function was requested or file system intervention is required before the driver can perform the requested I/O, then the FDT routine enters EXE$QIOACPPKT, in module SYSQIOREQ.

If the I/O request is valid and device action needs to be initiated, an FDT routine jumps to EXE$QIODRVPKT, in module SYSQIOREQ, to enter the driver's start I/O routine or invokes EXE$ALTQUEPKT, in module SYSQIOREQ, to enter its alternate start I/O routine.

22.2.1   Entering the Driver's Start I/O Routine

A traditional VMS device driver's FDT routine typically enters EXE$QIO-DRVPKT, which initiates I/O on the device if the device is idle. If the device is busy, it inserts the IRP on the wait queue of the unit control block (UCB). It invokes EXE$INSIOQ, in module SYSQIOREQ, to perform the following actions:

1. EXE$INSIOQ raises IPL to the fork IPL of the device, acquiring the fork lock, if any, specified in UCB$B_FLCK.
2. If the device unit is busy, as indicated by a set UCB$V_BSY bit in UCB$L_STS, EXE$INSIOQ invokes EXE$INSERTIRP, in module SYSQIOREQ, to insert the IRP on this unit's queue of pending I/O requests. The queue, whose listhead is at UCB$L_IOQFL, is ordered according to the base priority of the process that requested the I/O. When EXE$INSERTIRP returns, control is transferred to step 5.
3. If the device unit is idle, EXE$INSIOQ marks it busy by setting bit UCB$V_BSY in UCB$L_STS and initiates I/O on the device by invoking IOC$INITIATE, in module IOSUBNPAG.

IOC$INITIATE determines if the device on which the I/O was requested has affinity for the CPU that IOC$INITIATE is running on by examining the device's affinity mask, UCB$L_AFFINITY. If the device does not have affinity for this CPU, then IOC$INITIATE invokes SMP$SWITCH_CPU, in module SMPROUT. SMP$SWITCH_CPU creates a fork process on the CPU with the lowest physical CPU identification (ID) for which this device has affinity; this fork process invokes IOC$INITIATE again.

Running on a CPU for which the device has affinity, IOC$INITIATE performs the following steps:

a. It saves the IRP address in UCB$L_IRP.

b. IOC$INITIATE copies IRP$L_SVAPTE, IRP$W_BOFF, and IRP$W_BCNT to UCBL_SVAPTE, UCBW_BOFF and UCB$W_BCNT. This step is an optimization for direct I/O operations and is unnecessary for most buffered I/O operations.

c. It clears UCB$V_TIMOUT and UCB$V_CANCEL in UCB$L_STS. Table 22.1 explains the significance of these and other important flags in UCB$L_STS.

d. If a diagnostic buffer is associated with the current I/O request, IOC$INITIATE obtains its address and records the current system time in it as the operation start time.

e. It gets the address of the driver dispatch table (DDT) from the UCB, locates the driver's start I/O routine through DDT$L_START, and enters it with a JMP instruction.

4. The driver's start I/O routine eventually returns control to EXE$INSIOQ, as discussed in Section 22.3.2.

5. EXE$INSIOQ restores the IPL at entry, releasing any fork lock it acquired, and returns control to EXE$QIODRVPKT.

6. EXE$QIODRVPKT restores IPL to 0 and returns to the image that requested this I/O. The status returned in R0 indicates that the I/O request was queued to the driver successfully. The $QIO requestor cannot determine the status of the I/O operation until the VMS I/O postprocessing routine writes the I/O status block for this I/O request.

Table 22.1   Important Flags in UCB$L_STS

Flag	Meaning if Set
UCB$V_INT	An interrupt is expected from this device
UCB$V_TIM	This device has an I/O operation being timed
UCB$V_TIMOUT	This device has timed out
UCB$V_CANCEL	Current I/O on the device has been canceled
UCB$V_POWER	The system recovered from a power failure

22.2.2   **Entering the Driver's Alternate Start I/O Routine**

EXE$ALTQUEPKT enters the driver's alternate start I/O routine regardless of the setting of the UCB$V_BSY bit, as follows:

1. EXE$ALTQUEPKT raises IPL to the device's fork IPL, obtaining the unit's fork lock if appropriate.
2. It gets this CPU's physical CPU ID from the per-CPU database field CPU$L_PHY_CPUID and checks the device affinity mask in UCB$L_AFFINITY to determine if this device has affinity for the CPU. If it does not, then EXE$ALTQUEPKT invokes SMP$SWITCH_CPU, in module SMPROUT, to create a fork process on the CPU with the lowest physical CPU ID for which this device has affinity. This fork process invokes EXE$ALTQUEPKT again and resumes processing at step 1.
3. If this device does have affinity for this CPU, EXE$ALTQUEPKT gets the address of the driver's DDT from the UCB, locates its alternate start I/O routine through offset DDT$L_ALTSTART, and invokes it with a JSB instruction.
4. When the driver's alternate start I/O routine returns, EXE$ALTQUEPKT restores the IPL at entry, releasing any fork lock that was obtained earlier, and returns to its invoker, typically the $QIO requestor.

22.2.3   **Initiating File System I/O**

Some I/O requests require the involvement of the file system. This happens, for example, when the function requested is a file system function request, such as IO$_ACCESS, or when a window turn is required to map the requested virtual block number (VBN) to a logical block number (LBN). A window turn updates file retrieval information in the window control block (WCB), as discussed in Chapter 21. The file system may transform the I/O request into one more suitable for the device driver and queue it to the driver. Alternatively, it may request multiple I/O operations itself. In any case, when the file system has performed the request, it performs or initiates I/O postprocessing on the original IRP.

EXE$QIOACPPKT is entered by file system FDT routines in module SYSACPFDT when an I/O request requires action by a file system ancillary control process (ACP) or the Files-11 Extended QIO Processor (XQP). If the target device for the I/O is serviced by an ACP, then EXE$QIOACPPKT performs the following actions:

1. It locates the volume control block (VCB) of the device from the UCB. From the VCB, it locates the ACP queue block (AQB) and inserts the IRP into the tail of the interlocked I/O request queue at AQB$L_ACPIQ.
2. If the queue was not empty, EXE$QIOACPPKT returns a successful status indicating that the I/O request is queued. Control returns to the image following its service request.

3. If this IRP is the first to be inserted into the queue, EXE$QIOACPPKT gets the process ID (PID) of the ACP that services this device from AQB$L_ACPPID and invokes SCH$WAKE, in module SCHED, to wake up that ACP. If SCH$WAKE returns a success status, EXE$QIOACPPKT returns a success status for the $QIO request.

Later, when the ACP is placed into execution, it removes the request from its queue. It performs the requested function and initiates I/O postprocessing by queuing the IRP to the systemwide postprocessing queue. Section 22.3.4 and Chapter 21 discuss I/O postprocessing.

If, on the other hand, AQB$L_ACPPID is zero, then the XQP services this device, and EXE$QIOACPPKT enters EXE$QXQPPKT, in module SYSQIO-REQ. EXE$QXQPPKT generates a file system request in the context of the current process as follows:

1. It gets the address of the per-process XQP data area from CTL$GL_F11BXQP and inserts the IRP on the IRP queue in that area.
2. From the per-process XQP data area, EXE$QXQPPKT gets the address of the XQP routine DISPATCH, in module [F11X]DISPATCH, which is the asynchronous system trap (AST) procedure that initiates an XQP transaction. The XQP code resides in a system global section that is mapped into P1 space during process startup, as discussed in Chapter 25.
3. EXE$QXQPPKT, using the portion of the IRP that begins at offset IRP$L_IOQFL as an AST control block (ACB), stores the address of DISPATCH in ACB$L_AST.
4. EXE$QXQPPKT stores the address of the IRP itself in ACB$L_ASTPRM.
5. It then enters SCH$QAST, in module SCHED, to queue the IRP as a kernel mode AST to the current process.
6. When SCH$QAST returns, EXE$QXQPPKT lowers IPL to 0 and executes a RET instruction to return from EXE$QIO.

Before control returns to the $QIO requestor, the kernel mode AST is delivered and the procedure DISPATCH is called. DISPATCH queues the IRP to the per-process XQP queue in the XQP's data area. If the XQP is not busy servicing another IRP, DISPATCH calls DISPATCHER, in module [F11X]DISPAT, to service the request. DISPATCHER determines the function requested and calls the appropriate XQP procedure to perform the requested function.

When the XQP has serviced the request, DISPATCHER performs I/O postprocessing by invoking special entry points in IOC$IOPOST, in module IO-CIOPOST, which is the VMS I/O postprocessing routine.

22.3 DRIVER'S START I/O ROUTINE

The driver's start I/O routine must perform the user-requested function by interacting with the device. It typically initializes device registers, stalls

Example 22.1
Simple Start I/O Routine

```
STARTIO:
        .                               ;Set up device registers
        .                               ;Raise IPL to IPL$_POWER
        .                               ;Synchronize with powerfail recovery
        .                               ;Get transfer going by setting
                                        ; "GO" bit
        WFIKPCH  DEVTMO, #6             ;Wait for interrupt
        .                               ;Execution resumes here upon
                                        ; interrupt
        IOFORK                          ;Request to lower IPL to fork IPL
        .
        .
        REQCOM                          ;Complete request
```

until the device has performed the requested task and interrupted VMS,
resumes the I/O after the device interrupts, and initiates I/O request completion processing.

Example 22.1 shows the use of the three VMS-supplied macros, WFIKPCH,
IOFORK, and REQCOM, which essentially create a framework for a simple
driver's start I/O routine. These and other similar macros, documented in
the *VMS Device Support Manual*, are building blocks for the driver's start
I/O routine. The use of these macros allows the device driver writer to
orchestrate the carefully coordinated interplay between VMS and the device
driver.

This chapter discusses the expansion of the preceding three macros in the
context of this simple example and explains how and why VMS stalls and
resumes the driver's start I/O routine.

22.3.1   Initiating Device Action

Typically, the start I/O routine is entered when an image makes an I/O
request and the device is idle. Figure 22.1 shows the interaction between the
VMS executive and the appropriate device driver to initiate device action.
Note that in Figures 22.1, 22.2, and 22.3 portions of the start I/O routine
that are not relevant to the flow of control, but aid in understanding the
flow, are shaded.

The numbers in Figure 22.1 correspond to the numbered steps that follow:

①The system service routine EXE$QIO is called when the $QIO service is
requested.

②EXE$QIO validates the function-independent parameters of the request,
allocates and builds an IRP, and invokes the driver's FDT action routine
for the requested function.

③The FDT routine validates the function-dependent parameters of the request, sets up the necessary I/O buffers, and enters EXE$QIODRVPKT.

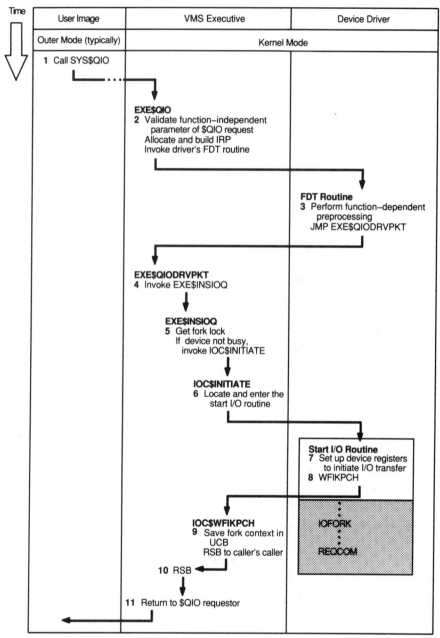

Figure 22.1
Entering the Start I/O Routine

④ EXE$QIODRVPKT invokes EXE$INSIOQ (see Section 22.2.1).

⑤ EXE$INSIOQ obtains the fork lock for the UCB and tests UCB$V_BSY. If the device is not busy, it invokes IOC$INITIATE.

⑥ IOC$INITIATE locates the start I/O routine and enters it.

⑦ The start I/O routine then sets up the device registers so that the device can perform the requested function. It initializes the device's control/status register (CSR), indicating to the device that it should perform the requested function and interrupt VMS when it is done. The start I/O routine manipulates device registers while holding the device spinlock to synchronize with device interrupts.

⑧ Once the device starts performing the requested function, the start I/O routine has to stall execution until the device interrupts. It does this by invoking the WFIKPCH macro.

The WFIKPCH macro has two arguments:

- The address of the timeout routine
- The number of seconds within which the interrupt should occur

If the interrupt occurs within the specified time, VMS resumes the start I/O routine at the instruction following the WFIKPCH. If it does not occur, VMS resumes the start I/O routine at the timeout routine specified.

The WFIKPCH macro invocation in the preceding example expands as follows:

```
PUSHL   #6
JSB     G^IOC$WFIKPCH
.WORD   DEVTMO - .
```

Note that the .WORD directive leaves a value, the offset to the timeout routine DEVTMO, in the instruction stream. By adding this value to its own address, code in the VMS executive computes the system virtual address of the device timeout routine when the need arises.

22.3.2   Waiting for the Device Interrupt

⑨ IOC$WFIKPCH, in module IOSUBNPAG, is invoked by a driver's start I/O routine through the WFIKPCH macro. It performs the following steps:

a. At entry to IOC$WFIKPCH, the return address that was left on the stack by the JSB instruction actually points to a value rather than to an instruction, as indicated previously. IOC$WFIKPCH adjusts the return address by adding 2 to it, in order to point past the word value.

b. It stores the adjusted return address, after removing it from the stack, in UCB$L_FPC.

c. It stores register R3 in UCB$L_FR3 and R4 in UCB$L_FR4.

d. It sets UCB$V_INT, to indicate that this device now expects an interrupt, and UCB$V_TIM, to indicate that this unit has I/O being timed.

e. It obtains the timeout value from the stack, adds it to the system uptime, EXE$GL_ABSTIM, and stores it in UCB$L_DUETIM. This value is the system uptime at which this request expires.

    f. IOC$WFIKPCH clears UCB$V_TIMOUT. If the interrupt does not occur within the specified time, EXE$TIMEOUT, in module TIME-SCHDL, will set the bit. Chapter 11 describes EXE$TIMEOUT.

    g. IOC$WFIKPCH releases the device spinlock and returns to the caller's caller.

Effectively, IOC$WFIKPCH saves the context of the driver's start I/O routine in the fork block contained within the UCB. It will be resumed when the device interrupts. IOC$WFIKPCH transfers control back to the VMS routine, EXE$INSIOQ. (EXE$INSIOQ used IOC$INITIATE to locate and invoke the start I/O routine. However, IOC$INITIATE entered the start I/O routine with a JMP instruction and did not leave a return address on the stack. As a result, the RSB instruction in IOC$WFIKPCH returns control to EXE$INSIOQ.)

⑩ EXE$INSIOQ returns to EXE$QIODRVPKT.

⑪ EXE$QIODRVPKT returns control to the image that requested this I/O operation, as discussed in Section 22.2.1.

22.3.3   Servicing the Device Interrupt

When the device has performed the requested function, it interrupts the processor. On a symmetric multiprocessing (SMP) system, it interrupts the primary processor. The mechanism by which VMS invokes a device's ISR when the device interrupts is known as interrupt dispatching (see Section 22.4).

Figure 22.2 shows the control flow when the ISR resumes the start I/O routine. The numbers in the figure correspond to the numbered steps outlined in this section.

① As part of VMS device interrupt dispatching, a few general registers, typically R0 through R5, are saved on the interrupt stack. VMS then invokes the driver's ISR.

② Example 22.2 shows a simple ISR for a device driver. Typically, an ISR relies on the fact that when it is entered, the top of the stack has a pointer to the interrupt dispatch block (IDB). The first two longwords of the IDB contain the addresses of the device CSR and the UCB of the device that requested the interrupt. The UCB contains the fork block that holds the context of the driver's start I/O routine.

The UCB also contains the address of the device lock. The device lock normally synchronizes access to controller and device registers and certain UCB fields. Every code thread that accesses these registers or UCB fields is expected to obtain that device lock first. A driver writer determines which registers and fields the device lock synchronizes based on the nature of the device and the interaction among driver routines like initialization, timeout, start I/O, and interrupt service routines.

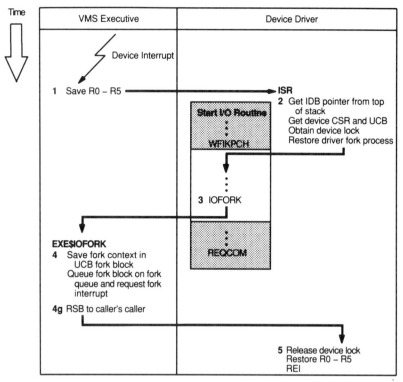

Figure 22.2
ISR Resumes the Start I/O Routine

Example 22.2
Simple Interrupt Service Routine

```
ISR:
        MOVQ    @(SP)+, R4              ;Get CSR in R4 and UCB in R5
        DEVICELOCK  -
          LOCKADDR=UCB$L_DLCK(R5),-     ;Obtain device lock
        BBCC    #UCB$V_INT, -
                UCB$L_STS(R5), 10$      ;If interrupt unexpected, go to 10$
        MOVL    UCB$L_FR3(R5), R3       ;Restore fork R3
        JSB     @UCB$L_FPC(R5)          ;Resume driver's start I/O routine
10$:    DEVICEUNLOCK  -
          LOCKADDR=UCB$L_DLCK(R5),-     ;Release device lock
        MOVQ    (SP)+, R0               ;Restore registers saved
        MOVQ    (SP)+, R2               ; during interrupt dispatching
        MOVQ    (SP)+, R4
        REI                             ;Dismiss interrupt
```

637

The ISR obtains the device lock and tests UCB$V_INT to determine if the interrupt is expected. If UCB$V_INT is clear, the ISR merely releases the device lock, restores R0 through R5, and dismisses the interrupt. Otherwise, the ISR resumes the start I/O routine at the instruction following its invocation of the WFIKPCH macro using the following instruction:

```
JSB    @UCB$L_FPC(R5)
```

③ When the start I/O routine determines that further processing for this I/O request may be performed at an IPL lower than the device IPL, it invokes the IOFORK macro. Since this part of the start I/O routine has been resumed from the ISR at device IPL, it may not explicitly lower the IPL. To do so would be in violation of the VAX architecture, which states that an interrupt thread of execution may not lower its IPL below that at which it was initiated.

The IOFORK macro is provided by VMS specifically for such purposes. This macro expands to the instruction JSB G^EXE$IOFORK.

④ EXE$IOFORK, in module FORKCNTRL, assumes that the fork block for the fork thread that invoked it resides in the UCB. It requests the resumption of the fork thread at its fork IPL as follows:

a. It clears bit UCB$V_TIM in UCB$L_STS to indicate that the device no longer has an I/O operation being timed.

b. It stores registers R3 and R4 in UCB$L_FR3 and UCB$L_FR4.

c. It gets the return address from the top of the stack and stores it in UCB$L_FPC. This is the address of the instruction following the invocation of IOFORK, the part of the start I/O routine that needs to be resumed at fork IPL.

d. It gets the fork IPL of this fork thread as follows:

On a uniprocessor system, from UCB$B_FIPL

On an SMP system, from the array SMP$AL_IPLVEC indexed by the contents of UCB$B_FLCK

e. EXE$IOFORK locates the head of the fork queue for this fork IPL in the per-CPU database for the processor on which it is running and inserts the fork block into this queue.

CPU$Q_SWIQFL in the per-CPU database is the array of listheads for the fork queues for IPLs 6 and 8 through 11. There is an unused listhead for IPL 7 as well.

f. If this fork block is the first to be inserted on this queue, EXE$IOFORK requests a software interrupt at the fork IPL for this queue.

g. EXE$IOFORK then executes an RSB instruction, effectively passing control to the caller's caller which, in this example, is the ISR.

⑤ The ISR simply releases the device lock, restores R0 through R5, and executes an REI instruction to dismiss the interrupt.

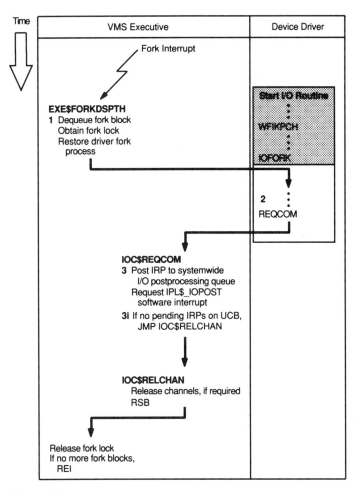

Figure 22.3
Fork Dispatcher Resumes the Start I/O Routine

22.3.4 **Requesting I/O Completion Processing**

Figure 22.3 shows the flow of control when the start I/O routine is resumed by the VMS fork dispatcher. The numbers in the figure correspond to the numbered steps in this section.

When processor IPL falls below the fork IPL of this device, the processor grants the requested software interrupt at that IPL. The software ISR is one of the EXE$FRKIPLxDSP routines in module FORKCNTRL, where x is 6, 8, 9, 10, or 11, one of the fork IPL values. All these routines converge in EXE$FORKDSPTH, also in module FORKCNTRL.

①EXE$FORKDSPTH removes one fork block at a time from the appropriate fork queue and performs the following steps:

639

   a. Running on an SMP system, it obtains the fork lock.

   b. It restores R3 and R4 from FKB$L_FR3 and FKB$L_FR4 of the fork block. For the UCB, these are the same as offsets UCB$L_FR3 and UCB$L_FR4.

   c. It executes a JSB instruction to FKB$L_FPC, thus resuming the fork process.

   d. When the fork process returns, EXE$FORKDSPTH releases the fork lock if it is running on an SMP system.

In Example 22.1, the JSB instruction in EXE$FORKDSPTH resumes the start I/O routine at the instruction following the invocation of the IOFORK macro, at the fork IPL for the device.

②The start I/O routine then checks for any errors and performs any device-dependent postprocessing of the I/O request. It constructs in R0 and R1 the I/O status block to be returned to the user image that requested the I/O. Finally, it invokes the REQCOM macro to complete the I/O request and initiate I/O postprocessing. VMS I/O postprocessing relays the final status of the I/O and the data, if any, to the $QIO requestor.

The REQCOM macro generates the instruction JMP G^IOC$REQCOM.

③IOC$REQCOM, in module IOSUBNPAG, queues the IRP to the systemwide postprocessing queue and requests an IPL$_IOPOST software interrupt by performing the following steps:

   a. If there is an error log buffer (if UCB$V_ERLOGIP in UCB$W_STS is set), IOC$REQCOM transfers the necessary information to the error log buffer and invokes ERL$RELEASEMB, in module ERRORLOG, to complete the error log activity for this I/O operation.

   b. It increments the I/O operation count in the UCB.

   c. It stores the final I/O status in IRP$L_IOST1 and IRP$L_IOST2.

   d. If the device is a tape and the request completed successfully, it invokes EXE$MNTVER_GEN_CRC, in module [SYSLOA]MOUNT-VER, to generate any needed cyclic redundancy check (CRC).

   e. If the I/O request completed with an error and the device is a disk or a tape, IOC$REQCOM checks if mount verification is pending or in progress (if UCB$V_MNTVERPND or UCB$V_MNTVERIP in UCB$L_STS is set). If either is true, it invokes EXE$MOUNTVER, in module [SYSLOA]MOUNTVER, to start mount verification.

     In the case of certain tape errors, IOC$REQCOM calls EXE$MNT-VER_GEN_CRC, as it does in the previous step, without checking the mount verification bits in UCB$L_STS.

   f. IOC$REQCOM tests and saves the current IPL. If it is not at least IPL$_IOPOST, it raises IPL to IPL$_IOPOST.

   g. IOC$REQCOM inserts the IRP in the interlocked systemwide I/O postprocessing queue, IOC$GQ_POSTIQ.

Running on a uniprocessor system, IOC$REQCOM simply requests an IPL$_IOPOST interrupt.

If this is an SMP system, and the I/O postprocessing queue was empty prior to the insertion of the IRP, IOC$REQCOM must request the IPL$_IOPOST software interrupt on the primary processor. If the current processor is the primary, IOC$REQCOM simply writes the appropriate value to PR$_SIRR. Otherwise, IOC$REQCOM requests an interprocessor interrupt to tell the primary to request an IPL$_IOPOST interrupt. Chapter 4 discusses software interrupts in more detail; Chapter 34 interprocessor interrupts.

h. IOC$REQCOM restores the saved IPL.

i. If mount verification is in progress, it tests UCB$V_MOUNTVER-PND:

If UCB$V_MOUNTVERPND is set and the I/O operation is being performed on a disk or a tape, then IOC$REQCOM clears UCB$V_MOUNTVERPND and invokes EXE$MOUNTVER without clearing the UCB$V_BSY bit. This occurs when a VAXcluster system has lost quorum; the result is to stall I/O until quorum is regained.

If UCB$V_MOUNTVERPND is clear, IOC$REQCOM simply enters IOC$RELCHAN, in module IOSUBNPAG, to release any device controllers to which the start I/O routine had obtained exclusive access. IOC$RELCHAN returns to the caller's caller.

j. If the unit has pending I/O requests, IOC$REQCOM removes the first one and branches to IOC$INITIATE, in module IOSUBNPAG, to initiate it. IOC$INITIATE, described in Section 22.2.1, enters the driver's start I/O routine. The start I/O routine typically invokes the WFIKPCH macro, resulting in the invocation of IOC$WFIKPCH, described in Section 22.3.2. IOC$WFIKPCH returns to the caller's caller, which in this example is the fork dispatcher, EXE$FORKDSPTH.

k. If there are no pending I/O requests for the unit, IOC$REQCOM clears the device unit busy flag (UCB$V_BSY in UCB$W_STS) and enters IOC$RELCHAN, in module IOSUBNPAG, to release any device controllers. IOC$RELCHAN returns to the caller's caller, which in this example is EXE$FORKDSPTH.

22.4 VMS INTERRUPT SERVICE ROUTINES

The following sections briefly describe how VMS dispatches some device and adapter interrupts to appropriate interrupt service routines and the actions typically taken by these routines. Chapter 20 presents an overview of the I/O database, the basis for interrupt dispatching. The *VMS Device Support Manual* describes the I/O database in more detail and provides a more complete discussion of driver interrupt service routines.

22.4.1   Servicing UNIBUS and Q22-Bus Interrupts

Each device on a UNIBUS or Q22-bus has one or more vector numbers and a bus request priority. The bus request priority enables the bus to be arbitrated among devices when multiple interrupts are requested.

On a UNIBUS, there are four bus request (BR) levels, called BR4, BR5, BR6, and BR7. BR7 is the highest priority. If interrupts are requested concurrently for multiple devices with the same BR level, the device electrically closest to the UNIBUS arbitration logic has the highest priority. On a Q22-bus, there are also four request levels, called bus interrupt request (BIRQ) levels. BIRQ7 is the highest priority.

In either case, the device IPL of the requested interrupt is the bus request level plus 16. For example, BR4 corresponds to IPL 20.

Interrupts from UNIBUS adapters (UBAs) may be vectored directly or indirectly, as discussed in the following sections. The difference between the two methods of vectoring is that there is an extra level of dispatching for indirectly vectored interrupts. When a device on an indirectly vectored UNIBUS interrupts, the adapter's ISR gains control, interrogates the device for its vector, and uses this vector to invoke the device's ISR.

22.4.1.1   Directly Vectored UNIBUS and Q22-Bus Interrupt Service Routines. VAX CPUs that implement directly vectored interrupts use additional pages of the system control block (SCB) for these interrupts.

SYSGEN is responsible for building the I/O database for devices and their drivers (see Chapter 20). For a device on a bus whose interrupts are directly vectored, SYSGEN initializes the SCB vector with the address of code that dispatches the interrupt to the ISR. This dispatching code is contained in the interrupt dispatch area within the channel request block (CRB) for the controller and resembles the following:

```
PUSHR   #^M⟨R0,R1,R2,R3,R4,R5⟩
JSB     @#driver_interrupt_service_routine
```

The second instruction dispatches to the driver ISR (see Figure 22.4). The longword following the JSB instruction contains the address of the IDB. Its address is pushed onto the stack as the return program counter (PC) for the JSB instruction. Control never returns there because that address is removed from the stack by the driver ISR, as are the saved registers.

After the JSB instruction in the CRB transfers control, the following events occur:

1. The driver ISR removes the IDB pointer from the stack and uses it to obtain the address of the device controller's CSR and the address of the UCB for the device generating the interrupt.
2. Having found the UCB, the ISR determines whether the interrupt is expected. If the interrupt is unsolicited, the interrupt service routine

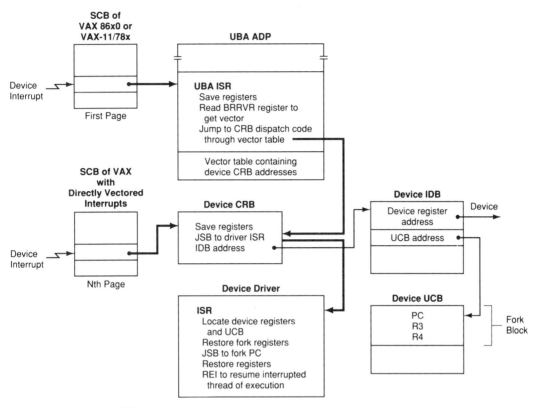

Figure 22.4
Control Flow in Servicing a UNIBUS or Q22-Bus Interrupt

may either take some appropriate action or simply dismiss the interrupt by restoring the saved registers and executing an REI.

3. If the interrupt is expected, the ISR restores the driver context saved in the UCB by the driver fork process. The driver ISR then executes a JSB instruction to transfer control to the saved PC.

4. The driver fork process transfers control back to the interrupt service routine. Most often, the driver fork process does this indirectly by forking or waiting for another interrupt. In either case, the fork process invokes a routine that saves the fork process context and returns to its caller by executing an RSB instruction. The driver ISR then restores the saved registers and dismisses the interrupt with an REI instruction.

22.4.1.2 **Indirectly Vectored UNIBUS Interrupt Service Routines.** When a device on an indirectly vectored UNIBUS requests an interrupt, the UBA receives the interrupt request and requests a CPU interrupt on behalf of the interrupting device. It is actually the UBA interrupt that is vectored through the SCB, using the interrupting device's IPL and the adapter's transfer request (TR) number, to an adapter ISR.

The adapter ISR saves registers R0 through R5, determines which device actually requested the interrupt, and then passes control to an ISR in the device driver for the interrupting device. The driver ISR can then respond to the interrupt in a device-dependent fashion. After servicing the interrupt, the registers saved by the adapter ISR must be restored and an REI instruction executed to dismiss the interrupt.

There are four ISRs for each UBA, one for each BR level at which UNIBUS devices request interrupts. They differ only in which internal UBA register they read to determine which device requested the interrupt. These ISRs are found in the adapter control block (ADP) that describes the UBA. The UBA ADP is created during system initialization by the CPU-specific routine INI$UBADP. The CPU-specific routine and the actual UBA ISRs are in module [SYSLOA]INIADP*xxx*, where *xxx* is either 780 for VAX-11/78*x* systems or 790 for VAX 86*x*0 systems.

Indirectly vectored UNIBUS interrupt servicing begins in one of four UNIBUS adapter ISRs. Each of these routines takes the following steps:

1. The routine saves registers R0 through R5 (see Figure 22.4).
2. A UBA internal register called the bus request receive vector register (BRRVR) is read to determine the identity of the interrupting device. Each BRRVR register contains either the vector number corresponding to the device interrupt or an indication that the UBA is interrupting on behalf of itself, not for some device. (There are four BRRVRs in the UBA, one for each BR level.)
3. The UBA interrupts on its own behalf to indicate an adapter error. Certain adapter errors result when a reference is made to a nonexistent address in UNIBUS I/O space. They can indicate a transient hardware error or a bug in a device driver. These errors are logged, up to a maximum of three in any given 15-minute period, and the interrupt is dismissed.

   Another possible error is that power on the UNIBUS or UBA is about to fail. Chapter 33 describes how adapter powerfail is handled.
4. For a device interrupt, the vector number is used as an index into a vector table, which is part of the ADP. The vector table contains a pointer to the JSB instruction in the CRB. The service routine transfers control by executing a JMP to the JSB instruction.

   The vector table entry pointing to the CRB and address fields in the CRB are initialized by SYSGEN in response to the CONNECT command.

The JSB instruction in the CRB transfers control to the driver ISR. The longword following the instruction contains the address of the IDB. This address is pushed onto the stack as the return PC for the JSB instruction. However, control is never returned there, because that address is removed from the stack by the driver ISR.

At this point, interrupt dispatching becomes identical to that on directly vectored systems, as described in the previous section. Device driver interrupt service routines are entered in the same way regardless of system type.

22.4.2 MASSBUS Adapter Interrupt Service Routine

MASSBUS adapter (MBA) interrupt dispatching is identical across all VAX CPUs that support an MBA. During system initialization, four SCB vectors for each MBA are initialized by the CPU-specific routine INI$MBADP, in module [SYSLOA]INIADPxxx, where xxx designates one of the CPU types listed in Appendix G. The SCB vectors contain an address within the MBA CRB. The CRB contains a PUSHR instruction to save R2 to R5 and a JSB instruction to transfer control to the MBA ISR, MBA$INT in [SYSLOA]ADPSUBxxx.

MBA interrupts are handled differently from UNIBUS interrupts, partly because one MBA interrupt may indicate that multiple devices on the adapter need servicing. The MBA ISR reads an attention summary register to determine its response to an interrupt.

If the interrupt enable bit in the MBA is set, an MBA interrupt can be caused by any of the following operations:

- Completion of a data transfer
- Assertion of an attention line while the MBA is not busy
- Occurrence of an MBA error while the MBA is not busy
- Power recovery on the MBA

A device on the MASSBUS asserts its attention line under the following circumstances:

- If an error occurs, whether or not a transfer is taking place
- When a mechanical motion such as a disk seek or tape rewind completes
- When a device changes its state

In general, a MASSBUS device driver does not request ownership of the MBA channel (controller) until it is needed to perform a transfer. MBA$INT assumes that if the MBA owner is expecting an interrupt, then the interrupt currently being serviced indicates that a transfer has completed or been aborted. That is, when an MBA interrupt occurs and the current owner of the MBA is expecting an interrupt, MBA$INT dispatches immediately to the owner's driver.

Because data transfer functions block the interrupts from nontransfer functions until the data transfer completes, MBA$INT always checks the MBA attention summary register after a driver ISR returns control. It tests whether another device on the MASSBUS requested an interrupt either while the MASSBUS owner was transferring data or while the current interrupt was being processed. The UCB list contained in the IDB allows MBA$INT to associate UCB addresses with devices that are requesting service.

MBA$INT responds to an interrupt in one of three ways (see Figure 22.5). It may perform all three of these actions to service multiple attention requests in response to a single interrupt.

- For an expected interrupt (bit UCB$V_INT set in UCB$W_STS) on a single-unit device, MBA$INT restores the driver fork process context and executes a JSB instruction to the fork PC. The driver fork process returns to MBA$INT when it has completed its work.
- For an unsolicited interrupt (bit UCB$V_INT clear in UCB$W_STS) on a single-unit device, MBA$INT executes a JSB instruction that transfers control to a driver-supplied unexpected ISR, which will return to MBA$INT.
- For a multidevice controller (a magnetic tape formatter), MBA$INT transfers control to the CRB for the device controller. The device controller CRB dispatches to a controller ISR that saves R2 to R5 and transfers control to the driver ISR. This service routine eventually returns control to MBA$INT.

MBA$INT uses the unit number of a device asserting attention as an index into the list IDB$L_UCBLIST. It identifies the type of the selected longword entry by checking its low-order bit. If the bit is set, then the entry is for a multidevice controller. If the bit is clear, the entry is the UCB address for a single-unit device. UCBs, like CRBs, are always longword-aligned (the low-order two bits are clear). When a CRB is created for a multidevice controller, and its address stored in the MBA IDB, the address is incremented by 1 so the low-order bit will be set. Control is actually transferred to the PUSHR instruction in the CRB with the following instruction, where R5 contains the MBA IDB entry:

```
JSB      -(R5)                    ;Autodecrement address to subtract 1
```

22.4.3   VAXBI Adapter Interrupt Service Routines

The dispatching of interrupts from VAX bus interconnect (VAXBI) adapters to the appropriate ISR varies according to the adapter type and the VAX system it is on.

Each adapter on a VAXBI bus is assigned four vectors in the SCB, corresponding to four interrupt levels. The VAXBI bus has 16 slots, or nodes, to connect adapters. Therefore, each VAXBI bus on a VAX system requires 64 interrupt vectors in the SCB to be reserved for adapter interrupts. Additional vectors are required for adapters such as the UNIBUS-to-VAXBI adapter (DW-BUA), as discussed in Section 22.4.3.1.

The 64 adapter interrupt vectors are organized in the appropriate page of the SCB as four contiguous arrays of 16 longwords each. The four arrays correspond to the four interrupt levels. This is similar to the organization of the upper half of the first page of the SCB, as discussed in Chapter 2.

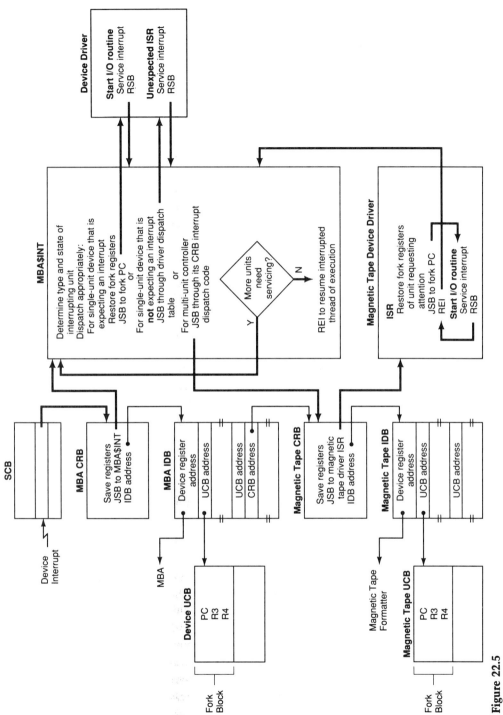

Figure 22.5
Control Flow in Servicing a MASSBUS Interrupt

647

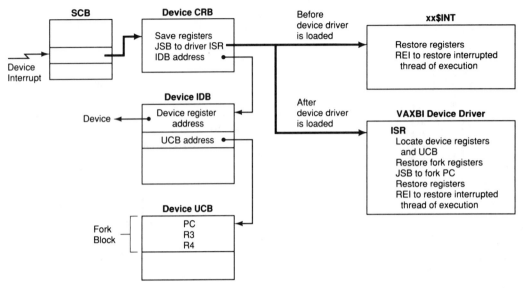

Figure 22.6
Control Flow in Servicing a VAXBI Adapter Interrupt

For example, the SCB vector for the lowest interrupt level for the adapter at node number 0 is at offset 100_{16} into the SCB page assigned to the VAXBI bus. The next three interrupt vectors for this adapter are at offsets 140_{16}, 180_{16}, and $1C0_{16}$, in the same page of the SCB. Sections 22.4.3.2 and 22.4.3.3 discuss the system-dependent assignment of an SCB page to a VAXBI bus.

The four SCB vectors assigned to each VAXBI adapter are used in an adapter-dependent manner. Adapter initialization procedures for all VAXBI adapters are in module [SYSLOA]INICOMBI.

Typically, the adapter initialization procedure connects a vector for an I/O adapter to the interrupt dispatch area in the CRB for that VAXBI adapter. The instructions in the CRB interrupt dispatch area are a PUSHR for R0 through R5 and a JSB. The IDB address follows the JSB instruction in the CRB (see Figure 22.6).

Initially, the JSB in the CRB transfers control to a skeleton ISR, such as CI$INT or BVP$INT, in module [SYSLOA]INICOMBI. This routine fields interrupts generated by the adapter prior to the loading of the device driver. It merely cleans off the stack and dismisses the interrupt.

When a VAXBI device driver is loaded, the destination of the JSB instruction is modified to the address of the ISR within the driver. From this point, interrupt dispatching is driver-dependent but generally resembles dispatching for directly vectored interrupts, as discussed in Section 22.4.1.1.

22.4.3.1   UNIBUS-to-VAXBI Adapters. Two adapters fit this description: the DW-BUA, which adapts the UNIBUS to the VAXBI bus, and the KLESI-B, which adapts the low-end storage interconnect (LESI) to the VAXBI bus. The KLESI-B is actually the functional equivalent of a DWBUA connected to a KLESI-U, which connects the LESI to the UNIBUS.

Each of these adapters on a VAX system is assigned a separate page of the SCB, because devices on the UNIBUS may generate any of the 128 possible vectors. Interrupts from devices on the UNIBUS and LESI are directly vectored through that assigned page.

An interrupt requested by the DWBUA or the KLESI-B adapter on its own behalf is vectored through one of the four vectors assigned for the adapter. On most systems, the last of these four vectors is used to service error interrupts requested by the adapter. The other vectors are unused and point to a routine that restores state and dismisses the interrupt.

The SCB entry for adapter error interrupts at offset $1C0_{16}$ in the appropriate page points to a JSB instruction within the ADP at offset ADP$L_UBASCB. The JSB invokes the routine EXE$UBAERR_INT, in module ADPERRxxx, where xxx is one of the CPU designations listed in Appendix G. EXE$BUA-ERR_INT and EXE$BLAERR_INT are synonyms for EXE$UBAERR_INT.

22.4.3.2   **VAXBI Adapters on VAX 8200 Family Systems.**   The VAX 8200 family includes the VAX 8200, VAX 8250, VAX 8300, VAX 8350, and the VAXstation 8000. On these systems, the VAXBI bus is the system bus as well as the primary I/O bus. This means that CPU modules and memory modules as well as I/O adapters connect to the VAXBI bus.

VAXBI adapter interrupts are vectored through the first page of the SCB on these systems. Additional pages of SCB may be assigned to adapters of the kind discussed in Section 22.4.3.1, if they are present.

22.4.3.3   **Other VAXBI Adapters.**   This category includes all VAXBI adapters on a VAXBI bus that is the primary I/O bus but not the system bus on a VAX system. It excludes those listed in Section 22.4.3.1. The VAXBI bus serves as the primary I/O bus on VAX 8800 family and VAX 6000 series systems.

These systems provide support for multiple VAXBI buses. Each VAXBI bus is assigned a separate page of the SCB. Additional pages of SCB may be assigned to adapters of the kind discussed in Section 22.4.3.1, if they are present. Chapter 3 explains the assignment of SCB pages for specific systems.

22.4.4   **CI Adapter Interrupt Service Routines**

Computer interconnect (CI) adapter interrupts are dispatched directly via the SCB. During system initialization, four SCB vectors for each CI port adapter are initialized by the CPU-specific routine INI$CIADP. INI$CIADP is in module [SYSLOA]INICOMBI for VAXBI-to-CI adapters and in module [SYSLOA]INIADPxxx for all other CI adapters.

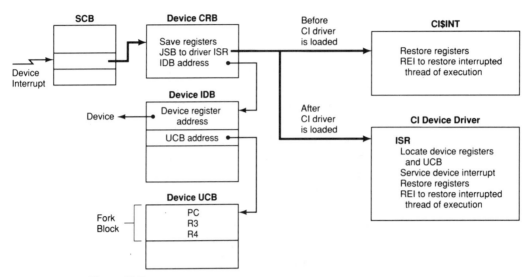

Figure 22.7
Control Flow in Servicing a CI Interrupt

Each of the four SCB vectors points to the interrupt dispatch area within the CI adapter's CRB. The interrupt dispatch area contains a PUSHR to save R2 to R5 and a JSB instruction to transfer control to the ISR.

Initially, the JSB in the CI adapter's CRB transfers control to routine CI$INT. CI$INT is in module [SYSLOA]ADPSUBxxx, where xxx is the CPU designation for VAX-11/750, VAX-11/78x, and VAX 86x0 systems. This routine simply performs the following operations:

1. Clears the adapter power-up and power-down bits in the CI control register
2. Sets the maintenance initialization bits in the CI control register
3. Restores registers R2 to R5
4. Executes an REI instruction to dismiss the interrupt

Actually, VAXBI-to-CI adapter interrupts are disabled until PADRIVER, the CI device driver, is loaded. CI$INT, a dummy ISR for VAXBI-to-CI adapters, is in module [SYSLOA]INICOMBI.

When PADRIVER is loaded, the destination of the JSB instruction is modified to the address of the interrupt service routine within the driver. There are several of these, one for each different type of CI port adapter. They are all in module [DRIVER]PAADP and have names such as INTERRUPT_CI780. They are very similar, differing primarily in their methods of testing for error conditions. The following list summarizes their actions, which are pictured in Figure 22.7:

1. The ISR removes the address of the IDB pointer from the stack, retrieving the address of the UCB.
2. The ISR examines various adapter registers to determine whether the CI port adapter interrupted because it queued a response packet to a formerly empty response queue or because an error occurred.
3. If there was no error, the ISR invokes the routine INT$FORK in module [DRIVER]PAINTR.
4. INT$FORK sets and tests a fork block interlock bit in the UCB. If the bit is already set, the UCB is already in use as a fork block and INT$FORK merely returns to the ISR. If the bit was not already set, INT$FORK forks, using the UCB. That is, a fork PC is stored in the UCB and the UCB is inserted on the IPL 8 fork queue.
5. INT$FORK returns to the ISR, which restores the registers saved on the stack and executes an REI instruction to dismiss the interrupt.
6. When the driver fork process is entered, it updates the maintenance timer on the CI port to indicate that the system is still active.
7. It then removes a response packet from the response queue and processes it. It continues dequeuing response packets and processing them until either the queue is empty or it has handled 100 response packets.

22.4.5   **DR32 Interrupt Service Routine**

DR32 interrupts are dispatched directly through the SCB. During system initialization, entries are made in the SCB to transfer control to locations in the CRB for the DR32. The instructions in the CRB are a PUSHR for R2 through R5 and a JSB instruction. The DR32 IDB address follows these instructions in the DR32 CRB (see Figure 22.8).

Initially, the JSB instruction in the DR32 CRB transfers control to routine DR$INT, in module [SYSLOA]ADPSUBxxx. This routine simply performs the following operations:

1. Clears the adapter power-up and power-down bits in a DR32 control register
2. Restores registers R2 to R5
3. Executes an REI instruction

When the DR32 driver, in module [DRIVER]XFDRIVER, is loaded by SYS-GEN, the destination of the JSB instruction is changed to the ISR in the driver. This routine performs the following operations:

1. Responds to the various types of DR32 interrupts
2. Restores registers R2 to R5
3. Executes an REI instruction

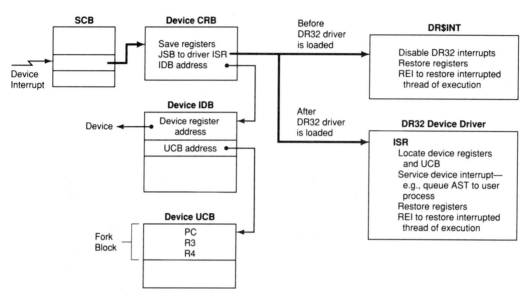

Figure 22.8
Control Flow in Servicing a DR32 Interrupt

22.5   CONNECT-TO-INTERRUPT MECHANISM

The connect-to-interrupt facility is an extension of the interrupt dispatching scheme. It enables a process to be notified of a UNIBUS or Q22-bus device interrupt by the delivery of an AST, setting of an event flag, or both. The process can also specify an interrupt service routine to respond to device interrupts.

A process with CMKRNL and PFNMAP privileges can respond to an interrupt by reading or writing device registers and possibly by initiating further device activity. However, to directly manipulate device registers, the process must first map the UNIBUS or Q22-bus space containing the registers for the device into its per-process space. The *VMS Device Support Manual* describes mapping UNIBUS I/O space and using the connect-to-interrupt capability. Chapter 15 of this book contains more detailed information on how the mapping is actually performed.

Note that the physical address range of UNIBUS I/O space differs on different types of VAX systems. The *VMS Device Support Manual* contains a list of symbols defined by the system-specific macros (for example, $IO730DEF) that define the physical addresses symbolically.

To use the connect-to-interrupt facility, the connect-to-interrupt driver, in module [DRIVER]CONINTERR, must be associated with the interrupt vector. The association is made using the SYSGEN command CONNECT, specifying all the following:

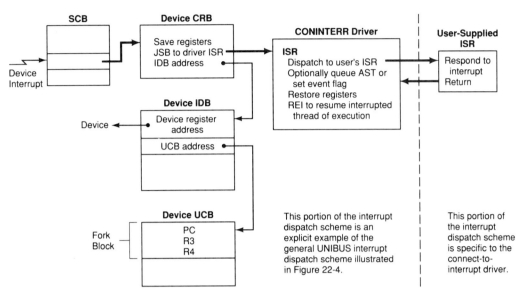

Figure 22.9
Extending Interrupt Dispatch Mechanism with the
Connect-to-Interrupt Facility

- Name for the device (used by the process connecting to the interrupt)
- CSR address of the device
- Interrupt vector at which the device generates interrupts
- CONINTERR driver, which initially responds to the device interrupts

When the device generates an interrupt, the normal UNIBUS or Q22-bus interrupt dispatching sequence is followed, as discussed in Section 22.4.1. However, the CONINTERR ISR transfers control to the user-supplied ISR at device IPL if one was supplied, using a JSB or CALL instruction, as requested by the user. This transfer is illustrated in Figure 22.9.

When the user-supplied ISR executes an RSB or RET instruction, the CONINTERR ISR regains control. Before restoring the registers and dismissing the interrupt, it creates an IPL$_QUEUEAST fork process to queue an AST, if requested, to the process to notify it that an interrupt has occurred. CONINTERR's AST routine sets an event flag, queues the user-requested AST, or both.

For the process-supplied ISR to be accessible to the CONINTERR ISR, the CONINTERR driver must double-map the user routine into system address space. The double mapping requires enough system page table entries (SPTEs) to map the user-supplied routines. These SPTEs must have been reserved through the REALTIME_SPTS SYSGEN parameter. When the process disconnects from the interrupt, the SPTEs used to map its routines are made available for similar use by other processes.

Note that the connect-to-interrupt driver has no provision for direct memory access I/O. It does not allocate map registers and data paths. Its fork IPL, IPL$_QUEUEAST, is lower than IPL 8, the IPL at which access to these adapter resources is arbitrated. Furthermore, the driver does not perform the tasks required to deal with VMS direct I/O buffers.

23   Mailboxes

Knowing how to answer one who speaks,
To reply to one who sends a message.
Amenemope, *The Instruction of Amenemope*

A VMS mailbox is a virtual I/O device for interprocess communication. One process writes a message to a mailbox for another process to read. A process reads or writes mailbox messages using standard VMS I/O mechanisms.

This chapter discusses mailboxes: the data structures that define them, the system services that create and delete them, and the driver that implements mailbox I/O. It briefly describes some examples of their use by the VMS executive and components.

23.1   OVERVIEW

VMS mailboxes are virtual I/O devices implemented in software. A mailbox is described by the same basic data structures as any other device. However, unlike those of a hardware device configured by SYSGEN, mailbox data structures are dynamically created in response to a process's Create Mailbox and Assign Channel ($CREMBX) system service request.

Mailboxes are read and written through the standard I/O mechanisms. However, messages written to a mailbox device are actually stored in non-paged pool until read. The mailbox driver, MBDRIVER, services Queue I/O ($QIO) system service requests to mailbox devices. Unlike most other drivers, the mailbox driver is implemented within a loadable executive image.

Processes sharing a mailbox generally identify it by an agreed-upon logical name. Since a mailbox exists in memory, it can be shared by any process running on a processor with access to that memory—either a uniprocessor or any CPU in a multiprocessing system. Because processes running on different VAXcluster system members do not share common memory, they must communicate by mechanisms other than mailboxes.

Processes typically use a mailbox as a one-way communication path between two or more processes; one process reads messages written to the mailbox by one or more other processes. The mailbox driver associates each write request with a single read request; mailbox messages are read in the order in which they are written. A message written to a mailbox cannot be broadcast; it is read by only one process. Although each mailbox read is paired with a mailbox write, VMS places no restrictions on the order in which read and write requests are issued.

A mailbox is created with a specified capacity to buffer messages written to it that have not yet been read. Thus, a process can write a message to a mailbox whether or not there is a pending read request. If there is a pending read request, the message is read immediately; otherwise, the message is buffered. A process can specify that its write request complete immediately. By default, a write request does not complete until another process reads the message.

When a process issues a read request to a mailbox, a buffered message may or may not be present. A process can request that if there is no buffered message, the read complete immediately. By default, a read request does not complete until another process writes a message to the mailbox. The *VMS I/O User's Reference Manual: Part I* provides more information on using mailboxes.

There are two kinds of mailboxes: temporary and permanent. A temporary mailbox is deleted automatically when no more processes have channels assigned to it. A permanent mailbox must be explicitly marked for deletion using the Delete Mailbox ($DELMBX) system service. Once marked for deletion, a permanent mailbox is deleted when no more processes have channels assigned to it.

A mailbox can also be created in MA780 multiport memory. This option loosely connects multiple VAX-11/780 processors or VAX-11/785 processors. Processes on all the processors sharing an MA780 memory can communicate through a mailbox in shared memory. At an application level, an MA780 shared memory mailbox differs from a local memory mailbox only in its name. At an implementation level, however, there are significant differences. This chapter describes only the implementation of local memory mailboxes.

23.2 LOGICAL NAMES OF MAILBOXES

Like any other I/O device, a mailbox has a device name specification in the form *ddcu*. The mailbox device type, *dd*, is MB. Its controller designation, *c*, is A. The unit number, *u*, is an integer from 1 to 9999.

Unlike those for other I/O devices, a particular unit number is not usually associated with a particular mailbox. The only mailboxes created with specific unit numbers are those permanently defined in the executive (see Section 23.3). When a mailbox is created, it is assigned the next available unit number. Its unit number cannot be determined before the mailbox is created.

Therefore, a process creating a mailbox usually also requests the creation of a logical name that translates to the mailbox device name. Other processes identify the mailbox by its logical name when they assign a channel to it. Although a user-specified logical name is not required, accessing a mailbox without one is difficult.

Every logical name is associated with a logical name table. The $CREMBX system service creates a logical name for a mailbox in one of two tables:

- The table LNM$TEMPORARY_MAILBOX for a temporary mailbox
- The table LNM$PERMANENT_MAILBOX for a permanent mailbox

LNM$TEMPORARY_MAILBOX is itself a logical name, whose default translation is LNM$JOB, the jobwide logical name table. The default translation of LNM$PERMANENT_MAILBOX is LNM$SYSTEM, the systemwide logical name table. Thus, temporary mailboxes, by default, can only be shared by processes in the same job tree. Processes not in the same job tree may share a temporary mailbox by redefining LNM$TEMPORARY_ MAILBOX to some shared logical name table. (For further information, see the *VMS System Services Reference Manual*.)

In addition to automatic logical name creation for a mailbox being created, VMS provides automatic logical name deletion for a mailbox being deleted.

Directed by the $CREMBX system service, the Create Logical Name ($CRELNM) system service stores the address of the logical name data structure in the mailbox UCB field UCB$L_LOGADR and the address of the mailbox UCB in the logical name data structure. (However, if the mailbox logical name is a process-private name, $CRELNM clears UCB$L_LOGADR to prevent possible race conditions at process deletion, when all process-private logical names are deleted.)

A mailbox in MA780 multiport memory is distinguished from a local memory mailbox by its logical name. The *VMS System Services Reference Manual* discusses the format of logical names for shared memory objects, including mailboxes.

23.3 MAILBOX DATA STRUCTURES

A mailbox device uses many of the same basic data structures that other I/O devices use. These include

- A device data block (DDB)
- A controller request block (CRB)
- A unit control block (UCB) for each unit
- An object rights block (ORB) for each unit

However, since a mailbox is not a physical device and does not service interrupts, it does not require an interrupt data block (IDB) or an adapter control block (ADP).

Chapter 20 contains a further description of these data structures.

Unlike those of most other devices, the mailbox DDB and CRB are assembled into the loadable executive image SYSTEM_PRIMITIVES, as are three mailbox UCBs and ORBs.

The first mailbox unit, MBA0, is the template from which $CREMBX clones all other mailboxes. (See Chapter 21 for a description of template device processing and IOC$CLONE_UCB.) Section 23.6 describes the use of the second and third mailbox units.

A mailbox UCB contains several device-specific fields:

- UCB$L_MB_MSGQ heads the queue of messages written to a mailbox device.

    The symbol UCB$L_MB_MSGQ, which is local to the driver, is the same offset as the symbol UCB$L_FQFL.

- UCB$L_LOGADR contains the address of the mailbox device's logical name block (LNMB).

- UCB$L_MB_R_AST and UCB$L_MB_W_AST head the read and write attention asynchronous system trap (AST) lists, where AST control blocks (ACBs) for attention ASTs are linked.

    Section 23.5.1.1 describes the mailbox driver's use of attention ASTs.

    The symbols UCB$L_MB_R_AST and UCB$L_MB_W_AST are local to the mailbox driver. They are the same offsets as UCB$L_ASTQFL and UCB$L_ASTQBL.

- UCB$W_INIQUO contains the maximum space allocation for messages written to the mailbox. No message written to the mailbox can be longer than this value.

    UCB$W_INIQUO is set to the $CREMBX argument BUFQUO if the argument is specified. Otherwise, the SYSGEN parameter DEFMBXBUFQUO is used.

- UCB$W_BUFQUO contains the space currently available for messages. Initially, UCB$W_BUFQUO contains the value stored in UCB$W_INIQUO. When a message is written to the mailbox, UCB$W_BUFQUO is reduced by the size of the message. When the message is read, its size is added to UCB$W_BUFQUO.

Figure 23.1 depicts a mailbox UCB.

A message written to a mailbox is stored in a nonpaged pool data structure called a message block. Figure 23.2 shows the layout of a mailbox message block.

23.4 MAILBOX CREATION AND DELETION

Two system services are related specifically to mailbox use: $CREMBX and $DELMBX.

23.4.1 $CREMBX System Service

The $CREMBX system service procedure, EXE$CREMBX in module SYS-MAILBX, runs in kernel mode. It creates a virtual mailbox device named MBA*n* and assigns an I/O channel to it or, if the mailbox already exists, merely assigns an I/O channel. $CREMBX has seven arguments:

MB__MSGQ		
MB__MSGQ + 4		
FLCK	TYPE	SIZE
MB__W__AST		
MB__R__AST		
MSGCNT		MSGMAX
INIQUO		BUFQUO
ORB		
CPID		
CRB		
(104 bytes)		
LOGADR		
SVAPTE		
(16 bytes)		

Figure 23.1
Mailbox Unit Control Block

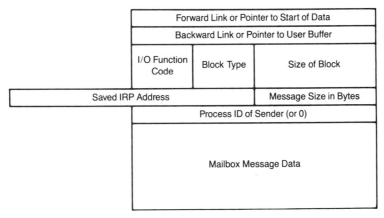

Figure 23.2
Layout of Mailbox Message Block

- PRMFLG, a flag specifying whether the mailbox is to be permanent or temporary
- CHAN, the address of a word in which the channel number assigned to the mailbox by EXE$CREMBX is written
- MAXMSG, the maximum size of a message that can be sent to the mailbox
- BUFQUO, the number of bytes of nonpaged pool that can be used to buffer messages sent to the mailbox
- PROMSK, the protection mask to be associated with the created mailbox
- ACMODE, the access mode to be associated with the channel to which the mailbox is assigned

659

- LOGNAM, the logical name to be assigned to a new mailbox or translated to locate an existing mailbox

The CHAN argument is required; all others are optional.
EXE$CREMBX takes the following initial steps:

1. It verifies that the CHAN argument is write-accessible.
2. If the LOGNAM argument is present, EXE$CREMBX invokes MMG$MBX-TRNLOG, in module SHMGSDRTN, to determine whether the mailbox is an MA780 shared memory mailbox.
3. EXE$CREMBX raises IPL to 2 to prevent process deletion and invokes IOC$FFCHAN to find a free channel control block (CCB). IOC$FFCHAN is discussed in Chapter 21.
4. It checks that the process has the necessary privilege to create the type of mailbox specified in the PRMFLG argument: PRMMBX for a permanent mailbox or TMPMBX for a temporary mailbox.
5. It locks the I/O database mutex for write access.
6. If the LOGNAM argument was omitted, EXE$CREMBX presumes that the mailbox does not exist and must be created. It creates the mailbox, as described in Section 23.4.1. It clears UCB$L_LOGADR to indicate that the mailbox has no associated logical name and continues with step 11.
7. If the LOGNAM argument was specified, EXE$CREMBX requests the Translate Logical Name ($TRNLNM) system service to obtain the address of the mailbox UCB, if one exists. It passes the following arguments to $TRNLNM:

   —The name of the mailbox logical name table
   —The logical name specified by the LOGNAM argument
   —The maximized access mode, that is, the less privileged of the access mode specified by the ACMODE argument and the access mode of the requestor
   —An item list element requesting the back pointer

8. If the logical name exists, EXE$CREMBX uses its back pointer contents as the UCB address and continues with step 11.
9. If the logical name does not exist, EXE$CREMBX presumes that the mailbox does not exist and must be created. It takes the steps described in Section 23.4.1.
10. EXE$CREMBX requests the Create Logical Name ($CRELNM) system service to create the logical name specified by the LOGNAM argument. It passes the following arguments to the $CRELNM system service:

    —The name of the mailbox logical name table
    —The logical name specified by the LOGNAM argument
    —The maximized access mode
    —An item list element directing the $CRELNM system service to store the address of the logical name block in UCB$L_LOGADR

11. EXE$CREMBX increments the reference count for that mailbox and assigns a channel to the mailbox by taking the following steps:

    a. It stores the mailbox UCB address in CCB$L_UCB.

    b. It stores the access mode at which the channel was assigned (plus 1) in CCB$B_AMOD. The access mode is biased by 1 because a 0 in CCB$B_AMOD indicates an unassigned channel. As usual, the access mode at which the channel is assigned is the less privileged of the access mode specified by the ACMODE argument and the access mode of the requestor.

12. EXE$CREMBX stores the channel number in the address specified by the CHAN argument. It unlocks the I/O database mutex, lowers IPL to 0, and returns the success status SS$_NORMAL to its requestor.

EXE$CREMBX can create a temporary or a permanent mailbox depending on the value of the PRMFLG argument. To create a temporary mailbox, a process must have sufficient byte count quota for the mailbox messages and UCB. The quota is charged at mailbox creation and returned at mailbox deletion. Because a permanent mailbox may survive the deletion of its creating process, quota is not charged for its creation. Instead, PRMMBX, a privilege less lightly granted than TMPMBX, is required for a process to create a permanent mailbox.

For a temporary mailbox, EXE$CREMBX invokes IOC$CHKMBXQUOTA, in module UCBCREDEL, to determine if the process buffered I/O byte count quota (JIB$L_BYTCNT) can accommodate both of the following with a margin of 256 bytes left:

- The size of a mailbox UCB.
- The space to buffer mailbox messages, the buffer quota. (This value is the BUFQUO argument if the argument was specified or the SYSGEN parameter DEFMBXBUFQUO if the BUFQUO argument is absent.)

IOC$CHKMBXQUOTA invokes EXE$DEBIT_BYTCNT_BYTLM_NW to charge the process buffered I/O byte count quota (JIB$L_BYTCNT) and byte limit (JIB$L_BYTLM) for the size of the mailbox UCB and the mailbox message buffer. If a quota is insufficient, IOC$CHKMBXQUOTA returns an error status to EXE$CREMBX, which returns the error to its caller.

EXE$CREMBX invokes IOC$CLONE_UCB, in module UCBCREDEL, to clone a new UCB and ORB from the template mailbox unit MBA0. IOC$CLONE_UCB allocates sufficient nonpaged pool to create a new UCB and ORB. It copies the template UCB and ORB to the newly allocated memory. It increments the value found in UCB$W_UNIT_SEED in the template UCB and checks whether that unit number exists. If so, the next value is tried. This continues until an available unit number is found or a maximum of 9999 is reached. If that occurs, the unit number wraps to 1 and the search continues.

IOC$CLONE_UCB initializes the new UCB as follows: it links the new UCB into the UCB list, sets the reference count to 1, marks the device online, and loads the new ORB address into the UCB's ORB pointer field.

EXE$CREMBX further initializes the cloned UCB:

1. It stores the buffer quota in the buffer quota and initial buffer quota fields, UCB$W_BUFQUO and UCB$W_INIQUO.
2. It clears the owner field, UCB$L_PID.
3. It modifies the ORB associated with the UCB to specify the system, owner, group, and world format protection mask, and stores the PROMASK argument in ORB$W_PROT.
4. It stores the current process's user identification code (UIC) in the ORB owner UIC field.
5. It stores the maximum message size in the UCB device buffer size field. This value is the MAXMSG argument if the argument is specified. Otherwise, it is the SYSGEN parameter DEFMBXMXMSG.
6. It clears the current message count, UCB$L_DEVDEPEND.
7. It stores the sum of the UCB size and the buffer quota in UCB$W_CHARGE.
8. If the mailbox is permanent, EXE$CREMBX sets bit UCB$V_PRMMBX in UCB$W_DEVSTS.
9. If the mailbox is temporary, EXE$CREMBX takes the following steps:

    a. It sets bit UCB$V_DELMBX in UCB$W_DEVSTS. This marks the mailbox for deletion on the last channel deassignment.
    b. It invokes IOC$DEBIT_UCB, in module UCBCREDEL, to copy the master PID charged for the UCB (JIB$L_MPID) into the charge PID field (UCB$L_CPID).

In earlier versions of VMS, IOC$DEBIT_UCB decremented the job information block (JIB) byte count quota and byte limit fields. In VMS Version 5, this function has been moved to EXE$DEBIT_BYTCNT_BYTLM_NW, which now charges quotas while holding the JIB spinlock.

Figure 23.3 shows the data structures associated with mailbox creation.

23.4.2 $DELMBX System Service

The $DELMBX system service marks a mailbox for deletion. Requesting $DELMBX to mark a temporary channel for deletion is superfluous; it can be deleted simply by deassigning the channel to it. The $DELMBX system service has only one argument: CHAN, the number of the channel assigned to the mailbox to be deleted.

The $DELMBX system service procedure, EXE$DELMBX in module SYSMAILBX, runs in kernel mode. EXE$DELMBX invokes IOC$VERIFYCHAN to verify the channel number and get the address of the CCB. Once it has

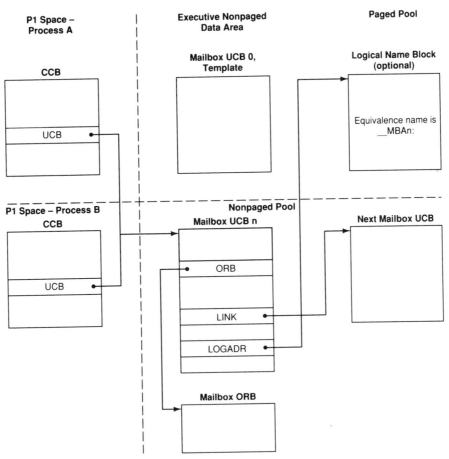

Figure 23.3
Data Structures Associated with Mailbox Creation

located the CCB, EXE$DELMBX gets the UCB address from CCB$L_UCB and then verifies the following:

- That the UCB is a mailbox (DEV$V_MBX in UCB$L_DEVCHAR is set)
- That, if the mailbox is permanent, the process has PRMMBX privilege

If these conditions are met, EXE$DELMBX marks a permanent mailbox for deletion by setting bit UCB$V_DELMBX in UCB$W_DEVSTS. The $CREMBX system service sets bit UCB$V_DELMBX for a temporary mailbox when the mailbox UCB is created.

The mailbox is actually deleted by IOC$DELETE_UCB, in module UCB-CREDEL, when the reference count goes to zero (after the last channel assigned to it has been deassigned). Last channel processing is performed by IOC$LAST_CHAN, in module IOSUBNPAG. IOC$LAST_CHAN invokes the driver cancel I/O routine with an appropriate cancellation reason code.

The mailbox driver, MBDRIVER, in module MBDRIVER, deletes the logical name, if any, as part of the last channel processing done by its cancel I/O routine. (See Chapter 21 for a discussion of last channel processing and Section 23.5.4 for details on the mailbox driver's cancel I/O routine.)

23.5 MAILBOX DRIVER

The following sections describe the functions of the mailbox driver, in module MBDRIVER. Note that mailboxes in MA780 multiport memory are supported by a separate, loadable driver, [DRIVER]MBXDRIVER, which this chapter does not discuss.

MBDRIVER uses IPL$_MAILBOX, the highest fork interrupt priority level (IPL) as its fork IPL. It does this to prevent possible synchronization problems with other drivers that reference mailboxes while in their fork processes (for example, to send a "device is off line" message to the operator's mailbox). It uses the MAILBOX spinlock as both the fork lock and the device lock.

23.5.1 Processing Set Mode Requests

A process uses the IO$_SETMODE function to request MBDRIVER to perform three different operations. The function modifier determines the specific operation.

- IO$M_READATTN—Request an attention AST when a read request is issued for the mailbox
- IO$M_WRTATTN—Request an attention AST when a write request is issued for the mailbox
- IO$M_SETPROT—Set the volume protection on the mailbox

Only one of the modifiers can be specified at one time. If no modifier is specified, MBDRIVER uses IO$M_WRTATTN by default.

23.5.1.1 AST Notification of Mailbox Read or Write Requests.
When an image requests a set mode function to establish either a read or a write attention AST, MBDRIVER's set mode FDT routine, FDTSET, takes the following steps:

1. It verifies that the process may access the mailbox.
2. It invokes COM$SETATTNAST, in module COMDRVSUB, to allocate, initialize, and queue an ACB to the appropriate listhead in the mailbox UCB. FDTSET passes the address of the listhead, either UCB$L_MB_W_AST for write attention AST requests or UCB$L_MB_R_AST for read attention AST requests. Chapter 7 provides more information on attention ASTs.
3. It acquires the MAILBOX spinlock, raising IPL to IPL$_MAILBOX, to synchronize access to the UCB.
4. It determines if the notification condition is met.

—If the request is for a write attention AST, there must be at least one message queued to the mailbox (UCB$W_MSGCNT is not equal to zero).

—If the request is for a read attention AST, the UCB must be busy (UCB$V_BSY in UCB$W_STS is set).

If the appropriate condition is met, FDTSET invokes COM$DELATTN-AST, in module COMDRVSUB, to queue the attention AST to the requesting process.

Otherwise, MBDRIVER later queues an attention AST to the process when a read or write request, as appropriate, is issued for the mailbox.

5. FDTSET releases the MAILBOX spinlock and jumps to EXE$FINISHIOC, in module SYSQIOREQ, to complete the I/O request (see Chapter 21).

23.5.1.2　**Specifying Access Protection of a Mailbox.** When an image requests a set mode function to set the protection on a mailbox, FDTSET takes the following steps:

1. It verifies that the requesting process either has BYPASS privilege or owns the UCB. It examines the mailbox ORB for ownership verification.

2. It acquires the MAILBOX spinlock, raising IPL to IPL$_MAILBOX, to synchronize access to the UCB.

3. It sets the flag specifying that the standard system, owner, group, world protection mask is valid (ORB$M_PROT_16 in ORB$B_FLAGS) and moves the P2 argument of the $QIO request to the protection mask word (ORB$W_PROT) of the ORB.

4. It releases the MAILBOX spinlock and transfers control to EXE$FINISH-IOC to complete the I/O request.

23.5.2　**Processing a Mailbox Write Request**

When an image requests the $QIO system service to request a mailbox write, MBDRIVER's write FDT routine, FDTWRITE, takes the following steps:

1. It invokes WRITECHECKIO, in module MBDRIVER, to validate the request. The following criteria must be met:

—The process must have write access to the mailbox as determined by EXE$CHKWRTACCES, in module EXSUBROUT.

—The message size must be less than or equal to the maximum message size for the mailbox (UCB$W_DEVBUFSIZ). If the message size exceeds the maximum, the request is aborted with a completion status of SS$_MBTOOSML.

—The process must have read access to the specified buffer (from which the mailbox message will be read) as determined by EXE$WRITECHK, in module SYSQIOFDT.

WRITECHECKIO saves the address of the specified buffer in IRP$L_MEDIA.

2. FDTWRITE invokes EXE$ALONONPAGED, in module MEMORYALC, to allocate a message block from nonpaged pool.
3. It initializes the block, as shown in Figure 23.2.
4. It loads the message block with the data found in the specified buffer.
5. It saves the current IPL and acquires the MAILBOX spinlock, raising IPL to IPL$_MAILBOX.
6. It determines if there is enough buffer quota remaining for the message. If not, it releases the spinlock, restores the saved IPL, and deallocates the message block to nonpaged pool. It then performs one of the following actions:

—If the message size is less than the total space allowed for messages (UCB$W_INIQUO) and resource wait mode is enabled, as it is unless the $QIO no-resource-wait modifier IO$M_NORSWAIT was specified, FDTWRITE transfers control to EXE$IORSNWAIT, in module SYSQIOFDT, to place the process into a RWMBX resource wait state. Chapter 12 gives details on resource waits.

—If the message size is less than the total space allowed for messages and resource wait mode is disabled (the no-resource-wait modifier, IO$M_NORSWAIT, was specified), FDTWRITE transfers control to EXE$ABORTIO, in module SYSQIOREQ, with a completion status of SS$_MBFULL.

—If the message size is larger than UCB$W_INIQUO, FDTWRITE transfers control to EXE$ABORTIO to abort the I/O request with a completion status of SS$_MBTOOSML.

7. If there is enough room for the message, FDTWRITE invokes INSMBQUEUE, in module MBDRIVER. INSMBQUEUE takes the following steps:

a. It increments the count of outstanding messages (UCB$W_MSGCNT) and saves a copy of the count in UCB$L_DEVDEPEND.
b. It subtracts the size of the new message from the buffer quota field UCB$W_BUFQUO.
c. If the UCB$V_BSY bit is set (if there is a read request outstanding), it jumps to FINISHREAD, in module MBDRIVER (see Section 23.5.3.3). FINISHREAD uses the message block to complete the outstanding read request, whose I/O request packet (IRP) it locates from UCB$L_IRP.
d. If the UCB is not busy, the message block must be queued to wait for a read request. The message block contains the address of the write request IRP and the actual data. INSMBQUEUE inserts the message block at the tail of the message queue, as shown in Figure 23.4.

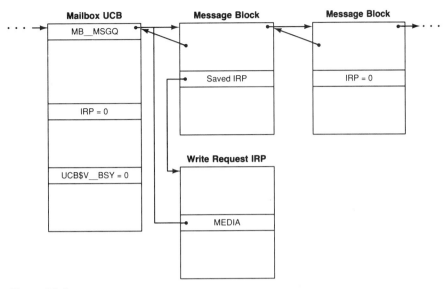

Figure 23.4
Queued Mailbox Messages

> e. INSMBQUEUE transfers control to COM$DELATTNAST to queue any write attention ASTs to the appropriate processes.

8. FDTWRITE releases the spinlock, restoring the saved IPL.

9. If the IO$M_NOW modifier was specified, FDTWRITE clears the saved IRP address field in the message block. It transfers control to EXE$FINISHIOC to record I/O status block (IOSB) information in the IRP and complete the I/O request through I/O postprocessing with a completion status of SS$_NORMAL.

10. If the IO$M_NOW modifier was not specified, FDTWRITE transfers control to EXE$QIORETURN, in module SYSQIOREQ, to complete the $QIO system service. The processing of the write request is stalled until a read request is issued.

23.5.3 Processing a Mailbox Read Request

MBDRIVER processes a read request in three phases: FDT preprocessing, start I/O processing, and request completion.

23.5.3.1 FDT Read Request Processing.

When an image requests the $QIO system service to read a message from a mailbox, MBDRIVER's read FDT routine, FDTREAD, takes the following steps:

> 1. It invokes READCHECKIO, in module MBDRIVER, to validate the request. The following criteria must be met:

—The process must have read access to the mailbox as determined by EXE$CHKRDACCES, in module EXSUBROUT.

—The message size must be less than or equal to the maximum message size for the mailbox (UCB$W_DEVBUFSIZ). If the message size exceeds the maximum, the request is aborted with a completion status of SS$_MBTOOSML.

—The process must have write access to the specified buffer (in which the mailbox message will be placed) as determined by EXE$READCHK, in module SYSQIOFDT.

READCHECKIO saves the address of the specified buffer in IRP$L_MEDIA.

2. FDTREAD sets the mailbox I/O bit in the IRP (IRP$V_MBXIO in IRP$W_STS). The I/O postprocessing special kernel mode AST routine announces the availability of the mailbox resource when it processes an I/O request with the mailbox I/O bit set.

3. If the IO$M_NOW modifier was not specified, FDTREAD transfers control to EXE$QIODRVPKT to queue the IRP. MBDRIVER's start I/O routine does the rest of the processing of this request.

4. If the IO$M_NOW modifier was specified, FDTREAD takes the following steps:

   a. It acquires the MAILBOX spinlock, raising IPL to IPL$_MAILBOX.

   b. If any message is available (UCB$W_MSGCNT is nonzero), it transfers control to EXE$QIODRVPKT to queue the IRP. MBDRIVER's start I/O routine does the rest of the processing of this request.

   c. If no message is available, it releases the spinlock and transfers control to EXE$FINISHIOC to complete the I/O operation with a final I/O status of SS$_ENDOFFILE.

23.5.3.2   Start I/O Read Request Processing. STARTIO, which is MBDRIVER's start I/O routine, performs the following steps while holding the MAILBOX spinlock:

1. It tries to dequeue a message written to the mailbox from the UCB listhead at UCB$L_MB_MSGQ.

2. If the message queue is empty, it transfers control to COM$DELATTN-AST to queue any pending read attention ASTs to the appropriate processes.

   The mailbox UCB busy bit remains set. As a result, subsequent read requests are queued to the UCB. The current read request does not complete until a write request is issued. When the current read request is completed, STARTIO processes the next read request in the queue.

3. If STARTIO dequeues a message, it transfers control to FINISHREAD.

23.5.3.3 **Read Request Completion.** STARTIO and INSMBQUEUE transfer control to FINISHREAD to complete the current read request by matching it with a message block built by a write request. STARTIO transfers control to FINISHREAD when it processes a read request and there is at least one message in the queue. INSMBQUEUE transfers control to FINISHREAD when a write request is to be queued and there is a read request waiting.

For each request, FINISHREAD loads IOSB information into the request's associated IRP and passes the IRP to a routine for insertion onto the I/O postprocessing queue. Since FINISHREAD matches a read request to a write request and each request has a unique IRP, it must handle both IRPs in this manner. It locates the read request's IRP from the current IRP field UCB$L_IRP and the write request's IRP from the message block.

FINISHREAD takes the following steps:

1. It obtains the read request's IRP from UCB$L_IRP.
2. It holds a message block, either a newly constructed one in the case of INSMBQUEUE or a dequeued one in the case of STARTIO. It stores the address of the message block (see Figure 23.2) in IRP$L_SVAPTE in the read request's IRP. The I/O postprocessing routine uses this field to determine the address of the message to be copied to the user's buffer. Chapter 21 provides more information on I/O postprocessing.
3. FINISHREAD initializes the first two longwords in the message block with the values expected by the I/O postprocessing routine. The first longword points to the message data, stored in the message block, and the second longword points to the user buffer, where the data will be copied by the I/O completion special kernel mode AST. It obtains the address of the user's buffer from IRP$L_MEDIA in the read request IRP.
4. It increases the message quota (UCB$W_BUFQUO) by the size of the message to reflect the delivery of this message.
5. It creates a fork thread to declare the availability of the mailbox resource if bit RSN$_MAILBOX is set in SCH$L_RESMASK, indicating that a process is waiting for the resource, and if the mailbox fork block is available.
6. It stores the final byte count in the read request IRP.
7. It decrements the message count in UCB$W_MSGCNT and copies that value to UCB$L_DEVDEPEND.
8. It obtains the write request's IRP address (or a zero) from the message block. If the write request specified the IO$M_NOW modifier, or if the message block was created by the internal routine EXE$WRTMAILBOX, no write request IRP exists. In these cases, FINISHREAD finds a zero in the message block and branches to step 11 to complete the read request IRP. Section 23.5.6 describes EXE$WRTMAILBOX.

Otherwise it places the process ID (PID) of the process that issued the read request in IRP$L_MEDIA + 4 so that it will become the high-order longword of the IOSB for the write request $QIO. It stores the SS$_NORMAL success code in the low-order word of the IOSB (IRP$L_MEDIA) of the write request IRP and the final byte count at IRP$L_MEDIA + 2.

9. It invokes COM$POST, in module COMDRVSUB, to insert the write request's IRP on the I/O postprocessing queue. FINISHREAD invokes this routine, rather than invoking the REQCOM macro, so that another IRP is not dequeued (because only read request IRPs are queued to the UCB waiting to enter the start I/O routine).

10. It places the PID of the process that issued the write request in R1. If the internal routine EXE$WRTMAILBOX built the message block, this PID may be inaccurate.

11. It stores the completion status and transfer count in R0. The completion status is either SS$_NORMAL or, if the message block function code is IO$_WRITEOF, SS$_ENDOFFILE.

12. To complete the read request, it invokes the REQCOM macro, which transfers control to IOC$REQCOM. The value in R1 becomes the high-order longword of the read request's IOSB and the value in R0 becomes the low-order longword. IOC$REQCOM dequeues the next request and the start I/O sequence is repeated. If no read request is outstanding, the busy bit is cleared.

Figure 23.5 shows the data structures involved in read request completion.

23.5.4 Mailbox Cancel I/O Routine

The mailbox driver's cancel I/O routine, CANCELIO, performs functions depending on one of three cancellation reason codes: CANC_CANCEL, CANC_AMBXDGN, or CAN$C_DASSGN.

- For a reason code of CAN$C_CANCEL, CANCELIO aborts the outstanding I/O for a particular process and channel on a mailbox unit. It then flushes the read and write attention AST queues (see Chapter 7) and declares the mailbox resource available if necessary.

- For a reason code of CAN$C_AMBXDGN, CANCELIO tests bit UCB$V_DELMBX. If it is set, CANCELIO synchronizes its access to the logical name table and deletes the mailbox logical name if one exists. It then deallocates all queued message blocks to nonpaged pool and marks the mailbox UCB for deletion.

- For a reason code of CAN$C_DASSGN, CANCELIO performs all the functions associated with the CAN$C_CANCEL reason code. Additionally, CANCELIO checks whether the mailbox's reference count has fallen to zero. If so, it performs all the functions associated with the CAN$C_AMBXDGN reason code.

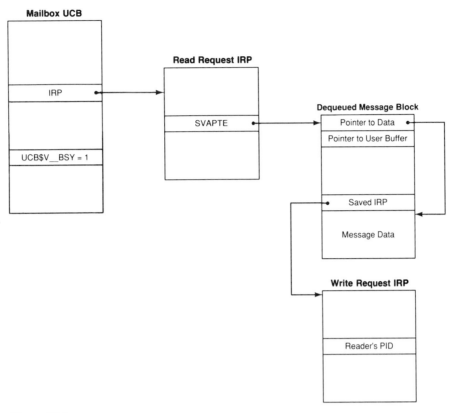

Figure 23.5
Read Request Completion

23.5.5   **Mailbox Messages from Drivers**

EXE$SNDEVMSG, in module MBDRIVER, builds a device-specific mailbox message and inserts it onto a message queue. VMS routines like drivers cannot assume process context and so cannot use the $QIO system service to write a message to a mailbox, in particular, to the mailbox of the operator communication process (OPCOM). Such routines use EXE$SNDEVMSG instead.

EXE$SNDEVMSG must be invoked at or below mailbox fork IPL, IPL$_MAILBOX. The driver provides its device UCB address, the address of a mailbox UCB to which to queue a message, and the type of message to create.

EXE$SNDEVMSG performs the following:

1. It acquires the MAILBOX spinlock, raising IPL to IPL$_MAILBOX.
2. It allocates space for the message on the stack.
3. It inserts a message code and device unit number into the message. System mailbox message codes are defined by the $MSGDEF macro.

671

4. It inserts the device name in the form *node$controller* into the message by invoking IOC$CVT_DEVNAM.

5. It invokes EXE$WRTMAILBOX (see Section 23.5.6) to allocate a message block, complete the message, and queue it to the appropriate mailbox unit.

6. EXE$SNDEVMSG cleans the stack and releases the MAILBOX spinlock before returning to its invoker.

23.5.6   **Alternative Mailbox Write Request Processing**

EXE$WRTMAILBOX performs message buffer allocation and message queuing, just as FDTWRITE does. However, EXE$WRTMAILBOX executes within the limitations of system context. In addition, it does not reference any IRP fields, so it is available to driver code that bypasses the $QIO system service and that has no IRP to describe its mailbox I/O request. System routines such as EXE$SNDEVMSG and EXE$SNDOPR invoke EXE$WRTMAILBOX to complete mailbox message processing.

EXE$WRTMAILBOX performs the following:

1. It acquires the MAILBOX spinlock.

2. It compares the message size to UCB$W_BUFQUO to ensure that there is enough remaining quota; if not, it returns the error status SS$_MBFULL.

3. It compares the message size to UCB$W_DEVBUFSIZ to ensure that the message does not exceed the maximum size; if the message exceeds the maximum size, EXE$WRTMAILBOX returns the error status SS$_MBTOOSML.

4. It verifies that the owner protection field in the ORB allows write access to the mailbox; if not, EXE$WRTMAILBOX returns the error status SS$_NOPRIV.

5. EXE$WRTMAILBOX invokes EXE$ALONONPAGED to allocate a message block from nonpaged pool.

6. It initializes the block, as shown in Figure 23.2. However, it clears the message block's packet address field because no IRP is associated with the request. The PID is obtained from the process control block (PCB) found in the per-CPU database field CPU$L_CURPCB. Since EXE$WRTMAILBOX might be executing in system context, this PID is not necessarily relevant.

7. It copies the data to be written to the mailbox into the message block.

8. It invokes INSMBQUEUE to insert the message onto the queue or to complete an outstanding read request. Section 23.5.2 describes INSMBQUEUE.

9. Finally, EXE$WRTMAILBOX releases one instance of MAILBOX spinlock ownership and returns to its caller.

23.6   **MAILBOX USE BY THE VMS EXECUTIVE AND COMPONENTS**

The VMS executive uses mailboxes in a number of different ways:

- A process establishes a termination mailbox to receive status information about a subprocess it creates. Chapters 25 and 28 offer more information on termination mailboxes.
- A process can monitor error logging activity as it happens through the use of an error log mailbox. Chapter 32 describes the error log mailbox mechanism.
- When a process assigns a channel to a nonshareable device, it can request an associated mailbox to receive device status information such as the arrival of unsolicited input. The description of the Assign I/O Channel ($ASSIGN) system service in Chapter 21 provides more information.

When a process spawns a subprocess through the Digital command language (DCL), DCL establishes a termination mailbox for the spawned subprocess. It also creates a mailbox to write logical names and symbol definitions to the subprocess and another mailbox to receive attach requests from the subprocess. Chapter 27 describes the use of these mailboxes in more detail.

The sections that follow describe the use of mailboxes to communicate with the job controller, with OPCOM, with the audit server, and with the file system.

23.6.1   **Job Controller Mailbox Use**

Symbiont processes and the VMS executive communicate with the job controller through the job controller's input mailbox, MBA1. Various modules in the executive pass information and requests to the job controller through this mailbox. System services that request information from the job controller, such as Send Job Controller ($SNDJBC) and Get Queue Information ($GETQUI), package their requests as mailbox messages. Unsolicited terminal input, unsolicited card reader input, connection manager notification that a node has left the VAXcluster, and notification of process termination are all events communicated to the job controller though messages to MBA1.

INI$DEVICE_DATABASE, in module PERMANENT_DEVICE_DATA-BASE, stores the UCB address of MBA1 into the field SYS$AR_JOBCTLMB during system initialization. The mailbox is defined with a reference count of 1, which protects it from allocation and deletion.

The job controller's initialization routine uses the symbol SYS$C_JOB-CTLMB, which has the value MBA1, to assign a channel to the input mailbox.

Before the job controller creates a symbiont process, it creates an input mailbox for that symbiont and obtains the new mailbox device name using the Get Device/Volume Information ($GETDVI) argument DVI$_DEVNAM.

Then it requests the actual Create Process ($CREPRC) system service, specifying the new mailbox as the symbiont's input device and the job controller's input mailbox as the symbiont's output device.

To communicate with a symbiont, the job controller routine SEND_SYMBIONT_MESSAGE writes to the symbiont's mailbox. It uses the $QIO modifiers IO$M_NOW and IO$M_NORSWAIT so that its I/O operations complete immediately.

23.6.2 Operator Communication Process Mailbox Use

A device or process communicates with OPCOM, the operator communication process, through OPCOM's input mailbox, MBA2. INI$DEVICE_DATABASE stores the address of the OPCOM mailbox's UCB in SYS$AR_OPRMBX during system initialization. This mailbox is defined with a reference count of 1 and cannot be allocated or deleted.

OPCOM's initialization routine assigns a channel to its mailbox and sets the mailbox protection. It posts an initial mailbox read request, specifying the AST procedure READ_MAILBOX, in module [OPCOM]OPCOMMAIN.

The AST is triggered by a write to OPCOM's mailbox. The AST procedure allocates a work queue element, reads the OPCOM mailbox, and copies the data from the mailbox into the work queue element. It inserts the element on OPCOM's work queue, wakes the main loop, and reissues the mailbox read request.

The main loop services the work queue, reading messages from it and servicing each based on its function code. Most messages come through the Send Message to Operator ($SNDOPR) system service, although device online/offline messages, for example, are sent through EXE$SNDEVMSG.

23.6.3 Audit Server Mailbox Use

Communication with AUDIT_SERVER, the audit server process, occurs via the audit server mailbox, MBA3. During system initialization, INI$DEVICE_DATABASE stores the UCB address of MBA3 into the field SYS$AR_AUDSRVMBX. The audit server's initialization routine assigns a channel to this mailbox and posts an initial mailbox read request, specifying the AST procedure AUDSRV$QUEUE_MESSAGE, in module [AUDSRV]AUD-SERVER.

[CLIUTL]SETAUDIT, which implements the DCL SET AUDIT command, passes information and requests to the audit server through this mailbox. It triggers the AST by writing to the mailbox. The AST procedure allocates a message queue element, reads the AUDIT_SERVER mailbox, and copies the data from the mailbox into the message queue element. It inserts the element on AUDIT_SERVER's work queue, wakes the main loop, and reissues the mailbox read request.

OPCOM's initialization routine also assigns a channel to the audit server mailbox. While security auditing is enabled, OPCOM inserts a message in the audit server mailbox whenever a security alarm is generated. The $NSADEF macro defines the format of both the security alarm messages and the SET AUDIT messages.

23.6.4   **File System Bad Block Mailbox**

File system initialization creates a permanent mailbox named ACP$BAD-BLOCK_MBX. This mailbox provides a path for communication with bad block recovery processes.

When a driver notifies the file system (through I/O postprocessing) of a suspected bad block, the file system flags the file header. When the file containing the detected bad block is deleted, another file system routine performs further processing. It assigns a channel to the bad block mailbox, writes a message to the mailbox indicating the device UCB and file ID number, and creates a process running the image BADBLOCK. The bad block process assigns a channel to the mailbox and reads the message for instructions. See Chapter 24 for more information on bad block processing.

24 Miscellaneous I/O Topics

Lull'd in the countless chambers of the brain,
Our thoughts are link'd by many a hidden chain;
Awake but one, and lo, what myriads arise!
Each stamps its image as the other flies.

Alexander Pope

This chapter presents a number of miscellaneous I/O-related topics. The first few sections highlight techniques used by selected device drivers, techniques that aid an understanding of the VMS I/O subsystem and that are not described in the *VMS Device Support Manual*. No attempt is made to discuss each VMS device driver, nor is every feature of a particular driver described. For detailed descriptions of the features and capabilities provided by each supported device driver, see the *VMS I/O User's Reference Volume*.

Additional topics, such as bad block processing for disks, the Breakthrough ($BRKTHRU) system service, and other informational system services, are covered in this chapter.

24.1 CLASS AND PORT DRIVERS

VMS uses a layered approach for certain device drivers. The class driver, which is the functional layer, handles operations on a certain class of device, such as disk, tape, or terminal. The port driver, which is the communications layer, handles operations that depend on the protocol and hardware used to communicate with the actual device and controller.

VMS class and port device drivers include the following:

- The terminal class driver, TTDRIVER
- Terminal port drivers, such as DZDRIVER and YIDRIVER
- The mass storage control protocol (MSCP) disk driver, DUDRIVER
- The tape MSCP (TMSCP) driver, TUDRIVER
- System communication services (SCS) port drivers, such as PADRIVER and PUDRIVER
- The small computer systems interface (SCSI) disk driver, DKDRIVER
- The SCSI tape driver, MKDRIVER
- SCSI port drivers, such as PKNDRIVER and PKSDRIVER

In each case, the class driver is bound to a specific port driver through a system data structure. Through this binding, the class driver is able to invoke routines in the port driver in a generic fashion, and vice versa.

For example, using the following instruction, the MSCP disk class driver invokes a port-specific routine to send a message over the port:

```
JMP     @PDT$L_SNDCNTMSG(R4)     ;Jump to PORT routine
```

In this example, the binding data structure is the port descriptor table (PDT), which contains pointers to port-specific routines for well-defined functions such as sending a message over the port. A port driver is really a set of port-specific subroutines for one or more class drivers.

Both the MSCP disk class driver and the TMSCP tape class driver support devices that communicate using a Digital protocol known as systems communication architecture (SCA). Figure 24.1 shows a conceptual diagram of SCA. A brief description of SCA follows in Section 24.1.1.

SCSI disk and tape class drivers implement many of the same features as their MSCP counterparts; however, they use a different protocol to communicate with the controllers. SCSI drivers are not discussed in this book.

The terminal class and port drivers differ substantially from the other drivers and are discussed in Section 24.2.

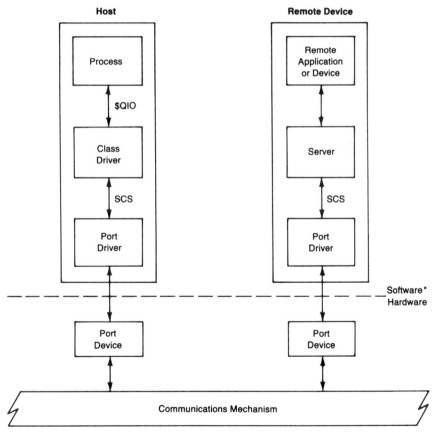

*It is possible for the remote device to implement the port driver and server in hardware.

Figure 24.1
Conceptual Diagram of Systems Communication
Architecture

24.1.1 Implementation of SCA on VMS

SCA defines a communications layer and the external interface to that layer. The VMS implementation of SCA is known as SCS. An SCA port driver implements SCS on a specific port device. VMS SCA port drivers include the following:

- PADRIVER for the computer interconnect (CI) adapters, such as the CI780, CI750, BCI750, and CIBCI
- PBDRIVER for the DEBNT, DEBNK, and TBK70 controllers
- PUDRIVER for UNIBUS port devices, such as UDA50 and TU81; Q22-bus port devices, such as RD52 and TK50; and VAXBI port devices, such as KDB50
- PEDRIVER, which implements SCA over the network interconnect (NI)
- PIDRIVER for Digital storage systems interconnect (DSSI) controllers, which are integrated with disks like the RF30 and RF71, and the KFQSA, which is the Q22-bus-to-DSSI adapter

An SCA class driver uses SCS as a communications medium for some higher level functions or protocols. A class driver implements the functional layer and performs operations on a user-visible device without regard for the SCA communications transport used.

Currently there are three protocols in the function layer that call SCS to communicate information:

- DECnet-VAX, which uses SCS for communication over the CI. The CI driver for DECnet is CNDRIVER.
- MSCP, a general protocol designed to describe all types of disk operation. It is implemented by controllers for Digital Storage Architecture (DSA) disks, such as the KDB50 and the HSC50, and by the software MSCP server supplied with VMS. The MSCP disk class driver is DUDRIVER.
- TMSCP, a general tape protocol designed to describe all types of tape operations. It is implemented by controllers for tape drives, such as the TA78, TU81, and TK50. The TMSCP class driver is TUDRIVER.

The disk class driver can communicate to an MSCP server through any SCA port driver. Similarly, the tape class driver can use any SCA port driver to communicate to a TMSCP device. The DECnet class driver uses the CI port driver exclusively.

24.1.2 I/O Processing

When a user application performs I/O through a class and port driver, a channel must be assigned to the class driver. The application requests I/O operations on that channel.

The following sequence illustrates how SCA class and port drivers communicate information from a process on a host system to a remote device. The disk class driver is used as an example.

1. The process on the host system requests an I/O operation of a class driver. The Queue I/O Request ($QIO) system service validates the I/O request and describes it in an I/O request packet (IRP). The $QIO system service passes the IRP to the class driver.

2. The class driver translates portions of the IRP to an MSCP request. Parameters of the MSCP request include the following:

   —Unit number of the device
   —Function code, such as read or write, of the operation requested
   —Starting logical block number
   —Number of bytes to transfer

   The class driver then initializes fields in a class driver request packet (CDRP). A CDRP contains information necessary for SCS operations. Figure 24.2 shows the layout of a CDRP. As a convenience to the $QIO/class driver interface, a CDRP is designed to be an extension of an IRP.

3. The class driver then invokes SCS to transmit the MSCP request to the MSCP server.

4. The SCS operations are interpreted by the port driver, which then communicates the I/O request to a remote port driver.

5. The remote port driver communicates the request to the MSCP server.

6. The server acts on the MSCP request and passes the I/O request to the remote application or device.

24.2   TERMINAL DRIVER

The VMS terminal driver is made up of one class driver and a number of device-specific port drivers. The terminal class driver consists of device-independent routines for terminal I/O processing. A terminal port driver contains routines that are specific to the actual transmission and reception of characters on a particular type of hardware. This section presents a brief overview of terminal I/O processing.

Note that the terminal class and port drivers do not communicate using the SCS protocol, nor do the terminal port devices conform to the SCA standards. The terminal class driver, TTDRIVER.EXE, contains function decision table (FDT) routines and other device-independent routines. The port drivers contain interrupt service routines and other controller-specific subroutines. The logical components of the terminal I/O subsystem are illustrated in Figure 24.3.

The class and port driver images are separate, loadable images. Support for a new terminal controller can be added in a new port driver. The following port drivers are currently supplied with VMS:

- DZDRIVER for DZ11 and DZ32 controllers
- YCDRIVER for DMF32 and DMZ32 controllers
- YFDRIVER for DHU11, DHV11, DSH32, DHQ11, and CX controllers

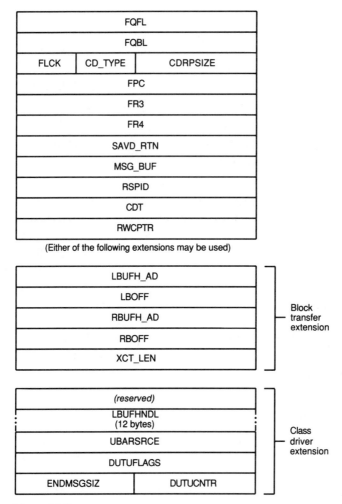

FQFL		
FQBL		
FLCK	CD_TYPE	CDRPSIZE
FPC		
FR3		
FR4		
SAVD_RTN		
MSG_BUF		
RSPID		
CDT		
RWCPTR		

(Either of the following extensions may be used)

LBUFH_AD
LBOFF
RBUFH_AD
RBOFF
XCT_LEN

Block transfer extension

(reserved)	
LBUFHNDL (12 bytes)	
UBARSRCE	
DUTUFLAGS	
ENDMSGSIZ	DUTUCNTR

Class driver extension

Figure 24.2
Class Driver Request Packet

- YIDRIVER for DMB32 and DHB32 controllers
- YEDRIVER for MicroVAX 2000 and 3100 family systems' serial lines
- Various CPU-specific console port drivers built into SYSLOA*xxx* images (see Section 24.4)

When the system is bootstrapped, the secondary bootstrap program, SYS-BOOT, reads the terminal class driver image into nonpaged pool. The executive initialization routine EXE$INIT, in module INIT, creates the necessary linkages between the terminal class driver and the console port driver. The device-specific extension of a terminal unit control block (UCB) contains pointers to the class and port vector dispatch tables. EXE$INIT locates the address of the dispatch tables for the two drivers and stores them in the console UCB.

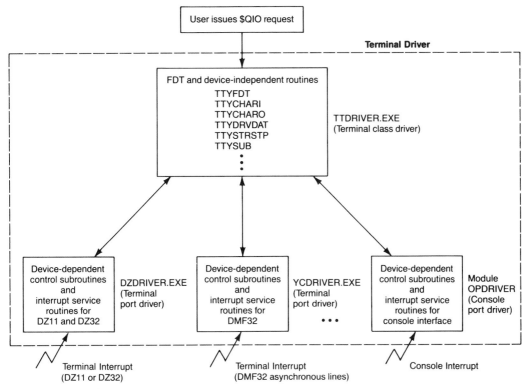

Figure 24.3
Terminal I/O System

Later in system initialization, during autoconfiguration, SYSGEN identifies the terminal controllers present and loads the appropriate port drivers. The controller and unit initialization routines of these port drivers initialize the UCB extensions.

The relations among the terminal class driver, console port driver, and the console UCB are shown in Figure 24.4, as an example of how the terminal class driver and its various port drivers are bound together.

The SYSGEN parameter TTY_CLASSNAME is initialized with the first two ASCII characters of the terminal class driver name to be loaded by SYSBOOT. This facilitates VMS debugging of new terminal class driver images. If a new terminal class driver image contains errors that prevent the system from completing its initialization sequence, TTY_CLASSNAME can be set conversationally to the first two ASCII characters of an alternative terminal class driver image during a system reboot.

VMS does not support user-written alternative terminal class drivers.

24.2.1 Full-Duplex Operation

The terminal driver implements partial full-duplex operation by default.

Full-duplex operation is based upon an alternate start I/O routine entry point to the terminal class driver. Whenever a write request is issued to a full-duplex terminal, the write FDT routine TTY$FDTWRITE, in module [TTDRVR]TTYFDT, allocates and initializes a write buffer packet to describe the write request. It then invokes EXE$ALTQUEPKT, in module SYSQIOREQ, to enter the alternate start I/O routine of the driver.

Normally, an FDT routine transfers to EXE$QIODRVPKT, in module SYSQIOREQ, to enter the driver's start I/O routine. EXE$QIODRVPKT tests whether the driver is already active for that unit. If the unit is already busy, EXE$QIODRVPKT queues the IRP to the UCB rather than entering the start I/O routine.

EXE$ALTQUEPKT differs from EXE$QIODRVPKT as follows:

- It does not test the UCB busy flag. The flag may be set as the result of a read request in progress. Full-duplex operation means that a read request can be interrupted by a write request.
- It does not clear the UCB$V_CANCEL and UCB$V_TIMOUT bits in UCB$W_STS because they may be in use by the current IRP for a read request.
- It does not copy the SVAPTE, BCNT, and BOFF fields from the IRP to the UCB because this would affect the current I/O operation if the UCB were busy.
- It enters the alternate start I/O routine in the driver rather than the regular start I/O routine.

For more information on EXE$QIODRVPKT and EXE$ALTQUEPKT, see Chapter 22.

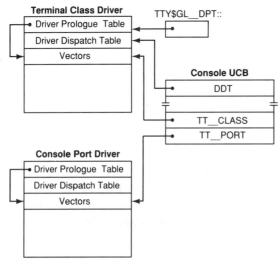

Figure 24.4
Terminal Driver Initialization

TTY$WRTSTARTIO, in module [TTDRVR]TTYSTRSTP, is the alternate start I/O routine entry point. It raises interrupt priority level (IPL) to device IPL, obtains the device spinlock to block device interrupts from the current I/O operation in case the device is busy, and processes the packet as follows:

1. If a write is currently in progress, the write buffer packet is queued.
2. If a read or a read with prompt operation is in progress but the I/O function modifier specifies write breakthrough (IRP$V_BREAKTHRU), the write is started.
3. If a read is occurring but no read data has echoed yet, the write is started.
4. Otherwise, the write buffer packet is queued to the UCB.

To complete a write I/O request for full-duplex operation, the driver's start I/O routine exits by invoking routine COM$POST, in module COM-DRVSUB. COM$POST places the IRP on the systemwide I/O postprocessing queue, requests an IPL$_IOPOST software interrupt, and returns. See Chapter 4 for details on the IPL$_POST software interrupt. Note that traditional drivers issue the REQCOM macro to complete I/O requests. REQCOM generates a transfer to IOC$REQCOM, in module IOSUBNPAG.

IOC$REQCOM is avoided for full-duplex write requests because it would attempt to initiate processing of the next IRP queued to the UCB while there is still an active IRP. However, all read requests and half-duplex writes are terminated through IOC$REQCOM, so that the next request of this type can be processed normally. For more information on IOC$REQCOM, see Chapter 22.

In full-duplex operation, the device can expect more than one interrupt at a time, one for a read request and one for a write request. Therefore, two fork program counters (PCs) must be stored. A traditional driver expects only one interrupt at a time and stores the fork PC in UCB$L_FPC. The terminal driver stores more than one fork PC by altering the value of R5, which normally points to the UCB, to point to the write buffer packet or the IRP before invoking the FORK macro.

A fork block is thereby formed in the write buffer packet or in the IRP. The fork block in the UCB is not used for read or write requests, although it is used at other times, for example, when a type-ahead buffer is allocated or when unsolicited input is being handled.

The technique of altering R5 before forking can be copied by any driver to allow more than one outstanding interrupt for a particular device. Any number of outstanding I/O requests could be handled by a driver entered at the alternate start I/O routine entry point. The driver, however, must be able to distinguish which interrupt is associated with which fork block and synchronize I/O operations. Such a driver might maintain queues for outstanding I/O requests and operate almost exclusively at device IPL, as the terminal port drivers do, blocking out device interrupts to achieve synchronization with multiple I/O request processing.

24.2.2   Channels and Terminal Controllers

The VMS terminal port drivers do not need to synchronize access to a terminal controller using the channel mechanism. Therefore, the terminal driver never requests or releases a controller channel with the REQCHAN and RELCHAN macros. The *VMS Device Support Manual* documents the use of these macros by traditional device drivers for arbitrating access to the controller. The locations normally used in the channel request block (CRB) as the controller wait queue for arbitrating fork processes are redefined and contain modem control status information.

24.2.3   Type-Ahead Buffer

TTDRIVER allocates a type-ahead buffer from nonpaged pool for each terminal device. Every character typed on the terminal is placed into this buffer whether a read request is active or not, unless the terminal is set pasthru and a read request is active. This ensures that characters typed at a terminal are not lost even if there is no application at the moment to read them.

The size of the type-ahead buffer is usually specified by the SYSGEN parameter TTY_TYPAHDSZ. This is the systemwide default and applies to all terminals that do not have the TT2$V_ALTYPEAHD characteristic. If the terminal has the characteristic TT2$V_ALTYPEAHD, then the SYSGEN parameter TTY_ALTYPAHD specifies the type-ahead buffer size.

If the terminal is in host-synchronous mode when the buffer is within eight characters of being full, the driver sends an XOFF character to the terminal to tell it to stop sending data. If the terminal has the alternative size type-ahead buffer, the SYSGEN parameter TTY_ALTALARM is the threshold for determining when to send an XOFF. When the buffer is emptied, the driver sends an XON character to the terminal to tell it to start sending data. This technique prevents loss of characters during block I/O transmission from high-speed terminals.

24.2.4   Virtual Terminal Support

A process that is associated with a virtual terminal device rather than a physical terminal may freely break and reestablish its connection to the virtual terminal. A virtual terminal device is associated with a physical terminal by the terminal driver upon process login. The connection between a physical terminal and the virtual terminal may be broken by a line disconnect caused by modem signals or broken local area terminal (LAT) server communication, or by the Digital command language (DCL) DISCONNECT command. This section explains how the terminal driver implements virtual terminal support.

When a terminal device that is not associated with any process receives unsolicited input, TTDRIVER forks to invoke the routine UNSOL, in module [TTDRVR]TTYSUB. UNSOL notifies the job controller of such an occurrence by sending a message to the job controller's permanent mailbox. The message contains the unsolicited data and the name of the terminal device. The name of the device can be that of the physical device or that of a virtual terminal, which is created by UNSOL.

If the terminal that received unsolicited data has the TT2$V_DISCON-NECT characteristic and if the device VTA0 exists on the system, UNSOL invokes CLONE_UCB, in module [TTDRVR]TTYSUB, to create a virtual device corresponding to the physical terminal.

CLONE_UCB clones the UCB for the virtual device from the UCB for VTA0. The virtual device is called VTA*n*, where *n* is the unit number. The virtual device UCB has a pointer, UCB$L_TL_PHYUCB, to the physical device's UCB. Similarly, the physical device's UCB has a pointer, UCB$L_TT_LOGUCB, to the virtual device's UCB.

UNSOL then passes the terminal device UCB to the job controller along with the unsolicited data notification.

When the job controller receives notification of unsolicited data on an unowned terminal, it creates a detached process running LOGINOUT.EXE, which begins a login session at the specified terminal. For more information on process creation by the job controller, see Chapter 25.

FDT routines in TTDRIVER operate on the terminal UCB regardless of whether it is a physical terminal or a virtual terminal. For a virtual terminal in a disconnected state, TTDRIVER queues any I/O requests to the UCB.

TTDRIVER's start I/O routine gets the physical device's UCB from offset UCB$L_TL_PHYUCB in the device UCB on which it operates. For a physical terminal, UCB$L_TL_PHYUCB points to itself (that is, the physical terminal's UCB). TTDRIVER's alternate start I/O routine operates in the same manner.

24.2.5   Local Area Terminal Server Support

Support for a LAT server such as the LAT11 is implemented in the framework of the same terminal port/class driver model. The terminal driver treats a LAT device as a physical terminal device. A LAT device has a name of the form LTA*n*, where *n* is the unit number. LTDRIVER, the driver for LAT terminal ports, interacts with TTDRIVER through the terminal driver port/class interface.

24.2.6   Remote Terminals

DECnet-VAX allows users to log in on a remote VMS system and perform operations on that remote system just as they would at the local system. The communication from the remote system to the controlling terminal is performed through a pseudo device on the remote system called a remote terminal. The driver for remote terminals is CTDRIVER.EXE.

Note that while DECnet-VAX can communicate with other Digital operating systems running DECnet, the focus of this discussion is on DECnet communication between two VAX systems running VMS Version 4 or a later version. If the remote VAX system is running a version of VMS prior to Version 4, a different protocol and a remote terminal driver named RTTDRIVER.EXE are used.

In addition to DECnet, three images are required to support remote terminals: the local system uses the image RTPAD.EXE; the remote system uses the images REMACP.EXE and CTDRIVER.EXE. REMACP.EXE is created from modules in facility [REM]. CTDRIVER.EXE and RTPAD.EXE are created from modules in facility [RTPAD].

The following list describes the sequence by which a user on a local system logs in on a remote system:

1. When a user on a local system issues the DCL command SET HOST, DCL runs the image RTPAD.EXE.
2. RTPAD uses DECnet-VAX to request a connection to a network object on the specified node. On a remote system running the VMS operating system, the object is REMACP.
3. The image REMACP, running on the remote system, creates a UCB for the remote terminal device whose name is of the form RTA*n*, where *n* is the unit number.
4. REMACP links the UCB into the driver tables by invoking CTDRIVER at its unsolicited input entry point.
5. REMACP returns information about the remote system to RTPAD.
6. RTPAD has routines for communicating with a number of different Digital operating systems, including RSTS/E, RSX-11M, TOPS-20, and VMS. Using the information returned from REMACP, RTPAD determines which operating system is communicating with the local system. On a remote system running VMS Version 4 or later, REMACP sends unsolicited data to CTDRIVER; sending this data to CTDRIVER is equivalent to pressing the RETURN key on a terminal that is not logged in.
7. CTDRIVER sends a message to the job controller's mailbox, located through the global location SYS$AR_JOBCTLMB, indicating that an unsolicited interrupt was received from the remote terminal.
8. The job controller creates a detached process running LOGINOUT on terminal RTA*n*. The user may now log in to the remote system.

RTPAD converts all I/O requests on the user's local terminal to messages it sends over the DECnet link. CTDRIVER does the same for all I/O requests on the remote terminal. The protocol for the exchange of messages between RTPAD and CTDRIVER is proprietary to Digital.

When the user logs off from the remote system, REMACP deletes the remote terminal UCB.

24.3   **PSEUDO DEVICES**

VMS supports a number of virtual devices, also called pseudo devices:

- Null device, NL:
- Network device, NET:
- Virtual terminal devices, VTA*n*:
- Remote terminal devices, RT*Cn*:
- Mailboxes, MBA*n*:

where *C* is the controller designation and *n* is the unit number.

A user can assign a channel to one of these devices and issue I/O requests just as though it were a real device. Chapter 23 discusses mailboxes. Section 24.2 discusses remote terminals and virtual terminals. The following sections highlight some features of the device drivers for other pseudo devices.

24.3.1   **Null Device Driver**

The null device driver, NLDRIVER, is assembled and linked with the executive image SYSDEVICE.EXE. It is a simple driver, consisting of two FDT routines, one to complete read requests and one to complete write requests. The read FDT routine responds to read requests by returning the status SS$_ ENDOFFILE. The write FDT routine responds to write requests by returning the status SS$_NORMAL. No data is transferred, nor are any privilege or quota checks made.

24.3.2   **Network Device Driver**

The network device (NET:) is best viewed as a mechanism for DECnet-VAX users to access network functions. An image requests the Assign I/O Channel ($ASSIGN) system service to assign a channel to the NET: device. EXE$ASSIGN, its system service procedure in module SYSASSIGN, clones a network UCB from the NET0: template device. EXE$ASSIGN gives this UCB a new unit number to produce a unique device name, such as NET100. The channel assigned points to the newly created UCB. This channel can then be used to perform access, control, and other I/O operations on the network. When the image deassigns the last channel to the network UCB, the UCB is deleted. Chapter 21 describes EXE$ASSIGN in more detail.

The following images are used for network communication:

- The network device driver, NETDRIVER
- The network ancillary control process, NETACP
- Network communication device drivers

NETDRIVER creates links to other systems, performs routing and switching functions, breaks user messages into manageable pieces for transmission, and reassembles the messages on reception. An appropriate communication device driver performs the actual I/O operations. Examples include XEDRIVER, which does network communication over the DEUNA/DELUA UNIBUS network adapters, and ETDRIVER, which does network communication over the DEBNT/DEBNI VAXBI network adapters.

NETACP performs the following tasks:

- Creates processes to accept inbound connects
- Parses network control blocks and supplies defaults when a user issues an IO$_ACCESS function code to create a logical link
- Transmits and receives routing messages to maintain a picture of the network
- Maintains the volatile network database

NETDRIVER and other communication drivers support two I/O request interfaces: $QIOs and internal IRPs.

- The $QIO interface is standard and works as it would for any VMS driver.
- Internal IRPs are built by kernel mode modules, such as other device drivers, and passed to the driver's alternate start I/O interface. This mechanism avoids the overhead of the $QIO system service procedure, which performs a number of validation checks that are considered unnecessary at this interface level.

For example, CTDRIVER, the remote terminal driver, uses the NETDRIVER internal IRP interface in communication across the network. NETDRIVER uses the internal IRP interface to pass I/O requests to lower level device drivers, such as ETDRIVER or XQDRIVER.

Figure 24.5 illustrates some network I/O functions. For more information on DECnet, see the *VMS Networking Manual* and the *VMS Network Control Program Manual*.

24.4 CONSOLE SUBSYSTEM

The console subsystem is the portion of the processor that initiates a bootstrap operation and permits microdiagnostics to execute. The details of the console subsystem are not specified by the VAX architecture, but are CPU-specific.

Some console features are common to most VAX systems. On these systems, there are at least four internal processor registers for communication with a console terminal. Table 24.1 lists these registers. On some systems, these registers also communicate with a console block storage device; on others there are additional registers.

Chapter 30 contains more details about the console subsystem of each VAX system.

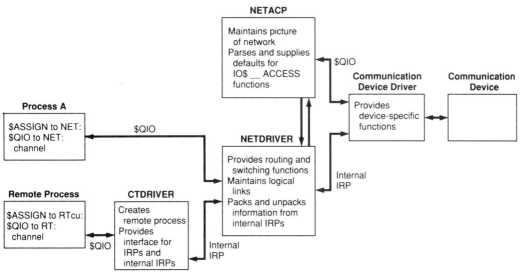

Figure 24.5
Processing Network I/O Requests

Table 24.1   VAX Console Processor Registers

Register Name	Use
PR$_RXCS	Console receive control and status register
PR$_RXDB	Console receive data buffer register
PR$_TXCS	Console transmit control and status register
PR$_TXDB	Console transmit data buffer register

24.4.1   Data Transfer Between the VAX CPU and Console Devices

Data is transferred to and from console devices through internal processor registers and, on certain systems, device registers in I/O space. No direct memory transfer is made between a VAX CPU and any console device.

The internal processor registers PR$_TXCS and PR$_RXCS are used for control and status information such as enabling interrupts and indicating that a device is ready. The other two internal processor registers, PR$_RXDB and PR$_TXDB, transfer data. For information about other CPU-specific internal processor registers that communicate with console devices, see the CPU-specific hardware documentation. The TX*xx* registers are used for transmit operations (with respect to the VAX CPU), while the RX*xx* registers are used for receive operations.

Most other device drivers treat device registers as if they were memory locations, using MOVB, MOVW, or MOVL instructions to read or write data in those registers. In the case of the console, the MTPR and MFPR instructions must be used to transmit and receive data, control, and status information.

Table 24.2   Special Uses of the Console PR$_TXDB Register

Register Contents	Meaning	Comments
F01	Software done	This value notifies the console program that a program started by means of a console command file has completed successfully.
F02	Reboot the CPU	This value is written to request a system reboot from the default boot device.
F03	Clear warm-start flag	This flag is maintained to prevent nested restart attempts.
F04	Clear cold-start flag	This flag is maintained to prevent nested bootstrap attempts.

For example, the following instructions on the VAX-11/780 transmit and receive data:

```
MTPR    data,#PR$_TXDB          ;Transmit data
MFPR    #PR$_RXDB,data          ;Receive data
```

The data is sent or received as a longword, with bits ⟨7:0⟩ containing the ASCII character and bits ⟨11:8⟩ identifying which console device (terminal or block storage device) is sending or receiving the data.

On some VAX systems, the distinction between devices is made by choice of register instead of by including a device code in a data buffer register. Note that all data is passed a character at a time, even to the block storage device.

The VAX architecture specifies that the PR$_TXDB register is also used for passing a message from code executing VAX instructions to the console subsystem. Some special uses of this register are listed in Table 24.2. Some VAX systems support additional uses.

24.4.2   Console Interrupt Dispatching

As the previous discussion of processor registers indicates, the terminal and console block storage device are treated slightly differently. On some systems, the block storage device has its own control registers and interrupt vectors. On others, the two devices are handled more as a single entity, with common routines distinguishing terminal operations from console block storage operations.

24.4.2.1   Console Terminal Interrupts.
When the system is bootstrapped, the system control block (SCB) is initialized from the SCB template in module [SYS]SCBVECTOR. The vectors at offsets $F8_{16}$ and FC_{16} dispatch to console interrupt service routines (ISRs), CON$INTDISI for console input and CON$INTDISO for console output, both in module [SYS]PERMANENT_DEVICE_DATABASE.

Both routines respond to an interrupt by saving registers R0 through R5 and transferring control to a console driver routine in the CPU-specific image SYSLOA*xxx*. Appendix G contains a list of VAX systems and their *xxx* designations. CON$INTINP is the routine invoked for console input, and CON$INTOUT is the routine invoked for console output. For many systems, these routines are in module [SYSLOA]OPDRIVER; on others, the console driver modules have names of the form OPDRV*xxx*.

Reading the data and console device identification from the PR$_RXDB register, CON$INTINP determines whether the interrupt was from the console terminal or block storage device. If the interrupt was from the console terminal, then CON$INTINP reads the character using the terminal driver's character buffering routine, whose address is stored in the console terminal UCB. CON$INTINP also echoes the character back to the console terminal by placing it in the PR$_TXDB register.

Routine CON$INTOUT transmits data to the console through the PR$_TXDB register and determines whether the resulting interrupt is from the console terminal or the console block storage device. If the interrupt was caused by the terminal, then CON$INTOUT invokes the terminal driver's character output routine, whose address is stored in the console terminal UCB.

Note that the handling of console terminal I/O is done by the normal terminal driver routines. Only the initial fielding of interrupts and the device registers that are read or written distinguish console terminal I/O from operations through the regular terminal subsystem.

Figure 24.4 shows how the console terminal UCB binds the terminal class driver and the console port driver.

24.4.2.2 **Console Block Storage Device I/O.** The device driver and associated database for the console block storage device are not loaded until an explicit CON-NECT CONSOLE command is issued to SYSGEN. At that time, the device driver and data structures appropriate to the specific system are loaded into memory and initialized.

A SYSGEN CONNECT CONSOLE command on a VAX-11/730 or VAX-11/750 causes DDDRIVER, the TU58 driver, to be loaded. Data structures for a device called CSA1 are built. On the VAX-11/730, a UCB for CSA2 is also created. In addition, two dedicated vectors in the SCB, at offsets $F0_{16}$ and $F4_{16}$, are loaded to point to interrupt dispatch code contained in the console device CRB.

DDDRIVER responds to console TU58 interrupts in exactly the same way it responds to interrupts generated by a TU58 on the UNIBUS. The only difference between the two interrupts is the device IPL at which each is dispatched. On a VAX-11/750, a console TU58 interrupt occurs at IPL 23, while UNIBUS TU58 interrupts and VAX-11/730 console TU58 interrupts occur at IPL 20.

A SYSGEN CONNECT CONSOLE command on a VAX-11/780 causes DXDRIVER, the console floppy disk driver, to be loaded and data structures for device CSA1 to be built. Because the console floppy interrupts through the same vectors used by the console terminal, no further SCB modification is required.

When a console interrupt occurs, CON$INTINP determines whether the interrupt is from the console terminal or from the block storage device. If the interrupt is from the block storage device, the console has been connected (a UCB exists for device CSA1), and the interrupt was expected, then the driver context is restored from the UCB and the driver process is resumed at the saved PC (UCB$L_FPC). Otherwise, the interrupt is considered spurious and is simply dismissed.

In response to the CONNECT CONSOLE command on a VAX 8600 or VAX 8650, SYSGEN loads the console RL02 driver, CVDRIVER, and builds data structures for CSA1. The SCB vector at offset $F0_{16}$ is initialized to point to interrupt dispatching code in the console CRB.

The VAX 8800 family is similar to the VAX 8600, except that the console block storage driver name is CWDRIVER and there are three block storage units. On the VAX 8200 and VAX 8300, the console block storage device is an RX50 and its driver is RXDRIVER.

24.4.2.3 **Double Mapping of Buffer Pages.** One notable feature of the console block storage device drivers is that they double-map a page in the user's data buffer into system address space so that data can be transferred directly to and from the user's buffer. Such a driver identifies its need for a reserved system page table entry to double-map a buffer by setting the DPT$V_SVP bit in the FLAGS argument of the DPTAB macro.

A user buffer page is not normally accessible to a driver routine running in system context, which cannot access process address space. By double mapping a buffer page as a system page, the driver can access the entire user buffer, one page at a time.

By making the user buffer accessible through system virtual addresses, a console block storage driver can implement VMS direct I/O, even though its device cannot perform direct memory access (DMA). Use of VMS direct I/O enables a console block storage driver to support virtual I/O requests, use VMS-supplied FDT routines, and use the virtual I/O postprocessing routines.

24.5 **BAD BLOCK PROCESSING ON DISKS**

24.5.1 **Static Bad Block Handling**

A non-DSA disk is typically tested to detect bad blocks before the disk is put into use. The bad blocks are allocated to a special file, [000000]BAD-

BLK.SYS, so that they cannot be allocated to user files. This is known as static bad block handling. As the disk is used, additional blocks may become bad. Dynamic bad block handling deals with those blocks.

24.5.2 Dynamic Bad Block Handling

Dynamic bad block handling is a cooperative effort among driver FDT routines, I/O postprocessing, and the Files-11 Extended QIO Processor (XQP). FDT routines for IO$_READVBLK and IO$_WRITEVBLK construct an IRP and set the IRP$V_VIRTUAL bit in IRP$W_STS. When the I/O postprocessing routine, in module IOCIOPOST, discovers a transfer error on a virtual I/O function, it routes the IRP to the XQP.

The XQP, using information in the IRP, calculates the bad block address and stores that information in the file [000000]BADLOG.SYS. This file contains a list identifying suspected bad blocks on the volume that are not currently contained in the volume's bad block file. In addition, the XQP sets a bit in the file control block to indicate the presence of a bad block. When the file is closed, an equivalent bit is set in the file's header on disk.

When such a file is deleted, the XQP creates a process running the image BADBLOCK.EXE to diagnose the file. It writes worst-case test patterns over the blocks of the file and reads them back, comparing the data to the original pattern. If a bad block is found, the image uses privileged file system functions to allocate the disk cluster containing the block to the bad block file [000000]BADBLK.SYS;1. (The smallest unit of file system allocation is the disk cluster.) In addition, the entry in the [000000]BADLOG.SYS file that describes this bad block is removed.

Note that a dynamic bad block is not discovered until it is already part of a file and is not allocated to the bad block file until that file is deleted. When a bad block is discovered while writing a file, the bad block information is recorded. A bit is set in the file control block (FCB) for the file, and an error indication is returned to the requesting process.

Dynamic bad block handling is restricted to virtual I/O functions (that is, file I/O). Processes performing logical or physical I/O functions must provide their own bad block handling.

24.5.3 Bad Block Replacement on DSA Disks

Dynamic bad block handling is performed only for non-DSA disks.

A DSA disk maintains a given set of logical block numbers (LBNs) regardless of bad blocks. It maintains a number of spare blocks that are used as replacement blocks for LBNs that are detected to be bad. If the disk controller detects that a given LBN has a nonrecoverable error, it initiates a procedure known as bad block replacement (BBR). BBR remaps the bad LBN to a good replacement block.

Some controllers, such as the UDA50 and the KDB50, require host assistance for BBR. Others, such as the HSC50, are capable of performing BBR without assistance.

A forced error flag is associated with each block on a DSA disk. When a read operation to a DSA disk block results in a nonrecoverable error, the block is reassigned to a replacement block on the disk and the forced error flag for this block is set. The forced error flag is a signal that the data in the block is questionable. When a block with this flag set is read, the status SS$_FORCEDERROR is returned by the driver to the image that requested the I/O operation. A subsequent successful write to the block clears the forced error flag.

Note that it is possible to have blocks assigned to [000000]BADBLK.SYS;1 on a DSA disk. This happens, for example, when the disk size in blocks is odd, and the disk cluster size is even. (The cluster size of a disk is the minimum unit of allocation on a disk in blocks and is specified by the DCL command INITIALIZE/CLUSTER_SIZE.) In that case, one or more of the last blocks on the disk become unusable.

24.5.4 Bad Block Replacement on SCSI Disks

The SCSI disk class driver (DKDRIVER) performs bad block replacement for SCSI disks. However, there is no forced error flag associated with SCSI disk blocks.

When a read operation to a SCSI disk results in a nonrecoverable error, the SCSI disk class driver returns the status SS$_PARITY to the requestor of the I/O operation. BBR does not occur for this block. This is because BBR at this point would result in undetected user data corruption, since there is no forced error flag associated with SCSI disk blocks.

The file system then performs the same bad block processing discussed in Section 24.5.2.

24.6 $BRKTHRU SYSTEM SERVICE

The $BRKTHRU system service sends a specified message to one or more terminals. All its eleven arguments except MSGBUF are optional.

- The number of the event flag to be set when the message has been written to the specified terminals, EFN
- The message buffer containing the text to be written, MSGBUF
- The name of the terminal or user name to which to send the text, SENDTO
- The type of terminal to which to send the message, SNDTYP
- The address of an I/O status block (IOSB) that will receive the I/O completion status of the $BRKTHRU system service, IOSB
- The carriage control to be used with the message, CARCON
- Options for the $BRKTHRU system service, FLAGS

- The class requestor identification, which identifies the application or image that is requesting the $BRKTHRU system service, REQID
- The number of seconds that must elapse before an attempted write by the $BRKTHRU system service is considered to have failed, TIMOUT
- The address of the AST procedure to be executed after the message has been sent to the specified terminals, ASTADR
- The AST parameter to be passed to the AST procedure specified by the ASTADR argument, ASTPRM

The $BRKTHRU system service procedure, EXE$BRKTHRU in module SYSBRKTHR, runs in kernel mode. Its processing consists of three major steps:

1. It allocates and initializes a breakthrough message descriptor block (BRK) for the request and stores the formatted message in the BRK, as discussed in Section 24.6.1. Figure 24.6 shows the format of a BRK.
2. It initiates a write to a given terminal, as discussed in Section 24.6.2.
3. It responds to the completion of a given write, as discussed in Section 24.6.3.

EXE$BRKTHRU sends two types of messages: the unformatted, user-specified message and the screen message. The screen message is a formatted version of the user-specified message that is sent to video terminals. It consists of the following fields, which are mainly escape sequences that envelop the message:

- Escape sequences to save the cursor's position and attributes, position it in column 1 of the correct line, and erase to the end of the line.
- One escape sequence for every line to be erased. The number of lines to be erased is specified by the low byte of the FLAGS argument.
- The text specified by the MSGBUF argument.
- An escape sequence to restore the cursor position and attributes.

24.6.1 Initial Processing

EXE$BRKTHRU begins by clearing the event flag specified by the EFN argument. Since the EFN argument is passed by value, it defaults to zero. If an IOSB is specified, EXE$BRKTHRU verifies that the caller has write access to it and clears it.

It verifies the accessibility of the message buffer specified by the MSGBUF argument.

It computes the size of the BRK needed for the request as the sum of the following items, rounded up to an integral number of longwords:

- The basic size (BRK$C_LENGTH) of the BRK
- Space for the name of the terminal to which to send the mailbox message (16 bytes)

Figure 24.6
Layout of a Breakthrough Message Descriptor Block

- The size of the unformatted message
- Space for the screen message (208 bytes plus the size of the unformatted message)
- Space for four $QIO context areas

Table 24.3 Meanings of the SNDTYP and SENDTO Arguments

SNDTYP	*SNDTO*	*Comments*
BRK$C_USERNAME	User name	Send message to a single user
BRK$C_DEVICE	Device name	Send message to a specific device
BRK$C_ALLUSERS	–	Send message to all users
BRK$C_ALLTERMS	–	Send message to all devices

It allocates space from the process allocation region in P1 space for the BRK and initializes it as follows:

1. It clears the BRK from BRK$Q_PRIVS up to BRK$T_MSGBUF.
2. It stores the size of the BRK in BRK$W_SIZE.
3. It locks the entire BRK structure in the process's working set through the Lock Pages in Working Set ($LKWSET) system service.
4. It stores the address of the $QIO context area in BRK$L_QIOCTX.
5. It stores the length of the screen message in BRK$L_SCRMSGLEN.
6. It stores the address of the requestor's PCB in BRK$L_PCB.
7. It stores the address of the IOSB in BRK$L_IOSB.
8. It stores the length of the unformatted message in BRK$W_MSGLEN and copies the unformatted message text to the buffer starting at BRK$T_MSGBUF.
9. It stores the address of the first byte after the message in BRK$L_SCRMSG. It will store the screen message at this address.
10. It validates the SNDTYP argument.
11. It sets up the BRK to reflect the SNDTYP and SENDTO arguments. Table 24.3 explains the meanings of these arguments.

   —If the SNDTYP argument is BRK$C_USERNAME or BRK$C_DEVICE, EXE$BRKTHRU invokes EXE$PROBER_DSC, in module [SYS]EXSUBROUT, to verify the accessibility of the user name or device specified by the SENDTO argument.

   —If the SNDTYP argument is BRK$C_USERNAME, it copies the SENDTO argument to BRK$T_SENDNAME and compares it with the current user name. If the two names are equal, it has completed this step. If they are not equal, it verifies that the process has OPER privilege.

   —If the SNDTYP argument is BRKC_DEVICE, EXEBRKTHRU requests the Get Device/Volume Information ($GETDVI) system service to get the physical name of the device. EXE$BRKTHRU copies the name returned to BRK$T_DEVNAM and sets BRK$V_CHKPRV in BRK$B_STS to indicate that it should check the process's privilege to send to the specified device at a later step.

   —If the SNDTYP argument is either BRK$C_ALLUSERS or BRK$C_ALLTERMS, EXE$BRKTHRU verifies that the process has OPER privilege.

12. If the TIMOUT argument was specified, EXE$BRKTHRU ensures that it is at least BRK_C_MINTIME (4 seconds). It converts the argument to clock ticks and stores the resulting quadword in BRK$Q_TIMEOUT.

13. It stores the default VAXcluster timeout value BRK_C_CLUTIMEOUT (15 seconds) in BRK$W_SECONDS.

14. EXE$BRKTHRU determines if the sender has BYPASS and SHARE privileges. This is to check if the sender has access to the target terminal. Even if the sender does not have either of these privileges, it is sufficient for the sender to have the OPER and WORLD privileges to use the $BRKTHRU system service. For a sender that does not have either or both of the BYPASS and SHARE privileges, EXE$BRKTHRU will later temporarily enable these privileges (see Section 24.6.2.4).

    In this step, EXE$BRKTHRU stores a privilege mask in BRK$Q_PRIVS. The mask has at most two bits, those corresponding to the BYPASS and SHARE privileges, set. The mask specifies which of the two privileges the process does not already have.

15. It copies the remaining $BRKTHRU arguments to the BRK.

16. It verifies that the REQID argument is less than or equal to 63.

17. It stores the success status SS$_NORMAL in BRK$W_STATUS.

18. It stores the mailbox prefix code MSG$_TRMBRDCST in BRK$W_TRM-MSG. Note that the BRK contains a mailbox message in fields BRK$W_TRMMSG through the end of the unformatted message stored at BRK$T_MSGBUF.

19. It stores the access mode from which the $BRKTHRU service was requested in BRK$B_PRVMODE.

20. It stores −1 in BRK$L_PIDCTX. This is the wildcard PID that will be passed as an argument to the Get Job/Process Information ($GETJPI) system service later.

21. It requests the Formatted ASCII Output ($FAO) system service to format the message. $FAO stores the length of the screen message in BRK$L_SCRMSGLEN and the screen message at the address in BRK$L_SCRMSG. At this point, the BRK contains the unformatted message starting at BRK$T_MSGBUF and the screen message immediately following it. BRK$L_SCRMSGLEN and BRK$L_SCRMSG constitute a descriptor for the screen message.

EXE$BRKTHRU is now ready to commence sending messages. It does so in the following steps:

1. It requests the Set AST Enable ($SETAST) system service to disable delivery of kernel mode ASTs. This is necessary to prevent image exit before the CCB$V_IMGTMP bit is set in the CCB of the channel through which EXE$BRKTHRU will write to a terminal. A channel with this bit set will be deassigned upon image exit, if it is not already deassigned, by

the image rundown procedure (see Section 24.6.2.4).

2. It attempts to initiate BRK_C_SIMULCAST (four) message writes, as discussed in Section 24.6.2.

3. If the system is a VAXcluster member and the BRK$V_CLUSTER flag was specified in the $BRKTHRU request, EXE$BRKTHRU invokes EXE$CSP_ BRKTHRU, in module [SYSLOA]CSPCLIENT, to send a clusterwide process services (CWPS) message to all other nodes in the VAXcluster system. The CLUSTER_SERVER process on each of the other nodes responds to such a message by invoking CSP$BRKTHRU, in module [SYSLOA]CSPBRKTHR. CSP$BRKTHRU requests the $BRKTHRU system service to broadcast the message on that system. Chapter 13 provides more information on this mechanism.

4. It checks if all writes have been completed. If so, it deallocates the BRK. The specific steps it takes are discussed in Section 24.6.3.3.

5. It requests the $SETAST system service to reenable kernel mode AST delivery.

The asynchronous form of the system service, $BRKTHRU, returns to its requestor. Its requestor can either wait for I/O completion or continue processing. The synchronous form of the system service, $BRKTHRUW, waits for the event flag associated with the request to be set and status to be returned. See Chapter 6 for more information concerning synchronous and asynchronous system services.

24.6.2 Writing the Breakthrough Message

EXE$BRKTHRU takes two major steps when it attempts to initiate writing a message: selecting the next terminal to which to write, and starting the actual I/O operation. If it does not find a terminal to which to write, it skips the second of these. Each time it finds an acceptable terminal UCB, it initiates a write.

The steps EXE$BRKTHRU takes to find the next terminal depend upon the SNDTYP argument.

24.6.2.1 Finding a Specific Terminal.
If the SNDTYP argument was BRKC_DEVICE, EXEBRKTHRU has already found the terminal when it requested the $GET-DVI system service to initialize the BRK. All that it does now is set BRK$V_ DONE in BRK$B_STS.

24.6.2.2 Finding All Terminals for a Specific User.
If the SNDTYP argument was BRK$C_USERNAME, EXE$BRKTHRU must find all terminals on which the given user is logged in. It accomplishes this by finding all processes belonging to that user and the terminal, if any, associated with each of those processes.

EXE$BRKTHRU requests the $GETJPI system service to perform a wild-card operation. The *VMS System Services Reference Manual* provides details on performing wildcard operations with $GETJPI. EXE$BRKTHRU stores the PID to be passed to $GETJPI in BRK$L_PIDCTX. The initial value of BRK$L_PIDCTX is −1, the value required to initiate a wildcard operation. On each request of $GETJPI, EXE$BRKTHRU requests the user name and the name of the process's login terminal. Each time $GETJPI returns, EXE$BRKTHRU verifies that the process is an interactive process and belongs to the correct user. If the process does not meet these criteria, EXE$BRKTHRU requests $GETJPI to get information about the next process.

Once EXE$BRKTHRU finds an interactive process belonging to the correct user, it invokes IOC$SEARCHDEV, in module IOSUBPAGD, to locate the UCB and the device data block (DDB) for the terminal. EXE$BRKTHRU then verifies that the UCB and the device it describes meet the following criteria:

- It is a terminal UCB.
- It is available.
- It is not a network device, a spooled device, or a detached terminal.
- It does not have the broadcast class specified by the REQID argument disabled.
- It does not have broadcasts disabled or passall enabled unless there is a broadcast mailbox associated with the UCB.

If the UCB does not meet these criteria, EXE$BRKTHRU requests the $GETJPI service to get information about the next process.

If the UCB meets these criteria, EXE$BRKTHRU verifies that the requestor has the privilege to access the device. If BRK$V_CHKPRIV in BRK$B_STS is clear, no further check is necessary. Otherwise, EXE$BRKTHRU verifies that at least one of the following conditions is met:

- The sender process's PID matches the owner PID, UCB$L_PID, of the terminal.
- The process is a descendant of the owner of the UCB. EXE$BRKTHRU follows the process control block (PCB) process owner chain until it finds a process whose PID matches the device owner. If the end of the process owner chain is reached without a match, then the next condition must be met.
- The process has OPER privilege.

If the process has the necessary privilege to access the device, EXE$BRKTHRU invokes IOC$CVT_DEVNAM, in module IOSUBNPAG, to convert the device name to the form *ddcn* and store the name starting at BRK$T_DEVNAM + 1. EXE$BRKTHRU stores the length of the name in BRK$T_DEVNAM, the unit number in BRK$W_TRMUNIT, and the contents of DDB$T_NAME in BRK$T_TRMNAME.

24.6.2.3   **Finding All Terminals and All Users.** If the SNDTYP argument was BRK$C_
ALLTERMS or BRK$C_ALLUSERS, EXE$BRKTHRU must find all terminals
on the system. It does this by invoking IOC$SCAN_IODB, in module IO-
SUBNPAG, to find each UCB in the system.

Any invoker of IOC$SCAN_IODB must pass a DDB and UCB address to it
at each invocation. From this context IOC$SCAN_IODB determines where
to start its search of the I/O database. If the addresses are zero, it starts at
the beginning of the I/O database.

EXE$BRKTHRU passes IOC$SCAN_IODB the addresses in BRK$L_UCB-
CTX and BRK$L_DDBCTX. These fields were cleared when the BRK was
initialized. EXE$BRKTHRU stores the results from invoking IOC$SCAN_
IODB in these fields. Each time IOC$SCAN_IODB finds a UCB, it returns a
success status. When IOC$SCAN_IODB reaches the end of the I/O database,
it returns a failure status.

After each successful call to IOC$SCAN_IODB, EXE$BRKTHRU makes
sure that the UCB is acceptable:

- It must be a terminal UCB.
- It must be online.
- If the terminal is not allocated, the terminal must not be set autobaud.

If the UCB is not acceptable, EXE$BRKTHRU invokes IOC$SCAN_IODB
to get another UCB. If IOC$SCAN_IODB finds one, EXE$BRKTHRU checks
that UCB. EXE$BRKTHRU continues this loop until it gets an accept-
able UCB or all UCBs have been found. When all UCBs have been found,
EXE$BRKTHRU sets BRK$V_DONE in BRK$B_STS.

24.6.2.4   **Performing the Breakthrough I/O.** EXE$BRKTHRU now has in the BRK the
information necessary to send the message to a specific terminal. It takes
the following steps to send the message:

1. If TT2$V_BRDCSTMBX in UCB$L_DEVDEPND2 is set and UCB$L_
   AMB is nonzero, EXE$BRKTHRU invokes EXE$WRTMAILBOX, in module MBDRIVER, to write the message to the associated mailbox. Note
   that the BRK contains the message already formatted for the mailbox
   write starting at BRK$W_TRMMSG.
2. It verifies that broadcasts to the terminal are not disabled and that the
   terminal is not in passall mode. There are two reasons for checking these
   bits now. If they were checked earlier, they could have changed since the
   earlier check was performed. If the terminal has an associated mailbox,
   EXE$BRKTHRU did not check these bits earlier.
3. If BRK$Q_PRIVS is nonzero, EXE$BRKTHRU requests the Set Privilege
   ($SETPRIV) system service to enable the privileges specified by BRK$Q_

PRIVS. The result of this step is to give the process BYPASS and SHARE privileges if it does not already have them.

4. It requests the $ASSIGN system service to assign a channel to the terminal UCB, with the CHAN argument specifying BRK2$W_CHAN. If BRK$Q_PRIVS is nonzero, after the $ASSIGN system service completes EXE$BRKTHRU requests $SETPRIV to disable the privileges specified by BRK$Q_PRIVS.

5. It sets CCB$V_IMGTMP in the CCB of the channel just assigned. As a result, SYS$RUNDWN will deassign this channel on image exit if the channel has not been deassigned previously. This ensures that the channel will be deassigned if the image exits before EXE$BRKTHRU completes. Image termination is discussed in Chapter 26.

6. It requests the $QIO system service to write the message to the terminal. Note that each concurrent write uses a different $QIO context area. Since there are four such areas, only four writes can be outstanding at any one time. The following arguments are specified:

   —If BRK$V_SCREEN was specified in the FLAGS argument and TT2$V_DECCRT in UCB$L_DEVDEPND2 is set, the screen message is written. The message length is the value in BRK$L_SCRMSGLEN; the message is the one at the address stored in BRK$L_SCRMSG; the carriage control is a zero.

   Otherwise, the unformatted message is written. The message length is the value in BRK$W_MSGLEN; the message is the one stored at BRK$T_MSGBUF; the carriage control is in BRK$L_CARCON.

   —The channel is the one specified by BRK2$W_CHAN.

   —The IOSB is the one at BRK2$Q_IOSB.

   —The AST procedure address is QIO_DONE, in module SYSBRKTHR. This procedure is discussed in Section 24.6.3.2.

   —The AST parameter is the address of the $QIO context area, BRK2$L_COMMON.

   —The function code is write virtual block, with the refresh, cancel CTRL/O, and breakthrough modifiers.

   —The event flag is BRK_C_EFN (31).

7. EXE$BRKTHRU increments BRK$W_OUTCNT to reflect another outstanding write request.

8. If the TIMOUT argument was specified, EXE$BRKTHRU requests the Set Timer ($SETIMR) system service, specifying QIO_TIMEOUT, in module SYSBRKTHR, as the AST procedure to be called when the timer expires and the value in BRK$Q_TIMEOUT as the time. QIO_TIMEOUT is discussed in Section 24.6.3.1.

EXE$BRKTHRU has now completed all the work necessary to initiate the writing of the breakthrough message to a given terminal.

24.6.3 **Completion Actions**

EXE$BRKTHRU performs three sets of actions related to completion:

- It responds to the expiration of a timer.
- It responds to the completion of a write to a terminal.
- It checks for completion of the $BRKTHRU system service.

It performs the first two within AST procedures. It performs the last in a subroutine.

24.6.3.1 **Timer Expiration.** If the timer expires before the I/O completion AST is executed, the executive calls the AST procedure QIO_TIMEOUT with an argument that is the address of the $QIO context area. QIO_TIMEOUT requests the $CANCEL system service to cancel the write request. This will result in QIO_DONE being invoked as part of completing the I/O request; any further processing required will be performed by QIO_DONE.

24.6.3.2 **I/O Completion AST.** The I/O completion AST procedure, QIO_DONE, is called when the I/O operation requested via the $QIO system service completes. Its one argument is the address of the $QIO context area for the completed write. QIO_DONE takes the following steps:

1. If BRK$Q_TIMEOUT is nonzero, QIO_DONE requests the Cancel Timer ($CANTIM) system service to cancel the timer requested through the $SETIMR system service. Note that the timer may have expired already.
2. It requests the $DASSGN system service to deassign the channel.
3. It decrements BRK$W_OUTCNT to reflect the completion of the write request.
4. It attempts to initiate another write operation by taking the steps described in Section 24.6.2.
5. It then checks for completion of the $BRKTHRU request by taking the steps described in Section 24.6.3.3.

24.6.3.3 **Completion Checks.** CHECK_COMPLETE is invoked to check for completion of the $BRKTHRU request:

1. It checks BRK$W_OUTCNT. If it is nonzero, there is at least one write request outstanding, and CHECK_COMPLETE exits.
2. It stores the final status in the IOSB if the requestor specified an IOSB.
3. If the $BRKTHRU request specified a completion AST, CHECK_COMPLETE requests the Declare AST ($DCLAST) system service, specifying the AST procedure and parameter recorded in the BRK.
4. It requests the Set Event Flag ($SETEF) system service to set the specified event flag.
5. It requests the Unlock Pages from Working Set ($ULWSET) system service to unlock the BRK from the working set.

6. Finally, it deallocates the BRK to the P1 allocation region.

24.7 BROADCAST SYSTEM SERVICE

The Broadcast ($BRDCST) system service sends messages to one or more terminals, even if an I/O operation is currently in progress on the terminal. The $BRDCST system service has been superseded by the $BRKTHRUW system service, which should be used for future software development. $BRDCST has four arguments:

- The message buffer containing the text to be written, MSGBUF
- The device to which to send the message, DEVNAM
- The carriage control to be used with the message, CARCON
- Options for the $BRDCST system service, FLAGS

The $BRDCST system service routine, EXE$BRDCST in module SYS-BRKTHR, runs in the access mode of the caller. EXE$BRDCST requests the $BRKTHRUW system service to perform the breakthrough operation equivalent to the requested broadcast operation. EXE$BRDCST specifies the following arguments to the $BRKTHRUW system service:

- The EFN argument is BRK_C_BRDCSTEFN, event flag 31.
- The $BRKTHRUW MSGBUF argument is the same as the $BRDCST MSGBUF argument.
- The SNDTYP argument is as follows:

  —If the DEVNAM argument is zero, the SNDTYP argument is BRK$C_ALL-TERMS.
  —If the DEVNAM argument is nonzero, it is taken as the address of a descriptor. If the descriptor specifies a length of zero, the SNDTYP argument is BRK$C_ALLUSERS. If the descriptor specifies a nonzero length, the SNDTYP argument is BRK$C_DEVICE.

- If the SNDTYP argument is BRK$C_DEVICE, the SENDTO argument is the same as the DEVNAM argument to the $BRDCST system service. Otherwise, the SENDTO argument is irrelevant.
- The $BRKTHRUW FLAGS argument is the same as the $BRDCST FLAGS argument, if the latter argument is specified. Otherwise, the $BRKTHRUW FLAGS argument is zero. Note that the $BRDCST FLAGS argument has no bits equivalent to the BRK$V_ERASE_LINES and BRK$V_CLUSTER bits of the $BRKTHRUW FLAGS argument.
- The $BRKTHRUW CARCON argument is the same as the $BRDCST CARCON argument, if the latter argument is specified. Otherwise, the $BRKTHRUW CARCON argument is an ASCII blank.
- The TIMOUT argument is 10, which specifies a timeout of 10 seconds.
- The IOSB argument specifies an IOSB allocated on the stack by EXE$BRD-CST.

Upon completion of the $BRKTHRUW system service, EXE$BRDCST examines the return status. If the status is an error, EXE$BRDCST returns that status to the caller. If the return status of the $BRKTHRUW system service is a success status, EXE$BRDCST returns the status in the IOSB to the caller. Note that if either return status is SS$_NOOPER, EXE$BRDCST replaces it with SS$_NOPRIV. This is done to maintain compatibility with previous implementations of $BRDCST.

24.8   **INFORMATIONAL SERVICES**

Images frequently require information about particular devices on the system. VMS provides several system services to obtain specific information about a particular device.

Device-independent information refers to information that is present for each device on the system, such as the device unit number, UCB$W_UNIT, device characteristics, UCB$L_DEVCHAR, and the device type, UCB$B_DEVTYPE. It is obtained by reading fields in the UCB that have the same interpretation for all devices on the system.

Device-dependent information refers to information that is present for each device on the system but whose interpretation is device-dependent, such as the device-dependent information fields UCB$L_DEVDEPEND and UCB$L_DEVDEPND2, or information that is present only for certain devices, such as the logical UCB address in a physical terminal UCB, UCB$L_TT_LOGUCB.

There are two sets of information, the primary and secondary device characteristics, for each device. These two sets are identical unless one of the following conditions holds:

- If the device has an associated mailbox, the primary characteristics are those of the assigned device and the secondary characteristics are those of the associated mailbox.
- If the device is spooled, the primary characteristics are those of the intermediate device and the secondary characteristics are those of the spooled device.
- If the device represents a logical link on the network, the secondary characteristics contain information about the link.

The $GETDVI system service, in module SYSGETDVI, obtains device-independent information about a device. See the *VMS System Services Reference Manual* for a listing of the fields that can be returned. $GETDVI uses an item list argument mechanism, which allows it to be extended in an upwardly compatible fashion.

The $DEVICE_SCAN system service, in module SYSGETDVI, returns the names of all devices that match a set of search criteria, such as those of a certain device class or type. Both $DEVICE_SCAN and $GETDVI are described in Chapter 36.

Support still exists for the Get I/O Channel Information ($GETCHN) and Get I/O Device Information ($GETDEV) system services, which are both in module SYSGETDVI. The $GETDVI system service supersedes the $GETCHN and $GETDEV system services and should be used in future software development.

The $QIO system service can be used to obtain device information. Two function codes, IO$_SENSEMODE and IO$_SENSECHAR, can be used to request the device driver to return device-dependent information to the caller. The specific information that can be returned depends on the device. See the *VMS I/O User's Reference Volume* manual for details about what information is returned by specific VMS device drivers.

PART VII / Life of a Process

25 Process Creation

All things in the world come from being.
And being comes from non-being.

Lao-tzu, *Tao Tê Ching*

The creation of a new process takes place in several phases:

1. Creation begins in the context of an existing process that requests the Create Process ($CREPRC) system service. The $CREPRC system service performs the following steps:

   a. It makes privilege and quota checks.

   b. It allocates and initializes the process control block (PCB); the job information block (JIB), unless it is creating a subprocess; and the process quota block (PQB), with explicit $CREPRC arguments and implicit parameters taken from the context of the creator.

   c. It places the new process into the scheduler database.

2. The initial scheduling state of the new process is computable outswapped (COMO). Thus, execution of the new process is suppressed until the swapper process moves the new process into the balance set. The following steps are performed in the context of the swapper process:

   a. The swapper moves the template for the new process context into the balance set from the shell, a module in the WORKING_SET_MANAGEMENT loadable executive image.

   b. It builds the process header (PHD) according to the values of SYSGEN parameters for this configuration.

   c. It requests that the new process be scheduled for execution.

3. The final steps of process initialization take place in the context of the new process in the routine EXE$PROCSTRT. EXE$PROCSTRT performs the following steps:

   a. It copies the arguments from the PQB to the PHD and various locations in P1 space.

   b. It requests the image activator to activate the image.

   c. It calls the image at its entry point.

Figure 25.1 shows these phases of process creation and the context within which each phase occurs.

25.1 CREATE PROCESS SYSTEM SERVICE

The $CREPRC system service establishes the parameters of the new process. Some of these parameters are passed to the system service by the caller. The

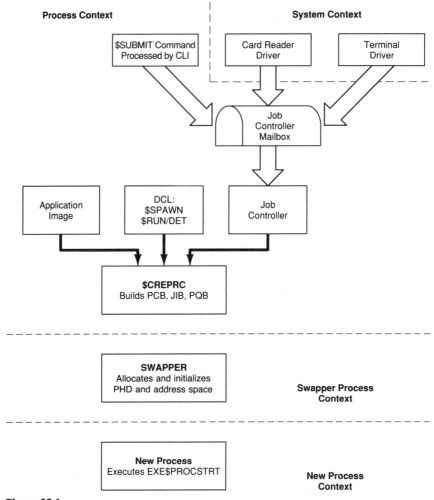

Figure 25.1
Process Creation

system service copies others from the context of the caller: the caller's PCB, PHD, JIB, and control region (see Figure 25.2).

The $CREPRC system service can copy information to the PCB or the JIB of the new process but cannot access its PHD or control region because neither exists at this stage of process creation. It stores the parameters to be copied to either the PHD or the control region in the PQB, a temporary data structure, until the new process comes into existence and has a virtual address space and PHD. Table 25.1 lists the contents of the PQB.

25.1.1 Control Flow of the Create Process System Service

The $CREPRC system service procedure, EXE$CREPRC in module SYSCRE-PRC, runs in kernel mode. It performs the following steps:

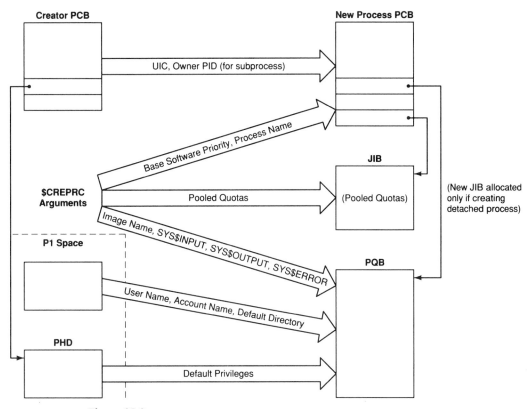

Figure 25.2
Sample Movement of Parameters in Process Creation

1. EXE$CREPRC verifies that the address specified in the PIDADR argument is accessible to the mode from which EXE$CREPRC was requested. If not, it returns the error status SS$_ACCVIO.

2. EXE$CREPRC creates either a top-level process, detached from its creator, or a subprocess, attached to its creator's job tree. EXE$CREPRC's actions depend on the UIC argument and the PRC$V_DETACH bit in the STSFLG argument.

   —If the requestor specified a nonzero UIC argument, EXE$CREPRC creates a top-level process. The process is further classified as interactive, network, batch, or detached based on EXE$CREPRC's STSFLG argument.
   —If the UIC argument is zero, the default, and the requestor did not set the PRC$V_DETACH bit in the STSFLG argument, EXE$CREPRC creates a subprocess.
   —If the UIC argument is zero, the default, but the requestor set the PRC$V_DETACH bit in the STSFLG argument, EXE$CREPRC creates a top-level, detached process with the same user identification code (UIC) as that of the requestor.

711

Table 25.1   Contents of the Process Quota Block

Item	Size (bytes)	Item	Size (bytes)
Privilege mask	8	Reserved	1
Size of PQB	2	Authorization file flags	4
Type code	1	Process creation flags	4
Status	1	Minimum authorized security class	20
AST limit	4	Maximum authorized security class	20
Buffered I/O limit	4	SYS$INPUT attributes	4
Buffered I/O byte limit [1]	4	SYS$OUTPUT attributes	4
CPU time limit	4	SYS$ERROR attributes	4
Direct I/O limit	4	SYS$DISK attributes	4
Open file limit [1]	4	CLI image name	32
Paging file quota [1]	4	CLI command table name	256
Subprocess limit [1]	4	Spawn CLI image name	32
Timer queue entry limit [1]	4	Spawn CLI command table name	256
Working set quota	4	Equivalence name for SYS$INPUT	256
Working set default	4	Equivalence name for SYS$OUTPUT	256
Lock limit	4	Equivalence name for SYS$ERROR	256
Working set extent	4	Equivalence name for SYS$DISK	256
Logical name table quota	4	Default directory string	256
Flags	2	Image name	256
Default message flags	1		

[1] This quota or limit is now pooled in the JIB; hence, the PQB is no longer used to transfer this value.

EXE$CREPRC tests whether the specified UIC is zero or the same as that of the requestor. If it is, no privilege is necessary to create a top-level process. Otherwise, the requestor needs either the DETACH or CMKRNL privilege. If the requestor requested creation of a top-level process without the necessary privilege, EXE$CREPRC returns the error status SS$_NOPRIV.

3. EXE$CREPRC allocates a PCB from nonpaged pool, raising interrupt priority level (IPL) to 2. It next allocates a PQB from either the PQB lookaside list or paged pool, and completely zeros the PCB and PQB, except for their headers.

Chapter 19 describes nonpaged pool, paged pool, and the PQB lookaside list.

EXE$CREPRC remains at IPL 2 or above from this point to prevent process deletion and the loss of allocated but unrecorded memory. If an error occurs, EXE$CREPRC deallocates the PCB, PQB, and JIB (if necessary) before returning the error status to the requestor.

4. JIB initialization for top-level processes differs from that for subprocesses:

—If EXE$CREPRC is creating a top-level process, it allocates a JIB from nonpaged pool. It initializes the JIB's jobwide list of mounted volumes as an empty list, then copies the account and user name fields from the creating process's JIB and zero-fills the JIB to its end.

—If EXE$CREPRC is creating a subprocess, no JIB allocation is necessary; the subprocess shares the JIB of its creator. However, processes sharing a JIB must access its fields in an interlocked manner, since the processes might execute concurrently on different members of a symmetric multiprocessing (SMP) system. Thus, EXE$CREPRC increments JIB$W_PRCCNT, the count of subprocesses in the job tree, with **ADAWI**, an interlocked instruction.

Before EXE$CREPRC accesses JIB$L_PGFLCNT, the process page file quota, it acquires the MMG spinlock, raising IPL to IPL$_MMG. It then charges JIB$L_PGFLCNT for the number of process page file pages contributed by the shell and releases the MMG spinlock, lowering IPL to 2.

If the job has insufficient page file quota, EXE$CREPRC deallocates the newly acquired data structures and returns the error status SS$_EXQUOTA to its requestor. Otherwise, it compares JIB$W_PRCCNT to JIB$W_PRCLIM, the maximum number of processes in the job tree. If JIB$W_PRCCNT exceeds JIB$W_PRCLIM, the job tree is at its maximum size. EXE$CREPRC deallocates the PCB and PQB and returns the error status SS$_EXQUOTA to its requestor. Figure 25.3 shows the relation between the JIB and the PCBs of several processes in the same job.

Note that the process count field within a PCB (PCB$W_PRCCNT) tracks the number of subprocesses created by one process. JIB$W_PRCCNT counts the total number of subprocesses in the entire job.

5. For both top-level processes and subprocesses, EXE$CREPRC stores the address of the JIB in PCB$L_JIB.

6. EXE$CREPRC initializes several fields in the PCB to nonzero values:

   a. It sets up the asynchronous system trap (AST) queue as an empty listhead and enables AST delivery to all access modes.

   b. It sets up the lock queue in the PCB as an empty listhead.

   c. It initializes the PCB current and permanent CPU capability requirement fields to the system default value found in SCH$GL_DEFAULT_PROCESS_CAP.

   d. It copies the default affinity skip value from SCH$GL_AFFINITY_SKIP to the PCB.

   e. If the system default capability mask enables implicit affinity, it copies the CPU ID of the processor for which the current process has affinity to the new process's PCB$L_AFFINITY field. Chapter 12 describes process affinity.

   f. It copies the default file protection from the system default file protection or the creating process's PCB.

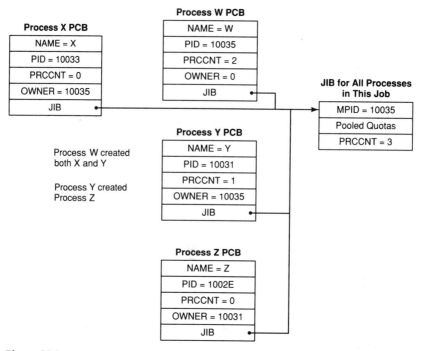

Figure 25.3
Relation Between the JIB and the PCBs of Several
Processes in the Same Job

g. It copies the entire access rights block (ARB) from the creating process's ARB. If the creator has an extended rights list, EXE$CREPRC allocates a nonpaged pool buffer into which it copies the extended rights list.

The ARB is currently located within the PCB. However, VMS routines that check a process's access rights use the ARB pointer, PCB$L_ARB, to locate the privilege mask and UIC. All programs should follow this convention, since the ARB may become an independent structure in the future. Any programs that do not use the ARB pointer will require modification when this occurs.

h. EXE$CREPRC copies the unit number of the termination mailbox from the MBXUNIT argument. The termination mailbox number is not used until the process is eventually deleted. At that time, the process deletion routine writes a termination message to the specified mailbox if the unit number is nonzero.

i. It initializes the process-private page count, PCB$W_PPGCNT, to the number of pages required for the new process header and the shell pages.

j. EXE$CREPRC copies the process name, if one exists, into the PCB.

7. It determines the process privileges of the new process and stores them in

the PQB. Table 26.2 summarizes the various privilege masks associated with a process.

If no privilege argument is present, EXE$CREPRC uses the current privileges of the creator.

If a privilege argument is present and the creator has SETPRV privilege, EXE$CREPRC uses the privilege argument with no modification.

If a privilege argument is present and the creator does not have SETPRV privilege, EXE$CREPRC stores the logical AND of the privileges of the creator and the privileges specified in the argument. In short, a created process cannot receive privileges that its creator does not have.

8. EXE$CREPRC determines the software priority of the new process and stores it in the PCB base priority and current priority fields. Because the BASPRI argument is passed by value, it is always present. The system service macro $CREPRC_S, used from VAX MACRO, specifies a default value of 2 for BASPRI. The default value for other languages is determined by the treatment of missing arguments by the language processor.

   If the creator has ALTPRI privilege, EXE$CREPRC uses the priority specified in the argument list. If the creator does not have ALTPRI privilege, EXE$CREPRC uses the smaller of the creator's base priority and the priority in the argument list.

9. EXE$CREPRC determines the UIC of the new process and stores it in the PCB. The UIC argument is used if the requestor specified that argument. Otherwise, EXE$CREPRC uses the UIC of the creator. Therefore, a subprocess always has the same UIC as its creator—if the UIC argument had been specified, EXE$CREPRC would have created a top-level process.

10. If the new process is a subprocess, EXE$CREPRC copies the internal process ID (IPID) of the creator to the PCB$L_OWNER field of the new PCB and the extended process ID (EPID) of the creator to the field PCB$L_EOWNER. Section 25.1.3.1 describes internal and extended process IDs.

    If the process is a top-level process, the PCB$L_OWNER and PCB$L_EOWNER fields remain zero.

11. EXE$CREPRC tests that the process name is unique within the UIC group. It examines the process name fields of all PCBs in the system with the same group number. If the process name is not unique, EXE$CREPRC returns the error status SS$_DUPLNAM to its requestor. Process name is always qualified by UIC group number.

12. EXE$CREPRC copies several text strings to the PQB, taking the image name and the equivalence names for SYS$INPUT, SYS$OUTPUT, and SYS$ERROR from the $CREPRC argument list. For most processes, the image is LOGINOUT.

13. It translates the logical name SYS$DISK in the table LNM$FILE_DEV and stores its equivalence name in the PQB. For compatibility with previous releases, SYS$DISK is translated once. Thus, its equivalence name must be either a shareable logical name or a physical device name.

14. EXE$CREPRC copies the minimum and maximum authorized security clearance records from the creator's PHD to the new process's PQB.

15. It copies the following information from the P1 space of the creator process:

   —Default directory string
   —Command language interpreter (CLI) name
   —Command table name
   —CLI name for use by spawned subprocesses
   —Command table name for use by spawned subprocesses

16. It copies the default message flags and flags from the authorization file record from the control region of the creator to the PQB.

17. It extracts the status flags for the new process from the $CREPRC argument list and sets the corresponding flags in the PCB and PQB. Table 25.2 describes the status flags. All PCB flags listed in the table are found in the field PCB$L_STS. The IMGDMP flag is eventually stored in the field PHD$W_FLAGS, but since the PHD does not exist yet, the PQB temporarily maintains the flag. EXE$CREPRC always propagates the flag PCB$V_SECAUDIT from the creator process. It checks the creator process's privilege mask for any flags requiring privilege.

18. If the process being created is not a subprocess, and it is not a batch, network, or interactive process, then it must be a true detached process. In that case, EXE$CREPRC copies JIB$W_MAXJOBS and JIB$W_MAX-DETACH from the JIB of the creator to that of the new process. If either count is nonzero, indicating a limit, EXE$CREPRC must check whether creation of this process would exceed one of those limits.

   It acquires the SCHED spinlock, raising IPL to IPL$_SCHED. Holding the spinlock, it scans all existing processes except for the swapper process. It looks for a process that is not a network process or a subprocess and that has the same user name as the process being created. If it finds one, it increments the total count of jobs with that user name. If the process is neither interactive nor batch, it also increments the total count of detached processes with that user name.

   After scanning all the processes, EXE$CREPRC releases the SCHED spinlock and restores IPL to 2. If either job limit has been exceeded, EXE$CREPRC returns the error status SS$_EXPRCLM to its requestor.

19. It determines the quotas for the new process and stores them in the PQB. Section 25.1.2 describes the steps taken to determine the quota list for the new process.

20. EXE$CREPRC processes the ITMLST argument, if one was supplied. This argument is reserved for VMS software, which uses it to pass logical name attributes for SYS$INPUT, SYS$OUTPUT, and SYS$ERROR to EXE$CREPRC. It in turn copies the attributes into the PQB.

21. EXE$CREPRC stores the address of the PQB in the field PCB$L_PQB.

Table 25.2   Status Flags Specified at Process Creation

Flag Argument	Meaning if Set	Destination
PRC$V_SSRWAIT	Disable system service resource wait mode	PCB$V_SSRWAIT
PRC$V_SSFEXCU	Enable system service exceptions for user mode	PCB$V_SSFEXCU
PRC$V_PSWAPM [1]	Inhibit process swapping	PCB$V_PSWAPM
PRC$V_NOACNT [2]	Suppress accounting	PCB$V_NOACNT
PRC$V_BATCH [3]	Batch (noninteractive) process	PCB$V_BATCH
PRC$V_HIBER	Hibernate process before calling image	PCB$V_HIBER
PRC$V_IMGDMP	Enable image dump	PHD$V_IMGDMP
PRC$V_NOUAF [4]	Log in without reading the authorization file	PCB$V_LOGIN
PRC$V_NETWRK	Process is a network connect object	PCB$V_NETWRK
PRC$V_DISAWS	Disable system initiated working set adjustment	PCB$V_DISAWS
PRC$V_DETACH [5]	Process is detached	PCB$V_DETACH
PRC$V_INTER	Process is interactive	PCB$V_INTER
PRC$V_NOPASSWORD	Disable prompt for user name and password	PCB$V_NOPASSWORD

[1] Requires PSWAPM privilege
[2] Requires NOACNT privilege
[3] Requires DETACH privilege
[4] Formerly PRC$V_LOGIN
[5] Flag ignored unless same UIC

PCB$L_PQB is the same longword as the event flag wait mask field, PCB$L_EFWM. The field PCB$L_PQB is available until the process executes in its own context and is placed into a resource or event flag wait state. At that time, its contents are overwritten by an event flag wait mask. Therefore, the initial instructions of EXE$PROCSTRT, the first code to run in the new process's context, are nonpageable and immediately copy the PQB address elsewhere. Section 25.3 describes EXE$PROCSTRT.

Earlier versions of VMS allocated space in the swap file for the process at this point. For VMS Version 5, swap file space allocation does not occur unless the process must actually be swapped from memory. Chapter 18 describes the circumstances under which this could occur.

22. EXE$CREPRC acquires the MMG and SCHED spinlocks, raising IPL to IPL$_MMG. It searches the PCB vector for an empty slot. If none is available, it returns the error status SS$_NOSLOT to its requestor after

releasing the SCHED and MMG spinlocks. The PCB vector is pictured in Figure 25.4. Section 25.1.3.1 describes the search process.

Otherwise, having found an available PCB vector slot, EXE$CREPRC tests the maximum process count. If the maximum process count has been exceeded (SCH$GW_PROCCNT's contents are larger than those of SCH$GW_PROCLIM), EXE$CREPRC returns the error status SS$_NOSLOT to its requestor after releasing the SCHED and MMG spinlocks. EXE$CREPRC increments SCH$GW_PROCCNT regardless of process type.

If the new process is an interactive one, EXE$CREPRC increments SYS$GW_IJOBCNT, the current interactive job count for the system. Since all interactive jobs begin by executing the LOGINOUT image, the comparison of SYS$GW_IJOBCNT to the SYSGEN parameter IJOBLIM is handled by LOGINOUT.

If the new process is a batch job, EXE$CREPRC increments SYS$GW_BJOBCNT, the current batch job count for the system.

23. EXE$CREPRC stores the new PCB address in the available PCB vector slot.

24. It fabricates internal and extended process IDs (see Section 25.1.3.1) and stores them in the PCB of the new process.

25. If the new process is not a subprocess, EXE$CREPRC stores its IPID in the master process ID field of the JIB (JIB$L_MPID).

26. EXE$CREPRC invokes the routine SCH$CHSE, in module RSE, to insert the process into the COMO scheduling queue. It specifies the priority increment class PRI$_TICOM to boost the base priority by 6.

27. If it is creating a subprocess, EXE$CREPRC increments the count of subprocesses owned by the creator (PCB$W_PRCCNT in the creator's PCB). In addition, if a CPU time limit is in effect for the creator, EXE$CREPRC deducts the amount of CPU time that is passed to the new process from the creator.

28. Finally, it returns the EPID of the new process to the requestor (if requested), releases the SCHED and MMG spinlocks, lowers IPL to 0, and returns control to its requestor.

25.1.2 Establishing Quotas for the New Process

The $CREPRC system service uses two tables in the executive to set up quotas for the new process: a minimum quota table and a default quota table. Each quota or limit in the system has an entry in both tables. The contents of the minimum table are determined by the SYSGEN parameters whose names are of the form PQL_M*quota-name*; the contents of the default table are of the form PQL_D*quota-name*. Following is a list of the steps EXE$CREPRC takes to determine the value for each quota or limit that is passed to the new process:

1. It places the default value for each quota into the PQB as initial value.
2. It replaces the default values in the PQB by any quotas specified in the argument list to the $CREPRC system service.
3. It forces each quota to at least its minimum value.
4. It checks to ensure that the creator possesses sufficient quota to cover the quota that it is giving to the new process. It performs this check as follows:

   a. If the creator has either DETACH or CMKRNL privilege and is creating a top-level process, quotas are unrestricted and no check is performed.

   b. If the creator has neither privilege and is creating a top-level process with the same UIC, then the new process quotas must be less than or equal to those of the creator.

   c. If a subprocess is being created and the quota is neither pooled nor deductible (the only deductible quota currently implemented is CPU time limit), then the subprocess quota must be smaller than or equal to the creator's quota.

   d. Pooled quotas require no special action when a subprocess is being created because they already reside in the JIB, a structure that is shared by all processes in the job (see Figure 25.3).

   e. If a subprocess is being created and the quota in question is the CPU time limit quota, EXE$CREPRC's actions depend on how much quota the creator process possesses. If the creator has an infinite CPU time limit, then no check is performed. If the creator has a finite CPU time limit and specifies an infinite CPU time limit for the subprocess, half of the creator's CPU time limit is passed to the subprocess. If the creator has a finite CPU time limit and specifies a finite CPU time limit for the subprocess, the amount passed to the subprocess must be less than the creator's original quota, or the creation is aborted.

5. EXE$CREPRC places pooled quotas directly into the newly allocated JIB. It places other quotas into the PCB or stores them temporarily in the PQB.

Table 25.3 lists the quotas that are passed to a new process when it is created, whether each quota is deductible or pooled, and where the limit is stored in the context of the new process. Further discussion of quotas can be found in the *Guide to Setting Up a VMS System* and in the *VMS System Services Reference Manual*.

With the exception of CPU time limit and subprocess count, all active counts start at their process limit values and decrement to zero. An active count of zero indicates no quota remaining. An active count equal to the corresponding process limit indicates no outstanding requests.

Table 25.3   Storage Areas for Process Quotas

Quota/Limit Name	Location of Active Count	Location of Process Limit	Count/Limit Stored by[1]
	NONDEDUCTIBLE QUOTAS		
AST limit	PCB$W_ASTCNT	PHD$W_ASTLM	C/P
Buffered I/O limit	PCB$W_BIOCNT	PCB$W_BIOLM	C/C
Direct I/O limit	PCB$W_DIOCNT	PCB$W_DIOLM	C/C
Working set quota	n/a[2]	PHD$L_WSQUOTA	/P
Working set default	n/a[2]	PHD$L_DFWSCNT	/P
Working set extent	n/a[2]	PHD$L_WSEXTENT	/P
	DEDUCTIBLE QUOTA		
CPU time limit	PHD$L_CPUTIM	PHD$L_CPULIM	P/P[3]
	POOLED QUOTAS (SHARED BY ALL PROCESSES IN THE SAME JOB)		
Buffered I/O byte limit	JIB$L_BYTCNT	JIB$L_BYTLM	[4]
Open file limit	JIB$W_FILCNT	JIB$W_FILLM	[4]
Page file page limit	JIB$L_PGFLCNT	JIB$L_PGFLQUOTA	[4]
Subprocess limit	JIB$W_PRCCNT	JIB$W_PRCLIM	[4]
Timer queue entry limit	JIB$W_TQCNT	JIB$W_TQLM	[4]
Enqueue limit	JIB$W_ENQCNT	JIB$W_ENQLM	[4]

[1] The slash (/) separates the count from the limit: C/ indicates that the count value is stored by EXE$CREPRC; /C indicates that the limit value is stored by EXE$CREPRC; P/ indicates that the count value is stored by EXE$PROCSTRT; /P indicates that the limit value is stored by EXE$PROCSTRT.

[2] Working set list quotas are handled differently from other quotas (see Chapter 17).

[3] CPUTIM starts at zero and increments for each clock tick that the process is current. If limit checking is in effect (CPULIM nonzero), then CPUTIM may not exceed CPULIM.

[4] The contents of the JIB are loaded by EXE$CREPRC when a detached process is created. Subprocess creation uses an existing JIB.

25.1.3   Process Identification

VMS provides two forms of process identifier (PID) for each process. The internal, traditional form—the IPID—identifies a process within the context of a single VMS system. The EPID is a compressed version of the IPID that additionally identifies the VAXcluster node of a process. In this book, the unqualified term *process ID* or *PID* refers to the internal, traditional form.

VMS routines use the IPID or EPID to locate a process's PCB. All process PCB addresses are stored in the PCB vector. The IPID or EPID provides an index into the PCB vector and a parallel array called the sequence vector. The number of entries in each array (and therefore the maximum number of processes allowed at a given time on a VMS system) is determined by the SYSGEN parameter MAXPROCESSCNT.

The VMS executive generally identifies a process internally by its IPID, although code such as the lock management system services and the cluster-wide process control system service may use both forms of PID. System services accept and return EPIDs, and system utilities display EPIDs, but the format of the EPID is subject to change in future versions of VMS. No program should attempt to partition the EPID fields. Instead, VMS supplies the following routines (in the module SYSPCNTRL) for transformation or manipulation of an EPID when necessary:

- EXE$EPID_TO_PCB—Convert an EPID to address of corresponding PCB
- EXE$EPID_TO_IPID—Convert an EPID to IPID
- EXE$IPID_TO_EPID—Convert an IPID to EPID
- EXE$IPID_TO_PCB—Convert an IPID to address of corresponding PCB

25.1.3.1   **Fabricating PIDs.** EXE$CREPRC fabricates a process's IPID and EPID after obtaining a free PCB vector slot (and implicitly the associated sequence vector slot).

The PCB vector is allocated from nonpaged pool during system initialization, and its address is stored in SCH$GL_PCBVEC. It contains a longword slot for each possible process in the system. The first entry in the vector contains the address of the null PCB. The second entry contains the address of the swapper process PCB. All other entries in the vector initially contain the address of the null PCB.

Note that in earlier versions of VMS, the null PCB was associated with an actual null process. In VMS Version 5, a null process became unnecessary. The null PCB remains, however, to serve as an indicator of an available slot in the PCB vector.

When EXE$CREPRC creates a process, it searches the PCB vector for an empty slot into which to insert the address of the new PCB it has built. It considers an entry that contains the address of the null PCB to be an empty slot. EXE$CREPRC excludes the first two PCBs (the null PCB and the swapper process) from its scan of the PCB vector. It begins the scan with the slot most recently allocated and wraps to the slot after the swapper process if it exceeds the maximum entry. The index of the maximum entry is stored in SCH$GL_MAXPIX.

Figure 25.4 provides an example of the contents of the PCB vector.

As processes are created and deleted on the system over time, the slots in the PCB vector are reused. The sequence vector tracks the reuse of these PCB vector slots.

All entries in the sequence vector are cleared during system initialization. Each time EXE$CREPRC uses a PCB vector slot, it increments the value in the corresponding sequence vector slot. This sequence number becomes the high-order word of the IPID. Thus, executive routines use the sequence number as a consistency check to determine that a number alleged to be an IPID corresponds to a real process in the system.

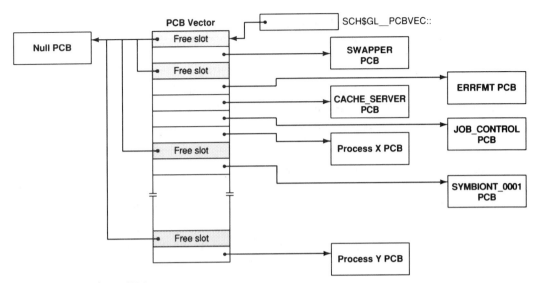

Figure 25.4
Sample PCB Vector

When a process is deleted, the executive stores the address of the null PCB in its PCB vector slot to indicate that the slot is available. The sequence number, however, is not incremented until the slot is reassigned by EXE$CREPRC.

The sequence number increments to 32,767, then cycles back to 0. Therefore, when IPIDs are interpreted as signed integers, they are never negative. This allows the I/O subsystem to treat a negative value in the IRP$L_PID field of an I/O request packet (IRP) in a special manner. The I/O postprocessing interrupt service routine interprets a negative IRP$L_PID value as the (system virtual) address of an internal I/O completion routine.

A PCB contains four fields related to process identification. EXE$CREPRC loads them all, because it has access to the PCB of the creator process and it fabricates the IPID and EPID of the new process.

- PCB$L_PID—Internal process ID
- PCB$L_EPID—Extended process ID
- PCB$L_OWNER—Internal process ID of process's creator
- PCB$L_EOWNER—Extended process ID of process's creator

25.1.3.2   **Internal PID.** The IPID is a longword value. Its low-order word contains an index into the PCB vector and the sequence vector, unique across the local system but not across the nodes of a VAXcluster system. Its high-order word is the sequence number from the sequence vector.

The executive uses the sequence number to check the validity of an IPID. The high-order word of the IPID must match the sequence number in the sequence vector offset indexed by the low-order word of the IPID. Additionally, the PCB vector slot must contain the address of a PCB other than the null PCB.

To optimize the IPID validity check, the VMS routines EXE$IPID_TO_PCB and EXE$NAMPID, in module SYSPCNTRL, rely on two PCB characteristics. First, a PCB contains its own IPID at offset PCB$L_PID. Second, the null PCB contains a zero in its PCB$L_PID field, and it is the only PCB whose IPID is zero. To verify that an IPID is valid, these routines index into the PCB vector using the low-order word of the IPID. They obtain the PCB and compare its PCB$L_PID to the IPID being checked. The test fails under two conditions:

- If the process specified has been deleted and the slot has been reused, the new PCB's IPID contains an incremented sequence number and does not match.
- If the process specified has been deleted but the slot has not been reused, the PCB vector contains the address of the null PCB. The null PCB contains zero in its PCB$L_PID field and can never match the IPID being checked.

Figure 25.5 shows how an IPID is constructed.

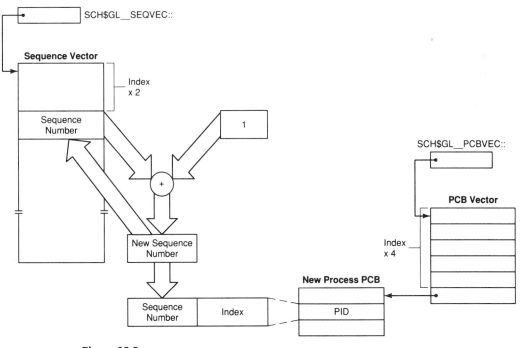

Figure 25.5
Fabrication of Internal Process IDs

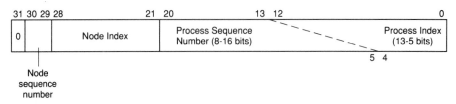

Figure 25.6
Layout of an Extended Process ID

25.1.3.3   **Extended PID.** The EPID serves as a VAXcluster-wide process identification. The EPID is currently constructed from the IPID. Figure 25.6 shows
its format. Its low-order 21 bits contain the IPID in two fields. The widths
of these two fields vary, depending on the value of the SYSGEN parameter
MAXPROCESSCNT. The first field, beginning at bit 0, contains the process
index. The size of the field is computed at system initialization and stored
in global location SCH$GL_PIXWIDTH. The second field contains the se-
quence number. Its size is 21 minus the size of the first field.

Bit 31 of the EPID is zero, preserving the rule that an EPID or IPID is never
negative. The other ten high-order bits identify the VAXcluster node. The
node identification is similar to process identification in that it consists of
an index into a node table and a sequence number that counts how many
times the index has been reused. On a system that is not a VAXcluster node,
these bits are all zero.

After a system becomes a VAXcluster member, the EPIDs of any existing
processes must be updated with the node information, which comes from the
node's cluster system identification (CSID). The low-order ten bits from the
global location SCH$GW_LOCALNODE are inserted into the field PCB$L_
EPID of each process and, if appropriate, into the field PCB$L_EOWNER.

25.2   **SHELL LAYOUT**

After EXE$CREPRC creates a new PCB and requests its placement in the
scheduler's database, the skeletal process exists in the COMO scheduling
state. When the swapper brings the new process into memory, it obtains the
initial pages from a special template called the shell rather than from a swap
file. The shell exists in a pageable portion of the loadable executive image
WORKING_SET_MANAGEMENT. The swapper locates the shell through
SWP$GL_SHELLBAS.

The actual contents of the shell are listed in Table 25.4. As shown in the
table, the swapper process copies eight pages from the shell when it creates
a new process: one page of PHD, three P1 page table pages, the P1 pointer
page, the Record Management Services (RMS) data page, and two pages that
contain the initialization code SWP$SHELINIT.

Table 25.4   Contents of the Shell Pages

Item	Size	Locked	Page Number
PHD (fixed)	1 [1]	Yes	1
P1 page table pages	3	Yes	2, 3, 4
P1 pointer page	1	Yes	5
RMS data area	1	No	6
SWP$SHELINIT	2	Yes	7, 8

[1] The ultimate size of the top of the PHD depends on the values of several SYSGEN parameters. See Appendix F for details on how the size of the PHD is calculated by SYSBOOT.

25.2.1   **Moving the Shell into Process Context**

The swapper takes the following steps in preparation for the inswap of any process:

1. It allocates physical memory for the process, the number of pages specified by PCB$L_PPGCNT plus PCB$L_GPGCNT.
2. It records the page frame numbers (PFNs) of these pages in its I/O map.
3. It allocates a balance slot, a place for the process's PHD.

In the case of a newly created process, EXE$CREPRC has initialized PCB$L_PPGCNT to the value in SWP$GL_SHELLSIZ. Computed during system initialization as a function of SYSGEN parameters and the shell constants, this value includes

- The fixed portion of the PHD
- The working set list
- The process section table (PST)
- The PHD page arrays and page table page arrays
- The shell pages

As the swapper allocates each physical page, it stores the PFN in its I/O map area. (Recall from Chapter 18 that the swapper's map area is also used as its P0 page table.) Each map entry doubles as a P0 page table entry (PTE). The swapper initializes each PTE as active, valid, with a protection code of ERKW.

After allocating a balance slot, the swapper examines PCB$L_WSSWP, the location of the outswapped process. A zero value in this field identifies a newly created process that must be initialized from the shell.

The swapper uses SWP$GL_SHELLBAS to locate the shell in system space. It tests whether all the pages of the shell are resident. If any page is not valid, the swapper reads all the pages from the image on disk rather than page fault several times. This optimization is effective at times when many processes are being created.

Once all the shell pages are resident, the swapper copies them into its own P0 address space with a MOVC instruction. The first eight PTEs, therefore, map the eight pages of the shell. The remaining PTEs map physical pages that the swapper has allocated for the new process but has not yet initialized.

The swapper then invokes a special subroutine contained within the shell, called SWP$SHELINIT, to configure the PHD before completing the final operations of inswap.

25.2.2 Configuration of the Process Header

When the loadable executive image WORKING_SET_MANAGEMENT is linked, the shell pages within it are constructed to resemble an outswapped process. However, a PHD cannot be entirely configured without taking into account several SYSGEN parameters, so part of the PHD configuration must occur dynamically (see Chapter 14).

To complete the configuration of the PHD, the swapper invokes the routine SWP$SHELINIT, in module SHELL. Since SWP$SHELINIT executes only during the creation of a new process, it is pageable and resides with the other shell pages. As described in the previous section, the swapper maps the physical pages containing SWP$SHELINIT in its P0 address space. It then invokes SWP$SHELINIT as a subroutine.

Running in kernel mode from the process context of the swapper, SWP$SHELINIT performs the following actions:

1. Since SWP$SHELINIT runs in the swapper's process context, it has access to the swapper's virtual address space and page table. It zeros the pages that the swapper allocated for the new process but did not read from the shell. None of the information destined for these pages is assembled into the WORKING_SET_MANAGEMENT image; EXE$PROCSTRT dynamically determines and stores their contents at a later stage.
2. SWP$SHELINIT calculates the address of the system page table entry (SPTE) that maps the start of the PHD. It copies the first entry in the swapper's P0 page table into this SPTE, thereby initializing it with the PFN of the first page read from the shell.

    It initializes subsequent SPTEs, mapping the working set list and PST from the swapper's P0PTEs that map pages zeroed in step 1.
3. SWP$SHELINIT skips the SPTEs that map the empty pages of the PHD (used for working set list expansion), leaving them as no-access pages.
4. It initializes the next SPTEs, which map the PHD page arrays and page table page arrays, from swapper P0PTEs that map pages zeroed in step 1.
5. It invalidates the translation buffer.
6. It stores the balance slot index in the PHD. This value indexes the PHD reference count array and the process index array, as well as the balance slots. Chapter 14 describes these arrays.

7. It stores the SYSGEN parameters that determine the default page fault cluster size and the default page table page fault cluster size in the PHD.
8. It requests the initial page file assignment for the new process and reserves enough pages in the page file for its PHD pages and the shell pages. It stores the page file and reservation count in the PHD.
9. It calculates and stores the index to the beginning of the working set list (PHD$L_WSLIST) and the pointer to the end of the PST (PHD$L_PSTBASOFF).
10. It calculates and stores PHDL_WSLX, PHDL_BAK, PHD$L_PTWSLE-LCK, and PHD$L_PTWSLEVAL, the pointers to the PHD page arrays and the page table page arrays (see Figure 14.10).

    The size of an entry in the PHD$L_WSLX array corresponds to the size of an entry in the PFN database working set list index (WSLX) array.

    The size of a WSLX entry depends on the amount of memory present on a particular system (see Chapter 14). On a system with more than 32 megabytes described by the PFN database, each WSLX array entry is a longword. On a system with less memory, each WSLX array entry is a word.
11. SWP$SHELINIT initializes the page table page arrays located by PHD$L_PTWSLELCK and PHD$L_PTWSLEVAL. These count the locked and valid PTEs in each page table page. Initializing the entries to −1 indicates that no pages are locked or valid. The next to last page table page in P1 space has its entries corrected to reflect the fact that it contains the PTEs for locked pages and valid pages.
12. The fixed portion of the PHD maintains four counters pertaining to page table pages: the number of page table pages with locked pages, the number with valid pages, the number of active page table pages, and the number of page table pages with nonzero entries. SWP$SHELINIT initializes the counters to the number of permanent P1 page table pages copied from the shell. For VMS Version 5, there are three permanent P1 page table pages.
13. The PHD page copied from the shell contains initial values for the three working set list longword index values (PHDL_WSLOCK, PHDL_WSDYN, and PHD$L_WSNEXT). SWP$SHELINIT adjusts the indexes to account for any additions to the permanent part of the working set. Note that for VMS Version 5, these fields are longwords.

    After altering the index to the dynamic portion of the working set (PHD$L_WSDYN), SWP$SHELINIT moves any dynamic working set list entries from their old location to the new location. In VMS Version 5, this affects only the working set list entry defined in the shell for the RMS data page.
14. SWP$SHELINIT updates the process working set list with the pages comprising the beginning of the PHD (fixed portion, working set list, PST, and page table page arrays). In addition, it updates the PFN database

arrays for the physical pages to indicate that these pages are active and modified (PFN STATE array) and page table pages (PFN TYPE array). It stores the working set list offset in the PFN WSLX array, the page file number in the PFN BAK array, and the PTE back pointer in the PFN PTE array.

15. It initializes the SPTEs for the process page table pages as demand zero pages with a protection code of ERKW.

16. It copies the swapper P0PTEs that map the three P1 page table pages defined in the shell into SPTEs. It locks these pages into the process working set list and updates the PFN arrays as in step 14.

17. SWP$SHELINIT calculates the offsets from the beginning of the PHD to the beginning of the P0 page table and the end of the P1 page table to reflect the size of the beginning of the PHD (see Chapter 14 and Appendix F). It adjusts the address of the first free virtual address in P1 space (stored in the PHD at offset PHD$L_FREP1VA) and the contents of the copy of the P1 length register (stored in the hardware PCB in the PHD) to reflect the size of the PHD that is mapped into P1 space.

18. It rearranges entries in the swapper P0 page table to reflect the state of the newly built working set list. It calculates the address of the P1 window to the PHD and stores it in location CTL$GL_PHD. The swapper can access the P1 address space of the newly created process because its pages are mapped as swapper P0 addresses. CTL$GL_PHD resides in the P1 pointer page copied from the shell. When SWP$SHELINIT returns control to the swapper for completion of the inswap, the swapper will complete PTE generation based on the working set list.

19. SWP$SHELINIT marks the PHD resident by setting bit PCB$V_PHDRES in PCB$L_STS.

20. It initializes the WSEXTENT and WSAUTHEXTENT indexes to reflect the value of the SYSGEN parameter WSMAX, and the WSQUOTA and WSAUTH indexes to reflect the value of WSMAX or 65,536 pages, whichever is smaller. It initializes PHD$L_WSFLUID to the value of the SYSGEN parameter MINWSCNT. The end of the working set list (WSLAST) and the default count (DFWSCNT) initially reflect the value of the SYSGEN parameter PQL_DWSDEFAULT. PHD$W_WSSIZE is initialized to the value of PQL_DWSDEFAULT.

21. The calculations in step 17 adjusted the values of the P0 and P1 base registers relative to the beginning of the PHD. The virtual address of the PHD is added to these two registers so that they contain the virtual addresses of the beginning of the P0 and P1 page tables, as required for address translation.

22. SWP$SHELINIT initializes the P1PTEs that map the system service vectors with the contents of the SPTEs that map the system service vectors in system space. The P1 mapping of the system service vectors enables

them to be replaced on a per-process basis, simply by modifying that process's P1PTEs.

SWP$SHELINIT returns control to the swapper's main inswap routine, which completes the remaining steps of the inswap operation. It generates the remaining PTEs based on the working set list. The pages containing the shell code become part of the kernel stack for the new process. They are not zeroed, so the initial content of the kernel stack is the shell code. As the final step, the swapper invokes the scheduler routine SCH$CHSEP, in module RSE, to change the state of the new process to executable and possibly trigger a rescheduling interrupt. These steps are described in Chapter 18.

25.3 PROCESS CREATION IN THE CONTEXT OF THE NEW PROCESS

The final steps of process creation take place in the context of the newly created process. The process's initial register context is contained within the PHD copied from the shell. When it becomes current, the process begins execution at the saved program counter (PC) in that PHD, the address of the routine EXE$PROCSTRT, in module PROCSTRT. The saved processor status longword (PSL) indicates kernel mode at IPL 2. Thus, the first code that executes in the context of a newly created process is the same for every process in the system.

25.3.1 Operation of EXE$PROCSTRT

When EXE$PROCSTRT begins execution, the PCB and the PHD have been created. In addition, information passed from the creator process has been copied into the PQB by EXE$CREPRC. EXE$PROCSTRT must copy the information from its temporary location in the PQB into the PHD and P1 space (see Figure 25.7). EXE$PROCSTRT then prepares for and activates the image specified by the creator process.

EXE$PROCSTRT begins execution in kernel mode at IPL 2. Later segments of the code execute in executive mode and user mode. Because the PCB$L_PQB field is an overlay of PCB$L_EFWM, the process cannot enter a resource or event flag wait state until the PQB address has been copied elsewhere. Since a page fault might cause a process to be placed in a resource wait state, the process cannot page fault until EXE$PROCSTRT has copied the PQB address. Therefore, the first three instructions of EXE$PROCSTRT are located in nonpageable memory. These instructions obtain the address of the process's PCB and copy the PQB address from the PCB to a register. The remainder of EXE$PROCSTRT is pageable.

EXE$PROCSTRT performs the following steps:

1. It obtains the PCB address from CTL$GL_PCB and copies the PQB address from the PCB to a register, as described previously.

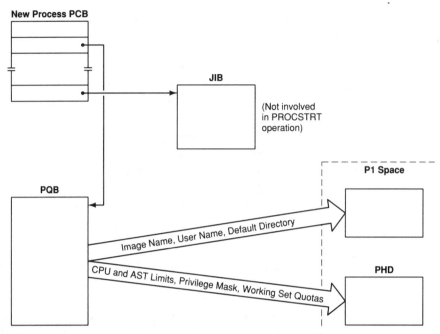

Figure 25.7
Removal of Process Parameters from the Process
Quota Block

2. It stores the addresses of the RMS dispatcher and the base of the control region in the P1 pointer page. The base of the control region, stored in CTL$GL_CTLBASVA, is the boundary between process-permanent and image-specific P1 space. EXE$PROCSTRT initializes CTL$GL_CTLBAS-VA to a value determined during system initialization but updates it with each expansion of process-permanent P1 virtual address space.

3. EXE$PROCSTRT initializes the dispatch vectors for kernel and executive mode user-written system services, as well as the vectors for user-written rundown handlers. Each of these vectors begins with a longword pointer to the next available entry, followed by the actual entries. EXE$PROC-STRT initializes each pointer with the offset to the second entry and stores an RSB instruction in the first entry. Each vector has an additional pointer to the first loaded entry, used for dispatching. EXE$PROCSTRT stores the address of the RSB instruction here.

4. It initializes the first longword of the message vector with the offset to the first entry and the message pointer with the address of that entry.

5. If the creator process requested an image dump, EXE$PROCSTRT propagates that flag to the PHD.

6. EXE$PROCSTRT initializes the kernel request packet (KRP) lookaside list (see Chapter 19), forming the space into KRPs and inserting them on the list.

7. It moves the CPU time limit and the AST limit from the PQB to the PHD (see Table 25.3).

8. EXE$PROCSTRT initializes the working set list pointers in the PHD to reflect the quotas passed from the creator. It minimizes the SYSGEN parameter WSMAX, the maximum working set size, with the number of potentially available physical pages. It then enforces the following restrictions on quotas:

   —Working set quota must be less than or equal to 64K, the maximum size of a swap slot.

   —Working set extent must be less than or equal to the maximum physical pages.

   —Working set quota must be less than or equal to working set extent.

   —Working set default must be less than or equal to working set quota.

9. EXE$PROCSTRT copies the process's base priority to PHD$B_AUTHPRI and PCB$B_AUTHPRI. Saving the base priority enables a process without ALTPRI privilege to lower its base priority and later raise it as high as the original base priority.

10. It copies the process privilege mask from the PQB to the first quadword of the PHD (PHD$Q_PRIVMSK), the permanent privilege mask (CTL$GQ_PROCPRIV in the P1 pointer page), and the authorized privilege mask (PHD$Q_AUTHPRIV). Chapter 26 describes the use of each of these privilege masks.

11. It copies the default message flags to P1 space.

12. It saves the login time in CTL$GQ_LOGIN.

13. EXE$PROCSTRT copies the minimum and maximum authorized security clearance records from the PQB to the PHD.

14. It initializes the following listheads as empty:

   —The Get Job/Process Information ($GETJPI) system service's context queue

   —The three image activator listheads (see Chapter 26): image control blocks (ICBs) representing activated images; ICBs representing work in progress; and the ICB lookaside list

   —The clusterwide process services (CWPS) queue in the PCB

     In Version 5 of VMS, processes are visible and can be manipulated clusterwide. CWPS supports system services in implementing this feature. Chapter 13 provides details.

   —The process scan queue in the PHD

     The $PROCESS_SCAN system service uses this queue to maintain its search context. Chapter 13 provides details.

15. EXE$PROCSTRT creates P1 virtual address space for four uses:

   —Channel control block table

   —Process allocation region

—Process I/O segment

—Image I/O segment

Appendix F describes these areas and the SYSGEN parameters that affect their size. EXE$PROCSTRT records the address of each portion and updates the process-permanent boundary address in CTL$GL_CTL-BASVA with the new, lower address.

16. It allocates and initializes space from the P1 allocation region for the process logical name hash table. EXE$PROCSTRT also allocates space for the process-private logical names and tables that it will create. Chapter 35 describes the logical name data structures and their use.

17. It initializes the process directory logical name table, LNM$PROCESS_DIRECTORY, and the process logical name table and inserts them into the hash table.

18. EXE$PROCSTRT creates the logical name table logical names LNMJOB, LNMGROUP, and LNM$PROCESS. It inserts them into the hash table and into LNM$PROCESS_DIRECTORY.

19. Using the equivalence strings and logical name attributes from the PCB, EXE$PROCSTRT creates the logical names SYS$INPUT, SYS$OUTPUT, SYS$ERROR, TT, and SYS$DISK.

20. If the process is not a subprocess, EXE$PROCSTRT creates the job and group logical name tables. (If the process is a subprocess, then the tables already exist.) Because multiple processes access the tables, they must be in system space. EXE$PROCSTRT allocates space for the tables from paged pool. It locks the logical name table mutex for write access and holds it while accessing the shareable logical name hash table. Chapter 8 describes mutexes.

    EXE$PROCSTRT initializes the two tables and inserts the job table into the shareable logical name hash table. It attempts to do the same with the group table. However, the group table may have already been created by some other process with the same UIC group number. If this is the case, the new table is unnecessary and EXE$PROCSTRT deallocates it back to paged pool. Otherwise, EXE$PROCSTRT inserts the group table into the shareable logical name hash table. In either case, it unlocks the logical name table mutex.

21. EXE$PROCSTRT then allocates space from the P1 allocation region for the process-private logical name table cache. It formats the space into a lookaside list of logical name cache entries.

22. It copies the image name from the PQB to the image header buffer for subsequent use by the image activator.

23. EXE$PROCSTRT copies the default directory string, if one exists, from the PQB to the control region. It also copies the two sets of CLI and command table information.

24. It copies the $CREPRC and user authorization file (UAF) flags from the PQB to control region flags.

25. It copies the user name and account name from the JIB into the P1 pointer page.

26. EXE$PROCSTRT deallocates the PQB by inserting it on the PQB lookaside list (see Chapter 19).

27. EXE$PROCSTRT invokes MMG$IMGRESET, which resets PHD$L_WSLAST, the pointer to the end of the working set list. MMG$IMGRESET also lowers IPL to 0, making it possible for the process to be deleted.

    Another, more philosophical, interpretation is that at this point in the creation of a process, there exists something that is capable of being deleted, a full-fledged process.

28. EXE$PROCSTRT initializes the shareable image list for the Address Relocation Fixup ($IMGFIX) system service to point to a dummy element. This system service is described in Chapter 26.

29. EXE$PROCSTRT merges the Files-11 Extended QIO Processor (XQP) into P1 space. During system initialization, a global section is created from the XQP image. It contains pure code and read-only data to be shared among all processes. EXE$PROCSTRT requests the Map Global Section ($MGBLSC) system service to map the shareable XQP section.

    EXE$PROCSTRT writes the lowest XQP address into CTL$GL_CTLBASVA to record the new P1 base virtual address. It dispatches to initialization code within the XQP image. The initialization code requests the Expand Program/Control Region ($EXPREG) system service to create a process-private copy of XQP impure area and space for the XQP's private kernel stack. The code then updates CTL$GL_CTLBASVA. After performing other Files-11 initialization, it returns to EXE$PROCSTRT.

30. EXE$PROCSTRT changes access mode to executive by fabricating a PSL and PC on the stack and executing an REI instruction. Execution of an REI instruction is the only way to get to an outer (less privileged) access mode.

    At this point, EXE$PROCSTRT has moved all the information from the creator to the context of the new process and is now ready to activate the image that will execute in the context of the new process. It must change mode to executive to request the image activator, which is an executive mode system service.

31. EXE$PROCSTRT requests the image activator to set up the page tables and perform the other steps necessary to activate the image. Image activation is described in Chapter 26.

32. EXE$PROCSTRT declares EXE$RMSEXH, an executive mode termination handler. This handler will be called when the Exit ($EXIT) system

service is requested from executive access mode, which usually happens when the process is deleted. When called, it calls SYS$RMSRUNDWN for each open file.

33. The address of a dummy CLI call back routine is stored in location CTL$AL_CLICALBK. If an image that was activated from EXE$PROC-STRT attempts to communicate with a nonexistent CLI, the dummy CLI call back routine will return the error status CLI$_INVREQTYP.

34. EXE$PROCSTRT changes access mode to user by fabricating a PSL and PC on the stack and executing an REI instruction.

35. It clears the frame pointer (FP), guaranteeing that the search of the user mode stack for a condition handler by the exception dispatcher will terminate (see Chapter 5).

36. EXE$PROCSTRT sets up an initial call frame on the user mode stack by executing a CALLG instruction to an inline procedure:

```
        CLRL    FP
        CALLG   (AP),B ^260$
        REI
260$:   .WORD   0                       ;Entry mask
        MOVAB   B^EXE$CATCH_ALL,(FP)
        .
        .                               ;Procedure code
```

37. EXE$PROCSTRT establishes EXE$CATCH_ALL, the catch-all condition handler, as the condition handler for this call frame and also as the last chance exception vector for user mode. The purpose and action of this handler are discussed in the next section.

38. EXE$PROCSTRT requests the $IMGFIX system service to perform address relocation for the image.

39. An argument list that is nearly identical to the one used by one of the CLIs (see Chapter 27) is built on the stack. This argument list allows an image to execute with no concern over whether it was activated from EXE$PROCSTRT or from a CLI.

40. EXE$PROCSTRT determines whether the process was created with the hibernate STSFLG. If the PCB$V_HIBER bit in PCB$L_STS is set, it requests the Hibernate ($HIBER) system service. EXE$PROCSTRT will continue when the process is awakened.

41. It calls the image at its initial transfer address. If the image subsequently terminates with a RET instruction (instead of requesting the $EXIT system service directly), control returns to EXE$PROCSTRT. If the process was created with the hibernate STSFLG, EXE$PROCSTRT places the process back into hibernation. When awakened, EXE$PROC-STRT calls the image again. An effect of this implementation is that the image is not exited and no exit handlers (user-declared or system-declared, such as EXE$RMSEXH) are called.

If the process was not created with the hibernate flag, EXE$PROC-STRT requests the $EXIT system service itself. In general, there is no difference between an image terminating with a RET instruction or with a request of the $EXIT system service. If the process was initially created with the hibernate flag, there is a difference between executing a RET instruction and requesting $EXIT. If a process is to be put into hibernation for future awakenings, it must use the RET instruction to return to EXE$PROCSTRT rather than terminate by requesting the $EXIT system service.

25.3.2   Catch-All Condition Handler

EXE$PROCSTRT and the CLIs establish the catch-all condition handler, EXE$CATCH_ALL, in module PROCSTRT, in the outermost call frame before calling an image. EXE$PROCSTRT also establishes it as the last chance exception vector for user mode through the Set Exception Vector ($SETEXV) system service. Any condition that is resignaled (not properly handled) by other handlers (or unfielded because no other handlers have been established) is eventually passed to this handler. The handler outputs a message using the Put Message ($PUTMSG) system service. Depending on the severity level of the condition, it may force image exit.

EXE$CATCH_ALL's arguments are the addresses of the signal and mechanism arrays. It performs the following actions:

1. It tests the condition in the signal array. If the condition is a system service failure, SS$_SSFAIL, EXE$CATCH_ALL disables system service failure mode to avoid an infinite loop.

2. If a call to LIB$SIGNAL generated the condition, EXE$CATCH_ALL removes the PC and PSL that LIB$SIGNAL fabricated from the signal array, leaving only those arguments passed to LIB$SIGNAL (see Chapter 5).

3. Unless system services are inhibited for this process, EXE$CATCH_ALL requests the $PUTMSG system service to write an error message to SYS$OUTPUT (and to SYS$ERROR if different from SYS$OUTPUT). The $PUTMSG system service is discussed in Chapter 36.

4. If EXE$CATCH_ALL was called as a last chance handler or if the error level is severe or greater (and if system services are not inhibited for this process), it calls EXE$EXCMSG to write an exception summary to SYS$OUTPUT. Chapter 36 describes EXE$EXCMSG.

   EXE$CATCH_ALL then dispatches to EXE$IMGDUMP_MERGE, described in Section 25.3.3, to write the process address space to a file for later analysis. When it returns, EXE$CATCH_ALL requests the $EXIT system service.

5. If it was not called as a last chance handler and if the error level is less than severe, EXE$CATCH_ALL returns the status SS$_CONTINUE to the exception dispatcher, which returns to the image.

25.3.3 Image Dump Facility

EXE$IMGDMP_MERGE, in module PROCSTRT, provides the capability to write a dump file of the process's address space in a format that can be mapped later for analysis by the debugger. It is invoked when the image terminates as the result of an exception that it cannot handle. EXE$IMGDMP_MERGE is normally invoked by the condition handler established by the Image Startup system service (see Chapter 26), but it can also be invoked from the last chance handler, EXE$CATCH_ALL.

If the exception occurred in a mode more privileged than user, then no dump may be taken and EXE$IMGDMP_MERGE returns to its invoker. If the exception occurred in user mode, the routine requests the $GETJPI system service to obtain process privileges, installed image privileges, and the PHD flags. EXE$IMGDMP_MERGE tests whether the PHD$V_IMGDMP flag is set. If it is clear, the process has not requested image dump and EXE$IMG-DMP_MERGE returns. This flag can be specified as part of the $CREPRC STSFLG argument and with the DCL commands SET PROCESS/DUMP and RUN/DUMP.

If the flag is set, EXE$IMGDMP_MERGE checks whether the image was installed with more privileges than the process has. If the image was installed with more privileges than the process, and the process has neither CMKRNL nor SETPRV privilege, no dump can be taken and EXE$IMGDMP_MERGE returns. Otherwise, it requests the $IMGACT and $IMGFIX system services to activate the image SYS$LIBRARY:IMGDMP.EXE and transfers control to the image.

26　Image Activation and Exit

> I would have you imagine, then, that there exists in the mind
> of man a block of wax . . . and that we remember and know
> what is imprinted as long as the image lasts; but when the
> image is effaced, or cannot be taken, then we forget or do not
> know.
>
> Plato, *Dialogs, Theaetetus* 191

Before an image can execute, the VMS operating system must take several steps to prepare the process. It must locate the correct image file on disk, set up process page tables and other data structures, and resolve address references among shareable images. The term *image activation* refers to the combination of these steps. In addition, if the debugger, Image Dump Utility, or traceback handler is expected to run when the image executes, VMS must incorporate the correct hooks to enable these images to be invoked.

At image exit, VMS must call exit handlers declared by itself or by the user. In any process that has had a command language interpreter (CLI) mapped by LOGINOUT, multiple images can execute one after another. All traces of the current image must be eliminated so that the next image can begin execution with no side effects from the execution of the previous image. This is referred to as image rundown.

This chapter describes the following system services related to image activation and exit:

- Image Activate ($IMGACT)
- Address Relocation Fixup ($IMGFIX)
- Image Startup ($IMGSTA)
- Declare Exit Handler ($DCLEXH)
- Exit ($EXIT)
- Rundown ($RUNDWN)

These system services, other than $DCLEXH and $EXIT, are reserved for the VMS operating system. Any other use is completely unsupported.

The chapter also describes the initialization and use of the various privilege masks maintained for each process.

26.1　IMAGE INITIATION

VMS initiates images via a private-to-Digital system service, $IMGACT, which is commonly known as the image activator. The image activator contains no special code to load images into memory for initial execution. Instead, it uses the page fault mechanism to bring in pages on demand from an image file. For this scheme to work, the process page tables must reflect the state of all the pages in the main image file and its shareable images' files. The image activator initializes the process page tables and makes other necessary preparations, such as creating address space for the user stack.

In this chapter, the term *main image* refers to a primary, controlling image that can be invoked by a user through the RUN command. A main image can be linked with multiple shareable images, which themselves can be linked with other shareable images. A shareable image is partly linked but has no transfer address. Thus it is not directly executable and must be linked with object modules or other shareable images to produce a main image.

Before control is transferred to a main image, the image activator resolves .ADDRESS and G^ references that point to locations within the shareable images that have been linked with the main image. This resolution is performed at activation time rather than at link time so that shareable images can change in size without requiring a relink of all images that use them.

The image activator transfers control to the main image by way of a special path in the executive that allows hooks to be inserted for later inclusion of a debugger, the Image Dump Utility, or the traceback facility. This path, called the debug bootstrap, always executes unless explicitly excluded at link time with a /NOTRACEBACK qualifier to the LINK command.

26.1.1 Image Activation

Although the concept of image activation is straightforward, there are several special cases of image activation. This section discusses some of these cases explicitly and mentions others only in passing.

The following types of image activation are discussed explicitly:

- Activation of a simple main image, one linked with no shareable images
  This is an artificial separation from the next case, simply to illustrate the difference in the image activator's actions.
- Activation of an image linked with one or more shareable images
  Because almost every high-level language processor generates calls to library routines implemented as shareable images, this case includes most images.
- Activation of a known image
  The activation of images that have been installed is streamlined by the data structures created by the Install Utility.
- Activation of a compatibility mode image
  When the image activator is called to activate a compatibility mode image, it actually activates the RSX-11M Application Migration Executive (AME) and passes the compatibility mode image name to the AME for further processing. (The RSX-11M AME is part of the optional software product VAX-11 RSX.)

There are several other special cases that the image activator must check for:

- Image activation at system initialization time

  During initialization of the system, image files must be opened without the support of either Record Management Services (RMS) or the file system. The image activator calls special code in the executive that performs the simpler file system operations in the absence of a file system. These routines are briefly described with system initialization in Chapters 30 and 31.

- Merged image activation

  A merged image activation occurs subsequent to the activation and transfer of control to a main image. This can be used for mapping a debugger, the Image Dump Utility, the traceback handler, a message file, or a CLI into an unused area of P0 or P1 space. It is also used to activate a shareable image when an already activated image calls the Run-Time Library procedure Find Universal Symbol in Shareable Image File (LIB$FIND_IMAGE_ SYMBOL).

  Rather than using the virtual address descriptors found in the merged image, the image activator simply uses the next available portion of P0 or P1 space. The user stack and image I/O segment are not mapped for a merged image. The RMS initialization routines are not called either, because an image is already executing and has RMS context that cannot be destroyed.

- Message sections

  Message sections add per-process or image-specific entries to the message facility.

- P0-only images

  The VMS Linker can produce images that map all temporary structures, including the user stack and the image I/O segment, in P0 space. The image activator must recognize this type of image and correctly map these two structures, usually located in the lowest address portion of P1 space.

  A P0-only image executes when the permanent part of the low-address end of P1 space must be extended without overwriting image structures. For example, the SET MESSAGE command causes a P0-only image called SETP0.EXE to execute. This image maps the indicated message section into the low-address end of P1 space and alters location CTL$GL_CTLBASVA to reflect the new boundary between the temporary and permanent parts of P1 space. This last step is critical if the message section is to remain mapped when later images terminate.

- Privileged shareable images

  Privileged shareable images implement user-written system services and rundown routines. System service procedures that are not part of the executive loadable images (for example, $MOUNT and $DISMOU) are implemented as privileged shareable images.

- Images that do not reside on a random access mass storage device

  The image activator can activate images from sequential devices (certain magnetic tape devices) and images located on another node of a network. An address space large enough to contain the entire image is first created. The image is then copied into this address space, thus requiring all image pages, including read-only pages, to be set up as writable.

26.1.1.1   Overview of the Image Activator. The image activator performs several steps to activate an image. First, it calls RMS to open the image file, which enables the system to perform all its file protection checks. Then it reads the image header (IHD). The IHD contains information about the virtual address space requirements of each section in the image. The image activator requests a memory management system service to map each image section.

26.1.1.2   Data Structures That Describe Images. An image consists of several variable-sized pieces, the first of which is the IHD. The IHD is followed by the image body, the actual program code and data; by a fixup table with information for address references that must be resolved at image activation; and, optionally, by symbol table information. Figure 26.1 shows the organization of an image.

The IHD itself consists of a number of variable-sized pieces. At the beginning of the IHD is the fixed portion, which contains some standard information about the image and pointers to the other parts of the IHD. Figure 26.1

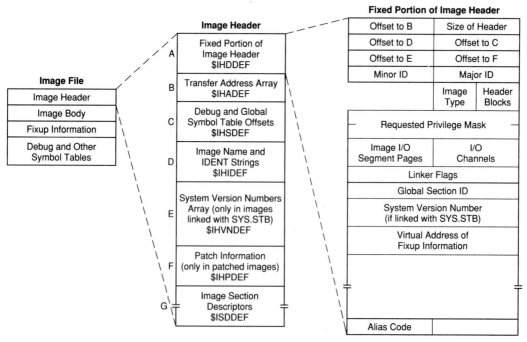

Figure 26.1
Contents of an Image Header

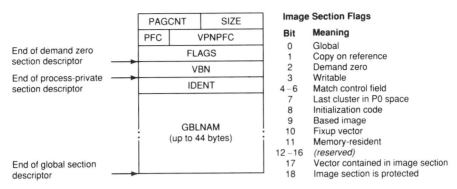

Figure 26.2
Layout of an Image Section Descriptor

shows the organization of the IHD and the layout of its fixed part. The macro $IHDDEF defines symbolic offsets for the fixed part. Offsets for the other parts are defined by the macros shown in Figure 26.1.

The IHD contains image section descriptors (ISDs), one for each section in the image. Each ISD describes a portion of the image and its location, in an image file and in virtual address space. Figure 26.2 shows the layout of the three types of ISD.

The three types of ISD are differentiated by flags in the field ISD$L_FLAGS and by the size of the data structure:

- Demand zero ISD. Identified by the flag ISD$V_DZRO, a demand zero ISD describes a range of virtual address space that begins as zero-filled pages. The image section will be mapped in virtual address space beginning at the virtual page number in ISD$L_VBNPFC. ISD$W_PAGCNT contains its length in pages.
- ISD for a private section. A private section ISD describes a range of virtual address space initially filled with code or data from the image file. This type of ISD may also describe a private mapping of a global section. The image section begins in the image file at the virtual block number in the field ISD$L_VBN; its length in pages is in ISD$W_PAGCNT. The image section will be faulted into virtual address space beginning at the virtual page number in ISD$L_VBNPFC.
- Global ISD. Identified by the flag ISD$V_GBL, a global ISD describes code or data stored in a shareable image. The global section name is stored as a counted string in the field ISD$T_GBLNAM. In the normal case, a nonbased shareable image, the field ISD$L_VBNPFC is zeroed by the linker, and the image activator maps the shareable image into the next available virtual address space.

A main image linked without any shareable images contains only the first two types of ISD.

A main image linked with a shareable image contains a global ISD that describes the shareable image. This type of ISD primarily serves to name the shareable image. The shareable image contains its own IHD and ISDs to describe its own virtual address space. Address space for the shareable image is not usually assigned when the main image is linked; that is, the shareable image is not normally based. Instead, the address space for the shareable image is assigned and allocated when it is activated. Thus, the size of the shareable image can change without requiring the main image to be relinked.

A shareable image linked with another shareable image contains a global ISD to point to the second shareable image. If the main image refers only to symbols in the first shareable image but not the second, it need not contain a global ISD for the second shareable image. The entire collection of shareable images implied by a main image is not determined until image activation. Thus, a shareable image can be relinked to reference additional shareable images without requiring the relink of the main image linked with it.

Activating a main image can result in the activation of many shareable images. After a main image has begun to execute, the image activator can be requested again to activate additional shareable images. The image activator keeps track of which images are activated, using a data structure called an image control block (ICB) to describe each image.

The image activator keeps two ICB lists—one for images already activated and one for images yet to be activated. ICBs are initially allocated from the P1 allocation region (see Chapter 19) but are deallocated to an ICB lookaside list for faster subsequent allocation. These doubly linked lists are located in P1 space at the following global locations:

- IAC$GL_ICBFL—Lookaside list
- IAC$GL_IMAGE_LIST—Activated images (known as the done list)
- IAC$GL_WORK_LIST—Images to be activated (known as the work list)

Figure 26.3 shows the layout of an ICB.

ICB$B_ACT_CODE describes how the image was activated—as a main image, a merged image, or a shareable image section. ICB$B_ACCESS_MODE contains the access mode specified in the $IMGACT request, maximized with the requestor's access mode. The image file is opened on a channel assigned in this access mode, and the pages that are mapped are owned by this mode. ICB$W_CHAN holds the channel number on which the image file is opened. The image's name is stored as a counted string in the field ICB$T_IMAGE_NAME, and the address range into which it was mapped is stored in ICB$L_STARTING_ADDRESS and ICB$L_END_ADDRESS. ICB$L_IHD points to the IHD of the image file, ICB$L_KFE locates the known file entry (KFE) associated with the image (if any), and ICB$L_CONTEXT points to the image activator local context block, a temporary structure that points to image activator buffers.

FLINK			
BLINK			
(reserved)	TYPE	SIZE	
CHAN		ACT__CODE	ACCESS__MODE
FLAGS			
IMAGE__NAME (40 bytes)			
(reserved)			
(reserved)			MATCH__CONTROL
MAJOR__ID		MINOR__ID	
STARTING__ADDRESS			
END__ADDRESS			
IHD			
KFE			
CONTEXT			
BASE__ADDRESS			
INITIALIZE			
ACTIVE__SONS			

Figure 26.3
Layout of an Image Control Block

26.1.1.3   **Data Structures That Describe Known Images.**   Several data structures describe known images. A known image has special properties that affect its
activation. The Install Utility is used to specify known images and their
properties. The *VMS Install Utility Manual* describes this utility and its
commands.

The known image mechanism has several functions. Its main purpose is
to identify executable images installed with privileges and images installed
to be shared in the virtual address space of multiple processes. A subsidiary
function is faster image activation.

An executable image that requires enhanced privileges but must execute in
nonprivileged process context (such as MOUNT, SET, or SHOW) is installed
with the /PRIVILEGE qualifier. When such an image is activated, the process
gains enhanced privileges temporarily. The enhanced privileges are removed
when the image is run down.

Several different types of image are installed with the /SHARE qualifier:

- A shareable or executable image with image sections that are to be shared
  by multiple processes
- A shareable image containing code that executes in an inner mode, such
  as a user-written system service or rundown routine
- A shareable or executable image whose shareable sections are to reside
  in MA780 multiport memory and be accessed by processes running on
  multiple VAX-11/780 or VAX-11/785 CPUs

An installed image is opened by its file ID rather than its file name, saving the overhead of a file lookup. Image activation can be further shortened if the image is installed /OPEN so that its file remains open. In this case, the image activator's $OPEN RMS request is essentially a null operation. If such an image is installed /HEADER_RESIDENT, its IHD is stored in paged pool. Keeping the IHD resident saves the additional read operations otherwise required to read it into memory every time the image is activated.

The Install Utility creates and manages the known image database (also called the known file database) to describe images that have been installed. RMS scans the known image database whenever a file is opened with the known file option. (Use of this option is reserved to the VMS operating system and unsupported for any other use.) All the known image data structures are in paged pool. The two major ones are the KFE and the known file directory (KFD).

The Install Utility allocates a KFE for each known image. The KFE contains information used by the image activator to locate and map the image. KFE$L_FID and KFE$L_WCB are different symbolic names for the same location in the KFE. If the image header is not memory-resident, three words beginning at KFE$L_FID contain the full file ID of the image, thus locating the file header on the disk. Otherwise, if the file header is already in memory, KFE$L_WCB contains the address of the file's window control block (WCB), which describes the disk location of the blocks of an open file. KFE$L_IMGHDR contains the address of the resident IHD.

The field KFE$W_FLAGS contains flag bits indicating the manner in which the image was installed—for example, if KFE$V_PROTECT is set, the image was installed /PROTECTED. An image installed with privileges has its privilege mask recorded in KFE$Q_PROCPRIV.

When a shareable image is installed with the /SHARE qualifier, the number of global sections it consists of is stored in KFE$W_GBLSECCNT. Its global section identifier is at KFE$L_IDENT, and the match control information supplied when the image was linked is stored in KFE$B_MATCHCTL. The image activator maintains a count of the number of processes sharing the image at KFE$L_USECNT. Figure 26.4 shows the layout of a KFE.

Although the file name of the installed image is stored in the KFE, the full device and directory names are stored in the KFD field KFD$T_DDTSTR. Typically, multiple known images are installed from the same device and directory combination and thus share the same KFD. Keeping the device and directory information in the KFD rather than in each KFE saves paged pool. The number of KFEs sharing a KFD is found in KFD$W_REFCNT. The KFEs themselves are linked together at KFD$L_KFELIST. Figure 26.5 shows the layout of a KFD. Figure 26.6 shows a KFD and its list of KFEs.

A data structure called a known file resident image header (KFRH) exists for each known image installed /HEADER_RESIDENT. The KFRH immedi-

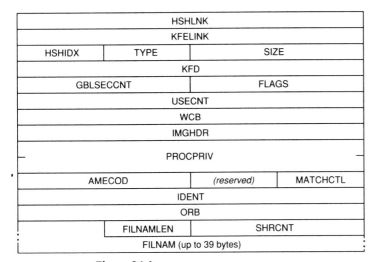

HSHLNK				
KFELINK				
HSHIDX	TYPE	SIZE		
KFD				
GBLSECCNT		FLAGS		
USECNT				
WCB				
IMGHDR				
PROCPRIV				
AMECOD		(reserved)	MATCHCTL	
IDENT				
ORB				
FILNAMLEN		SHRCNT		
FILNAM (up to 39 bytes)				

KFE Flags

Bit	Meaning
0	Installed/PROTECT
1	Shareable image
2	Installed/PRIVILEGE
3	Installed/OPEN
4	Image header resident
5	Shared image
6	Shared memory image
7	Compatibility mode image
8	Installed/NOPURGE
9	Image accounting enabled
10	Has writable sections
11	Execute access only

Figure 26.4
Layout of a Known File Entry

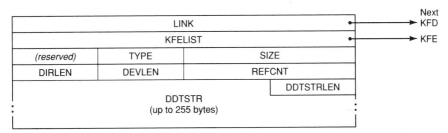

Figure 26.5
Layout of a Known File Directory

ately precedes the IHD, and space for the IHD is allocated with the KFRH. Figure 26.7 shows the layout of a KFRH.

A KFE hash table locates all the KFEs. A known image name is hashed to a number between 0 and 127, which is an index into the 128-entry hash table. If the table entry contains a zero, no KFE is associated with that hash index. Otherwise, the table entry is the address of a KFE. As a confirmation, the KFE contains its own hash index value at KFE$B_HSHIDX. KFEs with the same hash index are linked together through the field KFE$L_HSHLNK. The end of the list is a forward link of zero. Figure 26.8 shows the hash table and several KFEs linked to it.

There is one more known image data structure, the known file pointer block (KFPB). The KFPB contains the hash table address at KFPB$L_KFE-HSHTAB and the number of hash table entries at KFPB$W_HSHTABLEN. It also holds the head of the KFD list at KFPB$L_KFDLST and the KFD count

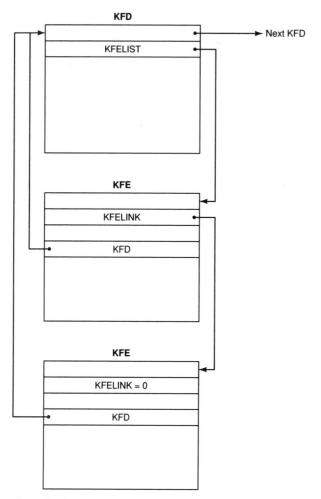

Figure 26.6
Known File Directory and Known File Entries

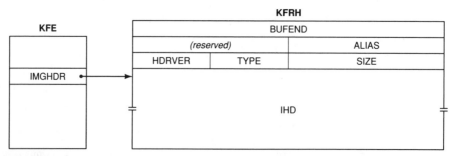

Figure 26.7
Layout of a Known File Resident Image Header

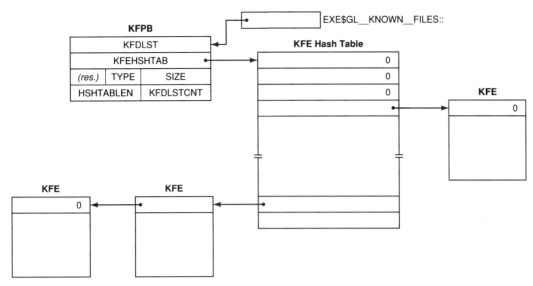

Figure 26.8
Layout of a Known File Pointer Block and a KFE
Hash Table

at KFPB$W_KFDLSTCNT. Figure 26.8 shows the layout of the KFPB and its relation to the other known image data structures.

26.1.1.4   **Implementation of the Image Activator.** The image activator is implemented as the $IMGACT system service. Direct requests to this system service are reserved for the VMS operating system. Direct requests by users are completely unsupported. Instead, users can request the image activator indirectly through any CLI command that runs an image and through the Run-Time Library procedure LIB$FIND_IMAGE_SYMBOL.

Table 26.1 shows the arguments to the $IMGACT system service.

26.1.1.5   **Activation of a Simple Main Image.** Most of the common operations that are performed by the image activator occur during the activation of a simple main image, that is, one linked with no shareable images. This section, therefore, follows the general flow through the image activator for simple main images, including those installed as header resident or shareable. Other forms of activation, described in later sections, are mentioned briefly in this section when appropriate.

The $IMGACT system service procedure, EXE$IMGACT, runs primarily in executive mode with some kernel mode subroutines. EXE$IMGACT is in the module SYSIMGACT; some of the procedures it calls are in modules IMGMAPISD, IMGDECODE, and SYSIMGFIX. EXE$IMGACT and the procedures it calls are known as the image activator.

To activate a simple main image, the image activator takes the following steps:

Table 26.1 Arguments to the Image Activator System Service

Argument Name	Meaning
NAME	Descriptor of image name to be activated.
DFLNAM	Descriptor of default file name.
HDRBUF	Address of 512-byte buffer in which the IHD and image file descriptor are returned. The first two longwords in the buffer are the addresses within the buffer of the IHD and the image file descriptor.
IMGCTL	Image activation control flags. These flags control the form that the activation will take. The options are the following: • IAC$V_MERGE—If set, the image activator is directed to merge an image into the address space of an already activated image. When this flag is set, the user stack and the image I/O segment are to be ignored. This flag must be set if the image activator is requested from user mode. • IAC$V_EXPREG—If set, the INADR argument does not give an actual address range but merely indicates P0 address space, which is expanded as required. This flag is only used during a merged image activation for a P0 image. • IAC$V_P1MERGE—If set, the image activator is directed to merge an executable image into P1 space. This flag is used when mapping a CLI into P1 space. This merge is performed in two parts: first the image is merged into P0 space, then into P1 space. The sole purpose of the merge into P0 space is to determine the size of the image. Once the size is determined, the correct starting address in P1 space can be calculated. • IAC$V_SETVECTOR—If set, the image activator only initializes the P1 vectors that dispatch to user-written system services, rundown routines, and message sections.
INADR	Address of a two-longword array containing the virtual address range into which the image is to be mapped. This argument is usually omitted, in which case the address ranges designated by the ISDs in the IHD are used or the image is mapped at the next available location.
RETADR	Address of a two-longword array to receive the starting and ending addresses into which the image was actually mapped.
IDENT	Address of a quadword containing the version number and matching criteria for a shareable image.
ACMODE	Access mode for page ownership and image channel assignment. This defaults to user mode. If specified, it is maximized with the access mode of the $IMGACT requestor.

1. It initializes its eight-page scratch area in P1 space.
2. It resets the P1 space vectors for user-written system services, rundown routines, and message sections.
3. It checks the accessibility of the system service argument list and its arguments and copies them for later use.
4. It invokes RM$RESET, in module RMSRESET, to initialize the image I/O segment.
5. It allocates and zeros an ICB.
6. It locks the known file database by requesting the Enqueue Lock Request

and Wait ($ENQW) system service. It locks the systemwide resource INSTALL$KNOWN FILE for protected read. This blocks any attempt at concurrent changes to the known file database by the Install Utility.

7. The image activator requests RMS to open the image for execute access, specifying the user-open, process-permanent file, sequential-only, and known file database search options. It requests a WCB containing complete mapping information for the file, thus avoiding later window turns.

   The image activator then stores the image name and channel number in the ICB. If RMS discovers the image in the known file database, it returns the address of the KFE in the CTX field of the file access block (FAB). The image activator stores the KFE address in the ICB as well. It takes note of whether the image was installed with the /PRIVILEGE, /ACCOUNT, /PROTECTED, /EXECUTE_ONLY, or /SHARE qualifiers.

8. The image activator tests whether the IHD is resident. A known image with its header resident in memory can be activated quickly because a header read operation is avoided. If the IHD is not resident, the image activator reads the image file and performs several consistency checks to determine that it has indeed found an IHD.

9. The image activator tests whether the image is an ordinary native mode image. The last word in the first block of the IHD, IHD$W_ALIAS, indicates whether the image is a native image produced by the VMS Linker, an image produced by some other linker, or an image that is a CLI. Depending on the value in IHD$W_ALIAS, another image might be activated before the current one.

   The only other linker supported is the RSX-11M Task Builder. It produces a compatibility mode image with a zero in IHD$W_ALIAS. When the image activator finds such an image, it instead activates SYS$SYSTEM:RSX.EXE. Further details about the activation of a compatibility mode image are found in Section 26.1.1.11.

   If the IHD specifies that the image is a CLI, the image activator instead activates LOGINOUT. Section 26.1.1.12 contains further details about the activation of a CLI.

10. The image activator copies information from the system service argument list into the ICB and inserts the ICB at the tail of its work list.

11. The image activator enters its main loop. It begins processing the work list by removing an ICB from the head of the list. The first ICB removed from the work list is the ICB describing the main image, which was inserted in step 10.

12. The image activator processes the ISDs in the image's header, which it locates through the ICB. Its main task is setting up the process page tables to reflect the address space produced by the linker. It reads each ISD in the IHD (see Figure 26.2) and determines the type of section described: private or demand zero for the simple main image in this

example; private, demand zero, or global for a main image linked with shareable images. It then requests the appropriate memory management system service to perform the actual mapping.

—The most common form of ISD describes a private section. A private section is either read-only or read/write, depending on the attributes of the program sections (PSECTs) that comprise the image section. Initial page faults for all pages in a private section are satisfied from the appropriate blocks in the image file.

To map a private section into process address space, the image activator normally requests the Create and Map Section ($CRMPSC) system service, using the contents of the ISD as input arguments. It always specifies the NO_OVERMAP flag, so that if pages exist in the desired virtual address range, they are not deleted.The result is a series of page table entries (PTEs) containing process section table indexes. Figure 26.9 shows the PTEs, the process section table entry, and the ISD. The number of PTEs is equal to the page count in the ISD. Notice that all the PTEs index the same process section.

If an image is installed /SHARE, however, the Install Utility has already processed its ISDs and has created global sections wherever image section characteristics allowed. When a process activates an image installed /SHARE, the image activator maps those existing global sections into process address space using the Map Global Section ($M-GBLSC) system service and only creates private sections for those ISDs whose characteristics do not allow sharing.

If the section is read-only and the image was installed /SHARE, the image activator requests the $MGBLSC system service. The result is a series of PTEs that are global page table indexes. Figure 26.10 shows the PTEs, global page table, and ISD.

If the section is writable and the image was installed /SHARE /WRITE, the image activator requests the $MGBLSC system service.

If the section is writable and copy-on-reference, it requests the $CRMPSC system service to create a private copy of the section.

If the section is read-only but not shared, it requests the $CRMPSC system service. An image section containing a .ASCID directive or .ADDRESS reference to a symbol in a shareable image cannot be shared except in a main image (see Section 26.1.2).

One special kind of private section is a fixup vector table, which describes addresses in the image that are resolved at image activation rather than at link time. Fixup vector processing is described in Section 26.1.2. When the image activator encounters an ISD describing a fixup vector table, it stores the base address of the current image into

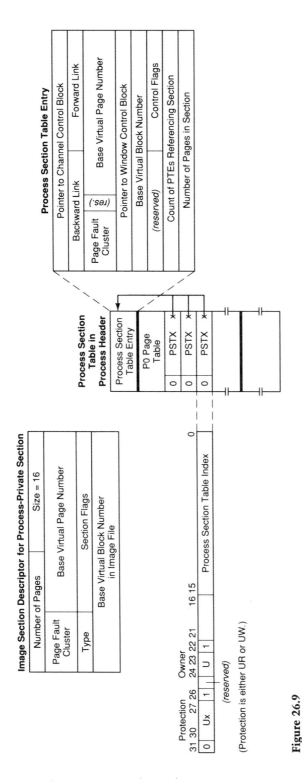

Figure 26.9
ISD and Page Table Entries for Process-Private Section

751

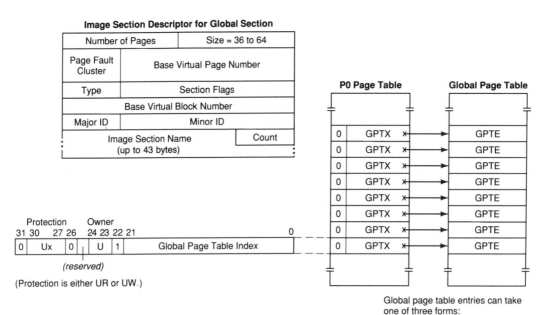

Figure 26.10
ISD and Page Table Entries for Global Section

the fixup vector table and adds it to the list of fixup vector tables to be processed later by the $IMGFIX system service.

—Another form of ISD is a demand zero section. The linker produces such a section whenever there are five (or some user-specified default number) consecutive uninitialized copy-on-reference pages in the image file. The image file does not contain demand zero section pages but merely an indication in the ISD that a certain range of virtual address space contains all zeros.

The image activator uses the contents of this type of ISD as input arguments to an internal interface to the Create Virtual Address Space ($CRETVA) system service. The $CRETVA system service creates new demand zero pages in the specified range of virtual addresses. By default, if it discovers any pages that already exist in the range, they are deleted. The internal interface allows the image activator to specify the NO_OVERMAP flag, overriding this default. The result is a series of demand zero page PTEs. The number of PTEs is equal to the page count in the ISD. Figure 26.11 shows the ISD and PTEs for the demand zero section.

Note that one such section is the area in P1 space that contains the user stack. The linker distinguishes this special demand zero section

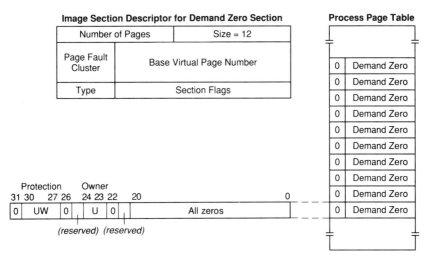

Figure 26.11
ISD and Page Table Entries for Demand Zero Section

from others by a special code byte in the type designator in the ISD. The image activator records the ISD page count and delays mapping the user stack until later in the activation.

—The third type of ISD, which would not be found in the simple main image of this example, is a global ISD. A global ISD indicates that the image activator must map a shareable image into a range of virtual address space. When the image activator encounters a global ISD, it builds an ICB to describe the shareable image and inserts it in its work list. Section 26.1.1.6 describes ICB insertion and the activation of a shareable image.

13. If the image is being activated from a sequential device (magnetic tape or across a network), then the address range is created and the entire image read from the sequential device into virtual address space. All future page faults are resolved from the page file.

14. In this example of a simple image (with no references to shareable images and thus no global ISDs), the only ICB on the work list has now been processed. The image activator continues with its end processing, described in Section 26.1.1.7.

In the case of an image linked with shareable images, the image activator would have found global ISDs while processing the main image ICB. Thus, additional ICBs were added to the work list. The image activator processes them as described in the following section.

26.1.1.6   **Activation of Shareable Images.** Whenever the image activator encounters a global ISD in the header of an image being activated, it allocates an ICB, copies the image name from the ISD into the ICB, and inserts the ICB onto the ICB work list. When the image activator completes the processing associated with, for example, the main image's ICB, it continues with the following steps. (In the case of a merged image activation request, perhaps initiated through the procedure LIB$FIND_IMAGE_SYMBOL, there would be no main image processing.)

1. The image activator attempts to remove an ICB from its work list. If there is none, activation is complete and the image activator proceeds with its end processing, described in Section 26.1.1.7.

2. It checks the done list to see whether the image named in the work list ICB has already been activated in the virtual address space. If so, the done list includes an ICB with the same name.

   Commonly referenced shareable images, such as LIBRTL, can appear on the work list multiple times. Activating an image linked with several shareable images, each linked with LIBRTL, causes multiple insertions of LIBRTL on the work list. No matter how many times a shareable image appears on the work list, it is only activated once because the image activator discovers it on the done list for all subsequent activation attempts.

   If the image activator discovers the image on the done list, it must ensure that the earlier activation matches current protection requirements. If an image is installed /PROTECTED, all shareable images with which it links must be installed. If several shareable images link with the same shareable image X, and only one of those shareable images is installed /PROTECTED, image X might possibly be activated before the /PRO-TECTED image, that is, before the image activator detects that image X must be an installed image. The image activator checks for this condition and returns the error status SS$_PRIVINSTAL if the image is not installed. Otherwise it deallocates the ICB and goes back to step 1 to process the next ICB on the work list.

3. If the image is not already activated, the image activator places the ICB to the right of a stack pointer maintained on the done list. This mechanism ensures that ICBs appear on the list in the proper order for image initialization (see Section 26.1.1.8).

4. The image activator requests RMS to open the image named by the ICB. It specifies a default file type of EXE and directory of SYS$SHARE, with file open options of user-open, process-permanent file, sequential-only, and known file database search. It requests a WCB containing complete mapping information for the file, thus avoiding later window turns. If the global ISD specified a writable global section, the image activator requests shared write access. Otherwise, it requests execute access.

   To locate the file, RMS attempts logical name translation of the file name part of the image name.

   When activating one of the following image types, the image activator specifies that RMS use only executive or kernel mode logical names to translate the image name:

—An image installed with privileges

—A main image installed /EXECUTE_ONLY and activated from user mode

—A main image invoked by a process with execute access but not read access to the image file

—An image installed as a protected image or having an ancestor installed as a protected image

5. If the image or any ancestor is protected, the image activator checks that the image returned by RMS is a known image. If not, the activation is aborted and the image activator returns the error status SS$_PRIVINSTALL.

   In addition, if a shareable image is not installed /EXECUTE_ONLY, and the process does not have both read and execute access to it, the activation is aborted and the image activator returns the error status SS$_ACCONFLICT.

6. If the image is not a known image with its header resident, the image activator reads in its header (see step 8 in Section 26.1.1.5).

7. It then checks that the match control information in the IHD is consistent with the match requested in the global ISD whose presence caused the activation of this shareable image. If there is a mismatch, the image activator aborts the activation and returns the error status SS$_SHRIDMISMAT.

8. If the IHD indicates that the shareable image has an initialization section, the image activator sets the ICB$V_INITIALIZE flag and records the address of the initialization section in ICB$L_INITIALIZE.

9. If the image was not header resident, the image activator invokes EXE$CHECK_VERSION, in module CHECK_VERSION, which checks whether an image linked against system global symbols is compatible with the versions of those symbols in the running system. Chapter 29 describes the compatibility check in detail.

   Since the Install Utility performs this check as well, the image activator skips the check if the image is header resident.

   For VMS Versions 5.0 and 5.1, version incompatibility caused the image activator to remove CMKRNL and CMEXEC privileges from the image but continue the activation. Beginning with VMS Version 5.2, the image activator aborts the activation and returns the fatal error status SS$_SYSVERDIF.

10. If the versions are compatible, the image activator processes the ISDs for each section in the shareable image.

    —If the ISD is a global ISD, representing a different shareable image, the image activator compares the portion of its name designating the image (that is, without the trailing *nnn*) to the name of the ICB most recently added to the work list. If the names are the same, the image activator does not add an ICB to the work list. The comparison prevents some ICB redundancy in the work list. An image referencing different image sections within a second image would have multiple global ISDs describing the second image. Without the comparison, multiple ICBs would be generated for the second image.

If the names are different, the image activator creates an ICB to describe the image. Before adding it to the work list, the image activator examines all existing work list entries for an entry whose name matches. If there is no match, the current ICB is inserted at the head of the work list. Otherwise, the ICB is inserted in place of the matching ICB, and the matching ICB is moved to the head of the work list. This ensures that the earliest reference to a based shareable image controls the mapping of the image.

—If the ISD is not a global ISD, the image activator maps the section into the process address space. Step 12 in Section 26.1.1.5 describes the processing of private ISDs and demand zero ISDs.

11. When all ISDs are disposed of, processing for the ICB is complete. If this ICB has added more ICBs to the work list, it becomes the top of the stack maintained on the done list. The image activator removes the next ICB from its work list and repeats the steps in this section.

After the last ICB is processed, the image activator performs the end processing described in Section 26.1.1.7.

26.1.1.7 **Image Activator End Processing.** If a main image was activated, the image activator performs the complete end processing described in this section. For a merged activation, it performs only steps 7 and 8.

The image activator's end processing consists of the following steps:

1. The image activator tests if the image was linked with an image I/O segment larger than the standard space allocated during process creation. The standard size is determined by the SYSGEN parameter IMGIOCNT, which has a default value of 64. However, the default can be overridden at link time with the following line in the linker options file:

   ```
   IOSEGMENT = n
   ```

   If an image I/O segment larger than the default value is requested, the image activator requests the $CRETVA system service to create a replacement image I/O segment.

   If a P0-only image is being activated, the image activator creates the image I/O segment at the high-address end of P0 space.

2. The address space for the user stack is created with the Expand Region ($EXPREG) system service. The usual location of the user stack is at the

low-address end of P1 space, where the automatic stack expansion can add user stack space as needed. The location of the user stack in P0-only images is at the high-address end of the P0 image.

The default size of the user stack is 20 pages. The following line in the linker options file can override this value:

```
STACK = n
```

The image activator creates a user stack with two extra pages for system use during exception processing in case the user stack is corrupted.

3. Running in kernel mode, the image activator stores the address of the high end of the user stack in the P1 pointer page, in the CTL$AL_STACK array. Reserving space for system use during exception processing, the image activator loads an address two pages below the high end of the stack into the processor register PR$_USP. This is the value loaded into the SP register when an REI instruction returns the process to user mode, which usually occurs following the return from the image activator.

4. The privileges that will be in effect while this image is executing are calculated. The logical AND of the privilege mask found in IHD$Q_PRIVREQS (which currently enables all privileges and so is effectively unused) with the process-permanent privilege mask at location CTL$GQ_PROCPRIV is then ORed with the privilege enhancements for a privileged known image, from KFE$Q_PROCPRIV.

   The result is stored in the process privilege mask in the access rights block (ARB) at offset ARB$Q_PRIV (also known as PCB$Q_PRIV) and in the process header (PHD) at offset PHD$Q_PRIVMSK. The mask at KFE$Q_PROCPRIV is copied to the PHD at offset PHD$Q_IMAGPRIV. The uses of the various privilege masks are described in Section 26.4.1.

5. The image activator stores the address of the IHD buffer in the global location CTL$GL_IMGHDRBF.

6. It checks whether image accounting was requested for this particular image or enabled for the system as a whole. If so, the image activator records various statistics, such as current CPU time, in their P1 locations.

7. If a known image is being activated, its use count must be incremented. If the image was installed /OPEN, the share count in its WCB must also be incremented. The image activator then sets the done bit in the ICB to indicate that it has been activated. The actions in this step are done for each image being activated.

8. At this point, the image activator has finished its work. It releases its lock on the known file list, loads a final status into R0, and returns to its requestor to allow the image itself to be called. The caller (EXE$PROC-STRT, LIB$FIND_IMAGE_SYMBOL, or a CLI) requests the $IMGFIX system service to perform address relocation. Section 26.1.2 describes $IMGFIX.

26.1.1.8 **Computing the Proper Order of Image Initialization.** As a by-product of its normal work, the image activator computes the order of initialization for multiple shareable images activated by a main image. The basic rule for image initialization is that if shareable image A calls shareable image B, then the initialization routine for image B must be called before the initialization routine for image A. This rule enables image A to call any routine in image B (or in any image that B calls) during A's own initialization.

The initialization routine for each activated image is called as part of image fixup (see Section 26.1.2.5). $IMGFIX first calls the initialization routine specified by the ICB that is at the tail of the done list. It proceeds towards the head of the done list. The image activator must create the correct order of ICBs on the done list by careful placement of ICBs on both the work and done list.

If image A calls image B, then at some point during the activation of image A, the image activator encounters a global ISD that references image B. The image activator builds an ICB to insert at the head of the work list. Inserting these ICBs at the head of the list ensures that these called, or son, images will be activated after the calling, or parent, image and generally before any siblings of the parent.

Before actually inserting the ICB on the work list, the image activator examines existing work list entries. If it finds an entry whose name matches that of the ICB to be added, it inserts the ICB after the matching ICB and then moves the matching ICB to the head of the work list. Since an image is only activated once no matter how many times it is referenced, this ensures that its mapping is controlled by the top-level accessor. Otherwise the current ICB is inserted at the head of the work list. This list generates a walk of the image call graph known as a preorder traversal.

A stack, implemented at the head of the done list, is used to convert the preorder traversal for image activation into a postorder traversal for image initialization. Basically, a parent node remains on the stack until its last son is activated. A stack pointer points to the top of this stack in the done list. (Initially, the stack pointer points to the queue header.) Figure 26.12 shows how the ICBs at the head of the done list form this stack.

To pop this stack, the stack pointer is simply moved to the left. The next ICB from the work list is always inserted to the right of the top of the stack. It becomes the new top of the stack if it has any sons. ICBs to the right of the top of the stack are always in the proper initialization order. ICBs at and to the left of the stack pointer are parent ICBs who still have descendants that have not been activated.

The stack is built to ensure that the sons and descendants of an image are always placed on the done list to the right of the ICB of the parent. Since the done list is processed in reverse order during initialization, this placement ensures that all images called directly or indirectly by some image are initialized before that image itself.

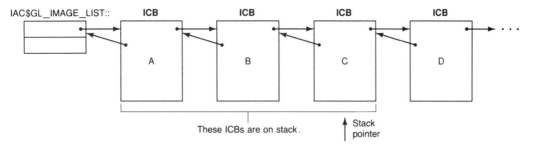

Figure 26.12
ICB Stack in the Done List

The manipulation of the work and done lists is controlled by the ICB$L_
ACTIVE_SONS count in each ICB. This field specifies how many of the
image's sons have not yet been activated (their ICBs are still on the work
list) and how many have been activated but still have active sons of their
own (these ICBs are on the stack in the done list). The ICBs to the right of
the stack in the done list have no active sons.

The following steps describe the image activator's manipulation of ICBs
on the done and work lists to generate the proper initialization order. The
details of image activation are described in Sections 26.1.1.5 and 26.1.1.6 and
are not repeated here.

1. The image activator tries to remove an ICB from the front of the work
   list. If there is none, it goes on to end processing (see Section 26.1.1.7).
2. If this is an image that was already activated (that is, on the done list) and
   still has active sons, then the image activator has detected a circularity.
   (The image is one of its own descendants, so no initialization order
   is possible.) In this rare case, all the images on the done list that are
   involved in the circularity must be marked. An error will be reported
   if a subsequent attempt is made to initialize one of those images. The
   images involved in the circularity are exactly those ICBs on the stack
   from the top of the stack down to and including the previously activated
   image.

   Regardless of whether there is a circularity, if the image was previously
   activated, the image activator deallocates the ICB and then continues at
   step 6.
3. Otherwise, this is a new image needing activation. The image activator
   inserts its ICB just to the right of the top of the stack in the done list
   and zeros its ICB$L_ACTIVE_SONS count.

   It then performs the detailed work of activation for this image (steps 4
   through 8 in Section 26.1.1.6). During those steps, each time the image
   activator creates a new global ICB (son), it places the new ICB at the front
   of the work list and increments ICB$L_ACTIVE_SONS in its parent's
   ICB. (After the parent image is activated but before its sons have been,

this field contains the total number of shareable images referenced by the image.)

4. If the field ICB$L_ACTIVE_SONS in the ICB to the right of the top of the stack is nonzero after the image has been activated, the image activator makes that ICB the top of the stack and continues with step 1. (This new parent remains on the stack until all its sons, which are located at the front of the work list, are activated and no longer have active sons of their own.)

5. Otherwise, the field ICB$L_ACTIVE_SONS in the ICB to the right of the top of the stack is zero, and the image activator continues with step 6.

6. This step is called a "decrement parent" operation. ICB$L_ACTIVE_ SONS in the parent ICB at the top of the stack must be decremented to indicate that one of its sons is activated. If its count becomes zero, this same step must be repeated for its parent, and so on.

   If the stack is empty, there is no parent to decrement. The image activator continues with end processing (see Section 26.1.1.7). Otherwise, it decrements ICB$L_ACTIVE_SONS in the ICB at the top of the stack.

7. If the count is still positive (the image still has active sons), the ICB remains at the top of the stack and the image activator continues with step 1. Otherwise, if ICB$L_ACTIVE_SONS is now zero, it must decrement the ICB$L_ACTIVE_SONS field in the parent of the ICB.

8. When it reaches the ICB at the top of the stack (the ICB that initiated the activations, and therefore has no parent), the image activator proceeds to its end processing. Otherwise, the image activator pops the stack by moving the stack pointer to the left in the done list and repeats step 6.

26.1.1.9 **Example Activation.** The details of activating an image linked with several shareable images can be illustrated with an example. The example main image references the shareable images A and LIBRTL, image A references the shareable images B and LIBRTL, and image B references LIBRTL.

At the beginning of the activation, an ICB representing the main image is placed on the work list. This first ICB is moved from the work list to the done list. As its ISDs are processed, work list items are added for A and LIBRTL as the result of references in the main image.

Work List	Done List	Stack Top
LIBRTL (main image)	Main image (2 sons)	⇐
A (main image)		

After mapping the sections of the main image, the image activator removes the ICB for LIBRTL from its work list. The ISD is processed and the main image's son count is decremented. Since LIBRTL has no sons, the main image remains at the top of the stack.

Work List	*Done List*	*Stack Top*
A (main image)	Main image (1 son)	⇐
	LIBRTL	

The image activator removes the ICB for image A from its work list. In processing A, work list items are added for B and LIBRTL. Since A has sons, it becomes the new stack top.

Work List	*Done List*	*Stack Top*
LIBRTL (A)	Main image (1 son)	
B (A)	A (2 sons)	⇐
	LIBRTL	

The image activator removes the ICB for LIBRTL from the work list, discovers the duplication, and discards the entry, decrementing A's son count.

Work List	*Done List*	*Stack Top*
B (A)	Main image (1 son)	
	A (1 son)	⇐
	LIBRTL	

The image activator removes the ICB for image B from its work list. In processing B, a work list item is added for LIBRTL. Since B has a son, it becomes the new stack top.

Work List	*Done List*	*Stack Top*
LIBRTL (B)	Main image (1 son)	
	A (1 son)	
	B (1 son)	⇐
	LIBRTL	

The image activator removes the ICB for LIBRTL from the work list, discovers the duplication, and discards the entry, decrementing B's son count. Since this brings B's count to zero, A (B's parent) becomes the stack top and its son count is decremented, again to zero. Thus the main image becomes the stack top, its count is decremented to zero, and the image activator performs its end processing. The done list is left in the correct order for image initialization.

Work List	*Done List*	*Stack Top*
	Main image	⇐
	A	
	B	
	LIBRTL	

26.1.1.10 **Activation of a Known Image.** When the image activator opens a known image, RMS places the address of the KFE in the CTX field of the FAB.

The activation of a known image proceeds in the same way as that of a regular image, although some of the work that the image activator must perform in the regular case is avoided. In particular, a known image that has its header resident is activated more quickly, because the header read operation is avoided.

In any case, the ISDs must still be processed and the PTEs set up so that the image can execute. In addition, the image activator must update the usage statistics for this known image (see Figure 26.4).

26.1.1.11 **Activation of a Compatibility Mode Image.** When the image activator determines from IHD$W_ALIAS that it is attempting to activate a compatibility mode image, it changes its course and instead activates the RSX-11M AME (SYS$SYSTEM:RSX.EXE).

An AME is itself a native mode image, responsible for mapping the compatibility mode image into the address range between 0 and 10000_{16}, passing control to that image while turning on the compatibility mode bit (with an REI instruction), and fielding all compatibility mode and other exceptions generated by the compatibility mode image. Currently, the RSX-11M AME is the only supported AME.

From the point of view of image activation, once the image activator determines that it is activating a compatibility mode image, it continues with activation, but activation of the AME and not the compatibility mode image. The name of the compatibility mode image is stored at location CTL$AG_CMEDATA, where it is retrieved by the AME.

26.1.1.12 **Activation of a Command Language Interpreter.** When the image activator determines that it is attempting to activate a CLI and the IAC$V_MERGE flag is clear, it activates instead the image LOGINOUT. First, the image activator closes the CLI image file, because LOGINOUT performs its own file open. Then it activates LOGINOUT and transfers control to it. LOGINOUT maps the CLI into P1 space and passes control to it. Chapter 27 describes this flow.

26.1.2 **$IMGFIX System Service**

The $IMGFIX system service procedure, EXE$IMGFIX in module SYSIMG-FIX, runs in the access mode from which it is requested. In cooperation with $IMGACT and the linker, EXE$IMGFIX enables the postponement of address assignment from link time to image activation. Delaying address assignment permits position independence within shareable images and the images that link with them. Because fixups modify pointers within images themselves, they are performed in the access mode from which the main image will run.

The exceptions are .ADDRESS fixups for privileged shareable images, which are performed from executive mode.

The linker creates fixup vector tables for executable images and for most shareable images. When EXE$IMGACT encounters an ISD describing a fixup vector table, it copies the base address of the current image to the fixup vector table and inserts the table at the head of the list pointed to by CTL$GL_FIXUPLNK. EXE$IMGFIX processes entries from the fixup vector list, created by EXE$IMGACT. This chapter refers to the image whose address EXE$IMGACT stores as the fixup image.

EXE$IMGFIX performs modifications to several forms of addressing:

- A Gˆ (general) reference to an address in a shareable image
- A .ADDRESS reference to a location within a nonbased shareable image
- A .ASCID directive within a nonbased shareable image

Resolution of a Gˆ reference is deferred until image activation so that the relative address is not affected by a change in the size of any intervening shareable image.

The .ADDRESS directive references a fixed address in virtual memory. Resolution of a .ADDRESS reference to a location in a shareable image is deferred so that the shareable image need not be loaded at a fixed base address. .ADDRESS references are fixed up after the base address of the shareable image is determined when it is activated. However, if the linker options file specifies a base address for an image, .ADDRESS references to locations within it are resolved at link time.

The .ASCID directive builds an ASCII string and a descriptor for it. It incorporates the equivalent of an .ADDRESS directive referencing the string. .ASCID directives within a nonbased shareable image are fixed up after the base address of the shareable image is determined. In the following sections, text references to .ADDRESS directives include those generated by .ASCID directives.

The *VMS Linker Utility Manual* explains in more detail the motivation for the $IMGFIX system service and the linker's action in preparing for image fixups.

An image linked under Version 3 or later of the VMS operating system includes a section called the fixup vector table. The table contains data that describes Gˆ references, a list of the shareable images referenced by the image, and data that describes .ADDRESS references. Figure 26.13 shows the layout of an image and its fixup vector table.

26.1.2.1   **Shareable Image List.** There is one shareable image list entry (SHL) for each shareable image referenced by the fixup image, plus one SHL for the fixup image itself. Each SHL contains the name of the associated shareable image. EXE$IMGFIX uses this name to match the SHL with an ICB on the done

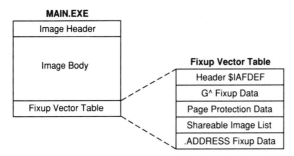

Figure 26.13
Image Layout with Fixup Vectors

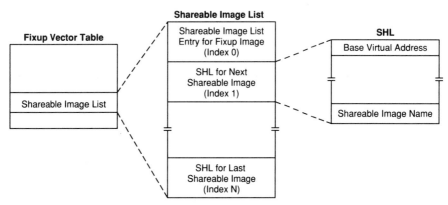

Figure 26.14
Shareable Image List

list. It then copies the base virtual address of the shareable image from the ICB into the SHL.

The SHL for the fixup image, which is the first shareable image list element (index 0), contains information used to resolve .ADDRESS locations. EXE$IMGACT stores the base virtual address of the image in this SHL. Figure 26.14 shows the layout of the shareable image list entries within the fixup vector table.

26.1.2.2 **Resolution of Gˆ Locations.** A section of each fixup vector table is reserved for Gˆ vectors. This Gˆ vector table is composed of multiple substructures, one for each shareable image containing the target of a Gˆ reference. The substructure consists of an entry count, the index of the SHL associated with the shareable image, and a longword entry for each target label. Figure 26.15 shows the layout of the Gˆ vector table and substructures.

When an image is linked, the linker tries to resolve Gˆ references by changing them to absolute addressing mode, @#. When it encounters a Gˆ reference to a location in a shareable image, however, the linker instead changes the addressing mode to longword relative deferred, @Lˆ. The displacement to the

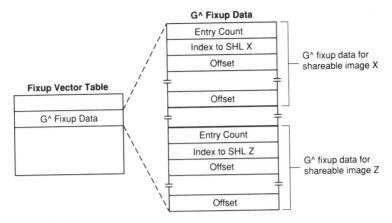

Figure 26.15
Gˆ Vector Table

operand address locates a longword entry in the Gˆ vector table substructure for the shareable image containing the target. The linker calculates the offset from the base of the shareable image to the target and stores this value in the substructure entry.

If there are multiple Gˆ references to the same target, the linker points all of them to the same substructure entry.

For each substructure in the Gˆ vector table, EXE$IMGFIX resolves Gˆ references by performing the following actions:

- It uses the index into the shareable image list to locate the SHL associated with the shareable image.
- From the SHL, it obtains the base virtual address of the shareable image.
- It adds the base address to each longword entry in the substructure.

When the image executes, the instruction's displacement to the operand address locates the appropriate entry within the Gˆ vector table substructure. The entry contains the corrected virtual address of the target label.

26.1.2.3 **Resolution of .ADDRESS Locations.** Like the Gˆ vector table, the .ADDRESS vector table is composed of multiple substructures, one for each shareable image referenced by a .ADDRESS directive. The .ADDRESS vector table also contains a substructure for the fixup image itself, if it is not a based image. A substructure consists of an entry count, the index of the SHL associated with the shareable image, and a longword entry for each .ADDRESS directive whose target is within the shareable image. The longword entry contains the offset from the base of the fixup image to the .ADDRESS directive. Figure 26.16 shows the layout of a .ADDRESS vector table.

The linker takes the following actions for each .ADDRESS directive:

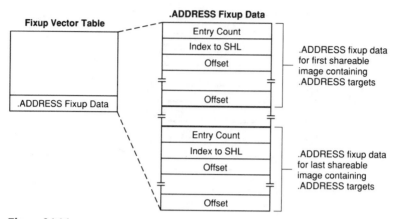

Figure 26.16
.ADDRESS Vector Table

1. It determines the offset of the target location from the base of its shareable image. It stores this offset in the longword reserved in the fixup image by the .ADDRESS directive.

2. It determines the offset of the .ADDRESS directive from the base of the fixup image. It stores this offset in the .ADDRESS vector table substructure associated with the shareable image that contains the target.

Figure 26.17 illustrates the resolution of the .ADDRESS directive by the linker. The target MTH$SQRT is within the shareable library MTHRTL. The .ADDRESS directive within MAIN.EXE contains the offset of the label MTH$SQRT from the base of MTHRTL.EXE. The entry in MTHRTL's .ADDRESS vector table substructure contains the offset of the .ADDRESS directive from the base of MAIN.

When EXE$IMGFIX resolves a .ADDRESS directive, it performs the following steps to obtain the actual address of the location:

1. It adds the base address of the fixup image (in the previous example, the image MAIN), to each entry in the .ADDRESS vector table substructure. Separating the offset and base address in this fashion allows the fixup image to be a position-independent shareable image.

2. Using the substructure entry to locate the .ADDRESS cell in the fixup image, it adds the base address of the shareable image (MTHRTL.EXE) to the contents of the .ADDRESS cell (the offset to the label MTH$SQRT).

3. It stores the resulting address in the .ADDRESS cell.

EXE$IMGFIX repeats this action for all .ADDRESS directives in all the linked images, except in images that have a specified starting base address. Note that an image section containing .ADDRESS or .ASCID references fixed

MAIN.EXE

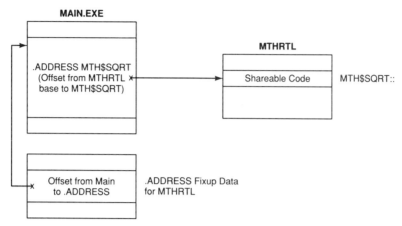

Figure 26.17
Resolution of the .ADDRESS Directive

up in this way cannot be shared among processes, since the resolutions of those directives are specific to the virtual address space in each process.

26.1.2.4 **Page Protection Fixup.** After address fixup is complete, EXE$IMGFIX adjusts page protection as specified in the page protection data area of the fixup vector table. The manner in which EXE$IMGFIX performs a .ADDRESS fixup requires that the page containing the .ADDRESS reference be writable. To allow a read-only image section to use .ADDRESS references, the section is originally defined as writable. The linker creates an entry in the page protection data area for each section of this type, specifying a new page protection of UR. After address fixup, EXE$IMGFIX requests the Set Protection on Pages ($SETPRT) system service for each entry in the page protection data area.

The final page protection entry alters the protection of the fixup vector section itself to UREW. The fixup vector pages are always protected from user mode modification because entries in the Gˆ vector table are referenced during image execution. Figure 26.18 shows the layout of the page protection area.

26.1.2.5 **Additional Functions of EXE$IMGFIX.** Following address fixup and page protection modification, EXE$IMGFIX tests whether any privileged shareable images have been activated. If so, it requests the $IMGACT system service, specifying the IAC$V_SETVECTOR flag. Running in executive mode, the image activator initializes the P1 space dispatch vectors for user-written system services, rundown routines, and message sections.

If any shareable image specified an initialization routine, EXE$IMGFIX scans the done list, ICBs representing activated images, from back to front. EXE$IMGFIX, running in user mode, calls the initialization routine of each shareable image that specified one.

767

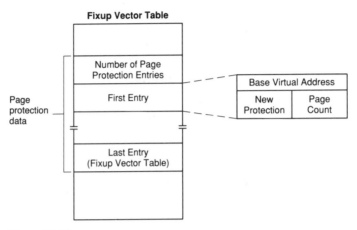

Figure 26.18
Page Protection Area

26.1.3 Image Startup

EXE$PROCSTRT or a CLI can request image activation and fixup, as described in Chapter 27. After successful image activation and fixup, the image is called at its transfer address. Depending on how the image was linked, the initial transfer of control may be to a debugger, a user-supplied initialization procedure, or the executable image itself.

26.1.3.1

Transfer Address Array. In addition to the ISDs previously discussed, the linker includes in the image header a data structure called a transfer address array. This array contains the user-supplied transfer address. It also provides the means for including a debugger or a traceback handler in the user image.

The format of the transfer address array is pictured in Figure 26.19. If a debugger transfer address is specified or implied, it appears first in the list. An image-specific initialization procedure, if specified, occurs next. The last entry in the list is the transfer address of the user image, either the argument of a .END directive for a VAX MACRO program or the first statement of a main program written in a high-level language. A fourth entry containing a zero is the end of list indication, no matter what options were passed to the linker.

The initialization transfer address is described in the *VMS Run-Time Library Routines Volume* and is not discussed here.

If the Digital command language (DCL) command LINK/DEBUG=*file-spec* is used to link an image, the explicit file specification is the name of a particular debugger object module. The linker places the transfer address found in the specified debugger file into the first element in the transfer address array. If the /NOTRACEBACK option is included (and not overridden implicitly by including an explicit /DEBUG option), then there is no debug transfer address. In all other cases (including the DCL command LINK/DEBUG, which does not specify an explicit debugger module), the linker places the address of

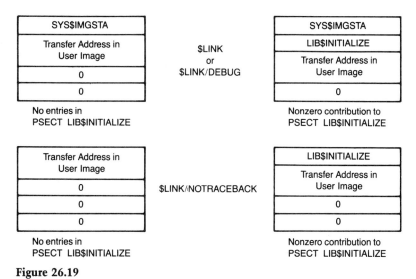

Figure 26.19
Transfer Address Array

SYS$IMGSTA (found in the system service vector area) in the first element of the transfer address array.

26.1.3.2 **$IMGSTA System Service.** Unless explicitly suppressed (with the /NO-TRACEBACK qualifier), all images execute the Image Startup ($IMGSTA) system service, sometimes called the debugger bootstrap. The system service procedure, EXE$IMGSTA in module SYSIMGSTA, runs in user mode. This procedure examines link and CLI flags to determine whether to start the user image directly or to map the debugger (identified by translating the logical name LIB$DEBUG) into the user's P0 space and transfer control to it.

EXE$IMGSTA first tests whether it should map a debugger into P0 space. The mapping is done if either of the following conditions is true:

- If the program was linked with the DCL command LINK/DEBUG and simply run (that is, not run with a RUN/NODEBUG command)
- If the program was run with the DCL command RUN/DEBUG, independent of whether the debugger was requested at link time

The debugger is not mapped if the image was run with a RUN/NODEBUG command or if the /DEBUG qualifier was omitted from both the LINK command and the RUN command.

If a debugger is to be mapped, EXE$IMGSTA requests the Translate Logical Name ($TRNLOG) system service to translate the logical name LIB$DEBUG. If there is no translation, EXE$IMGSTA uses the string DEBUG as the debugger name. EXE$IMGSTA then requests the $IMGACT system service to activate the debugger image. It specifies flags for a merged activation in P0 space, so that the debugger will be mapped at addresses just higher than the main image and its shareable images. EXE$IMGSTA then requests the $IMGFIX system service and finally transfers control to the debugger image through a self-relative offset at the beginning of the image. The debugger, in response to user commands, transfers control to the image.

If no debugger is mapped, EXE$IMGSTA establishes a condition handler in the current call frame. This condition handler, BOOT_HANDLER, gains control on signals that the image does not handle directly. After gaining control, the condition handler invokes the debugger, invokes the traceback handler, or resignals.

Whether or not a debugger is mapped, EXE$IMGSTA alters the argument list to point to the next address in the transfer vector array and passes control to the next transfer address. This is either the Run-Time Library procedure LIB$INITIALIZE or the transfer address of the user image.

26.1.3.3 **Exception Handler for Traceback.** BOOT_HANDLER, the condition handler established by EXE$IMGSTA before the image was called, has two functions:

- It invokes a debugger if a DEBUG command is typed after an image is interrupted with a CTRL/Y.
- If an unfielded condition occurs, it causes an image dump, if one was requested, and invokes the traceback handler to produce a symbolic stack dump.

If a user interrupts execution of a nonprivileged image by typing CTRL/Y and DEBUG, the DCL or monitor console routine (MCR) CLI generates the signal SS$_DEBUG. (Privileged images are simply run down in response to this command sequence.) If all handlers established by the image resignal the SS$_DEBUG exception, the debugger boot handler eventually gains control. Its response to an SS$_DEBUG signal is to map the debugger specified by the logical name LIB$DEBUG (if it is not already mapped) and transfer control to it. Note that an image that was neither linked nor run with the debugger can still be debugged, albeit without a debug symbol table, if the image reaches some undesirable state, such as an infinite loop.

The second function of the condition handler is to field any error conditions (where the severity level is WARNING, ERROR, or SEVERE) and pass them on to the traceback facility. If an image dump was requested, the handler dispatches to EXE$IMGDMP_MERGE (see Chapter 25) to create an image dump. When EXE$IMGDMP_MERGE returns, the handler maps the traceback facility, denoted by the logical name LIB$TRACE, into P0 space. If the condition has a severity level of either SUCCESS or INFO, the handler merely resignals it. The condition is then handled by the catch-all condition handler established by either EXE$PROCSTRT or the CLI that called the image.

26.2   **IMAGE EXIT**

When an image has completed its work, it passes control back to VMS, either by requesting the $EXIT system service or by returning to its caller, which requests the $EXIT system service. $EXIT calls whatever exit handlers have been declared by the image and then requests the Delete Process ($DELPRC) system service.

Exit handlers are described in the next section, which is followed by a description of the operations of the $EXIT system service.

26.2.1   **Exit Handlers and Related System Services**

An exit handler is an optional, user-declared procedure that performs image cleanup. To use this option, an image running in a process builds a data structure called an exit control block and passes its address to the $DCLEXH system service. Exit handlers can be declared for user, supervisor, and executive access modes. The access mode from which the service is requested is the mode in which the exit handler is to execute.

An exit control block contains the address of the exit handler and its arguments. The exit handler's first argument is the address of a longword to receive the final image status. The declarer of the exit handler defines any additional arguments and their use. An exit control block also contains a forward link field. This field contains the address of the next exit control block or, if there is none, zero. The $DCLEXH system service links together all the exit control blocks for an access mode. Each list is ordered with the most recently declared exit handlers' control blocks first.

The exit handler listheads are in a three-longword array. Another three-longword array contains the number of exit control blocks in each list. Each array is indexed by access mode. Figure 26.20 shows these arrays and exit control blocks.

Both arrays are in P1 space and modifiable only from kernel mode. Exit control blocks, however, are defined by the image in the per-process address space that it controls. Therefore, the system services that access these lists must exercise particular care. An exit control block corrupted through program error could destroy the integrity of its list.

When inserting or removing an exit control block, for example, each system service must test the accessibility of affected forward links. The count array is used to prevent infinite loops that might otherwise result from multiple declarations of the same exit control block.

Two system services other than $DCLEXH access exit control blocks: Cancel Exit Handler ($CANEXH) and $EXIT (see Section 26.2.2). An image requests the $CANEXH system service to delete a particular exit control block or all those for one access mode.

The $DCLEXH and $CANEXH system service procedures, EXE$DCLEXH and EXE$CANEXH, in module SYSDCLEXH, both execute in kernel mode.

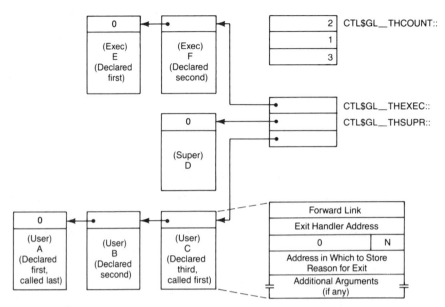

Figure 26.20
Sample Exit Handler Lists

26.2.2 Flow of the $EXIT System Service

The $EXIT system service procedure, EXE$EXIT in module SYSEXIT, runs in kernel mode. It also executes in outer modes, calling exit handlers.

EXE$EXIT is called with a single argument, the final status of the image. It stores the status in the P1 pointer page, at global location CTL$GL_FINALSTS, where it can be copied for image or process accounting. It clears the force exit pending flag, PCB$V_FORCPEN in the processor status longword (PCB$L_STS).

If EXE$EXIT was called from kernel mode, it requests the $DELPRC system service, and the process is deleted. If EXE$EXIT was called from any other access mode, it examines the exit handler listheads (see Figure 26.20). It begins with the one for the mode from which it was called and proceeds to those of inner (more privileged) access modes.

If EXE$EXIT finds a nonzero listhead, it saves the listhead contents and the number of exit control blocks in the list, and clears both the listhead and the count longwords. EXE$EXIT then empties the kernel stack and executes an REI instruction to enter the outer access mode from which it was invoked.

Running in the outer mode, EXE$EXIT removes the first exit control block from the list; saves the address of the next handler, final image status, and count of remaining handlers on the stack; and zeros the list pointer. It writes the final image status to the address specified in the exit control block and calls the exit handler. When (if) that handler returns, EXE$EXIT calls the

next handler in the list. This continues until the list is exhausted or until
EXE$EXIT has exhausted the count of exit handlers.

Once all the exit handlers for a given access mode have been called,
EXE$EXIT must return to a more privileged access mode. It changes access
mode by requesting the $EXIT system service. If none of the exit handlers
in the list just processed has done anything extraordinary (such as declaring
another exit handler), then the list for that mode is still empty and EXE$EXIT
proceeds to the next inner access mode in its search for more exit handlers.

When EXE$EXIT reaches kernel mode, that is, when it has called all
existing handlers, it requests $DELPRC to delete the process.

26.2.3   **Example of Exit Handler List Processing**

To illustrate the processing of exit handlers, suppose that a process has its
exit handler lists set up as shown in Figure 26.20. When the image requests
the $EXIT system service from user mode, EXE$EXIT takes the following
steps:

1. EXE$EXIT finds a nonzero listhead for user mode exit control blocks.
   The listhead points to the exit control block for procedure C, the most
   recently declared user mode exit handler.
2. EXE$EXIT stores this address in R0 and clears the listhead. It then ex-
   ecutes an REI instruction to change access mode to user and then calls
   procedure C. When C returns, EXE$EXIT calls procedure B and finally
   procedure A. When A returns, EXE$EXIT determines that the user mode
   list is exhausted (because the forward pointer in the last exit handler
   is zero). EXE$EXIT, running in user mode, requests the $EXIT system
   service.
3. As in step 1, the search for exit handlers begins with user mode but this
   list is now empty. EXE$EXIT continues with the supervisor mode list,
   which has the single exit control block for handler D. The supervisor
   listhead is cleared, access mode is changed to supervisor, and procedure
   D is called. When D returns, EXE$EXIT again requests the $EXIT system
   service, this time from supervisor mode.
4. Now the search for exit handlers begins with supervisor mode, whose list
   is empty. The list for executive mode contains two exit handlers, F and
   E, which are called from executive mode. When they return, the $EXIT
   system service is again requested, this time from executive access mode.
   The search that now begins with the executive mode listhead fails and
   the process is deleted.

The logic illustrated here shows how a process can prevent image exit
through the use of exit handlers. Suppose EXE$EXIT called a supervisor mode
handler that redeclared itself. When EXE$EXIT exhausted the exit handler
list and requested the $EXIT system service again, the handler would be back

on the supervisor mode exit handler list and would be reentered to redeclare itself again.

In fact, this use of exit handlers is just the mechanism employed by the DCL and MCR CLIs to allow multiple images to execute, one after another, in the same process. This mechanism is discussed in more detail in Chapter 27.

Note that an exit handler that is declared later (which implies that it will be called earlier) can prevent previously declared handlers for the same access mode from even being called by simply requesting the $EXIT system service. In the previous example, procedure C could prevent exit handlers B and A from being called by requesting $EXIT itself.

26.3 IMAGE AND PROCESS RUNDOWN

In any process that has had a CLI mapped by LOGINOUT, multiple images can execute one after another. Several steps must be taken to prevent a later image from inheriting either enhancements (such as elevated privileges) or degradations (such as a reduced working set) from a previous image. In addition, when a process is deleted, all traces of it must be eliminated from the system data structures and all reusable resources returned to the system.

The $RUNDWN system service serves both those needs. (Note that use of the $RUNDWN system service is reserved to the VMS operating system. Any other use is completely unsupported.)

$RUNDWN is called with one argument, access mode. This argument enables $RUNDWN to distinguish between image rundown and process rundown. The service is requested with an argument of user mode by both the DCL and MCR CLIs to clean up between image executions. $RUNDWN is also requested from the $DELPRC system service (see Chapter 28) with an argument of kernel mode to remove traces of a process being deleted.

The $RUNDWN system service performs much of its work by requesting other system services. $RUNDWN passes its access mode argument to these services to allow them to determine how much work to do. For example, the Dequeue Lock Request ($DEQ) system service (see Chapter 10) can be requested with an access mode argument to release all locks for that access mode and all outer modes. If $RUNDWN is requested with an argument of user mode, its $DEQ request cancels only user mode locks. If $RUNDWN is requested with an argument of kernel mode, then all process locks are dequeued.

The $RUNDWN system service procedure, EXE$RUNDWN in module SYSRUNDWN, runs in kernel mode. It first maximizes the access mode argument with the access mode of its caller. That is, the less privileged access mode is passed to other system services. Used in the following list, the phrase "based on access mode" means "perform this operation for this access mode and all outer (less privileged) access modes."

The following steps describe its actions:

1. EXE$RUNDWN clears any previously requested powerfail asynchronous system trap (AST) and returns AST quota to the process.
2. If any per-process or systemwide executive mode rundown routines are defined, EXE$RUNDWN invokes them from executive mode.
3. It requests the Set Resource Wait Mode ($SETRWM) system service, enabling resource wait mode to ensure that image rundown completes successfully.
4. EXE$RUNDWN invokes any per-process or systemwide kernel mode rundown routines. Such a routine might perform cleanup for user-written system services.
5. It invokes the License Management Facility (LMF) rundown routine to release any license units granted to the exiting image or process.
6. It resets the process's current CPU capability and affinity requirements to their permanent values. Chapter 12 explains these requirements.
7. If image accounting is enabled, an image deletion message is written to the accounting log file.
8. EXE$RUNDWN increments the image counter (PHD$L_IMGCNT). This counter prevents the delivery of ASTs to an image that has exited. The use of this synchronization technique in the operation of the Get Job/Process Information ($GETJPI) system service is described in Chapter 13.
9. The four P1 space vectors for user-written system services, user-written rundown routines, and image-specific message sections are reset to contain RSB instructions.
10. EXE$RUNDWN requests the Set Page Fault Monitoring ($SETPFM) system service to disable any monitoring of process page faults.
11. EXE$RUNDWN searches the channel control block table for channels to deassign. It compares the access mode of each assigned channel to that of the rundown. For each channel assigned in the same or an outer mode, EXE$RUNDWN requests the Deassign Channel ($DASSGN) system service. The deassign completes unless the channel has an open file. The access mode comparison prevents process-permanent files from being closed when an image is being run down ($RUNDWN from user mode). Other channels that are not deassigned at this stage of image rundown include the image file and any other file that is mapped to a range of virtual addresses.

    If the channel's assigned mode is more privileged, EXE$RUNDWN makes an additional check of the flag CCB$V_IMGTMP to see whether the channel is associated with the Breakthrough ($BRKTHRU) system service. If it is, EXE$RUNDWN deassigns the channel so that broadcast operations are aborted at image exit.

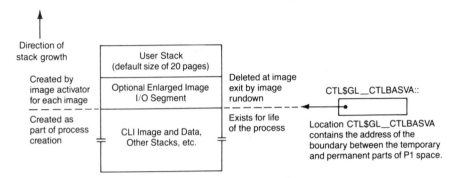

Figure 26.21
Low-Address End of P1 Space That Is Deleted at
Image Exit

12. The rights database identifier table is deallocated to the P1 process allocation region.

13. EXE$RUNDWN requests the Cancel Timer ($CANTIM) and the Cancel Wakeup ($CANWAK) system services to cancel any requests made from this and outer access modes.

14. It requests the $DEQ service to release locks for this and outer access modes.

15. EXE$RUNDWN invokes MMG$IMGRESET, in module PHDUTL, to reset the image pages. MMG$IMGRESET performs the image cleanup associated with memory management:

   a. MMG$IMGRESET invokes RM$RESET, in module RMSRESET, to reset the image I/O segment.

   b. It invokes EXE$PSCAN_IMGRESET, in module PROCESS_SCAN, to remove and deallocate process scan blocks, restoring the context of the Process Scan ($PROCESS_SCAN) system service.

   c. It returns memory management working set peak checking to its previous state.

   d. MMG$IMGRESET releases all ICBs that describe currently mapped images and places them on the ICB lookaside list. If any ICBs remain on the work list, it places them on the ICB lookaside list as well.

   e. All of P0 space is deleted. This frees the main image file and any other image file currently mapped. Physical pages are released, and blocks in the page files assigned to the process are deallocated.

   f. The nonpermanent parts of P1 space are deleted. These are the user stack and an optional enlarged image I/O segment (see Figure 26.21). Any expansions to P1 space (at smaller virtual addresses than the user stack) are also deleted, as well as VAX DEBUG dynamic memory.

   g. The working set list is reset to its default value, undoing any previous expansion or contraction performed by the Adjust Working Set Limit

($ADJWSL) system service. Working set size changes are described in Chapter 17.

h. MMG$IMGRESET raises IPL to 2 and invokes MMG$SECTBLRST, which compresses the process section table.

i. The process privilege masks in the process header and PCB are reset to their permanent value, found at location CTL$GQ_PROCPRIV. This step eliminates any privilege enhancements to the process resulting from the execution of an image installed with privilege. Section 26.4 describes the various privilege masks.

j. The global location CTL$GL_IMGHDRBF is cleared to indicate that no image is active.

k. If the process was the last accessor of a global section, releasing the process address space may make the global section deletable. If so, the global sections are deleted under the protection of the global section mutex. The associated WCB is released as well.

l. The pointer to the end of the active working set list (PHD$W_WSLAST) is reset to the end of the minimum working set list.

16. The channel deassignment loop performed in step 11 is executed again. However, because the image file and other mapped files have now been dissociated from virtual address space, the channels associated with those files will also be deassigned. As in step 11, this deassignment is based on access mode, so that process-permanent files are unaffected by image rundown.

17. EXE$RUNDWN requests the Deallocate Device ($DALLOC) system service to deallocate devices allocated from this and outer access modes.

18. It requests the Disassociate Common Event Flag Cluster ($DACEFC) system service to dissociate clusters 2 and 3.

19. EXE$RUNDWN acquires the SCHED spinlock, elevating IPL to IPL$_SCHED.

20. EXE$RUNDWN checks the system error log mailbox queue EXE$AQ_ERLMBX. EXE$RUNDWN deassigns each error log mailbox belonging to this process. The method for declaring an error log mailbox is described in Chapter 32.

21. All pending AST control blocks (ACBs) are removed from the list in the process control block (PCB), based on access mode. If user AST quota was charged for the AST, the quota is returned. If the ACB is deletable, it is deallocated to nonpaged pool. This operation starts at the tail of the list and proceeds toward the head of the list until an ACB is found with a more privileged (smaller) access mode than the $RUNDWN access mode or until the AST pending queue is empty. (Recall from Chapter 7 that ASTs are enqueued in order of increasing access mode.)

22. Any change mode handlers for this and outer access modes are eliminated. Because change mode handlers only exist for user and supervisor

modes, this step results in elimination of a change-mode-to-user handler every time an image exits and the elimination of a change-mode-to-supervisor handler when the process is deleted.

23. Any exit handlers for this and outer access modes are canceled.

24. Exception handlers found in the primary, secondary, and last chance vectors are eliminated for this and outer access modes.

25. The AST active bits for this and outer access modes are cleared. The AST enable bits for this and outer access modes are set.

26. System service failure exceptions are disabled for this and outer access modes.

27. Any compatibility mode handler that has been declared is canceled.

28. A new value of ASTLVL is calculated by routine SCH$NEWLVL, in module ASTDEL, to reflect the change in the AST queue resulting from step 21.

29. The force exit pending (PCB$V_FORCPEN) and wake pending (PCB$V_WAKEPEN) flags in the PCB are cleared. After clearing these flags, EXE$RUNDWN releases the SCHED spinlock, lowering IPL to 2.

30. It reenables AST delivery to user mode by clearing CTL$GB_SOFT_AST_DISABLE and CTL$GB_REENABLE_ASTS.

31. EXE$RUNDWN deletes all process logical names based on access mode. At image exit, all user mode logical names are deleted. At process deletion, all process logical names are deleted.

32. EXE$RUNDWN resets any P0 extension made to the process allocation region (see Chapter 19).

33. Resource wait mode is returned to its previous state, normal completion status is set, and control is returned to the requestor.

26.4 PROCESS PRIVILEGES

The VMS executive prevents unauthorized use of the system through process privileges. One or more of these privileges are required to perform particular system services, execute certain commands, or use privileged utilities.

26.4.1 Process Privilege Masks

A process has three sets of privileges available to it: privileges available while executing a particular image, privileges available to the current process context, and privileges from which the process can selectively alter its current context. Each set of privileges is represented by a quadword bit mask. A set bit means the process has the privilege corresponding to that bit.

VMS maintains the following privilege masks for processes and images. Table 26.2 summarizes the use of the masks.

- PCB$Q_PRIV exists in the access rights block, which is currently a part of the software PCB. It is also referenced by the symbol ARB$Q_PRIV.

Table 26.2   Process Privilege Masks

Symbolic Name	Use of This Mask	Modified by	Referenced by
PCBQ_PRIV, ARBQ_PRIV	Working privilege mask	EXE$PROCSTRT, LOGINOUT, $SETPRV, Image activator, MMG$IMGRESET	Device drivers, XQP, ACPs, System services requiring privilege
PHD$Q_PRIVMSK	Duplicate of ARB mask	Same as PCB$Q_PRIV	Some system services requiring privilege
CTL$GQ_PROCPRIV	Records permanently enabled privileges	EXE$PROCSTRT, LOGINOUT, $SETPRV	Image activator, SET/SHOW commands, MMG$IMGRESET
PHD$Q_AUTHPRIV	Records privileges from authorization file	EXE$PROCSTRT, LOGINOUT	$SETPRV, $GETJPI
PHD$Q_IMAGPRIV	Records privileges of installed image	Image activator	$SETPRV, LOGINOUT, $GETJPI
UAF$Q_PRIV	Records privileges in authorization file	AUTHORIZE	LOGINOUT
UAF$Q_DEF_PRIV	Records default privileges in authorization file	AUTHORIZE	LOGINOUT
KFE$Q_PROCPRIV	Records privileges with which an image is installed	Install Utility	Image activator
IHD$Q_PRIVREQS	Currently unused	Linker	Image activator

PCB$Q_PRIV contains the working privilege mask, sometimes called an image-specific privilege mask. This mask is checked by most system services that require privilege, and by the file system. At image activation, the mask is initialized to the combination of the privileges of the image and the privileges of the current process context. It can be altered by the Set Privileges ($SETPRV) system service, either during image execution or from DCL level. It is reset at image rundown to the current process privileges.

- The other image-specific privilege mask is PHD$Q_PRIVMSK in the process header. It is a duplicate of the privilege mask in the ARB and is altered in the same manner. Some older system services reference this mask rather than ARB$Q_PRIV.

- Current process privileges (also called process-permanent privileges) are stored in the P1 pointer page at global location CTL$GQ_PROCPRIV. This mask is initialized at process creation from the UAF default privilege mask; from the privilege mask argument passed to the $CREPRC system service; or, for a subprocess, from the creator's current privilege mask. It can be altered by the $SETPRV system service, either during image execution or from DCL level. Its contents are copied to the working privilege mask at image rundown.

- The authorized privilege mask, PHD$Q_AUTHPRIV, does not change over the life of the process. It allows a process to remove a privilege from its current privilege mask with the $SETPRV system service and to later regain that privilege. The authorized privilege mask is initialized at process creation from the UAF privilege mask; the privilege mask argument passed to the $CREPRC system service; or, for a subprocess, the creator's current privilege mask.
- Each user's authorization file record contains the two privilege masks UAF$Q_DEF_PRIV and UAF$Q_PRIV. UAF$Q_DEF_PRIV contains the default privileges that LOGINOUT copies to CTL$GQ_PROCPRIV, PCB$Q_PRIV, and PHD$Q_PRIVMSK when an interactive user logs in. UAF$Q_PRIV contains the authorized privileges that LOGINOUT copies to PHD$Q_AUTHPRIV.
- KFE$Q_PROCPRIV records the privileges with which a known executable image has been installed. When a process runs such an image, those privileges are temporarily granted to the process as part of the working privilege mask.
- PHD$Q_IMAGPRIV contains a copy of the KFE$Q_PROCPRIV mask of the privileged known image while that image is executing in process context. This mask is used by the $SETPRV system service to allow an image installed with privilege to invoke the $SETPRV service without losing privileges.

26.4.2 $SETPRV System Service

The $SETPRV system service enables a process to alter its image-specific (PCB$Q_PRIV and PHD$Q_PRIVMSK) privilege masks or its image-specific and process-permanent (CTL$GQ_PROCPRIV) privilege masks, gaining or losing privileges as a result. In addition, the service can return the previous settings of either the image-specific or process-permanent privileges, if requested.

The $SETPRV system service procedure, EXE$SETPRV in module SYS-SETPRV, runs in kernel mode.

The path through EXE$SETPRV that disables privileges requires no special privilege and clears the requested privilege bits in the image-specific and, optionally, the process-permanent privilege masks.

The code path that enables privileges requires the requested privilege to be already included in the mask of privileges authorized for this process (PHD$Q_AUTHPRIV). If a process tries to acquire a privilege that is not in its authorized mask, the requested privilege is still granted if any one of the following three conditions holds:

- The process has SETPRV privilege in its authorized mask. A process with this privilege can acquire any other privilege with either the $SETPRV system service or the DCL command SET PROCESS/PRIVILEGES (which requests the $SETPRV system service).
- The system service was requested from executive or kernel mode. This condition allows either VMS or user-written system services to acquire whatever privileges they need without regard for whether the current process has SETPRV privilege. Such procedures must disable privileges granted in this fashion as part of their return path.
- The privilege is being acquired temporarily (enabled in the two image-specific privilege masks) and is included in the mask of privileges authorized for the image (PHD$Q_IMAGPRIV), or the SETPRV privilege is included in this mask. This allows an image to acquire a privilege without permanently granting the new privilege to the process. When the image exits, image rundown copies the process-permanent mask to the image-specific masks, removing privileges acquired temporarily.

Note that the implementation of the $SETPRV system service does not return an error if a nonprivileged process attempts to add unauthorized privileges. In such a case, the service clears all unauthorized bits in the requested privilege mask, loads the modified privilege mask, and returns the alternative success status SS$_NOTALLPRIV.

781

27 Process Dynamics

In my end is my beginning.

Motto of Mary, Queen of Scots

The three other chapters in Part VII, Life of a Process, describe the steps of process creation, image activation, and process deletion. This chapter describes the manner in which VMS components create processes on a user's behalf. It examines the circumstances under which the various components are invoked and the resulting process types.

In addition, this chapter describes the VMS mechanisms supporting the most common situation, a process that executes several images consecutively. Because this mode of operation occurs in all interactive and batch processes, these two process types are discussed in detail.

27.1 PROCESS CLASSIFICATION

A process can be classified by several characteristics:

- It is either a subprocess and part of its creator's job tree, sharing the job information block (JIB), or it is detached from its creator, a top-level process with an independent job tree of its own.
- It either interacts with a user and receives input from a terminal, or it is noninteractive and receives input from a file or device.
- It includes a command language interpreter (CLI) and can make the transition from one image to another, or it executes only one image and exits when the image does.

27.2 THE ROLE OF VMS COMPONENTS

Various VMS components initiate process creation by requesting the Create Process ($CREPRC) system service. They include

- The job controller for interactive and batch processes
- The Digital command language (DCL) CLI for subprocesses and noninteractive processes
- NETACP for network processes

Arguments to the $CREPRC system service determine process characteristics, particularly the arguments UIC, STSFLG, INPUT, and IMAGE. Chapter 25 discusses this system service and its arguments in detail. Tables 27.1, 27.2, and 27.3 provide examples of arguments passed to the $CREPRC system service by VMS components.

Some VMS components that implement portions of process startup execute in the context of the new process. When the process is created, the creator specifies an image later activated by EXE$PROCSTRT, as described in Chapter 25. This is generally the LOGINOUT image. One of LOGINOUT's functions is to map a CLI, generally DCL, into the process's P1 space. The CLI enables the process to execute successive images, accomplishing the transition from one image to the next. This mode of operation occurs in all interactive and batch processes, and is optional but common for detached and network processes. Sections 27.5 and 27.6 provide more information on LOGINOUT and CLIs. The total operation of a CLI, however, is beyond the scope of this chapter.

27.3   THE JOB CONTROLLER AND PROCESS CREATION

The job controller process manages the creation of nearly all interactive and batch processes. It creates an interactive process in response to unsolicited terminal input and a batch process as a result of the CLI response to the SUBMIT command. Unsolicited card reader input results in the creation of a batch input symbiont.

The terminal class driver and card reader driver notify the job controller of unsolicited input via the job controller mailbox. The CLI, in response to a SUBMIT command, notifies the job controller of a batch process creation request. The job controller creates an appropriate process for each input source. The sections that follow describe these steps in more detail.

The process created by the job controller executes the image LOGINOUT. The actions that LOGINOUT takes, especially mapping a CLI into P1 space, differentiate processes that can execute multiple images in succession, such as interactive and batch processes, from processes that exit after the execution of a single image.

27.3.1   Unsolicited Terminal Input

The common terminal driver character-processing routine takes special action for unsolicited terminal input:

- If the terminal has the characteristic NO_TYPEAHEAD, the driver ignores the unsolicited input and dismisses the interrupt.
- If the terminal is owned, the driver inserts the character into the type-ahead buffer. If the owner process had requested notification of unsolicited input, the driver notifies the owner process.
- If the terminal is unowned and has the characteristic SECURE, it is attached to a secure server. The terminal driver inserts the character into the type-ahead buffer.
- If the terminal is unowned and has the AUTOBAUD characteristic, the driver tests the incoming character. It senses the baud rate and sets it as appropriate. If the character is a standard terminator recognized by the driver, the driver sends a message to the job controller mailbox, notifying the job controller that an unowned terminal has received an unsolicited

Table 27.1   Arguments Resulting in Interactive Process Creation

Argument Passed to $CREPRC	Value
Process name	_ttcu:
UIC	[1,4]
Image name	SYS$SYSTEM:LOGINOUT.EXE
SYS$INPUT	ttcu:
SYS$OUTPUT	ttcu:
SYS$ERROR	ttcu:
Base priority	DEFPRI (SYSGEN parameter)
Privilege mask	TMPMBX, NETMBX, SETPRV
Status flags	PRC$V_INTER

interrupt. The driver then inserts the input character into the type-ahead buffer.

In a sense, the job controller is the default owner of all otherwise unclaimed terminals.

If the type-ahead buffer does not exist when the driver attempts to insert a character, the driver initiates a fork thread to create the buffer. The current character, however, is discarded.

The job controller routine that responds to unsolicited terminal input simply requests the $CREPRC system service. Table 27.1 shows the arguments it passes to the system service.

The string *ttcu:* indicates the controller and unit of the terminal where the unsolicited input was typed. The terminal device type can be an actual physical device; an LT device, if the terminal is connected through a DECserver; an RT device, if the terminal is remote; a VT device, if virtual terminal support is enabled; or a TW device for DECwindows.

Note that the job controller creates each interactive process with a process name indicating its input device and LOGINOUT as the image to be executed. The creation of an interactive process is pictured schematically in Figure 27.1.

27.3.2   SUBMIT Command

When the SUBMIT command is entered, the CLI activates the SUBMIT.EXE image. SUBMIT sends messages to the job controller mailbox via the Send to Job Controller ($SNDJBC) system service. The job controller reads the mailbox messages and creates a job record in its data file, JBCSYSQUE.DAT. It inserts the job record onto an internal list of pending requests for the desired batch execution queue or generic queue. When the number of active jobs in a batch execution queue drops below its maximum value, the job

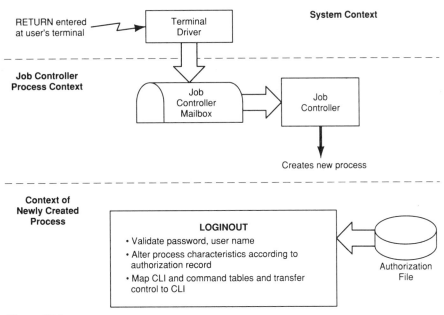

Figure 27.1
Creation of an Interactive Process

controller selects the queue's highest priority pending request. It requests the $CREPRC system service to create a process for that request, specifying LOGINOUT as the image to be executed.

The job controller specifies _NLA0: as the SYS$INPUT value and the string BATCH_ plus queue entry number as the process name, SYS$OUTPUT, and SYS$ERROR value. LOGINOUT later redefines SYS$INPUT to be the name of the batch command procedure, and SYS$OUTPUT and SYS$ERROR to be the name of a log file in an appropriate directory. Because LOGINOUT maps the appropriate CLI into the process P1 space, the batch input file can contain a series of command language statements. Figure 27.2 shows the processing of the SUBMIT command. Table 27.2 shows the arguments that the job controller passes to $CREPRC for a batch process.

27.3.3 Unsolicited Card Reader Input

An alternative method for starting a batch process uses the "hot" card reader feature implemented in the card reader driver interrupt service routine. Like the terminal driver, the card reader driver informs the job controller that an unsolicited interrupt has occurred on an unowned device. The job controller creates a process to service the unsolicited interrupt. The process executes an input symbiont, the image INPSMB.EXE, rather than LOGINOUT. Table 27.3 shows the arguments passed to the $CREPRC system service by the job controller.

The letter c represents the controller number. The unit number is always

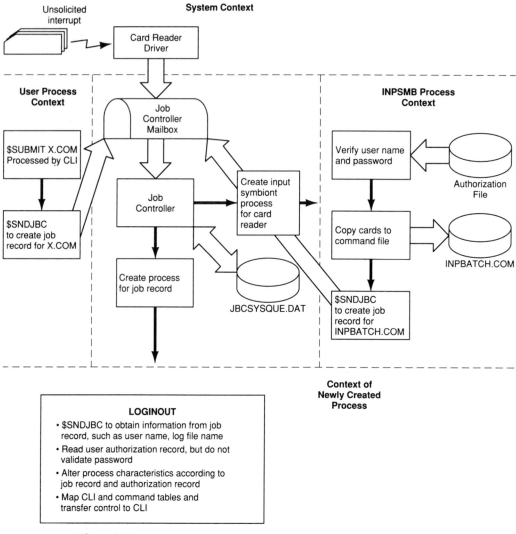

Figure 27.2
Creation of a Batch Process

zero because the card reader controller supports only one unit. The fact that this process has a card reader for its output device is irrelevant, because the input symbiont does not write to either SYS$OUTPUT or SYS$ERROR.

The input symbiont reads the $JOB and $PASSWORD cards and performs a validation similar to the one performed by LOGINOUT. After determining the user's default directory from the authorization record, the input symbiont opens a file in that directory and reads the rest of the job cards into that file. By default, it names the file INPBATCH.COM. Terminating conditions of this read are an end of file, an $EOJ card, or another $JOB card.

Once the input stream has been read into the user's directory, the input

Table 27.2   Arguments Resulting in Batch Process
Creation

Argument Passed to $CREPRC	*Value*
Process name	BATCH_nnn
UIC	[1,4]
Image name	SYS$SYSTEM:LOGINOUT.EXE
SYS$INPUT	_NLA0:
SYS$OUTPUT	BATCH_nnn
SYS$ERROR	BATCH_nnn
Base priority	DEFPRI (SYSGEN parameter)
Privilege mask	All
Status flags	PRC$V_BATCH

Table 27.3   Arguments Resulting in Input Symbiont
Process

Argument Passed to $CREPRC	*Value*
Process name	_CRc0:
UIC	[1,4]
Image name	SYS$SYSTEM:INPSMB.EXE
SYS$INPUT	CRc0:
SYS$OUTPUT	CRc0:
SYS$ERROR	CRc0:
Base priority	DEFPRI (SYSGEN parameter)
Privilege mask	TMPMBX, NETMBX, SETPRV
Status flags	None

symbiont sends a message to the job controller to create a job record for the stream. The operation proceeds from this point in exactly the same manner as for the SUBMIT command. That is, the job controller and LOGINOUT collaborate to produce a process with the card file as SYS$INPUT and a log file as SYS$OUTPUT and SYS$ERROR. Figure 27.2 shows this flow.

27.4   SPAWN AND ATTACH

DCL provides two commands to create and connect with interactive subprocesses. The DCL command SPAWN creates interactive subprocesses. The ATTACH command transfers terminal control from one process to another within the same job. The module [DCL]SPAWN contains the code for both commands. The Run-Time Library procedures LIB$SPAWN and LIB$ATTACH make the SPAWN and ATTACH functions available to an image by passing the request back to the DCL CLI. The major difference between the two ways of requesting the function is the method of passing parameters. From DCL level, the command line is parsed to obtain the parameters. The Run-Time Library procedures use an argument list.

27.4.1   SPAWN

Spawning a subprocess primarily involves copying process context information from the creating process to the subprocess. This information includes the process CLI symbols, process-private logical names, current privileges, out-of-band asynchronous system trap (AST) settings, verify flag settings, prompt string, default disk and directory, keypad definitions and states, and the command line that was passed to SPAWN (if one exists).

In response to a SPAWN request, DCL performs the following operations:

1. It parses the command line to determine what qualifiers are present. It validates the qualifiers and copies them to a temporary data structure.
2. It temporarily disables the current process's out-of-band ASTs, blocking CTRL/Y ASTs during a critical section of code.
3. It creates or locates a termination mailbox and requests an attention AST if a message is written to the mailbox.

    Termination information from the subprocess is written to the termination mailbox when the subprocess is eventually deleted. The attention AST is delivered to the subprocess's creator at that time. Because four spawned subprocesses can share the same termination mailbox, DCL checks for an available one that the new subprocess can share before creating a new mailbox.
4. DCL records the name of the subprocess's CLI and command table files in P1 space locations. The $CREPRC system service later copies them to the process quota block (PQB). When LOGINOUT eventually runs in the context of the new subprocess, this is the CLI that it will invoke. The default, if no CLI is specified, is the creator's CLI.
5. For CLIs supplied by Digital, DCL creates a second mailbox, called the communication mailbox, through which further context information is transferred to the spawned subprocess, as described in step 10.
6. DCL creates an attach request mailbox for the current process with a jobwide logical name of the form DCL$ATTACH_*pid*, where *pid* is the extended process ID. Other processes in the job tree can attach to this process by writing attach requests to this mailbox.
7. DCL requests the Get Job/Process Information ($GETJPI) system service to determine the current process's nondeductible quotas. From these quotas, it builds a quota list to be used in the creation of the spawned subprocess.
8. If the process name was not specified in the command line or argument list, DCL creates one by appending _*n* to the user name string, where *n*

is a value from 1 to 255. If the new name is a duplicate, DCL increments *n* and tries again.

9. DCL requests the $CREPRC system service to create the subprocess. It specifies LOGINOUT as the IMAGE argument and the name of the communication mailbox from step 5 as the ERROR argument. If the creating process does not specify input and output files to the SPAWN command, DCL uses the creating process's SYS$INPUT and SYS$OUTPUT file specifications as the INPUT and OUTPUT arguments. It specifies the termination mailbox from step 3 to the $CREPRC service to receive a process deletion message from the subprocess. Because the request does not include a privilege mask for the subprocess, the $CREPRC system service creates the subprocess with the current privileges of the current process (see Chapter 25).

10. When LOGINOUT runs in the context of the newly spawned subprocess, it maps the specified CLI, DCL in this example, and passes control to it. DCL determines that it is running in the context of a subprocess and translates the logical name SYS$ERROR. If there is a supervisor mode translation with a mailbox name as the equivalence string, DCL recognizes that a SPAWN operation is in progress and that it must read context information from the creating process.

    At this point, both the creating process and the spawned subprocess are executing DCL routines. The creating process passes context information to the spawned subprocess in the following manner:

    a. The spawned subprocess assigns a channel to the communication mailbox and issues read requests to it.

    b. The creating process writes context information to the mailbox, one record at a time. Each record has a type code identifying its contents. When the subprocess receives the information, it adds the information to its context.

    c. The first transferred record contains the permanently enabled privilege mask (CTL$GQ_PROCPRIV), verify flag setting, out-of-band AST flag settings, and prompt string.

       The spawned subprocess reads the record and initializes the process accordingly. It requests the Set Privilege ($SETPRV) system service to disable all privileges, then resets the process privileges from those transferred in the record. Thus, the working, permanently enabled (current), and authorized privilege masks of the subprocess contain the privileges its creator possessed when the spawn occurred. This enables a privileged image to tailor the environment in a spawned subprocess.

    d. Next, the creating process transfers the SPAWN command string (if one was specified).

    e. The creating process then scans the process logical name directory,

789

which contains a list of process logical name table names. It copies all table names that were defined in user or supervisor mode and that do not have the CONFINE attribute. It then copies all the logical names defined in those tables. The spawned subprocess creates the corresponding logical name tables and their logical names.

f. The creating process then transfers the contents of the symbol table, one symbol at a time, followed by terminal keypad definitions. The spawned subprocess receives each symbol and places it into the symbol table. Note that the creating process's potentially modified DCL command tables are not transferred to the subprocess.

11. Once it has transferred all information to the subprocess, the creating process tests whether it should wait for the subprocess. If so, it requests a write attention AST on the attach request mailbox and hibernates. Otherwise it restores out-of-band ASTs and resumes normal processing.

12. The spawned subprocess deletes the supervisor mode logical name SYS$ERROR, leaving the executive mode logical name. It restores out-of-band ASTs and, if the subprocess is interactive, issues a special I/O request to the terminal driver to declare the subprocess the terminal owner. It then continues normal DCL processing.

When a subprocess created by the SPAWN command is deleted, a termination message is written to its creator's termination mailbox. As a result, a write attention AST is queued to the creator. The AST procedure simply performs cleanup work pertaining to the deleted subprocess. It deassigns the channels to the attach and termination mailboxes and deletes the mailboxes. If the subprocess was created by a call to LIB$SPAWN and if an event flag or AST procedure was specified in the call, the event flag is set or the AST is delivered.

27.4.2 ATTACH

The DCL ATTACH request transfers terminal control from the process that issues the command to a target process. The operation of the DCL ATTACH routine is as follows:

1. From the context of the issuing process, DCL first disables out-of-band ASTs, blocking delivery of CTRL/Y ASTs. It then obtains the name or process identification (PID) of the target process. It verifies that the target process is not itself and that it is a process in the same job tree.

2. DCL creates an attach request mailbox and logical name for the issuing process. Since interactive input will be detached from the issuing process and attached to the target process, the issuing process must have an attach mailbox to accept attach requests later. Otherwise, the terminal cannot be reattached to it.

3. DCL locates the target process's attach mailbox and writes the name of

the current output stream (usually the equivalence name of SYS$INPUT) to the mailbox. Since the target process had declared a write attention AST on its attach mailbox, it is notified of the message placed in the mailbox. The original process then issues a read request on the target process's attach mailbox in anticipation of a message from the target.

4. The target process wakes in response to the write attention AST. The AST procedure determines whether the target process is already attached to a terminal. If not, it writes an affirmative response (a longword with a value of 1) to the attach mailbox. Otherwise, it writes a zero longword to refuse the attach request and reenables the write attention AST for the attach mailbox.

5. Once it receives the affirmation, DCL in the original process deassigns its channel to the target process's attach mailbox. It requests a write attention AST for its own attach mailbox so it can be notified of any incoming attach requests. It then hibernates.

6. The AST procedure in the target process issues a wake request to return control to the target process.

27.5 THE LOGINOUT IMAGE

The LOGINOUT image provides three major functions:

1. It validates a user's access to the system, checking password information in the authorization file.
2. It adjusts various process quotas and defaults based on information from the authorization file or from the job controller.
3. It maps a CLI into P1 space.

LOGINOUT need not perform all these functions for every process. Its actions are based on the original arguments passed to the $CREPRC system service, stored in the process control block (PCB), process header (PHD), and P1 space. For example, it does not perform password validation if the $CREPRC STSFLG argument PRC$V_NOUAF was specified.

The LOGINOUT image is installed with privileges, which it enables and disables based on the current function. The image executes primarily in user mode, with some executive and kernel mode procedures.

Normally, the $CREPRC IMAGE argument specifies LOGINOUT and the image is activated by EXE$PROCSTRT. However, under certain conditions, the image activator independently invokes LOGINOUT. Chapter 26 contains further details.

The LOGINOUT modules are located in the facility [LOGIN].

27.5.1 LOGINOUT and Interactive Processes

When the LOGINOUT image executes in an interactive process created in response to unsolicited terminal input, it must verify that the user has access to the system before proceeding with the rest of its operations. It performs the following steps:

1. It establishes a user mode call frame condition handler to service any exceptions or software conditions that occur while LOGINOUT is executing. Should this handler be called, it first requests the Put Message ($PUTMSG) system service to write an error message. It then checks the type and severity of the condition. If the status code has not already been stored in P1 space, the handler stores it in preparation for writing the code to the termination mailbox.

   If the condition is a severe error, the handler requests the Exit ($EXIT) system service from executive mode, causing the process to be deleted. Otherwise, it returns, and LOGINOUT continues execution.

   LOGINOUT declares this same condition handler for many of its executive mode procedures.

2. LOGINOUT requests the $GETJPI system service to obtain the user name, process status flags, job type, and process owner.

3. LOGINOUT requests the Get Device Information ($GETDVI) system service to obtain the name and characteristics of SYS$INPUT.

4. It translates the logical names SYS$INPUT, SYS$OUTPUT, and SYS$ERROR in the LNM$PROCESS table and saves the resultant strings for later use.

5. LOGINOUT initializes the process-permanent data (PPD) region in P1 space. This region is shared by LOGINOUT and the CLI it maps.

6. LOGINOUT classifies the process as one of the following five mutually exclusive types and performs type-specific initialization:

   —Batch—The batch bit is set in CTL$GL_CREPRC_FLAGS, a copy of the flags specified to the $CREPRC system service.

   —Network—The network bit is set in CTL$GL_CREPRC_FLAGS.

   —Subprocess—The parent PID is nonzero.

   —Interactive—The interactive bit is set and the nopassword bit is clear in CTL$GL_CREPRC_FLAGS.

   A DECwindows process is an interactive process whose input device type is DC$_WORKSTATION.

   —Detached—Anything not covered by the previous types.

7. For an interactive process, typically one created in response to unsolicited input from a terminal, LOGINOUT performs the following steps:

   a. It initializes the user name and account name fields in the JIB and P1 space to the string <login>.

   b. It creates process-permanent files for the input and output devices through calls to Record Management Services (RMS). LOGINOUT redefines the logical names SYS$INPUT and SYS$OUTPUT in the LNM$PROCESS table. It defines the logical names SYS$ERROR and

SYS$COMMAND with the same equivalence strings as SYS$OUT-PUT and SYS$INPUT. It prefixes the equivalence names for these logical names by four bytes: an escape ($1B_{16}$), a null character (00_{16}), and the two-byte internal file identifier (IFI) returned by RMS. When RMS receives such a string as a result of logical name translation, it uses the IFI as an index into one of its internal tables. Accessing by IFI allows fast access to these commonly used files.

c. In the case of an interactive login, the input device must be a terminal device. Otherwise, LOGINOUT exits with the error message "invalid SYS$INPUT for interactive login."

d. If the terminal line has modem control enabled, LOGINOUT requires the TT$V_REMOTE bit to be set. This bit notifies the driver that the process must be logged off or disconnected if the modem signals disappear.

e. LOGINOUT determines whether the job type is local, dialup, or remote, based on the characteristics of the SYS$INPUT terminal. It stores this status in the JIB, at offset JIB$B_JOBTYPE, and copies the terminal name to PCB$T_TERMINAL.

It marks an interactive DECwindows process as local but does not store a terminal name for it.

f. LOGINOUT determines whether there is a system password and whether it applies to this terminal. If there is, it issues a timed, no-echo read to the terminal and checks the password entered by the user.

g. It then translates the logical name SYS$ANNOUNCE and writes the announcement message defined by the system manager.

h. LOGINOUT checks whether autologins are enabled for the terminal that is logging in. If they are, LOGINOUT looks up the terminal name in SYS$SYSTEM:SYSALF.DAT to determine the user name associated with the terminal. It then reads the user authorization file (UAF) record associated with the user and stores the user name in the JIB and in CTL$T_USERNAME in P1 space.

LOGINOUT prompts for, reads, and verifies the password, if one is required. If there is a secondary password for the account, it prompts for, reads, and verifies that as well.

i. If autologins are not enabled for the SYS$INPUT terminal, LOGIN-OUT prompts on it for the user name. It reads and parses the input, noting the presence of qualifiers, such as /CONNECT and /CLI. It opens the system authorization file and reads the record associated with that user, if any. LOGINOUT stores the user name in the JIB and in CTL$T_USERNAME.

Whether the desired UAF record exists or not, LOGINOUT always prompts for the password. It reads and verifies the password and, if there is a secondary password for the account, prompts for, reads, and verifies that as well.

  j. If the account is captive or restricted, LOGINOUT checks that the user did not include login qualifiers to change aspects of the process environment fixed for that account.

  k. LOGINOUT then performs a scan of the intrusion database in non-paged pool. The type of scan performed depends on the success of user validation.

      If a user validation error (such as invalid user name or password) has occurred, a suspect scan is performed. If evasion is in effect, the user name is set and a break-in audit is performed. Otherwise, the failed password count is incremented in the user's UAF record, and a corresponding intrusion record is either created or updated.

      If the login was valid, an intruder scan is performed. If the user is found to be an intruder, a break-in audit is performed and the login terminates.

  l. If SYS$INPUT is not a remote terminal and reconnection is allowed for the account, LOGINOUT then checks whether the user has disconnected from a process that still exists. It performs a wildcard $GETJPI, looking for a process with the same user name and user identification code (UIC) and a disconnected terminal. It displays any matches and asks the user to which process, if any, the terminal should be connected. It records the answer for later use.

  m. If the user does not have OPER privilege, LOGINOUT checks that the interactive process count would not be exceeded by the logging in of this process, and that logins are not currently disabled.

8. LOGINOUT records some of the process attributes extracted from the authorization file in their proper places, overwriting the attributes placed there when the process was created:

—Default disk and directory string
—User name
—Base scheduling priority
—UIC

9. After the process's correct UIC has been set, LOGINOUT recreates the job logical name table and, possibly, the group logical name table.

10. LOGINOUT completes the local rights list entries based on the process charactistics and the identifiers associated with the UIC.

11. LOGINOUT copies the remaining attributes extracted from the authorization file to their proper places.

—It moves process quotas and limits, testing each to ensure that it is not less than the minimum.

—It copies the default privilege mask from the UAF record into PHD$Q_
AUTHPRIV and CTL$GQ_PROCPRIV.

—It initializes ARB$Q_PRIV and PHD$Q_PRIVMSK as the default privilege mask ORed with the image privilege mask.

—It copies information about primary and secondary day restrictions.

12. LOGINOUT attempts to change the process name from _ttcu: to the user
    name. This attempt fails if another process in the same group already
    has the same name. (A common cause of user name duplication is a user
    logged in at more than one terminal.) In the case of failure, the process
    retains its name (_ttcu:), guaranteed to be unique for a given system.

13. LOGINOUT checks a number of other fields in the authorization file
    record. These include the user or account job limit, the primary and
    secondary password expiration flags, the DISUSER flag, the account expi-
    ration time, and the account hourly restrictions. These checks are waived
    in the case of the SYSTEM account logging in on the console terminal.

14. LOGINOUT begins initialization for a CLI. It creates user mode logical
    names PROC0 through PROC9, each equated to the file specification of a
    command procedure (or indirect command file) to be executed before the
    CLI enters its input loop. Currently, only PROC0 and PROC1 are used.
    PROC0 is equated to the system name table translation of the logical
    name SYS$SYLOGIN.

    PROC1 is equated to the file specified by the LGICMD field of the
    user's UAF record or the file specified by the login qualifier /COMMAND
    at login time (by an authorized user). If the contents of the LGICMD
    field are null and no /COMMAND qualifier was present on the login
    command, PROC1 is equated to the string LOGIN. The LGICMD field
    should indicate the null device (using the string NL:) to provide a default
    of no login command file.

    When the CLI later executes its initialization code, it will translate
    these logical names and execute the command procedures (or indirect
    command files).

15. LOGINOUT requests a merged image activation of the selected CLI to
    map the CLI into the low-address end of P1 space. The procedure LIB$P1_
    MERGE first merges the CLI into P0 space to determine its size, deletes
    the P0 space, and maps the correct amount of P1 space. Next, the CLI's
    command table is mapped into P1 space, using the same procedure.

    Network and DECwindows processes always use DCL and DCL-
    TABLES as the CLI name and command table name. A restricted user
    receives the CLI name and command table name specified in the UAF
    record. However, an unrestricted interactive user can specify /CLI and
    /TABLE on the login command line to choose a particular CLI and com-
    mand table. If the login command line does not contain a /CLI qualifier,

LOGINOUT assigns the first nonzero CLI name in the following list to an unrestricted user:

—CTL$AG_CMEDATA, the CLI name specified by the image activator
—CTL$GT_SPAWNCLI, the CLI name specified by a parent process for a spawned subprocess
—The default CLI specified in the UAF record
—CTL$GT_CLINAME, the CLI name of the parent process
—DCL and DCLTABLES

16. LOGINOUT calls a kernel mode procedure to change the owner and protection of the CLI and command table pages. It changes the owner access mode for each page to supervisor and alters the protection on all writable pages to prevent writes from user mode.

17. To accommodate the CLI symbol table, LOGINOUT requests the Expand Process/Control Region ($EXPREG) system service to expand P1 space by a number of pages equal to the SYSGEN parameter CLISYMTBL. It updates the global location CTL$GL_CTLBASVA to reflect the new low-address end of P1 space.

18. If the DISWELCOME flag is clear in the UAF record, LOGINOUT writes to SYS$OUTPUT, announcing successful login. It first translates the logical name SYS$WELCOME and writes the welcome message defined by the system manager. If SYS$WELCOME is not defined, LOGINOUT writes the following message, obtaining the version number from the global location SYS$GQ_VERSION and the node name by translating the logical name SYS$NODE:

```
Welcome to VAX/VMS version V5.2 on node FOOBAR
```

19. If the DISREPORT flag is clear in the UAF record, LOGINOUT also writes the dates of the last interactive and noninteractive logins and the number of login failures since the last successful login. If the DISNEW-MAIL flag is clear, it writes the number of new mail messages for the user.

20. LOGINOUT creates the logical names SYS$LOGIN, SYS$LOGIN_DE-VICE, and SYS$SCRATCH in the process's job logical name table. The equivalence name for these logical names is the default disk and directory specified by the user's UAF record. (To override the default disk, follow the user name portion of the login sequence with the qualifier /DISK=ddcu:.)

    For a DECwindows terminal emulation window, LOGINOUT creates the logical name DECW$DISPLAY, with the workstation device name as the equivalence name. For a remote login, it creates the logical name SYS$REM_NODE, the remote node's name or address, and SYS$REM_ID, the remote user name.

21. LOGINOUT checks whether the primary or secondary password lifetime

has ended. If so, it marks the password as expired in the UAF record. If the DISFORCE flag is clear in the UAF record or if the user specified the /NEW_PASSWORD qualifier on the login command line, LOGINOUT forces the user to set a new password before continuing. If the DISFORCE flag is set, LOGINOUT informs the user that the password has expired, but allows the login to continue.

If the lifetime of either the primary or secondary password has not ended but is due to expire within five days, LOGINOUT warns the user of that fact.

22. LOGINOUT records the time of login in the UAF record. It notifies the security audit subsystem of the login.

23. At this point, LOGINOUT has finished its work and must pass control to the CLI. To pass control to the CLI, LOGINOUT calls an executive mode routine that performs the following actions:

    a. It changes the protection on pages in the PPD region so that the pages can only be accessed from supervisor and inner access modes.

    b. It copies the transfer address of the CLI from CTL$AG_CLIMAGE into the program counter (PC) from the Change Mode to Executive (CHME) exception.

    c. It modifies the processor status longword (PSL) in the exception PSL so that the current and previous mode fields contain supervisor mode.

    d. It returns to the change mode dispatcher, which exits from executive mode by executing an REI instruction. This returns the process to supervisor mode with the PC pointing to the first instruction in the CLI, its initialization routine.

27.5.2   LOGINOUT and Batch Processes

Many of the operations performed by LOGINOUT for an interactive process are also necessary for a batch process. For example, LOGINOUT must open the input and output streams and map the CLI. However, LOGINOUT does not perform password verification—either the input symbiont has already checked it or, in the case of a SUBMIT command, it is not necessary.

Rather than describing the steps performed by LOGINOUT again, the following list simply specifies those that are different for a batch process:

1. When the batch flag is set in CTL$GL_CREPRC_FLAGS, a copy of the flags originally specified to the $CREPRC system service, LOGINOUT takes actions to create a batch process.

2. It initializes the account name fields in the JIB and P1 space to the string <batch>.

3. LOGINOUT requests the $SNDJBC system service to obtain information about the batch process, for example, its user name, process priority, and working set information.

The prompted reads of user name and password, and the system announcements that occur in the login of an interactive process, are unnecessary for a batch process.

4. LOGINOUT opens the batch input file and log file as process-permanent files through calls to RMS. It defines the logical names SYS$INPUT and SYS$COMMAND with the batch input file name prefaced by the file IFI (returned by RMS) as the equivalence string. It defines the logical names SYS$OUTPUT and SYS$ERROR with the batch log file name prefaced by the file IFI (returned by RMS) as the equivalence string.

5. LOGINOUT reads the authorization file record for this user. It obtains process attributes to supplement information specified during batch queue creation and job submission. These values from the authorization file are minimized with the values returned by the job controller.

6. The job parameters, P1 through P8, if present, are defined as user mode logical names, which the CLI later translates.

The procedures of mapping the CLI and transferring control are exactly the same as if the process were interactive. In both cases, if SYS$SYLOGIN is defined as a system logical name, the first commands that execute are the commands in the site-specific login command file. If the UAF does not specify a user login command file, the command file SYS$LOGIN:LOGIN.COM is executed next (if the CLI is DCL).

27.5.3   LOGINOUT and Network Processes

The NETACP image requests the $CREPRC system service to create a network process. Many of the operations performed by LOGINOUT for a network process are similar to those for an interactive process. The major difference is that LOGINOUT does not necessarily map a CLI for a network process.

NETACP specifies the $CREPRC INPUT, OUTPUT, and ERROR arguments as follows:

- The INPUT argument is the name of a command procedure or executable image to be invoked by LOGINOUT.
- The OUTPUT argument is a flag indicating whether a proxy login is allowed, followed by access control information.
- The ERROR argument is the address of a network control block (NCB) for the connection.

LOGINOUT obtains the network logical link number from the NCB and stores the remote node name, address, and ID in P1 space. It checks to see whether the network process should use proxy login and performs validation of the access control information accordingly. It creates an executive mode logical name SYS$NET, which locates the NCB.

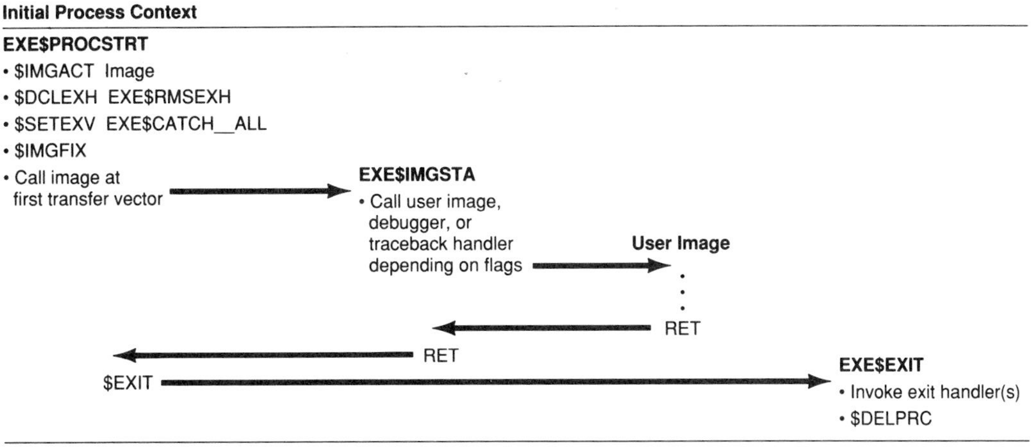

Initial Process Context

Figure 27.3
Process That Executes a Single Image

If the INPUT argument specified a file of type EXE rather than COM, LOG-INOUT activates the executable image from a small code segment in P1 space. Since no CLI is mapped, this process will be deleted when its image exits. This optimization decreases network process activation time. Otherwise, if the file type is COM, LOGINOUT activates a CLI to execute the file's commands and creates a log file.

27.6   CLIS AND IMAGE PROCESSING

Digital provides four CLIs that run under the VMS operating system: DCL, monitor console routine (MCR), DEC/Shell, and CSHELL. DCL is supplied with the VMS software. MCR, once a VMS component, is now part of the optional product VAX-11 RSX. This section describes features of DCL and MCR. The other CLIs are beyond the scope of this book.

After the DCL or MCR CLI gains control and performs some initialization, it reads and processes successive records from SYS$INPUT. This section describes those operations that result in image execution, to contrast interactive and batch processes with processes that do not map a CLI. The operations that DCL and MCR perform to activate an image are nearly identical. Any differences are explicitly mentioned.

One of the important steps that either CLI performs is the declaration of a supervisor mode exit handler. It is this handler that prevents process deletion following image exit and allows the successive execution of multiple images within the same process.

Figure 27.3 shows the flow of control in a process that does not map a CLI and thus executes only one image. Figure 27.4 shows the flow of control in a process that maps a CLI and thus can execute multiple images.

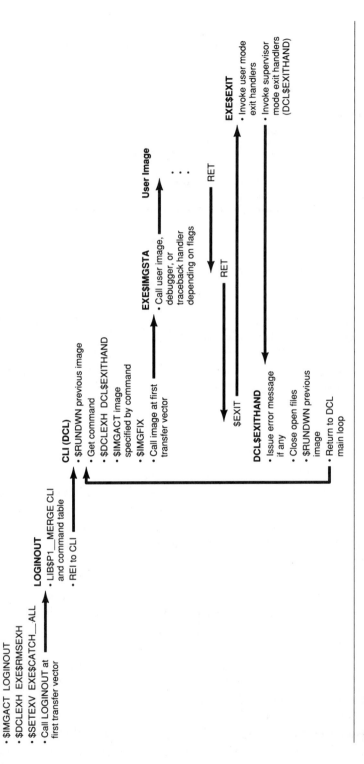

Figure 27.4
Process That Executes Multiple Images

27.6.1   **CLI Initialization**

The DCL CLI's initialization code is the routine DCL$STARTUP in module [DCL]INITIAL. For the MCR CLI, the initialization code is the routine MCR$STARTUP in module [MCR]MCRINIT. Running in supervisor mode, the initialization code performs the following steps before entering the main command processing loop:

1. The CLI clears the FP register and then calls itself, creating an initial call frame on the supervisor stack. This initial call frame therefore contains a zero in the saved FP, terminating the call frame chain. The CLI calls itself again and establishes a call frame condition handler.

2. The CLI writes the address of its CLI callback service routine in the global location CTL$AL_CLICALBK. Callback is a mechanism an image uses to obtain services from the CLI, such as symbol creation and lookup.

3. The CLI initializes its work area from internal variables transferred by LOGINOUT to the PPD region. It also initializes the CLI symbol table data structures.

4. For a batch process, the CLI translates the logical names for parameters P1 through P8. It creates symbols whose values are the equivalence names.

5. The CLI translates PROC0 through PROC9 and saves their equivalence names to identify the command procedures it must execute.

6. The CLI requests the Rundown ($RUNDWN) system service with an argument of user mode to run down the LOGINOUT image.

7. The CLI validates the structure of its command table.

8. It issues a special I/O request to the terminal driver, naming the process as the terminal owner.

9. DCL enables CTRL/Y and out-of-band ASTs on the terminal. MCR enables CTRL/Y ASTs. (CTRL/Y ASTs are not enabled if the UAF record had the DISCTLY flag set.)

10. The CLI calls the Declare Change Mode Handler ($DCLCMH) system service to establish a change-mode-to-supervisor handler. This handler allows the CLI to enter supervisor mode from user mode when it needs to access write protected data structures. One instance where this is required is in symbol definition, because CLI symbol tables are protected from write access by user mode.

11. Finally, the CLI branches to the first instruction of the main command processing loop (routine DCL$RESTART or MCR$RESTART).

27.6.2   **Command Processing Loop**

In the main command processing loop, the CLI reads a record from SYS$IN-PUT and takes whatever action is dictated by the command. The CLI can perform some actions directly. Others require the execution of a separate

Table 27.4   General Actions Performed by a Command Language Interpreter

General CLI Operations	Sample Commands
Commands that the CLI can execute internally (see Table 27.5)	EXAMINE, SET DEFAULT
Commands that require external images	COPY, LINK, some SET commands, some SHOW commands
Commands that require internal processing and an external image	LOGOUT, MCR, RUN
Foreign command definition	command_string :== $image-file-spec
Other operations that destroy an image	STOP, EXIT, invoking a command procedure
Other internal operations	Symbol definition

image. Table 27.4 lists the general operations performed by the CLI and indicates those actions that require an external image.

A simplified flow of control through a CLI is pictured in Figure 27.5.

After the CLI reads a record from the input stream and recognizes a command, it either performs the requested action itself or activates an external image. DCL or MCR can execute some commands without destroying a currently executing image. Table 27.5 lists these commands but does not include special commands used by the MCR indirect command file processor. Any other command either requires an image to execute (such as COPY or LINK) or directly affects the currently executing image (such as STOP).

27.6.3   Image Initiation by a CLI

When the CLI determines that an external image is required, it first performs some command-specific steps. It then enters a common routine to activate and call the image. The steps that it takes are nearly identical to the steps performed by EXE$PROCSTRT, described in Chapter 25:

1. The CLI requests the $RUNDWN system service, which removes any traces of a previously executing image, if one exists. If the previous image terminated normally, this request is unnecessary. However, if the user typed CTRL/Y followed by an external command, the normal image termination path is bypassed; the CLI must perform this extra step to ensure that the previous image is eliminated before another is activated.

2. The CLI declares an internal routine as a supervisor mode exit handler to regain control when the image exits. Recall from Chapter 26 that an exit handler must be redeclared after each use.

3. To activate the image, the CLI requests the Image Activate ($IMGACT) system service, described in Chapter 26.

4. If the activation succeeds, the CLI builds a PSL with a current mode

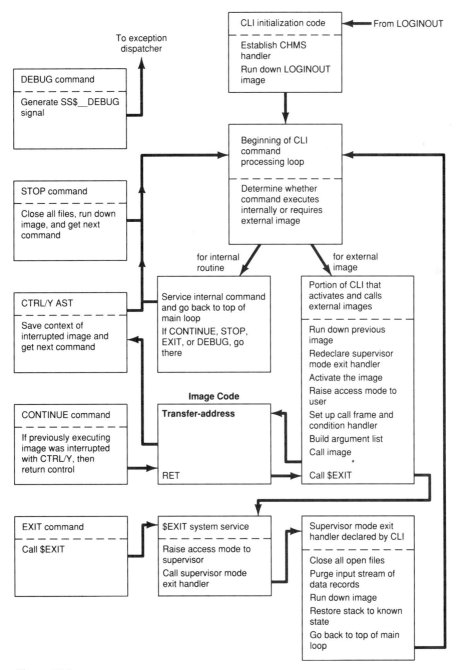

Figure 27.5
Simplified Control Flow Through a Command
Language Interpreter

803

Table 27.5   Commands Handled by CLI Internal Procedures

Command	Description
=	Create/modify a symbol
ALLOCATE	Allocate a device
ASSIGN[1]	Create a logical name
ATTACH	Transfer control to another process in job
CALL[1]	Transfer control to a labeled subroutine in a command procedure
CANCEL	Cancel scheduled wakeups for a process
CLOSE[1]	Close a process-permanent file
CONNECT[1]	Connect the physical terminal to a virtual terminal of another process
CONTINUE	Resume interrupted image
CREATE/NAME_TABLE	Create a new logical name table
DEALLOCATE	Deallocate a device
DEASSIGN	Delete a logical name
DEBUG	Invoke the symbolic debugger
DECK[1]	Delimit the beginning of an input stream
DEFINE	Create a logical name
DEFINE/KEY	Associate a character string and attributes with a terminal key
DELETE/KEY	Delete a key definition
DELETE/SYMBOL[1]	Delete a symbol definition
DEPOSIT	Modify a memory location
DISCONNECT[1]	Disconnect a physical terminal from a virtual terminal
EOD[1]	Delimit the end of an input stream
EOJ	Delimit the end of batch job submitted through card reader
EXAMINE	Examine a memory location
EXIT	Exit a command procedure
	Run down an image after invoking exit handlers
GOSUB[1]	Transfer control to a labeled subroutine in a command procedure
GOTO	Transfer control within a command procedure
IF/THEN/ELSE/ENDIF[1]	Conditional command execution
INQUIRE[1]	Interactively assign a value to a symbol
ON	Define conditional action
OPEN[1]	Open a process-permanent file
READ[1]	Read a record into a symbol
RECALL[1]	Display previously entered commands for possible reissue
RETURN[1]	Terminate a GOSUB subroutine procedure
SET CONTROL	Determine responses to CTRL/C, CTRL/Y,and CTRL/T
SET DEFAULT	Define default directory string
SET KEY	Change current terminal key definition state
SET [NO]ON	Determine error processing

(continued)

Table 27.5 Commands Handled by CLI Internal Procedures *(continued)*

Command	Description
SET OUTPUT_RATE	Set rate at which output is written to a batch job log file
SET PROMPT [1]	Change the CLI's prompt string
SET PROTECTION	Define default file protection
SET SYMBOL [1]	Alter scope of a symbol
SET UIC	Change process UIC and default directory string
SET [NO]VERIFY	Determine echoing of command procedure commands
SHOW DEFAULT	Display default directory string
SHOW KEY	Display terminal key definitions
SHOW PROTECTION	Display default file protection
SHOW QUOTA	Display current disk file usage
SHOW STATUS	Display status of currently executing image
SHOW SYMBOL	Display value of symbol(s)
SHOW TIME	Display current time
SHOW TRANSLATION	Show translation of single logical name
SPAWN	Create a subprocess and transfer control to it
STOP	Run down an image bypassing exit handlers
WAIT [1]	Wait for specified interval to elapse
WRITE [1]	Write the value of a symbol to a file

[1] These commands are available in the DCL CLI but not in the MCR CLI.

of user and pushes it onto the stack. It copies an internal CLI address onto the stack as a PC. It then executes an REI instruction, entering an internal routine with its access mode changed to user.

5. It clears the argument pointer (AP) and frame pointer (FP) registers and calls another internal routine, creating an initial call frame on the user stack. Because the saved FP in the call frame is zero, it will act as a terminator for a future user mode call frame chain.

6. It establishes the catch-all condition handler as the handler for this call frame and as the last chance exception handler.

7. It requests the Address Relocation Fixup ($IMGFIX) system service to relocate image addresses.

8. The CLI builds an argument list on the user stack to pass to the image and to any intervening procedures such as SYS$IMGSTA. Figure 27.6 shows the argument list.

9. The CLI calls the image at the first address in the transfer address array, described in Chapter 26. Unless the image was linked with the /NO-TRACEBACK qualifier, the first transfer address entry is the address of the Image Startup ($IMGSTA) system service. This service establishes the traceback exception handler and maps the debugger, if requested.

10. Later, the image terminates itself by issuing a RET instruction or by requesting the $EXIT system service. Since the CLI instruction stream

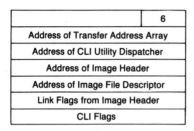

		6
Address of Transfer Address Array		
Address of CLI Utility Dispatcher		
Address of Image Header		
Address of Image File Descriptor		
Link Flags from Image Header		
CLI Flags		

Figure 27.6
Argument List Passed to an Image by EXE$PROCSTRT
or a CLI

requests the $EXIT system service anyway, the termination method chosen by the image is generally irrelevant. However, for an image that might be called as a procedure from another image, a RET instruction is the preferred method of image termination.

27.6.4 Normal Image Termination

When an image in a process with a CLI terminates normally, the $EXIT system service eventually calls the supervisor mode exit handler established by the CLI before it called the image. DCL's exit handler DCL$EXITHAND or MCR's exit handler MCR$EXITHAND performs several cleanup steps:

1. If the image exited with an error status in R0, the handler stores the error in the symbol $STATUS. It then writes the corresponding error message.
2. It calls SYS$RMSRUNDWN, closing any files left open by the image and the image file itself.
3. It discards any data records in the input stream (records that do not begin with a dollar sign for DCL or a right angle bracket for MCR) and issues a warning message.
4. It runs down the terminated image by requesting the $RUNDWN system service with an argument of user mode.
5. Finally, it transfers control to the beginning of the main command loop so that the CLI can read and process the next command.

27.6.5 Abnormal Image Termination

A user can interrupt an image by typing CTRL/Y or CTRL/C; an image can interrupt itself through the pause capability supplied by the VMS Run-Time Library procedure LIB$PAUSE. Further execution of the image depends on the sequence of commands issued while the image is interrupted.

27.6.5.1 CTRL/Y Processing.
When CTRL/Y is typed at the terminal, the terminal driver transfers control to the AST procedure established by the CLI during its initialization. The AST procedure first reestablishes itself, enabling future CTRL/Ys to be passed to the same AST procedure. It then checks whether the

process has disabled CTRL/Ys through the SET NOCONTROL=Y command. If so, the AST procedure returns, dismissing the CTRL/Y. Otherwise, its actions depend on the access mode interrupted by the CTRL/Y.

If the previous mode was supervisor, the AST procedure actions depend on whether an ON CONTROL_Y command was issued previously, specifying a particular command to be executed in response. If so, the AST procedure sets a flag to request that the command be executed and returns. If not, the CLI is restored to its initial state (with no nesting of indirect levels) and control transfers to the beginning of the main command loop.

If the previous mode was user, then the CTRL/Y interrupted an image. If the image was installed with enhanced privileges, the CLI saves those privileges and resets the process privileges to those in use before the image was activated. After setting a flag, the CLI returns to command processing. If, at this point, the user enters the DCL commands ATTACH, CONTINUE, or SPAWN (or the MCR command CONTINUE), the appropriate action is taken and the image is not run down. Any other command causes the CLI to run down a privileged image before executing the command; a nonprivileged image may continue (see Section 27.6.5.3). Issuing a STOP command for a nonprivileged image causes the CLI to terminate the image without calling user mode exit handlers (see Section 27.6.5.7). However, because a privileged image is run down before the STOP command is processed, its exit handlers are called.

27.6.5.2   **Pause Capability.** The VMS Run-Time Library procedure LIB$PAUSE provides the capability to interrupt an image under program control. An image executing in the context of an interactive process can invoke LIB$PAUSE to interrupt itself and transfer control to the CLI at the beginning of its main command loop.

27.6.5.3   **State of Interrupted Images.** When a nonprivileged image is interrupted, the image context is saved and control transfers to the beginning of the CLI's main command loop, allowing the user to execute commands. If the command is one that the CLI can perform internally (see Table 27.5), the image context is not destroyed and the image can be continued.

However, execution of any command that requires an external image destroys the context of the interrupted image. In addition, executing an indirect command file destroys an interrupted image, even if the commands in the indirect command file can be performed internally by the CLI.

Six commands that the user can enter when an image has been interrupted by CTRL/Y have special importance. These commands are ATTACH, CONTINUE, DEBUG, EXIT, SPAWN, and STOP. ATTACH and SPAWN are described in Section 27.4. The other commands are described in the following sections.

27.6.5.4   **CONTINUE Command.** If a CONTINUE command is typed and the previous mode was user, the CLI dismisses the AST and returns control to the image at the point where it was interrupted.

27.6.5.5   **DEBUG Command.** As described in Chapter 26, a DEBUG command causes the CLI to generate an SS$_DEBUG signal, which is eventually fielded by the condition handler established by the $IMGACT system service. (If the image was linked with the /NOTRACEBACK qualifier, the handler was never established and the image exits.) This handler responds to the SS$_ DEBUG signal by mapping the debugger (if it is not already mapped) and transferring control to it. This technique enables the debugger to be used, even if the image was not linked with the /DEBUG qualifier.

27.6.5.6   **EXIT Command.** The EXIT command invokes the $EXIT system service from user mode. Exit handlers are called and the image is run down.

27.6.5.7   **STOP Command.** The STOP command performs essentially the same clean-up operations that occur for a normally terminating image. However, STOP does its own work and does not call the $EXIT system service. Thus, user mode exit handlers are not called when an image terminates with a CTRL/Y STOP sequence.

The STOP command processor first determines whether an image or a process is being stopped. (The various STOP commands are described in the *VMS DCL Dictionary*.) If an image is being stopped, all open files are closed by calling SYS$RMSRUNDWN. The image itself is then run down through the $RUNDWN system service. Finally, control transfers to the beginning of the main command loop.

Note that STOP performs nearly identical operations to the CLI exit handler called as a result of an $EXIT system service request or an EXIT command. The only difference between the EXIT sequences and the STOP command is that user mode exit handlers are not called first. Thus, in most cases, the STOP and EXIT commands are interchangeable. One useful aspect of the STOP command is that it can eliminate an image containing a user mode exit handler that is preventing that image from completely going away, either intentionally or as a result of an error.

27.7   **LOGOUT OPERATION**

LOGINOUT, the image that performs the initialization of an interactive or batch process, also eventually executes to delete such a process. When LOGINOUT executes, it performs login, logout, or batch job step initialization. (When a batch process is submitted with more than one command procedure specified, each procedure is handled as a separate batch job step.) LOGINOUT determines whether the process is logged in already by the existence of the PPD region, used to communicate between LOGINOUT and the CLI.

If the PPD region exists, LOGINOUT's actions depend on whether the process is interactive or batch. For an interactive process, LOGINOUT performs the following steps:

1. LOGINOUT copies the IFIs for SYS$INPUT and SYS$OUTPUT from PPD locations into RMS data structures. This restores definitions of SYS$INPUT and SYS$OUTPUT made at login.

2. LOGINOUT notifies the security audit subsystem of the logout.

3. If the user specified the /[NO]HANGUP qualifier on the LOGOUT command, LOGINOUT checks whether it is appropriate to change the terminal characteristics. If the process is interactive and not a subprocess, and the terminal is local, LOGINOUT reads the current terminal characteristics and resets them, altering the hangup bit.

4. LOGINOUT writes the logout message to the restored SYS$OUTPUT. (Thus, it cannot be redirected via a logical name definition.) If the user asked for a full logout message, LOGINOUT requests the $GETJPI system service to get information, such as CPU time, number of page faults, and number of I/O requests.

5. It closes SYS$INPUT and SYS$OUTPUT.

6. Finally, LOGINOUT requests the $EXIT system service from executive mode. As described in Chapter 26, this limits the search for exit handlers to the executive mode list, bypassing the supervisor mode exit handler established by the CLI to prevent process deletion following image exit.

7. After the executive mode exit handler has performed its work, the $EXIT system service requests the $DELPRC system service, which removes the logged out process from the system.

If the process is a batch process, LOGINOUT first closes SYS$INPUT. It requests the $SNDJBC system service again to determine if there is another job step. If the batch process was submitted with multiple command procedures specified, LOGINOUT opens the new SYS$INPUT, reinitializes the batch process environment, and reenters the CLI.

If the previous batch job step failed, or the message that is returned from the job controller indicates that the process should be terminated, LOGINOUT terminates it through the following steps:

1. It writes a logout message to the log file.

2. It closes the log file.

3. If the log file is to be printed, then LOGINOUT requests $SNDJBC again, this time to queue the file to a print queue.

4. It then requests the $EXIT system service from executive mode. After the executive mode exit handler has performed its work, the $EXIT system service requests the $DELPRC system service, which removes the process from the system.

28 Process Deletion

... for dust you are and unto dust you shall return.

Genesis 3:19

When a process is to be deleted, a series of cleanup actions are necessary:

- All traces of the process must be removed from the system.
- All resources in the process's custody must be returned to the system.
- Accounting information must be sent to the job controller.
- Any subprocesses of the process being deleted must be deleted.
- If the process being deleted is a subprocess, all quotas and limits taken from its parent (owner) process must be returned.
- Finally, if the owner requested notification of the subprocess's deletion through a termination mailbox, the deletion message must be sent.

A process can delete itself or any other process in the VAXcluster system that it has the capability to affect. Process deletion occurs in two stages, the first in the context of the process requesting the deletion, and the second in the context of the process being deleted.

28.1 PROCESS DELETION IN CONTEXT OF CALLER

Process deletion is implemented by the Delete Process ($DELPRC) system service. Its initial operation occurs in the context of the process requesting the system service. This part of the operation performs a simple set of privilege checks and then queues a kernel mode asynchronous system trap (AST) that will cause the deletion to continue in the context of the process being deleted. Chapter 7 describes the queuing and delivery of ASTs.

The $DELPRC system service procedure, EXE$DELPRC in module SYS-DELPRC, runs in kernel mode. If the requesting process is the process to be deleted, no arguments are required; otherwise the requesting process can specify either the process name or the extended process ID (EPID) of the process to be deleted.

EXE$DELPRC performs the following steps:

1. It immediately invokes EXE$NAMPID, in module SYSPCNTRL, to locate the process control block (PCB) of the process to be deleted.

   EXE$NAMPID determines whether the input arguments specify a target process on this VAXcluster node or on another node. In the former case, EXE$NAMPID confirms the existence of the target process and the ability of the current process to delete it. (Chapter 13 describes the possible relation between the two processes and the privileges required in each case.) If the process is identified as one on another VAXcluster node,

EXE$NAMPID cannot make those checks; it can only confirm that the VAXcluster node identification is valid.

If further action is possible, EXE$NAMPID returns at IPL$_SCHED with the SCHED spinlock held; otherwise it returns at IPL 0. In either case, it returns an appropriate status.

2. If EXE$NAMPID returns the status SS$_REMOTE_PROC, indicating that the process may exist on another VAXcluster node, EXE$DEL-PRC transfers control to the clusterwide process service (CWPS) routine CWPS$PCNTRL, in module SYSPCNTRL. CWPS$PCNTRL transmits the deletion request to the appropriate VAXcluster node and places the process into a wait state. A cooperating CWPS routine on the other node processes the request and transmits status back to this node. Through mechanisms described in Chapter 13, control returns to a CWPS routine running in the context of the $DELPRC requestor. This routine exits from the $DELPRC system service, returning the status transmitted from the other node.

3. If EXE$NAMPID returns any other error status, EXE$DELPRC simply exits, returning the error status to its requestor.

4. If EXE$NAMPID returns a status indicating that the target process exists on this node and that the requesting process may affect it, EXE$DELPRC continues.

5. EXE$DELPRC tests the flag PCB$V_NODELET in PCB$L_STS. VMS uses this flag to prevent deletion of system processes such as the swapper and NETACP. If the flag is set, EXE$DELPRC does not delete the process but instead releases the SCHED spinlock, lowers IPL, and returns the error status SS$_NODELETE. Use of the PCB$V_NODELET flag is reserved to Digital. Any other use is completely unsupported.

6. EXE$DELPRC must queue a kernel mode AST to the target process. It allocates and initializes an AST control block (ACB) to describe the kernel AST.

7. It marks the target process for deletion by setting the flag PCB$V_DELPEN in PCB$L_STS. If the bit is found already set, deletion is underway for the target process. EXE$DELPRC releases the SCHED spinlock, lowers IPL, deallocates the ACB, and returns the success status SS$_NORMAL. However, if an executive mode rundown routine is entered as a result of process deletion and it rerequests the $DELPRC system service, EXE$DELPRC ignores PCB$V_DELPEN and continues as though the process were not marked for deletion.

8. EXE$DELPRC sets the target process's PCB$V_RESPEN bit and reports a resume event for the process. This event is significant only for a process in scheduling state SUSP or SUSPO and causes such a process to be resumed. This mechanism is necessary because no ASTs can be delivered to a process suspended in kernel mode, including the delete process kernel mode AST.

9. EXE$DELPRC initializes the ACB with the process ID (PID) of the target process and the address of the kernel mode AST procedure that performs the actual process deletion, routine DELETE in module SYSDELPRC.

10. It queues the AST to the target process, with a potential boost of PRI$_RESAVL to its software priority.

Queuing the AST to the target process makes it computable. Eventually, the scheduler selects that process for execution.

28.2 PROCESS DELETION IN CONTEXT OF PROCESS BEING DELETED

Most of process deletion occurs in the context of the process being deleted. If the process has no pending special kernel mode or other kernel mode ASTs, the process deletion AST procedure executes immediately. Note that a process executing or waiting at IPL 2 or above cannot be deleted because ASTs cannot be delivered.

Deleting a process in its context means that its address space and process header are readily accessible. The DELETE AST procedure is therefore able to request standard system services, such as Delete Virtual Address Space ($DELTVA) and Deassign I/O Channel ($DASSGN). Special cases, such as the deletion of a process that is outswapped, are avoided by ensuring that the process is first made resident.

28.2.1 DELETE Kernel Mode AST

The DELETE AST procedure performs the following steps:

1. DELETE first enables resource wait mode by clearing PCB$V_SSRWAIT in PCB$L_STS.

2. It then searches for per-process or systemwide executive mode rundown routines to perform image-specific cleanup. Use of executive mode rundown routines is reserved to Digital. Any other use is strongly discouraged by Digital and completely unsupported.

   If executive mode rundown is not already active and executive mode rundown routines exist, DELETE sets a flag indicating that executive mode rundown is active and queues an executive mode AST to the process, specifying EXEC_RUNDOWN_AST as the AST address. DELETE then exits, allowing the executive mode AST to be delivered.

   EXEC_RUNDOWN_AST, in module SYSDELPRC, invokes the per-process executive mode rundown routines and the systemwide executive mode rundown routines if any exist. It then requests the Change to Kernel Mode ($CMKRNL) system service to resume processing in the original DELETE code path at step 4, in kernel mode.

3. If no executive mode rundown routines need to be invoked, DELETE clears the PCB$B_ASTACT bit to indicate that no kernel mode AST is active. It invokes SCH$NEWLVL to determine the mode of the most

important pending AST. Taking these steps enables another kernel mode AST to interrupt the DELETE AST. Although interruption of an AST by another at the same mode is usually prohibited, it may be necessary before process deletion can complete.

4. DELETE checks whether the process has a Files-11 operation in progress. This must complete before DELETE can proceed. If PCB$B_DPC is non-zero, indicating this condition, DELETE places the process into a resource wait state for resource RSN$_ASTWAIT. When the queuing and delivery of a kernel mode AST ends the resource wait, DELETE repeats its check. When PCB$B_DPC is zero, the DELETE procedure can continue. Chapter 7 documents the field PCB$B_DPC and its use in stalling process deletion.

5. If per-process or systemwide user-specified kernel mode rundown routines exist, they are invoked to perform image-specific cleanup.

6. DELETE then reinitializes the P1 cells that control dispatching to privileged shareable images and user-specified rundown routines.

7. It calls SYS$RMSRUNDWN to perform Record Management Services (RMS) rundown. The service routine, RMS$RMSRUNDWN in module [RMS]RMS0RNDWN, aborts RMS I/O for the process and transfers control to the routine RM$LAST_CHANCE, in module [RMS]RMS0LSTCH, to perform the actual rundown.

   RM$LAST_CHANCE scans the process's open disk files and detaches any file that uses global buffers from the global buffer pool. No further rundown is performed on files that are journaled.

   For a sequential file, RM$LAST_CHANCE writes the current buffer operated on by the process to disk if the buffer has been modified. This attempt to preserve the last data records written to the file may help a subsequent attempt to analyze process action prior to deletion. This feature is intended for problem analysis rather than for minimizing data loss.

   RM$LAST_CHANCE deaccesses any file open for exclusive access to update the RMS record attributes in its file header, particularly the end-of-file pointer.

   During RMS rundown no attempt is made to write all modified data buffers to disk. User applications not using journaling must be able to handle potential data loss resulting from forced process deletion.

8. If the process has any subprocesses (if its PCB$W_PRCCNT field is nonzero), they must be deleted before deletion of the owner process can continue. Section 28.2.2 contains an example of deleting a process with subprocesses.

   The following steps are performed to delete the subprocesses:

   a. DELETE scans the PCB vector for all PCBs whose PCB$L_OWNER field specifies the PID of the process being deleted. DELETE requests the $DELPRC system service to delete each of these subprocesses.

b. DELETE again checks the subprocess count PCB$W_PRCCNT. If it is greater than zero, the process is placed into a resource wait state (MWAIT) for resource RSN$_ASTWAIT. This parent process becomes computable again when the RETQUOTA special kernel mode AST returns CPU time quota from one of the subprocesses (see step 17) and control returns to DELETE. DELETE repeats this step until the subprocess count is zero. At that point, all subprocesses have been deleted and the DELETE procedure can continue.

9. DELETE requests the $RUNDWN system service to run down the process from kernel mode (see Chapter 26).

10. For each section still mapped to the process virtual address space, DELETE requests the $DELTVA system service to delete those virtual pages. The process section table entry is checked before the deletion. If the SEC$V_INPROG flag is set in the process section table entry, the section was being created when the delete process AST was delivered. In this case, DELETE invokes MMG$DECSECREFL to correct the section reference count.

If any pages are actually deleted, the $RUNDWN system service is requested once again to complete the deassignment of open channels.

11. The channel control blocks (CCBs) are scanned to ensure that all channels have been deassigned. If any is still assigned, DELETE generates a fatal FILCNTNONZ bugcheck.

12. If the current process is not a subprocess (if the PCB$L_OWNER field is zero) DELETE dismounts each jobwide mounted volume.

If the current process is a subprocess, DELETE reassigns any volumes allocated by the subprocess to the owner process. DELETE stores the owner process's PID in UCB$L_PID and sets the UCB$V_DEADMO bit to ensure that the volume will be deallocated when it is eventually dismounted by the owner process.

13. DELETE ensures that all outstanding process I/O requests have completed. It compares PCB$W_DIOLM to PCB$W_DIOCNT and PCB$W_BIOLM to PCB$W_BIOCNT. The difference between the first two fields is the number of outstanding direct I/O requests; the difference between the latter two is the number of outstanding buffered I/O requests.

14. If the current process is not a subprocess, DELETE decrements one of two system process counts. If the process is interactive (if PCB$V_INTER in PCB$L_STS is set), DELETE decrements the number of interactive jobs, SYS$GW_IJOBCNT. If the process is a batch job (if PCB$V_BATCH in PCB$L_STS is set), DELETE decrements the number of batch jobs, SYS$GW_BJOBCNT.

15. If the current process is not a subprocess, DELETE deletes the jobwide logical name table.

16. DELETE resets the process name string in the PCB by zeroing the count byte.

17. If the current process is a subprocess, any remaining deductible quotas must be returned to the owner process. The following steps are taken:

    a. An I/O request packet (IRP) is allocated for use as an ACB.

    b. The address of the return quota special kernel mode AST (routine RETQUOTA in module SYSDELPRC) and the PID of the owner process are stored in the ACB.

    c. The only quota that must be returned to the owner process, unused CPU time, is stored in the portion of the IRP immediately following the ACB. All other quotas are either pooled or nondeductible (see Chapter 25).

    d. Finally, the special kernel mode AST is queued to the owner process, giving it a priority boost of PRI$_RESAVL.

18. If the current process is a subprocess and the owner process requested a termination mailbox message, a termination message is constructed on the stack. DELETE requests the Queue I/O Request ($QIO) system service to send the termination message to the mailbox unit specified by PCB$W_TMBU. The message contents are listed in Table 28.1. The message size is specified by ACC$C_TERMLEN.

19. EXE$PRCDELMSG, in module ACCOUNT, is invoked to send an accounting message to the job controller. It sends the message unless accounting is inhibited for this process (the NOACNT flag was specified at process creation) or process termination accounting is disabled for the entire system. The contents of this message are used to fill in all relevant fields of the accounting identification and resource packets. The data structures used by the Accounting Utility are described in the *VMS Accounting Utility Manual*.

20. After IPL is raised to 2 to prevent AST delivery, most of the remainder of P1 space is deleted. However, the P1 pages permanently locked into the working set list, the kernel stack, for example, are not deleted. Some of P1 space, including the user stack, may have already been deleted as a result of a previous image reset call.

21. DELETE releases the process page table pages to the head of the free page list and deallocates the associated page file space. It acquires the MMG and SCHED spinlocks to synchronize access to the memory management and scheduler databases.

    At this point, DELETE executes a SVPCTX instruction to remove the process from execution. Executing this instruction switches stacks; DELETE is now running on the interrupt stack.

Table 28.1   Contents of the Termination Mailbox
Message Sent to the Owner Process

Field in Message Block	*Source of Information*
Message type	MSG$_DELPROC [1]
Final exit status	CTL$GL_FINALSTS
Process ID	PCB$L_EPID
Job ID	Not currently used
Logout time	EXE$GQ_SYSTIME
Account name	CTL$T_ACCOUNT
User name	CTL$T_USERNAME
CPU time	PHD$L_CPUTIM
Number of page faults	PHD$L_PAGEFLTS
Peak paging file usage	Not currently used
Peak working set size	CTL$GL_WSPEAK
Buffered I/O count	PHD$L_BIOCNT
Direct I/O count	PHD$L_DIOCNT
Count of mounted volumes	CTL$GL_VOLUMES
Login time	CTL$GQ_LOGIN
EPID of owner	PCB$L_EOWNER

[1] MSG$_DELPROC is a constant, indicating that this is
a process termination message.

22. If the process capability mask indicates explicit affinity to a particular
    CPU, DELETE decrements that CPU's explicit affinity count.
23. DELETE stores the address of the null PCB in the per-CPU database field
    CPU$L_CURPCB and in the PCB vector slot formerly occupied by the
    process being deleted, thus freeing the slot for future use.
24. The pages in process space that were permanently locked into the work-
    ing set, for example, the kernel stack and the P1 pointer page, are deleted
    and placed at the head of the free page list. The process header pages that
    are a permanent part of the working set will be deleted by the swapper
    when the process header is deleted.
25. Each remaining ACB is removed from the PCB queue and deallocated to
    nonpaged pool unless its ACB$V_NODELETE bit is set. If the ACB$V_
    NODELETE bit is set, the ACB is assumed to be part of another data
    structure whose deletion is not desirable.
26. DELETE removes any pending CWPS structures from the PCB$Q_CWPS-
    SRV_QUEUE queue of the process being deleted. It inserts them on the
    swapper's PCB$Q_CWPSSRV_QUEUE queue.
        These structures cannot be deleted until the stalled fork thread that
    expects to access them is resumed by the arrival of a response from
    another VAXcluster member. When the response arrives, the fork thread

determines that the requestor process was deleted and deallocates the structures.

27. If the process had an extended rights list, it is deallocated to nonpaged pool.

28. The process count field in the job information block (JIB) is decremented in an interlocked manner. If the process being deleted is a detached process (the PID of the process being deleted is equal to the master PID field in the JIB), the JIB is deallocated.

29. If the process being deleted is a subprocess, its owner's subprocess count (PCB$W_PRCCNT) is decremented. If the owner process is also being deleted, the owner is currently in a wait state, waiting for the contents of this field to become zero. DELETE makes the owner process computable so that it can check the value of PCB$W_PRCCNT. If the value is now zero, the owner can continue with its own deletion.

30. The PCB is deallocated to nonpaged pool.

31. The number of processes in the balance set, SWP$GW_BALCNT, is decremented.

32. The routine SCH$SWPWAKE is invoked to awaken the swapper because there is a process header to be removed from the balance slot area (see Chapter 18).

33. The scheduler's process count, SCH$GW_PROCCNT, is decremented.

34. Finally, the DELETE AST procedure releases the MMG spinlock and exits by jumping to the scheduler at entry SCH$SCHED, holding the SCHED spinlock. The scheduler selects the next process for execution and releases the SCHED spinlock (see Chapter 12).

28.2.2   **Deletion of a Process That Owns Subprocesses**

When a process owns subprocesses, the deletion of the owner process must be delayed until all its subprocesses are deleted. The prior deletion of subprocesses ensures that any quotas taken from the owner process are returned. In early versions of VMS prior to the existence of the JIB and its jobwide pooled quotas (see Chapter 25), several quotas were charged against a process when it created a subprocess. At deletion of the subprocess, the subprocess returned those quotas. All the quotas treated in this way are now pooled except for CPU time limit, which is the only quota returned at subprocess deletion.

During the execution of the DELETE AST procedure, a check is made to see if the process being deleted owns any subprocesses. If it does, these processes must be located and deleted.

As Figure 28.1 shows, there are no forward pointers in the JIB or PCB of an owner process to indicate which subprocesses it has created. The only indication that a process has created subprocesses is a nonzero value in PCB$W_PRCCNT. The process's subprocesses can only be located by

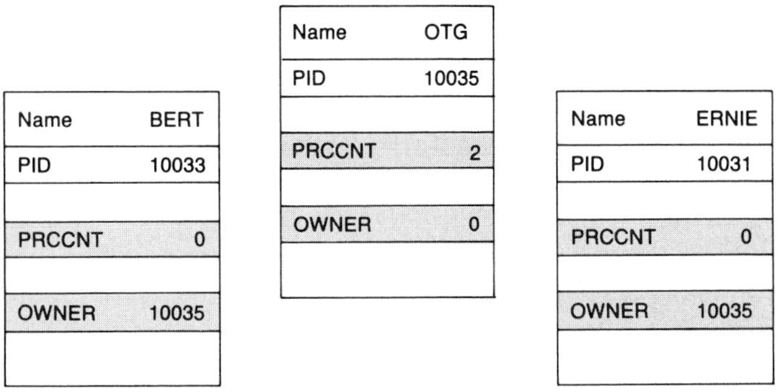

Name	OTG
PID	10035
PRCCNT	2
OWNER	0

Name	BERT
PID	10033
PRCCNT	0
OWNER	10035

Name	ERNIE
PID	10031
PRCCNT	0
OWNER	10035

Figure 28.1
Sample Job to Illustrate Process Deletion with
Subprocesses

scanning all the PCBs in the system until each PCB is located whose owner field contains the PID of interest.

28.2.3   Example of Process Deletion with Subprocesses

The details of this situation can best be illustrated with an example. Figure 28.1 shows a process whose process ID equals 10035 and whose name is OTG. The process OTG owns two subprocesses: the first has a process ID of 10033 and the name BERT; the second has a process ID of 10031 and the name ERNIE.

Neither of these subprocesses owns any further subprocesses. The following steps occur as a result of the process OTG being deleted. Assume that the priorities are such that the processes execute in the order OTG, BERT, and ERNIE.

1. The deletion of process OTG proceeds normally until it is determined that this process has created two subprocesses. The PCB vector is scanned until the two PCBs containing 10035 in the PCB$L_OWNER field are located. These two processes are marked for deletion. This means that the DELETE kernel mode AST is queued to the two subprocesses and they are made computable. Process OTG is placed into a wait state because its count of owned subprocesses is nonzero (actually 2, at this point).

2. The previous assumption about priorities implies that process BERT executes next. Its deletion proceeds past the point where process OTG stopped because it owns no subprocesses. However, the next step in the DELETE AST procedure determines that process BERT is a subprocess and must return quotas to its owner. The return of quotas is accomplished by queuing a special kernel mode AST (RETQUOTA) to process OTG, changing its state back to computable. When BERT has finished with all actions that require the presence of the JIB, it decrements the

process count in OTG's PCB$W_PRCCNT and declares a resource availability event, which awakens OTG. However, the count of owned subprocesses is still not zero (down to 1 now), so process OTG is put back into the resource wait state. Process BERT continues to execute until it disappears entirely from the system.

3. Process ERNIE now begins execution of the DELETE AST procedure. Again, the check for owned subprocesses indicates none, but the check for being a subprocess is positive. A RETQUOTA AST is again queued to process OTG and the count of owned subprocesses decremented (finally to zero).

4. Now process OTG resumes execution as a result of the delivery of the RETQUOTA AST and subsequently finds that the count of owned subprocesses has gone to zero. In fact, process OTG continues to be deleted at this point, even though process ERNIE has not been entirely deleted. This overlapping is simply a result of the timing in this example. The process ERNIE is well on the way to being deleted and is no longer of any concern to process OTG. The important point is that the quotas given to process ERNIE have been returned to OTG. Once OTG's PCB$W_PRCCNT is equal to zero, it is irrelevant which process executes next. Because ERNIE and BERT have finished work that depended on the presence of the JIB, OTG and the JIB can be deleted totally.

In the general case of a series of subprocesses arranged in a tree structure, the deletion of some arbitrary process requires that each subprocess further down in the tree must execute the process deletion step, which returns quota to its owner.

PART VIII / Life of the System

29 The Modular Executive

Non sunt multiplicanda entia praeter necessitatem.
[Entities should not be multiplied beyond necessity.]
William of Occam

The VMS executive consists of a base image and a number of separately loadable images. Some of these images are loaded on all systems, while others support features unique to particular system configurations.

The base image connects requests for services with the routines that provide the services. That is, the base image consists mostly of very small routines whose addresses are fixed and that dispatch to service-providing routines in separately loadable images. It also contains data and pointers to data in loadable images.

This chapter describes the organization of the base image and various types of loadable image, and the connections among them. It concentrates on the base image and loadable executive images, which are new to VMS Version 5. It describes more briefly the other types of loadable image, such as the CPU-specific code supplied in the SYSLOA*xxx*.EXE images.

29.1 OVERVIEW

The VMS executive has always been partitioned into multiple images. As VMS has supported more features and CPU types, the number of images has grown. In previous versions of VMS, much of the executive was in SYS.EXE, the system image. Features not common to all system configurations were supported in separate images, such as device drivers and the SYSLOA*xxx*.EXE images.

In VMS Version 5, the executive has been further partitioned. There are two major reasons for this change: to simplify subsequent changes to the executive, and to reduce the number of system-dependent images that require relinking when some part of the executive changes. Changing SYS.EXE formerly meant applying complex patches to it or rebuilding it. Rebuilding has had the undesirable side effect of requiring a subsequent relinking of all images linked against SYS.STB, both VMS- and user-supplied.

The concept underlying the reorganized executive is similar to that of a shareable image, which contains transfer vectors and routines. A transfer vector is a pointer or a very small number of instructions, placed at a location that does not change when the image containing it is modified, recompiled, or relinked. It serves as an indirect address, or transfer, to code or data whose location may change. A transfer vector's unchanging location provides a stable target for references from external code and frees such code from the need to relink whenever the destination of the transfer vector moves.

The system image has been split into a base image, named SYS.EXE, and a number of other images called loadable executive images. Unlike shareable image transfer vectors, executive transfer vectors are collected in an image of their own, the base image. The routines themselves are in other images, mostly in loadable executive images. The base image also contains pointers to systemwide data in loadable executive images. Each loadable executive image contains related routines and data. For example, the loadable executive image LOGICAL_NAMES.EXE contains all the routines and much of the data related to support for logical names. Section 29.3.1 describes extensions to the implementation of shareable images required for loadable executive images.

The reorganization of the executive makes it less likely that SYS.EXE will need to be rebuilt when corrections or enhancements are made to loadable executive images. Under VMS Version 5, it is possible to replace a loadable executive image with no impact on SYS.EXE. The replacement image might be a corrected or enhanced one or it might be an alternative version. For example, there are three versions of the system synchronization image. During system initialization, the version appropriate to the configuration is selected and loaded.

The reorganization of the executive also simplifies system initialization. Initialization code specific to a feature is now part of the appropriate loadable executive image. Furthermore, initialization routines can be invoked multiple times at different phases of system initialization.

As part of the reorganization, all executive images have been moved from the directory SYS$SYSTEM to the directory SYS$LOADABLE_IMAGES.

Several problems were addressed to reorganize the system image:

- Creating address space for the executive with appropriate pageability and protection characteristics
- Developing a mechanism to load executive images
- Enabling one loadable executive image to call routines or access data in another
- Connecting the transfer vectors in the base image to routines and data in loaded executive images
- Maintaining the position independence of a loadable executive image that contains .ADDRESS or .ASCID directives
- Controlling executive version identification and compatibility
- Allocating and deallocating system address space

The solutions to these problems are described throughout the rest of this chapter.

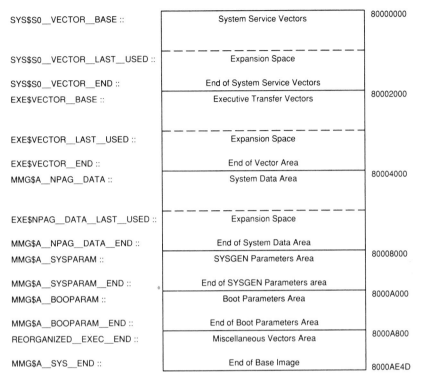

Figure 29.1
Layout of the Base Executive Image

29.2   **SYS.EXE, THE BASE IMAGE**

The base image, SYS.EXE, is the only executive image linked to a fixed address. Its base address is 80000000_{16}, the lowest address in system space. It contains almost no executable code other than instructions in transfer vectors.

The base image is the pathway to routines and data in loadable executive images and in previously existing loaded images such as SYSLOA*xxx*.EXE. The base image symbol table, SYS.STB, is linked with all images that need resolutions for references to its global symbols. For example, each loadable executive image is linked with SYS.STB to resolve references to other executive images' transfer vectors, to data and parameters in SYS.EXE, and to transfer vectors for routines in loaded images such as SYSLOA*xxx*.EXE.

SYS.EXE provides a fixed address space so that the addresses of transfer vectors and data cells within it will be constant. Having fixed values for these addresses makes it unnecessary to relink an image that references them. Address space is reserved for expansion so that transfer vectors and data cells can be added without affecting the addresses of existing ones.

Figure 29.1 shows the layout of SYS.EXE, as defined by the module EXEC‗ LAYOUT. It contains the following areas:

- Transfer vectors to system service procedures
- Transfer vectors to routines in loadable executive images
- Commonly accessed data and pointers to data structures in executive images
- SYSGEN parameters area
- Boot parameters area
- Transfer vectors to routines in loaded images such as SYSLOA*xxx*.EXE

These areas are described separately in the sections that follow.

29.2.1   System Service Vectors

System service vectors occupy the lowest pages of system space. Their addresses are constant for all versions of VMS so that existing user programs will not have to be relinked for a new version of VMS. A system service vector contains a minimal procedure that executes in the mode of the caller and that dispatches to the actual procedures implementing the service request. The actual procedures are within loadable executive images and typically execute in an inner access mode.

A typical system service vector is eight bytes and contains the following:

```
SYS$service_name::
        .WORD   entry_mask
        CHMx    I^#service_specific_code
        RET
        .BYTE   0
```

An image requests a particular system service by executing a CALLx instruction to SYS$*service_name*, the global label at its system service vector. The linker resolves system service vector names using global definitions from a module in the library SYS$LIBRARY:STARLET.OLB, which it searches by default.

The change mode exception service routines use the operand of the CHMx instruction to dispatch to the requested service. The operand serves as an index into several tables, one of which contains the addresses of the actual system service procedures.

In earlier versions of VMS, each system service vector was initialized with a register save mask and a CHMx instruction; a change mode operand number was assigned at assembly time. In VMS Version 5, each system service vector is initialized to JMP @#EXE$LOAD_ERROR at assembly time. EXE$LOAD_ERROR contains a HALT instruction.

Change mode operand numbers are not assigned until executive image load time and can vary with the order in which system services are loaded, possibly from one system boot to another. This means, for example, that a user program using a hard-coded CHMx instruction rather than a CALLx to a system service vector is very unlikely to work correctly.

As an executive image is loaded, each system service in it that executes in an inner access mode is assigned a change mode operand number. Its system service vector is reinitialized with the appropriate register save mask and change mode instruction. The table entries selected by that change mode operand number are reinitialized with values appropriate to that system service. The system service vector for a mode of caller service is reinitialized with the appropriate register save mask and a JMP instruction that transfers control to the service procedure.

The address space reserved for system service vectors is nonpageable. This address space also contains the code used for testing the completion of synchronous services such as Queue I/O Request and Wait ($QIOW) and Enqueue Lock Request and Wait ($ENQW). It is defined in the module EXEC_ LAYOUT and by the macro $SYSVECTORDEF.

Chapter 6 contains further information about system service vectors, change mode dispatching, and synchronous system services. Section 29.5.4.3 describes the initialization of system service vectors.

29.2.2 Executive Transfer Vectors

An executive transfer vector is similar to a system service vector or a transfer vector in a shareable image. Unlike a system service vector, an executive transfer vector contains no instruction to change access mode. These vectors are used by routines already running in the appropriate mode, typically kernel.

Each executive transfer vector contains a JMP instruction whose destination is in a loadable executive image. The address of a transfer vector is independent of the address of its destination and independent of which loadable executive image contains the destination.

An executive transfer vector is eight bytes long. For a called procedure, it takes the form

```
exec_entry_point::
        .WORD   entry-mask
        JMP     @#routine
```

For a routine entered through a JSB instruction, it takes the form

```
exec_entry_point::
        JMP     @#routine
        NOP
        NOP
```

An image invokes a particular executive routine by executing a CALLx or JSB instruction to *exec_entry_point*, the global label of the routine's executive transfer vector. The image must be linked with SYS.STB for the linker to resolve the global executive transfer vector name.

Executive transfer vectors are defined in module SYSTEM_ROUTINES, through its macros DEFINE_ROUTINE_JSB and DEFINE_ROUTINE_CALL.

Example 29.1
Definition of Executive Transfer Vectors

```
; Transfer vectors from SYSTEM_ROUTINES
        DEFINE_ROUTINE_CALL -
                RMS$RESTART_THREAD,-
                VERSION_MASK=<VOLATILE,FILES_VOLUMES>
        .ALIGN  QUAD
        RMS$RESTART_THREAD == .
        .WORD   0
        JSB     @#EXE$LOAD_ERROR
        .
        .
        .
        DEFINE_ROUTINE_JSB -
                EXE$ALLOCIRP,-
                VERSION_MASK=<MEMORY_MANAGEMENT>
        .ALIGN  QUAD
        EXE$ALLOCIRP == .
        JSB     @#EXE$LOAD_ERROR
```

Their dispatch instructions are initialized to JSB @#EXE$LOAD_ERROR at assembly time. A transfer vector for a called routine is initialized to begin with a register save mask. Example 29.1 shows two such macro invocations and the code they generate. Section 29.6 describes the use of the VERSION_MASK keyword.

When a loadable executive image is mapped and loaded into system space, its base image transfer vectors are reinitialized to point to their corresponding routines in the loaded executive image. For a called procedure, the entry mask in the transfer vector is also initialized. See Section 29.4.1 for more information on the initialization of executive transfer vectors.

The address space used for executive transfer vectors is nonpageable.

29.2.3 System Data Area

The system data area contains some, but not all, of the data formerly in SYS.EXE. Its cells are accessed by multiple loadable executive images and by other images linked against SYS.STB. Data cells accessed by only a limited set of routines typically reside in the same loadable executive image as the routines. A data cell in one loadable image used by another must have a pointer in the base image. If the data cell is small, the cell itself resides in the base image (to save on overhead).

A data cell or structure in this area must be of fixed size. A structure whose size may change from version to version, such as the system disk unit control block (UCB), is placed in a loadable executive image, where its variable size cannot affect fixed addresses in the base image.

Some locations in this area are pointers to data in loaded executive images. Such a location is modified to contain the loaded address of the data. Its global symbol has a type of AR to indicate that it contains the address

828

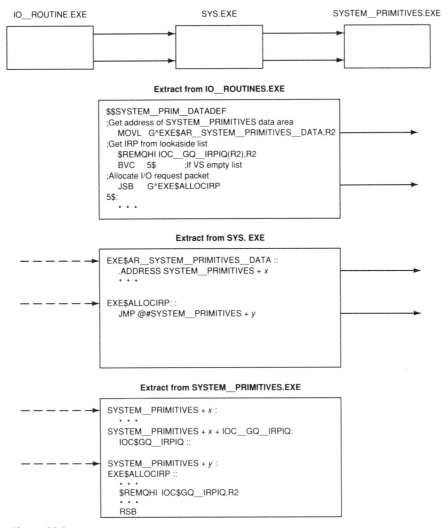

Figure 29.2
An Example of Loadable Executive Image Address
Resolution

of a record or a structure. For example, LNM$AR_SYSTEM_DIRECTORY
contains the address of the logical name table system directory, once part of
SYS.EXE, now part of LOGICAL_NAMES.EXE.

In some cases, a pointer contains the address of a block of moved data
cells whose layout is defined by a macro. For example, EXE$AR_SYSTEM_
PRIMITIVES_DATA contains the address of data relating to the nonpaged
pool lookaside lists. The macro $$SYSTEM_PRIM_DATADEF defines sym-
bols for the fields in this area, such as IOC_GQ_IRPIQ, the I/O request
packet lookaside listhead. Figure 29.2 shows an example of a reference using
EXE$AR_SYSTEM_PRIMITIVES_DATA and symbolic offsets.

Example 29.2
Definition of Executive Data Cells

```
; SYSTEM_PRIMITIVES private data area
        DEFINE_DATA_CELL -
                EXE$AR_SYSTEM_PRIMITIVES_DATA,-
                VERSION_MASK=<MEMORY_MANAGEMENT>
                .LONG 0
        .
        .

; Head of executive loaded image data block list
        DEFINE_DATA_CELL -
                LDR$GQ_IMAGE_LIST,-
                VERSION_MASK=<MEMORY_MANAGEMENT>
                .LONG .,.-4
```

The local macro DEFINE_DATA_CELL is invoked for each data cell or structure, along with a VAX MACRO directive to allocate and possibly initialize storage for the cell or structure. Example 29.2 shows two examples of the use of this macro. Section 29.6 describes the use of the VERSION_MASK keyword.

When a loadable executive image is mapped and loaded into system space, the base image pointers to its universal symbols are reinitialized to point to their corresponding data structures in the loaded executive image. Like the address of a transfer vector, the location of a pointer to data in a loaded executive image is fixed, while the data to which it points can change location or even executive image.

The system data area is defined in module SYSTEM_DATA_CELLS and is nonpageable.

Section 29.3.2 describes other criteria for locating a piece of system data in the base image or in a particular loadable executive image.

29.2.4 SYSGEN Parameters Area

This area contains all the SYSGEN parameters. To coordinate with SYS-BOOT, which copies the current parameters to this area during system boot, all SYSGEN parameters are virtually contiguous and in an area that can be extended to add new parameters.

SYSGEN parameters are kept in the base image rather than in a loadable executive image so that they can be referenced directly. There is no one loadable executive image that references them most often; they are widely referenced from most loadable executive images and other images linked with SYS.STB.

The SYSGEN parameters area is defined in module SYSPARAM and is nonpageable.

29.2.5   Boot Parameters Area

The boot parameters area passes information from SYSBOOT to later stages of system initialization. It is defined in module BOOPARAM and is non-pageable. Chapter 30 provides further information on its contents.

29.2.6   Miscellaneous Vectors Area

The miscellaneous vectors area consists primarily of transfer vectors to images that are not loadable executive images, namely SYSLOA*xxx*.EXE, SCSLOA.EXE, and CLUSTRLOA.EXE. Each set of transfer vectors has its own expansion space. This area includes the routines that connect the transfer vectors to their loaded routines and data. Section 29.7.1 contains more information about the form of these transfer vectors.

The area is nonpageable and is primarily defined in the modules SYS-LOAVEC, SCSVEC, and CLUSTRVEC, with some contributions from SYS-TEM_ROUTINES_MASK and LINKVEC.

29.3   LOADABLE EXECUTIVE IMAGES

The base image contains almost no executable code. Its system service vectors, executive transfer vectors, and miscellaneous area vectors dispatch to routines in separately loadable images. Most of these images are loadable executive images.

A loadable executive image is a type of shareable image. Each loadable executive image consists of data and routines related to each other and of initialization code specific to the image's functions and features. In most cases, to simplify maintenance and enhancement, routines supporting related functions and features are collected into an image. In some cases, routines used early in system initialization are combined into a loadable executive image, for example, EXEC_INIT.EXE and PRIMITIVE_IO.EXE. Table 29.1 lists the loadable executive images and summarizes their contents.

29.3.1   Structure of a Loadable Executive Image

A loadable executive image is implemented as a form of shareable image. Like any other shareable image, it has a global symbol table, image section descriptors, and address fixup section. The internal structure of a loadable executive image is more constrained than that of a typical shareable image. Like a nonbased shareable image, a loadable executive image must be position-independent because its system space address range is not determined until load time.

A loadable executive image is allowed at most one image section of each of the following types and no others:

- Nonpageable read-only, for code, read-only data, and patches
- Nonpageable read/write, for read/write data and for .ADDRESS and .ASCID directives

Table 29.1   Loadable Executive Images

Image Name	Description
	Description
PART A–IMAGES LOADED BY SYSBOOT.EXE	
ERRORLOG.EXE	Error logging routines and system services
EXEC_INIT.EXE	Routines required for executive initialization
PRIMITIVE_IO.EXE	Primitive console I/O and file system routines
SYSTEM_DEBUG.EXE	XDELTA (optional)
SYSTEM_PRIMITIVES.EXE	Basic system support routines
One of the following:	
SYSTEM_SYNCHRONIZATION.EXE	Symmetric multiprocessing (SMP) synchronization routines with debug support
SYSTEM_SYNCHRONIZATION_MIN.EXE	SMP synchronization routines
SYSTEM_SYNCHRONIZATION_UNI.EXE	Uniprocessor synchronization routines
PART B–IMAGES LOADED BY EXEC_INIT.EXE (EXE$INIT)	
CPULOA.EXE	Tables of CPU data
EVENT_FLAGS_AND_ASTS.EXE	Event flag and AST routines and system services
EXCEPTION.EXE	Exception service routines and system services, bugcheck routines
IMAGE_MANAGEMENT.EXE	Image activation services and routines
IO_ROUTINES.EXE	I/O-related routines and system services
LMF$GROUP_TABLE.EXE	Tables of license data
LOCKING.EXE	Lock management routines and system services
LOGICAL_NAMES.EXE	Logical name routines and system services
MESSAGE_ROUTINES.EXE	Message routines and system services
PAGE_MANAGEMENT.EXE	Page fault service routine, related routines, virtual address space system services
PROCESS_MANAGEMENT.EXE	Scheduling routines and process creation and control system services
SECURITY.EXE	Security-related routines and system services
SYSDEVICE.EXE	Pseudo device drivers and mailbox system services
SYSGETSYI.EXE	$GETSYI system service
SYSLICENSE.EXE	$LICENSE system service
WORKING_SET_MANAGEMENT.EXE	Swapper and supporting routines, related system services
PART C–IMAGES LOADED BY SYSINIT.EXE	
DDIF$RMS_EXTENSION.EXE	Support for Digital Document Interchange Format (DDIF) file operations
RMS.EXE	Record Management Services (RMS)
RECOVERY_UNIT_SERVICES.EXE	RMS recovery services
SYSMSG.EXE	System message file
SYSLDR_DYN.EXE	Dynamic loading of loadable executive images

- Pageable read-only, for code, read-only data, and patches
- Pageable read/write, for read/write data and for .ADDRESS and .ASCID directives
- Initialization routine section
- Address fixup section

The first five of these image sections are defined as program sections (PSECTs) within the modules of a loadable executive image, and the last is created by the linker. The address fixup section (see Chapter 26) contains information needed to transform .ADDRESS and .ASCID references to locations within the loaded image.

The first four sections allow for the combinations of pageability and protection required for executive code and data. Because they have different virtual memory characteristics, each must begin at a page boundary. On average, this results in half a page unused at the end of each image section. Constraining the number of image sections limits the potential unused space to an average of two pages per image. (The initialization routine and address fixup sections are deleted during system initialization.) It also simplifies the loading mechanism.

Most modules invoke the DECLARE_PSECT macro to define standard loadable executive PSECT names and attributes. Each image is built with a linker options file that collects and orders the image sections. Table 29.2 lists the clusters and PSECTs that make up a typical loadable executive image. It shows some of the modules that make contributions to the PSECTs. This information is extracted from the image map of IO_ROUTINES.EXE.

In VMS Version 5, several additions and extensions were made to the shareable image mechanism to support the reorganization of the executive.

A new type of universal symbol, a *vectored* universal symbol, has two values: the relative address of the symbol in the loadable executive image, and the absolute value of the symbol's transfer vector in the base image. These are described by new global symbol table records.

The linker VECTOR option specifies that all universal symbols in the loadable executive image are vectored and identifies the name of the base image symbol table file, SYS.STB.

The image header now contains space for an array of version numbers, described in Section 29.6.

The linker COLLECT option has a new qualifier, /ATTRIBUTES. The possible values for the qualifier are RESIDENT, to designate a nonpageable image section, and INITIALIZATION_CODE, to designate the initialization image section. These values initialize the new image section descriptor flags ISD$V_RESIDENT and ISD$V_INITIALCODE.

29.3.2 Data in a Loadable Executive Image

A data cell private to routines in a loadable executive image resides in that

Table 29.2   Organization of IO_ROUTINES.EXE, a Typical Loadable Executive Image

Cluster Name	*PSECT Name*	*Modules*
NONPAGED_READONLY_PSECTS	EXEC$NONPAGED_CODE	BUFFERCTL
		.
		PATA_NONPAGED
NONPAGED_READWRITE_PSECTS	EXEC$NONPAGED_DATA	MMDAT
		.
PAGED_READONLY_PSECTS	EXEC$PAGED_CODE	IOSUBPAGD
		.
		PATA_PAGED
PAGED_READWRITE_PSECTS	EXEC$PAGED_DATA	IOSUBPAGD
		.
INITIALIZATION_PSECTS	EXEC$INIT_000	SYS$DOINIT
	EXEC$INIT_001	SYS$DOINIT
		MMDAT
		.
	EXEC$INIT_002	SYS$DOINIT
	EXEC$INIT_CODE	SYS$DOINIT
		MMDAT
		.
		PATA_NONPAGED
		PATA_PAGED
	EXEC$INIT_PFNTBL_000	SYS$DOINIT
	EXEC$INIT_PFNTBL_001	SYS$DOINIT
	EXEC$INIT_PFNTBL_002	SYS$DOINIT
	EXEC$INIT_SSTBL_000	SYS$DOINIT
	EXEC$INIT_SSTBL_001	SYS$DOINIT
		SYSASSIGN
		.
	EXEC$INIT_SSTBL_002	SYS$DOINIT
	[Fixup vectors]	

image. A data cell accessed by routines in multiple loadable executive images
may be placed in the base image or in one of the loadable executive images. If
the data itself is not in the base image, the base image must contain a pointer
to it for use by the other loadable executive images. That is, a routine in one
loadable executive image cannot directly reference data in another and must
make an indirect reference through a base image pointer.

Certain data cells reside in loadable executive images even though they
are small and unlikely to change size. A data cell that is referenced primarily

by routines within the image is typically in the image itself, to reduce the access overhead for the most frequent references.

A data structure whose size is likely to vary from version to version is stored in a loadable executive image, where its varying size and movement cannot affect the location of base image transfer vectors and pointers. A cell in the base image points to the structure if it is referenced from other loadable executive images.

Writable data cells referenced by commonly executed code paths are stored in the image with the most time-critical accesses.

Read-only data cells referenced by commonly executed code paths in multiple loadable executive images are defined in the module MMDAT. Several different loadable executive images include MMDAT by linking with it to reference these cells locally. The local reference often saves an instruction that would otherwise be needed for using a postindex operand specifier with these cells. MMDAT defines, for example, the cells MMG$GL_SPTBASE, which contains the base address of the system page table, and SCH$GL_PCBVEC, which contains the address of the software process control block vector. MMDAT includes an initialization routine; each image that includes MMDAT initializes these cells from the values computed earlier in system initialization.

29.3.3 Symbol Resolution in a Loadable Executive Image

A vectored universal symbol has two definitions. Each vectored universal symbol must be defined as a global in the base image, where its value is a system space address. It must also be defined as a universal symbol in a loadable executive image. This definition has two values—the absolute system space address of the base image global and the relative offset of the symbol within the loadable executive image. The procedure that loads loadable executive images (see Section 29.4.1) uses the relative offset in calculating the loaded address of the symbol; it stores this loaded address at the base image global address.

A universal symbol in a loadable executive image is defined through one of several macros:

- For a system service, the macro SYSTEM_SERVICE, which generates a .ENTRY directive and other code, described in Section 29.5.4.3
- For a routine entered through a CALLx instruction, the macro UNIVERSAL_ENTRY, which generates a .ENTRY directive
- For a routine entered through a JSB instruction, the macro UNIVERSAL_SYMBOL, which generates a .TRANSFER directive
- For a data structure whose address is stored in a base image global, the macro UNIVERSAL_SYMBOL, which generates a .TRANSFER directive

Figure 29.2 shows how references from one loadable executive image to another are resolved at run time through SYS.EXE.

The code extracted from the image IO_ROUTINES.EXE is part of the Queue I/O ($QIO) system service. It tries to allocate an I/O request packet (IRP) from the IRP lookaside list. If the list is empty, the $QIO system service procedure invokes EXE$ALLOCIRP either to expand the lookaside list or to allocate one from the nonpaged variable-length list.

Both the IRP lookaside list and the routine EXE$ALLOCIRP are in the image SYSTEM_PRIMITIVES.EXE. The IRP lookaside list is part of a larger structure whose fields are defined symbolically by the macro $$SYSTEM_PRIM_DATADEF. The base image global EXE$AR_SYSTEM_PRIMITIVES_DATA points to this larger structure. Example 29.2 shows its definition. The base image contains an executive transfer vector for the routine EXE$ALLOCIRP. Example 29.1 shows its definition.

The image SYSTEM_PRIMITIVES.EXE defines the vectored universal symbols EXE$AR_SYSTEM_PRIMITIVES_DATA and EXE$ALLOCIRP, as shown in Example 29.3. When the image is loaded, the executive image loader relocates their base image globals.

Thus, at run time, the instruction MOVL G^EXE$AR_SYSTEM_PRIMITIVES_DATA,R2 stores the effective address of the loaded SYSTEM_PRIMITIVES.EXE data structure in R2. The instruction JSB G^EXE$ALLOCIRP transfers control to the base image transfer vector, which then transfers control to the routine in the loaded SYSTEM_PRIMITIVES.EXE. Note that EXE$ALLOCIRP itself can refer directly to IOC$GQ_IRPIQ, the IRP lookaside listhead, without referring to the base image pointer, since they are in the same loadable executive image.

29.4 EXECUTIVE IMAGE LOADING

Loadable executive images are loaded or initialized at several well-defined stages in system initialization. An image is loaded at only one particular stage. However, it may potentially execute initialization code at that and succeeding stages of initialization. In general, loading of executive images is deferred to the later stages of system initialization, if possible, for simplicity.

The major stages of system initialization at which images are loaded or initialized are

1. SYSBOOT.EXE
2. EXEC_INIT.EXE (routine EXE$INIT)
3. The swapper process
4. The SYSINIT process

Chapters 30 and 31 describe these and other stages of system initialization in detail. This section is concerned only with their role in the loading and initialization of loadable executive images.

These stages are more finely subdivided, primarily for initialization of loadable images. The system global EXE$GL_STATE describes these finer divisions with a bit set to represent each substage that has been reached. The

Example 29.3
Definition of Vectored Universal Symbols

```
        UNIVERSAL_SYMBOL -                  ;Make pointer to lookaside lists
EXE$AR_SYSTEM_PRIMITIVES_DATA               ; universal
;
; I/O packet lookaside listhead
        .ALIGN   QUAD
IOC_BASE:
        ASSUME   IOC_GQ_IRPIQ EQ 0
IOC$GQ_IRPIQ::
        .QUAD    0
        ASSUME   IOC_GL_IRPREM EQ .-IOC_BASE
IOC$GL_IRPREM::
        .LONG    0                          ;Address of partial packet
        ASSUME   IOC_GL_IRPCNT EQ .-IOC_BASE
IOC$GL_IRPCNT::                             ;
        .LONG    0                          ;Current count of allocated
                                            ; packets
        ASSUME   IOC_GL_IRPMIN EQ .-IOC_BASE
IOC$GL_IRPMIN::                             ;Minimum size to take from list
        .LONG    <<IRP$C_LENGTH*2>/3>
        .
        .
        UNIVERSAL_SYMBOL EXE$ALLOCIRP
;EXE$ALLOCIRP::                             ;Allocate I/O packet -
                                            ; conditional wait
        ASSUME   IRP$B_TYPE EQ IRP$W_SIZE+2
        PUSHL    <DYN$C_IRP@16>!-           ;Set data structure type
                 <IRP$C_LENGTH+EXE$C_ALCGRNMSK>&<^C<EXEC$C_ALCGRNMSK>>
                                            ;Set size of buffer required
        BRB      20$
        .
        .
```

macro $BOOSTATEDEF defines symbolic values for these bits. Table 29.3 lists them in the order in which their states occur.

Loadable executive images are mapped and loaded at several different stages of system initialization by LDR$LOAD_IMAGE, in module SYSLDR. LDR$LOAD_IMAGE executes as part of the following images and stages:

1. SYSBOOT.EXE, the secondary bootstrap program, which initializes system space and loads the base image, the minimal set of executive images listed in part A of Table 29.1, and various other images (see Chapter 30)
2. EXEC_INIT.EXE, the loadable executive image that performs initialization after memory management has been enabled and that loads most of the rest of the executive images, as shown in Table 29.1, part B
3. SYSINIT.EXE, which runs in the SYSINIT process and loads the images listed in Table 29.1, part C

Table 29.3   States in System Initialization

Bit Name	Set By	Meaning
BOOSTATE$V_SYSBOOT	(Unused)	
BOOSTATE$V_INIT	EXE$INIT	EXE$INIT has begun
BOOSTATE$V_MAPPED	EXE$INIT	Memory management has been enabled
BOOSTATE$V_CONSOLE	EXE$INIT	Console I/O routines are available
BOOSTATE$V_PFN_INIT	EXE$INIT	Page frame number (PFN) database is initialized
BOOSTATE$V_POOL_INIT	EXE$INIT	Nonpaged pool allocation is possible
BOOSTATE$V_SWAPPER	EXE$SWAPINIT	Swapper process has begun
BOOSTATE$V_SYSINIT	SYSINIT	SYSINIT process has begun
BOOSTATE$V_RMS	SYSINIT	RMS has been loaded
BOOSTATE$V_XQP	SYSINIT	File system has been mapped
BOOSTATE$V_STARTUP	SYSINIT	Startup process has been created

The loading and initialization of loadable executive images are described in the sections that follow.

In addition, after system initialization is complete, a loadable executive image can be loaded through the LDR$LOAD_IMAGE procedure built as part of SYSLDR_DYN.EXE, a loadable executive image.

29.4.1   Actions of LDR$LOAD_IMAGE

LDR$LOAD_IMAGE must effectively activate an executive image and establish connections between the transfer vectors and pointers in the base image and their targets in the loaded image. This section describes the basic operations of LDR$LOAD_IMAGE, with some details of the differences that arise from its execution in different initialization stages. (Note that SYSBOOT.EXE is linked with module SYSLDR_SYSBOOT, and SYSLDR_DYN.EXE with module SYSLDR_DYN. These modules contain slightly different versions of LDR$LOAD_IMAGE.)

LDR$LOAD_IMAGE is called with the name of a loadable executive image and a flag indicating whether the image should be loaded with its pageable sections resident. The flag is based on the value of bit S0PAGING$V_EXEC (bit 0) of the SYSGEN parameter S0_PAGING.

LDR$LOAD_IMAGE takes the following steps:

1. It opens the image file using whatever mechanism is available at this stage, either minimal file system routines or the full file system. A window control block (WCB) is created for a file opened with the minimal file system routines. Later, after SYSINIT has mapped the file system

and loaded RMS, SYSINIT opens the file and leaves it open so that, for example, normal file system checks will prevent the file's deletion.

Running in process context and after system initialization is complete, LDR$LOAD_IMAGE in module SYSLDR_DYN is entered in executive mode and uses RMS to open the image. It then requests the Change to Kernel Mode ($CMKRNL) system service and performs the rest of its processing in kernel mode.

2. LDR$LOAD_IMAGE reads the first block of the file, its image header, and checks that the executive versions with which the file was linked are compatible with the current system.

3. If the versions are incompatible, LDR$LOAD_IMAGE does not load the executive image and returns the severe error status SS$_SYSVERDIF.

   If the versions are compatible, LDR$LOAD_IMAGE allocates a loadable image data block (LDRIMG) from nonpaged pool. (Running with SYSBOOT, LDR$LOAD_IMAGE builds the LDRIMG in local storage and subsequently copies it to pool.) It initializes the LDRIMG, copying information from the image header, such as image file name, link time, and address of the initialization routine. Figure 29.3 shows the layout of the LDRIMG.

4. LDR$LOAD_IMAGE in module SYSLDR_DYN locks the base image mutex, EXE$GL_BASIMGMTX, for write access. It searches the LDRIMG list to see if a loadable executive image with the same name has already been loaded.

   —If one exists, LDR$LOAD_IMAGE deallocates the LDRIMG, unlocks the mutex, and returns the error status SS$_DUPLNAM to its caller.

   —If one does not, LDR$LOAD_IMAGE sets LDRIMG$V_PART_LOAD to indicate that image loading is not complete, inserts the LDRIMG at the front of the list, and unlocks the mutex.

5. Scanning the image section descriptors (ISDs), LDR$LOAD_IMAGE initializes the appropriate LDRIMG fields to describe the location and size in bytes of each section. For example, it initializes the fields LDRIMG$L_NONPAG_W_BASE and LDRIMG$L_NONPAG_W_LEN to describe the resident writable section.

6. LDR$LOAD_IMAGE allocates contiguous system page table entries (SPTEs) for the pages of all the image sections (see Section 29.8.1). It computes the system address represented by the lowest SPTE as the base address of the image, stores it in the LDRIMG, and relocates the initialization routine address by the base address.

7. It invokes LDR$LOAD_NONPAGED, in module SYSLDR, twice—once to map and load the nonpaged read-only code section and once for the writable one. Section 29.4.2 describes LDR$LOAD_NONPAGED.

8. It invokes a local routine, LOAD_PAGED, to map pageable read-only and then pageable writable sections. (The images loaded by SYSBOOT

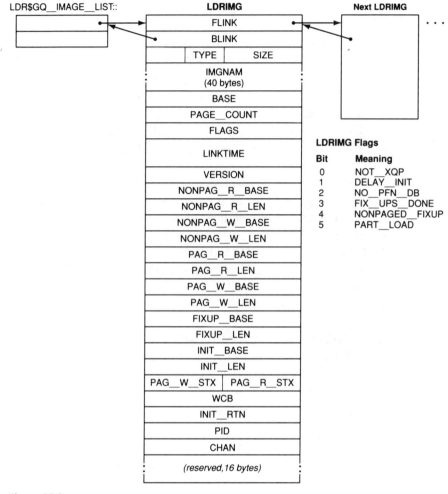

Figure 29.3
Layout of a Loadable Image Data Block (LDRIMG)

have no pageable code or data, so this routine is never invoked during SYSBOOT.) Section 29.4.3 describes LOAD_PAGED.

9. LDR$LOAD_IMAGE invokes LDR$LOAD_NONPAGED twice more— once to map and load the fixup section and once for the initialization section.

10. LDR$LOAD_IMAGE in module SYSLDR_DYN changes the protection on the pages containing the system service vectors to permit writes from kernel mode.

11. It scans the image's global symbol table for vectored universal symbol and entry point records. Each of these records contains the symbol's two values and, for a universal entry point, the procedure register save mask.

LDR$LOAD_IMAGE adds the loaded image base address to the symbol's relative offset to form its effective address.

If the symbol is an entry point, it could be a system service vector or an executive transfer vector for a routine entered through a CALLx instruction. LDR$LOAD_IMAGE stores in the loaded base image the symbol's register save mask and a JMP to the effective address in the loaded image. (Section 29.5.4.3 describes how the JMP instruction is overwritten with instructions for inner mode system services.) Otherwise, it examines the word at the symbol's system space address to determine whether the symbol is a transfer vector or a pointer to data. (A transfer vector that is not an entry point starts with a JSB or JMP instruction.) LDR$LOAD_IMAGE stores the effective address of the symbol as the destination of a transfer instruction or as the pointer value.

12. LDR$LOAD_IMAGE in module SYSLDR_DYN restores the original protection on the pages containing the system service vectors.

13. If LDR$LOAD_IMAGE is not running as part of SYSBOOT, it invokes LDR$INIT_SINGLE to call the image's initialization routine, if there is one (see Section 29.5.1). Otherwise, if it is running as part of SYSBOOT and there is an initialization routine, it sets the flag LDRIMG$V_DELAY_INIT in LDRIMG$L_FLAGS so that the routine will be invoked at a later stage of initialization.

14. If LDR$LOAD_IMAGE is running as part of SYSBOOT, it allocates nonpaged pool and copies the local storage LDRIMG to the pool. If LDR$LOAD_IMAGE is running as part of SYSBOOT, EXE$INIT, or SYSINIT, it inserts the LDRIMG at the head of the list of LDRIMGs, LDR$GQ_IMAGE_LIST.

    If LDR$LOAD_IMAGE is running after system initialization is complete, as part of SYSLDR_DYN, it locks the base image mutex, clears LDRIMG$V_PART_LOAD to indicate that loading is complete, unlocks the base image mutex, and returns from the kernel mode procedure.

15. LDR$LOAD_IMAGE returns to its caller.

29.4.2 Actions of LDR$LOAD_NONPAGED

LDR$LOAD_NONPAGED is invoked with arguments specifying the address of the LDRIMG, base and length of the section, and protection for the section's pages. LDR$LOAD_NONPAGED performs the following steps:

1. For each page of the section, it does the following:

   a. Unless it is running as part of SYSBOOT, it acquires the MMG spinlock.

   b. It allocates a page of physical memory.

   c. It initializes the SPTE for that section page with the allocated PFN, owner mode of kernel, valid bit set, and a protection of KW. KW is required so that the page can be overwritten with the contents of the image file. Its protection is changed later.

    d. If the physical page is described by the PFN database, LDR$LOAD_NONPAGED records information about the page, such as the address of the page table entry (PTE) that contains it, and its state and type.

    e. If it has acquired the MMG spinlock, it now releases the spinlock.

2. It reads the image section into the allocated space.

3. It changes the protection in the section's SPTEs to the appropriate value. If LDR$LOAD_NONPAGED is not executing as part of SYSBOOT, this operation requires that the MMG spinlock be held and that any entries in the translation buffer for these SPTEs be invalidated.

4. It returns to LDR$LOAD_IMAGE.

29.4.3   Actions of LOAD_PAGED

LOAD_PAGED is invoked with the same arguments as is LDR$LOAD_NONPAGED. Its arguments include a flag that indicates whether the image should be loaded with its pageable sections resident. It performs the following steps:

1. If pageable sections are to be made resident, LOAD_PAGED invokes LDR$LOAD_NONPAGED to load the section and returns.

2. Otherwise, LOAD_PAGED first forms prototype PTE contents suitable for mapping each page of the section. The protection, passed as an argument, is either UR for a read-only or URKW for a writable section. The page owner is kernel mode. The type bits in the PTE are set to indicate that the page is part of a section and currently in the image file.

3. LOAD_PAGED tests and sets the shared bit in the image's WCB. If the bit was clear (if the file had been opened with primitive file routines), LOAD_PAGED initializes its reference count to 2. If the bit was set, LOAD_PAGED increments its reference count. These steps make the WCB look like any other WCB describing a section file, even if it had been created by primitive file routines, and ensure that the file is permanently open.

4. LOAD_PAGED, running as part of SYSLDR_DYN, locks the global section mutex for write access.

5. It allocates and initializes a section table entry from the system header.

6. LOAD_PAGED, running as part of SYSLDR_DYN, unlocks the global section mutex.

7. LOAD_PAGED stores the index number of the section table entry in the prototype PTE contents. It records information such as the WCB address, number of section pages, section base system virtual page number, and a flag indicating whether the section is writable.

8. LOAD_PAGED writes the prototype PTE to the SPTEs previously allocated for the section by LDR$LOAD_IMAGE. The section's pages will

be read in later from the loadable executive image in response to page faults, possibly during image initialization when address fixups are done or later during image execution.

9. It triggers invalidation of its own processor's translation buffer and that of any other SMP members.
10. It returns to LDR$LOAD_IMAGE.

29.4.4 Loading of Optional Images

If the value of the special SYSGEN parameter LOAD_SYS_IMAGES is 1, its default, the loading of optional images is enabled. The images to be loaded are listed in SYS$LOADABLE_IMAGES:VMS$SYSTEM_IMAGES.DATA. Each entry specifies the name of a loadable executive image and in which phase, EXE$INIT or SYSINIT, the image should be loaded.

This mechanism provides for the loading of

- Optional VMS-supplied executive images
- Executive images that are part of optional software products
- Site-specific images containing custom versions of the Magnetic Tape Accessibility ($MTACCESS) and Get Security Erase Pattern ($ERAPAT) system services

Both EXE$INIT and SYSINIT call LDR$ALTERNATE_LOAD, in module ALTERNATE_LOAD. LDR$ALTERNATE_LOAD takes the following steps:

1. It tests the value of LOAD_SYS_IMAGES.
2. If the value is zero, the procedure returns. Otherwise, it opens and reads SYS$LOADABLE_IMAGES:VMS$SYSTEM_IMAGES.DATA.
3. For each record in the file, LDR$ALTERNATE_LOAD tests whether it is running during the specified initialization phase. If it is not, LDR$ALTERNATE_LOAD reads the next record.
4. If the current initialization phase matches that in the record, LDR$ALTERNATE_LOAD opens the specified image and reads its image header. It then invokes LDR$LOAD_IMAGE to map the image.
5. When LDR$ALTERNATE_LOAD reaches the end of the file, it closes the file and returns to its caller.

Introduction to VMS System Services documents the procedure for building a site-specific version of the $MTACCESS system service. Apart from replacements for the $ERAPAT and $MTACCESS system services, use of this mechanism is reserved to Digital and completely unsupported.

29.5 INITIALIZATION OF A LOADABLE EXECUTIVE IMAGE

Each loadable executive image contains its own initialization routines that perform a variety of functions. Some are specific to the features and functions supported by the image; others are required by all loadable executive images.

An initialization routine may need to execute in an environment that does not exist when the routine's executive image is first loaded. There is a mechanism, therefore, to provide for delayed and multiple invocations of initialization routines. Initialization routines can be invoked, for example, after the PFN database has been created or once paging is possible. The space occupied by these routines is deallocated when initialization is complete.

Initialization routines are described by an initialization routine table in each loadable executive image. Each table entry is a quadword. The first longword specifies the location of an initialization routine, containing either the system space address of a routine in the base image or a self-relative offset to a routine within the loadable executive image. The second longword contains flags that describe the initialization routine and its state.

Each loadable executive image (except SYSMSG.EXE) is linked with the module DOINIT, which includes an initialization routine dispatcher, INI$DOINIT. Each image linked with DOINIT specifies INI$DOINIT as its transfer address. LDR$LOAD_IMAGE copies the transfer address from the image header to the field LDRIMG$L_INIT_RTN. INI$DOINIT is invoked multiple times during system initialization. It scans the initialization routine table and invokes the specified routines. Each routine can examine the flags in EXE$GL_STATE to identify the current phase of system initialization and determine whether its execution is appropriate.

The DOINIT module defines a number of PSECTs, all of which are clustered into the initialization image section. Three of the PSECTs build the initialization routine table: EXEC$INIT_000 defines its start and names it INI$A_VECTOR_TABLE; EXEC$INIT_001 defines its body; EXEC$INIT_002 defines its end with an entry of zero. Modules in the loadable executive image, including DOINIT itself, make entries in the body of the table by invoking the macro INITIALIZATION_ROUTINE. The other PSECTs and their uses are described in subsequent sections.

The macro $INIRTNDEF defines symbolic values for the flags in the initialization table. INIRTN$V_SYSRTN, when set by the INITIALIZATION_ROUTINE macro, means that the routine address is within the base image. INIRTN$V_CALLED, when set, means that INI$DOINIT has invoked the initialization routine. INIRTN$V_NO_RECALL, when set, means that the initialization routine should not be invoked again. The use of these flags is described in Section 29.5.3.

The module DOINIT itself contains INITIALIZATION_ROUTINE macros that create table entries for three common initialization routines used by most loadable executive images:

- LOADER$FIXUP_DOT_ADDRESS, which performs address fixups for the image
- INI$PFN_FIXUP, which alters the image's instructions that reference the PFN database

- INI$SYSTEM_SERVICE, which performs initialization for any system services in the image

These initialization routines are described in later sections.

29.5.1 **Initialization Sequence**

LDR$INIT_SINGLE and LDR$INIT_ALL are the routines that trigger loadable executive image initialization. LDR$INIT_SINGLE initializes a single loadable executive image. LDR$INIT_ALL scans the LDRIMG list, which contains image data blocks for the images loaded thus far, and invokes LDR$INIT_SINGLE for each of them. Both these routines are in the SYSLDR, SYSLDR_SYSBOOT, and SYSLDR_DYN modules and are linked with SYS-BOOT.EXE, EXEC_INIT.EXE, SYSINIT.EXE, and SYSLDR_DYN.EXE.

These routines can be invoked multiple times during system initialization:

1. In the case of an image loaded by SYSBOOT, LDR$LOAD_IMAGE sets the flag LDRIMG$V_DELAY_INIT so that the routine will be reinvoked at a later stage. At this stage, memory management is off.

2. After memory management has been enabled and the system control block (SCB) has been established, EXE$INIT invokes LDR$INIT_ALL to perform further initialization of those images loaded by SYSBOOT.

3. After nonpaged pool and the PFN database are initialized, EXE$INIT sets flags in EXE$GL_STATE to indicate their initialization and invokes LDR$INIT_ALL again to perform further initialization of the images loaded by SYSBOOT.

4. EXE$INIT loads the set of loadable executive images listed in Table 29.1, part B. For each, EXE$INIT invokes LDR$LOAD_IMAGE, which invokes LDR$INIT_SINGLE.

5. EXE$INIT then invokes LDR$INIT_ALL to perform further initialization of all the images loaded thus far. This additional initialization is done in case actions in one image's initialization routine depend on actions taken in another image's initialization routine.

6. The swapper process sets a flag in EXE$GL_STATE, to indicate that the swapper is running, and initializes paged pool. It invokes LDR$INIT_ALL. Now that paging is possible, address fixups in pageable sections of loadable executive images can be done and system services can be connected.

7. The SYSINIT process loads several loadable executive images through LDR$LOAD_IMAGE, which invokes LDR$INIT_SINGLE for each of them.

In addition, LDR$INIT_SINGLE can be invoked to initialize a loadable executive image that is loaded dynamically after system initialization is complete.

29.5.2 Actions of LDR$INIT_SINGLE

LDR$INIT_SINGLE performs the following steps:

1. It tests whether the value of LDRIMG$L_INIT_RTN is zero. If it is, the routine returns.
2. Otherwise, it calls the routine whose address is in LDRIMG$L_INIT_RTN. It passes one argument, the address of the LDRIMG. Although this mechanism allows for other possibilities, LDRIMG$L_INIT_RTN currently always contains the address of INI$DOINIT.
3. If INI$DOINIT returns an error status, LDR$INIT_SINGLE returns to its invoker.
4. Otherwise, it tests the flag LDRIMG$V_FIX_UPS_DONE, which is set by LOADER$FIXUP_DOT_ADDRESS when all address fixups have been done. If the flag is set, LDR$INIT_SINGLE deallocates the address space occupied by the image fixup section, unless the space has already been deallocated. Section 29.8.2 gives information on the deallocation of system space.
5. LDR$INIT_SINGLE tests the flag LDRIMG$V_DELAY_INIT, which is set by INI$DOINIT when an initialization routine specifies that it must be reinvoked. If the flag is clear, LDR$INIT_SINGLE deallocates the address space occupied by the initialization section, unless it has already been deallocated.
6. It returns to its invoker.

29.5.3 Actions of INI$DOINIT

INI$DOINIT is the initialization routine dispatcher. It performs the following steps:

1. It clears the LDRIMG flag LDRIMG$V_DELAY_INIT to implement its default of not scanning the initialization table again.
2. It scans the table.
3. For each entry, it tests and sets the INIRTN$V_NO_RECALL flag to implement the default of invoking a routine only once. If the flag was already set, it goes on to the next entry.
4. If the flag was clear, it invokes the routine with a JSB instruction.
5. If the routine determines that it should be reentered at a later state of system initialization, it clears the INIRTN$V_NO_RECALL flag.
6. When the routine returns, INI$DOINIT sets INIRTN$V_CALLED to record that the routine was invoked and tests INIRTN$V_NO_RECALL. If the flag is clear, INI$DOINIT sets LDRIMG$V_DELAY_INIT to ensure that LDR$INIT_SINGLE does not deallocate the initialization section and that INI$DOINIT will be recalled at a later point in system initialization.

29.5.4   **Initialization Routines**

An image-specific initialization routine might do a number of things, including, but not limited to, the following:

- Store the absolute address of an interrupt or exception service routine in an appropriate SCB vector
- Initialize base image (SYS.EXE) globals
- Initialize data in a loadable executive image
- Allocate pool for a data structure

For the details of what happens in the initialization of a particular loadable executive image, see Chapters 30 and 31 and any chapters that describe that specific image.

The following sections describe the three common initialization routines that are part of most loadable executive images.

29.5.4.1   **Address Relocation Fixups.** LOADER$FIXUP_DOT_ADDRESS relocates the addresses in any .ADDRESS and .ASCID directives within the loadable executive image. These references from the image to locations within itself cannot be position-independent unless they are relocated after the load address of the image is determined. Chapter 26 gives a more detailed description of address fixups.

LOADER$FIXUP_DOT_ADDRESS uses a table in the address fixup image section. It takes the following steps:

1. As a sanity check, it tests that the address fixup section in the loadable executive image represents only one image and that it contains no G^ reference fixups, that is, it contains no outbound calls other than through the base image. If either test fails, the routine returns with an error status and without having relocated address fixups.

2. It examines the fixup section to see if there are any address fixups required. If not, it sets LDRIMG$V_FIX_UPS_DONE in LDRIMG$L_FLAGS and returns.

3. It tests a flag in EXE$GL_STATE to determine whether paging is possible yet.

4. If paging is not possible, the routine tests further to see whether memory management has been enabled.

   If memory management has not been enabled, the routine clears the flag INIRTN$V_NO_RECALL, so that the routine will be entered in a later initialization stage, and returns.

   If memory management is enabled, LOADER$FIXUP_DOT_ADDRESS performs address fixups in the nonpageable section, unless it already has, and sets the flag LDRIMG$V_NONPAGED_FIXUP to indicate that they are done. If there are pageable fixups yet to be done, the routine clears

INIRTN$V_NO_RECALL before returning, so that the routine will be entered in a later initialization stage.

5. If paging is possible, all address fixups can be done. LOADER$FIXUP_DOT_ADDRESS performs both paged and nonpaged fixups, unless it already has, and sets the flags LDRIMG$V_NONPAGED_FIXUP and LDRIMG$V_FIX_UPS_DONE. It returns without clearing INIRTN$V_NO_RECALL. When control returns to LDR$INIT_SINGLE with the flag LDRIMG$V_FIX_UPS_DONE set, LDR$INIT_SINGLE deallocates the fixup section.

For each address fixup (each .ADDRESS or .ASCID directive), the linker has created a table entry in the fixup section. In that entry, it has placed the offset into the image of the location whose address must be made absolute. In the location itself, the linker has placed the offset into the image of the target address. To perform an address fixup, LOADER$FIXUP_DOT_ADDRESS first adds the image's base address to the offset in the fixup table entry, thus calculating the address of the location to be fixed. It then adds the image's base address to the contents of that location. If LOADER$FIXUP_DOT_ADDRESS is only performing nonpaged or paged fixups, it must first determine that the longword is located in a nonpageable or pageable part of the image.

29.5.4.2   **PFN Fixups.** On a CPU with more than 32 MB of memory described in the PFN database (see Chapter 14), the forward and back link arrays in the database must have longword, rather than word, elements. Many of the instructions that reference these arrays use context indexing. Thus, their opcodes are sensitive to the array element size and cannot be determined at assembly time. INI$PFN_FIXUP replaces word context opcodes with longword context opcodes in these instructions.

INI$PFN_FIXUP is table-driven, using a PFN opcode replacement table within each loadable executive image. The module DOINIT defines three PSECTs that build the table: EXEC$INIT_PFNTBL_000 defines its start and names it MMG$AL_FIXUPTBL; EXEC$INIT_PFNTBL_001 defines its body; and EXEC$INIT_PFNTBL_002 defines its end with an entry of zero. Modules in the loadable executive image make entries in the body of the table by invoking the macro PFN_REFERENCE.

PFN_REFERENCE only makes entries for instructions within nonpageable PSECTs. (For instructions in pageable PSECTs, it generates in-line alternative code paths and a branch selecting the appropriate one.) Each entry consists of the following three fields:

- A longword containing the self-relative offset into the image of the instruction that may need modification
- A byte containing the word context opcode
- A byte containing the longword context opcode

INI$PFN_FIXUP tests MMG$GW_BIGPFN to determine if fixup is necessary. By default, the instructions are assembled with word context opcodes. If MMG$GW_BIGPFN is zero, fixups are not necessary and INI$PFN_FIXUP returns. Otherwise, it scans the table.

For each entry, it calculates the effective address of the instruction. As a sanity check, it tests that the byte at that address is the word context opcode in the table entry. If not, it generates a fatal PFNFIXUP bugcheck. Otherwise, it replaces the opcode with the longword context opcode in the table entry. When INI$PFN_FIXUP reaches the end of the table, it constructs a program counter/processor status longword (PC/PSL) pair and executes an REI instruction to flush the processor's instruction lookahead buffer. It then returns.

29.5.4.3   **System Service Initialization.** INI$SYSTEM_SERVICE connects any system services in the loadable executive image to their system service vectors and assigns change mode codes for inner access mode services. It is table-driven, using INI$A_BUILD_TABLE, a table of system service descriptor blocks within the image. The module DOINIT defines three PSECTs that build the table: EXEC$INIT_SSTBL_000 defines its start; EXEC$INIT_SSTBL_001 defines its body; and EXEC$INIT_SSTBL_002 defines its end with an entry of zero. Modules in the loadable executive image make entries in the body of the table by invoking the macro SYSTEM_SERVICE. The macro initializes the fields in a system service descriptor block.

Each system service descriptor block contains the following fields:

- The absolute address of the system service vector
- The self-relative offset to the system service procedure in the loadable executive image
- The number of arguments to the system service
- The minimum number of arguments required
- The system service filter group (see Chapter 6)
- A code indicating the access mode in which the system service procedure executes
- A value indicating what wait routine, if any, is required for synchronous system services
- A value indicating what kind of additional exit processing, if any, is required after the system service returns

The macro $SSDESCRDEF defines symbolic offsets for these fields.

INI$SYSTEM_SERVICE takes the following steps:

1. Because INI$SYSTEM_SERVICE requires process context to execute, it first tests a flag in EXE$GL_STATE to determine whether the swapper process has executed yet. If not, the routine clears INIRTN$V_NO_

RECALL so that the routine will be entered in process context, when paging is possible, and returns. If the swapper process has begun to execute, INI$SYSTEM_SERVICE proceeds.

2. It changes the protection on the pages containing the system service vectors, making them writable so that it can modify vectors.

3. It scans the system service initialization table. For each entry it finds, it calls EXE$CONNECT_SERVICES, in module SYSTEM_SERVICE_LOADER, passing it the address of the system service descriptor block.

4. When INI$SYSTEM_SERVICE reaches the end of the table, it makes the system service vector pages read-only again and returns.

EXE$CONNECT_SERVICES takes the following steps:

1. It determines whether the service is kernel mode, executive mode, or mode of caller.

2. For a mode-of-caller service, it checks that the information in the system service vector, already initialized by the loading of the loadable executive image, matches the information in the system service descriptor block. If the information does not match, it generates the fatal bugcheck BADVECTOR.

3. For an inner access mode service, EXE$CONNECT_SERVICES does the following:

   a. It acquires write ownership of a mutex called the change mode mutex, which prevents multiple processes from adding system services concurrently.

   b. It tests whether the instruction in the system service vector is a JMP or a change mode instruction. If it is already a change mode instruction, the service is being reloaded; EXE$CONNECT_SERVICES takes the actions described in steps 3e, 3f, and 3g. (Reloading is only used and supported for $MTACCESS and $ERAPAT.)

   c. If the instruction is a JMP, the service is being loaded for the first time. EXE$CONNECT_SERVICES checks that the register save mask and JMP destination in the vector match the information in the descriptor block and generates the fatal bugcheck BADVECTOR if they do not match. (LDR$LOAD_IMAGE stored the register save mask as part of processing the system service procedure's .ENTRY universal symbol.)

   d. If they match, EXE$CONNECT_SERVICES gets the change mode operand number to be assigned to this service (contents of CMOD$GW_CHMK_LIMIT for kernel mode, CMOD$GW_CHME_LIMIT for executive) and tests that the number is less than or equal to 255, the maximum operand number. If it is not, EXE$CONNECT_SERVICES generates the fatal bugcheck SSVECFULL.

   e. If it is less than or equal to 255, EXE$CONNECT_SERVICES constructs the system service vector contents as the concatenation of the register save mask, the appropriate change mode instruction, a RET, and a byte of 0. It ORs R2 and R4 into the register save mask to reflect their use by the change mode dispatcher.

f. It builds a PC/PSL pair and executes an REI instruction to flush the processor's instruction lookahead buffer in case any of the altered instructions were in a CPU instruction pipeline.

g. EXE$CONNECT_SERVICES records information from the system service descriptor block in arrays used by the change mode dispatchers. One set of arrays describes kernel mode system services; another set decribes executive mode services. Each array is indexed by the change mode operand number of the service. Chapter 6 describes these arrays and their uses.

h. EXE$CONNECT_SERVICES increments CMOD$GW_CHMx_LIMIT. The change mode dispatcher compares the contents of that cell against the operand of a change mode instruction to test its validity. A valid operand must be less than the contents. It then releases the change mode mutex.

4. For either type of service, EXE$CONNECT_SERVICES tests whether the service has a synchronous form (for example, $QIOW is the synchronous form of $QIO). If so, it initializes the system service vector (and following bytes, if necessary) for its synchronous form, copying the wait code for the service as well.

5. It returns to its caller.

29.6   VERSION NUMBERS

Versions of VMS have always been identified externally by a two-part number of the form *M.N*, for example, Version 4.6. *M* represents the major version and *N* represents the minor version. The major version identified a linked version of the system image, SYS.EXE, and its symbol table, SYS.STB, and changed only when SYS.EXE was relinked. The minor version identified a patch revision level of SYS.EXE.

An image linked with SYS.STB to resolve references to system globals contained an internal form of the major system version number in its image header, at field IHD$L_SYSVER.

The image activator compared the version in the image header to the running system's value. If the two were different, the image activator inhibited kernel and executive mode execution in the image. To run under a version of VMS with a new SYS.EXE, the image minimally had to be relinked to resolve global references with the new SYS.EXE's addresses and to alter the system version number in its image header. Algorithmic changes and reassembly might also be required as the result of system data structure or routine interface changes. The system version number, however, did not convey that

Table 29.4 Executive Version Categories

Category Name	Number	Description
BASE_IMAGE	0	Base image transfer vectors
MEMORY_MANAGEMENT	1	Memory management and dynamic pools
IO	2	I/O data structures and routines
FILES_VOLUMES	3	RMS and file system
PROCESS_SCHED	4	Process control, scheduling, and structure; layout of P1 space; timer events, ASTs, and event flags
SYSGEN	5	SYSGEN parameters
CLUSTERS_LOCKMGR	6	VAXcluster connection manager, lock manager, and other clusterwide facilities
LOGICAL_NAMES	7	Logical names
SECURITY	8	Security subsystem
IMAGE_ACTIVATOR	9	Image activation and image file interpretation
NETWORKS	10	DECnet and support for datalink drivers
COUNTERS	11	Cells that are interpreted as counts
STABLE	12	Routines and data structures expected to be stable
MISC	13	Miscellaneous
CPU	14	CPU-specific support
VOLATILE	15	Routines and data structures expected to change in the next release
SHELL	16	The layout of the SHELL module and P1 space

type of information, and care was required to ensure that the image was still compatible with the system routines and data structures it referenced.

The intent of the Version 5 executive reorganization is to minimize the frequency with which images linked with SYS.STB must relink. A change to a loadable executive image does not alter the addresses of its vectored universal symbols in SYS.EXE. However, data structure and routine interface changes within it may require algorithmic changes and reassembly of any images using its routines and data.

VMS Version 5 implements a more detailed form of internal system version identifier, which can denote data structure and routine interface changes. This number is independent of the external VMS version number. The executive reorganization does not tie a routine to a particular loadable executive image. Therefore, a version number for each loadable executive image is not a good solution. Instead, the executive has been divided into conceptual categories, such as I/O or memory management, each with its own version number. Table 29.4 lists these conceptual categories, each of which is identified by a number. The $SYSVERSIONDEF macro defines symbols for these numbers.

Each base image global symbol specifies the conceptual categories with which it is associated, using the VERSION_MASK keyword in the macro that defines it. Each bit in the mask corresponds to the number of a conceptual category. The macros that define base image data cell and transfer vector globals can also generate a mask global for each global. A module such as SYSTEM_DATA_CELLS is conditionally assembled to generate its mask globals and linked with the system image.

For example, the routine EXE$ALLOCIRP, invoked to allocate an IRP, is associated with the category MEMORY_MANAGEMENT. The symbol EXE$AR_SYSTEM_PRIMITIVES_DATA is also associated with the category MEMORY_MANAGEMENT. Extracts from SYSTEM_ROUTINES and SYSTEM_DATA_CELLS that define those symbols and their masks are shown in Examples 29.1 and 29.2.

Each category version number is a longword, with major ID in the high-order word and minor ID in the low-order word. Each is defined by a symbol named SYS$K_*category-name*. The category version numbers are defined in SYS.STB.

The version number for a category changes when an interface in that category changes. The minor ID changes for an upwardly compatible change; the major ID changes for an incompatible change. For example, if a routine's input arguments or a data structure's fields are redefined, then images referencing that routine or data structure will not execute properly unless they are changed. In such a case, the major ID is incremented. Examples of an upwardly compatible change are the addition of optional arguments to a routine and the use of data structure fields that had previously been defined as spare.

The format of an image header has been expanded in VMS Version 5 to include an array for category version numbers. The first longword of the array contains a mask identifying which categories are relevant to the image. The image header field IHD$L_SYSVER still contains the overall system version number, with the major version number in the high-order byte and the minor version number in the low-order three bytes. When an image referencing an executive global is linked, the linker ORs the value of the corresponding mask global into the image's category mask longword. When all globals are resolved, the mask has a bit set for each conceptual category relevant to the image. Starting from bit 0, the linker stores the relevant category version numbers from SYS.STB into the subsequent longwords of the version array. There are no entries in the version array for categories not relevant to that image.

The following is extracted from the output of the command ANALYZE /IMAGE SYS$SYSTEM:SDA.EXE.

```
SYS$COMMON:[SYSEXE]SDA.EXE;1
IMAGE HEADER

Fixed Header Information

image format major id: 02, minor id: 05
header block count: 2
image type: executable (IHD$K_EXE)
I/O channel count: default
I/O page count: default
linker flags:
        (0)  IHD$V_LNKDEBUG   0
        (1)  IHD$V_LNKNOTFR   0
        (2)  IHD$V_NOPOBUFS   0
        (3)  IHD$V_PICIMG     1
        (4)  IHD$V_POIMAGE    0
        (5)  IHD$V_DBGDMT     1
system version (major/minor): 1.0
system version array information:
        SYS$K_MEMORY_MANAGEMENT : (1.1 / 1.1)
        SYS$K_PROCESS_SCHED : (1.1 / 1.1)
        SYS$K_SYSGEN : (1.1 / 1.1)
        SYS$K_STABLE : (1.1 / 1.2)
        SYS$K_VOLATILE : (1.1 / 1.1)
```

The BASE_IMAGE category describes the layout of SYS.EXE rather than any particular conceptual category. The BASE_IMAGE minor ID is altered when a new transfer vector or data cell is added so that an image using the new symbol cannot run on an older version. Altering the BASE_IMAGE major ID forces a relink of all images linked with SYS.STB. Required when the layout of the base image changes, this is expected to be rare.

The overall system version, SYS$K_VERSION, has for its major ID the major ID of the BASE_IMAGE category. Its minor ID represents the particular release or build; its use is reserved to VMS.

Base image global SYS$GL_VERSION begins a 32-longword array of version numbers generated from the assembly of module VERSION_NUMBERS. When an image linked with SYS.STB is activated, the routine EXE$CHECK_VERSION, in module CHECK_VERSION, is invoked to compare the array of version numbers in its image header with the versions of the running executive. All of the following must be true:

- The major ID of the image must match the major ID of the running system.
- The minor ID must be less than or equal to that of the running system.
- The first longword of the IHD version array contains a mask of conceptual executive categories relevant to the image. For each bit set in the mask, the major ID of the executive category at the time the image was linked

must be equal to that of the category in the running system. The minor ID must be less than or equal to that of the category in the running system.

In VMS Versions 5.0 through 5.1, if the versions are incompatible, the image activator inhibits kernel and executive mode execution in the image by removing CMEXEC and CMKRNL privileges. In VMS Version 5.2, the image activator aborts the activation and returns the fatal error status SS$_SYSVERDIF.

29.7   OTHER KINDS OF LOADABLE EXECUTIVE IMAGE

During the evolution of VMS, the number of executive images grew. Several different loading mechanisms were implemented to deal with different types of executive image.

VMS Version 1 supported one CPU type, the VAX-11/780, and a number of I/O devices. Most of the executive was in the system image, SYS.EXE, which contained CPU-specific support. Separate device driver images loaded into nonpaged pool provided most I/O device support. The device driver structure and loading mechanism were designed to be extensible to user-written device drivers. The SYSGEN utility was designed to build I/O data structures and load both VMS and user-written device drivers.

VMS Version 2 supported a second CPU type, the VAX-11/750. Requiring all systems to load code required for both CPU types was not desirable. Instead, the CPU-specific routines were moved into separately loadable images named SYSLOA*xxx*.EXE, where *xxx* designates the CPU type. VMS Version 2 included a mechanism for loading SYSLOA*xxx*.EXE into nonpaged pool and a method of dispatching into its routines.

VMS Version 3 added support for a new storage system protocol, system communication services (SCS). Support for it and its first devices required a disk class device driver, two different port drivers, and SCS support routines that provided an interface between a class and port driver. The SYSLOA loading and dispatching mechanism was extended to SCS support routines, which were built in the SCSLOA.EXE image.

VMS Version 4 added support for VAXcluster systems and for MicroVAX processors. VAXcluster-specific routines were built in the CLUSTRLOA.EXE image, which used the SYSLOA loading and dispatching mechanism. Two images that contained instruction emulation routines were added: VAXEMUL.EXE contained support for emulating VAX instructions not implemented in MicroVAX microcode; FPEMUL.EXE contained support for floating-point data types not supported by microcode on all CPU types. The instruction emulation images were loaded into nonpaged pool.

The rest of this section briefly describes some of the loading mechanisms used for these executive images that existed prior to VMS Version 5. The *VMS Device Support Manual* describes the driver loading mechanism.

29.7.1 CPU-Dependent and Other Loadable Routines

The CPU-specific images have names of the form SYSLOA*xxx*.EXE. (Appendix G lists SYSLOA images.) SYSBOOT uses the CPU type, CPU subtype, and, in some cases, type of console device, to select the SYSLOA image appropriate to the configuration. The SYSLOA images are in directory SYS$LOADABLE_IMAGES.

SYSBOOT opens the image and reads the image header and the first block of the image body. It invokes EXE$CHECK_VERSION to check that the running system has compatible software for all conceptual executive categories relevant to the SYSLOA image. If the versions are incompatible, SYSBOOT writes an error message on the console terminal and halts.

Otherwise, SYSBOOT allocates nonpaged pool from the high end of the variable-length region for the image. The first block of the image body begins with a dynamic data structure header; the longword at offset 0 and the word at offset 8 both specify the size of the image to be loaded into nonpaged pool. Offset 4 in the data structure header contains the offset from the beginning of the image to a routine within the image that performs image-specific initialization. SYSBOOT loads the image into nonpaged pool and records its starting address and size for EXE$INIT. The image must be position-independent code, since its location in pool is indeterminate at link time.

The miscellaneous vectors area of the base image includes vectored entry points to routines in a SYSLOA image. These entry points are defined as base image globals in the module SYSLOAVEC. A typical entry point is a JMP instruction whose initial target is EXE$LOAD_ERROR, the address of a HALT instruction.

The source for this module is conditionally assembled to build the module LOAVEC, a table containing a self-relative offset into the image for each CPU-dependent transfer vector. LOAVEC is linked into each SYSLOA*xxx* image. During system initialization, the LOAVEC table in the loaded SYSLOA*xxx* image is used to relocate the targets of the SYSLOA transfer vectors in the base image.

Each element in the table is five bytes long: the first byte identifies its type; the next longword is a self-relative offset into the image of the transfer vector's target. A type code of 1 identifies a longword-aligned transfer vector, which is a simple pointer to data in the loaded image. A type code of 2 identifies a transfer vector that must be longword-aligned because it is an interrupt or exception service routine. A type code of 3 identifies a simple JMP instruction transfer vector.

EXE$INIT invokes EXE$LINK_VEC, in module LINKVEC, to perform this relocation. EXE$LINK_VEC scans the table twice. The first time, it checks that the table is well formed and has no inconsistent data. The second time, it calculates the effective destination of each transfer vector in the loaded image and stores it in the transfer vector. Each destination is the sum of the base address of the loaded SYSLOA image, the offset of its table entry, and the offset of the corresponding routine or data. Figure 29.4 illustrates this linkage.

EXE$INIT subsequently invokes the initialization routine in the loaded SYSLOAxxx image.

SCSLOA is loaded on every system with any disk or magnetic tape controllers that use mass storage control protocol (MSCP). If the system has a computer interconnect (CI) adapter, if its system disk is an MSCP device, or if the SYSGEN parameter VAXCLUSTER is nonzero, SYSBOOT loads SCSLOA in the same manner as it does SYSLOA. SYSBOOT records its starting address and size for EXE$INIT.

SCSLOA's transfer vectors are defined in the base image module SCS-VEC. The source for this module is conditionally assembled to build the module [SYSLOA]SCSVEC, which contains the table of self-relative offsets into SCSLOA. During system initialization, the SCSVEC table in the loaded SCSLOA image is used to relocate the SCSLOA transfer vectors in the base image.

If EXE$INIT finds that SCSLOA has been loaded, it invokes EXE$LINK_VEC to relocate the SCSLOA transfer vectors. It then invokes the SCSLOA initialization routine.

It is possible for SCSLOA to be loaded after system initialization by the SYSGEN utility. If SYSGEN configures an MSCP disk and tape and finds that SCSLOA has not been loaded yet, SYSGEN loads it. It invokes EXE$LINK_VEC to relocate the SCSLOA transfer vectors and then invokes the SCSLOA initialization routine.

The transfer vectors for CLUSTRLOA are defined in the base image module CLUSTRVEC. The source for this module is conditionally assembled to build the module [SYSLOA]CLUSTRLOA, which contains the table of self-relative offsets into CLUSTRLOA. During system initialization, the table in the loaded CLUSTRLOA image is used to relocate the transfer vectors in the base image.

SYSBOOT loads CLUSTRLOA into nonpaged pool on every node of a VAX-cluster system. SYSBOOT records its address and size. EXE$INIT invokes EXE$LINK_VEC to relocate the CLUSTRLOA transfer vectors and then invokes the initialization routine within CLUSTRLOA.

29.7.2   Instruction Emulators

SYSBOOT determines whether either or both types of instruction emulation are required on a particular system. The VAXEMUL.EXE and FPEMUL.EXE images are in directory SYS$LOADABLE_IMAGES.

If either is needed, SYSBOOT opens the image file and reads its image header and the first block of the image body, just as it does for SYSLOA. It

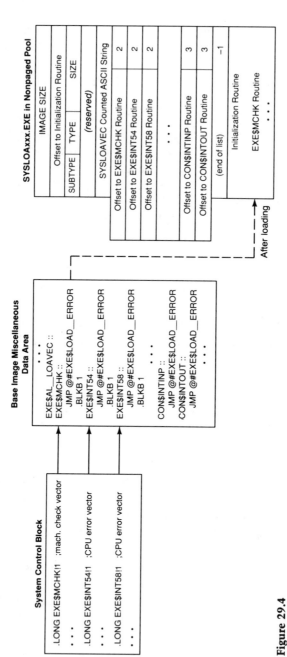

Figure 29.4
Linkage and Control Flow Example for CPU-Dependent
Routines

858

checks that the running system has compatible software for all conceptual executive categories relevant to the emulation image.

The first block of the image body begins with a dynamic data structure header; the longword at offset 0 and the word at offset 8 both specify the size of the image to be loaded into nonpaged pool. Offset 4 in the data structure header contains the offset from the beginning of the image to a routine within the image that performs image-specific initialization. SYSBOOT loads the image into nonpaged pool and records its starting address and size for EXE$INIT. The image must be position-independent code, since its location in pool is indeterminate at link time.

EXE$INIT tests whether SYSBOOT has loaded the emulation images. If an emulation image has been loaded, EXE$INIT invokes its initialization routine. The initialization routine stores the addresses of the image's exception service routines in the appropriate SCB vectors.

29.8   DYNAMIC ALLOCATION AND DEALLOCATION OF SPTES

VMS Version 5 implements dynamic allocation and deallocation of SPTEs. This enables space to be allocated for a loadable executive image when it is loaded and for its initialization and fixup sections to be deallocated after they are no longer needed. The address space thus freed can be reused. This replaces a simpler mechanism used in earlier versions of VMS, which permitted only the allocation of free SPTEs.

As described in Chapter 30 and Appendix F, SYSBOOT defines the layout of system space, based largely on SYSGEN parameter values. SYSBOOT defines the high end of system space for areas such as the system page table and nonpaged pool. Its layout is fixed. SYSBOOT reserves the lowest pages of system space for the base image. The area dynamically allocated and deallocated begins immediately above the base image.

Two routines in module PTALLOC maintain a list of available pages in this area:

- LDR$ALLOC_PT, which allocates SPTEs
- LDR$DEALLOC_PT, which deallocates SPTEs

Their actions are described in Sections 29.8.1 and 29.8.2.

The list of available pages of system space is kept within the available SPTEs themselves. Figure 29.5 shows the form of the list. Each element on the list is a group of adjacent available SPTEs. The smallest group is one SPTE.

The listhead is at global cell LDR$GL_FREE_PT, which points to the first element on the list. A list element is typically two longwords: the first points to the next set of free SPTEs; the second is the number of SPTEs in this group. A group of free SPTEs is identified by its byte offset from the beginning of the system page table. For example, if LDR$GL_FREE_PT contained $3BC0_{16}$,

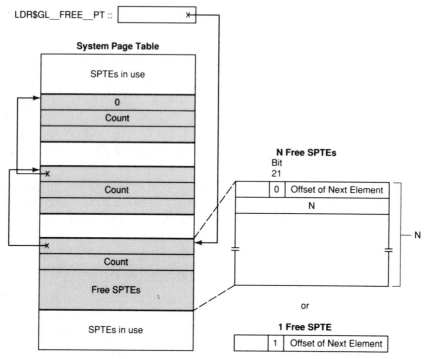

Figure 29.5
List of Available SPTEs

the next SPTE available for allocation would be at offset $3BC0_{16}$ from the base of the system page table. The number of SPTEs in that group would be at offset $3BC4_{16}$.

The offset is stored in the low-order 21 bits of the SPTE. The high-order 11 bits are zero. Thus, to memory management microcode, such an SPTE has no read or write access and an owner mode of kernel.

Two SPTEs are required to describe a group of two adjacent available SPTEs. A single available SPTE contains, in its low-order 21 bits, the offset of the next group. Bit 21 is set to identify the SPTE as the sole member of its group.

The SPTE allocation algorithm is first-fit and takes the higher end of a group of SPTEs if the group is larger than needed. SPTE deallocation keeps the list ordered from larger offset to smaller, that is, from higher system virtual page number to lower.

Much SPTE allocation occurs during system initialization, in EXE$INIT and SYSBOOT.EXE. These only execute on the primary CPU of an SMP system and at interrupt priority level (IPL) 31. When LDR$ALLOC_PT and LDR$DEALLOC_PT are invoked at later stages of initialization, they synchronize their accesses to the SPTE list by acquiring the MMG spinlock.

29.8.1   **Actions of LDR$ALLOC_PT**

LDR$ALLOC_PT is invoked with the number of SPTEs to be allocated. It takes the following steps:

1. If it is running after the swapper process has begun, it acquires the MMG spinlock, raising IPL to IPL$_MMG.
2. It scans the list of available SPTEs, starting with the group whose offset is stored in LDR$GL_FREE_PT, looking for a large enough group.
3. If it finds a group exactly the right size, it removes that group from the list by changing the forward pointer of the predecessor group to point to the next group.
4. If it finds a group larger than needed, it subtracts the number of SPTEs needed from the count longword. If the count is reduced to 1, LDR$AL-LOC_PT sets bit 21 in the single available SPTE. It allocates the SPTEs at the high end of the group, so that it does not have to copy the pointer and count longwords and to alter the longword pointing to the beginning of the group.
5. It zeros the allocated SPTEs and returns to its invoker the address of the lowest SPTE in the allocated group and a status of SS$_NORMAL.
6. If it cannot make the allocation, it returns the error status SS$_INSFSPTS to its invoker.
7. In either case, it releases the MMG spinlock and lowers IPL.

29.8.2   **Actions of LDR$DEALLOC_PT**

LDR$DEALLOC_PT is invoked with the address of the lowest SPTE in the group to be deallocated and the number of SPTEs. The invoker must have already deallocated any physical memory associated with the SPTEs and zeroed the SPTEs. It takes the following steps:

1. If it is running after the swapper process has begun, it acquires the MMG spinlock, raising IPL to IPL$_MMG.
2. It first checks that the SPTEs are all zero. If they are not, it releases the spinlock, lowering IPL, and returns the error status LOADER$_PTE_ NOT_EMPTY to its invoker.
3. Otherwise, it scans the list of available SPTEs, looking for the first group whose address is less than that of the group being deallocated.
4. It inserts the group being deallocated at that point and checks whether it can be merged with the group on either side of it. It makes whatever merges are possible, altering pointers and count longwords as appropriate.
5. It releases the spinlock, lowering IPL, and returns the status SS$_NOR-MAL to its invoker.

30   Bootstrap Procedures

Ante mare et terras et quod tegit omnia caelum unus erat toto
naturae vultus in orbe, quem dixere chaos: rudis indigestaque
moles.
[Before the sea was, and the lands, and the sky that hangs
over all, the face of Nature showed all alike, which state has
been called chaos: a rough unordered mass of things.]

Ovid, *Metamorphoses* I, 5–7

Before the VMS operating system can assume control of a VAX system, some
initialization or bootstrap programs must execute to configure the system
and read the executive into memory. Parts of the bootstrap operation are
specific to the type of VAX processor. Others are common across all VAX
family members.

This chapter first summarizes all phases of system initialization and then
describes those that occur before the system base image (SYS.EXE) and loadable executive images execute. Chapter 31 describes the later phases of
system initialization, and Chapter 34 describes the portions of system initialization specific to multiprocessors.

30.1   OVERVIEW OF SYSTEM INITIALIZATION

VMS system initialization requires a number of programs. Some of them run
prior to an operating system environment; others execute in system context
with memory management enabled; others execute in process context. In
general, VMS postpones an initialization task to as late a stage of initialization as possible. The following list summarizes the system initialization
programs:

- The console subsystem is CPU-specific. Regardless of its implementation,
  the subsystem must initialize the CPU, locate physically contiguous good
  memory, and load a VMB image into that memory.
- VMB, the primary bootstrap program, runs stand-alone on a VAX processor
  with memory management disabled. In a symmetric multiprocessing (SMP)
  system, VMB runs on the processor selected to be primary by the console
  subsystem. It provides a bootstrap that is independent of the operating
  system. It sizes memory, initializes context for the adapter and device
  unit containing the secondary bootstrap program, and loads the secondary
  bootstrap.
- SYSBOOT, the secondary bootstrap program for the VMS software, also
  runs stand-alone with memory management disabled. It reads SYSGEN
  parameters and lays out system virtual address space based on their values.

862

SYSBOOT loads the system base image, SYS.EXE, and several loadable executive images into memory. It also loads the system device driver, the port driver, auxiliary drivers, the SYSLOA image, and VAXcluster code, as needed. SYSBOOT transfers control to EXE$INIT, in the loadable executive image EXEC_INIT.

- After turning on memory management, EXE$INIT runs at interrupt priority level (IPL) 31 on the interrupt stack. It performs initialization tasks that require memory management but must occur before process context is available. EXE$INIT invokes the initialization routines of the images loaded by SYSBOOT, including the SYSLOA routines that perform processor-specific initialization. It loads most of the remaining loadable executive images and invokes their initialization routines. The loadable executive images initialize the scheduler, memory management, spinlock, and I/O databases, among other operations. EXE$INIT then configures and starts secondary CPUs. It REIs to the scheduling routine SCH$SCHED, described in Chapter 12, which places the swapper process into execution.
- EXE$SWAPINIT, the swapper initialization routine, performs the minimum tasks that must complete in process context before any other processes can be created. Because it is pageable code, it eventually disappears from the system working set and thus occupies no physical space. Its tasks include initializing paged pool and the pageable logical name database, and invoking loadable executive image initialization routines that require process context in order to execute. EXE$SWAPINIT creates the SYSINIT process.
- The SYSINIT process performs initialization tasks that must be done in process context and that do not lend themselves to Digital command language (DCL) commands. These include initializing the swap and page files and opening the Files-11 Extended QIO processor (XQP) as a global section. The SYSINIT process creates the startup process.
- The startup process has a full process context; it maps DCL and can thus execute a series of DCL commands. It executes the command procedure SYS$SYSTEM:STARTUP.COM, which processes other command procedures and data files in the SYS$STARTUP directory. The various command procedures create system processes, such as OPCOM, the job controller, and the SMISERVER. They create systemwide logical names, run SYSGEN to autoconfigure the I/O database, and install images specified by the VMSIMAGES.DAT data file. The startup process executes a series of site-specific command procedures and finally enables interactive logins.

From SYSBOOT onward, the files and programs used in bootstrap operations are primarily independent of processor type. Table 30.1 lists the processor-independent bootstrap programs and processes, the files they access, and the reason for the access. Subsequent sections list processor-dependent bootstrap files.

Table 30.1   Processor-Independent Bootstrap Files

Files Accessed	*Reason for Access*
	SYSBOOT
VAXVMSSYS.PAR and other parameter files	Configure system
SYSDUMP.DMP	System dump file, located and sized for later use
PAGEFILE.SYS	Primary page file, located and sized if dump file not found
SYS.EXE	System base image, loaded into memory
TTDRIVER.EXE	Terminal class driver, loaded into nonpaged pool
*xx*DRIVER.EXE	System device driver, loaded into nonpaged pool
*yy*DRIVER.EXE	Port driver, conditionally loaded into nonpaged pool
*zz*DRIVER.EXE	Auxiliary device driver, conditionally loaded into nonpaged pool
SYSLOA*xxx*.EXE	CPU-specific routines, loaded into nonpaged pool
SCSLOA.EXE	System communication services, conditionally loaded into nonpaged pool
CLUSTRLOA.EXE	VAXcluster support, conditionally loaded into nonpaged pool
FPEMUL.EXE	Floating-point emulation code, conditionally loaded into nonpaged pool
VAXEMUL.EXE	String and other emulated instruction code, conditionally loaded into nonpaged pool
SYSTEM_SYNCHRONIZATION_ *xxx*.EXE	SMP synchronization image, one of three
SYSTEM_PRIMITIVES.EXE	Basic system support routines
PRIMITIVE_IO.EXE	Primitive console I/O and file system routines
ERRORLOG.EXE	Error logging routines and system services
SYSTEM_DEBUG.EXE	System debugger (XDELTA), conditionally loaded
EXEC_INIT.EXE	Next image in bootstrap sequence
	EXEC_INIT
CPULOA.EXE	Tables of CPU data
EVENT_FLAGS_AND_ASTS.EXE	Event flag and AST routines and system services
EXCEPTION.EXE	Exception service routines and system services, bugcheck routines
IMAGE_MANAGEMENT.EXE	Image activation services and routines
IO_ROUTINES.EXE	I/O-related routines and system services
LMF$GROUP_TABLE.EXE	Tables of license data
LOCKING.EXE	Lock management routines and system services
LOGICAL_NAMES.EXE	Logical name routines and system services
MESSAGE_ROUTINES.EXE	Message routines and system services
PAGE_MANAGEMENT.EXE	Page fault service routine, related routines, virtual address space system services
PROCESS_MANAGEMENT.EXE	Scheduling routines and process creation and control system services
SECURITY.EXE	Security-related routines and system services

(continued)

Table 30.1   Processor-Independent Bootstrap Files *(continued)*

Files Accessed	*Reason for Access*
	EXEC_INIT
SYSDEVICE.EXE	Pseudo device drivers and mailbox system services
SYSGETSYI.EXE	$GETSYI system service
SYSLICENSE.EXE	$LICENSE system service
WORKING_SET_ MANAGEMENT.EXE	Swapper and supporting routines, related system services
	SYSINIT PROCESS
SYSMSG.EXE	System message file
RMS.EXE	Record Management Services (RMS)
F11BXQP.EXE	File system, mapped as global section
QUORUM.DAT	VAXcluster system quorum file
RECOVERY_UNIT_SERVICES.EXE	RMS recovery services
DDIF$RMS_EXTENSION.EXE	Support for Digital Document Interchange Format (DDIF) file operations
SYSLDR_DYN.EXE	Dynamic loading of loadable executive images
	STARTUP PROCESS
STARTUP.COM	SYS$INPUT for startup process
LOGINOUT.EXE	First image that runs in startup process
DCL.EXE	CLI, mapped into P1 space to interpret and execute commands
DCLTABLES.EXE	Command tables, mapped into P1 space and used by DCL.EXE
VMS$PHASES.DAT	Startup phase definition data file
VMS$VMS.DAT	Procedure definition data file for VMS
VMS$LAYERED.DAT	Procedure definition data file for layered products
Various	Procedures and images defined by previous two data files
SWAPFILE.SYS	System swap file opened and initialized
PAGEFILE.SYS	System page file opened and initialized
SATELLITE_PAGE.COM	VAXcluster satellite page file installation
SYPAGSWPFILES.COM	Site-specific page and swap files
SYLOGICALS.COM	Site-specific logical names
SYCONFIG.COM	Site-specific device configuration command procedure
SYSTARTUP_V5.COM	Site-specific startup command procedure
	INSTALL UTILITY, IN CONTEXT OF STARTUP PROCESS
VMSIMAGES.DAT	List of images to be installed
All installed images	Set up as known images
	SYSGEN, IN CONTEXT OF STARTUP PROCESS
VAXVMSSYS.PAR	Written to record SYSGEN parameters
Various device drivers	Loaded into nonpaged pool, they perform I/O database and device initialization

865

30.2 PROCESSOR-SPECIFIC INITIALIZATION

The preliminary steps in the initialization of a VMS system depend on the particular VAX processor being booted. The console subsystem is the portion of the processor that initiates a bootstrap operation and permits microdiagnostics and macrodiagnostics to execute. Not all details of the console subsystem are specified by the VAX architecture; some are CPU-specific. The installation and technical guides for a particular VAX processor contain a detailed description of its console subsystem, and Chapter 24 describes console registers and communication.

The next sections describe the various VAX systems and the processor-specific steps that occur before VMB gains control and begins execution. In all processors, the following steps occur:

1. An error-free, page-aligned, and contiguous block of physical memory is located.
2. VMB is loaded into the second page of the memory.
3. The bootstrap device code, other bootstrap flags, and additional information are passed to VMB using registers R0 through R5, R7, and R10 through AP.
4. VMB executes.

The main differences in the initiation of VMB on various VAX processors are the following:

- Location of VMB—console block storage device, system device, or read-only memory (ROM)
- Method for determining system device
- Contents of R0 through R5 and R7
- Program that loads and passes control to VMB

The amount of error-free memory located by the console subsystem is specified by the VAX architecture, which was amended in 1987. VAX processors announced after 1987 locate a 256K-byte block of memory; earlier VAX processors locate a 64K-byte or 128K-byte block. The manner in which error-free memory is located is CPU-dependent. The register contents are also somewhat CPU-dependent, but the most obvious processor-specific item that affects the bootstrap operation is the console configuration. Figure 30.1 summarizes the bootstrap sequence, and the following sections describe the various consoles.

Note that all descriptions assume the console terminal is in local enable mode, able to receive command input.

30.2.1 MicroVAX CPUs with ROM-based VMB

The MicroVAX processors implement a subset VMB in ROM. The actual VMB code differs only slightly from one MicroVAX to another and evolved from the MicroVAX II VMB. The following sections describe the console

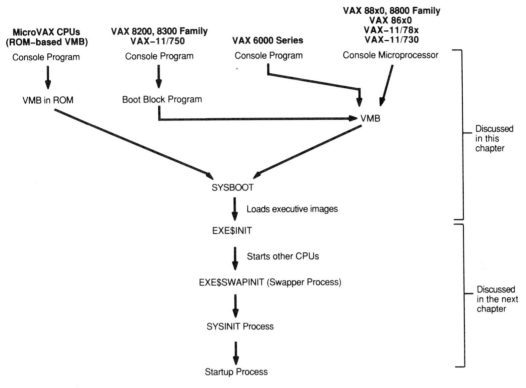

Figure 30.1
Sequence of Initialization Events

subsystems and bootstrap operations of the various MicroVAX CPUs. Note that most of the MicroVAX CPUs are also available in VAXstation configurations. The description of MicroVAX initialization applies to its VAXstation configuration as well.

30.2.1.1 **MicroVAX II Console Subsystem and Initial Bootstrap Operation.** The console subsystem on the MicroVAX II consists of a console program and a console terminal. The MicroVAX II console program is written in VAX MACRO instruction code. Because the MicroVAX II has no console block storage device, the console program is stored in ROM in the processor's local I/O space. A subset version of VMB.EXE, specific to the MicroVAX II, is also stored in ROM, along with the power-up diagnostics.

When the console program has control, the MicroVAX II processor executes the console program's VAX instructions rather than user or system instructions. The console program gains control of the processor whenever any halt condition occurs, such as execution of a HALT instruction.

The MicroVAX II has four internal processor registers for communication with the console terminal.

There are several circumstances in which a bootstrap sequence is initiated:

Table 30.2   Processor-Dependent Programs Used to Bootstrap the MicroVAX II

Program Executing	Location of Program	Purpose of Program
CPU initialization microcode	MicroVAX II CPU	Pass control to the console program
Console program	I/O address space ROM in MicroVAX II CPU	Size physical memory, locate block of good memory, load VMB from ROM into memory, and pass control to it
VMB.EXE	I/O address space ROM in MicroVAX II CPU	Locate secondary bootstrap, load it into memory, and pass control to it

---

- The system is powered on, and halts are disabled through the Halt Enable switch on the CPU patch panel insert, mounted inside the rear of the CPU cabinet. Chapter 33 describes the significance of this switch in more detail.
- The B(oot) command is entered while the system is in console mode.
- The halt action field in the console program mailbox (CPMBX) is set to 2 by the operating system.
- An attempt to restart the system after an error halt fails, and the console program mailbox has its default contents.

When a MicroVAX II system is initialized, several programs execute before VMB. These are summarized in Table 30.2.

The steps of initial bootstrap are as follows:

1. Following power recovery, the processor performs hardware initialization, writes a power-up code into the AP register, and passes control to the console program in ROM.
2. On power-up, the console program checks its own integrity by computing the checksum of its own code and comparing it to the expected value stored within ROM. The console then looks for a small piece of contiguous good physical memory. It scans from high memory addresses downward. It requires two pages for use as a stack and writable data area and the rest for a bitmap of available memory.
3. The console program performs some additional checks, including determination of the console terminal type. It then executes diagnostics, which are also located in ROM, to test the processor and memory. The memory test diagnostic records the memory it finds in the bitmap. A set bit indicates a present page of memory. The first bit in the map corresponds to the first page of memory. The bitmap does not map itself or the other pages of memory reserved for the console program's use. The address of the bitmap and its size will be passed to VMB.
4. To perform a bootstrap, the console program searches for a 64K-byte

block of good memory. It initializes the Q22-bus I/O map registers to map to the first four megabytes of MicroVAX II memory.

5. The console does not process command files. It must construct the contents of R0 through R5 from the combination of boot device and bootstrap command. Table 30.3 shows the register arguments.

6. The console program copies VMB from the console program ROM into the piece of good memory, starting at the second page, and passes control to it.

The MicroVAX II VMB is based upon the full VMB that runs on other VAX processors. There are, however, a number of significant differences between the two, which are summarized in the following list. For a detailed description of the MicroVAX II VMB, see the *MicroVAX 630 CPU Module User's Guide*. Section 30.3 gives a detailed description of the full VMB.

- The register arguments are different; contrast Table 30.20 with Table 30.3.
- Full VMB sizes memory itself if necessary. The MicroVAX II VMB requires an available memory bitmap built by the memory diagnostic.
- Full VMB.EXE tries to boot a system from the system device specified by its register arguments. MicroVAX II VMB has several possibilities:

  —In response to a B(oot) command with no device specification, MicroVAX II VMB searches for a bootable disk. In searching for a bootable disk, VMB tries each disk drive of all possible mass storage control protocol (MSCP) controllers. Furthermore, if it does not locate SYSBOOT, it checks whether the first logical block of the disk (LBN 0) is a boot block. It then searches for a TK50 magnetic tape to boot. If that fails, it scans memory for the signature of programmable read-only memory (PROM). Last, it looks for a DEQNA or DELQA controller to request a down-line

---

Table 30.3   Register Input to MicroVAX II VMB

Register	Contents
R0	Zero or ASCII name of bootstrap device
R1	Contents of MicroVAX II boot and diagnostic register
R2	Memory bitmap size in bytes
R3	Address of memory bitmap
R4	Unused
R5	Software boot control flags
R10 [1]	Halt program counter (PC)
R11 [1]	Halt processor status longword (PSL)
AP [1]	Halt code
SP	Address of 64K bytes of good memory plus 200_{16}

---

[1] The console program sets up these registers after a halt condition. VMB does not use these values.

bootstrap. If there is no response in 30 seconds, VMB retransmits its request every 30 seconds. If no response is received after 12 retransmits, VMB doubles the timeout interval. It retransmits 12 times with a 60-second timeout. It continues in this manner, up to a maximum delay of 60 minutes.

—In response to a boot command with a device specification, it searches the specified device for the secondary bootstrap.

30.2.1.2 **MicroVAX 2000 Console Subsystem and Initial Bootstrap Operation.** The console subsystem on the MicroVAX 2000 consists of a console program and a console terminal port. The MicroVAX 2000 console program is written in VAX MACRO instruction code and resides on the system module ROM. A subset version of VMB.EXE, specific to the MicroVAX 2000, is also stored in ROM, along with the diagnostic code.

When the console program has control, the MicroVAX 2000 processor executes the console program's VAX instructions. The console program gains control of the processor whenever any halt condition occurs, such as execution of a HALT instruction.

The console program's actions are determined in part by the current contents of the following three areas of nonvolatile random access memory (NVR):

- The console program mailbox contains the default recovery setting (halt action), the restart-in-progress flag, and the boot-in-progress flag.
- The boot device (BOOT_DEV) area stores the name of the default boot device.
- The boot flag (BOOT_FLG) area contains the default boot flags, passed to VMB in R5.

The console utility programs TEST 51 and TEST 52 load the boot device and boot flag areas, respectively. The console utility program TEST 53 alters the default recovery setting in the console program mailbox. The recovery setting determines the console action when the processor halts, as follows:

- If the setting is 0 or 1, restart. If that fails, boot. If boot fails, halt.
- If the setting is 2, boot. If that fails, halt.
- If the setting is 3, halt at the console prompt.

Note that if the halt button is pressed, the console halts at the console prompt and ignores the recovery setting.

A bootstrap sequence is initiated for the MicroVAX 2000 under the following conditions:

- The system is powered on, and the recovery setting is 0, 1, or 2.
- The B(oot) command is entered while the system is in console mode.
- The operating system sets the halt action field in the console program mailbox to 2.

The MicroVAX 2000 bootstrap proceeds in the following manner:

1. When the processor recovers power, it performs hardware initialization, saves a restart code that is later passed to VMB, and transfers control to the console program in ROM.

2. The console program performs some checks, including determination of the console terminal type. It then executes diagnostics, which are also located in ROM, to test the processor and memory. The memory test diagnostic records the memory it finds in a bitmap. The first bit in the map corresponds to the first page of memory. A set bit indicates that the page of memory is present and usable. The bitmap itself and the pages reserved for the console program's use are marked as bad in the bitmap. The address of the bitmap and its size are later passed to VMB.

3. The console does not process command procedures. To perform a bootstrap, the console program constructs the contents of R0 through R5 as shown in Table 30.4. If a boot device is specified on the command line or in the boot device area, the console loads R0 from that information.

4. The console program then searches for a 128K-byte block of good memory. Reserving the first page of good memory for the restart parameter block (RPB), it copies VMB into the memory starting at the second page. The console program transfers control to VMB.

MicroVAX 2000 VMB evolved from MicroVAX II VMB. It differs from full VMB, used by larger VAX CPUs that do not store VMB in ROM, in the following ways:

- MicroVAX 2000 VMB uses different register arguments and only recognizes a subset of the R5 boot flags.

Table 30.4 Register Input to MicroVAX 2000 VMB

Register	Contents
Register	*Contents*
R0	Zero or ASCII name of bootstrap device
R1	Address of configuration table
R2	Memory bitmap size in bytes
R3	Address of memory bitmap
R4	Unused
R5	Software boot control flags
R10[1]	Halt PC
R11[1]	Halt PSL
AP[1]	Halt code
SP	Address of 128K bytes of good memory plus 200_{16}

[1] The console program sets up these registers after a halt condition. VMB does not use these values.

Table 30.5 MicroVAX VMB Boot Flags (Contents of R5)

Bit Position	Symbolic Name	Meaning
0	RPB$V_CONV	Conversational boot. If set, SYSBOOT solicits parameters from the console terminal.
3	RPB$V_BBLOCK	Secondary boot from boot block. If set, VMB reads LBN 0 of the boot device. If it is a boot block, the block is executed. VMB makes no search for a Files-11 secondary bootstrap file.
4	RPB$V_DIAG	Diagnostic boot. If set, secondary bootstrap is image [SYS*n*.SYSMAINT]DIAGBOOT.EXE.
5	RPB$V_BOOBPT	Bootstrap breakpoint. If set, VMB and SYSBOOT_XDELTA execute BPT instructions to transfer control to XDELTA.
6	RPB$V_HEADER	Image header. If set, VMB transfers control to an address specified in the secondary bootstrap's file image header. If clear, VMB transfers control to the first byte of the secondary boot file.
8	RPB$V_SOLICT	Solicit file name. If set, VMB prompts for the name of a secondary bootstrap file. Used to load SYSBOOT_XDELTA.
9	RPB$V_HALT	Halt before transfer. If set, VMB executes a HALT instruction before transferring control to the secondary bootstrap.
⟨31:28⟩	RPB$V_TOPSYS	Specifies the top-level directory number for a system disk with multiple system roots.

Table 30.5 describes the VMB boot flags used by MicroVAX CPUs and the manner in which the flags influence the search for a secondary bootstrap image.

- Rather than size memory itself, VMB initializes the RPB page frame number (PFN) bitmap pointer to point to the bitmap built by the console memory diagnostic routine.
- If a boot device is not specified as an input argument, either from the command line or from the default boot device area, MicroVAX 2000 VMB's "sniffer boot" searches a priority ordered sequence of potential boot devices until it discovers one from which it can boot.

The sniffer boot mechanism exists because the MicroVAX I and MicroVAX II did not have NVR available in which to save a default bootstrap device. All MicroVAX CPUs from the MicroVAX 2000 onward contain NVR, preserved by battery backup across power outages, and thus can maintain a default bootstrap device.

The sniffer boot search for a secondary bootstrap image begins with disk drives. If no disk provides a bootstrap, VMB searches for a TK50 magnetic tape drive. Finally, it looks for a network device to request a down-line load of the secondary boot image. If none of these devices provide a bootstrap, VMB displays a message and retries the last entry, the network device.

Note that the MicroVAX 2000 supports one PROM bootstrap, the system exerciser.

30.2.1.3   **MicroVAX 3100 Console Subsystem and Initial Bootstrap Operation.** The console subsystem on the MicroVAX 3100 consists of a console program and a console terminal port. The MicroVAX 3100 console program is written in VAX MACRO instruction code and resides on the system module ROM. A subset version of VMB.EXE, specific to the MicroVAX 3100, is also stored in ROM, along with the diagnostic code and drivers.

When the console program has control, the MicroVAX 3100 processor executes the console program's VAX instructions. The console program gains control of the processor when a halt condition occurs, such as execution of a HALT instruction.

The console program's actions are determined in part by the current contents of the following areas of NVR:

- The console program mailbox contains the default recovery setting (halt action), the restart-in-progress flag, and the boot-in-progress flag.
- The boot device area stores the name of the default boot device.
- The boot flag area contains the default boot flags.

The console command SET BOOT stores a default boot device in the boot device area. The SHOW DEVICE command displays the known devices, and the SHOW BOOT command displays the current default boot device.

The console command SET BFLG loads the boot flag area, passed to VMB in R5.

The console command SET HALT sets the default recovery setting in the console program mailbox. The recovery setting determines the console action when the processor halts, as follows:

- If the setting is 0 or 1, restart. If that fails, boot. If boot fails, halt.
- If the setting is 2, boot. If that fails, halt.
- If the setting is 3, halt at the console prompt.

Note that if the halt button is pressed, the console halts at the console prompt and ignores the recovery setting.

A bootstrap sequence is initiated for the MicroVAX 3100 in the following circumstances:

- The system is powered on, and the power-on action is not defined as "halt."
- The B(oot) command is entered while the system is in console mode.
- The operating system sets the halt action field in the console program mailbox to 2.

The MicroVAX 3100 bootstrap proceeds in the following manner:

Table 30.6   Register Input to MicroVAX 3100 VMB

Register	Contents
Register	*Contents*
R0	Address of descriptor specifying boot device name [1]
R1	Reserved
R2	Memory bitmap size in bytes
R3	Address of memory bitmap
R4	Unused
R5	Software boot control flags
R10 [2]	Halt PC
R11 [2]	Halt PSL
AP [2]	Halt code
SP	Address of 256K bytes of good memory plus 200_{16}

---

[1] Thus, the boot device name may contain more than four characters.

[2] The console program sets up these registers after a halt condition. VMB does not use these values.

1. When the processor recovers power, it performs hardware initialization, saves a restart code that is later passed to VMB, and transfers control to the console program in ROM.
2. The console program performs some checks, including determination of the console terminal type. It then executes diagnostics, which are also located in ROM, to test the processor and memory. The memory test diagnostic records the memory it finds in a bitmap. The first bit in the map corresponds to the first page of memory. A set bit indicates that the page of memory is present and usable. The bitmap itself and the two pages reserved for the console program's use are marked as bad in the bitmap. The address of the bitmap and its size are passed to VMB. The MicroVAX maintains a checksum on the bitmap. For subsequent reboots, it does not execute the memory test diagnostic or rebuild the bitmap unless a checksum mismatch indicates that a new bitmap is needed.
3. The console does not process command procedures. To perform a bootstrap, the console program constructs the contents of R0 through R5 as shown in Table 30.6. If a boot device is specified on the command line or in the boot device area, it loads R0 from that information. Otherwise it loads R0 with a value identifying its default boot device, the network device.
4. The console program then searches for a 256K-byte block of good memory. Reserving the first page of good memory for the RPB, it copies VMB into the memory starting at the second page. The console program transfers control to VMB.

MicroVAX 3100 VMB is based upon MicroVAX 2000 VMB. It differs from full VMB, used by larger VAX CPUs that do not store VMB in ROM, in the following ways:

- MicroVAX 3100 VMB uses different register arguments and only recognizes a subset of the R5 boot flags, described in Table 30.5.
- Rather than size memory itself, VMB initializes the RPB PFN bitmap pointer to point to the bitmap built by the console memory diagnostic routine.

The MicroVAX 3100 supports one PROM bootstrap, the system exerciser.

30.2.1.4 **MicroVAX 3200/3500/3600 Console Subsystem and Initial Bootstrap Operation.** The console subsystem on MicroVAX 3200, 3500, and 3600 processors consists of a console program and a console terminal port. The console program is written in VAX MACRO instruction code and resides on the system module erasable programmable read-only memory (EPROM). A subset version of VMB.EXE is also stored in ROM, along with the diagnostic code and drivers.

When the console program has control, the processor executes the console program's VAX instructions. The console program gains control of the processor when a halt condition occurs, such as execution of a HALT instruction.

The console program's actions are determined in part by the current contents of the following three areas of NVR:

- The console program mailbox contains the halt action setting, the restart-in-progress flag, and the boot-in-progress flag.
- The boot device area stores the name of the default boot device.
- The boot flag area contains the default boot flags.

The halt action setting determines the console action when the processor halts. It is used by the operating system to force a particular console action, regardless of the setting of the Halt Enable switch. Its values are the following:

- If the setting is 0, restart. If that fails, boot. If boot fails, halt.
- If the setting is 1, restart. If that fails, halt.
- If the setting is 2, boot. If that fails, halt.
- If the setting is 3, halt at the console prompt.

The console command SET BOOT sets an alternative boot device in the boot device area. The SHOW DEVICE command displays the known devices.

The console command SET BFLG loads the boot flag area, passed to VMB in R5.

A bootstrap sequence is initiated in the following circumstances:

- The system is powered on, and the power-on action is not defined as "halt."
- The B(oot) command is entered while the system is in console mode.

- The operating system sets the halt action field in the console program mailbox to 2.

The MicroVAX 3200/3500/3600 bootstrap proceeds as follows:

1. When the processor recovers power, it performs hardware initialization, saves a restart code that is later passed to VMB, and transfers control to the console program in ROM.
2. The console program performs some checks, including determination of the console terminal type. It then executes diagnostics, which are also located in ROM, to test the processor and memory. The memory test diagnostic records the memory it finds in a bitmap. The first bit in the map corresponds to the first page of memory. A set bit indicates that the page of memory is present and usable. The bitmap itself and the pages reserved for the console program's use are marked as bad in the bitmap. The address of the bitmap and its size are passed to VMB.

   Note that the MicroVAX maintains a checksum on the bitmap. For subsequent reboots, it does not execute the memory test diagnostic or rebuild the bitmap unless a checksum mismatch indicates that a new bitmap is needed.
3. The console does not process command procedures. To perform a bootstrap, the console program constructs the contents of R0 through R5 as shown in Table 30.7. If a boot device is specified on the command line or in the boot device area, it loads R0 from that information.

   In later versions of the console, if no boot device is specified on the command line and no default boot device exists, the MicroVAX displays the names of available boot devices and prompts for input. If it does not receive a boot device name within its timeout period, it attempts to boot from the network device.

Table 30.7   Register Input to MicroVAX 3200/3500/3600 VMB

Register	Contents
R0, R1	Boot device name
R2	Memory bitmap size in bytes
R3	Address of memory bitmap
R4	Unused
R5	Software boot control flags
R10[1]	Halt PC
R11[1]	Halt PSL
AP[1]	Halt code
SP	Address of 128K bytes of good memory plus 200_{16}

---

[1] The console program sets up these registers after a halt condition. VMB does not use these values.

876

4. The console program then searches for a 128K-byte block of good memory. Reserving the first page of good memory for the RPB, it copies VMB into the memory starting at the second page. The console program transfers control to VMB.

MicroVAX 3200/3500/3600 VMB is based on MicroVAX II VMB. In early versions of this console subsystem, if no boot device is specified on the command line or in the boot device area, MicroVAX 3200/3500/3600 VMB uses a sniffer boot mechanism, which searches a priority ordered sequence of potential boot devices until it discovers one from which it can boot. If none of these devices provide a bootstrap, VMB displays a message and retries the last entry, the network device. Later versions omit the sniffer boot mechanism.

30.2.1.5 **MicroVAX 3300/3400 and 3800/3900 Console Subsystem and Initial Bootstrap Operation.** Although the console subsystem and VMB for MicroVAX 3300/3400 processors differ slightly from those of MicroVAX 3800/3900 CPUs, they are alike in the details presented in this section.

The console subsystem on these processors consists of a console program and a console terminal port. The console program is written in VAX MACRO instruction code and resides on the system module ROM. A subset version of VMB.EXE is also stored in ROM, along with the diagnostic code and drivers.

When the console program has control, the processor executes the console program's VAX instructions. The console program gains control of the processor when a halt condition occurs, such as execution of a HALT instruction.

The console program's actions are determined in part by the current contents of the following three areas of NVR:

- The console program mailbox contains the halt action setting, the restart-in-progress flag, and the boot-in-progress flag.
- The boot device area stores the name of the default boot device.
- The boot flag area contains the default boot flags, passed to VMB in R5.

The halt action setting determines the console action when the processor halts. It is used by the operating system to force a particular console action regardless of the setting of the Halt Enable switch. Its values are the following:

- If the setting is 0, restart. If that fails, boot. If boot fails, halt.
- If the setting is 1, restart. If that fails, halt.
- If the setting is 2, boot. If that fails, halt.
- If the setting is 3, halt at the console prompt.

The console command SET BOOT sets an alternative boot device in the boot device area. The SHOW DEVICE command displays the known devices.

The console command SET BFLG loads the boot flag area. The console also supports the SHOW VERSION command, which displays the console and VMB version numbers.

A bootstrap sequence is initiated in the following circumstances:

- The system is powered on, and the power-on action is not defined as "halt."
- The B(oot) command is entered while the system is in console mode.
- The operating system sets the halt action field in the console program mailbox to 2.

The bootstrap for these processors proceeds in the following manner:

1. When the processor recovers power, it performs hardware initialization, saves a restart code that is later passed to VMB, and transfers control to the console program in ROM.

2. The console program performs some checks, including determination of the console terminal type. It then executes diagnostics, which are also located in ROM, to test the processor and memory. The memory test diagnostic records the memory it finds in a bitmap. The first bit in the map corresponds to the first page of memory. A set bit indicates that the page of memory is present and usable. The bitmap itself and the pages reserved for the console program's use are marked as bad in the bitmap. The address of the bitmap and its size are passed to VMB.

   Note that the MicroVAX maintains a checksum on the bitmap. For subsequent reboots, it does not execute the memory test diagnostic or rebuild the bitmap unless a checksum mismatch indicates that a new bitmap is needed.

3. The console does not process command procedures. To perform a bootstrap, the console program constructs the contents of R0 through R5 as shown in Table 30.8. If a boot device is specified on the command line

---

Table 30.8   Register Input to MicroVAX 3300/3400 and 3800/3900 VMB

Register	Contents
R0	Address of descriptor specifying boot device name [1]
R1	Reserved
R2	Memory bitmap size in bytes
R3	Address of memory bitmap
R4	Value of PR$_TODR
R5	Software boot control flags
R10 [2]	Halt PC
R11 [2]	Halt PSL
AP [2]	Halt code
SP	Address of 128K bytes of good memory plus 200_{16}

---

[1] Thus, the boot device name may contain more than four characters.

[2] The console program sets up these registers after a halt condition. VMB does not use these values.

or in the boot device area, it loads R0 from that information. Otherwise it loads R0 with a value identifying its default boot device, the network device.

4. The console program searches for a 128K-byte block of good memory. Reserving the first page of good memory for the RPB, it copies VMB into the memory starting at the second page. The console program transfers control to VMB.

VMBs for these processors evolved from MicroVAX 3200/3500/3600 VMB.

30.2.1.6   **VAXstation 35x0 Console Subsystem and Initial Bootstrap Operation.** VAXstation 35x0 systems support multiple CPUs per system, currently two or four. One CPU acts as the primary and performs the main work of booting VMS. VMS directs the initialization of the remaining secondary CPUs, as described in Chapter 34.

The console subsystem of VAXstation 35x0 processors consists of a console program and a console terminal port. The console program, implemented in BLISS-32 and VAX MACRO code, resides in ROM on the CPU module. Each CPU has a private EPROM.

The console program runs on the VAX processor rather than on a separate console processor. It can read and interpret commands typed on the console terminal, allowing an operator to examine or modify the state of the machine and boot the operating system. In a multiprocessor system, each CPU runs the console program, although only the primary processor is allowed to perform I/O directly to the console terminal. These multiple instances of the console program communicate with the primary processor and cooperate to control the system. The console program reserves a segment of main memory called the console communications area (CCA) for communication among the processors while they are in console mode. This area is also visible to VMS and may contain items such as hardware revision levels, machine check functions, and CPU model information.

The console program initiates the boot sequence under the following conditions:

• The console command B(oot) is entered on the console terminal while it is in console mode and the control panel is enabled.
• The control panel is locked into secure mode or is enabled with auto start selected, and one of the following occurs:

—Power is restored to the system.
—The primary processor attempts to restart and fails.
—A secondary processor attempts to restart, fails, and the bit CCA$Q_SECSTART pertaining to that secondary is clear.

• The Restart switch is pressed and the console is enabled.

- Kernel mode code requests a reboot by setting the bit CCA$V_REBOOT in the CCA$B_HFLAGS byte and halting the primary node.

VAXstation 35x0 systems execute the following in response to a power-up or system reset:

1. Each CPU initializes itself to a known state and transfers control to the console program.
2. The console program directs a self-test and participates in the selection of a primary processor. The CPU that has passed self-test and has the lowest node ID becomes the primary processor unless it has been disabled through the SET CPU/NOPRIMARY console command.
3. Each CPU performs an extended self-test. In addition, the primary configures the CCA, tests main memory, and prints the results of the various tests on the console terminal.
4. The primary processor's console program configures memory, determining how much is present and which pages have uncorrectable errors. It allocates pages from the high end of physical memory for the CCA and for a bitmap that will inform VMS which physical pages are usable and which are not. In the bitmap, the console program marks as unusable any pages found bad. In addition, it marks as unusable those pages that CCA and the bitmap itself occupy to prevent VMS from attempting to put them to a second concurrent use.

   The console program locates 256K bytes of good physical memory and copies VMB from ROM into the second page of good memory, reserving the first for the RPB.
5. The console does not process command procedures. To perform a bootstrap, the console program constructs the contents of R0 through R5 as shown in Table 30.9. If a boot device is specified on the command line or in the boot device area, it loads R0 from that information.
6. The primary processor transfers control to VMB.

The VAXstation 35x0 VMB is similar to that of the MicroVAX 3100.

30.2.2 VAX CPUs with Console Microprocessors

Some VAX processors communicate with an external console microprocessor system by means of a special interconnect, or incorporate an internal microprocessor. On these VAX CPUs, the console program executes on the console microprocessor, which has independent access to VAX memory. Because the console program executes on a separate processor, the console subsystem can perform a number of functions while the VAX CPU is executing instructions, without halting the VAX CPU. The console processor can also monitor the running VAX and perform diagnostic tests.

The console subsystem includes a block storage device, which the console processor can access. In particular, it reads a bootstrap command procedure

Table 30.9   Register Input to VAXstation 35x0 VMB

Register	Contents
R0	Address of descriptor specifying boot device name [1]
R1	Reserved
R2	Memory bitmap size in bytes
R3	Address of memory bitmap
R4	Address of CCA
R5	Software boot control flags
R10 [2]	Halt PC
R11 [2]	Halt PSL
AP [2]	Halt code
SP	Address of 256K bytes of good memory plus 200_{16}

[1] Thus, the boot device name may contain more than four characters.

[2] The console program sets up these registers after a halt condition. VMB does not use these values.

and executes its commands to boot the system. A bootstrap command procedure identifies the system device and other characteristics of the bootstrap operation by loading general registers R0 through R5 with parameters that will be interpreted by the primary bootstrap program, VMB.

VAX processors with console microprocessors include the VAX 86x0, the VAX 88x0, the VAX 8800 family, the VAX-11/780 and VAX-11/785, and the VAX-11/730.

30.2.2.1   **VAX 86x0 Console Subsystem and Initial Bootstrap Operation.** The console subsystem on VAX 8600 and VAX 8650 processors consists of a separate PDP-11 (T-11) microcomputer, an RL02 disk console block storage device, the console terminal, and a remote diagnosis port. The T-11 runs a modified version of the RT-11 operating system; VAX console support is provided by the console program, ED0AA. The console disk is an RT-11 directory-structured device.

The VAX 8600 or VAX 8650 CPU has six internal processor registers to communicate with the two console devices, four for the console terminal and two for the disk.

There are several circumstances in which a bootstrap sequence is initiated:

- The VAX processor is powered on, and the system control panel Restart Control switch is in the BOOT position.
- The console command B(oot) is typed while the console terminal is in console mode and the VAX processor is halted.
- A bootstrap command procedure is invoked while the console terminal is in console mode and the VAX processor is halted.
- The following instruction is executed in kernel mode:

```
MTPR    #^XF02,#PR$_TXDB
```

- While the Restart Control switch is in the RESTART/BOOT position, a CPU halt condition occurs and auto restart fails.
- While the Restart Control switch is in the BOOT position, a powerfail or error halt condition occurs.

In the bootstrap sequence, the console subsystem must execute a series of programs to load and execute VMB. Table 30.10 lists these programs.

The initial bootstrap programs are console microprocessor programs. The bootstrap steps are as follows:

1. When the console is powered on, code in the console PROM executes. It initializes the console microprocessor and performs self-tests. At successful completion of its self-tests, the PROM code performs some diagnosis of the path to the RL02 and reads the boot block.
2. The boot block program boots the modified RT-11 monitor.
3. The monitor automatically locates and loads the console program. It turns on the power for the VAX CPU.
4. The console program executes the command procedure LOAD.COM, initializes the CPU, I/O adapters, and physical memory map, and invokes the execution of ULOAD.COM.
5. The console program executes the command procedure ULOAD.COM, which loads microcode from the RL02 into the various CPU microstores.
6. The console program then clears the system cache. The console tests the Restart Control switch. If it is in the RESTART/BOOT position, the console attempts a warm restart. If that fails, the console then initiates a boot.
7. The three console commands that bootstrap a VMS system cause the execution of command procedures located on the console RL02. Table 30.16 shows the commands and their command procedure file names. A boot initiated other than through console command uses the default bootstrap command procedure DEFBOO.COM.
8. Each bootstrap command procedure contains the following command to initiate a search for a 64K-byte block of good VAX memory:

```
FIND/MEMORY
```

9. Each contains the following three commands. These commands cause the primary bootstrap program, VMB, to be loaded from the RL02 into the good block of VAX memory, leaving the first page free for the RPB. The START command transfers control to VMB at its first location.

```
EXAMINE SP
LOAD/START:@ VMB
START @
```

VMB is described in Section 30.3.

Table 30.10   Processor-Dependent Programs Used to Bootstrap VAX 86x0 Processors

Program Executing	*Location of Program*	*Purpose of Program*
	EXECUTES ON CONSOLE MICROPROCESSOR	
Console microprocessor PROM bootstrap	PROM in console subsystem	Read RL02 boot block into memory and execute code contained there
RL02 boot block program	LBN 0 on console RL02	Locate monitor program, read it into memory, and pass control to it
RT-11-based monitor program	Console RL02	Locate ED0AA, read it into memory, and pass control to it
ED0AA	Console RL02	Initialize VAX CPU, load general registers, and execute the next several command procedures
LOAD.COM	Console RL02	Initialize VAX CPU, start execution of ULOAD.COM
ULOAD.COM	Console RL02	Load VAX CPU microcode from RL02
	EXECUTES ON VAX 86x0 PROCESSOR	
VMB.EXE	Console RL02	Size physical memory, locate secondary bootstrap, load it into memory, and pass control to it

30.2.2.2   **VAX 88x0 Console Subsystem and Initial Bootstrap Operation.** The VAX 88x0 processors are multiprocessing members of the VAX 8800 family. The dual, triple, and quad CPU systems are composed of VAX 8700 CPUs and a special bus configuration. In these systems, CPUs connect to one VAX 88x0 memory interconnect (NMI) bus, memory modules connect to a second NMI bus, and the two NMI buses communicate via an interconnect called the NMI bus window.

The console subsystem for the VAX 88x0 systems consists of a MicroVAX II processor with a TK50 tape drive, an RD53 fixed disk, a console terminal, and an LA75 printer. The MicroVAX II communicates with the VAX 88x0 CPUs via a Q22-bus module that connects to the console interface module (CIM) in the VAX 88x0 backplane. Through the CIM, the console subsystem controls the VAX 88x0 processor. It can load system microcode, access system registers, transfer files, and control the system clock. It also monitors environmental conditions and can shut down the system if tolerances are exceeded.

The MicroVAX II console processor runs a modified version of VMS, with a dedicated process running a console program. Its subprocesses perform environmental monitoring and control the printer.

There are several circumstances in which a bootstrap sequence is initiated:

- The console processor is powered on, and the software key switches AUTO_POWERON and AUTO_BOOT are both enabled.
- The console command B(oot) is typed while the console terminal is in console mode and the larger VAX processor is halted.
- A bootstrap command procedure is invoked while the console terminal is in console mode and the larger VAX processor is halted.
- The following instruction is executed in kernel mode:

```
MTPR    #^XF02,#PR$_TXDB
```

- While the software key switches AUTO_RESTART and AUTO_BOOT are enabled, a CPU halt condition occurs and restart fails.

In the bootstrap sequence, the console subsystem must execute a series of programs to load and execute VMB. Table 30.11 lists these programs. Note that the foregoing description of the bootstrap sequence does not include booting the secondary processors of an SMP system; see Chapter 34.

The initial bootstrap programs are console programs. The steps of initial bootstrap are as follows:

1. The system power-up sequence causes the console MicroVAX and the environmental monitoring modules (EMMs) to perform self-test.

Table 30.11   Processor-Dependent Programs Used to Bootstrap VAX 88x0 Systems

Program Executing	Location of Program	Purpose of Program
EXECUTES ON CONSOLE PROCESSOR		
Console processor microcode	ROM in console subsystem	Perform self-test, read VMS into memory, and pass control to it
Console VMS	Console fixed disk	Locate console program, PO-LARIS, read it into memory, and transfer control to it
POLARIS.EXE	Console fixed disk	Initialize console database, open log file, and execute SYSINIT.COM and bootstrap command procedures
EXECUTES ON VAX 88x0 PROCESSOR		
Console support microcode	Console fixed disk	Initialize VAX CPUs, NMI, NMI-to-VAXBI adapter (NBI), and memory; locate 256K-byte block of good memory
VMB.EXE	Console fixed disk	Size physical memory, locate secondary bootstrap, load it into memory, and pass control to it

---

2. The MicroVAX boots console VMS from its fixed disk, then executes the console program.

3. The console program, POLARIS, optionally opens a log file to record all console input and output (the terminal is a video monitor). It starts up the subprocess that controls communication with the VAX CPU. It then reads the command procedure SYSINIT.COM (not to be confused with the SYSINIT process) from the console fixed disk and executes it.

4. The SYSINIT.COM command procedure turns on the VAX processor's power if AUTO_POWERON is enabled and checks that hardware modules are correctly placed. It loads VAX CPU microcode from the fixed disk into the control store of each enabled CPU and checks hardware and microcode revisions. It checks that the revisions are at least the minimum supported and also compatible with one another.

5. Each CPU starts, controlled by its CPU microcode. The SYSINIT.COM command procedure initializes the CPUs and the NMIs to a known state.

6. SYSINIT.COM then tests the software key switches AUTO_RESTART and AUTO_BOOT, both of which are most likely on. SYSINIT.COM thus tries auto restart first. If restart fails, it initiates a boot.

7. The three console commands that bootstrap a VMS system cause the execution of command procedures located on the fixed disk. Table 30.16 shows the commands and their command procedure file names. A boot initiated other than through console command uses the default bootstrap command procedure DEFBOO.COM.

8. Each bootstrap command procedure contains the following three commands. They cause VMB to be loaded from the fixed disk into the good block of VAX memory located by the console, leaving the first page free for the RPB. The START command transfers control to VMB at its first location.

```
EXAMINE SP
LOAD /MAINMEMORY /START:@ VMB.EXE
START @
```

Section 30.3 describes VMB.

30.2.2.3 **VAX 8800 Family Console Subsystem and Initial Bootstrap Operation.** The VAX 8800 family includes the VAX 8500, VAX 8530, VAX 8550, VAX 8700, and VAX 8800. The console subsystem on a VAX 8800 family member consists of a separate PDP-11 microprocessor, three block-addressable storage devices (two floppy RX50 diskettes and a fixed head disk), a console terminal, and a remote diagnosis port. The microprocessor runs the P/OS operating system; VAX console support is provided by an application task under P/OS. The fixed head disk is an ODS-1 directory-structured device. The floppies are either ODS-1 or ODS-2, depending on their use.

Table 30.12   Processor-Dependent Programs Used to Bootstrap VAX 8800 Family Processors

Program Executing	Location of Program	Purpose of Program
EXECUTES ON CONSOLE MICROPROCESSOR		
Console micropro-cessor microcode	ROM in console subsystem	Perform self-test, read P/OS into memory, and pass control to it
Console P/OS	Console fixed disk	Locate console program, CON-SOL.TSK (formerly called N16PRO.TSK), read it into memory, and transfer control to it
CONSOL.TSK	Console fixed disk	Initialize console database, open log file, and execute SYSINIT.COM and bootstrap command procedures
EXECUTES ON VAX 8800 FAMILY PROCESSOR		
Console support microcode	Console fixed disk	Initialize VAX CPUs, NMI, NBI, and memory; locate 64K-byte block of good memory
VMB.EXE	Console fixed disk	Size physical memory, locate secondary bootstrap, load it into memory, and pass control to it

Each VAX 8800 family member has four internal processor registers to communicate with all the console devices. The device ID is encoded into control bits to distinguish among the devices.

There are several circumstances in which a bootstrap sequence is initiated:

- The console is powered on, and the software key switches AUTO_POWER-ON and AUTO_BOOT are both enabled.
- The console command B(oot) is typed while the console terminal is in console mode and the VAX processor is halted.
- A bootstrap command procedure is invoked while the console terminal is in console mode and the VAX processor is halted.
- The following instruction is executed in kernel mode:

```
MTPR    #^XF02,#PR$_TXDB
```

- While the software key switches AUTO_RESTART and AUTO_BOOT are enabled, a CPU halt condition occurs and restart fails.

In the bootstrap sequence, the console subsystem must execute a series of programs to load and execute VMB. Table 30.12 lists these programs. Note that the foregoing description of the bootstrap sequence does not include booting the secondary processors of an SMP system; see Chapter 34.

The initial bootstrap programs are console microprocessor programs. The steps of initial bootstrap are as follows:

1. When the console microprocessor is turned on, it performs a self-test, loads P/OS from the fixed disk, and starts it.

2. P/OS loads the console program from the fixed disk and transfers control to it.

3. The console program opens a log file to record all console input and output (the terminal is a video monitor) and starts up the real-time interface (RTI) driver, which controls communication with the VAX CPU. It reads the command procedure SYSINIT.COM (not to be confused with the SYSINIT process) from the console fixed disk and executes it.

4. The SYSINIT.COM command procedure turns on the VAX CPU's power if AUTO_POWERON is enabled and checks that hardware modules are correctly placed. It loads VAX CPU microcode (including console support microcode) from the fixed disk, and checks hardware and microcode revisions. It checks that the revisions are at least the minimum supported and also compatible with one another. The command procedure initializes the NMI, NBIs, and the memory.

5. SYSINIT.COM then tests the software key switches AUTO_RESTART and AUTO_BOOT, both of which are most likely on. SYSINIT.COM thus tries auto restart first. If that fails, it initiates a boot.

6. The three console commands that bootstrap a VMS system cause the execution of bootstrap command procedures located on the fixed disk. Table 30.16 shows the commands and their associated command procedure file names. A boot initiated other than through console command procedures uses the default bootstrap command procedure DEFBOO.COM.

7. Each bootstrap command procedure contains the following three commands. They cause VMB to be loaded from the fixed disk into the good 64K-byte block of VAX memory, leaving the first page free for the RPB. The START command transfers control to VMB at its first location.

```
EXAMINE SP
LOAD /MAINMEMORY /START:@ VMB.EXE
START @
```

Section 30.3 describes VMB.

30.2.2.4 **VAX-11/78x Console Subsystem and Initial Bootstrap Operation.** The console subsystem on VAX-11/780 and VAX-11/785 processors consists of a separate LSI-11 microcomputer, a block-addressable RX01 floppy diskette, a console terminal, and an optional remote diagnosis port. The console program executes on the LSI-11, and the console devices are on the LSI-11 bus.

A VAX-11/780 or VAX-11/785 CPU has four internal processor registers for communication with both console devices. The device ID is encoded into control bits to distinguish between the two devices. In fact, the console program reads the registers and performs the appropriate I/O function to the appropriate device.

There are several circumstances in which a bootstrap sequence is initiated:

- The B(oot) command is entered while the system is in console mode, or the Boot switch is pressed.
- A bootstrap command procedure is invoked while the system is in console mode.
- The following instruction is executed in kernel mode:

```
MTPR    #^XF02,#PR$_TXDB
```

- An attempt to restart the system after a power failure recovery or any other halt condition does not succeed, and the Auto Restart switch is in the ON position.

In the bootstrap sequence, the console subsystem must execute a series of programs to load and execute VMB on a VAX-11/78x processor. The initial bootstrap programs run on the LSI-11 and execute PDP-11 instructions without VAX instructions. Table 30.13 lists these programs and those that run on the VAX processor.

Table 30.13   Processor-Dependent Programs Used to Bootstrap VAX-11/780 and VAX-11/785 Processors

Program Executing	Location of Program	Purpose of Program
EXECUTES ON LSI-11 MICROCOMPUTER		
LSI-11 ROM bootstrap	LSI-11 I/O space	Read floppy boot block into memory and execute code contained there
Floppy boot block program	LBN 0 on console floppy	Locate CONSOL.SYS, read it into memory, and pass control to it
CONSOL.SYS	Console floppy	Initialize VAX-11/78x CPU, load general registers, and invoke memory locator program; load VMB into VAX memory and transfer control to it
EXECUTES ON VAX-11/78x PROCESSOR		
ISP ROM	ROM in memory controller	Locate 64K-byte block of error-free memory
VMB.EXE	Console floppy	Size physical memory, locate secondary bootstrap, load it into memory, and pass control to it

---

The steps of initial bootstrap are as follows:

1. The first program that executes in the LSI-11 after self-test is a bootstrap program located in ROM. It loads the boot block program located on LBN 0 of the console floppy (sectors 1, 3, 5, and 7) into LSI memory.

2. The boot block program at LBN 0 is a copy of the bootstrap program used by the RT-11 operating system. The RT-11 bootstrap, which understands the RT-11 file system, looks for a specific file (the monitor), loads it into memory, and transfers control to it.

   The boot block program found on the console floppy diskette looks for a program called CONSOL.SYS.

3. On the VAX 11/780, CONSOL.SYS loads the file WCSxxx.PAT from the floppy diskette into the VAX writable control store. The VAX 11/785 loads the file SSUxxx.WCS. CONSOL.SYS then prompts >>> on the console terminal. It verifies that the versions of the microcode are consistent with one another. If there is a version mismatch between the writable control store (WCS) and either the PROM control store (PCS) or the field programmable logic array (FPLA), an error message is displayed on the console terminal.

4. The three console commands that bootstrap a VMS system cause the execution of command procedures located on the console floppy. Table 30.16 shows the commands and their command procedure file names. A boot initiated other than through a console command uses the default bootstrap command procedure DEFBOO.CMD.

5. Each bootstrap command procedure contains the following commands:

   ```
   START    20003000
   WAIT     DONE
   ```

   These two commands cause a program located in ROM in the first memory controller on the synchronous backplane interface (SBI) to execute. The command procedure waits until the memory ROM program completes before executing its next command. The memory ROM program signals the console program that it is done by writing the "software done" signal with the following instruction:

   ```
   MTPR     #^XF01,#PR$_TXDB
   ```

   The program in the memory controller ROM performs a primitive memory sizing operation in an effort to locate 64K bytes of error-free, page-aligned, contiguous physical memory that can be used by the remaining bootstrap programs. The output of this program is an address 200_{16} bytes beyond the beginning of the first good page. This address is loaded into SP. In a typical system with no errors in the first 64K bytes, the contents of SP are 200_{16}.

6. Each bootstrap command procedure contains the following three commands. They cause VMB to be loaded from the floppy diskette into the

good 64K-byte block of VAX memory, leaving the first page free for the RPB. The START command transfers control to the first byte of VMB.

```
EXAMINE SP
LOAD VMB.EXE/START:@
START @
```

Section 30.3 describes VMB.

30.2.2.5   **VAX-11/730 Console Subsystem and Initial Bootstrap Operation.** The console subsystem on the VAX-11/730 consists of a console microprocessor, a terminal, two block-addressable storage devices (TU58 cartridge devices), and an optional remote diagnosis port. The console TU58 is an RT-11 directory-structured device. The console program executes on the console microprocessor. When the console program has control, the VAX-11/730 cannot execute VAX instructions.

A VAX-11/730 CPU has eight internal processor registers for communication with the console devices: four for the console terminal and four for the TU58s.

There are several circumstances in which a bootstrap sequence is initiated:

- A power-on occurs (the Boot switch is pressed or the processor is turned on).
- The console command B(oot) is typed while the processor is in console mode.
- A bootstrap command procedure is invoked while the system is in console mode.
- The following instruction is executed in kernel mode:

```
MTPR    #^XF02,#PR$_TXDB
```

- While the Auto Restart switch is in the ON position, a CPU halt condition occurs and auto restart fails.

In the bootstrap sequence, the console subsystem must execute a series of programs to load and execute VMB. Table 30.14 lists these programs.

The initial bootstrap programs are console microprocessor programs. The steps of initial bootstrap are as follows:

1. After performing a self-test, the microprocessor locates the TU58 that contains the boot block (trying DD1 first and, if that fails, then DD0) and loads blocks 0 through 5 from the tape into microprocessor memory. The code in the boot block locates the main console microcode program CONSOL.EXE on the console TU58.
2. CONSOL.EXE executes two command procedure files, POWER.CMD and CODE0*n*.CMD. POWER.CMD loads several microcode files into the CPU, including one called POWER.CPU. POWER.CPU initializes the machine, searches for a page-aligned 64K-byte block of good memory,

Table 30.14   Processor-Dependent Programs Used to Bootstrap a VAX-11/730 Processor

Program Executing	Location of Program	Purpose of Program
EXECUTES ON CONSOLE MICROPROCESSOR		
Console micro-processor ROM bootstrap	ROM in console subsystem	Read TU58 boot block into memory and execute code contained there
TU58 boot block program	LBN 0 on console TU58	Locate CONSOL.EXE, read it into memory, and pass control to it
CONSOL.EXE	Console TU58	Initialize VAX-11/730 CPU, load general registers, and execute command procedures
EXECUTES ON VAX-11/730 PROCESSOR		
VMB.EXE	Console TU58	Size physical memory, locate secondary bootstrap, load it into memory, and pass control to it

Table 30.15   VAX-11/730 Bootstrap Command Procedures

Command File	Hardware Configuration
CODE00.CMD	No floating-point accelerator (FPA), no integrated disk controller (IDC)
CODE01.CMD	No FPA, with IDC
CODE02.CMD	With FPA, no IDC
CODE03.CMD	With FPA, with IDC

and checks the configuration of the machine. When POWER.CPU exits, it returns an address 200_{16} bytes beyond the beginning of the first good page. This address is loaded into SP. In a typical system with no errors in the first 64K bytes, the contents of SP are 200_{16}.

Each possible configuration of the VAX-11/730 is assigned a value. Whichever value POWER.CPU returns is substituted into the file name CODE0n.CMD. The CODE0n.CMD command procedures load the normal run-time microcode for the appropriate processor configuration. Table 30.15 lists the command procedures used with specific processor configurations.

3. The Auto Restart switch is checked. If it is in the OFF position, the processor enters console mode and prints the console command prompt >>>.

891

4. If the Auto Restart switch is in the ON position, the console executes the commands in the default bootstrap command procedure DEFBOO.CMD.

5. The three console commands that bootstrap a VMS system cause the execution of command procedures located on the console TU58. Table 30.16 shows the commands and their command procedure file names. A boot initiated other than through a console command uses the default bootstrap command procedure DEFBOO.CMD.

6. Each bootstrap command procedure contains the following three commands. They display the contents of SP (to identify the starting address in physical memory). They then load the primary bootstrap program, VMB, from the TU58 into the good 64K-byte block of VAX memory, leaving the first page available for the RPB. The S command transfers control to the first byte of VMB.

```
E SP
L/P/S:@ VMB.EXE
S @
```

Section 30.3 describes VMB.

30.2.3 VAX CPUs Without Console Microprocessors

VAX CPUs without console microprocessors include the VAX 6000 series, the VAX 8200 family, and the VAX-11/750. On these types of VAX CPU, the console program is implemented either in CPU microcode or in VAX MACRO instructions and executes on the VAX processor itself. When the CPU is in console mode, the console program (and nothing else, such as a user program or VMS itself) executes.

30.2.3.1 VAX 6000 Series Console Subsystem and Initial Bootstrap Operation. The VAX 6000 model 200, 300, and 400 systems are collectively referred to as the VAX 6000 series.

Table 30.16   Commands to Boot VAX Processors

Command	Command Procedure [1]
B	DEFBOO.CMD or DEFBOO.COM
B *dev*	*dev*BOO.CMD or *dev*BOO.COM
@*filespec*	*filespec*.CMD or *filespec*.COM

---

[1] The file type of a console bootstrap command procedure depends on the particular processor and console subsystem. CMD is used by the VAX-11/730 and VAX-11/78*x* processors and by BOOT58.EXE. COM is used by VAX 8800 family, VAX 88*x*0, and VAX 86*x*0 processors.

The VAX 6000 series machines support multiple CPUs per system. One CPU acts as the primary and performs the main work of booting VMS. VMS directs the initialization of the remaining secondary CPUs, as described in Chapter 34.

The console subsystem for a VAX 6000 series system consists of a console program, a console terminal port, and a block storage device (a TK50 or TK70 tape drive) to which the console state can be saved. Each CPU has a console ROM and an electrically erasable programmable read-only memory (EEPROM) as dedicated console memory.

The console program, written in VAX MACRO and Bliss-32, resides in ROM. For each possible boot device, the ROM also contains a routine that can read the boot block of its associated boot device and use information in the boot block to locate VMB. This routine is known as a boot primitive. Console patches, parameters, and bootstrap information are stored in the EEPROM.

The console program runs on the VAX processor rather than on a separate console processor. It can read and interpret commands typed on the console terminal, allowing an operator to examine or modify the state of the machine and boot the operating system. In a multiprocessor system, each CPU runs the console program, although only the primary processor is allowed to perform I/O directly to the console terminal. These multiple instances of the console program communicate with the primary processor and cooperate to control the system. The console program reserves a segment of main memory called the CCA for communication among the processors while they are in console mode. This area is also visible to VMS and may contain items such as hardware revision levels, machine check functions, and CPU model information.

The console program initiates the boot sequence under the following conditions:

- The console command B(oot) is entered on the console terminal while it is in console mode and the control panel is enabled.
- The control panel is locked into secure mode or is enabled with auto start selected, and one of the following occurs:

  —Power is restored to the system.
  —The primary processor attempts to restart and fails.
  —A secondary processor attempts to restart, fails, and the bit CCA$Q_SECSTART pertaining to that secondary is clear.

- The Restart switch is pressed and the console is enabled.
- Kernel mode code requests a reboot by setting the bit CCA$V_REBOOT in the CCA$B_HFLAGS byte and halting the primary node.

The console subsystem uses a series of programs to load and execute VMB. Table 30.17 lists these programs.

Table 30.17   Processor-Dependent Programs Used to Bootstrap VAX 6000 Series Processors

Program Executing	Location of Program	Purpose of Program
Console program	ROM in VAX CPU	Initialize CPU, load boot parameters from EEPROM, load boot primitive from ROM, locate block of good memory, determine action to take, and pass control to boot primitive
Boot primitive	ROM	Load LBN 0 of boot device into memory and pass control to it
Boot block code	LBN 0 of boot device	Load primary bootstrap program from system device and pass control to it
VMB.EXE	Specific LBN on system device	Size physical memory, locate secondary bootstrap, load it into memory, and pass control to it

VAX 6000 series systems execute the following in response to power-up or system reset:

1. Each CPU begins execution of console code. It initializes itself to a known state and performs appropriate actions based on the control panel setting. Assuming that auto start is selected, it performs the steps that follow.
2. The console program directs a self-test and participates in the selection of a primary processor. The CPU that has passed self-test and has the lowest VAX 6000 series memory interconnect bus (XMI) node ID becomes the primary processor unless it has been disabled through the SET CPU/NOPRIMARY console command.
3. The primary prints the results of the self-test on the console terminal.
4. The CPUs perform an extended self-test, specifically verifying their ability to access main memory.
5. In case the CPU originally chosen as the primary fails the extended self-test, the primary selection process occurs again. The CPU that passes all self-tests and has the lowest XMI node ID becomes the primary processor unless disabled through the SET CPU/NOPRIMARY console command. The console program, executing on the CPU selected as the primary, performs the remaining bootstrap operations, while the secondary CPUs wait for permission to proceed.
6. The primary performs further testing and prints results on the console. The primary processor's console program configures memory, determining how much is present and which pages have uncorrectable errors. It

allocates pages from the high end of physical memory for the CCA and for a bitmap that will inform VMS which physical pages are usable and which are not. In the bitmap, the console program marks as unusable any pages found bad. In addition, it marks as unusable those pages that CCA and the bitmap itself occupy to prevent VMS from attempting to put them to a second concurrent use.

The console program also locates 256K bytes of good physical memory for VMB.

7. The console program running on the primary searches the EEPROM and ROM for parameters describing the boot device and bootstrap options. It locates a matching boot primitive, loads the processor registers as required by the boot parameters and the boot device, and transfers control to the boot primitive.

8. The action of the boot primitive depends upon the type of boot device:

—For a disk device, the boot primitive reads the first logical block of the disk (the boot block, LBN 0) into the first good page of memory. The boot block contains the size and location of the VMB image on the disk. Code in the boot block and in the boot primitive load VMB into memory, as described in Section 30.2.3.3.1. Note that a VAX 6000 series system never uses the BOOT58 program.

—For a tape device, the boot primitive rewinds the tape and reads the first block into the first good page of memory. If the block size is 80 bytes, the tape is assumed to be a standard ANSI labeled tape. The first file after the tape label is assumed to be VMB; the boot primitive copies it into memory starting at the second good page and transfers control. Otherwise, the boot primitive reads the remaining blocks until it encounters a tapemark, then transfers control to the loaded image at offset 12 from the base of good memory.

—For an Ethernet device, the boot primitive causes the adapter to request a tertiary load, similar to the method described in Section 30.3.4.

9. Through one of these methods, the primary processor transfers control to VMB.

30.2.3.2 **VAX 8200 Family Console Subsystem and Initial Bootstrap Operation.** The VAX 8200 family consists of the VAX 8200, VAX 8250, VAX 8300, and VAX 8350. The VAX 8200 family console subsystem includes two block-addressable storage devices (RX50 floppy diskettes), an optional remote diagnosis port, and the console program. The console program is implemented as microcode in the VAX CPU. When the CPU is in console mode, the console program (and nothing else, such as a user program or VMS itself) executes. The console program gains control of the processor whenever any halt condition occurs, such as execution of a HALT instruction.

The VAX 8200 and VAX 8250 CPUs have four internal processor registers to communicate with the console terminal. Communication with the disk drives is through device registers in I/O space.

On the multiprocessor members of the family, the VAX 8300 and VAX 8350, only the primary CPU can communicate with the console terminal (using the same four internal processor registers as a VAX 8200 CPU). The secondary CPU communicates with the console terminal via the primary CPU. The primary and secondary CPUs use the internal processor register PR8SS$_RXCD to transfer console data to each other. The primary CPU uses the previously mentioned four internal processor registers to communicate with the console terminal on behalf of the secondary CPU.

There are several circumstances in which a bootstrap sequence is initiated:

- The system is powered on or the RESTART button on the control panel is pressed, and the lower key switch on the CPU control panel is in the AUTO START position.
- The B(oot) command is typed while the system is in console mode.
- The following instruction is executed in kernel mode:

```
MTPR    #^XF02,#PR$_TXDB
```

- An attempt to restart the system after a power failure recovery or some other halt condition does not succeed, and the lower key switch is in the AUTO START position.

When a VAX 8200 family member is initialized, the console program is the first in a series of programs that execute before VMB executes. These programs are summarized in Table 30.18. Note that this description does not include booting the attached processor of an SMP system; see Chapter 34.

The steps of initial bootstrap are as follows:

1. The console program initializes the CPU. It locates 64K bytes of contiguous, error-free, page-aligned memory and loads the bootstrap code from the EEPROM into a boot random access memory (RAM).
2. The console program does not process command procedures. Instead, it must construct the contents for R0 through R5 from the combination of default boot device and the bootstrap command itself. The system manager identifies the default boot device by running a stand-alone diagnostic to load its name into the EEPROM.
3. The console program passes control to the bootstrap code loaded from the EEPROM.
4. The bootstrap code consists of two main pieces, a dispatch routine and device-specific routines. The dispatch routine parses the boot device name passed from the console microcode and selects the corresponding device-specific routine. The device-specific routine simply reads LBN 0 of the selected device into the first page of good memory and passes control to it (at an address 12 bytes past the beginning of the program).

Table 30.18 Processor-Dependent Programs Used to Bootstrap VAX 8200 Family Processors

Program Executing	*Location of Program*	*Purpose of Program*
Console program	ROM in VAX CPU	Initialize CPU, load bootstrap code from EEPROM into boot RAM, locate block of good memory, determine action to take, and pass control to bootstrap code
Bootstrap code	EEPROM	Load LBN 0 of boot device into memory and pass control to it
Boot block code	LBN 0 of boot device	Load primary bootstrap program from system device or BOOT58 from console RX50 and pass control to it
VMB.EXE	Specific LBN on system device	Size physical memory, locate secondary bootstrap, load it into memory, and pass control to it
BOOT58.EXE	Specific LBN on console RX50	Process command procedures or enhanced console commands, boot from a hierarchical storage controller (HSC) system device

5. The boot block program reads VMB or BOOT58 from the boot device into memory. Section 30.2.3.3.1 describes the boot block program, Section 30.2.3.3.2 describes BOOT58, and Section 30.3 describes VMB.

30.2.3.3 **VAX-11/750 Console Subsystem and Initial Bootstrap Operation.** The console subsystem on the VAX-11/750 consists of a terminal, a TU58 cartridge device, an optional remote diagnosis port, and console microcode in the VAX-11/750 processor. The console program is implemented in CPU microcode and stored in ROM within the CPU. When the console program has control, that is, when the CPU is in console mode, the VAX-11/750 processor executes console microcode rather than user or system instructions.

A VAX-11/750 processor has eight internal processor registers for communication with the console devices: four for the terminal and four for the TU58 console block storage device.

There are several circumstances in which a bootstrap sequence is initiated:

- The system is powered on or the RESET front panel button is pressed, and the Power-on Action switch is in the BOOT position.
- The B(oot) command is entered while the system is in console mode.
- A HALT instruction is executed or some other halt condition occurs, and the Power-on Action switch is in the BOOT position.

Table 30.19   Processor-Dependent Programs Used to Bootstrap a VAX-11/750 Processor

Program Executing	Location of Program	Purpose of Program
Console program	ROM in VAX-11/750 CPU	Initialize CPU, locate block of good memory, determine boot device, and pass control to device-specific ROM
Device-specific ROM code	I/O address space of VAX-11/750 CPU	Load LBN 0 of boot device into memory and pass control to it
Boot block code	LBN 0 of boot device	Load primary bootstrap program from system device or BOOT58 from console TU58 and pass control to it
VMB.EXE	Specific LBN on system device	Size physical memory, locate secondary bootstrap, load it into memory, and pass control to it
BOOT58.EXE	Specific LBN on console TU58	Process indirect command files or enhanced console commands, boot from an HSC system device

- The following instruction is executed in kernel mode:

```
MTPR    #^XF02,#PR$_TXDB
```

- An attempt to restart the system after a power failure recovery or some other halt condition does not succeed, and the Power-on Action switch is in the RESTART/ BOOT position.

In the bootstrap sequence, the console subsystem must execute a series of programs to load and execute VMB. Table 30.19 lists these programs.

The steps of initial bootstrap are as follows:

1. The console program initializes the CPU and locates a page-aligned 64K-byte block of good memory. It loads the first 128 map registers in the UNIBUS adapter to address this block of memory (a step not taken when the TU58 is used as a bootstrap device). The console program on the VAX-11/750 does not process command procedures. Instead, it must construct the contents for R0 through R5 from the device selected by the Boot Device switch and the bootstrap command itself. It then passes control to the device-specific ROM selected either by the bootstrap device selector switch on the CPU cabinet front panel or by the B(oot) command.

2. The device-specific ROM program is a VAX MACRO instruction program. It consists of two main pieces, a control routine and a device-specific subroutine. This program simply reads the boot block, LBN 0, of

the selected device into the first page of good memory and passes control to it (at an address 12 bytes past the beginning of the program).

3. The code in the boot block reads VMB or BOOT58 from the console device into memory. The boot block program is described in more detail in Section 30.2.3.3.1. Section 30.3 describes VMB.

4. BOOT58 executes a command procedure that reads VMB from the system device into memory. BOOT58 is described in more detail in Section 30.2.3.3.2.

30.2.3.3.1 *Boot Block Program.* The boot block program loads a single program into memory and passes control to it. The boot block program does not contain any I/O support. It uses the driver subroutine (or boot primitive) from the device ROM program. The boot block program on a system device loads VMB. The boot block program on a console device can load an enhanced command processor program, called BOOT58, for some CPUs. The boot block program on a stand-alone Backup console device loads VMB.

The boot block program resides in the first logical block (LBN 0) of the boot device. Three longwords of header information precede the body of the boot block program. These longwords contain the following:

- The size of the bootstrap program to be loaded by the boot block program
- The starting LBN of the bootstrap program to be loaded
- A relative offset into the block of good memory where this program is to be loaded

The boot block is written during normal VMS system operation by the Writeboot Utility. It uses the file system to look up a user-specified file (VMB.EXE or BOOT58.EXE) on a user-specified device. WRITEBOOT determines values for the three header longwords and writes the boot block program into LBN 0. Note that the boot block program has the LBN of the bootstrap program hard coded into the block. If the position of the bootstrap program on the volume changes, the Writeboot Utility must be run again to rewrite the boot block with new information.

Note that the location of VMB by the boot block program is one of the few cases in the VMS system of a file being located by an LBN coded into another program. Thus, VMB on the system device of a VAX CPU without a console microprocessor is one of the few files that is not free to move or be superseded by a newer version without some external intervention such as running WRITEBOOT.

30.2.3.3.2 *BOOT58.* The block-addressable storage device on a VAX CPU without a console processor is not necessarily used during a normal bootstrap operation. However, an alternative bootstrap path uses the device to provide the following:

- Command procedure capability

- An enhanced console command language
- The ability to bootstrap a system if the boot block on the system device is corrupted
- The ability to bootstrap a system from an HSC disk

The stand-alone program BOOT58 is an enhanced console command processor loaded from the block-addressable storage device that provides the features previously listed. BOOT58 is loaded by selecting the console block storage device (DDA0:) as the bootstrap device, either by the device selector switch or with the following command:

```
>>>B    DDA0:
```

Note that the drive DDA0: must contain an RT-11 structured medium with console command files and BOOT58.EXE.

The boot block on the device boots BOOT58. Once BOOT58 prompts, commands or command procedure file specifications can be entered at the console terminal. BOOT58 accepts the commands shown in Table 30.16.

There is no device-specific ROM on a VAX-11/750 processor or VAX 8200 family member that supports loading LBN 0 from an HSC disk through a computer interconnect (CI) adapter and then loading VMB. BOOT58 makes it possible to load VMB from the console. VMB does contain device support for the CI and HSC disks. It first loads volatile CI microcode from the console device into the CI device and volatile CPU microcode into the processor.

30.3 PRIMARY BOOTSTRAP PROGRAM (VMB)

The first program that is common to VAX systems, generally independent of CPU type, is the primary bootstrap program, VMB. VMB exists in two forms:

- Full VMB is located on the system device or console medium and is used by systems such as VAX 6000 series, VAX-11/750, and VAX 86x0 processors. Section 30.3.1 describes the operation of full VMB.
- ROM-based VMB is a VMB subset stored in processor ROM. All MicroVAX processors boot via this general method, with the actual VMB code differing slightly between MicroVAX implementations. ROM-based VMB links with a processor-specific subset of the normal boot drivers, includes a minimal version of the XDELTA debugger, and interprets register contents differently than does full VMB. Section 30.2.1.2 provides an example of ROM-based VMB.

VMB performs the following two major steps:

1. It locates and determines the size of physical memory on the system unless the console subsystem has previously sized memory, as is the case with all MicroVAX processors.

2. It locates a secondary bootstrap program, loads it into memory, and transfers control to it.

VMB and the secondary bootstrap program, SYSBOOT, are conceptually one program. The VAX-11/780 initialization (initially implemented for Version 1.0 of the VMS operating system) required that the initial bootstrap program reside on the console floppy diskette, whose capacity of 512 blocks was also used for microcode, the console program, and command procedures. Rather than impose artificial restrictions on the size of the bootstrap program, the designers divided the program into two pieces:

- A primary piece that resides on the floppy diskette or in ROM, one of whose major purposes is to locate the secondary piece
- A secondary piece that resides on the system device (with no real limits on its size) that performs the bulk of the bootstrap operation

Once this division was achieved, VMB became a more flexible tool that could be used to load programs other than VMS. To preserve this flexibility, the division of the bootstrap into primary and secondary pieces was continued in subsequent versions of the VMS operating system.

VMB is a general-purpose bootstrap program. In addition to loading SYSBOOT to initialize a VMS system, the default, VMB can perform the following three options:

- VMB can load the diagnostic bootstrap [SYSMAINT]DIAGBOOT.EXE instead of SYSBOOT.
- VMB can prompt for the name of any stand-alone program to be loaded into VAX memory. This program might be a stand-alone diagnostic program, an alternative secondary bootstrap, or another operating system. The file system routines and control transfer mechanism used by VMB place some restrictions on this file:
  —The system device containing the file to be loaded by VMB must be an ODS-2 Files-11 volume.
  —The file must be contiguous.
  —The code in the program must be position-independent.
- VMB can load the contents of a bootstrap block from the system disk and execute the program that it finds there. In general, this boot block is LBN 0 on the volume. The VAX-11/78x bootstrap sequences allow an alternative boot block number to be passed to VMB in R4. VMS only supports an alternative boot block number for a VAX-11/78x system.

  The ability to pass control to a boot block program makes VMB a flexible tool. One possible use for such a program is support for a file system other than Files-11, such as that of ULTRIX-32.

If none of these listed options is selected through the corresponding flags in R5, VMB enters its default path, which loads SYSBOOT into memory and transfers control to it.

VMB is enhanced in each version of the VMS software. These enhancements include support for new processor types, support for new devices, and changes to the argument list passed to SYSBOOT. Because a user might attempt to bootstrap a VMS system with an old version of VMB, it is desirable to maintain forward and backward compatibility between versions of VMB and SYSBOOT. SYSBOOT checks the version of VMB that loaded it and takes appropriate action, depending on the relative versions. Compatibility is maintained by not removing functionality from VMB that is required by older versions of SYSBOOT.

30.3.1 Operation of VMB

VMB receives control running in the following environment:

- In kernel mode
- On the boot stack (SP = RPB base plus 200_{16})
- With memory management disabled
- At IPL 31

Most modules that make up full VMB.EXE are from facility [BOOTS]. VMB modules include minimal drivers for boot devices, VAX instruction emulation routines, test routines for various types of memory, primitive file access routines, and the XDELTA debugger.

VMB interprets the contents of registers R0 through R5 and R7 to determine the type of bootstrap being performed and the identity of the boot device.

Tables 30.20 and 30.21 summarize the input parameters passed to VMB. VMB saves these parameters in the RPB (see Table 30.22) for use by later steps in system initialization.

The steps that VMB takes to load SYSBOOT into memory follow. Note that this list describes full VMB rather than ROM-based VMB and does not include error paths. It focuses on booting VMS from a system device and does not discuss booting stand-alone Backup.

1. VMB creates a one-page system control block (SCB) with most interrupt and exception vectors pointing to a single service routine, a fault handler (see Figure 30.2). It loads the vectors for TBIT and BPT exceptions with the addresses of exception service routines in XDELTA, linked as a part of the VMB image. It loads the vectors for OPCDEC and OPCDEC_FPD exceptions with the addresses of minimal character string instruction emulation routines for processors that require emulation.

2. VMB reads the processor ID register (PR$_SID) to determine the CPU type. It uses the CPU type in several places to choose the appropriate section of CPU-dependent code to execute. SYSBOOT later performs

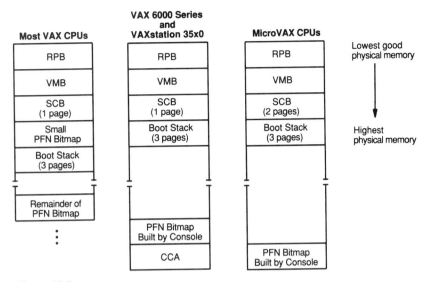

Figure 30.2
Physical Memory Layouts Used by VMB and SYSBOOT

a similar step for the use of both SYSBOOT and the executive. If the processor type is unknown, VMB prints an error message and halts.

3. If the R5 bootstrap breakpoint flag, RPB$V_BOOBPT, is set, VMB executes a BPT instruction, which transfers control to XDELTA, linked as a part of the VMB image. This breakpoint is useful in debugging problems that prevent a system from booting.

4. VMB stores some of its input parameters and the physical addresses of the boot device driver in the RPB (see Table 30.22).

5. VMB switches to a three-page stack, either in the physical pages immediately following the SCB or four pages beyond the SCB, depending on the location of the bitmap described in the next step.

6. SYSBOOT requires a bitmap describing all physical memory that is to be used as main memory. Each possible page is represented by one bit. If the page is free from error, the bit representing it is set. If the page does not exist or has errors, its bit is clear. SYSBOOT uses the bitmap as the basis for the creation of the PFN database.

Memory test and bitmap construction is performed by VMB or, on many VAX systems, by the VAX console. Either the console reserves pages of memory in high physical address space for the bitmap (and for additional CPU-specific structures such as the CCA), or VMB reserves the four pages immediately beyond the SCB to describe up to eight megabytes of physical memory, and allocates further pages as more memory is discovered.

If the console tests memory and loads the bitmap, it marks the pages containing the bitmap (and CPU-specific structures) as unavailable in

Table 30.20   Register Input to VMB

Register	Contents
R0	Bootstrap device type code

Bit Field	Meaning
⟨31:16⟩	MASSBUS—mbz [1]
	UNIBUS—Optional vector address; if zero, use default vector
⟨15:8⟩	mbz
⟨7:0⟩	Bootstrap device code (decimal) from $BTDDEF

Value	Meaning
0	MASSBUS device (RM03/5, RP04/5/6/7, RM80)
1	RK06/7
2	RL01/2
3	IDC on VAX-11/730
4–16	Reserved for UNIBUS devices
17	UDA
18	TK50
19–31	Reserved
32	HSC on CI
33	KDB50
34	KRBTA
35	DEBNK (tape)
36–42	VAXstation 2000 and 3100 DSSI and SCSI devices
43–63	Reserved
64	Console block storage device
65–95	Reserved
96	DEQNA
97	DEUNA
98	DEBNK (Ethernet)
99	VAXstation 2000 and 3100 Ethernet
100–103	Reserved
104	DEBNI
105–127	Reserved for network boot devices
128	Disk served by an LAVc host

R1	Bootstrap device bus address

CPU	Bit Field	Meaning
VAX-11/730,	⟨31:4⟩	mbz
VAX-11/78x	⟨3:0⟩	TR number of adapter
VAX-11/750	⟨31:24⟩	mbz
	⟨23:0⟩	Address of I/O page for boot device's UNIBUS
VAX 86x0	⟨31:6⟩	mbz
	⟨5:4⟩	A-bus adapter number
	⟨3:0⟩	TR number of adapter
VAX 8200	⟨31:4⟩	mbz
family	⟨3:0⟩	VAXBI node number of adapter

(continued)

Table 30.20   Register Input to VMB *(continued)*

Register	Contents
R1	Bootstrap device bus address

CPU	Bit Field	Meaning
VAX 8800,	⟨31:6⟩	mbz
88x0	⟨5:4⟩	VAXBI bus number
family	⟨3:0⟩	VAXBI node number of adapter
VAX 6000	⟨31:8⟩	mbz
series	⟨7:4⟩	XMI or DWMBA TR number
	⟨3:0⟩	VAXBI node number of adapter

Register	Contents
R2	Bootstrap device controller information

Bus Type	Bit Field	Meaning
Other buses	⟨31:24⟩	Bus type
UNIBUS	⟨31:18⟩	mbz
	⟨17:0⟩	UNIBUS address of the device's CSR
MASSBUS	⟨31:4⟩	mbz
	⟨3:0⟩	Adapter's controller/formatter number
CI	⟨31:16⟩	mbz
	⟨15:8⟩	HSC port number
	⟨7:0⟩	Alternative HSC port number

Register	Contents
R3	Boot device unit number
R4	LBN of boot block (VAX-11/780 and VAX-11/785 only)
R5	Software boot control flags (see Table 30.21)
R7	CCA address
R10[2]	Halt PC
R11[2]	Halt PSL
AP[2]	Halt code
SP	Address of 64K bytes of good memory plus 200_{16}

[1] mbz stands for "must be zero."
[2] The console subsystem sets up these registers after a halt condition. VMB does not use these values.

the bitmap itself so that VMS does not overwrite them. However, they are not counted as bad pages. If VMB tests memory and loads the bitmap with a CPU-specific routine, it marks the bitmap pages available to VMS, and they are eventually reused.

If the memory test fails on 10 percent or more of the physical pages, VMB writes a message to that effect on the console terminal and halts.

Figure 30.2 illustrates the layout of physical memory after VMB begins execution. Note that the RPB resides at the lowest physical address available.

Table 30.21 VMB Boot Control Flags (Contents of R5)

Bit Position	Symbolic Name	Meaning
0	RPB$V_CONV	Conversational boot. If set, SYSBOOT solicits parameters from the console terminal. On a VAX-11/730, if this and RPB$V_DIAG are set, the diagnostic supervisor enters MENUTEST mode.
1	RPB$V_DEBUG	Debug. If set, SYSBOOT loads the SYSTEM_DEBUG loadable executive image.
2	RPB$V_INIBPT	Initial breakpoint. If it and RPB$V_DEBUG are set, EXE$INIT executes one BPT instruction after turning on memory management. It enables other breakpoints specified in the SYSGEN BREAKPOINT parameter.
3	RPB$V_BBLOCK	Secondary boot from boot block. If set, secondary bootstrap is a single 512-byte block. On a VAX-11/78x, its LBN can be specified in R4. On other processors, the boot block is LBN 0. On MicroVAX CPUs, this bit causes VMB to bypass its search for a Files-11 secondary bootstrap file.
4	RPB$V_DIAG	Diagnostic boot. If set, secondary bootstrap is image [SYSn.SYSMAINT]DIAGBOOT.EXE.
5	RPB$V_BOOBPT	Bootstrap breakpoint. If set, VMB and SYSBOOT_XDELTA execute BPT instructions to transfer control to XDELTA.
6	RPB$V_HEADER	Image header. If set, VMB takes the transfer address of the secondary bootstrap image from that file's image header. If clear, VMB transfers control to the first byte of the secondary boot file.
7	RPB$V_NOTEST	Memory test inhibit. If set, VMB does not test memory pages.
8	RPB$V_SOLICT	Solicit file name. If set, VMB prompts for the name of a secondary bootstrap file. Used to load SYSBOOT_XDELTA.
9	RPB$V_HALT	Halt before transfer. If set, VMB executes a HALT instruction before transferring control to the secondary bootstrap.
10	RPB$V_NOPFND	No PFN deletion (not currently used).
11	RPB$V_MPM	Multiport memory (not currently used).
12	RPB$V_USEMPM	If set, specifies that the memory bitmap is to include both multiport memory and local memory for later use by VMS, as though both were one single pool of pages (not used by VMS).
13	RPB$V_MEMTEST	If set, specifies that a more extensive algorithm is to be used when testing main memory for uncorrectable hardware errors.
14	RPB$V_FINDMEM	Reserved.

(continued)

Table 30.21 VMB Boot Control Flags (Contents of R5) *(continued)*

Bit Position	Symbolic Name	Meaning
15	RPB$V_AUTOTEST	On a VAX-11/730, if this and RPB$V_DIAG are set, the diagnostic supervisor enters AUTOTEST mode.
16	RPB$V_CRDTEST	If set, specifies that memory pages with correctable errors are not to be used by VMS.
17	RPB$V_DIFSYSDEV	If set, indicates that the system device is different from the boot device, which is magnetic tape. Used for booting stand-alone Backup from magnetic tape.
18	RPB$V_BOOTLOG	Reserved.
⟨31:28⟩	RPB$V_TOPSYS	Specifies the top-level directory number for a system disk with multiple system roots.

Table 30.22 Contents of the Restart Parameter Block

Field Name	Contents	Size in Bytes	Loaded by	Special Uses
RPB$L_BASE	Physical base address of block	4	VMB	Identifies RPB
RPB$L_RESTART	Physical address of EXE$RESTART	4	EXE$INIT	Locates restart routine
RPB$L_CHKSUM	Checksum of first 31 longwords of EXE$RESTART	4	EXE$INIT	Consistency check on RPB and EXE$RESTART
RPB$L_RSTSTFLG	Restart in progress flag	4	Console, EXE$INIT, EXE$RESTART	Prevents nested restarts
RPB$L_HALTPC	PC at HALT/restart	4	VMB	
RPB$L_HALTPSL	PSL at HALT/restart	4	VMB	
RPB$L_HALTCODE	Reason for restart	4	VMB	
RPB$L_BOOTRx	Saved bootstrap parameters (R0 through R5)	24	VMB	
RPB$L_IOVEC	Address of bootstrap driver	4	VMB, EXE$INIT	Loads system images, writes crash dump
RPB$L_IOVECSZ	Size (in bytes) of bootstrap driver	4	VMB	
RPB$L_FILLBN	LBN of secondary bootstrap file	4	VMB	

(continued)

Table 30.22   Contents of the Restart Parameter Block *(continued)*

Field Name	Contents	Size in Bytes	Loaded by	Special Uses
RPB$L_FILSIZ	Size in blocks of secondary bootstrap file	4	VMB	
RPB$Q_ PFNMAP	Descriptor of PFN bitmap	8	VMB	Used by SYSBOOT to locate bitmap
RPB$L_ PFNCNT	Count of physical pages	4	VMB, SYSBOOT	
RPB$L_SVASPT	System virtual address of system page table	4	EXE$INIT	Used by EXE$RESTART
RPB$L_ CSRPHY	Physical address of UBA device CSR	4	VMB	Locates boot device
RPB$L_CSRVIR	Virtual address of UBA device CSR	4	INIADP*xxx*	Locates boot device
RPB$L_ ADPPHY	Physical address of adapter configuration register	4	VMB	Locates boot device
RPB$L_ADPVIR	Virtual address of adapter configuration register	4	INIADP*xxx*	Locates boot device
RPB$W_UNIT	Bootstrap device unit number	2	VMB	
RPB$B_ DEVTYP	Bootstrap device type code	1	VMB	
RPB$B_SLAVE	Bootstrap device slave unit number	1	VMB	
RPB$T_FILE	Secondary bootstrap file name (counted ASCII string)	40	VMB	
RPB$B_ CONFREG	Byte array of adapter types	16	VMB[1]	
RPB$B_ HDRPGCNT	Count of header pages in secondary bootstrap image	1	VMB	
RPB$W_ BOOTNDT	Type of boot adapter	2	VMB	Used by boot driver
RPB$B_FLAGS	Miscellaneous flag bits	1		
RPB$L_MAX_ PFN	Absolute highest PFN	4	VMB	Formerly RPB$L_ISP
RPB$L_SPTEP	System space PTE prototype register	4		Formerly RPB$L_ PCBB

(continued)

908

Table 30.22   Contents of the Restart Parameter Block *(continued)*

Field Name	Contents	Size in Bytes	Loaded by	Special Uses
RPB$L_SBR	Saved system base register	4	EXE$INIT, EXE$POWERFAIL	Restored by EXE$RESTART
RPB$L_CPUDBVEC	Physical address of per-CPU database vector or primary's per-CPU database	4	EXE$INIT	Formerly RPB$L_SCBB
RPB$L_CCA_ADDR	Physical address of CCA	4	VMB	Formerly RPB$L_SISR
RPB$L_SLR	Saved system length register	4	EXE$INIT, EXE$POWERFAIL	Restored by EXE$RESTART
RPB$L_MEMDSC	Longword array of memory descriptors	64	VMB	Used by BUG-CHECK to dump physical memory
RPB$L_SMP_PC	SMP boot page physical address	4	EXE$INIT	Formerly RPB$L_BUGCHK
RPB$B_WAIT	Bugcheck loop code for attached processor	4	VMB, SMP initialization	VAX 8800 or 88x0 secondary processor started at this location
RPB$L_BADPGS	Number of bad pages found in memory scan	4	VMB	
RPB$B_CTRLLTR	Controller letter designation	1	VMB	
RPB$B_SCBPAGCT	SCB page count	1	SYSBOOT	
Reserved		6		
RPB$L_VMB_REVISION	VMB revision level	4	MicroVAX VMBs	Format varies

[1] The byte array of adapter types is loaded by VMB only on VAX-11/750 and VAX-11/78x processors. The system configuration is determined at a later stage of system initialization on other processors.

7. If VMB finds a CI port adapter that requires loadable microcode, such as the CIBCA-A, it looks up and reads the microcode from the console block storage device. The microcode file for a CI780, CI750, or BCI750 adapter is called CI780.BIN; the file for a CIBCA is called CIBCA.BIN.

If the system is a VAX 8800 processor or VAX 88x0 family member, the microcode is on CSA3. For a VAX 6000 series system, VMB reads the CIBCA-A microcode from the TK50/70 tape drive.

If VMB finds a CI750 on a VAX-11/750 CPU, VMB must check that the CPU revision level is at or above the minimum level required for

CI support. It also tests whether the level is high enough to require the loading of volatile CPU microcode. If it is, VMB locates the file PCS750.BIN on the console TU58, reads it into memory, and loads it into the CPU microstore.

VMB sets the flag VMB$V_LOAD_SCS in the SYSBOOT argument list to indicate that SYSGEN must load the system communication services (SCS) code.

8. VMB relocates the boot driver (see Section 30.3.2).

9. Depending on processor and bus type, VMB initializes the bus and the bus adapter for the system device. If necessary, it initializes the bootstrap device. The CI port adapter initialization routine loads the CI microcode.

10. VMB identifies the secondary bootstrap image by flags and values in R5 and, optionally, information solicited from the console terminal. The following order holds in choosing a secondary bootstrap image:

    a. If the R5 flag RPB$V_BBLOCK is set, VMB reads the boot block program from the system device. On VAX-11/780 or VAX-11/785 processors, R4 contains the logical number of the disk block that contains the secondary bootstrap image.

    b. If the R5 flag RPB$V_SOLICT is set, VMB prompts for the name of the secondary bootstrap image on the console terminal.

    c. If the R5 flag RPB$V_DIAG is set, VMB loads the diagnostic bootstrap image, the file [SYSMAINT]DIAGBOOT.EXE, which activates the diagnostic supervisor.

    d. SYSBOOT.EXE is used as the secondary bootstrap image in the absence of any other option. To locate SYSBOOT, VMB first checks the system root directory, specified in the high four bits of R5. VMB searches [SYS*n*.SYSEXE] and [SYS*n*.SYSCOMMON.SYSEXE], where *n* is the root number. For example, using the default root of 0, VMB would search [SYS0.SYSEXE], then [SYS0.SYSCOMMON.SYSEXE], for SYSBOOT. If it does not find SYSBOOT and the root directory is 0, VMB searches [SYSEXE] for compatibility with older versions of VMS.

11. VMB records the file name of the secondary bootstrap image in the field RPB$T_FILE.

12. It disables XDELTA exceptions and moves the SCB, bitmap, and current stack.

13. VMB opens the file and reads the secondary bootstrap image into memory. SYSBOOT overlays much of VMB, to fit into known good memory.

14. If the R5 flag RPB$V_HALT is set, VMB executes a HALT instruction before passing control to the secondary bootstrap image. This feature enables use of the console subsystem to debug the secondary bootstrap.

15. VMB passes control to the secondary bootstrap image at its transfer address, normally the first byte in SYSBOOT. However, if an image

other than SYSBOOT is being loaded and the flag RPB$V_HEADER in R5 is set, VMB uses the transfer address stored in the image header of the secondary bootstrap program (provided that the secondary bootstrap image was produced by the VMS Linker).

30.3.2   Bootstrap Driver and I/O Subroutines

VMB contains a skeleton Queue I/O Request ($QIO) procedure and device driver to perform its I/O. SYSBOOT later copies this driver and routine into nonpaged pool for possible later use by the bugcheck code, described in Chapter 32.

The VMB image actually includes simple drivers for all boot devices. Once it has determined the name of the bootstrap device from register contents, VMB moves the driver code for the selected device so that it is adjacent to the $QIO procedure, thus allowing the entire bootstrap I/O system to be moved with a single MOVC3 instruction.

This simple operation by VMB prevents nonpaged pool from being loaded with a set of bootstrap device drivers that are never used. That is, the only bootstrap driver preserved for the life of a VMS system is the bootstrap device driver for the system device, which is selected through input to VMB. All other bootstrap drivers are linked into the VMB image but disappear along with the rest of VMB when VMS is completely initialized. By locating the $QIO procedure and driver in the low-address end of VMB, much of VMB can be overlaid by SYSBOOT code. Thus, more efficient use is made of the pretested block of memory into which SYSBOOT must fit.

The combined $QIO procedure and bootstrap device driver begin with a boot driver dispatch vector area (BQO), offsets in which are defined by the macro $BQODEF. VMB records the location of the BQO in the RPB at the offset RPB$L_IOVEC. It records the size of the $QIO procedure plus the driver at the offset RPB$L_IOVECSZ. SYSBOOT and EXE$INIT locate through the RPB pointer to the BQO.

30.3.3   File Operations

The bootstrap operation must locate files before the file system itself is in full operation. Many files must be looked up before the Files-11 Extended QIO Processor (XQP) has been loaded into memory and initialized by SYSINIT. Two special object modules, FILEREAD and FILERWIO, exist for this purpose. The modules contain subroutines that can perform some primitive file operations on a Files-11 ODS-2 volume. VMS links these modules in the loadable executive image PRIMITIVE_IO. One of these modules, FILEREAD, is also part of the VMB, SYSBOOT, NISCS_LOAD, and EXEC_INIT images.

VMB and SYSBOOT call FIL$OPENFILE in FILEREAD, a file open procedure, to look up files such as SYS.EXE. To improve its performance,

FIL$OPENFILE caches information about directories used in file lookup. For example, to locate SYS.EXE might require looking up and reading the master file directory, SYS*n*.DIR, and SYSEXE.DIR.

In order to avoid repeated lookups and directory and subdirectory reads, FIL$OPENFILE records directory file IDs, size in blocks, starting LBN, and also caches blocks from directory files. While VMB and SYSBOOT run, the cache is physically based. SYSBOOT copies the cache to nonpaged pool for use by EXE$INIT and the SYSINIT process until the XQP is operational.

30.3.4 Booting a VAXcluster Member over the Ethernet

Digital's Maintenance Operations Protocol (MOP) allows a processor to request the down-line loading of a program from an Ethernet service node into the requestor's memory. VMS uses this mechanism to allow a processor to boot over the Ethernet and join a VAXcluster system. Note that to boot in this manner, both VMS systems must be members of the same VAXcluster; booting an independent VMS system over the Ethernet is not implemented.

A servicing processor, called a host, identifies a requesting processor, called a satellite, by the satellite's unique Ethernet address. A network database on the host, SYS$SYSTEM:NETNODE_REMOTE.DAT, contains an entry for each valid satellite. The satellite's database entry includes the name of the VAXcluster system disk and root directory in which its files reside.

A satellite can request a specific program from the host, accept a default program defined in the host's database, or request the activation of the load assist agent defined in the host's database. In this case, the host transfers control to the load assist agent, a program which directs further communication with the satellite.

The ability to boot over the Ethernet must exist in the satellite's console program or its ROM-based VMB, and its Ethernet device. When a satellite executes local ROM-based VMB, VMB performs the steps described in Section 30.3.4.1 if it discovers that the boot device is an Ethernet adapter.

30.3.4.1 Obtaining the Secondary Bootstrap.

ROM-based VMB on the satellite must obtain the secondary boot file over the network. It therefore issues a multicast MOP message requesting that an operating system be loaded into its memory. The MOP message includes the satellite's Ethernet address.

Ethernet hosts receive the message and check their network databases for an entry whose Ethernet address matches that of the incoming message. If a host finds a match, it activates the load assist agent defined in the database entry, SYS$SYSTEM:NISCS_LAA.EXE.

NISCS_LAA receives one value from the network database entry. This load assist parameter defines the system disk and VAXcluster root directory from which the satellite should boot. If NISCS_LAA does not find a SYSGEN parameter file, VAXVMSSYS.PAR, in the specified root directory, or if the parameter file indicates that the node will not attempt to become a member of the VAXcluster, the boot aborts. Otherwise, NISCS_LAA obtains the cluster group authorization number and password from the cluster authorization file, CLUSTER_AUTHORIZE.DAT. It constructs a parameter block containing the password, the cluster group number, and information from the parameter file such as SCSNODENAME. NISCS_LAA appends the parameter block to the image SYS$SYSTEM:NISCS_LOAD and down-line loads both to the satellite.

The image and parameter block are stored in a known location in satellite memory. Once the satellite recognizes that the down-line load is complete, it transfers control to the loaded image, NISCS_LOAD. NISCS_LOAD can be thought of as a VMB extension. It contains a minimal class driver and several Ethernet datalink drivers. Using the class driver and the appropriate datalink driver, the satellite can access the secondary bootstrap file, normally SYSBOOT, on the system disk served by the host. The minimal class driver and Ethernet datalink driver present a standard disk interface, allowing SYSBOOT and the rest of the boot procedure to execute as though performing a normal disk boot.

30.4   SECONDARY BOOTSTRAP PROGRAM (SYSBOOT)

The secondary bootstrap program, SYSBOOT, executes when VMB is directed to load a VMS system. VMB, having already tested main memory, reads SYSBOOT into memory and transfers control. (When booting over the Ethernet, VMB loads NISCS_LOAD and NISCS_LOAD loads SYSBOOT.)

Most of the modules that make up SYSBOOT are from facility [BOOTS]. There is little CPU-dependent code in SYSBOOT, as most of the CPU-dependent requirements have already been taken care of by VMB. However, SYSBOOT does load the CPU-dependent code that is used during normal VMS system execution.

When SYSBOOT gains control, R11 points to the beginning of the RPB. VMB passes an argument list to SYSBOOT using the AP. The count and definition of arguments depends upon the VMB version number. The BQO, located through RPB$L_IOVEC, contains the VMB version number at the offset BQO$W_VERSION.

Table 30.23 lists the arguments that VMB Version 15, for VMS Version 5.2, passes to SYSBOOT.

SYSBOOT performs three major functions:

1. It configures the system by loading a set of adjustable SYSGEN parameters. By default, it uses the parameters stored in the file [SYS*n*.SYSEXE] VAXVMSSYS.PAR, managed by the SYSGEN utility. In a conversational bootstrap, SYSBOOT prompts on the console terminal. The person booting the system can change the value of specific parameters, select a whole different set of parameters from a different file, or use a set of default

Table 30.23   Argument List Passed from VMB to SYSBOOT

Argument Name	Size	Description
VMB$Q_FILECACHE	Quadword	FILEREAD cache descriptor
VMB$L_LO_PFN	Longword	Lowest PFN found by VMB
VMB$L_HI_PFN	Longword	Highest PFN exclusive
VMB$Q_PFNMAP	Quadword	PFN bitmap descriptor
VMB$Q_UCODE	Quadword	Loaded microcode descriptor
VMB$B_SYSTEMID	6 bytes	SCS system ID
Reserved	2 bytes	
VMB$L_FLAGS	Longword	VMBV_LOAD_SCS, VMBV_TAPE, and VMB$V_VOLSWIT flags
VMB$L_CI_HIPFN	Longword	Highest PFN used by CI code
VMB$Q_NODENAME	Quadword	Booting node name
VMB$Q_HOSTADDR	Quadword	Host node address
VMB$Q_HOSTNAME	Quadword	Host node name
VMB$Q_TOD	Quadword	Time of day in MOP format
VMB$L_XPARAM	Longword	Address of extra MOP parameters
VMB$L_BVP_PGTBL	Longword	Address of port page table

values built into SYSBOOT and SYSGEN. SYSBOOT calculates other system parameters whose values depend on the values of the adjustable parameters.

2. SYSBOOT maps system virtual address space. The sizes of many of the pieces of system address space depend on the values of one or more SYSGEN parameters. The calculations that SYSBOOT performs and the results of these calculations are detailed in Appendix F. In addition to sizing the pieces of system space, SYSBOOT also sets up the system page table (SPT) to map many of the pieces of the nonpaged and paged executive. In a related step, SYSBOOT prepares a P0 page table that allows memory management to be turned on (see Chapter 31).

3. The last major SYSBOOT step is to allocate physical memory and read the various portions of SYS.EXE into those pages. SYSBOOT also locates a number of other files (see Table 30.1) and reads them into nonpaged pool. Their locations in pool are passed on to EXE$INIT in a bootstrap parameter block, defined by module BOOPARAM (see Table 30.24).

30.4.1   Operation of SYSBOOT

SYSBOOT runs in the environment established by the console subsystem and VMB:

- In kernel mode
- On the boot stack
- With memory management disabled
- At IPL 31

Table 30.24   Information Passed from SYSBOOT to INIT

Global Location	Size	Description
BOO$GL_DSKDRV	Longword	Address of bootstrap device driver in nonpaged pool
BOO$GL_SYSLOA	Longword	Address of CPU-dependent image in nonpaged pool
BOO$GL_TRMDRV	Longword	Address of terminal class driver in nonpaged pool
BOO$GL_NPAGEDYN	Longword	Size of nonpaged pool remaining (in bytes)
BOO$GL_SPLITADR	Longword	Base address of I/O request packet (IRP) lookaside list
BOO$GL_IRPCNT	Longword	Number of IRPs to be initialized
BOO$GL_LRPSIZE	Longword	Size of large request packets (LRPs) in bytes
BOO$GL_LRPMIN	Longword	Minimum size of request that can be allocated an LRP
BOO$GL_LRPSPLIT	Longword	Base address of LRP lookaside list
BOO$GL_LRPCNT	Longword	Number of LRPs to be initialized
BOO$GL_SRPSPLIT	Longword	Base address of small request packet (SRP) lookaside list
BOO$GL_SRPCNT	Longword	Number of SRPs to be initialized
BOO$GQ_FILCACHE	Quadword	Pool descriptor for FIL$OPENFILE cache
BOO$GL_BOOTCB	Longword	Address of boot control block in pool
BOO$GT_TOPSYS	40 bytes	Top-level system directory (ASCIC string)
BOO$GB_SYSTEMID	6 bytes	48-bit SCS system ID of boot device port
BOO$GL_PRTDRV	Longword	Address of port driver in pool
BOO$GL_SUBPRTDRV	Longword	Address of subport driver in pool
BOO$GL_UCODE	Longword	Address of port microcode in pool
BOO$GL_SCSLOA	Longword	Address of SCS loadable code in pool
BOO$GL_CLSLOA	Longword	Address of cluster loadable code in pool
BOO$GB_NODENAME	8 bytes	ASCII name of the node containing boot device
BOO$GL_VAXEMUL	Longword	Address of instruction emulation loadable code in pool
BOO$GL_FPEMUL	Longword	Address of floating-point emulation loadable code in pool
BOO$GL_DEVNAME	Longword	ASCII boot device name
BOO$GL_VMB_FLAGS	Longword	Boot flags from VMB
BOO$GL_BOOPTE	Longword	SVAPTE of page table entries (PTEs) temporarily allocated for BOO$MAP
BOO$GL_BOOPTECNT	Longword	Count of PTEs temporarily allocated for BOO$MAP
BOO$GL_PDDATAPTR	Longword	Pointer to address and size of loaded PSEUDOLOA.EXE
BOO$GL_SPARE1	Longword	Reserved
BOO$GL_SPARE2	Longword	Reserved
BOO$GL_SPARE3	Longword	Reserved
BOO$GL_SPARE4	Longword	Reserved

Beginning with VMS Version 5.0, SYSBOOT no longer links with XDELTA. With XDELTA, SYSBOOT would have been too large to fit into the guaranteed 64K-byte block of good memory available on older systems. Instead, VMS provides a separate image, SYSBOOT_XDELTA.EXE, which is loaded by booting with the RPB$V_SOLICT flag set in R5 and specifying SYSBOOT_XDELTA at the prompt.

SYSBOOT_XDELTA performs the same functions as SYSBOOT, except for the following:

- It alters the SCB vectors for the TBIT and BPT exceptions to dispatch to exception service routines in the XDELTA code.
- If the bootstrap breakpoint flag, RPB$V_BOOBPT in R5, is set, SYSBOOT_XDELTA executes a BPT instruction. The exception transfers control to the XDELTA code.

Note that the flag RPB$V_BOOBPT controls breakpoint execution in both VMB and SYSBOOT_XDELTA. The flag can be used to locate a hardware problem or other problem that prevents system initialization.

The following steps describe the operation of SYSBOOT:

1. SYSBOOT reinitializes the SCB created by VMB so that most vectors contain the address of a service routine in SYSBOOT. It modifies the machine check vector to point to a customized exception service routine. Some VAX processors emulate certain instructions rather than supporting them in CPU microcode. For these processors, execution of an instruction such as MOVTC causes an exception. SYSBOOT initializes subset instruction emulation vectors in the SCB to dispatch to service routines within SYSBOOT, until the appropriate software emulation routines are loaded.

2. SYSBOOT reads the system identification processor register, PR$_SID, to determine the CPU type. It stores this information in the field EXE$GB_CPUTYPE. On some processors, such as the MicroVAX II and the VAX 6000 series machines, SYSBOOT reads an additional register called the extended system ID or system type register to determine the CPU subtype. SYSBOOT copies this information to the 16 bytes beginning at EXE$GB_CPUDATA. Code whose execution depends on a specific CPU type can check EXE$GB_CPUTYPE and EXE$GB_CPUDATA to determine the environment. The CPUDISP macro, described in the *VMS Device Support Manual*, selects portions of CPU-specific code at execution time (with suitable test-and-branch instructions).

   SYSBOOT employs the CPU type and subtype to determine the following items:

   —Pieces of CPU-dependent code within SYSBOOT that execute; for example, SYSBOOT must check whether the hardware revision level is at least the minimum required to support the VMS software. Its test is processor-specific.

—Name of the file containing CPU-specific support, SYSLOA*xxx*.EXE, where *xxx* designates the CPU type. Appendix G lists CPU types and their corresponding SYSLOA*xxx* image names.

—Size of the SCB. Appendix F lists the sizes required by various VAX processors.

3. For certain processors whose console, rather than VMB, creates the PFN bitmap, SYSBOOT moves a copy of the bitmap to the area of memory immediately following SYSBOOT's location, if sufficient error-free contiguous memory exists. SYSBOOT alters the bitmap as it allocates physical memory. If SYSBOOT works from a copy of the bitmap, preserving the original, the MicroVAX console subsystems that maintain a checksum on the original bitmap need not execute memory test diagnostics and rebuild the bitmap on subsequent reboots.

4. SYSBOOT checks the BQO field BQO$W_VERSION to determine which version of VMB executed. Older versions of VMB do not perform many of the operations that newer versions incorporate. SYSBOOT compensates for these older versions by performing the operations missing from the older VMB version or by performing its own operations in alternative ways. This step allows backward compatibility for earlier versions of VMB. The following items are checked at this point:

—Bootstrap adapter device type
—Support for more than eight megabytes of memory
—Presence and contents of the SYSBOOT argument list
—Presence of the FIL$OPENFILE cache
—Presence of memory descriptors in the RPB
—Presence of CI microcode read into memory
—Presence of a system root directory name

5. SYSBOOT allocates memory for a boot control block and a buffer to contain retrieval pointers for special files that it opens, such as the system dump file.

The boot control block, offsets in which are defined by the macro $BOODEF, ultimately resides in nonpaged pool and is pointed to by EXE$GL_BOOTCB. It contains information that must be available in the event of a fatal bugcheck, such as the mapping information for SYSDUMP.DMP. SYSBOOT loads all fields in the boot control block except for BOO$L_BUG_WCB and BOO$L_BUG_LBN. The initialization routine for the loadable executive image EXCEPTION, which contains the bugcheck code, stores the window control block (WCB) mapping the nonresident bugcheck code and the first LBN of the code into these fields.

Figure 30.3 shows the structure of the boot control block.

6. For each loadable executive image to be opened, SYSBOOT allocates a block of memory for file mapping information. SYSBOOT maintains a statistics block for each file that it must potentially load. A statistics

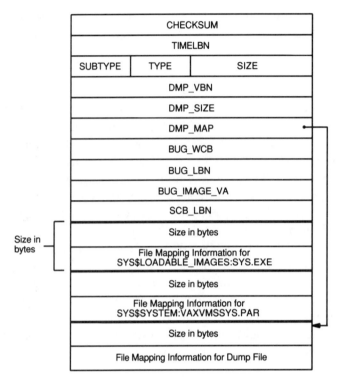

Figure 30.3
Boot Control Block

block contains the file name and context information required by the routines that open and read the file, LDR$OPEN_FILE and LDR$READ_FILE. The statistics block also contains a pointer to the file mapping information. Chapter 29 describes loadable executive images and the manner in which they are loaded.

When SYSBOOT discovers that a file for which it has a statistics block is not, in fact, to be loaded, it clears the file name field in the statistics block.

7. When the STABACKIT.COM file creates a bootable VMS tape, it copies a file called OPEN_INDEX.DAT onto the tape following SYSBOOT. For each file on the tape, OPEN_INDEX.DAT contains the file name, file size, and tape position. If SYSBOOT determines that the boot device was a tape, it allocates memory, reads this file, and uses the information to optimize tape access.

8. SYSBOOT checks whether NISCS_LOAD determined that an auxiliary device driver is needed; if so, it creates a statistics block for the driver.

9. Based on the CPU type and subtype, SYSBOOT performs the following:

—It checks that the hardware and microcode revisions are appropriate for the VMS version being loaded and issues a warning message if not.

—It determines the name of the SYSLOA*xxx* image containing CPU-specific code to be loaded. Appendix G lists CPU types and their corresponding SYSLOA*xxx* image names.

—It determines the number of pages in the SCB.

—For an SMP system, SYSBOOT records the ID of the CPU on which it is executing, the primary CPU.

10. For console devices and small disk devices, the boot files may require more space than is available. For these devices, SYSBOOT sets the bit VMB$V_VOLSWIT in BOO$GL_VMB_FLAGS. If this bit is set, SYSBOOT and EXE$INIT allow the boot medium to be removed and another volume substituted.

11. SYSBOOT locates the system base image, SYS.EXE. It first checks the specified root directory (defaulting to root 0). If it does not find SYS.EXE and the root directory was 0, SYSBOOT also checks [SYSEXE]. This maintains compatibility with earlier versions of VMS.

    During this check, SYSBOOT switches volumes if it is both necessary and allowed.

12. If the system device is a disk, SYSBOOT records the LBN of the first block of the storage bitmap file, BITMAP.SYS, in the boot control block at offset BOO$L_SCB_LBN. This block, which is called the storage control block, contains shadow set generation information for shadow set members.

13. SYSBOOT reads VAXVMSSYS.PAR, the file containing the current SYSGEN parameters. Chapter 31 describes in detail the movement of parameter information during the initialization sequence.

14. SYSBOOT tests whether the operator requested a conversational bootstrap by setting the R5 flag RPB$V_CONV. If so, SYSBOOT prompts to allow interactive alteration of the parameter values. In any case, SYSBOOT enters the next step with a set of adjustable parameters.

15. If the system device is a disk, SYSBOOT opens the system dump file, [SYS*n*.SYSEXE]SYSDUMP.DMP, and records the file mapping information for use in the event of a bugcheck.

    If SYSBOOT does not find the dump file, it opens and maps the primary page file, [SYS*n*.SYSEXE]PAGEFILE.SYS, and sets the flag EXE$V_PAGFILDMP in EXE$GL_DEFFLAGS. The first blocks of the page file, if one exists, are used as an alternative dump file when the system bugchecks. When the SYSINIT process runs (see Chapter 31), it will look in the page file instead of the dump file for saved error log messages to restore.

    SYSBOOT saves the size of the dump or page file in the boot control block at the offset BOO$L_DMP_SIZE. In BOO$L_DMP_MAP, it stores a pointer to the area of the boot control block that contains the file map information.

16. Using the system device information saved in the RPB, SYSBOOT determines the name of the full driver for the system device. It looks in the boot driver data structure to determine the name of any auxiliary driver needed, for example, a CI port driver.

17. SYSBOOT determines whether SCSLOA.EXE and CLUSTRLOA.EXE must be loaded, based on the SYSGEN parameters VAXCLUSTER and NISCS_LOAD_PEA0 and on the boot device.

18. SYSBOOT then tests which types of instructions, if any, must be emulated in software. Not all VAX processors implement all types of instructions. In particular, certain types of floating-point instructions may not be present. For example, the MicroVAX II does not implement many string and decimal instructions. SYSBOOT must decide whether the images VAXEMUL.EXE, FPEMUL.EXE, or both must be loaded for string and decimal instruction emulation and floating-point instruction emulation. Bits in EXE$GL_ARCHFLAG record the various types of emulation required.

19. SYSBOOT tests the boot parameters to determine if XDELTA, in the image SYSTEM_DEBUG.EXE, is to be loaded. If not, it clears the statistics block for the image.

20. SYSBOOT then constructs the name of the terminal class driver, prefixing the value of the parameter TTY_CLASSNAME to the string DRIVER.

21. SYSBOOT determines the PFN of the highest usable page of memory, taking into account the value of the SYSGEN parameter PHYSICAL-PAGES, and stores it in MMG$GL_MAXMEM. If the parameter is set artificially low, specifying only partial use of the memory, the lower physical pages are used.

22. SYSBOOT calculates the size of a process header and the sizes of the other pieces of system address space, including the SCB. In particular, it calculates the size of the SPT. Appendix F describes the details of these calculations.

23. SYSBOOT allocates and zero-fills pages of contiguous physical memory at the highest physical addresses for the SCB, SPT, and system header.

24. It loads the first page of the SCB with the contents of module SCBVEC-TOR, which contains the entry points for the architecturally defined interrupt and exception service routines. Vectors in additional pages of the SCB, if present, are loaded with the address of ERL$UNEXP, an unexpected interrupt handler. For some processors, interrupt vectors used for passive releases are initialized with the address of ERL$VEC_RETURN.

25. SYSBOOT configures the system header. At this time, it fills in all entries in the system header whose contents depend on configuration parameters. This step is analogous to the process header configuration performed by code in the shell as a part of process creation (see Chapter 25).

26. It initializes system page table entries (SPTEs) to map the pages of the SPT and system header.

27. It initializes demand zero SPTEs for the global page table.
28. It initializes SPTEs for the SCB.
29. It allocates physical memory and initializes SPTEs for the primary's per-CPU data area, which includes the interrupt stack and the boot stack.
30. It allocates physical memory for the initial sizes of the three nonpaged pool lookaside lists, loads the corresponding SPTEs, and records the size and address of each list.
31. It allocates nonpaged pool for the device drivers listed in step 37 and the FIL$OPENFILE cache.
32. It allocates physical memory and initializes SPTEs to map the system base image.
33. SYSBOOT determines the size of the PFN database, which must map any remaining unassigned physical pages. It allocates and zero-fills physical memory for the PFN database and initializes the SPTEs that map it. The physical pages allocated for the nonpaged portions of the executive are not accounted for in the PFN database, because their state will never change. The pages occupied by the PFN database itself are also not accounted for in the PFN database.
34. SYSBOOT initializes an SPTE for the RPB. Since the RPB is already present in a physical page, SYSBOOT merely stores its page number in the new SPTE and the virtual address in EXE$GL_RPB.
35. SYSBOOT reads the system base image, SYS.EXE, into memory. From the base image, it obtains a private copy of the system version array. These version numbers are used in step 37 to check that the loadable images are compatible with the system base image.
36. SYSBOOT determines which synchronization image to use, as described in Chapter 8.
37. SYSBOOT invokes the boot driver with a list of loadable images to read into nonpaged pool or system virtual address space. These files include the following:

    —EXEC_INIT.EXE, the next piece of initialization code
    —SYSTEM_DEBUG.EXE, the XDELTA image, if requested
    —SYSTEM_PRIMITIVES.EXE, containing primitive system routines
    —SYSTEM_SYNCHRONIZATION_*xxx*.EXE, as determined by step 36
    —PRIMITIVE_IO.EXE, the primitive file system routines
    —ERRORLOG.EXE, the error logging routines and system services
    —The system device driver and, if applicable, its port driver
    —Terminal class driver
    —SCSLOA.EXE, if needed
    —SYSLOA*xxx*.EXE
    —CLUSTRLOA.EXE, if needed
    —FPEMUL.EXE, if needed
    —VAXEMUL.EXE, if needed

38. SYSBOOT copies the contents of its internal parameter table to the portion of the memory image of SYS.EXE that contains the adjustable parameters. This step makes the current parameter settings available for the remaining system initialization routines and preserves them (because SYSBOOT is exiting) until SYSINIT writes them back to the disk (see Chapter 31).

39. SYSBOOT copies the FIL$OPENFILE cache into nonpaged pool, where it will facilitate file lookups until the file system is initialized. (If the boot was from tape, SYSBOOT copies the cached OPEN_INDEX.DAT file instead. OPEN_INDEX.DAT contains the name, size, and tape position of every file on the tape and thus optimizes tape access.)

40. It copies the boot control block, boot driver, and any microcode associated with the boot device to nonpaged pool, and modifies RPB$L_IOVEC to reflect the virtual address of the boot driver.

41. SYSBOOT copies the argument list it built for EXE$INIT into the bootstrap parameter block in the memory image of SYS.EXE (see Table 30.24).

42. SYSBOOT loads the base and length registers for the P0 and system page tables so that EXE$INIT can turn on memory management (see Chapter 31).

43. Finally, SYSBOOT transfers control to module EXE$INIT. This transfer must be done to a physical location, because memory management is not yet enabled.

31 Operating System Initialization and Shutdown

Had I been present at the creation, I would have given some
useful hints for the better ordering of the universe.

Alfonso the Wise

Several components contribute to the second phase of system initialization:

- Routine EXE$INIT in module INIT, in the EXEC_INIT image
- The initialization routines of loadable executive images
- A special process, SYSINIT, created to complete those pieces of initialization that require process context to execute

EXE$INIT turns on memory management, configures the I/O adapters, and initializes scheduling and memory management data structures. It maps loadable executive images and invokes their initialization routines.

The initialization routines of loadable executive images execute in various phases of system initialization, and an initialization routine may be invoked several times. These routines perform initialization that logically relates to the function of the associated image.

SYSINIT opens system files, creates system processes, loads the Record Management Services (RMS) and system message loadable executive images, among others, and creates a process to execute the startup command procedure.

31.1 INITIAL EXECUTION OF THE EXECUTIVE

The final instruction in SYSBOOT transfers control to the physical address of EXE$INIT. EXE$INIT begins execution in an environment set up by SYS-BOOT. It executes on the interrupt stack at interrupt priority level (IPL) 31. It immediately modifies its environment by turning on memory management.

In a symmetric multiprocessing (SMP) system, SYSBOOT and EXE$INIT execute on the BOOT CPU, a CPU with full access to the console subsystem. In VMS Version 5.2, the BOOT CPU is the primary processor; the other CPUs are called secondary processors.

31.1.1 Turning on Memory Management

The first and perhaps most important step that EXE$INIT takes is to turn on memory management. Actions previously taken by SYSBOOT make this possible. SYSBOOT allocates physical memory and system page table entries

(SPTEs) for the EXEC_INIT image, initializes the SPTEs, and reads EXEC_INIT into memory.

Before SYSBOOT transfers control to EXE$INIT, it constructs a P0 page table that has only one valid page table entry (PTE). The PTE maps the first physical page of EXE$INIT to a P0 virtual address with a virtual page number identical to its physical page number. Thus, EXE$INIT can be referenced by its physical address before memory management is turned on, by a P0 virtual address that translates to the identical physical address, and by its system virtual address.

31.1.1.1   **Mapping of EXE$INIT by SYSBOOT.** P0 space is used for the double mapping of EXE$INIT because the P0 address range (0 to $3FFFFFFF_{16}$) is the maximum physical address range permitted by the VAX architecture. That is, even on a VAX processor with the maximum possible physical memory, a P0 address range with identical addresses exists.

SYSBOOT must be able to account for the placement of EXE$INIT anywhere in physical memory, that is, it must be able to map every P0 address. A page table page can map 128 pages of virtual address space. Constructing a page table large enough to map all 2,097,152 pages of P0 space would be rather inefficient, particularly since SYSBOOT only needs to create one valid PTE. Instead, SYSBOOT constructs a one-page P0 page table and loads the P0 base register, PR$_P0BR, which normally contains the system virtual address of the first page in the P0 page table, with a computed value derived as follows:

1. SYSBOOT computes the offset within a complete P0 page table that would contain the PTE mapping EXE$INIT's address. It determines the required number of PTEs (the last PTE maps the first page of EXE$INIT) and the offset of the desired PTE from the start of the last page table page.
2. In its one-page P0 page table, at the latter offset, it stores a valid PTE mapping EXE$INIT.
3. Since it will reference only the last page table page, SYSBOOT subtracts the amount of virtual address space that would be occupied by the missing PTEs from the system virtual address of its one-page P0 page table. It stores the resulting value in PR$_P0BR. Thus, to the address translation hardware/microcode, EXE$INIT's page table appears to be complete.

As an example, suppose EXE$INIT begins at physical address $20BA00_{16}$. In a complete P0 page table, its P0 address (also $20BA00_{16}$) would be mapped by PTE 4189, or the ninety-third PTE of the thirty-third P0 page table page. At the ninety-third PTE in its one-page P0 page table, SYSBOOT constructs a valid PTE containing EXE$INIT's page frame number (PFN). SYSBOOT subtracts (4096 * 4) from the system virtual address of its P0 page table to account for the missing PTEs and stores the result in PR$_P0BR.

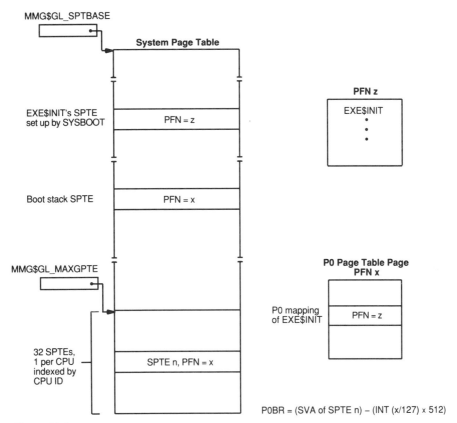

Figure 31.1
Mapping EXE$INIT

31.1.1.2 **Accessing EXE$INIT.** The net result of SYSBOOT's mapping is that the physical page containing EXE$INIT can and will be accessed in three different ways. These different mappings are listed here in order of mapping complication, not in the order in which they are used. EXE$INIT can be accessed in the following ways:

- As a physical address
- As a system virtual address mapped by the system page table (SPT)
- As a P0 virtual address translated by the combination of computed P0BR and one-page P0 page table

Figure 31.1 shows the mapping set up by SYSBOOT.

31.1.1.3 **Instructions That Turn On Memory Management.** When EXE$INIT begins execution, memory management is disabled. The program counter (PC) contains the physical address of EXE$INIT. In the following example, the instruction sequence executes in three different address contexts. The numbers in the example correspond to numbers in the list that follows.

```
EXE$INIT:
        MOVL    RPB$L_BOOTR5(R11),FP          ①
        MTPR    #1,S^#PR$_MAPEN               ②
        JMP     FIRST_SYS_VA(R1)              ③
        FIRST_SYS_VA = . - EXE$INIT
10$:    INVALIDATE_TB ENVIRONMENT=UNMAPPED    ④
```

① The first instruction executes in physical space. Its effect is not related to enabling memory management.

② This instruction actually enables memory management. All address references from this point are translated. Note that the MTPR instruction does not cause a transfer of control to an instruction stream at a different physical location. The PC is simply incremented by 3, the number of bytes in the instruction. However, the next PC reference will be translated, because memory management is enabled.

The incremented (physical) PC, the address of the JMP instruction, is seen as a P0 virtual address by the address translation hardware/microcode. Because of the mapping set up by SYSBOOT, translating it as a P0 address results in the correct physical address.

③ This instruction is the only instruction that executes with a P0 PC. R1 contains the system virtual address of the base of EXE$INIT, passed to EXE$INIT by SYSBOOT.

FIRST_SYS_VA is the offset from the base of EXE$INIT to the instruction following the JMP instruction, calculated at assembly time. When this offset is added to the system virtual address in R1, it results in the system virtual address of the next instruction in EXE$INIT. Translating this address using the SPT results in the physical address of the next instruction, which is the first instruction to execute with a system PC.

④ With the INVALIDATE_TB macro, EXE$INIT flushes stale virtual address translations from the translation buffer. Chapter 14 describes the translation buffer.

Thus, these instructions execute in three different mapping contexts. The mapping set up by SYSBOOT results in the selection of successive instructions from the same physical page.

31.1.1.4   **Secondary Processors and Memory Management.** Each secondary CPU in an SMP system must also turn on memory management using the same basic sequence as the primary processor. To make this possible, SYSBOOT reserves the highest 32 SPTEs, one for each potential CPU in the SMP system. A CPU uses the SPTE indexed by its CPU ID number to map its one-page P0 page table. SYSBOOT reserves the highest system virtual address space for the page tables to guarantee that the PR$_P0BR values resulting from the subtraction described in Section 31.1.1.1 are always virtual addresses in system space.

A secondary processor uses the same physical page for both its P0 page table and its boot stack. Figure 31.1 shows the mapping. Chapter 34 describes secondary processor initialization.

31.1.2 Initialization of the Executive

Once EXE$INIT has turned on memory management, it can refer to system addresses. In particular, it can now initialize dynamic data structures whose listheads are in global locations in system space. Some of these steps involve allocation from nonpaged pool. Table 31.1 lists some of the nonpaged pool space allocated by EXE$INIT, and the SYSGEN parameters that control allocation size.

EXE$INIT takes the following steps once memory management has been turned on:

1. It sets the INIT and MAPPED flags in EXE$GL_STATE, indicating that memory management is enabled and EXE$INIT is running.
2. It switches to the primary CPU's interrupt stack by storing its address in the stack pointer (SP) register.
3. EXE$INIT tests flags in EXE$GL_ARCHFLAG, initialized by SYSBOOT,

Table 31.1   Allocation of Nonpaged Pool by EXE$INIT

Item	Global Name of Pointer	Factors That Affect Size
Real-time bitmap	EXE$GL_RTBITMAP	RBM$K_LENGTH+(4*REALTIME_SPTS)
Lock ID table	LCK$GL_IDTBL	12 + (4 * LOCKIDTBL)
Resource hash table	LCK$GL_HASHTBL	12 + (4 * RESHASHTBL)
Deadlock detection process bitmap	LCK$GL_PRCMAP	13 + (MAXPROCESSCNT/8)
Process control block (PCB) and sequence number vectors	SCHGL_PCBVEC, SCHGL_SEQVEC	12 + (6 * (MAXPROCESSCNT + 1))[1]
Process header vectors	PHVGL_PIXBAS, PHVGL_REFCBAS	12 + (4 * (BALSETCNT + 1))[2]
Network window control block (WCB)	NET$AR_WCB	WCB$K_LENGTH
Page-and-swap-file vector	MMG$GL_PAGSWPVC	4 * (PAGFILCT + SWPFILCT + 1) + 16

[1] Each array contains one extra slot for the system process, which has a process index of MAXPROCESSCNT.

[2] Each array contains one extra slot for the system header, which has a balance slot index of BALSETCNT.

to determine whether the processor needs subset instruction or floating-point emulation. If so, SYSBOOT has already loaded VAXEMUL.EXE or FPEMUL.EXE (or both) into nonpaged pool, and EXE$INIT invokes the initialization routine of either or both emulators.

4. EXE$INIT stores the physical address of the system control block (SCB) into the SCB base register (PR$_SCBB).

5. EXE$INIT allocates an SPTE and stores its virtual page number and corresponding virtual address in MMG$GL_FREE_NO_PFN_DB_PTE and in MMG$GL_FREE_NO_PFN_DB_VA. The SPTE temporarily maps an available physical page to manipulate a list of pages not described in the PFN database.

6. EXE$INIT calls LDR$INIT_ALL, in module SYSLDR, to invoke the initialization routines for the loadable executive images loaded by SYSBOOT. The routines for SYSTEM_PRIMITIVES, SYSTEM_SYNCHRONIZATION, ERRORLOG, and, if requested, SYSTEM_DEBUG, execute (see Section 31.2).

7. EXE$INIT performs its SMP-related initialization, which is described in Chapter 34.

8. SYSBOOT determined which SYSLOA*xxx*.EXE image was appropriate for the processor type and loaded the image into nonpaged pool (*xxx* is one of the CPU designations listed in Appendix G).

EXE$INIT invokes EXE$LINK_VEC, in module LINKVEC, to connect the routines in the SYSLOA image to vectors in the system base image, SYS.EXE. Chapter 29 describes EXE$LINK_VEC, the system images loaded into nonpaged pool, and the system base image.

CPU-specific support for the console terminal, which is part of SYSLOA, is needed to print the announcement message (and any other messages).

9. EXE$INIT initializes the console terminal and prints the announcement message and system version number. Note that this important milestone, while not very far into EXE$INIT, indicates that the base image and several loadable executive images have been read into memory and that memory management has been turned on, both significant steps in initializing the executive.

10. It initializes the nonpaged pool variable list, described in Chapter 19.

11. The restart parameter block (RPB) contains the boot flags passed to VMB in R5. If the boot flag RPB$V_DEBUG was specified, SYSBOOT loaded the optional loadable executive image SYSTEM_DEBUG, the XDELTA debugger. If the initial breakpoint flag, RPB$V_INIBPT, was specified, EXE$INIT executes a JSB instruction to the location INI$BRK, a BPT instruction that causes entry into XDELTA.

XDELTA prompts on the console terminal and responds to any commands entered. In response to a continue command, XDELTA returns to INI$BRK, which returns to EXE$INIT.

EXE$INIT also copies the BREAKPOINT SYSGEN parameter to the global location EXE$GL_BRKMSK. This parameter controls other breakpoints later in EXE$INIT.

If the boot flag RPB$V_DEBUG was not specified, EXE$INIT replaces the BPT instruction at INI$BRK with a NOP instruction.

12. EXE$INIT establishes a tentative value for the maximum number of processes.

13. It sets the values for the high and low thresholds of the modified page list.

14. It places the remaining physical pages represented in the PFN bitmap on the free page list. Each page of the PFN bitmap must be virtually mapped before it can be accessed; one SPTE is used for this purpose.

15. EXE$INIT initializes the SPTEs for paged pool. By default, this pool will page (if the POOLPAGING SYSGEN parameter is set); EXE$INIT initializes the SPTEs as demand zero format PTEs with a protection code of ERKW. If pool paging is disabled, EXE$INIT allocates a physical page for each page of pool; it stores a PFN in each SPTE, sets the protection code to ERKW, sets the valid bit, and initializes the PFN database entry for the page.

    EXE$INIT flushes the translation buffer to remove obsolete translations based on the earlier contents of altered PTEs.

16. EXE$INIT sets the POOL_INIT bit in EXE$GL_STATE, indicating that nonpaged pool allocation is enabled. (Paged pool must be initialized in process context.) Once again, EXE$INIT invokes the initialization routines of the loadable executive images loaded by SYSBOOT.

17. EXE$INIT sets up the FIL$OPENFILE cache pointers and the top-level system directory name string for FILEREAD. SYSBOOT initialized these global parameters.

18. EXE$INIT initializes the permanent local system block. The SYSGEN parameters SCSSYSTEMID, SCSSYSTEMIDH, and SCSNODE determine the system ID and VAXcluster node name.

19. EXE$INIT flushes the temporary boot device mapping from the buffer.

20. EXE$INIT invokes a SYSLOA*xxx* initialization routine from module [SYSLOA]INIADP*xxx*. This processor-specific routine determines which adapters are present on the system and initializes the adapters and their data structures. Section 31.1.3 describes adapter initialization.

21. SYSBOOT may have loaded one or both of the following images into nonpaged pool:

    —SCSLOA.EXE, if the system has a computer interconnect (CI) adapter or system communication services (SCS) type system device

    —CLUSTRLOA.EXE, if the system is to participate in a VAXcluster system

    EXE$INIT invokes EXE$LINK_VEC for the images, to connect their vectors in the system base image to the actual code in nonpaged pool. It then executes each image's initialization routine. Chapter 29 describes this process in detail.

22. EXE$INIT invokes LDR$DEALLOC_PT, in module PTALLOC, to deallocate the SPTEs that mapped I/O space for the temporary use of the boot driver.

23. EXE$INIT reserves a page of physical memory (the "black hole" page) for adapter powerfail. It stores the PFN in global location EXE$GL_BLAKHOLE. When power failure occurs, for example, on a UNIBUS, all virtual pages mapped to UNIBUS adapter (UBA) registers or UNIBUS I/O space (24 pages in all) are remapped to this physical page. This remapping prevents drivers for UNIBUS devices from generating multiple machine checks while the power is off for the UBA. Powerfail operations are discussed in more detail in Chapter 33.

24. EXE$INIT invokes LDR$LOAD_IMAGE, in module SYSLDR, for each loadable executive image in its list, to load the image into memory and invoke its initialization routine. If the value of SYSGEN parameter S0_PAGING disables paging of the executive images, LDR$LOAD_IMAGE maps all image sections as nonpageable. Chapter 29 describes its actions in detail.

25. EXE$INIT calls LDR$ALTERNATE_LOAD, also described in Chapter 29, to load optional images, for example, site-specific images containing custom versions of the Magnetic Tape Accessibility ($MTACCESS) and Get Security Erase Pattern ($ERAPAT) system services. LDR$ALTERNATE_LOAD opens [SYSx.SYS$LDR]VMS$SYSTEM_IMAGES.DATA and loads any images flagged for the current boot phase. (LDR$ALTERNATE_LOAD executes later during the SYSINIT phase as well.)

26. EXE$INIT initalizes the first page file control block (PFL), called the null page file block, to access the shell process. Since the shell is part of the loaded executive image WORKING_SET_MANAGEMENT, EXE$INIT locates the address of the WCB mapping WORKING_SET_MANAGEMENT and stores it in the PFL. It also stores the virtual block number (VBN) of the shell within the image file.

27. EXE$INIT invokes the CPU-specific routine SMP$SETUP_SMP (see Chapter 34) to initialize the multiprocessing environment if the configuration is a suitable one.

28. If the SYSGEN parameter REALTIME_SPTS is nonzero, EXE$INIT allocates the number of SPTEs that it specifies. It calculates the size of the real-time bitmap control block, allocates it from nonpaged pool, and stores its address in the global location EXE$GL_RTBITMAP. The connect-to-interrupt driver, described in Chapter 22, uses these SPTEs and the bitmap.

29. EXE$INIT allocates three lock management data structures from nonpaged pool: the lock ID table, the resource hash table, and a process

bitmap used for deadlock detection. The map has one bit for each possible process.

30. It allocates the PCB and sequence number vectors from nonpaged pool. Chapter 25 describes these structures.

    The initialization routine for the PROCESS_MANAGEMENT loadable executive image, module SYSTEM_PCBS_AND_PHDS, initialized three PCBs: a system PCB used by the page fault handler to read faulted pages into the system working set, the swapper PCB for the swapper process, and a null PCB used as a placeholder.

    EXE$INIT stores the address of the swapper PCB in the second slot of the PCB vector. It initializes all other PCB vector slots to contain the address of the null PCB. The PCB vector has one extra entry, where EXE$INIT stores the address of the system PCB. It initializes all entries in the sequence number vector to zero.

31. EXE$INIT calculates an extended process ID for the swapper process and the null PCB, then invokes SCH$CHSE, in module RSE (see Chapter 12), to make the swapper process computable.

32. From nonpaged pool, it allocates the process header (PHD) vectors. These are the reference count array and the process index array, which contain an entry for each balance slot. Chapter 14 describes these vectors.

    Each element in the reference count array is initialized to contain −1.

    The null PCB (with a process index of zero) does not require a balance slot. An index of zero can thus be used for another purpose, namely to indicate a free balance slot. Thus, to indicate free balance slots, the process index array is zeroed.

    As Appendix F illustrates, the system header and SPT immediately follow the balance slot area in system address space. In fact, portions of the memory management subsystem treat the system header as the occupant of an additional balance slot, one with a slot number equal to the SYSGEN parameter BALSETCNT. The two PHD vector arrays have one extra entry at the end to reflect this feature.

33. The entries in the PFN database arrays for the page occupied by the RPB are initialized.

34. EXE$INIT allocates a WCB from nonpaged pool and initializes its header. Despite its name, NET$AR_WCB, the structure serves as a header for a kernel mode work queue used by the network logging monitor.

35. It initializes the page-and-swap-file vector. Each array element is the address of a PFL for a page or swap file recognized by the system. It stores the address of the null page file block, initialized in step 26, in the first array element.

36. The maximum depth of the lock manager resource name tree is calculated. The size of the tree is based on the size of the interrupt stack.

37. It stores the boot time in the primary's per-CPU database.

38. EXE$INIT stores the process index and the address of the system header in the system PCB.

39. EXE$INIT calls LDR$INIT_ALL to invoke any remaining loadable executive image initialization routines.

40. It invokes EXE$INI_TIMWAIT, in module [SYSLOA]ERRSUB*xxx*. This initializes CPU$L_TENUSEC and CPU$L_UBDELAY, the timed wait count variables used in timed wait loops generated by the TIMEWAIT and TIMEDWAIT macros. These variables count iterations of instruction loops that are executed, in part, to wait for a minimum amount of time to elapse. These counts are used, for example, during powerfail recovery, to wait for disk drives to come back online. These counts also control the length of time a processor spins waiting to acquire a spinlock. They are not constants because they vary with CPU type and therefore are calibrated during system initialization by EXE$INI_TIMWAIT. In earlier versions of VMS, these counts were systemwide globals. SMP support requires that they be CPU-specific and thus capable of being changed, for example, to reflect cache disabling on one CPU. Therefore, the counts now reside in the per-CPU databases.

CPU$L_TENUSEC is the number of times a prototype loop executes in 10 microseconds. The prototype loop includes an inner loop that is simply a SOBGTR instruction. CPU$L_UBDELAY is the number of times the SOBGTR instruction executes in 3 microseconds. In actual use, the prototype loop is likely to be replaced by code that polls a device register. The delay represented by the inner SOBGTR loop is incorporated so as to introduce a 3-microsecond gap between successive references to the UNIBUS or other I/O bus that contains the device register.

41. EXE$INIT inserts the driver prolog table (DPT) for the console terminal in the driver list at the listhead IOC$GL_DPTLIST.

42. From nonpaged pool, it allocates Create Logical Name ($CRELNM) argument lists for SYS$DISK and SYS$SYSDEVICE. The swapper process accesses this area in nonpaged pool and creates the logical names after it initializes paged pool and the logical name database.

43. SYSBOOT loaded the terminal class driver into nonpaged pool. EXE$INIT invokes IOC$INITDRV, in module RELOCDRV, to initialize its data structures as directed by the DPT (defined by the driver's invocations of the DPT_STORE macro). Then EXE$INIT inserts the DPT into the list at IOC$GL_DPTLIST, relocates the terminal class vector table, and connects it to the console port driver data structures. SYSGEN establishes data structures for additional terminals later.

44. EXE$INIT completes the configuration of the I/O database for the system device. Based on information in the driver or drivers' DPTs, EXE$INIT allocates and initializes driver data structures if necessary and links the drivers into the I/O database. It scans the list of adapter control blocks

(ADPs) to locate the boot adapter and obtains the boot device controller letter and the device unit number from the RPB.

EXE$INIT processes the subport driver, if one exists; proceeds to the port driver, if one exists; and finally processes the system device driver. For each driver, it performs the following actions:

a. EXE$INIT inserts the driver's DPT into the driver list.

b. It then allocates a complete set of driver data structures from non-paged pool, including a device data block (DDB), a unit control block (UCB), an object rights block (ORB), a channel request block (CRB), an interrupt data block (IDB), and a device spinlock. It initializes these structures and connects them to each other and the rest of the I/O database. (The system device driver data structures, within the loadable executive image SYSTEM_PRIMITIVES, are initialized by the SYSTEM_PRIMITIVES initialization routine.)

c. EXE$INIT invokes IOC$INITDRV to initialize the data structures as directed by the DPT.

d. For a MicroVAX with Q22-bus multilevel interrupts enabled and a system device on a Q22-bus adapter, EXE$INIT inserts instructions into the CRB to ensure that the system operates only with a correct bus configuration, and to adjust the IPL at each device interrupt.

e. It invokes SMP$INIT_SPL, in module SPINLOCKS, with the address of the device spinlock allocated in step b. SMP$INIT_SPL stores the appropriate IPL, rank, and timeout interval, among other items, in the new device spinlock.

f. If the driver specifies a fork IPL rather than a fork spinlock, EXE$INIT sets a flag indicating the presence of a device driver unable to function correctly in an SMP environment. VMS will not enable SMP operation while a driver of this type is loaded.

45. If the device is a subport, EXE$INIT marks its UCB as a template and sets its status to online. Otherwise, the UCB is marked valid.

46. EXE$INIT constructs a name for the system device unit using information passed from VMB and the driver name, then stores the device and driver names in the system DDB, SYS$AR_BOOTDDB.

47. It stores the system device UCB address in EXE$GL_SYSUCB.

48. Loadable executive images reside on the system device. EXE$INIT scans the list of loadable images at LDR$GQ_IMAGE_LIST. If a loadable executive image contains a pageable image section, EXE$INIT stores the system device UCB address in the image's associated WCB.

49. It allocates an SPTE, if requested, for the system device and stores its number in UCB$L_SVPN.

50. Once the system device name is determined, the equivalence names for SYS$DISK and SYS$SYSDEVICE are stored in the $CRELNM argument lists allocated in step 42 for later use by the swapper process.

51. If the system is a VAXcluster member and requested a remote bootstrap over its network device, BOO$GB_NODENAME contains the node name of the remote system serving the system disk. EXE$INIT creates a system block for this node.

52. All loaded drivers are then invoked at their controller and unit initialization entry points.

53. EXE$INIT invokes EXE$INIPROCREG, a CPU-specific routine within the SYSLOA image, to initialize processor registers, for example, to enable interval timer interrupts.

54. It allocates two SPTEs for tape mount verification and stores the virtual address of the first SPTE at EXE$GL_TMV_SVAPTE.

55. It allocates a page of physical memory and an SPTE to map it for mount verification. The virtual address of the SPTE is stored in EXE$GL_SVAPTE.

56. It allocates an SPTE, computes the associated system virtual address, and stores that address in MMG$GL_DZRO_VA. This is used to optimize global demand zero page deletion.

57. It allocates two pages of physical memory and two SPTEs to map them. These become the system erase pattern buffer and a pseudo page table mapping the buffer. The virtual addresses are stored in EXE$GL_ERASE-PB and EXE$GL_ERASEPPT. These optimize erasure of disk blocks during the deletion of an erase-on-delete file.

58. EXE$INIT adjusts the maximum allowable working set (if necessary) to reflect the amount of available physical memory. It subtracts the number of physical pages used by the executive from the amount of available physical memory.

59. It clears the warm start inhibit and cold start inhibit flags, which are used by the restart mechanism. Chapter 33 describes these flags.

60. It allocates a page of physical memory and an SPTE to map it to use as an executive mode data page. It clears the page and stores its address in EXE$AR_EWDATA.

61. It allocates two pages of physical memory and two SPTEs to map them. The first page becomes the swapper's only P1 page, the P1 pointer page, described in Appendix C. EXE$INIT stores the address of the swapper PCB in that page at the offset CTL$GL_PCB.

   The second page becomes the swapper P1 page table page, required to map the P1 pointer page.

62. EXE$INIT removes itself from the override set and determines SMP status (enabled or disabled) from the SYSGEN parameter MULTIPROCESSING and the information described in step 44f. If SMP is enabled, EXE$INIT sets the start flag, indicating that secondary CPU initialization may proceed. Chapter 34 describes these flags and SMP initialization.

63. Finally, EXE$INIT builds a PC/processor status longword (PSL) pair on the stack and REIs, passing control to the scheduler routine SCH$SCHED

at IPL$_SCHED, on the interrupt stack. The memory that EXE$INIT occupies is deallocated later by the SYSINIT process.

31.1.3   I/O Adapter Initialization

A CPU-specific routine in module [SYSLOA]INIADPxxx determines the location of external adapters and initializes the adapters for later use by SYSGEN.

Although some of the initialization that INIADPxxx performs depends on the nature of the external I/O adapter, there are several general steps that are taken for each adapter:

1. INIADPxxx allocates an ADP from nonpaged pool and initializes it. The ADP identifies the adapter and contains information about how the adapter's internal registers are mapped.
2. It allocates SPTEs to map to the I/O space addresses for internal adapter registers and other I/O space assignments.
3. It initializes the adapter hardware.

INIADPxxx records information about the hardware configuration in three parallel arrays in nonpaged pool, which are indexed by nexus number (the contents of EXE$GL_NUMNEXUS specify the number of elements in each array):

- MMG$GL_SBICONF contains the address of a longword array. Each element contains the starting virtual address to which its adapter registers are mapped.
- EXE$GL_CONFREG contains the address of a byte array that specifies the type code of each adapter, as defined by the $NDTDEF macro in LIB.MLB. Processors such as VAX-11/78x and VAX 86x0 CPUs, whose adapter type codes are one byte long, use this format.
- EXE$GL_CONFREGL contains the address of a longword array that also specifies the type code of each adapter. Processors such as VAX 8200 family systems, whose type codes are a longword in length and include a bus code, use this format.

Table 31.2 lists the differences in ADP size and mapping requirements for many of the possible external adapters.

INIADPxxx also checks for the presence of UNIBUS or Q22-bus memory. If this memory exists, INIADPxxx disables the associated map registers.

31.2   LOADABLE EXECUTIVE IMAGE INITIALIZATION ROUTINES

Chapter 29 describes the general mechanism by which loadable executive image initialization routines are invoked. The actions of these routines are constrained by the current phase of system initialization, represented by the flags in EXE$GL_STATE. For instance, a routine that needs to allocate

Table 31.2   External Adapter Initialization

Adapter Type	Size of ADP (in bytes)	Number of System Virtual Pages Mapped for Adapter
Local memory	None exists	1 (or 0 on some CPUs)
MA780 shared memory	132	1
UNIBUS adapter	608 or 1248 [1]	24 [2]
Q22-bus adapter	1128	24 [2]
MASSBUS adapter	56	8
DR32 interface	56	4
CI interface	66	16
KDB50	600	8
KLESI-B	600	8
DMB32 interface	56	2
DRB32	56	16
DEBNI	152	16
Generic VAXBI device	56	16
Unoccupied slot	None exists	1 to allow access
DWMBA	88	1

[1] An ADP for a UBA with indirect vectors also contains the interrupt service routines for the UBA and 128 longword vectors, corresponding to UNIBUS vectors from 0 to 774_8.

[2] Eight pages map the UBA internal registers, such as mapping registers and data path registers. Sixteen pages map the UNIBUS I/O page to allow virtual access to device control/status registers, data registers, and so on.

nonpaged pool cannot do so before EXE$INIT sets the POOL_INIT flag. An initialization routine unable to perform its tasks in the current phase returns a status to its invoker indicating that it should be reinvoked at a later phase. When the initialization routine completes all its tasks, it is deallocated.

Each initialization routine performs initialization that logically relates to the function of its associated image. For instance, the SYSTEM_PRIMITIVES image contains the interrupt service routines (ISRs) that handle fork dispatching. The SYSTEM_PRIMITIVES initialization routine stores the address of these ISRs in the appropriate SCB vectors.

The following paragraphs describe some of the actions of the loadable executive image initialization routines invoked from EXE$INIT, the swapper process, and the SYSINIT process. Note that these routines can be invoked multiple times and thus may not perform all listed functions in the same system initialization phase.

The SYSTEM_PRIMITIVES initialization routine formats and links the nonpaged pool lookaside list packets, as described in Chapter 19. It builds the I/O database structures for the system, console, and mailbox devices and stores the addresses of the fork ISRs into the appropriate SCB vectors.

It inserts two permanent system timer queue entries into the timer queue and stores the addresses of the interval timer and software timer ISRs in the appropriate SCB vectors.

The SYSTEM_DEBUG initialization routine stores the address of the X-DELTA ISR in its SCB vector.

The SYSTEM_SYNCHRONIZATION initialization routine initializes the static spinlock vector area. It initializes spinwait timeout values; assigns device spinlocks to the null device, console device, and permanent mailbox devices; and initializes the buffer pool used by SMP$FORK_TO_PRIMARY.

The ERRORLOG initialization routine allocates and initializes error log allocation buffers and initializes the global cells that describe them.

The EVENT_FLAGS_AND_ASTS initialization routine copies the contents of frequently referenced data cells such as SCH$GL_PCBVEC from the system base image into cells local to itself to improve access time. It initializes the IPL 2 SCB vector with the address of its ISR, SCH$ASTDEL. It connects system services, including the Set Event Flag ($SETEF) and Clear Event Flag ($CLREF) system services to their system service vectors.

The PROCESS_MANAGEMENT initialization routine similarly copies the contents of frequently referenced data cells from the system base image into local cells. It stores the address of the system logical name table in the group and job templates used for process creation. It initializes the swapper PCB and PHD, the system PCB, and the null PCB. It stores the address of SCH$RESCHED, the IPL 3 ISR, in the SCB vector. It connects the process control system services, including the Create Process ($CREPRC), Delete Process ($DELPRC), Get Job/Process Information ($GETJPI), and Set Process Priority ($SETPRI) system services.

The IO_ROUTINES initialization routine similarly copies the contents of frequently referenced data cells from the system base image into local cells. It stores the address of the IPL 4 ISR, IOC$IOPOST, in the SCB vector. It enables system restart by storing the physical address of the system restart routine, EXE$RESTART, in the RPB at RPB$L_RESTART and the checksum of the first 31 longwords of the restart routine at RPB$L_CHKSUM. It stores the address of the powerfail ISR, EXE$POWERFAIL, in the SCB vector.

The WORKING_SET_MANAGEMENT initialization routine creates the swapper process's P0 page table. It similarly copies the contents of frequently referenced data cells from the system base image into local cells. It connects the working set control system services, including the Adjust Working Set Limit ($ADJWSL) and Lock Working Set ($LKWSET) system services.

The PAGE_MANAGEMENT initialization routine stores the address of the page fault exception service routine (ESR) in the SCB vector. It ensures that modified page writer SYSGEN parameters are sensible; for instance, it checks that MPW_WAITLIMIT is not less than MPW_HILIMIT and adjusts it if necessary. MPW_IOLIMIT specifies the number of concurrent I/O operations that the modified page writer can have in progress. The initialization routine allocates that many I/O request packets (IRPs) and inserts them on a private lookaside list.

The EXCEPTION initialization routine stores the addresses of its ESRs, such as the reserved operand ESR, EXE$ROPRAND, and the access violation ESR, EXE$ACVIOLAT, in the SCB. It stores the addresses of the change mode to kernel (CHMK) and change mode to executive (CHME) ESRs in the SCB. It saves the address of the EXCEPTION image's loadable image data block (LDRIMG) and WCB in the boot control block for use during bugcheck processing. If the SYSGEN parameter DUMPSTYLE is 1, it allocates 127 SPTEs used to write a selective dump.

The IMAGE_MANAGEMENT initialization routine stores the address of the known file entry resource name string and its size in the global location EXE$GQ_KFE_LCKNAM.

31.3   INITIALIZATION IN PROCESS CONTEXT

The remaining steps in system initialization must be performed by a process. For instance, system services can only be called from process context and a command language interpreter (CLI) can only be mapped into P1 space by code executing in process context.

The process phase of system initialization is divided into several parts: the swapper initialization routine EXE$SWAPINIT, in swapper process context; the SYSINIT process; and the startup process.

31.3.1   Swapper Process

EXE$INIT transfers control to SCH$SCHED, in module SCHED, which selects the highest priority computable process for execution. Since only one process is computable at this time, the choice is easy: the scheduler selects the swapper process.

Several routines cooperate to initialize the swapper's process context. An initialization routine in the PROCESS_MANAGEMENT loadable executive image initializes the swapper PCB, PHD, and kernel stack. An initialization routine in the WORKING_SET_MANAGEMENT loadable executive image allocates nonpaged pool to use as the swapper's P0 page table, described in Chapter 14. (The page table's address is stored in the global location SWP$GL_MAP, and pages mapped in the swapper map are accessible as P0 virtual pages when the swapper is the current process.) EXE$INIT allocates a P1 page table page and the P1 pointer page.

The swapper PHD contains the address of EXE$SWAPINIT as the saved PC, so the swapper executes EXE$SWAPINIT when it is placed into execution for the first time. The saved PSL contains zeros, causing the swapper process to run in kernel mode at IPL 0.

EXE$SWAPINIT contains system initialization code, executed only once during the life of the system. It performs the minimum initialization that requires process context. In particular, it initializes paged pool, invokes loadable executive image initialization routines once again, and initializes the logical name database.

EXE$SWAPINIT begins by setting the swapper bit in EXE$GL_STATE to indicate that process context is available. EXE$INIT already initialized demand zero PTEs for all of paged pool. EXE$SWAPINIT now initializes the paged pool forward link and count fields in the first page of the pool. The resulting page fault requires process context. EXE$SWAPINIT invokes LDR$INIT_ALL to invoke loadable executive image initialization routines and to perform address fixups for pageable image sections in loadable executive images. The loadable executive image initialization routines execute in the context of the swapper process with paged pool available for allocation.

EXE$SWAPINIT then performs the following steps to initialize the logical name database, described in Chapter 35:

1. It allocates paged pool for the shareable logical name hash table.
2. It zeros the allocated area, initializes its header, and stores its address in the longword pointed to by LNM$AL_HASHTBL.
3. It initializes the logical name table header (LNMTH) of the system directory. It records the hash table address in the LNMTH. It then hashes the system directory name and inserts it into the appropriate hash chain of the shareable hash table.
4. EXE$SWAPINIT initializes the system logical name table, recording the hash table address in its LNMTH. It invokes LNM$INSLOGTAB, in module LNMSUB, to insert the system table into the database.
5. The swapper requests the $CRELNM system service to create the following logical names:

   —LNM$DIRECTORIES, whose equivalence names are the shareable and per-process shareable directories
   —The executive mode table name LNM$FILE_DEV
   —The supervisor mode table name LNM$FILE_DEV
   —The table names that provide upward compatibility from VMS Version 3: LOG$PROCESS, LOG$GROUP, LOG$SYSTEM, TRNLOG$_GROUP_SYSTEM, TRNLOG$_PROCESS_GROUP, TRNLOG$_PROCESS_SYSTEM, and TRNLOG$_PROCESS_GROUP_SYSTEM
   —The table names LNM$PERMANENT_MAILBOX and LNM$TEMPORARY_MAILBOX
   —The table name LNM$SYSTEM
   —The executive mode names SYS$DISK and SYS$SYSDEVICE in the LNM$SYSTEM table

6. It deallocates the nonpaged pool used by EXE$INIT to pass information needed for the creation of SYS$DISK and SYS$SYSDEVICE.

EXE$SWAPINIT creates the SYSINIT process, which performs more of the system initialization requiring process context. EXE$SWAPINIT exits by jumping to the swapper main loop.

31.3.2 SYSINIT Process

In one sense, SYSINIT is an extension of the swapper process. However, the initialization code is isolated to prevent encumbering the swapper with more code that only executes once during the life of a system. This isolation is one of several techniques used during system initialization and process creation to cause seldom-used code to disappear after it executes. A list of such techniques appears in Appendix B.

SYSINIT performs the following major functions:

- It loads RMS and other loadable executive images.
- It initializes VAXcluster software for a VAXcluster node.
- It opens the swap and page files and records their extents.
- It activates F11BXQP.EXE, the Files-11 Extended QIO Processor (XQP) image, as a system global section.
- It loads the system message file.
- It creates the startup process.

31.3.2.1 Pool Allocation by SYSINIT.
SYSINIT, like EXE$INIT, allocates nonpaged pool. It also allocates some paged pool. However, the sizes of various blocks are not directly related to SYSGEN parameters. Structures that are allocated from nonpaged pool as a result of the execution of SYSINIT include the following:

- Four security audit structures
- PFL structures and bitmaps for the page and swap files
- Lock and resource blocks
- File control blocks (FCBs) and WCBs for all opened files
- Space to copy the contents of the error log allocation buffers from the crash dump file

31.3.2.2 Detailed Operation of SYSINIT.
SYSINIT is a normal process, scheduled and placed into execution in the ordinary way. Its main module is [SYSINI]SYS-INIT. SYSINIT begins execution in user mode but performs much of its work in kernel and executive modes.

SYSINIT takes the following steps:

1. It changes mode to kernel and sets the SYSINIT bit in EXE$GL_STATE to indicate that the SYSINIT process context is available.
2. It expands the kernel stack and invokes LDR$UNLOAD_IMAGE, in module SYSLDR, to release the physical pages and address space occupied by EXE$INIT.

3. SYSINIT allocates four security audit vectors from nonpaged pool. It initializes the structure headers and the pointers to these structures: NSAAR_ALARM_VECTOR, NSAAR_AUDIT_VECTOR, NSA$AR_ALARM_FAILURE, and NSA$AR_AUDIT_FAILURE.

4. SYSINIT invokes the loader to activate the following loadable executive images and execute their initialization routines:

   RMS.EXE
   RECOVERY_UNIT_SERVICES.EXE
   DDIF$RMS_EXTENSION.EXE
   SYSLDR_DYN.EXE

   If paging of RMS and related images is disabled, LDR$LOAD_IMAGE places them in nonpaged pool.

   SYSINIT sets the RMS bit in EXE$GL_STATE to indicate that RMS is loaded. RMS cannot be used, however, until the XQP is mapped.

5. From user mode, SYSINIT invokes LDR$ALTERNATE_LOAD, previously invoked by EXE$INIT, to load optional images. LDR$ALTERNATE_LOAD opens the file [SYSx.SYS$LDR]VMS$SYSTEM_IMAGES. DATA and loads those images requesting to be loaded during the current boot phase.

6. SYSINIT changes mode to kernel to create a system-specific root resource. It requests the Enqueue Lock Request ($ENQ) system service to create an executive mode system resource and acquire an exclusive lock on it. The resource name is the string SYS$SYS_ID concatenated with the system's SCS system ID (SYSGEN parameters SCSSYSTEMID and SCSSYSTEMIDH). The name is therefore unique within the VAXcluster system.

   SYSINIT locks the root resource with a system-owned lock so that the lock survives the deletion of SYSINIT. SYSINIT stores the lock ID in EXE$GL_SYSID_LOCK. The lock is always mastered on the local VAXcluster system, since each VAXcluster node locks its own unique name. Any sublocks of this lock are guaranteed to be mastered locally. Thus, VMS components use this lock as a parent for locks whose scope is limited to the local VAXcluster node. Appendix H provides more information on the system ID lock, and Chapter 10 describes lock management in general.

7. SYSINIT changes mode to kernel to set the system time. It invokes the routine EXE$INIT_TODR in the SYSLOA image. Chapter 11 describes EXE$INIT_TODR and altering the system time.

8. SYSINIT changes mode to kernel to initialize cluster connection management. If this system expects to participate in a VAXcluster system, SYSINIT locates the incarnation file, SYS$SYSTEM:SYS$INCARNATION.DAT. It opens the file, reads the first block, and stores the WCB address and the data in the cluster incarnation block (CLUICB).

SYSINIT creates the stand-alone configure process, STACONFIG. This process autoconfigures disks and SCS communication ports. If the SYSGEN parameter DISK_QUORUM indicates there is to be a quorum disk, STACONFIG starts SCS polling to discover remote mass storage control protocol (MSCP) disk servers. Connection to the quorum disk may be necessary for the node to join the VAXcluster system. SYSINIT sets a flag to tell the VAXcluster connection manager to proceed with cluster formation and prints the following message on the console terminal:

```
Waiting to form or join VAXcluster
```

It waits for 100 milliseconds, during which time the STACONFIG process and the VAXcluster connection manager run, and then tests whether the quorum disk has been found.

If it has, SYSINIT assigns a channel to it, opens the quorum file, and starts the quorum disk polling routine to run every QDISKINTERVAL seconds. It then checks whether the system is a member of a VAXcluster system yet. If not, SYSINIT waits again.

When the system is a member, SYSINIT takes out a concurrent read lock on the system device and resets the time to correspond to the clusterwide time.

9. If the system disk is to be a member of a disk shadow set, SYSINIT changes mode to kernel and establishes the shadow set.

10. Back in user mode, SYSINIT recreates executive mode logical names for SYS$SYSDEVICE and SYS$DISK in the system logical name table. (In the case of an MSCP system disk, their equivalence names are not quite right. At the time EXE$INIT created them, the allocation class of the system disk was not yet known. When SYSINIT runs, the MSCP server for the system disk has communicated its allocation class and SYSINIT can form an equivalence name that contains the allocation class.)

SYSINIT also creates the following logical names:

SYS$SYSROOT
SYS$COMMON
SYS$SHARE
SYS$MESSAGE
SYS$SYSTEM
SYS$LOADABLE_IMAGES

The creation of these names occurs here because they are needed as a part of the creation of the startup process. The name of the image that STARTUP initially executes is SYS$SYSTEM:LOGINOUT, and SYS$SYSTEM is defined in terms of SYS$SYSROOT and SYS$COMMON. LOGINOUT performs a merged image activation to map the Digital command language (DCL) CLI into P1 space. The image activator uses logical name SYS$SHARE to locate the shareable image DCL-TABLES.EXE, which contains the command database for the DCL CLI.

11. If the SYSGEN parameter UAFALTERNATE is set, SYSINIT creates the executive mode logical name SYSUAF in the system table. Its equivalence name is SYS$SYSTEM:SYSUAFALT.DAT. This feature allows an alternative authorization file to be used. If the alternative authorization file does not exist, logins are enabled only from the console terminal.

12. In kernel mode, SYSINIT uses the primitive file I/O routines to open the following files on the system disk:

   —[SYS*n*.SYSEXE]PAGEFILE.SYS, if not already open
   —[SYS*n*.SYSEXE]SWAPFILE.SYS, if SYSGEN parameter SWPFILCNT is nonzero
   —[SYS*n*.SYSEXE]SYSDUMP.DMP

   It ensures that the file highwater mark is set to the end of each of these files. A highwater mark prevents access to file blocks that are allocated but not yet written. These blocks may have previously belonged to another file, now deleted, and may still contain data from the other file. A highwater mark is one way to prevent access to this data. However, SYSINIT adjusts the highwater mark to the end of the file for the page file, swap file, and system dump file, since the mechanism is not appropriate for these special-purpose files.

13. SYSINIT changes mode to kernel and invokes LDR$LOAD_IMAGE to open the loadable executive image SYS$MESSAGE:SYSMSG.EXE, the system message file.

14. It calls a kernel mode procedure that performs the following functions:

   a. It initializes the global page table entry (GPTE) list.

   b. The dump file (or the page file if no dump file exists) contains the contents of the error log allocation buffers at the time of the crash or shutdown. These buffers were written by the bugcheck code, described in Chapter 32, so their contents would not be lost. SYSINIT attempts to locate saved error log buffers and record their contents.

      It multiplies the number of buffers by the number of pages per buffer, adds sufficient space for a header and an extra buffer for the bugcheck error log entry, and allocates this amount of nonpaged pool. It stores the address of this area in EXE$GL_SAVED_EMBS. It copies the error log buffers from the dump or page file to the area and records the number of buffers copied in EXE$GW_SAVED_EMBS_COUNT. Eventually, the messages will be written to SYS$ERROR-LOG:ERRLOG.SYS.

   c. The kernel routine initializes the page file data structures; it allocates a PFL and a bitmap from nonpaged pool to describe the page file and the availability of each block in the file. The bitmap is initialized to all 1's to indicate that all blocks are available. If the page file contains a valid dump and the SYSGEN parameter SAVEDUMP is set to 1, the blocks in the page file that contain the dump are marked unavailable. The address of the page file WCB, the page file size, the bitmap address, the free page count, and other items are stored in the PFL, whose address is then stored in the page-and-swap-file vector.

Note that page file blocks marked unavailable because they contain a crash dump may be reclaimed by copying them to another file using the System Dump Analyzer (SDA) command COPY, or released with the command ANALYZE/CRASH_DUMP/RELEASE. However, releasing the blocks deletes the crash dump.

d. If present, the swap file is initialized. The routine allocates a PFL and a bitmap from nonpaged pool to describe the swap file and the availability of each block in the file. It initializes the bitmap to all 1's, indicating that all blocks are available. The address of the swap file WCB, the swap file size, the bitmap address, the free page count, and other items are stored in the PFL, whose address is then stored in the page-and-swap-file vector.

Chapter 14 describes the page-and-swap-file vector.

e. The kernel mode routine stores the address of RMS in the P1 pointer page at the location CTL$GL_RMSBASE.

f. So that the error log entry describing a bugcheck is not lost if the error log buffers are full at the time of the crash, the VMS bugcheck code writes it in the first block of the dump file. After a crash, SYSINIT copies this error log entry from the dump file into the last error log buffer in the area pointed to by EXE$GL_SAVED_EMBS. It logs a cold start in the system error log.

15. SYSINIT exits the kernel mode procedure, returning to user mode, and changes mode to executive. It requests the Image Activate ($IMGACT) and Image Fixup ($IMGFIX) system services to activate the XQP in SYSINIT's P1 space. After setting the XQP flag in EXE$GL_STATE, it transfers control to kernel mode initialization routine in the XQP. From this point on, the file system is available for SYSINIT's file operations.

16. In user mode, SYSINIT assigns a channel to the system disk. In executive mode, it calls a procedure to mount the system disk.

17. SYSINIT requests the Set Time ($SETIME) system service to record the system time in the system image.

18. SYSINIT disables the FIL$OPENFILE cache and deallocates its pages to nonpaged pool.

19. It creates the logical name SYS$TOPSYS.

20. SYSINIT reads the XQP's image header, changes mode to kernel, and calls a procedure to create global sections for the XQP's image sections. If the SYSGEN parameter ACP_XQP_RES is set, SYSINIT creates resident

global sections so that the pages of the XQP are always in physical memory.

21. SYSINIT opens the page file, swap file, dump file, and all loadable executive image files. From kernel mode, each WCB is converted into a shared window by clearing the WCB$L_PID field, setting the WCB$V_SHRWCB flag, and incrementing its reference count to 2. Thus, an attempt to delete one of these files will only mark the file for deletion.

22. Finally, SYSINIT creates the startup process, specifying that it execute the LOGINOUT image, which maps the DCL CLI into P1 space. Chapter 27 describes LOGINOUT.

31.3.3 Startup Process

The startup process created by SYSINIT completes system initialization. This process is the first in the system to include a CLI. The inclusion of DCL allows the operation of this process to be directed by a DCL command procedure, SYS$SYSTEM:STARTUP.COM.

31.3.3.1

STARTUP.COM. For VMS Version 5.0, the STARTUP command procedure was reorganized. It now directs the execution of other command procedures that perform the actual work, using input from three data files in the SYS$STARTUP directory.

- VMS$PHASES lists eight startup phases from INITIAL to END. It sequences the invocation of the command procedures and executable images defined in the other two data files.

- VMS$VMS is reserved for use by the operating system. Each record contains the name of a VMS-supplied command procedure or executable image, the startup phase in which it executes, a flag through which execution is enabled or disabled, and a mode field defining the manner in which the file executes (for instance, mode "b" signifies that the file should be submitted as a batch job).

   By convention, the file name in each VMS$VMS record begins with the string VMS$, followed by the name of the phase in which the image or procedure executes. For instance, the command procedure VMS$INITIAL-050_VMS.COM executes in the INITIAL phase.

- VMS$LAYERED is reserved for the use of customers and layered products. A customer or layered product installation procedure uses SYSMAN to insert the name of the layered product startup file, its execution phase, and the flag, mode, and other fields, as in VMS$VMS, into a VMS$LAYERED record. STARTUP executes the command procedure in the specified phase and manner.

VMSVMS, VMSLAYERED, and all files that they specify reside in the SYS$STARTUP directory. STARTUP processes them as follows:

1. It reads the first phase defined in VMS$PHASES and stores it as the current phase.
2. For records in VMS$VMS whose phase matches the current phase, it executes the associated image or command procedure if it is enabled. When no more records in VMS$VMS match the current phase, STARTUP executes each image or command procedure defined in VMS$LAYERED whose phase matches the current phase.
3. STARTUP waits for all batch processes and subprocesses to complete.
4. When no more records exist for the current phase, STARTUP reads the next phase from VMS$PHASES and processes records from VMS$VMS and VMS$LAYERED that match the new phase.
5. Finally, when no more phases remain, STARTUP exits.

Some of the more important command files and their actions follow. Note that this section describes the full set of STARTUP actions, some of which are disabled when the SYSGEN parameter STARTUP_P1 has the value MIN.

VMS$INITIAL-050_VMS.COM, the first command procedure invoked by STARTUP, performs these actions:

1. It creates the following system logical names:

   SYS$SPECIFIC
   SYS$SYSDISK
   SYS$ERRORLOG
   SYS$EXAMPLES
   SYS$HELP
   SYS$INSTRUCTION
   SYS$LIBRARY
   SYS$MAINTENANCE
   SYS$MANAGER
   SYS$UPDATE
   SYS$TEST

2. It preserves SYSGEN parameters. If the SYSGEN parameter WRITESYS-PARAMS is set, it runs SYSGEN to execute WRITE CURRENT, which records the parameters in SYS$SYSTEM:VAXVMSSYS.PAR.
3. It installs MTHRTL.EXE or UVMTHRTL.EXE, whichever is the appropriate math library.
4. It makes privileged and shareable images known to the system by running the Install Utility with input taken from the file SYS$MANAGER:VMS-IMAGES.DAT.
5. VMS$INITIAL-050_VMS.COM creates the CONFIGURE process for VAXcluster members, so that page and swap files on disks other than the system disk can be located and installed.
6. It installs the page file and swap file if they exist, either from the node's root directory or, for satellite VAXcluster nodes, from local disks.

7. It invokes SYPAGSWPFILES.COM to install secondary page and swap files.

VMS$INITIAL-050_LIB.COM defines logical names and name tables for the Text Processing Utility (TPU), the debugger (DBG), and RMS. It also invokes SYLOGICALS.COM for site-specific logical name creation.

VMS$CONFIG-050_VMS.COM invokes the DECwindows startup procedure, which in this initial invocation performs the subset of its operations that are appropriate for all nodes.

VMS$CONFIG-050_ERRFMT.COM creates the error logger (ERRFMT) process.

VMS$CONFIG-050_CACHE_SERVER.COM creates the Files-11 XQP cache server (CACHE_SERVER) process for VAXcluster nodes.

VMS$CONFIG-050_CSP.COM creates the cluster server (CLUSTER_SERVER) process for VAXcluster nodes.

VMS$CONFIG-050_OPCOM.COM creates the operator communication (OPCOM) process.

VMS$CONFIG-050_AUDIT_SERVER.COM executes the site-specific security procedure, SYSECURITY.COM, if it exists. It then creates the audit server (AUDIT_SERVER) process.

VMS$CONFIG-050_JOBCTL.COM creates the job controller (JOB_CONTROL) process.

VMS$CONFIG-050_LMF.COM loads software licenses from the license database.

VMS$SYSFILES-050_VMS.COM directs device configuration:

1. It stops the CONFIGURE process, created earlier to locate page and swap files.
2. It invokes the site-specific command procedure if it exists. This command procedure, SYS$MANAGER:SYCONFIG.COM, can configure user-written device drivers prior to VMS autoconfiguration or disable autoconfiguration by clearing the DCL symbol STARTUP$AUTOCONFIGURE.
3. Unless disabled by the the SYSGEN parameter NOAUTOCONFIG or the STARTUP$AUTOCONFIGURE symbol, the command procedure runs SYSGEN to configure external I/O devices.
4. Unless disabled by the SYSGEN parameter NOAUTOCONFIG or the STARTUP$AUTOCONFIGURE symbol, the command procedure creates the CONFIGURE process for VAXcluster nodes with paging enabled.

VMS$BASEENVIRON-050_VMS.COM configures the operator's console as appropriate for the system and determines the message classes that will be logged to the console and the operator log file.

947

VMS$BASEENVIRON-050_SMISERVER.COM creates the system management server (SMISERVER) process for VAXcluster members and larger standalone systems.

VMS$LPBEGIN-050_VMS.COM performs miscellaneous tasks:

1. It invokes the site-specific command procedure SYS$MANAGER:SY-STARTUP_V5.COM if it exists.
2. If the SCSNODE SYSGEN parameter is not blank and the rights database is in use, the command procedure creates the node-specific identifier (the string SYS$NODE_ concatenated with the node name).
3. It enables interactive logins.

VMS$LPBEGIN-050_STARTUP.COM invokes the DECwindows startup procedure, which in this invocation starts the windowing software.

31.3.3.2 **Site-Specific Startup Command Procedure.** The site-specific command procedure SYS$MANAGER:SYSTARTUP_V5.COM is typically edited by the system manager to do the following:

- Start batch and print queues
- Set terminal speeds and other device characteristics
- Create site-specific system logical names
- Install additional privileged and shareable images
- Load user-written device drivers
- Mount volumes other than the system disk
- Load the console block storage driver (if desired) with a CONNECT CONSOLE command to SYSGEN and mount the console medium
- Start DECnet (if present on the system)
- Produce an error log report
- Announce system availability

31.4 **SYSTEM GENERATION UTILITY (SYSGEN)**

SYSGEN fits into the initialization sequence in two unrelated ways: SYSBOOT may use parameter files produced by SYSGEN to define system characteristics, and STARTUP.COM invokes SYSGEN directly to autoconfigure the external I/O devices.

SYSGEN's role in autoconfiguring the I/O system is described in the *VMS Device Support Manual*. Table 31.3 briefly compares the operations that SYSGEN and SYSBOOT perform on parameter files.

31.4.1 **SYSGEN Parameters**

SYSGEN parameters are defined in the source module SYSPARAM.MAR. Through different settings of conditional assembly parameters, this source module produces two object modules: SYSPARAM, which links into the

Table 31.3   Comparison of SYSGEN and SYSBOOT

SYSGEN	*SYSBOOT*

PURPOSE

SYSGEN has four unrelated purposes: • It creates parameter files for use in future bootstrap operations. • It modifies dynamic parameters in the running system with the WRITE ACTIVE command. • It loads device drivers and builds their associated data structures. • It creates and installs additional page and swap files.	SYSBOOT configures the system using parameters from VAXVMSSYS.PAR or another parameter file.

USE IN SYSTEM INITIALIZATION

During initialization, SYSGEN can be invoked to autoconfigure all I/O devices and record the current SYSGEN parameters.	SYSBOOT is the secondary bootstrap program that executes after VMB and before control is passed to the executive.

ENVIRONMENT

SYSGEN executes in the normal environment of a utility program. The driver and swap/page functions require CMKRNL privilege. A WRITE ACTIVE command also requires CMKRNL privilege. The parameter file operations are protected through the file system.	SYSBOOT runs in a stand-alone environment with no file system, memory management, process context, or any other environment provided by VMS.

VALID COMMANDS

USE	USE
USE FILE-SPEC	USE FILE-SPEC
USE CURRENT	USE CURRENT
USE DEFAULT	USE DEFAULT
USE ACTIVE	No equivalent command
SET	SET
SHOW	SHOW
EXIT (CONTINUE)	EXIT (CONTINUE)
WRITE	No equivalent command
Commands associated with device drivers	No equivalent commands
Commands associated with additional page and swap files	No equivalent commands

INITIAL CONDITIONS

Implied USE ACTIVE	Implied USE CURRENT

system base image, and PARAMETER, which links into both SYSGEN and SYSBOOT.

The SYSPARAM source module invokes a macro named PARAMETER to define each adjustable parameter. The macro $PRMDEF, in LIB.MLB, defines the fields of the data structures created by PARAMETER. Table 31.4 lists these fields and flags. For each parameter, the macro also creates a Get System Information ($GETSYI) item code in the form SYI$_ followed by parameter name. The following code demonstrates the PARAMETER macro invocation that defines the SYSGEN parameter GBLPAGES.

```
PARAMETER          ADDRESS=SGN$GL_MAXGPGCT,-
                   DEFAULT=10000,-
                   MIN=512,-
                   NAME=GBLPAGES,-
                   SIZE=LONG,-
                   TYPE=<SYSGEN,SYS,MAJOR>,-
                   UNIT=Pages,-
                   VERSION_MASK=[SYSGEN]
```

In an initialized system, each parameter occupies a cell in a table of active values stored within the address space reserved for the system base image. A parameter's virtual address within the base image does not change across minor version releases of VMS, although new parameters may be added to reserved address space at the end of the parameter area. Appendix C lists the contents of this area.

When SYSBOOT or SYSGEN executes, it maintains a private table of working parameters. It is manipulated by the following SYSGEN and SYS-BOOT commands:

- Displayed by SHOW *parameter-name* commands
- Altered by SET *parameter-name value* commands
- Overwritten in memory by a USE command
- Written to the file VAXVMSSYS.PAR by the SYSGEN WRITE CURRENT command
- Written to a selected file by the SYSGEN WRITE *file-spec* command
- Dynamic parameters are written to the executive's memory image by the SYSGEN WRITE ACTIVE command

31.4.2 Use of Parameter Files by SYSBOOT

Figure 31.2 shows the flow of parameter value data during a bootstrap operation. The numbers in the figure correspond to the following steps:

①SYSBOOT first locates the file VAXVMSSYS.PAR in SYS$SYSROOT:[SYSEXE] and reads its parameter settings into SYSBOOT's working table. In the language of SYSBOOT and SYSGEN commands, this step is an implied command:

```
USE CURRENT
```

This initializes the system with the parameter settings saved in VAX-VMSSYS.PAR, either during the last boot of the system as shown in step 5, through the AUTOGEN command procedure, or from an explicit SYSGEN command, WRITE CURRENT.

Prior to VMS Version 4, the current parameters were stored in SYS.EXE. However, to support sharing of SYS.EXE by multiple members of a VAXcluster system, the parameters were moved into a separate file, VAXVMS-SYS.PAR. Each member has its own version of this file.

Table 31.4 Information Stored for Each Adjustable Parameter by SYSGEN and SYSBOOT

Item	Size of Item
Parameter address in base image [1]	Longword
Parameter default value	Longword
Minimum value that the parameter can assume	Longword
Maximum value that the parameter can assume	Longword
Parameter type flags	Longword

Parameter Type	Display Command	
DYNAMIC	SHOW /DYN	
STATIC		
SYSGEN	SHOW /GEN	
ACP	SHOW /ACP	
JBC	SHOW /JOB	
RMS	SHOW /RMS	
SYS	SHOW /SYS	
SPECIAL	SHOW /SPECIAL	
DISPLAY		
CONTROL		
MAJOR	SHOW /MAJOR	
PQL	SHOW /PQL	
NEG		
TTY	SHOW /TTY	
SCS	SHOW /SCS	
CLUSTER	SHOW /CLUSTER	
ASCII		
LGI	SHOW /LGI	
MULTIPROCESSING	SHOW /MULTIPROCESSING	

Parameter size	Byte
Bit position (if parameter is a flag)	Byte
Parameter's SYSGEN name (counted ASCII string)	16 bytes
Units of allocation (counted ASCII string)	12 bytes

[1] The working value of each parameter is found not only in internal tables in SYSBOOT and SYSGEN but also in the executive itself. In fact, the parameter address (first item) stored for each parameter symbolically locates the working value of each parameter in the memory image of the system base image.

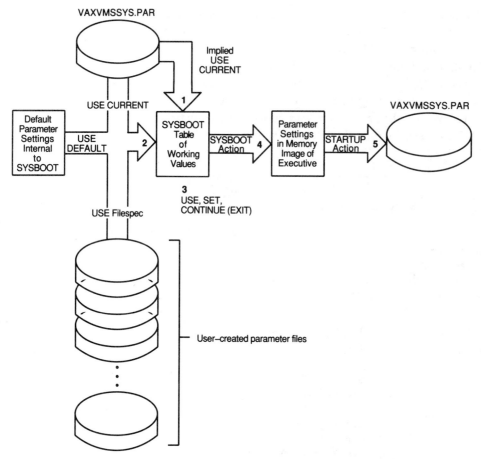

Figure 31.2
Movement of Parameter Data by SYSBOOT and
STARTUP

②When a conversational bootstrap is selected (R5⟨0⟩ is set as input to VMB),
SYSBOOT prompts for commands to alter current parameter settings. A
USE command at the SYSBOOT prompt results in the working table's
being overwritten with an entire set of parameter values. There are three
possible sources of these values:

—USE *file-spec* directs SYSBOOT to the indicated parameter file for a
new set of values.
—USE DEFAULT causes the working table in SYSBOOT to be filled with
the default values for each parameter.
—USE CURRENT causes the parameter values in VAXVMSSYS.PAR to
be loaded into SYSBOOT's working table. A USE CURRENT command
is redundant if it is the first command issued to SYSBOOT.

③Once the initial conditions are established, individual parameters can be altered with SET commands. The conversational phase of SYSBOOT ends with a CONTINUE (or EXIT) command.

④ After SYSBOOT calculates the sizes of the various pieces of system space but before it transfers control to EXE$INIT, it copies the contents of its working table to the corresponding table in the memory image of the executive.

⑤ One of the steps performed by the startup process copies the parameter table from the memory image of the executive to SYS$SYSTEM:VAX-VMSSYS.PAR if the WRITESYSPARAMS parameter is set. SYSBOOT sets this parameter automatically when another parameter is altered in a conversational boot. Since SYSBOOT always uses VAXVMSSYS.PAR unless directed otherwise, subsequent bootstraps will use the latest parameter settings even if no conversational bootstrap is selected.

31.4.3   Use of Parameter Files by SYSGEN

SYSGEN's actions, pictured in Figure 31.3, closely correspond to those of SYSBOOT. The numbers in the figure correspond to the following steps:

① The initial contents of SYSGEN's working table are the values taken from the memory image of the executive. The data movement pictured in Figure 31.3 is a movement from one memory area to another rather than the result of an I/O operation. In any event, SYSGEN begins its execution with an implied command:

        USE ACTIVE

This copies the parameter table from the memory image of the executive into SYSGEN's working table.

The ACTIVE parameters in the base image in memory do not differ from the CURRENT parameters in VAXVMSSYS.PAR on disk unless SYSGEN is run and parameters are written to either CURRENT (VAXVMSSYS.PAR) or ACTIVE (memory).

② Alternatively, SYSGEN can load its working table from the same sources available to SYSBOOT.

③ SET commands alter individual parameter values. SET only alters the parameter in SYSGEN's working table; the setting disappears on exit from SYSGEN unless preserved with a WRITE command.

④ The WRITE command preserves the contents of SYSGEN's working table in the following way:

—WRITE *file-spec* creates a new parameter file that contains the contents of SYSGEN's working table.

—WRITE CURRENT alters the copy of SYS$SYSTEM:VAXVMSSYS.PAR. The next bootstrap operation uses the updated values automatically.

—Several parameters determine the size of portions of system address space. Other parameters determine the size of blocks of pool space allocated by EXE$INIT. These parameters cannot be changed in a running

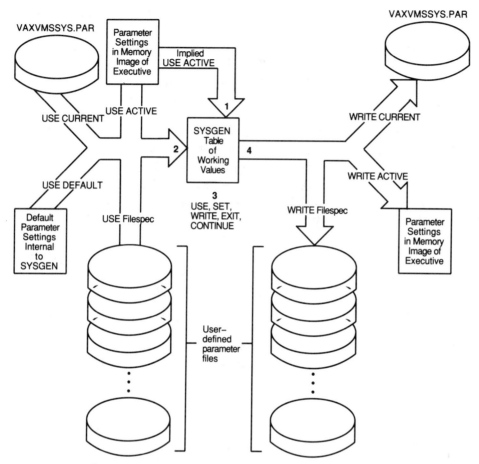

Figure 31.3
Movement of Parameter Data by SYSGEN

system. However, many parameters are not used in configuring the system. These parameters are designated DYNAMIC (see Table 31.4).

A WRITE ACTIVE command to SYSGEN alters the settings only of dynamic parameters, and only in the memory image of the executive.

A word of caution is in order here. Before experimenting with a new configuration, save the parameters from a working system in a parameter file. If the new configuration creates an unusable system, the system can be restored to its previous state by rebooting with the saved parameters.

31.5   SYSTEM SHUTDOWN

VMS provides two mechanisms to shut down a system in a controlled fashion. The preferred method, SYS$SYSTEM:SHUTDOWN.COM, provides a warning of the shutdown to system users and performs extensive house-keeping. The alternative method, SYS$SYSTEM:OPCCRASH.EXE, performs minimal cleanup.

31.5.1 SHUTDOWN.COM

SHUTDOWN.COM is a VMS-supplied command procedure that performs extensive cleanup and shuts down a VMS system in a controlled fashion. It requires the privileges CMKRNL, EXQUOTA, LOG_IO, NETMBX, OPER, SECURITY, SYSNAM, SYSPRV, TMPMBX, and WORLD to execute successfully, and will enable them automatically for a user with the SETPRV privilege. SHUTDOWN's tasks include the following:

- Optionally saving AUTOGEN feedback information to SYS$SYSTEM: AGEN$FEEDBACK.DAT
- Disabling interactive logins
- Shutting down DECnet
- Stopping the job controller's queue operations
- Stopping user processes
- Dismounting mounted volumes
- Stopping secondary processors on a multiprocessing system
- Removing installed images
- Invoking the site-specific shutdown procedure SYSHUTDWN.COM
- Closing the operator's log file
- Stopping the AUDIT_SERVER and ERRFMT processes
- Recalibrating the system time from the time-of-year clock and recording the change in the base image

If a shutdown is requested in an AUTOGEN command procedure parameter, AUTOGEN defines the logical name SHUTDOWN$AUTOGEN_SHUTDOWN before executing the SHUTDOWN command procedure. This notifies SHUTDOWN that the shutdown is coordinated from AUTOGEN and the standard shutdown questions need not be asked.

In addition, SHUTDOWN allows a reboot consistency check to be performed without actually shutting down the system. If a translation exists for the logical name SHUTDOWN$LOG_REBOOT_CHECK, SHUTDOWN creates the file REBOOT_CHECK_*nodename*.LOG, where *nodename* is the name of the system on which SHUTDOWN is executing. The following factors determine the files required to reboot:

- VAXcluster membership
- MSCP requirements
- Processor type
- Multiprocessing versus single-CPU system
- System boot device (remote boot over the network)

SHUTDOWN's reboot consistency check verifies the existence of files required to reboot. Defining SHUTDOWN$LOG_REBOOT_CHECK causes SHUTDOWN to write the verified file names to the log file and discontinue the shutdown.

SHUTDOWN runs the OPCCRASH program to actually shut down the system. It passes parameters to OPCCRASH via logical names.

The *Guide to Setting Up a VMS System* describes other actions of SHUT-DOWN and its use of the following logical names:

> SHUTDOWN$MINIMUM_MINUTES
> SHUTDOWN$TIME
> SHUTDOWN$INFORM_NODES

31.5.2 OPCCRASH

OPCCRASH.EXE, in module [OPCOM]OPCCRASH, performs the minimal tasks required to shut down a VMS system. Typically it is invoked as the final step of the SHUTDOWN.COM procedure, described in the previous section, but it can be executed directly in an emergency.

OPCCRASH performs the following:

1. It flushes the file system caches for the system disk (or multiple disks for a volume set) by marking the UCB for dismount and requesting a dismount Queue I/O ($QIO) system service. If the logical name OPC$UN-LOAD evaluates as true, OPCCRASH also marks the UCB for unload. When OPCCRASH is executed from SHUTDOWN, SHUTDOWN sets this parameter based on the user's answer to the question, Do you want to spin down the disk volumes?

2. If the logical name OPC$REBOOT evaluates as true, OPCCRASH sets the EXE$V_REBOOT flag in EXE$GL_FLAGS. This determines whether EXE$BUG_CHECK, in modules BUGCHECKBT and BUGCHECKLD, halts the system or invokes a processor-dependent routine that directs the console to attempt a reboot. When OPCCRASH is executed from SHUTDOWN, SHUTDOWN sets this parameter based on the user's answer to the question, Should an automatic system reboot be performed?

3. If the logical name OPC$NODUMP evaluates as true, OPCCRASH sets the low-order bit in EXE$GL_DUMPMASK. This determines whether EXE$BUG_CHECK writes the contents of memory to the dump file. When OPCCRASH is executed from SHUTDOWN, SHUTDOWN passes this parameter as true. Thus, although EXE$BUG_CHECK writes the error log buffers and header, no memory dump occurs for an operator-requested shutdown.

4. OPCCRASH raises IPL to IPL$_SYNCH, acquires the MMG and SCHED spinlocks, forces the modified page list to be written, and releases the MMG spinlock. It places the process into the resource wait state RSN$_MPLEMPTY, where it remains until the modified page list is completely

empty. When the process is taken out of the wait state, it resumes execution at IPL 0 with no spinlocks held.

5. If the system is a VAXcluster node, OPCCRASH translates the logical name OPC$CLUSTER_SHUTDOWN. When OPCCRASH is executed from SHUTDOWN, SHUTDOWN sets this parameter based on the shutdown option CLUSTER_SHUTDOWN. If the logical name evaluates as true, OPCCRASH raises IPL to IPL$_SYNCH, acquires the SCS spinlock, and invokes the connection manager routine CNX$SHUTDOWN, in module [SYSLOA]CONMAN. This routine coordinates a clusterwide shutdown. OPCCRASH lowers IPL to 0 and hibernates; the connection manager ultimately crashes the system with a bugcheck.

6. If the system is a VAXcluster node, OPCCRASH translates the logical name OPC$REMOVE_NODE. When OPCCRASH is executed from SHUTDOWN, SHUTDOWN sets this parameter based on the shutdown option REMOVE_NODE. If the logical name evaluates as true, OPCCRASH raises IPL to IPL$_SYNCH, acquires the SCS spinlock, and invokes CNX$SHUTDOWN to communicate the shutdown to the VAXcluster connection manager on this and the other nodes. It computes a new value for expected votes by subtracting this node's votes from the current expected votes and invokes the connection manager routine CNX$ADJ_EXPT_VOTES, in module [SYSLOA]CONMAN, to communicate the new value to the remaining VAXcluster nodes. It releases the SCS spinlock and waits until quorum is adjusted.

7. Finally, OPCCRASH crashes the system by issuing the BUG_CHECK macro, specifying a bugcheck type of OPERATOR and the keyword FATAL. Chapter 32 describes this macro, bugcheck processing, and the actions of EXE$BUG_CHECK.

32 Error Handling

There is always something to upset the most careful of
human calculations.

Ihara Saikaku, *The Japanese Family Storehouse*

This chapter discusses the mechanisms used for reporting systemwide errors in VMS. Process-specific and image-specific errors are handled by the exception mechanism described in Chapter 5.

Systemwide error-reporting mechanisms include

- The error logging subsystem, by which device drivers and other system components record errors and other events for later inclusion in an error log report
- The bugcheck mechanism, by which VMS shuts down the system and records its state when internal inconsistencies or other unrecoverable errors are detected
- Machine checks and error interrupts, by which the processor indicates that it has detected CPU-specific errors

32.1 ERROR LOGGING

The error logging subsystem records device errors, CPU-detected errors, and other noteworthy events, such as volume mounts, system startups, system shutdowns, and bugchecks.

32.1.1 Overview of the Error Logging Subsystem

The error logging subsystem uses a set of buffers called error log allocation buffers, created at system initialization. Logging an error occurs in the following steps:

1. A thread of execution, such as a device driver, invokes an executive routine to reserve a portion of an error log allocation buffer. The reserved portion is called an error message buffer.
2. The thread of execution writes information into the error message buffer and then invokes another executive routine to indicate that the buffer is valid, containing a completed message.
3. The ERRFMT process is awakened to copy the contents of error log allocation buffers to the error log file, SYS$ERRORLOG:ERRLOG.SYS.

Subsequently, the system manager can run the Error Log Utility to analyze the contents of the error log file and produce a formatted report.

If the system is shut down or crashes, the error log allocation buffers are copied to the dump file to prevent the loss of error log messages. On the next system boot, the SYSINIT process copies the error log allocation buffers saved in the dump file to nonpaged pool. When ERRFMT runs, it scans them for valid messages to write to the error log file. In this way, no error log information is lost across a system crash or shutdown.

32.1.2 Error Log Data Structures

During system initialization, a group of buffers is allocated in contiguous nonpageable system address space. The number of buffers allocated is specified by the SYSGEN parameter ERRORLOGBUFFERS. Their starting address is recorded in global location EXE$AL_ERLBUFADR. Prior to VMS Version 5.0, the number of error log allocation buffers was fixed at two.

The number of pages in each error log allocation buffer is specified by the SYSGEN parameter ERLBUFFERPAGES, whose default value is two pages. Prior to VMS Version 5.2, each error log allocation buffer was one page.

The group of buffers is treated as a ring. Initially, error message buffers are reserved in the first allocation buffer. When it fills, error message buffers are reserved in the second allocation buffer. After an allocation buffer fills, the ERRFMT process is awakened to copy the buffer's contents to the error log file so that the buffer can be reused. By the time the last allocation buffer becomes full, the first allocation buffer should be reusable.

The global location EXE$GW_ERLBUFTAIL contains the number of the allocation buffer in which error message buffers are currently being reserved. EXE$GW_ERLBUFHEAD contains the number of the allocation buffer whose contents should be written to the error log file next. These pointers replace ERL$GB_BUFIND used in earlier versions of VMS.

The address of a particular error log allocation buffer is computed as follows:

$$address = @EXE\$AL\_ERLBUFADR$$
$$+ (@EXE\$GB\_ERLBUFPAGES * 512 * buffer\_number)$$

A header at the beginning of each error log allocation buffer describes its state. The macro $ERLDEF defines symbolic names for fields in the buffer header. The following fields are of particular interest:

- ERL$B_BUSY contains the number of pending messages in the buffer, messages for which space has been reserved but which have not been completely written.
- ERL$B_MSGCNT contains the number of completed messages.
- ERL$B_FLAGS has one defined flag, ERL$V_LOCK, set to inhibit further allocation in the buffer while ERRFMT is copying the buffer contents.
- ERL$L_NEXT points to the first available space in the buffer.
- ERL$L_END points to the first byte past the end of the buffer and is used to test whether the buffer is full.

959

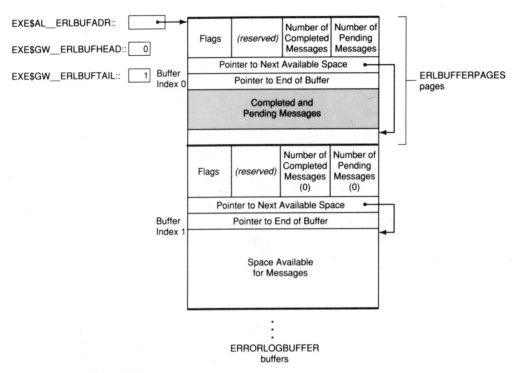

EXE$AL__ERLBUFADR::

EXE$GW__ERLBUFHEAD:: 0

EXE$GW__ERLBUFTAIL:: 1

Figure 32.1
Error Log Allocation Buffers

Figure 32.1 shows these data structures and globals. In this figure, buffer 0 has been filled. Error message buffers will be allocated from buffer 1 next.

The format and length of an error message buffer vary with its type. Each error message buffer has a header that contains type identification and information common to all types of message. The macro $EMBHDDEF defines fields in the header. The macro $EMBETDEF defines the error message types. Most of the common information in the header is written by the routine that reserves the error message buffer. Information specific to the error type is written by the component logging the error.

Each message is uniquely identified by a systemwide error sequence number, the contents of global location ERL$GL_SEQUENCE. The number is incremented on each attempt to reserve an error message buffer, whether or not it is successful. Sequence number gaps in an error log file may indicate the loss of error messages. (However, they may also indicate deleted time stamp messages; see Section 32.1.6).

32.1.3   Operation of the Error Logger Routines

The routines that manage the error log allocation buffers are

- ERL$ALLOCEMB—Invoked to reserve an error message buffer

- ERL$RELEASEMB—Invoked to release a completed error message buffer

Both are in module ERRORLOG.

ERL$ALLOCEMB is invoked with the size of the requested error message buffer. It takes the following steps:

1. It first acquires the EMB spinlock, raising interrupt priority level (IPL) to 31, to synchronize access to the allocation buffer data structures.
2. It tests whether the message is larger than will fit into an empty allocation buffer and, if so, returns an error status.
3. ERL$ALLOCEMB calculates the address of the allocation buffer indicated by EXE$GW_ERLBUFTAIL.
4. It tests whether the lock flag of that allocation buffer is clear (the usual state). If it is, ERL$ALLOCEMB tests whether the message fits into the unused space in the buffer.
5. If the lock flag is set or if the message does not fit, ERL$ALLOCEMB forces a wakeup of the ERRFMT process. It switches to the next allocation buffer, incrementing EXE$GW_ERLBUFTAIL.

   If the next available allocation buffer is still full of error messages not yet written to the error log file, ERL$ALLOCEMB advances to the next allocation buffer, wrapping back to the beginning of the buffer ring if necessary. If it fails to find room for the message buffer, ERL$ALLOC-EMB continues in this way until it reaches its starting point, the buffer whose number is in EXE$GW_ERLBUFHEAD. ERL$ALLOCEMB then increments ERL$GL_SEQUENCE; releases the EMB spinlock, restoring IPL; and returns an error status. Incrementing the error sequence number for each attempt to log an error facilitates the detection of messages lost in this way.

6. If the message fits into an allocation buffer, ERL$ALLOCEMB reserves an error message buffer of the requested size, advances the ERL$L_NEXT pointer, and increments the pending message count.

   In the error message buffer, it records information such as CPU ID, SCS node name, the size of the message buffer, number of its allocation buffer, contents of ERL$GL_SEQUENCE, and system time. It then increments the sequence number; releases the EMB spinlock, restoring IPL; and returns a success status, the error sequence number, and the address of the reserved message buffer.

When the component logging the error has written its information in the message buffer, it invokes ERL$RELEASEMB.

ERL$RELEASEMB takes the following steps:

1. It first acquires the EMB spinlock, raising IPL to 31, to synchronize access to the allocation buffer data structures.
2. It sets a flag in the error message buffer to indicate that this buffer is valid.

3. It extracts the number of the allocation buffer in which the message buffer was reserved and computes its address.

4. It subtracts 1 from the allocation buffer pending message count and adds 1 to the completed message count.

5. If the ERRFMT process is hibernating and there are ten or more completed messages in the allocation buffer, ERL$RELEASEMB forces a wakeup of the ERRFMT process.

6. It releases the EMB spinlock, restoring the previous IPL, and returns.

The routine ERL$WAKE, in module ERRORLOG, is invoked to wake the ERRFMT process. It is invoked once a second from EXE$TIMEOUT (see Chapter 11). ERL$WAKE does not necessarily wake the ERRFMT process. Rather, it decrements a counter at global location ERL$GB_BUFTIM and only wakes ERRFMT when the counter reaches zero.

When the counter reaches zero, it is reset to its starting value of 30. This value is an assembly time parameter, not a SYSGEN parameter. Thus, a maximum of 30 seconds can elapse before ERRFMT is awakened. This ensures that error messages are written to the error log file at reasonable intervals, even on systems with very few errors.

Both ERL$ALLOCEMB and ERL$RELEASEMB exploit this timing mechanism to force a wakeup of ERRFMT. These routines simply set ERL$GB_BUFTIM to 1 so that the next invocation of ERL$WAKE will wake ERRFMT. ERL$WAKE must acquire the SCHED spinlock to synchronize access to the scheduler database (see Chapters 8 and 12). Thus, it cannot be invoked with a higher ranking spinlock held or from an IPL higher than IPL$_SCHED. ERL$ALLOCEMB and ERL$RELEASEMB run at higher IPLs, holding the EMB spinlock, and are thus unable to invoke ERL$WAKE directly.

ERL$ALLOCEMB forces a wakeup whenever the current error log allocation buffer fills and it must switch to the next one. ERL$RELEASEMB forces a wakeup if the current message buffer contains ten or more messages.

If the ERRFMT process is not running, there is no way for error log messages to be written to the error log file. Initially, attempts to log errors by reserving error message buffers would be successful. However, once the error log allocation buffers fill with messages, any subsequent attempt to reserve an error message buffer fails. System operation is otherwise normal.

32.1.4 Device Driver Error Logging

It is not mandatory for device drivers to log errors, although, under most circumstances, it is good practice. To facilitate driver error logging, VMS provides several routines in module ERRORLOG that a driver can invoke to log errors. To use these routines, the driver and its tables must satisfy certain prerequisites, which are described in the *VMS Device Support Manual*.

Two commonly used routines are ERL$DEVICERR and ERL$DEVICTMO. Each of these logs an error associated with a particular I/O request. A

driver invokes ERL$DEVICERR to report a device-specific error and ERL$DE-
VICTMO to report a device timeout.

Each routine executes the following sequence:

1. The routine determines whether an error should be logged by testing that
   error logging is enabled on the device (bit DEV$V_ELG set in unit control
   block field UCB$L_DEVCHAR) and that error logging is not inhibited for
   this I/O request (bit IO$V_INHERLOG clear in UCB$W_FUNC). If either
   of these tests fails, the routine returns.
2. The routine increments UCB$W_ERRCNT, the cumulative number of
   errors that have occurred on the unit.
3. The routine then tests whether an error message is already in progress
   on the device (bit UCB$V_ERLOGIP set in UCB$W_STS) and returns if
   one is.
4. The routine invokes ERL$ALLOCEMB to reserve a message buffer. The
   size of the message buffer is device driver-specific and defined in the
   driver dispatch table field DDT$W_ERRORBUF. If the reservation fails,
   the routine returns. Otherwise, it records the address of the message
   buffer in UCB$L_EMB and sets bit UCB$V_ERLOGIP to indicate that an
   error message is in progress.
5. The routine records information common to all devices in the error message buffer, for example, unit number, device name, count of completed
   operations, error count, and I/O function.
6. The routine then invokes the device driver's register dump routine to
   write device-specific information in the error message buffer. Typically,
   this information consists of device register contents at the time of the
   error.
7. When the driver register dump routine returns, the error logging routine returns control to the device driver. When the device driver finishes
   processing the I/O request, it invokes IOC$REQCOM, in module IOSUB-
   NPAG.
8. IOC$REQCOM, finding that there is an error log message in progress,
   records the final I/O request status, device status, and error retry counters
   in the error log buffer. It then invokes ERL$RELEASEMB to indicate that
   the error message buffer has been completely written.

   Some device drivers report conditions that are not associated with a par-
ticular I/O request; such conditions are called device attention errors. The
CI port driver (PADRIVER), for example, reports an error if the port's mi-
crocode is not at the required revision level. To log such an error, a driver
invokes ERL$DEVICEATTN. This routine is similar to ERL$DEVICERR and
ERL$DEVICTMO in that it reserves and fills in an error message buffer.
However, the routine itself, rather than IOC$REQCOM, invokes ERL$RE-
LEASEMB to indicate that the message buffer is completely written.

In addition to ERL$DEVICEATTN, the system communication services (SCS) port and class drivers use several other error log routines:

- ERL$LOGSTATUS—Used by the disk and tape class drivers to log an error status code returned in a mass storage control protocol (MSCP) end packet. The end packet itself is written to the error log buffer with ERL$LOGMESSAGE.

- ERL$LOGMESSAGE—Used by the port and class drivers to log an error condition associated with a command packet, for example, a packet that contains invalid data or a hierarchical storage controller (HSC) error log datagram.

- ERL$LOG_DMSCP—Used by the disk class drivers (DUDRIVER and DSDRIVER) to log controller errors and resets.

- ERL$LOG_TMSCP—Similar to ERL$LOG_DMSCP, this is used by the tape class driver (TUDRIVER) to log controller errors and resets.

32.1.5 Other Error Log Messages

VMS uses the error log subsystem to record events other than device errors. Other kinds of entries written to the error log include the following:

- Warm start, a successful recovery from a power failure
- Cold start, a successful system bootstrap
- Fatal and nonfatal bugchecks (see Section 32.2)
- Machine check
- Memory and other CPU-specific errors
- Volume mount and dismount
- A user-requested message written by the Send Message to Error Logger ($SNDERR) system service (see Chapter 36)
- Time stamp (see Section 32.1.6)

32.1.6 The ERRFMT Process

During system initialization, the detached ERRFMT process is created with user identification code [1,6] and several privileges, including CMKRNL. ERRFMT runs in kernel and user mode. In kernel mode, it can access the error log allocation buffers and copy their contents to its own process space. In user mode, it scans the copied buffer contents for valid messages and writes them to the error log file SYS$ERRORLOG:ERRLOG.SYS.

When ERRFMT is first started, it enters kernel mode, using the Change to Kernel Mode ($CMKRNL) system service. It tests whether there are any error log allocation buffers restored from the dump file to be processed. If global location EXE$GL_SAVED_EMBS has nonzero contents, ERRFMT initializes several variables to indicate that there are saved error buffers that require processing in a later step.

It requests the Set Timer ($SETIMR) system service to request an asynchronous system trap (AST) notification in ten minutes. Its AST procedure invokes ERL$ALLOCEMB, writes a time stamp message containing the time of day, invokes ERL$RELEASEMB, and requests the $SETIMR system service again. Thus, every ten minutes, ERRFMT's kernel mode AST procedure writes a time stamp message to indicate that ERRFMT is executing and that the system is operational.

After kernel mode initialization is complete, ERRFMT returns to user mode and executes the following loop to process an error log allocation buffer:

1. ERRFMT changes mode to kernel and, in its kernel mode procedure, tries to select an error log allocation buffer to process:

   a. If there are multiple buffers restored from the dump file to be processed, it selects the first one in the buffer ring, advances the ring pointer, copies the buffer contents to P0 space, decrements the count of restored unprocessed buffers, and returns.

   b. If there is only one restored buffer left to be processed, ERRFMT copies its contents, deallocates the nonpaged pool occupied by the restored buffers, clears EXE$GL_SAVED_EMBS, and returns.

   c. If there are no restored buffers to be processed, ERRFMT acquires the EMB spinlock, raising IPL to 31. It determines the next error log allocation buffer to be processed and sets the lock flag in it to prevent any further reservations.

   d. It tests the pending message counter in the allocation buffer to determine whether there are error messages for which space has been reserved and not yet released.

   If there are pending messages, ERRFMT releases the EMB spinlock, lowering IPL to 0. It sets a timer and waits for half a second before testing the counter again. ERRFMT repeats its wait and test sequence until there are no more pending messages or until it has waited 255 times. It then reacquires the EMB spinlock.

   e. ERRFMT then copies the error log allocation buffer contents to its own P0 space and compares the copy to the original to detect any changes that might have occurred during the copy. If the two are not equal, ERRFMT repeats the copy, trying to get a consistent copy of the buffer contents. If necessary, it repeats the copy and compare sequence 255 times. This sequence is an alternative to copying the buffer contents with the EMB spinlock held and at IPL 31. If 255 attempts fail to get a consistent copy, ERRFMT uses the copy it has.

   f. Once ERRFMT has copied the allocation buffer contents, it reacquires the EMB spinlock, clears the pending and completed message counts in the copied buffer, and clears its lock flag. It updates EXE$GW_ERLBUFHEAD to point to the next allocation buffer, advancing it to the beginning of the ring if necessary. It releases the EMB spinlock, restoring the previous IPL.

      g. ERRFMT then returns to user mode with a status indicating whether there are any completed messages in the copied buffer.

2. In user mode, ERRFMT checks whether there are any completed messages to process. If there are none, ERRFMT hibernates until it is awakened through ERL$WAKE and then returns to the first step to select an error log allocation buffer.

3. If there are messages, ERRFMT processes the messages in the buffer, writing valid ones to the error log file. Whenever ERRFMT finds one of its time stamp messages, it checks whether the previous message written to the error log file is also a time stamp. If so, ERRFMT updates the record containing the older time stamp with the newer one. This avoids filling the error log file with time stamps and ensures that the newest time stamp is recorded. Note, however, that this can cause a sequence number gap in the error log file messages.

4. If ERRFMT detects a volume mounted or dismounted message in the error log buffer, it checks the SYSGEN parameter MOUNTMSG or DISMOUMSG. If the appropriate parameter is set, ERRFMT sends a volume mounted or dismounted message to terminals enabled as disk or tape operators. By default, the SYSGEN parameters are zero, disabling the sending of these messages to operator terminals.

5. If any process has declared an error log mailbox (see Section 32.1.7), ERRFMT writes every message in the error log buffer to that mailbox.

6. ERRFMT proceeds to the first step to select an error log allocation buffer.

32.1.7 Error Log Mailbox

The error logging subsystem provides the capability for up to five processes to monitor error logging activity as it happens, rather than wait for offline processing with the Error Log Utility. This capability is provided through the undocumented Declare Error Log Mailbox ($DERLMB) system service. This system service is provided for use only by Digital's software, such as the optional software products VAXsim and VAXsimPLUS, and is unsupported for any other use.

To assign an error log mailbox, a process with DIAGNOSE privilege requests the $DERLMB system service with the unit number of a mailbox to receive error log messages. A process requests this service with a unit number of zero to cancel its use of an error log mailbox.

The $DERLMB system service procedure, EXE$DERLMB in module SYSDERLMB, runs in kernel mode. It first tests whether the process has DIAGNOSE privilege; if it does not, the system service returns the error status SS$_NOPRIV. If it does, EXE$DERLMB scans the array of error log mailbox descriptors, which begins at EXE$AQ_ERLMBX. It synchronizes access to the array by acquiring the SCHED spinlock, raising IPL to IPL$_SCHED.

If the process is trying to assign an error log mailbox, EXE$DERLMB tries to find a free descriptor. If it finds one, it stores the unit number in the first word of the mailbox descriptor and the internal process ID (IPID) of the requesting process in the second longword. It releases the SCHED spinlock and returns the status SS$_NORMAL. Otherwise, if no descriptor is free, EXE$DERLMB releases the SCHED spinlock and returns the error status SS$_DEVALLOC.

If the process is trying to cancel use of an error log mailbox, EXE$DERLMB scans the descriptor array for the one associated with this process's IPID. If it finds one, it clears it. The Image Rundown ($RUNDWN) system service (see Chapter 26) performs a similar scan to ensure that error log mailbox use is canceled at image rundown.

32.2 SYSTEM CRASHES (FATAL BUGCHECKS)

When VMS detects an internal inconsistency, such as a corrupted data structure or an unexpected exception, it generates a bugcheck. If the inconsistency is not severe enough to prevent continued system operation, the bugcheck generated is nonfatal and merely results in an error log entry.

If the error is serious enough to jeopardize system operation and data integrity, a fatal bugcheck is generated. This generally results in aborting normal system operation, recording the contents of memory to a dump file for later analysis, and rebooting the system.

32.2.1 Bugcheck Mechanism

Source code generates a bugcheck by invoking the BUG_CHECK macro. The macro has one required argument, the bugcheck type, and one optional argument, the keyword FATAL. This macro expands into the two-byte opcode $FEFF_{16}$ and a one-word operand that identifies the bugcheck type and, in bits $\langle 2:0 \rangle$, its severity. If the keyword FATAL is present, the severity is set to the value STS$K_SEVERE; otherwise, it is zero.

This fatal bugcheck example is extracted from SCH$SCHED, in module SCHED:

```
QEMPTY: BUG_CHECK   QUEUEMPTY,FATAL
```

Its invocation generates the following code:

```
.WORD   ^XFEFF
.WORD   BUG$_QUEUEMPTY!4
```

The execution of the bugcheck opcode results in a reserved instruction exception (SS$_OPCDEC, opcode reserved to Digital), causing control to be transferred through the system control block (SCB) to the service routine for that exception, EXE$OPCDEC in module EXCEPTION.

EXE$OPCDEC checks whether the reserved opcode is either $FEFF_{16}$ or $FDFF_{16}$. The two-byte opcode $FEFF_{16}$ indicates that the bugcheck operand is a word. The two-byte opcode FDFF$_{16}$ indicates that the bugcheck operand is a longword. VMS does not currently use longword bugcheck operands.

If either opcode is present, EXE$OPCDEC interprets this exception as a bugcheck and transfers control to routine EXE$BUG_CHECK, in module BUGCHECKBT. Otherwise, the illegal opcode exception is treated in the usual manner, described in Chapter 5.

The actions of EXE$BUG_CHECK vary, depending on the access mode in which the bugcheck occurred and the severity of the bugcheck. EXE$BUG_CHECK first saves all the general registers on the stack. It then confirms the read accessibility of the bugcheck operand from the mode that generated the bugcheck and advances the exception program counter (PC) saved on the stack to point to the instruction following the bugcheck. (As a result, the bugcheck PC shown in a dump is an address four bytes higher than the actual bugcheck.) EXE$BUG_CHECK then determines in which access mode the bugcheck occurred.

32.2.2 Bugchecks from User and Supervisor Modes

VMS itself generates few bugchecks from user or supervisor mode. It provides the mechanism for use by other software. When a bugcheck is generated from either user or supervisor mode code running in a process with BUG-CHK privilege, EXE$BUG_CHECK writes an error log message, invoking ERL$ALLOCEMB and ERL$RELEASEMB. The error message resembles that shown in Table 32.2 but has an entry type of user-generated bugcheck and lacks the contents of CPU-specific registers.

If the bugcheck is fatal, EXE$BUG_CHECK restores the saved registers, executes an REI instruction to return to the access mode of the bugcheck, and requests the Exit ($EXIT) system service. The value SS$_BUGCHECK is the final image status. What happens as a result of this service request depends on whether the process is executing a single image (without a command language interpreter, CLI, to establish a supervisor mode exit handler) or is an interactive or batch job.

- If the process is executing a single image, a fatal bugcheck from user or supervisor mode typically results in process deletion.
- With the current use of supervisor mode exit handlers, a fatal bugcheck generated from an interactive or batch job causes the currently executing image to exit and control to be passed to the CLI to read the next command.

In either case, the only difference between user and supervisor mode is that user mode exit handlers are not called if a fatal bugcheck is generated from supervisor mode.

If the bugcheck is not fatal, EXE$BUG_CHECK restores the saved registers and executes an REI instruction. Execution continues with the instruction following the BUG_CHECK macro.

The SYSGEN parameter BUGCHECKFATAL has no effect on bugchecks generated from user or supervisor mode. The severity field in the bugcheck operand determines whether a given bugcheck is fatal. User and supervisor mode bugchecks affect only the current process.

32.2.3 Bugchecks from Executive and Kernel Modes

Various VMS components generate bugchecks from executive and kernel modes.

If an executive or kernel mode bugcheck operand is not fatal and the SYSGEN parameter BUGCHECKFATAL is zero, EXE$BUG_CHECK proceeds as it does for nonfatal bugchecks for the outer two access modes. It writes an error log entry, restores the general registers, and dismisses the exception, passing control back to the instruction following the BUG_CHECK macro.

The error log entry for a nonfatal bugcheck is identical to that for a fatal bugcheck (see Table 32.2) except that it has an entry type of system-generated bugcheck and lacks the contents of CPU-specific registers.

Typically, execution continues with no further effects. However, the routine that detects the error and generates the bugcheck can take further action. One example of such a routine is the last chance handler for executive mode exceptions. It generates the nonfatal bugcheck SSRVEXCEPT (unexpected system service exception). On the presumption that process data structures are inconsistent, it then requests the $EXIT system service. Exiting from executive mode results in process deletion.

In the case of a fatal bugcheck, EXE$BUG_CHECK's most important function is to record the contents of the error log allocation buffers and memory in the dump file. Later, during system initialization, error log messages in the dump file are copied to nonpaged pool for processing by the ERRFMT process. The dump file can be examined subsequently with the System Dump Analyzer (SDA) to determine the cause of the crash. EXE$BUG_CHECK also prevents any further system operations in case they might lead to data corruption. It halts the system and initiates a reboot.

If BUGCHECKFATAL is 1, any executive or kernel mode bugcheck is treated as fatal, independent of the severity bits in the bugcheck operand. By default, BUGCHECKFATAL is 0, which means that a nonfatal inner access mode bugcheck does not cause the system to crash. If either BUGCHECK-FATAL is 1 or the bugcheck is fatal, EXE$BUG_CHECK performs fatal bugcheck processing.

Section 32.2.4 describes the contents of the dump file, and Section 32.2.5 provides details about fatal bugcheck processing.

32.2.4 System Dump File

System initialization code locates and opens the dump file. The dump file must be in directory SYS$SPECIFIC:[SYSEXE] on the system disk so that each member of a VAXcluster system has a unique dump file. By default, the dump file is SYSDUMP.DMP. In its absence, VMS instead writes a dump to PAGEFILE.SYS, if it exists. (Subsequent analysis of a dump written to the page file requires that the SYSGEN parameter SAVEDUMP be 1.)

The dump file is divided into several distinct pieces:

1. The dump header is written to the first block of the file, virtual block number (VBN) 1. The dump header includes information that enables SDA to determine the state of the dump file and locate key information in it. The contents of this data structure are shown in Table 32.1. Symbolic offsets for the dump header field names are defined by the macro $DMPDEF in SYS$LIBRARY:STARLET.MLB.

2. The error log allocation buffers are written to the next blocks. The SYSGEN parameter ERLBUFFERPAGES specifies the number of blocks in each buffer. The SYSGEN parameter ERRORLOGBUFFERS specifies how many buffers there are.

3. The rest of the dump file is filled with memory contents.

Note that the dump header includes an error log entry. The entry associated with a fatal bugcheck is recorded in the header to avoid loss of information in case the error log allocation buffers are full when the bugcheck occurs.

Table 32.2 shows the contents of an error log entry for a fatal bugcheck. The macros $EMBHDDEF and $EMBCRDEF define symbolic offsets for fields in this error log entry.

After the system reboots, SYSINIT (see Chapter 31) copies the fatal bugcheck error log entry to nonpaged pool, along with the error log allocation buffers saved in the dump file. It stores their starting address in global location EXE$GL_SAVED_EMBS. Later, the ERRFMT process will record them in the error log file.

In earlier versions of VMS, a dump was always a dump of physical memory. A physical dump generally requires that all physical memory be written to the dump file to ensure the presence of the system page table (SPT). In a typical VMS configuration, the SPT, required for virtual address translation, is allocated in high physical memory (see Chapter 30). Since a dump of physical memory is written in order by memory addresses, with lowest first, an undersized dump file is likely to lack the SPT.

A partial dump without the SPT is useless and cannot be analyzed by SDA. The size of the file required for a complete dump of physical memory is the sum of one block for the header, ERRORLOGBUFFERS times ERLBUFFERPAGES blocks for the error log buffers, and as many blocks as there are physical pages of memory being used. If MA780 shared memory is present on the system, the dump file must be large enough to include its contents as well.

VMS Version 5.0 introduces an alternative form of crash dump—a dump

Table 32.1 Contents of the Dump Header

Description	Size
Last error log sequence number	Longword
Dump file flags	Word

Meaning if Set	*Bit Position*
Dump file has been analyzed	0
Dump has no valid data	1
Error occurred writing header	2
Error occurred writing error log buffers	3
Error occurred writing memory	4
Error occurred writing system page table	5
Dump completely written	6
Header and error log buffers completely written	7
Dump style	8–11
0 = full physical memory dump	
1 = selective memory dump	
Unused	12–15

Unused	Byte
Number of pages in each error log buffer	Byte
Contents of SBR, SLR, KSP, ESP, SSP, USP, ISP	7 longwords
Quadword descriptors for eight memory controllers	8 quadwords
• Page count	3 bytes
• Transfer request number for this controller	Byte
• Base page frame number (PFN) for this controller	Longword
System version number	Longword
One's complement of previous longword	Longword
Dump file version (contains 0520_{16} for VMS Version 5.2)	Word
Number of error log allocation buffers	Word
Index of error log buffer ring head	Word
Index of error log buffer ring tail	Word
Last I/O status from writing the dump	Longword
Number of errors that occurred writing the dump	Longword
Number of pages of memory in the dump	Longword
Number of processes written in selective dump	Longword
Error log entry for fatal bugcheck (see Table 32.2)	78 longwords

of selected virtual address space. This alternative makes possible a dump of a system with more physical memory than dump file space.

In a selective dump, related pages of virtual address space are written to the dump file as a unit called a logical memory block (LBN). For example, one logical memory block consists of the system and global page tables; another is the address space of a particular process. Those logical memory

Table 32.2   Contents of Error Log Entry for Fatal Bugcheck (CRASH CPU)

Description	Size
Error message buffer header	5 bytes
• Size in bytes of buffer	Word
• Allocation buffer number	Word
• Error message valid indicator	Byte
System ID of CRASH CPU	Longword
Error message header revision level (contains FFFC$_{16}$)	Word
Extended system ID information from CRASH CPU	Longword
ID of CRASH CPU	Longword
Device class (unused)	Byte
Device type (unused)	Byte
SCS node name	16 bytes
Flags	Word
Operating system ID	Byte
Header size	Byte
Entry type (contains EMB$K_CR = 25$_{16}$)	Word
System time when crash occurred (from EXE$GQ_SYSTIME)	Quadword
Error log sequence number (low-order word of ERL$GL_ SEQUENCE)	Word
Software version	Quadword
Error type mask	Longword
Contents of KSP, ESP, SSP, USP, ISP from CRASH CPU	5 longwords
Contents of R0 to R11, AP, FP, SP, PC, PSL from CRASH CPU	17 longwords
Contents of P0BR, P0LR, P1BR, P1LR, SBR, SLR, PCBB, SCBB, ASTLVL, SISR, ICCS from CRASH CPU	11 longwords
Contents of CPU-specific registers from CRASH CPU	24 longwords
Bugcheck operand on CRASH CPU	Longword
ID of process current on CRASH CPU	Longword
Name of process current on CRASH CPU	16 bytes

blocks likely to be most useful in crash dump analysis are written first. Section 32.2.5.2 describes logical memory blocks in more detail.

A value of 1 for the SYSGEN parameter DUMPSTYLE specifies a selective crash dump; the parameter's default value is 0. If DUMPSTYLE is 1, 127 system page table entries (SPTEs) are allocated during system initialization for later use in writing a selective dump. If these SPTEs cannot be allocated, DUMPSTYLE is zeroed to specify that a physical dump be taken.

32.2.5 Fatal Bugcheck Processing

The code that performs fatal bugcheck processing and its data are not resident and are not referenced during normal system operation. They are within the pageable part of the executive image EXCEPTION.EXE. When needed, they are read into memory, overlaying nonpaged read-only executive code.

The decision that fatal bugcheck code be nonresident saves a considerable amount of memory during normal operations. It results, however, in some added complexity during the infrequent occurrence of a fatal bugcheck. Another implication is that the executive code overlaid by the fatal bugcheck code cannot subsequently be examined in the dump. It is thus possible that some part of the causal sequence that led to the crash may be unavailable. However, this is judged to be a low-probability event relative to the frequency with which the extra memory is useful.

The fatal bugcheck overlay includes the nonresident portion of EXE$BUG_CHECK, in module BUGCHECKLD; a table of all bugcheck codes; and two pages containing the bugcheck message text associated with the fatal bugcheck. One additional page of executive is used as a data buffer. The bugcheck overlay and its data buffers are shown in Figure 32.2.

EXE$BUG_CHECK does not use standard I/O mechanisms to read the fatal bugcheck overlay or write the dump because they may be affected by the system inconsistency that triggered the fatal bugcheck. Instead, it calls the bootstrap system device driver for all its I/O. The bootstrap system device driver is the one used during system initialization (see Chapter 30). Furthermore, EXE$BUG_CHECK cannot request the file system to look up the image containing the fatal bugcheck code or the dump file. Instead, it uses information about their locations that was recorded and checksummed at system initialization.

Before reading the fatal bugcheck overlay, EXE$BUG_CHECK takes the following steps:

1. It validates the checksum of the boot control block, the data structure containing the locations of the bugcheck overlay and dump file. If the boot control block checksum is no longer valid, EXE$BUG_CHECK clears a flag tested in a later step.
2. On a symmetric multiprocessing (SMP) system, the first CPU to execute EXE$BUG_CHECK is called the CRASH CPU. It informs the other CPUs

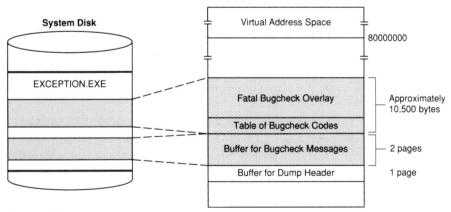

Figure 32.2
Fatal Bugcheck Overlay

that a fatal bugcheck is in progress and takes a number of steps to ensure that a consistent system state can be saved. After these steps, the primary CPU in the system assumes the context of the CRASH CPU and completes fatal bugcheck processing. Chapter 34 contains further details on fatal bugcheck processing in an SMP system.

3. EXE$BUG_CHECK invokes SCS$SHUTDOWN, in module [SYSLOA] SCSLOA, to shut down any SCS circuits.

4. It invokes EXE$SHUTDWNADP to shut down all adapters and invokes EXE$INIBOOTADP to initialize the adapter containing the system device. These routines are in the CPU-specific module [SYSLOA]ERR-SUB*xxx*, where *xxx* identifies the CPU type (see Appendix G).

5. It invokes INI$WRITABLE to change the protection of the pages containing nonpaged read-only sections of loaded executive images so that they can be overwritten by the bugcheck overlay.

6. It calls the device initialization routine in the bootstrap driver.

7. EXE$BUG_CHECK scans the list of loaded executive images for one containing a nonpaged code section large enough for the bugcheck overlay and its data buffers. It skips over those executive images that contain routines used by the bugcheck overlay.

8. EXE$BUG_CHECK then tests whether the boot control block was found to be valid. If not, it reboots the system.

EXE$BUG_CHECK calls the bootstrap driver to read the first page of the nonresident bugcheck code and transfers control to a routine within it which reads the rest of the overlay. (For simplicity, the name EXE$BUG_CHECK is used here to refer to both the resident and nonresident bugcheck code.) If an I/O error occurs while the nonresident bugcheck code is being read, EXE$BUG_CHECK writes an error message on the console terminal and reboots the system.

Before writing to the dump file, the routine takes the following steps:

1. It determines the block number in EXCEPTION.EXE that contains the start of the bugcheck message associated with the bugcheck type. It reads that block and, in case the message spans blocks, the next block.

2. It builds the error log message in the dump header buffer, invoking the CPU-specific routine EXE$DUMPCPUREG, in module [SYSLOA] ERRSUB*xxx*, to copy CPU-specific processor registers to the error log message.

3. If this is an operator-requested shutdown bugcheck, EXE$BUG_CHECK skips the next step.

4. EXE$BUG_CHECK writes information about the bugcheck to the console terminal. This information includes the bugcheck message, addresses of the loaded executive images, current process name, and contents of general registers and stacks relevant to the crash. On an SMP

system, EXE$BUG_CHECK writes additional information, such as which CPUs are active and which CPU incurred the fatal bugcheck.

The console output is written before the dump file and should not be interrupted by halting the VAX processor from the console terminal. Such an interruption prevents the dump file from being written.

5. Next, EXE$BUG_CHECK determines whether a dump is to be written and, if so, what kind of dump:

    —If the SYSGEN parameter DUMPBUG is 0, no dump is written. (Its default value is 1.)

    —If the boot control block was found to be invalid, no dump is written.

    —If neither SYSDUMP.DMP nor PAGEFILE.SYS existed in the directory SYS$SPECIFIC:[SYSEXE] at boot time, no dump is written.

    —If this is an operator-requested shutdown generated through the system shutdown command procedure, only the dump header and error log allocation buffers are written to the dump file. (This behavior is new with VMS Version 5.0.)

    —If the parameter DUMPSTYLE is 1, memory is dumped selectively; otherwise, a full memory dump is written. (The default value of this parameter is 0.)

6. If no dump is to be written, EXE$BUG_CHECK concludes with the steps described in Section 32.2.5.3.

7. If any type of dump is to be written, EXE$BUG_CHECK next writes the dump header and the contents of the error log allocation buffers to the dump file. After successfully writing the error log buffers, it rewrites the dump header with a status indicating that the dump contains them.

8. If the system is being shut down and no further dump is necessary, EXE$BUG_CHECK concludes with the steps in Section 32.2.5.3. Otherwise, it determines whether a physical or selective dump is to be written. The following two sections describe its actions in writing these different types of memory dumps.

32.2.5.1   **Physical Memory Dump.** EXE$BUG_CHECK uses the memory descriptors in the restart parameter block constructed by VMB (see Chapter 30) to provide an accurate description of physical address space. It uses the contents of the global MMG$GL_MAXMEM as the largest PFN that should be written to the dump file. This global is initialized as the highest page in use by VMS. If the SYSGEN parameter PHYSICALPAGES has been set to fewer pages of memory than are available, VMS only uses the lowest PHYSICALPAGES of memory.

Writing 127 physical pages at a time, EXE$BUG_CHECK writes memory contents to the dump file. It begins writing to the block following the dump header and error log allocation buffers and continues until it gets to the end

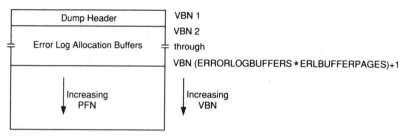

Figure 32.3
Layout of a Physical Memory Dump

of the dump file or until it has written all of the physical memory in use by
VMS. Figure 32.3 shows the layout of a physical memory dump.

32.2.5.2 **Selective Memory Dump.** In a selective dump, related pages of virtual
address space are written to the dump file as a unit called a logical memory
block. A list in EXE$BUG_CHECK explicitly specifies the order in which
logical memory blocks are written to the dump file, as follows:

1. The system and global page tables.
2. System space. This excludes the system and global page tables and those
   pages overwritten by the bugcheck overlay and its data. It includes any
   system transition pages, pages that are invalid but on the free or modified
   list.
3. Global pages in use at the time of the crash.
4. The per-process address space of the process current at the time of the
   crash, excluding global pages and including any of its pages on the free
   and modifed lists. (On an SMP system, the address space of the process
   current on the CRASH CPU is written in this step.)
5. The per-process address spaces of the following processes, in the order
   specified:

   a. MSCPmount
   b. NETACP
   c. REMACP
   d. LES$ACP
   e. On an SMP system, processes current on other active CPUs
   f. Other resident processes, in order by process index

Following the dump header and error log allocation buffers, EXE$BUG_
CHECK writes logical memory blocks to the dump file until it is full or the
end of the list is reached.

Each logical memory block in a dump begins with a descriptor that identifies the block and gives its size. The range of addresses to be included in a
block is determined by the particular address space being dumped.

Not all virtual addresses in the range spanned by a logical memory block are necessarily included in it. Because nonresident pages (those not currently in memory) are not dumpable, a nonresident page is a hole in the address space. In the case of a process logical memory block, a global page is also a hole, because global pages are all dumped together in the global page logical memory block.

A logical memory block with holes in its address space contains a hole table, which lists the pages of address space not present in the dump. The rest of the block consists of pages of address space in order by ascending address. Figure 32.4 shows the organization of a logical memory block and the layout of a typical selective dump.

EXE$BUG_CHECK's general sequence in writing a logical memory block is the following:

1. It writes a logical memory block descriptor in the next block of the dump.
2. It scans the page tables that describe the address space to be dumped, looking for invalid pages that are not transition pages. It writes an entry in a hole table for each such sequence of pages found. It writes the hole table to the next block (or blocks) of the dump. (Chapter 14 describes the different PTE forms.)
3. EXE$BUG_CHECK scans the page tables again, filling in its 127 SPTEs with information from each valid or transition PTE found. That is, it double-maps those pages so that it can write 127 virtually noncontiguous pages in one I/O request.
4. When EXE$BUG_CHECK has written all the valid and transition pages in a particular logical memory block to the dump file, it rewrites the block containing the descriptor with correct information about the number of holes in the address space and the number of data blocks (valid and transition pages) in the logical memory block.

Generally, EXE$BUG_CHECK reaches the end of a file sized for selective dumps before it reaches the end of the logical memory block list. When it does, it rewrites the descriptor of the current logical memory block with the hole count and actual number of data blocks written. It then rewrites the dump header, filling in status information such as number of I/O errors encountered writing the dump file, whether the SPT was dumped, how many process logical memory blocks were written, and so on.

Note that a selective dump to the page file is not likely to survive system initialization. For a dump in a page file to remain intact until it can be copied, there must be 452 additional blocks in the page file available for paging. If there are not, SYSINIT releases for paging the blocks occupied by the dump. Because EXE$BUG_CHECK typically continues to write a selective dump until there is no more room, there is no way for the system manager to ensure that 452 blocks of page file will remain unoccupied by the dump.

In writing a selective dump, EXE$BUG_CHECK must defend against the

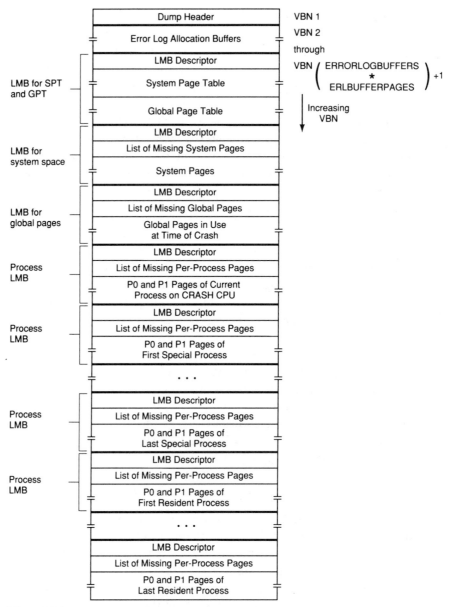

Figure 32.4
Layout of a Selective Memory Dump

possibility that whatever error led to the bugcheck corrupted the data structures necessary to write virtual address space. It replaces the page fault and access violation exception service routines with its own routines to prevent recursive bugchecks if either of those errors occur. It also performs consistency checks on certain key data structures. For example, it checks that an address presumed to be that of a process header is "syntactically" correct;

that is, it must be within known address boundaries and at an integral number of process headers from the beginning of the address range.

32.2.5.3   **Final Fatal Bugcheck Processing.** The last step in EXE$BUG_CHECK either loops or reboots the system. If the SYSGEN parameter BUGREBOOT is 0, EXE$BUG_CHECK writes a message on the console terminal and loops at IPL 31, waiting for a command to be entered at the console terminal. If BUGREBOOT is 1, its default value, EXE$BUG_CHECK reboots the system by invoking the routine CON$SENDCONSCMD, in module OPDRIVER, to send a special boot command to the console and halt. When the HALT instruction is executed, the console subsystem gains control and processes the boot command.

32.3   **MACHINE CHECK MECHANISM**

A machine check is an exception that is reported when CPU microcode detects an internal error during the attempted execution of an instruction. Machine check errors are CPU-specific; possible types of machine checks include memory cache parity error, translation buffer parity error, and CPU timeout. Many, but not all, machine checks are caused by some sort of hardware condition. Some hardware conditions are transient; others are persistent.

During a machine check exception, CPU microcode logs information, called the machine check frame, on the interrupt stack. The machine check frame identifies the type of machine check and includes the contents of relevant CPU registers. Its exact form varies on each type of CPU. Consult CPU-specific literature for information on the form of the machine check frame and the layout of the associated CPU registers.

A machine check exception is dispatched through the SCB to a machine check exception service routine. The exception is serviced on the interrupt stack at IPL 31. On an SMP system, the machine check exception service routine acquires the MCHECK spinlock as needed, for example, to serialize access to VAX bus interconnect (VAXBI) or memory controller registers.

The actual exception service routine is contained in the CPU-specific image SYSLOA*xxx* and is loaded during system initialization. The module name has the form MCHECK*yyy*. Appendix G describes the possible values for these CPU- and system-specific suffixes.

The actual processing of a machine check exception is CPU-specific. This section contains only an overview of machine check handling common to all CPU types.

VMS determines from the machine check frame what type of machine check occurred. Although VMS treats each type of machine check somewhat differently, its general response is to log an error and increment the global counter EXE$GL_MCHKERRS. The Digital command language command SHOW ERROR displays the contents of this counter as CPU errors.

VMS then determines whether the error is recoverable. Recoverability depends on whether the machine check exception was a fault or an abort. In the case of a fault, register and memory operands have been restored to their state prior to the attempted execution of the instruction. In the case of an abort, they cannot be restored, and it is therefore impossible to restart the instruction. Recoverability also depends on whether the instruction is a resumable one. The details of recoverability are CPU-specific.

The basic philosophy of the machine check service routine is to keep the system running if possible. How serious a particular machine check is depends upon whether it is recoverable and the access mode in which the machine check occurred. If the machine check is recoverable, the service routine takes any needed recovery action, removes the machine check frame from the interrupt stack, and executes an REI to dismiss the exception and return control to the instruction that incurred the exception.

If the machine check is not recoverable, the action taken by the machine check handler depends on the access mode in which the machine check occurred. If the previous mode was supervisor or user, a machine check exception is reported to that access mode. (Unless the process has declared a condition handler for this type of exception, this step results in image exit.) If the previous mode was executive or kernel, the machine check service routine generates the fatal bugcheck MACHINECHK.

On some CPUs, some machine checks are asynchronous, such that the actual PC and access mode at the time of the error cannot be determined. In such a case, VMS, acting to protect the integrity of the system, makes the conservative assumption that the access mode was kernel or executive and bugchecks. One example of such an error is a memory parity error on a MicroVAX II processor.

32.3.1 Machine Check Protection Mechanism

VMS provides the capability for a block of kernel mode code to protect itself from machine checks while executing and to discover whether a machine check occurred during the protected sequence of code. For example, this feature is used if an interrupt is generated from a previously unconfigured adapter. The code that services the interrupt must access the adapter's registers. If the interrupt is spurious, this may mean referencing nonexistent I/O space. In this context, a machine check caused by such a reference must not result in a system crash.

The code to be protected is called a machine check recovery block. There are several restrictions on such a block:

- It must be executing in kernel mode.
- The stack cannot be used across the entry into or the exit out of the recovery block. This restriction exists because a co-routine mechanism

is used to pass control between the recovery block and the VMS routines that establish it.

• Because VMS elevates IPL to 31, only a limited number of instructions should be included in the block. Note that no spinlock acquisition is required; the code is protecting against a possible machine check on the same CPU on which it executes.

• The contents of R0 are overwritten by the mechanism.

The basis for the machine check protection mechanism is several routines in the module EXCEPTION_PRIMITIVES and two data cells in the per-CPU database. The kernel mode code to be protected must invoke the two macros described in the following paragraphs.

The first macro generates code that dispatches to EXE$MCHK_PRTCT to define the beginning of the block:

```
$PRTCTINI    LABEL,MASK
```

The label argument is identical to the label argument associated with the second macro that defines the end of the block. This macro generates code that returns to EXE$MCHK_PRTCT to define the end of the block:

```
$PRTCTEND    LABEL
```

If no error occurred while the protected code was executing, R0 contains the success status SS$_NORMAL. Otherwise, R0 contains the error status SS$_MCHECK.

The mask argument allows the block of code to protect itself from different classes of errors. The $MCHKDEF macro defines the following specific types of protection:

Protection Name	Description
MCHK$M_LOG	Inhibit error logging for the error
MCHK$M_MCK	Protect against machine checks
MCHK$M_NEXM	Protect against nonexistent memory
MCHK$M_UBA	Protect against UNIBUS adapter error interrupts

Invoking the following macro enables kernel mode code to determine whether a recovery block is in effect and to take action accordingly:

```
$PRTCTEST    ADDRESS,MASK
```

This macro invokes the routine EXE$MCHK_TEST, which returns status in R0. The low bit set in R0 indicates that a recovery block is in effect and that the specified mask is being used. This routine is typically used to determine whether a machine check should be logged in the error log.

Another related routine, EXE$MCHK_BUGCHK, is invoked from a machine check exception service routine to determine whether a recovery block is in effect. If no block is in effect, the routine returns, usually to code that generates a bugcheck. If a block is in effect, the routine returns control to the end of the protected block, with R0 containing an error code of SS$_ MCHECK.

32.4 CPU-SPECIFIC ERROR INTERRUPTS

Five vectors in the SCB, at offsets 50_{16} through 60_{16}, are reserved for CPU-specific system bus and memory errors. These interrupts occur at CPU-specific IPLs within the range 18_{16} through $1D_{16}$. Not all processors implement all five interrupts.

VMS services these interrupts in the CPU-specific image SYSLOA*xxx*. The actual interrupt service routines are contained in the CPU-specific module MCHECK*yyy*. Appendix G describes the possible values for these CPU- and system-specific suffixes.

In general, VMS servicing of these interrupts is done at IPL 31 and includes logging an error to the error log. On an SMP system, a CPU-specific error interrupt service routine acquires the MCHECK spinlock as needed, for example, to serialize access to VAXBI or memory controller registers. This serializes access among a CPU-specific error interrupt service routine running on one CPU and both CPU-specific error interrupt and machine check exception service routines running on other CPUs.

33 Power Failure and Recovery

For there are moments when one can neither think nor feel.
And if one can neither think nor feel, she thought, where
is one?

Virginia Woolf, *To the Lighthouse*

Powerfail recovery support enables a suitably equipped VMS system to survive power fluctuations and power outages of short duration with no loss of operation. The support is provided by hardware features (battery backup) and VMS software routines.

VMS support includes a powerfail service routine that saves the volatile state of the machine when the power fails, a restart routine that restores that state when the power is restored, CPU-specific initialization code, and device-specific code within many VMS device drivers. The VMS software also provides process notification by means of power recovery asynchronous system traps (ASTs).

33.1 POWERFAIL SEQUENCE

When the CPU hardware detects a drop in operating voltage, it requests a powerfail interrupt at interrupt priority level (IPL) 30. The VAX architecture specifies that this interrupt dispatch through the vector at offset $0C_{16}$ in the system control block (SCB). This vector contains the address of the VMS powerfail interrupt service routine, EXE$POWERFAIL in module POWERFAIL. Because powerfail is an interrupt rather than an exception, code executing at IPL 30 or 31 can block powerfail notification. Some VMS routines deliberately execute at IPL 31 for short instruction sequences to avoid potential synchronization problems.

Main memory is preserved by battery backup. EXE$POWERFAIL saves the volatile machine state, those registers whose contents are not preserved by some sort of battery backup, in main memory. EXE$POWERFAIL itself saves registers common to all types of VAX processors. To save CPU-specific registers, it invokes the routine EXE$REGSAVE, in module [SYSLOA]ERRSUB*xxx*, part of the CPU-specific image SYSLOA*xxx*. Appendix G contains the SYSLOA image names for particular processors.

Some of a CPU's registers are saved on its interrupt stack, some in its per-CPU database, and some in the restart parameter block (RPB). The CPU's interrupt stack pointer (ISP) is the last value saved. Checking the value of the saved ISP in the per-CPU database, the restart routine can determine whether the interrupt service routine preserved all the required registers.

Once the registers have been saved, EXE$POWERFAIL waits at IPL 31 in the following tight loop until the CPU ceases all operations:

```
10$:     BRB      10$
```

The BRB instruction was chosen over an explicit HALT to avoid triggering a restart before the CPU stops.

Tables 33.1 and 33.2 list the registers preserved by EXE$POWERFAIL and restored at powerfail recovery.

33.2 POWER RECOVERY

The console subsystem power recovery logic performs validity checks in a CPU-dependent fashion and then passes control to the VMS restart routine on the primary CPU. This routine restores the saved state of the machine, restarts the secondary CPUs that were active prior to the power failure, and notifies each device driver in the system that power has failed and been restored, so that the drivers can take device-specific action to restore interrupted I/O requests.

33.2.1 Initial Step in Power Recovery

The initial step in recovery from a power failure is performed by the CPU-specific console subsystem. It performs the following tasks:

1. Initializes the CPU
2. Verifies that the contents of memory survived the power outage
3. Locates the restart routine through the RPB
4. Passes control to that routine

The RPB is a page of physical memory whose first four longwords contain the physical address of the RPB, the physical address of the restart routine, the checksum of the first 31 longwords in the restart routine, and a warm restart inhibit flag. On most systems, the RPB is located at physical address 0.

When searching for the RPB, the console subsystem looks for a longword on a page boundary that contains its own address. The console subsystem examines the second longword to determine that it contains a valid physical address (and not zero, in case a page of zeros passes the first test). If the address is acceptable, the checksum of the first 31 longwords of the restart routine is calculated. The checksum is then compared to the checksum in the RPB. If the two checksums are equal, the page contains an RPB and the restart routine is intact.

The sections that follow contain further information about power recovery on each type of VAX processor. Many VAX processors have two control panel switches whose settings affect powerfail recovery: a Console Enable switch and a Restart Action switch. The Console Enable switch allows or inhibits command entry on the local console terminal. The descriptions that follow assume that the local console terminal is enabled.

Table 33.1   Data Saved by EXE$POWERFAIL and Restored During
Power Recovery

The elements in Group A are restored before memory management is
reenabled. The RPB is accessed through its physical address.

GROUP A

Element	*Where Stored*
System base register (SBR)	RPB
System length register (SLR)	RPB
System control block base register (SCBB)	Per-CPU database

The elements in Group B are restored after memory management has been
reenabled, which allows the RPB, interrupt stack, and per-CPU database to
be accessed through system virtual addresses.

GROUP B

Element	*Where Stored*
Interrupt stack pointer	Per-CPU database
Process control block base register (PCBB)	Per-CPU database
Software interrupt summary register (SISR)	Per-CPU database
P1 length register (P1LR)	Interrupt stack
P1 base register (P1BR)	Interrupt stack
P0 length register (P0LR)	Interrupt stack
P0 base register (P0BR)	Interrupt stack
AST level register (ASTLR)	Interrupt stack
Four per-process stack pointers	Interrupt stack
CPU-specific processor registers (see Table 33.2)	Interrupt stack

The elements in Group C are not restored until the other power recovery
steps described in the text are performed and the powerfail interrupt is
dismissed. The program counter (PC) and processor status longword (PSL)
are restored by the REI instruction that dismisses the interrupt.

GROUP C

Element	*Where Stored*
General registers (R0 through FP)	Interrupt stack
Interrupt PC	Interrupt stack
Interrupt PSL	Interrupt stack

Table 33.2 CPU-Specific Registers Saved at Powerfail

Register[1]	*CPU*
Performance monitor enable register	VAX-11/730
Performance monitor enable register	VAX-11/750
Translation buffer disable register	VAX-11/750
Memory cache disable register	VAX-11/750
Performance monitor enable register	VAX-11/78x
Synchronous backplane interconnect (SBI) maintenance register	VAX-11/78x
Performance monitor enable register	VAX 8200 family
Translation buffer disable register	VAX 8200 family
Memory cache disable register	VAX 8200 family
Performance monitor enable register	VAX 86x0
Cache state register	VAX 86x0
Fbox state register	VAX 86x0
Performance monitor enable register	VAX 8800 family, VAX 88x0
Cache on register	VAX 8800 family, VAX 88x0
Cache disable register	VAX 6000 model 200/300
None[2]	VAX 6000 model 400
None	VAXstation 3520/40
None[3]	MicroVAX processors

[1] These CPU-specific processor registers are saved on and restored from the per-CPU interrupt stack.

[2] In VMS Version 5.2, the register save routine for a VAX 6000 model 400 CPU clears the bit corresponding to its CPU ID in CCA$Q_RESTARTIP.

[3] Power failure recovery is not implemented on MicroVAX processors.

Chapter 30 provides more detail on the various implementations of the console subsystem.

33.2.1.1 **Power Recovery on a VAX-11/730 Processor.** When power is restored on a VAX-11/730 processor, the console subsystem tests whether the Auto Restart/Boot switch on the front of the processor cabinet is in the OFF position. If it is, the console subsystem simply prompts on the console terminal and waits for input. (Note that the Auto Restart/Boot switch on the front panel should be switched off when first turning on a VAX-11/730 system to avoid an unnecessary restart attempt.)

If the Auto Restart/Boot switch is in the ON position, the console subsystem searches through physical memory for a valid RPB. In searching for the RPB, it tests whether the contents of memory survived the power outage. Memory contents can fail to be backed up for two reasons:

- Because the system does not have battery backup, the contents of memory are lost when the power fails.

- Because the power is off for longer than the battery backup could preserve memory contents, the contents of memory are lost when the battery backup fails. (This time depends on the amount of memory present but is generally not shorter than ten minutes.)

If the RPB is not located, the restart fails and the console subsystem attempts to bootstrap the system by executing the command procedure DEFBOO.CMD.

If the RPB is located, the warm restart inhibit flag (bit ⟨0⟩ in the fourth longword of the RPB) is checked. If set, it indicates that a warm restart was attempted and failed. In that case, the console subsystem then executes the command procedure DEFBOO.CMD to bootstrap the system.

If the warm restart inhibit flag is clear, the console subsystem performs the following steps:

1. Sets the warm restart inhibit flag to prevent a second restart attempt before the first has succeeded
2. Loads the stack pointer (SP) register with the address of the RPB plus 200_{16}
3. Loads the argument pointer (AP) register with a value indicating the cause of the halt
4. Loads R10 and R11 with the PC and PSL at the time of the halt for use in servicing error halt conditions other than powerfail
5. Transfers control to the restart routine whose address is in the second longword of the RPB

33.2.1.2 **Power Recovery on a VAX-11/750 Processor.** When power is restored on a VAX-11/750 processor, the console subsystem tests the setting of the Power-on Action switch on the front of the processor cabinet. If the switch is in either the HALT or BOOT position, the console subsystem performs the designated action. If the switch is in either the RESTART/BOOT or RESTART/HALT position, the console subsystem attempts a restart. The second option (BOOT or HALT) is used only if the restart fails.

For a restart, the console subsystem first tries to locate the RPB. In searching for the RPB, it tests whether the contents of memory survived the power outage.

If a valid RPB cannot be located or if the warm restart inhibit flag is set, the restart attempt fails and the console subsystem takes its alternative option. For the BOOT alternative, the console subsystem executes bootstrap read-only memory (ROM) code for unit 0 of the device identified by the device switch on the cabinet. The ROM code reads the boot block, block 0, from that device and then transfers control to it. Chapter 30 provides more information.

If a valid RPB is located, the console subsystem transfers control to the restart routine, as described in Section 33.2.1.1.

987

33.2.1.3   **Power Recovery on VAX-11/780 and VAX-11/785 Processors.** When power is restored on a VAX-11/780 or VAX-11/785 processor, the console subsystem (LSI-11) performs the same sequence as when a system is being initialized (see Chapter 30). If power is also being restored on the LSI-11, CONSOL.SYS is loaded from the console floppy into the LSI-11 memory. No state for the LSI-11 is preserved across a power failure.

The console subsystem then tests the Auto Restart switch on the front of the processor cabinet. If it is in the OFF position or if the warm restart inhibit flag is set, the console subsystem simply prompts on the console terminal and waits for input.

If the Auto Restart switch is in the ON position and the warm restart inhibit flag is clear, the console subsystem executes the command procedure RESTAR.CMD, located on the console floppy. Before it executes RESTAR.CMD, it reloads the CPU microcode writable control store (WCS) contents from the console floppy (from file WCSxxx.PAT). WCS is not preserved by memory battery backup.

The standard RESTAR.CMD command procedure contains commands designed to restart a running VMS system. RESTAR.CMD generally contains the following lines:

```
HALT                        ! Halt processor
INIT                        ! Initialize processor
DEPOSIT/I 11 20003800       ! Set address of SCB base
DEPOSIT R0 0                ! Clear unused register
DEPOSIT R1 3                ! TR number for UNIBUS adapter
DEPOSIT R2 0                ! Clear unused register
DEPOSIT R3 0                ! Clear unused register
DEPOSIT R4 0                ! Clear unused register
DEPOSIT R5 0                ! Clear unused register
DEPOSIT FP 0               ! No machine check expected
START 20003004              ! Start restart referee
```

On systems with more than two memory controllers, the UNIBUS adapter (UBA) is not located at TR 3. For such a system, RESTAR.CMD must be altered so that R1 is loaded with the TR number of the UBA. This step is necessary because the UBA map registers are used by ROM restart code as temporary storage.

The START command passes control to the same ROM program that is used during system initialization except that the program is entered at its restart entry point. The ROM program determines whether the contents of main memory are valid. If they are, the ROM program attempts to locate the RPB.

If a valid RPB cannot be found or if the warm restart inhibit flag in the RPB is set, the ROM program sends a Boot (cold start) command to the console subsystem by executing the following instruction:

```
MTPR    #^XF02,#PR$_TXDB
```

988

The special uses of the PR$_TXDB register for communication from the VAX CPU to the console program are described in Chapter 24.

If a valid RPB is found, the ROM program passes control to the restart routine as described in Section 33.2.1.1.

33.2.1.4   **Power Recovery on VAX 8200 Family Processors.** When power is restored on a VAX 8200 family member, the console subsystem tests the settings of the upper and lower key switches on the front of the processor cabinet. If the upper switch is in either the ENABLE or SECURE position and the lower switch is in the AUTO START position, the console subsystem attempts a restart.

The console microcode tests and sets its restart-in-progress flag. It also tests its bootstrap-in-progress flag. If either flag is already set, the restart attempt is aborted. If the bootstrap-in-progress flag is clear, the console subsystem initiates a boot; otherwise, it halts. Chapter 30 provides more information.

The console subsystem next tries to locate the RPB. In searching for the RPB, it tests whether the contents of memory survived the power outage. If a valid RPB cannot be located or if the RPB warm restart inhibit flag is set, the restart attempt fails and the console subsystem initiates a boot. If a valid RPB is located, the console subsystem initiates execution of the restart routine, described in Section 33.2.1.1, on the primary processor. The secondary processor, if present, remains in console mode and is restarted by software, as described in Chapter 34.

33.2.1.5   **Power Recovery on VAX 8600 and VAX 8650 Processors.** When power is restored to the console microprocessor of a VAX 86x0 processor, the console microprocessor initializes itself and the VAX CPU as described in Chapter 30.

In the case of a warm restart, the console program tests the Restart Control switch, which has four positions:

> BOOT
> HALT
> RESTART/BOOT
> RESTART/HALT

If the switch is in the BOOT position, the console program invokes the DEFBOO.COM command procedure. If it is in the HALT position, the console program halts.

If it is in one of the two RESTART positions, the console program confirms that the battery backup unit was still operational when the power was restored. It tests its warm-start-in-progress flag. A set flag indicates a previously unsuccessful attempt at warm restart. If the flag is clear, the console commands the VAX 86x0 console support microcode to locate the RPB.

If the RPB is located, the console program sets the warm-start-in-progress flag and transfers control to the restart routine (see Section 33.2.1.1).

If restart cannot be attempted and the Restart Control switch is in the RESTART/BOOT position, the console program invokes the DEFBOO.COM command procedure. If the switch is in the RESTART/HALT position, the console program halts the processor.

33.2.1.6   **Power Recovery on VAX 8800 Family Processors.** The VAX 8800 family consists of VAX 8500, VAX 8530, VAX 8550, VAX 8700, and VAX 8800 CPUs. This family's console program executes on a separate console microprocessor, as an application task under the P/OS operating system. One family member, the VAX 8800, is a multiprocessor. It supports two CPUs per system, one of which acts as the primary and performs the main work of booting VMS. VMS directs the initialization of the other, secondary CPU, as described in Chapter 34.

When power is restored to the console microprocessor of a VAX 8800 family member, its P/OS operating system boots and runs the console program. The console program restores its own state, which was saved in a log file. It determines whether the power failure included the VAX CPUs. If so, the console program executes SYSINIT.COM, described in Chapter 30. If the AUTO_RESTART software key switch is set, SYSINIT.COM invokes the command procedure RESTAR.COM. If it is clear but the AUTO_BOOT software key switch is set, SYSINIT.COM invokes DEFBOO.COM.

After an error halt, the console program executes the command procedure RESTAR.COM. If the AUTO_RESTART switch is set, RESTAR.COM deposits the halt code, PC, and PSL into AP, R10, and R11, initializes the CPU, clears R0 through R5, and searches for an RPB. If it locates a valid RPB, RESTAR.COM initiates execution of the restart routine, described in Section 33.2.1.1, on the primary processor. The secondary processor, if present, remains in console mode and is restarted by software, as described in Chapter 34.

If the AUTO_RESTART switch is clear or a valid RPB is not found, RESTAR.COM tests the setting of the AUTO_BOOT switch. If it is set, the procedure DEFBOO.COM is executed.

33.2.1.7   **Power Recovery on VAX 88x0 Processors.** VAX 88x0 processors are multiprocessing members of the VAX 8800 family. The VAX 88x0 console program executes on a separate MicroVAX II processor, which communicates with the VAX 88x0 CPUs via a console interface module (CIM).

One CPU acts as the primary and performs the main work of booting VMS. VMS directs the initialization of the remaining secondary CPUs, as described in Chapter 34.

The MicroVAX II console runs console VMS; the console program is an application running from a dedicated process. When power is restored to the console microprocessor of a VAX 88x0 family member, console VMS boots and executes the console program. The console program restores its own state, which was saved in a data file. It determines whether the power failure included the VAX CPUs. If so, the console program executes SYSINIT.COM, described in Chapter 30.

SYSINIT.COM tests the software key switch AUTO_RESTART. If it is set, SYSINIT.COM invokes the command procedure RESTAR.COM. If it is clear but the AUTO_BOOT switch is set, SYSINIT.COM invokes DEFBOO.COM.

After an error halt, the console program executes the command procedure RESTAR.COM. If the AUTO_RESTART switch is set, RESTAR.COM deposits the halt code, PC, and PSL into AP, R10, and R11, initializes the CPU, clears R0 through R5, and searches for an RPB. If it locates a valid RPB, RESTAR.COM initiates execution of the restart routine, described in Section 33.2.1.1, on the primary processor. The secondary processors, if present, remain in console mode and are restarted by software, as described in Chapter 34.

If the AUTO_RESTART switch is clear or a valid RPB is not found, RESTAR.COM tests the setting of the AUTO_BOOT switch. If it is set, the procedure DEFBOO.COM is executed; otherwise, RESTAR.COM exits and leaves the system halted.

33.2.1.8   Power Recovery on VAX 6000 Series Systems. The VAX 6000 model 200, 300, and 400 systems are collectively referred to as the VAX 6000 series. Some models support multiple CPUs per system. One CPU acts as the primary and performs the main work of booting VMS. VMS directs the initialization of the remaining secondary CPUs, as described in Chapter 34.

When power is restored on a VAX 6000 series system, the console subsystem, executing on each CPU, directs that CPU to perform a series of self-tests. The CPUs select a primary processor, as described in Chapter 30.

The console program, executing on the primary processor, tests the settings of the upper and lower key switches on the front of the processor cabinet. These recovery settings determine the action of the primary processor. Unless the upper switch is in the ENABLE position and the lower switch is in the AUTO START position, or unless the upper key switch is in the SECURE position, the system halts at the console prompt.

Otherwise, the actions of the console depend upon the field CCA$Q_RESTARTIP in the console communications area (CCA). CCA$Q_RESTART-IP contains a restart-in-progress flag for each potential processor.

To restart, the console program tests and sets the restart-in-progress flag corresponding to the processor's CPU ID. If the flag is already set, the restart fails. Otherwise, the console program tries to locate the RPB. If it succeeds, the console subsystem initiates execution of the restart routine, described in Section 33.2.1.1, on the primary processor.

If the console cannot locate a valid RPB, the restart attempt fails and the primary processor initiates a boot.

A secondary processor can attempt a restart only following an error halt. For all other halt conditions, including power failure, the primary processor and operating system are responsible for restarting the secondary. Chapter 34 describes restart of secondary processors.

Following an error halt, a secondary processor tests and sets the bit corresponding to its CPU ID in CCA$Q_RESTARTIP. It searches for the RPB and transfers control to the restart routine if a valid RPB is located.

If a valid RPB is not located, the console program examines the bit corresponding to the secondary processor's CPU ID in the field CCA$Q_SECSTART. If the bit is clear, the console forces a reboot. Otherwise, the processor enters console mode. CCA$Q_SECSTART is set and cleared by the operating system, which uses it to avoid repeatedly forcing the boot of a secondary processor.

If a different processor is selected as the primary following a power failure, the VMS powerfail recovery routine detects the difference and forces a boot rather than a restart.

33.2.1.9   **Power Recovery on a MicroVAX II Processor.** A MicroVAX II processor has no battery backup for memory. Therefore, when the power recovers, it is not possible to resume normal system operation. Instead, the console program tests the setting of the Halt Enable switch. The Halt Enable switch is on the CPU patch panel insert, mounted inside the rear of the CPU cabinet. If the switch is down, the normal setting, halts are disabled. Otherwise, they are enabled.

Following power recovery, the console tests the Halt Enable switch. If halts are enabled, the console performs a diagnostic self-test and halts the processor. Otherwise, after the self-test, it boots the processor. If the boot attempt fails, the console halts the processor.

Following an error halt, the console tests the Halt Enable switch and halt action bits in the console program mailbox (CPMBX) register. VMS does not set the bits (except when it initiates a boot directly), so the bits remain at their initialized value of zero. If halts are enabled, the console halts the processor. Otherwise, it tests and sets the console program mailbox restart-in-progress flag. If the flag was already set, the restart fails. If the flag was clear, the console tries a restart, followed by a boot; if both fail, it halts the processor.

For a restart, the console first tries to locate the RPB. If a valid RPB is located, the console subsystem transfers control to the restart routine, described in Section 33.2.1.1.

33.2.1.10   **Power Recovery on MicroVAX 2000 and 3100 Processors.** MicroVAX 2000 and 3100 processors have no battery backup for memory. Therefore, when the power recovers, it is not possible to resume normal system operation, and the system performs its normal boot actions, described in Chapter 30.

Following an error halt rather than a power failure, the actions of the console depend upon the default recovery setting (halt action) and the restart-in-progress flag, both in the console program mailbox area of nonvolatile random access memory (NVR).

The recovery settings affect the console actions as follows:

• If the setting is 0 or 1, restart. If that fails, boot. If the boot fails, halt.
• If the setting is 2, boot. If that fails, halt.
• If the setting is 3, halt at the console prompt.

A restart attempt succeeds if the console finds the restart-in-progress flag clear and is able to set it, and if the console locates a valid RPB. The console subsystem transfers control to the restart routine, described in Section 33.2.1.1.

The recovery setting is specified as follows:

• On the MicroVAX 2000, the console utility program TEST53 alters the default recovery setting in the console program mailbox.
• On the MicroVAX 3100, the console command SET HALT sets the default recovery setting.

33.2.1.11 **Power Recovery on VAXstation 35x0 Systems.** VAXstation 35x0 systems have no battery backup for memory. Therefore, when the power recovers, they cannot resume normal system operation. Instead, the console program initiates a boot sequence, described in Chapter 30.

Following an error halt rather than a power failure, the actions of the console depend upon several fields, including the halt code, the default recovery setting in the console program mailbox area of NVR, and the flag CCA$V_REBOOT in CCA$B_HFLAGS.

If CCA$V_REBOOT is set, the primary processor attempts to boot the operating system using the default boot device. On failure, it enters console mode.

Otherwise, if CCA$V_REBOOT is clear, the primary processor's actions are controlled by the recovery setting:

• If the setting is 0, restart. If that fails, boot. If the boot fails, halt.
• If the setting is 1, restart. If that fails, halt.
• If the setting is 2, boot. If that fails, halt.
• If the setting is 3, halt at the console prompt.

The primary processor tests and sets the bit corresponding to its CPU ID in CCA$Q_RESTARTIP. If it locates a valid RPB, it transfers control to the restart routine.

A secondary processor halts at the console prompt if the recovery setting is 3; otherwise it attempts to restart. It tests and sets the bit corresponding to its CPU ID in CCA$Q_RESTARTIP. If it locates a valid RPB, it transfers control to the restart routine. Otherwise, if the bit corresponding to the secondary processor's CPU ID in the field CCA$Q_SECSTART is clear, the console forces a boot. If the bit is set, the processor enters console mode. VMS controls the setting of CCA$Q_SECSTART and uses it to avoid repeatedly forcing the boot of a secondary processor.

33.2.1.12   Power Recovery on Other MicroVAX Processors. This section describes the operations of MicroVAX 3200, 3300, 3400, 3500, 3600, 3800, and 3900 processors.

These MicroVAX processors have no battery backup for memory. Therefore, when the power recovers, it is not possible to resume normal system operation. Instead, the console program tests the setting of the Break Enable/Disable switch (sometimes referred to as the Halt Enable switch). If the switch is set to ENABLE, the system performs a self-test and halts. Otherwise, if the switch is set to DISABLE, the system performs a self-test and automatically reboots the processor. Note that a restart is not possible.

Following an error halt the actions of the console depend upon the default recovery setting and the restart-in-progress flag, both in the console program mailbox in NVR.

The recovery settings determine the console action when the processor halts:

- If the setting is 0, restart. If that fails, boot. If the boot fails, halt.
- If the setting is 1, restart. If that fails, halt.
- If the setting is 2, boot. If that fails, halt.
- If the setting is 3, halt at the console prompt.

A restart attempt succeeds if the console finds the restart-in-progress flag clear and is able to set it, and if the console locates a valid RPB. The console subsystem transfers control to the restart routine, described in Section 33.2.1.1.

33.2.2   Operations of the Restart Routine

In a symmetric multiprocessing (SMP) system, the console subsystem restarts the primary processor. The secondary processors remain halted until restarted by software. This section describes the general powerfail recovery sequence. Chapter 34 describes in detail the steps taken by the VMS restart routine, EXE$RESTART in module POWERFAIL, that are specific to restarting a primary processor. It also describes the steps by which a secondary processor is restarted.

The VMS restart routine, EXE$RESTART, receives control with the following environment:

- In kernel mode

- On the boot-time interrupt stack (SP = RPB base plus 200_{16})
- With memory management disabled
- At IPL 31

These initial conditions are similar to the entry to VMB, except that the RPB has already been initialized. Another similarity is that the SP register contains the high-address end of the RPB, which serves two purposes. First, the SP specifies the location of the RPB. Second, the last several longwords in the page containing the RPB are used as stack space by EXE$RESTART until the per-CPU boot stack pointer is restored.

EXE$RESTART branches to EXE$RESTART_ATT, also in POWERFAIL, which first restores information saved in the RPB and per-CPU database by EXE$POWERFAIL (see Table 33.1, Group A). Most of this information is necessary to turn memory management back on. A dummy P0 page table is created (just like the one set up by SYSBOOT) so that the page containing the restart routine is mapped as a P0 virtual address that, when translated, yields the identical physical address.

After the P0 page table is set up, EXE$RESTART_ATT enables memory management in the same manner as EXE$INIT:

```
        MTPR    #1,#PR$_MAPEN
        JMP     FIRST_SYSTEM_VA(R2)

        FIRST_SYSTEM_VA = . - EXE$RESTART
10$:
```

Chapter 31 shows how the contents of PR$_P0BR are determined to produce the identity mapping and describes in detail the instruction sequence that enables memory management.

Once memory management has been enabled, EXE$RESTART_ATT checks whether the restart was initiated as part of powerfail recovery or in response to another error halt condition detected by the console subsystem.

If an error halt caused the restart, EXE$RESTART_ATT generates a reason-specific fatal bugcheck. This will result in a cold start, a bootstrap, if the SYSBOOT flag BUGREBOOT is set. By causing a crash, EXE$RESTART_ATT preserves information about the error condition in the crash dump file. One example of such an error halt is an invalid interrupt stack. The CPU microcode causes this halt if the interrupt stack pointer points to a page which is not valid or to which kernel mode does not have write access when an interrupt or exception must be serviced.

If this is a power recovery, EXE$RESTART_ATT clears two warm restart inhibit flags, the use of which is discussed in Section 33.3.2.

Each processor in an SMP system saves its own state and can detect the success or failure of the endeavor by the condition of its saved ISP. However, a mechanism is required to detect the failure of any processor to save state, because an SMP system must boot rather than restart in that case. The field

POWERDWN_L_DONE, defined in module POWERFAIL, serves this purpose. Each CPU sets a bit corresponding to its CPU ID in POWERDWN_L_DONE upon completion of the powerfail sequence. When power returns and EXE$RESTART_ATT executes on the primary CPU, it compares SMP$GL_ACTIVE_CPUS, the CPUs active at the time of the powerfail, to the mask in POWERDWN_L_DONE. Unless all processors saved their state, EXE$RESTART_ATT generates the fatal bugcheck STATENTSVD, software state not saved during powerfail. It also generates this bugcheck if EXE$POWERFAIL does not save the ISP in the per-CPU database. Otherwise, it copies the saved ISP value to R6 and to the SP register.

EXE$RESTART_ATT restores the registers listed in Table 33.1, Group B. It does not use the SP register to restore this data from the stack. Instead, it uses a scratch register (R6) to reference the stack. Because the SP register is left pointing to the end of the saved information, the data on the stack will not be overwritten if another power failure occurs while the data is being restored. Using a scratch register allows the restart routine to be repeated as many times as necessary without special action.

The restoration of the SISR is also affected by the possibility of another power failure. If an interrupt is requested during powerfail recovery, and another power failure occurs before the recovery is complete, the interrupt would be lost. Thus, EXE$RESTART_ATT sets all fork level interrupt bits (IPL 6 and IPL 8 through 11) in the restored SISR to guarantee that no interrupts are lost. As each request is granted, the fork interrupt service routine merely dismisses the interrupt if no packet exists on its work queue.

EXE$RESTART_ATT invokes the routine EXE$REGRESTOR to restore the CPU-specific registers saved by EXE$REGSAVE. EXE$REGRESTOR resides in module [SYSLOA]ERRSUB*xxx*, part of the CPU-specific image SYSLOA*xxx*.

It initializes processor registers by invoking the CPU-specific routine EXE$INIPROCREG, also in module [SYSLOA]ERRSUB*xxx*.

At this point, only the general registers remain to be restored. Each processor sets the bit corresponding to its CPU ID in POWERUP_L_DONE, defined in module POWERFAIL. A secondary processor pauses here until the primary directs it to continue. It then restores its general registers and returns control to the instruction sequence interrupted by the power failure.

The primary processor takes the following steps:

1. It reads the battery backed up time-of-year clock by invoking the CPU-specific routine EXE$READP_LOCAL_TODR, in module [SYSLOA]ERR-SUB*xxx*.
2. It computes the restart time plus three minutes and stores the value in the global location EXE$GL_PWRDONE. This value represents the time it may take all hardware components to become fully operational again. Device drivers can use the routine EXE$PWRTIMCHK, in module

POWERFAIL, to make sure that these three minutes have passed before restarting I/O operations. Devices such as disks may take as long as three minutes to become operational.

3. It computes the duration of the powerfail and stores the result in global location EXE$GL_PFATIM.

4. It corrects the system time, at global location EXE$GQ_SYSTIME, by adding to it the duration of the powerfail.

5. It clears the timestamp validating the lock manager's process bitmap, used to detect multiple resource deadlocks. Clearing the timestamp has the effect of discarding the deadlock search in progress.

6. It scans the timer queue for timer queue entries (TQEs) that have expired. For each expired TQE, it changes the absolute due time to the corrected system time. This substitution allows periodic timer requests to reestablish internal synchronization.

   For example, suppose that a periodic timer request is declared with a period of one minute and the power is off for three minutes. With no adjustment of the absolute due time, the request would expire immediately three times following power recovery. The readjustment causes one request to come due immediately, with the next request not occurring until one minute later.

   Note that relative synchronization between several requests may be lost as a result of a power failure. For example, if one request is due to expire in two minutes, a second is due to expire in five minutes (or three minutes after the first), and the power is off for more than five minutes, then both requests will be delivered at the same time. A power recovery AST might be used to allow multiple requests to reestablish their relative synchronization.

7. A power recovery entry is made in the error log.

8. EXE$RESTART_ATT invokes CNX$POWER_FAIL. If the system is a VAXcluster member, this notifies the VAXcluster connection manager of power recovery.

9. EXE$RESTART_ATT initializes external adapters by invoking the CPU-specific routine EXE$STARTUPADP in [SYSLOA]ERRSUB*xxx*.

10. Device drivers are notified that a power failure and recovery sequence have occurred. This step is detailed in Section 33.2.3.

11. The console device unit initialization routine causes the console subsystem to initialize and restart secondary CPUs. Chapter 34 describes this process.

    EXE$RESTART_ATT waits for the secondary CPUs active at the time of the power failure to restart. The secondary CPUs are restarted here, rather than later at a lower IPL, to avoid the possibility of deadlock. If a secondary CPU holds a spinlock for which the primary CPU is waiting at the time of the power failure, the primary CPU executes EXE$RE-START_ATT and returns to the spinwait loop when power is recovered.

Thus, the secondary CPUs must be restarted before the primary exits EXE$RESTART_ATT.

12. EXE$RESTART lowers IPL to 29 to allow any pending powerfail interrupt to occur, then raises IPL back to 31. Section 33.3.1 explains the reason for this step.

13. EXE$RESTART_ATT clears POWERDWN_L_DONE.

14. On a system with multiprocessing enabled, EXE$RESTART_ATT sets the start flag to notify secondary CPUs that they may proceed.

15. EXE$RESTART then clears EXE$GL_PFAILTIM.

16. Each CPU modifies its SP to point to the saved general registers on the interrupt stack and restores them.

17. Each clears its last sanity check flag, the saved interrupt stack pointer, CPU$L_SAVED_ISP. EXE$RESTART_ATT will find the pointer zero if the state is incompletely saved in a subsequent power failure (see Section 33.3.1).

18. EXE$RESTART_ATT dismisses the powerfail interrupt by executing an REI instruction. Control returns to the code that was interrupted by the power loss notification.

33.2.3 Device Notification

EXE$RESTART_ATT invokes the routine EXE$INIT_DEVICE, also in module POWERFAIL, to initialize devices and device drivers after a powerfail recovery.

While IPL is still at 31 to block all interrupts, EXE$INIT_DEVICE scans the I/O database. It sets the powerfail bit, UCB$V_POWER, in the status word of each unit control block (UCB) it finds, except for mailbox UCBs.

For each controller it finds, EXE$INIT_DEVICE invokes the controller initialization routine. If that routine returns successfully, EXE$INIT_DEVICE invokes the unit initialization routine for each unit of that controller. The powerfail bit enables these initialization routines to differentiate between power recovery and ordinary initialization.

EXE$INIT_DEVICE checks each unit to see whether its driver fork process is expecting an interrupt or has I/O being timed. If either is true, EXE$INIT_DEVICE clears its interrupt-expected bit, sets its timeout-expected bit, and sets its due time to zero. These actions cause each such device to time out. Later, when the driver's timeout routine runs, it can differentiate between ordinary timeout and power failure by checking the powerfail bit.

The check for device timeout occurs within EXE$TIMEOUT, the system subroutine that executes once a second (see Chapter 11). EXE$TIMEOUT cannot execute until later, after both of the following occur:

- The interval timer interrupts (which means that IPL has dropped below 22 or 24, depending on CPU type).

- The software timer interrupt service routine executes. (This will not happen until IPL drops below 7.)

In VMS, most of the work done to recover from a power failure occurs in drivers. VMS disk drivers and magnetic tape drivers are capable of restarting whatever request they were processing when the power failed in such a way that the power failure is totally transparent to them. (If a magnetic tape unit lost vacuum, operator intervention is required to reestablish the vacuum and rewind the tape. Once that is done, the driver automatically restarts the I/O request that was in progress when the power failed.)

33.2.4   Process Notification

If so requested, VMS will notify a process of powerfail recovery by queuing an AST to it. A process requests this notification by requesting the Set Power Recovery AST ($SETPRA) system service.

33.2.4.1 $SETPRA System Service.
The $SETPRA system service procedure, EXE$SETPRA in module SYSSETPRA, runs in kernel mode. It performs two steps:

1. Stores the address of the AST in global location CTL$GL_POWERAST and the access mode in which the AST is to be delivered in location CTL$GB_PWRMODE
2. Sets the power AST flag (PCB$V_PWRAST) in the process control block (PCB) status longword

The effect of this system service is canceled by the delivery of the power recovery AST or by image rundown (see Chapter 26).

33.2.4.2   Delivery of Power Recovery ASTs.
The delivery of a power recovery AST occurs in several distinct steps:

1. EXE$RESTART_ATT stores the duration of the power failure in location EXE$GL_PFATIM. (This value is simply the current contents of the time-of-year clock minus EXE$GL_PFAILTIM, the time at which the power failed.) Nonzero contents in this location act as a trigger to the swapper the next time that it runs.

   Note that no special action is taken at this point to wake up the swapper. In fact, because this routine is running at IPL 31, the swapper scheduling state could not be changed without potential synchronization problems.
2. The swapper's main loop (see Chapter 18) invokes routine EXE$POWERAST, in module SYSSETPRA, if location EXE$GL_PFATIM contains a nonzero value.

999

3. EXE$POWERAST scans the PCB vector and queues a special kernel mode AST to each process that has the PCB$V_PWRAST flag set. It then clears the flag, disabling further power recovery ASTs to the process, to prevent multiple ASTs in case another powerfail occurs before the process executes. A special kernel mode AST is required because the address and access mode of the recovery AST are stored in the P1 space of the requesting process. When EXE$POWERAST completes its scan of the PCB vector, it clears EXE$GL_PFATIM.

4. The special kernel mode AST copies the address and access mode from their P1 space locations into the AST control block and queues the recovery AST to the requesting process.

5. Finally, the recovery AST itself is delivered to the requesting process. The AST parameter is the duration of the power failure in 10-millisecond units.

To receive notification of a subsequent powerfail recovery, a process must "rearm" the AST by requesting the $SETPRA system service again.

33.3 MULTIPLE POWER FAILURES

Hardware and software flags exist in combination to prevent infinite looping or related problems in response to a power failure that occurs while either the powerfail service routine or the restart routine is executing.

33.3.1 Nested Powerfail Interrupts

Caution is necessary where power failure is concerned. Fluctuating voltages can cause the power to repeatedly fail and be restored. VMS must provide for the possibility of a second powerfail interrupt before an earlier one is dismissed.

The powerfail interrupt code is only guaranteed a brief interval between the powerfail interrupt request and the total loss of power. If the powerfail interrupt is blocked while the CPU is running at IPL 30 or 31, EXE$POW-ERFAIL will have that much less time to save the volatile machine state.

A second powerfail interrupt can be blocked for a considerable time while EXE$RESTART restores state from a previous interrupt. If the second interrupt were not granted until EXE$RESTART completed restoration and dismissed the first powerfail interrupt, there could be insufficient time to save the processor state. An additional consideration for an SMP system is that the state of all CPUs active at the time of power loss must be saved for a recovery to succeed.

VMS uses a combination of three things to defend against nested powerfail interrupts: CPU$L_SAVED_ISP; preserving the processor state saved on the stack; and temporarily lowering IPL in EXE$RESTART.

One of the first steps EXE$POWERFAIL takes is to check the contents of CPU$L_SAVED_ISP, the saved interrupt stack field in the per-CPU database.

This location retains nonzero contents until just before EXE$RESTART executes its REI instruction, dismissing the powerfail interrupt. If a powerfail interrupt occurs while this location contains a nonzero value (indicating that another failure/recovery is already in progress), EXE$POWERFAIL does not save the processor state.

Volatile machine state has already been saved as a result of the first powerfail interrupt. That state will be restored eventually by EXE$RESTART. Any state saved at the time of the second interrrupt would merely reflect the interruption of EXE$RESTART's attempts to restore state after the first interrupt. This check prevents nested powerfail interrupts on a system experiencing some obscure behavior that would otherwise be extremely difficult to diagnose.

One more bit of caution is evident in the manner in which EXE$RESTART restores data from the interrupt stack. A scratch register rather than the SP register is used to traverse the stack. If another powerfail interrupt were to occur while data was being restored, the saved PC and PSL would not overlay the previously saved data.

When EXE$RESTART is nearly done but CPU$L_SAVED_ISP is still nonzero and the stack is still intact, it deliberately lowers IPL to 29 to allow any pending powerfail interrupt to be granted. If one is pending and granted, EXE$POWERFAIL sees that CPU$L_SAVED_ISP is nonzero and saves no state. It branches to itself, awaiting the power failure. When the power recovers and EXE$RESTART is reentered, it again restores machine state from the RPB and the state saved on the stack.

If there is no pending powerfail interrupt, EXE$RESTART raises IPL back to 31, clears POWERDWN_L_DONE and EXE$GL_PFAILTIM, and notifies secondary CPUs that they may proceed. Each CPU modifies its SP to point to the saved general registers on the interrupt stack and restores the registers. Each clears its last sanity check flag, the saved interrupt stack pointer, CPU$L_SAVED_ISP. Each then executes an REI instruction to dismiss the interrupt.

33.3.2 Prevention of Infinite Restart Loop

There are two flags whose purpose is to prevent an infinite restart loop such as the following:

1. An error halt condition occurs.
2. The console subsystem locates the RPB and transfers control to EXE$RESTART.
3. Prior to restoring or crashing the system, EXE$RESTART incurs an error halt condition.
4. The console subsystem locates the RPB and transfers control to EXE$RESTART.
5. EXE$RESTART incurs the same error halt condition. . . .

The first flag is the low bit of RPB$L_RSTRTFLG, located in the RPB. During system initialization, the initialization routine for the loadable executive image IO_ROUTINES, invoked from EXE$INIT, clears the flag after there is enough of VMS to restart.

The flag is tested and set by the console subsystem during restart after it finds a valid RPB. If it locates an otherwise valid RPB with this flag set, it aborts the restart attempt. Either the RPB is in error or an earlier restart attempt has incurred an error halt.

A second flag, called the warm start inhibit flag or the restart-in-progress flag, is maintained by the console subsystem on some types of VAX CPU. It functions in a similar manner to RPB$L_RSTRTFLG. The console sets the flag at the beginning of the restart. EXE$RESTART initiates the clearing of it by sending a command to the console subsystem. On some CPUs, the following instruction sends the command:

```
MTPR    #^XF03,#PR$_TXDB
```

If the console subsystem detects that this flag is set while attempting a restart, it aborts the restart and takes the same processor-specific action it would if the RPB flag were set.

Multiprocessing systems must implement a flag of this type for each potential CPU. Some do this by designating a bit per CPU in the CCA field CCA$Q_RESTARTIP. This bit is cleared by EXE$REGRESTOR after it restores any saved processor-specific registers.

33.3.3 Device Driver Action

Drivers do not have to concern themselves directly with the multiple restart problem. Even though the bulk of driver recovery is done in response to an IPL 7 software timer interrupt, when a second power failure is possible, drivers are protected by one of the following situations:

- The driver controller and unit initialization routines are invoked at IPL 31 before CPU$L_SAVED_ISP is cleared. Drivers are protected here by the same sanity checks that VMS uses for itself.
- If the driver does not get invoked at its timeout entry point before the power fails again, the preserved driver state indicates a unit that has already timed out. When power is finally restored permanently, the driver will be invoked at its timeout entry point.
- If the driver is in the middle of its timeout routine, it still appears to the system as a unit that has timed out. It will be invoked at its timeout entry point again when the machine finally stabilizes.
- The driver may succeed in returning control to the operating system with, for example, one of the following macro invocations: WFIxxCH, IOFORK, or REQCOM.

If the operating system has received control, the request has either been completed or the driver is back into a state (such as expecting an interrupt) where the power recovery logic will cause the driver to be invoked at its timeout entry point when the power is finally restored.

33.4   FAILURE OF EXTERNAL ADAPTER POWER

Certain adapters can experience a power failure independently of the processor. These adapters are the following:

- UNIBUS adapter on VAX-11/78x, VAX 86x0 processors
- Second UNIBUS adapter on a VAX-11/750 processor
- MASSBUS adapter on VAX-11/78x, VAX 86x0 processors
- CI780, CI750, and CIBCI port adapters

These adapters notify VMS of power loss or power restoration by interrupting. VMS provides service routines for their interrupts.

A key problem is that a reference to the registers or I/O space of a powerfailed adapter causes a machine check. If the reference is made in kernel mode, for example, by a device driver trying to access device registers, the machine check would result in a fatal bugcheck.

One method that VMS uses to prevent such machine checks is to remap the system virtual address space reserved for the adapter to point to the "black hole" page, EXE$GL_BLAKHOLE. This page is a physical page of memory allocated at system initialization for this purpose. This mapping technique prevents subsequent machine checks or related errors from device drivers that reference a powerfailed adapter.

An adapter on an SMP system, however, requires a different method. Remapping to the black hole page requires that the translation buffer (TB) entry for the former adapter virtual address be invalidated on all CPUs. TB invalidation involves an interprocessor interrupt, which is serviced at a lower priority than the power failure processing. Thus, beginning with VMS Version 5.0, adapters available for systems that support SMP use an alternative technique, described in Section 33.4.3.

33.4.1   UNIBUS Power Failure

A UNIBUS failure on a VAX-11/780, VAX-11/785, VAX 8600, or VAX 8650 processor does not necessarily indicate that the entire system is in error. VMS allows UNIBUS errors, including UNIBUS power failure caused by turning off the power to the UBA or the BA-11K, to occur without crashing the entire system.

When such an error occurs, the UBA interrupts on its own behalf. The interrupt service routine for the affected UBA detects that a UBA interrupt (rather than a UNIBUS device interrupt) has occurred and transfers control to an error routine that does the following:

1. Checks that the interrupt is a result of the power failure of the UBA or UNIBUS
2. Writes an error log entry
3. Remaps the system virtual addresses that previously mapped the UBA itself and the UNIBUS I/O page (24 pages in all) so that these pages now point to the black hole page reserved at initialization time
4. Modifies the interrupt vector to point to a power-up routine

If the UNIBUS is not responding, either because the power was turned off or for some other reason, devices that were waiting for I/O completion will time out. The program that issued the initial I/O request will receive an appropriate error notification, assuming that no driver is in a tight loop at device IPL waiting for a status bit to change state.

When the power is restored, the system virtual pages are remapped to point to the UBA registers and UNIBUS I/O space. EXE$INIT_DEVICE is invoked to reinitialize all devices on the recovered UBA. Its actions in reinitializing devices are described in Section 33.2.3. If any devices were removed while the power was turned off, they will be marked offline as part of the power recovery operation. The interrupt vector is restored to its usual contents.

It is also possible for power to fail on the second UNIBUS interface of a VAX-11/750 processor without failing on the entire system. VMS responds as it does on the systems previously described. The UBA interrupts to indicate powerfail through the vector at SCB offset $1E4_{16}$.

33.4.2 Support for Power Failure of MASSBUS Adapters

A MASSBUS adapter (MBA) power failure on a VAX-11/78x or VAX 86x0 processor does not necessarily indicate that power is being lost for the entire system. VMS services MBA powerfail on those processors as it does UBA powerfail. It maps the system virtual address space corresponding to the MBA registers to the black hole page. When the power is restored, the address space is mapped back to the MBA registers, the MBA is initialized, and EXE$INIT_DEVICE is invoked to reinitialize the devices on the adapter.

33.4.3 Support for Power Failure of Computer Interconnect Adapters

Certain computer interconnect (CI) adapters (CI780, CI750, and CIBCI) can lose power independently of the rest of the system. Before VMS Version 5.0, the CI device driver, PADRIVER, mapped the system virtual address space corresponding to the CI registers to the black hole page. Since the CIBCI adapter is supported on some VAX multiprocessor models, PADRIVER was changed to access all CI registers through pointers in the port definition table (PDT).

If a power failure occurs, the CI adapter interrupts on its own behalf. The interrupt service routine transfers control to a power-down routine that stores the virtual address of a private black hole location within the driver into the PDT pointers. Thus, any subsequent register access references a different virtual address. This alternative to remapping the same virtual address to a different physical address does not require TB invalidation.

When power returns to the CI adapter, the driver again loads each PDT pointer with the virtual address of a device register, reloads the volatile CI microcode, and reinitializes the CI.

34 Symmetric Multiprocessing

> Virtue can only flourish amongst equals.
>
> Mary Wollstonecraft, *A Vindication of the Rights of Men*

Version 5 of the VMS operating system adds support for tightly coupled symmetric multiprocessing (SMP). This chapter describes

- Communication and cooperation among the members of an SMP system
- Initialization of the SMP environment
- Addition and removal of a member

34.1 OVERVIEW

A VMS multiprocessing system consists of two or more CPUs that address common memory and that can execute instructions simultaneously. If all CPUs in the system execute the same copy of the operating system, the multiprocessing system is said to be tightly coupled. If all CPUs have equal access to operating system functions, the system is said to be symmetric.

In most respects the members of a VMS SMP system are symmetric. Each member can perform the following tasks:

- Initiate an I/O request
- Service exceptions
- Service software interrupts
- Service hardware interrupts (other than from I/O devices), such as interprocessor, interval timer, and powerfail interrupts
- Execute process context code in any access mode

One CPU can be executing process context code while another services a software interrupt. Section 34.4 describes the changes in VMS Version 5 that enable this concurrency.

VMS characterizes the various members of an SMP system in several ways. One important characteristic is that of primary CPU. During system operation, the primary CPU has several unique responsibilities:

- System timekeeping
- Servicing I/O device interrupts and their concomitant software interrupts
- Writing messages to the console terminal and accessing other I/O devices that are not accessible to all members

All device interrupts are serviced on the primary CPU. Section 34.6.2 describes this division of labor. An SMP configuration may include some devices that are not accessible from all SMP members. The console terminal, for example, may be accessible only from the primary processor. Section 34.6.3 describes a mechanism called device affinity by which VMS supports such devices.

Booting the system is initiated on a CPU with full access to the console subsystem, called the BOOT CPU. The BOOT CPU controls the bootstrap sequence and boots the other available CPUs. In VMS Version 5.2, the BOOT CPU and the primary CPU are always the same; the others are called secondary or attached processors. (The terms *CPU* and *processor* are used interchangeably in this chapter and throughout the book.)

The booted primary and all currently booted secondary processors are called the active set. These processors actively participate in system operations and respond to interprocessor interrupts, which coordinate systemwide events. Section 34.5.2 contains more information on the use of interprocessor interrupts.

VMS imposes little binding between a process and a particular CPU. That is, in general, each CPU is equally able to execute any process. However, a process may need capabilities possessed only by certain CPUs or may have populated the memory and translation buffer caches of a specific CPU. For those cases, VMS implements a mechanism by which a process may be bound to one or more CPUs. Chapter 12 describes the implementation of process affinity and processor capabilities.

As described in Chapter 4, VMS performs many key system functions through software interrupts. On an SMP system, each processor services its own software interrupt requests, of which the most significant are the following:

- When a process receives an interrupt priority level (IPL) 2 interrupt because of a pending asynchronous system trap (AST), the AST delivery interrupt service routine runs on the same processor as the process. Chapter 7 describes IPL 2 interrupts and their servicing.
- When a current process is preempted by a higher priority computable resident process, the IPL 3 rescheduling interrupt service routine, running on that processor, takes the current process out of execution and switches to the higher priority process. Chapter 12 describes scheduling in more detail and the circumstances under which the rescheduling interrupt is requested.
- When a device driver completes an I/O request, an IPL 4 I/O postprocessing interrupt is requested: some completed requests are queued to a CPU-specific postprocessing queue and are serviced on that CPU; others are queued to a systemwide queue and serviced on the primary CPU. Section 34.6.4 describes the different postprocessing queues and their uses. Chapter 21 describes the I/O postprocessing interrupt service routine.
- When the current process has used its quantum of CPU time, the IPL 7 software timer interrupt service routine, running on that CPU, performs

quantum-end processing. Another function of this interrupt service routine, servicing the timer queue, is only performed on the primary CPU. Chapter 11 describes software timer interrupts and their servicing.

- Software interrupts at IPLs 6 and 8 through 11 are requested to execute fork processes. Each processor services its own set of fork queues. A fork process generally executes on the same CPU from which it was requested. However, since many fork processes are requested from device interrupt service routines, which currently execute only on the primary CPU, more fork processes execute on the primary than on other processors. Chapter 4 describes fork interrupts and their servicing.

SMP support was added to VMS Version 5 with the following goals:

- One version of VMS. As part of the standard VMS product, SMP support does not require its own version of VMS. The enhanced version of VMS runs on all VAX processors. The synchronization methodology and the interface to synchronization routines are the same on all systems. However, as described in Chapter 8, there are different versions of the synchronization routines themselves. Partly for that reason, SMP support imposes relatively little additional overhead on a uniprocessor system.
- Parallelism in kernel mode. SMP support might have been implemented such that any single processor could execute kernel mode code, but not more than one at a time. However, more parallelism was required for a solution that would support configurations with more CPUs. The members of an SMP system can be executing different portions of the executive concurrently. The executive has been divided into different critical regions, each with its own lock, called a spinlock.
- Flexibility in the granularity of the locking mechanisms. The spinlock mechanism allows for the creation of additional static spinlocks in future versions of the VMS operating system. The IOLOCK8 spinlock, for example, could be subdivided to allow increased parallelism.

34.2 SMP HARDWARE CONFIGURATIONS

SMP supports a theoretical maximum of 32 CPUs, each of which has a unique ID between 0 to 31. For any particular processor type, the actual maximum is likely to be smaller. The manner in which the CPU ID is determined also varies with processor type:

- On a VAX 83x0 system, the CPU ID is taken from the system ID processor register. It is the CPU's VAXBI bus node ID, which is determined by a plug on the VAXBI backplane slot where the node is inserted.
- On a VAX 88x0 or VAX 8800 system, the CPU ID is taken from the system ID processor register.
- On a VAX 6000 series processor, the CPU ID is taken from a location in XMI bus node-private space.

- On a VAXstation 3520 or VAXstation 3540 system, the CPU ID is taken from a CPU-specific processor register.

Some SMP support is processor-type-specific, for example, CPU initialization routines and the routines that request interprocessor interrupts. These routines are implemented in CPU-specific modules in the [SYSLOA] facility that are linked into the various SYSLOA*xxx* images. The *xxx* varies with CPU type; for example, SYSLOA8NN supports VAX 8800 systems. Appendix G contains a list of CPU types and their corresponding SYSLOA*xxx* names.

VMS SMP requires a hardware configuration of multiple CPUs of the same model type. Each processor can execute an instruction stream independently of the others. An interprocessor interrupt mechanism enables kernel mode software running on one processor to interrupt one or more of the others.

The CPUs access common physical memory through the same physical addresses. The CPUs' memory caches are invalidated as needed by the hardware without software involvement. This feature is called cache coherency. As required for any VAX processor, the memory supports interlocked access. That is, if one CPU accesses memory with an interlocked instruction, for example, BBSSI, the memory controller must block any attempt at interlocked access to that location by another CPU.

In addition, the CPUs must be at the same hardware and microcode revision levels. If one has a floating-point accelerator or optional microcode, such as G-floating-point and H-floating-point support, all must have it. These requirements exist because a process running on one CPU can be taken out of execution in the middle of certain instructions and resumed on another processor.

The primary processor must be able to access all I/O peripherals. All CPUs must be able to access most I/O peripherals. On many types of configuration, the console devices may not be accessible other than to the primary processor.

The following sections describe the systems on which VMS Version 5.2 supports SMP.

34.2.1 VAX 8300 and VAX 8350 Systems

The VAX 8300 system consists of two VAX 8200 processors on a common backplane interconnect, the VAXBI bus. The VAX 8350 system has two VAX 8250 processors. The processor in the second physical VAXBI backplane slot is connected to the console. It is booted as the primary processor; the other CPU is booted as the secondary processor. The processors access common memory on the VAXBI bus. The VAXBI bus provides an interprocessor interrupt capability. Both processors are physically capable of accessing any I/O adapters connected to the VAXBI bus.

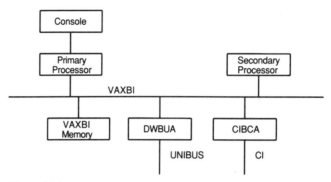

Figure 34.1
Hardware Layout of a VAX 83x0 System

Any VAXBI node that implements a cache, such as a CPU, must monitor the bus for writes to locations whose contents are in its cache and invalidate them as required. Because both processors and the memory are on the same bus, this mechanism is sufficient to maintain the validity of both processors' caches. The cache implements a write-through policy; that is, when a CPU modifies a cached location, the new contents are immediately written to memory.

Figure 34.1 shows the hardware configuration of an example VAX 83x0 system with two I/O adapters: a VAXBI-to-UNIBUS adapter (DWBUA), and a VAXBI-to-CI adapter (CIBCA).

A VAX 83x0 system has one physical console terminal. By default, console commands are intended for the primary processor. CPU console microcode can pass commands and messages between the physical console and the logical console of the secondary processor. Commands and messages can also be passed to and from the logical console of the secondary processor through processor registers accessed with MTPR and MFPR instructions.

34.2.2 VAX 8800 and VAX 88x0 Family

The VAX 8800 system consists of two VAX 8700 processors on a common backplane, the VAX 8800 memory interconnect (NMI). The processors access common memory on the NMI. The NMI provides an interprocessor interrupt capability. A processor is either the LEFT or the RIGHT processor, depending on its physical position in the CPU cabinet. A console command allows either processor to be selected as the primary processor. By default, the LEFT processor is the BOOT CPU and primary processor.

Both CPUs and the memory are on the NMI. Each CPU has its own cache of recently referenced locations and their contents. Logic in the cache monitors the bus for modifications to memory whose contents are cached. The cache is a write-through cache and invalidates itself whenever appropriate. This, however, is not sufficient to ensure the validity of the data in another processor's cache or in memory, since each processor's writes to memory locations are buffered temporarily in a "write buffer." The write buffer can combine several CPU writes into a single bus transaction, reducing bus traffic. Execution of an interlocked instruction, however, forces the write buffer to be emptied, completing writes to memory. Other instructions, such as REI and SVPCTX, and interrupt or exception initiation also force emptying of the write buffer. As the other processor's cache monitors the NMI, it sees the memory writes and invalidates itself as appropriate.

A VAX 8800 NMI-to-VAXBI adapter (NBIA) connects one or two VAXBI buses to the NMI. Both processors are physically capable of accessing any I/O adapters connected to the NMI or VAXBI bus.

Figure 34.2 shows a possible VAX 8800 hardware configuration: a VAX 8800 system with one NBIA connecting one VAXBI bus.

The VAX 88x0 family is a follow-on to the VAX 8800 system. Its multiprocessor members, the VAX 8820, VAX 8830, and VAX 8840 systems, consist of two, three, or four VAX 8700 processors on an NMI backplane. In a dual-CPU configuration, processors and memory are on the same NMI. In a configuration with more processors, the memory controllers are on a second NMI.

Each processor is identified by a number from 0 to 3. A console command allows any processor to be selected as the primary processor. By default, the processor with the lowest number is the BOOT CPU and primary processor.

34.2.3   VAX 6000 Series Systems

VAX 6000 series systems support different processor types in otherwise similar configurations. Processors, memories, and DWMBA I/O adapters connect as nodes to a backplane called the XMI bus. There can be up to 14 nodes on

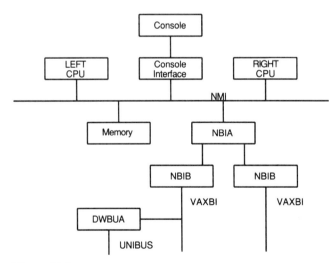

Figure 34.2
Hardware Layout of a VAX 8800 System

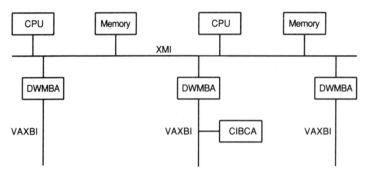

Figure 34.3
Hardware Layout of a VAX 6000 Series System

the XMI bus. The DWMBA is an XMI-to-VAXBI adapter. All I/O peripherals except for the console terminal are on a VAXBI bus. Figure 34.3 shows the configuration of an example VAX 6000 series system.

By default, the processor with the lowest CPU ID that passes self-test is the primary processor.

Each CPU has its own write-through cache that monitors the XMI for memory writes to locations it has cached. Each CPU has a write buffer similar to that on a VAX 8700 processor.

Each processor runs its own console program. That is, the console subsystem is implemented in VAX instructions that execute on the CPU itself rather than on a separate console processor. The consoles communicate with each other through an area in memory called the console communications area (CCA). Each processor has a buffer of its own in the CCA. The executive, running on the primary processor, communicates with a secondary processor's console program by testing status bits in and writing messages to the secondary processor's CCA buffer.

34.2.4 VAXstation 3520 and 3540 Systems

The VAXstation 3520 system consists of two CVAX processors connected through a cache and bus interface to a common backplane, the M-bus. The VAXstation 3540 system has four processors. The processors access common memory on the M-bus. Each processor is interfaced to the bus through a cache that monitors the M-bus for other CPUs' memory references. Disk devices connect to a small computer system interface (SCSI) bus, which interfaces to the M-bus through the I/O adapter. An optional Q22-bus adapter module allows connection of additional peripherals, such as magnetic tape. Figure 34.4 shows a sample VAXstation 3520 configuration.

Each cache can determine whether a particular memory location is cached exclusively in itself or shared in at least one other cache. This makes possible a write-back policy for unshared locations and a write-through policy for shared locations. That is, when a CPU modifies a memory location cached

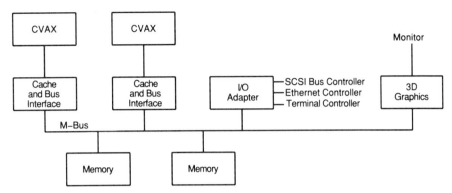

Figure 34.4
Hardware Layout of a VAXstation 3520 System

only in its own cache, only the cache is changed. The memory location is not modified until that cache entry must be reused for a different memory location not currently cached or until some other CPU reads the memory location. When a CPU modifies a shared location, the cache initiates a write on the M-bus to update the memory; monitoring the bus and seeing the write, the other CPUs' caches update their own entries if necessary.

An interprocessor interrupt capability is provided. The console capability is identical to that described in Section 34.2.3.

34.3   DATA STRUCTURES RELATED TO SMP SUPPORT

Two longwords, SMP$GL_FLAGS and EXE$GL_TIME_CONTROL, contain flags controlling SMP operations. These flags are accessed with interlocked instructions. Symbolic names for the bits in SMP$GL_FLAGS are defined by the $SPLCODDEF macro. These bits are

- SMP$V_ENABLED—When set, indicates that SMP operation is enabled
- SMP$V_START_CPU—When set, indicates that the primary CPU has finished initialization
- SMP$V_CRASH_CPU—When set, indicates that a member has initiated a fatal bugcheck
- SMP$V_TODR—When set, indicates that SMP$GL_PROPOSED_TODR, described in Section 34.5.2, is in use
- SMP$V_UNMOD_DRIVER—When set, indicates that a driver has been loaded that has not been modified for SMP operation
- SMP$V_TODR_ACK—When set, indicates that the primary CPU has completed its part in an SMP time-of-year clock access
- SMP$V_SYNCH—When set, indicates that an SMP synchronization image has been loaded
- SMP$V_BENIGN—When set, indicates that a benign state, described in Section 34.5.4, has been requested

Symbolic names for the bits in EXE$GL_TIME_CONTROL are defined in module SYSPARAM. Those relevant for SMP are

- EXE$V_NOSMPSANITY—When set, disables SMP sanity timeouts
- EXE$V_NOSPINWAIT—When set, disables SMP spinwait timeouts

SMP supports a maximum of 32 CPUs, each of which has a unique ID between 0 to 31. Kernel mode code running at an IPL above 2 can identify the CPU on which it is executing by examining its per-CPU database, described later in this section.

The global cell SMP$GL_PRIMID contains the ID of the primary processor. When the system crashes, the ID of the CPU that initiates the bugcheck, the CRASH CPU, is recorded in the global cell SMP$GL_BUGCHKCP.

A number of global cells describe the various members of the SMP system. Each is a longword with one bit for each CPU; when set, bit 0, for example, indicates that the CPU whose ID is 0 has the characteristic described by the cell.

- SMP$GL_CPUCONF identifies the available set, those physically present processors that have passed the power-on hardware diagnostics and are available for booting into the SMP system.
- SMP$GL_ACTIVE_CPUS identifies the active set, those CPUs that are participating in the SMP system and responding to interprocessor interrupt requests.
- Generally, SCH$GL_IDLE_CPUS identifies the idle set, those CPUs without a process to execute. (However, whenever a resident computable process becomes available, the bits representing idle CPUs on which the process can run are cleared as a signal that those CPUs should reschedule.)
- XDT$GL_BENIGN_CPUS identifies those CPUs in the benign state (see Section 34.5.4).
- SMP$GL_OVERRIDE identifies the override set (see Section 34.5.5).
- SMP$GL_ACK_MASK identifies those CPUs that have responded to a translation buffer invalidate request (see Section 34.5.3).
- EXE$GL_AFFINITY contains the default device affinity mask, which is normally all 1's to specify that a device can be accessed from all SMP members. This mask is copied to the unit control block field UCB$L_AFFINITY of each device unit when it is created.
- SMP$GL_BUG_DONE identifies those CPUs that have completed fatal bugcheck processing (see Section 34.10).

The spinlock-related data structures are described in Chapter 8. The CPU mutex is described in Section 34.5.

XDT$GW_INTERLOCK and XDT$GW_OWNER_ID, cells related to the use of XDELTA, are described in Section 34.5.4.

The use of cell SMP$GL_INVALID is related to invalidation of a single translation buffer entry, described in Section 34.5.3.

Each member of an SMP system has memory for data that describes the state of that CPU. Referred to as the per-CPU data area, this memory consists of the following adjacent pieces:

- The per-CPU database
- A one-page stack, called the boot stack
- An interrupt stack
- No-access guard pages at each end of both stacks to detect stack overflow and underflow

The VAX architecture defines five stacks: four per-process stacks for the different access modes and one systemwide interrupt stack. Executing in process context, a processor runs on an access mode stack private to that process. Executing in system context in earlier versions of VMS, a processor used the systemwide interrupt stack. On an SMP system, more than one processor can execute in system context at the same time. Simultaneous use of a stack by more than one processor is clearly not viable; VMS therefore provides system-context interrupt and boot stacks for each processor's exclusive use.

Each processor executes on its own boot stack during bootstrap and halt-restarts, including powerfail recovery. Under some circumstances, the processor accesses the stack physically with memory management disabled and, under others, virtually. In earlier versions of VMS, the space at the high end of the page containing the restart parameter block (RPB) served this purpose.

Each processor has its own interrupt stack for use when memory management is enabled; the SYSGEN parameter INTSTKPAGES specifies the stack size in pages. The processor runs on this stack while executing in system context, servicing interrupts.

SYSBOOT sums the sizes of the per-CPU database, the boot and interrupt stacks, and the guard pages to determine how many pages are actually required for the per-CPU data area. It rounds up that page count to the next power of 2. Each per-CPU data area begins on a virtual page boundary aligned to that power of 2. Later in system initialization, the rounded size in bytes minus 1 will be stored in global SMP$GL_BASE_MSK.

34.3.1   Locating the Per-CPU Data Area

Because of the alignment of each per-CPU data area, any virtual address within it can be transformed to the base address of the area. The low-order bits of the address are simply cleared against the mask in SMP$GL_BASE_ MSK. Thus it is possible to locate the per-CPU data area for a processor based on the contents of its interrupt stack pointer.

The FIND_CPU_DATA macro serves this function. An example invocation and expansion follow:

```
; Macro invocation
;
        FIND_CPU_DATA R4                ;Get per-CPU database address
;
; Macro expansion
;
        MFPR    S^#PR$_ISP,R4
        BICL2   G^SMP$GL_BASE_MSK,R4
```

Note that use of this macro is restricted to code that executes in kernel mode with memory management enabled. Furthermore, the code must run at an IPL above 2 between invoking the macro and using the returned address. Code running in process context at IPL 2 or below is subject to rescheduling and subsequent execution on another processor whose per-CPU data area is at a different address.

The array called the CPU data vector begins at global SMP$GL_CPU_DATA. This 32-longword array contains the addresses of the per-CPU data areas. It is indexed by CPU ID number to get the address of the area for a particular processor. Figure 34.5 shows the organization of a per-CPU data area and its relation to the CPU data vector.

Fields in the first page of the per-CPU database and the boot stack may be accessed using physical addresses during bootstrap and halt-restarts. Section 34.8.3 describes these accesses.

34.3.2 The Per-CPU Database

The per-CPU database contains processor-specific information such as the process control block (PCB) address of its current process, the address of its interrupt stack, and its fork queues. Figure 34.6 shows the layout of the per-CPU database, which is currently two pages long.

CPU$L_CURPCB contains the PCB address of the process currently executing on this processor. CPU$B_CUR_PRI contains the process's current

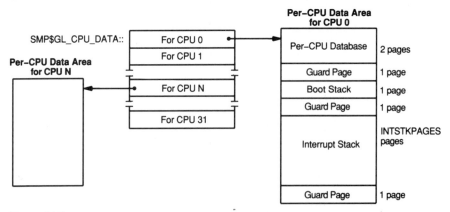

Figure 34.5
CPU Data Vector and Per-CPU Data Area

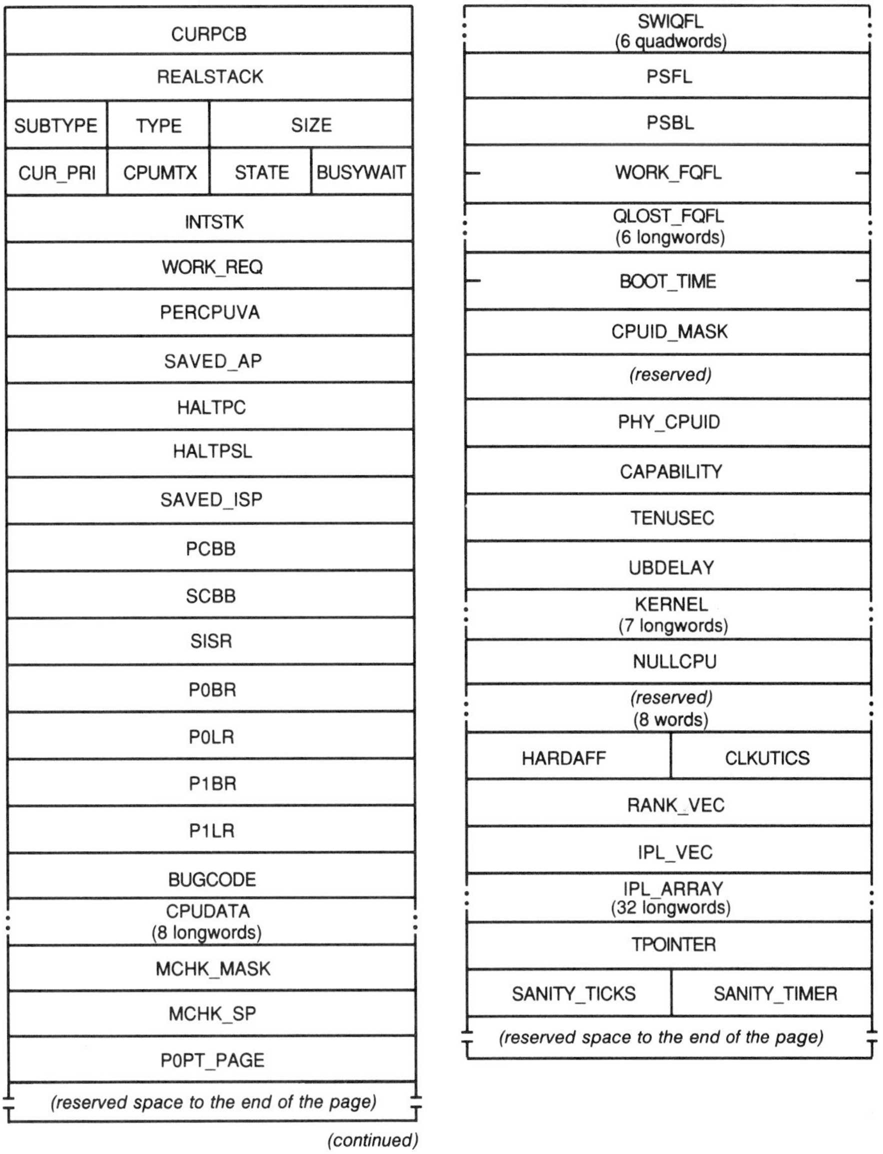

CURPCB			
REALSTACK			
SUBTYPE	TYPE	SIZE	
CUR_PRI	CPUMTX	STATE	BUSYWAIT
INTSTK			
WORK_REQ			
PERCPUVA			
SAVED_AP			
HALTPC			
HALTPSL			
SAVED_ISP			
PCBB			
SCBB			
SISR			
P0BR			
P0LR			
P1BR			
P1LR			
BUGCODE			
CPUDATA (8 longwords)			
MCHK_MASK			
MCHK_SP			
P0PT_PAGE			
(reserved space to the end of the page)			

SWIQFL (6 quadwords)	
PSFL	
PSBL	
WORK_FQFL	
QLOST_FQFL (6 longwords)	
BOOT_TIME	
CPUID_MASK	
(reserved)	
PHY_CPUID	
CAPABILITY	
TENUSEC	
UBDELAY	
KERNEL (7 longwords)	
NULLCPU	
(reserved) (8 words)	
HARDAFF	CLKUTICS
RANK_VEC	
IPL_VEC	
IPL_ARRAY (32 longwords)	
TPOINTER	
SANITY_TICKS	SANITY_TIMER
(reserved space to the end of the page)	

(continued)

Figure 34.6
Layout of the Per-CPU Database

priority. When the CPU is idle, CPU$L_CURPCB contains the address of the null PCB, and CPU$B_CUR_PRI contains −1.

CPU$L_REALSTACK contains the physical address of the high end of the boot stack, and CPU$L_INTSTK contains the virtual address of the high end of the interrupt stack. CPU$L_PERCPUVA contains the virtual address of the per-CPU data area.

CPUW_SIZE, CPUB_TYPE, and CPU$B_SUBTYPE contain the standard dynamic data structure header fields.

CPU$B_BUSYWAIT is nonzero while the processor is spinning, trying to acquire a spinlock, as described in Chapter 8. While this field is nonzero, the interval timer interrupt service routine does not charge a timer tick against the quantum of the current process (see Chapter 11).

CPU$B_STATE identifies the processor's current state (as distinct from process state). Section 34.7 describes the different states and the transitions among them.

CPU$B_CPUMTX is the number of nested times the CPU mutex has been acquired by the processor.

CPU$L_WORK_REQ is a bitmask describing outstanding work requests made by other processors of this processor. Section 34.5.2 describes these requests and their handling.

The per-CPU database contains several fields used in halt-restarts. CPUL_SAVED_AP, CPUL_HALTPC, and CPU$L_HALTPSL record information passed from the console subsystem after a halt.

CPU$L_SAVED_ISP records the value of the stack pointer after registers have been saved on the stack during a powerfail or fatal bugcheck.

During a powerfail, the current contents of various volatile processor registers are stored in the per-CPU database so that they can be restored during restart. Section 34.9 describes their use. These fields and their contents are

- CPU$L_PCBB—The physical address of the current process's hardware PCB
- CPU$L_SCBB—The physical address of the system control block (SCB)
- CPU$L_SISR—The software interrupt summary register
- CPU$L_P0BR—The base address of the current process's P0 page table
- CPU$L_P0LR—The length of the current process's P0 page table
- CPU$L_P1BR—The base address of the current process's P1 page table
- CPU$L_P1LR—The length of the current process's P1 page table

These fields also record information about the context at the time of a fatal bugcheck. The bugcheck code for the processor is stored in CPU$L_BUGCODE. Section 34.10 describes the use of these fields.

CPU$L_PHY_CPUID contains the ID of the processor, a number from 0 to 31. CPU$L_CPUID_MASK is a mask of 31 zeros with a single bit set in the bit position corresponding to the CPU ID number.

The eight longwords beginning at CPU$B_CPUDATA contain CPU-type-specific hardware data. The first longword is the contents of the system ID register; the rest of this area varies with each CPU type.

CPU$L_MCHK_MASK and CPU$L_MCHK_SP help implement machine check recovery blocks, described in Chapter 32.

CPU$L_P0PT_PAGE contains the system virtual address of the page reserved to this processor for use as a P0 page table when memory management is being enabled. Its use is described in Section 34.8.1.

The rest of the first page of the per-CPU database is reserved for future additional fields that might be referenced with physical addresses.

The processor's fork dispatching queues begin at CPU$Q_SWIQFL. Chapter 4 describes fork dispatching and the use of fork queues. The per-processor I/O postprocessing queue is at CPU$L_PSFL and CPU$L_PSBL. Its use is described in Section 34.6.4.

CPU$Q_WORK_FQFL is a work queue for switching fork processes from other processors to this one. Section 34.5.2 describes the use of this field.

Beginning at CPU$L_QLOST_FQFL is a data structure used to stall the CPU when quorum is lost. Section 34.5.2 describes its use.

CPU$Q_BOOT_TIME contains the system time at which the CPU was booted.

CPU$L_CAPABILITY is a bit mask with bits set to represent the capabilities of this processor. The low bit, when set, means that this CPU is the primary processor. The macro $CPBDEF defines symbolic values for the bits in this field. CPU$W_HARDAFF is the number of processes that have explicit affinity for this CPU. Chapter 12 describes processor capabilities and process affinity.

The per-CPU database contains two CPU-specific counts, referred to as the timed wait counts. These count iterations of instruction loops that are executed, in part, to wait for a minimum amount of time to elapse. These counts are used, for example, during powerfail recovery, to wait for disk drives to come back online. These counts also control the length of time a processor spins waiting to acquire a spinlock, as described in Section 34.5.6. They are not constants because they vary with CPU type and therefore are calibrated during system initialization. In earlier versions of VMS, these counts were systemwide globals. SMP support requires that they be CPU-specific and thus capable of being changed, for example, to reflect cache disabling on one CPU.

CPU$L_TENUSEC is the number of times a prototype loop executes in 10 microseconds. The prototype loop includes an inner loop that is simply a SOBGTR instruction. CPU$L_UBDELAY is the number of times the SOBGTR instruction executes in 3 microseconds. In actual use, the prototype loop is likely to be replaced by code that polls a device register. The delay represented by the inner SOBGTR loop is incorporated so as to introduce a 3-microsecond gap between successive references to the UNIBUS or other I/O bus that contains the device register.

Beginning at field CPU$L_KERNEL is a seven-longword array that records the amount of time the processor executes in each mode. CPU$L_NULLCPU records the amount of time spent in the scheduler idle loop. These counts are maintained by the interval timer interrupt service routine, described in Chapter 11.

Each bit, excluding bit 31, set in the field CPU$L_RANK_VEC corresponds to a static spinlock held by the processor; its position identifies the rank of the spinlock. Each bit set in the field CPU$L_IPL_VEC corresponds to an IPL at which the processor holds one or more spinlocks. The IPL representation is inverted. When a processor acquires a spinlock, the IPL of the spinlock is subtracted from 31. The bit in CPU$L_IPL_VEC corresponding to that number is set. The field thus represents the current set of (inverted) spinlock IPLs active on the processor. The inverted number is also used as an index into the 32-longword array at CPU$L_IPL_ARRAY, which records the number of different spinlocks held at each IPL. These fields are used only with the full-checking version of the spinlock routines, described in detail in Chapter 8.

The fields CPU$L_TPOINTER, CPU$W_SANITY_TIMER, and CPU$W_SANITY_TICKS are part of the SMP sanity timeout mechanism, which is described in Section 34.5.7.

The remainder of the second page of the per-CPU database is reserved for future use.

34.4 THE IMPLICATIONS OF SHARING MEMORY

All memory is physically accessible to all members of an SMP system. Because a process executes on only one CPU at a time, its per-process space is mapped on only that CPU and is not accessed concurrently from multiple processors. Thus, SMP support generally requires no additional synchronization of access to per-process space. (Note, however, that multiprocessing applications sharing a writable global section must synchronize possible concurrent accesses to the global section from processes running on different processors.)

However, all processors use the same system page table (SPT) and thus share system space. This has several important implications for system operation. First, because multiple processors can execute kernel mode threads and make concurrent access to system space data, SMP requires additional synchronization beyond that available with earlier versions of VMS. This section summarizes these changes.

Second, if code running on one processor changes a valid system page table entry (SPTE), it must inform all the other active SMP members, so that they will flush the cached contents of that SPTE, now stale, from their translation buffers. This mechanism is described in more detail in Section 34.5.3.

Third, multiple processors concurrently accessing pageable system space affect the movement of pages into and out of the system working set list. As a result, the "poor man's lockdown" technique used in earlier versions of VMS no longer works to force pages into the system working set list. This technique writes an IPL from the page to be locked into the PR$_IPL register. For the instruction to complete, the pages containing it and the IPL source must be faulted into memory and made valid. On a uniprocessor system with IPL raised high enough to block rescheduling, no further changes in the system working set list due to paging are possible. On an SMP system, however, the system working set list can change as the result of other processors' paging. Appendix B describes the method used to lock pages in VMS Version 5.

Earlier versions of the VMS executive used two different synchronization methods: IPL and mutual exclusion (mutex) semaphores. Since many important system functions are performed by software interrupt service routines, it was possible to synchronize access to shared system data by raising IPL to block the highest priority interrupt whose service routine accessed that data. In cases where raising IPL would be inappropriate (for example, access to pageable shared data), the need to acquire a mutex prevented access by more than one process at a time. No synchronization was required for shared system data accessed only by single uninterruptible instructions. For example, a processor executing an INSQUE instruction to insert an element at the tail of a lookaside list makes the multiple memory references required without allowing interrupts.

In an SMP system, processors execute concurrently; raising IPL on one processor blocks interrupts only on that processor and has no effect on the others. At an architectural or hardware level, the basic multiprocessing synchronization primitive is accessing shared memory with an interlocked instruction that reads and writes a location while blocking interlocked access to it from other processors. Using this primitive, VMS has implemented spinlocks, an extension to the IPL-based synchronization of previous versions. In its simplest form, a spinlock is a bit that describes the state of a set of shared data; the bit is set to indicate that a processor is accessing the data. The state of the bit is tested and changed with interlocked instructions.

In VMS Version 5, shared system data has been divided into a number of subsets, each with an associated IPL and spinlock. To access one of these subsets, a thread of execution raises IPL to the associated level and acquires the spinlock. The acquired spinlock synchronizes access from threads of execution on other processors. It could also synchronize the access of other threads of execution on the same processor, except that VMS allows any processor to reacquire a spinlock that it already holds. For that reason, elevated IPL is used, as in previous releases, to synchronize the access of threads of execution on the same processor. When done, the thread of execution releases the spinlock and typically restores the previous IPL.

During the development of VMS Version 5, each shared piece of data or resource needing synchronization was identified and an appropriate synchronization method determined.

- To certain synchronization IPLs, a corresponding spinlock was added; for example, use of IPL 6 now also requires that the QUEUEAST spinlock be owned. In contrast, the use of IPL$_SYNCH was subdivided into six different spinlocks, increasing the amount of parallelism possible.

- Single noninterruptible instructions of a read-modify-write type (for example, INCL or BBSS) that access shared data were converted to interlocked instructions, or the shared data was protected by a spinlock.
- A shared queue was either converted to an interlocked (self-relative) queue or accessed under protection of a spinlock. Accesses to the head or tail of a shared queue can be synchronized with interlocked queue instructions. A spinlock is required to synchronize access to a queue whose elements can be inserted or removed anywhere in the queue.

Some queues, such as fork queues, are local to a CPU and accessed only by threads of execution running on that CPU. For these, synchronization is achieved by accessing the head or tail of the queue with noninterlocked queue instructions or raising IPL to scan the queue.

Chapter 8 describes the use and implementation of synchronization mechanisms in more detail.

34.5 INTERPROCESSOR COOPERATION

The members of an SMP system that are participating in system operation make up the active set. The cell SMP$GL_ACTIVE_CPUS identifies these members with a bit set corresponding to the CPU ID of each. The primary, by definition, is a member of the active set. A secondary processor becomes a member during its initialization (see Section 34.8.4) and leaves when it is shut down (see Section 34.8.5).

A semaphore called the CPU mutex controls entry into the active set. Despite its name, the CPU mutex is a simplified form of spinlock, not an ordinary VMS mutex. An executive routine acquires and releases the CPU mutex semaphore using the LOCK and UNLOCK macros, as it would a spinlock.

A member of the active set must be responsive to interprocessor interrupts. VMS may interrupt a particular CPU to request a specific task, or it may interrupt all active set members to coordinate a systemwide action that requires all to cooperate. The following sections describe the interprocessor interrupt mechanism and the different work requests and their handling.

Some of the work requests are not urgent and are not acknowledged, for example, reschedule, I/O post, and quorum-lost work requests. In fact, a member typically responds to them by requesting a software interrupt at a priority lower than that of the interprocessor interrupt.

Several work requests, however, require timely response to prevent processor hangs and system deadlocks or crashes. These are a request to enter the benign state, a request to bugcheck, a request for the primary to serve the console terminal to a secondary, a request to invalidate a single translation buffer entry, and a request for the primary to access its time-of-year clock. Some of these requests involve a timed interprocessor dialogue to complete. Some require all members to respond. A processor executing for an extended period at an IPL at or above that of the interprocessor interrupt must check for and service certain of the requests.

A member of the active set must also release held spinlocks in a timely fashion. When a processor loops, using the SPINWAIT macro (described in Section 34.5.6) to wait for a spinlock to be released, it loops a finite number of times. Typically, the loop count is based on the timed wait counts from the per-CPU database and one of the two SYSGEN parameters SMP_SPINWAIT or SMP_LNGSPINWAIT. If the loop count is exhausted before the other member releases the spinlock, the waiting processor may presume the other member is hung and crash the system.

Sanity, spinlock wait, and busy wait timeouts exist to prevent the entire system, and the VAXcluster system of which it may be a part, from hanging when one member of the active set becomes unresponsive. Section 34.5.7 describes the sanity timer mechanism. Section 34.5.6 describes the need for processor responsiveness to certain interprocessor interrupt requests.

34.5.1 Requesting Interprocessor Interrupts

VMS provides several macros that request an interprocessor interrupt. The most commonly used are

- IPINT_ALL, to interrupt all other members of the active set
- IPINT_CPU, to interrupt a particular CPU

Each of these macros is typically invoked with an argument identifying the reason for the interrupt request. The macro generates code that sets the corresponding bit in CPU$L_WORK_REQ in the per-CPU databases of the processors to be interrupted. A work request bit is set, tested, and cleared with an interlocked instruction to serialize access to it. Some interprocessor interrupt requests, however, are identified by means other than a work request bit.

Table 34.1 lists the possible work request bits. Prefaced by CPU$V_ or CPU$M_, these symbols are defined by the macro $CPUDEF. The functioning of these bits is discussed in further detail in the following sections.

The following is an example of the invocation and expansion of the IPINT_CPU macro:

```
; Macro invocation
;
        IPINT_CPU IOPOST,G^SMP$GL_PRIMID ;Tell the primary to request
                                         ; a software interrupt
; Macro expansion
;
        PUSHL   R0
        MOVL    G^SMP$GL_PRIMID,R0
        PUSHL   R1
        MOVAL   G^SMP$GL_CPU_DATA,R1
        MOVL    (R1)[R0],R1
```

```
        BBSSI   S^#CPU$V_IOPOST,CPU$L_WORK_REQ(R1),30010$
30010$:
        POPL    R1
        JSB     G^SMP$INTPROC
        POPL    R0
```

The generated code invokes SMP$INTPROC, in module [SYSLOA]SMPINT_
xxx. (For the VAXstation 3520 and VAXstation 3540 systems, the module
name is SMPINT_60; the module SMPINT supports all other processors.)

SMP$INTPROC requests an interprocessor interrupt on the CPU whose ID
is in R0 and returns. The method for requesting an interprocessor interrupt
is CPU-dependent and generally requires writing to a processor register or a
location in node private address space. For example, the following instruction
interrupts the other processor of a VAX 8800 system:

```
        MTPR    #1,#PR8NN$_INOP         ;Write to interprocessor
                                        ; interrupt register
```

There are actually four slightly different routines, all of them in module
[SYSLOA]SMPINT_*xxx*, for requesting interprocessor interrupts of all active
set members. The IPINT_CPU macro selects one of the following routines
based on its arguments:

- SMP$INTALL—Interrupt each other active set member
- SMP$INTALL_BIT—Set the specified work request bit in each other active
  set member's per-CPU database and interrupt it
- SMP$INTALL_ACQ—Acquire the CPU mutex, interrupt all other active
  set members, and release the CPU mutex
- SMP$INTALL_BIT_ACQ (the default)—Acquire the CPU mutex, set the
  specified work request bit in each other active set member's per-CPU
  database and interrupt it, and release the CPU mutex

Table 34.1   Interrupt Work Request Bits

Name	Meaning
INV_TBS	Invalidate a specific translation buffer entry
INV_TBA	Invalidate all translation buffer entries
TBACK	Acknowledge a translation buffer invalidate request
BUGCHK	Generate a fatal bugcheck
BUGCHKACK	Unused
RECALSCH	Unused
UPDASTLVL	Update current process's PR$_ASTLVL
UPTODR	Access the primary's time-of-year clock
WORK_FQP	Service requests on the interprocessor fork queue
QLOST	Stall until VAXcluster quorum is regained
RESCHED	Request an IPL 3 reschedule interrupt
VIRTCONS	Unused
IOPOST	Request an IPL 4 I/O postprocessing interrupt

34.5.2   **Servicing Interprocessor Interrupts and Work Requests**

SMP$INTSR, in module [SYSLOA]SMPINT_*xxx*, is the interprocessor inter-
rupt service routine. It runs at IPL 20 or 22, depending on the CPU type:
on VAX 88x0 and VAX 83x0 systems, the IPL is 20; on VAX 6000 series,
VAXstation 3520, and VAXstation 3540 systems, the value is IPL 22.

After saving registers, SMP$INTSR tests system global cells and the pro-
cessor's work request bits to determine what actions are appropriate responses to the interrupt request. Note that the service routine may have
to respond to multiple requests. It tests and clears each work request bit
with a BBCCI instruction.

It tests XDT$GW_OWNER_ID to see if a processor executing XDELTA has
requested the other processors to stall. If so, it raises IPL to 31 and enters a
benign state, as described in Section 34.5.4. Afterward, SMP$INTSR restores
the previous IPL, that of the interprocessor interrupt.

SMP$INTSR checks whether it is running on the primary processor. If so,
it invokes SMP$VIRTCONS_SERVER, in module [SYSLOA]SMPINT_*xxx*, in
case there is a virtual console request to be serviced. The need to service one
is indicated by a secondary's having acquired the VIRTCONS spinlock.

A secondary processor performing I/O to the console terminal requires
the assistance of the primary. User-level I/O requests are queued through
a driver to a device that has affinity for the primary. However, requests
made from system context do not go through a device driver; instead, they
are performed by direct manipulation of the processor registers that interface to the console subsystem. Only the primary processor can access these
registers. SMP$VIRTCONS_SERVER serves the console terminal to the sec-
ondary processors. When the secondary processor releases the spinlock, the
routine returns to SMP$INTSR. (More typically, during normal operations,
a secondary invokes SMP$WRITE_OPA0, in module SMPROUT, to perform
console output.)

The previous two tasks, entry into the benign state and serving the console
terminal, are not requested through work request bits. Each of them is a
request for the processor to continue to perform an action until told to stop.
The signal to stop is a change in value in the relevant system global cell.

SMP$INTSR tests CPU$L_WORK_REQ to see if another processor has
incurred a fatal bugcheck and is requesting this processor to bugcheck. If
so, it restores the registers, returning the stack to its state at the start of
the interrupt service routine, and generates the fatal bugcheck CPUEXIT.
Section 34.10 describes how fatal bugchecks are processed on an SMP system.

If a single translation buffer entry invalidation was requested, SMP$INTSR
invokes SMP$INVALID_SINGLE, in module [SYSLOA]SMPINT_*xxx*. Sec-
tion 34.5.3 describes this routine and its requests in more detail.

If an I/O postprocessing interrupt was requested, SMP$INTSR requests an
IPL 4 software interrupt. Executive code running on a secondary that queues
an I/O request packet to the systemwide I/O postprocessing queue makes

this work request of the primary. Later, when IPL drops, IOC$IOPOST, running on the primary processor, will service its queue. Section 34.6.4 discusses the need for systemwide and per-CPU I/O postprocessing queues.

If there is a work request to invalidate the entire translation buffer, SMP$INTSR takes that action by writing to the PR$_TBIA register. The work request is made through the INVALIDATE_TB macro. This macro is invoked, for example, when the swapper process deletes or fills a process header slot, or when the protection is changed on the nonpaged pool pages occupied by floating-point or character string emulation images.

If there is a work request to update the AST level for this processor's current process, SMP$INTSR clears PR$_ASTLVL and its copy in the hardware PCB. Clearing them sets the AST level to kernel mode and catalyzes an AST delivery interrupt request when control returns to the process. Although there may be no AST deliverable to the process's current mode, its AST level will still be recomputed. This work request is made when SCH$QAST, in module ASTDEL, running on another processor, queues an AST to a process current on this processor.

SCH$QAST has no direct way to update another processor's PR$_ASTLVL register. Furthermore, there is a potential synchronization problem in the update of PHD$B_ASTLVL, which is the high byte of PHD$L_P0LRASTL, the hardware PCB copy of PR$_P0LR. PHD$L_P0LRASTL is updated from process context by memory management code that alters the size of P0 space. If such a routine's update were concurrent with SCH$QAST's altering PHD$B_ASTLVL, the update to PHD$B_ASTLVL would be lost. Therefore, SCH$QAST makes an interprocessor interrupt request. SMP$INTSR is running at too high an IPL to synchronize access to the AST queue, so it merely forces the AST interrupt by clearing both PR$_ASTLVL and PHD$B_ASTLVL.

If there is a work request indicating a fork process to be moved from another processor to this one, SMP$INTSR executes a REMQHI instruction to remove the first fork block from the queue at CPU$Q_WORK_FQFL. It invokes EXE$FORK, in module FORKCNTRL. EXE$FORK inserts the fork block in the fork queue on this processor corresponding to the appropriate IPL. (FKB$B_FIPL contains either an IPL or the index of a spinlock from which the IPL is taken.) SMP$INTSR repeats this for each fork block in the per-CPU database fork work queue.

Two routines in module SMPROUT make interprocessor fork work requests: SMP$FORK_TO_PRIMARY and SMP$SWITCH_CPU. The first is typically invoked from SMP$WRITE_OPA0, running on a secondary processor, to broadcast a message to the console terminal. The second is invoked to queue an I/O request to a device with affinity for a CPU other than the current processor. Section 34.6.3 describes device affinity.

If there is a work request to access the time-of-year clock, SMP$INTSR checks whether it is running on the primary. If not, it ignores the request. With guaranteed access to the console subsystem, which is the location of the time-of-year clock on some processors, the primary has the role of timekeeper. The value in its time-of-year clock is the basis for initializing system time after a boot or power failure. The clocks on secondary processors are set to the same value as the primary's clock, because, on some systems, the role of primary can shift to a different CPU after a reboot. During normal system operation, secondary processors' clocks are used only for measuring rates of certain CPU errors.

Associated with this work request are two bits in SMP$GL_FLAGS:

- SMP$V_TODR, which a secondary tests and sets to ensure that only one secondary at a time engages in this dialogue
- SMP$V_TODR_ACK, for whose setting a secondary waits as a signal that the cell SMP$GL_NEW_TODR contains valid data

SMP$GL_PROPOSED_TODR describes the type of clock access desired:

- On a VAX 83x0 system, −1 forces a read of the console watch chip. On other processors, it has the same effect as a value of 0.
- In response to a value of 0, the primary reads the time of year, typically from the clock processor register.
- In response to any other value, the primary writes this value to the clock.

The primary writes the new value of the time-of-year clock into SMP$GL_NEW_TODR.

The software interrupt request to access the clock is made from a secondary executing one of the following routines:

- EXE$INIT_TODR, in module [SYSLOA]INIADP*xxx*, which is invoked by the SYSINIT process
- EXE$READ_TODR or EXE$WRITE_TODR, in module [SYSLOA]ERR-SUB*xxx*

Accessing the primary's time-of-year clock from a secondary processor requires an interprocessor dialogue, whose general sequence is as follows:

1. Prior to requesting the interprocessor interrupt, each of the previously listed routines tests and sets bit SMP$V_TODR, writes SMP$GL_PRO-POSED_TODR, requests an interprocessor interrupt of the primary, and waits for bit SMP$V_TODR_ACK to be set.
2. Depending on the value in SMP$GL_PROPOSED_TODR, SMP$INTSR invokes EXE$READP_LOCAL_TODR or EXE$WRITEP_LOCAL_TODR in module [SYSLOA]ERRSUB*xxx*. EXE$WRITEP_LOCAL_TODR, on some processor types, broadcasts the new time to all secondary processors by requesting on each an interprocessor interrupt with a processor-type-specific work request.

3. SMP$INTSR then writes the time value to SMP$GL_NEW_TODR and sets SMP$V_TODR_ACK.

4. Once SMP$V_TODR_ACK has been set, the requesting secondary clears SMP$V_TODR_ACK, copies the time from SMP$GL_NEW_TODR, and clears SMP$V_TODR.

For further information on timekeeping and the role of the time-of-year clock, see Chapter 11.

If there is a work request indicating that VAXcluster quorum has been lost, SMP$INTSR stalls system operations on this processor until quorum has been regained. This work request is made by the VAXcluster connection manager, from routine CNX$CHECK_QUORUM, in module [SYSLOA]CONUTIL. The stall is implemented by the continuous requeuing of a packet onto the per-CPU I/O postprocessing queue. The packet, which begins at field CPU$L_QLOST_FQFL in the per-CPU database, contains the address of a system routine (called an end action routine) at offset IRP$L_PID rather than a process ID. IOC$IOPOST distinguishes the two by the sign of the value: an end action routine address is in system space; a process ID is always a positive number.

When IOC$IOPOST removes a packet specifying an end action routine, it invokes the end action routine. The quorum-lost end action routine, which is in module [SYSLOA]SMPINT_*xxx*, tests whether there is quorum. If there is, it merely returns to IOC$IOPOST. If not, the routine requeues its packet onto the per-CPU I/O postprocessing queue and requests another I/O post-processing interrupt.

If there is a work request for a rescheduling interrupt, SMP$INTSR requests an IPL 3 interrupt. Chapter 12 describes the circumstances under which this interrupt is requested. Briefly, they are

- When a resident process becomes computable whose priority allows it to preempt a process current on another CPU
- When a current process's priority is changed by a thread of execution running on a different CPU and there is a computable resident process of higher priority
- When a current process acquires explicit affinity for a different CPU
- When a capability has been removed from a CPU that is needed by its current process

Four bits are reserved for processor-type-specific requests. After servicing all other work requests, SMP$INTSR tests whether any work request bits are still set. If so, SMP$INTSR invokes SMP$SPEC_IPINT, in module [SYSLOA]MCHECK*xxx*, to handle them. On a VAX 8800, for example, the primary processor interrupts the secondary when an NMI bus fault machine check occurs. Each processor logs an error with the contents of various processor registers and its NMI silo. On a VAX 6000 series processor, the primary processor makes a CPU-specific work request of a secondary processor that the secondary processor disable a part of its cache that has received a certain number of errors. On a VAX 6000 model 400 processor, one CPU-specific work request is for a secondary processor to reset its time-of-year clock.

When no more work request bits are set, SMP$INTSR restores saved registers and dismisses the interrupt.

34.5.3   Translation Buffer Invalidation

A translation buffer (TB) is a CPU component that caches the result of recent successful virtual address translations of valid pages: the virtual page numbers and their corresponding page table entries (PTEs). Subsequent translations of cached addresses are quicker. On VAX processors supported by VMS Version 5.2, VAX microcode automatically removes, or flushes, cached per-process entries whenever a process is placed into execution with a LDPCTX instruction.

Kernel mode software can invalidate either a single TB entry by writing its virtual address to the processor register PR$_TBIS or all entries by writing a zero to the processor register PR$_TBIA. An attempt to invalidate an entry that is not cached is simply ignored. The VMS executive ensures the consistency of the TB by invalidating the TB entry corresponding to a valid PTE that it is changing, for example, during virtual address space deletion. Since the PTEs of invalid pages are not cached, the VMS executive does not invalidate TB entries when it alters a PTE for an invalid page.

On an SMP system, each processor has its own TB, which is filled with entries as the result of instruction stream execution on that processor. Since all members share the SPT, if one member is to change a valid SPTE, it must ensure that no other member is attempting to change the same SPTE and that all other members invalidate their TB entries for it. Another complication is a requirement for synchronization with VAX microcode, which sets the modify bit in a PTE when it writes to a page. To meet these requirements, an active set member changing a valid SPTE must request interprocessor interrupts of the others to put them into a quiescent state in which they cannot execute instructions that write the page in question. The possibility also exists that at the time of the interprocessor interrupt request a member might be executing a relatively lengthy sequence, at an IPL higher than that of the interprocessor interrupt, during which it could not tolerate any asynchronous PTE changes. Consequently, VMS has a multistep interprocessor dialogue for changing SPTEs.

A kernel mode routine changes a PTE using the macro INVALIDATE_TB, one of whose arguments is the address mapped by the PTE. (Another of its arguments identifies the environment in which the system is running. The description that follows assumes a full VMS environment with multiprocessing enabled.) If the address argument is omitted, the macro flushes the entire translation buffer and requests an interprocessor interrupt to do the same on each active member, as described in Section 34.5.2. Flushing the entire translation buffer is a preferred alternative to flushing a number of pages within a loop that includes the interprocessor dialogue described in the following paragraphs.

If the address argument is present on the macro invocation, the macro generates code to test in which address space the address argument lies. In the case of a process space address, the macro generates instructions from its arguments that actually change the PTE and then generates a simple write to the PR$_TBIS register. Since the same per-process space is not accessed concurrently by multiple processors, nothing further is necessary. In the case of a system space address, the macro generates instructions to implement the TB invalidation in three phases:

1. Invoke SMP$INVALID, in module SMPROUT. SMP$INVALID requests interprocessor interrupts to quiet all active members and executes a co-routine return to its invoker to change the SPTE.
2. Change the SPTE through instructions supplied as macro arguments.
3. Co-routine return to SMP$INVALID, which sets a bit in the per-CPU database of each active member to tell it to remove the SPTE from its TB.

INVALIDATE_TB invokes SMP$INVALID in the following circumstances:

- When MMG$FREWSLX, in module PAGEFAULT, removes a previously valid page from the system working set list
- When adapter configuration code, for example, in module [SYSLOA]INI-ADP8PS, clears an SPTE that was in use to map a potential page of adapter registers
- When a device driver clears an SPTE that was double-mapping a page of a direct I/O buffer

The following steps describe the sequence of a system space TB invalidation as it might occur concurrently on the CPU requesting the invalidation and the active set members. The numbers in Figure 34.7 correspond to the following steps, not all of which are represented in the figure.

The sequence begins with SMP$INVALID, in module SMPROUT, which runs on the processor changing the SPTE:

①It acquires the INVALIDATE spinlock, raising IPL to 1 less than the interprocessor interrupt IPL.
②It acquires the CPU mutex to block entry of new members into the active set.
③It stores the address to be invalidated in SMP$GL_INVALID.
④It stores a mask with only its CPU ID bit set in SMP$GL_ACK_MASK.
⑤It requests an interprocessor interrupt of all other active set members with a work request type of INV_TBS. In response, each member should

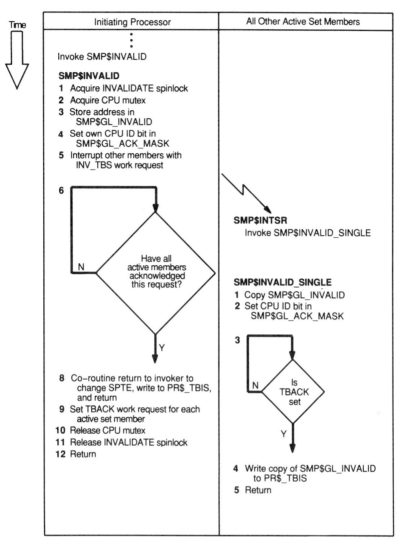

Figure 34.7
Invalidation of a Single TB Entry

copy SMP$GL_INVALID and set its own CPU ID bit in SMP$GL_ACK_
MASK.

⑥ Within a loop, SMP$INVALID compares SMP$GL_ACK_MASK to the
active set mask and checks for a request to bugcheck. When all active set
members have responded, it goes on to step 8.

7. If SMP$INVALID exceeds the loop count before all active members have
responded, SMP$INVALID invokes SMP$TIMEOUT, described in Section 34.5.7, to determine whether the lack of response is serious enough
to warrant crashing the system. If that routine returns, SMP$INVALID
resets the loop count and continues with step 6. The loop count is the

product of the two per-CPU database timed wait counts and the SYSGEN parameter SMP_SPINWAIT.

⑧ All other active members are now in a quiescent state, waiting for the signal to invalidate their TB entries. SMP$INVALID executes a co-routine return to allow its invoker to execute instructions that alter the PTE, do a local TB invalidate, and perform a co-routine return to SMP$INVALID.

⑨ SMP$INVALID sets the bit CPU$V_TBACK in each active member's work request longword as the signal for which they have been waiting. In response, each should write its copy of SMP$GL_INVALID to PR$_TBIS.

⑩ SMP$INVALID releases the CPU mutex.

⑪ It releases the INVALIDATE spinlock, restoring the previous IPL.

⑫ It returns to its invoker.

In response to the INV_TBS interprocessor interrupt described in step 5, the routine SMP$INTSR, in module [SYSLOA]SMPINT_*xxx*, runs on each other active set member and invokes the routine SMP$INVALID_SINGLE, in the same module.

SMP$INVALID_SINGLE takes the following steps:

① It copies SMP$GL_INVALID.

② It sets the processor's CPU ID bit in SMP$GL_ACK_MASK.

③ Within a loop, it waits for its work request TBACK to be set. When the bit is set, it goes on to step 4. Within the loop, it also checks for requests to enter the benign state and to bugcheck. The timed loop is generated by the BUSYWAIT macro, described in Section 34.5.6.

④ It writes its copy of SMP$GL_INVALID to PR$_TBIS.

⑤ It returns to SMP$INTSR, which checks for other work requests and finally executes an REI instruction to dismiss the interrupt.

34.5.4 Benign State and XDELTA

When one member of the active set requires that all other members temporarily cease their normal operations, it initiates the benign state. All the other members are quiescent until the initiating member terminates the benign state. While in a benign state, a processor loops at IPL 31, checking whether the state has been terminated. The benign state is currently used only when one processor executes XDELTA code; the other CPUs effectively pause rather than continue with operations that might disrupt or confuse the debugging session.

When a processor enters XDELTA, through a breakpoint or T-bit exception, the processor executes code within XDELTA that makes it the sole user of XDELTA:

1. It raises IPL to 31.
2. It repeatedly tests the low bit of XDT$GW_INTERLOCK, the XDELTA interlock bit, until it finds the bit clear.

3. It executes a BBSSI instruction to test and set the bit. If the bit was set, the processor returns to step 2. Otherwise, its exclusive access to the XDELTA owner cell, XDT$GW_OWNER_ID, is now guaranteed.

4. It tests the high bit of that cell to see whether any processor owns XDELTA.

   —If the bit is set, this processor writes its own CPU ID into the cell, clears the interlock bit, and proceeds with XDELTA.

   —If the bit is clear, indicating that some processor owns XDELTA, and the owner ID is that of this processor, it clears the interlock bit and proceeds with XDELTA.

   —If the bit is clear and the owner ID is that of another processor, the processor clears the interlock bit and invokes the benign state routine.

5. Proceeding with XDELTA, the processor requests an interprocessor interrupt of all the other members of the active set. As they execute SMP$INTSR, each finds XDELTA owned and enters the benign state by invoking the benign state routine.

6. When XDELTA is done, before it restores the thread of execution that incurred the exception, it acquires the XDELTA owner interlock bit, writes −1 to XDT$GW_OWNER_ID, and releases the owner interlock bit.

The benign state routine, XDT$CPU_WAIT in module [DELTA]XDELTA, takes the following steps:

1. To record its entry into the benign state, the processor sets the bit corresponding to its ID in XDT$GL_BENIGN_CPUS.

2. The processor tests whether it is the primary processor.

3. If it is not the primary processor, it continually tests the high bit of XDT$GW_OWNER_ID, waiting for the bit to be clear. When the bit is clear, the processor clears its bit in XDT$GL_BENIGN_CPUS. It invalidates the entire TB. It pushes a program counter/processor status longword (PC/PSL) pair so that it can return control with an REI instruction, flushing any prefetch of instructions that might have been altered by XDELTA commands or actions.

4. The primary processor is responsible for performing XDELTA console terminal I/O on behalf of a secondary processor. This mechanism is similar to the one described in Section 34.5.2, but not identical; the primary assumes the need to serve the console and does not check the state of the VIRTCONS spinlock. The primary saves the state of the physical console interface. It then communicates to the secondary processor through memory locations that look like a console port to the secondary. The primary serves the console by relaying data between the real console port and the virtual console port.

   When the secondary processor leaves XDELTA, the primary processor restores the saved state of the physical console interface. It then leaves the benign state in the same manner as the other processors.

There is provision for an alternative entry into and exit from the benign state, through routines SMP$INITIATE_BENIGN and SMP$TERMINATE_BENIGN, in module SMPROUT. SMP$INTSR tests for this form of the benign state and loops, checking for concurrent bugcheck and translation buffer invalidate requests. No current use is made of this form of benign state.

34.5.5   The Override Set

The override set consists of all processors currently in the override state. The override state allows a thread of execution to inhibit any change in its IPL when that change would be awkward for the algorithm and when its synchronization is not in doubt. The processor may be executing a code sequence beyond question, such as initialization code, or the processor may be executing code that confirms that local synchronization is not at issue. The machine check exception service routine is an example of a code thread that temporarily joins the override set to acquire a spinlock from high IPL, after checking that the code that incurred the exception was executing at IPL 2 or below, that is, that no lower IPL code thread would be desynchronized by this action.

A processor enters the override set when it must perform a synchronization operation that otherwise might be considered illegal. It sets its CPU ID bit in SMP$GL_OVERRIDE and leaves the override set when it clears the bit. While in the override set, a processor's IPL is not changed when the processor acquires a spinlock. Furthermore, the spinlock acquisitions and releases of a member of the override set are not subject to the IPL checks in the full-checking SMP synchronization image, which test that local CPU synchronization is not being violated.

Some examples of circumstances under which a processor joins the override set are

- During bootstrap and initialization, while the processor is executing at IPL 31
- During IPL 31 servicing of read data substitute machine checks, when the MMG spinlock must be acquired
- During fatal bugcheck processing

Note that widespread use of this mechanism is not supported or recommended. In many cases where it might seem like a good solution, a better structured alternative usually exists, for example, creating a lower IPL fork process.

34.5.6   **Spinwaits and Busy Waits**

The SPINWAIT and BUSYWAIT macros enable a processor to wait a finite length of time for another processor to take some action. Both generate loops with an iteration count based on the per-CPU database timed wait counts. The SPINWAIT macro generates a test for the availability of a spinlock within the loop, while the BUSYWAIT macro allows the user to specify the test to be made. If the loop count is exhausted before the test succeeds, the code generated by both macros invokes SMP$TIMEOUT to determine whether the system should be crashed.

The SPINWAIT macro is defined in the SPINLOCKS_xxx module and only used from within that module. It generates the following instruction sequence:

1. Establish a loop count based on the spinlock's timeout count and the per-CPU database timed wait counts.
2. Use instructions specified by the macro invoker to test whether the spinlock is available. If so, leave this loop.
3. If the current IPL is not blocking interprocessor interrupts, go to step 9.
4. If another processor has begun to execute XDELTA (if the high bit of XDT$GW_OWNER_ID is zero), invoke XDT$CPU_WAIT to enter the benign state, as described in Section 34.5.4.
5. If a bugcheck work request has been made, generate a fatal CPUEXIT bugcheck.
6. If the processor is not a member of the override set (described in Section 34.5.5), go to step 9.
7. If the processor is the primary, invoke SMP$VIRTCONS_SERVER to check whether there is a secondary that needs virtual console service.
8. If a work request to invalidate a single translation buffer entry has been made, invoke SMP$INVALID_SINGLE.
9. If the spinlock does not become available within retry count iterations and the spinlock owner has not changed, invoke SMP$TIMEOUT to determine whether to generate a SPINWAIT fatal bugcheck.
10. If SMP$TIMEOUT returns, continue with step 1.

SMP$TIMEOUT, in module SMPROUT, invokes SMP$CONTROLP_CPUS (see Section 34.5.7) to determine if any active set member has been halted through the console. If an active set member is halted, SMP$TIME-OUT returns. If no active set member is halted, SMP$TIMEOUT tests bit EXE$V_NOSPINWAIT in EXE$GL_TIME_CONTROL. This bit is set on a system booted with XDELTA and also set during the execution of certain CPU error routines and the IPL 12 interrupt service routine. If the bit is clear, SMP$TIMEOUT generates the fatal bugcheck CPUSPINWAIT. If the bit is set, SMP$TIMEOUT returns.

Even while spinwaiting, a processor must be responsive to certain interprocessor work requests to prevent deadlocks. If the processor is looping at an IPL below that of the interprocessor interrupt, its loop can be interrupted to service a work request. However, if it is looping at a higher IPL, it cannot be interrupted and must minimally check for work requests to bugcheck or to enter the benign state.

An incomplete dump or deadlock would result if such a spinwaiting processor were unresponsive to a bugcheck request and if, when its spinwait count was exhausted, SMP$TIMEOUT returned rather than crashing. If a fatal bugcheck were initiated in these circumstances, regardless of which active set member owned the spinlock of interest, it is likely that the spinlock would not be released and that the spinwaiting processor would simply continue to spinwait and fail to save its context in the dump. If the spinwaiting processor were the primary processor and failed to respond to the bugcheck request, the system would hang, deadlocked. Section 34.10 describes how fatal bugchecks are handled on an SMP system.

A deadlock could result if a primary processor spinwaiting at an IPL equal to or above that of the interprocessor interrupt were unresponsive to a request to enter the benign state. Once the benign state is initiated, whether the initiator or a processor already in the benign state owns the spinlock, it is likely that the spinlock would not be released and that the spinwait would continue. (Because the system has been booted with XDELTA, a spinwait crash would not result at the end of the spinwait loop.) The system would deadlock as soon as the benign state initiator required the primary processor to service secondary processor console I/O. Section 34.5.4 describes the benign state in more detail.

A processor that spinwaits at an IPL above that of the interprocessor interrupt and that is not in the override set is trying to acquire a spinlock whose IPL is above that of any associated with an urgent interprocessor request. In other words, the processor cannot be waiting for the INVALIDATE or VIRTCONS spinlocks. (The INVALIDATE spinlock's IPL is defined to be 1 less than that of the interprocessor interrupt; the VIRTCONS spinlock's IPL is equal to that of the interrupt.) Thus, for example, even if there is an active set member initiating an interprocessor dialogue for translation buffer invalidation, that processor cannot also be holding the higher ranked spinlock that the spinwaiting processor is trying to acquire. Thus there can be no deadlock between that processor and the spinwaiting one.

If, on the other hand, the processor is in the override set, the value of its IPL is not necessarily the IPL of the spinlock for which it is waiting. The SPINWAIT macro, therefore, also generates explicit tests for whether a processor in the override set should service requests to invalidate a single translation buffer entry or, as the primary, serve the console terminal to a secondary. Additionally, for a processor that is primary, the SPINWAIT macro should check whether there is an UPTODR request to service. This last test, however, is absent in VMS Version 5.2.

By default, the BUSYWAIT macro does not generate any tests for outstanding work requests that should be serviced. Any code that invokes the BUSYWAIT macro from IPLs at or above that of the interprocessor interrupt service routine should include the same tests as the SPINWAIT macro.

34.5.7   Sanity Timer Mechanism

The sanity timer mechanism enables detection of a member of the SMP system that is hung or otherwise nonfunctional. It acts as a check that each member is responding to interval timer interrupts. Each of the members of the active set monitors one other member, creating a sanity timer chain. A member monitors the one with the next lower ID than its own. The CPU with the lowest ID monitors the one with the highest ID, forming a circular list. When a CPU is booted and joins the active set, it inserts itself into the sanity timer chain.

The following fields in the per-CPU database are related to the sanity timer mechanism:

- CPU$W_SANITY_TIMER, initialized to the value of the SYSGEN parameter SMP_SANITY_CNT, is the number of interval timer ticks until this CPU times out. Its default value is 300.
- CPU$W_SANITY_TICKS, initialized to the value of the SYSGEN parameter SMP_TICK_CNT, is the number of interval timer ticks until the next time the processor monitors its neighbor in the sanity timer chain. Its default value is 30.
- CPU$L_TPOINTER contains the address of CPU$W_SANITY_TIMER in the per-CPU database of the active set member with the next lower ID.

The sanity timer mechanism is implemented as part of the interval timer interrupt service routine. Each processor resets its own sanity timer and monitors one other member's sanity timer, periodically decrementing it. If a processor decrements the watched CPU's sanity timer to zero, that means the watched CPU has not reset its sanity timer.

The interval timer interrupt service routine, EXE$HWCLKINT in module TIMESCHDL, running on each member of an SMP system, takes the following steps to implement the sanity timer mechanism:

1. It tests the low bit of SMP$GL_FLAGS to determine whether the system is multiprocessing. If the bit is clear, EXE$HWCLKINT bypasses all the sanity timer related code.
2. It resets the current processor's sanity timer in such a way as not to lose the refresh in case there is a concurrent decrement from the next CPU in the sanity timer chain.
3. It decrements CPU$W_SANITY_TICKS, the number of ticks until the next time it should check its neighbor's sanity timer. If the number has

reached zero, it resets CPU$W_SANITY_TICKS from SMP_TICK_CNT and subtracts the value of the SYSGEN parameter from its neighbor's sanity timer.

Note that EXE$HWCLKINT resets its own sanity timer at each interval timer interrupt but decrements its neighbor's sanity timer less frequently, giving its neighbor ample opportunity to reset its own sanity timer.

4. If its neighbor's timer is now less than or equal to zero, the routine makes several tests to determine how serious the situation is:

—If bit EXE$V_NOSMPSANITY in EXE$GL_TIME_CONTROL is set to indicate that sanity timeout is disabled, then the routine merely resets its neighbor's sanity timer and continues.

On a system booted with XDELTA, sanity timeouts are disabled in this way. During extended execution at high IPL in certain machine checks and the IPL 12 (IPC) interrupt service routine (see Chapter 4), the service routine sets EXE$V_NOSMPSANITY and then clears it when done.

—It checks the timer again and if the timer is now positive, indicating that its neighbor has resumed normal operations, it continues.

—It invokes SMP$CONTROLP_CPUS, in module [SYSLOA]ERR-SUBxxx, to see whether any active set members are at present halted via the console. On a CPU type whose console is unable to identify which processors are halted, this routine returns the entire active set. On other CPUs (VAX 6000 series and VAXstation 3520 or 3540 systems), it returns just those active CPUs that are halted.

If SMP$CONTROLP_CPUS returns any nonzero value, EXE$HW-CLKINT merely resets its neighbor's sanity timer and continues, since the halted CPU could have triggered the timeout. For example, if the halted CPU holds a high-IPL spinlock for which another CPU is spin-waiting at an IPL high enough to block interval timer interrupts, the first CPU's being halted too long can trigger sanity timeout of the second CPU. EXE$HWCLKINT therefore resets the sanity timer. If the second CPU's timeout was merely coincident with the first CPU's halt, the second CPU is likely to time out again.

5. If all the tests fail, EXE$HWCLKINT generates the fatal bugcheck CPU-SANITY.

34.6 I/O CONSIDERATIONS

A number of issues specific to I/O support arise under SMP, some of them software and some hardware:

- Synchronizing access to the device controller and device data structures from the asynchronous threads of execution that make up a device driver

- Impact of devices' interrupting all SMP members
- Access to a device by a subset of SMP members
- Order in which I/O requests complete

These issues are described further in the following sections.

34.6.1   **Synchronizing Driver Routines**

The various routines that comprise a driver are essentially independently activated threads of execution:

- Function decision table (FDT) action routines and cancel routines are entered in response to processes' system service requests.
- Some routines trigger others; for example, an FDT routine that jumps to EXE$QIODRVPKT eventually causes entry to the driver's start I/O routine.
- Device interrupt service routines are entered in response to various device interrupts.
- Some routines are entered by the executive in response to events such as powerfail recovery and expected interrupt timeout.

On a uniprocessor system, some of these routines can interrupt others. The device unit control block (UCB) has state bits that specify, for example, whether a fork process is active on that device unit (UCB$V_BSY in UCB$W_STS), whether an interrupt is expected (UCB$V_INT in UCB$W_STS), and whether there is a time limit for the interrupt's arrival (UCB$V_TIM in UCB$W_STS). The state bits help control the activation of driver threads. An important additional synchronization technique is raising IPL to block interrupts, either to fork level (UCB$B_FIPL) or to device level (UCB$B_DIPL). These techniques continue to be used, but they are not sufficient for the concurrency possible on an SMP system and have been augmented by spinlocks.

Each device controller has its own dynamic spinlock, called a device lock, that synchronizes access to the controller's registers and extends the concept of raising IPL to UCB$B_DIPL. Each device UCB identifies a static spinlock, called a fork lock, that synchronizes access to the UCB and extends the synchronization formerly achieved by raising IPL to UCB$B_FIPL. VMS enters a driver's start I/O and cancel I/O routines with the appropriate fork lock held. It enters the timeout routine holding both the fork lock and the device lock. The start I/O routine acquires the device lock as necessary. The interrupt service routine, to which the hardware may dispatch directly, must acquire the device lock immediately. (See Chapter 8 for a detailed description of spinlocks and the *VMS Device Support Manual* for a detailed description of when each is used.) On an SMP system, multiple processes can be executing FDT action routines or canceling I/O requests concurrently with interrupt service routine and fork process execution.

34.6.2 Device Interrupts

VMS and current processors that support SMP have mechanisms to pass device interrupts on to every system member. If these mechanisms were enabled, the first member to respond to the interrupt would service it, and the others would dismiss the interrupt. Currently, however, interrupts are not distributed; device interrupts are delivered to and serviced by only the primary processor.

Performance studies have shown no improvement from distributing interrupts and, in some cases, significantly increased overhead, as a result of several factors. If interrupt requests are distributed, on some current processor types, each member must interrupt what it is currently doing and perform bus transactions to determine the source of the interrupt. The first member to respond to the device would continue with interrupt processing; the others would receive passive releases and dismiss their interrupts. On some systems, the superfluous bus transactions would make a noticeable difference in bus throughput. On all such systems, all but the first member would have interrupted what they were doing to execute an unproductive thread of execution, with potential losses from their memory caches and TBs.

A further issue is that a typical device interrupt service routine requests a fork interrupt on the current processor. Distributing device interrupts thus requires distributing fork interrupts and fork processing. Time spent in the device interrupt service routine is small compared to fork processing time. Although a number of spinlocks are used as fork locks, the IOLOCK8 spinlock is used more heavily and would become a bottleneck if fork interrupts were distributed as a result of distributing device interrupts. As a result, processors that could otherwise have executed applications while the primary processor serviced device and fork interrupts would spend time spinwaiting for IOLOCK8.

While splitting IOLOCK8 into several spinlocks to enable more parallelism is possible in a future release of VMS, thus far the current scheme has not been a problem.

34.6.3 Device Affinity

Many devices can be accessed equally by every processor of an SMP system, but some can be accessed by only a subset of the processors. The SMP design for device support must take that into account.

- The console terminal and block storage device are typically accessible only from the primary.
- An application design might require that a particular device be accessed from a subset of available processors.

Software-implemented device affinity supports these hardware limitations by providing a mechanism to restrict device access to a subset of the system's processors.

Each device UCB has a longword mask in field UCB$L_AFFINITY that specifies a device affinity set, those processors from which its device registers may be accessed. By default, the mask is all 1's, enabling access from all processors. For console devices, the mask is zero, a value that means only the primary processor can access the device registers. In theory, the device affinity mask can express the idea that access from the primary is prohibited. However, in practice, under the current version, the primary processor is always presumed to be a member of every device's affinity set.

Before VMS enters any driver routine, it must ensure that the routine will run on a processor that is part of the device's affinity set. The major driver entry points are

- FDT action routines
- Start I/O and alternate start I/O routines
- Interrupt service routine
- Register dumping routine
- Device timeout routine
- Unit and controller initialization routines
- Cancel I/O routine

FDT action routines preprocess an I/O request and are expected not to access device registers. Thus, they can execute on any processor regardless of device affinity.

Before entering a device driver at either its start I/O or alternate start I/O routine, the executive tests whether it is running on a processor for which the device has affinity. If not, the executive invokes routine SMP$SWITCH_CPU, in module SMPROUT, which stores fork process context in reserved fields in the I/O request packet (IRP). It identifies the processor with the lowest CPU ID for which the device has affinity, queues the IRP to that processor's per-CPU database, and requests an interprocessor interrupt of work request type WORK_FQP (see Sections 34.5.1 and 34.5.2). The interprocessor interrupt service routine queues the IRP/fork block to the appropriate fork queue and requests a fork interrupt. When the fork interrupt is granted, the fork dispatcher acquires the appropriate fork lock and then enters the driver start I/O or alternate start I/O routine.

As previously described, device interrupt service routines always run on the primary processor. After the interrupt service routine forks, the fork process (generally, the reentered start I/O routine) executes on the primary processor. At that point, to run on a different processor in its affinity set, the fork process could itself invoke SMP$SWITCH_CPU.

A register dumping routine is entered indirectly by the start I/O routine when it invokes IOC$DIAGBUFILL or logs an error and thus runs on the same processor as the start I/O routine.

A device timeout routine is entered at device IPL from EXE$TIMEOUT, which runs on the primary as part of the IPL 7 software timer interrupt service routine. To run on another processor in its affinity set, the timeout routine must invoke SMP$SWITCH_CPU.

Unit and controller initialization routines run when a device is configured by SYSGEN and during powerfail recovery. Running in process context in kernel mode, SYSGEN calls SCH$REQUIRE_CAPABILITY, in module SCHED, to ensure that SYSGEN executes only on the primary processor during device configuration and similar operations. Power recovery code executes on the primary processor as part of system restart following system powerfail and recovery or as part of an adapter interrupt service routine following adapter powerfail and recovery.

A driver cancel routine is entered from process context code, either EXE$CANCEL, in module SYSCANCEL, the Cancel I/O on Channel ($CANCEL) system service procedure, or IOC$LAST_CHAN, in module IOSUBNPAG. Both check whether the device's affinity mask is the same as the default mask. If not, these routines call SCH$REQUIRE_CAPABILITY to ensure execution on the primary before invoking the cancel routine.

34.6.4 I/O Postprocessing

An SMP system has one systemwide I/O postprocessing queue and one in each CPU's per-CPU database. Most IRPs are queued to the systemwide queue. Since only the primary processor services this queue, the sequence in which requests complete is preserved, even if they complete on different processors, and a process receives AST notification of I/O completion in the order in which the requests complete.

Without the systemwide queue, AST notifications of the completion of asynchronous I/O requests could occur out of order. This might happen to requests made of a driver able to complete I/O requests on a secondary. To complete an I/O request on a secondary processor, a driver would need to have unrestricted device affinity and be able to complete a request in the start I/O routine without the need for a device interrupt. Synchronous I/O requests, made through the Queue I/O Request and Wait ($QIOW) system service are processed one at a time and cannot complete out of order.

With multiple processor-specific I/O postprocessing queues rather than a single systemwide one, problems such as the following can occur. A process requests several small asynchronous reads to a communications driver. The first read causes a device operation, whose interrupt service routine runs on the primary. The driver, in fact, receives a large transmission of data, sufficient to satisfy several small reads. The IRP of the first read is queued to the primary's I/O postprocessing queue. Before IPL drops low enough on the primary for the I/O postprocessing interrupt to be granted, several subsequent read requests from the process could complete on a secondary and their IRPs could be queued to its I/O postprocessing queue. If the secondary's I/O postprocessing interrupt is serviced first, the process receives AST notification of the later requests before the first one.

VMS provides several routines that are commonly invoked from device drivers. Each routine queues an IRP to the systemwide queue. If the routine is running on the primary, it requests an I/O postprocessing interrupt. Otherwise, it sets the primary's I/O postprocessing work bit and requests an interprocessor interrupt. These routines are

- COM$POST and COM$POST_NCNT, in module COMDRVSUB, for completed and canceled requests
- IOC$REQCOM, in module IOSUBNPAG, for completed requests

EXE$ABORTIO and EXE$FINISHIO[C] are routines invoked from device driver FDT action routines to complete an I/O request at FDT level. Each queues the IRP to the per-CPU I/O postprocessing queue and, running at IPL 2, requests an I/O postprocessing interrupt, which typically is granted immediately. Postprocessing such a request on the same processor enables it to complete immediately, synchronously with the system service, as it would have with earlier versions of VMS.

As described in Section 34.5.2, a special IRP is queued to each processor's per-CPU I/O postprocessing queue to stall during loss of VAXcluster quorum.

34.7 PROCESSOR STATES

A secondary SMP member can be characterized by its state, stored in the per-CPU database field CPU$B_STATE. Prefaced by CPU$C_, the state symbols are defined by the macro $CPUDEF. Table 34.2 lists the possible state values and a brief description of each.

The primary processor itself is always in the RUN state. A secondary processor participating in the SMP system is in the RUN state. Most of the other states are stages through which a secondary passes on its way to or from the RUN state. Figure 34.8 shows the transitions among them. These are summarized here and described in detail in subsequent sections.

When SMP$SETUP_CPU, described in Section 34.8.3, first initializes the environment for each secondary processor, it sets each CPU's state to INIT.

Table 34.2   Processor States

Name	Meaning
INIT	CPU is initializing
RUN	CPU is running
BOOTED	CPU is booted and waiting for go bit
STOPPED	CPU has stopped
TIMOUT	CPU has timed out during boot
BOOT_REJECTED	CPU was booted but refused to join the active set

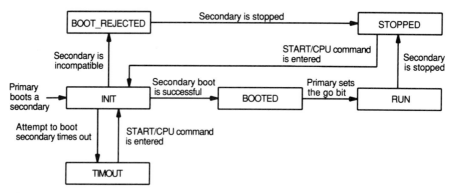

Figure 34.8
State Transitions of a Secondary Processor

SMP$SETUP_CPU makes three attempts to boot a secondary by sending a message to the console subsystem. If all fail, it sets the CPU's state to TIMOUT.

Routine CPU_START, described in Section 34.8.4, running on each secondary, makes the other transitions from the INIT state.

- It changes the CPU's state to BOOT_REJECTED if the CPU's revision or type is inconsistent with those of the BOOT CPU.
- It changes the CPU's state to BOOTED when it begins to loop, waiting for the BOOT CPU to set the go bit. Once the go bit is set, it changes the CPU's state to RUN.

SMP$SHUTDOWN_CPU, described in Section 34.8.5, makes the transitions to the STOPPED state.

34.8 INITIALIZATION

An SMP system initially boots as a uniprocessor. Based on hardware-specific criteria, the console subsystem selects a processor to be the BOOT CPU. The BOOT CPU does most of the work of system initialization, loading the executive into memory and performing the tasks involved in bootstrapping a single-processor system.

The exact initialization sequence varies from system to system. In particular, the ways in which the BOOT CPU is initialized and the primary (initial) bootstrap program, VMB.EXE, is loaded into it differ on each CPU type. However, the steps from the beginning of the execution of VMB are basically the same on all systems.

SMP-related initialization is performed in several phases of bootstrap:

1. SYSBOOT, the secondary bootstrap, runs on the BOOT CPU. It sizes the SPT to accommodate the per-CPU data areas and allocates that of the BOOT CPU.

2. EXE$INIT, running on the BOOT CPU, turns on memory management and performs CPU-independent SMP initialization.

3. The CPU-dependent routines SMP$SETUP_SMP and SMP$SETUP_CPU run on the BOOT CPU to perform further SMP initialization and boot the secondary processors.

4. Bootstrap code, running on each secondary, initializes processor registers, enables memory management, and adds the processor to the active set.

Chapter 30 provides a detailed description of CPU initialization, loading and execution of VMB, and the execution of SYSBOOT. Chapter 31 provides a detailed description of EXE$INIT and further steps in system initialization.

The following sections describe those parts of each bootstrap phase specifically related to SMP and the operations of the Digital command language (DCL) commands START/CPU and STOP/CPU. Figure 34.9 shows the major steps in these phases.

34.8.1   Initialization by SYSBOOT

SYSBOOT runs on the BOOT CPU in kernel mode at IPL 31 with memory management disabled.

SYSBOOT tests whether the CPU type supports SMP. On one that does, SYSBOOT includes SMP-related needs in its sizing of system space. First, it calculates the required size of the per-CPU data area and rounds that number up to the next power of 2. It multiplies the rounded size by 1 plus the number of CPUs in the SMP system. For some CPU types, it uses the maximum number of CPUs possible in an SMP configuration of that type. For others, it uses the number actually present in the hardware configuration. SYSBOOT adds the result to the total number of pages of system space. Adding pages equal to the size of one more per-CPU data area ensures that the areas needed can be allocated starting with a system space address aligned to the same power of 2 as the size of the area.

In addition, SYSBOOT adds 32 pages to the total number of system pages, one for each of the maximum possible number of CPUs, to double-map the per-CPU boot stack. Recall that to enable memory management it is necessary to execute code on a page whose physical and virtual addresses are the same (see Chapter 30). On current VAX processors, any physical address has the form of a P0 virtual address. Thus the virtual address required for the transition is a P0 address. The boot stack page will form one page of a temporary P0 page table. The P0 base register contents will be calculated such that the boot stack page is the page of the page table that contains the PTE of the page with the code that enables memory management.

The virtual address of the per-CPU data area, of which the boot stack is a part, is so low in system space that the calculated base address of the temporary P0 page table could fall below the start of system space (an illegal value). Therefore the boot stack page must be given a second (that is, doubly

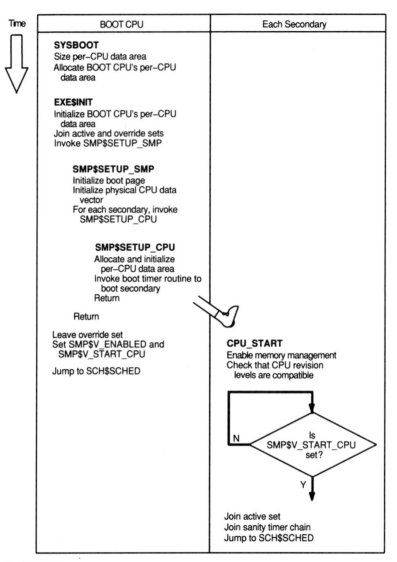

Figure 34.9
Major Steps in SMP Bootstrap

mapped) system space virtual address. SYSBOOT allocates the 32 SPTEs from the high end of system space for this double mapping and stores the system virtual address mapped by the first SPTE in SMP$GL_POPT_MAP. It allocates a separate SPTE for each CPU to allow for the possibility that multiple secondary processors are concurrently using their boot stack pages.

SYSBOOT allocates physical pages of memory for all of the BOOT CPU's per-CPU data area except the guard pages. It allocates and initializes SPTEs for the entire area. It also initializes the SPTE that double-maps the per-CPU boot stack.

SYSBOOT determines which version to load of the executive image that supports synchronization by testing the SYSGEN parameter MULTIPRO-CESSING in combination with the number of CPUs that are present in the configuration:

- If MULTIPROCESSING is 0, it selects the uniprocessor version, SYSTEM_SYNCHRONIZATION_UNI.EXE.
- If MULTIPROCESSING is 1 and multiple CPUs are present, SYSBOOT selects the full-checking multiprocessing version, SYSTEM_SYNCHRO-NIZATION.EXE. If only one CPU is present, it selects the uniprocessor version.
- If MULTIPROCESSING is 2, it selects the full-checking multiprocessing version.
- If MULTIPROCESSING is 3 and there are multiple CPUs present, it selects the streamlined multiprocessing version, SYSTEM_SYNCHRONIZA-TION_MIN.EXE. If only one CPU is present, it selects the uniprocessor version.

If SYSBOOT loads a multiprocessing version, it sets bit SMP$V_SYNCH in SMP$GL_FLAGS to indicate that SMP synchronization is required.

SYSBOOT stores the ID number of the BOOT CPU in SMP$GL_PRIMID. It calculates the system virtual address corresponding to the alternative mapping of the CPU's boot stack. Using this address, it builds a P0 page table that maps the beginning of EXE$INIT at a virtual address equal to its physical address. Chapter 31 explains the purpose of this page table in more detail.

SYSBOOT loads the P0 base and length registers to describe the page table and invalidates the translation buffer. It then jumps to EXE$INIT.

34.8.2   Initialization by EXE$INIT

This section describes SMP-related initialization in EXE$INIT. Unless otherwise noted, all of it takes place on each CPU type. EXE$INIT runs on the BOOT CPU in kernel mode at IPL 31. Its first actions include enabling memory management.

1. If the BOOT CPU is a VAX 6000 series processor, EXE$INIT maps the first page of its node-private space, which contains the CPU ID.
2. It initializes SMP$GL_BASE_MSK for subsequent use with the FIND_CPU_DATA macro and invokes the macro to get the address of the BOOT CPU's per-CPU data area.
3. EXE$INIT initializes the BOOT CPU's per-CPU data area:
   a. It zeros the per-CPU database.
   b. It saves the CPU ID in CPU$L_PHY_CPUID.
   c. It stores the address of the per-CPU data area in the CPU data vector entry for this CPU and in the field CPU$L_PERCPUVA.

    d. It stores the system virtual address of this CPU's P0 page table page in CPU$L_P0PT_PAGE.

    e. It stores a mask with a single bit set to represent the BOOT CPU in CPU$L_CPUID_MASK.

    f. It copies 16 bytes of CPU-specific hardware data obtained by SYS-BOOT to the per-CPU database and initializes CPU$L_CURPCB to the address of the null PCB.

    g. It stores the value BUG$_CPUCEASED in CPU$L_BUGCODE.

    h. It initializes the per-CPU I/O postprocessing queue and fork queues as empty lists.

    i. It copies the SYSGEN parameter SMP_SANITY_CNT, the number of interval timer ticks until SMP sanity timeout, to CPU$W_SANITY_TIMER, the BOOT CPU's sanity timer. It stores the address of the BOOT CPU's sanity timer in CPU$L_TPOINTER. When a secondary processor boots and inserts itself into the sanity timer chain, the BOOT CPU's CPU$L_TPOINTER will be altered to point to the secondary's sanity timer. For further details, see Section 34.5.7.

    j. It initializes CPU$L_INTSTK to the virtual address of the high end of the CPU's interrupt stack and CPU$L_REALSTACK to the physical address of the high end of the boot stack.

    k. It copies the physical address of the SCB to CPU$L_SCBB.

    l. It initializes CPU$L_TENUSEC and CPU$L_UBDELAY from the system global values so that any necessary busy, spin, or timed wait durations can be calculated on a CPU-specific basis.

4. It initializes the available set mask to the same value as CPU$L_CPUID_MASK, that is, a configuration with the BOOT CPU available, and copies it to the active, idle, and override set masks.

5. EXE$INIT initializes EXE$GL_AFFINITY, the default device affinity mask, to all 1's, so that, by default, device access is not limited to a subset of the SMP members.

6. It sets the processor's CPU$B_STATE field to RUN.

7. EXE$INIT stores the physical address of the BOOT CPU's per-CPU data area in the restart parameter block field RPB$L_CPUDBVEC and clears the bit RPB$V_PERCPU_VEC in RPB$B_FLAGS to describe the field's use. Later in initialization, after the system has been found to be capable of a multiprocessing configuration, the field will be reinitialized to its other use.

8. It defines the BOOT CPU's capabilities to be the capability PRIMARY plus the default ones in SCH$GL_DEFAULT_CPU_CAP, currently zero.

9. After initializing the SYSLOA*xxx* image and invoking its initialization routine, EXE$INIT invokes the CPU-specific routine SMP$SETUP_SMP, in module [SYSLOA]SMPSTART_*xxx*. The actions of SMP$SETUP_SMP are described in the next section.

10. EXE$INIT stores the time at which the system booted in CPU$Q_BOOT_TIME.

11. It invokes EXE$INI_TIMWAIT, in module [SYSLOA]ERRSUBxxx, to calibrate the timed wait counts in the processor's per-CPU database.

12. It clears the BOOT CPU ID bit in SMP$GL_OVERRIDE, leaving the override set. After this, to acquire a spinlock, the processor must first lower IPL.

13. EXE$INIT tests a combination of the MULTIPROCESSING SYSGEN parameter and the available set as described by SMP$GL_CPUCONF (reinitialized within SMP$SETUP_SMP) to determine whether to enable multiprocessing. If any of the following combinations is true, EXE$INIT does not enable multiprocessing:

   —MULTIPROCESSING is 0
   —MULTIPROCESSING is either 1 or 3 and SMP$GL_CPUCONF indicates no other CPUs present

14. If other CPUs are present or if MULTIPROCESSING is 2, EXE$INIT sets SMP$V_ENABLED and SMP$V_START_CPU in SMP$GL_FLAGS. The latter is known as the go bit, for whose setting the secondary processors wait, as described in Section 34.8.4.

34.8.3 Initialization by CPU-Dependent Routines

SMP$SETUP_SMP runs on the BOOT CPU in kernel mode at IPL 31 with memory management enabled. For a CPU type incapable of multiprocessing, this routine consists merely of an RSB instruction. For a CPU type that can be configured as a multiprocessor, the CPU-specific routine SMP$SETUP_SMP, in module [SYSLOA]SMPSTART_xxx, initializes the SMP environment. The following description is based upon the routine in SMPSTART_8NN for a VAX 8800 system; the routines for other CPU types execute similar steps.

1. SMP$SETUP_SMP first establishes device affinity to the primary for the console terminal by clearing its unit control block field UCB$L_AFFINITY.

2. It initializes the global EXE$GL_IPINT_IPL to the priority level of the interprocessor interrupt on this CPU type. It invokes the routine SMP$ADJUST_IPL, in module SPINLOCKS, to modify the spinlock database accordingly. That routine establishes the IPL for the INVALIDATE spinlock as 1 less than that of the interprocessor interrupt and the IPL for the HW-CLK spinlock as the IPL of the interval timer interrupt. (On processors whose interprocessor interrupt IPL is 22, SMP$SETUP_SMP adjusts the IPL of the VIRTCONS spinlock to 22 from its default value of 20.) It adjusts spinlocks' ranks as required to ensure that rank and IPL ordering result in the same sequence. Chapter 8 contains more information on the spinlock database.

3. SMP$SETUP_SMP then checks whether to establish an SMP environment. If the BOOT CPU is a uniprocessor or if there are no other CPUs available, the routine returns.

4. To establish an SMP environment, the routine first initializes the global SMP$GL_CPUCONF, the CPU configuration bitmask, using information from the console about what CPUs are actually present.

5. It initializes the interprocessor interrupt vector in the SCB with the address of the routine SMP$INTSR, in module [SYSLOA]SMPINT_*xxx*.

6. It allocates a page of physical memory, called the boot page, for CPU initialization code and data accessed by a secondary processor prior to its enabling memory management. If there is space (as there is, in VMS Version 5.2), the boot page also contains a physically based version of the CPU data vector. Otherwise, the vector is in a second physical page of memory. It updates the corresponding page frame number (PFN) database to describe the new state of the page or pages of memory and initializes SPTEs to map the memory while it is being initialized.

   SMP$SETUP_SMP copies the CPU initialization code into the boot page. It initializes the physical CPU data vector, stores its physical address in RPB$L_CPUDBVEC, and sets bit RPB$V_PERCPU_VEC in RPB$B_FLAGS. SMP$SETUP_SMP also initializes several other pointers for secondary processors' booting and restart:

   —The field RPB$L_SMP_PC, to the physical address of the routine CPU_START in the boot page code

   —In the boot page, at OFF_STRTVA, the system virtual address of the routine SMP$STRTVA in the boot page code

   —In the boot page, at OFF_RPBBASE, the physical address of the RPB

   —In the boot page, at OFF_RESTART, the physical address of the restart routine for secondary processors, EXE$RESTART_ATT

   Figure 34.10 shows the relations among the RPB, the physical CPU data vector, and the boot page. Section 34.8.4 describes how VMS uses these structures.

7. Systemwide SMP initialization is complete. SMP$SETUP_SMP compares the available set mask and the SYSGEN parameter SMP_CPUS to determine which CPUs are to be booted. The default value of the parameter is −1, a mask with all bits set, indicating that all available CPUs should be booted. It can be modified to block the automatic booting of particular CPUs. An available CPU not booted automatically can be brought online later with the DCL command START/CPU.

   For each secondary processor in the available set whose bit in SMP_CPUS is set, SMP$SETUP_SMP invokes SMP$SETUP_CPU to perform CPU-specific initialization. It then returns to its invoker.

SMP$SETUP_CPU is invoked with a register argument containing the

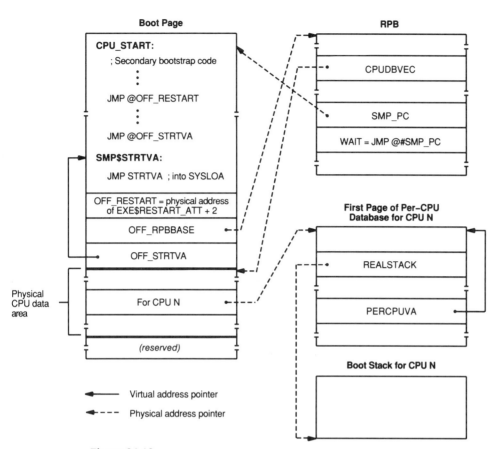

Figure 34.10
Relations among the RPB, Boot Page, and Physical
CPU Data Vector

CPU ID of the processor to be booted. Typically, it is invoked from SMP$SET-UP_SMP but can also be invoked with the DCL START/CPU command. The following description is based on the routine in SMPSTART_8NN for a VAX 8800 system; the routines for other CPU types perform much the same.

1. SMP$SETUP_CPU acquires the MMG spinlock. (This step is not necessary in the environment in which EXE$INIT runs, that of a uniprocessor, but is needed when SMP$SETUP_CPU is invoked in response to a later START/CPU command.)
2. It tests whether a per-CPU database area already exists for this processor. If this routine is running as part of EXE$INIT, there is none, and control proceeds to step 3.
   If this routine is running later, it is possible that the CPU has been booted once and is being restarted or that there are multiple concurrent attempts to start it. If the processor has a per-CPU data area and is in

1051

the INIT state, SMP$SETUP_CPU clears the processor's bug done bit in SMP$GL_BUG_DONE and transfers control to step 10.

Otherwise, the processor is being started by another process. The routine releases the MMG spinlock and returns to its invoker.

3. It clears the processor's bug done bit in SMP$GL_BUG_DONE.

4. SMP$SETUP_CPU calculates the number of pages required for the per-CPU data area, rounds that to the next power of 2, and invokes LDR$ALLOC_PT to allocate one fewer than twice that many SPTEs. This many SPTEs ensures that the per-CPU data area can be aligned at an address boundary somewhere within the allocation that is suitable for the FIND_CPU_DATA calculation described in Section 34.3.1.

If the allocation is unsuccessful, SMP$SETUP_CPU releases the MMG spinlock and returns the error status to its caller.

Otherwise, it calculates the placement of the per-CPU data area and deallocates the unneeded SPTEs on either or both sides of it.

5. It then allocates physical pages of memory for the interrupt stack, boot stack, and per-CPU database. If there is not enough physical memory available and the routine is running as part of EXE$INIT, it generates the fatal bugcheck INCONSTATE; when running in process context, it places the process into a free page wait.

If the pages allocated are described in the PFN database (see Chapter 14), it modifies the PFN database arrays to reflect the new state of the pages.

6. SMP$SETUP_CPU stores the physical address of the per-CPU data area in the physical CPU data vector entry for the processor. Bit 0 is set in the address as a flag indicating that the area is not fully initialized.

7. It initializes the SPTEs that map these pages as valid, owned by kernel mode, and writable only by kernel mode. The per-CPU database pages allow user mode read access, and the interrupt and boot stack pages allow executive mode read access. It initializes the guard pages' SPTEs as invalid no-access pages.

It also initializes the SPTE reserved for this processor's use as a P0 page table page. The SPTE double-maps the boot stack page; it will be used when the processor first enables memory management.

8. As described in Section 34.8.2, SMP$SETUP_CPU clears the per-CPU database pages and initializes many of the database fields. It initializes the processor's state to INIT. Initialization of some per-CPU database fields is deferred until step 10.

9. It stores the virtual address of the per-CPU data area in the CPU data vector.

10. Beginning at local routine RESTART, SMP$SETUP_CPU stores the physical address of the SCB in CPU$L_SCBB.

11. It clears bit 0 in the physical CPU data vector entry for the processor to indicate that the per-CPU data area is initialized.

12. It invokes the local routine BOOT_TIMER, part of SMPSTART_*xxx*. BOOT_TIMER sends a command to the console subsystem to boot a particular secondary CPU.

    For example, the primary processor of a VAX 8800 system writes the value F05$_{16}$ to the console transmit data processor register. In response to that particular command, the console subsystem executes the command procedure SECBOO.COM, which starts the secondary executing at the instruction RPB$B_WAIT, a JMP whose destination is the CPU_START routine in the boot page.

    The primary processor of a VAX 6000 series model 400 system invokes routine CON$BOOT_CPU, in module [SYSLOA]OPDRV9RR, to communicate with the console subsystem through the console communications area of the CPU to be booted.

    Booting another CPU is not instantaneous and may not be successful the first time. To permit a retry, BOOT_TIMER initializes a timer queue entry (TQE) specific to that secondary CPU to describe a system subroutine with a due time of 30 seconds from the current time. Because the routine is running with a higher ranking spinlock than the TIMER spinlock and at too high an IPL, it first forks, using the TQE as a fork block and the TIMER spinlock as fork lock. The fork routine queues the TQE. (Chapter 11 describes TQEs and timer system subroutines.)

    When the TQE comes due, its system subroutine, the routine TIMER_WAKE, local to SMPSTART_*xxx*, checks whether that secondary is still in the INIT state. If not, it exits. If it is, the routine invokes BOOT_TIMER again. If, after three attempts, the secondary has failed to boot, its state is changed to TIMOUT and a failure message is written to the console terminal.

13. SMP$SETUP_CPU releases the MMG spinlock and returns to its invoker.

34.8.4 **Secondary Bootstrap Code**

Each secondary processor begins executing in kernel mode at IPL 31 and with memory management disabled. The PC and stack pointer (SP) are established in a console-specific way. A secondary processor may begin executing in the boot page; at EXE$RESTART, the VMS halt-restart routine; or at the JMP instruction in the RPB. Its SP may initially be at the high end of the page containing the RPB or the boot stack page. Several examples follow:

- On a VAX 6000 series system, SMP$SETUP_CPU sends commands, byte by byte, to the console subsystem of a secondary processor being booted: it establishes the SP as the high-address end of the boot stack page and the PC as the physical address of EXE$RESTART, described in Section 34.9. EXE$RESTART transfers control to CPU_START.

- On a VAX 83*x*0 system, SMP$SETUP_CPU sends commands, byte by byte, to the secondary processor's logical console: it establishes the SP as the high-address end of the boot stack page and the PC as the physical address of the beginning of the boot page, the copy of the routine CPU_START.

- On a VAX 88*x*0 or VAX 8800 system, SMP$SETUP_CPU's boot timer routine issues a console command, in response to which the console executes the command procedure SECBOO.COM. The command procedure establishes the SP as the high-address end of the RPB page. It establishes the PC as the address of the RPB JMP instruction, whose destination is the copy of CPU_START in the boot page.

A secondary of any CPU type eventually executes the boot page copy of local routine CPU_START, in module [SYSLOA]SMPSTART_*xxx*. The description that follows is based upon the routine in SMPSTART_8NN for a VAX 8800 system; the routines for other CPU types execute similar steps.

1. CPU_START first sends a message to the console subsystem to enable restart, in case of an error halt.
2. It determines its own CPU ID and, through RPB$L_CPUDBVEC, the physical address of the first page of its per-CPU database, as shown in Figure 34.10.
3. If the address is 0 (a pathological condition), the CPU loops rather than halt and interfere with potential normal operations.
4. Under normal circumstances, it switches to its own boot stack.
5. If the CPU's state is RUN, this is a restart rather than a boot. With memory management still disabled, CPU_START dispatches through OFF_RESTART to EXE$RESTART_ATT + 2, described in Section 34.9.
6. If the CPU's state is not RUN, this is a boot. CPU_START loads its PR$_SBR, PR$_SLR, and PR$_SCBB from the contents of the RPB, preparatory to enabling memory management.
7. Enabling memory management, CPU_START goes through the same basic sequence as that of EXE$INIT, described in Chapter 31.

   a. It initializes its P0 mapping registers to describe a mostly nonexistent P0 page table with one real PTE, whose virtual address is the same as the physical address of the boot page.
   b. It invalidates its translation buffer (whose contents are indeterminate on some VAX CPU types while memory management is disabled) and then enables memory management.
   c. The updated PC, translated as a P0 space address, is the same as its physical address. It is the address of a JMP instruction. The instruction's destination is the system virtual address corresponding to the next physical instruction. Executing this JMP instruction, CPU_START moves the PC to system space, to the loaded SYSLOA*xxx* image.
   d. The next instruction is also a JMP. Its destination is the continuation of CPU_START elsewhere in the loaded SYSLOA*xxx* image. (Recall

that the physically accessed part of CPU_START must fit within the single boot page.)

8. At local label STRVA, the routine switches to the processor's interrupt stack and invalidates the TB to remove the cached POPTEs.

9. It joins the override set by setting its CPU bit in SMP$GL_OVERRIDE.

10. It acquires and stores CPU-specific revision information in the per-CPU database. It checks that the CPU type is a known one, that its subtype is the same as that of the boot CPU, that the CPU and microcode are at or above the minimium required revision level, and at the same level as the primary.

11. If any check fails, it writes an error message on the console terminal and changes the CPU state to BOOT_REJECTED. It raises IPL to 31 and loops.

12. If the checks pass, it records the current system time in CPU$Q_BOOT_TIME.

13. It invokes EXE$INI_TIMWAIT and EXE$INIPROCREG, routines in [SYSLOA]ERRSUBxxx, to reinitialize the timed wait counts and to initialize processor registers, for example, the interval timer.

14. It sets the CPU's state to BOOTED.

15. CPU_START then loops, testing the "go" bit, SMP$V_START_CPU in SMP$GL_FLAGS, set by the primary at the end of EXE$INIT.

16. When the bit is set, it writes a message to the console terminal indicating that it has joined the primary in multiprocessor operation.

17. It lowers IPL to 29 to permit any pending powerfail interrupt to be granted. Such an interrupt might have been blocked for a sufficiently long time by the continuous IPL 31 execution that there is not enough time to save software state before the power fails altogether. Rather than risk the powerfail after joining the active state, when a failure to save state would prevent the system's powerfail recovery, this routine lowers IPL now. If a powerfail were to occur, when the primary restarts, its boot timer will time out, causing it to reboot this secondary.

18. It raises IPL back to 31 and acquires the CPU mutex.

19. It changes the processor's state to RUN and sets the bit corresponding to its ID in SMP$GL_ACTIVE_CPUS, joining the active set.

20. It invokes SMP$INIT_SANITY, in module SMPROUT, to initialize the processor's sanity timer. Section 34.5.7 gives a description of the sanity timer mechanism.

21. CPU_START releases the CPU mutex.

22. It acquires the SCHED spinlock; calls SCH$ADD_CPU_CAP, in module SCHED, to initialize the processor's entry in the capabilities array; and releases the SCHED spinlock.

23. Clearing its CPU ID bit in SMP$GL_OVERRIDE, it leaves the override set.

24. It sets its CPU ID bit in SCH$GL_IDLE_CPUS to indicate that the processor needs a process to run.

25. CPU_START constructs a PC/PSL pair and executes an REI instruction that transfers control to SCH$SCHED, in module SCHED, at IPL$_SCHED. SCH$SCHED tries to schedule a process on this CPU.

34.8.5 Operation of START/CPU and STOP/CPU Commands

Several DCL commands support SMP:

- START/CPU [/ALL] [*cpu-id,...*]
- STOP/CPU [/ALL/OVERRIDE_CHECKS] [*cpu-id,...*]
- SHOW CPU [/ALL] [*cpu-id,...*]

For a complete description of the commands and their qualifiers, not all of which are listed here, see the *VMS DCL Dictionary*. All three commands are implemented by the single-module image [MP]SMPUTIL. This section describes the implementation of the first two commands.

In response to a START/CPU command, the SMPUTIL image checks that each specified CPU is available and not already a member of the active set. It then checks each CPU's state to see if it can be started: the CPU must have never been started or it must be in either the TIMOUT or STOPPED state.

In kernel mode, the image confirms that SMP is enabled, exiting if not. If a CPU has been started and thus has a per-CPU database, the image changes the CPU's state to INIT. It calls SCH$REQUIRE_CAPABILITY, in module SCHED, to ensure that the process in which it is running is executing on the primary processor. As a result, the process may be taken out of execution and then rescheduled on the primary. Running in kernel mode on the primary, it invokes SMP$SETUP_CPU, described in Section 34.8.3, to initialize each specified secondary CPU. It then calls SCH$RELEASE_CAPABILITY to remove the requirement that the process execute on the primary and returns.

In response to a STOP/CPU command, the SMPUTIL image checks that each specified CPU is available and a member of the active set. Running in kernel mode, it invokes SMP$SHUTDOWN_CPU, in module SMPROUT, once for each CPU. It passes a register argument based on the presence or absence of the /OVERRIDE_CHECKS qualifier, which specifies whether checks for loss of CPUs required for process affinity needs should be made. SMP$SHUTDOWN_CPU takes the following steps:

1. It invokes the CPU-specific routine SMP$STOP_CPU, in module [SYSLOA]SMPSTART_*xxx*, passing it the address of the per-CPU database of the target CPU. SMP$STOP_CPU checks the CPU's state.

   —If it is BOOT_REJECTED, the routine sets the state to STOPPED and returns. If the secondary did not boot, nothing further needs to be done.

—Otherwise, in the case of a VAX 6000 series CPU, the routine disables XMI bus interrupts directed at the CPU and then returns. In the case of other SMP CPU types, the routine simply returns.

2. SMP$SHUTDOWN_CPU checks the CPU state:

—If the CPU has just been put into the STOPPED state, it simply returns.

—If the CPU is in the BOOT_REJECTED state, the routine changes its state to STOPPED.

—If the CPU is in any other state than RUN, or if it is in RUN but not a member of the active set, SMP$SHUTDOWN_CPU returns to its invoker with the error status SS$_DEVOFFLINE; only a running active set member can be stopped.

3. It calls SCH$REQUIRE_CAPABILITY, in module SCHED, to ensure that the process in which it is running is executing on the processor to be stopped. As a result, the process may be taken out of execution and then rescheduled on the target processor.

4. Running on the target processor, SMP$SHUTDOWN_CPU raises IPL to IPL$_SCHED to block rescheduling. It then calls SCH$RELEASE_CAPABILITY to remove the explicit affinity requirement.

5. It acquires the SCHED spinlock to serialize access to the data structures describing processor capabilities and process affinities.

6. If affinity checks are required (that is, if they are not to be overridden), SMP$SHUTDOWN_CPU checks whether any process has explicit affinity for this processor. If any does, it cannot continue the shutdown. Instead, it releases the SCHED spinlock and returns an error status to its invoker.

7. If affinity checks are overridden or if no process has explicit affinity, SMP$SHUTDOWN_CPU calls SCH$REMOVE_CPU_CAP, in module SCHED, to remove the CPU from the capability database.

8. It then invokes SCH$CUR_TO_COM, in module RSE, to take the current process out of execution. Its context is saved such that when it is placed into execution on another processor, it will return a success status to the invoker of SMP$SHUTDOWN_COM. That is, two threads of execution diverge from this point: one continues in process context on another CPU, and one continues on the interrupt stack of the CPU to be shut down.

9. Running on the interrupt stack of the CPU to be shut down, SMP$SHUT-DOWN_COM releases the SCHED spinlock.

10. It creates a fork process to execute on the primary processor and write to the console terminal a message about this CPU's being shut down.

11. It raises IPL to 31 and sets its CPU ID bit in SMP$GL_OVERRIDE, joining the override set.

12. It clears its CPU ID bit in SMP$GL_ACTIVE_CPUS, leaving the active set.

13. It acquires the CPU mutex, removes itself from the sanity timer chain, and releases the CPU mutex.

14. It sets the CPU state to STOPPED.

15. It leaves the override set and invokes the routine SMP$HALT_CPU, in module [SYSLOA]SMPSTART_*xxx*.

16. SMP$HALT_CPU resets the stack pointer to the high end of the interrupt stack.

17. It cannot execute a HALT instruction, since that would trigger halt-restart processing and a system crash. Instead, it loops at IPL 31 with memory management still enabled, continually testing whether CPU$B_STATE has changed to the INIT state as the result of the DCL command START/CPU.

    If the state changes to INIT, SMP$HALT_CPU transfers control to STRVA, described in Section 34.8.4, to effect a reboot.

SMP$SHUTDOWN_CPU can also be invoked from interrupt service routines in modules [SYSLOA]MCHECK9CC and MCHECK9RR in response to certain types of CPU errors, such as correctable main memory errors and bus or cache parity errors. When either the cumulative number of such errors or the error rate exceeds a given threshold and the most recent error occurred in process context, the service routine fabricates a PC/PSL pair and executes an REI instruction to return to process context. Running in process context at IPL 3 to block rescheduling, it invokes SMP$SHUTDOWN_CPU.

34.9 POWERFAIL AND RECOVERY

When the power fails, each CPU is interrupted and executes EXE$POWER-FAIL, the interrupt service routine in module POWERFAIL. As described in Chapter 33, each CPU saves general and processor registers in memory, some in the per-CPU database and some on the interrupt stack. (Battery backup only protects the contents of memory; it has no effect on the contents of volatile CPU registers and temporaries.) It then saves the SP in CPU$L_SAVED_ISP and executes a BBSSI instruction to set its CPU ID bit in the local cell POWERDWN_L_DONE. The interlocked instruction has the side effect of forcing any pending writes to memory to complete. The CPU then loops, waiting for the power to cease.

When the power is restored, the console subsystem restarts the primary processor, using methods specific to that console subsystem. The console initializes the processor to be at IPL 31, with memory management disabled, the interrupt stack bit in the PSL set, and the SP pointing to the high-address end of the RPB page. Its PC contains the physical address of EXE$RESTART, obtained from the field RPB$L_RESTART. The secondary processors remain halted.

Chapter 33 describes the general powerfail recovery sequence. This section describes the steps that EXE$RESTART, in module POWERFAIL, takes that are specific to restarting a primary processor; it also describes the steps by which a secondary is restarted.

1. EXE$RESTART tests RPB$L_CPUDBVEC. If it contains a zero, the processor is being restarted prior to the creation of its per-CPU database, and EXE$RESTART executes a HALT instruction.

2. Otherwise, it determines the CPU type and ID of the processor and gets the address of its per-CPU database.

   If none has been created (a pathological case), EXE$RESTART loops endlessly rather than halt and confuse the restart sequence on other processors presumed to exist.

3. On a VAX 6000 series processor, EXE$RESTART tests that this CPU was the primary prior to the powerfail. If not, EXE$RESTART sends a message to the console to force a reboot and issues a node reset to trigger a halt, since VMS Version 5.2 does not support dynamic switching of primaries.

4. It switches to the boot stack and branches to EXE$RESTART_ATT, also in POWERFAIL.

5. EXE$RESTART_ATT enables memory management in much the same way as done by EXE$INIT, described in Section 34.8.4.

6. In the case of a halt-restart resulting from a powerfail, it compares SMP$GL_ACTIVE_CPUS to the mask in POWERDWN_L_DONE to see if all members saved their state. If not, it generates the fatal bugcheck STATENTSVD.

7. It tests CPU$L_SAVED_ISP as a further check that it has saved its own state and, if zero, generates the fatal bugcheck STATENTSVD.

8. After restoring various registers, EXE$RESTART_ATT sets the bit corresponding to its CPU ID in POWERUP_L_DONE.

9. It performs the standard powerfail recovery sequence, calculating the system time, recalibrating timer queue entry expiration times, and logging powerfail recovery.

10. It clears SMP$V_START_CPU in SMP$GL_FLAGS to block any secondary processors from execution until all of them are restarted.

11. It invokes EXE$INIT_DEVICE, in module POWERFAIL, which initializes devices, among them the console.

    CON$INITLINE, in [SYSLOA]OPDRV*xxx*, the console unit initialization routine, scans the CPU data vector for secondary processors that were in the RUN state when the power failed. In a console-specific way, it sends a message to the console subsystem to initialize and then restart each of them. The primary processor of a VAX 8800, for example, writes the message $F07_{16}$ to the console data transmit processor register. In response to that particular command, the console subsystem executes a command procedure directed at the secondary.

12. EXE$RESTART_ATT then executes a BUSYWAIT loop, waiting up to 30 seconds for the masks in POWERUP_L_DONE and SMP$GL_ACTIVE_

CPUS to be equal. If the masks still differ, it invokes SMP$TIMEOUT to determine whether to generate a fatal bugcheck.

13. After all the secondary processors have restarted, EXE$RESTART_ATT clears the mask in POWERDWN_L_DONE and sets bit SMP$V_START_CPU, for whose setting the secondary processors have been waiting.

14. It completes the last steps of powerfail recovery and executes an REI instruction to resume system operations.

To restart a secondary, EXE$RESTART takes the following steps:

1. As previously described, it locates the processor's physical per-CPU database and switches to the boot stack.

2. At label EXE$RESTART_ATT, it tests whether the processor was in the RUN state and, if not, dispatches through RPB$L_SMP_PC to boot page code, described in Section 34.8.4. (This is the path by which secondary processors of some CPU types boot.)

3. It enables memory management and tests CPU$L_SAVED_ISP to see if this processor has saved its state, generating the fatal bugcheck STATENTSVD if not.

4. Otherwise, it restores various processor registers and sets its bit in POWERUP_L_DONE.

5. EXE$RESTART_ATT loops, waiting for the primary to set bit SMP$V_START_CPU.

6. It completes the last steps of powerfail recovery and executes an REI instruction to resume system operations.

34.10 FATAL BUGCHECK PROCESSING

When one member of an SMP system incurs a fatal bugcheck, all members crash; the VMS executive takes the conservative approach that an inconsistency severe enough that operations on one CPU should cease is likely to be systemwide. All members of the active set participate in fatal bugcheck processing.

The CRASH CPU, the CPU that first incurs a fatal bugcheck, drives the crash, informing the other active CPUs that a bugcheck sequence has been initiated. In response, the other active CPUs crash with the fatal bugcheck CPUEXIT. The primary CPU performs most of the rest of fatal bugcheck processing.

Chapter 32 describes in detail the uniprocessor bugcheck sequence; this section describes the steps in fatal bugcheck processing specific to an SMP system.

Figure 34.11 shows the sequence of some of the steps in fatal bugcheck processing as they might occur concurrently on the CRASH CPU (which, as pictured, is not the primary processor), the primary processor, and the other active set members. Note that steps shown in different columns but on the same line do not necessarily execute at the same time on all CPUs. The

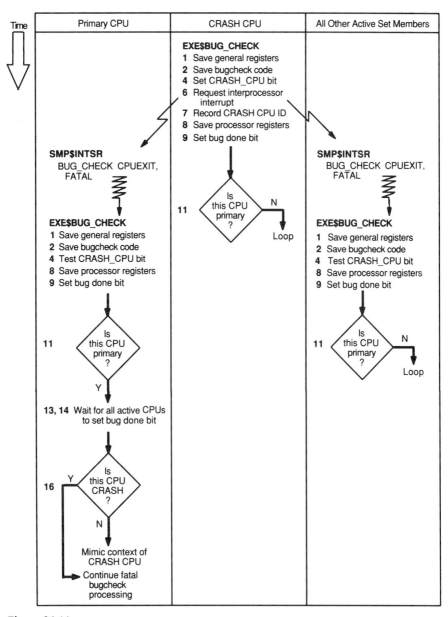

Figure 34.11
Fatal Bugcheck Processing on an SMP System

numbers in the figure correspond to the following steps, not all of which are represented in the figure.

EXE$BUG_CHECK, in module BUGCHECKBT, initially runs on the CRASH CPU and subsequently on other SMP members. It takes the following steps:

① As described in Chapter 32, it saves the general registers on the current stack, either the interrupt stack or the kernel stack of the current process. It then determines whether the bugcheck is fatal. For a fatal bugcheck, it performs several sanity checks to confirm that fatal bugcheck processing is possible.

②It raises IPL to 31 and stores the bugcheck code in the per-CPU database field CPU$L_BUGCODE.

3. It tests whether it is a member of the active set. If not (a pathological and unlikely case), it proceeds to step 8 rather than taking any steps that might interfere with SMP operations.

④If it is a member of the active set, it then tests and sets the bit SMP$V_CRASH_CPU in SMP$GL_FLAGS. Only the first CPU to crash actually sets this bit and thus becomes the CRASH CPU.

If the bit is already set, EXE$BUG_CHECK continues with step 8. Use of the bit prevents confusion during concurrent independent crashes.

5. It acquires the CPU mutex to prevent any other processors from joining the active set.

⑥It requests an interprocessor interrupt of each member of the active set, specifying bugcheck as the work request type (see Section 34.5.2).

⑦It records its own ID in SMP$GL_BUGCHKCP as the CRASH CPU.

⑧It invokes EXE$SAVE_CONTEXT, in module [SYSLOA]ERRSUBxxx, to save volatile processor registers on the current stack. After saving the contents of CPU-specific processor registers, the number of registers saved, the interval timer control register, the five stack pointers, and the AST level register, it records the current stack pointer in CPU$L_SAVED_ISP. EXE$SAVE_CONTEXT stores the contents of PR$_PCBB, PR$_SCBB, PR$_SISR, and the per-process mapping registers in the per-CPU database, and returns.

⑨EXE$BUG_CHECK then sets its ID bit in SMP$GL_BUG_DONE to indicate that it has saved its context.

10. If it owns the XDELTA lock (if its ID is in XDT$GW_OWNER_ID), it breaks the lock, releasing other active set members from the benign state so that each can respond to the interprocessor interrupt and save its own context. Section 34.5.4 describes XDELTA processing and the benign state.

⑪EXE$BUG_CHECK compares its CPU ID to that in SMP$GL_PRIMID to determine whether it is executing on the primary. If it is not, it loads the address of its per-CPU boot stack into the SP and loops, awaiting a later reboot. All members of the active set except the primary should eventually execute this loop. A crashing CPU that is not a member of the active set also executes this loop.

12. This and later steps execute only on the primary processor because it is the only member guaranteed access to the console terminal.

EXE$BUG_CHECK sets its CPU ID in SMP$GL_OVERRIDE, adding itself to the override set. As a member of the override set, its spinlock acquisitions and releases are not subject to the normal IPL checks.

(13) EXE$BUG_CHECK waits, up to a maximum of 30 seconds, for all active members to save their context. Under normal circumstances, much of this wait does not occur. However, if one member is restarting following a halt, it could take the member a significant time to complete that and respond to the interprocessor interrupt requesting bugcheck processing. If the time passes before all are done, EXE$BUG_CHECK proceeds.

It continues with steps common to fatal bugcheck processing on a uniprocessor system, reading the fatal bugcheck overlay into memory. The steps that follow are from the overlay, which is module BUGCHECK-LD. For simplicity, this chapter uses the name EXE$BUG_CHECK to refer to that code.

(14) Still running on the primary, EXE$BUG_CHECK tests if the CRASH CPU has saved its register context, waiting for up to 1 second beyond the earlier wait.

15. It uses the bugcheck code in the CRASH CPU's per-CPU database to select the bugcheck message text. This field is initialized to BUG$_CPUCEASED, in case a problem on the CRASH CPU prevents it from recording the real bugcheck code.

(16) The primary checks whether it is the CRASH CPU. If not, it checks whether the CRASH CPU completed saving its context. If it has, the primary mimics the CRASH CPU's context, enabling the use of the standard fatal bugcheck routine. It adopts the CRASH CPU's processor registers, copying them from its per-CPU database and stack. These registers include PR$_SCBB, PR$_PCBB, PR$_SISR, the per-process mapping registers, the stack pointers, PR$_ASTLVL, and the interval timer control register. (The translation buffer invalidation necessary for the primary to reference possible per-process addresses on the CRASH CPU is done in an earlier step by a routine invoked to make system space writable so that the bugcheck overlay can be loaded.)

This switch simplifies writing crash information to the console terminal, which may be accessible only from the primary processor. It also simplifies the sequence in which registers are written to the dump header block.

Running on the primary, EXE$BUG_CHECK continues with steps common to fatal bugcheck processing on a uniprocessor.

PART IX / Miscellaneous Topics

35 Logical Names

Call things by their right names. . . . Glass of brandy and
water! That is the current but not the appropriate name: ask
for a glass of liquid fire and distilled damnation.

Robert Hall, *Olinthus Gregory, Brief Memoir of the Life of Hall*

A logical name definition is a mapping of a string to zero or more replacement strings. A replacement string is called an equivalence name. A logical name can represent a node name, file specification, device name, application-specific information, or another logical name. Replacing an occurrence of the logical name with an equivalence string is called logical name translation.

VMS provides automatic logical name translation for a name used in a file specification or device name. A logical name that refers to a device or file enables transparent device independence and I/O redirection. For example, a program or command procedure can refer to a disk volume by logical name rather than by the name of the specific drive on which the disk volume is mounted.

A user can define a logical name as a shorthand way to refer to a file or directory that is referenced frequently.

This chapter first summarizes the characteristics of logical names. It then describes the data structures that implement logical names and internal operation of the system services related to logical names:

- Create Logical Name ($CRELNM)
- Create Logical Name Table ($CRELNT)
- Delete Logical Name ($DELLNM)
- Translate Logical Name ($TRNLNM)

Logical name concepts are described in the *VMS DCL Concepts Manual*. The *Introduction to VMS System Services* manual and *VMS System Services Reference Manual* document the use of the logical name system services.

35.1 GOALS OF LOGICAL NAME SUPPORT

The goals of VMS support for logical names are as follows:

- Independent name spaces for logical names. A logical name of a given access mode must be unique in any given table. VMS allows for creation of an arbitrarily large number of logical name tables, reducing the likelihood of logical name collisions.

- User control over the order in which logical name tables are searched. Each request to translate a logical name can determine which tables are to be searched by specifying a logical name whose multiple translations are the tables to be searched.
- Provision of a basis for Record Management Services (RMS) search lists. A multivalued logical name enables an ordered list of equivalence names to be associated with a single logical name. An RMS search list is a multivalued logical name, supplied as part or all of a file specification. Through its multiple equivalence names, a logical name can refer to multiple file specifications.
- Control over sharing of logical names. VMS provides a number of possibilities, ranging from no sharing to sharing based on access control lists (ACLs). Degree of shareability is specified when a shareable table is created. A process can control its sharing by partitioning its logical names into different tables.
- Upward compatibility for VMS Version 3 and earlier logical names and their system services. VMS provides the superseded system services as jacket routines for calls to the newer services. It automatically defines system, group, and process logical name tables whose properties are similar to those of older tables.

35.2 CHARACTERISTICS OF LOGICAL NAMES

A logical name is uniquely identified by the combination of the logical name string, the logical name table that contains its definition, and its access mode. That is, two otherwise identical name strings that have different access modes or that are defined in different logical name tables are different logical names.

A logical name string is from 1 to 255 bytes long.

The scope of a logical name varies. A logical name definition can be any of the following:

- Private to one process
- Handed down from a process to its spawned subprocesses
- Shared among a detached process and all its subprocesses (job tree)
- Shared among all the processes with the same user identification code (UIC) group code
- Shared among all the processes on the system
- Shared among a subset of processes on the system as specified by an ACL

A logical name definition cannot be shared among processes on different nodes of a VAXcluster system.

The scope of a logical name is determined primarily by the logical name table in which it is defined. By default, a name in a shareable table is shareable. A logical name in a process-private table can only be used by the process and, by default, handed down to any subprocess it spawns through the Digital command language (DCL). When a subprocess is spawned, each logical name created without the CONFINE attribute is copied to the spawned subprocess. That is, the logical name definitions current at the time of the spawn are copied; any subsequent changes to the definitions are not shared.

The access mode of a logical name can be specified when it is defined. If not specified, access mode defaults to that of the requestor of the $CRELNM system service. If the ACMODE argument is specified and if the process has the privilege SYSNAM, the logical name is created with the specified access mode. If a name of the same mode already exists, it is superseded. Otherwise, if the process lacks the privilege, the argument is maximized with (made no more privileged than) the mode of the system service requestor.

A logical name table can contain multiple definitions of the same logical name with different access modes. These are called aliases. When a request to translate such a logical name specifies the ACMODE argument, any definition made at a less privileged mode is ignored.

The access mode of a logical name specifies an integrity level. Because kernel and executive access mode logical names can only be created by the system manager or someone of equivalent privilege, they are used where the security of the system is at stake. For example, during certain system operations, such as the activation of an image installed with privilege, only executive and kernel mode logical names are used.

A process-private user mode logical name is deleted at the next image rundown. Shareable user mode names, however, survive image exit and process deletion.

A logical name can be created with several attributes:

- The CONFINE attribute indicates that DCL should not propagate the logical name to a spawned subprocess. Logical names of files created with the DCL OPEN command have the CONFINE attribute.
- The NO_ALIAS attribute indicates that the existence of this logical name precludes another definition for that name in the same logical name table and with an outer access mode. When a NO_ALIAS logical name is created, any definition for the name made in an outer mode is deleted, as well as any definition in the same mode.
- The CRELOG attribute indicates that the logical name was defined through the superseded $CRELOG system service. RMS uses this attribute to ensure translation compatible with VMS Version 3 and earlier versions. Use of this attribute is reserved to VMS. Section 35.9 briefly describes support for the superseded logical name system services.

Two other attributes, TABLE and NODELETE, are described in later sections.

A logical name can have more than one equivalence name. In that case, it is called a multivalued logical name, and its equivalence names are treated as an ordered list.

35.3 CHARACTERISTICS OF LOGICAL NAME TABLES

A logical name table is a container for logical names. Each table defines an independent name space. The characteristics of a logical name table are the following:

- Scope—Whether it is shareable or process-private
- Access mode
- Name
- Parent logical name table
- Access control in the case of a shareable logical name table
- Quota to limit the amount of pool occupied by its logical names

During system initialization, several shareable logical name tables are created. During the creation of each process, several other tables, shareable and process-private, are created. Section 35.3.1 documents these default tables. The $CRELNT system service enables a process to create additional tables at will. Process-private name tables are created in P1 space. Shareable tables are created in system space.

The access mode of a logical name table can be specified when it is created. If not specified, the mode defaults to that of the requestor of the $CRELNT system service. If the ACMODE argument is specified and if the process has the privilege SYSNAM, the logical name table is created with the specified access mode. Otherwise, the argument is maximized with the mode of the system service requestor.

A logical name table can contain logical names of its own and less privileged access modes. A logical name table can be a parent table to another table of the same or a less privileged access mode.

A logical name table is identified by its name, which is itself a logical name. The name of a logical name table has the logical name attribute TABLE. In fact, the name table data structure is a special form of equivalence name. As a logical name, each logical name table name must be contained within a logical name table. Two special logical name tables called directories exist as containers for logical name table names. A logical name that is to translate directly or iteratively to the name of a logical name table must be contained in a directory table. That is, there are only two name spaces for the names of logical name tables.

The system directory, LNM$SYSTEM_DIRECTORY, contains the names of all shareable tables. The process directory, LNM$PROCESS_DIRECTORY, contains the names of all process-private tables for that process. Each directory contains its own table name. Each directory table name has the logical name attributes TABLE, NO_ALIAS, and NODELETE. The NODELETE attribute prevents the deletion of a directory table name.

The address of either directory table can be determined, indirectly, through the two-longword array at LNM$AL_DIRTBL. Its first longword points to a longword containing the address of the system directory. Its second longword points to CTL$GL_LNMDIRECT, which contains the address of the process directory. Each process has its own process directory.

Any logical name in a directory table, including a logical name table name, is restricted to a length no longer than 31 characters. It can only consist of the characters $, _, the digits, and uppercase alphabet. The bytes of a logical name string in any other table can have any value.

All logical name tables are in one of two hierarchies. The system directory is the ancestor of the tables in one hierarchy. For each process, its process directory is the ancestor of the other. That is, each logical name table, except for the directory tables, has a parent logical name table. A directory anchors the quota and access hierarchy for its name space. The hierarchical structure enables finer control over quota allocation and access to logical name tables. When a logical name table is deleted, all its descendant tables are deleted.

The parent of a logical name table is not necessarily a directory table. That is, this hierarchical structure is distinct from the location of logical name table names. Consider the logical name table A, created by the following DCL command:

```
$ CREATE/NAME_TABLE/PARENT=LNM$PROCESS A
```

The parent table of logical name table A is the process-private logical name table LNM$PROCESS. A's table name, however, like all table names, is contained in a directory; in this case, it is contained in LNM$PROCESS_ DIRECTORY, the same directory that contains the name of its parent table.

There is a quota on how much memory the names in a logical name table may occupy. The quota is managed in a hierarchical fashion; a newly created name table inherits quota through its parent. At the top of the inheritance tree are the two logical name directories. Each of them has "infinite" memory quota, the largest possible positive longword number.

A table that manages or holds its own quota is called a quota holder table. The two directories are the quota holder tables at the top of the hierarchy.

When a new name table is created, its memory quota can be specified as limited or pooled. A nonzero $CRELNT QUOTA value indicates that the quota is limited; a zero value indicates that it is pooled.

When a name table is created with limited quota, it subtracts its quota from the quota of its parent or of the most recent ancestor that is a quota holder table. It then becomes a quota holder table itself.

If the quota is specified as pooled, the name table does not hold its own quota but shares quota with its parent. If its parent was created with pooled quota, the new table and its parent share quota with the grandparent table. Sharing continues upward in the hierarchy to the most recent ancestor to hold its own quota.

A shareable logical name table has UIC-based protection. Each class of user (system, owner, group, and world) can be granted four types of access:

- Read (R) access allows the user to read the contents of the logical name table, that is, to translate logical names.
- Write (W) access allows the user to modify the contents of the table, for example, delete or alter logical name translations. Write access to a directory table enables the user to delete the logical name table names in the directory.
- Enable (E) access allows the user to withdraw quota from the table when creating a descendant logical name table.
- Delete (D) access allows the user to delete the table itself, including all its logical names and descendant tables and their names. A logical name table is deleted when it or its parent table is deleted.

The default protection mask for a table created through the $CRELNT system service allows RWED access to system and owner users and no access to group or world users.

A logical name table can also be given ACL-based protection. An ACL for a logical name table enables fine-tuning of UIC-based protection. The DCL command SET ACL/OBJECT=LOGICAL_NAME_TABLE creates or modifies access control entries. The *VMS DCL Concepts Manual* provides further information.

To provide compatibility with earlier versions of VMS, a suitably privileged process can read and write certain logical name tables even if UIC- and ACL-based mechanisms would otherwise prohibit access. That is, a process with GRPNAM privilege can access its group table, LNM$GROUP_*gggggg*, to translate, create, or delete logical names, regardless of UIC- and ACL-based protection. A process with SYSNAM can similarly access the system table, LNM$SYSTEM_TABLE.

35.3.1 Default Logical Name Tables

Table 35.1 lists the default tables created by VMS. All names of logical name tables must be in one of the two directories. A directory table can contain other types of logical names as well.

The system directory and table are created during system initialization by initialization code running in the swapper process. The process directory and table are created during process creation by code in EXE$PROCSTRT, in module PROCSTRT. When creating a top-level process, EXE$PROCSTRT invokes EXE$CRE_JGTABLE, also in module PROCSTRT, to create the job table and, if it does not already exist, the group table. LOGINOUT, the first image to run in many processes, also invokes EXE$CRE_JGTABLE so that any changes in the process's UIC are reflected in its tables.

A number of predefined logical names for logical name tables are used in particular VMS contexts for translating and creating logical names. By convention, these names have the prefix LNM$. For example, RMS and other

Table 35.1   Default Logical Name Tables

Table Name	Directory	Use
LNM$PROCESS_ DIRECTORY	Process	Contains definitions of process-private logical name table names and names that translate iteratively to these table names
LNM$PROCESS_ TABLE	Process	Contains process-private logical names, such as SYS$DISK and SYS$INPUT
LNM$SYSTEM_ DIRECTORY	System	Contains definitions of shareable logical name table names and names that translate iteratively to these table names
LNM$SYSTEM_ TABLE	System	Contains names shared by all processes in the system, for example, SYS$LIBRARY and SYS$SYSTEM
LNM$JOB_ *xxxxxxxx* [1]	System	Contains names shared by all processes in the job tree, for example, SYS$LOGIN and SYS$SCRATCH
LNM$GROUP_ *gggggg* [2]	System	Contains names shared by all processes with that UIC group

[1] The string *xxxxxxxx* represents an eight-digit hexadecimal number that is the address of the job information block.

[2] The string *gggggg* represents a six-digit octal number containing the process's UIC group number.

VMS components specify the table LNM$FILE_DEV for file specification and device name translations. Table 35.2 lists some of the default logical names that translate to table names.

Some of these table names are normally referenced indirectly, through predefined logical names. Typically, for example, LNM$JOB is specified as a logical name for the table, rather than the actual name, LNM$JOB_*xxxxxxxx*. The indirection enables a generic and transparent reference to a process's job table rather than to the very specific and transient name LNM$JOB_ *xxxxxxxx*. In addition, indirections make it possible for users to redefine some of the predefined names to modify the search order or the tables to be used. LNM$PROCESS, for example, can be redefined as a multivalued logical name to subsume other tables into the process table.

Some table names exist to allow for user redefinition. For example, the table name LNM$DCL_LOGICAL is used for the SHOW LOGICAL and SHOW TRANSLATION DCL commands and for the logical name lexical functions. By default, as defined in LNM$SYSTEM_DIRECTORY, the name LNM$DCL_LOGICAL translates to LNM$FILE_DEV. However, a user interested in displaying names and translations in the directory tables themselves might define a new translation for LNM$DCL_LOGICAL, as shown in the following example:

```
$ SHOW LOGICAL TRNLOG$_PROCESS_GROUP
%SHOW-S-NOTRAN, no translation for logical name TRNLOG$_PROCESS_GROUP
$ !
$ ! Since LNM$DCL_LOGICAL is to be a name that translates to a
$ ! table name, it must be defined in a directory.
$ !
$ DEFINE/SUPERVISOR/TABLE=LNM$PROCESS_DIRECTORY LNM$DCL_LOGICAL -
_$ LNM$FILE_DEV,LNM$PROCESS_DIRECTORY,LNM$SYSTEM_DIRECTORY
$ !
$ SHOW LOGICAL TRNLOG$_PROCESS_GROUP
   "TRNLOG$_PROCESS_GROUP" = "LOG$PROCESS" (LNM$SYSTEM_DIRECTORY)
        = "LOG$GROUP"
```

Table 35.2   Default Logical Names That Translate to Logical Name Table Names

Logical Name	Equivalence Name
LNM$PROCESS	LNM$PROCESS_TABLE
LNM$JOB	LNM$JOB_*xxxxxxxx* [1]
LNM$GROUP	LNM$GROUP_*gggggg* [2]
LNM$SYSTEM	LNM$SYSTEM_TABLE
LNM$DCL_LOGICAL	LNM$FILE_DEV
LNM$FILE_DEV (supervisor mode)	LNM$PROCESS,
	LNM$JOB,
	LNM$GROUP,
	LNM$SYSTEM
LNM$FILE_DEV (executive mode)	LNM$SYSTEM
LNM$PERMANENT_MAILBOX	LNM$SYSTEM
LNM$TEMPORARY_MAILBOX	LNM$JOB
LOG$PROCESS [3]	LNM$PROCESS,
	LNM$JOB
LOG$GROUP [3]	LNM$GROUP
LOG$SYSTEM [3]	LNM$SYSTEM
TRNLOG$_GROUP_SYSTEM [3]	LOG$GROUP,
	LOG$SYSTEM
TRNLOG$_PROCESS_GROUP [3]	LOG$PROCESS,
	LOG$GROUP
TRNLOG$_PROCESS_SYSTEM [3]	LOG$PROCESS,
	LOG$SYSTEM
TRNLOG$_PROCESS_GROUP_SYSTEM [3]	LOG$PROCESS,
	LOG$GROUP,
	LOG$SYSTEM

[1] The string *xxxxxxxx* represents an eight-digit hexadecimal number that is the address of the job information block.

[2] The string *gggggg* represents a six-digit octal number containing the process's UIC group number.

[3] This table provides upward compatibility for tables used by the superseded logical name services.

```
1  "LOG$PROCESS" = "LNM$PROCESS" (LNM$SYSTEM_DIRECTORY)
       = "LNM$JOB"
2  "LNM$PROCESS" = "LNM$PROCESS_TABLE" (LNM$PROCESS_DIRECTORY)
2  "LNM$JOB" = "LNM$JOB_80471670" (LNM$PROCESS_DIRECTORY)
1  "LOG$GROUP" = "LNM$GROUP" (LNM$SYSTEM_DIRECTORY)
2  "LNM$GROUP" = "LNM$GROUP_000100" (LNM$PROCESS_DIRECTORY)
```

Because TRNLOG$_PROCESS_GROUP is defined in LNM$SYSTEM_DIRECTORY, the first SHOW LOGICAL command fails to find it. After the new definition of LNM$DCL_LOGICAL to include both directory tables, SHOW LOGICAL can translate TRNLOG$_PROCESS_GROUP. It can translate iteratively all its equivalence names as well, because they are defined in one of the two directory tables. For a description of the SHOW LOGICAL and DEFINE commands, see the *VMS DCL Dictionary*.

35.4   **CHARACTERISTICS OF LOGICAL NAME TRANSLATION**

A logical name with only one equivalence name has only one translation. A multivalued logical name has multiple equivalence names, up to a maximum of 128. An equivalence name is from 1 to 255 bytes long. Each byte can have any value. Each equivalence name is uniquely identified by a number called an index number.

An equivalence name can be defined with several attributes. Each equivalence name of a multivalued logical name can have different attributes.

- The CONCEALED attribute means that the equivalence name should not be displayed in system output. Typically, this is used to foster device independence by displaying logical names rather than the names of specific devices. It is also used in the creation of logical names for rooted directories.
- The TERMINAL attribute means that the equivalence name should not itself be treated as a logical name and translated further.

When a logical name is translated, the translation attribute CASE_BLIND can be specified. This attribute means that the search for that logical name is independent of the case (uppercase or lowercase) in which the logical name was originally defined and the case in which the logical name was specified to the $TRNLNM system service.

When access mode is specified for a logical name translation, it applies to both the translation of the name and of the name tables involved. For example, if executive access mode translation is requested, then all outer mode logical names and table names are ignored.

Logical name translation has two dimensions:

- Breadth. A logical name can have multiple equivalence strings.
- Depth. One logical name can translate to another logical name, which, in turn, translates to another logical name, and so on.

These dimensions apply to the name of a logical name table as well as to a logical name. To translate a logical name, VMS must also translate the name of the tables in which to look for the logical name. The translation for a logical name table name, done implicitly as part of translating a logical name, is different from that for a logical name.

35.4.1 Dimensions of Logical Name Translation

Logical name translation, as performed by the logical name system services, deals with the breadth of a name, but not its depth. That is, if requested by the user, the $TRNLNM system service returns multiple equivalence strings when it translates a logical name. One of the $TRNLNM arguments is an item list through which multiple equivalence names can be returned. For the user to receive multiple equivalence names, the item list must include entries and buffer addresses for them.

However, when the $TRNLNM system service translates a logical name, it does not translate iteratively. That is, it does not check whether an equivalence name is itself a logical name. Further translation must be requested explicitly; the equivalence name returned must be supplied as the logical name argument in another $TRNLNM request. Certain system services, such as Assign Channel ($ASSIGN), make iterative $TRNLNM requests to translate a logical name as deeply as possible, up to a maximum iteration count, typically of nine translations.

RMS has a more complex form of iteration. It parses a file specification and requests the $TRNLNM system service iteratively to translate certain components of it. For more details, see the *Guide to VMS File Applications*.

35.4.2 Dimensions of Logical Name Table Name Translation

Each of the logical name system services must translate a logical name table name to perform its main function. A table name can be one of the following:

- A logical name whose single translation is the table data structure itself rather than an equivalence name (see Section 35.5.2)
- A name whose equivalence name is itself a logical name that translates to the table data structure after one or more iterations
- A multivalued logical name, each of whose equivalence names is a logical name that translates iteratively to a table data structure

Unlike logical name translation, table name translation must deal with both the depth and the breadth of the name. To locate a particular logical name, for example, a table name and all its equivalence names might have to be translated iteratively. In the $TRNLNM system service, and sometimes the $DELLNM system service as well, translation of a table name continues until one is found that contains the target logical name. In the system services $CRELNT, $CRELNM, and under some circumstances (see

Section 35.8.5) $DELLNM, translation of a table name only goes as far as finding the first table.

The table name translation sequence is depth-first. That is, the first equivalence name is translated until it translates to a table data structure or can be translated no further. If the table name found does not contain the logical name of interest, the next equivalence name is translated, and so on. This is a simplified description of the algorithm, which is described in more detail in Section 35.7.

35.5 **LOGICAL NAME DATA STRUCTURES**

The logical name database consists of the following kinds of structures:

- Logical name blocks (LNMBs), describing the logical names that are defined
- Logical name translation blocks (LNMXs), which contain equivalence names
- Logical name table headers (LNMTHs), which describe logical name tables
- Hash tables that locate the LNMBs (LNMHSHs)
- Table name cache blocks (LNMCs)

The macro $LNMSTRDEF defines symbolic offsets for all these data structures. The data structures are described in the sections that follow.

35.5.1 **Logical Name Blocks and Logical Name Translation Blocks**

Each defined logical name is described by an LNMB. An LNMB contains the logical name counted string in field LNMB$T_NAME, its access mode in LNMB$B_ACMODE, and its attributes in LNMB$B_FLAGS.

The LNMB field LNMB$L_TABLE specifies the address of the header of the logical name table in which the logical name is defined. An LNMB also has two longwords, LNMB$L_FLINK and LNMB$L_BLINK, which link it into a hash chain of LNMBs whose logical names have the same hash value.

Each LNMB is immediately followed by at least one LNMX. An LNMX contains flags for the equivalence name attributes in LNMX$B_FLAGS, an index identifying the equivalence name in LNMX$B_INDEX, and a counted string equivalence name, LNMX$T_XLATION. LNMX$W_HASH contains the result of hashing the logical name. It is used only for table names. There is one LNMX for each equivalence name defined for the logical name. The series of LNMXs associated with a given LNMB concludes with a one-byte LNMX containing only the FLAGS byte with the bit LNMX$V_XEND set.

Figure 35.1 shows the layouts of the LNMB and LNMX data structures. The field LNMB$W_SIZE contains the size of the LNMB, including the sizes of the LNMXs that follow it. Before the memory for the LNMB and the LNMXs is allocated, the size required for the sum of all the strings plus the fixed size is rounded up to the next quadword. As a result, although an

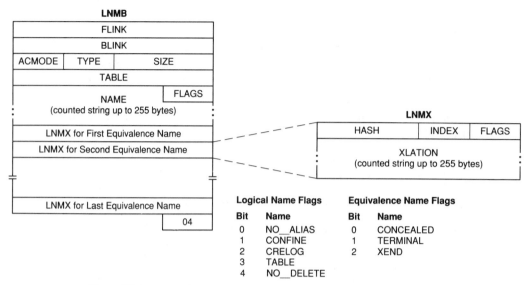

Figure 35.1
Layouts of Logical Name Blocks and Logical Name
Translation Blocks

LNMB and its LNMXs are of variable length, the combined data structure is always an integral number of quadwords.

Translation to a particular equivalence name can be requested by specifying its index. The index of an equivalence name is a one-byte signed number. By default, the first equivalence name is assigned an index value of 0, the second a value of 1, and so forth.

The positive values 0 to 127 are available for users. The negative values -1 to -128 are reserved for system use. Currently, VMS uses two special index values. The value 82_{16}, or -126, indicates that the equivalence string is a logical name table header. The value 81_{16}, or -127, indicates that the equivalence string is a back pointer, the address of another data structure. A back pointer can be used to link a mailbox unit control block (UCB) with the LNMB that contains its logical name. It can also be used to connect a mounted volume list entry and its LNMB. Only shareable logical names can have back pointers.

It is possible for the creator of a logical name explicitly to assign an index value to each equivalence name. Translation indexes can be sparse. For example, a particular logical name might have translations 1, 3, 5, and 10. VMS uses this feature itself to create back pointer logical names. Any general use of this feature is discouraged, however, because RMS and other VMS components assume that equivalence names have dense ascending indexes.

A process-private LNMB is allocated from the process allocation region. An LNMB for a shareable logical name must be accessible by multiple processes and is allocated from paged pool.

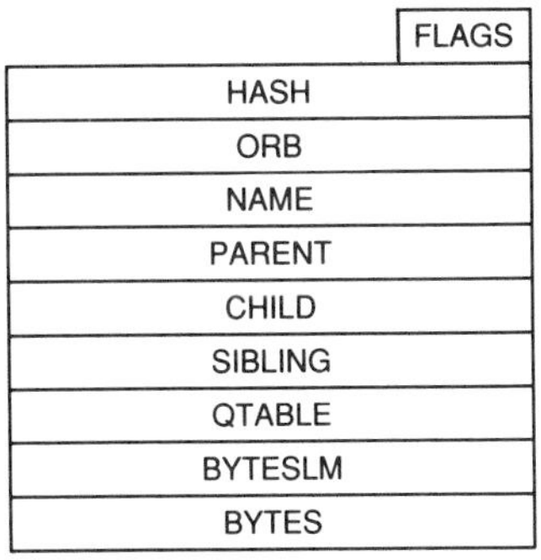

Flags

Bit	Name
0	SHAREABLE
1	DIRECTORY
2	GROUP
3	SYSTEM

Figure 35.2
Layout of Logical Name Table Header

35.5.2 Logical Name Table Headers

The data structure describing a logical name table is an LNMB whose first LNMX has the index value 82_{16} to indicate that it contains an LNMTH instead of an equivalence name. The second LNMX merely flags the end of the data structure.

An LNMTH describes a logical name table. Figure 35.2 shows its layout. The field LNMTH$L_HASH contains the address of either the shareable hash table or the process-private hash table, depending on whether the logical name table is shareable or process-private. Section 35.5.3 describes the use of logical name hash tables.

For a shareable table, LNMTH$L_ORB contains the address of the object rights block (ORB) associated with the table. The ORB defines the protection information for the logical name table: its system-owner-group-world protection mask and any access control entries that have been defined. For a process-private table, the field is unused. LNMTH$L_NAME contains the address of the beginning of the LNMB that contains this header; that is, it points back to the beginning of the data structure, an address impossible to compute from the LNMTH address, given the counted logical name string between them.

The fields LNMTH$L_PARENT, LNMTH$L_CHILD, and LNMTH$L_SIBLING contain addresses of other LNMTHs and link logical name tables into a quota and access hierarchy. The hierarchy consists of singly linked lists. A zero value in a pointer indicates the end of the list.

Figure 35.3 shows the hierarchical relations between several logical name tables: tables A and B are siblings whose parent is table R; R's parent is LNM$PROCESS_TABLE. For simplicity, the figure shows only LNMTHs and omits LNMBs. LNMTH$L_CHILD in table R contains the address of table A's header. Table A's LNMTH$L_PARENT field contains the address of table R's LNMTH. Because table R has another child table, A's field LNMTH$L_SIBLING contains the address of R's next child, table B.

LNMTH$L_QTABLE contains the LNMTH address of the table's quota

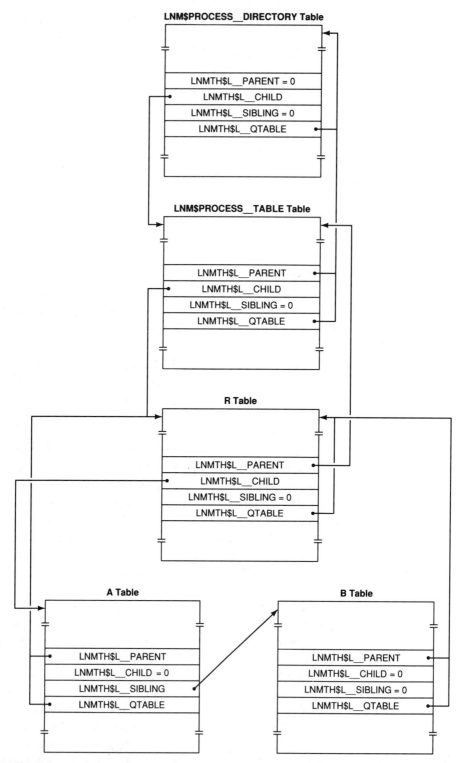

Figure 35.3
Hierarchical Relations Between Logical Name Tables

holder table. In the case of a table with limited quota, the table is its own quota holder, and the field contains the address of the start of the table's own header. For a table with limited quota, LNMTH$L_BYTESLM and LNMTH$L_BYTES contain the initial quota given to the table at its creation and the amount left. These fields are unused for a table whose quota is pooled. Figure 35.3 shows table R as its own quota holder and also the holder for tables A and B.

Note that an LNMTH contains no listhead for LNMBs. The intuitive view of the relation between a logical name and its containing table is different from the implementation. A logical name table contains logical names in an abstract sense, but it is not possible to examine a table header to locate logical names in that table. The only connection between a logical name and its containing table is from the LNMB to the table header; the field LNMB$L_TABLE contains the address of the LNMTH. Every LNMB of the appropriate hash table must be examined to determine which ones are in the table of interest.

A logical name directory is described by an LNMTH whose LNMTH$V_DIRECTORY flag is set and whose LNMTH$L_PARENT field is zero.

In a logical name table name, the field LNMB$L_TABLE always contains the address of its directory table's LNMTH. The directory's LNMB$L_TABLE also points to the directory's LNMTH.

Figure 35.4 shows the relations between the process directory; a particular logical name table, LNM$PROCESS_TABLE; and a particular logical name, SYS$LOGIN. For simplicity, Figure 35.4 omits hash table links, which are pictured in Figure 35.5.

35.5.3   **Logical Name Hash Tables**

Locating a translation for a particular logical name requires first hashing the logical name in the appropriate hash table and then determining whether the name found matches the name of interest.

Each process has its own hash table to locate all process-private logical names. All shareable logical names are hashed in the shareable hash table.

A hash table consists of a 12-byte header and a number of longword entries. Each entry in the hash table is either zero or a pointer to a hash chain of LNMBs with the same hash value. The chain is doubly linked through the fields LNMB$L_FLINK and LNMB$L_BLINK. The last LNMB in a chain has a forward pointer of zero.

The order of LNMBs in a hash chain is determined by the following criteria:

1. Length of the logical name, with shorter strings first
2. Alphabetical order, according to the ASCII collating sequence, of the logical name string for LNMBs that have logical names of the same length

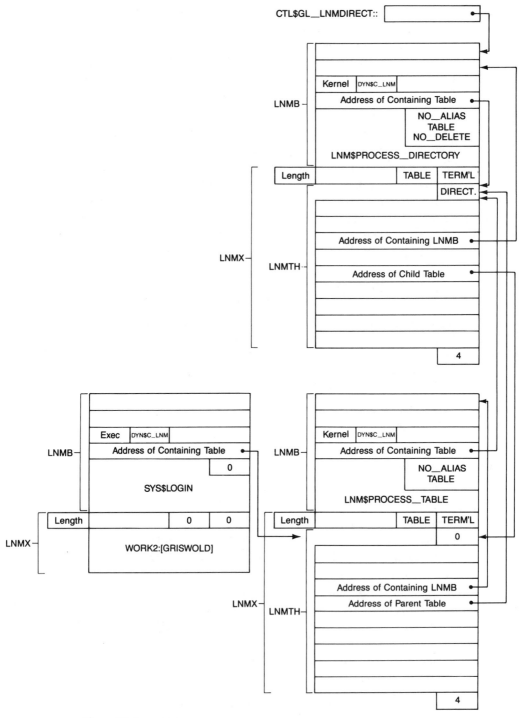

Figure 35.4
Relation Between Logical Name Table and
Directory Table

3. Address of the containing table address, with lowest address first, for LNMBs with the same logical name

4. Access mode of the logical name, with outermost access mode first, for LNMBs with the same logical name string in the same table

Recall that a logical name can be defined in different name tables and at different access modes. Translating a logical name means locating the first definition that satisfies containing table and access mode constraints. The last criterion supplies the mechanism by which an outer mode definition for a name can override an inner mode definition.

The SYSGEN parameter LNMPHASHTBL specifies the number of longword entries in the process-private hash table. During process creation, EXE$PROCSTRT allocates it from the process allocation region and initializes its header. Because the process allocation region consists of demand zero pages, the table's longword entries are zeroed as a side effect of allocating space from the region for the first time.

The SYSGEN parameter LNMSHASHTBL specifies the number of longword entries in the shareable hash table. The shareable hash table is allocated from paged pool, its header built, and longword entries cleared by the swapper process during system initialization.

The address of either hash table can be determined indirectly through the two-longword array at global location LNM$AL_HASHTBL. Its first longword points to a longword containing the address of the shareable hash table. Its second longword points to CTL$GL_LNMHASH, which contains the address of the process hash table. The field LNMTH$L_HASH in each logical name table contains the address of the hash table for its logical names.

Figure 35.5 shows this array, the two hash tables, and two hash chains.

The algorithm used to hash the logical names was chosen to be relatively fast and provide a good distribution within the hash table. It is implemented by the routine LNM$HASH, in module LNMSUB.

The hashing algorithm is as follows:

1. The size of the logical name string is moved to a longword. This is the base hash value.

2. Starting at the beginning of the string, four bytes are converted to uppercase and XORed into the hash longword. The hash is then rotated by nine bits to the left.

3. Step 2 is repeated with the next four bytes until there are fewer than four bytes remaining in the string.

4. The remaining bytes are XORed into the hash longword, one byte at a time. After each XOR, the hash is rotated by 13 bits.

5. The hash longword is then multiplied by an eight-digit hexadecimal number (71279461_{16}).

6. A number of high-order bytes in the hash longword are cleared against the mask in LNMHSH$L_MASK.

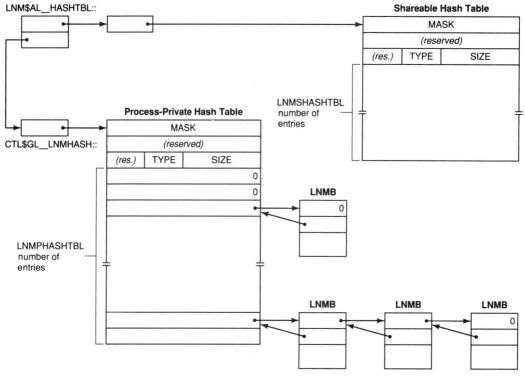

Figure 35.5
Logical Name Hash Tables and Logical Name Blocks

The result is a number no larger than the number of entries in the hash table minus 1. It is used as a longword index into the hash table. The hash value for a logical name table name is stored in its field LNMX$W_ HASHVAL and used to speed up translation of table names.

35.5.4   Logical Name Table Name Cache Blocks

To speed up logical name translation, information about logical name tables is cached. Every logical name translation entails translating a table name. If the table name translates to another logical name or is a multivalued logical name, iterative translation of multiple names may be required, as described in Section 35.7.

A cache block records the result of a particular table name translation for subsequent use. Figure 35.6 shows the layout of the logical name table cache block.

A cache block contains the address of the LNMB of the table name in field LNMC$L_TBLADDR and addresses of up to 25 LNMTHs obtained from translating that table name. As a fixed-size data structure, a cache block can hold the addresses of only 25 LNMTHs. A table name that resolves to more

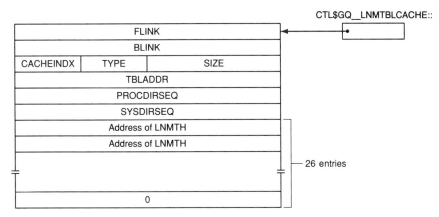

Figure 35.6
Layout of Logical Name Table Cache Block

than 25 table headers cannot be cached. As a table name is translated, table header addresses are stored in its cache block.

If a particular logical name is located in a table whose name requires iterative translation and the name's table is found before the table name is exhaustively translated, the cache block contains valid but incomplete data. The valid entries are followed by a zero longword. If the cache block describes the complete translation of the table name, the valid entries are followed by a longword containing −1. An incomplete list of table headers can be extended during later resolutions of the logical table name that require more translations. LNMC$B_CACHEINDX contains the index of the current entry, the one most recently entered or examined.

Each time the contents of a logical name table directory change, the sequence number associated with it is incremented. For example, when a process-private logical name table is created or deleted, global location CTL$GL_LNMDIRSEQ is incremented. It is also incremented if a logical name in the process directory is changed, for example, through the definition of an outer mode alias or the definition of a name that supersedes the old one. The sequence number for the shareable directory, LNM$GL_SYSDIRSEQ, is similarly incremented whenever the system directory is altered.

The cache block fields LNMC$L_PROCDIRSEQ and LNMC$L_SYSDIR-SEQ record the sequence numbers of the process and system directories current when a table name translation is cached. The fields are used as a validity check on the cached LNMTH addresses. During translation of that table name, the cached sequence numbers are checked against the current ones. The data cached in the block is valid only if both its sequence numbers are current. If one of the sequence numbers is out-of-date, it is possible that there have been changes in the directory contents that affect the cached translations.

1085

Each process has its own cache with blocks for the most recently referenced logical name table names. During process startup, EXE$PROCSTRT, in module PROCSTRT, allocates cache blocks from the process allocation region. It initializes and inserts them in a doubly linked list whose head is at CTL$GQ_LNMTBLCACHE. The amount of space used for cache blocks is approximately twice that used for the process hash table. Each cache block is 128 bytes. The number of cache blocks is related to the SYSGEN parameter LNMPHASHTBL in the following way:

$$\text{number\_of\_cache\_blocks} = \frac{\text{LNMPHASHTBL} * 8}{128}$$

35.5.5 Synchronization of Access to the Logical Name Database

A single mutex named LNM$AL_MUTEX provides synchronization to the shareable logical name database. Chapter 8 describes the use of mutexes.

The $TRNLNM system service locks the mutex for read access. Multiple processes can lock the mutex for concurrent read access and logical name translation. The other logical name system services all modify the database and therefore lock the mutex for write access, blocking any concurrent access by another process.

35.6 SEARCHING FOR A LOGICAL NAME

To search for a logical name, the $TRNLNM and $DELLNM logical name system services invoke the routine LNM$SEARCHLOG, in module LNM-SUB. LNM$SEARCHLOG invokes a number of other routines, some of which are invoked directly from the $CRELNM system service.

LNM$SEARCHLOG must first hash the name in both logical name hash tables to find out whether it exists. These hashes are independent of the containing table and are performed to find out whether the logical name has been defined at all. Because many file specifications are translated to check whether they are logical names, attempted logical name translation is most frequent. That is, most translations fail. The data structures and search algorithm were designed to optimize the determination that a particular string is not a logical name.

If LNM$SEARCHLOG determines that one or more names with a matching logical name string exist, it must locate the first one whose containing table and access mode match the routine's input arguments. This requires that LNM$SEARCHLOG translate its input table name to one or more name table header addresses.

LNM$SEARCHLOG takes the following steps:

1. It initializes a stack local data structure called a name translation block (NT) to describe the state of the name translation.

2. It then invokes LNM$PRESEARCH, in module LNMSUB, with the address of the process-private hash table. If the current process is the swapper, which has no process-private logical names, LNM$SEARCHLOG begins with the shareable logical name hash table.

   LNM$PRESEARCH and its associated routines, all in module LNMSUB, take the following steps:

   a. LNM$PRESEARCH invokes LNM$HASH to hash the logical name. The resulting value is used as an index into the hash table. The hash table entry located by the index is a listhead of LNMBs with that hash value, a hash chain.

   b. LNM$PRESEARCH invokes LNM$CONTSEARCH to search the hash chain for one with a matching logical name.

   c. Beginning with the first LNMB in the chain, LNM$CONTSEARCH compares the length of the logical name with the length of the target logical name. Comparing logical name lengths eliminates the overhead of a string comparison instruction that is bound to fail if the lengths differ. If the logical name in the LNMB is shorter, LNM$CONTSEARCH skips that LNMB and goes on to the next. If the name in the LNMB is longer, the search has passed the possible LNMBs, and the routine returns the error status SS$_NOLOGNAM. If the names are the same length, the routine compares them.

   d. If the names are identical, LNM$CONTSEARCH returns a success status and the address of the LNMB with the matching name.

   e. If the names differ, but the search is case-blind, one in which the uppercase version of both names must be compared, LNM$CONTSEARCH converts the names one character at a time and compares them. It continues converting and comparing until it reaches the end of the names or a character comparison fails.

      If it reaches the end of the names, the names are identical. It returns a success status and the address of the LNMB with the matching name.

   f. If the search is not case-blind or the converted names differ, it tests whether the name in the LNMB is alphabetically lower than the target logical name. If it is higher, the search has passed the last possible LNMB. LNM$CONTSEARCH returns the error status SS$_NOLOGNAM to its invoker.

   g. If the name is alphabetically lower, the routine continues the search until it reaches the end of the hash chain, an LNMB containing a name of a different length, an LNMB containing a name higher in the sort sequence, or an LNMB with a matching name. In the first three circumstances, LNM$CONTSEARCH returns the error status SS$_NOLOGNAM to its invoker.

3. Regardless of the outcome, LNM$SEARCHLOG initializes a second data

structure and invokes LNM$PRESEARCH again, this time with the address of the shareable hash table.

4. If there was no match in either hash table, LNM$SEARCHLOG returns the error status SS$_NOLOGNAM to its invoker.

5. If at least one logical name matched in either hash table, LNM$SEARCH-LOG must check whether the containing table and access mode also match.

   LNM$SEARCHLOG invokes LNM$SETUP to confirm that the target logical name's table name exists and to initialize logical name table processing. Section 35.7 describes table name resolution in detail.

   —If the table name does not exist, LNM$SETUP returns the error status SS$_NOLOGNAM, which LNM$SEARCHLOG returns to its invoker.

   —If the table name does exist, LNM$SETUP returns the address of the first LNMTH to which the table name resolves. Recall that a table name can be a multivalued logical name with equivalence names that are themselves logical names.

6. LNM$SEARCHLOG invokes LNM$CONTSEARCH, this time with the address of the containing table header.

7. Beginning at a point determined by the previous searches, LNM$CONT-SEARCH scans the hash chain for a matching logical name. If the table is shareable, LNM$CONTSEARCH looks in the shareable hash table chain; otherwise, it checks the process-private one.

   This time, however, when it finds a match, it also compares containing table name addresses.

   —If the LNMTH address in the hash chain LNMB is higher, the search has failed, since LNMBs with the same logical name are ordered by LNMTH address.

   —If the LNMTH address is lower, LNM$CONTSEARCH goes on to the next LNMB.

   —If the LNMTH addresses match, the routine must also check the access mode. If the LNMB access mode is greater (less privileged) than the requested mode, it goes on to the next LNMB. If the LNMB mode is equal to or less than the requested mode, the LNMB matches, and LNM$CONTSEARCH returns a success status and the address of the LNMB to LNM$SEARCHLOG.

8. If there is a matching logical name, LNM$SEARCHLOG returns the success status SS$_NORMAL and the address of the target LNMB.

9. If there is no matching name in the first table, the next table to which the table name resolves must be checked. LNM$SEARCHLOG invokes LNM$TABLE to continue the table processing begun with the invocation of LNM$SETUP. LNM$TABLE returns the address of the next LNMTH. LNM$SEARCHLOG invokes LNM$CONTSEARCH again, as in step 6, with that address.

This sequence continues until the first matching logical name is found or there are no more tables to check. If no match is found in any table, LNM$SEARCHLOG returns the failure status SS$_NOLOGNAM to its invoker.

System services other than logical name services, such as the $ASSIGN system service, invoke the routine LNM$SEARCH_ONE. LNM$SEARCH_ONE locks the logical name database mutex for read access. It invokes LNM$SEARCHLOG to find the LNMB and extracts the translation with index zero. It unlocks the mutex and returns to its invoker.

The SHOW LOGICAL utility builds an NT structure and invokes the routines LNM$PRESEARCH and LNM$CONTSEARCH directly. In contrast to the use of LNM$SEARCHLOG, where locating the first matching logical name is sufficient, the utility must be able to generate every possible match.

35.7   **LOGICAL NAME TABLE NAME RESOLUTION**

To resolve a logical name table name, the logical name system services and routines and the DCL SHOW LOGICAL command invoke either the routine LNM$FIRSTTAB or the combination of LNM$SETUP and LNM$TABLE. These three routines are all in module LNMSUB.

LNM$FIRSTTAB is called to return only the first table in the translation of a table name. A typical use of it is to identify the table in which to create a new logical name. LNM$FIRSTTAB itself invokes LNM$SETUP.

LNM$SETUP and LNM$TABLE perform iterative and potentially exhaustive translations of a table name. LNM$SETUP is invoked first to initialize the search context and return the address of the first table header. Subsequently, LNM$TABLE is invoked again and again, to return the next table header address, potentially until the table name has been exhaustively translated in a depth-first sequence.

When LNM$SETUP is entered, its invoker has allocated and partially initialized a stack local data structure called a recursive table translation block (RT). Its fields include recursion depth, recursion tries, access mode of the request, address of the associated table name cache block, and ten longwords in which to maintain search context. The recursion depth is an index into these ten longwords.

LNM$SETUP takes the following steps:

1. It initializes the recursion depth to zero and the number of remaining recursion tries to 255.
2. It invokes LNM$LOOKUP to confirm that the table exists.

    Invoking LNM$PRESEARCH, LNM$LOOKUP checks the process directory and, if that fails, the system directory for the starting table name. Recall that all logical names involved in the translation of table names must be contained in one of the two directories.

—If the table name does not exist, LNM$LOOKUP returns the error status SS$_NOLOGNAM, which LNM$SETUP returns to its invoker.

—If the table name exists, LNM$LOOKUP returns the address of the LNMB that defines it.

3. If the name exists, LNM$SETUP saves the address of its LNMB$T_ NAME field in the RT's top search context longword as the starting point of the translation.

4. It then scans for a valid table name cache block describing this table name.

—If one is found, its cache entries contain the addresses of some (possibly all) of the table headers to which the table name resolves.

—If a valid table name cache block is not found, the least recently used one is selected for reuse and initialized. Its first cache entry is cleared to indicate that it contains no valid entries.

5. LNM$SETUP saves the address of the cache block in the RT structure. It initializes the cache block index to -1 to indicate no cache entries have been examined yet and enters the routine LNM$TABLE.

Each time LNM$TABLE is entered to resolve the table name, it increments the cache index. It then checks whether the index selects a valid entry, one whose value is nonzero.

- If the longword is nonzero, LNM$TABLE returns it as the address of the next table header to its invoker.
- If the longword is zero, the valid cached data has been exhausted. In that case, LNM$TABLE invokes LNM$TABLE_SRCH to expand the resolution of the table name and add entries to the end of the cache block.

LNM$TABLE_SRCH contains the fundamental recursion loop in resolving a table name. It uses the RT data structure to keep track of the breadth and depth of its position in resolving the table name.

At the beginning of the loop, it decrements the number of remaining recursion tries. If none is left, LNM$TABLE_SRCH returns the error status SS$_TOOMANYLNAM to its invoker. This check prevents the code, for example, from looping endlessly trying to resolve a circular logical name table definition.

LNM$TABLE_SRCH examines the next equivalence name at the current recursion depth to determine what to do. There are several possibilities:

a. If the equivalence name is an ordinary string, LNM$TABLE_SRCH updates the contents in the stack longword to point to the equivalence name following it.

b. It tests that the maximum recursion depth (10) has not been exceeded. If

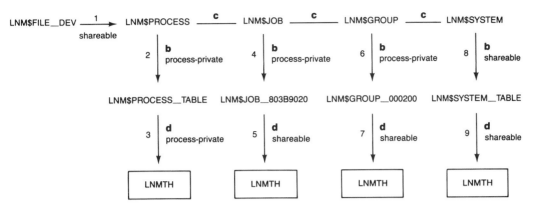

Figure 35.7
Example Resolution of a Logical Name Table Name

the depth has been exceeded, LNM$TABLE_SRCH returns the error SS$_
TOOMANYLNAM.

Otherwise, it increments the recursion depth and invokes the routine
LNM$LOOKUP to find the LNMB associated with the string. It positions
to the name string in the LNMX and examines its equivalence name,
beginning the loop again.

c. If there are no more equivalence names, LNM$TABLE_SRCH decrements
the recursion depth and selects the corresponding RT search longword.
It begins the loop again.

d. If the equivalence name is a table header (desired result), LNM$TABLE_
SRCH decrements the recursion depth and returns the address of the
table header to its invoker.

Figure 35.7 is an example showing complete resolution of the logical name
LNM$FILE_DEV. The first step is translating LNM$FILE_DEV, a shareable
name found in the system directory with four equivalence names. The second step is translating the "leftmost" equivalence name, LNM$PROCESS.
It is a process-private name whose equivalence name is LNM$PROCESS_
TABLE. The third step translates LNM$PROCESS_TABLE to its equivalence
name, the first table header for LNM$FILE_DEV.

In the figure, the numbers indicate the sequence of translations. The letters on each step correspond to the possible actions in the recursion loop
previously listed.

In this example, each equivalence name of LNM$FILE_DEV is translated
as deeply as required to reach a table header. In practice, during logical
name translation or deletion, table name resolution stops as soon as the first
table that contains the logical name is found. During logical name creation,
table resolution stops with the first table, in this example, LNM$PROCESS_
TABLE.

35.8   **LOGICAL NAME SYSTEM SERVICES**

The logical name system service procedures all run in kernel mode. The procedures themselves are in the module SYSLNM. Logical name subroutines that they use are in module LNMSUB.

Before describing the specific system service procedures, this section describes some checks common to the services.

35.8.1   **Privilege and Protection Checks**

Each of the system services has an access mode argument. If the requestor explicitly specifies it and has the privilege SYSNAM, the desired access mode is used with no further check. If the requestor specifies it but does not have the privilege, the access mode is maximized with the mode from which the system service was requested. That is, the less privileged of the two is used.

Any string argument passed to the services must be probed to test accessibility from the mode of the system service requestor. An input string is tested for read accessibility and an output string for write accessibility. An item list must be probed for read accessibility and each buffer in it must also be probed.

The logical name system services must check a process's access to a shareable table. (A process always has access to a process-private table, although it may be constrained by access mode considerations.) The system services use standard VMS protection checks. That is, they invoke the routine LNM$CHECK_PROT, which calls an internal entry point of the Check Access Protection ($CHKPRO) system service.

The $CHKPRO system service determines whether the process, given its rights and privileges, can access the table. The system service's checks encompass the process UIC, the protection mask of the table, any ACLs defined for the table, and whether the process has any of the following privileges:

> SYSPRV
> GRPPRV
> BYPASS
> READALL

If the $CHKPRO system service returns a failure status, LNM$CHECK_ PROT makes two checks of its own to provide compatibility with earlier versions of VMS. If the intended access is read or write, LNM$CHECK_ PROT tests whether the table of interest is either a group table or the system table. If this is the group table and the process has the privilege GRPNAM, its access is allowed. If this is the system table and the process has the privilege SYSNAM, its access is allowed.

35.8.2 Logical Name Translation

The $TRNLNM system service procedure, EXE$TRNLNM, takes the following steps to translate a logical name:

1. It first confirms the presence and accessibility of its required arguments: descriptors for the logical name string and name of its containing table.
2. It locks the logical name database mutex for read access.
3. It invokes LNM$SEARCHLOG to locate the first logical name that meets the table name and access mode constraints, as described in Section 35.6.

   If LNM$SEARCHLOG returns the error status SS$_NOLOGNAM, indicating that the logical name does not exist, EXE$TRNLNM unlocks the logical name database mutex and passes the error status back to its requestor.
4. If the logical name exists, LNM$SEARCHLOG returns the address of the LNMB of the first matching logical name.

   EXE$TRNLNM examines its address to determine whether it is a process-private or a shareable name.
5. If the name is shareable (a system space LNMB), EXE$TRNLNM invokes LNM$CHECK_PROT to determine whether the process has read access to the containing table. If the process does not have access, EXE$TRNLNM unlocks the logical name database mutex and returns the error status SS$_NOPRIV to its requestor.
6. If the name is a process-private one or a shareable one to whose table the process has access, EXE$TRNLNM processes the item list, which contains the list of specific information to be returned. EXE$TRNLNM probes any specified output buffers for write access and copies information from the LNMB, its LNMXs, and the LNMTH of its containing table, as requested.
7. EXE$TRNLNM then unlocks the logical name database mutex and returns to its requestor.

   If there was insufficient space in the output buffers for all requested information, EXE$TRNLNM returns the success status SS$_BUFFEROVF. Otherwise, it returns the success status SS$_NORMAL.

35.8.3 Logical Name Creation

The $CRELNM system service procedure, EXE$CRELNM, takes the following steps to create a logical name:

1. It confirms the presence of its required arguments: the descriptors for the logical name string and the name of its containing table.
2. If the requestor specified the address of an item list containing equivalence strings and their attributes, EXE$CRELNM scans the list to determine their cumulative size. The item list is not a required argument, but

there is little purpose served in creating a logical name with no translations, other than perhaps the creation of a logical name whose existence or nonexistence serves as an on-off flag.

3. EXE$CRELNM raises interrupt priority level (IPL) to 2 and allocates enough paged pool for the LNMB and all its LNMXs. The assumption is that the logical name is shareable and will thus require paged pool rather than space in the process allocation region. Until the containing table is located, EXE$CRELNM cannot determine whether the name is process-private or shareable. If there is insufficient paged pool, EXE$CRELNM returns the error status SS$_INSFMEM to its caller.

4. EXE$CRELNM then locks the logical name database mutex for write access and invokes LNM$FIRSTTAB (see Section 35.7) to translate the name of the containing logical name table. A new logical name is always created in the first table of a table name search list.

   If LNM$FIRSTTAB returns the error status SS$_NOLOGTAB to indicate that the containing table name did not translate to any existing table, EXE$CRELNM unlocks the logical name database mutex and deallocates the paged pool. It returns the error status to its requestor.

5. If the search is successful, LNM$FIRSTTAB returns the address of the containing table's LNMTH. EXE$CRELNM examines a flag in the LNMTH to determine whether it is a shareable table.

   —If the table is process-private, EXE$CRELNM deallocates the paged pool and allocates the same amount from the process allocation region. If there is insufficient process allocation region, EXE$CRELNM unlocks the mutex and returns the error status SS$_INSFMEM to its requestor.

   —If the table is shareable, EXE$CRELNM invokes LNM$CHECK_PROT to determine whether the process has write access to the containing table (see Section 35.3). If the process does not have access, EXE$CRELNM unlocks the mutex, deallocates the pool, and returns the error status SS$_NOPRIV to its requestor.

6. If the table is process-private or a shareable one to which the process has access, EXE$CRELNM then checks that there is sufficient quota for the LNMB in the table that holds the quota for the containing table (LNMTH$L_QTABLE). If there is not, EXE$CRELNM deallocates the pool, unlocks the mutex, and returns the error status SS$_EXLNM-QUOTA to its requestor.

7. EXE$CRELNM then begins to fill in the LNMB. If the containing table is one of the directories, EXE$CRELNM tests that the length of the logical name string is less than 32 characters and that it contains no characters other than those allowed for logical names contained in a directory. (Note that if a logical name is being created that is not a table name but whose containing table is one of the directories, it must meet

those same requirements.) If the logical name string does not meet those requirements, EXE$CRELNM deallocates the pool, unlocks the mutex, and returns the error status SS$_IVLOGNAM to its requestor.

8. EXE$CRELNM copies the logical name string to the LNMB. It then begins processing the item list, building LNMXs as specified by the requestor.

9. EXE$CRELNM invokes LNM$INSLOGTAB to insert the LNMB into the logical name database.

   LNM$INSLOGTAB scans any LNMBs with the same name and containing table until there are no more or it encounters one with a more privileged access mode. It compares their access modes to that of the logical name being created and examines the NO_ALIAS attribute of the new name to determine what to do:

   —If an LNMB has the same access mode, the old LNMB is deleted and superseded by the new one.
   —If one has a more privileged mode and the NO_ALIAS attribute, the new logical name cannot be inserted. LNM$INSLOGTAB returns the error status SS$_DUPLNAM to EXE$CRELNM. EXE$CRELNM deallocates the LNMB to pool, unlocks the mutex, and returns the error status to its requestor.
   —If there is one with a more privileged mode and without the NO_ALIAS attribute, the new logical name can be created.
   —If one or more is found with a less privileged mode and the new name has the NO_ALIAS attribute, the outer mode logical names are deleted and the new one is inserted. Section 35.8.5 describes the possible side effects of logical name deletion.

   LNM$INSLOGTAB charges the size of the LNMB against the containing table's quota holder. If the containing table is a directory, LNM$INSLOGTAB increments the appropriate directory sequence number as part of the cache invalidation mechanism. Section 35.5.4 describes the use of logical name caches.

10. If the containing table is a directory, EXE$CRELNM computes and stores a hash value for each of the equivalence names of the newly created logical name. The assumption behind this is that the logical name translates to one or more name table names, whose hash values will be needed whenever a table search involving this name is performed.

11. EXE$CRELNM unlocks the mutex and returns to its requestor.

35.8.4   Logical Name Table Creation

The $CRELNT system service procedure, EXE$CRELNT, takes the following steps to create a logical name table:

1. It confirms the presence and accessibility of the descriptor for the name of the parent table, its one required argument.
2. If the requestor omits the name of the table to be created, EXE$CRELNT supplies a default name. The form of default name is LNM$*xxxxxxxx-eeeeeeee*, where *xxxxxxxx* is the address of the LNMB of the table and *eeeeeeee* is the process's extended process ID (EPID). Using a default table name ensures that the name of a table does not conflict with any other defined table.
3. EXE$CRELNT raises IPL to 2 and allocates enough paged pool for the LNMB, its single LNMX and LNMTH, the trailer byte flagging the end of translations, and an ORB. The assumption is that the logical name table is shareable and thus requires paged pool rather than process allocation region space. Until the parent table is located, EXE$CRELNT cannot determine whether the new table is process-private or shareable.
4. EXE$CRELNT then locks the logical name database for write access and invokes LNM$FIRSTTAB (see Section 35.7) to translate the name of the parent logical name table. If the parent table is a table name search list, its first table name becomes the parent of the new table.

   If LNM$FIRSTTAB returns the error status SS$_NOLOGTAB to indicate that the parent table name does not translate to any existing table, EXE$CRELNT unlocks the logical name database mutex and deallocates the paged pool. It returns the error status to its requestor.
5. If the parent table name does translate, LNM$FIRSTTAB returns the address of the parent table's LNMTH.

   —If the parent table is process-private, EXE$CRELNT deallocates the paged pool and allocates space from the process allocation region. The process allocation does not include space for the ORB, because a process-private table does not need an ORB.

   —If the parent table is shareable, EXE$CRELNT calls LNM$CHECK_PROT to determine whether the process has enable access to the parent table and can thus withdraw quota from it. If the process does not have access, EXE$CRELNT deallocates the pool, unlocks the mutex, and returns the error status SS$_NOPRIV to its requestor.

   If the parent table is shareable and the process specified the name of the table to be created, EXE$CRELNT checks whether the process has write access to the system directory. If a default table name was constructed, the process does not need write access to the system directory. On error, EXE$CRELNT deallocates the pool, unlocks the mutex, and returns the error status SS$_NOPRIV to its requestor.
6. EXE$CRELNT checks that there is sufficient quota for the table name (its LNMB, LNMX, and LNMTH) in the directory table. If a quota for the new table was specified, then it also checks that the parent table's quota holder has sufficient quota for the names that will be contained in the

new table. If it does not, EXE$CRELNT deallocates the pool, unlocks the mutex, and returns the error status SS$_EXLNMQUOTA to its requestor.

7. If there is sufficient quota, EXE$CRELNT fills in the LNMB and translation blocks. If the requestor specified the name of the table to be created, EXE$CRELNT tests that it is a legal table name. If the table is shareable, EXE$CRELNT initializes its ORB.

8. EXE$CRELNT then invokes LNM$INSLOGTAB to insert the LNMB into the logical name database.

LNM$INSLOGTAB scans all LNMBs with the same name and containing table until there are no more or it encounters one with a more privileged access mode. Its actions depend on the NO_ALIAS attribute of the new name and any old ones, the access modes of the new and old names, and the presence or absence of the CREATE_IF ATTR argument. The CREATE_IF attribute means that the table should be created only if there is not already one with the same name and access mode.

—If there is an LNMB with the same access mode and CREATE_IF was not specified, the old LNMB is deleted and superseded by the new one. Deleting an LNMB whose equivalence name is an LNMTH means that all the logical names contained in that table must be deleted. Any descendant tables and their logical names must also be deleted.

—If there is an LNMB with the same access mode and CREATE_IF was specified, LNM$INSLOGTAB returns the status SS$_NORMAL and the address of the old LNMB. EXE$CRELNT deallocates the new LNMB to pool.

—If there is an LNMB with a more privileged mode and the NO_ALIAS attribute, the new LNMB cannot be inserted. LNM$INSLOGTAB returns the error status SS$_DUPLNAM to EXE$CRELNT, which deallocates the new LNMB to pool.

—If there is an LNMB with a more privileged mode and without the NO_ALIAS attribute, LNM$INSLOGTAB can insert the new LNMB. It returns the status SS$_LNMCREATED.

—If one or more LNMBs are found with a less privileged mode and the new name has the NO_ALIAS attribute, the outer mode LNMBs are deleted. The new LNMB is inserted. LNM$INSLOGTAB returns the status SS$_SUPERSEDE.

To insert the new LNMB (and its table), LNM$INSLOGTAB inserts the LNMB into the hash chain and the LNMTH into the name table hierarchy as the first child of its parent table. If there already was one, LNM$INSLOGTAB stores the address of its LNMTH in the new table's LNMTH$L_SIBLING. If this table is to be its own quota holder, quota is withdrawn from the parent's quota holder and allocated to the new table. Otherwise, the table's LNMTH$L_QTABLE is set to the same value as that of its parent table. Quota for the table's LNMB is withdrawn from the appropriate directory table. LNM$INSLOGTAB increments the appropriate directory sequence number.

9. EXE$CRELNT unlocks the logical name database mutex and returns to its requestor, passing back the status from LNM$INSLOGTAB, and, if requested, the name of the newly created table.

35.8.5   Logical Name Deletion

The $DELLNM system service procedure, EXE$DELLNM, takes the following steps to delete a logical name:

1. It confirms the presence of the descriptor for the name of the table containing the names to be deleted, its one required argument.

   The LOGNAM argument is the logical name to be deleted; it can be a logical name table name. The absence of the logical name argument is a request to delete all the table's logical names with access mode equally or less privileged than that of the request.

2. EXE$DELLNM raises IPL to 2 and locks the logical name database mutex for write access.

3. If the requestor requested deletion of a particular logical name, EXE$DEL-LNM invokes LNM$SEARCHLOG, described in Section 35.6, to determine whether the name exists. If the name is not found or if its access mode is more privileged than that of the service request, EXE$DELLNM unlocks the mutex and returns the error status SS$_NOLOGNAM to its requestor.

4. If the name found is shareable, EXE$DELLNM invokes LNM$CHECK_PROT to ensure that the requestor has write access to the containing logical name table. If the requestor does not, but the name being deleted is a table name, delete access to the table being deleted is sufficient.

   If the requestor does not have access, EXE$DELLNM unlocks the mutex and returns the error status SS$_NOPRIV to its requestor.

5. EXE$DELLNM invokes LNM$DELETE_LNMB to remove the logical name and any of its outer access mode aliases from the database. If the name is not the name of a table, deleting it is straightforward and consists of the following steps for each alias:

   a. Remove the LNMB and those of any outer mode aliases from the hash chain.

   b. Return the quota charged for them.

   c. Deallocate them to the process allocation region or paged pool.

   If, however, the LNMB is a table name, deleting it also requires deleting each LNMB contained within it, and any descendant tables and their logical names. LNM$DELETE_LNMB removes the LNMB from its hash chain and inserts it into a holding list. It then invokes a routine called DELETE_TABLE to delete the table.

DELETE_TABLE examines the table header to determine whether this table has any descendants. If it does, DELETE_TABLE finds the first one, removes it from its hash chain, inserts it into the holding list, and branches back to itself. DELETE_TABLE is now one level lower in the logical name table hierarchy. It continues recursively, until it reaches a childless level.

It then invokes DELETE_NAMES to delete all the logical names in that table. This requires scanning the appropriate hash table and examining each LNMB to see whether it is contained within the table. Each such LNMB is removed from its hash chain and deallocated to its pool, with quota returned to the containing table. If the table is shareable, the LNMB is deallocated to paged pool. Otherwise, it is deallocated to the process allocation region. DELETE_NAMES checks that the NODELETE flag is clear in each LNMB before deleting it, to ensure that it does not delete either directory table.

After all its names are deleted, the table is then removed from the table hierarchy, its table quota is returned to its quota holder, and the LNMB quota is returned to the appropriate directory. The appropriate directory sequence number is incremented and the LNMB deallocated to its pool.

DELETE_TABLE then processes the first LNMB in the holding list, the parent of the one just deleted. DELETE_TABLE examines the table header of that LNMB to see whether it still has descendants. If it does not, then all the logical names in that table and the table itself are deleted. If it still has descendants, DELETE_TABLE places the LNMB for the first child into the holding list and branches back to itself. Eventually, DELETE_TABLE empties the holding list and returns.

6. EXE$DELLNM unlocks the mutex and returns to its requestor.

If EXE$DELLNM is called without the logical name argument, it invokes LNM$FIRSTTAB to find the first table header to which the table name resolves. If the table is shareable, it invokes LNM$CHECK_PROT to confirm that the process has delete access to the table or write access to the directory. DELETE_NAMES is invoked to delete all the names in that table.

As described previously, it scans the appropriate hash table, looking for LNMBs with a matching table header address and an access mode equally or less privileged than that of the delete request. Each such LNMB is removed from the hash chain, its quota is returned, and it is deallocated to pool.

When all the names of suitable access mode in that table are deleted, EXE$DELLNM unlocks the mutex and returns to its requestor.

When an image exits, the Rundown Image ($RUNDWN) system service must delete all process-private logical names with an access mode less or equally privileged to the exit mode.

The $RUNDWN system service invokes the routine LNM$DELETE_HASH, specifying the exit access mode and the address of the process-private hash table. LNM$DELETE_HASH locks the logical name table mutex and invokes DELETE_NAMES with the address of the hash table. Many of its logical names, of course, are names of tables. Deleting each of them requires the steps previously described to delete a table, its descendant tables, and its logical names. When all the names are deleted, LNM$DELETE_HASH unlocks the mutex and returns to the $RUNDWN system service, whose details are described in Chapter 26.

35.9 SUPERSEDED LOGICAL NAME SYSTEM SERVICES

The current logical name system services supersede several system services from VMS Version 3 and earlier versions:

- Create logical name ($CRELOG)
- Delete logical name ($DELLOG)
- Translate logical name ($TRNLOG)

VMS supports these services to provide upward compatibility for software written for earlier versions. Table 35.3 shows the correspondence between the table numbers used in earlier versions and the table names that currently implement them. Table 35.2 shows the translation of those table names.

It is possible for users of the superseded logical name system services to make some use of current features without reprogramming. By defining aliases to the table names used by these system services, a process can access tables other than the standard process, group, and system logical name tables. In fact, VMS defines the name LOG$PROCESS to equate to both the process and jobwide logical name tables. This enables translation of logical names within the jobwide logical name table by default.

The superseded system service procedures are in module SYSLOGNAM and are mode-of-caller services. Each service confirms that the minimum number of arguments expected is present and that the argument list is accessible. Each service then transforms its argument list and invokes the equivalent replacement system service.

The arguments for each superseded service include access mode and table number. Each service checks that its table number argument is valid and converts it to the corresponding logical name table name. Table 35.3 shows this correspondence and also the access mode associated with each table.

For the process table, any access mode specified by the requestor is used. If the argument is omitted, the requestor's access mode is used. The access mode is passed as an argument to the replacement logical name system service, which checks that the process has suitable privileges.

The following paragraphs supply a few specific additional details about the implementation of the $CRELOG and $TRNLOG system services.

A name created with the $CRELOG system service has only one translation, the equivalence name supplied to $CRELOG. The logical name has the CRELOG attribute. The equivalence name is assigned translation index 0.

Table 35.3 Correspondence Between Table Numbers
and Logical Name Table Names

Table Number	Table Name	Access Mode
0	LOG$SYSTEM	Executive
1	LOG$GROUP	User
2	LOG$PROCESS	Mode of caller

If the equivalence name begins with a leading underscore, the underscore is removed and the equivalence name has the TERMINAL attribute.

The $TRNLOG system service returns translation number 0 of the specified logical name. If the translation has the TERMINAL attribute, $TRNLOG prefixes an underscore to the equivalence name. This manipulation enables most logical names, including file names, to be created and used through either the old or new system services.

Two arguments to the $TRNLOG system service control its actions: the TABLE and DSBMSK arguments. The TABLE argument is the address to receive the translation table number. The DSBMSK argument specifies which subset of the process, group, and system tables is to be searched. (The mask is a disable mask; by identifying which tables to omit, it indirectly identifies those to be searched.)

If the TABLE argument is zero, EXE$TRNLOG transforms the DSBMSK argument into a table name search list with the names of the tables to be searched. It selects one of the logical name table names whose name begins with the string TRNLOG$. It requests the $TRNLNM system service and transforms its return arguments into forms compatible with the Version 3 interface.

A nonzero TABLE argument means that EXE$TRNLOG must return the number of the containing table. To determine the table, EXE$TRNLOG requests the $TRNLNM system service once for each table to be searched, until the logical name is found or the end of the table subset is reached.

36 Miscellaneous System Services

... Of shoes—and ships—and sealing wax—
Of cabbages—and kings—
And why the sea is boiling hot—
And whether pigs have wings.
Lewis Carroll, *Through the Looking Glass*

This chapter briefly discusses a number of system services not mentioned in the previous chapters. Although these services do not generally make extensive use of the internal structures and mechanisms of the VMS executive, some of their descriptions are provided as an informational aid to users of the services and for completeness. The *VMS System Services Reference Manual* contains detailed discussions of these services and their arguments, return status codes, required process privileges, and options.

36.1 COMMUNICATION WITH SYSTEM PROCESSES

VMS performs some of the operations often associated with an operating system from independent processes rather than from code in the system base image or loadable executive images. Examples of this type of system activity include the following:

- Managing print and batch jobs and queues
- Gathering accounting information about utilization of system resources
- Communicating with one or more system operators
- Reporting device errors

36.1.1 Services Supported by the Job Controller

The job controller is a system process named JOB_CONTROL, which executes the image JOBCTL.EXE. The job controller supports several system services. It performs many different functions, including the following:

- As the queue manager of the batch/print subsystem, the job controller is responsible for all transactions to and from the queue file, typically SYS$SYSTEM:JBCSYSQUE.DAT. On a VAXcluster system, the job controllers running on every node can access a single, common queue file. These transactions include the creation and deletion of queues, and the creation, modification, and dispatching of batch and print jobs.

  To manage print jobs, the job controller directs the activity of one or more print symbiont processes. A print symbiont process executes a standard image supplied with VMS, such as PRTSMB.EXE or LATSMB.EXE, an image supplied with a VMS layered product, or a user-written image that links with SMBSRVSHR.EXE.

- As the system accounting manager, the job controller records the use of system resources in the file SYS$SYSTEM:ACCOUNTNG.DAT. On a VAXcluster system, each job controller accesses a node-specific accounting file.
- As the job manager, the job controller directs the creation of interactive and batch processes.

  —To create an interactive process, the job controller initiates a detached process running the image LOGINOUT.EXE in response to unsolicited terminal input.

  —To schedule a batch job to run from an execution queue, it creates a process running the image LOGINOUT.EXE. The new process makes a special job controller request to receive its job parameters.

  —In response to unsolicited card reader input, the job controller creates an input symbiont process, running the image INPSMB.EXE. The input symbiont reads the card deck and submits a batch job.

    Chapter 13 describes the job controller's actions as the job manager.

The job controller communicates with other processes on the system through mailbox messages. It receives messages as the result of system service requests, notification of process deletion, and messages from print symbionts, the terminal driver, and the card reader driver. The job controller sends messages to print symbionts and batch processes during login. Chapter 23 provides more details about the job controller's mailbox.

Several VMS system services, described in the following sections, enable processes to communicate with the job controller in its roles as queue manager and accounting manager:

- Send Message to Job Controller ($SNDJBC[W])
- Get Queue Information ($GETQUI[W])
- Send Message to Account Manager ($SNDACC, obsolete since VMS Version 4)
- Send Message to Symbiont Manager ($SNDSMB, obsolete since VMS Version 4)

36.1.1.1 **$SNDJBC System Service.** The $SNDJBC[W] system service requests that the job controller create, stop, or manage queues and the batch and print jobs in those queues. In addition, it issues requests to turn accounting on and off.

The $SNDJBC system service makes requests of the job controller by writing messages into its mailbox. A user typically requests the $SNDJBC system service indirectly through Digital command language (DCL) commands, for example, PRINT, SUBMIT, INITIALIZE/QUEUE, STOP/QUEUE, and DELETE/QUEUE. The arguments to the $SNDJBC system service include the following:

- The event flag number to set when the request completes
- The function code specifying which function $SNDJBC is to perform
- A place-holding null argument
- The address of an item list, each entry of which includes an item code appropriate for the function code, the size and address of a buffer to receive information from $SNDJBC or pass information to $SNDJBC, and a location to store the size of information returned from $SNDJBC
- An I/O status block (IOSB) to receive final status information
- The entry point and parameter for an asynchronous system trap (AST) procedure to call when the request completes

The $SNDJBC system service procedure, EXE$SNDJBC in module SYS-SNDJBC, executes in executive mode. It performs the following operations:

1. EXE$SNDJBC checks the IOSB, if specified, for write access. It clears the IOSB.
2. It validates the function code specified in the $SNDJBC argument list.
3. It allocates a message buffer on the current stack, the executive mode stack.
4. EXE$SNDJBC checks each item in the item list for correctness: its item code must be valid; its buffer descriptor and buffer must be readable or writable as appropriate. It checks each specified file for appropriate protection. It stores the following information in the message buffer, using code common to the $GETQUI system service:

   —Items in the item list
   —Function code
   —Address of the AST procedure and parameter
   —IOSB address
   —Event flag number
   —Image counter (PHD$L_IMGCNT)
   —System time (EXE$GQ_SYSTIME)
   —Terminal name of the requesting process (PCB$T_TERMINAL)
   —Extended owner process ID (PCB$L_EOWNER)
   —Process status longword (PCB$L_STS)
   —Extended process ID (PCB$L_EPID)
   —Access mode of system service requestor
   —Process base priority (PCB$B_PRIB)
   —Process user name and account name (CTL$T_USERNAME, CTL$T_ACCOUNT)
   —Longword reserved for the access rights block (ARB) address
   —Message type, in this case MSG$_SNDJBC

5. This common code requests the Change to Kernel Mode ($CMKRNL) system service. The kernel mode procedure called performs the following operations:

a. It clears the specified event flag.

b. The procedure checks and charges the process's AST quota if AST notification is requested. If the AST quota is insufficient, EXE$SNDJBC returns the status SS$_EXASTLM and does not queue the message to the job controller.

c. After raising interrupt priority level (IPL) to 2, the procedure invokes EXE$COPY_ARB, in module IMPERSONATE, to create a private copy of the ARB. It stores the address of this ARB in the longword reserved in step 4.

d. The procedure invokes EXE$SENDMSG, in module SYSSNDMSG, which writes the message buffer to the job controller mailbox, whose address is in SYS$AR_JOBCTLMB.

Many system services that communicate with system processes invoke EXE$SENDMSG. EXE$SENDMSG verifies that the target mailbox has a process reading messages written to the mailbox. It raises IPL to 2 and sets a flag in the process header (PHD) to block swapper trimming and automatic working set limit adjustment that could perturb the working set. It faults the message, still on the executive stack, into the process's working set. It then invokes EXE$WRTMAILBOX, part of the mailbox device driver, to perform the I/O operation. Because EXE$WRTMAILBOX runs at IPL$_MAILBOX, IPL 11, the pages containing the message must be valid; page faults are not allowed at IPLs above 2. When EXE$WRTMAILBOX returns, EXE$SENDMSG clears the PHD flag.

Chapter 23 describes the operation of EXE$WRTMAILBOX.

6. The asynchronous form of the system service, $SNDJBC, returns to the requestor. The requestor can either wait for the information to be returned or continue processing. The synchronous form of the system service, $SNDJBCW, waits for the event flag associated with the request to be set and status to be returned. See Chapter 6 for more information concerning synchronous and asynchronous system services.

Section 36.1.1.4 describes how information is returned to the user.

36.1.1.2 **$GETQUI System Service.** The $GETQUI[W] system service obtains information about the queues and jobs initiated and managed by the job controller. The $GETQUI system service shares common code with the $SNDJBC system service, described in Section 36.1.1.1, and thus performs the same operations. The minor difference is that $GETQUI messages have a message type of MSG$_GETQUI. DCL commands such as SHOW QUEUE and SHOW ENTRY request the $GETQUI service to obtain information for the user.

Section 36.1.1.4 describes how the $SNDJBC and $GETQUI system services return information to the user.

36.1.1.3 **$GETQUI Wildcard Support.** A $GETQUI request causes the job controller to create a $GETQUI context block (GQC) in which it stores the requestor's context information. The job controller maintains a linked list of GQCs in its process space. Unless the $GETQUI request specifies wildcard mode, the job controller deallocates the GQC when the service completes.

The job controller maintains a linked list of GQCs, and locates a process's GQC by an offset containing the requestor process ID (PID). The GQC describes the current wildcard context. The *VMS System Services Reference Manual* describes wildcard mode and its use.

36.1.1.4 **$SNDJBC and $GETQUI Special Kernel AST.** The job controller queues a special kernel AST to the process when its request completes. An extended AST control block (ACB) describes the AST. The ACB contains any data requested by the process, plus information about the amount of data to return and where to store the data. The special kernel AST routine, EXE$JBCRSP in module SYSSNDJBC, uses this information to return status and any requested data from the $SNDJBC and $GETQUI services to the process. Chapter 7 describes the implementation of special kernel ASTs.

EXE$JBCRSP first tests that the process is still executing the image that requested the system service. It compares the process's current PHD$L_IMGCNT against its value at the time of the service request. At each image rundown, PHD$L_IMGCNT is incremented, as described in Chapter 26. If the two values are different, the process is executing a different image. Thus, addresses from the previous image, such as that of the AST procedure or IOSB, are no longer valid. In this case, EXE$JBCRSP deallocates the extended ACB, returning AST quota to the process, if appropriate, and returns.

If the process is still executing the image that requested the system service, EXE$JBCRSP completes the request through the following actions:

1. It sets the specified event flag by invoking routine SCH$POSTEF with a null priority class increment (see Chapters 12 and 13).
2. It stores a status value in the IOSB if specified.
3. It stores data in any output buffer items from the original request.
4. If the user did not request AST notification, EXE$JBCRSP deallocates the ACB and returns.
5. If the user requested AST notification, EXE$JBCRSP invokes SCH$QAST to queue the ACB as a completion AST and returns.

36.1.2 **Superseded System Services**

The $SNDJBC system service supersedes two system services from versions of VMS prior to Version 4:

- Send Message to Accounting Manager ($SNDACC)
- Send Message to Symbiont Manager ($SNDSMB)

All functions provided by these services are available through $SNDJBC, which is the recommended interface. VMS Version 5.2 supports these services only for compatibility with earlier versions.

36.1.2.1 **$SNDACC System Service.** The $SNDACC system service sends requests to the accounting manager through the job controller's mailbox. A user requests the $SNDACC service to request actions normally available through the DCL command SET ACCOUNTING and to send messages directly to the accounting manager.

The $SNDACC system service procedure, EXE$SNDACC in module SYS-SNDMSG, runs in executive and kernel modes. It performs the following operations:

1. It defines the mailbox message type as MSG$_SNDACC and the target mailbox as the job controller's mailbox, whose address is in SYS$AR_JOBCTLMB.

2. It checks the request for possible errors, such as too large a message or inaccessible data references. The user privilege OPER is required to create a new log file or enable or disable accounting.

3. It allocates the message buffer on the current stack, which is the executive mode stack, and places the following information in the message buffer:

   —Mailbox message type
   —Reply mailbox channel, if specified as an optional argument
   —Privilege mask, user identification code (UIC), user name, and account name
   —Process base priority
   —Extended process ID (PCB$L_EPID)
   —Process status (PCB$L_STS)
   —Extended owner PID (PCB$L_EOWNER)
   —Terminal name (PCB$T_TERMINAL)
   —Current system time (EXE$GQ_SYSTIME)
   —User-supplied accounting message type that specifies which function is to be performed
   —User-defined message text

4. EXE$SNDACC requests the $CMKRNL system service to call the local procedure SENDMSG.

5. SENDMSG performs the following operations:

   a. It validates the process's reply channel, if one was specified as an optional argument.
   b. It verifies that the target mailbox has read/write access.
   c. It invokes routine EXE$SENDMSG. Section 36.1.1.1 describes the actions of EXE$SENDMSG.

36.1.2.2 **$SNDSMB System Service.** The $SNDSMB system service sends requests to the symbiont manager via the job controller's mailbox. A user requests the $SNDSMB service to request actions normally available through DCL commands, such as PRINT, SUBMIT, and DELETE/ENTRY.

The $SNDSMB and $SNDACC system services share common code. Thus, $SNDSMB performs exactly the same operations as $SNDACC, described in Section 36.1.2.1, except that the message type is defined to be MSG$_SNDSMB and a $SNDSMB message buffer includes a copy of the ARB.

36.1.3 **Operator Communications**

The system process OPCOM handles operator communications. OPCOM executes the image OPCOM.EXE, and performs the following functions:

- It selects the terminals used as operator terminals and the class of activity, such as disk or tape operations, for which the operator terminals receive messages.
- It replies to or cancels a user request to an operator.
- It manages the operator log file.

The Send Message to Operator ($SNDOPR) system service sends a request to OPCOM through OPCOM's mailbox. A user requests the $SNDOPR service to request actions normally available through the DCL command REQUEST and the operator command REPLY.

The $SNDOPR system service requires that a user have the OPER privilege to enable a terminal as an operator's terminal, reply to or cancel a user's request, or initialize the operator log file.

The $SNDOPR system service shares common code with the $SNDACC and $SNDSMB system services, described in Section 36.1.2. However, it uses a different mailbox, the one whose address is in SYS$AR_OPRMBX, and a different message type, MSG$_OPRQST, and it does not include the extended process ID, process status, extended owner PID, terminal name, and current system time fields in the message buffer.

Chapter 23 describes the OPCOM mailbox.

36.1.4 **Error Logger**

As described in Chapter 32, the error logging subsystem contains three pieces:

- The executive contains routines that maintain a set of error message buffers. These routines are called by device drivers and other components that log errors so that error messages can be written to some available space in one of these buffers.
- The error formatting process, process ERRFMT running the image ERRFMT.EXE, is awakened to copy the contents of these error message buffers to the error log file for subsequent analysis.

- The Error Log Utility reads the error messages in the error log file and produces an error log report, based on the contents of the error log file and the options selected when the utility executes.

A user can request the Send Message to Error Logger ($SNDERR) system service to send messages to the error logger (put messages into one of the error message buffers for later transmission to the error log file). Using this system service requires the BUGCHK privilege.

Unlike the $SNDJBC and $SNDOPR system services, the $SNDERR system service has the following characteristics:

- It executes entirely in kernel mode rather than in executive and kernel mode.
- It writes a message to an error message buffer rather than sending a mailbox message.

The $SNDERR system service procedure, EXE$SNDERR in module SYS-SNDMSG, performs the following actions:

1. It checks the request for access and privilege violations.
2. It invokes ERL$ALLOCEMB, in module ERRORLOG, to allocate an error message buffer.
3. It fills the message buffer with the message type (EMB$C_SS), the message size, and the message text. An error log sequence number and the current time are also a part of every error message.
4. It invokes ERL$RELEASEMB, also in ERRORLOG, to release the buffer to the error logging routines for subsequent output to the error log file.

Chapter 32 contains a discussion of the error log routines and a brief description of the ERRFMT process.

36.2   **SYSTEM MESSAGE FILE SERVICES**

VMS provides three levels of message file capability: image-specific message files, a process-permanent message file, and a system message file.

The creation and declaration of image-specific and process-permanent message files is discussed in the *VMS Message Utility Manual* and the *VMS DCL Dictionary*. The following list provides a brief overview:

- The Message Utility compiles a message source file, producing an object file that can be linked with a main program. When the resulting executable image is activated, the image activator maps the image-specific message file, which remains available until image rundown.
- In response to the command SET MESSAGE, DCL maps a process-specific message file, available for the life of the process or until the command is reissued specifying a different message file name.

- During system initialization, SYSINIT maps the system message file, SYS$MESSAGE:SYSMSG.EXE, into system address space as a pageable section. Chapter 31 describes SYSINIT actions.

Two system services allow a user to locate and display messages from the various message files:

- The Get Message ($GETMSG) system service searches for a message text corresponding to a given message code.
- The Put Message ($PUTMSG) system service writes one or more message texts to SYS$OUTPUT.

VMS uses a third procedure, EXE$EXCMSG in module EXCEPTMSG, as part of condition handling. It does not use the various message files but formats and displays a process's signal arguments and general registers.

36.2.1 Data Structures Related to Message Files

When it compiles a message file, the Message Utility produces an object module that contains a message section header and as many message sections as necessary.

The $PLVDEF macro defines a message section header. The Message Utility creates a message section header for the message file and sets its type code to PLV$C_TYP_MSG. At the offset PLV$L_MSGDSP + 6, it stores the instruction JSB (R5). The instruction merely identifies the section header; it is not executed. The offset to the first message section follows this instruction, then offsets to other message sections, if any. A longword of zero determines the end of the message section offsets.

The $MSCDEF macro defines a message section. The first byte of this structure, MSC$B_TYPE, contains either a 0, indicating a normal message section, or a 1, indicating an indirect message section.

Linking a normal message file, which includes text, with user object modules generates a normal message section within the executable image.

In a normal message section, the field MSC$L_INDEX_OFF contains an offset to an index structure defined by the $MIDXDEF macro and MSC$L_FAC_OFF is an offset to the table of facility codes.

Rather than incorporate a message file within an executable image, a user image can establish a pointer to a nonexecutable message file. The message file can then be changed without recompiling and relinking the image. Compiling an indirect message file with the Message Utility produces a pointer object module to link with user modules and a nonexecutable message file that contains the message data.

In an indirect message section, the MSG$B_TYPE field contains a 1. The field MSC$T_INDNAME contains the name of the associated message file, for example, PRGDEVMSG. At runtime, the $GETMSG system service uses the flag MSC$V_MAPPED to indicate whether the message file has been mapped into virtual memory. The *VMS Message Utility Manual* describes normal and indirect message files.

Three global symbols locate message section headers:

- CTL$GL_GETMSG locates image-specific message section headers
- CTL$GL_PPMSG locates a process-permanent message section header
- EXE$GL_SYSMSG locates the system message section header

CTL$GL_GETMSG contains the address of a message dispatch vector in P1 space, which follows the dispatch vectors for user-written system services and rundown routines. When the image activator activates an image that includes a message section, it loads the next available entry in this dispatch vector with the address of an offset in the message section header.

CTL$GL_PPMSG and EXE$GL_SYSMSG each contain the address of a message section header, or zero if no process-permanent or system message section is defined.

Figure 36.1 shows the layout of the message dispatch vector, message section headers, and message sections.

36.2.2   **$GETMSG System Service**

The $GETMSG system service procedure, EXE$GETMSG in module SYS-GETMSG, executes in its requestor's access mode. It is requested with the following arguments:

- The numeric identification of the desired message, called the message code
- A location in which EXE$GETMSG stores the length of the returned message
- A buffer in which EXE$GETMSG stores the returned message
- A FLAGS argument defining the message components to return
- An optional array containing, among other items, the Formatted ASCII Output ($FAO) argument count for the returned message

EXE$GETMSG searches each message section until it locates one containing a matching message code, at which point its search terminates, or until it processes all message sections. It begins with image-specific message sections, then process-permanent message sections, and finally system message sections.

The following list describes EXE$GETMSG's message search. If a matching message is found at any time, this search terminates.

1. From the process's message dispatch vector, whose address is found in CTLGL_GETMSG, EXEGETMSG obtains the first entry, the address of an image-specific message section header.
2. The header contains a list of message sections. EXE$GETMSG searches each section in order until it either encounters a matching message or processes all sections.

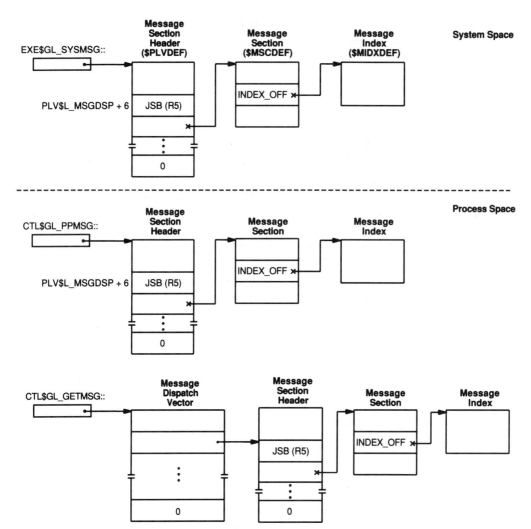

Figure 36.1
Message Vector, Section Headers, and Sections

For each normal message section, EXE$GETMSG calculates the starting address and length of the message section index. It then performs a binary search of the message section index to determine if it contains the specified message code.

For an indirect message section, one with the MSG$B_TYPE field containing a 1, EXE$GETMSG tests the flag MSC$V_MAPPED. If the flag is clear, the file is not yet mapped. EXE$GETMSG sets the flag and invokes the image activator to perform a merged activation of the indirect message section.

The image activator maps the nonexecutable image named in the file specification into the user's virtual address space. It adds the address of the new message section header to the end of the message dispatch vector; thus, all sections located by the message section header are processed later in the search. The search for the message code continues normally.

3. If no matching message is found, EXE$GETMSG locates the next image-specific message section header from the next entry in the process's message dispatch vector and searches its message sections as in step 2.

4. When all image-specific message section headers in the message dispatch vector have been processed and the search has not been successful, EXE$GETMSG proceeds to the process-permanent message section header. If one exists, CTL$GL_PPMSG contains its address; otherwise, CTL$GL_PPMSG contains a zero.

5. EXE$GETMSG searches each process-permanent message section located by the message section header until it finds a matching message or has no more process-permanent message sections.

6. If the search is not successful, EXE$GETMSG proceeds to the system message section header. If one exists, EXE$GL_SYSMSG contains its address; otherwise, EXE$GL_SYSMSG contains a zero.

7. EXE$GETMSG searches each system message section located by the message section header until it finds a matching message or has no more system message sections.

8. If no message section exists or no matching message code is found, the service returns the status code SS$_MSGNOTFND and a message declaring that the message file does not contain the desired code.

   Otherwise, if it discovers a matching message code, EXE$GETMSG copies selected information into the user-defined buffer.

   —If the FLAGS argument is not specified, $GETMSG uses the process default message flags (CTL$GB_MSGMASK) to select the information.

   —If the combine bit is set in the FLAGS argument (bit 4), EXE$GETMSG returns only the information selected by both the FLAGS argument and by CTL$GB_MSGMASK.

   —Otherwise, EXE$GETMSG returns the information selected by the FLAGS argument.

9. Control returns to the requestor of the $GETMSG system service.

36.2.3 $PUTMSG System Service

The $PUTMSG system service provides the ability to write one or more error messages to SYS$ERROR (and SYS$OUTPUT if it is different from SYS$ERROR). It executes in the access mode of its requestor and requests the $GETMSG system service to retrieve the associated text for a particular message code.

The $PUTMSG system service is requested with four arguments:

• A message argument vector describing the messages in terms of message codes, message field selection flag bits, and $FAO arguments (see Section 36.5.2).

- An optional action routine to call before writing the message texts.
- An optional facility name to associate with the first message written. If not specified, the $PUTMSG system service uses the default facility name associated with the message.
- An optional parameter to pass to the requestor's action routine. If not specified, it defaults to zero.

The *VMS System Services Reference Manual* discusses the construction of the message argument vector. The *VMS Run-Time Library Routines Volume* describes other uses of the $PUTMSG service.

The $PUTMSG system service procedure, EXE$PUTMSG in module SYSPUTMSG, processes each argument of the message argument vector as follows:

1. It determines whether the facility code of the request is a system, Record Management Services (RMS), or standard facility code. Standard facility codes can require $FAO arguments. System messages (facility code 0) and RMS messages (facility code 1) do not use associated $FAO arguments in the message argument vector. System exception messages require $FAO arguments to follow immediately after the message identification in the message vector.
2. It requests the $GETMSG system service with the message code and field selections based upon the selection bits and $FAO arguments.
3. If the message flags indicate at least one $FAO argument, EXE$PUTMSG requests the $FAOL system service (see Section 36.5.2) to assemble all the portions of the message (supplied facility code, optionally specified delimiters, output from $GETMSG).
4. EXE$PUTMSG invokes the user's action routine, if one was specified.
5. If the action routine returns an error status, EXE$PUTMSG does not write the message. Otherwise, it uses an RMS $PUT request to write the formatted message to SYS$OUTPUT, if it is informational, or to SYS$ERROR, if it is an error. In the latter case, it also writes the formatted error message to SYS$OUTPUT if SYS$ERROR is different from SYS$OUTPUT.

When all the arguments in the message argument vector have been processed, the $PUTMSG system service returns to its requestor.

36.2.4 Procedure EXE$EXCMSG

The catch-all condition handler uses EXE$EXCMSG, in module EXCEPT-MSG, internally to report a condition that has not been properly handled by any condition handlers further up the call stack. EXE$EXCEPTION also calls

EXE$EXCMSG to write the contents of the general registers to SYS$OUT-PUT if a condition is not handled in any other way. See Chapter 5 for information on condition handling.

EXE$EXCMSG requires two input arguments: the address of an ASCII string, and the address of the exception argument list passed to the condition handlers (see Chapter 5).

The procedure writes a formatted dump of the general registers, signal array, and stack, as well as the caller's message text, to SYS$OUTPUT (and to SYS$ERROR if different from SYS$OUTPUT). This message appears for all fatal errors that occur in images that were linked without the traceback handler. Note that most images shipped with VMS are linked without the traceback handler.

Although this procedure has an associated entry point in the system service vector area, it cannot be conveniently called from any languages except VAX MACRO and VAX BLISS-32. The specification of the second argument requires access to the argument pointer (AP), a capability denied to most high-level languages.

36.3 SYSTEM INFORMATION SYSTEM SERVICES

The Get System Information ($GETSYI[W]) system service provides selected information about the running system or about a target node in the VAXcluster system. Although VMS provides synchronous and asynchronous forms of the service, both forms complete synchronously under VMS Version 5.2. Currently, the only information available for other VAXcluster members is the information that already resides in the nonpaged pool data structures on the local system.

$GETSYI arguments include the following:

- An event flag to set when the request completes
- The address of the Cluster System Identification (CSID) of the target system
- The node name of the target system
- The address of an item list that includes (for each requested item) the type of information to return (item code), the size and address of a buffer to hold the information, and a location to receive the actual size of the returned information
- The address of an IOSB to receive the final request status
- An entry point and parameter for an AST procedure to call when the request completes

36.3.1 Operation of the $GETSYI System Service

The $GETSYI system service procedure, EXE$GETSYI in module SYSGET-SYI, executes in kernel mode and performs the following actions:

1. It invokes its local routine NAMCSID to validate the node name/CSID pair. NAMCSID tests CLU$GL_CLUB to determine whether the running system is a VAXcluster member.

   —If the system is a VAXcluster member, NAMCSID (after resolving a wildcard reference) invokes another local routine, EXE$NAMCSID, to obtain the address of the cluster system block (CSB) specified by CSID or node name. EXE$NAMCSID returns the address of the CSB or, if no CSB is located, the error status SS$_NOSUCHNODE. EXE$GETSYI returns this status to its requestor.

   —If the system is not a VAXcluster member and the user specified a CSID, NAMCSID returns the error SS$_NOMORENODE, which EXE$GETSYI returns as system service status.

   —If the system is not a VAXcluster member and the user specified a node name, NAMCSID checks that the node name is that of the running system. If it is, NAMCSID returns successfully with the address of the system block (SB). If the node name is not that of the running system, NAMCSID returns the error status SS$_NOSUCHNODE, which EXE$GETSYI returns as system service status.

2. If an IOSB is specified, EXE$GETSYI checks it for write access and clears it.

3. It clears the event flag.

4. If AST notification is requested, EXE$GETSYI checks that the process has sufficient AST quota and charges the quota.

5. EXE$GETSYI checks each item in the list for the following conditions:

   —The buffer descriptor is readable and the buffer writable.
   —The requested item is a recognized one.

6. If these conditions are met, EXE$GETSYI retrieves the requested information and copies it to the user-defined buffer. Under VMS Version 5.2, all available information can be obtained immediately in the context of the requesting process. If the target is not the local system, EXE$GET-SYI only returns information contained in the CSB or SB for that target. For the local system, EXE$GETSYI obtains additional information from various system global locations.

7. When no information remains to be gathered, the system service returns to its requestor after performing the following actions:

   a. Setting the specified event flag
   b. Queuing requested AST notification to the process
   c. Writing status information to an IOSB, if one was specified

36.3.2 $GETSYI Wildcard Support

The $GETSYI system service provides the ability to obtain information about all members of a VAXcluster system, that is, to perform a wildcard search of the cluster vector table. The cluster vector table is a table of CSB addresses, indexed by the low word of the CSID. The global location CLU$GL_CLUSVEC contains its address.

A negative CSID argument to the $GETSYI system service indicates a wildcard request. EXE$GETSYI recognizes a wildcard request and passes information back to the requestor about the first system described in the cluster vector table.

In addition, it alters the cluster system identification field of the requestor's CSID argument to contain the target system's node index. When the service requestor requests $GETSYI again, the negative sequence number (in the high-order word of the CSID) indicates that a wildcard operation is in progress. The positive node index (in the low-order word of the cluster system ID) indicates the cluster vector table offset where the search resumes. Note that the user program will not work correctly if it alters the value of the CSID argument between requests to $GETSYI.

The user program repeatedly requests the $GETSYI system service until it receives the status SS$_NOMORENODE, indicating that the cluster vector table has been completely searched.

36.4   DEVICE INFORMATION SYSTEM SERVICES

Images frequently require information about particular devices on the system. VMS provides several system services to identify and obtain specific information about a particular device. Two important device information services are the Get Device/Volume Information ($GETDVI[W]) system service and the Scan for Devices ($DEVICE_SCAN) system service.

Support still exists for two obsolete services, Get I/O Channel Information ($GETCHN) and Get I/O Device Information ($GETDEV), both in module SYSGETDVI, but the $GETDVI system service supersedes both and should be used in future software development.

36.4.1 $DEVICE_SCAN System Service

Introduced in VMS Version 5.2, the $DEVICE_SCAN system service searches for devices that match user-specified search criteria. The search criteria, specified in an item list, include the device type, the device class, and the wildcarded device name. The *VMS Version 5.2 New Features Manual* describes this service.

In response to an initial request, the $DEVICE_SCAN system service searches for the first occurrence of a device that matches the search criteria. It maintains context information so that on subsequent $DEVICE_SCAN requests, it can return other matching device names, until no more matching devices exist. At that time, the service returns the error status SS$_NOMOREDEV.

$DEVICE_SCAN arguments include the following:

- The address of a buffer in which $DEVICE_SCAN returns the name of a matching device
- A location to contain the length of the returned device name
- The name of a device for which to search, which can include the standard wildcard characters
- The address of an item list, in which each entry includes an item code, an input buffer address and length, and a reserved field
- The address of a context quadword, initially zeroed, where $DEVICE_SCAN maintains search context information across service requests

The $DEVICE_SCAN system service procedure, EXE$DEVICE_SCAN in module SYSGETDVI, executes in kernel mode. It performs the following operations:

1. It checks each item in the item list for correctness: its item code must be valid; its buffer descriptor and buffer must be readable. The $DVS-DEF macro defines two legal item codes, one indicating that the buffer contains a device class (defined by the $DCDEF macro) and one indicating that the buffer contains a device type (also defined by $DCDEF) for which to search.
2. It restores the search context information, either zeros on the first service request or the unit number and the device data block (DDB) of the matching device located in the previous search.
3. It invokes SCH$IOLOCKR, in module MUTEX, which raises IPL to 2 to prevent process deletion and obtains the I/O database mutex. Thus, the I/O database does not change until $DEVICE_SCAN releases the mutex. Chapter 20 describes the I/O database.
4. EXE$DEVICE_SCAN invokes IOC$SCAN_IODB_USRCTX, in module IOSUBNPAG, which sequentially scans the I/O database. EXE$DEVICE_SCAN tests each returned device and reinvokes IOC$SCAN_IODB_USR-CTX if the device type and class do not match the search criteria.
5. Otherwise, it invokes IOC$CVT_DEVNAM, in module IOSUBNPAG, to convert the matching device's name and unit number to a physical device name string. If the device allocation class is nonzero and the device is file-oriented, it returns a string of the form $*device_allocation_class*$ddCn, where *dd* is the device name, *C* is the controller designation, and *n* is the unit number. Otherwise, it returns a string in the form *VAXcluster_nodename*$ddCn.
6. If the user specified a device name in the search criteria, EXE$DEVICE_SCAN invokes EXE$MATCH_NAME, also in module IOSUBNPAG, to perform the wildcard comparison.
7. When it locates a device that matches all criteria, EXE$DEVICE_SCAN returns its device name and length to the requestor after storing the unit number and DDB address in the context block and unlocking the I/O database mutex, lowering IPL to 0.

36.4.2   **$GETDVI System Service**

The $GETDVI system service and its synchronous counterpart $GETDVIW
obtain device-independent information about a device. Device-independent
information refers to information that is present for each device on the system, such as the device unit number, UCB$W_UNIT, device characteristics,
UCB$L_DEVCHAR, and the device type, UCB$B_DEVTYPE. It is obtained
by reading fields in the unit control block (UCB) that have the same interpretation for all devices on the system. The *VMS System Services Reference
Manual* contains a complete description of the values that the service can
return.

The $GETDVI system service is requested with the following arguments:

- The event flag number to set when the request completes
- The number of an I/O channel assigned to the device
- The device name (possibly obtained via the $DEVICE_SCAN system ser-
  vice), used if no channel number is specified
- The address of an item list, each entry of which includes an item code, the
  size and address of a buffer to receive information, and a location to store
  the size of the information returned
- An IOSB to receive final status information
- The entry point and parameter for an AST procedure to call when the
  request completes
- A place-holding null argument

The $GETDVI system service returns information about primary and sec-
ondary device characteristics. These two sets of characteristics are identical
unless one of the following conditions holds:

- If the device has an associated mailbox, the primary characteristics are
  those of the assigned device and the secondary characteristics are those of
  the associated mailbox.
- If the device is spooled, the primary characteristics are those of the intermediate device and the secondary characteristics are those of the spooled
  device.
- If the device represents a logical link on the network, the secondary characteristics contain information about the link.

The $GETDVI system service procedure, EXE$GETDVI in module SYS-
GETDVI, executes in kernel mode. It performs the following operations:

1. EXE$GETDVI clears the specified event flag.
2. It checks the IOSB, if specified, for write access and clears the IOSB.
3. It checks and charges the process's AST quota if AST notification is
   requested. If the AST quota is insufficient, it returns the status SS$_
   EXASTLM.

4. If a channel number is specified, EXE$GETDVI verifies the channel and obtains the UCB of the device accessed on the channel. It invokes SCH$IOLOCKR to lock the I/O database mutex for read access.

5. Otherwise, if a device name is specified, EXE$GETDVI invokes SCH$IO-LOCKR to lock the I/O database mutex for read access and then invokes IOC$SEARCHDEV, in module IOSUBPAGD, to search the I/O database for the specified device and return the device UCB and DDB.

   If the request is for secondary device characteristics, EXE$GETDVI locates the appropriate structures at this point.

6. For each item, EXE$GETDVI performs the following:

   a. It checks each item in the item list for correctness: its item code must be valid; its buffer size, buffer, and return length must be readable or writable as appropriate.

   b. It processes the item code, locating the appropriate structure and offset and copying the desired information into the user buffer.

7. EXE$GETDVI unlocks the I/O database mutex.

8. It sets the specified event flag by invoking routine SCH$POSTEF, in module POSTEF.

9. It stores a status value in the IOSB, if specified.

10. If the user requested AST notification, EXE$GETDVI requests the Declare AST ($DCLAST) system service to queue the ACB as a completion AST and returns.

11. If the user did not request AST notification, EXE$GETDVI returns.

36.5 FORMATTING SUPPORT

The final group of system services described in this chapter provides conversion support for time-related requests and formatted I/O of ASCII character strings.

36.5.1 Time Conversion Services

Module SYSCVRTIM contains the time conversion system services. The Convert Binary Time to Numeric Time ($NUMTIM) system service executes in executive mode and converts a binary quadword time value in system time format (described in Chapter 11) into the following seven numerical word-length fields:

- Year (AD)
- Month of year
- Day of month
- Hour of day
- Minute of hour
- Second of minute
- Hundredths of seconds

The $NUMTIM system service converts a positive time argument into the corresponding absolute system time. It interprets a negative time argument as a delta time, the current system time plus a time interval. A zero-valued time argument requests the conversion of the current system time.

The Convert Binary Time to ASCII String ($ASCTIM) system service executes in the access mode of its requestor. It converts a system time format quadword into an ASCII character string. It passes the input binary time argument to the $NUMTIM system service and converts the seven fields returned into ASCII character fields. The input time format (absolute or delta) and the conversion flag determine the field selection. The conversion flag can be set to request conversion of day and time or only the time portion.

The $ASCTIM system service uses the $FAO system service (described in Section 36.5.2) to concatenate and format the string components before returning the string to the caller.

The Convert ASCII String to Binary Time ($BINTIM) system service executes in the access mode of its requestor. It converts an ASCII time string into a quadword absolute or delta time. If the input string expresses an absolute time, the service requests the $NUMTIM system service to convert the current system time to supply any fields omitted in the ASCII string. The $BINTIM system service converts each ASCII field to numerical values and stores the values in the seven-word $NUMTIM format. It then combines the seven word fields into a binary quadword value. It negates the resulting value if the ASCII string specifies a delta time.

36.5.2   Formatted ASCII Output System Services

The $FAO and $FAOL system services format and convert binary and ASCII input parameters into a single ASCII output string. The two system services, in module SYSFAO, execute in the access mode of the requestor and use common code. The only difference between them is whether the parameters are passed individually ($FAO) or as the address of the first parameter in a list ($FAOL).

The common routine, FAO, parses the control string character by character. It copies information not preceded by the control character ! into the output string without further action. When it encounters a control character and operation code in the control string, it executes the appropriate conversion routine to process zero, one, or two of the system service input parameters. When the control string is completely and correctly parsed, the service returns to the requestor with a normal status code. It returns a buffer overflow error if the output string length is exceeded.

The description of the $FAO system service in the *VMS System Services Reference Manual* describes the proper manner in which to specify $FAO requests.

Appendixes

A System Processes and Privileged Images

While this book describes much of the VMS executive in detail, it omits most of the components that make up a full VMS system. This appendix identifies those components that are most closely related to the executive, either because they link against SYS.STB or perform privileged operations.

Table A.1   System Processes

Image Name	Linked with SYS.STB	Description
F11AACP.EXE	Yes	Files-11 ODS-1 ancillary control process (ACP)
MTAAACP.EXE	Yes	Magnetic tape ACP
REMACP.EXE	Yes	Remote terminal ACP
NETACP.EXE	Yes	Network ACP
MAIL_SERVER.EXE	No	Network Mail Utility server
ERRFMT.EXE	Yes	Error log buffer format process
INPSMB.EXE	Yes	Card reader input symbiont
JOBCTL.EXE	Yes	Job controller/queue manager
OPCOM.EXE	Yes	Operator communication facility
PRTSMB.EXE	No	Print symbiont
FILESERV.EXE	Yes	VAXcluster Files-11 XQP cache server process
CSP.EXE	Yes	VAXcluster server process
CONFIGURE.EXE	Yes	Configure VAXcluster devices
SMISERVER.EXE	Yes	VMS system management facility
AUDIT_SERVER.EXE	Yes	Security audit server process

Table A.2   Images Installed with Privilege on a Standard VMS System

Image Name	Linked with SYS.STB	Description
ANALIMDMP.EXE	Yes	Image Dump Analyzer Utility
AUTHORIZE.EXE	Yes	Authorize Utility
CDU.EXE	Yes	Command Definition Utility
INIT.EXE	Yes	Volume Initialization Utility
INSTALL.EXE	Yes	Known Image Installation Utility
LOGINOUT.EXE	Yes	Login/logout image
MAIL.EXE	No	Mail Utility
MAIL_SERVER.EXE	No	Network Mail Utility server
MONITOR.EXE	Yes	System Statistics Utility
PHONE.EXE	No	Phone Utility
REQUEST.EXE	No	Operator request facility
RTPAD.EXE	No	Remote Terminal Utility
SET.EXE	Yes	SET command processor
SETP0.EXE	Yes	SET command processor
SETRIGHTS.EXE	No	SET RIGHTS_LIST command processor
SHOW.EXE	Yes	SHOW command processor
SHWCLSTR.EXE	Yes	SHOW CLUSTER command processor
SUBMIT.EXE	No	Batch and print job submission facility
SYSMAN.EXE	Yes	VMS system management facility command interface
VPM.EXE	Yes	Remote performance data collector server

Table A.3   Images Requiring Privilege That Are Typically Not Installed

Image Name	Linked with SYS.STB	Description
CIA.EXE	Yes	Show Intrusion Utility
LALOADER.EXE	Yes	LPA-11K microcode loader
LATCP.EXE	Yes	Local area transport control program
MSCP.EXE	Yes	VAXcluster disk server
NCP.EXE	No	Network control program
OPCCRASH.EXE	Yes	System shutdown facility
QUEMAN.EXE [1]	No	Queue manipulation command processor
REPLY.EXE	No	Message broadcasting facility
RUNDET.EXE	No	RUN [process] command processor
SDA.EXE	Yes	System Dump Analyzer Utility
SETAUDIT.EXE	Yes	SET AUDIT command processor
SMPUTIL.EXE	Yes	Multiprocessing Utility
STOPREM.EXE	Yes	Stop REMACP Process Utility
SYSGEN.EXE	Yes	System Generation and Configuration Utility
XFLOADER.EXE	Yes	DR32 microcode loader

[1] Although this image is installed, it is not installed with privilege.

Table A.4   Images Whose Operations Are Protected by System User Identification Code or Volume Ownership

Image Name	Linked with SYS.STB	Description
AUTHORIZE.EXE	Yes	Authorize Utility
BACKUP.EXE	Yes	Backup Utility
BADBLOCK.EXE	Yes	Bad block locator
DISKQUOTA.EXE	Yes	Disk Quota Utility
DISMOUNT.EXE	No	Volume Dismount Utility
ERF*.EXE	No	Error Log Formatting Utility and CPU-specific extensions
INIT.EXE	Yes	Volume Initialization Utility
VERIFY.EXE	No	File Structure Verification Utility
VMOUNT.EXE	No	Volume Mount Utility

Table A.5   Miscellaneous Other Images Linked with SYS$SYSTEM:SYS.STB

Image Name [1]	*Description*
AGEN$FEEDBACK.EXE	AUTOGEN feedback data reader
ANALAUDIT.EXE	Security Auditing Analysis Utility
ANALYZOBJ.EXE	Analyze Object Module Utility
CHECKSUM.EXE	Checksum File or Image Utility
CLUSTRLOA.EXE	VAXcluster support
DBGSSISHR.EXE	System service interceptor shareable image for VAX DEBUG and VAX PCA
DCL.EXE	Digital command language interpreter
DELTA.EXE	Executive debugger
DISMNTSHR.EXE	Dismount system service shareable image
DUMP.EXE	File Dump Utility
DYNSWITCH.EXE	Switch terminal port to asynchronous Digital Data Communications Message Protocol (DDCMP)
ERRSNAP.EXE	VAX 86x0 error log copy program
F11BXQP.EXE	ODS-2 file system
FORRTL2.EXE	FORTRAN parallel processing support run-time library
FPEMUL.EXE	Floating-point instruction emulation
IMGDMP.EXE	Write Image Dump Utility
MAILSHR.EXE	Callable Mail Utility shareable image
MAILSHRP.EXE	Callable Mail Utility protected shareable image
MOM.EXE	Network management maintenance operations process
MOUNTSHR.EXE	Mount system service shareable image
MSCP.EXE	Mass storage control protocol server
NISCS_LAA.EXE	Local area VAXcluster system downline load assist agent
NISCS_LOAD.EXE	Local area VAXcluster downline load secondary bootstrap
PATCH.EXE	Patch Utility
PFMFILWRT.EXE	Page Fault Monitor Utility
RECOVER.EXE	RECOVER/RMS_FILE command processor
S0DELTA.EXE	Executive debugger
SCSLOA.EXE	System communication services
SECURESHR.EXE	Security system services shareable image
SECURESHRP.EXE	Security system services protected shareable image
SETSHOACL.EXE	SET/SHOW access control list (ACL) Utility
SMBSRVSHR.EXE	Print symbiont shareable image
SPISHR.EXE	Get System Performance Information system service (undocumented) shareable image; used by MONITOR
SYSLOA*xxx*.EXE	CPU-specific support (see Appendix G)
TFFSHR.EXE	Terminal fallback facility shareable image
VAXEMUL.EXE	Subset instruction emulation
*xx*DRIVER.EXE	All device drivers

---

[1] The loadable executive images are also linked with SYS.STB but not listed in this table. They are described in Chapter 29.

B   Use of Listing and Map Files

This book presents a detailed overview of the VMS executive. However, the ultimate authority on how the executive or any other component of the system works is the source code for that component. This appendix shows how you can use the listing and map files produced by the language processors and the linker with other tools to investigate further how a given component works. The appendix assumes that you are familiar with the VAX instruction set, the VAX MACRO assembler, and the linker.

B.1   READING THE EXECUTIVE LISTINGS

Digital provides listing kits on magnetic tape, compact disk read-only memory (CD-ROM), and microfiche to customers who purchase and sign a source license agreement. The kits include listings and maps for most components but exclude certain proprietary modules, such as the License Management Facility. In addition, the microfiche listings include some source files:

- Macro and constant definition files written in VAX MACRO and VAX BLISS-32
- Command definition language (CLD) files
- Structure definition language (SDL) files

Most of the modules described in this book, those that make up the executive and initialization routines, are written in VAX MACRO. This appendix suggests how to read these modules as well as modules written in VAX BLISS-32, VAX C, VAX PL/I, VAX Pascal, and other languages.

B.1.1   VMS Listing Structure

Building a VMS system from source also produces the VMS listings. A directory structure divides and organizes the more than 4,000 VMS modules into more than 100 facilities. A facility consists of related modules and has a directory. Examples of facility directories include [SYS], [RMS], [JOBCTL], [DCL], and [COPY]. Each directory consists of a set of subdirectories, most of which are used only when a VMS system is built from source.

The system build procedure places the listing and map files into the appropriate [*facility*.LIS] subdirectory of the result disk volume. The result disk is often referenced by a logical name like RESD.

B.1.1.1   VMS Online Listing Structure.
An online listing kit contains only the listing subdirectories created by the system build procedure. A listing kit CD-ROM contains all the distributed files for a given version of VMS (such as Version

1129

5.0) and those files that have been changed or added since that version was released (such as Versions 5.0-1, 5.0-2, and 5.1). A top-level directory for each version contains subdirectories for each facility. The listing kit magnetic tape is a BACKUP saveset of such a disk.

B.1.1.2 **VMS Microfiche Listing Structure.** The microfiche listings are similar in organization and content to the online listings except that they also include some source files.

The last microfiche sheet in the set contains an index. The index is organized by facility, and within each facility by file name. For each file, the index identifies the microfiche sheet number and frame coordinates of the beginning of the file. In addition, each microfiche sheet contains its own table of contents in its last frame. A complete set of microfiche, including index, is distributed after each major VMS release.

Digital updates the microfiche listings for minor VMS releases by distributing update sets. Each update set replaces the old index sheet. Each update set begins with the sheet number of the old index sheet and contains a new index sheet at its end. The remaining new sheets contain new and replaced listings. Note that the out-of-date listings remain in the resulting set of sheets but are simply not referenced by the new index. Microfiche users may wish to retain the old index sheets to facilitate locating previous versions' listings.

B.1.1.3 **Locating a Listing File.** Locating an address or symbol involves identifying both the facility and the file name. First, you must narrow the search to one or a few facilities. Next, since each facility contains a small number of map files, you can search each map file for the address or global symbol of interest. Once you find the address or symbol in a map file, you can see which module defines it and read the corresponding listing file.

You should become somewhat familiar with the facilities that contain the listings read most often. The [SYS] facility contains the system services and most of the other executive routines described in this book. Most of the system service listing file names are in the form SYS*servicename*.LIS. The [BOOTS] facility contains most of the initialization listings and maps, including VMB, SYSBOOT, and SYSGEN.

Many utilities have their own facilities, such as [MOUNT] and [OPCOM]. Some facility names are abbreviations of their associated facilities, such as [F11X] for the Files-11 Extended $QIO Processor (XQP) and [PRTSMB] for the print symbiont.

If online listings are available, VMS utilities can help locate the modules of interest. For example, to search for a particular module without knowing the facility or exact file name, use wild card directory searches. The following Digital command language (DCL) command helps locate event-flag-related files:

```
$ DIRECTORY RESD:[V50.*.LIS]*EVENT*.*,*EVT*.*
```

Use the DCL SEARCH command to search several listing or map files for a particular routine, data cell, or comment. The following example locates the module that defines EXE$ALLOCIRP, the routine that allocates I/O request packets from the lookaside list:

```
$ SEARCH RESD:[V50.SYS.LIS]*.MAP EXE$ALLOCIRP
```

Use an editor to peruse the file:

```
$ EDIT/READ_ONLY RESD:[V50.SYS.LIS]MEMORYALC.LIS
```

B.1.1.4   **Locating a DCL Command Routine.** Some DCL commands are implemented by routines within DCL and others are implemented by external images or routines. When you need to identify the module that implements a particular DCL command, first determine whether it is an internal routine (sometimes also called an internal image) by examining the second and third tables built by the INTIMAGES macro in [DCL]COMMAND.LIS. (The first table contains the first eight characters of each command.) The second table is a CASE table, and the third is a list of the internal routine names. (Internal routines have names of the form DCL$*command*.) Examine [DCL]DCL.MAP to identify the module that contains the internal routine of interest.

If the command is not implemented within DCL itself, find the command definition file that defines the command. Many command definition file listings are combined in [CLD]DCLTABLE*x*.LIS; others reside in the same facility as their related listings and maps. A command definition file associates one or more commands with either the image or the routine that implements each command. Locate the DEFINE VERB or DEFINE SYNTAX statement for the command of interest.

A command definition file either modifies the system or process command table or is linked with a related program. The presence of a ROUTINE statement indicates that the file is linked with a related program. The MODULE statement assigns a name to the object module that contains the command table, and the ROUTINE statement specifies the routine in the related program that implements the command. The following example from [INSTAL]INSCMD.LIS defines two of the commands for the Install Utility:

```
module INSCMD
.
.
.
define verb CREATE
        routine INS$CREATE_VERB
.
.
define verb LIST
        routine INS$LIST_VERB
```

Look for a map file that contains the object module named by the `MODULE` statement, and in it find the module that defines the symbol named by the `ROUTINE` statement. Read the routine in the module's listing. The following example is part of [INSTAL]INSTALL.MAP:

```
                    +------------------------+
                    ! Object Module Synopsis !
                    +------------------------+
Module Name     Ident     Creator
-----------     -----     -------
INSMAIN         X-9   ...  VAX Bliss-32 V4.5-862
  .
  .
  .
INSCMD          0-0   ...  VAX/VMS Command Definition Utility
                    +------------------------+
                    ! Symbol Cross Reference !
                    +------------------------+
Symbol              Value        Defined By    Referenced By ...
------              -----        ----------    -----------------
  .
  .
INS$CREATE_VERB     00000B18-R   INSMAIN       INSCMD
  .
  .
INS$LIST_VERB       0000113D-R   INSMAIN       INSCMD
```

If a command definition file does not contain a `ROUTINE` statement, then it modifies a command table and uses the `IMAGE` statement to specify the name of the image that implements the command. (Most command definition files explicitly specify the image name. If it is missing, it defaults to the command verb.) Look in the image's map file to identify the modules to read. The following example from [CLD]DCLTABLE1.LIS defines three of the DCL ANALYZE commands:

```
define syntax ANALYZE_CRASH_DUMP
  image SDA
  qualifier CRASH_DUMP,default
  qualifier SYSTEM
  .
  .
define syntax ANALYZE_DISK_STRUCTURE
  image VERIFY
  qualifier DISK_STRUCTURE,default
  qualifier REPAIR
  .
  .
define verb ANALYZE
  image ANALYZOBJ
  qualifier CRASH_DUMP,nonnegatable,syntax=ANALYZE_CRASH_DUMP
  qualifier DISK_STRUCTURE,nonnegatable,syntax=ANALYZE_DISK_STRUCTURE
  qualifier OBJECT,default,nonnegatable
```

The *VMS Command Definition Utility Manual* gives more information on command definition files.

B.1.2   **Data Structure Offset, Constant, and Macro Definitions**

Some data structure offset, constant, and macro definitions are contained in facility source modules. Others reside in several libraries in SYS$LIBRARY:. These libraries are supplied as part of the VMS binary distribution and are used by the operating system as well as privileged and nonprivileged applications. There are separate VAX MACRO and VAX BLISS-32 libraries. Several SDL source files contribute definitions to each library file. This section discusses these and other libraries and the source files that contribute to them.

SYS$LIBRARY:STARLET.MLB, the default macro library that is automatically searched by the assembler, defines offsets, constants, and macros that are used in system services and other public interfaces. SYS$LIBRARY: STARLET.REQ defines these in VAX BLISS-32. The STARLET definitions are primarily intended for use in nonprivileged applications.

Most of the offsets, constants, and macros used by the executive are not public, that is, they are subject to change. These are defined in VAX MACRO in a special library called SYS$LIBRARY:LIB.MLB, and in VAX BLISS-32 in SYS$LIBRARY:LIB.REQ. Applications such as user-written device drivers and user-written system services using this library must be reassembled or recompiled with each new release of LIB, which usually occurs with each major release of the VMS operating system.

B.1.2.1   **Locating Data Structure Offset and Constant Definitions.** One set of SDL files contributes data structure offset and constant definitions to the STARLET libraries. These files are in the [VMSLIB] facility and have names of the form STARDEF*xx*.SDL, where *xx* is AE, FL, MP, or QZ. Another set contributes to the LIB libraries. These are in the [SYS] facility and have names of the form SYSDEF*xx*.SDL. In addition, various VAX MACRO source files contribute definitions to these libraries. An SDL source file can yield definitions in both VAX MACRO and VAX BLISS-32. However, only the VAX BLISS-32 files retain the comments from the SDL statements.

Section B.4 briefly discusses SDL files. Appendix E lists many of the data structures described in this book. It also describes some of the SDL files that contribute to the LIB and STARLET libraries.

Since the VAX BLISS-32 versions of the LIB and STARLET REQUIRE files retain the comments, they are particularly helpful. Even readers unfamiliar with VAX BLISS-32 can read the comments about the data structures, fields, and constants. Use an editor to search for the section of interest:

```
$ EDIT/READ_ONLY SYS$LIBRARY:LIB.REQ
```

The VMS Librarian Utility can extract modules from SYS$LIBRARY: STARLET.MLB or SYS$LIBRARY:LIB.MLB but not from the VAX BLISS-32 REQUIRE files. An editor or the VAX BLISS-32 compiler can extract modules from the VAX BLISS-32 REQUIRE files. The following example illustrates extracting the macro that defines the unit control block (UCB) offset definitions from LIB.MLB:

```
$ LIBRARY/MACRO/EXTRACT=$UCBDEF/OUTPUT=SYS$OUTPUT: -
_$ SYS$LIBRARY:LIB.MLB
```

B.1.2.2 **The $xyzDEF Macros.** Most executive modules begin by invoking a series of macros that define symbolic offsets into data structures referenced by the module. The general form of these macros is $xyzDEF, where *xyz* represents the data structure whose offsets are required.

For example, a module that deals with the I/O subsystem probably invokes the $IRPDEF and $UCBDEF macros to define offsets into I/O request packets (IRPs) and UCBs. Some of the $xyzDEF macros, such as $SSDEF, $IODEF, and $PRDEF, define constants (system service status returns, I/O function codes and modifiers, and processor register definitions) rather than offsets into data structures.

The symbol table at the end of an assembly listing lists the symbol definitions resulting from these macros. However, the assembly listing includes only those symbols referenced by the module and not necessarily all the symbols defined by a $xyzDEF macro. The following sequence of DCL commands produces a complete list of symbols:

```
$ CREATE xyzDEF.MAR
        .TITLE xyzDEF
        $xyzDEF GLOBAL
        .END
^ Z
$ MACRO xyzDEF+SYS$LIBRARY:LIB.MLB/LIBRARY
$ LINK/NOEXECUTABLE/MAP/FULL xyzDEF
$ PRINT xyzDEF.MAP
```

This command sequence produces a single object module that contains all the symbols produced by the $xyzDEF macro. The argument GLOBAL makes all the symbols produced by the macro global. (This argument must appear in uppercase to be properly interpreted by the assembler's macro processor.) That is, the assembler passes the symbol names and values to the linker so that they appear on whatever map the linker produces. The full map contains two lists of symbol definitions, one in alphabetical order and one in numeric order.

The System Dump Analyzer (SDA) Utility can read the resulting object file to add symbols to its symbol table.

B.1.2.3   **Instructions That Reference Data Structures.** Data structure references are usually made using displacement mode addressing. For example, the following instruction loads the contents of R3 (presumably the address of an IRP) into the IRP pointer field (a longword) in a UCB pointed to by R5:

```
MOVL    R3,UCB$L_IRP(R5)
```

Such instructions are practically self-documenting. You do not need to know the overall arrangement of data in a particular structure to understand such instruction references.

B.1.2.4   **Locating Macro Definitions.**   Commonly used instruction sequences are often coded as macros. Other instruction sequences, particularly those that read or write internal processor registers, are more readable if hidden in a macro. However, because macros are rarely expanded as a part of the assembler listing, you must sometimes be able to locate the macro definitions to understand the invoking code. Macros fall into three classes:

- Macros that are local to a module are defined in the module. Such macros are often used to generate data tables used by a single module.
- Macros that are part of a specific facility are defined in a separate file and appear with the listings for that facility. For example, the DCL listings include the macros that are used to assemble the DCL images in [DCL]CLIMAC.MAR. Sometimes there are related facilities, such as [CLI-UTL], that contain related listings and macro definitions.
- Macros that are used by many components of the operating system are defined in the LIB or STARLET libraries.

Many macro definition files reside in the [SYS] and [VMSLIB] facilities. For example, the [SYS] facility contains SYSMAR.MAR, EXEC_REORG_MACROS.MAR, and LOADER_MACROS.MAR. SYSMAR.MAR defines macros for many common instruction sequences that appear in several components. [VMSLIB]UTLDEFM.MAR defines macros commonly used in structure and constant definitions. [VMSLIB]STARMISC.MAR defines macros for common instruction sequences. Other facilities also contain macro source definition files.

Code written in languages other than VAX MACRO may have associated macro definition files. These appear in the same facility as the associated code. For example, the volume initialization utility, which is written in VAX BLISS-32, has a common definitions file, [INIT]INIDEF.B32. Use the techniques described in Section B.1.2.1 to search for a particular macro.

B.1.2.5   **The ASSUME Macro.** The ASSUME macro checks assumed relations and issues an assembly time error if an assumption is not true. Sometimes assumptions are made about the relative location of fields within a data structure.

- A single instruction could move two or more adjacent fields. For example, a single MOVQ instruction could move two adjacent longword fields.
- Autoincrement or autodecrement addressing could be used to traverse a structure.

Changes in the data structure could cause these instructions to fail. For example, to clear three adjacent fields in a UCB, a device driver uses the following instruction and macro sequence to prevent subtle errors if the layout of the UCB changes in the future:

```
CLRQ    UCB$L_SVAPTE(R5)
ASSUME  UCB$W_BOFF EQ (UCB$L_SVAPTE + 4)
ASSUME  UCB$W_BCNT EQ (UCB$L_SVAPTE + 6)
```

Sometimes assumptions are made about the arithmetic relation between various quantities, for example, interrupt priority levels (IPLs) or spinlock ranks. The ASSUME macro can also check these relations. For example, the nonpaged pool expansion routine, EXE$EXTENDPOOL in module MEM-ORYALC, assumes that the MMG spinlock's rank is 1 higher than the rank of the SCHED spinlock:

```
ASSUME  SPL$C_MMG EQ SPL$C_SCHED+1
```

SYS$LIBRARY:STARLET.MLB defines the ASSUME macro; its source, including comments, is contained in [VMSLIB]UTLDEFM.MAR. Examine the definition of the ASSUME macro to determine what options are available with it. The VAX BLISS-32 macro $ASSUME plays a similar role and is defined in SYS$LIBRARY:STARLET.REQ.

The ASSUME and $ASSUME macros produce no executable code. Since they perform their checks at assembly or compile time, there is no execution performance penalty for using them.

B.1.3 Executive Assembler Listings

The modules that make up the base image and the loadable executive images are all written from a common template that includes a module header describing each routine in the module. The *VAX MACRO and Instruction Set Reference Manual* describes the general format of a VAX MACRO listing file. The comments in this section should aid you in reading the executive assembler listings.

In general, the routines that make up the executive are coded according to standards resulting in more easily maintained code. For someone attempting to learn how the VMS operating system works, this also produces code that is easier to read.

B.1.3.1 Register Conventions. Each of the major subsystems of the executive uses a set of register conventions in its main routines. That is, the same registers

are used to hold the same contents from routine to routine. Some of the more common conventions are listed here.

- R4 usually contains the address of the process control block (PCB) of the current process. Nearly all system service procedures and scheduling routines use this convention. In fact, the change-mode-to-kernel system service dispatcher loads the address of the PCB of the caller into R4 before passing control to the service-specific procedure.
- When it is necessary to store a process header (PHD) address, R5 is usually chosen. R5 usually contains the address of the P1 window to the PHD. However, during the execution of the swapper and certain memory management code that executes at IPL$_SYNCH, R5 contains the system space address of the PHD.
- The memory management subsystem uses R2 to contain an address on an invalid page and R3 to contain the system virtual address of the page table entry (SVAPTE) that maps the page. After a physical page is associated with the page, its page frame number (PFN) is stored in R0.
- The I/O subsystem uses two nearly identical conventions, depending on whether it is executing in process context (in the Queue I/O Request, $QIO, system service and in device driver function decision table, FDT, routines) or in response to an interrupt. The most common register contents are the current IRP address stored in R3 and the UCB address in R5. In process context, R4 contains the address of the PCB of the requesting process. Within interrupt service routines, R4 contains the virtual address that maps one of the command and status registers (CSRs) of the interrupting device. The *VMS Device Support Manual* provides a more complete list of register use by device drivers and the I/O subsystem.
- The synchronization routines generally store a spinlock structure address or a spinlock index in R0. Many invocations of these routines are enveloped in macros, some of which set up R0 before passing control to the synchronization routine. For the convenience of the invoking code, these macros optionally preserve and restore the previous value of R0 with the PRESERVE= argument.

B.1.3.2   **CPU-Dependent Routines.** The VMS executive uses two different methods for incorporating CPU-dependent code. When there are only a few instructions or data references that depend on the specific CPU type, the code includes the instruction or data sequences for all CPUs. The CPUDISP macro uses the contents of global location EXE$GB_CPUTYPE to select the appropriate instructions or data. SYSBOOT initializes this location with the contents of the PR$_SID register. On some processor types, the CPUDISP macro uses an additional level of dispatch based on the CPU subtype stored in global location EXE$GB_CPUDATA + 15. The CPUDISP macro is described in the *VMS Device Support Manual* and is defined in SYSMAR.MAR.

When many instructions or data references depend on the specific CPU type, they are linked together into a set of CPU-dependent images (see Section B.2.3).

B.1.4   VAX Instruction Set and Addressing Mode Use

The VAX instruction set contains instructions with a natural number of operands. Thus, there are two- and three-operand forms of the arithmetic instructions ADD, SUB, MUL, and DIV. There are also bit manipulation instructions, a calling standard, character string instructions, and so on. All of these allow the assembly language programmer to produce code that is not only efficient but also readable.

However, there are certain places in the executive where the most obvious choice of instruction or addressing mode is not used because a shorter or faster alternative is available. Interrupt service routines, routines that execute at elevated IPL, and commonly executed code paths, such as the system service dispatcher and the main paths in the pager, are all examples where clarity of the source code is sacrificed for execution speed.

There are at least two reasons for concern over instruction length, even though the VAX architecture supports a very large virtual address space. Most areas where instruction size is an issue are within the nonpaged executive. This portion of the system consumes a fixed amount of physical memory. Keeping instruction size small is one way to keep this real memory cost to a minimum.

More important, VAX processors make use of an instruction lookahead buffer that contains the next few bytes in the instruction stream. Its size varies on different processors but is at least eight bytes on all current processor types. If the buffer empties, the next instruction or operand cannot be evaluated until the buffer is replenished. Keeping instructions small in key areas avoids this wait. The instruction buffer is filled in parallel with other CPU operations.

B.1.4.1   Techniques for Increasing Instruction Speed.

This section lists some of the techniques employed to reduce instruction size or increase execution speed. The list is hardly exhaustive, but a pattern emerges here that can be applied to other modules in the executive that are not explicitly mentioned. Each list element describes a general technique and may also contain a specific example, including the name of the module that employs the technique:

- Aligning data on "natural" boundaries is the most universally applied technique to reduce access time. Naturally aligned data begins at certain address boundaries, for example, aligned longwords begin at addresses that are multiples of four. Aligned reads and writes to memory are faster than unaligned transfers because of the way memory controllers are organized and the way processors access memory controllers. There are several manifestations of this technique:

—The VAX MACRO .PSECT directive and the DECLARE_PSECT macro, and the VAX BLISS-32 PSECT statement specify code and data program section (PSECT) alignments. (EXEC_REORG_MACROS.MAR defines the DECLARE_PSECT macro.)

—The VAX MACRO .ALIGN directive aligns data and code.

—Fields within data structures are ordered so that they begin on natural boundaries. Every structure allocated from pool is at least quadword-aligned. Sometimes dummy fields are included to force subsequent fields to natural boundaries.

—Many frequently invoked routines are aligned because longword-aligned branch targets increase transfer speed. For example, system service vectors and executive transfer vectors are all longword-aligned. Each set of vectors begins on a page boundary, and each vector is padded with NOP instructions or .BYTE 0 directives to make it a multiple of four bytes long. In addition, the beginnings of some loops are aligned.

• When two successive writes to memory occur, on many types of VAX processors the second write must wait for the first to complete. If successive write operations can be overlapped with register-to-register operations, instruction stream references, or other operations that do not generate writes to memory, then some other instruction can begin execution while the memory write completes.

Several executive routines use this technique. The three examples that follow are among the most commonly executed code paths in the system:

—The page fault handler saves R0 through R5 with PUSHL instructions interspersed among instructions that do not write to memory.

—The $QIO system service procedure intersperses writes to memory (initializing an IRP) with reads from its argument list and register operations.

—The change mode dispatchers for executive and kernel modes build customized call frames on their stacks. The writes to memory (the stack operations) are overlapped with register and instruction stream references.

• A pipeline design processor, such as the VAX 86x0 CPU, can have several instructions at varying stages of completion at any point in time. The overlapped instruction execution has several implications for coding style.

—The most common code path is in line. Code is arranged to minimize branching and maximize "falling through" to the next instruction or routine. Linear code executes faster than code that branches because after a branch the pipe is empty, losing the advantages of overlapped execution.

—Unrelated instructions are inserted between two instructions if the second instruction depends on the result of the first. If the first instruction has not completed, the dependent instruction stalls. Inserting unrelated instructions allows the first instruction to complete before the dependent instruction begins.

- There are three ways to push registers onto the stack: a PUSHR mask instruction, a series of MOVQ instructions to –(SP), or a series of PUSHL instructions. Instruction implementation is sufficiently different on various VAX processors to make generalization about performance of these instructions difficult. However, the PUSHR instruction is seldom used in time-critical places because it is slower than either MOVQ or PUSHL unless there are four or more registers to save. PUSHR must interpret its bit mask operand and then push the registers accordingly. PUSHR, however, does not alter condition codes and is used when their settings must be retained across saving registers.

- When it is necessary to include a test-and-branch operation, a decision as to which sense of the test to branch on and which sense to allow to continue in line is required. One basis for this decision is to allow the common (usually error-free) case to continue in line, only requiring the (slower) branch operation in unusual cases.

B.1.4.2 **Unusual Instruction and Addressing Mode Use.** There are several instances in the executive where the purpose of an instruction is not at all obvious. This list includes some of the common occurrences of unusual instruction set and addressing mode use.

- There are many instances of the following instruction sequence where the initial setting of the bit has no effect on the flow of control:

```
        BBSS    bit arguments, 10$
10$:
```

This sequence sets the bit identified by a bit number or bit position. An equivalent instruction sequence using BBCC clears the specified bit.

In some cases the BBxx instructions are preferred to the BISx or BICx instructions. The BIxx instructions require a mask with a 1 in the designated position. Creating such a mask requires either two instructions or an immediate mask that might occupy a longword. The only exception to this involves a bit in the first six positions, where a short literal constant can contain the mask.

Note that a BBCS instruction is equivalent to a BBSS instruction when the branch destination is the next instruction. There are some occurrences of BBCS where a BBSS would seem to accomplish the same purpose. The usual sense of the bit in question influences the instruction choice so as to avoid the branch in the usual case.

- There are several instances of autoincrement deferred addressing where the need for the increment of the register is not apparent. For example, both of the following instructions occur in the rescheduling interrupt service routine in module SCHED:

```
INSQUE  (R1),@(R2)+
;
REMQUE  @(R2)+,R4
```

In both cases, before the instruction executes, R2 contains the address of the listhead of a doubly linked list. Its contents after the instruction executes are irrelevant.

In fact, the increment is totally unnecessary; only double deferral from a register is needed. In other words, the addressing mode @0(R2) would be equally appropriate, since the final contents of R2 are not important. (The VAX architecture defines no @(Rx) double deferral addressing mode without a displacement.) However, deferred byte displacement addressing costs an extra byte to hold the displacement. In this commonly executed code path, saving one byte is extremely important.

It is worth noting that there is no similar problem when a single level of deferral from a register is required. The assembler generates simple register deferred mode (code 6) when it encounters byte displacement mode with a displacement of zero (0(Rn)) in the source code.

- The MOVAx and PUSHAx instructions combined with displacement mode addressing are equivalent to an ADDLx instruction. For example, the following two instructions are equivalent:

```
PUSHAB  12(R3)
;
ADDL3   #12,R3,-(SP)
```

However, the PUSHAB instruction is one byte shorter and executes faster than the ADDL3 instruction.

- The use of MOVAx and PUSHAx described in the previous item can be combined with indexed mode addressing to accomplish a multiply by 2, 4, or 8. For example, the following instruction multiplies the contents of R1 by 4, adds the value of the symbol LNMHSH$K_BUCKET to the product, and places the result back into R1:

```
MOVAL   @#LNMHSH$K_BUCKET[R1],R1
```

EXE$PROCSTRT, in module PROCSTRT, uses this instruction during process creation to calculate the size of a logical name hash table from the number of entries.

- The following instruction, found in routine EXE$ALLOCATE in module MEMORYALC, serves two purposes:

```
MOVAB   (R0)+,R2
```

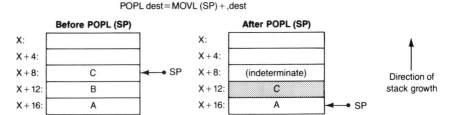

Figure B.1
Stack Modification due to POPL (SP) Pseudo
Instruction

Its ostensible purpose is to place the address of the allocated block of memory into R2, where it is later picked up by the invoker. However, because the allocated block is always at least quadword-aligned, the byte context of the instruction forces an increment of R0 by 1, setting the low bit of R0. The invoker interprets this set bit as a success indicator.

- The permanent symbol table of the VAX MACRO assembler recognizes the mnemonic POPL, even though there is no POPL instruction in the VAX instruction set. The code generated for the following instructions is identical:

```
POPL    dst
;
MOVL    (SP)+,dst
```

The mnemonic generates two bytes (one for the instruction opcode and the other for the source operand specifier) plus whatever is required to specify the destination operand.

For example, the following pseudo instruction (the first instruction in the change-mode-to-kernel dispatcher in the module SYSTEM_SERVICE_DISPATCHER) removes the change mode code from the stack (so that a subsequent REI will work correctly) and loads it into R0:

```
POPL    R0
```

A combination of the POPL instruction with an unusual addressing mode occurs in the exception dispatcher for change-mode-to-supervisor and change-mode-to-user exceptions where it is necessary to remove the second longword from the stack. The following instruction has the effect of removing the next-to-last item from the stack and discarding it, leaving the stack in the state pictured in Figure B.1:

```
POPL    (SP)
```

- The VAX instruction set does not include a TSTQ instruction. However, the following instruction sets the condition codes as a TSTQ instruction would:

```
MOVQ    R0,R0
```

The Set Timer ($SETIMR) and Schedule Wakeup ($SCHDWK) system services, in module SYSSCHEVT, use this instruction.

B.1.4.3 **REI Instruction Use.** The REI instruction most commonly dismisses an interrupt or exception at the end of an interrupt or exception service routine. However, other routines also use it. It is the only means of reaching a less privileged access mode from a more privileged mode. Two slightly different techniques accomplish this mode change. The most general technique of going to a less privileged access mode alters the flow of execution at the same time. The RSX-11 Application Migration Executive (AME), part of the optional product VAX-11 RSX, uses this technique to get into compatibility mode and transfer control to the PDP-11 code. The following instruction sequence accomplishes the desired result:

```
PUSHL   new-PSL
PUSHL   new-PC
REI
```

Note that the many protection checks built into the REI instruction (see Chapter 2) prevent the REI instruction from being used by a nonprivileged user to get into a more privileged access mode or to elevate IPL, two operations that would allow such a user to damage the system.

A second technique changes the access mode but not the flow of control. The instruction sequence listed here (patterned after code contained in module PROCSTRT) shows this second technique:

```
        PUSHL   executive-mode-PSL
        BSBB    DOREI
        .                               ;Do processing in
        .                               ; executive access mode
        PUSHL   user-mode-PSL
        BSBB    DOREI
        .                               ;Do processing in
        .                               ; user access mode
        BRB     somewhere_else
DOREI:  REI                             ;REI uses pushed PSL, and the PC
        .                               ; that BSBB put on the stack
        .
```

B.1.5 **Elimination of Seldom-Used Code**

Several different techniques are used to eliminate code and data that are not used very often. For example, none of the programs used during the initialization of a VMS system remains after its work is accomplished. The VMS executive uses several techniques that allow these routines to do their work as efficiently as possible and yet eliminate them after they have done their work.

B.1.5.1   **Bootstrap Programs.** The following list illustrates some of the techniques used to remove system initialization code from memory after it has done its work:

- Both VMB and SYSBOOT execute in physical pages whose use is not recorded anywhere. When module EXEC_INIT places all physical pages except those occupied by the permanently resident executive on the free page list, it includes the pages used by VMB and SYSBOOT. Their contents are overwritten the first time that each physical page is used.
- After the initialization of a loadable executive image is complete, the address space occupied by its fixup and initialization sections is deallocated.
- The SYSINIT process deallocates to the free page list the physical pages occupied by EXEC_INIT (see Chapter 31). As part of this deallocation, the system page table entries (SPTEs) mapping EXEC_INIT are also deallocated.
- Part of system initialization takes place in process context. The swapper creates the SYSINIT process, which in turn creates the startup process. Because both SYSINIT and startup are separate processes, they disappear when they are deleted, that is, after they have completed their work.

B.1.5.2   **Infrequently Used System Routines.** The simplest and most common technique used to prevent infrequently used code and data from permanently occupying memory is to put them into one of the pageable image sections of a loadable executive image. Chapter 29 describes loadable executive images, their image sections, and their loading. The normal operation of system working set replacement eventually forces infrequently referenced pages out of the system working set.

Process creation employs an additional technique to eliminate code from the system after a process is created. The swapper invokes a special subroutine when it brings a process into memory from SHELL. This subroutine is located in several of the SHELL pages that the swapper brings into memory. These pages become the kernel stack of the new process, once the swapper changes the process state to computable and resident. Because of the way that the swapper does its I/O, these pages are mapped as P0 pages in the swapper's address space.

B.1.6   **Locking Code or Data into Memory**

While infrequent use may lead to a routine's being placed in a pageable image section, other considerations may require that the code be nonpageable. For example, the page fault handler assumes that page faults do not occur above IPL 2; it enforces this assumption by generating a fatal bugcheck if it is violated.

Several infrequently used and thus pageable system services (including the Create Process, $CREPRC, system service) elevate IPL to IPL$_SYNCH (for example, as a result of acquiring a spinlock while synchronizing access to the scheduler database) and thus need to lock some code pages into memory. Several different techniques are used to lock pages into memory.

B.1.6.1   **Placing Code into the Nonpaged Executive.** Code and data in the executive images reside in pageable and nonpageable image sections. The minimum amount possible is placed into the PSECTs that comprise the nonpageable image sections. A branch or subroutine call transfers control from the paged to the nonpaged code. The following variation on a routine within the Get Job/Process Information ($GETJPI) system service illustrates the technique. The entire routine cannot exist in a pageable image section because the routine EXE$NAMPID returns at IPL$_SYNCH and thus may not incur a page fault.

```
        .PSECT  EXEC$PAGED_CODE
        .ENABLE LOCAL_BLOCK
        .                               ;Processing begins
        .                               ; in paged code
        JSB     25$
        .

        .SAVE_PSECT
        .PSECT  EXEC$NONPAGED_CODE
25$:    JSB     G^ EXE$NAMPID           ;This is the only
                                        ; nonpaged piece
        SETIPL  #0
        RSB
        .RESTORE_PSECT
        .                               ;Processing continues
        .                               ; in paged code
```

B.1.6.2   **Dynamically Locking Pages into the System Working Set.** The preceding piece of code only contributes seven bytes to the nonpaged executive. The $CREPRC system service must execute many more instructions at IPL$_ SYNCH. It employs a technique that dynamically locks pages into the system working set. (The Lock Pages in Working Set, $LKWSET, system service cannot lock pages into the system working set.)

The PMLREQ and PMLEND macros, new with VMS Version 5, expand into code that dynamically locks and unlocks a set of pages in the system working set and optionally changes the IPL. Typically the macros appear at the beginning and end of a code sequence that may not incur a page fault. However, a larger range of pages may be specified with macro arguments. This range may include data as well as code.

The instructions generated by the PMLREQ macro push the size and starting address of the group of pages to be locked. If not explicitly specified, the starting address is a location within the macro. The ending address must be specified. An instruction generated by the macro transfers control to MMG$LOCK_SYSTEM_PAGES, in module LOCK_SYSTEM_PAGES, as a co-routine.

MMG$LOCK_SYSTEM_PAGES performs several functions for each page to be locked:

1. It checks that the page is in system space. If it is not, the routine generates the NOTSYSVA bugcheck.
2. It faults the page into the system working set, if it is not already in the system working set.
3. If the page's PFN is described in the PFN database, the routine increments the share count (PFN$Ax_SHRCNT) in the PFN database and sets the locked in working set flag (WSL$V_WSLOCK) in the page's working set list entry (WSLE). These steps ensure that the page remains locked in memory.

MMG$LOCK_SYSTEM_PAGES then returns to instructions generated by the PMLREQ macro as a co-routine. The size and starting address of the locked pages remain on the stack. If a new IPL was specified in the macro invocation, PMLREQ now sets the IPL. The pages in the specified range are now valid and will remain so until the instructions generated by the PMLEND macro are invoked.

The PMLEND macro generates instructions that optionally change the IPL and then transfer to MMG$UNLOCK_SYSTEM_ENTRY, in module LOCK_SYSTEM_PAGES, as a co-routine. MMG$UNLOCK_SYSTEM_ENTRY uses the size and starting address information left on the stack. It decrements the share count in the PFN database and clears WSL$V_WSLOCK for each locked page. After cleaning up the stack, MMG$UNLOCK_SYSTEM_ENTRY returns. The following example illustrates the use of these macros:

```
        PMLREQ  END=2300$               ;Lock pages between here and 2300$
;++
; NB: Co-routine address + 2 LWs have been placed on top of stack
;--
                .                        ;This code incurs no page faults
                .
        PMLEND                          ;Through with locked pages
;++
; NB: Co-routine address + 2 LWs have been removed from top of stack
;--
                .
                .
2300$:
```

B.1.6.3   **Dynamically Locking Pages into the Process Working Set.** Privileged utilities and other code that executes in process context may need to lock pages into the process working set when running at elevated IPL. Two techniques are available, depending on the number of pages to be locked. The $LKWSET system service can lock any number of pages into the process working set, limited only by the process quotas and the amount of free memory.

A process can lock one or two pages into its working set with a simple technique known as "poor man's lock down." Once the desired pages are in the working set, the process raises the IPL to IPL$_SYNCH or higher, blocking quantum-end processing and, in particular, the working set limit adjustment.

```
        .                               ;Processing begins in paged code
        .
BEGIN_LOCK:
        DSBINT  LOCK_IPL
        .                               ;No page faults will occur here
        .

        ENBINT
        .                               ;Page faults can occur again
        .

        BRB     END_LOCK
LOCK_IPL:
        .LONG   IPL$_SYNCH
END_LOCK:
        ASSUME  ⟨END_LOCK-BEGIN_LOCK⟩ LE 512
```

The DSBINT macro expands to the following instructions:

```
        MFPR    #PR$_IPL,-(SP)
        MTPR    src,#PR$_IPL
```

The key to this technique is that the second instruction generated by the DSBINT macro cannot successfully complete until both the page containing the instruction and the page containing the source operand are valid. (The instruction faults these pages into the working set if they are not already valid.) Once the instruction completes, implying that both pages are valid, IPL is set at IPL$_SYNCH, preventing quantum end and further working set list manipulation until the IPL is lowered (with the ENBINT macro).

The ASSUME macro ensures that the DSBINT macro and source operand are not more than one page apart. This prevents the possibility of an invalid page existing between the two valid pages, an occurrence that would not only subvert this technique but might also lead to a PGFIPLHI fatal bugcheck.

Several processes, such as the error formatter process (ERRFMT), use this technique.

B.2   MAP FILES

The map files produced when a VMS system is built from source are indispensable to readers of listing files. The listing kit contains map files for many images, including the base image, loadable images, device drivers, and utilities. (Chapter 29 describes the base image and loadable executive images.) Most map files reside in the same facility as their related listing files.

Table B.1   Selected Map File Locations

Map File	Facility
Base image (SYS.MAP)	[SYS]
Most loadable executive images	[SYS]
CPU-specific loadable images (SYSLOA*xxx*.MAP)	[SYSLOA]
CLUSTRLOA.MAP and CSP.MAP	[SYSLOA]
SCSLOA.MAP	[SYSLOA]
CPULOA.MAP	[CPULOA]
SYSTEM_DEBUG.MAP	[DELTA]
DDIF$RMS_EXTENSION.MAP	[RMSEXT]
RECOVERY_UNIT_SERVICES.MAP	[RUF]
RMS.MAP	[RMS]
SYSMSG.MAP	[MSGFIL]
VMB.MAP, SYSGEN.MAP, and SYSBOOT.MAP	[BOOTS]
Most device drivers	[DRIVER], [COMM_DRIVER], or [TTDRVR]
Other device drivers	[RTPAD], [LAT], [NETACP], [DUP], or [TFF]
DCL.MAP	[DCL]

For example, the base image and most loadable executive image map files reside in the [SYS] facility. Table B.1 lists the location of selected map files.

Map files list the value of each global symbol. These symbols include routine and data cell locations as well as some data structure offset, bit field, and other constant definitions. The base image map file lists the system virtual addresses of the executive transfer vectors, data cell pointers, and data cells in SYS.EXE. The loadable image map files list the locations of routines and data cells as offsets from the beginning of the image. The system virtual addresses of locations within loadable images are not determined until the images are loaded. The utility map files list the virtual addresses of routines and data cells.

It is often necessary to identify which module defines a given symbol. Because of the modular construction of VMS, many symbols referenced by one routine are defined in some other module. Many images are built from a large number of modules, so the map file alphabetical cross-reference listing is particularly valuable. It identifies the modules that define and reference each global symbol.

The techniques described for using the executive image map files are also applicable to other map files. Map files for device drivers are necessary for debugging a new device driver. This section also describes map files for DCL and certain other loadable images because these images are not activated in the usual way but rather are mapped into process or system virtual address space.

B.2.1 VMS Executive Map Files

Fundamentally, the map files enable you to correlate system virtual addresses and their locations in listing files. For example, when the system crashes, the addresses that are reported on either the console terminal or in the system dump file must be related to actual routines and data cells in system address space.

B.2.1.1

Locating a System Address in the Listings. The list of loadable executive images and their addresses reported on the console terminal and in the system dump file help identify which executive image contains the offending reference. Compare the address in question with the base and end addresses for each loadable image to find the correct range. (System addresses less than MMG$A_SYS_END are in the base image.)

In the following example, output from the System Dump Analyzer, the location $80132F20_{16}$ is in the loadable executive image EXCEPTION.EXE:

```
Image                   Base      End       Length
SYSMSG                  800C9C00  800F2A00  00028E00
.
.
.
SYSDEVICE               8011E600  8011FC00  00001600
MESSAGE_ROUTINES        80120200  80122800  00002600
EXCEPTION               80132C00  8013B200  00008600
LOGICAL_NAMES           8013BC00  8013D600  00001A00
SECURITY                8013DC00  8013F400  00001800
.
.
```

Subtract the image's base address from the address in question to get its offset within the loadable image. Continuing the previous example, calculate the offset of the location in question:

```
 80132F20    Location in question
-80132C00    Base address of loadable executive image EXCEPTION
---------
      320    Location's offset within EXCEPTION
```

The identified image's map file then helps correlate addresses to PSECTs. In its program section synopsis, a map file lists the PSECTs that contribute to an image and lists each PSECT's address range. A loadable image's base address is not determined until the image is loaded, so addresses in its map file are offsets from the beginning of the image.

Compare the offset in question with each PSECT address range until you find the PSECT that contains the offset. Note the PSECT's name, since it is required later. From the following fragment of EXCEPTION.MAP, you can see that offset 320_{16} is in PSECT EXEC$NONPAGED_CODE:

```
                    +---------------------------+
                    ! Program Section Synopsis !
                    +---------------------------+
Psect Name      Module Name            Base      End
----------      -----------            ----      ---
EXEC$NONPAGED_CODE                     00000000  000004FF
                BUGCHECKBT             00000000  00000039
                EXCEPTION              0000003C  0000021A
                SYSTEM_SERVICE_DISPATCHER
                                       00000220  000003F6
                SYSTEM_SERVICE_EXIT
                                       000003F8  0000047E
                PATA_NONPAGED          00000480  000004FF
EXEC$NONPAGED_DATA                     00000600  00001FE7
```

Often, several modules contribute to a given PSECT. The map file's program section synopsis lists the beginning and ending address of each module's contribution to the PSECT. Compare the offset in question with each module's contribution to the identified PSECT to find the module that defines the location. In this example, the module SYSTEM_SERVICE_DISPATCHER contributes offset 320_{16}.

Subtract the beginning address of the identified module's contribution to the PSECT from the offset of interest to produce an offset into the correct module and PSECT:

```
 00000320    Location's offset within EXCEPTION
-00000220    Base of EXEC$NONPAGED_CODE in SYSTEM_SERVICE_DISPATCHER
---------
      100    PSECT offset within module SYSTEM_SERVICE_DISPATCHER
```

This is the offset, within module SYSTEM_SERVICE_DISPATCHER's contribution to PSECT EXEC$NONPAGED_CODE, of the instruction or data reference in question. You must ensure that you locate the correct PSECT within the listing, since there may be several PSECTs. The following fragment is from SYSTEM_SERVICE_DISPATCHER.LIS:

```
0000   163   DECLARE_PSECT   EXEC$NONPAGED_CODE,ALIGNMENT=QUAD
 .
 .
 .
0100   573 EXE$CMODKRNL::
0100   574   POPL R0                      ;Retrieve CHMK code from stack
```

If the address in question is within the base image, the calculations are somewhat simpler. The addresses in SYS.MAP are system addresses, so compare the address in question directly with the address ranges in the program section synopsis to identify the PSECT and contributing module. Subtract the beginning address of the identified module's contribution to the PSECT from the address in question to produce an offset within the assembler listing. Exercise care to read the correct PSECT in the listing.

In general, this technique, transforming an address into an offset within a module's contribution to a PSECT, can be applied to any type of image. However, associating a system space address with a particular image may be more difficult for images other than the base image and loadable executive images. Other system space images include dynamically loaded images like device drivers, or one of the other loadable images like the CPU-dependent images. Global pointers identify most dynamically mapped portions of system address space. Examine the contents of these locations to determine the component that contains the offending address. Chapter 29 contains a description of some of these loadable routines and the loading mechanism.

B.2.1.2 **Relocatable and Vectored Symbols.** A symbol whose value must be adjusted to account for an image's base address is identified as a relocatable symbol in a map file, indicated by R after the symbol's value:

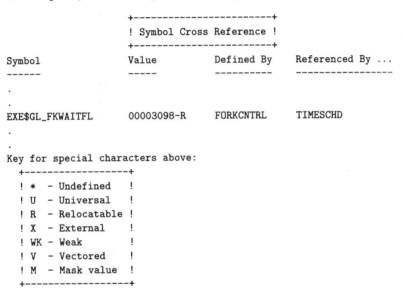

```
                          +------------------------+
                          ! Symbol Cross Reference !
                          +------------------------+
    Symbol                Value           Defined By       Referenced By ...
    ------                -----           ----------       -----------------
    .
    .
    EXE$GL_FKWAITFL       00003098-R      FORKCNTRL        TIMESCHD
    .
    .

    Key for special characters above:
        +------------------+
        ! *  - Undefined   !
        ! U  - Universal   !
        ! R  - Relocatable !
        ! X  - External    !
        ! WK - Weak        !
        ! V  - Vectored    !
        ! M  - Mask value  !
        +------------------+
```

Executive code refers to routines and data cells in other loadable images through executive transfer vectors and data cell pointers in the base image. The vectors and pointers are filled in with the correct addresses when the corresponding images are loaded. A map file identifies the symbols for these routines and data cells as vectored universal symbols, indicated by V after the symbol's value. A universal symbol is one that can be interpreted outside the image that defined it.

Vectored universal symbols appear twice in a map file. In the first occurrence, the symbol's value equals its offset from the beginning of the image that defines the symbol. The linker creates a second symbol, indicated by (V) after the symbol's name in the map file. The second symbol's value equals the executive transfer vector's or data cell pointer's address in the base image.

For example, the routine EXE$DEANONPAGED resides in module MEM-ORYALC, part of the loadable executive image SYSTEM_PRIMITIVES.EXE. (Module EXSUBROUT invokes this routine directly, since EXSUBROUT is also part of SYSTEM_PRIMITIVES.EXE.) The following fragment is from SYSTEM_PRIMITIVES.MAP:

```
Symbol                  Value         Defined By    Referenced By ...
------                  -----         ----------    ------------------
EXE$DEANONPAGED         0000051A-RV   MEMORYALC     EXSUBROUT
EXE$DEANONPAGED (V)     80002338
```

Each loadable executive image is linked with the base image's symbol table (SYS.STB) to resolve references to externally defined vectored universal symbols, such as routines in other images. These universal symbols appear twice in the resulting map file. In the first occurrence, the symbol's value equals its location within the image that defines the symbol, in this case, its address in the base image (the same address as its vector or pointer). As previously described, the linker creates a second symbol whose value equals the vector's or pointer's address in the base image.

Continuing the previous example, module ASTDEL (part of the loadable executive image EVENT_FLAGS_AND_ASTS.EXE) invokes EXE$DEANONPAGED. The following fragment is from EVENT_FLAGS_AND_ASTS.MAP:

```
Symbol                  Value         Defined By    Referenced By ...
------                  -----         ----------    ------------------
EXE$DEANONPAGED         80002338      SYS           ASTDEL
                                                    POSTEF
                                                    SYSASCEFC

EXE$DEANONPAGED (V)     80002338
```

A relocatable symbol that is referenced by other loadable images is generally a vectored universal symbol. Relocatable symbols that are referenced only by modules within the same loadable image are not vectored universal symbols.

Symbols for constants like data structure offsets, IPLs, and the sizes of preallocated buffers are not affected by the ultimate location of a loadable image. These symbols are therefore not relocatable:

```
Symbol                  Value         Defined By    Referenced By ...
--------                -----         ----------    ------------------
PQL$C_SYSPQLLEN         00000046      SWAPPER       SWAPPER_INIT
```

Some base image global symbols have an associated version mask. The map file identifies these mask value symbols with M after the symbol values. The map file lists the symbol values, not the mask values:

Symbol	Value	Defined By	Referenced By ...
EXE$DUMPCPUREG	8000A868-RM	SYSLOAVEC	SYSLOAVEC_MASK
EXE$V_BUGREBOOT	0000000B-M	SYSPARAM	SYSPARAM_MASK

B.2.2   **DCL.MAP**

A command language interpreter (CLI) is mapped into a virtual address range that is not known until the mapping occurs. The first longword at global location CTL$AG_CLIMAGE in the P1 pointer page contains the base address of any CLI. Because DCL is linked with a base address of zero, the contents of this location can be used to relate an address extracted from the map with a virtual address in a running system.

For example, if the location of interest is $7FF720CC_{16}$ in P1 space and the contents of the first longword at CTL$AG_CLIMAGE is $7FF71200_{16}$, then the difference between these two numbers equals the offset into the DCL image. Obviously, if this difference is larger than the size of the DCL image, then the address is not in DCL:

```
 7FF720CC    Location of interest
-7FF71200    Base address of DCL
---------
      ECC    Location's offset within DCL image
```

Compare the location's offset within DCL to the address ranges listed in [DCL]DCL.MAP to determine which PSECT and module contain the location of interest. Subtract the beginning address of the identified module's contribution to the PSECT from the offset within DCL to produce an offset into the correct module and PSECT. This offset then locates in the listing file the routine or data cell of interest.

To calculate the P1 space address of a data cell or instruction in a DCL module, start with the location as shown in the module's listing. Add to it the base address of the module's contribution to the correct PSECT (taken from [DCL]DCL.MAP) to form the offset into the DCL image. Add this sum to the contents of global location CTL$AG_CLIMAGE to form the P1 address of the location in question.

B.2.3   **CPU-Dependent Routines**

Entire routines or modules that are CPU-dependent, such as the machine check service routine, are linked together into a set of CPU-dependent images. The images have names of the form SYSLOA*xxx*.EXE, where *xxx* identifies the CPU type (see Appendix G). SYSBOOT uses the CPU type and subtype to determine which SYSLOA image to load into nonpaged pool. Segregating CPU-dependent routines into separate images minimizes the number of CPU-dependent decisions that are made at execution time and reduces the size of the executive.

SYSBOOT stores the base address of the CPU-dependent code in the global location MMG$GL_SYSLOA_BASE (see Chapter 31). The map files for the CPU-dependent images have names of the form [SYSLOA]SYSLOA*xxx*.MAP. Perform address calculations using the techniques described in Section B.2.1.1.

B.2.4   **Device Driver Map Files**

SYSGEN loads device drivers into nonpaged pool. The SYSGEN command SHOW/DEVICE displays the address range into which the driver images are loaded. Each driver is linked with a base address of 0. The starting address displayed by SDA corresponds to offset 0 in the image. The address of the driver dispatch table (DDT) displayed by SDA usually corresponds to PSECT $$$115_DRIVER in the driver map. The *VMS Device Support Manual* discusses debugging device drivers in more detail.

B.2.5   **Other Map Files**

You can use other map files for the cross-reference capabilities already mentioned. In addition, many other components of the operating system execute as regular images, so no base addresses have to be used to locate addresses in virtual address space. The addresses on the map correspond to the virtual addresses that are used for an executable image. However, the map file does not include the base address of nonbased, position-independent code shareable images; their base addresses are determined at image activation time.

As the image activator processes an image and its references to other images, the image activator builds image control blocks (ICBs) (see Chapter 26). An ICB includes the image name and the starting and ending addresses of the image. The ICBs for activated images form a doubly linked list starting at the listhead IAC$GL_IMAGE_LIST. You may be able to examine this list of ICBs with SDA (in conjunction with the map file's image section synopsis) to determine what images are mapped into P0 space. The listhead and the ICBs are pageable, so they may not be present in a system dump file.

B.3   **SYSTEM DUMP ANALYZER**

SDA allows you to analyze a running system or examine the contents of a dump file. Map files can only supply addresses of static data storage areas in the system, not their contents. In addition, many data structures are dynamically constructed. With SDA you can examine these data structures, other memory locations, and the hardware context of each processor.

The *VMS System Dump Analyzer Utility Manual* describes how to use SDA. This section mentions several of the many SDA commands that are especially useful when studying how the operating system works.

B.3.1   **Symbols**

SDA maintains a symbol table that it uses to interpret memory addresses
and contents. SDA reads certain symbols, including SYS$SYSTEM:SYS.STB
and a small subset of SYS$SYSTEM:SYSDEF.STB, into its symbol table when
it first executes. You can add symbols to SDA's table with the DEFINE and
READ commands. Since SYS$SYSTEM:SYSDEF.STB contains many com-
mon data structure definitions, reading it into SDA's symbol table is frequently useful. Use the following command:

```
SDA> READ SYS$SYSTEM:SYSDEF.STB
```

Many of the dynamic data structures are located through global pointers in
the base image. These static locations are loaded when these structures are
created or modified, either as a part of system initialization or some other
loading mechanism.

The SDA command SHOW SYMBOLS/ALL is one way to display these
global pointers. It shows both the addresses and the contents of all locations
for which SDA has symbols in its symbol table. This list, together with the
map files, enables you to locate any data structure in system address space if
you know the global name that locates the structure. Alternatively, use the
EXAMINE command to determine the contents of particular global pointers.
The SHOW SYMBOLS/ALL command produces a very long list. The SHOW
SYMBOLS/ALL *xyz* command lists only those symbols that begin with *xyz*.

The READ/EXECUTIVE command reads the definitions of universal symbols from the loadable executive images and adds the appropriate image's
base address to each relocatable symbol. Before such a command is issued,
SDA interprets references to vectored universal symbols as their base image
executive transfer vectors or data cell pointers. In the example, note that
SDA has defined the symbol SYSTEM_PRIMITIVES to be the base address
of the loadable image:

```
SDA> SHOW SYMBOL EXE$ALLOCIRP
EXE$ALLOCIRP = 80002160 :   A4109F17
SDA> EXAMINE/INSTRUCTION EXE$ALLOCIRP     !Executive transfer vector
EXE$ALLOCIRP:  JMP     @#SYSTEM_PRIMITIVES+00010
```

After reading a loadable executive image's symbol table, SDA interprets
references to vectored universal symbols as their locations within the loadable executive image. SDA creates new symbols (prefixed with V_) for the
vectors or pointers in the base image. In the example, note that SDA now
displays the JMP instruction destination as EXE$ALLOCIRP:

```
SDA> READ/EXECUTIVE
       .
       .
       .
```

```
%SDA-I-READSYM, reading symbol table SYS$COMMON:[SYS$LDR]RMS.EXE;7
%SDA-I-READSYM, reading symbol table SYS$COMMON:[SYS$LDR]CPULOA.EXE;4
   .
   .
   .
SDA> SHOW SYMBOL EXE$ALLOCIRP
EXE$ALLOCIRP = 8018A410 :   00B08FDD
SDA> SHOW SYMBOL V_EXE$ALLOCIRP
V_EXE$ALLOCIRP = 80002160 :   A4109F17
SDA> EXAMINE/INSTRUCTION EXE$ALLOCIRP     !Location in loadable image
EXE$ALLOCIRP:  PUSHL    #000A00B0
SDA> EXAMINE/INSTRUCTION V_EXE$ALLOCIRP   !Executive transfer vector
V_EXE$ALLOCIRP:  JMP      @#EXE$ALLOCIRP
```

The SDA command SHOW EXECUTIVE produces a list of the loadable executive images, their starting and ending addresses, and their sizes. Section B.2.1.1 describes the use of this list in conjunction with the executive map files. SDA defines symbols for the base addresses of the loadable executive images and a number of other loadable images. These symbols include the following:

- CLUSTRLOA—Base address of VAXcluster system support
- xxDRIVER (xx is typically a device name)—Base address of device driver
- FPEMUL—Base address of floating-point emulation code
- MSCP—Base address of the mass storage control protocol (MSCP) server
- SCSLOA—Base address of system communication services (SCS) image
- SYSLOA—Base address of CPU-specific code
- VAXEMUL—Base address of string emulation code

With these symbols you can form simple address expressions to specify a particular location in any of these images. For example, the following SDA command examines offset 100_{16} in PAGE_MANAGEMENT:

```
EXAMINE PAGE_MANAGEMENT + 100
```

The symbol table files read by SDA contain only global symbols. (In the case of loadable executive images, they contain only universal symbols.) Sometimes it is helpful to add some of a module's local symbols to SDA's symbol table. You can create a local symbol definition file for SDA. Start with the map file that includes the module in question. For example, SYS-TEM_PRIMITIVES.MAP reveals that module TIMESCHDL's contribution to PSECT EXEC$NONPAGED_CODE begins at offset $10B0_{16}$ from the beginning of the loadable image:

```
                   +---------------------------+
                   ! Program Section Synopsis  !
                   +---------------------------+
Psect Name      Module Name      Base       End
----------      -----------      ----       ---

EXEC$NONPAGED_CODE               00000000   00001F5F
                MEMORYALC        00000000   00000BC5
                INIRDWRT         00000BC8   00000C58
```

```
MUTEX                 00000C5C   00000F5E
FORKCNTRL             00000F60   000010AE
TIMESCHDL             000010B0   000017C1
```

Next, examine the list of symbols and their values located at end of the module's listing file. The following fragment is from TIMESCHDL.LIS:

```
CHECK_SANITY_TIMER     00000000 R          05
CHKTMQ                 000001BC R          05
  .
  .


                       +----------------+
                       ! Psect synopsis !
                       +----------------+
PSECT name             Allocation         PSECT No.  Attributes
----------             ----------         ---------  ----------
  .

  .
EXEC$NONPAGED_CODE      00000712 ( 1810.)  05 (  5.)  ...
```

If an online listing is available, use an editor to manipulate a copy of it into a local symbol definition file. If only a microfiche listing is available, manually create a local symbol definition file. In either case, phrase each definition as an SDA DEFINE command. Begin by defining a symbol whose value equals the starting address of the PSECT that contains the code or data of interest. The following fragment is from a user-created symbol definition file called TIMESCHDL_LOCALS.COM:

```
DEFINE PSECT_BASE = SYSTEM_PRIMITIVES + 10B0
DEFINE CHECK_SANITY_TIMER = PSECT_BASE + 00000000
DEFINE CHKTMQ = PSECT_BASE + 000001BC
```

Invoke the local symbol definition file from SDA. Notice that SDA then uses the local symbol CHKTMQ:

```
SDA> EXAMINE/INSTRUCTION SYSTEM_PRIMITIVES + 10B0 + 275
SYSTEM_PRIMITIVES+01325:  BRW       SYSTEM_PRIMITIVES+0126C

SDA> @TIMESCHDL_LOCALS.COM

SDA> EXAMINE/INSTRUCTION SYSTEM_PRIMITIVES + 10B0 + 275
CHKTMQ+000B9:  BRW       CHKTMQ

SDA> EXAMINE/INSTRUCTION CHKTMQ
CHKTMQ:  BLBC      @#SMP$GL_FLAGS,CHKTMQ+00012
```

Section B.1.2.2 describes a technique for adding data structure offset and other symbols to SDA's symbol table.

B.3.2   Address Space Layout

You can also use SDA to create a picture of P1 and system address space.

As Figure 1.8 shows, many of the pieces of system address space are constructed at initialization time. SYSGEN parameters determine the sizes of the various pieces (see Appendix F). In response to the command SHOW PAGE_TABLE/SYSTEM, SDA lists the contents of the entire system page table. This listing, the symbol table, the list of loadable executive images and their starting addresses, and the system map files allow you to draw a sketch of system virtual address space.

The output from the SDA SHOW PAGE_TABLE/P1 command, together with the information in Figure 1.2 and Table F.6, allows you to draw a layout of P1 address space.

B.4 INTERPRETING SDL FILES

Most data structures and other systemwide constants used by the executive and other system components are defined with SDL files. SDL enables data structures to be defined in a language-independent way. SDL can generate language-specific versions of the same structure in any of several languages.

When a VMS system is built from source, the SDL preprocessor reads and processes system data structure definitions written in SDL. It produces a set of macro definitions for use by the VAX MACRO assembler and another set for the VAX BLISS-32 compiler.

In particular, there are SDL files that generate the macros that define data structures and constants in the VAX MACRO libraries SYS$LIBRARY: LIB.MLB and STARLET.MLB and the VAX BLISS-32 files SYS$LIBRARY: LIB.REQ and STARLET.REQ. The VMS listing kit includes these SDL files. The SDL definition of a data structure typically includes comments describing the fields of the structure. The SDL definition can thus be a source of information about the meaning of system data structure fields. These comments are not propagated to LIB.MLB and STARLET.MLB, although they do appear in LIB.REQ and STARLET.REQ.

This section shows how the SDL description of a data structure relates to both the resulting VAX MACRO definition and a picture of the structure. Its sole purpose is to assist in the interpretation of SDL files supplied with the VMS listing kit. Note that SDL is an internal Digital tool. Any other use is completely unsupported.

B.4.1 A Sample Structure Definition

To see how a structure is defined, look at the resultant symbol definitions and compare the SDL definition of a given structure with the resultant VAX MACRO or VAX BLISS-32 symbols. Any listing that uses the structure in question includes these symbols. Alternatively, use the command procedure listed in Section B.1.2.2.

Example B.1 shows the SDL definition of the AST control block (ACB) and the comments that accompany each field definition. Figure 7.1 shows the

Example B.1
SDL Definition of AST Control Block

```
module $ACBDEF;
/* +
/* AST CONTROL BLOCK DEFINITIONS
/* AST control blocks exist as separate structures and as
/* substructures within larger control blocks such as I/O
/* request packets and timer queue entries.
/*
/*-
aggregate ACBDEF structure prefix ACB$;
  ASTQFL longword unsigned;                 /*AST queue forward link
  ASTQBL longword unsigned;                 /*AST queue backward link
  SIZE word unsigned;                       /*Structure size in bytes
  TYPE byte unsigned;                       /*Structure type code
  RMOD_OVERLAY union fill;
    RMOD byte unsigned;                     /*Request access mode
    RMOD_BITS structure fill;
      MODE bitfield length 2;               /*Mode for final delivery
      FILL_1 bitfield length 2 fill prefix ACBDEF tag $$;  /*Spare
      PKAST  bitfield mask;                 /*Piggyback
                                            /*  special kernel AST
      NODELETE bitfield mask;               /*Don't delete ACB on
                                            /*  delivery
      QUOTA bitfield mask;                  /*Account for quota
      KAST bitfield mask;                   /*Special kernel AST
    end RMOD_BITS;
  end RMOD_OVERLAY;
  PID longword unsigned;                    /*Process ID of request
  AST longword unsigned;                    /*AST routine address
  ASTPRM longword unsigned;                 /*AST parameter
  KAST longword unsigned;                   /*Internal kernel mode
                                            /*  transfer address
  constant <quote>(LENGTH) equals . prefix ACB$ tag K;  /*Length of block
  constant <quote>(LENGTH) equals . prefix ACB$ tag C;  /*Length of block
end   ACBDEF;
end_module $ACBDEF;
```

layout of an ACB. Table B.2 lists each SDL directive in the ACB definition, its meaning, the symbol it creates, and the value of that symbol. The following sections briefly describe the individual SDL directives.

B.4.2   **Commonly Used SDL Statements**

An SDL statement consists of SDL keywords, user-specified names, and expressions. A semicolon terminates an SDL statement. It can be followed by a comment to be included in the output macro. The comment must begin with the character pair /*.

Valid SDL expressions can contain any of the following:

• Numeric constants

Table B.2   SDL Directives and Resultant VAX MACRO Symbol Definitions for AST Control Block

SDL Directive	Directive Meaning	Resultant Symbol	Symbol Value
module $ACBDEF	Begin $ACBDEF macro		
aggregate ACBDEF structure prefix ACB$	Begin ACB structure		
ASTQFL longword unsigned	Longword field	ACB$L_ASTQFL	0
ASTQBL longword unsigned	Longword field	ACB$L_ASTQBL	4
SIZE word unsigned	Word field	ACB$W_SIZE	8
TYPE byte unsigned	Byte field	ACB$B_TYPE	10
RMOD_OVERLAY union fill	Begin overlay structure		
RMOD byte unsigned	Byte field	ACB$B_RMOD	11
RMOD_BITS structure fill	Begin RMOD_BITS structure		
MODE bitfield length 2	Bit field of length 2	ACB$V_MODE ACB$_MODE	0 2
FILL_1 bitfield length 2 fill prefix ACBDEF tag $$	Skip two spare bits		
PKAST bitfield mask	Single bit field	ACB$V_PKAST ACB$M_PKAST	4 10_{16}
NODELETE bitfield mask	Single bit field	ACB$V_NODELETE ACB$M_NODELETE	5 20_{16}
QUOTA bitfield mask	Single bit field	ACB$V_QUOTA ACB$M_QUOTA	6 40_{16}
KAST bitfield mask	Single bit field	ACB$V_KAST ACB$M_KAST	7 80_{16}
end RMOD_BITS	End RMOD_BITS structure		
end RMOD_OVERLAY	End the overlay structure		
PID longword unsigned	Longword field	ACB$L_PID	12
AST longword unsigned	Longword field	ACB$L_AST	16
ASTPRM longword unsigned	Longword field	ACB$L_ASTPRM	20
KAST longword unsigned	Longword field	ACB$L_KAST	24
constant "LENGTH" equals . prefix ACB$tag K	Define a constant	ACB$K_LENGTH	28
constant "LENGTH" equals . prefix ACB$tag C	Define a constant	ACB$C_LENGTH	28
end ACBDEF	End ACB structure		
end_module $ACBDEF	End $ACBDEF macro		

- Local symbols
- Special offset location symbols: period (.), colon (:), and circumflex (ˆ)
- Arithmetic, shift, and logical operators
- Parentheses to define the order of evaluation

The next sections describe the SDL statements commonly employed to define structures used by VMS. They emphasize the SDL files used to build the system. A complete syntax of each statement is not given.

B.4.2.1   **MODULE Statement.** A MODULE statement groups related symbols and data structures. It defines a collection of SDL statements to be processed. Typically, each VMS data structure is defined within its own module. The name of the module is the name of the generated macro. For example, the following statement from Example B.1 defines the beginning of the module that defines the ACB data structure:

```
module  $ACBDEF;
```

B.4.2.2   **AGGREGATE Statement.** An AGGREGATE declaration defines a single data structure within a module. There are two types of AGGREGATE declaration:

- STRUCTURE
- UNION

The fields in a STRUCTURE occupy consecutive storage locations; the fields in a UNION reuse the same storage location.

The period character symbolizes the current byte offset within an AGGREGATE declaration.

Each VMS data structure definition begins with an AGGREGATE STRUCTURE statement. This statement includes a PREFIX keyword that specifies the prefix characters in each symbol definition. For example, the following statement from Example B.1 defines the beginning of the ACB structure, each of whose symbol definitions begins with the characters ACB$:

```
aggregate ACBDEF structure prefix ACB$;
```

B.4.2.3   **Data Structure Fields.** Each field in a data structure is defined in a statement consisting of a name and one or more keywords. A keyword can identify the type of data or its size. For example, the keywords BYTE, WORD, LONGWORD, QUADWORD, and OCTAWORD specify integer fields of those sizes. A keyword can specify some attribute of a field. For example, the keyword SIGNED specifies that an integer field is signed. The default is unsigned. Many other keywords are used to define VMS data structures. Examples are F_FLOATING, BITFIELD, and CHARACTER.

The value of the symbol name is set equal to the current value of an internal offset counter. In general, as each field definition is processed, the internal counter value is increased by the size of the field (1, 2, 4, or 8).

B.4.2.4   **Symbol Names.** The naming conventions that apply to VMS symbols defined through SDL are listed in Appendix D. In general, a data structure symbol has the form *structure$type_field-name*. *Structure* identifies its data structure. *Type* identifies the type of data. *Field-name* names the field.

A data structure symbol name is formed from a combination of the following elements:

- PREFIX keyword value, which includes a dollar sign ($) to indicate a Digital-defined symbol
- Letter indicating type. Data type keywords of BYTE, WORD, LONG-WORD, QUADWORD, or OCTAWORD generate characters B, W, L, Q, or O. A CONSTANT statement usually specifies a TAG value of C or K.
- Underscore (_)
- Field name from the data type statement

B.4.2.5   **Symbol Values.** It is possible for the user to assign values directly to a symbol defined as part of an SDL structure (for example, with the DEFAULT keyword). Normally, however, SDL assumes that a symbol will be used as an offset from the beginning of its data structure. SDL keeps track of the current offset from the start of the structure, and SDL assigns that value to the symbol.

B.4.2.6   **UNION Statement.** It is often desirable to give a field multiple names. In addition, subfields within a field often exist. The UNION statement defines the beginning of a substructure whose members reuse the same storage locations. The following extract from Example B.1 shows a UNION substructure:

```
RMOD_OVERLAY union fill;
    RMOD byte unsigned;
    RMOD_BITS structure fill;
        .
        .
        .
    end RMOD_BITS;
end RMOD_OVERLAY;
```

This extract defines both the symbol ACB$B_RMOD and the structure ACB$R_RMOD_BITS to be the value of the current byte offset. The FILL qualifier indicates that no symbol is to be generated in the VAX MACRO and VAX BLISS-32 expansions of the structure definition.

B.4.2.7   **CONSTANT Statement.** The CONSTANT statement defines a constant. Depending on what TAG argument is supplied, the CONSTANT statement produces symbols of the form *xyz*$C_*name*, *xyz*$K_*name*, or *xyz*$_*name*. By convention, symbols with C in the type field of the symbol name define ASCII character constants, while symbols with K in the type field define other constants. Early versions of VMS used only the C type for both character and other constants, and these symbols are still in use. Table B.2 illustrates one use of the CONSTANT statement:

```
constant "LENGTH" equals . prefix ACB$ tag K;
```

This statement defines the symbol ACB$K_LENGTH equal to the value of the period character, the current byte offset in the ACB structure.

There are several other examples of constant definitions in both the SYS-DEF and STARDEF SDL files. The definitions of the DYN$ symbols describe dynamically allocated structures. The JPI$ symbols describe an information list to the $GETJPI system service.

B.4.2.8   **BITFIELD Statement.** Bit fields require two numbers to completely describe them, a bit position and a size. SDL always defines a bit position (indicated by V in the type field of the symbol name). The bit position is specified by the current bit offset. The circumflex character (^) symbolizes the current bit offset within the current subaggregate.

The size of a field (indicated by S in the type field of the symbol name) is defined when the field size is specified explicitly with the LENGTH keyword. It is often useful to define a mask symbol (indicated by M in the type field of the symbol name) that has 1's in each bit position defined by the bit field and zeros elsewhere. SDL defines such a symbol if the MASK keyword is present in the BITFIELD statement.

Because this section merely tries to show what symbols result from a given SDL definition, the simplest way to describe the bit field syntax is with some examples. Table B.2 includes SDL BITFIELD statements extracted from the definition of the ACB.

B.4.2.9   **END and END_MODULE Statements.** The structure definition is terminated with an END statement. The module is terminated with an END_MODULE statement.

C Executive Data Areas

The writable executive consists of various dynamically allocated tables as well as statically allocated data structures that are a part of the base system image SYS.EXE. This appendix summarizes the major dynamic data areas and emphasizes the static base image data.

Most of the information presented in this appendix is from the specific source modules that comprise SYS.EXE. In general, it does not include data areas private to any loadable executive images. Names that appear in the Global Symbol column in lowercase type represent local symbols, which are only used within the module in which they are defined.

C.1 THE BASE IMAGE

This section describes the global cells that make up the base image. Its organization, defined by the module EXEC_LAYOUT, is shown in Figure 29.1. Each subsection describes a different area in the base image and lists the source modules that contribute to that area. Program section names (PSECT names) are included in each section title.

C.1.1 System Service Vector Area ($$$000_SYSTEM_SERVICE_VECTORS)

The first 16 pages of system virtual address space are reserved for system service vectors. These pages are read-only except when system services are being loaded. The global label SYS$S0_VECTOR_END, defined in module EXEC_LAYOUT, represents the high-address end of the system service vector pages. Chapter 6 gives more information on this section.

C.1.2 Nonpaged Executive Transfer Vectors ($$$$$NONPAGED_CODE)

Most of this area consists of transfer vectors to routines in loadable executive images. Each vector is a quadword. Most vectors contain a JMP instruction whose target is within a loadable executive image. In a few cases, a routine itself is in this area. The table that follows identifies these cases as "routine body." Module SYSTEM_ROUTINES defines this area. Chapter 29 gives more information on this section.

Global Symbol	Size	Description of Routine
ACP$ACCESS	Quadword	Function decision table (FDT) routine for IO$_ ACCESS and IO$_CREATE to files-oriented device
ACP$ACCESSNET	Quadword	FDT routine for IO$_ACCESS to network device
ACP$DEACCESS	Quadword	FDT routine for IO$_DEACCESS to files-oriented device
ACP$MODIFY	Quadword	FDT routine for IO$_ACPCONTROL, IO$_ DELETE, IO$_MODIFY to files-oriented device
ACP$MOUNT	Quadword	FDT routine for IO$_MOUNT to files-oriented device
ACP$READBLK	Quadword	FDT routine for IO$_READxBLK to files-oriented device
ACP$WRITEBLK	Quadword	FDT routine for IO$_WRITExBLK to files-oriented device
BUG$BUILD_HEADER	Quadword	Write bugcheck information into error log message buffer
BUG$DUMP_REGISTERS	Quadword	Store processor register contents in a buffer
BUG$FATAL	Quadword	Reserved
BUG$READ_ERR_RETRY	Quadword	Reserved
BUG$REBOOT	Quadword	Reboot after bugcheck processing
COM$DELATTNAST	Quadword	Deliver attention ASTs from specified list
COM$DELATTNASTP	Quadword	Deliver attention ASTs from specified list to a specific process
COM$DELCTRLAST	Quadword	Deliver out-of-band ASTs from specified list
COM$DELCTRLASTP	Quadword	Deliver out-of-band ASTs from specified list to a specific process
COM$DRVDEALMEM	Quadword	Deallocate nonpaged pool
COM$FLUSHATTNS	Quadword	Flush specified attention AST list
COM$FLUSHCTRLS	Quadword	Flush specified out-of-band AST list
COM$POST	Quadword	Queue an IRP to systemwide I/O postprocessing queue
COM$POST_NOCNT	Quadword	Queue an IRP to systemwide I/O postprocessing queue without incrementing UCB$L_OPNT
COM$SETATTNAST	Quadword	Enable or disable attention ASTs
COM$SETCTRLAST	Quadword	Enable or disable out-of-band ASTs
DTSS$TIMESERVICE_ HOOK	Quadword	Hook for distributed time service optional software
ERL$ALLOCEMB	Quadword	Allocate and initialize an error message buffer
ERL$COLDSTART	Quadword	Allocate and initialize an error message buffer for a boot message
ERL$DEVICEATTN	Quadword	Allocate and initialize an error message buffer for a device attention condition
ERL$DEVICERR	Quadword	Allocate and initialize an error message buffer for a device error
ERL$DEVICTMO	Quadword	Allocate and initialize an error message buffer for a device timeout
ERL$GETFULLNAME	Quadword	Copy device name including system communication services node name to a buffer
ERL$LOGMESSAGE	Quadword	Allocate and initialize an error message buffer for an error associated with a command packet

Global Symbol	Size	Description of Routine
ERL$LOGSTATUS	Quadword	Allocate and initialize an error message buffer for an error returned in a mass storage control protocol (MSCP) end packet
ERL$LOG_DMSCP	Quadword	Allocate and initialize an error message buffer for a disk MSCP controller error
ERL$LOG_TMSCP	Quadword	Allocate and initialize an error message buffer for a tape MSCP controller error
ERL$RELEASEMB	Quadword	Release a filled-in error log message buffer
ERL$UNEXP	Quadword	Unexpected interrupt service routine that generates a nonfatal bugcheck
ERL$VEC_RETURN	Quadword	Unexpected interrupt service routine that increments counter
ERL$WAKE	Quadword	Conditionally wake ERRFMT process
ERL$WARMSTART	Quadword	Allocate and initialize an error message buffer for a restart
EXE$ABORTIO	Quadword	Abort an I/O request from function decision table action routine
EXE$ACVIOLAT	Quadword	Access violation exception service routine
EXE$ALLOCATE	Quadword	Allocate dynamic memory from specified variable-length list
EXE$ALLOCBUF	Quadword	Allocate and initialize nonpaged pool for a buffer
EXE$ALLOCCEB	Quadword	Allocate and initialize nonpaged pool for a common event block
EXE$ALLOCIRP	Quadword	Allocate and initialize nonpaged pool for an IRP
EXE$ALLOCJIB	Quadword	Allocate and initialize nonpaged pool for a job information block
EXE$ALLOCPCB	Quadword	Allocate and initialize nonpaged pool for a PCB
EXE$ALLOCTQE	Quadword	Allocate and initialize nonpaged pool for a timer queue entry
EXE$ALONONPAGED	Quadword	Allocate nonpaged pool
EXE$ALONPAGVAR	Quadword	Allocate nonpaged pool from the variable-length list
EXE$ALONPAGWAIT	Quadword	Allocate nonpaged pool and conditionally wait if pool not available
EXE$ALONPAGWAITS	Quadword	Alternative entry point to EXE$ALONPAGWAIT
EXE$ALOP1IMAG	Quadword	Allocate memory from process allocation region for duration of image
EXE$ALOP1PROC	Quadword	Allocate memory from process allocation region
EXE$ALOPAGED	Quadword	Allocate paged pool
EXE$ALOPHYCNTG	Quadword	Allocate and map physically contiguous memory
EXE$ALOSHARED	Quadword	Allocate a block of MA780 shared memory
EXE$ALTQUEPKT	Quadword	Queue an IRP to a driver's alternate start I/O entry point
EXE$ARITH	Quadword	Arithmetic error exception service routine
EXE$ASTDEL	Quadword	Call AST procedure
EXE$ASTFLT	Quadword	Signal stack access failure during AST delivery
EXE$BLDPKTGSR	Quadword	Build I/O packet for shared memory global section read
EXE$BLDPKTGSW	Quadword	Build I/O packet for shared memory global section write

Global Symbol	Size	Description of Routine
EXE$BLDPKTMPW	Quadword	Build I/O packet for modified page writer
EXE$BLDPKTSWPR	Quadword	Build I/O packet for swap read
EXE$BLDPKTSWPW	Quadword	Build I/O packet for swap write
EXE$BOOTCB_CHK	Quadword	Check validity of boot control block
EXE$BREAK	Quadword	Breakpoint exception service routine
EXE$BUG_CHECK	Quadword	Process a bugcheck
EXE$BUILDPKTR	Quadword	Build I/O packet for page read
EXE$BUILDPKTW	Quadword	Build I/O packet for page write
EXE$CANCELN	Quadword	Internal entry point for $CANCEL system service
EXE$CARRIAGE	Quadword	Interpret I/O carriage control specifier
EXE$CATCH_ALL	Quadword	Catch-all condition handler procedure
EXE$CEBREFLCK	Quadword	Acquire SHMCEB reference count lock
EXE$CHECKACL	Quadword	Search an access control list for an entry granting requested rights
EXE$CHECKACMODE	Quadword	Perform access mode protection check
EXE$CHECKCLASS	Quadword	Perform nondiscretionary security check
EXE$CHECKPROT	Quadword	Perform system-owner-group-world protection check using expanded protection mask
EXE$CHECKPROT_16	Quadword	Perform system-owner-group-world protection check using 16-bit mask
EXE$CHECK_BYPASS	Quadword	Check for either BYPASS privilege or READALL privilege and read access
EXE$CHKCREACCES	Quadword	Check that process has create access to an object
EXE$CHKDELACCES	Quadword	Check that process has delete access to an object
EXE$CHKEXEACCES	Quadword	Check that process has execute access to an object
EXE$CHKIMAGNAME	Quadword	Check access to image name in image header buffer
EXE$CHKLOGACCES	Quadword	Check that process has logical I/O function access to an object
EXE$CHKPHYACCES	Quadword	Check that process has physical I/O function access to an object
EXE$CHKPRO_INT	Quadword	Internal entry point to the $CHKPRO system service
EXE$CHKRDACCES	Quadword	Check that process has read access to an object
EXE$CHKWAIT2	Quadword	Check whether event flag wait condition is satisfied
EXE$CHKWRTACCES	Quadword	Check that process has write access to an object
EXE$CLEANUP_ORB	Quadword	Delete all structures referenced by an object rights block
EXE$CLI_UTILSRV	Quadword	Dummy command language interpreter callback procedure
EXE$CLOSE_MSG	Quadword	Close files opened by EXE$OPEN_MSG for SYS$OUTPUT and SYS$ERROR
EXE$CLOSE_RDB	Quadword	Close the rights database file and zero the rights identifier table
EXE$CMODSUPR	Quadword	Change mode to supervisor exception service routine
EXE$CMODUSER	Quadword	Change mode to user exception service routine
EXE$COMPAT	Quadword	Exception service routine for compatibility mode faults

Global Symbol	*Size*	*Description of Routine*
EXE$CONNECT_SERVICES	Quadword	Initialize system service vector and array entries for a newly loaded system service
EXE$CONTSIGNAL	Quadword	Continue from exception
EXE$CRE_GTABLE	Quadword	Create group logical name table
EXE$CRE_JGTABLE	Quadword	Create job and group logical name tables
EXE$DEALLOCATE	Quadword	Deallocate dynamic memory to specified variable-length list
EXE$DEANONPAGED	Quadword	Deallocate nonpaged pool
EXE$DEANONPGDSIZ	Quadword	Deallocate nonpaged pool block whose size is in R1
EXE$DEAP1	Quadword	Deallocate memory to P1 allocation region
EXE$DEAPAGED	Quadword	Deallocate paged pool
EXE$DEAPGDSIZ	Quadword	Deallocate paged pool block whose size is in R1
EXE$DEASHARED	Quadword	Deallocate a block of MA780 shared memory
EXE$EPID_TO_IPID	Quadword	Convert extended process ID to internal process ID
EXE$EPID_TO_PCB	Quadword	Convert extended process ID to PCB address
EXE$EXCEPTION	Quadword	Common exception servicing routine
EXE$EXCPTNE	20 bytes	Routine body—executive mode last chance exception handler
EXE$EXCPTN	6 bytes	Routine body—kernel mode last chance exception handler
EXE$EXIT_IMAGE	Quadword	Procedure to invoke $EXIT at end of image execution
EXE$EXPANDSTK	Quadword	Expand user stack
EXE$EXTENDPOOL	Quadword	Extend nonpaged pool areas
EXE$FINDACL	Quadword	Search specified access control list segment for an entry of specified type
EXE$FINISHIO	Quadword	Complete an I/O operation at function decision table level
EXE$FINISHIOC	Quadword	Complete an I/O operation at function decision table level, zeroing second longword of status
EXE$FORK	Quadword	Insert fork process on specified queue
EXE$FORKDSPTH	Quadword	Dispatch fork processes from a given queue
EXE$FORK_WAIT	Quadword	Insert fork process on fork and wait queue
EXE$FRKIPL10DSP	Quadword	IPL 10 interrupt service routine, fork dispatching
EXE$FRKIPL11DSP	Quadword	IPL 11 interrupt service routine, fork dispatching
EXE$FRKIPL6DSP	Quadword	IPL 6 interrupt service routine, fork dispatching
EXE$FRKIPL8DSP	Quadword	IPL 8 interrupt service routine, fork dispatching
EXE$FRKIPL9DSP	Quadword	IPL 9 interrupt service routine, fork dispatching
EXE$HWCLKINT	Quadword	Interval timer interrupt service routine
EXE$IMGDELMSG	Quadword	Send image purge message to job controller
EXE$IMGDMP_EXEC	Quadword	Merge image dump facility after executive, supervisor, or user mode error and call it
EXE$IMGDMP_MERGE	Quadword	Merge image dump facility after user mode error and call it
EXE$IMGPURMSG	Quadword	Send image termination message to job controller
EXE$INIT_DEVICE	Quadword	Call device drivers' controller and unit initialization routines
EXE$INSERTIRP	Quadword	Insert IRP by priority order in unit control block queue

Global Symbol	Size	Description of Routine
EXE$INSIOQ	Quadword	Insert IRP in unit control block pending-I/O queue or invoke IOC$INITIATE
EXE$INSTIMQ	Quadword	Insert entry in time-ordered timer queue entry list
EXE$IOFORK	Quadword	Insert fork process on specified queue, disabling timeouts from the device
EXE$IORSNWAIT	Quadword	Place process in resource wait, backing out $QIO request
EXE$IPAPBKAST	Quadword	Reserved
EXE$IPCONTROL	Quadword	IPL 12 interrupt service routine, console intervention
EXE$IPID_TO_EPID	Quadword	Convert internal process ID to extended process ID
EXE$IPID_TO_PCB	Quadword	Convert internal process ID to PCB address
EXE$JBCRSP	Quadword	Special kernel mode AST routine for receiving response from $SNDJBC system service
EXE$KERSTKNV	Quadword	Invalid kernel stack exception service routine
EXE$LCLDSKVALID	Quadword	Function decision table routine for local disk valid function
EXE$LDB_SYNCH	Quadword	Reserved
EXE$LOAD_ERROR	1 byte	Routine body—HALT routine
EXE$MAXACMODE	Quadword	Maximize a specified access mode with previous mode in processor status longword
EXE$MCHECK	Quadword	Signal unrecoverable machine check to outer mode
EXE$MCHK_BUGCHK	Quadword	Handle machine checks for which protection is desired
EXE$MCHK_PRTCT	Quadword	Enable recovery block for machine check exceptions
EXE$MCHK_TEST	Quadword	Test machine check recovery block for mask match
EXE$MODIFY	Quadword	Function decision table routine for direct I/O modify functions
EXE$MODIFYLOCK	Quadword	Check I/O buffer for write accessibility and lock in memory
EXE$MODIFYLOCKR	Quadword	Check I/O buffer for read accessibility and lock in memory, returning via co-routine on error
EXE$MULTIQUOTA	Quadword	Check multiunit resource request and conditionally wait the process
EXE$NAMPID	Quadword	Translate process name to internal process ID
EXE$NETSNDERL	Quadword	Send a network message to the error logger
EXE$NULLPROC	Quadword	Reserved
EXE$ONEPARM	Quadword	Function decision table routine for I/O request with one parameter
EXE$OPCCUS	Quadword	Opcode reserved to customer exception service routine
EXE$OPCDEC	Quadword	Reserved instruction exception service routine
EXE$OPEN_MSG	Quadword	Open files for SYS$OUTPUT and SYS$ERROR
EXE$OPEN_RDB	Quadword	Open the rights database as necessary
EXE$OPRSNDERL	Quadword	Send an operator message to the error logger
EXE$OUTBLANK	Quadword	Write blank to specified device

Global Symbol	Size	Description of Routine
EXE$OUTCHAR	Quadword	Write character to specified device
EXE$OUTCRLF	Quadword	Write carriage return and line feed to specified device
EXE$OUTCSTRING	Quadword	Write counted string to specified device
EXE$OUTHEX	Quadword	Convert longword to hexadecimal digits and write to specified device
EXE$OUTBYTE	Quadword	Convert byte to hexadecimal digits and write to specified device
EXE$OUTZSTRING	Quadword	Write zero-terminated string to specified device
EXE$PAGRDERR	Quadword	Signal page read error fault
EXE$POWERAST	Quadword	Queue a special kernel mode AST to each process that requested notification of power recovery
EXE$POWERFAIL	Quadword	Powerfail interrupt service routine
EXE$PRCDELMSG	Quadword	Send process termination message to job controller
EXE$PRCPURMSG	Quadword	Send process purge message to job controller
EXE$PROBER	Quadword	Check read accessibility of user buffer
EXE$PROBER_DSC	Quadword	Check read accessibility of user buffer specified by descriptor
EXE$PROBEW	Quadword	Check write accessibility of user buffer
EXE$PROBEW_DSC	Quadword	Check write accessibility of user buffer specified by descriptor
EXE$PROCIMGACT	Quadword	Startup code for processes such as stand-alone SYSGEN
EXE$PROCSTRT	Quadword	Standard process startup code
EXE$PWRTIMCHK	Quadword	Check for reasonable interval since power recovery
EXE$QIOACPPKT	Quadword	Queue an IRP to an ancillary control process or the Files-11 Extended QIO Processor (XQP)
EXE$QIODRVPKT	Quadword	Queue an IRP to a driver's start I/O entry point
EXE$QIORETURN	Quadword	Return from $QIO system service with success status
EXE$QXQPPKT	Quadword	Insert an IRP in the XQP queue and conditionally enter the XQP dispatcher
EXE$RADRMOD	Quadword	Reserved addressing mode exception service routine
EXE$READ	Quadword	Function decision table routine for direct I/O read functions
EXE$READCHK	Quadword	Check buffer for write access and abort I/O on error
EXE$READCHKR	Quadword	Check buffer for write access
EXE$READLOCK	Quadword	Check I/O buffer for write access and lock in memory
EXE$READLOCKR	Quadword	Check I/O buffer for write access and lock in memory, returning via co-routine on error
EXE$REFLECT	Quadword	Reflect an exception from a mode other than kernel
EXE$RESETVEC	Quadword	Reset privileged library vectors
EXE$RESTART	Quadword	Warm restart following power recovery and error halts
EXE$RESTART_ATT	Quadword	Warm restart a secondary processor following power recovery and error halts

Global Symbol	*Size*	*Description of Routine*
EXE$RMSEXH	Quadword	Executive mode exit handler procedure
EXE$RMVTIMQ	Quadword	Remove entry from timer queue entry list
EXE$ROPRAND	Quadword	Reserved operand exception service routine
EXE$SEARCH_RIGHT	Quadword	Search specified rights segment for a given identifier
EXE$SENDMSG	Quadword	Write a message to specified mailbox
EXE$SENSEMODE	Quadword	Function decision table (FDT) routine for IO$_SENSEMODE and IO$_SENSECHAR functions
EXE$SETCHAR	Quadword	FDT routine for IO$_SETCHAR and IO$_SETMODE functions
EXE$SETIME_INT	Quadword	Internal entry point to $SETIME system service
EXE$SETMODE	Quadword	FDT routine for IO$_SETCHAR and IO$_SETMODE functions queued to a driver
EXE$SETOPR	Quadword	Enable specified device as an operator terminal
EXE$SET_RDIPTR	Quadword	Store the address of the rights identifier block in P1 space
EXE$SET_PAGES_READ_ONLY	Quadword	Set protection on system service vector pages to read-only
EXE$SET_PAGES_WRITABLE	Quadword	Set protection on system service vector pages to kernel-write
EXE$SHMCEBDEL	Quadword	Delete (release) master common event block in MA780 shared memory
EXE$SIGTORET	Quadword	Condition handler procedure that turns an exception into an error return
EXE$SNDEVMSG	Quadword	Send device-specific message to specified mailbox
EXE$SNGLEQUOTA	Quadword	Check single-unit resource request and conditionally wait the process
EXE$SSFAIL	Quadword	Signal system service failure exception
EXE$SWAPINIT	Quadword	Initialization code that runs in swapper process
EXE$SWTIMINT	Quadword	IPL 7 interrupt service routine, software timer
EXE$TBIT	Quadword	Trace fault exception service routine
EXE$TIMEOUT	Quadword	Perform periodic functions, including scan for device timeouts
EXE$UBCLKINT	Quadword	Clock interrupt service routine
EXE$VAL_IDNAME	Quadword	Validate identifier name
EXE$WRITE	Quadword	Function decision table routine for direct I/O write functions
EXE$WRITECHK	Quadword	Check buffer for read access and abort I/O on error
EXE$WRITECHKR	Quadword	Check buffer for read access
EXE$WRITELOCK	Quadword	Check I/O buffer for read access and lock in memory
EXE$WRITELOCKR	Quadword	Check I/O buffer for read access and lock in memory, returning via co-routine on error
EXE$WRTMAILBOX	Quadword	Write specified message to mailbox
EXE$ZEROPARM	Quadword	Function decision table routine for I/O request with no parameters
FIL$CVT_DTB	Quadword	Convert decimal to binary
FIL$CVT_HTB	Quadword	Convert hexadecimal to binary
FIL$CVT_OTB	Quadword	Convert octal to binary
FIL$CVTFILNAM	Quadword	Convert file name from ASCII to RAD50

Executive Data Areas

Global Symbol	Size	Description of Routine
FIL$INIWCB	Quadword	Allocate and initialize window control block
FIL$OPENFILE	Quadword	Open file using primitive I/O
FIL$OPENFILE_1	Quadword	Assign device and open file using primitive I/O
FIL$RDWRTLBN	Quadword	Read or write specified logical block from device
IMG$DECODE_IHD	Quadword	Read and decode image header
IMG$GET_NEXT_ISD	Quadword	Get next image section descriptor
INI$ALLOC_CRB	Quadword	Allocate and partly fill a controller request block and spinlock
INI$ALONONPAGED	Quadword	Allocate nonpaged pool; used by EXE$INIT
INI$ALONPAGVAR	Quadword	Allocate nonpaged pool from the variable-length list; used by EXE$INIT
INI$BRK	2 bytes	Routine body—has BPT known to XDELTA
INI$MASTERWAKE	4 bytes	Routine body—awakens XDELTA
INI$RDONLY	Quadword	Change protection on read-only sections of loadable executive images to read-only
INI$WRITABLE	Quadword	Change protection on read-only sections of loadable executive images to kernel-write
IOC$ALOUBAMAP	Quadword	Allocate map registers for transfer described in unit control block fields
IOC$ALOUBAMAPN	Quadword	Allocate specified number of map registers
IOC$ALOUBAMAPSP	Quadword	Allocate a specific set of map registers
IOC$ALOUBMAPRM	Quadword	Permanently allocate map registers
IOC$ALOUBMAPRMN	Quadword	Permanently allocate specified number of map registers
IOC$ALTREQCOM	Quadword	Alternative entry to I/O request complete
IOC$APPLYECC	Quadword	Apply error correction code correction to data read from a disk
IOC$BROADCAST	Quadword	Broadcast to a single local terminal
IOC$BUFPOST	Quadword	Files-11 XQP buffered I/O completion routine
IOC$CANCELIO	Quadword	Cancel I/O on channel
IOC$CHKMBXQUOTA	Quadword	Check quota for creating mailbox
IOC$CHKUCBQUOTA	Quadword	Check quota for creating a unit control block
IOC$CLONE_UCB	Quadword	Copy a template to create a new unit control block and connect it
IOC$CONBRDCST	Quadword	Broadcast emergency message to console
IOC$COPY_UCB	Quadword	Copy a given unit control block
IOC$CREATE_UCB	Quadword	Create a mailbox or network unit control block and link it into the I/O database
IOC$CREDIT_UCB	Quadword	Return quota charged for deleted unit control block
IOC$CTRLINIT	Quadword	Call driver controller initialization routine
IOC$CVTLOGPHY	Quadword	Conditionally convert logical block to physical address
IOC$CVTLOGPHYU	Quadword	Unconditionally convert logical block to physical address
IOC$CVT_DEVNAM	Quadword	Convert a device name and unit number to a physical device name string
IOC$DALLOC_DEV	Quadword	Deallocate device clusterwide
IOC$DALLOC_DMT	Quadword	Deallocate device on dismount
IOC$DEBIT_UCB	Quadword	Record master process ID charged for created unit control block

Global Symbol	Size	Description of Routine
IOC$DELETE_UCB	Quadword	Delete unit control block if its reference count is zero
IOC$DIAGBUFILL	Quadword	Write final device information into diagnostic buffer
IOC$DIRPOST1	Quadword	Alternative entry point to direct I/O special kernel mode AST
IOC$DISMOUNT	Quadword	Dismount a mounted mass storage volume
IOC$FFCHAN	Quadword	Search the I/O channel table for a free channel
IOC$FILSPT	Quadword	Fill system page table entry with page table entry mapping user buffer
IOC$FREE_UCB	Quadword	Deallocate nonpaged pool for a unit control block being deleted and its associated object rights block
IOC$GETBYTE	Quadword	Get one byte of data from user buffer
IOC$INITBUFWIND	Quadword	Initialize one-page window into user buffer
IOC$INITDRV	Quadword	Initialize database for a specific device driver
IOC$INITIATE	Quadword	Initiate next I/O request on device
IOC$IOPOST	Quadword	IPL 4 interrupt service routine, I/O postprocessing
IOC$LAST_CHAN	Quadword	Handle deassignment of last channel to a device
IOC$LAST_CHAN_AMBX	Quadword	Handle deassignment of last channel to a mailbox associated with a device
IOC$LINK_UCB	Quadword	Link a new unit control block to device data block chain
IOC$LOADMBAMAP	Quadword	Load MASSBUS adapter map registers to describe I/O buffer
IOC$LOADUBAMAP	Quadword	Load UNIBUS adapter map registers to describe I/O buffer
IOC$LOADUBAMAPA	Quadword	Alternative entry point to IOC$LOADUBAMAP
IOC$LOADUBAMAPN	Quadword	Load UNIBUS adapter map registers specified by register input
IOC$LOCK_DEV	Quadword	Take out clusterwide device lock
IOC$LUBAUDAMAP	Quadword	Load UNIBUS adapter map registers for UDA port
IOC$MAPVBLK	Quadword	Map virtual block number to logical block number
IOC$MNTVER	Quadword	Assist driver with mount verification
IOC$MOVFRUSER	Quadword	Move data from user buffer
IOC$MOVFRUSER1	Quadword	Internal entry point to IOC$MOVFRUSER
IOC$MOVFRUSER2	Quadword	Internal entry point to IOC$MOVFRUSER
IOC$MOVTOUSER	Quadword	Move data to user buffer
IOC$MOVTOUSER1	Quadword	Internal entry point to IOC$MOVTOUSER
IOC$MOVTOUSER2	Quadword	Internal entry point to IOC$MOVTOUSER
IOC$PARSDEVNAM	Quadword	Parse device name string
IOC$PTETOPFN	Quadword	Get page frame number associated with invalid page table entry
IOC$PUTBYTE	Quadword	Write one byte of data to user buffer
IOC$QNXTSEG	Quadword	Queue next segment of virtual I/O request
IOC$QNXTSEG1	Quadword	Alternative entry point to IOC$QNXTSEG
IOC$REINITDRV	Quadword	Reinitialize driver database after reloading a device driver
IOC$RELCHAN	Quadword	Release device's controller
IOC$RELDATAP	Quadword	Release buffered data path

Global Symbol	Size	Description of Routine
IOC$RELDATAPUDA	Quadword	Release buffered data path specified by class driver request packet
IOC$RELMAPREG	Quadword	Release map registers
IOC$RELMAPUDA	Quadword	Release map registers described by class driver request packet
IOC$RELOC_DDT	Quadword	Relocate the driver dispatch table
IOC$RELSCHAN	Quadword	Release device's secondary controller
IOC$REQCOM	Quadword	Complete a device's I/O request and start the next
IOC$REQDATAP	Quadword	Request buffered data path
IOC$REQDATAPNW	Quadword	Request buffered data path and return if unavailable
IOC$REQDATAPUDA	Quadword	Request buffered data path using information in class driver request packet and return if unavailable
IOC$REQMAPREG	Quadword	Request map registers for transfer described by unit control block fields
IOC$REQMAPUDA	Quadword	Request map registers for transfer described by class driver request packet fields
IOC$REQPCHANH	Quadword	Allocate device's primary controller with high priority
IOC$REQPCHANL	Quadword	Allocate device's primary controller with low priority
IOC$REQSCHANH	Quadword	Allocate device's secondary controller with high priority
IOC$REQSCHANL	Quadword	Allocate device's secondary controller with low priority
IOC$RETURN	Quadword	Null routine consisting of RSB
IOC$SCAN_IODB	Quadword	Scan the I/O database and return next block
IOC$SCAN_IODB_2P	Quadword	Scan the I/O database, including dual-path information, and return next block
IOC$SEARCH	Quadword	Search the I/O database for specified device
IOC$SEARCHALL	Quadword	Do a generic search of the I/O database for a local device
IOC$SEARCHCONT	Quadword	Continue a device search started by IOC$SEARCHINT
IOC$SEARCHDEV	Quadword	Search the I/O database for a specific physical device
IOC$SEARCHINT	Quadword	Search the I/O database for specified device
IOC$SENSEDISK	Quadword	Function decision table routine for IO$_SENSECHAR and IO$_SENSEMODE to a disk
IOC$SEVER_UCB	Quadword	Unlink a unit control block from its device data block and controller request block
IOC$TESTUNIT	Quadword	Check unit control block against search rules
IOC$THREADCRB	Quadword	Insert controller request block into controller request block timeout list
IOC$TRANDEVNAM	Quadword	Translate logical device name
IOC$UNITINIT	Quadword	Call driver unit initialization routine
IOC$UNLOCK	Quadword	Unlock the I/O database mutex
IOC$UNLOCK_DEV	Quadword	Release the clusterwide device lock

1174

Global Symbol	Size	Description of Routine
IOC$UPDATRANSP	Quadword	Update transfer parameters after a partly successful I/O transfer
IOC$VERIFYCHAN	Quadword	Verify an I/O channel number
IOC$WAKACP	Quadword	Queue an IRP to an ancillary control process or the Files-11 XQP and wake it if the queue was empty
IOC$WFIKPCH	Quadword	Wait for interrupt, not releasing the device controller
IOC$WFIRLCH	Quadword	Wait for interrupt, releasing the device controller
LCK$BREAK_DEADLOCK	Quadword	Break a lock deadlock
LCK$CHECK_RSB	Quadword	Deallocate a resource block if necessary
LCK$COMP_GGMODE	Quadword	Compute lock group grant mode
LCK$CVTNOTQED	Quadword	Requeue a granted lock whose convert request cannot be granted
LCK$CVT_GRANTED	Quadword	Grant a lock conversion
LCK$DEALLOC_RSB	Quadword	Deallocate a resource block with no locks
LCK$DEQLOCK	Quadword	Dequeue a lock
LCK$DLCKEXIT	Quadword	Return from lock deadlock detection
LCK$EXTEND_IDTBLW	Quadword	Extend the lock ID table, waiting if there is insufficient nonpaged pool
LCK$GRANTCVTS	Quadword	Try to grant locks in the wait or conversion queue
LCK$GRANTWTRS	Quadword	Try to grant waiting locks
LCK$GRANT_LOCK	Quadword	Grant a lock request
LCK$GRANT_LOCK_ALT	Quadword	Alternative entry point to LCK$GRANT_LOCK
LCK$GRANT_REM	Quadword	Grant a remote lock request
LCK$LOCAL_CVT	Quadword	Convert a local lock that is the only one in granted or conversion queue
LCK$LOCAL_LOCK	Quadword	Handle local lock requests
LCK$NOT_QUEUED	Quadword	Deallocate lock ID and return
LCK$QUEUECVT	Quadword	Insert a lock on the conversion queue
LCK$QUEUED_EXIT	Quadword	Return after successfully queuing a lock request
LCK$QUEUEWAIT	Quadword	Insert a lock on the wait queue
LCK$QUEUE_BLKAST	Quadword	Queue local blocking ASTs
LCK$QUEUE_BLOCKAST	Quadword	Queue local blocking ASTs or send message to other system
LCK$QUEUE_REM	Quadword	Insert a remote lock request on a wait queue
LCK$SEARCHDLCK	Quadword	Search and break lock deadlocks
LCK$SRCH_HSHTBL	Quadword	Search hash table for matching resource name
LCK$SRCH_RESDLCK	Quadword	Search for resource deadlocks
LCK$SYNC_EXIT	Quadword	Complete a synchronously granted lock request
LKI$SEARCH_BLOCKEDBY	Quadword	Search for locks blocked by the current lock
LKI$SEARCH_BLOCKING	Quadword	Search for locks blocking the current lock
LNM$CHECK_PROT	Quadword	Check access to a logical name table
LNM$CONTSEARCH	Quadword	Find the next logical name that might match
LNM$DELETE_HASH	Quadword	Delete all logical names in a hash table
LNM$DELETE_LNMB	Quadword	Delete a logical name block
LNM$FIRSTTAB	Quadword	Search for the first logical name table name that matches
LNM$HASH	Quadword	Hash a logical name
LNM$INSLOGTAB	Quadword	Insert a logical name in a logical name table

Global Symbol	*Size*	*Description of Routine*
LNM$LOCKR	Quadword	Lock the logical name table mutex for read access
LNM$LOCKW	Quadword	Lock the logical name table mutex for write access
LNM$PRESEARCH	Quadword	Find the first logical name that might match
LNM$SEARCH_ONE	Quadword	Search for a specified logical name and return translation
LNM$SETUP	Quadword	Initialize recursive logical name table name processing
LNM$TABLE	Quadword	Translate a logical name table name
LNM$UNLOCK	Quadword	Unlock the logical name table mutex
MMG$ALCPHD	Quadword	Allocate space in the process header for a section table entry or working set list entries
MMG$ALCSTX	Quadword	Allocate a section table index from specified section table
MMG$ALC_PGFLVBN	Quadword	Allocate a specific set of blocks in a page file
MMG$ALLOCONTIG	Quadword	Allocate physically contiguous pages
MMG$ALLOCPAGFIL1	Quadword	Allocate a cluster of pages from specified file, maintaining the reserved page count
MMG$ALLOCPAGFIL2	Quadword	Allocate the first contiguous set of blocks from specified page file, maintaining the reserved page count
MMG$ALLOCPFN	Quadword	Allocate a page from the free page list
MMG$ALLOCSWPAREA	Quadword	Allocate a swap area in a swap or page file
MMG$ALOSHMGSD	Quadword	Allocate an MA780 shared memory global section descriptor
MMG$ALOSHMPAG	Quadword	Allocate MA780 shared memory pages for a global section
MMG$CALCSWAPSIZE	Quadword	Calculate process swap size
MMG$CEFTRNLOG	Quadword	Translate a logical name for a common event cluster
MMG$CLR_BITMAP	Quadword	Clear bits in the MA780 shared memory global page bitmap
MMG$CREDEL	Quadword	Common per-page loop for creation/deletion /lock/unlock
MMG$CREPAG	Quadword	Create a page of process address space
MMG$CRETVA	Quadword	Internal entry point to $CRETVA system service
MMG$DALCBAKSTORE	Quadword	Free a page's backing store
MMG$DALCPAGFIL	Quadword	Deallocate specified page in specified page file
MMG$DALCSTX	Quadword	Deallocate a section table entry
MMG$DALCSTXSCN	Quadword	Scan a given process header for section table entries that can be deallocated
MMG$DALCSTXSCN1	Quadword	Scan the system header for section table entries that can be deallocated
MMG$DALLOCPFN	Quadword	Deallocate a page of physical memory
MMG$DEALLOCPAGFIL	Quadword	Deallocate specified blocks in a page file, maintaining the reserved page count
MMG$DECPHDREF	Quadword	Decrement the process header reference count
MMG$DECPHDREF1	Quadword	Subentry point to MMG$DECPHDREF
MMG$DECPTREF	Quadword	Decrement the reference count for specified page table entry
MMG$DECSECREF	Quadword	Decrement a section table reference count

Global Symbol	*Size*	*Description of Routine*
MMG$DECSHMREF	Quadword	Decrement an MA780 shared memory global section descriptor page table entry reference count
MMG$DELCONPFN	Quadword	Delete former virtual contents of a page of physical memory
MMG$DELGBLSEC	Quadword	Delete a global section
MMG$DELGBLWCB	Quadword	Deaccess section files on the deleted section window control block list
MMG$DELPAG	Quadword	Delete a page of process address space
MMG$DELPFNLST	Quadword	Remove a page frame number from page list and delete its former virtual contents
MMG$DELSHMGS	Quadword	Delete an MA780 shared memory global section
MMG$DELWSLEPPG	Quadword	Delete specified process page working set list entry
MMG$DELWSLEX	Quadword	Delete specified working set list entry
MMG$QUEUE_GSD_ CLEAN	Quadword	Queue an AST to a process to clean up delete-pending global section descriptor queue
MMG$EXPKSTK	Quadword	Expand the kernel stack
MMG$EXPREG	Quadword	Internal entry point to $EXPREG system service
MMG$EXTRADYNWS	Quadword	Calculate extra dynamic working set count
MMG$FAST_CREATE	Quadword	Expand the process or control region by the requested size, all at once
MMG$FIND1STGSD	Quadword	Find first MA780 shared memory global section based on translating the shared memory logical name
MMG$FINDGSDPFN	Quadword	Find the global section descriptor (GSD) that maps a specific MA780 shared memory page frame number
MMG$FINDGSNOTRN	Quadword	Find the GSD when the normal search path has failed
MMG$FINDSHB	Quadword	Find the MA780 shared memory block for a specific MA780 shared memory
MMG$FINDSHD	Quadword	Find the MA780 shared memory containing a particular GSD
MMG$FREEGSD	Quadword	Release any MA780 shared memory GSDs no longer in use
MMG$FREWSLE	Quadword	Select a working set list entry and release the page that occupied it
MMG$FREWSLX	Quadword	Free specified working set list entry
MMG$FRE_TRYSKIP	Quadword	Subentry point to MMG$FREWSLX
MMG$GETGSNAM	Quadword	Get a global section name and MA780 shared memory name
MMG$GETNXTGSD	Quadword	Get the next GSD in the search sequence
MMG$GETPTIPAG	Quadword	Get page table information for specified page
MMG$GSDMTXULK	Quadword	Unlock the GSD mutex
MMG$GSDSCN	Quadword	Scan the GSD queue for a section with specified name
MMG$GSDTRNLOG	Quadword	Translate a global section logical name
MMG$IMGRESET	Quadword	Reset the process section table and working set list and invoke RM$RESET after deleting image pages

Global Symbol	*Size*	*Description of Routine*
MMG$INADRINI	Quadword	Get the input address range and initialize the return address range argument
MMG$INCPTREF	Quadword	Increment the reference count for specified page table entry
MMG$INCSHMREF	Quadword	Increment an MA780 shared memory global section descriptor page table entry reference count
MMG$INIBLDPKT	Quadword	Perform initialization for EXE$BLDPKT*xx* routines
MMG$ININEWPFN	Quadword	Allocate a page of physical memory and initialize its page frame number (PFN) database fields
MMG$INSPFNH	Quadword	Insert a PFN at head of specified list
MMG$INSPFNT	Quadword	Insert a PFN at tail of specified list
MMG$IN_REGION	Quadword	Test whether address space overlaps existing space
MMG$IOLOCK	Quadword	Lock an I/O buffer into memory
MMG$IOLOCKPAG	Quadword	Lock a page of an I/O buffer into memory
MMG$LCKULKPAG	Quadword	Lock/unlock single page in working set or memory
MMG$LOCKPGTB	Quadword	Lock a page table page by incrementing its reference count
MMG$MAKEWSLE	Quadword	Make a working set list entry for specified virtual page
MMG$MBXTRNLOG	Quadword	Translate a logical name for a mailbox
MMG$MOVPTLOCK	Quadword	Lock into the working set list a page table page with window page table entry
MMG$MOVPTLOCK1	Quadword	Alternative entry point to MMG$MOVPTLOCK
MMG$MPWCHECK	Quadword	Test whether modified page writing should start
MMG$PAGEFAULT	Quadword	Translation-not-valid exception service routine
MMG$PAGETYPE	Quadword	Determine page type from page table entry bits
MMG$PGFLTWAIT	Quadword	Insert the PCB into specified wait queue following a page fault
MMG$PTEADRCHK	Quadword	Return the system virtual address of the page table entry corresponding to a given address
MMG$PTEINDX	Quadword	Return the longword postindex into the process header corresponding to a given virtual address
MMG$PTEINDXCHK	Quadword	Alternative entry to MMG$PTEINDX that bugchecks if address is not mapped
MMG$PTEREF	Quadword	Return the system virtual address of the page table entry corresponding to a given address, faulting the page table page if necessary
MMG$PURGWSSCN	Quadword	Scan the working set list for pages in specified address range to be deleted
MMG$READ_GSD	Quadword	Read from disk the pages of a newly created MA780 shared memory global section
MMG$REFCNTNEG	Quadword	Generate REFCNTNEG fatal bugcheck
MMG$RELPFN	Quadword	Release a page frame number (PFN) to the modified or free page list
MMG$REMPFN	Quadword	Remove a specific PFN from specified page list
MMG$REMPFNH	Quadword	Remove a PFN from head of specified page list
MMG$RESRCWAIT	Quadword	Place the process into a wait for a resource needed for its faulted page to become valid
MMG$RETADRINI	Quadword	Initialize a return address range argument

Global Symbol	Size	Description of Routine
MMG$RETRANGE	Quadword	Return address range information and perform common exit processing
MMG$RET_BYT_QUOTA	Quadword	Return byte count quota to file owner for a window control block converted to a shared one
MMG$RLPFNSAVPTE	Quadword	Release the page frame number from a global demand zero page
MMG$SCNWSLX	Quadword	Scan working set list for specified virtual address
MMG$SETPRTPAG	Quadword	Set protection on specified page
MMG$SET_BITMAP	Quadword	Set bits in the MA780 shared memory global page bitmap
MMG$SHMTXLK	Quadword	Lock the MA780 shared memory mutex for write access and acquire shared memory bit lock
MMG$SHMTXULK	Quadword	Unlock the MA780 shared memory mutex access and release shared memory bit lock
MMG$SHRCNTNEG	Quadword	Generate a SHRCNTNEG fatal bugcheck
MMG$SHRINKWS	Quadword	Shrink specified working set list
MMG$SUBSECREF	Quadword	Subtract a given number from section table reference count
MMG$SVAPTECHK	Quadword	Return system virtual address of page table entry corresponding to specified virtual address
MMG$SVPCTX	Quadword	Save process context following an unsatisfied page fault
MMG$SWAPWSLE	Quadword	Swap working set list entries
MMG$TRY_ALL	Quadword	Test whether region can be expanded to requested size and adjust page file quota
MMG$ULKGBLWSLE	Quadword	Unlock a global page from working set
MMG$UNIQUEGSD	Quadword	Check that an MA780 shared memory global section descriptor is unique
MMG$UNLOCK	Quadword	Unlock I/O buffer pages
MMG$UPDSECAST	Quadword	$UPDSEC system service I/O completion special kernel mode AST
MMG$VALIDATEGSD	Quadword	Validate an MA780 shared memory global section descriptor
MMG$VFYSECFLG	Quadword	Verify that section flags contain only user-definable flags
MMG$WRITE_GSD	Quadword	Write to disk the pages of an MA780 shared memory global section
MMG$WRTMFYPAG	Quadword	Write pages from the modified page list
MMG$WRTPGSBAK	Quadword	Write section pages to disk, part of $UPDSEC system service
MMG$WSLEPFN	Quadword	Get page frame number from working set list entry
MMG$WSPEAKCHK	Quadword	Enable or disable working set peak checking
MT$CHECK_ACCESS	Quadword	Check for write access to a magtape
NSA$ARGLST_IMGNAM	Quadword	Insert the image name packet entry in caller's argument list
NSA$EVENT_AUDIT	Quadword	Write a journal record for an auditable system event
PFM$GETBUF	Quadword	Return a buffer of page fault monitoring information to caller

Global Symbol	Size	Description of Routine
PFM$MON	Quadword	Record information about a page fault being monitored
PFM$PURGE	Quadword	Deallocate to nonpaged pool process page fault monitoring buffers
PMS$ABORT_RQ	Quadword	Record aborting of I/O request in performance data buffer
PMS$END_IO	Quadword	Record end of I/O transaction in performance data buffer
PMS$END_RQ	Quadword	Record end of I/O request in performance data buffer
PMS$START_IO	Quadword	Record start of I/O transaction in performance data buffer
PMS$START_RQ	Quadword	Record start of I/O request in performance data buffer
RM$DIRCACHE_BLKAST	Quadword	System blocking AST routine for RMS directory cache
RM$RESET	Quadword	Reset process's image I/O segment
RM$SET	Quadword	Initialize process's image I/O segment
SCH$ASTDEL	Quadword	IPL 2 interrupt service routine, AST delivery
SCH$CHSE	Quadword	Change process scheduling state to computable
SCH$CHSEP	Quadword	Change process scheduling state to computable and set priority as specified
SCH$CLREF	Quadword	Clear specified event flag
SCH$CLREFR	Quadword	Clear specified event flag and return via RSB
SCH$FORCEDEXIT	Quadword	Queue $FORCEX AST to process
SCH$GETEFC	Quadword	Compute address of event flag cluster
SCH$IOLOCKR	Quadword	Lock the I/O database mutex for read access
SCH$IOLOCKW	Quadword	Lock the I/O database mutex for write access
SCH$IOUNLOCK	Quadword	Unlock the I/O database mutex
SCH$LOCKR	Quadword	Lock a specified mutex for read access
SCH$LOCKW	Quadword	Lock a specified mutex for write access
SCH$LOCKWNOWAIT	Quadword	Lock a mutex for write access; do not wait if it is not free
SCH$NEWLVL	Quadword	Compute AST level for the current process
SCH$OSWPSCHED	Quadword	Select processes to shrink or outswap
SCH$PIXSCAN	Quadword	Give selected computable processes a priority boost
SCH$POSTEF	Quadword	Set specified event flag
SCH$QAST	Quadword	Queue an AST to a process
SCH$QEND	Quadword	Perform quantum-end processing for the current process
SCH$RAVAIL	Quadword	Declare scheduling resource available for waiting processes
SCH$REMOVACB	Quadword	Remove an AST control block queued to a process
SCH$RESCHED	Quadword	IPL 3 interrupt service routine, rescheduling
SCH$RSE	Quadword	Report scheduling event for a process
SCH$RWAIT	Quadword	Place a process into resource wait
SCH$SCHED	Quadword	Schedule new process for execution
SCH$SWAPACBS	Quadword	Replace one enqueued AST control block with another
SCH$SWPWAKE	Quadword	Conditionally wake the swapper process

Global Symbol	Size	Description of Routine
SCH$UNLOCK	Quadword	Unlock specified mutex
SCH$UNWAIT	Quadword	Remove a PCB from a scheduling wait queue
SCH$WAIT	Quadword	Clean kernel stack, insert PCB in wait queue, and place process into a wait state
SCH$WAITK	Quadword	Subentry point of SCH$WAIT
SCH$WAITL	Quadword	Subentry point of SCH$WAIT
SCH$WAITM	Quadword	Subentry point of SCH$WAIT
SCH$WAKE	Quadword	Wake specified process
XDT$BPT	Quadword	XDELTA breakpoint fault handler entry
XDT$IBRK	Quadword	Address of initial breakpoint
XDT$TBIT	Quadword	XDELTA TBIT handler
XDT$LOADBASE	Quadword	Base of loadable CPU-dependent code
XQP$BLOCK_ROUTINE	Quadword	Block further XQP activity
XQP$DEQBLOCKER	Quadword	Dequeue blocking lock
XQP$FCBSTALE	Quadword	Blocking routine to mark file control block as stale
XQP$REL_QUOTA	Quadword	Release quota cache entry
XQP$UNLOCK_CACHE	Quadword	Release cache contents and unlock
XQP$UNLOCK_QUOTA	Quadword	Release lock on quota cache entry
LDR$ALLOC_PT	Quadword	Allocate system page table entries
LDR$DEALLOC_PT	Quadword	Deallocate system page table entries
LDR$LOAD_NONPAGED	Quadword	Load nonpaged section of loadable executive image
LDR$LOAD_IMAGE	Quadword	Map and load a loadable executive image
LDR$INIT_ALL	Quadword	Invoke initialization routines of all loaded executive images
MMG$INCSECREFL	Quadword	Acquire MMG spinlock and increment section reference count
MMG$ADDSECREFL	Quadword	Acquire MMG spinlock and add to section reference count
MMG$DECSECREFL	Quadword	Acquire MMG spinlock and decrement section reference count
MMG$SUBSECREFL	Quadword	Acquire MMG spinlock and subtract from section reference count
SMP$ACQUIRE	Quadword	Acquire a spinlock or fork lock and force synchronization
SMP$ACQUIREL	Quadword	Acquire a device lock and force synchronization
SMP$RESTORE	Quadword	Conditionally release a spinlock or fork lock
SMP$RESTOREL	Quadword	Conditionally release a device lock
SMP$RELEASE	Quadword	Release a spinlock or fork lock
SMP$RELEASEL	Quadword	Release a device lock
SMP$REI_CHECK	Quadword	Check spinlock database consistency
SMP$NOLOCKS	Quadword	Make sure no spinlocks are held
SMP$CHKLOCK	Quadword	Make sure spinlock is owned before proceeding
SMP$ALLOC_SPL	Quadword	Allocate a spinlock
SMP$INIT_SPL	Quadword	Initialize a spinlock
SMP$GET_CURPCB	Quadword	Return current PCB address
SMP$SWITCH_CPU	Quadword	Switch to another CPU based on device affinity
SMP$IOPOST_IRP	Quadword	Place IRP on per-processor I/O postprocessing queue
SMP$INVALID	Quadword	Invalidate a single translation buffer entry

Global Symbol	Size	Description of Routine
EXE$INSIOQC	Quadword	Insert IRP in unit control block pending-I/O queue or invoke IOC$INITIATE and release fork lock
SMP$ACQNOIPL	Quadword	Acquire a device lock and assume IPL is already at the correct level
LCK$EXTEND_IDTBL	Quadword	Extend the lock ID table
SMP$ADJUST_IPL	Quadword	Adjust the IPL of a lock
XDT$CPU_WAIT	Quadword	Wait for release of XDELTA interlock
MMG$LOCK_SYSTEM_PAGES	Quadword	Dynamically lock pages into system working set for a bounded code segment
SCH$LOCKWEXEC	Quadword	From system context, lock the specified mutex for write access
SCH$LOCKREXEC	Quadword	From system context, lock the specified mutex for read access
SCH$UNLOCKEXEC	Quadword	From system context, unlock the specified mutex
SMP$CALCAFF	Quadword	Calculate process affinity mask
SMP$CALCAFF_INCLUSIVE	Quadword	Calculate process affinity mask, including PCB$L_CPU_ID in calculation if PCB$V_HARDAFF is set
SMP$SETAFF	Quadword	Set/clear hard affinity for process
SMP$SETCAP	Quadword	Set/clear capability-based affinity for process
EXE$CHECK_VERSION	Quadword	Check for mismatch of image linked with SYS.STB against current running system
IOC$CHECK_HWM	Quadword	Do highwater mark processing for a write request
EXE$DVI_FREEBLOCKS	Quadword	Fetch device free block count from volume lock block
MMG$ALLOCPFN_NO_DB	Quadword	Allocate a page frame number from the list of pages not described in the page frame number database
LMF$RUNDOWN	Quadword	Reserved
MMG$DALCPAGFIL-DUMP	Quadword	Deallocate page file pages formerly occupied by a crash dump
MPW$ALLOCPAGFIL1	Quadword	Allocate a cluster of pages from specified page file
MPW$ALLOCPAGFIL2	Quadword	Allocate the first contiguous set of blocks from specified page file
MPW$DEALLOCPAGFIL	Quadword	Deallocate specified blocks in a page or swap file
MMG$ASNPRCPGFL	Quadword	Assign an additional page file to a process
MMG$ASNPRCPGFLP	Quadword	Assign the first page file to a process
MMG$RASNPRCPGFL	Quadword	Reassign a process to other page files
MMG$RSRVPRCPGFL	Quadword	Reserve pages from the process's current page file unless it is overcommitted
MMG$RSRVPRCPGFL2	Quadword	Reserve pages from the process's current page file
MMG$DASNPRCPGFL	Quadword	Deassign specified process page file
MMG$DASNPRCPGFLS	Quadword	Deassign all process page files
MMG$DALCPRCPGFL	Quadword	Deallocate specified page to specified page file, updating page file accounting information
ARCH$PTOLEMY_HOOK	Quadword	Reserved
LKI$SEARCH_LOCKS	Quadword	Search for all locks on a given resource
LKI$STANDARD_INFO	Quadword	Collect standard information on a lock
SCH$ONE_SEC	Quadword	Perform periodic scheduling functions
MMG$SWITCH_PRCPGFL	Quadword	Select process page file and reserve space after a failure to assign backing store

Global Symbol	Size	Description of Routine
LDR$ALTERNATIVE_LOAD	Quadword	Conditionally load executive images listed in VMS$SYSTEM_IMAGES.DATA file
WP$CREATE_WATCHPOINT	Quadword	Create specified watchpoint
WP$DELETE_WATCHPOINT	Quadword	Delete an existing watchpoint
SMP$INIT_SANITY	Quadword	Initialize symmetric multiprocessing sanity timer pointer in CPU database
EXE$JIB_WAIT	Quadword	Place a process into wait for job information block resource
EXE$JIB_AVAIL	Quadword	Declare job information block resource available for waiting processes
EXE$DEBIT_BYTCNT_ALO	Quadword	Debit JIB$L_BYTCNT, waiting if insufficient quota, and allocate pool
EXE$DEBIT_BYTCNT_BYTLM_ALO	Quadword	Debit JIB$L_BYTCNT and JIB$L_BYTLM, waiting if insufficient quota, and allocate pool
EXE$DEBIT_BYTCNT	Quadword	Debit JIB$L_BYTCNT, waiting if insufficient quota
EXE$DEBIT_BYTCNT_BYTLM	Quadword	Debit JIB$L_BYTCNT and JIB$L_BYTLM, waiting if insufficient quota
EXE$CREDIT_BYTCNT	Quadword	Return JIB$L_BYTCNT quota charge
EXE$CREDIT_BYTCNT_BYTLM	Quadword	Return quota charged to JIB$L_BYTCNT and JIB$L_BYTLM
SMP$TIMEOUT	Quadword	SMP timeout processing routine
EXE$DEBIT_BYTCNT_NW	Quadword	Debit JIB$L_BYTCNT, returning error if insufficient quota
EXE$DEBIT_BYTCNT_BYTLM_NW	Quadword	Debit JIB$L_BYTCNT and JIB$L_BYTLM, returning error if insufficient quota
MMG$ADDPRCPGFL	Quadword	Assign a process to an additional page file
MMG$LOCK_SYSTEM_PAGES_CALL	Quadword	Dynamically lock pages into the system working set for a bounded code sequence, using call interface
MMG$UNLOCK_SYSTEM_PAGES_CALL	Quadword	Unlock pages from the system working set, using call interface
SMP$SHUTDOWN_CPU	Quadword	Final actions associated with stopping a CPU
MMG$DEALLOCSWP-AREA	Quadword	Deallocate a process's swap space
SMP$INITIATE_BENIGN	Quadword	Initiate a benign state
SMP$TERMINATE_BENIGN	Quadword	Leave a benign state
SMP$ENTER_BENIGN	Quadword	Reserved
MMG$ALLOCSWPAREA2	Quadword	Allocate swap space using free space description built by MMG$ALLOCPFLMAP
MMG$ALLOCPFLMAP	Quadword	Allocate and initialize a page and swap file mapping window that describes free space
MMG$DEALLOCSWP-AREA2	Quadword	Deallocate swap space using free space description built by MMG$ALLOCPFLMAP
EXE$RESETVEC1	Quadword	Reset privileged library vectors
IOC$POST_IRP	Quadword	Insert IRP on I/O postprocessing queue and request interrupt
RMS$GET_SPACE	Quadword	Get virtual memory for an RMS extension

Global Symbol	Size	Description of Routine
RMS$RETURN_SPACE	Quadword	Return virtual memory from an RMS extension
RMS$GET_EF	Quadword	Get the synchronization event flag
RMS$STALL_THREAD	Quadword	Stall current execution thread
RMS$RESTART_THREAD	Quadword	Reserved
RMS$LOCK_RECORD	Quadword	Lock designated record
RMS$UNLOCK_RECORD	Quadword	Unlock designated record
RMS$IS_RECORD_ LOCKED	Quadword	Check for conflicting lock
RMS$IS_RECORD_ WRITELOCKED	Quadword	Check for conflicting lock
RMS$GET_BUFFER	Quadword	Get a data buffer
RMS$RELEASE_BUFFER	Quadword	Release a previously obtained buffer
RMS$OPEN_JOURNAL	Quadword	Open a journal file
RMS$CLOSE_JOURNAL	Quadword	Close a journal file
RMS$WRITE_JOURNAL_ ENTRY	Quadword	Write a journal entry
RMS$FLUSH_JOURNAL_ ENTRIES	Quadword	Flush stacked journal data
RMS$INIT_EXTENSION	Quadword	Register an RMS extension with the base RMS
RMS$DELETE_REC_AT_ RP	Quadword	Delete current record
RMS$FIND_REC_AT_NRP	Quadword	Find next record
RMS$GET_REC_AT_NRP	Quadword	Get next record
RMS$PUT_REC_AT_NRP	Quadword	Insert next record
RMS$SCAN_XAB_CHAIN	Quadword	Scan extended attribute blocks
RMS$UPDATE_REC_AT_ RP	Quadword	Update current record
RMS$UNSUPPORTED	Quadword	Declare operation unsupported
EXE$PROC_ADP_ INTVEC	Quadword	Reserved
EXE$PROC_ADP_CRB	Quadword	Reserved
EXE$PROC_LOAD_ VOLUME	Quadword	Reserved
ACF$PROC_ADP	Quadword	Reserved
EXE$NETWORK_ASSIGN	Quadword	Assign channel to network device
MMG$INIT_PGFLQUOTA	Quadword	Charge page count against job information block page file quota
MMG$MORE_PGFL- QUOTA	Quadword	Alternative entry point to MMG$INIT_ PGFLQUOTA
MMG$RET_PGFLQUOTA	Quadword	Return charged page file quota to job information block
EXE$READ_SYSTIME	Quadword	Reserved
EXE$WRITE_SYSTIME	Quadword	Reserved
SMP$SETUP_PFORK	Quadword	Set up for fork to primary
SMP$FORK_TO_ PRIMARY	Quadword	Migrate work packet to primary CPU
EXE$COPY_ARB	Quadword	Create a copy of an access rights block (ARB)
EXE$CLEANUP_ARB	Quadword	Deallocate any external structures from an ARB
EXE$DELETE_ARB	Quadword	Delete an ARB
EXE$HOOKUP_ARB	Quadword	Connect an ARB to a PCB
SMP$WRITE_OPA0	Quadword	Fork routine to broadcast message to console

Global Symbol	Size	Description of Routine
8 reserved vectors	Quadword	Reserved
SCH$REQUIRE_ CAPABILITY	Quadword	Add a capability to a process's required list
SCH$RELEASE_ CAPABILITY	Quadword	Remove a capability from a process's required list
SCH$ADD_CPU_CAP	Quadword	Add a capability to a CPU's capability list
SCH$REMOVE_CPU_CAP	Quadword	Remove a capability from a CPU's capability list
SCH$ACQUIRE_ AFFINITY	Quadword	Acquire implicit affinity for a specific CPU
SCH$REMOVE_AFFINITY	Quadword	Remove a process's implicit affinity for a specific CPU
SCH$CHANGE_CUR_ PRIORITY	Quadword	Modify the priority of the current process
SCH$CUR_TO_COM	Quadword	Make the current process computable
CWPS$PARSE_PRCNAM	Quadword	Separate a process name into its component parts
EXE$ALOP0IMAG	Quadword	Allocate memory from process allocation region
EXE$CHECK_PCB_PRIV	Quadword	Check the ability of one process to affect another
EXE$PSCAN_CHECKCTX	Quadword	Validate process scan context block
EXE$PSCAN_DEALCTX	Quadword	Deallocate process scan context block
EXE$PSCAN_IMGRESET	Quadword	Reset process scan context block
EXE$PSCAN_LOCKCTX	Quadword	Lock process scan context block
EXE$PSCAN_NEXT_PID	Quadword	Scan for next process
IOC$SCAN_IODB_ USRCTX	Quadword	Scan I/O database for next device
EXE$MATCH_NAME	Quadword	Wildcard string match
DDTM$GET_CURRENT_ TID	Quadword	Reserved
DDTM$SET_CURRENT_ TID	Quadword	Reserved
IMG$ADD_PRIVILEGED_ VECTOR	Quadword	Install a change mode, rundown, or message vector
NET$VEC_RESERVE1	Quadword	First of 32 quadwords reserved for DECnet/VAX
LDR$UNLOAD_IMAGE	Quadword	Remove executive image from memory
LDR$FINAL_UNLOAD	Quadword	Reserved
MMG$DINSPAGSWPFIL	Quadword	Deinstall a page or swap file
EXE$PROC_IDLE	Quadword	Reserved
ERL$DEVINFO	Quadword	Log an error message without updating unit control block error count
LNM$SEARCHLOG	Quadword	Search for a logical name
2 reserved vectors	Quadword	Reserved
EXE$EMULAT_REFLECT	Quadword	Reflect an exception from a mode other than kernel
exe_success_rsb	8 bytes	Local routine body—to return success status

C.1.3   **Nonpaged System Data Area ($$$$$NONPAGED_DATA)**

Module SYSTEM_DATA_CELLS defines this area.

Global Symbol	Size	Description of Data
PFN$AL_HEAD	3 longwords	Pointers to the heads of the free, modified, and bad page lists
PFN$AL_TAIL	3 longwords	Pointers to the tails of the free, modified, and bad page lists
SCH$GL_FREECNT	Longword	Free page count
SCH$GL_MFYCNT	Longword	Modified page count
PFN$AL_COUNT+8	Longword	Bad page count
PFN$GL_PHYPGCNT	Longword	Number of available physical pages
SCH$GL_FREEREQ	Longword	Free pages required by the swapper
SCH$GL_MFYLIM	Longword	Modified page list high limit
PFN$AL_HILIMIT+8	Longword	Bad page list high limit
SCH$GL_FREELIM	Longword	Free page list low limit
SCH$GL_MFYLOLIM	Longword	Modified page list low limit
PFN$AL_LOLIMIT+8	Longword	Bad page list low limit
PHV$GL_PIXBAS	Longword	Address of process index array
PHV$GL_REFCBAS	Longword	Address of process header reference count array
MMG$GL_PAGSWPVC	Longword	Address of vector of page/swap file control blocks
SCH$GL_PCBVEC	Longword	Address of PCB vector of longwords
SCH$GL_SEQVEC	Longword	Address of sequence vector of words
MPW$GL_BADPAG-TOTAL	Longword	Number of pages on the bad page list
MMG$GL_MAXPFIDX	Longword	Maximum page file index currently in use
MMG$GW_MINPFIDX ⎫	Word	Minimum page file index in use
SGN$GW_SWPFILCT ⎭		Number of swap file slots
MB$AR_DPT	Longword	Address of mailbox driver
MB$AR_DDT	Longword	Address of mailbox driver dispatch table
NL$AR_DPT	Longword	Address of null device driver
NL$AR_DDT	Longword	Address of null driver dispatch table
SCH$GL_MFYLIMSV	Longword	Saved high-limit threshold of modified page list
SCH$GL_MFYLOSV	Longword	Saved low-limit threshold of modified page list
PMS$GL_FAULTS	Longword	Number of page faults
PMS$GL_PREADS	Longword	Number of page reads
PMS$GL_PREADIO	Longword	Number of I/O requests to read pages
PMS$GL_PWRITES	Longword	Number of modified pages written
PMS$GL_PWRITIO	Longword	Number of I/O requests to write modified pages
PMS$GL_DZROFLTS	Longword	Number of demand zero page faults
PMS$GL_DPTSCN	Longword	Number of dead page table scans
PMS$GL_GVALID	Longword	Number of global valid page faults
MPW$GL_IOPAGCNT	Longword	Modified pages in transit to disk
MPW$L_COUNT	Longword	Reserved
EXE$GQ_SYSDISK	Quadword	Descriptor for SYS$DISK
LDR$GQ_IMAGE_LIST	Quadword	Listhead of loaded image data blocks
MMG$GL_PFNLOCK	Longword	Countdown counter of pages remaining that may be locked in memory

Global Symbol	Size	Description of Data
SWP$GL_SWTIME	Longword	Earliest time for next exchange swap
EXE$GL_PWRDONE	Longword	End time for power recovery interval
EXE$GL_PWRINTVL	Longword	Allowable recovery interval in 10-millisecond units
SWP$GW_BALCNT	Word	Number of processes in balance set excluding swapper and process
SCH$GW_SWPFCNT	Word	Number of successive outswap schedule failures
LNM$AR_SYSTEM_DIRECTORY	Longword	Address of system logical name directory
LNM_AR_SYSTEM_DIR_LNMTH	Longword	Address of system directory table header
PQL$AR_SYSPQL	Longword	Address of system process quota list
PQL$GL_SYSPQLLEN	Longword	Length of system process quota list
ERL$GB_BUFFLAG	Byte	Buffer status flags
	Byte	Spare for alignment
ERL$GB_BUFTIM	Byte	Format process wakeup timer
ERL$GL_ERLPID	Longword	Process ID of error format process
ERL$GL_SEQUENCE	Longword	Systemwide error sequence number
EXE$AR_SYSTEM_PRIMITIVES_DATA	Longword	Address of SYSTEM_PRIMITIVES private data area; offsets defined by $$SYSTEM_PRIM_DATADEF macro
EXE$AR_IO_ROUTINES_DATA	Longword	Address of IO_ROUTINES private data area; offsets defined by $$IO_ROUTINES_DATADEF macro
EXE$AR_FORK_WAIT_QUEUE	Longword	Address of fork and wait queue
EXE$AB_HEXTAB	16 bytes	Hexadecimal conversion table
BUG$L_BUGCHK_FLAGS	Longword	Flags used by bugcheck code
BUG$L_FATAL_SPSAV	Longword	Fatal bugcheck in progress stack pointer
EXE$A_ID_UPCASE	Longword	Address of table to translate lowercase to uppercase
IOC$GL_ADPLIST	Longword	Listhead of adapter control blocks
IOC$GL_DPTLIST	Quadword	Listhead of driver prolog tables (DPTs)
TTY$GL_DPT	Longword	Address of terminal class driver DPT
NO$GL_DPT	Longword	Address of asynchronous class driver DPT
TTY$GL_JOBCTLMB	Longword	Address of job controller mailbox
SYS$GL_UIS	Longword	Address of loaded UIS code
UIS$GL_USB	Longword	Address of UIS context block
SYS$GL_FALLBACK	Longword	Reserved
EXE$GL_CPUNODSP	Longword	Virtual address that maps CPU node private space
EXE$GL_CONFREGL	Longword	Address of nexus device type longword array
EXE$GL_CONFREG	Longword	Address of nexus device type byte array
MMG$GL_SBICONF	Longword	Address of a longword array containing nexus slot virtual addresses
EXE$GL_NUMNEXUS	Longword	Maximum nexus number possible
MMG$GL_RMSBASE	Longword	Base address of RMS image
MMG$GL_FPEMUL_BASE	Longword	Base address of floating-point instruction emulator
MMG$GL_SYSLOA_BASE	Longword	Base address of SYSLOAxxx.EXE

Global Symbol	Size	Description of Data
MMG$GL_VAXEMUL_BASE	Longword	Base address of decimal/string instruction emulator
MMG$GL_GBLSECFND	Longword	Last global section table entry found when deleting page file backing store addresses
MMG$GL_GBLPAGFIL	Longword	Remaining page file available for global sections
SCH$GL_MAXPIX	Longword	Maximum process index for this system
SCH$GL_PIXLAST	Longword	Last process index created
SCH$GL_PIXWIDTH	Longword	Width of process index field determined by MAXPROCESSCNT parameter
SCH$GW_LOCALNODE	Word	ID for local VAXcluster node
	Word	Spare for alignment
PMS$GL_DIRIO	Longword	Number of direct I/O operations
PMS$GL_BUFIO	Longword	Number of buffered I/O operations
PMS$GL_SPLIT	Longword	Number of split I/O transfers
PMS$GL_HIT	Longword	Number of disk transfers not requiring window turns
PMS$GL_LOGNAM	Longword	Number of logical name translations
PMS$GL_MBREADS	Longword	Number of mailbox read operations
PMS$GL_MBWRITES	Longword	Number of mailbox write operations
PMS$GL_TREADS	Longword	Number of terminal read operations
PMS$GL_TWRITES	Longword	Number of terminal write operations
PMS$GL_IOPFMPDB	Longword	Address of performance data block
PMS$GL_IOPFMSEQ	Longword	Master I/O packet sequence number
PMS$GL_ARRLOCPK	Longword	Number of local packets arriving
PMS$GL_DEPLOCPK	Longword	Number of local packets departing
PMS$GL_ARRTRAPK	Longword	Number of arriving packets
PMS$GL_TRCNGLOS	Longword	Cumulative transit congestion loss
PMS$GL_RCVBUFFL	Longword	Number of receiver buffer failures
PMS$GL_ENQNEW_LOC	Longword	Number of local new lock requests
PMS$GL_ENQNEW_IN	Longword	Number of incoming new lock requests
PMS$GL_ENQNEW_OUT	Longword	Number of outgoing new lock requests
PMS$GL_ENQCVT_LOC	Longword	Number of local conversion requests
PMS$GL_ENQCVT_IN	Longword	Number of incoming conversion requests
PMS$GL_ENQCVT_OUT	Longword	Number of outgoing conversion requests
PMS$GL_DEQ_LOC	Longword	Number of local dequeues
PMS$GL_DEQ_IN	Longword	Number of incoming dequeues
PMS$GL_DEQ_OUT	Longword	Number of outgoing dequeues
PMS$GL_ENQWAIT	Longword	Number of $ENQ requests waiting
PMS$GL_ENQNOTQD	Longword	Number of $ENQ requests not queued
PMS$GL_BLK_LOC	Longword	Number of local blocking ASTs queued
PMS$GL_BLK_IN	Longword	Number of incoming blocking ASTs queued
PMS$GL_BLK_OUT	Longword	Number of outgoing blocking ASTs queued
PMS$GL_DIR_IN	Longword	Number of incoming directory operations
PMS$GL_DIR_OUT	Longword	Number of outgoing directory operations
PMS$GL_DLCKMSGS_IN	Longword	Number of incoming deadlock detection messages
PMS$GL_DLCKMSGS_OUT	Longword	Number of outgoing deadlock detection messages
PMS$GL_DLCKSRCH	Longword	Number of deadlock searches performed
PMS$GL_DLCKFND	Longword	Number of deadlocks found

Global Symbol	Size	Description of Data
PMS$GL_FLAGS	Longword	Flags used in disk queue length monitoring
PMS$GL_QLEN_SCANS	Longword	Number of I/O database scans for monitoring queue length
PMS$GL_QLEN_TOINT	Longword	Timeout interval for disk queue monitoring
PMS$GL_QLEN_TOCTR	Longword	Timeout down counter for disk queue monitoring
PMS$GL_RESERVED1	18 longwords	Reserved
PMS$GL_CHMK	Longword	Number of CHMK exceptions
PMS$GL_CHME	Longword	Number of CHME exceptions
PMS$GL_PAGES	Longword	Number of physical pages of memory in configuration
PMS$GW_BATCH	Word	Number of current batch jobs
	Word	Spare for alignment
PMS$GW_INTJOBS	Longword	Number of interactive users
PMS$GL_READCNT	Longword	Total number of terminal characters read since bootstrap
PMS$GL_WRTCNT	Longword	Total number of terminal characters written since bootstrap
PMS$GL_PASSALL	Longword	Number of reads in PASSALL mode
PMS$GL_RWP	Longword	Number of read-with-prompt reads
PMS$GL_LRGRWP	Longword	Number of read-with-prompt reads of more than 12 characters
PMS$GL_RWPSUM	Longword	Total number of characters read in prompt mode
PMS$GL_NOSTDTRM	Longword	Number of reads not using standard terminators
PMS$GL_RWPNOSTD	Longword	Number of read-with-prompt reads not using standard terminators
PMS$GL_TTY_CODE1	Longword	Performance code vector 1
PMS$GL_TTY_CODE2	Longword	Performance code vector 2
PMS$GL_LDPCTX	Longword	Reserved
PMS$GL_SWITCH	Longword	Number of switches from the current process
PMS$GB_PROMPT	4 bytes	RTE input prompt
EXE$AR_EWDATA	Longword	Address of the exec-writable file system measurement data
PMS$GL_DOSTATS	Longword	Flags to turn statistics code on and off
SCH$GL_COMQS	Longword	Queue summary longword for computable state
SCH$GL_COMOQS	Longword	Queue summary longword for computable outswapped state
SCH$GB_SIP	Byte	Swapper flags
• SCH$V_MPW	Bit	Modified page writer active
• SCH$V_SIP	Bit	Swap in progress
SCH$GB_RESCAN	Byte	Queue reordering notification flags
• SCH$V_REORD	Bit	RELPFN has reordered the queue
MMG$GB_FREWFLGS	Byte	Swapper/MMG$FREWSLE communication flags
• MMG$V_NOWAIT	Bit	MMG$FREWSLE may not enter resource wait for pages from the modified list
• MMG$V_NOLASTUPD	Bit	MMG$FREWSLE may not update WSLAST
	3 bytes	Spare for alignment

Global Symbol	Size	Description of Data
SCH$GW_PROCCNT	Word	Process count excluding the swapper process
SCH$GW_PROCLIM	Word	Maximum number of processes on the system
SWP$GL_SLOTCNT	Longword	Obsolete
SCH$GQ_CEBHD	Quadword	Listhead for common event blocks
SCH$GW_CEBCNT	Word	Number of common event blocks
SCH$GW_DELPHDCT	Word	Number of process headers of already deleted processes
SWP$GL_SHELL	Longword	Shell process swap address
SWP$GL_INPCB	Longword	PCB address of process being swapped into memory
SWP$GL_ISPAGCNT	Longword	Inswap page count
SWP$GW_IBALSETX	Word	Balance set slot index for inswap process
SWP$GB_ISWPRI	Byte	Priority of inswap process
	3 bytes	Spare for alignment
SWP$GL_ISWPPAGES	Longword	Number of inswapped pages
SWP$GL_ISWPCNT	Longword	Number of inswaps performed
SWP$GL_OSWPCNT	Longword	Number of outswaps performed
SWP$GL_HOSWPCNT	Longword	Number of header outswaps
SWP$GL_HISWPCNT	Longword	Number of header inswaps
SWP$GL_MAP	Longword	Address of swapper's I/O page table
SCH$GL_RESMASK	Longword	Resource wait mask vector
EXE$GL_FLAGS	Longword	System flags longword loaded from EXE$GL_DEFFLAGS (see Section C.1.4)
EXE$GL_STATE_FLAGS	Longword	State of system control flags
EXE$AQ_ERLMBX	5 quadwords	Descriptors of error log mailboxes
EXE$GL_VAXEXCVEC	Longword	Address for intercept VAX CPU exception dispatching, used by instruction emulation
EXE$GL_FPEXCVEC	Longword	Address for intercept of floating exception dispatching
EXE$GL_USRCHMK	Longword	Address of systemwide user-written change-mode-to-kernel dispatcher
EXE$GL_USRCHME	Longword	Address of systemwide user-written change-mode-to-executive dispatcher
SWI$GL_FQFL	6 quadwords	Fork queue listheads for IPLs 6 through 11; IPL 7 used only as a place holder
LNM$AL_MUTEX	Longword	Mutex for shareable logical names
LNM$GL_SYSDIRSEQ	Longword	Sequence number for cache of system logical name table translations
EXE$GL_SYSUCB	Longword	Address of system disk unit control block
FIL$GT_DDDEV	16 bytes	Counted ASCII string of default device (SYS$SYSDEVICE)
FIL$GT_TOPSYS	40 bytes	Counted ASCII string of top-level system directory on default device
FIL$GQ_CACHE	Quadword	File read cache descriptor
EXE$GQ_BOOTCB_D	Quadword	Descriptor for boot control block
EXE$GL_SAVEDUMP	Longword	Number of page file blocks to release when dump is copied from page file
EXE$GL_ERASEPB	Longword	Address of an erase pattern buffer containing zeros
EXE$GL_ERASEPPT	Longword	Address of a pseudo page table that maps the erase pattern buffer filled in by INIT

Global Symbol	Size	Description of Data
NET$GL_DIAG_BUF	Longword	Address of network diagnostic tool common buffer
EXE$GQ_PQBIQ	Quadword	Listhead for process quota block lookaside list
IOC$GL_AQBLIST	Longword	Ancillary control process queue block listhead
IOC$GQ_MOUNTLST	Quadword	Systemwide mounted volume list
IOC$GQ_BRDCST	Quadword	Reserved
IOC$GL_CRBTMOUT	Longword	List of controller request blocks to scan for timeouts
IOC$GL_DU_CDDB	Longword	Listhead of class driver data blocks for disk class driver connections
IOC$GL_TU_CDDB	Longword	Listhead of class driver data blocks for tape class driver connections
IOC$GL_HIRT	Longword	Address of host-initiated replacement table (used by mass storage control protocol disks)
IOC$GL_SHDW_WRK	Longword	Address of area used for processing shadow set generation number comparisons
EXE$GL_GSDGRPFL EXE$GL_GSDGRPBL	2 longwords	Listhead for group global section descriptor (GSD) list
EXE$GL_GSDSYSFL EXE$GL_GSDSYSBL	2 longwords	Listhead for system GSD list
EXE$GL_GSDDELFL EXE$GL_GSDDELBL	2 longwords	Listhead for GSD block delete pending list
EXE$GQ_WCBDELIQ	Quadword	Listhead for window control block delete queue for GSD windows
EXE$GQ_SYSWCBIQ	Quadword	Listhead for system window control blocks
IOC$GQ_POSTIQ	Quadword	Systemwide sequential I/O postprocessing queue
EXE$GQ_RIGHTSLIST	Quadword	Systemwide rights list descriptor
PMS$GL_KERNEL	6 longwords	Reserved
EXE$GL_ABSTIM	Longword	Seconds elapsed since system booted
	Longword	Spare for alignment
EXE$GQ_SYSTIME	Quadword	System time in units of 100 nanoseconds
EXE$GQ_SYSTIME2	Quadword	Number of 100-nanosecond units elapsed since system boot
EXE$GQ_BOOTTIME	Quadword	Base time of last boot
EXE$GL_SYSTICK	Longword	Amount to be added to EXE$GQ_SYSTIME
EXE$GL_TIMEADJUST	Longword	Number of ticks necessary to adjust time
EXE$GL_TICKADJUST	Longword	Tick adjustment
EXE$GL_TICKLENGTH	Longword	Total length of a tick
EXE$GL_DTSFLAG	Longword	Time service flags
EXE$GL_PFAILTIM	Longword	Contents of time-of-year clock at last power failure
EXE$GL_PFATIM	Longword	Duration of most recent power failure in 10-millisecond units
IOC$GL_MUTEX	2 words	I/O database mutex
EXE$GL_CEBMTX	2 words	Common event block list mutex
SMP$GL_CPU_MUTEX	Longword	Special mutex to freeze active CPU set
EXE$GL_PGDYNMTX	2 words	Paged dynamic memory mutex
EXE$GL_GSDMTX	2 words	Global section descriptor list mutex

1191

Global Symbol	Size	Description of Data
EXE$GL_SHMGSMTX	2 words	MA780 shared memory global section descriptor list mutex
EXE$GL_SHMMBMTX	2 words	MA780 shared memory mailbox list mutex
EXE$GL_ENQMTX	2 words	Reserved
EXE$GL_ACLMTX	2 words	Reserved
EXE$GL_SYSID_LOCK	Longword	System parent lock ID
EXE$GL_KNOWN_FILES	Longword	Address of hash table for known file entries
EXE$GL_GPT	Longword	Address of first free global page table entry
	Longword	Dummy count of number of global page table entries in listhead
SYS$GQ_VERSION	Quadword	ASCII string containing system version number
	Longword	Reserved
SYS$GW_IJOBCNT	Word	Current count of interactive logins
SYS$GW_BJOBCNT	Word	Current count of batch logins
SYS$GW_NJOBCNT	Word	Current count of network logins
	2 bytes	Spare for alignment
EXE$GL_SYSMSG	Longword	Address of systemwide message section
EXE$GL_USRUNDWN	Longword	Address of systemwide user rundown service vector
EXE$GL_NONPAGED	Longword	IPL at which nonpaged pool allocation occurs
	Longword	Address of first free block of nonpaged pool
	Longword	Dummy size of zero for listhead
EXE$GL_SPLITADR	Longword	Address of boundary between large request packet and intermediate request packet lookaside lists
EXE$GL_PAGED	Longword	Address of first free block of paged pool
	Longword	Dummy size of zero for listhead
EXE$GL_SHBLIST	Longword	Address of MA780 shared memory control block list
EXE$GL_RTBITMAP	Longword	Address of real-time system page table entry bitmap
EXE$GL_MCHKERRS	Longword	Number of machine checks since bootstrap
EXE$GL_MEMERRS	Longword	Number of memory errors since bootstrap
IO$GL_UBA_INT0	Longword	Number of UNIBUS adapter interrupts through vector 0
EXE$GL_BLAKHOLE	Longword	Physical page used to remap addresses of adapters that have lost power
IO$GL_SCB_INT0	Longword	Number of unexpected system control block interrupts
EXE$GL_TENUSEC	Longword	Number of times loop executed in 10 microseconds in TIMEDWAIT macro
EXE$GL_UBDELAY	Longword	Number of times to execute a 3-microsecond loop delay in TIMEDWAIT macro
EXE$GL_MP	Longword	Obsolete
EXE$GL_SITESPEC	Longword	Longword available to privileged users for site-specific purposes
EXE$GL_INTSTKLM	Longword	Top of primary CPU's interrupt stack
LCK$AR_COMPAT_TBL	Longword	Address of lock mode compatibility table
LCK$GL_IDTBL	Longword	Address of lock ID table
LCK$GL_NXTID	Longword	Address of next lock ID to use
LCK$GL_MAXID	Longword	Maximum lock ID

Global Symbol	Size	Description of Data
LCK$GL_HASHTBL	Longword	Address of resource hash table
LCK$GL_HTBLCNT	Longword	Number of entries in resource hash table (expressed as a power of 2)
LCK$GL_TIMOUTQ	Quadword	Listhead for lock timeout queue
LCK$GL_DIRVEC	Longword	Address of directory vector
LCK$GL_PRCMAP	Longword	Address of process bitmap
LCK$GQ_BITMAP_EXP	Quadword	Process bitmap expiration timestamp (exact time)
LCK$GQ_BITMAP_ EXPLCL	Quadword	Process bitmap expiration timestamp (approximate local time)
LCK$GB_HTBLSHFT	Byte	Number of entries in hash table (expressed as a shift count)
LCK$GB_MAXDEPTH	Byte	Maximum number of sublocks allowed
LCK$GB_STALLREQS	Byte	Stall lock request flag
LCK$GB_REBLD_STATE	Byte	Lock rebuild state flag
EXE$GL_ACMFLAGS	Longword	Accounting manager control flags
EXE$GL_SVAPTE	Longword	System virtual address of page table entry that maps the black hole page
XQP$GL_SECTIONS	Longword	Number of Files-11 XQP global sections
XQP$GL_DZRO	Longword	Size of XQP demand zero section
XQP$GL_FILESERVER	Longword	Process ID of CACHE_SERVER
XQP$GL_FILESERV_ ENTRY	Longword	AST entry point of CACHE_SERVER process
SYS$GQ_PWD	Quadword	Encrypted system password
CIA$GL_MUTEX	2 words	Mutex for system intruder lists
CIA$GQ_INTRUDER	2 longwords	Listhead of known and suspected intruders
EXE$GL_BADACV_T	Longword	Time of the last spurious access violation
EXE$GL_BADACV_C	Longword	Number of spurious access violations
EXE$EXCEPTABLE	Longword	Address of exception table
SMP$AR_SPNLKVEC	Longword	Address of spinlock vector
SMP$GW_SPNLKCNT	Word	Number of entries in spinlock vector
SMP$GW_MIN_INDEX	Word	Value of first spinlock index
EXE$GQ_1ST_TIME	Quadword	Expiration time for first timer queue entry
SMP$GL_BASE_MSK	Longword	Per-CPU data area access mask
SMP$GL_CPUCONF	Longword	Bit mask of available CPUs
SMP$GL_ACTIVE_CPUS	Longword	Bit mask of members of active set
SMP$GL_OVERRIDE	Longword	Bit mask of members of override set
SMP$GL_ACK_MASK	Longword	Bit mask of CPUs to wait for acknowledgment
SMP$GL_BUG_DONE	Longword	Bit mask of CPUs that have completed state saving during bugcheck
SMP$GL_INVALID	Longword	Contains system virtual address to invalidate in the translation buffer
SMP$GL_FLAGS	Longword	Symmetric multiprocessing control flags
SMP$GL_BUGCHKCP	Longword	CPU ID of bugcheck initiator (CRASH CPU)
SMP$GL_TODR	Longword	TODR value for EXE$WRITE_TODR
SMP$GL_PRIMID	Longword	Primary CPU ID
SMP$GL_CPU_DATA	64 longwords	Per-CPU data area pointer array
SMP$GL_PROPOSED_ TODR	Longword	Proposed new value for TODRs
SMP$GL_NEW_TODR	Longword	Most recent contents of primary's TODR
XDT$GW_INTERLOCK	Word	XDELTA entry interlock (low bit)

Global Symbol	Size	Description of Data
XDT$GW_OWNER_ID	Word	CPU ID of XDELTA owner
XDT$GL_BENIGN_CPUS	Longword	Mask of CPUs in XDELTA-controlled benign state
CLU$GB_CLUVER	Byte	VAXcluster version number for rolling upgrade
	3 bytes	Spare for alignment
MMG$GL_DZRO_PTE	Longword	Address of system page table entry for zeroing demand zero global pages during address space deletion
MMG$GL_DZRO_VA	Longword	Address corresponding to system page table entry for zeroing demand zero global pages during address space deletion
EXE$GL_ABSTIM_TICS	Longword	Number of 10-millisecond ticks elapsed since boot
PMS$GL_NPAGDYNEXPS	Longword	Number of successful attempts to expand pool
PMS$GL_NPAGDYNEXPF	Longword	Number of unsuccessful attempts to expand pool
PMS$GL_PAGDYNF	Longword	Number of paged pool allocation failures
PMS$GL_PROCCNTMAX	Longword	Maximum number of concurrent processes
SMP$GL_CAPABILITIES	32 quadwords	Per-capability bit mask of CPUs
SMP$GW_AFFINITY_COUNT	32 words	Per-capability count of users of capability
EXE$GA_LES_TABLE	Longword	Address of main low-end system data structure
EXE$GL_AFFINITY	Longword	Default device affinity value
EXE$GL_TMV_SVAPTE	Longword	Address of first page table entry used to map tape mount verify buffer
EXE$GL_TMV_SVABUF	Longword	Address of 1024-byte area for tape mount verify
EXE$GL_IPINT_IPL	Longword	IPL of interprocessor interrupts
EXE$GA_WP_CRE	Longword	Address of create watchpoint routine
EXE$GA_WP_DEL	Longword	Address of delete watchpoint routine
EXE$GA_WP_WPRE	Longword	Address of start of watchpoint restore entries array
EXE$GA_HWNAME	Longword	Address of start of hardware name table
EXE$GA_HWTYPE	Longword	Address of start of hardware type table
EXE$GL_USRUNDWN_EXEC	Longword	Vector for systemwide executive mode rundown
SYS$GL_VERSION	33 longwords	Array of system version numbers
MMG$GL_FREE_NO_PFN_DB_LIST	Longword	Address of list of free pages not described in the page frame number (PFN) database
MMG$GL_FREE_NO_PFN_DB_VA	Longword	Address to map free page not described in the PFN database
MMG$GL_FREE_NO_PFN_DB_PTE	Longword	System page table entry to map free page not described in the PFN database
LMF$GL_RESERVED	Longword	Reserved
CLU$GW_QUORUM	Word	Contains quorum for use by $GETSYI
SYS$GL_S0_VECTOR_LAST_USED	Longword	End of system service vector area
EXE$GL_VECTOR_LAST_USED	Longword	End of system routine area
EXE$GL_NPAG_DATA_LAST_USED	Longword	End of nonpageable data area
	2 bytes	Spare for alignment

Global Symbol	Size	Description of Data
PMS$GL_NPAGDYNF	Longword	Count of nonpaged pool allocation failure epochs
PMS$GL_NPAGDYNF-PAGES	Longword	Failed nonpaged pool pages accumulator
PMS$GL_PAGDYNF-PAGES	Longword	Failed paged pool pages accumulator
PMS$GL_NPAGDYNREQ	Longword	Number of nonpaged pool allocation requests
PMS$GL_NPAGDYN-REQF	Longword	Number of failed nonpaged pool allocation requests
PMS$GL_PAGDYNREQF	Longword	Number of failed paged pool allocation requests
PMS$GL_XRPFAIL	3 longwords	Number of request packet lookaside list allocation failures
	3 longwords	Reserved
SYS$GL_UIS_FLAGS	Longword	Address of UIS flags field
SYS$GL_UISBG_EPID	Longword	Address of UIS background process ID
UIS$GL_LTRC_BUF	Longword	Address of UIS lock event trace buffer
UIS$GL_LTRC_END	Longword	Address of UIS lock event trace buffer end
UIS$GL_LTRC_PTR	Longword	Position in UIS lock event trace buffer
UIS$GL_LTRC_SPARE	Longword	Reserved for UIS
	Quadword	Terminates outswap scheduling scan
SCH$AQ_COMH	32 quadwords	Listheads for computable processes at all software priority levels
SCH$AQ_COMOH	32 quadwords	Listheads for computable outswapped processes at all software priority levels
SCH$AQ_WQHDR	176 bytes 176 = 16 * 12	Wait queue headers for 11 wait states with headers reserved
PMS$AL_TRANSFLT	60 longwords	Array for recording page faults out of transition states
NSA$AR_ALARM_VECTOR	Longword	Address of security alarm event vector
NSA$AR_AUDIT_VECTOR	Longword	Address of security audit event vector
NSA$AR_ALARM_FAILURE	Longword	Address of security alarm failure vector
NSA$AR_AUDIT_FAILURE	Longword	Address of security audit failure vector
SCS$AR_LOCALSB	Longword	Address of the local system block
NET$AR_WCB	Longword	Address of window control block for network pseudo device
MMG$AR_NULLPFL	Longword	Address of the null page file structure
SCH$AR_NULLPCB	Longword	Address of the null PCB
SCH$AR_SWPPCB	Longword	Address of the swapper PCB
MMG$AR_SYSPCB	Longword	Address of the system PCB, used for system paging
EXE$AR_UPCASE_DAT	Longword	Address of the DEC multinational upcase table
IOC$GL_DEVLIST	Longword	Listhead of device data blocks of all devices (part of system block)
MB$AR_DDB	Longword	Address of mailbox device data block
MB$AR_ORB1	Longword	Address of object rights block (ORB) for MBA1
MB$AR_ORB2	Longword	Address of ORB for MBA2
MB$AR_UCB1	Longword	Address of unit control block (UCB) for MBA1

Global Symbol	Size	Description of Data
SYS$AR_JOBCTLMB	Longword	Address of job controller mailbox UCB for MBA1
MB$AR_UCB2	Longword	Address of UCB for MBA2
SYS$AR_OPRMBX	Longword	Address of OPCOM mailbox UCB for MBA2
MB$AR_ORB0	Longword	Address of ORB for template mailbox UCB
MB$AR_UCB0	Longword	Address of template mailbox UCB
NL$AR_DDB	Longword	Address of null device data block
NL$AR_ORB0	Longword	Address of null device ORB
NL$AR_UCB0	Longword	Address of null device UCB
OPA$AR_DDB	Longword	Address of console terminal device data block
OPA$AR_ORB0	Longword	Address of console terminal device ORB
OPA$AR_UCB0	Longword	Address of console terminal device UCB
OPA$AR_CRB	Longword	Address of console terminal device controller request block
OP$AR_DPT	Longword	Address of console terminal device driver
OPA$AR_SPL	Longword	Address of console terminal spinlock
OPA$AR_IDB	Longword	Address of console device interrupt dispatch block
ARCH$GQ_PTOLEMY_CELL	Quadword	Reserved
SWP$GL_SHELLBAS	Longword	Address of beginning of SHELL
LNM$AL_HASHTBL	3 longwords	Addresses of logical name hash tables
	2 longwords	Reserved
LNM$AL_DIRTBL	2 longwords	Addresses of logical name directories
	1 longword	Reserved
SCH$GL_SWPPID	Longword	Process ID of swapper
SWP$AL_SWAPPER_STACK	Longword	Address of the swapper's stack
SWP$GL_SWAPPER_STACK_SIZE	Longword	Size of swapper's stack
SYS$AR_BOOTUCB	Longword	Address of system device unit control block
SYS$AR_BOOTORB	Longword	Address of system device object rights block
SYS$AR_BOOTDDB	Longword	Address of system device data block
EXE$AR_UAFC_HASH_TABLE	Longword	Reserved
EXE$AR_ARBC_HASH_TABLE	Longword	Reserved
EXE$GL_HWNAME_LENGTH	Longword	Length of hardware name table
EXE$GL_HWTYPE_LENGTH	Longword	Length of hardware type table
SMP$AL_IPLVEC	31 longwords	Spinlock IPL vector postindexed with negative numbers
EXE$AR_TQENOREPT	Longword	Address of permanent timer queue entry
EXE$GL_SAVED_EMBS	Longword	Address of saved error message buffer pointers
EXE$GW_SAVED_EMBS_COUNT	Word	Saved error message buffer count
OPA$AR_VECTOR	Longword	Address of console port driver dispatch vector
SYS$GW_MBXUCBSIZ	Word	Size of mailbox template unit control block
EXE$AL_ERLBUFADR	Longword	Address of array of error log allocation buffers

Global Symbol	Size	Description of Data
EXE$GW_ERLBUFHEAD	Word	Number of next error log allocation buffer to copy to file
EXE$GW_ERLBUFTAIL	Word	Number of current error log allocation buffer
	6 bytes	Spare for alignment
EXE$GL_TQFL	Quadword	Timer queue listhead
EXE$GQ_KFE_LCKNAM	Quadword	String descriptor of known file entry lock name
EXE$GL_BRKMSK	Longword	Mask of INI$BRK invokers that cause XDELTA breakpoint
CLU$GB_QUORUM_LOST	Byte	Cluster quorum lost flag
	3 bytes	Spare for alignment
SMP$AR_PRIMID_COPY	Longword	Address of copy of primary CPU ID
EXE$GL_XPCA	Longword	Reserved
MMG$GL_FPEMUL_END	Longword	End address of floating-point emulator
MMG$GL_VAXEMUL_END	Longword	End address of decimal/string emulator
PAT$A_NONPAGED	Longword	Dummy cell for the system loader
PAT$A_PAGED	Longword	Dummy cell for the system loader
SCH$GL_IDLE_CPUS	Longword	Bit mask of idle CPUs
	Longword	Reserved
DECW$GL_VECTOR	Longword	Address of array used by DECwindows device drivers
EXE$GW_CLKUTICS	Word	Reserved
EXE$GW_CLKUTICR	Word	Reserved
EXE$GL_ABSTIM_UTICS	Longword	Reserved
LMF$AR_GROUPTBL	Longword	Reserved
EXE$AR_DUMP_PTES	Longword	Address of system page table entries allocated for selective dump
EXE$GL_DUMPMASK	Longword	Dump type flags
VMS$GL_LICENSE_VERSION	Longword	Reserved
VMS$GQ_LICENSE_DATE	Quadword	Reserved
MMG$GL_VVIEF_BASE	Longword	Reserved
MMG$GL_VVIEF_END	Longword	Reserved
MMG$GL_VVIEF_ADDR	Longword	Reserved
MMG$GL_VAXEMUL_EXIT	Longword	Address of character instruction emulation exit
SMP$GL_P0PT_MAP	Longword	Address of array of virtual pages used to double-map CPUs' boot stack pages
EXE$GL_NS_FLAGS	Longword	Vector processing flags
EXE$GL_MMG_FLAGS	Longword	Reserved
NET$GL_ATM_RCVPKT	Longword	Reserved
NET$GL_ATM_XMTPKT	Longword	Reserved
NET$GL_ATM_FWDPKT	Longword	Reserved
SMP$GL_PFORK_POOL	Longword	Address of pool for forking to primary
SMP$GB_PFORK_POOL_SIZE	Byte	Size in pages of PFORK_POOL
SCH$GL_DEFAULT_PROCESS_CAP	Longword	Default capabilities required by newly created processes

Global Symbol	Size	Description of Data
SCH$GL_DEFAULT_CPU_CAP	Longword	Default capabilities granted to every CPU
SCH$AR_CAP_PRIV	Longword	Reserved
SCH$GL_ACTIVE_PRIORITY	Longword	Mask of current CPU priorities
SCH$GL_CPU_CAP_SUM	Longword	Summary of all capabilities on all CPUs
DDTM$AR_PERFOR-MANCE_CELLS	Longword	Reserved
NET$GQ_CTF_WRK_Q	Quadword	Reserved
NET$GQ_CTF_REG_Q	Quadword	Reserved
PMS$GL_GBLSECTCNT	Longword	Current number of mapped global sections
PMS$GL_GBLSECTMAX	Longword	Maximum number of mapped global sections
PMS$GL_GBLPAGCNT	Longword	Current number of mapped global pages
PMS$GL_GBLPAGMAX	Longword	Maximum number of mapped global pages
SYS$GL_EXITRET	Longword	Return address of $EXIT system service
PMS$GL_CWPS_MSGS_IN	Longword	Count of inbound Clusterwide Process Server (CWPS) messages
PMS$GL_CWPS_MSGS_OUT	Longword	Count of outbound CWPS messages
PMS$GL_CWPS_BYTES_IN	Longword	Count of inbound CWPS bytes
PMS$GL_CWPS_BYTES_OUT	Longword	Count of outbound CWPS bytes
PMS$GL_CWPS_GETJPI_IN	Longword	Count of inbound CWPS $GETJPI requests
PMS$GL_CWPS_GETJPI_OUT	Longword	Count of outbound CWPS $GETJPI requests
PMS$GL_CWPS_PCNTRL_IN	Longword	Count of inbound process control requests
PMS$GL_CWPS_PCNTRL_OUT	Longword	Count of outbount process control requests
PMS$GL_CWPS_RSRC_SEND	Longword	Count of resource failure messages sent
PMS$GL_CWPS_RSRC_RECV	Longword	Count of resource failure messages received
MB$AR_UCB3	Longword	Address of audit server mailbox unit control block
MB$AR_ORB3	Longword	Address of audit server mailbox object rights block
SYS$AR_AUDSRVMBX	Longword	Address of audit server mailbox unit control block
EXE$GL_XMI_NEXUS_ARRAY	Longword	Address of XMI device type array
EXE$GL_XMI_CSR_ARRAY	Longword	Address of XMI node space pointer array
EXE$GL_XMI_STRUCTURE_ARRAY	Longword	Address of XMI primary data structure pointer array
PSX$GL_STATE	Longword	Reserved
SMP$GQ_PRIMARY_WORKQ	Quadword	Primary CPU's work queue
LCK$GL_RRSFL	Quadword	Listhead of all root resource blocks

Global Symbol	Size	Description of Data
PMS$GL_RM_QUOTA_WAIT	Longword	Number of lock remaster quota waits
PMS$GL_RM_UNLOAD	Longword	Number of resource trees moved to another node
PMS$GL_RM_ACQUIRE	Longword	Number of resource trees moved to this node
PMS$GL_RM_FINISH	Longword	Number of remaster operations completed
PMS$GL_RM_REQ_NAK	Longword	Number of proposed new mastership declines
PMS$GL_RM_MSG_SENT	Longword	Number of remaster messages sent
PMS$GL_RM_MSG_RCV	Longword	Number of remaster messages received
PMS$GL_RM_RBLD_SENT	Longword	Number of remaster rebuild messages sent
PMS$GL_RM_RBLD_RCVD	Longword	Number of remaster rebuild messages received
LCK$GB_DLCK_INCMPLT	Byte	Number of incomplete deadlock searches
NET$GQ_CTF_TB_Q	Quadword	Reserved
EXE$GL_BASIMGMTX	Longword	Loadable executive image mutex
EXE$GL_LDR_SEQ	Longword	Loaded image queue sequence number
EXE$GL_LDR_CNT	Longword	Number of loadable executive images
IOC$GL_INTERRUPTS	Longword	Number of CPUs that accept I/O interrupts
EXE$GL_NUM_XMI_NEXUS	Longword	Number of active array elements in EXE$GL_XMI_NEXUS_ARRAY
NET$GL_RESERVED1	7 longwords	Reserved
NET$GL_NSA_FWDPKT	Longword	Reserved
EXE$GL_FT_FLAGS	Longword	Reserved
EXE$GL_SYS_SPECIFIC	16 longwords	Reserved

C.1.4   Table of Adjustable SYSGEN Parameters ($$$$$SYSPARAM_DATA)

As described in Chapter 31, the system image contains a copy of the working value of each SYSGEN parameter. This table of values is written into the loaded base image of the executive by SYSBOOT. Global label MMG$A_SYSPARAM, defined in module EXEC_LAYOUT, locates the beginning of the parameters area. Global label EXE$A_SYSPARAM, defined in module SYSPARAM, has the same value.

The following table lists all the global symbols that make up this area. The name of each parameter is included as a part of its description.

Global Symbol	Size	Description of Data
EXE$GQ_TODCBASE	Quadword	Base value in time-of-day clock in system time format (not a parameter)
EXE$GL_TODR	Longword	Base value in time-of-year clock (not a parameter)
SGN$GW_DFPFC	Word	Default page fault cluster size (PFCDEFAULT)
SGN$GB_PGTBPFC	Byte	Default page table page fault cluster size (PAGTBLPFC)
SGN$GB_SYSPFC	Byte	Page fault cluster factor for system paging (SYSPFC)

Global Symbol	*Size*	*Description of Data*
SGN$GB_KFILSTCT	Byte	Reserved
	Byte	Spare for alignment
SGN$GW_GBLSECNT	Word	Global section count (GBLSECTIONS)
SGN$GL_MAXGPGCT	Longword	Global page count (GBLPAGES)
SGN$GL_GBLPAGFIL	Longword	Global page file page limit (GBLPAGFIL)
SGN$GW_MAXPRCCT	Word	Maximum process count (MAXPROCESSCNT)
SGN$GW_PIXSCAN	Word	Maximum number of processes to scan for priority boosting (PIXSCAN)
SGN$GL_SMP_CPUS	Longword	Mask of CPUs to boot automatically during system initialization; defaults to any that exist (SMP_CPUS)
SGN$GL_SMP_CPUSH	Longword	Reserved
SGN$GB_MULTI-PROCESSING	Byte	Controls loading of system synchronization image (MULTIPROCESSING)
SGN$GW_SMP_SANITY_CNT	Word	Number of symmetric multiprocessing sanity timer cycles before timeout (SMP_SANITY_CNT)
SGN$GW_SMP_TICK_CNT	Word	Number of clock ticks between SMP sanity timer cycles (SMP_TICK_CNT)
SGN$GL_SMP_SPINWAIT	Longword	Normal SMP busy wait timeout interval (SMP_SPINWAIT)
SGN$GL_SMP_LNG-SPINWAIT	Longword	Long SMP busy wait timeout interval (SMP_LNGSPINWAIT)
SGN$GW_MAXPSTCT	Word	Process section count (PROCSECTCNT)
SGN$GL_MINWSCNT	Longword	Minimum working set size (MINWSCNT)
SGN$GW_PAGFILCT	Word	Number of page files (PAGFILCNT)
SGN$GW_SWPFILES	Word	Number of swap files (SWPFILCNT)
SGN$GL_SYSDWSCT	Longword	Maximum size of system working set (SYSMWCNT)
SGN$GW_ISPPGCT	Word	Size in pages of interrupt stack (INTSTKPAGES)
LCK$GL_EXTRASTK	Longword	Amount of interrupt stack that must remain free when performing deadlock searches (DLCKEXTRASTK)
SGN$GL_BALSETCT	Longword	Balance set count (BALSETCNT)
SGN$GL_IRPCNT	Longword	Initial number of preallocated intermediate request packets (IRPCOUNT)
SGN$GL_IRPCNTV	Longword	Maximum number of intermediate request packets (IRPCOUNTV)
SGN$GL_MAXWSCNT	Longword	Maximum process working set size (WSMAX)
SGN$GL_NPAGEDYN	Longword	Initial number of bytes of nonpaged pool (NPAGEDYN)
SGN$GL_NPAGEVIR	Longword	Maximum size of nonpaged pool (NPAGEVIR)
SGN$GL_PAGEDYN	Longword	Number of bytes of paged pool (PAGEDYN)
SGN$GL_MAXVPGCT	Longword	Maximum per-process virtual page count (VIRTUALPAGECNT)
SGN$GL_SPTREQ	Longword	Number of additional system page table enties to reserve (SPTREQ)
SGN$GL_EXUSRSTK	Longword	Reserved (EXUSRSTK)
SGN$GL_LRPCNT	Longword	Initial number of large request packets (LRPs) in lookaside list (LRPCOUNT)

Global Symbol	Size	Description of Data
SGN$GL_LRPCNTV	Longword	Maximum number of LRPs (LRPCOUNTV)
SGN$GL_LRPSIZE	Longword	Size of an LRP (LRPSIZE)
SGN$GL_LRPMIN	Longword	Minimum request that can be allocated an LRP (LRPMIN)
SGN$GL_SRPCNT	Longword	Initial number of small request packets (SRPs) in lookaside list (SRPCOUNT)
SGN$GL_SRPCNTV	Longword	Maximum number of SRPs (SRPCOUNTV)
SGN$GL_SRPSIZE	Longword	Size of an SRP (SRPSIZE)
SGN$GL_SRPMIN	Longword	Minimum request that can be allocated an SRP (SRPMIN)
SGN$GW_PCHANCNT	Word	Permanent I/O channel count (CHANNELCNT)
SGN$GW_PIOPAGES	Word	Size of process I/O segment in pages (PIOPAGES)
SGN$GW_CTLPAGES	Word	Size of process allocation region in pages (CTLPAGES)
SGN$GW_CTLIMGLIM	Word	Limit on use of the process allocation region by image requests (CTLIMGLIM)
SGN$GW_IMGIOCNT	Word	Default number of pages mapped for image I/O segment (IMGIOCNT)
SCH$GW_QUAN	Word	Length in 10-millisecond units of quantum (QUANTUM)
MPW$GW_MPWPFC	Word	Modified page writer cluster factor (MPW_WRTCLUSTER)
MPW$GW_HILIM	Word	High-limit threshold of modified page list (MPW_HILIMIT)
MPW$GW_LOLIM	Word	Low-limit threshold of modified page list (MPW_LOLIMIT)
MPW$GB_IOLIM	Byte	Maximum number of concurrent I/O transfers initiated by the modified page writer (MPW_IOLIMIT)
MPW$GB_PRIO	Byte	Priority at which modified page writes are queued (MPW_PRIO)
SWP$GB_PRIO	Byte	Priority at which swapper I/O requests are queued (SWP_PRIO)
MPW$GL_THRESH	Longword	Limit below which modified page writer does not reclaim pages (MPW_THRESH)
MPW$GL_WAITLIM	Longword	Limit above which processes creating modified pages must wait until pages have been released from modified page list (MPW_WAITLIMIT)
MPW$GL_LOWAITLIM	Longword	Modified page writer busy wait low limit (MPW_LOWAITLIMIT)
SGN$GW_WSLMXSKP	Word	Number of working set list entries to skip in modified scan of working set list (TBSKIPWSL)
MMG$GL_PHYPGCNT	Longword	Maximum number of physical pages to use (PHYSICALPAGES)
SCH$GL_PFRATL	Longword	Low-limit page fault rate threshold (PFRATL)
SCH$GL_PFRATH	Longword	High-limit page fault rate threshold (PFRATH)

Global Symbol	Size	Description of Data
SCH$GL_PFRATS	Longword	Page fault rate threshold for system paging (PFRATS)
SCH$GL_WSINC	Longword	Working set list increment (WSINC)
SCH$GL_WSDEC	Longword	Working set list decrement (WSDEC)
SCH$GL_AWSMIN	Longword	Minimum value of automatic working set limit adjustment (AWSMIN)
SCH$GL_AWSTIME	Longword	Working set measurement interval in 10-millisecond units (AWSTIME)
SCH$GL_SWPRATE	Longword	Swap rate for compute-bound jobs (SWPRATE)
SWP$GL_SWPPGCNT	Longword	Target number of pages for a working set about to be outswapped (SWPOUTPGCNT)
SWP$GW_SWPINC	Word	Swap file allocation increment value (SWPALLOCINC)
SCH$GW_IOTA	Word	Amount of time in 10-millisecond units charged against quantum when process goes into wait state (IOTA)
SCH$GW_LONGWAIT	Word	Amount of elapsed time for a LEF or HIB process to be scheduled as a long wait process (LONGWAIT)
SCH$GW_DORMANT-WAIT	Word	Number of seconds to wait before marking computable process dormant (DORMANTWAIT)
SCH$GW_SWPFAIL	Word	Number of outswap failures to happen before modifying selection algorithm (SWPFAIL)
SGN$GL_VMSD1	Longword	Reserved (VMSD1)
SGN$GL_VMSD2	Longword	Reserved (VMSD2)
SGN$GL_VMSD3	Longword	Reserved (VMSD3)
SGN$GL_VMSD4	Longword	Reserved (VMSD4)
SGN$GL_VMS5	Longword	Reserved (VMS5)
SGN$GL_VMS6	Longword	Reserved (VMS6)
SGN$GL_VMS7	Longword	Reserved (VMS7)
SGN$GL_VMS8	Longword	Reserved (VMS8)
SGN$GL_JOBCTLD	Longword	Job controller error processing control flags (JOBCTLD)
SGN$GL_PU_OPTIONS	Longword	PUDRIVER trace enable options (PU_OPTIONS)
SGN$GL_WPTTE_SIZE	Longword	Number of trace table entries that WPDRIVER allocates from nonpaged pool (WPTTE_SIZE)
SGN$GW_WPRE_SIZE	Word	Number of pages that WPDRIVER allocates from nonpaged pool for watchpoint restore entries (WPRE_SIZE)
SGN$GB_QBUS_MULT_INTR	Word	Q22-bus Multilevel interrupt control (QBUS_MULT_INTR)
SGN$GW_ERLBUFCNT	Word	Number of error log allocation buffers (ERRORLOGBUFFERS)
SGN$GL_DUMP_STYLE	Longword	Bit mask specifying the crash dump style option, either full physical memory or a selective dump (DUMPSTYLE)
SGN$GL_USERD1	Longword	Parameter reserved for users (USERD1)
SGN$GL_USERD2	Longword	Parameter reserved for users (USERD2)
SGN$GL_USER3	Longword	Parameter reserved for users (USER3)

Global Symbol	Size	Description of Data
SGN$GL_USER4	Longword	Parameter reserved for users (USER4)
SGN$GL_EXTRACPU	Longword	Extra CPU time given a process after CPU time expiration (EXTRACPU)
EXE$GL_SYSUIC	Longword	Maximum group code for system user identification code (MAXSYSGROUP)
IOC$GW_MVTIMEOUT	Word	Time before abandoning mount verification attempt (MVTIMEOUT)
IOC$GW_TAPE_ MVTIMEOUT	Word	Maximum time for a tape device to wait in mount verification (TAPE_MVTIMEOUT)
IOC$GW_MAXBUF	Word	Maximum buffered I/O request size (MAXBUF)
IOC$GW_MBXBFQUO	Word	Default buffer quota for mailbox creation (DEFMBXBUFQUO)
IOC$GW_MBXMXMSG	Word	Default maximum message size for mailbox creation (DEFMBXMXMSG)
SGN$GL_FREELIM	Longword	Low-limit threshold of free page list (FREELIM)
SGN$GL_FREEGOAL	Longword	Target free page list size when memory is reclaimed (FREEGOAL)
SCH$GL_GROWLIM	Longword	Minimum number of pages on the free page list for a process to expand its working set above WSQUOTA (GROWLIM)
SCH$GL_BORROWLIM	Longword	Minimum number of pages on the free page list for a process to extend its working set list above WSQUOTA (BORROWLIM)
EXE$GL_LOCKRTRY	Longword	Number of retries allowed to lock a multiprocessor data structure (LOCKRETRY)
IOC$GW_XFMXRATE	Word	Maximum DR780 data rate (XFMAXRATE)
IOC$GW_LAMAPREG	Word	Number of UNIBUS map registers to preallocate for LPA11 (LAMAPREGS)
EXE$GL_RTIMESPT	Longword	Number of preallocated system page table entries for connect-to-interrupt driver (REALTIME_SPTS)
EXE$GL_CLITABL	Longword	Number of pages for command language interpreter symbol table (CLISYMTBL)
LCK$GL_IDTBLSIZ	Longword	Size of the lock ID table (LOCKIDTBL)
LCK$GL_IDTBLMAX	Longword	Maximum size of lock ID table (LOCKIDTBL_MAX)
LCK$GL_HTBLSIZ	Longword	Size of the resource hash table (RESHASHTBL)
LCK$GL_WAITTIME	Longword	Deadlock detection timeout period (DEADLOCK_WAIT)
SCS$GW_BDTCNT	Word	Number of buffer descriptor table entries allocated for system communication services (SCS) (SCSBUFFCNT)
SCS$GW_CDTCNT	Word	Number of connection descriptor table entries allocated for SCS (SCSCONNCNT)
SCS$GW_RDTCNT	Word	Number of response descriptor table entries allocated for SCS (SCSRESPCNT)
SCS$GW_MAXDG	Word	Maximum SCS datagram size (SCSMAXDG)
SCS$GW_MAXMSG	Word	Maximum SCS sequenced message size (SCSMAXMSG)
SCS$GW_FLOWCUSH	Word	SCS flow control cushion (SCSFLOWCUSH)

Global Symbol	Size	Description of Data
SCS$GB_SYSTEMID SCS$GB_SYSTEMIDH	Quadword	48-bit SCS system ID (SCSSYSTEMID and SCSSYSTEMIDH)
SCS$GB_NODENAME	Quadword	SCS system node name (SCSNODE)
SCS$GW_PRCPOLINT	Word	SCA process poller - polling interval (PRCPOLINTERVAL)
SCS$GW_PASTMOUT	Word	Wakeup interval for computer interconnect (CI) port driver (PASTIMOUT)
SCS$GW_PAPPDDG	Word	Number of datagram buffers to queue for START (PASTDGBUF)
SCS$GB_PANPOLL	Byte	Number of CI ports to poll each interval (PANUMPOLL)
SCS$GB_PAMXPORT	Byte	Maximum port number to poll each interval (PAMAXPORT)
SCS$GW_PAPOLINT	Word	Time between polls (PAPOLLINTERVAL)
SCS$GW_PAPOOLIN	Word	Time between checks for SCS applications waiting for pool (PAPOOLINTERVAL)
SCS$GB_PASANITY	Byte	CI port flags including sanity timer enable/disable (PASANITY)
SCS$GB_PANOPOLL	Byte	CI remote port polling enable/disable flags (PANOPOLL)
SGN$GL_PE1	Longword	Reserved (PE1)
SGN$GL_PE2	Longword	Reserved (PE2)
SGN$GL_PE3	Longword	Reserved (PE3)
SGN$GL_PE4	Longword	Reserved (PE4)
SGN$GL_PE5	Longword	Reserved (PE5)
SGN$GL_PE6	Longword	Reserved (PE6)
SGN$GW_TPWAIT	Word	Amount of time to wait for the time of day to be entered when booting (TIMEPROMPTWAIT)
EXE$GW_CLKINT	Word	Reserved
SCS$GB_UDABURST	Byte	Maximum number of longwords that the host is willing to accept per transfer (UDABURSTRATE)
LNM$GL_HTBLSIZS	Longword	Size of shareable logical name hash table (LNMSHASHTBL)
LNM$GL_HTBLSIZP	Longword	Size of process logical name hash table (LNMPHASHTBL)
EXE$GL_DEFFLAGS	Longword	System flags longword (copied to EXE$GL_FLAGS; not a parameter itself)
. EXE$V_BUGREBOOT	Bit	Automatic reboot on bugcheck (BUGREBOOT)
. EXE$V_CRDENABL	Bit	Corrected read data error enable (CRDENABLE)
. EXE$V_BUGDUMP	Bit	Write system dump on bugcheck (DUMPBUG)
. EXE$V_FATAL_BUG	Bit	Make all bugchecks fatal (BUGCHECKFATAL)
. EXE$V_MULTACP	Bit	Create separate ancillary control process for each volume (ACP_MULTIPLE)
. EXE$V_NOAUTOCNF	Bit	Inhibit autoconfiguration of I/O devices (NOAUTOCONFIG)
. EXE$V_NOCLUSTER	Bit	Inhibit page read clustering (NOCLUSTER)
. EXE$V_POOLPGING	Bit	Enable paging of paged pool (POOLPAGING)
. EXE$V_SBIERR	Bit	Enable detection of synchronous backplane interconnect errors (SBIERRENABLE)

Global Symbol	Size	Description of Data
• EXE$V_SETTIME	Bit	Prompt for system time in SYSBOOT (SETTIME)
• EXE$V_SHRF11ACP	Bit	Enable sharing of file ancillary control process (ACP_SHARE)
• EXE$V_SAVEDUMP	Bit	Save dump from page file (SAVEDUMP)
• EXE$V_SSINHIBIT	Bit	Inhibit system services on a per-process basis (SSINHIBIT)
• EXE$V_SYSUAFALT	Bit	Select alternative authorization file (UAFALTERNATE)
• EXE$V_SYSWRTABL	Bit	Leave executive images in memory writable (WRITABLESYS)
• EXE$V_RESALLOC	Bit	Enable resource allocation checking (RESALLOC)
• EXE$V_CONCEALED	Bit	Enable use of concealed devices (CONCEAL_DEVICES)
EXE$GL_TIME_CONTROL	Longword	Time control flag (TIME_CONTROL)
• EXE$V_NOCLOCK	Bit	Do not turn on clock
• EXE$V_NOSMPSANITY	Bit	Disable symmetric multiprocessing sanity timer timeouts
• EXE$V_NOSPINWAIT	Bit	Disable symmetric multiprocessing spin/busy wait timeouts
SGN$GL_BRKMSK	Longword	Determines initial breakpoint callers (BREAKPOINTS)
EXE$GL_DYNAMIC_FLAGS	Longword	Dynamic system flags (not a parameter itself)
• EXE$V_CLASS_PROT	Bit	Perform mandatory access control protection check (CLASS_PROT)
• EXE$V_WRITE-SYSPARAMS	Bit	Set by SYSBOOT if a USE DEFAULT, USE "file," or a SET command is executed (WRITESYSPARAMS)
• EXE$V_BRK_TERM	Bit	Use the terminal name in the association string used in LOGIN's break-in detection (LGI_BRK_TERM)
• EXE$V_BRK_DISUSER	Bit	If enabled, set the DISUSER flag in the user authorization file record if a break-in attempt is detected (LGI_BRK_DISUSER)
• EXE$V_NOPGFLSWP	Bit	Disallow swapping into page files (NOPGFLSWP)
EXE$GL_MSGFLAGS	Longword	Mount message flags (not a parameter itself)
• EXE$V_DISMOUMSG	Bit	Inform operator console of dismounts (DISMOUMSG)
• EXE$V_MOUNTMSG	Bit	Inform operator console of mounts (MOUNTMSG)
SGN$GL_LOADFLAGS	Longword	System load flags (not a parameter itself)
• SGN$V_LOAD_SYS_IMAGES	Bit	Enables loading of optional loadable executive images (LOAD_SYS_IMAGES)
TTY$GL_DELTA	Longword	Delta time for dialup line timer scan (TTY_SCANDELTA)

Global Symbol	Size	Description of Data
TTY$GB_DIALTYP	Byte	Dialup flag bits (TTY_DIALTYPE)
	. Bit	0 = Bell standard protocol
		1 = CCITT standard protocol
	. Bit	0 = disable use of RING signal
		1 = require RING signal before setting DTR
	. Bit	0 = enable 30-second timeout for channel assignment
		1 = disable timeout
	. 2 bits	Reserved
	. Bit	0 = VWS 77 dots per inch monitor
		1 = VWS 100 dots per inch monitor
	. Bit	Reserved for DECwindows
	. Bit	0 = VWS disable square pixel monitor
		1 = VWS enable square pixel monitor
TTY$GB_DEFSPEED	Byte	Default speed for terminals (TTY_SPEED)
TTY$GB_RSPEED	Byte	Default receive speed (TTY_RSPEED)
TTY$GB_PARITY	Byte	Default parity (TTY_PARITY)
TTY$GW_DEFBUF	Word	Default terminal line width (TTY_BUF)
TTY$GL_DEFCHAR	Longword	Default terminal characteristics (TTY_DEFCHAR)
TTY$GL_DEFCHAR2	Longword	Default terminal characteristics (second longword) (TTY_DEFCHAR2)
TTY$GW_TYPAHDSZ	Word	Size of type-ahead buffer (TTY_TYPAHDSZ)
TTY$GW_ALTYPAHD	Word	Alternative type-ahead buffer size (TTY_ALTYPAHD)
TTY$GW_ALTALARM	Word	Alternative type-ahead buffer alarm size (TTY_ALTALARM)
TTY$GW_DMASIZE	Word	Direct memory access size (TTY_DMASIZE)
TTY$GW_PROT	Word	Default terminal allocation protection (TTY_PROT)
TTY$GL_OWNUIC	Longword	Default device owner user identification code (TTY_OWNER)
TTY$GW_CLASSNAM	Word	Default terminal class driver name prefix (TTY_CLASSNAME)
TTY$GB_SILOTIME	Byte	Default silo timeout value for DMF-32 (TTY_SILOTIME)
TTY$GL_TIMEOUT	Longword	Default disconnected terminal timeout value (TTY_TIMEOUT)
TTY$GB_AUTOCHAR	Byte	Autobaud rate recognition character (TTY_AUTOCHAR)
TTY$GL_DEFPORT	Longword	Default port characteristics (TTY_DEFPORT)
SYS$GB_DFMBC	Byte	Default multiblock count (RMS_DFMBC)
SYS$GB_DFMBFSDK	Byte	Default multibuffer count for sequential disk I/O (RMS_DFMBFSDK)
SYS$GB_DFMBFSMT	Byte	Default multibuffer count for magtape I/O (RMS_DFMBFSMT)
SYS$GB_DFMBFSUR	Byte	Default multibuffer count for unit record devices (RMS_DFMBFSUR)
SYS$GB_DFMBFREL	Byte	Default multibuffer count for relative files (RMS_DFMBFREL)

Global Symbol	Size	Description of Data
SYS$GB_DFMBFIDX	Byte	Default multibuffer count for indexed files (RMS_DFMBFIDX)
SYS$GB_DFMBFHSH	Byte	Reserved (RMS_DFMBFHSH)
SYS$GB_RMSPROLOG	Byte	Default structure level for indexed files (RMS_PROLOGUE)
SYS$GW_RMSEXTEND	Word	Default extend quantity for RMS files (RMS_EXTEND_SIZE)
SYS$GW_FILEPROT	Word	Default system-owner-group-world file protection (RMS_FILEPROT)
SYS$GW_GBLBUFQUO	Word	Maximum number of global buffers that may be in concurrent use (RMS_GBLBUFQUO)
SYS$GB_DFNBC	Byte	Default number of blocks for RMS DAP network record-mode transfers; defines maximum network record size (RMS_DFNBC)
PQL$AL_DEFAULT+4	12 longwords	Table of process quota list default values (see Table 25.3)
PQL$AL_MIN+4	12 longwords	Table of process quota list minimum values (see Table 25.3)
PQL$AB_FLAG+1	12 bytes	Table of process quota flags
ACP$GW_MAPCACHE	Word	Number of blocks in bitmap cache (ACP_MAPCACHE)
ACP$GW_HDRCACHE	Word	Number of blocks in file header cache (ACP_HDRCACHE)
ACP$GW_DIRCACHE	Word	Number of blocks in file directory cache (ACP_DIRCACHE)
ACP$GW_DINDXCACHE	Word	Number of pages in file system directory index cache (ACP_DINDXCACHE)
ACP$GW_WORKSET	Word	Ancillary control process working set size (ACP_WORKSET)
ACP$GW_FIDCACHE	Word	Number of cached index file slots (ACP_FIDCACHE)
ACP$GW_EXTCACHE	Word	Number of cached disk extents (ACP_EXTCACHE)
ACP$GW_EXTLIMIT	Word	Fraction of disk to cache (ACP_EXTLIMIT)
ACP$GW_QUOCACHE	Word	Number of quota file entries to cache (ACP_QUOCACHE)
ACP$GW_SYSACC	Word	Default directory access. Not used on disks managed by Files-11XQP (ACP_SYSACC)
ACP$GB_MAXREAD	Byte	Maximum number of blocks to read at once for directories (ACP_MAXREAD)
ACP$GB_WINDOW	Byte	Default window size for system volumes (ACP_WINDOW)
ACP$GB_WRITBACK	Byte	Enable deferred cache write back (ACP_WRITEBACK)
ACP$GB_DATACHK	Byte	Ancillary control process (ACP) data check enable flags (ACP_DATACHECK)
• ACP$V_READCHK	Bit	Do data check on reads
• ACP$V_WRITECHK	Bit	Do data check on writes
ACP$GB_BASEPRIO	Byte	ACP base software priority (ACP_BASEPRIO)
ACP$GB_SWAPFLGS	Byte	ACP swap flags (ACP_SWAPFLGS)

Global Symbol	Size	Description of Data
• ACP$V_SWAPSYS	Bit	Swap ACPs for /SYSTEM volumes
• ACP$V_SWAPGRP	Bit	Swap ACPs for /GROUP volumes
• ACP$V_SWAPPRV	Bit	Swap ACPs for private volumes
• ACP$V_SWAPMAG	Bit	Swap magnetic tape ACPs
EXE$GL_STATIC_FLAGS	Longword	Static system control flags (not a parameter itself)
• EXE$V_XQP_RESIDENT	Bit	Files-11 XQP memory resident (ACP_XQP_RES)
• EXE$V_REBLDSYSD	Bit	System disk rebuild flag (ACP_REBLDSYSD)
• EXE$V_SHADOWING	Bit	Load the volume shadowing driver (SHADOWING)
SYS$GB_DEFPRI	Byte	Default priority for job initiations (DEFPRI)
SYS$GW_IJOBLIM	Word	Limit for interactive jobs (IJOBLIM)
SYS$GW_BJOBLIM	Word	Limit for batch jobs (BJOBLIM)
SYS$GW_NJOBLIM	Word	Limit for network jobs (NJOBLIM)
SYS$GW_RJOBLIM	Word	Limit for remote terminal jobs (RJOBLIM)
SYS$GB_DEFQUEPRI	Byte	Default queue priority (DEFQUEPRI)
SYS$GB_MAXQUEPRI	Byte	Maximum queue priority (MAXQUEPRI)
SYS$GB_PWD_TMO	Byte	Number of seconds that a dialup user has to enter system password before LOGINOUT exits (LGI_PWD_TMO)
SYS$GB_RETRY_LIM	Byte	Number of retries an interactive user has before the process is deleted (LGI_RETRY_LIM)
SYS$GB_RETRY_TMO	Byte	Number of seconds user has to attempt another login before process is deleted (LGI_RETRY_TMO)
SYS$GB_BRK_LIM	Byte	Number of consecutive login failures before LOGINOUT begins evasive action (LGI_BRK_LIM)
SYS$GL_BRK_TMO	Longword	Number of seconds that a suspect must be free of login failures before it is taken off the suspect list (LGI_BRK_TMO)
SYS$GL_HID_TIM	Longword	Number of seconds that LOGINOUT should practice evasive action on an intruder (LGI_HID_TIM)
CLU$GB_VAXCLUSTER	Byte	Controls loading of VAXcluster code; node cannot participate in a VAXcluster unless code is loaded (VAXCLUSTER) 0 = never load 1 = load if SCSLOA is being loaded 2 = always load and also load SCSLOA
CLU$GW_EXP_VOTES	Word	Maximum number of votes that are expected to be in the cluster (EXPECTED_VOTES)
CLU$GW_VOTES	Word	Number of votes this system contributes to quorum (VOTES)
CLU$GW_RECNXINT	Word	Interval during which to attempt reconnection to a VAXcluster member (RECNXINTERVAL)
CLU$GB_QDISK	Octaword	VAXcluster quorum disk name (DISK_QUORUM)

Global Symbol	Size	Description of Data
CLU$GW_QDSKVOTES	Word	Number of votes contributed by quorum disk (QDSKVOTES)
CLU$GW_QDSK-INTERVAL	Word	Disk quorum interval (QDSKINTERVAL)
CLU$GL_ALLOCLS	Longword	Device allocation class for system (ALLOCLASS)
CLU$GW_LCKDIRWT	Word	Determines portion of lock manager directory entries that will be handled by this system (LOCKDIRWT)
CLU$GL_SGN_FLAGS	Longword	Static cluster flags (not a parameter itself)
. CLU$V_NISCS_CONV_BOOT	Bit	Allow remote conversational boot (NISCS_CONV_BOOT)
. CLU$V_NISCS_LOAD_PEA0	Bit	Load the NISCS module PEDRIVER (NISCS_LOAD_PEA0)
CLU$GL_NISCS_PORT_SERV	Longword	Flags for port service (NISCS_PORT_SERV)
CLU$GL_MSCP_LOAD	Longword	Load mass storage control protocol (MSCP) server (MSCP_LOAD)
CLU$GL_MSCP_SERVE_ALL	Longword	Controls MSCP server defaults (MSCP_SERVE_ALL) 0 = do not serve any disks 1 = serve all available disks 2 = serve only locally attached (not hierarchical storage controller) disks
CLU$GL_MSCP_BUFFER	Longword	Amount of nonpaged pool to allocate for the MSCP server (MSCP_BUFFER)
CLU$GL_MSCP_CREDITS	Longword	Number of MSCP send credits for each granted connection (MSCP_CREDITS)
SGN$GB_TAILORED	Byte	Indicates if system is tailored (TAILORED)
EXE$GL_WSFLAGS	Longword	Workstation SYSGEN flags (not a parameter itself)
. EXE$V_OPA0	Bit	If set, reserve the first 23 scan lines for an OPA0 window (WS_OPA0)
SGN$GB_STARTUP_P1	Longword	Passes information to the system startup procedure (STARTUP_P1)
SGN$GB_STARTUP_P2	Longword	Passes information to the system startup procedure (STARTUP_P2)
SGN$GB_STARTUP_P3	Longword	Passes information to the system startup procedure (STARTUP_P3)
SGN$GB_STARTUP_P4	Longword	Passes information to the system startup procedure (STARTUP_P4)
SGN$GB_STARTUP_P5	Longword	Passes information to the system startup procedure (STARTUP_P5)
SGN$GB_STARTUP_P6	Longword	Passes information to the system startup procedure (STARTUP_P6)
SGN$GB_STARTUP_P7	Longword	Passes information to the system startup procedure (STARTUP_P7)
SGN$GB_STARTUP_P8	Longword	Passes information to the system startup procedure (STARTUP_P8)
EXE$GL_S0_PAGING	Longword	Bit mask enabling paging of system code (S0_PAGING)

Global Symbol	Size	Description of Data
SGN$GL_PSEUDOLOA	Longword	Size of pseudo device (PSEUDOLOA)
EXE$GL_POOLCHECK	Longword	Control flags for poolcheck code (POOLCHECK)
SCH$GL_CTLFLAGS	Longword	Reserved
SCH$GB_MINCLASSPRI	Byte	Reserved
SCH$GB_MAXCLASSPRI	Byte	Reserved
SCH$GB_MINPRPRI	Byte	Reserved
MMG$GL_RSRVPAGCNT	Longword	Number of pages to reserve/escrow in process page file (RSRVPAGCNT)
EXE$GL_WINDOW_SYSTEM	Longword	Default windowing system for a workstation (WINDOW_SYSTEM) 0 = no windowing system defined 1 = use DECwindows 2 = use VWS
SCH$GL_AFFINITY_SKIP	Longword	Number of times that a computable process waits for CPU for which it has implicit affinity (AFFINITY_SKIP)
SCH$GL_AFFINITY_TIME	Longword	Reserved (AFFINITY_TIME)
EXE$GB_ERLBUFPAGES	Byte	Number of pages per error log buffer (ERLBUFFERPAGES)
CLU$GL_TAPE_ALLOCLS	Longword	Tape device allocation class (TAPE_ALLOCLASS)

The rest of module SYSPARAM consists of other systemwide parameters, the values of which are not directly adjustable with SYSBOOT or SYSGEN. Rather, their values depend directly on the values of one or more adjustable parameters.

Global Symbol	Size	Description of Data
SWP$GL_SHELLSIZ	Longword	Pages required for shell process
SWP$GW_BAKPTE	Word	Number of process header (PHD) pages for process header page arrays
SWP$GW_EMPTPTE	Word	Number of empty PHD pages for working set list expansion
SWP$GW_WSLPTE	Word	Number of PHD pages for fixed area, working set list, and process section table
SWP$GB_SHLP1PT	Byte	Number of P1 page table pages required for SHELL
	Byte	Spare for alignment
SWP$GL_BSLOTSZ	Longword	Size in pages of balance slot
SWP$GL_MAP	Longword	Address of swapper's I/O page table
SWP$GL_PHDBASVA	Longword	Base address of PHD window
SGN$GL_PHDAPCNT	Longword	Number of SHELL header pages
SGN$GL_PHDLWCNT	Longword	Number of longwords in PHD
SGN$GL_P1LWCNT	Longword	Number of longwords to end of P1 page table
SGN$GL_PHDPAGCT	Longword	Number of all PHD pages excluding page table pages

Global Symbol	Size	Description of Data
SGN$GL_PTPAGCNT	Longword	Number of page table pages
MMG$GL_CTLBASVA	Longword	Initial low-address end of P1 space
EXE$GL_INTSTK	Longword	Address of primary processor's interrupt stack base
MMG$GL_GPTBASE	Longword	Base address of global page table
MMG$GL_GPTE	Longword	Address of first global page table entry at end of system page table (SPT)
MMG$GL_MAXGPTE	Longword	Highest global page table entry address
MMG$GL_MAXSYSVA } MMG$GL_FRESVA	Longword	Highest system virtual address (plus 1)
MMG$GL_SPTBASE	Longword	Base virtual address of SPT
LDR$GL_SPTBASE	Longword	Base address of SPT—physical or virtual as required by SYSLDR
MMG$GL_SPTLEN	Longword	Length of SPT
MMG$GL_SYSPHD	Longword	Virtual address of system header
MMG$GL_SYSPHDLN	Longword	Size in bytes of system header
SWP$GL_BALBASE	Longword	Base virtual address of balance set slots
SWP$GL_BALSPT	Longword	Base virtual address in SPT for mapping balance slots
MMG$GL_SBR	Longword	Physical address of SPT
MMG$GL_NPAGEDYN	Longword	Virtual address of beginning of nonpaged pool
MMG$GL_NPAGNEXT	Longword	Next virtual address for nonpaged pool variable-length list extension
MMG$GL_IRPNEXT	Longword	Next virtual address for intermediate request packet list extension
MMG$GL_LRPNEXT	Longword	Next virtual address for large request packet list extension
MMG$GL_SRPNEXT	Longword	Next virtual address for small request packet list extension
MMG$GL_PAGEDYN	Longword	Virtual address of beginning of paged pool
MMG$GL_MAXPFN	Longword	Maximum page frame number (PFN) accounted for in PFN database
MMG$GL_MINPFN	Longword	Minimum PFN in PFN database
MMG$GL_MAXMEM	Longword	Highest PFN mapped by SYSBOOT (includes pages not in PFN database)
EXE$GL_RPB	Longword	Virtual address of restart parameter block
EXE$GL_SCB	Longword	Virtual address of system control block
EXE$GL_ARCHFLAG	Longword	Architectural flags (bits defined by $ARCDEF)
EXE$GL_STATE	Longword	Flags describing bootstrap progression
LDR$GL_FREE_PT	Quadword	Listhead of free system page table entry database
EXE$GB_CPUDATA	16 bytes	System-specific information
EXE$GB_CPUTYPE	Byte	CPU type read from PR$_SID
EXE$GW_CPUMODEL	Word	CPU model number
CLU$GB_NISCS_COMM } CLU$GQ_NISCS_AUTH	Quadword	NISCS communications region NISCS authorization quadword from CLUSTER_AUTHORIZE.DAT
CLU$GL_NISCS_GROUP	Longword	NISCS group code from CLUSTER_AUTHORIZE.DAT
	12 bytes	Spare for NISCS extensions
PFN$GB_LENGTH	Byte	Number of bytes per page in PFN database

Executive Data Areas

Global Symbol	Size	Description of Data
MMG$GW_BIGPFN	Word	Flag to indicate size of PFN FLINK, BLINK
EXE$GW_PGFL_FID	3 words	File ID of PAGEFILE.SYS
PFN$A_BASE	8 longwords	Base address of eight PFN database array pointers
. PFN$AL_PTE	Longword	Address of page table entry array
. PFN$AL_BAK	Longword	Address of backing store address array
. PFN$AW_REFCNT	Longword	Address of reference count array of words
. PFN$AX_FLINK	Longword	Address of combined forward link
. PFN$AX_SHRCNT		Global share count array of words
. PFN$AX_BLINK	Longword	Address of combined backward link
. PFN$AX_WSLX		Working set list index array of words
. PFN$AW_SWPVBN	Longword	Address of swap image virtual block number array of words
. PFN$AB_STATE	Longword	Address of STATE array of bytes
. PFN$AB_TYPE	Longword	Address of TYPE array of bytes
EXE$GT_STARTUP	33 bytes	Counted ASCII string of name of startup command procedure file

The following table lists the SYSGEN parameters alphabetically and indicates the names of the cells where each parameter is stored.

SYSGEN Parameter	Cell Name
ACP_BASEPRIO	ACP$GB_BASEPRIO
ACP_DATACHECK	ACP$GB_DATACHK
ACP_DINDXCACHE	ACP$GW_DINDXCACHE
ACP_DIRCACHE	ACP$GW_DIRCACHE
ACP_EXTCACHE	ACP$GW_EXTCACHE
ACP_EXTLIMIT	ACP$GW_EXTLIMIT
ACP_FIDCACHE	ACP$GW_FIDCACHE
ACP_HDRCACHE	ACP$GW_HDRCACHE
ACP_MAPCACHE	ACP$GW_MAPCACHE
ACP_MAXREAD	ACP$GB_MAXREAD
ACP_MULTIPLE	EXE$V_MULTACP (EXE$GL_DEFFLAGS)
ACP_QUOCACHE	ACP$GW_QUOCACHE
ACP_REBLDSYSD	EXE$V_REBLDSYSD (EXE$GL_STATIC_FLAGS)
ACP_SHARE	EXE$V_SHRF11ACP (EXE$GL_DEFFLAGS)
ACP_SWAPFLGS	ACP$GB_SWAPFLGS
ACP_SYSACC	ACP$GW_SYSACC
ACP_WINDOW	ACP$GB_WINDOW
ACP_WORKSET	ACP$GW_WORKSET
ACP_WRITEBACK	ACP$GB_WRITBACK
ACP_XQP_RES	EXE$V_XQP_RESIDENT (EXE$GL_STATIC_FLAGS)
AFFINITY_SKIP	SCH$GL_AFFINITY_SKIP
AFFINITY_TIME	SCH$GL_AFFINITY_TIME
ALLOCLASS	CLU$GL_ALLOCLS
AWSMIN	SCH$GL_AWSMIN
AWSTIME	SCH$GL_AWSTIME
BALSETCNT	SGN$GL_BALSETCT
BJOBLIM	SYS$GW_BJOBLIM

SYSGEN Parameter	*Cell Name*
BORROWLIM	SCH$GL_BORROWLIM
BREAKPOINTS	SGN$GL_BRKMSK
BUGCHECKFATAL	EXE$V_FATAL_BUG (EXE$GL_DEFFLAGS)
BUGREBOOT	EXE$V_BUGREBOOT (EXE$GL_DEFFLAGS)
CHANNELCNT	SGN$GW_PCHANCNT
CLASS_PROT	EXE$V_CLASS_PROT (EXE$GL_DYNAMIC_FLAGS)
CLISYMTBL	EXE$GL_CLITABL
CLOCK_INTERVAL	EXE$GW_CLKINT
CONCEAL_DEVICES	EXE$V_CONCEALED (EXE$GL_DEFFLAGS)
CRDENABLE	EXE$V_CRDENABL (EXE$GL_DEFFLAGS)
CTLIMGLIM	SGN$GW_CTLIMGLIM
CTLPAGES	SGN$GW_CTLPAGES
DEADLOCK_WAIT	LCK$GL_WAITTIME
DEFMBXBUFQUO	IOC$GW_MBXBFQUO
DEFMBXMXMSG	IOC$GW_MBXMXMSG
DEFPRI	SYS$GB_DEFPRI
DEFQUEPRI	SYS$GB_DEFQUEPRI
DISK_QUORUM	CLU$GB_QDISK
DISMOUMSG	EXE$V_DISMOUMSG (EXE$GL_MSGFLAGS)
DLCKEXTRASTK	LCK$GL_EXTRASTK
DORMANTWAIT	SCH$GW_DORMANTWAIT
DUMPBUG	EXE$V_BUGDUMP (EXE$GL_DEFFLAGS)
DUMPSTYLE	SGN$GL_DUMP_STYLE
ERLBUFFERPAGES	EXE$GB_ERLBUFPAGES
ERRORLOGBUFFERS	SGN$GW_ERLBUFCNT
EXPECTED_VOTES	CLU$GW_EXP_VOTES
EXTRACPU	SGN$GL_EXTRACPU
EXUSRSTK	SGN$GL_EXUSRSTK
FREEGOAL	SGN$GL_FREEGOAL
FREELIM	SGN$GL_FREELIM
GBLPAGES	SGN$GL_MAXGPGCT
GBLPAGFIL	SGN$GL_GBLPAGFIL
GBLSECTIONS	SGN$GW_GBLSECNT
GROWLIM	SCH$GL_GROWLIM
IJOBLIM	SYS$GW_IJOBLIM
IMGIOCNT	SGN$GW_IMGIOCNT
INTSTKPAGES	SGN$GW_ISPPGCT
IOTA	SCH$GW_IOTA
IRPCOUNT	SGN$GL_IRPCNT
IRPCOUNTV	SGN$GL_IRPCNTV
JOBCTLD	SGN$GL_JOBCTLD
KFILSTCNT	SGN$GB_KFILSTCT
LAMAPREGS	IOC$GW_LAMAPREG
LGI_BRK_DISUSER	EXE$V_BRK_DISUSER (EXE$GL_DYNAMIC_FLAGS)
LGI_BRK_LIM	SYS$GB_BRK_LIM
LGI_BRK_TERM	EXE$V_BRK_TERM (EXE$GL_DYNAMIC_FLAGS)
LGI_BRK_TMO	SYS$GL_BRK_TMO
LGI_HID_TIM	SYS$GL_HID_TIM
LGI_PWD_TMO	SYS$GB_PWD_TMO
LGI_RETRY_LIM	SYS$GB_RETRY_LIM
LGI_RETRY_TMO	SYS$GB_RETRY_TMO

SYSGEN Parameter	Cell Name
LNMPHASHTBL	LNM$GL_HTBLSIZP
LNMSHASHTBL	LNM$GL_HTBLSIZS
LOAD_SYS_IMAGES	SGN$V_LOAD_SYS_IMAGES (SGN$GL_LOADFLAGS)
LOCKDIRWT	CLU$GW_LCKDIRWT
LOCKIDTBL	LCK$GL_IDTBLSIZ
LOCKIDTBL_MAX	LCK$GL_IDTBLMAX
LOCKRETRY	EXE$GL_LOCKRTRY
LONGWAIT	SCH$GW_LONGWAIT
LRPCOUNT	SGN$GL_LRPCNT
LRPCOUNTV	SGN$GL_LRPCNTV
LRPMIN	SGN$GL_LRPMIN
LRPSIZE	SGN$GL_LRPSIZE
MAXBUF	IOC$GW_MAXBUF
MAXCLASSPRI	SCH$GB_MAXCLASSPRI
MAXPROCESSCNT	SGN$GW_MAXPRCCT
MAXQUEPRI	SYS$GB_MAXQUEPRI
MAXSYSGROUP	EXE$GL_SYSUIC
MINCLASSPRI	SCH$GB_MINCLASSPRI
MINPRPRI	SCH$GB_MINPRPRI
MINWSCNT	SGN$GL_MINWSCNT
MOUNTMSG	EXE$V_MOUNTMSG (EXE$GL_MSGFLAGS)
MPW_HILIMIT	MPW$GW_HILIM
MPW_IOLIMIT	MPW$GB_IOLIM
MPW_LOLIMIT	MPW$GW_LOLIM
MPW_LOWAITLIMIT	MPW$GL_LOWAITLIM
MPW_PRIO	MPW$GB_PRIO
MPW_THRESH	MPW$GL_THRESH
MPW_WAITLIMIT	MPW$GL_WAITLIM
MPW_WRTCLUSTER	MPW$GW_MPWPFC
MSCP_BUFFER	CLU$GL_MSCP_BUFFER
MSCP_CREDITS	CLU$GL_MSCP_CREDITS
MSCP_LOAD	CLU$GL_MSCP_LOAD
MSCP_SERVE_ALL	CLU$GL_MSCP_SERVE_ALL
MULTIPROCESSING	SGN$GB_MULTIPROCESSING
MVTIMEOUT	IOC$GW_MVTIMEOUT
NISCS_CONV_BOOT	CLU$V_NISCS_CONV_BOOT (CLU$GL_SGN_FLAGS)
NISCS_LOAD_PEA0	CLU$V_NISCS_LOAD_PEA0 (CLU$GL_SGN_FLAGS)
NISCS_PORT_SERV	CLU$GL_NISCS_PORT_SERV
NJOBLIM	SYS$GW_NJOBLIM
NOAUTOCONFIG	EXE$V_NOAUTOCNF (EXE$GL_DEFFLAGS)
NOCLOCK	EXE$V_NOCLOCK (EXE$GL_TIME_CONTROL)
NOCLUSTER	EXE$V_NOCLUSTER (EXE$GL_DEFFLAGS)
NOPGFLSWP	EXE$V_NOPGFLSWP (EXE$GL_DYNAMIC_FLAGS)
NOSMPSANITY	EXE$V_NOSMPSANITY (EXE$GL_TIME_CONTROL)
NOSPINWAIT	EXE$V_NOSPINWAIT (EXE$GL_TIME_CONTROL)
NPAGEDYN	SGN$GL_NPAGEDYN
NPAGEVIR	SGN$GL_NPAGEVIR
PAGEDYN	SGN$GL_PAGEDYN
PAGFILCNT	SGN$GW_PAGFILCT
PAGTBLPFC	SGN$GB_PGTBPFC
PAMAXPORT	SCS$GB_PAMXPORT

SYSGEN Parameter	*Cell Name*
PANOPOLL	SCS$GB_PANOPOLL
PANUMPOLL	SCS$GB_PANPOLL
PAPOLLINTERVAL	SCS$GW_PAPOLINT
PAPOOLINTERVAL	SCS$GW_PAPOOLIN
PASANITY	SCS$GB_PASANITY
PASTDGBUF	SCS$GW_PAPPDDG
PASTIMOUT	SCS$GW_PASTMOUT
PE1	SGN$GL_PE1
PE2	SGN$GL_PE2
PE3	SGN$GL_PE3
PE4	SGN$GL_PE4
PE5	SGN$GL_PE5
PE6	SGN$GL_PE6
PFCDEFAULT	SGN$GW_DFPFC
PFRATH	SCH$GL_PFRATH
PFRATL	SCH$GL_PFRATL
PFRATS	SCH$GL_PFRATS
PHYSICALPAGES	MMG$GL_PHYPGCNT
PIOPAGES	SGN$GW_PIOPAGES
PIXSCAN	SGN$GW_PIXSCAN
POOLCHECK	EXE$GL_POOLCHECK
POOLPAGING	EXE$V_POOLPGING (EXE$GL_DEFFLAGS)
PQL_DASTLM	PQL$GDASTLM
PQL_DBIOLM	PQL$GDBIOLM
PQL_DBYTLM	PQL$GDBYTLM
PQL_DCPULM	PQL$GDCPULM
PQL_DDIOLM	PQL$GDDIOLM
PQL_DENQLM	PQL$GDENQLM
PQL_DFILLM	PQL$GDFILLM
PQL_DJTQUOTA	PQL$GDJTQUOTA
PQL_DPGFLQUOTA	PQL$GDPGFLQUOTA
PQL_DPRCLM	PQL$GDPRCLM
PQL_DTQELM	PQL$GDTQELM
PQL_DWSDEFAULT	PQL$GDWSDEFAULT
PQL_DWSEXTENT	PQL$GDWSEXTENT
PQL_DWSQUOTA	PQL$GDWSQUOTA
PQL_MASTLM	PQL$GMASTLM
PQL_MBIOLM	PQL$GMBIOLM
PQL_MBYTLM	PQL$GMBYTLM
PQL_MCPULM	PQL$GMCPULM
PQL_MDIOLM	PQL$GMDIOLM
PQL_MENQLM	PQL$GMENQLM
PQL_MFILLM	PQL$GMFILLM
PQL_MJTQUOTA	PQL$GMJTQUOTA
PQL_MPGFLQUOTA	PQL$GMPGFLQUOTA
PQL_MPRCLM	PQL$GMPRCLM
PQL_MTQELM	PQL$GMTQELM
PQL_MWSDEFAULT	PQL$GMWSDEFAULT
PQL_MWSEXTENT	PQL$GMWSEXTENT
PQL_MWSQUOTA	PQL$GMWSQUOTA
PRCPOLINTERVAL	SCS$GW_PRCPOLINT

SYSGEN Parameter	*Cell Name*
PROCSECTCNT	SGN$GW_MAXPSTCT
PSEUDOLOA	SGN$GL_PSEUDOLOA
PU_OPTIONS	SGN$GL_PU_OPTIONS
QBUS_MULT_INTR	SGN$GB_QBUS_MULT_INTR
QDSKINTERVAL	CLU$GW_QDSKINTERVAL
QDSKVOTES	CLU$GW_QDSKVOTES
QUANTUM	SCH$GW_QUAN
REALTIME_SPTS	EXE$GL_RTIMESPT
RECNXINTERVAL	CLU$GW_RECNXINT
RESALLOC	EXE$V_RESALLOC (EXE$GL_DEFFLAGS)
RESHASHTBL	LCK$GL_HTBLSIZ
RJOBLIM	SYS$GW_RJOBLIM
RMS_DFMBC	SYS$GB_DFMBC
RMS_DFMBFHSH	SYS$GB_DFMBFHSH
RMS_DFMBFIDX	SYS$GB_DFMBFIDX
RMS_DFMBFREL	SYS$GB_DFMBFREL
RMS_DFMBFSDK	SYS$GB_DFMBFSDK
RMS_DFMBFSMT	SYS$GB_DFMBFSMT
RMS_DFMBFSUR	SYS$GB_DFMBFSUR
RMS_DFNBC	SYS$GB_DFNBC
RMS_EXTEND_SIZE	SYS$GW_RMSEXTEND
RMS_FILEPROT	SYS$GW_FILEPROT
RMS_GBLBUFQUO	SYS$GW_GBLBUFQUO
RMS_PROLOGUE	SYS$GB_RMSPROLOG
RSRVPAGCNT	MMG$GL_RSRVPAGCNT
S0_PAGING	EXE$GL_S0_PAGING
SAVEDUMP	EXE$V_SAVEDUMP (EXE$GL_DEFFLAGS)
SBIERRENABLE	EXE$V_SBIERR (EXE$GL_DEFFLAGS)
SCH_CTLFLAGS	SCH$GL_CTLFLAGS
SCSBUFFCNT	SCS$GW_BDTCNT
SCSCONNCNT	SCS$GW_CDTCNT
SCSFLOWCUSH	SCS$GW_FLOWCUSH
SCSMAXDG	SCS$GW_MAXDG
SCSMAXMSG	SCS$GW_MAXMSG
SCSNODE	SCS$GB_NODENAME
SCSRESPCNT	SCS$GW_RDTCNT
SCSSYSTEMID	SCS$GB_SYSTEMID
SCSSYSTEMIDH	SCS$GB_SYSTEMIDH
SETTIME	EXE$V_SETTIME (EXE$GL_DEFFLAGS)
SHADOWING	EXE$V_SHADOWING (EXE$GL_STATIC_FLAGS)
SMP_CPUS	SGN$GL_SMP_CPUS
SMP_CPUSH	SGN$GL_SMP_CPUSH
SMP_LNGSPINWAIT	SGN$GL_SMP_LNGSPINWAIT
SMP_SANITY_CNT	SGN$GW_SMP_SANITY_CNT
SMP_SPINWAIT	SGN$GL_SMP_SPINWAIT
SMP_TICK_CNT	SGN$GW_SMP_TICK_CNT
SPTREQ	SGN$GL_SPTREQ
SRPCOUNT	SGN$GL_SRPCNT
SRPCOUNTV	SGN$GL_SRPCNTV
SRPMIN	SGN$GL_SRPMIN
SRPSIZE	SGN$GL_SRPSIZE

SYSGEN Parameter	*Cell Name*
SSINHIBIT	EXE$V_SSINHIBIT (EXE$GL_DEFFLAGS)
STARTUP_P1	SGN$GB_STARTUP_P1
STARTUP_P2	SGN$GB_STARTUP_P2
STARTUP_P3	SGN$GB_STARTUP_P3
STARTUP_P4	SGN$GB_STARTUP_P4
STARTUP_P5	SGN$GB_STARTUP_P5
STARTUP_P6	SGN$GB_STARTUP_P6
STARTUP_P7	SGN$GB_STARTUP_P7
STARTUP_P8	SGN$GB_STARTUP_P8
SWPALLOCINC	SWP$GW_SWPINC
SWPFAIL	SCH$GW_SWPFAIL
SWPFILCNT	SGN$GW_SWPFILES
SWPOUTPGCNT	SWP$GL_SWPPGCNT
SWPRATE	SCH$GL_SWPRATE
SWP_PRIO	SWP$GB_PRIO
SYSMWCNT	SGN$GL_SYSDWSCT
SYSPFC	SGN$GB_SYSPFC
TAILORED	SGN$GB_TAILORED
TAPE_ALLOCLASS	CLU$GL_TAPE_ALLOCLS
TAPE_MVTIMEOUT	IOC$GW_TAPE_MVTIMEOUT
TBSKIPWSL	SGN$GW_WSLMXSKP
TIMEPROMPTWAIT	SGN$GW_TPWAIT
TTY_ALTALARM	TTY$GW_ALTALARM
TTY_ALTYPAHD	TTY$GW_ALTYPAHD
TTY_AUTOCHAR	TTY$GB_AUTOCHAR
TTY_BUF	TTY$GW_DEFBUF
TTY_CLASSNAME	TTY$GW_CLASSNAM
TTY_DEFCHAR	TTY$GL_DEFCHAR
TTY_DEFCHAR2	TTY$GL_DEFCHAR2
TTY_DEFPORT	TTY$GL_DEFPORT
TTY_DIALTYPE	TTY$GB_DIALTYP
TTY_DMASIZE	TTY$GW_DMASIZE
TTY_OWNER	TTY$GL_OWNUIC
TTY_PARITY	TTY$GB_PARITY
TTY_PROT	TTY$GW_PROT
TTY_RSPEED	TTY$GB_RSPEED
TTY_SCANDELTA	TTY$GL_DELTA
TTY_SILOTIME	TTY$GB_SILOTIME
TTY_SPEED	TTY$GB_DEFSPEED
TTY_TIMEOUT	TTY$GL_TIMEOUT
TTY_TYPAHDSZ	TTY$GW_TYPAHDSZ
UAFALTERNATE	EXE$V_SYSUAFALT (EXE$GL_DEFFLAGS)
UDABURSTRATE	SCS$GB_UDABURST
USER3	SGN$GL_USER3
USER4	SGN$GL_USER4
USERD1	SGN$GL_USERD1
USERD2	SGN$GL_USERD2
VAXCLUSTER	CLU$GB_VAXCLUSTER
VIRTUALPAGECNT	SGN$GL_MAXVPGCT
VMS5	SGN$GL_VMS5
VMS6	SGN$GL_VMS6

SYSGEN Parameter	Cell Name
VMS7	SGN$GL_VMS7
VMS8	SGN$GL_VMS8
VMSD1	SGN$GL_VMSD1
VMSD2	SGN$GL_VMSD2
VMSD3	SGN$GL_VMSD3
VMSD4	SGN$GL_VMSD4
VOTES	CLU$GW_VOTES
WINDOW_SYSTEM	EXE$GL_WINDOW_SYSTEM
WPRE_SIZE	SGN$GW_WPRE_SIZE
WPTTE_SIZE	SGN$GL_WPTTE_SIZE
WRITABLESYS	EXE$V_SYSWRTABL (EXE$GL_DEFFLAGS)
WRITESYSPARAMS	EXE$V_WRITESYSPARAMS (EXE$GL_DYNAMIC_FLAGS)
WSDEC	SCH$GL_WSDEC
WSINC	SCH$GL_WSINC
WSMAX	SGN$GL_MAXWSCNT
WS_OPA0	EXE$V_OPA0 (EXE$GL_WSFLAGS)
XFMAXRATE	IOC$GW_XFMXRATE

C.1.5 Boot Parameters Area ($$$$$Z_BOOPARAM)

The boot parameters area passes information from SYSBOOT to later stages of system initialization. The global label MMG$A_BOOPARAM, defined in module EXEC_LAYOUT, locates the beginning of the boot parameters area. Global label BOO$A_BOOPARAM, defined in module BOOPARAM, has the same value. These labels mark the beginning of nonpageable storage reserved for boot parameters. The actual parameters are defined in module BOOPARAM. Chapter 30 gives further information on its contents.

C.1.6 Entry Points for CPU-Dependent Routines ($$$500)

Module SYSLOAVEC contains an entry point for each CPU-dependent routine. Each entry point is a JMP instruction with absolute addressing. The destination of each JMP is changed to a routine in the CPU-dependent image SYSLOA*xxx*.EXE, loaded into nonpaged pool during system initialization. Chapter 29 gives further information.

There are two types of routines in this area. Those routines that are entered through the SCB must have their entry points longword-aligned. Each of these routines has two spare bytes to preserve longword alignment. Other routines can have the six-byte JMP instructions packed together. The area also contains several pointers to CPU-specific data cells.

This program section also has contributions from modules SCSVEC and CLUSTRVEC. Module SCSVEC contains entry points for the loadable system communication services (SCS) code (see Chapter 22). Module CLUSTRVEC describes the entry points for the VAXcluster connection manager and distributed lock manager.

Global Symbol	Size	Description of Routine
		MODULE SYSLOAVEC
EXE$AL_LOAVEC	8 bytes	Address of start of vectors
EXE$MCHK		Machine check exception service routine
EXE$INT54	8 bytes	Interrupt service routine for system control block (SCB) vector 54_{16}
EXE$INT58	8 bytes	Interrupt service routine for SCB vector 58_{16}
EXE$INT5C	8 bytes	Interrupt service routine for SCB vector $5C_{16}$
EXE$INT60	8 bytes	Interrupt service routine for SCB vector 60_{16}
UBA$UNEXINT	8 bytes	Interrupt service routine for unexpected UNIBUS interrupts
EXE$EXTRA1	8 bytes	Extra jump vector; currently targeted to halt in ERRSUB
EXE$EXTRA2	8 bytes	Extra jump vector; currently targeted to halt in ERRSUB
EXE$EXTRA3	8 bytes	Extra jump vector; currently targeted to halt in ERRSUB
EXE$EXTRA4	8 bytes	Extra jump vector; currently targeted to halt in ERRSUB
EXE$EXTRA5	8 bytes	Extra jump vector; currently targeted to halt in ERRSUB
ECC$REENABLE	6 bytes	Reenable memory error timers
EXE$INIBOOTADP	6 bytes	Initialize boot device adapter
EXE$SAVE_CONTEXT	6 bytes	Save processor's context in BUGCHECK
EXE$DUMPCPUREG	6 bytes	Write CPU-specific registers in error log buffer
EXE$REGRESTOR	6 bytes	Restore CPU-specific registers on power recovery
EXE$REGSAVE	6 bytes	Save CPU-specific registers at power failure
EXE$INIPROCREG	6 bytes	Initialize processor registers
EXE$TEST_CSR	6 bytes	Test UNIBUS console/status register for existence
IOC$PURGDATAP	6 bytes	Purge UNIBUS buffered data path
INI$MPMADP	6 bytes	Initialize MA780 shared memory
EXE$STARTUPADP	6 bytes	Start up any adapters
EXE$SHUTDWNADP	6 bytes	Shut down any (all) adapters
MA$RAVAIL	6 bytes	MA780 shared memory resource available
MA$REQUEST	6 bytes	MA780 shared memory request
MA$INITIAL	6 bytes	MA780 shared memory initialization
CON$STARTIO	6 bytes	Console start I/O
CON$SET_LINE	6 bytes	Set console line
CON$DS_SET	6 bytes	Console data set
CON$XON	6 bytes	Send XON to console
CON$XOFF	6 bytes	Send XOFF to console
CON$STOP	6 bytes	Stop console output
CON$STOP2	6 bytes	Stop console output for 2 seconds
CON$ABORT	6 bytes	Abort console I/O
CON$RESUME	6 bytes	Resume console output
CON$SET_MODEM	6 bytes	Set console modem
CON$NULL	6 bytes	Null routine
CON$DISCONNECT	6 bytes	Console disconnect routine
CON$INITIAL	6 bytes	Initialize console controller
CON$INITLINE	6 bytes	Initialize console line
CON$INTINP	6 bytes	Console input interrupt

Global Symbol	Size	Description of Routine
		MODULE SYSLOAVEC
CON$INTOUT	6 bytes	Console output interrupt
CON$$SENDCONSCMD	6 bytes	Send CPU-dependent command to console
SYSL$CLRSBIA	6 bytes	Clear synchronous backplane interconnect adapter error bits
CON$OWNCTY	6 bytes	Set up to talk directly to console
CON$RELEASECTY	6 bytes	Restore normal console interface
CON$GETCHAR	6 bytes	Get a character from the console
CON$PUTCHAR	6 bytes	Put a character out to the console
CON$INIT_CTY	6 bytes	Initialization routine for the console
EXE$READ_TODR	6 bytes	Read time-of-year clock
EXE$WRITE_TODR	6 bytes	Write time-of-year clock
EXE$INIT_TODR	6 bytes	Initialize system time-of-year clock
INI$CONSOLE	6 bytes	Initialize console device data structures
EXE$INI_TIMWAIT	6 bytes	Initialize TIMEDWAIT macro loop data cells
EXE$READP_LOCAL_ TODR	6 bytes	Read physical time-of-year clock
EXE$WRITEP_LOCAL_ TODR	6 bytes	Write physical time-of-year clock
EXE$MOUNTVER	6 bytes	Mount verification main entry point
EXE$MNTVERSIO	6 bytes	Mount verification start I/O request
EXE$MNTVERSHDOL	6 bytes	Mount verification online shadow unit
EXE$CLUTRANIO	6 bytes	Mount verification VAXcluster state transition block I/O
EXE$UPDGNERNUM	6 bytes	Mount verification update shadow set generation number
EXE$MNTVER_GEN_ CRC	6 bytes	Mount verification generate cyclical redundancy checks for magtape devices
EXE$MNTVERSP1	6 bytes	Mount verification spare transfer vector
EXE$MNTVERSP2	6 bytes	Mount verification spare transfer vector
EXE$GL_MVMSLBAS	Longword	Mount verification message list base address
SMP$INTPROC	6 bytes	Interrupt specified CPU
SMP$INTALL	6 bytes	Interrupt all CPUs
SMP$INTALL_BIT	6 bytes	Interrupt all CPUs and set work bit
SMP$INTALL_ACQ	6 bytes	Acquire CPU mutex and interrupt all CPUs
SMP$INTALL_BIT_ACQ	6 bytes	Acquire CPU mutex, set work bit, and interrupt all CPUs
SMP$SETUP_CPU	6 bytes	Initialize symmetric multiprocessing environment for an individual CPU
SMP$SETUP_SMP	6 bytes	Initialize systemwide symmetric multiprocessing context before any individual secondary processor boots
CON$SAVE_CTY	6 bytes	Save console terminal context
CON$RESTORE_CTY	6 bytes	Restore console terminal context
IOC$ALOALTMAP	6 bytes	Allocate alternative map registers (unit control block specified)
IOC$ALOALTMAPN	6 bytes	Allocate alternative map registers (argument specified)
IOC$ALOALTMAPSP	6 bytes	Allocate a specific set of alternative map registers
IOC$REQALTMAP	6 bytes	Request a set of alternative map registers

Global Symbol	Size	Description of Routine
		MODULE SYSLOAVEC
IOC$LOADALTMAP	6 bytes	Load alternative map registers
IOC$RELALTMAP	6 bytes	Release alternative map registers
EXE$READ_LOCAL_ TODR	6 bytes	Read time-of-year clock
SMP$START_CPU	6 bytes	CPU-specific kernel mode code for $START/CPU
SMP$STOP_CPU	6 bytes	CPU-specific kernel mode code for $STOP/CPU
SMP$SHOW_CPU	6 bytes	CPU-specific kernel mode code for $SHOW/CPU
SMP$HALT_CPU	6 bytes	CPU-specific code for completely halting a CPU
SMP$CONTROLP_CPUS	6 bytes	Return a bit mask of CPUs halted by explicit console command
SMP$INVALID_SINGLE	6 bytes	Invalidate translation buffer entry
SMP$VIRTCONS_SERVER	6 bytes	Serve virtual console request from secondary CPU
EXE$SNAPSHOT_BI	6 bytes	Log VAXBI errors
EXE$LOGMEM	6 bytes	Log memory control and status registers to error log buffer
EXE$ISSUE_ADP_STOP	6 bytes	Issue a VAXBI stop to KRBTA adapters
CON$VCINP	6 bytes	Workstation keyboard driver entry point to OPA0 input routines
EXE$EXTRA7	6 bytes	Extra jump vector; currently targeted to halt in ERRSUB
EXE$EXTRA8	6 bytes	Extra jump vector; currently targeted to halt in ERRSUB
EXE$EXTRA9	6 bytes	Extra jump vector; currently targeted to halt in ERRSUB
EXE$EXTRA10	8 bytes	Extra jump vector; currently targeted to halt in ERRSUB
EXE$MCHK_ERRCNT	Longword	Address of error counters in machine check routine
EXE$FRAME_BLOX	Longword	Address of local copies of machine check frames
EXE$LOAD_NOP	Byte	RSB instruction (initial destination of JMP instructions in vectors)
EXE$LOAD_KDISP ⎫ EXE$LOAD_KCJF ⎭	6 bytes	Reserved; currently targeted to EXE$LOAD_NOP
EXE$LOAD_KRUF	6 bytes	Reserved; currently targeted to EXE$LOAD_NOP
EXE$LOAD_KSPR1	6 bytes	Reserved; currently targeted to EXE$LOAD_NOP
EXE$LOAD_KSPR2	6 bytes	Reserved; currently targeted to EXE$LOAD_NOP
	Byte	RSB instruction
EXE$LOAD_EDISP	6 bytes	Reserved; currently targeted to EXE$LOAD_NOP
EXE$LOAD_ESPR1	6 bytes	Reserved; currently targeted to EXE$LOAD_NOP
EXE$LOAD_ESPR2	6 bytes	Reserved; currently targeted to EXE$LOAD_NOP
	Byte	RSB instruction
		MODULE SCSVEC
SCS$GQ_CONFIG	Quadword	Listhead for system descriptor blocks
SCS$GQ_DIRECT	Quadword	Listhead for directory of processes in VAXcluster system
SCS$GQ_POLL	Quadword	Listhead of system communication architecture poller process blocks giving process names

1221

Global Symbol	Size	Description of Routine
		MODULE SCSVEC
SCS$GL_BDT	Longword	Buffer descriptor table for system communication services (SCS) block transmissions
SCS$GL_CDL	Longword	Connection descriptor table pointing to list of SCS connections
SCS$GL_RDT	Longword	Response descriptor table
SCS$GL_MCLEN	Longword	Reserved
SCS$GL_MCADR	Longword	Address of computer interconnect port microcode in nonpaged pool
SCS$GL_MSCP	Longword	Address of mass storage control protocol (MSCP) server
SCS$GL_MSCP_MV	Longword	MSCP server mount verification routine
SCS$GL_MSCP_NEWDEV	Longword	MSCP server new device handling
SCS$GL_PDT	Longword	Listhead of port descriptor blocks
SCS$GA_DFLTMSK	Word	Mask of SCS system applications to enable when new systems appear
SCS$GW_NEXTBIT	Word	Next bit available for assignment
SCS$GA_EXISTS	Longword	Address of SCSLOA
SCS$AL_LOAVEC	6 bytes	Address of start of SCS vectors
SCS$ACCEPT		Perform SCS accept
SCS$ALLOC_CDT	6 bytes	Allocate a connection descriptor table
SCS$ALLOC_RSPID	6 bytes	Allocate a response ID
SCS$CONFIG_PTH	6 bytes	Configure with path to remote system
SCS$CONFIG_SYS	6 bytes	Configure with system ID
SCS$CONNECT	6 bytes	Perform SCS connect
SCS$DEALL_CDT	6 bytes	Deallocate a connection descriptor table
SCS$DEALL_RSPID	6 bytes	Deallocate a response ID
SCS$DISCONNECT	6 bytes	Perform SCS disconnect
SCS$ENTER	6 bytes	Insert an entry in SCS directory
SCS$LISTEN	6 bytes	Perform an SCS listen operation
SCS$LOCLOOKUP	6 bytes	Look up a path block
SCS$REMOVE	6 bytes	Remove an entry in SCS directory
SCS$RESUMEWAITR	6 bytes	Resume when controller request block is dequeued
SCS$UNSTALLUCB	6 bytes	Resume when unit control block is dequeued
SCS$LKP_RDTCDRP	6 bytes	Search a response descriptor table for a class driver request packet (CDRP)
SCS$LKP_RDTWAIT	6 bytes	Search a response ID wait queue for a CDRP
SCS$RECYL_RSPID	6 bytes	Recycle a response ID
SCS$FIND_RDTE	6 bytes	Locate and validate the response descriptor table entry for a given response ID
SCS$LKP_MSGWAIT	6 bytes	Send credit wait queues for CDRP with given connection descriptor table
SCS$DIR_LOOKUP	6 bytes	Search for processes on remote node
SCS$NEW_SB	6 bytes	Called when a system block is created or reused
SCS$POLL_PROC	6 bytes	Declare a process name to the poller
SCS$POLL_MODE	6 bytes	Enable/disable polling of a process
SCS$POLL_MBX	6 bytes	Declare a mailbox to receive poll notifications
SCS$CANCEL_MBX	6 bytes	Cancel notifications to a mailbox
SCS$SHUTDOWN	6 bytes	Shut down all SCS virtual circuits

Global Symbol	Size	Description of Routine
		MODULE CLUSTRVEC
CLU$GL_CLUB	Longword	Address of cluster block
CLU$GL_CLUSVEC	Longword	Address of cluster system vector
CLU$GW_MAXINDEX	Word	Maximum index+1 in cluster system vector
clu_rsb	Byte	Local RSB instruction used to make unloaded entry a NOP
CLU$AL_LOAVEC ⎫ CLS$AL_LOAVEC ⎬ CLU$GL_LOA_ADDR ⎭	Longword	Contains cluster code load address
LCK$SND_CVTREQ	6 bytes	Send a conversion request to remote system
LCK$SND_LOCKREQ	6 bytes	Send a lock request to remote system
LCK$SND_GRANTED	6 bytes	Send a lock granted message
LCK$SND_DEQGR	6 bytes	Send a dequeue lock message to master system (lock is in granted state)
LCK$SND_DEQCV	6 bytes	Send a dequeue lock message to master system (lock is in conversion wait state)
LCK$SND_DEQWT	6 bytes	Send a dequeue lock message to master system (lock is in wait state)
LCK$SND_BLKING	6 bytes	Send a blocking message
LCK$SND_RMVDIR	6 bytes	Send a remove directory entry message
LCK$SND_TIMESTAMP_RQST	6 bytes	Send a timestamp request
LCK$SND_SRCHDLCK	6 bytes	Send a deadlock search message
LCK$SND_DLCKFND	6 bytes	Send a deadlock found message
LCK$SND_REDO_SRCH	6 bytes	Send a redo deadlock search message
LCK$CVT_ID_TO_LKB	6 bytes	Convert a lock ID to lock block address
CNX$ALLOC_CDRP	6 bytes	Allocate a class driver request packet (CDRP) and convert cluster system ID
CNX$ALLOC_CDRP_ONLY	6 bytes	Allocate a CDRP
CNX$ALLOC_WARMCDRP	6 bytes	Allocate a CDRP with response ID and message buffer
CNX$ALLOC_WARMCDRP_CSB	6 bytes	Allocate a warm CDRP using cluster system block (CSB)
CNX$DEALL_MSG_BUF_CSB	6 bytes	Deallocate a message buffer using a CSB
CNX$DEALL_WARMCDRP_CSB	6 bytes	Deallocate a warm CDRP using a CSB
CNX$INIT_CDRP	6 bytes	Initialize a CDRP
CNX$SEND_MNY_MSGS	6 bytes	Send acknowledged messages to all nodes
CNX$SEND_MSG	6 bytes	Send an acknowledged message
CNX$SEND_MSG_CSB	6 bytes	Send a message using a CSB
CNX$SEND_MSG_RESP	6 bytes	Send a message and recycle message buffer
CNX$SEND_MSG_RSPID	6 bytes	Send a message with a response ID
CNX$BLOCK_XFER	6 bytes	Initiate a block transfer request
CNX$BLOCK_XFER_IRP	6 bytes	Initiate a block transfer request with an IRP
CNX$PARTNER_INIT_CSB	6 bytes	Initialize partner portion of a block transfer
CNX$BLOCK_READ	6 bytes	Partner block read
CNX$BLOCK_READ_IRP	6 bytes	Partner block read with an IRP

Global Symbol	Size	Description of Routine
		MODULE CLUSTRVEC
CNX$BLOCK_WRITE	6 bytes	Partner block write
CNX$BLOCK_WRITE_IRP	6 bytes	Partner block write with an IRP
CNX$PARTNER_FINISH	6 bytes	Complete partner's end of a block transfer
CNX$PARTNER_RESPOND	6 bytes	Send a block transfer completed response
CNX$ADJ_EXPT_VOTES	6 bytes	Adjust expected votes
CNX$SHUTDOWN	6 bytes	Request a cluster shutdown
CNX$POWER_FAIL	6 bytes	Powerfail recovery entry
CNX$DISK_CHANGE	6 bytes	Quorum disk connection state change
CNX$BUGCHECK_CLUSTER	6 bytes	Bugcheck local cluster
EXE$ALLOC_CSD	6 bytes	Allocate and initialize a cluster server data block
EXE$DEALLOC_CSD	6 bytes	Deallocate cluster server data block or mark it for deletion
EXE$CSP_BRDCST	6 bytes	Send a cluster server process request to all nodes
EXE$CSP_CALL	6 bytes	Send a request message to local or remote cluster server process
EXE$CSP_COMMAND	6 bytes	Receive command from cluster server process
EXE$CSP_BRKTHRU	6 bytes	Send a breakthrough message throughout cluster
LKI$SND_STDREQ	6 bytes	Send a standard information request message
LKI$SND_BLKING	6 bytes	Send a request for list of blocking locks
LKI$SND_BLKBY	6 bytes	Send a request for list of blocked locks
LKI$SND_LOCKS	6 bytes	Send a request for list of all locks
CNX$CREATED_INCRNF	6 bytes	Incarnation file creation
CWPS$ALLOCATE_SRV	6 bytes	Allocate a clusterwide process service (CWPS) block
CWPS$COPY_NODE_INFO	6 bytes	Obtain information about all current VAXcluster nodes
CWPS$SSND_CREPRC_RQST	6 bytes	Send CWPS $CREPRC request to partner node
CWPS$SSND_GETJPI_RQST	6 bytes	Send CWPS $GETJPI request to partner node
CWPS$SSND_PCNTRL_RQST	6 bytes	Send CWPS process control request to partner node
CWPS$SSND_GETSYI_RQST	6 bytes	Send CWPS $GETSYI request to partner node
CWPS$SSND_GETDVI_RQST	6 bytes	Send CWPS $GETDVI request to partner node

C.2   **DYNAMICALLY ALLOCATED EXECUTIVE DATA**

Many of the data structures and areas of system address space are not part of the base image but instead are constructed when the system is initialized. The sizes of some of these areas depend on the values of SYSGEN parameters; those of others, on the particular physical configuration.

C.2.1   **Restart Parameter Block**

The restart parameter block (RPB) is filled in at initialization time with bootstrap parameters. The power failure interrupt service routine loads the volatile machine state into the RPB before the system halts. During power recovery, the console subsystem examines the RPB to determine whether memory contents survived the power outage. The use of the RPB is discussed in Chapters 30 and 33.

C.2.2   **Page Frame Number Database**

The page frame number (PFN) database consists of several arrays, the contents of which describe the state of pages of physical memory. The PFN arrays are described in Chapter 14. Their use during page fault resolution is discussed in Chapter 16. PFN array manipulation during swapper operations is discussed in Chapter 18.

C.2.3   **Paged Pool**

Paged pool contains systemwide dynamically allocated structures that do not have to be permanently resident. Typical structures allocated from paged pool are listed in Chapter 19.

C.2.4   **Nonpaged Pool**

Nonpaged pool contains dynamically allocated structures and loaded code modules that must not page. There are several nonpaged pool areas:

- A variable-length list area that can accommodate blocks of any size
- Three lookaside lists containing preformed fixed-length blocks, which can be quickly allocated or deallocated

The organization and uses of the areas of nonpaged pool are described in Chapter 19.

C.2.5   **Interrupt Stack**

The interrupt stack is used to service all hardware interrupts and all software interrupts except asynchronous system trap (AST) delivery. Each CPU has its own interrupt stack, located within the CPU's per-CPU data area.

C.2.6   **System Control Block**

The system control block (SCB) contains vectors through which the processor dispatches exceptions and interrupts to the appropriate service routines. SCB size varies with processor type and configuration. All processors have at least one page, which is defined by the VAX architecture. EXE$GL_SCB contains the starting virtual address of the SCB. Chapter 2 contains information on the architecturally defined page, and Chapter 3, information on the use of any additional pages.

C.2.7   **Balance Set Slot Area**

The balance set slot area is an array of process headers (PHDs). Each resident process has its PHD in one of the balance set slots. Balance set slots are described in Chapter 14. Their use by the swapper is discussed in Chapter 18.

C.2.8   **System Header**

The system header is a system analog to PHDs. It is used in the paging of system code. The major structures within the system header are the system working set list and the system section table, which describes mapped global sections.

C.2.9   **System Page Table**

The system page table (SPT) maps system space. It is sized and initialized by SYSBOOT to reflect system needs and SYSGEN parameters. It is altered during system operation to reflect changes in system space caused by the following events, among others:

- Loading of executive images
- Process creation, outswap, and inswap
- Use of paged pool
- System space paging

C.2.10   **Global Page Table**

The global page table is a pseudo extension of the SPT that allows global page table entries (GPTEs) to be accessed with system virtual page numbers (SVPNs). The global page table is altered when global sections are created and deleted. In addition, GPTEs can change as a result of page faults. The global page table is described in Chapter 14.

C.3   **PROCESS-SPECIFIC EXECUTIVE DATA**

Some process-specific data is stored in the PHD. That data is accessible (subject to synchronization considerations) whenever the process is resident. Most other process-specific data is kept in P1 space. P1 space is only accessible when the process is current. The executive queues an AST to execute in process context when it is necessary to acquire or modify such data from a process that is not current.

This section lists the contents of P1 space.

C.3.1 **P1 Pointer Page**

The P1 pointer page is a permanent member of the process working set and is defined in executive module SHELL.

Global Symbol	Size	Description of Data
CTL$GW_NMIOCH	Word	Number of I/O channels
CTL$GW_CHINDX	Word	Maximum channel index
CTL$GL_LNMHASH	Longword	Process logical name hash table pointer
CTL$GL_LNMDIRECT	Longword	Process logical name directory pointer
	Longword	Maximum extent (low-address limit) of kernel stack
CTL$AL_STACK	4 longwords	Array of stack pointer values
	. Longword	Initial value of kernel stack pointer
	. Longword	Initial value of executive stack pointer
	. Longword	Initial value of supervisor stack pointer
	. Longword	Initial value of user stack pointer
CTL$GQ_LNMTBL-CACHE	2 longwords	Listhead for logical name translation cache
CTL$GL_CMSUPR	Longword	Address of change mode to supervisor handler
CTL$GL_CMUSER	Longword	Address of change mode to user handler
CTL$GL_CMHANDLR	Longword	Address of compatibility mode handler
CTL$AQ_EXCVEC	8 longwords	Addresses of primary and secondary exception handlers for each of the four access modes
CTL$GL_THEXEC	Longword	Executive mode exit handler listhead
CTL$GL_THSUPR	Longword	Supervisor mode exit handler listhead
CTL$GQ_COMMON	Quadword	Descriptor (size and address) of per-process common area
CTL$GL_GETMSG	Longword	Address of per-process message dispatcher
CTL$AL_STACKLIM	4 longwords	Lowest stack value for each access mode
CTL$GL_CTLBASVA	Longword	Low-address end of permanent part of P1 space
CTL$GL_IMGHDRBF	Longword	Address of image header buffer
CTL$GL_IMGLSTPTR	Longword	Address of image control block list (for debugger)
CTL$GL_PHD	— Longword	Address of P1 window that double-maps the process header
CTL$GQ_ALLOCREG	2 longwords	Address of process allocation region and size
CTL$GQ_MOUNTLST	Quadword	Listhead for the process-private mounted volume list
CTL$T_USERNAME	12 bytes	User name for process (blank-filled ASCII string)
CTL$T_ACCOUNT	8 bytes	Account name for process (blank-filled ASCII string)
CTL$GQ_LOGIN	Quadword	System time at process creation
CTL$GL_FINALSTS	Longword	Exit status of latest image to execute
CTL$GL_WSPEAK	Longword	Peak working set size for process

Global Symbol	Size	Description of Data
CTL$GL_VIRTPEAK	Longword	Peak page file used
CTL$GL_VOLUMES	Longword	Number of mounted volumes
CTL$GQ_ISTART	Quadword	Image activation time
CTL$GL_ICPUTIM	Longword	Initial image CPU time
CTL$GL_IFAULTS	Longword	Initial image page fault count
CTL$GL_IFAULTIO	Longword	Initial image page fault I/O count
CTL$GL_IWSPEAK	Longword	Image working set peak
CTL$GL_IPAGEFL	Longword	Image page file peak usage
CTL$GL_IDIOCNT	Longword	Initial image direct I/O count
CTL$GL_IBIOCNT	Longword	Initial image buffered I/O count
CTL$GL_IVOLUMES	Longword	Initial image volume mount count
CTL$T_NODEADDR	7 bytes	Remote node address
CTL$T_NODENAME	7 bytes	Remote node name
CTL$T_REMOTEID	17 bytes	Remote node ID
	Byte	Spare for alignment
CTL$GQ_PROCPRIV	Quadword	Permanent process privilege mask
CTL$GL_USRCHMK	Longword	Address of per-process change mode to kernel dispatcher
CTL$GL_USRCHME	Longword	Address of per-process change mode to executive dispatcher
CTL$GL_POWERAST	Longword	Address of power recovery AST for process
CTL$GB_PWRMODE	Byte	Access mode for power recovery AST
CTL$GB_SSFILTER	Byte	System services inhibit filter mask
CTL$GB_REENABLE_ASTS	Byte	Low bit set by SCH$ASTDEL to notify user mode code that it must request $SETAST to reenable user mode ASTs
	Byte	Spare for alignment
CTL$AL_FINALEXC	4 longwords	Address of last chance exception handlers for each of the four access modes
CTL$GL_CCBBASE	Longword	Address of base of I/O channel area
CTL$GQ_DBGAREA	Quadword	Descriptor (size and address) of debug symbol table
CTL$GL_RMSBASE	Longword	Address of base of RMS image
CTL$GL_PPMSG	2 longwords	Address of process-permanent message section
CTL$GB_MSGMASK	Byte	Default message display flags
CTL$GB_DEFLANG	Byte	Default message language
CTL$GW_PPMSGCHN	Word	Channel to process-permanent message section
CTL$GL_USRUNDWN	Longword	Per-process vector to user rundown service
CTL$GL_PCB	Longword	Address of process control block
CTL$GL_RUF	Longword	Address of recovery unit process block
CTL$GL_SITESPEC	Longword	Site-specific per-process cell
CTL$GL_KNOWNFIL	Longword	Process known file list pointer
CTL$AL_IPASTVEC	8 longwords	Reserved
CTL$GL_CMCNTX	Longword	Address of the AME context page
CTL$GL_IAFLNKPTR	Longword	Address of image activator fixup list (used by the debugger)
CTL$GL_F11BXQP	Longword	Address of Files-11 XQP data area
CTL$GQ_P0ALLOC	Quadword	Header of P0 extension to process allocation region
CTL$GL_PRCALLCNT	Longword	Number of bytes of process allocation region usable by image requests

Global Symbol	Size	Description of Data
CTL$GL_RDIPTR	Longword	Address of rights database identifier
CTL$GL_LNMDIRSEQ	Longword	Sequence number for cache of process logical name table translations
CTL$GQ_HELPFLAGS	Quadword	Help flags
CTL$GQ_TERMCHAR	Quadword	Reserved
CTL$GL_KRPFL	Quadword	Listhead for kernel request packet lookaside list
CTL$GL_KRPBL		list
CTL$GL_CREPRC_FLAGS	Longword	$CREPRC flags used to create this process
CTL$GL_THCOUNT	3 longwords	Number of exit handlers for executive, supervisor, and user modes
CTL$GQ_CWPS_Q1	Quadword	Reserved
CTL$GQ_CWPS_Q2	Quadword	Reserved
CTL$GL_CWPS_L1	Longword	Reserved
CTL$GL_CWPS_L2	Longword	Reserved
CTL$GL_CWPS_L3	Longword	Reserved
CTL$GL_CWPS_L4	Longword	Reserved
	Quadword	Spare for alignment
CTL$GL_PRCPRM_ KDATA2	Longword	Address of kernel mode data extension area
CTL$GL_USRUNDWN_ EXEC	Longword	Address of executive mode user rundown service

C.3.2   Other P1 Space Data Areas

The layout of P1 space is described in Appendix F. Table F.6 lists the global labels that delimit each area in P1 space. The remainder of this section lists data locations in specific P1 areas that are defined in module SHELL. The areas are presented in order of decreasing P1 virtual addresses. That is, the command language interpreter (CLI) data pages, presented first, occupy the highest P1 address range. The RMS data area, listed last, occupies the lowest P1 address range of the areas presented here.

C.3.2.1   Data Pages for Command Language Interpreter. Module SHELL sets aside an area for the generic CLI data pages.

Global Symbol	Size	Description of Data
CTL$AL_CLICALBK	2 longwords	Call back vector for command language interpreter (CLI)
CTL$AG_CLIMAGE	2 longwords	Virtual address range of CLI
CTL$GL_UAF_FLAGS	Longword	Flags from authorization record
CTL$GT_CLINAME	32 bytes	CLI name (file name only)
CTL$GT_TABLENAME	256 bytes	CLI table name (full file specification)
CTL$GT_SPAWNCLI	32 bytes	Spawn CLI name (file name only)
CTL$GT_SPAWNTABLE	256 bytes	Spawn CLI table name (full file specification)
CTL$AG_CLIDATA		Rest of CLI data area

C.3.2.2 **Process Allocation Region.** The process allocation area is a per-process pool area constructed exactly like paged and nonpaged dynamic memory. Chapter 19 gives further information.

Global Symbol	Size	Description of Data
CTL$GQ_ALLOCREG	Longword	Process allocation region pointer
	Longword	Initial size of region

C.3.2.3 **Compatibility Mode Context Page.** Another P1 data area for which module SHELL defines symbols is the page used by the compatibility mode exception service routine.

Global Symbol	Size	Description of Data
CTL$AL_CMCNTX	10 longwords	General register contents stored by exception service routine
	• 7 longwords	Saved R0 through R6
	• 1 longword	Saved compatibility mode exception code
	• 2 longwords	Saved exception program counter and processor status longword
	Rest of page	Used by compatibility mode emulator

C.3.2.4 **RMS Data Area.** This area contains the RMS context that exists for the life of the process. It includes impure areas to describe process-permanent and image I/O files.

Global Symbol	Size	Description of Data
PIO$GL_FMLH	2 longwords	Free memory listhead for process I/O segment
PIO$GL_IIOFSPLH	2 longwords	Free memory listhead for image I/O segment
PIO$GW_STATUS	Word	RMS overall status
PIO$GT_ENDSTR	16 bytes	End-of-data string
PIO$GW_DFPROT	Word	Default file protection
PIO$GB_DFMBC	Byte	Default multiblock count
PIO$GB_DFMBFSDK	Byte	Default multibuffer count for sequential disk I/O
PIO$GB_DFMBFSMT	Byte	Default multibuffer count for magnetic tape I/O
PIO$GB_DFMBFSUR	Byte	Default multibuffer count for unit record devices
PIO$GB_DFMBFREL	Byte	Default multibuffer count for relative files

Global Symbol	Size	Description of Data
PIO$GB_DFMBFIDX	Byte	Default multibuffer count for indexed files
PIO$GB_DFMBFHSH	Byte	Reserved
PIO$GB_DFNBC	Byte	Default network block count
PIO$GB_RMSPROLOG	Byte	Default structure level for indexed files
PIO$GW_RMSEXTEND	Word	Default extend quantity for RMS files
PIO$GB_JNL_STALL_ CNT	Byte	Count of stalled journal threads
PIO$GL_DIRCACHE	2 longwords	Directory cache listhead
PIO$GL_DIRCFRLH	Longword	Free list for directory cache nodes
PIO$GL_RUB_FLINK	2 longwords	RMS Recovery Unit Block listhead
PIO$GL_RUB_BLINK		
PIO$GL_NXTIRBSEQ	Longword	Next sequence number for IRB$L_IDENT
PIO$GW_PIOIMPA	9 longwords	Impure area descriptor for process I/O segment
	4 bytes	Spare for alignment
PIO$GW_IIOIMPA	41 longwords	Impure area descriptor for image I/O segment
PIO$AL_RMSEXH	4 longwords	RMS exit handler control block
PIO$GQ_IIODEFAULT	Quadword	Default image I/O area
PIO$GL_LNKCSHADR	Longword	Logical link cache entry listhead
PIO$GL_RU_HANDLER_ ID	Longword	Default recovery unit handler ID
PIO$GL_RU_FAILURE_ COUNT	Longword	Recovery unit failure count
PIO$GL_RU_WAIT_Q_ FLINK	2 longwords	Recovery unit wait queue listhead
PIO$GL_RU_WAIT_Q_ BLINK		
PIO$GQ_NTRUB_LH	Quadword	Reserved
PIO$GL_NT0_RM_ID	Longword	Reserved
PIO$GL_RESERVED0	Longword	Reserved
PIO$GQ_RUF_TSB_LH	Quadword	Reserved
PIO$GL_RESERVED1	Longword	Reserved
PIO$GL_RESERVED2	Longword	Reserved
PIO$GL_RESERVED3	Longword	Reserved
PIO$GL_RESERVED4	Longword	Reserved
PIO$GL_RESERVED5	Longword	Reserved
PIO$GL_RESERVED6	Longword	Reserved
PIO$GT_DDSTRING	256 bytes	Default directory string

D Naming Conventions

The conventions described in this appendix were adopted to aid implementors in producing meaningful public names. Public names are names that are global (known to the linker) or that appear in parameter or macro definition files. Public names follow these conventions for the following reasons:

- Using reserved names ensures that customer-written software will not be invalidated by subsequent releases of Digital products that add new symbols.
- Using definite patterns for different uses tells someone reading the source code what type of object is being referenced. For example, the form of a macro name is different from that of an offset, which is different from that of a status code.
- Using length codes within a pattern associates the size of an object with its name, increasing the likelihood that reference to this object will use the correct instructions.
- Using a facility code in symbol definitions gives the reader an indication of where the symbol is defined. Separate groups of implementors choose facility code names that will not conflict with one another.

To fully conform with these standards, local synonyms should never be defined for public symbols. The full public symbol should be used in every reference to give maximum clarity to the reader.

D.1 PUBLIC SYMBOL PATTERNS

All Digital symbols contain a dollar sign. Thus, customers and applications developers are strongly advised to use underscores instead of dollar signs to avoid future conflicts.

Public symbols should be constructed to convey as much information as possible about the entities they name. Frequently, private names follow a similar convention. The private name convention is then the same as the public one, with the underscore replacing the dollar sign in symbol names. Private names are used both within a module and globally between modules of a facility that is never in a library. All names that might ever be bound into a user's program must follow the rules for public names. In the case of internal names, a double dollar sign convention can be used, as shown in item 4 in the following list of formats:

1. System service and Record Management Services (RMS) VAX MACRO names are of the form

    $*service-name*

In a system service VAX MACRO name, a trailing _S or _G distinguishes the stack form from the separate argument list form. Details about the names of system service macros can be found in the *Introduction to VMS System Services*.

These names appear in the system macro library STARLET.MLB and represent a call to one of the VMS system services or RMS services. The following examples show this form of symbol name:

$ASCEFC_S	Associate common event flag cluster
$CLOSE	Close a file
$TRNLNM_G	Translate logical name

2. Facility-specific public macro names are of the form

   $*facility_macro-name*

   The executive does not use any symbol names of this form.
3. System macros using local symbols or macros always use names of the form

   $*facility*$*macro-name*

   This is the form to be used both for symbols generated by a macro and included in calls to it, and for internal macros that are not documented. The executive does not use any symbol names of this form.
4. Global entry point names are of the form

   facility$*entry-name*

   The following examples show this form of symbol name:

EXE$ALOPAGED	Allocate paged dynamic memory
IOC$WFIKPCH	Wait for interrupt and keep channel
MMG$PAGEFAULT	Page fault exception handler

Global entry point names that are intended for use only within a set of related procedures but not by any calling programs outside the set are of the form

   facility$$*entry-name*

The executive contains few symbol names of this form. However, the Run-Time Library contains several examples of symbol names that follow this convention, for example:

BAS$$NUM_INIT	Initialize the BASIC NUM function
FOR$$SIGNAL_STO	Signal a FORTRAN error and call LIB$STOP
OTS$$GET_LUN	Get logical unit number

5. Global entry point names that have nonstandard invocations (JSB entry point names) are of the following form, where _R*n* indicates that R0 through R*n* are not preserved by the routine:

   facility$*entry-name*_R*n*

   Note that the invoker of such an entry point must include at least registers R2 through R*n* in its own entry mask so that a stack unwind will restore all registers properly.

   The executive does not use this convention for its JSB entry points, but the Run-Time Library contains several examples of its use, for example:

COB$CVTFP_R9	Convert floating to packed
MTH$SIN_R4	Single precision sine function
STR$COPY_DX_R8	JSB entry to general string copying routine

6. Status codes and condition values are of the form

   facility$_*status*

   The following examples show this form of symbol name:

RMS$_FNF	File not found
SS$_ILLEFC	Illegal event flag cluster
SS$_WASCLR	Flag was previously clear

7. Global variable names are of the form

   facility$G*t*_*variable-name*

   The letter G indicates a global variable. The letter *t* represents the type of variable (see Section D.2). The following examples show this form of symbol name:

CTL$GQ_PROCPRIV	Process privilege mask
EXE$GL_NONPAGED	First free block in nonpaged pool
SCH$GL_FREECNT	Number of pages on the free page list

8. Addressable global arrays use the letter A (instead of the letter G) and are of the form

   facility$A*t*_*array-name*

   The letter A indicates a global array. The letter *t* indicates the type of array element (see Section D.2). In some uses, the symbol's value is the address of the beginning of the array; in other uses, the symbol is the name of a variable that contains the address of the beginning of the array. The following examples show both uses of this form of symbol name:

CTL$AQ_EXCVEC	Array of primary and secondary exception vectors
CTL$AL_STACK	Array of stack limits
PFN$AX_FLINK	Address of array of forward links for page frame number lists
EXE$AL_ERLBUFADR	Address of array of error log allocation buffers

9. The letter A, along with the letter R, indicates a pointer to a structure. This use, new with VMS Version 5, describes a vectored universal symbol in the base image that contains the address of a structure in a loadable executive image. Chapter 29 describes the modular organization of the VMS executive in detail. The following examples show this form of symbol name:

EXE$AR_SYSTEM_ PRIMITIVES_DATA	Address of data related to nonpaged pool allocation
SMP$AR_SPNLKVEC	Address of table of spinlock control blocks
SYS$AR_JOBCTLMB	Address of job controller's mailbox unit control block

10. Public structure definition macro names are of the form

   $*facility_structure*DEF

Invoking this macro defines all symbols of the form *structure*$*xxxxxx*.

Most of the public structure definitions used by the VMS operating system do not include the string "facility_" in the macros that define structure offsets. Rather, macros of the following form are used to define *structure*$*xxxxxx* symbols:

   $*structure*DEF

The following examples show the $*structure*DEF form of the macro:

$ACBDEF	Offsets into asynchronous system trap (AST) control block
$PCBDEF	Offsets into software process control block
$PHDDEF	Offsets into process header

Many of the macros of this form are contained in the macro libraries LIB.MLB or STARLET.MLB. These macros are initially defined in a language-independent structure definition language (see Appendix B).

11. VAX MACRO public structure offset names are of the form

   structure$*t_field-name*

The letter *t* indicates the data type of the field (see Section D.2). The value of the public symbol is the byte offset to the start of the data element in the structure. The following examples show this form of symbol name:

CEB$L_EFC	Event flag cluster (in common event block)
GSD$W_GSTX	Global section table index (in global section descriptor)
PCB$B_PRI	Current process priority (in software process control block)

12. VAX MACRO public structure bit field offsets and single bit names are of the form

    structure$V_*field-name*

    The value of the public symbol is the bit offset from the start of the field that contains the data, not from the start of the control block. The following examples show this form of symbol name:

ACB$V_QUOTA	Charge AST to process AST quota
PSL$V_CURMOD	Current access mode
UCB$V_CANCEL	Cancel I/O on this unit

13. VAX MACRO public structure bit field size names are of the form

    structure$S_*field-name*

    The value of the public symbol is the number of bits in the field. The following examples show this form of symbol name:

ACB$S_MODE	Access mode of requestor (2 bits)
PSL$S_CURMOD	Current access mode (2 bits)
PTE$S_PROT	Memory protection on page (4 bits)

14. For BLISS, the functions of the symbols in the previous three items are combined into a single name used to reference an arbitrary datum. Names are of the following form, where x is the same as t for standard-sized data (B, W, L, and Q) and x stands for V for arbitrary and bit fields:

    structure$x_*field-name*

    The macro includes the offset, position, size, and sign extension suitable for use in a BLISS field selector. Most typically, this name is defined by the following BLISS statement:

```
    MACRO
structure$V_field-name=
        structure$t_field-name,
        structure$V_field-name,      !VAX MACRO V
                                     ! bit field definition

        structure$S_field-name,
        (sign extension) %;
```

15. Public structure mask names are of the form

    structure$M_*field-name*

    The value of the public symbol is a mask with bits set for each bit in the field. This mask is not right-justified. Rather, it has *structure*$V_*field-name* zero bits on the right. The following examples show this form of symbol name:

PCB$M_RES	Bit set to indicate process residency
PSL$M_CURMOD	Current access mode
PTE$M_PROT	Memory protection on page

16. Public structure constant names are of the form

    structure$K_*constant-name*

    The following examples show this form of symbol name:

PCB$K_LENGTH	Length (in bytes) of software process control block
SRM$K_FLT_OVF_F	Code for floating overflow fault
STS$K_SEVERE	Fatal error code

    For historical reasons, many of the constants used by the executive have the letter C instead of K to indicate that the object data type is a constant. Examples of this form of symbol name are

DYN$C_PCB	Structure type is software process control block
EXE$C_CMSTKSZ	Size of stack space added by change mode handler
PTE$C_URKW	Protection code of user read, kernel write

17. PSECT names are of the form

    facility$*mnemonic*

    When these names are put into a library, they have the form

    _*facility*$*mnemonic*

    The following examples show symbols of the form *facility*$*mnemonic*:

COPY$COPY_FILE	File copying main routine program section
DCL$ZCODE	Program section that contains most code for the Digital command language interpreter
DBG$CODE	Program section containing VAX debugger routines

This convention is not adhered to as strictly as the other naming conventions because PSECT names control the way that the linker allocates virtual address space. Names are often chosen to affect the relative locations of routines and the data they reference.

Some sample PSECT names from the Run-Time Library show examples of the form _facility$mnemonic:

_LIB$CODE	General library (read-only) code section
_MTH$DATA	Data section in mathematics library
_OTS$CODE	Code portion of language-independent support library

The VMS base image, SYS.EXE, does not use this convention in its PSECT names. Rather, it uses names that cause the desired sections to be placed in a particular order. The following examples show PSECT names that are used in the base image:

$$$$$000_SYSTEM_SERVICE_VECTORS	The first program section in the base image
$$$$$NONPAGED_CODE	Program section containing transfer vectors to loadable executive images
_Z_SYS$END	Last program section

D.2 OBJECT DATA TYPES

Table D.1 shows some of the letters used to indicate data types or reserved for various other purposes. N, P, and T strings are typically variable-length. In structures or I/O records, they frequently contain a byte-sized digit or character count preceding the string. If so, the location or offset is to the count. Counted strings cannot be passed in procedure calls. Instead, a string descriptor must be generated.

D.3 FACILITY PREFIX TABLE

Table D.2 lists some of the facility prefixes used by Digital-supplied software. This list is not inclusive and is intended to show examples of several facility prefixes. Each facility name has a unique facility code.

Note that bit ⟨27⟩, the customer facility bit, is clear in all the facility codes listed here. Customers are free to use any of the facility codes listed here, provided that they set bit ⟨27⟩. The default action of the message compiler is to set this bit.

The location of the facility code within a status code and the meaning of the other fields in the status code are described in the *VMS Utility Routines Manual*.

Individual products such as compilers also have unique facility codes formed from the product name.

Table D.1   Letters and the Data Types They Indicate

Letter	Data Type or Use
A	Address
B	Byte integer
C	Character[1]
D	Double precision floating
E	Reserved to Digital
F	Single precision floating
G	G_floating-point values
H	H_floating-point values
I	Reserved for integer extensions
J	Reserved to customers for escape to other codes
K	Constant
L	Longword integer
M	Field mask
N	Numeric string (all byte forms)
O	Reserved to Digital as an escape to other codes
P	Packed string
Q	Quadword integer
R	Reserved for records (structure)
S	Field size
T	Text (character) string
U	Smallest unit of addressable storage
V	Field position (VAX MACRO)
	Field reference (BLISS)
W	Word integer
X	Context-dependent (generic)
Y	Context-dependent (generic)
Z	Unspecified or nonstandard

[1] In many of the symbols used by VMS, C is used as a synonym for K. Although K is the preferred indicator for constants, many constants used by VMS are indicated by a C in their name. Some constants, such as lengths of data structures, have both a C form and a K form.

Structure name prefixes are typically local to a facility. Refer to the individual facility documentation for its structure name prefixes. Individual facility structure names do not cause problems, because these names are not global and are therefore not known to the linker. They become known at assembly or compile time only by explicit invocation of the macro defining the facility structure.

For example, the macro $FORDEF defines all the status codes that can be returned from the VAX FORTRAN support library. The facility code of 24 is included in the upper 16 bits of each of the status codes defined with this macro.

Table D.2   Facility Names and Their Prefixes

Prefix	Description	Condition ⟨27:16⟩
	EXECUTIVE AND SYSTEM PROCESSES	
SS	System service status codes	0
CLI	Command language interpreters	3
JBC	Job controller	4
OPC	Operator communication	5
ERF	Error logger format process	8
	RUN-TIME LIBRARY COMPONENTS	
SMG	Screen management routines	18
LIB	General-Purpose Library	21
MTH	Mathematics Library	22
OTS	Language-independent object time system	23
FOR	VAX FORTRAN Run-Time Library	24
SORT	VAX SORT	28
STR	String manipulation procedures	36
	UTILITIES AND COMPILERS	
DBG	Symbolic debugger	2
LIN	VMS Linker	100
DIF	File Differences Utility	108
PAT	VAX Image File Patch Utility	109
LAT	Local area terminal	374

Digital provides a registration service for customer facility names. For information on this service, contact

> Digital Equipment Corporation
> VMS Product Registrar—ZKO2-1/N20
> 110 Spit Brook Road
> Nashua, New Hampshire 03062-2698

E Data Structure Definitions

This book has described the VMS operating system in terms of the data structures used by various components of the executive. This appendix summarizes those data structures.

E.1 LOCATION OF DATA STRUCTURE DEFINITIONS

The data structures used by VMS are defined in a language called structure definition language (SDL), which is briefly described in Appendix B. Two sets of four files each contain most SDL definitions.

Four files contain most structure and constant definitions used internally by the VMS executive. They have names of the form [SYS]SYSDEF*xx*.SDL, where *xx* represents the letters AE, FL, MP, or QZ. The two letters indicate the range of initial letters of all the data structures contained in that file. The VAX MACRO definitions based on these files are stored in the file LIB.MLB. The BLISS-32 definitions based on these files are stored in the file LIB.REQ. Many components of VMS are built with the definitions in these files. They are also available to users for special applications such as user-written device drivers and system services.

Four files named [VMSLIB]STARDEF*xx*.SDL contain all structure and constant definitions available for general applications, such as system service calls. Again, *xx* represents the letters AE, FL, MP, or QZ. The definitions based on these files are stored in the files STARLET.MLB and STARLET.REQ.

The distinction between the files in SYSDEF*xx*.SDL and STARDEF*xx*.SDL is that a structure or constant defined in STARDEF is considered an external interface and usually does not change from release to release. A structure or constant defined in SYSDEF is considered an internal interface and is subject to change. Consequently, VAX MACRO programs that use LIB.MLB or BLISS-32 programs that use LIB.REQ (or LIB.L32) must be reassembled and relinked with each major release of the VMS operating system.

E.2 OVERVIEW

Table E.1 lists the data structures and constants summarized in this appendix. The majority of them are defined in the SYSDEF*xx* modules. The following classes of structures are in the table:

- Data structures used by memory management, the scheduler, and other components of the system image. At least one figure or table in this book describes each of these structures.

Table E.1   Summary of Data Structures in
Appendix E

SYSTEMWIDE DATA STRUCTURES

ACB	ACL [1]	ARB	CEB
CPU	FKB	GSD	ISD
JIB	KFD	KFE	KFPB
KFRH	LKB	LNMB	LNMC
LNMHSH	LNMTH	LNMX	MTX
ORB	PCB	PHD	PQB
RPB	RSB	SPL	TQE

STRUCTURES USED BY THE I/O AND FILE SUBSYSTEMS

ADP	BRK	CCB	CDDB
CDRP	CRB	DDB	DDT
DPT	FCB	IDB	IRP
TAST	UCB	WCB	

SYMBOLIC CONSTANTS

BTD	CA	DYN	IO*xxx*
IPL	NDT	PR	SPL

---

[1] This structure is defined in module STARDEF*xx*.

- Data structures used by the I/O and file subsystems.
- Constants such as data structure types, interrupt priority levels (IPLs), and processor register definitions.

E.3   **EXECUTIVE DATA STRUCTURES**

This section contains a brief summary of each of the data structures described in this book. Three data structures, the software process control block (PCB), the process header (PHD), and the job information block (JIB), are partly described in several places throughout the book. They are illustrated here in their entirety, with references to other partial descriptions.

E.3.1   **ACB—Asynchronous System Trap (AST) Control Block**

Purpose	Describes a pending AST for a process.
Usual location	AST queue with listhead in software PCB.
Allocated from	Nonpaged pool.
Reference	Figure 7.1.
Special notes	ACBs are usually a part of a larger structure, such as an I/O request packet (IRP) or timer queue entry (TQE).

1242

FLINK		
BLINK		
(reserved)	TYPE	SIZE
LIST		

Figure E.1
Layout of an Access Control List

E.3.2 ACL—Access Control List

Purpose	List of entries that grant or deny access to a particular system resource.
Usual location	ACL queue with listhead in resource's object rights block (ORB$L_ACLFL).
Allocated from	Paged pool.
Reference	Figure E.1.
Special notes	An ACL contains access control entries (ACEs) beginning at offset ACL$L_LIST.

E.3.3 ADP—Adapter Control Block

Purpose	Defines characteristics and current state of an I/O adapter.
Location	Pointed to by CRB (CRB$L_INTD + VEC$L_ADP).
Allocated from	Nonpaged pool.
Reference	Figure E.2.

E.3.4 ARB—Access Rights Block

The ARB is currently a part of the software PCB. The ARB pointer (PCB$L_ARB) points to this overlaid data structure. Figure E.14 shows an ARB within a software PCB. Program references that use the ARB pointer in the software PCB to locate the ARB or any fields within the ARB (such as the privilege mask) will continue to work without modification should the ARB become an independent data structure in a future release of the VMS operating system.

Purpose	Defines process access rights and privileges.
Location	Currently a part of the software PCB.
References	Table 26.2, Figures E.3, E.14.

E.3.5 BRK—Breakthrough Message Descriptor Block

Purpose	Used to send asynchronous messages to one or more terminals.

(continued)

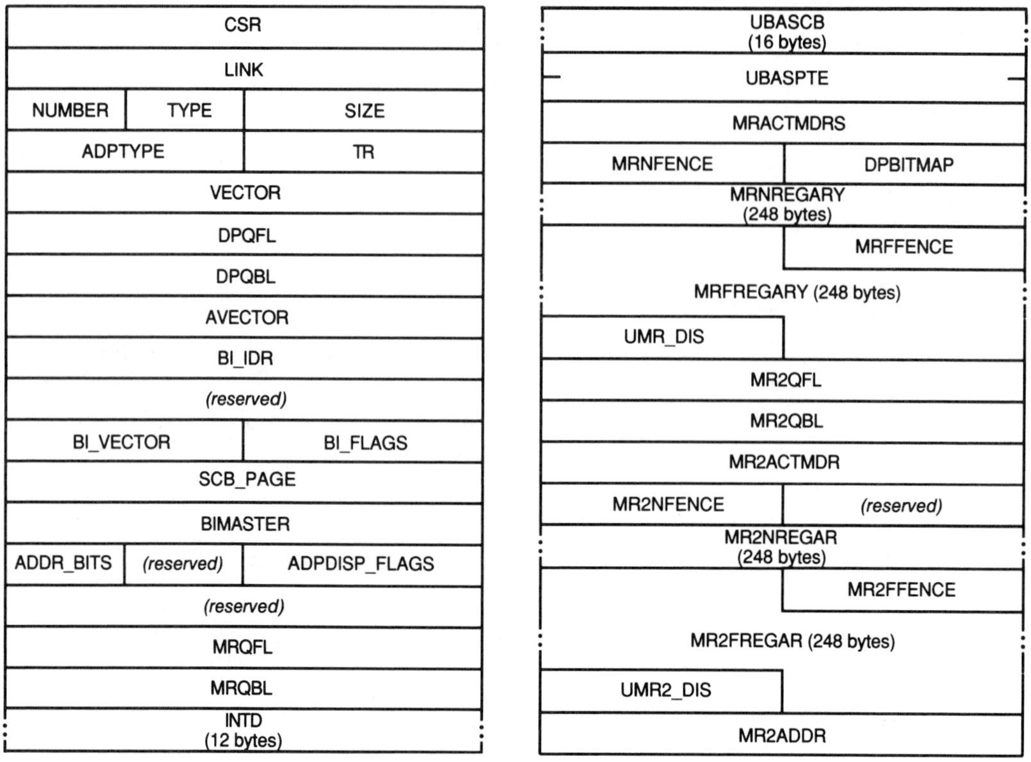

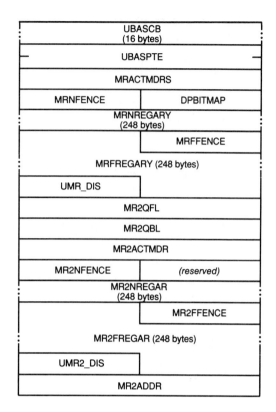

Figure E.2
Layout of an Adapter Control Block

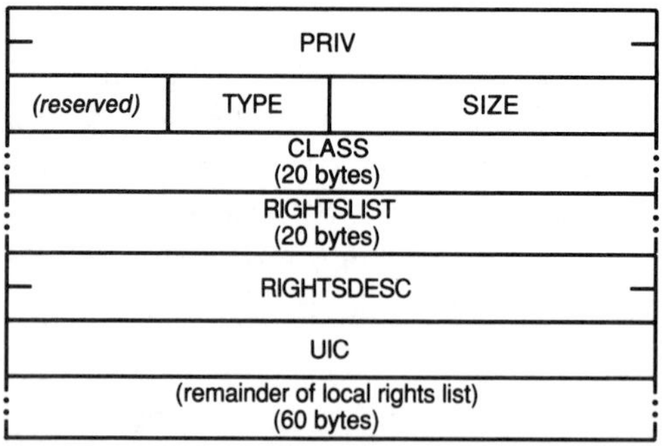

Figure E.3
Layout of an Access Rights Block

Allocated from	Nonpaged pool.
Reference	Figure 24.6.

E.3.6   CCB—Channel Control Block

Purpose	Describes the logical path between the process and the UCB of the specific device.
Location	Within per-process space table, pointed to by CTL$GL_CCBBASE.
Reference	Figure 21.2.

E.3.7   CDDB—Class Driver Data Block

Purpose	Auxiliary data structure for each system communication services (SCS) connection between a disk or tape class driver and a remote mass storage control protocol (MSCP) server.
Usual location	Pointed to by CRB$L_AUXSTRUC.
Allocated from	Nonpaged pool.
Reference	Figure E.4.
Special notes	There is one CDDB per MSCP controller.

E.3.8   CDRP—Class Driver Request Packet

Purpose	Data structure used to communicate between SCS and a class driver.
Usual location	Linked into CDDB listhead (CDDB$L_CDRPQFL).
Allocated from	Nonpaged pool.
Reference	Figure 24.2.
Special notes	Contains within it, at negative offsets, a full IRP.

E.3.9   CEB—Common Event Block

Purpose	Contains description and wait queue for common event flag cluster.
Location	In list whose head is at SCH$GQ_CEBHD. (Master CEBs are located in shared memory and pointed to by a field in the slave CEB located in the CEB list on each processor.)
Allocated from	Nonpaged pool. (Master CEBs are allocated from a CEB table located in shared memory.)
References	Figures 9.1, 9.2, 9.3.

E.3.10   CPU—Per-CPU Database

Purpose	Records processor-specific information. There is one CPU structure for every CPU in the system.

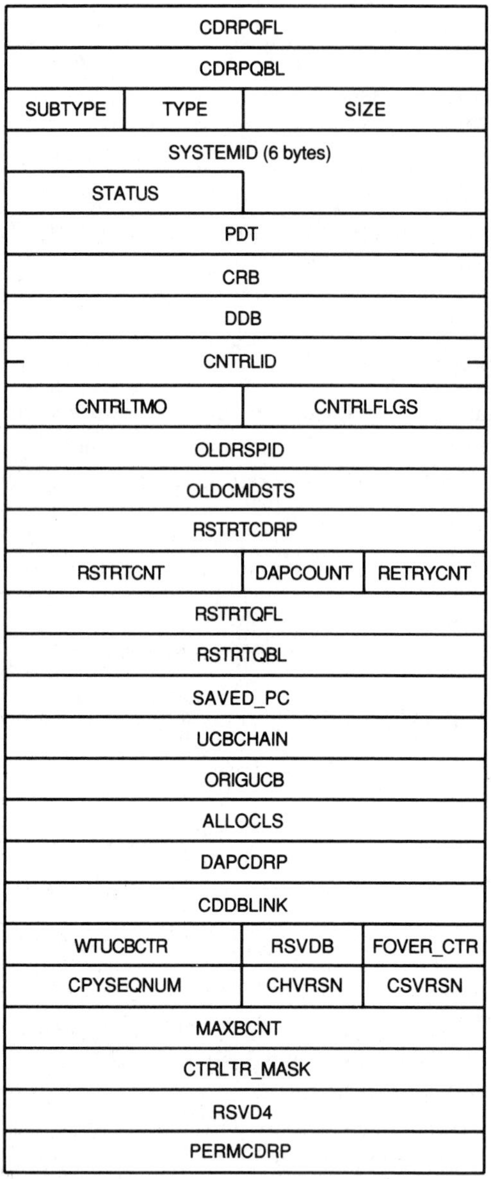

CDRPQFL			
CDRPQBL			
SUBTYPE	TYPE	SIZE	
SYSTEMID (6 bytes)			
STATUS			
PDT			
CRB			
DDB			
CNTRLID			
CNTRLTMO		CNTRLFLGS	
OLDRSPID			
OLDCMDSTS			
RSTRTCDRP			
RSTRTCNT		DAPCOUNT	RETRYCNT
RSTRTQFL			
RSTRTQBL			
SAVED_PC			
UCBCHAIN			
ORIGUCB			
ALLOCLS			
DAPCDRP			
CDDBLINK			
WTUCBCTR		RSVDB	FOVER_CTR
CPYSEQNUM		CHVRSN	CSVRSN
MAXBCNT			
CTRLTR_MASK			
RSVD4			
PERMCDRP			

Figure E.4
Layout of a Class Driver Data Block

1246

Usual location	At a known offset from the interrupt stack pointer for the CPU. The FIND_CPU_DATA macro should be used.
Allocated from	Statically allocated pages of system space.
References	Figures 34.5, 34.6.

E.3.11 CRB—Channel Request Block

Purpose	There is one CRB for each set of devices whose access to a controller must be synchronized.
Location	Pointed to by the unit control block (UCB$L_CRB).
Allocated from	Nonpaged pool.
Reference	Figure E.5.

E.3.12 DDB—Device Data Block

Purpose	There is one DDB for each controller in a system.
Location	Linked into device listhead (IOC$GL_DEVLIST).
Allocated from	Nonpaged pool.
Reference	Figure E.6.

E.3.13 DDT—Driver Dispatch Table

Purpose	Specifies driver entry points for various I/O functions.
Location	Pointed to by DDB$L_DDT and UCB$L_DDT.
Allocated from	Nonpaged pool.
Reference	Figure E.7.

E.3.14 DPT—Driver Prolog Table

Purpose	Defines the identity and the size of the driver to the system routine that loads the driver into virtual memory.
Location	Beginning of the driver image. All DPTs on the system are linked in a list. Listhead is in IOC$GL_DPTLIST.
Allocated from	Nonpaged pool.
Reference	Figure E.8.
Special notes	The size of the DPT is the size of the entire driver, including the DPT itself.

E.3.15 FCB—File Control Block

Purpose	Describes a uniquely accessed file on a volume; provides a means for controlling shared access to a file.

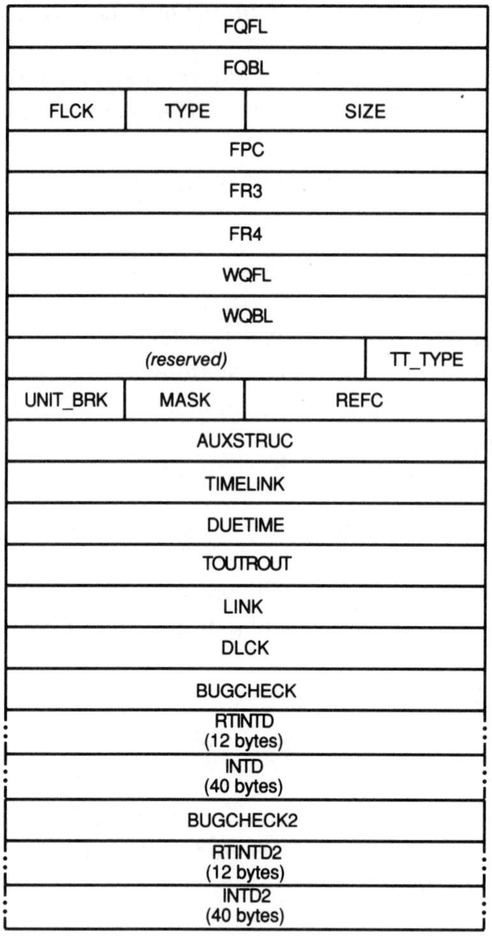

FQFL		
FQBL		
FLCK	TYPE	SIZE
FPC		
FR3		
FR4		
WQFL		
WQBL		
(reserved)		TT_TYPE
UNIT_BRK	MASK	REFC
AUXSTRUC		
TIMELINK		
DUETIME		
TOUTROUT		
LINK		
DLCK		
BUGCHECK		
RTINTD (12 bytes)		
INTD (40 bytes)		
BUGCHECK2		
RTINTD2 (12 bytes)		
INTD2 (40 bytes)		

Figure E.5
Layout of a Channel Request Block

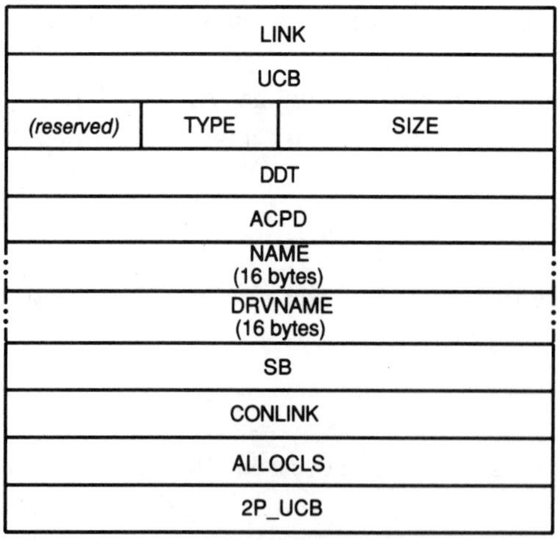

LINK		
UCB		
(reserved)	TYPE	SIZE
DDT		
ACPD		
NAME (16 bytes)		
DRVNAME (16 bytes)		
SB		
CONLINK		
ALLOCLS		
2P_UCB		

Figure E.6
Layout of a Device Data Block

START
UNSOLINT
FDT
CANCEL
REGDUMP

ERRORBUF	DIAGBUF

UNITINIT
ALTSTART
MNTVER
CLONEDUCB

(reserved)	FDTSIZE

MNTV_SSSC
MNTV_FOR
MNTV_SQD
AUX_STORAGE
AUX_ROUTINE

Figure E.7
Layout of a Driver Dispatch Table

FLINK			
BLINK			
REFC	TYPE	SIZE	
UCBSIZE		(reserved)	ADPTYPE
FLAGS			
REINITTAB		INITTAB	
MAXUNITS		UNLOAD	
DEFUNITS		VERSION	
VECTOR		DELIVER	
NAME (12 bytes)			
LINKTIME			
ECOLEVEL			
UCODE			
LMF_1 (64 bytes)			
	DECW_SNAME		

Figure E.8
Layout of a Driver Prolog Table

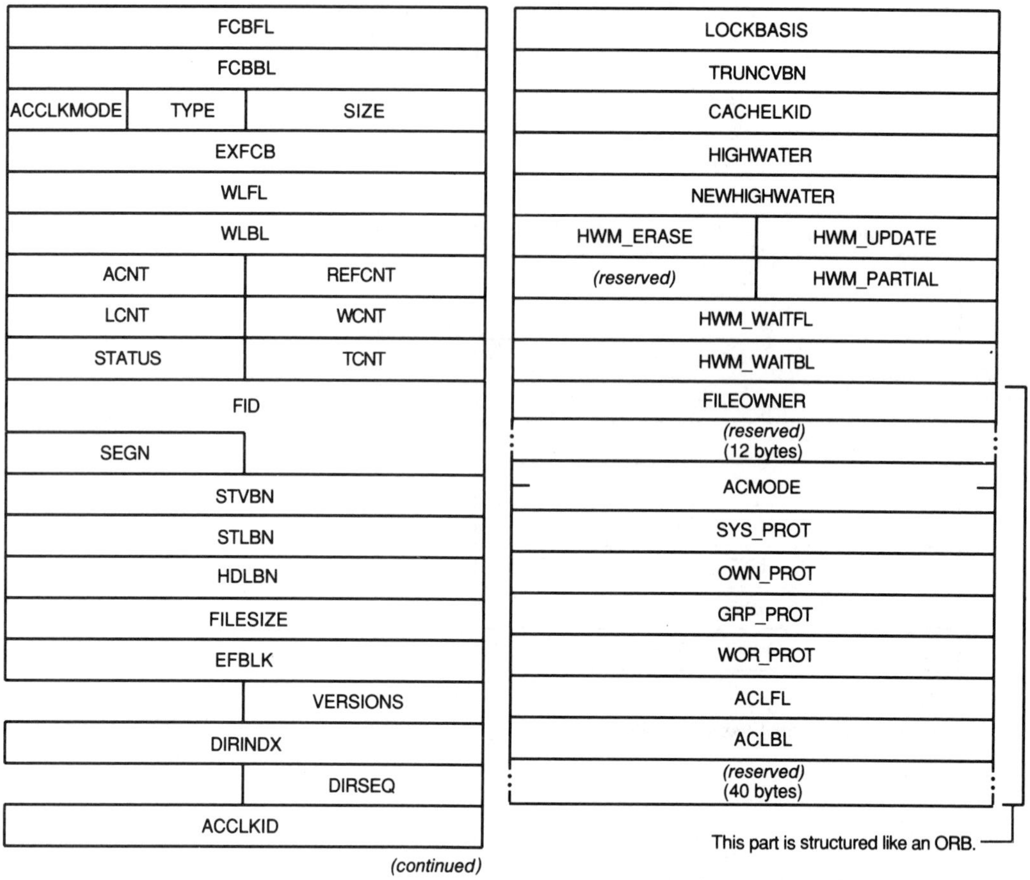

FCBFL		
FCBBL		
ACCLKMODE	TYPE	SIZE
EXFCB		
WLFL		
WLBL		
ACNT		REFCNT
LCNT		WCNT
STATUS		TCNT
FID		
SEGN		
STVBN		
STLBN		
HDLBN		
FILESIZE		
EFBLK		
		VERSIONS
DIRINDX		
		DIRSEQ
ACCLKID		

LOCKBASIS	
TRUNCVBN	
CACHELKID	
HIGHWATER	
NEWHIGHWATER	
HWM_ERASE	HWM_UPDATE
(reserved)	HWM_PARTIAL
HWM_WAITFL	
HWM_WAITBL	
FILEOWNER	
(reserved) (12 bytes)	
ACMODE	
SYS_PROT	
OWN_PROT	
GRP_PROT	
WOR_PROT	
ACLFL	
ACLBL	
(reserved) (40 bytes)	

This part is structured like an ORB.

(continued)

Figure E.9
Layout of a File Control Block

Usual location	Linked into the volume control block listhead (VCB$L_FCBFL).
Allocated from	Nonpaged pool.
Reference	Figure E.9.

E.3.16   FKB—Fork Block

Purpose	Stores minimum context for a fork process.
Usual location	First six longwords of unit control block (UCB) and CDRP.
Allocated from	Nonpaged pool.
References	Figures 4.1, 4.2.

E.3.17   GSD—Global Section Descriptor

Purpose	Contains identifying information about a global section.

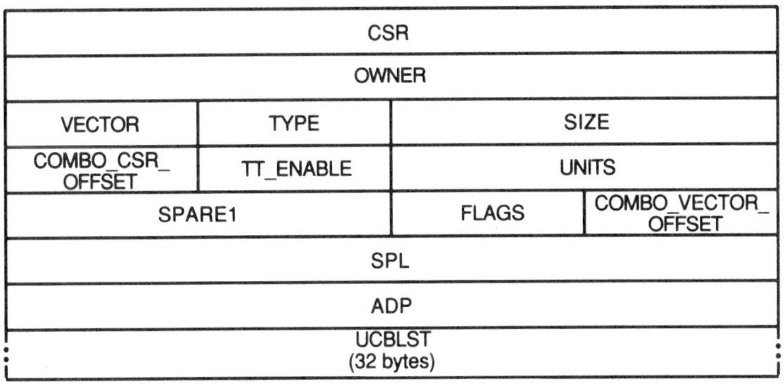

CSR			
OWNER			
VECTOR	TYPE	SIZE	
COMBO_CSR_ OFFSET	TT_ENABLE	UNITS	
SPARE1		FLAGS	COMBO_VECTOR_ OFFSET
SPL			
ADP			
UCBLST (32 bytes)			

Figure E.10
Layout of an Interrupt Dispatch Block

Location	Group or system GSD list.
Allocated from	Paged pool.
Reference	Figure 14.17.
Special notes	There are two types of GSD: a normal GSD and a GSD for page frame number (PFN) mapped section.

E.3.18   **IDB—Interrupt Dispatch Block**

Purpose	Provides the information for a controller-specific interrupt dispatcher to dispatch an interrupt to the appropriate driver for that device unit.
Location	Pointed to by CRB$L_INTD + VEC$L_IDB.
Allocated from	Nonpaged pool.
Reference	Figure E.10.

E.3.19   **IRP—I/O Request Packet**

Purpose	Constructed by the Queue I/O Request ($QIO) system service to describe an I/O function to be performed on a device unit.
Usual location	All IRPs pending for a particular device unit are linked together, typically at UCB$L_IOQFL.
Allocated from	Nonpaged pool.
Reference	Figure E.11.

E.3.20   **ISD—Image Section Descriptor**

Purpose	Describes virtual address range and corresponding information (virtual block range, global section name) to the image activator.
Location	Image header.
References	Figures 26.2, 26.9, 26.10, 26.11.

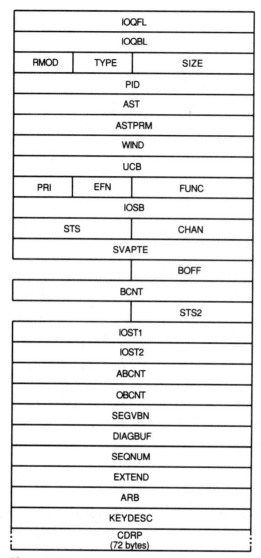

Figure E.11
Layout of an I/O Request Packet

E.3.21   JIB—Job Information Block

The JIB appears in several figures in this book. Figure E.12 shows all the fields currently defined in this structure.

Purpose	Contains quotas pooled by all processes in the same job.
Location	Pointed to by PCB$L_JIB field of all PCBs in the same job.
Allocated from	Nonpaged pool.
Reference	Figure E.12.

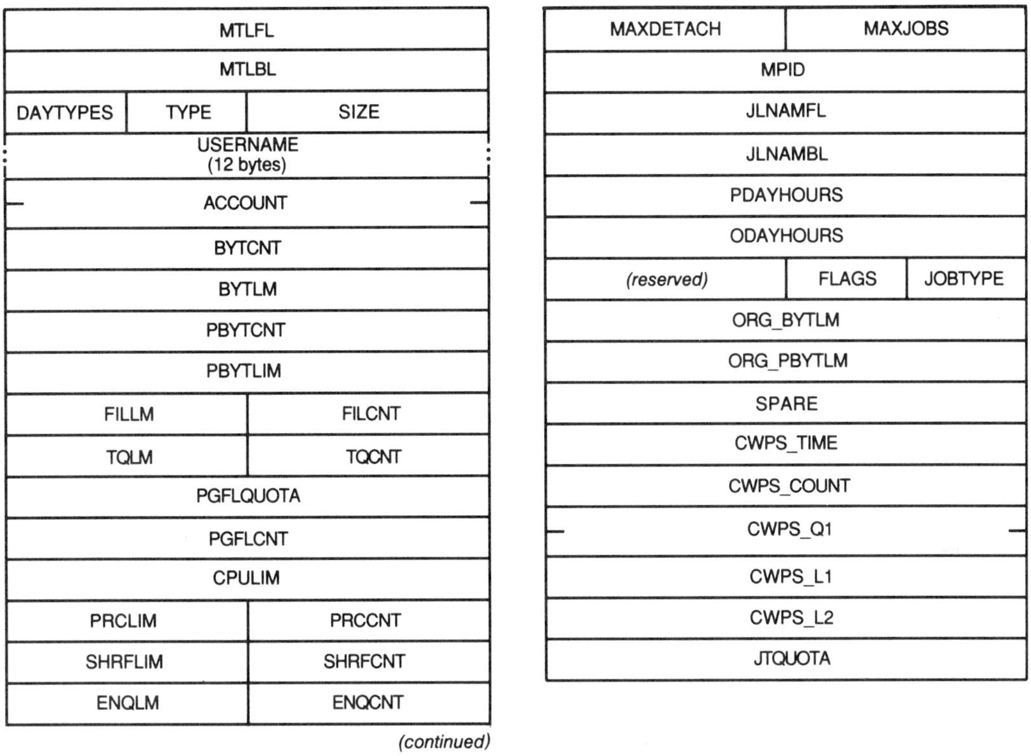

MTLFL		
MTLBL		
DAYTYPES	TYPE	SIZE
USERNAME (12 bytes)		
ACCOUNT		
BYTCNT		
BYTLM		
PBYTCNT		
PBYTLIM		
FILLM		FILCNT
TQLM		TQCNT
PGFLQUOTA		
PGFLCNT		
CPULIM		
PRCLIM		PRCCNT
SHRFLIM		SHRFCNT
ENQLM		ENQCNT

MAXDETACH		MAXJOBS
MPID		
JLNAMFL		
JLNAMBL		
PDAYHOURS		
ODAYHOURS		
(reserved)	FLAGS	JOBTYPE
ORG_BYTLM		
ORG_PBYTLM		
SPARE		
CWPS_TIME		
CWPS_COUNT		
CWPS_Q1		
CWPS_L1		
CWPS_L2		
JTQUOTA		

(continued)

Figure E.12
Layout of a Job Information Block

E.3.22   **KFD—Known File Device and Directory Block**

Purpose	Contains the file device and directory names associated with an image. Multiple known images share the same KFD.
Location	Pointed to by the known file pointer block (KFPB$L_ KFDLST).
Allocated from	Paged pool.
Reference	Figure 26.5.

E.3.23   **KFE—Known File Entry Block**

Purpose	Identifies the file name of the image and its properties.
Location	Pointed to by the KFPE hash table, whose address is contained in the known file pointer block (KFPB$L_ KFEHSHTAB).
Allocated from	Paged pool.
References	Figures 26.4, 26.6.

E.3.24   **KFPB—Known File Pointer Block**

Purpose   Contains the address of KFE hash table and the
                     listhead for the KFDs.
Location   Pointed to by EXE$GL_KNOWN_FILES.
Allocated from   Paged pool.
Reference   Figure 26.8.

E.3.25   **KFRH—Known File Resident Image Header**

Purpose   Exists for each known image installed /HEADER_
                     RESIDENT.
Location   Immediately precedes the IHD and specifies its size
                     and version number.
Allocated from   Paged pool.
Reference   Figure 26.7.

E.3.26   **LKB—Lock Block**

Purpose   Contains information about a request to the Enqueue
                     Lock ($ENQ) system service.
Location   All lock blocks may be located through the lock ID
                     table, whose address is found in global location
                     LCK$GL_IDTBL.
Allocated from   Nonpaged pool.
Reference   Figure 10.4.

E.3.27   **LNMB—Logical Name Block**

Purpose   Contains the logical name string, its access mode, and
                     attributes.
Location   Chained from the shared logical name hash table or a
                     process-private hash table.
Allocated from   Paged pool for shared logical names or process
                     allocation region for process logical names.
References   Figures 35.1, 35.5.

E.3.28   **LNMC—Logical Name Table Name Cache Block**

Purpose   Facilitates logical name translation.
Location   Doubly linked from a P1 space listhead (CTL$GQ_
                     LNMTBLCACHE).
Allocated from   Process allocation region.
Reference   Figure 35.6.

E.3.29   **LNMHSH—Logical Name Hash Table**

Purpose   Locates all logical names.

Location	Indirectly pointed to by the array of addresses at LNM$AL_HASHTBL.
Allocated from	Paged pool and process allocation region.
Reference	Figure 35.5.

E.3.30 LNMTH—Logical Name Table Header

Purpose	Describes a logical name table.
Allocated from	Paged pool for the shared table or process allocation region for process tables.
Reference	Figure 35.2.

E.3.31 LNMX—Logical Name Translation Block

Purpose	Describes an equivalence name for a logical name.
Location	Follows an LNMB.
Allocated from	Paged pool for shared names or process allocation region for process names.
Reference	Figure 35.1.

E.3.32 MTX—Mutex (Mutual Exclusion Semaphore)

Purpose	Controls process access to protected data structures.
Usual location	Statically allocated longwords in system space.
Reference	Figure 8.3.

E.3.33 ORB—Object Rights Block

Purpose	Defines the protection information for various objects within the system.
Usual location	Linked to a data structure, such as a UCB, via offset *xxx*$L_ORB.
Allocated from	Paged pool.
Reference	Figure E.13.

E.3.34 PCB—Process Control Block

The term *process control block* can refer to two different structures in the VAX literature. All software documentation, including this book, refers to the software process control block as simply the PCB and always prefixes a reference to the hardware process control block with "hardware."

E.3.34.1 Software Process Control Block

Purpose	Contains the permanently resident information about a process.

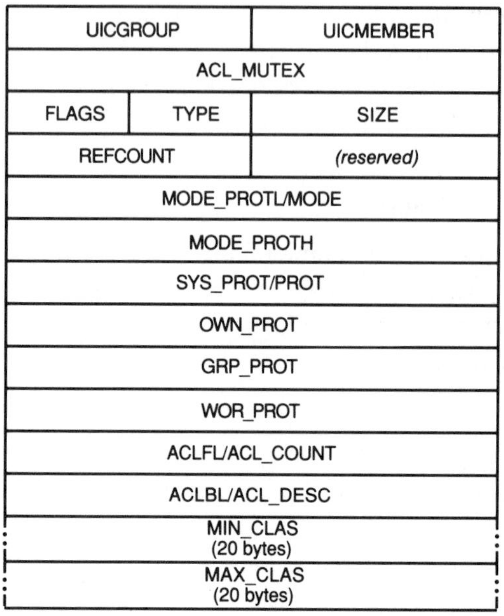

UICGROUP		UICMEMBER	
ACL_MUTEX			
FLAGS	TYPE	SIZE	
REFCOUNT		(reserved)	
MODE_PROTL/MODE			
MODE_PROTH			
SYS_PROT/PROT			
OWN_PROT			
GRP_PROT			
WOR_PROT			
ACLFL/ACL_COUNT			
ACLBL/ACL_DESC			
MIN_CLAS (20 bytes)			
MAX_CLAS (20 bytes)			

Figure E.13
Layout of an Object Rights Block

Location	Linked into a scheduling state queue; also pointed to by one of the PCB vector elements.
Allocated from	Nonpaged pool.
Reference	Figure E.14.

E.3.34.2 **Hardware Process Control Block**

Purpose	Contains hardware context of a process while it is not executing.
Location	Part of the fixed portion of the process header.
References	Figures 12.10, 12.11.

E.3.35 **PHD—Process Header**

Purpose	Contains process context data that must reside in system space but can be outswapped.
Location	Balance slot area in system space. (PHD pages that are not page table pages are double-mapped by a range of P1 space addresses.)
References	Figures E.15, 14.5, 14.6, 14.8, 14.10, 14.22.
Special notes	The process's hardware PCB is contained in the PHD, beginning at field PHD$L_PCB and ending just before PHD$L_WSEXTENT.

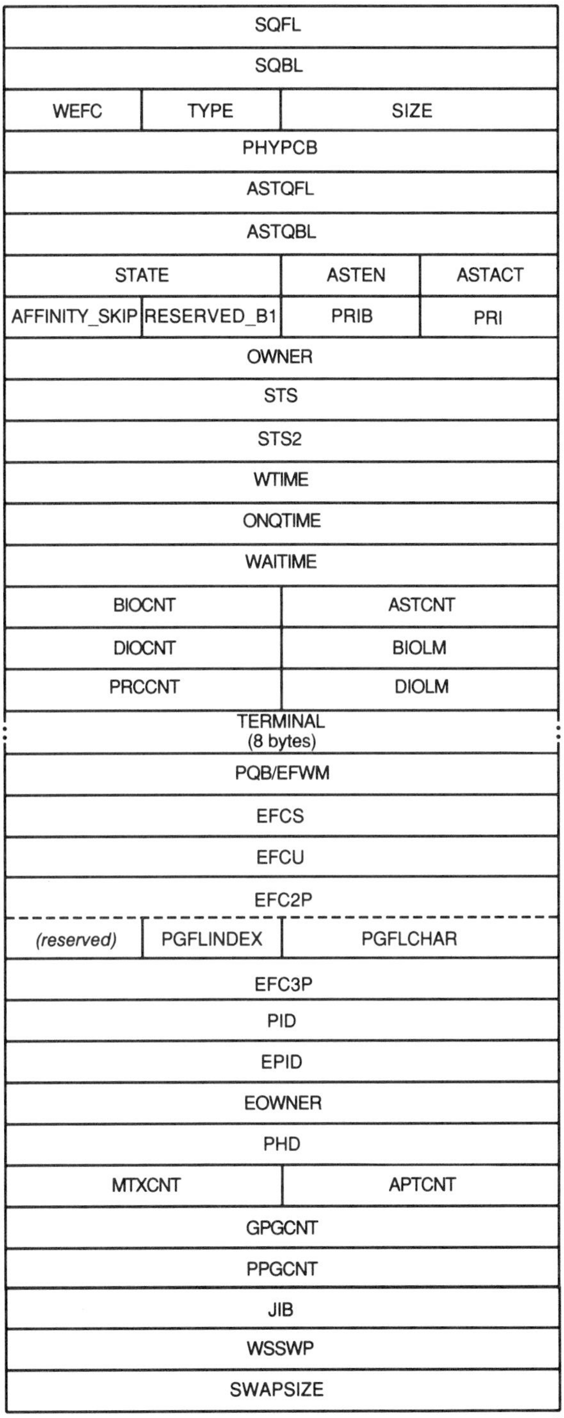

SQFL			
SQBL			
WEFC	TYPE	SIZE	
PHYPCB			
ASTQFL			
ASTQBL			
STATE		ASTEN	ASTACT
AFFINITY_SKIP	RESERVED_B1	PRIB	PRI
OWNER			
STS			
STS2			
WTIME			
ONQTIME			
WAITIME			
BIOCNT		ASTCNT	
DIOCNT		BIOLM	
PRCCNT		DIOLM	
TERMINAL (8 bytes)			
PQB/EFWM			
EFCS			
EFCU			
EFC2P			
(reserved)	PGFLINDEX	PGFLCHAR	
EFC3P			
PID			
EPID			
EOWNER			
PHD			
MTXCNT		APTCNT	
GPGCNT			
PPGCNT			
JIB			
WSSWP			
SWAPSIZE			

(continued)

Figure E.14
Layout of a Software Process Control Block

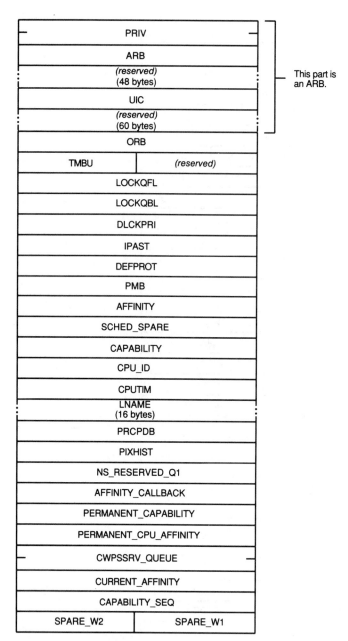

Figure E.14 *(continued)*
Layout of a Software Process Control Block

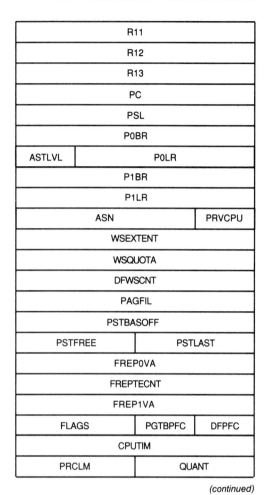

PRIVMSK			
SPARE_1	TYPE	SIZE	
WSLIST			
WSLOCK			
WSDYN			
WSNEXT			
WSLAST			
PCB/KSP			
ESP			
SSP			
USP			
R0			
R1			
R2			
R3			
R4			
R5			
R6			
R7			
R8			
R9			
R10			

(continued)

R11			
R12			
R13			
PC			
PSL			
P0BR			
ASTLVL	P0LR		
P1BR			
P1LR			
ASN		PRVCPU	
WSEXTENT			
WSQUOTA			
DFWSCNT			
PAGFIL			
PSTBASOFF			
PSTFREE	PSTLAST		
FREP0VA			
FREPTECNT			
FREP1VA			
FLAGS	PGTBPFC	DFPFC	
CPUTIM			
PRCLM	QUANT		

(continued)

Figure E.15
Layout of a Process Header

E.3.36   PQB—Process Quota Block

Purpose	Used during process creation to store new process parameters that are copied to the PHD and P1 space after those areas are accessible.
Location	Pointed to by PCB$L_EFWM.
Allocated from	Paged pool.
Reference	Figure E.16.

E.3.37   RPB—Restart Parameter Block

Purpose	Contains volatile processor state during power failure; locates the bootstrap I/O driver and associated subroutines.

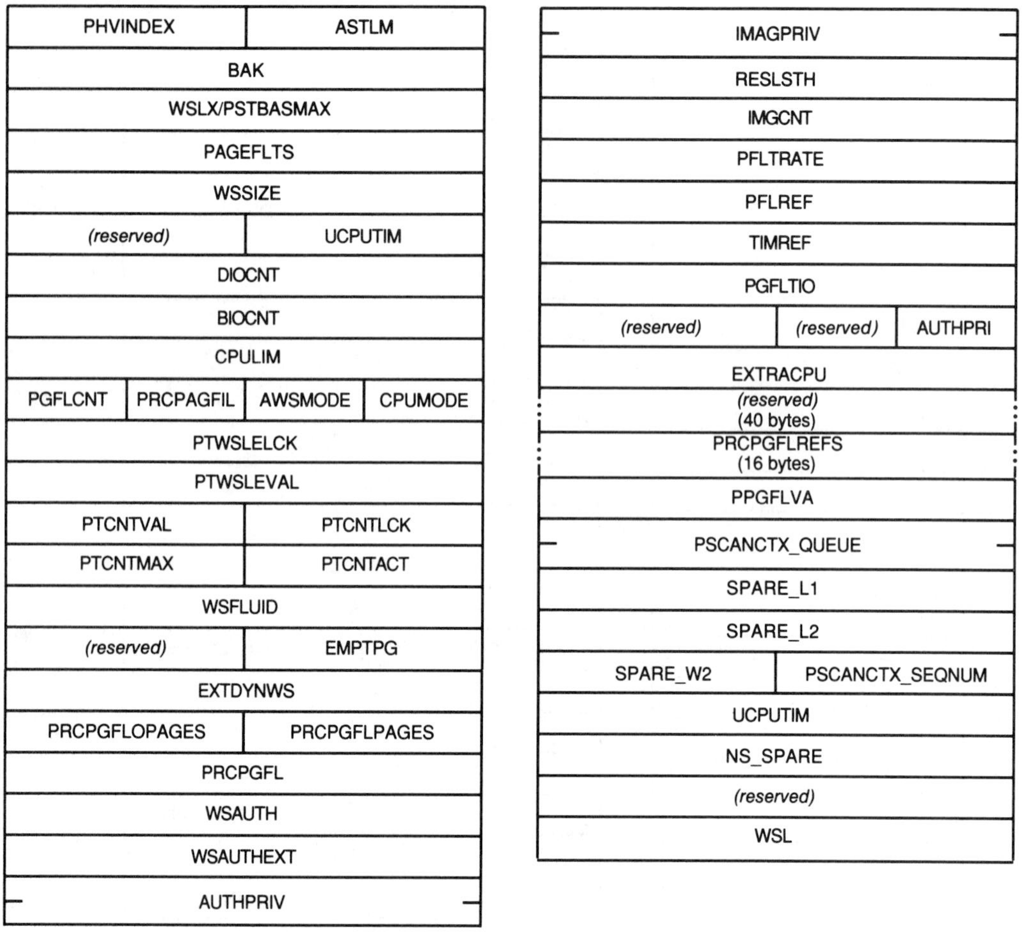

PHVINDEX		ASTLM	
BAK			
WSLX/PSTBASMAX			
PAGEFLTS			
WSSIZE			
(reserved)		UCPUTIM	
DIOCNT			
BIOCNT			
CPULIM			
PGFLCNT	PRCPAGFIL	AWSMODE	CPUMODE
PTWSLELCK			
PTWSLEVAL			
PTCNTVAL		PTCNTLCK	
PTCNTMAX		PTCNTACT	
WSFLUID			
(reserved)		EMPTPG	
EXTDYNWS			
PRCPGFLOPAGES		PRCPGFLPAGES	
PRCPGFL			
WSAUTH			
WSAUTHEXT			
AUTHPRIV			

IMAGPRIV		
RESLSTH		
IMGCNT		
PFLTRATE		
PFLREF		
TIMREF		
PGFLTIO		
(reserved)	(reserved)	AUTHPRI
EXTRACPU		
(reserved) (40 bytes)		
PRCPGFLREFS (16 bytes)		
PPGFLVA		
PSCANCTX_QUEUE		
SPARE_L1		
SPARE_L2		
SPARE_W2		PSCANCTX_SEQNUM
UCPUTIM		
NS_SPARE		
(reserved)		
WSL		

(continued)

Figure E.15 *(continued)*
Layout of a Process Header

Usual location	Physical page zero on system with no bad memory in the first 64K bytes.
Reference	Table 30.22.

E.3.38   RSB—Resource Block

Purpose	Contains information about a resource defined to the lock management system services.
Location	All resource blocks can be located through the resource hash table, pointed to by LCK$GL_HASHTBL.
Allocated from	Nonpaged pool.
References	Figures 10.1, 10.3.

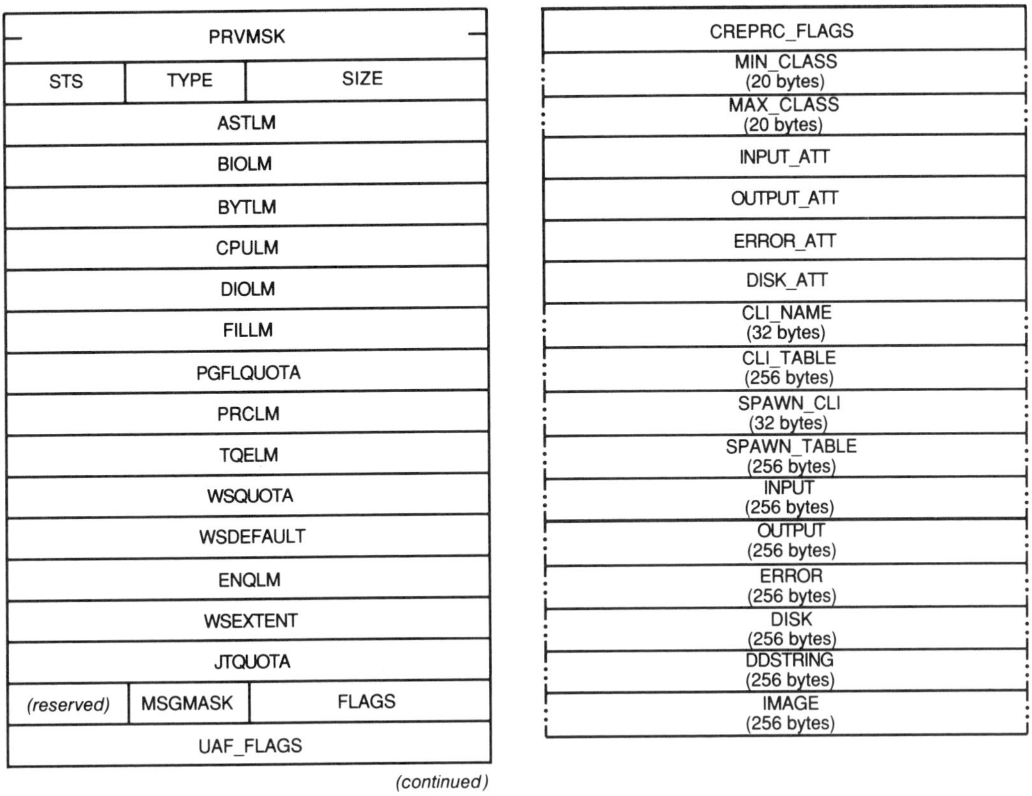

PRVMSK		
STS	TYPE	SIZE
ASTLM		
BIOLM		
BYTLM		
CPULM		
DIOLM		
FILLM		
PGFLQUOTA		
PRCLM		
TQELM		
WSQUOTA		
WSDEFAULT		
ENQLM		
WSEXTENT		
JTQUOTA		
(reserved)	MSGMASK	FLAGS
UAF_FLAGS		

CREPRC_FLAGS
MIN_CLASS (20 bytes)
MAX_CLASS (20 bytes)
INPUT_ATT
OUTPUT_ATT
ERROR_ATT
DISK_ATT
CLI_NAME (32 bytes)
CLI_TABLE (256 bytes)
SPAWN_CLI (32 bytes)
SPAWN_TABLE (256 bytes)
INPUT (256 bytes)
OUTPUT (256 bytes)
ERROR (256 bytes)
DISK (256 bytes)
DDSTRING (256 bytes)
IMAGE (256 bytes)

(continued)

Figure E.16
Layout of a Process Quota Block

E.3.39 **SPL—Spinlock Control Block**

Purpose	Synchronization tool for multiprocessing.
Usual location	A static spinlock is identified by the position of its address in SMP$AR_SPNLKVEC, a table of static spinlock addresses.
	A dynamic (device) spinlock is pointed to by the field CRB$L_DLCK in the CRB that describes the device's controller, and by the field UCB$L_DLCK in the device's UCB.
Allocated from	Static spinlocks are allocated statically. Dynamic spinlocks are allocated from nonpaged pool.
References	Figures 8.1, 8.2.

E.3.40 **TAST—Terminal AST Block**

Purpose	Contains information for delivery of out-of-band character ASTs.
Usual location	Queued to the terminal UCB via TAST$L_LINK.

Allocated from   Nonpaged pool.
References   Figures 7.5, 7.6, 7.7.

E.3.41   TQE—Timer Queue Entry

Purpose   Describes pending timer or scheduled wakeup
                    request.
Location   Linked to the timer queue at EXE$GL_TQFL.
Allocated from   Nonpaged pool.
Reference   Figure 11.1.

E.3.42   UCB—Unit Control Block

Purpose   Describes the status, characteristics, and current state
                    of a device unit.
Location   Linked from DDB$L_UCB.
Allocated from   Nonpaged pool.
Reference   Figure E.17.
Special notes   Figure E.17 shows the part of the UCB common to all
                    device units. See the *VMS Device Support Manual*
                    for information on extensions to the common part
                    of the UCB.

E.3.43   WCB—Window Control Block

Purpose   Describes the virtual to logical correspondence for the
                    blocks of a file.
Location   Contained in FCB list at FCB$L_WLFL.
Allocated from   Nonpaged pool.
Reference   Figure E.18.

E.4   SYMBOLIC CONSTANTS

The files [SYS]SYSDEF*xx*.SDL and [VMSLIB]STARDEF*xx*.SDL define many systemwide symbolic codes that identify structures, resources, quotas, priorities, and so on. Many of these constants are listed in the *VMS System Services Reference Manual* and the *VMS I/O User's Reference Volume*. Those that are most closely tied to the material in this book but not listed in those manuals are listed here.

E.4.1   BTD—Bootstrap Device Codes

The bootstrap device codes (see Table E.2) are used by VMB, the primary bootstrap program, and by SYSBOOT, the secondary bootstrap program, to interpret the contents of the RPB$B_DEVTYP field, which specify the boot device.

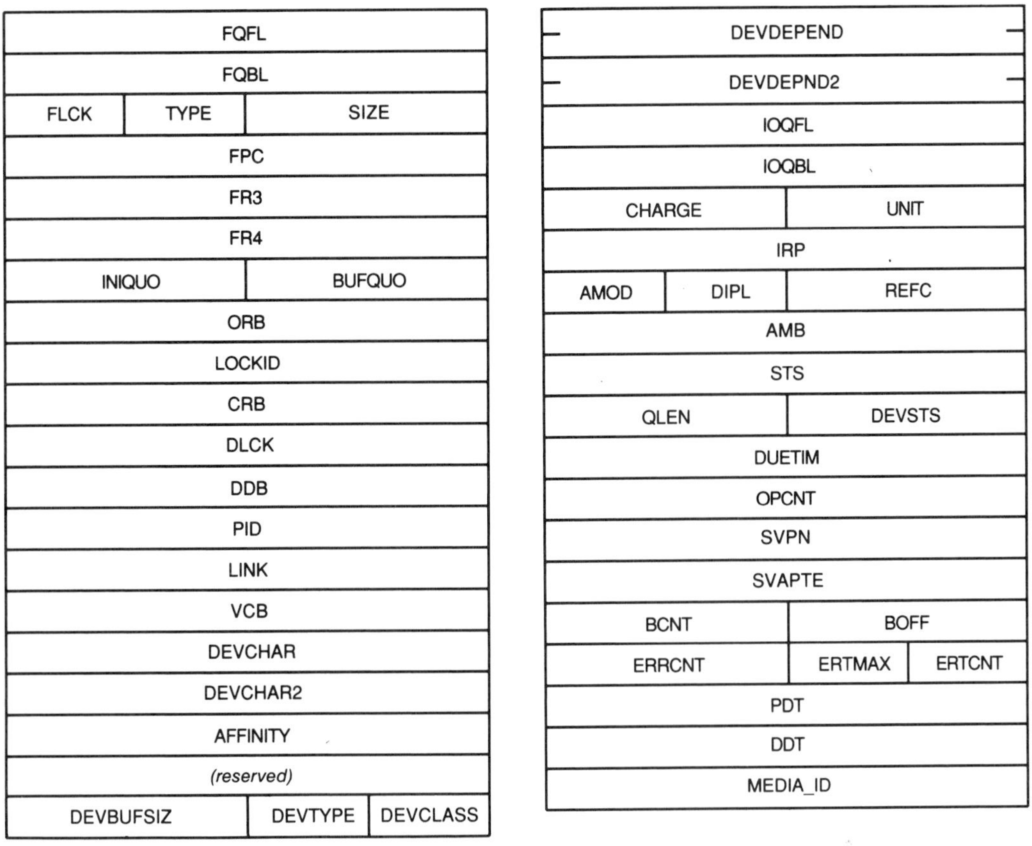

FQFL			
FQBL			
FLCK	TYPE	SIZE	
FPC			
FR3			
FR4			
INIQUO		BUFQUO	
ORB			
LOCKID			
CRB			
DLCK			
DDB			
PID			
LINK			
VCB			
DEVCHAR			
DEVCHAR2			
AFFINITY			
(reserved)			
DEVBUFSIZ		DEVTYPE	DEVCLASS

DEVDEPEND			
DEVDEPND2			
IOQFL			
IOQBL			
CHARGE		UNIT	
IRP			
AMOD	DIPL	REFC	
AMB			
STS			
QLEN		DEVSTS	
DUETIM			
OPCNT			
SVPN			
SVAPTE			
BCNT		BOFF	
ERRCNT		ERTMAX	ERTCNT
PDT			
DDT			
MEDIA_ID			

(continued)

Figure E.17
Layout of a Unit Control Block

E.4.2 CA—Conditional Assembly Parameters

The conditional assembly parameters (see Table E.3) control whether certain code is included when components of VMS are assembled. The first parameter was important during the initial development of VMS but is no longer used. All measurement code (used by the Monitor Utility) is always included.

E.4.3 DYN—Data Structure Type Definitions

Most structures allocated from nonpaged and paged pool have a unique code in the type field, at offset *xxx*$B_TYPE (see Table E.4). The System Dump Analyzer (SDA) uses the contents of this field when formatting dumps of pool and in automatic formatting of a data structure with the FORMAT command.

Codes that have numeric values greater than or equal to DYN$C_SUB-TYPE are subtypable codes. Each subtypable code refers to a generic function.

1263

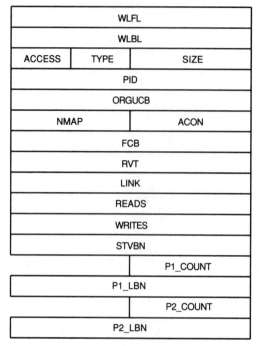

WLFL			
WLBL			
ACCESS	TYPE	SIZE	
PID			
ORGUCB			
NMAP		ACON	
FCB			
RVT			
LINK			
READS			
WRITES			
STVBN			
		P1_COUNT	
P1_LBN			
		P2_COUNT	
P2_LBN			

Figure E.18
Layout of a Window Control Block

Different data structures related to the same generic function have the same value in the type field but different values in the subtype field. The subtype field is at offset *xxx*$B_SUBTYPE within a subtypable data structure. For example, the system block (SB) and the path block (PB) are data structures used by SCS. Both structures have the value DYN$C_SCS in their type field; the SB has the value DYN$C_SCS_SB in its subtype field, whereas the PB has the value DYN$C_SCS_PB in its subtype field. SDA can interpret the subtype fields of standard system data structures.

E.4.4 IOxxx—I/O Address Space Definitions

The LIB.MLB $IO*xxx*DEF macros define the layout of I/O space for each CPU. Appendix G lists the values of *xxx*.

E.4.5 IPL—Interrupt Priority Level Definitions

IPLs that are used by VMS for synchronization and other purposes are given the symbolic names listed in Tables 3.1 and 4.1.

E.4.6 NDT—Nexus Device Type

Each external adapter has an associated code that is used by VMB, INIT,

Table E.2 Bootstrap Device Codes

Symbolic Name	Code	Device
BTD$K_MB	0	MASSBUS device
BTD$K_DM	1	RK06/7
BTD$K_DL	2	RL02
BTD$K_DQ	3	RB02/RB80
BTD$K_PROM	8	PROM (not copied)
BTD$K_PROM_COPY	9	PROM (copied)
BTD$K_UDA	17	UDA
BTD$K_TK50	18	TK50
BTD$K_KFQSA	19	KFQSA adapter
BTD$K_HSCCI	32	HSC on a CI
BTD$K_BDA	33	KDB50, VAXBI disk adapter
BTD$K_BVPSSP	34	KRBTA
BTD$K_AIE_TK50	35	DEBNK (tape)
BTD$K_KA410_DISK	36	VAXstation 2000 ST506 disk
BTD$K_KA420_DISK	36	VAXstation 3100 ST506 disk
BTD$K_ST506_DISK	36	VAXstation 3100 ST506 disk
BTD$K_KA410_TAPE	37	VAXstation 2000 SCSI tape
BTD$K_KA420_TAPE	37	VAXstation 3100 SCSI tape
BTD$K_SCSI_5380_TAPE	37	VAXstation 3100 SCSI tape
BTD$K_SII	39	Embedded DSSI controller
BTD$K_SHAC	41	Single chip DSSI adapter
BTD$K_SCSI_5380_DISK	42	VAXstation 3100 SCSI disk
BTD$K_CONSOLE	64	Console block storage device
BTD$K_NET_DLL	96	Start of network boot devices
BTD$K_QNA	96	DEQNA
BTD$K_UNA	97	DEUNA
BTD$K_AIE_NI	98	DEBNK (Ethernet)
BTD$K_KA410_NI	99	VAXstation 2000 Ethernet
BTD$K_KA420_NI	99	VAXstation 3100 Ethernet
BTD$K_LANCE	99	LANCE NI chip
	100–103	Reserved
BTD$K_DEBNI	104	DEBNI
	105–127	Reserved for network boot devices
BTD$K_NISCS	128	Disk served by a local area VAXcluster host

Table E.3 Conditional Assembly Parameters

Symbolic Name	Code	Feature
CA$_SIMULATOR	1	VMS running on simulator
CA$_MEASURE	2	Accumulate statistics for Monitor Utility
CA$_MEASURE_IOT	4	Accumulate I/O statistics for Monitor Utility

Table E.4   Data Structure Type Definitions

Symbolic Name	Code	Structure Type
DYN$C_ADP	1	Adapter control block
DYN$C_ACB	2	AST control block
DYN$C_AQB	3	ACP queue block
DYN$C_CEB	4	Common event block
DYN$C_CRB	5	Channel request block
DYN$C_DDB	6	Device data block
DYN$C_FCB	7	File control block
DYN$C_FRK	8	Fork block
DYN$C_IDB	9	Interrupt dispatch block
DYN$C_IRP	10	I/O request packet
DYN$C_LOG	11	Logical name block
DYN$C_PCB	12	Software process control block
DYN$C_PQB	13	Process quota block
DYN$C_RVT	14	Relative volume table
DYN$C_TQE	15	Timer queue entry
DYN$C_UCB	16	Unit control block
DYN$C_VCB	17	Volume control block
DYN$C_WCB	18	Window control block
DYN$C_BUFIO	19	Buffered I/O buffer
DYN$C_TYPAHD	20	Terminal type-ahead buffer
DYN$C_GSD	21	Global section descriptor
DYN$C_MVL	22	Magnetic tape volume list
DYN$C_NET	23	Network message block
DYN$C_KFE	24	Known file entry
DYN$C_MTL	25	Mounted volume list entry
DYN$C_BRDCST	26	Broadcast message block
DYN$C_CXB	27	Complex chained buffer
DYN$C_NDB	28	Network node descriptor block
DYN$C_SSB	29	Logical link subchannel status block
DYN$C_DPT	30	Driver prolog table
DYN$C_JPB	31	Job parameter block
DYN$C_PBH	32	Performance buffer header
DYN$C_PDB	33	Performance data block
DYN$C_PIB	34	Performance information block
DYN$C_PFL	35	Page file control block
DYN$C_PFLMAP	36	Page file mapping window
DYN$C_PTR	37	Pointer control block
DYN$C_KFRH	38	Known file image header
DYN$C_DCCB	39	Data cache control block
DYN$C_EXTGSD	40	Extended global section descriptor
DYN$C_SHMGSD	41	Shared memory global section descriptor
DYN$C_SHB	42	Shared memory control block
DYN$C_MBX	43	Mailbox control block
DYN$C_IRPE	44	Extended I/O request packet
DYN$C_SLAVCEB	45	Slave common event block

(continued)

Table E.4 Data Structure Type Definitions *(continued)*

Symbolic Name	Code	Structure Type
DYN$C_SHMCEB	46	Shared memory master common event block
DYN$C_JIB	47	Job information block
DYN$C_TWP	48	Terminal driver write packet ($TTYDEF)
DYN$C_RBM	49	Real-time system page table entry bitmap
DYN$C_VCA	50	Disk volume cache block
DYN$C_CDB	51	X25 low-end system (LES) channel data block
DYN$C_LPD	52	X25 LES process descriptor
DYN$C_LKB	53	Lock block
DYN$C_RSB	54	Resource block
DYN$C_LKID	55	Lock ID table
DYN$C_RSHT	56	Resource hash table
DYN$C_CDRP	57	Class driver request packet
DYN$C_ERP	58	Error log packet
DYN$C_CIDG	59	CI datagram buffer
DYN$C_CIMSG	60	CI message buffer
DYN$C_XWB	61	DECnet logical link context block
DYN$C_WQE	62	DECnet work queue block
DYN$C_ACL	63	Access control list queue entry
DYN$C_LNM	64	Logical name block
DYN$C_FLK	65	Fork lock request block
DYN$C_RIGHTSLIST	66	Rights list
DYN$C_KFD	67	Known file device directory block
DYN$C_KFPB	68	Known file list pointer block
DYN$C_CIA	69	Compound intrusion analysis block
DYN$C_PMB	70	Page fault monitor control block
DYN$C_PFB	71	Page fault monitor buffer
DYN$C_CHIP	72	Internal check protection block
DYN$C_ORB	73	Object rights block
DYN$C_QVAST	74	QVSS AST block
DYN$C_MVWB	75	Mount verification work buffer
DYN$C_UNC	76	Universal context block
DYN$C_DCB	77	DECnet control block for chained I/O
DYN$C_DLL	78	General DECnet datalink block
DYN$C_SPL	79	Spinlock control block
DYN$C_ARB	80	Access rights block
DYN$C_SUBTYPE	96	Beginning of subtypable codes
DYN$C_SCS	96	SCS control block
DYN$C_CI	97	CI port structure
DYN$C_LOADCODE	98	Loadable code
DYN$C_INIT	99	Structure set up by INIT
DYN$C_CLASSDRV	100	Class driver structure
DYN$C_CLU	101	VAXcluster structure
DYN$C_PGD	102	Paged pool structure

(continued)

Table E.4 Data Structure Type Definitions *(continued)*

Symbolic Name	Code	Structure Type
DYN$C_DECW	103	DECwindows structure
DYN$C_VWS	104	VAX Workstation Software structure
DYN$C_DSRV	105	Disk server structure
DYN$C_MP	106	Multiprocessing-related structure
DYN$C_NSA	107	Nondiscretionary security audit structure
DYN$C_CWPS	108	Clusterwide process services
DYN$C_SPECIAL	128	Code that defines beginning of special dynamic memory types
DYN$C_SHRBUFIO	128	Shared memory buffered I/O buffer

and the power recovery routine to determine which adapter-specific action should be taken to (re)initialize each adapter (see Table E.5).

E.4.7 PR—Processor Register Definitions

The macro $PRDEF, in LIB.MLB, defines symbolic names for the processor registers that are common to all types of VAX processor. For each CPU type, a second LIB.MLB macro, $PR*xxx*DEF, defines symbolic names for the CPU's additional processor registers. Appendix G lists the values of *xxx*.

E.4.8 SPL—Static Spinlock Definitions

Symbolic names such as SPL$C_SCHED for the static spinlocks used by VMS are listed in Table 8.2.

Table E.5 Nexus Device Types

Symbolic Name	Code	Adapter
NDT$_MEM4NI	8	Memory, 4K, not interleaved
NDT$_MEM4I	9	Memory, 4K, interleaved
NDT$_MEM16NI	16	Memory, 16K, not interleaved
NDT$_MEM16I	17	Memory, 16K, interleaved
NDT$_MEM1664NI	18	Memory, 16K and 64K mixed
NDT$_MB	32	MBA 0, 1, 2, or 3
NDT$_UB0	40	UNIBUS adapter or interconnect 0
NDT$_UB1	41	UNIBUS adapter 1
NDT$_UB2	42	UNIBUS adapter 2
NDT$_UB3	43	UNIBUS adapter 3
NDT$_DR32	48	DR32
NDT$_CI	56	CI750, CI780
NDT$_MPM0	64	Multiport memory 0

(continued)

Table E.5 Nexus Device Types *(continued)*

Symbolic Name	Code	Adapter
NDT$_MPM1	65	Multiport memory 1
NDT$_MPM2	66	Multiport memory 2
NDT$_MPM3	67	Multiport memory 3
NDT$_MEM64NIL	104	64K memory, not interleaved, lower controller
NDT$_MEM64EIL	105	64K memory, externally interleaved, lower controller
NDT$_MEM64NIU	106	64K memory, not interleaved, upper controller
NDT$_MEM64EIU	107	64K memory, externally interleaved, upper controller
NDT$_MEM64I	108	64K memory, internally interleaved
NDT$_MEM256NIL	112	256K memory, not interleaved, lower controller
NDT$_MEM256EIL	113	256K memory, externally interleaved, lower controller
NDT$_MEM256NIU	114	256K memory, not interleaved, upper controller
NDT$_MEM256EIU	115	256K memory, externally interleaved, upper controller
NDT$_MEM256I	116	256K memory, internally interleaved
NDT$_KA410	128	VAXstation 2000 processor
NDT$_KA420	128	VAXstation 3100 processor
NDT$_KA640	129	MicroVAX 3300/3400 processor
NDT$_SCORMEM	80000001_{16}	VAX 8200 memory
NDT$_BIMFA	80000101_{16}	DRB32 adapter
NDT$_BUA	80000102_{16}	VAXBI UNIBUS adapter
NDT$_BLA	80000103_{16}	KLESI-B
NDT$_KA810	80000105_{16}	KA810 processor
NDT$_NBI	80000106_{16}	VAX 8800 VAXBI adapter
NDT$_XBIB	80002107_{16}	VAXBI-to-XMI adapter
NDT$_BCA	80000108_{16}	CIBCA adapter
NDT$_BICOMBO	80000109_{16}	DMB32 adapter
NDT$_DSB32	$8000010A_{16}$	DSB32 adapter
NDT$_BCI750	$8000010B_{16}$	CIBCI adapter
NDT$_BDA	$8000010E_{16}$	VAXBI disk adapter
NDT$_DEBNT	$8000410F_{16}$	DEBNT adapter
NDT$_DEMNA	$00000C03_{16}$	DEMNA adapter
NDT$_CIXCD	$00000C05_{16}$	CIXCD adapter
NDT$_XCP	00008001_{16}	VAX 6000 models 200/300 processor
NDT$_XRP	00008082_{16}	VAX 6000 model 400 processor
NDT$_XMA	00004001_{16}	XMI memory
NDT$_XBI	00002001_{16}	XMI-to-VAXBI adapter

F   Size of System and P1 Virtual Address Spaces

Many of the VMS data structures are not created until the system is bootstrapped, so that the structure sizes can be determined from the appropriate SYSGEN parameters. This appendix describes the relations among these parameters and the resulting use of virtual address space.

In the equations that appear in this appendix, two common features dominate. The first is division by 512, the number of bytes in a page. This division, actually an arithmetic shift by -9, converts an input parameter expressed as a number of bytes, such as the SYSGEN parameter NPAGEDYN, into a page count. Adding 511 to a byte expression before the integer division takes place rounds up to the next highest page boundary.

The second feature is the number 128, which appears in expressions that convert a page count into the number of page table pages required to map that page count. Since a page table entry (PTE) is four bytes long, each page table page can contain 128 PTEs, mapping 128 pages. Division by 128, actually an arithmetic shift by -7, converts an input parameter expressed as a number of pages (and therefore the same number of PTEs) into a count of page table pages. In this case, 127 is added as the rounding factor.

F.1   PROCESS HEADER

The SYSBOOT image, executing in the early stages of system initialization, reads SYSGEN parameters and sizes the various portions of address space. SYSBOOT's first calculation of this type determines the size of the process header (PHD) from related SYSGEN parameters. Six segments compose the PHD:

- Fixed portion, including the register save area and offsets to the other segments
- Working set list (WSL)
- Process section table (PST)
- Empty pages reserved for WSL expansion
- Two PHD page arrays and two page table page arrays, each containing one entry per page of the PHD
- P0 and P1 page tables

Most of the calculations in this appendix treat the PHD fixed portion, working set list, and the PST as a unit.

Table F.1 lists the PHD segments, the global locations where segment sizes

Table F.1   Discrete Portions of the Process Header

PHD Segment	Symbolic Name Used in Calculations	Global Location Containing Segment Size	Parameters Affecting Size
Fixed portion, WSL, PST	PHD(Fixed, WSL, PST)	SWP$GW_WSLPTE	PHD$C_LENGTH, PROCSECTCNT, PQL_DWSDEFAULT
Empty pages for WSL expansion	PHD(Expansion_Pages)	SWP$GW_EMPTPTE	WSMAX, PQL_DWSDEFAULT
PHD and page table page arrays	PHD(Page_Arrays)	SWP$GW_BAKPTE	Number of PHD pages
P0 and P1 page tables	PHD(Page_Tables)	SGN$GL_PTPAGCNT	VIRTUALPAGECNT

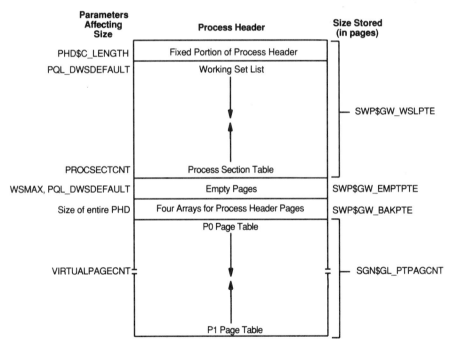

Figure F.1
Process Header and SYSGEN Parameters

are stored, and the SYSGEN parameters that affect segment sizes. The table also introduces the notation used in this section to describe the segments of the PHD. Figure F.1 shows the layout of the PHD and the relations among the segments described in Table F.1.

The following global locations contain the sums of various segments listed in Table F.1:

$$\text{SGN\$GL\_PHDAPCNT} = \text{PHD(Fixed, WSL, PST)} + \text{PHD(Page\_Arrays)}$$

$$\text{SGN\$GL\_PHDPAGCT} = \text{PHD(Fixed, WSL, PST)}$$
$$+ \text{PHD(Expansion\_Pages)} + \text{PHD(Page\_Arrays)}$$

$$\text{SWP\$GL\_BSLOTSZ} = \text{PHD(Fixed, WSL, PST)} + \text{PHD(Expansion\_Pages)}$$
$$+ \text{PHD(Page\_Arrays)} + \text{PHD(Page\_Tables)}$$

F.1.1 Process Page Tables

The P0 and P1 page tables compose most of the PHD. The total number of pages allocated for the process page tables depends on the parameter VIRTUALPAGECNT:

$$\text{PHD(Page\_Tables)} = \frac{\text{VIRTUALPAGECNT} + 127}{128} \tag{F1}$$

F.1.2 Working Set List and Process Section Table

The PHD begins with the fixed portion. Immediately following the fixed portion are the WSL and PST, which grow toward each other. The SYSGEN parameter PROCSECTCNT determines the PST size. The WSL size depends on the WSMAX parameter. In most systems, however, the working set of an average process is much smaller than the allowed maximum. Therefore, the parameter PQL_DWSDEFAULT determines the initial WSL size, and the difference between WSMAX and PQL_DWSDEFAULT is reserved for WSL expansion.

To determine the initial size of the PHD fixed portion, WSL, and PST, SYSBOOT first uses WSMAX to establish the maximum number of pages for that area, and then it determines the extra space reserved for WSL expansion. The difference between these two numbers is the number of pages initially available for the fixed portion, WSL, and PST. In the following, 4 is the size in bytes of a working set list entry, and 32 is the size in bytes of a process section table entry.

$$\text{Temp} = \frac{\left[\begin{array}{l} \text{PHD\$C\_LENGTH} + (4 * \text{WSMAX}) \\ + (32 * \text{PROCSECTCNT}) + 511 \end{array} \right]}{512}$$

$$\text{PHD(Expansion\_Pages)} = \frac{\text{WSMAX} - \text{PQL\_DWSDEFAULT}}{128}$$

$$\text{PHD(Fixed, WSL, PST)} = \text{Temp} - \text{PHD(Expansion\_Pages)} \tag{F2}$$

F.1.3 **Process Header and Page Table Page Arrays**

The PHD contains two PHD page arrays, the working set list index (WSLX) array, and the backing store (BAK) array. The swapper stores information about PHD pages in these arrays while the header is outswapped. The BAK array entries are longwords. The size of an entry in the WSLX array varies: if 32 or more megabytes of memory are described by the page frame number (PFN) database, each WSLX array entry is one longword in length; otherwise, each entry is one word.

The PHD also contains two arrays of one-byte entries that describe each page table page. However, to simplify the calculation of the memory required for these arrays, each array contains an entry for each page in the PHD, as the WSLX and BAK arrays do. Since the page tables constitute approximately 90 percent of the PHD in a typical system, this algorithm results in a good approximation.

Thus, each page of the PHD requires an entry in each of four parallel arrays. This requires ten bytes of memory per PHD page on a system with 32 or more megabytes of memory described by the PFN database, eight bytes per page otherwise.

Because the page arrays reside within the PHD, their size must be included in the PHD page count. That is, each page array must contain an entry for each page in the PHD, including the pages within which the page arrays themselves reside. Thus, the space allocated for this area depends on its own size. SYSBOOT's calculation of this portion of the PHD proceeds iteratively.

1. SYSBOOT computes the size of the PHD in bytes, excluding the page arrays and page tables, and adds 511.

$$\text{PHD\_Byte\_Count} = 512 * \text{PHD(Fixed, WSL, PST)}$$
$$+ 512 * \text{PHD(Expansion\_Pages)}$$
$$+ 511 \qquad \text{(F3)}$$

2. It calculates the number of PHD pages except for the page arrays themselves. This is the approximate number of entries needed in each page array. SYSBOOT multiplies this count by eight or ten bytes, producing the approximate size of the page arrays in bytes.

$$\text{Page\_Array\_Byte\_Count} = \text{Entry\_Size} * \text{PHD(Fixed, WSL, PST)}$$
$$+ \text{Entry\_Size} * \text{PHD(Expansion\_Pages)}$$
$$+ \text{Entry\_Size} * \text{PHD(Page\_Tables)}$$
$$\text{(F4)}$$

3. SYSBOOT adds the approximate size of the page arrays to the PHD size calculated in step 1.

$$\text{PHD\_Byte\_Count} = \text{PHD\_Byte\_Count}$$
$$+ \text{Page\_Array\_Byte\_Count} \qquad \text{(F5)}$$

4. It converts the approximate page array size from step 2 into a page count. This is the estimated number of additional page array entries required for the page arrays themselves.

$$\text{Page\_Array\_Page\_Count} = \frac{\text{Page\_Array\_Byte\_Count}}{512} \qquad (F6)$$

Note that SYSBOOT converts bytes to pages by integer division. Therefore, the resulting page count is zero if the byte count is less than 512 (one page).

If the page count is nonzero, SYSBOOT multiplies the page count by eight or ten, depending on system memory configuration. This produces the number of additional bytes required in the page array to describe its own pages. SYSBOOT adds this number to the approximate PHD size calculated in step 3. It converts these additional bytes to a page count and repeats this step until the page count falls to zero.

5. Once the page count falls to zero, SYSBOOT converts the accumulated size of the PHD from bytes to pages. It stores the result in SGN$GL_PHDPAGCT.

$$\text{SGN\$GL\_PHDPAGCT} = \frac{\text{PHD\_Byte\_Count}}{512} \qquad (F7)$$

Thus, SGN$GL_PHDPAGCT contains the number of pages in the PHD fixed portion, WSL, PST, expansion pages, and page arrays. SGN$GL_PT-PAGCNT, initialized from VIRTUALPAGECNT, determines the page table size. SYSBOOT adds SGN$GL_PHDPAGCT and SGN$GL_PTPAGCNT to obtain the total size of the PHD in pages, which it stores in SWP$GL_BSLOTSZ.

F.2   SYSTEM VIRTUAL ADDRESS SPACE

Once SYSBOOT has calculated the size of the PHD, it computes the size of system virtual address space. System virtual address space must be large enough to include the system base image and loadable executive images, the variable-size pieces primarily defined by SYSGEN parameters, and other variable-size pieces based on CPU and I/O space configuration.

Figure F.2 shows system virtual address space prior to the loading of loadable executive images. Much of this address space is not cataloged in the PFN database; instead, SYSBOOT itself permanently allocates physical memory and initializes system page table entries (SPTEs) for these pages. The section labeled Available System Pages is the area of virtual address space available for mapping I/O space, loading executive images, loading EXE$INIT, and similar functions. The global location LDR$GL_FREE_PT contains the offset from the base of the system page table (SPT) to the

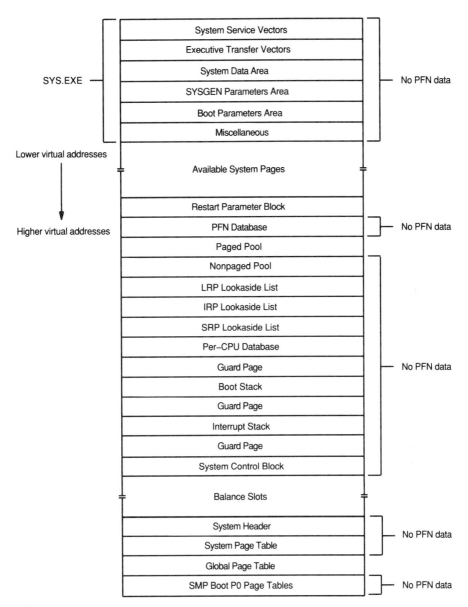

Figure F.2
Initial Layout of System Virtual Address Space

first available SPTE in this address range; the actual contents are system-dependent.

Many pieces of system address space vary in size, depending on one or more SYSGEN parameters or on a particular CPU configuration. Table F.2 lists the pieces of system space in the order in which they are configured (mapped from high to low virtual address by SYSBOOT), the global location of the pointer to the start of each piece, and the factors that affect the size.

1275

Table F.2 Layout of System Virtual Address Space

Item	Global Location [1]	Factors That Affect Size	Protection	Pageable
High end of system space	@MMG$GL_MAXSYSVA			
Reserved for symmetric multiprocessing (SMP) boot P0 page tables		32 pages	ERKW	No
Global page table	@MMG$GL_GPTE	GBLPAGES	URKW	Yes [2]
System page table	@MMG$GL_SPTBASE	Everything	ERKW	No
System PHD	@MMG$GL_SYSPHD	SYSMWCNT, GBLSECTIONS	ERKW	No
Balance slot area	@SWP$GL_BALBASE	BALSETCNT, Size of a PHD	ERKW	Yes, no [3]
System control block	@EXE$GL_SCB	CPU configuration	ERKW	No
No access guard page	@EXE$GL_INTSTK	1 page	No access	No
Interrupt stack	@EXE$GL_INTSTKLM	INTSTKPAGES	ERKW	No
No access guard page		1 page	No access	No
Boot stack		1 page	ERKW	No
No access guard page		1 page	No access	No
Per-CPU database	@SMP$GL_CPU_DATA[*cpu_id*]	2 pages	URKW	No
Small request packet (SRP) lookaside list	@IOC$GL_SRPSPLIT	SRPCOUNT, SRPCOUNTV, SRPSIZE	ERKW	No
Intermediate request packet (IRP) lookaside list	@EXE$GL_SPLITADR	IRPCOUNT, IRPCOUNTV	ERKW	No
Large request packet (LRP) lookaside list	@IOC$GL_LRPSPLIT	LRPCOUNT, LRPCOUNTV, LRPSIZE	ERKW	No
Nonpaged pool variable-length list	@MMG$GL_NPAGEDYN	NPAGEDYN, NPAGEVIR	ERKW	No
Paged pool	@MMG$GL_PAGEDYN	PAGEDYN	ERKW	Yes
PFN database	@PFN$A_BASE	Everything	ERKW	No
Restart parameter block (RPB)	@EXE$GL_RPB	1 page	URKW	No

(continued)

Table F.2   Layout of System Virtual Address Space *(continued)*

Item	Global Location [1]	Factors That Affect Size	Protection	Pageable
Available system virtual address space [4]	LDR$GL_FREE_PT [5]	Everything	No access	
System base image (SYS.EXE) [6]	SYS$S0_VECTOR_BASE	88 pages [7]	UR and URKW [8]	No

[1] If the symbol @ does not precede the global location name, the name's value is the starting address of the area in question. If the symbol @ precedes the global location name, the global location contains the address of the area.

[2] Global page table pages are initially configured as demand zero pages and are pageable. However, every global page table page containing at least one valid global PTE is locked into the system working set.

[3] Each PHD in the balance slot area is part of a process working set. Some portions of the PHD do not page, but those physical pages are accounted for in a process working set and do not count toward the executive's use of memory.

[4] All loadable executive images eventually reside in this area.

[5] This location contains the offset from MMG$GL_SPTBASE to the first available SPTE.

[6] See Chapter 29 for a detailed picture of the system base image layout.

[7] This includes virtual address space reserved for expansion.

[8] Four system service vector pages are protected UR; the remaining pages, including one modifiable vector page, are protected URKW.

It also shows the protection and pageability of each piece; the owner access mode of all system space pages is kernel.

Except for the system base image, the sizes of most pieces of system address space listed in Table F.2 are simply based on one or two SYSGEN parameters. SYSBOOT computes their sizes in a straightforward manner. The system page table and the PFN database are more complicated. The next sections discuss their sizes.

F.2.1   System Page Table

The SPT contains an SPTE for each page of system virtual address space, including the SPT pages themselves. Thus, the space allocated for this area depends in part on its own size. To calculate the size of the SPT, SYSBOOT determines the actual sizes of some segments of system virtual address space from SYSGEN parameters, estimates the size of the PFN database, and adds 1,024 SPTEs.

SYSBOOT performs the following calculations and sums the resulting values to arrive at the SPTE count:

1. It determines the size of the area devoted to balance slots by multiplying the size of a PHD in pages, described in Section F.1, by the SYSGEN

parameter BALSETCNT. The area devoted to balance slots constitutes more than half of system virtual address space in a typical configuration.

2. The SYSGEN parameter PAGEDYN is the number of bytes reserved for paged pool. SYSBOOT converts PAGEDYN to a page count, rounding downward, to get the number of SPTEs required to map paged pool.

3. Two SYSGEN parameters exist for each lookaside list and the nonpaged variable-length list; one defines the initial size of the list and one defines the maximum size to which the list can expand. SYSBOOT reserves enough virtual address space for the maximum list size.

   For each lookaside list, SYSBOOT performs the following:

   a. It determines the size of a request packet in the list, specified as a SYSGEN parameter for SRPs and LRPs and as a constant, IRP$C_LENGTH, for IRPs. It rounds the size upward to a 16-byte boundary, the granularity of pool allocation. (For simplicity, Equation F8 does not show this rounding.)

   b. It multiplies the larger of the initial and maximum list size parameters by the size of a request packet. It converts the result to a page count, rounding upward, to get the lookaside list size in pages. For example, for the IRP lookaside list,

   $$\text{Temp} = \max(\text{IRPCOUNT}, \text{IRPCOUNTV})$$

   $$\text{IRP\_List} = \frac{(\text{IRP\$C\_LENGTH} * \text{Temp}) + 511}{512} \tag{F8}$$

   SYSBOOT converts the larger of the SYSGEN parameters NPAGEDYN and NPAGEVIR to a page count, rounding downward, to get the size of the nonpaged variable-length list. Note that SYSBOOT rounds the size of the nonpaged variable-length list downward to an integral number of pages whereas it rounds the size of each lookaside list upward.

   Although SYSBOOT reserves enough virtual address space for the maximum size of each list, it allocates only as much physical memory as the initial list size. This initial physical memory is not cataloged in the PFN database. During system operations, each list can expand to its maximum size, but the physical pages allocated for expansion are generally pages with PFN database entries.

4. SYSBOOT uses a simple estimate for the number of SPTEs to reserve for the PFN database. It ignores the fact that some system pages will not have entries in the PFN database and calculates the virtual address space reserved for the PFN database as though every available page of memory will have an entry.

   This estimate errs on the high side in allocating SPTEs for the PFN database. However, physical page allocation for the PFN database is not based on this computation but on the more accurate computation described in Section F.2.2. Thus, there is no large waste of physical memory.

5. The SYSGEN parameter SPTREQ includes sufficient additional SPTEs to map all loadable executive images and the system base image. SYSBOOT adds this value to its tally.

6. SYSBOOT also adds the value specified by the parameter REALTIME_SPTS, a count of pages used by the connect-to-interrupt driver.

7. It adds 1,024 to its tally as an estimated I/O space requirement.

8. If the SYSGEN parameter DUMPSTYLE is set to 1 (a selective dump is enabled), SYSBOOT allocates 127 extra SPTEs. EXE$BUG_CHECK uses these SPTEs to double-map noncontiguous pages of memory so that they can be transferred to the crash dump file in a single I/O request. Chapter 32 describes this process.

9. The system header calculation is similar to the calculation of PHD size, described in Section F.1. However, since the size of the system working set should not vary dramatically, the optimization technique for empty working set expansion pages is not used. Also, since the system header will never swap, it need not contain page arrays. The size of the SPT is calculated separately, so the system header contains only a fixed portion, a WSL, and a PST. Two SYSGEN parameters, SYSMWCNT and GBLSEC-TIONS, control the size of these areas. In the following equation, 4 is the size in bytes of a working set list entry, and 32 is the size in bytes of a section table entry.

$$\text{SYSPHD} = \frac{\left\lceil \begin{array}{c} \text{PHD\$C\_LENGTH} + (4 * \text{SYSMWCNT}) \\ + (32 * \text{GBLSECTIONS}) + 511 \end{array} \right\rceil}{512} \tag{F9}$$

10. SYSBOOT adds the size of the interrupt stack in pages, the SYSGEN parameter INTSTKPAGES, to the number of pages required for the per-CPU database, currently two. It adds one page for the CPU boot stack and three pages for guard pages, and rounds the result to the next highest power of 2.

    The page protection code of guard pages is set to permit no access. These pages cause an "interrupt stack not valid" processor halt on either stack overflow or stack underflow.

    On nonmultiprocessing systems, SYSBOOT adds the computed value to its tally.

    On an SMP system, SYSBOOT multiplies this value by the number of actual or potential CPUs.

    —For VAX 8200 family processors, the value is multiplied by 16.

    —For VAX 8800 family processors, the value is multiplied by 2.

    —For VAX 88x0 processors, SYSBOOT multiplies the value by 4.

    —For the VAX 6000 series processors, SYSBOOT multiplies the value by the actual number of CPUs available. It adds 80 additional SPTEs for CPU-specific space requirements.

—For VAXstation 3520 and 3540 processors, SYSBOOT multiplies the value by 6. It adds 2,664 additional SPTEs for CPU-specific space requirements.

11. On an SMP system, SYSBOOT allocates 32 additional SPTEs, one per potential CPU. A CPU uses the SPTE indexed by its CPU ID to double-map its boot stack. The same page serves as a P0 page table page mapping EXE$INIT, allowing EXE$INIT to be referenced by a P0 address in the process of turning on memory management. Chapter 34 describes the boot stack. Chapter 31 describes turning on memory management.

12. SYSBOOT calculates the amount of system virtual address space to reserve for the global page table based on SYSGEN parameter GBLPAGES:

$$\text{Global\_Page\_Table} = \frac{\text{GBLPAGES} + 127}{128} \qquad \text{(F10)}$$

13. SYSBOOT adds the size of the system control block (SCB), a number between 1 and 32, to its tally. The size of the SCB is CPU-dependent. All processors have at least a one-page architecturally defined SCB, but the bus and device configuration of a particular processor may require more SCB pages.

—VAX-11/780 and VAX-11/785 processors use only one page of architecturally defined SCB.

—VAX-11/730 and MicroVAX II processors use a second page for dispatching UNIBUS or Q22-bus interrupts.

—VAX-11/750 processors use one additional page for each UNIBUS interface on the system. This results in either a two-page or a three-page SCB.

—VAX 8200 family processors use an additional page for each VAXBI-to-UNIBUS adapter (DWBUA).

—VAX 8800 family and VAX 88x0 processors use a 32-page SCB to support the theoretical maximum number of directly vectored adapters.

—VAX 8600 and VAX 8650 processors use a four-page SCB to support the maximum configuration of four synchronous backplane interface (SBI) adapters.

—VAX 6000 series processors use an additional SCB page for each XMI-to-VAXBI bus adapter (XBI) found on the XMI bus. The processors search each VAXBI and use an additional page for each DWBUA on the VAXBI.

—MicroVAX 2000 processors use a two-page SCB.

—MicroVAX 3100 processors use a two-page SCB for dispatching small computer system interface (SCSI) bus interrupts.

—MicroVAX 3300, 3400, and 3800 processors use a two-page SCB for dispatching DSSI and Q22-bus interrupts.

—MicroVAX 3200, 3500, and 3600 processors use a two-page SCB for dispatching Q22-bus interrupts.

—MicroVAX 3900 processors use a two-page SCB for dispatching Q22-bus interrupts.

—VAXstation 3520 and 3540 processors use a two-page SCB for dispatching SCSI and Q22-bus interrupts.

The sum of items 1 through 13 represents the approximate number of SPTEs needed, except those for the SPT pages themselves. SYSBOOT rounds the SPTE count upward and divides it by 128, obtaining the number of SPT pages that will themselves need SPTEs. It adds that number to the original SPTE count and divides by 128, obtaining the number of SPT pages required.

$$\text{Temp} = \frac{\text{SPTE\_Count} + 127}{128}$$

$$\text{SPT\_Pages} = \frac{\text{SPTE\_Count} + \text{Temp}}{128} \qquad \text{(F11)}$$

SYSBOOT does not count the single page required for the RPB when determining the initial size of the SPT. It assumes that page rounding or one of the approximations will add the single SPTE required to map the RPB.

F.2.2 PFN Database

The PFN database describes each page of physical memory except for certain nonpaged portions of system space. This nonpaged area includes the area where the PFN database itself resides. Thus, the size of the PFN database depends in part on itself.

The PFN database includes either 18 or 22 bytes of information for each page of physical memory it describes. If 32 or more megabytes of memory require PFN database entries, the global variable MMG$GW_BIGPFN contains the value 1 and the PFN database contains 22 bytes of information per page. Otherwise, MMG$GW_BIGPFN contains the value 0, and the PFN database contains 18 bytes of information per page. Chapter 14 describes the PFN database and the reason for the differing amounts of information.

In Equation F12, PFN_Entry_Size represents either 18 or 22. Available_Pages represents the number of pages of available physical memory, the lesser of actual physical memory and the SYSGEN parameter PHYSICAL-PAGES. No_PFN_Entries represents the nonpaged portions of system space not accounted for in the PFN database, listed in Equation F13.

$$\text{PFN\_DB\_Size} = \frac{\left\lfloor \begin{array}{c} \text{PFN\_Entry\_Size} * \\ (\text{Available\_Pages} - \text{No\_PFN\_Entries}) + 511 \end{array} \right\rfloor}{512} \qquad \text{(F12)}$$

No_PFN_Entries = System base image
+ PFN database
+ Initial allocation, nonpaged variable-length list
+ Initial allocation, lookaside lists
+ Interrupt stack
+ Per-CPU database and boot stack
+ SCB
+ System header
+ System page table   (F13)

F.2.3   Available System Virtual Address Space

After SYSBOOT calculates the size of system virtual address space, it allocates physical memory and initializes SPTEs for the portions of system space not cataloged in the PFN database. It maps the SPT at the high end of virtual address space, allocating its pages from the high end of physical memory. It then assigns the system header, SCB, and so on at decreasing addresses, as in Figure F.2. Finally, at the low end of system address space, it maps the system base image, SYS.EXE.

The remaining SPTEs (the section labeled Available System Pages in Figure F.2) represent a contiguous area of system virtual address space. This area initially includes the entire region between the RPB and the system base image. SYSBOOT loads the global location LDR$GL_FREE_PT with the offset from the base of the SPT to the first available SPTE. At the next higher SPTE, it places the count of available SPTEs. The routine LDR$ALLOC_PT, described in Chapter 29, allocates virtual address space from this area, from high to low virtual addresses. SYSBOOT, EXE$INIT, and SYSINIT use this space to map I/O space, load executive images, and for similar functions.

This address space is reusable; for instance, SYSBOOT maps EXE$INIT into this region. When EXE$INIT completes, its address space is deallocated and becomes available to the next invoker of LDR$ALLOC_PT. Loadable executive images, also described in Chapter 29, can contain paged and non-paged image sections as well as image sections that are deallocated after use. In addition, a system might not include every loadable executive image. Thus, the contents as well as the size of this area are system-dependent, and part of the address space may be pageable.

Table F.3 lists the items allocated from this area, the order in which they are allocated, and the page protection. The owner access mode of all these pages is kernel. Note that the loadable executive images loaded by SYSBOOT contain no pageable sections. The System Dump Analyzer (SDA) command SHOW EXECUTIVE displays the location and size of every image currently loaded and thus provides a fairly complete picture of this area.

Figure F.3 shows the address space on a typical system after the completion of system initialization. For the sake of simplicity, the figure does not

Table F.3   System Virtual Address Area

Item	Global Location [1]	Protection
MAPPED FROM HIGH TO LOW VIRTUAL ADDRESS FROM AVAILABLE SYSTEM SPACE AREA BY SYSBOOT		
Temporary I/O space for boot driver		(deallocated)
EXEC_INIT.EXE		(deallocated)
SYSTEM_DEBUG.EXE [2]		UR/URKW
SYSTEM_PRIMITIVES.EXE		UR/URKW
SYSTEM_SYNCHRONIZATION.EXE [3]		UR/URKW
PRIMITIVE_IO.EXE		UR/URKW
ERRORLOG.EXE		UR/URKW
MAPPED FROM AVAILABLE SYSTEM SPACE AREA BY EXE$INIT		
Page to map pages without PFN database entry	@MMG$GL_FREE_NO_ PFN_DB_VA	KW
Temporary page (VAX 6000 series)	@EXE$GL_CPUNODSP	KW
Mapping for I/O adapters	@(@MMG$GL_SBICONF) [4]	KW
PROCESS_MANAGEMENT.EXE		UR/URKW
IO_ROUTINES.EXE		UR/URKW
EVENT_FLAGS_AND_ASTS.EXE		UR/URKW
IMAGE_MANAGEMENT.EXE		UR/URKW
WORKING_SET_MANAGEMENT.EXE		UR/URKW
PAGE_MANAGEMENT.EXE		UR/URKW
LOCKING.EXE		UR/URKW
SECURITY.EXE		UR/URKW
LOGICAL_NAMES.EXE		UR/URKW
EXCEPTION.EXE		UR/URKW
MESSAGE_ROUTINES.EXE		UR/URKW
SYSDEVICE.EXE		UR/URKW
SYSGETSYI.EXE		UR/URKW
SYSLICENSE.EXE		UR/URKW
LMF$GROUP_TABLE.EXE		UR/URKW
CPULOA.EXE		UR/URKW
Connect-to-interrupt pages	@(@EXE$GL_RTBITMAP) [5]	No access [6]
Tape mount verification buffer (two pages)	@EXE$GL_TMV_SVABUF	KR
Mount verification buffer	EXE$GL_SVAPTE [7]	KW
Demand zero optimization page	@MMG$GL_DZRO_VA	KW
Erase pattern buffer page	@EXE$GL_ERASEPB	KW
Erase pattern page table page	@EXE$GL_ERASEPPT	UR
Executive data page	@EXE$AR_EWDATA	UREW
Swapper page table page	@SWP$GL_MAP	ERKW
Swapper P1 vector page		KW

(continued)

1283

Table F.3 System Virtual Address Area *(continued)*

Item	Global Location [1]	Protection
MAPPED FROM AVAILABLE SYSTEM SPACE AREA BY THE SYSINIT PROCESS		
DDIF$RMS_EXTENSION.EXE		UR/URKW
SYSLDR_DYN.EXE		UR/URKW
RECOVERY_UNIT_SERVICES.EXE		UR/URKW
RMS.EXE	@MMG$GL_RMSBASE	UR/URKW
SYSMSG.EXE	@EXE$GL_SYSMSG	UR/URKW

[1] If the symbol @ does not precede the global location name, the name's value is the starting address of the area in question. If the symbol @ precedes the global location name, the global location contains the address of the area.

[2] Optionally loaded based on boot parameters.

[3] One of three possible synchronization images loaded.

[4] An element in the longword array @MMG$GL_SBICONF contains the system virtual address of the first page of an adapter's I/O space. The number and type of adapters present determine the size of this area. The global EXE$GL_NUMNEXUS contains the number of adapters.

[5] This location contains a system virtual page number, not a system virtual address. REALTIME_SPTES determines the number of pages allocated.

[6] Initialization maps the connect-to-interrupt pages as "no access." Allocation alters the protection.

[7] This location contains the system virtual address of a PTE, not a system virtual address.

show the areas of available virtual address space between loadable executive images. These areas originally contained the image initialization and fixup routines, deallocated by the time system initialization is complete. The Miscellaneous sections represent pages allocated individually by EXE$INIT and loadable executive images.

F.2.4 Nonpaged Pool

SYSBOOT loads the boot driver and boot control block into nonpaged pool. Some executive images such as SYSLOA*xxx*.EXE, whose format differs from that of loadable executive images like SYSTEM_PRIMITIVES.EXE, are loaded into nonpaged pool by SYSBOOT and later initialized by EXE$INIT. SYSBOOT also loads any necessary device drivers and any emulation images. Table F.4 shows the initial use of nonpaged pool.

F.3 VMS PHYSICAL MEMORY REQUIREMENTS

The physical memory requirement of the VMS executive, that is, the number of pages not available for user processes, is the sum of the nonpaged areas, the system working set, the low-limit thresholds for the free and modified page lists, the Files-11 Extended QIO Processor (XQP), and the working sets of memory-resident system processes:

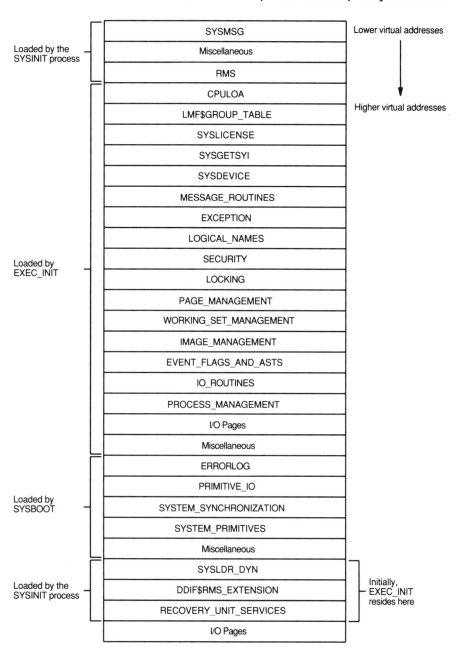

Figure F.3
Typical System Virtual Address Assignment

Table F.4   Loaded into Nonpaged Pool by SYSBOOT

Item	Description
Boot driver	Primitive system disk driver
Boot control block	Information for use during initialization and crashing
System disk driver	
Port driver	Optional
Terminal driver	
SCSLOA.EXE	Optional system communication services (SCS) image
SYSLOA*xxx*.EXE	CPU-dependent image
CLUSTRLOA.EXE	Optional VAXcluster image
VAXEMUL.EXE	Optional instruction emulation
FPEMUL.EXE	Optional instruction emulation

$$\text{System\_Memory} = \text{Nonpaged} + \text{SYSMWCNT} + \text{FREELIM}$$
$$+ \text{MPW\_LOLIMIT} + \text{XQP} + \text{System\_Processes}$$

(F14)

$$\text{Available\_Memory} = \text{Total\_Physical\_Memory} - \text{System\_Memory}$$

(F15)

F.3.1   Nonpaged Areas

The nonpaged areas on a given system include the physical pages not cataloged in the PFN database (see Equation F12), the permanently mapped pages for mount verification and similar items, and the nonpageable image sections of the loadable images selected by local SYSGEN parameters:

$$\text{Nonpaged} = \text{No\_PFN\_Entries pages} + \text{Miscellaneous pages}$$
$$+ \text{Nonpageable image sections}$$
$$\text{of loadable executive images}$$

(F16)

As shown in this appendix, much depends on SYSGEN parameters. They determine the size of executive data areas and whether the normally pageable portions of the executive are made nonpageable. They influence the choice of loadable executive images, which contribute to both paged and nonpaged memory use.

Table F.5 lists the paged and nonpaged portions of the executive. Where possible, the table includes either the size in pages or a reference to the section of this appendix that describes the size computation. However, the table does not include the sizes of the loadable executive image sections. Chapter 29 describes the loadable executive image structure in detail; note that each image is allowed two pageable and two nonpageable image sections.

(This appendix ignores the initialization section and fixup section, since they are deallocated by the time system initialization completes.) The amount of physical memory used by a loadable image is the sum of the sizes of its two nonpageable image sections. The Analyze/Image Utility displays each image section, its characteristics, and its size.

Paged pool, the paged portions of the loadable executive images, and the global page table pages also require physical memory. However, it is reasonable to assume that the system working set is full at all times, so that the physical memory requirements of the paged portions are simply SYSMWCNT pages.

Two other items must be taken into account when calculating the number of physical pages used by the executive: the SYSGEN parameters FREELIM and MPW_LOLIMIT set, which set low-limit thresholds on the number of pages on the free and modified page lists; and the Files-11 XQP, which is mapped in the P1 space of each process. When the SYSGEN parameter ACP_XQP_RES is 1 (its default value), SYSINIT maps the XQP as a resident global section, which means that all its shareable pages are permanently resident. For VMS Version 5.2, a resident XQP contributes approximately 131 pages to the total memory requirements.

F.3.2   System Processes

The working sets of memory-resident system processes can also be included in the total memory requirements of VMS. Some of the following processes are not required; however, all are considered to be system processes:

- Job controller
- Print symbionts
- Error logger format process (ERRFMT)
- Operator communication process (OPCOM)
- Magnetic tape ancillary control processes (ACPs)
- Network ACP (NETACP)
- Remote terminal ACP (REMACP)
- Audit collection process (AUDIT_SERVER)
- System Management Utility process (SMISERVER)
- Network event logger (EVL)

Several other system processes exist on a VAXcluster node:

- Cluster cache server process (CACHE_SERVER)
- Cluster server process (CLUSTER_SERVER)
- Cluster device configuration process (CONFIGURE)

The Digital command language (DCL) command SHOW SYSTEM lists the physical memory in use by each of these processes at a given time. However, the amount of memory varies over time for these reasons:

Table F.5 Division of System Virtual Address Space into Nonpaged and
Paged Pieces

Item	*Size*

SYSBOOT permanently maps the following portions of system address space. The
PFN database does not contain entries for the physical pages that these portions
occupy.

System base image	34 physical pages, from MMG$A_SYS_END to SYS$S0_VECTOR_SPACE
PFN database	Equation F13
Initial portion of nonpaged pool	Item 3 in Section F.2.1
Initial portion of lookaside lists	Item 3 in Section F.2.1
Interrupt stack	Item 10 in Section F.2.1
Per-CPU database and boot stack	3 pages
System control block	Item 13 in Section F.2.1
System header	Equation F9
System page table	Equation F11

Other nonpageable system virtual address space.

RPB	1 page
All nonpaged image sections in loadable executive images [1,2]	
Page to map pages without PFN database entry	1 page
Temporary page (VAX 6000 series)	1 page
Tape mount verification buffer	2 pages
Mount verification buffer	1 page
Demand zero optimization page	1 page
Erase pattern buffer	1 page
Erase pattern page table	1 page
Executive data page	1 page
Swapper page table page	1 page
Swapper P1 vector page	1 page

This system address space is pageable. A maximum of SYSMWCNT pages of this
area can be resident at a given time.

Pageable image sections of loadable executive images [1]	
Paged executive data	1 page
Paged pool	Item 2 in Section F.2.1
Global page table pages	Equation F10

(continued)

Table F.5   Division of System Virtual Address Space into Nonpaged and
Paged Pieces *(continued)*

Item	Size
This system address space does not require physical memory.	
I/O space mapping	I/O addresses
Balance slot area	PHD pages and page table pages are charged to process working sets

[1] Not all loadable executive images are required.
[2] The SDA command SHOW EXECUTIVE displays loadable images.

- The memory the process consumes is its working set. Automatic working set limit adjustment changes the size of the process working set over time. (This assumes that the process reaches its working set limit, a reasonable assumption for a system process.)
- A system process can be outswapped, temporarily reducing its physical memory requirement to zero.

Because many system processes are optional and because their physical memory requirements vary over time, this appendix cannot describe their memory use. Use the Monitor Utility and the DCL command SHOW SYSTEM to obtain the process working set size and other characteristics. Use the DCL command SHOW MEMORY/PHYSICAL to obtain the number of pages allocated to VMS and not cataloged in the PFN database.

F.4   SIZE OF P1 SPACE

P1 space includes both fixed and dynamically configured areas. The SHELL module defines the fixed-size area. The many dynamic areas are configured by other modules based on SYSGEN parameters, image sizes, and other variables. Table F.6 describes the fixed and dynamic areas of P1 space and the size of each. Note that the first module maps the low-address end of P1 space and subsequent modules describe P1 space toward higher virtual addresses. The highest P1 address range is the fixed-size portion defined in SHELL, which is the initial P1 mapping for every process.

1. The SHELL module initially defines P1 space. It constructs a skeleton P1 page table, mapping a predetermined virtual address range. It also creates the P1 window to the PHD, which maps all PHD virtual pages except the page table pages. Section F.1 shows each segment of the PHD and the SYSGEN parameter that controls its size.

2. Following SHELL, EXE$PROCSTRT dynamically configures more of P1 space. It primarily determines the sizes from SYSGEN parameters. It also expands P1 space to map the Files-11 XQP into the P1 space of each

Table F.6 Layout of P1 Space

Item	Global Location[1]	Factors That Affect Size[2]	Protection	Owner	Pageable
MAPPED BY THE IMAGE ACTIVATOR					
Low-address end of P1 space	@((@CTL$GL_PHD) +PHD$L_FREP1VA)				
User stack	@(CTL$AL_STACK+0C)[3]	ISD$K_ USRSTACK (20-page default)	UW	U	Yes
Extra user stack pages		2 pages	UW	U	Yes
Extra image I/O segment		IOSEGMENT link option	UREW	E	Yes
Boundary between process-permanent and image-specific P1 space	@CTL$GL_CTLBASVA[4]				
MAPPED BY THE DCL COMMAND SET MESSAGE					
Per-process message section	@CTL$GL_PPMSG	Size of section	UR	E	Yes
MAPPED BY LOGINOUT					
CLI symbol table	@(CTL$AG_CLIDATA+10)	CLISYMTBL	SW	S	Yes
CLI command tables	@CTL$AG_CLITABLE	Size of command tables	UR	S	Yes
CLI image	@CTL$AG_CLIMAGE	Size of CLI image	UR	S	Yes
MAPPED BY EXE$PROCSTRT					
Files-11 XQP data and stack	@(@CTL$GL_F11BXQP+18)		KW	K	Yes, no[5]
Files-11 XQP image	@(@CTL$GL_F11BXQP+10)	Size of F11BXQP	ER	E	Yes, no[5]
Image I/O segment	@(PIO$GQ_IIODEFAULT+4)	IMGIOCNT	UREW	K	Yes
Process I/O segment		PIOPAGES	UREW	K	Yes
Process allocation region		CTLPAGES	UREW	K	Yes
Channel control block table	@CTL$GL_CCBBASE[6]	CHANNEL-CNT	UREW	K	Yes
Initial end of P1 space for each process	@MMG$GL_CTLBASVA[7]				

(continued)

Table F.6   Layout of P1 Space *(continued)*

Item	Global Location [1]	Factors That Affect Size [2]	Protection	Owner	Pageable
		FIXED SIZE PORTION — DEFINED IN SHELL			
P1 window to PHD	@CTL$GL_PHD	Size of the PHD	URKW, ERKW	K	No
VWS area	CTL$A_VWS	2 pages	UW	K	Yes
RMS pointer page	PIO$GL_FMLH	1 page	UREW	E	No
RMS pointer page extension		1 page	UREW	E	Yes
RMS directory cache	PIO$A_DIRCACHE	4 pages	UREW	E	Yes
RMS internal structures		1 page	UREW	E	Yes
Per-process common for users	PIO$A_RMS_PIOEND	4 pages	UW	K	Yes
Per-process common for Digital	CTL$A_COMMON	4 pages	UW	K	Yes
Compatibility mode data pages	CTL$AG_CMEDATA	2 pages	UW	K	Yes
Security audit data pages	NSA$T_IDT	3 pages	KW	K	Yes
Image activator context page	CTL$GL_IAFLINK	1 page	UREW	E	Yes
Generic CLI data pages	CTL$AL_CLICALBK	12 pages	URSW	S	Yes
Image activator scratch pages	IAC$AL_IMGACTBUF	8 pages	UREW	E	Yes
Debugger context pages		4 pages	UW	U	Yes
Vectors for user-written system services and messages	CTL$A_DISPVEC	3 pages	UREW	K	Yes
Image header buffer	MMG$IMGHDRBUF	1 page	URSW	E	Yes
Kernel request packet lookaside list	CTL$GL_KRP	4 pages	URKW	K	Yes
No access guard page		1 page	No access	K	
Kernel stack expansion pages	CTL$GL_KSTKBASEXP	4 pages	No access	K	
Kernel stack	CTL$GL_KSTKBAS	3 pages	SRKW	K	No
Executive stack	CTL$AL_STACK+4 [3]	16 pages	SREW	E	Yes
Supervisor stack	@(CTL$AL_STACK+8) [3]	32 pages	URSW	S	Yes

(continued)

1291

Table F.6   Layout of P1 Space *(continued)*

Item	Global Location [1]	Factors That Affect Size [2]	Protec-tion	Owner	Page-able
	FIXED SIZE PORTION — DEFINED IN SHELL				
VMS kernel mode data pages	CTL$A_PRCPRM_DATA	2 pages	URKW	K	Yes
VMS user mode data page	CTL$GL_DCLPRSOWN	1 page	UW	K	Yes
System service vectors	P1SYSVECTORS	5 pages	UR	K	No
Reserved for system service vector expansion		11 pages	No access	K	
P1 pointer page	CTL$GL_VECTORS	1 page	URKW	K	No
VAX DEBUG dynamic memory	@(CTL$GQ_DBGAREA+4)	128 pages	UW	U	Yes

[1] Numbers in address expressions are hexadecimal. If the symbol @ precedes the global location name, the global location contains the address of the area. If the symbol @ does not precede the global location name, the name's value is the starting address of the area.

[2] These sizes are in decimal.

[3] Global location CTL$AL_STACK is the address of a four-longword array whose elements contain the initial values of the four per-process stack pointers. An array element is indexed by access mode.

[4] Global location CTL$GL_CTLBASVA contains the address of the boundary between the image-specific portion of P1 space (deleted at image exit by routine MMG$IMGRESET) and the process-permanent portion of P1 space.

[5] The XQP stack and some of its data pages are accessed at elevated interrupt priority levels (IPLs). Therefore, they are locked into the process's working set list and are not pageable. If the SYSGEN parameter ACP_XQP_RES is 1, the default, the XQP is mapped as a resident global section.

[6] CTL$GL_CCBBASE points to the high-address end of the channel control block table.

[7] SYSBOOT sizes the PHD (and thus the P1 window to the PHD) and initializes global location MMG$GL_CTLBASVA to the next available P1 space virtual address. Each time the process-permanent portion of P1 space expands, to map the CCBs or the XQP for instance, CTL$GL_CTLBASVA is updated to reflect the changes.

> process. It then calls initialization code within the XQP, which creates additional P1 space to use as the XQP impure area and private kernel stack. The size of the image F11BXQP.EXE and its data area determine the space required for the file system.
>
> 3. A process typically executes LOGINOUT next. LOGINOUT maps a selected command language interpreter (CLI), expanding P1 space to include the CLI, CLI command tables, and CLI symbol table. The size of these images and the SYSGEN parameter CLISYMTBL determine the P1 virtual address space requirements.
>
> 4. The DCL command SET MESSAGE maps a message file into P1 space as a process-permanent message section.

5. The mapping and configuration of the remaining P1 space alters with the activation of each new image. This area is bounded by PHD$L_FREP1VA, the next available P1 space virtual address, and CTL$GL_CTLBASVA, which divides the area from permanently allocated P1 space. The image size and link options determine the size of this area.

F.4.1 Selected Dynamic P1 Areas

The following list expands the description of selected dynamic portions of P1 space:

- The channel control block (CCB) table has SYSGEN parameter CHAN-NELCNT elements, each 16 bytes long. CTL$GL_CCBBASE points to the high-address end of the table. A particular CCB is identified by its negative byte displacement from the contents of CTL$GL_CCBBASE.
- The process allocation region is a P1 space dynamic memory pool (see Chapter 19). The SYSGEN parameter CTLPAGES determines its size in pages.
- The process I/O segment contains Record Management System (RMS) data structures describing process-permanent files, those which can and usually do remain open across image activations. The SYSGEN parameter PIOPAGES determines its size.
- The SYSGEN parameter IMGIOCNT specifies the default number of pages created by EXE$PROCSTRT for the image I/O segment, the RMS impure area for files opened during the execution of a specific image.

  The following line in the link time option file overrides the default number of image I/O segment pages for a specific image:

  ```
  IOSEGMENT = n
  ```

  If the IOSEGMENT option specifies more pages than the IMGIOCNT parameter, the image activator allocates an alternative image I/O segment of size IOSEGMENT.
- The image activator allocates two extra pages adjacent to the user stack. These pages allow the operating system to recover if the user stack is corrupted.
- The default user stack size is 20 pages. The following option in the link options file overrides the default user stack size at link time:

  ```
  STACK = n
  ```

  Because the system's access violation handler automatically expands the user stack on overflow, the link option is generally unnecessary. One possible exception might be an image that requires a large amount of stack space but cannot afford the overhead required for automatic run-time stack expansion.

G VAX CPU Designations

Most parts of VMS are independent of CPU type. There are, however, certain CPU-specific components. The names of these components contain CPU designations in the positions shown as *xxx* or *yyy*. Table G.1 lists the CPU designation for each CPU type.

The CPU-specific components include the following:

- The set of macros $PR*yyy*DEF
- The set of macros $IO*yyy*DEF
- The set of macros $KA*yyy*DEF
- The loadable images SYSLOA*xxx*.EXE

The macro $PRDEF, in STARLET.MLB, defines symbolic names for the processor registers that are common to all types of VAX processors. For most CPU types, a second LIB.MLB macro, $PR*yyy*DEF, defines symbolic names for the CPU's additional processor registers.

The LIB.MLB $IO*yyy*DEF macros define symbolic names for the physical addresses of CPU-specific registers.

The LIB.MLB $KA*yyy*DEF macros define symbolic names for the offsets from the address stored in EXE$GL_CPUNODSP to CPU-specific registers, as defined in $IO*yyy*DEF. There is not necessarily a $KA*yyy*DEF macro for each CPU type.

The loadable SYSLOA*xxx* images contain support for CPU-specific implementation details, such as machine check exceptions, memory and bus error interrupts, I/O adapter initialization, and console terminal support. The SYSLOA*xxx* image names and the names of their CPU-specific source modules contain a CPU designation. Certain VAX processors, such as the MicroVAX II, support sufficiently different console terminals that a different SYSLOA*xxx* image is required for each type of console terminal. Table G.1 lists the names of the SYSLOA*xxx* images. Chapters 30 and 31 describe the manner in which the SYSLOA*xxx* images are loaded and used.

Table G.1   VAX CPU Designations

yyy	*SYSLOAxxx*	*System Types*
UV2	SYSLOAUV2.EXE	MicroVAX II
UV2	SYSLOAWS2.EXE	VAXstation II
UV2	SYSLOAWSD.EXE	VAXstation II/GPX
410	SYSLOA410.EXE	MicroVAX 2000
410	SYSLOA41W.EXE	VAXstation 2000 (monochrome)
410	SYSLOA41D.EXE	VAXstation 2000/GPX
420	SYSLOA420.EXE	MicroVAX 3100
420	SYSLOA42W.EXE	VAXstation 3100 (monochrome) models 30/40/38/48
420	SYSLOA42D.EXE	VAXstation 3100/GPX models 30/40/38/48
60	SYSLOA60.EXE	VAXstation 3520/3540
640	SYSLOA640.EXE	MicroVAX 3300, MicroVAX 3400
650	SYSLOA650.EXE	MicroVAX 3200, MicroVAX 3500, MicroVAX 3600, MicroVAX 3800, MicroVAX 3900
650	SYSLOA65D.EXE	VAXstation 3200, VAXstation 3500
730	SYSLOA730.EXE	VAX-11/730
750	SYSLOA750.EXE	VAX-11/750
780	SYSLOA780.EXE	VAX-11/780, VAX-11/785
790	SYSLOA790.EXE	VAX 8600, VAX 8650
8SS	SYSLOA8SS.EXE	VAX 8200, VAX 8250, VAX 8300, VAX 8350
8NN	SYSLOA8NN.EXE	VAX 8500, VAX 8530, VAX 8550, VAX 8700, VAX 8800
8PS	SYSLOA8PS.EXE	VAX 8810, VAX 8820, VAX 8830, VAX 8840
9CC	SYSLOA9CC.EXE	VAX 6000 series model 200, model 300
9RR	SYSLOA9RR.EXE	VAX 6000 series model 400

H Lock and Resource Use by VMS Components

Many VMS facilities use lock management system services to coordinate their own activities, both locally and within a VAXcluster system. This appendix examines a number of those facilities and describes their lock use. The aim is to demonstrate a variety of locking techniques and to provide examples of situations where specific techniques are beneficial.

This appendix is by no means a complete description of VMS lock use or of the various facilities mentioned. It assumes that the reader is familiar with Chapter 10 of this book and with the description of the VMS lock management system services found in the *VMS System Services Reference Manual*.

H.1 ASPECTS OF RESOURCE AND LOCK USE

The data structure that represents the entity being locked is a resource block, commonly referred to as a resource. A resource is uniquely identified by the combination of its resource name string, scope, access mode, and parent resource, if any.

A lock on a resource is characterized by its lock mode, the extent to which it allows shared access with other locks on the same resource. Chapter 10 lists the different lock modes: concurrent read/write (CR, CW), protected read/write (PR, PW), null (NL), and exclusive (EX). The context of a lock is also relevant: locks on some resources are owned by the system rather than by a particular process. For convenience in describing resources and their associated locks, the discussion often mentions only the lock; in these cases, the resource is implied.

The resource name string of a resource created by VMS for its own use typically begins with a facility code. The remainder of the string further identifies the specific resource, for example, SCSNODE, device name, or file ID.

Table H.1 lists some VMS facilities, their associated facility codes, and the sections in this appendix that further describe the facility's lock use.

The scope of a resource, and of its locks, is the extent to which the resource name is available to processes sharing the resource. By default, VMS includes as part of a resource name the user identification code (UIC) group of the process creating the resource. Processes belonging to other UIC groups cannot share such a resource.

To share resources throughout a VAXcluster system independent of UIC,

Table H.1   VMS Facility Codes

Facility	Code	Section
VMS executive	SYS$	Section H.2
$MOUNT system service	MOU$	Section H.3
$DISMOU system service	DMT$	Section H.4
Volume shadowing	SHAD$	Section H.5
File system (Files-11 XQP)	F11B$	Section H.6
Record Management Services (RMS)	RMS$	Section H.7
Image activator and Install Utility	INSTALL$	Section H.8
DECnet—VAXcluster alias	CLU$	Section H.9.1
DECnet—proxy	NET$	Section H.9.2
Job controller	JBC$	Section H.10
System Generation (SYSGEN) Utility	SYSGEN$	Section H.11
System Management (SYSMAN) Utility	SMISERVER$	Section H.12

many VMS facilities specify the Enqueue Lock Request ($ENQ) system service flag LCK$V_SYSTEM. (A process not in kernel or executive mode requires the SYSLCK privilege to specify this flag.) The flag causes VMS to omit the UIC group from the resource name. Thus, a process belonging to any UIC group can share the resource if it specifies the LCK$V_SYSTEM flag in its lock request. Such a resource is usually characterized as being systemwide. To avoid confusion with the characteristic system-owned, this chapter refers to the scope of these resources and locks as UIC-independent.

Other VMS facilities, such as the job controller, require a process on each VAXcluster node. The processes are created in a controlled fashion and belong to the same UIC group. Each process synchronizes access to private structures and files using a protocol shared by its counterparts on other nodes. These processes do not use the LCK$V_SYSTEM flag in their lock requests; thus, their resources and locks are available only to members of the same UIC group. This chapter refers to the scope of these resources and locks as UIC-specific.

The lock manager deallocates a resource block (RSB) when its last lock is dequeued. Locks are dequeued and lock blocks deallocated when their creating process is deleted. To guarantee the survival of an important lock so that its resource block and especially its value block remain available, a VMS facility enqueuing a lock can declare its context to be system-owned rather than process-owned. The use of system-owned locks is reserved to Digital. Any other use is strongly discouraged by Digital and completely unsupported.

A parent resource is used to create a logical lock grouping or, in the case of the System ID lock, to restrict resource mastership to a particular node (see Section H.2.1).

Other significant aspects of VMS lock use include a lock's value block; the presence or absence of a blocking asynchronous system trap (AST) and the trigger for delivery of a blocking AST; and the name of any symbol used to locate the lock or define the resource name. Blocking ASTs are described in Chapter 10.

Every lock description in this appendix begins with a table of the lock's significant attributes.

H.2   VMS EXECUTIVE LOCK USE

H.2.1   System ID Lock

Resource name string	"SYS$SYS_ID" + SCSSYSTEMID
Symbol	EXE$GL_SYSID_LOCK
Mode of acquisition	EX
Scope	UIC-independent
Access mode	Executive
Parent	None
Value block	None
Blocking AST	None
Context	System-owned

The System ID lock guarantees a unique identity for each VAXcluster node by enforcing the requirement that the SYSGEN parameter SCSSYSTEMID be unique within the VAXcluster system.

During system initialization, every VMS system requests an EX lock on a resource whose name is based on its own SCSSYSTEMID. Since SCSSYS-TEMID is required to be unique in a VAXcluster system, the lock should be granted immediately. If the lock request is successful, the numeric lock ID is stored in the cell EXE$GL_SYSID_LOCK. If the lock request fails, an identical SCSSYSTEMID exists in the VAXcluster system. An error message is generated and further system initialization is prevented.

Since each VAXcluster node builds and locks a unique resource, the System ID lock is always mastered on the local system. Therefore, any sublock of the System ID lock is mastered on the local system. Many VMS facilities take advantage of this feature and use the lock ID in EXE$GL_SYSID_LOCK as a parent for locks to be mastered locally and for locks whose range is limited to a specific VAXcluster node rather than to the entire VAXcluster system.

H.2.2   Set Time Lock

Resource name string	"SYS$CWSETIME"
Symbol	None
Mode of acquisition	EX

Scope	UIC-independent
Access mode	Kernel
Parent	None
Value block	None
Blocking AST	None
Context	Process-owned

The Set Time lock serializes concurrent SET TIME/CLUSTER operations. The image that runs in response to this Digital command language (DCL) command acquires an EX mode lock on the resource SYS$CWSETIME. Even if more than one process enters the SET TIME/CLUSTER command simultaneously, only one process acquires the lock while the others wait. Therefore, the same time value is broadcast to all VAXcluster nodes during this interval. When the owning process releases the lock, a waiting process may acquire it and broadcast its own time value. This mechanism ensures that time is broadcast consistently across all VAXcluster nodes.

H.2.3   **Device Lock**

Resource name string	"SYS$" + allocation class device name
Symbol	UCB$L_LOCKID
Modes of acquisition	CR, PW, EX
Scope	UIC-independent
Access mode	Kernel
Parent	None
Value block	Yes
Blocking AST	None
Context	System-owned

Device locks propagate the standard VMS properties for device allocation throughout a VAXcluster system. They manage the availability of devices visible clusterwide. The Deallocate Device ($DALLOC), Assign I/O Channel ($ASSIGN), Mount Volume ($MOUNT), Dismount Volume ($DISMOU), and Deassign I/O Channel ($DASSGN) system services, among others, acquire and release Device locks either directly or using the routines IOC$LOCK_DEV and IOC$UNLOCK_DEV in module IOSUBPAGD.

A VAXcluster node actually has at most one Device lock enqueued per device, with a resource name based on the allocation class device name as returned by the Get Device/Volume Information ($GETDVI) system service argument DVI$_ALLDEVNAM. Its lock ID is stored in the device's unit control block (UCB) at UCB$L_LOCKID.

A Device lock is enqueued or converted for a device visible to the VAXcluster system when the device is explicitly allocated, when the $MOUNT system service implicitly allocates the device for a private mount request, when the $MOUNT system service must ensure that the device is available and not allocated for a shareable request, when the $ASSIGN system service creates the first channel to a device that is available clusterwide, and through other code paths as well.

The lock mode varies depending on the operation and its arguments:

- At device allocation, an EX mode lock is requested.
- For a private mount, the $MOUNT system service requests an EX mode lock.
- For a system or group mount, the $MOUNT system service initially requests a PW mode lock with the LCK$V_NOQUEUE flag. If the device is already allocated or mounted privately, an EX mode lock exists, the PW request fails, and the $MOUNT system service returns an error. If the device is already mounted in a shareable fashion by any other VAXcluster nodes, only CR mode locks exist. The PW mode lock is granted and eventually converted to CR mode.
- The $ASSIGN system service requests a CR mode lock.

The value block of a Device lock contains such information as a device's mount state, protection, ownership, shadow set membership, and write lock state. It coordinates these attributes across the cluster.

System services like $DALLOC, $DASSGN, and $DISMOU invoke the routine IOC$UNLOCK_DEV to dispose of the Device lock correctly:

- If the device remains allocated by a process, the lock is not dequeued until device deallocation.
- If channels remain open to a dismounted device, the lock is converted to CR mode and eventually dequeued during the closing of the last channel.
- Otherwise, the lock is dequeued.

H.3 $MOUNT LOCK USE

The $MOUNT system service establishes a lock to guard against concurrent mount requests for a particular device or volume from the local node or from other VAXcluster nodes. In addition, it acquires the system-owned Device lock (see Section H.2.3) to synchronize clusterwide device access with the $DISMOU, $DALLOC, and $ASSIGN system services, among others. The $MOUNT system service uses the file system's Volume Allocation lock (see Section H.6.1) to synchronize its accesses to mounted volumes with those of the file system. It compares the mount context information in the value blocks of the Device lock and the Volume Allocation lock to ensure that volume labels are unique within a VAXcluster system.

H.3.1   Label Lock

Resource name string   "MOU$" + CSID or zero + volume label as specified in $MOUNT argument

Symbol	None
Mode of acquisition	EX
Scope	UIC-independent
Access mode	Executive
Parent	None
Value block	None
Blocking AST	None
Context	Process-owned

The Label lock serializes shareable mount requests for the same volume from multiple processes on the same system. In response to a request to mount a volume to be shared, for example, among all UIC-group members, the $MOUNT system service requests this lock in EX mode. It includes the VAXcluster system ID (CSID) to make the Label lock node-specific. If the system is not a VAXcluster node, a CSID of zero is used.

For a shareable mount request, the $MOUNT system service searches the local I/O database to ensure that no other volume has been mounted with the same volume label and shareability. It holds the Label lock for the duration of local mount processing to prevent other processes running on the same node from trying to mount the same volume on other devices.

The $MOUNT system service cannot use either of the other two locks involved in mount processing to accomplish that purpose. The Mount Device lock (see Section H.3.2) is based on device name, not volume label, so its use would not detect simultaneous attempts to mount a volume with the same label on different devices. Neither would the use of the system-owned Device lock, which is only acquired for devices available clusterwide.

The $MOUNT system service does not acquire the Label lock for a private mount request, because process-private use of a particular volume name cannot conflict with that of any other use.

H.3.2 Mount Device Lock

Resource name string	"MOU$" + allocation class device name
Symbol	None
Mode of acquisition	EX
Scope	UIC-independent
Access mode	Executive
Parent	None
Value block	None
Blocking AST	None
Context	Process-owned

The Mount Device lock synchronizes simultaneous mount requests for the same device. The $MOUNT system service first locates the device to be mounted and reserves it with the system-owned Device lock. It then attempts to acquire the Mount Device lock in EX mode. If the Mount Device lock cannot be immediately acquired, because another $MOUNT request is proceeding concurrently on the same device, the $MOUNT system service releases the system-owned Device lock and queues for the Mount Device lock in EX mode. When the Mount Device lock is granted, the $MOUNT system service releases it and repeats its attempt to acquire the system-owned Device lock.

Thus, mount attempts in a VAXcluster wait for the Mount Device lock rather than the system-owned Device lock when the system-owned Device lock is not immediately available. A process cannot wait for a system-owned lock.

The Mount Device lock's resource name is based on the allocation class device name as returned in the $GETDVI system service argument DVI$_ALLDEVNAM.

H.4 $DISMOU LOCK USE

H.4.1 Dismount Lock

Resource name string	"DMT$" + allocation class device name
Symbol	None
Mode of acquisition	EX
Scope	UIC-independent
Access mode	Executive
Parent	None
Value block	None
Blocking AST	None
Context	Process-owned

The $DISMOU system service acquires an EX mode Dismount lock to synchronize simultaneous dismount requests for the same volume from processes on the local system and on other VAXcluster nodes. The Dismount lock's resource name is based on the allocation class device name returned in the $GETDVI system service argument DVI$_ALLDEVNAM.

In addition to the Dismount lock, the $DISMOU system service acquires, converts, and releases the system Device lock to update the value block. The $DISMOU system service also dequeues file system locks for Files-11 volumes and the Shadow lock for shadow sets.

H.5 VOLUME SHADOWING LOCK USE

H.5.1 Shadow Lock

Resource name string	"SHAD$" + allocation class device name of virtual unit

Symbol	VCB$L_SHAD_LKID
Modes of acquisition	NL, CR, PW, EX
Scope	UIC-independent
Access mode	Kernel
Parent	None
Value block	Yes
Blocking AST	Yes
Context	System-owned and process-owned

The Shadow lock manages clusterwide consistency of shadow set membership knowledge using the following lock modes:

Lock Mode	Meaning
EX	Holder is rebuilding the shadow set
CR	Holder has current access to the shadow set and believes that its knowledge of the membership is accurate
NL	Holder does not have access to the shadow set

This arrangement ensures that only one VAXcluster node can rebuild the shadow set at any given time and that no other node can access the shadow set while it is being rebuilt.

The Shadow lock has two ancillary purposes:

- It manages updates to the shadow generation information.
- It provides a doorbell mechanism by which a VAXcluster node can cause all other nodes to check their knowledge of shadow set membership.

To alter shadow set membership generation information, a VAXcluster node acquires the Shadow lock in PW mode.

To initiate a clusterwide review of shadow set membership, a VAXcluster node raises its CR mode lock to EX mode temporarily, causing delivery of a blocking AST to each other VAXcluster node holding the Shadow lock. The blocking AST procedure verifies shadow set membership by invoking mount verification.

The Shadow lock is initially acquired when a shadow set is mounted. The $MOUNT system service enqueues a process-owned lock on a resource whose name is based on the allocation class device name of the virtual unit returned in the $GETDVI system service argument DVI$_ALLDEVNAM. Before exiting, it converts the lock to a CR mode system-owned lock with a blocking AST enabled. The $MOUNT system service loads the lock ID into the volume control block (VCB) of the virtual unit at the field VCB$L_SHAD_LKID. Normally, all VAXcluster nodes that mount the shadow set hold a CR mode lock on the resource.

The $DISMOU system service dequeues the Shadow lock.

H.6 FILE SYSTEM LOCK USE

The file system uses locks to arbitrate access to volumes and files as well as access to local cache structures and their contents. In a VAXcluster system, all locks described in this section are necessary for proper synchronization. In a stand-alone system, the volume locks and File Serialization lock are required for synchronization of local processes, but the File Access Arbitration and Cache locks are unnecessary.

H.6.1 Volume Allocation Lock

Resource name string	"F11B$v" + VCB$T_VOLCKNAM or RVT$T_VLSLCKNAM
Symbol	VCB$L_VOLLKID or RVT$L_STRUCLKID
Modes of acquisition	CR, PW
Scope	UIC-independent
Access mode	Kernel
Parent	EXE$GL_SYSID_LOCK if private mount
Value block	Yes
Blocking AST	Yes
Context	System-owned

The Volume Allocation lock synchronizes volume space allocation by coordinating access to the storage and file header bitmaps. Each volume has a unique volume allocation resource name. Every VAXcluster node acquires a PW mode lock on that resource when it mounts the volume through the $MOUNT system service. The resource name string is based on the contents of VCB$T_VOLCKNAM or, for volume sets, the volume set name contained in relative volume table (RVT) field RVT$T_VLSLCKNAM:

- For a privately mounted volume, the resource name string is based on the name of the system issuing the $MOUNT request and that system's UCB address for the device. The Volume Allocation lock is a sublock of the lock ID stored in EXE$GL_SYSID_LOCK.
- For a shareable native volume, the resource name string is based on the volume label.
- For a shareable volume set, the resource name string is the volume set name.

The naming convention for shareable volumes guarantees that volume labels are unique in a VAXcluster system.

The Volume Allocation lock is converted to CR mode by each VAXcluster node when the $MOUNT system service completes. The lock ID is stored in VCB$L_VOLLKID (or, for volume sets, RVT$L_STRUCLKID). This lock is held in CR mode for as long as the volume remains mounted. The $DISMOU system service dequeues it. In addition, any code path that allocates or deallocates space on the volume (that is, accesses the index file bitmap or the storage bitmap) acquires an additional lock in PW mode. This is compatible with the CR mode locks but would block another PW mode lock; thus, it allows multiple readers but only one writer.

H.6.2   **Volume Blocking Lock**

Resource name string	"F11B$b" + VCB$T_VOLCKNAM or RVT$T_VLSLCKNAM
Symbol	VCB$L_BLOCKID or RVT$L_BLOCKID
Modes of acquisition	CR, PW, EX
Scope	UIC-independent
Access mode	Kernel
Parent	None
Value block	None
Blocking AST	Yes
Context	System-owned and process-owned

The Volume Blocking lock enables exclusive access to a volume by utilities such as the Analyze/Disk Structure Utility. Its lock ID is stored in VCB$L_BLOCKID or RVT$L_BLOCKID as appropriate.

The Volume Blocking lock is normally held by all nodes in CR mode. To lock the volume, a utility requests an EX mode process-owned lock on the resource. This causes a blocking AST to be delivered to each VAXcluster node holding a Volume Blocking lock, including the node on which the utility is executing. The lock manager dispatches to the blocking AST procedure at IPL$_SCS while holding the SCS spinlock.

The blocking AST procedure clears VCB$L_BLOCKID. The field VCB$W_ACTIVITY reflects the state of the Volume Blocking lock. The field is initialized to 1, and the volume remains usable as long as the field is odd. Normal file system activity on the volume increments the VCB$W_ACTIVITY count by 2, and decrements it by 2 on completion. The blocking AST procedure decrements VCB$W_ACTIVITY by 1, making its value even, and thus blocks further file system requests for the volume. If this decrement of VCB$W_ACTIVITY brings its value to zero, the routine requests a kernel AST to dequeue the Volume Blocking lock from the context of the swapper process. Otherwise, as each outstanding file system request completes, it decrements VCB$W_ACTIVITY by 2. When VCB$W_ACTIVITY eventually falls to zero, the completing file system request dequeues the CR mode lock. This allows the EX mode lock to be granted so that the operation requiring exclusive access can proceed.

After the EX mode lock is released, the next file system request reacquires the Volume Blocking lock before accessing the volume.

H.6.3 **File Access Arbitration Lock**

Resource name string	"F11B$a" + volume lock name + FCB$L_LOCKBASIS
Symbol	FCB$L_ACCLKID
Modes of acquisition	All
Scope	UIC-independent
Access mode	Kernel
Parent	None
Value block	Yes
Blocking AST	Yes
Context	System-owned

The file system provides access arbitration for files; users can open files for read or write operations and specify whether others may open the file concurrently. The Access Arbitration lock extends the scope of file arbitration to be clusterwide. Its resource name string uniquely identifies a particular file by including the volume lock name from VCB$T_VOLCKNAM or RVT$T_VLSLCKNAM, and the file's ID number and relative volume number from the file control block (FCB) field FCB$L_LOCKBASIS. Each VAXcluster node on which at least one process has that file open holds one system-owned Access Arbitration lock. Each lock represents the state of all accesses to the file from a given node. Thus, a VAXcluster node acquires the lock in the most restrictive mode in which any of its local processes have opened the file.

The Access Arbitration lock's blocking AST synchronizes access to its associated FCB, which contains information from the file header, such as protection and size. Each VAXcluster node accessing the file has an FCB and an Access Arbitration lock for the file. When a node alters an FCB in its memory, it also requests an EX mode Access Arbitration lock. This causes execution of the blocking AST procedure on every node accessing the file, causing each to mark its FCB as stale. Each node rebuilds its FCB on the next local access.

H.6.4 **File Serialization Lock**

Resource name string	"F11B$s" + FCB$L_LOCKBASIS
Symbol	None
Modes of acquisition	NL, PW
Scope	UIC-independent
Access mode	Kernel
Parent	VCB$L_VOLLKID or RVT$L_STRUCLKID
Value block	Yes
Blocking AST	None
Context	System-owned when NL, process-owned when PW

A File Serialization lock synchronizes access to a file on a particular volume. The file's ID number and relative volume number from FCB$L_LOCKBASIS make up the resource name string; its parent is a Volume Allocation lock. The file system, running in local process context, requests a File Serialization lock in PW mode for the duration of a single file operation, such as create, extend, or truncate. A process must hold the lock before accessing a file header or associated data in a file system cache. The lock value block contains two sequence numbers, one for the file header and one for associated data.

Upon completion of the file operation, the file system converts the lock to a NL mode system-owned lock, rewrites the sequence numbers into the value block, and records them in a cache descriptor. The system-owned lock is maintained until the cache entry is removed from cache or reused as described in the following paragraph.

If a process on this VAXcluster node requests a subsequent access to the file, the file system acquires the File Serialization lock in PW mode and obtains the sequence numbers in its value block. It compares the sequence numbers to the stored values in the cache descriptor. If the values match, the cached information is still accurate. Otherwise, another VAXcluster node acquired a PW mode lock while this node held a NL mode lock, and performed a file operation that updated a sequence number. The information in the local cache is no longer accurate and must be reread.

H.6.5   Cache Locks

Cache locks synchronize access to the per-volume caches that exist on each VAXcluster node for each mounted volume: the file ID cache, extent cache, and disk quota cache. This section describes the general mechanism used to cause each VAXcluster node in turn to flush a particular cache's contents to disk. Sections H.6.5.1, H.6.5.2, and H.6.5.3 describe the individual locks. The file system flushes all per-volume caches when a volume is dismounted. It flushes an individual cache when the cache becomes full, when a privileged user attempts to access the associated cache disk file directly, when one VAXcluster node's cache is empty, and on similar occasions.

Each cache type has a defined cache flush resource name. Each VAXcluster node that mounts a volume acquires a lock on each of the three cache flush resources for the volume. These locks are normally system-owned and held in PR mode.

To flush cache entries back to disk, a VAXcluster node writes its own cache back under the protection of a PW mode Volume Allocation lock. It then marks the particular cache invalid, lowers the system-owned PR mode Cache lock to NL mode, and lowers the Volume Allocation lock back to CR mode, rewriting the value block. The node then requests an additional process-owned CW mode lock on the cache flush resource.

This causes blocking AST delivery to all other VAXcluster nodes holding PR mode Cache locks. Since these are system-owned locks, the lock manager dispatches to the blocking AST routine at IPL$_SCS while holding the SCS spinlock. The AST parameter identifies which volume and cache to flush. Each blocking AST routine uses an AST control block (ACB) built into the cache data structure to deliver an AST to the CACHE_SERVER process. The CACHE_SERVER process requests the Queue I/O ($QIO) system service with the function code IO$_ACPCONTROL and a parameter identifying the device and cache.

The file system, running in the context of the CACHE_SERVER process, requests a PW mode Volume Allocation lock on the appropriate volume. Only one VAXcluster node's request for this lock is granted; the other nodes wait. The node that successfully acquires the Volume Allocation lock flushes its cache, marks the cache invalid, and lowers its PR mode Cache lock to NL mode. Next it converts the Volume Allocation lock back to CR mode, rewriting the value block. One waiting Volume Allocation lock request from another node is granted, and that node flushes its cache. This sequence is repeated until each node in turn has flushed its cache.

While the cache flush is in progress, the cache is marked invalid. If the file system accesses it and finds it invalid, the file system requests conversion of the NL mode Cache lock back to PR mode.

When the last VAXcluster node completes and converts its PR mode Cache lock to NL mode, the original CW mode request is granted and immediately dequeued, and the cache flush is complete.

H.6.5.1 File ID Cache Lock

Resource name string	"F11B$c" + lock basis of INDEXF.SYS
Symbol	VCA$L_FIDCLKID
Modes of acquisition	NL, CW, PR
Scope	UIC-independent
Access mode	Kernel
Parent	VCB$L_VOLLKID or RVT$L_STRUCLKID
Value block	Yes
Blocking AST	Yes
Context	System-owned

Each VAXcluster node maintains its own cache of available file headers for each mounted volume. This cache is filled primarily by file deletion on the local node. Any file identification numbers (FIDs) held in the cache are still marked "in-use" in the disk file number bitmap. A cache flush requires each VAXcluster node to write all entries in its local cache back to the file number bitmap on disk. The File ID Cache lock arbitrates this cache flush across the VAXcluster system, as described in Section H.6.5.

H.6.5.2   **Extent Cache Lock**

Resource name string	"F11B$c" + lock basis of BITMAP.SYS
Symbol	VCA$L_EXTCLKID
Modes of acquisition	NL, CW, PR
Scope	UIC-independent
Access mode	Kernel
Parent	VCB$L_VOLLKID or RVT$L_STRUCLKID
Value block	Yes
Blocking AST	Yes
Context	System-owned

Each VAXcluster node maintains its own cache of available disk space for each mounted volume. Any disk blocks held in this cache are still marked "in-use" in the disk storage allocation bitmap. A cache flush requires each VAXcluster node to write all entries in its local cache back to the storage allocation bitmap on disk. The Extent Cache lock arbitrates this cache flush across the VAXcluster system, as described in Section H.6.5.

H.6.5.3   **Disk Quota Cache Lock**

Resource name string	"F11B$c" + lock basis of QUOTA.SYS
Symbol	VCA$L_QUOCLKID
Modes of acquisition	NL, CW, PR
Scope	UIC-independent
Access mode	Kernel
Parent	VCB$L_VOLLKID or RVT$L_STRUCLKID
Value block	Yes
Blocking AST	Yes
Context	System-owned

If disk quotas are enabled for a volume, a disk quota cache and Disk Quota Cache lock are created when the volume is mounted.

Each VAXcluster node maintains its own cache of quota entries. It must sometimes flush all valid entries back to disk, for example, before dismounting the device. The Disk Quota Cache lock arbitrates this cache flush across the VAXcluster system, as described in Section H.6.5.

H.6.5.4   **Quota Cache Entry Lock**

Resource name string	"F11B$q" + VCB$T_VOLCKNAM or RVT$T_VLSLCKNAM + quota record UIC
Symbol	VCA$L_QUOLKID
Modes of acquisition	CR, PW, EX
Scope	UIC-independent
Access mode	Kernel

Parent	None
Value block	Yes
Blocking AST	Yes
Context	System-owned

To acquire a user's quota information, a VAXcluster node enqueues a PW mode system-owned Quota Cache Entry lock. On the first access to a specific quota cache entry, the user's quota information is read from disk into a cache block. The dynamic portion of the user's quota information is shared among VAXcluster nodes through the value blocks of the Quota Cache Entry locks for that user.

When another VAXcluster node needs the same user's quota information, it requests its own PW mode system-owned Quota Cache Entry lock. This request causes a blocking AST to be delivered to the original lock owner. The blocking AST procedure, running in the swapper's process context, marks the local cache entry invalid. It converts the PW mode lock to CR mode, updating the value block with the shared quota information. The other node's PW mode lock request is granted, and it receives this quota information from the value block.

An EX mode lock on a quota cache entry causes VAXcluster nodes to remove the entry from the quota cache. This is used when a quota record is deleted.

H.7 RMS LOCK USE

RMS uses lock management system services to protect files and records. When a file is accessed in a shareable fashion with write access allowed, RMS uses locks to coordinate the actions of the file sharers. The locks that it requests depend on a file's organization, the presence of global buffers, and numerous file-sharing and record-locking options specified by the user application. This section describes some of the more common RMS locks, sometimes in a simplified manner. It does not include locks used for RMS journaling.

RMS runs in a process's context and maintains private data structures in process space. It requires a file access block (FAB) for each initial access (open) of a file and a record access block (RAB) for each stream connected to a FAB. It creates internal copies of FABs and RABs called IFABs and IRABs (in data structures named IFB$ and IRB$) as well as many internal structures mentioned briefly in this appendix.

A process can optionally open a file multiple times (with multiple FABs). The term *accessor*, as used in this appendix, indicates an entity in process context that has opened the file; for example, a file opened twice by process A and once by process B would have three accessors. Additionally, each accessor can optionally connect multiple record streams to the file (multiple RABs to each FAB). RMS therefore must synchronize file access among accessors and record streams from the same process through a variety of mechanisms. The focus of this appendix, however, is primarily on the synchronization that RMS provides among independent processes sharing a file on a local system or in a VAXcluster.

RMS transfers a bucket of data on a process's behalf from a file into a buffer in memory. An RMS local buffer is mapped in process space and is available to only one process. A global buffer is mapped in system space within a VMS global section and can be shared by any process on the system. Global buffers, however, cannot be shared by processes on different VAXcluster nodes.

RMS performs some functions that affect the internal file structure, such as altering the end-of-file marker; some functions that affect internal bucket or buffer structure or contents; and some functions that affect only record contents. It uses locks of different scope to protect these different functions. RMS enforces a strict hierarchy in the acquisition of locks to ensure that deadlocks do not occur. Thus, for locks other than Record locks, RMS can safely specify the LCK$V_NODLCKWT and LCK$V_NODLCKBLK flags in its $ENQ system service requests. Chapter 10 gives more information on these flags.

A user application has no direct control over most RMS locks. However, it can directly control record locking. Therefore, RMS does not use the $ENQ flags mentioned above when requesting Record locks.

With the exception of Record locks, RMS holds locks in restrictive lock modes only for the duration of an RMS service request. To operate more efficiently and to preserve lock value block information, especially the sequence number, RMS typically converts a lock to NL mode rather than releasing it altogether.

H.7.1 File Lock

Resource name string	"RMS$" + file ID + device name
Symbol	SFSBL_LOCK_ID, IFBL_PAR_LOCK_ID
Modes of acquisition	NL, PW
Scope	UIC-independent
Access mode	Executive
Parent	None
Value block	Yes
Blocking AST	Yes
Context	Process-owned

A File lock's resource name identifies one specific file. Locks on that resource serialize access to the file—clusterwide, interprocess, and intraprocess. When an accessor opens a file, it tells RMS how it wishes to access the file and the type of access that it will allow to other accessors. RMS creates a File lock for a file opened in a shareable fashion where the opener either specifies write access for itself or allows write access from others.

The File lock provides a consistent view of the file through the information in its value block, which includes the current end-of-file marker and the length of the longest record. RMS always uses the File lock as the parent lock of a file's Record locks (see Section H.7.4). It stores the lock ID of the File lock in IFB$L_PAR_LOCK_ID when global buffers are not present, so the File lock sometimes serves as the parent lock of Bucket locks as well (see Section H.7.2).

RMS builds the File lock resource name string from the six-byte file identifier plus the device identifier returned in the $GETDVI argument DVI$_DEVLOCKNAM. The device identifier is normally the mount type code followed by the volume name from VCB$T_VOLCKNAM or RVT$T_VLSLCKNAM. The mount type code is 1 for a privately mounted device or 2 for a device mounted in a shareable fashion.

When an accessor uses RMS to open a shareable, writable file, RMS acquires a File lock in PW mode and declares an RMS procedure as the associated blocking AST procedure. The accessor retains the lock in PW mode until another accessor requires an RMS file-level service on the same file and requests the File lock in PW mode.

The lock request causes the blocking AST to be delivered to the accessor holding the PW mode lock. The blocking AST procedure converts the PW mode File lock to NL mode. This allows RMS to acquire the lock in PW mode for the new accessor, again declaring an RMS procedure as the associated blocking AST procedure.

Therefore, only one accessor of the file holds the File lock in PW mode. Every other accessor either holds a NL mode File lock, is waiting for a new PW mode lock, or is waiting for its NL mode lock to be converted to PW mode.

When a file accessor requests the File lock in PW mode and cannot obtain it immediately, it stalls. When an accessor closes a file, RMS dequeues its File lock.

RMS creates a shared file synchronization block (SFSB) in process space for each accessor using a File lock. The SFSB describes the accessor's File lock: its resource name, lock ID, lock value block contents, and other items. An SFSB also contains three status bits identifying the lock state:

Bit Field Name	Meaning if Set
SFSB$V_TAKEN	File lock is held in PW mode
SFSB$V_INUSE	File lock is currently in use by a record stream
SFSB$V_WANTED	File lock is wanted by another accessor

RMS uses these status bits to support file sharing by multiple record streams associated with one accessor (when multistreaming is selected) as well as among multiple accessors.

For example, when RMS acquires the File lock in PW mode for a record stream, it sets the SFSB$V_TAKEN and SFSB$V_INUSE bits in the process's SFSB. When the record stream finishes the operation requiring the File lock, RMS clears the SFSB$V_INUSE bit. The accessor still holds the File lock in PW mode.

If a record stream from a different accessor now requires the PW mode lock, RMS requests the $ENQ system service and stalls the stream awaiting $ENQ completion.

The accessor holding the PW mode lock must lower the lock to NL mode before the stalled stream can proceed. It receives blocking AST notification that another accessor has requested the lock. The blocking AST procedure tests the SFSB$V_INUSE bit. If the File lock is not in use, it lowers the lock to NL mode and clears the SFSB$V_TAKEN bit.

Otherwise, the blocking AST procedure sets the SFSB$V_WANTED bit and exits. When the current operation completes, RMS will discover that the SFSB$V_WANTED bit is set, convert the File lock to NL mode, and clear the SFSB$V_TAKEN bit.

In either case, the lock is eventually converted to NL mode and the stalled stream's outstanding PW mode request is granted. RMS now sets the SFSB$V_TAKEN and SFSB$V_INUSE bits in this accessor's SFSB.

When the RMS multistreaming option is selected, there may be more than one record stream for a given file access (an accessor may have multiple RABs for one FAB). If a record stream needs a File lock that is already held by another record stream sharing its FAB, the requesting stream stalls by inserting its context on a wait queue without requesting the $ENQ system service. When the other record stream finishes with the File lock, it checks this wait queue and resumes the stalled stream through the Declare AST ($DCLAST) system service. There is no need to convert the File lock unless a record stream from a different FAB requests it.

H.7.2   Bucket Lock

Resource name string	Bucket virtual block number
Symbol	BLB$L_LOCK_ID
Modes of acquisition	NL, PW, EX
Scope	UIC-independent
Access mode	Executive
Parent	IFB$L_PAR_LOCK_ID
Value block	Yes
Blocking AST	Sometimes
Context	System-owned, process-owned

RMS Bucket locks ensure the integrity of buckets held in local or global buffers. The resource name string of the Bucket lock identifies the first virtual block number of the bucket data within the file. Because RMS must acquire an EX mode process-owned Bucket lock for an accessor before it can read or write the bucket, it can maintain a consistent picture of the bucket contents clusterwide.

RMS reads a bucket into either an I/O buffer in a process's address space or an RMS global I/O buffer in a VMS global section in system space. It protects buckets in both locations through Bucket locks. One difference between Bucket locks for buckets in local and in global buffers is the parent lock. The IFB$L_PAR_LOCK_ID cell identifies the Bucket lock's parent: the File lock for a local buffer, or the Global Buffer Master lock (see Section H.7.3.1) if global buffers are being used.

RMS I/O buffers are a limited commodity; both local and global buffers are used and reused under the control of an RMS cache replacement algorithm. RMS maintains information about local buffer entries that are in use through buffer descriptor blocks (BDBs) and buffer lock blocks (BLBs). Before a process fills a local buffer from a bucket, it obtains a BDB and, if RMS locking is being performed, a BLB. It then acquires an EX mode, process-owned Bucket lock.

RMS stores information regarding the Bucket lock in the BLB, including the lock ID, an identifier for the record stream that owns the lock, the lock status block, the lock value block, the lock resource name, and the associated BDB address. The BDB contains, among other items, the actual address of the buffer and a saved clusterwide sequence number for the bucket that currently resides in the buffer.

The Bucket lock value block contains a sequence number for the bucket. A process must own the Bucket lock in EX mode before modifying the bucket, so that it can increment the sequence number in the lock. This invalidates any buffer containing an earlier version of the bucket. For example, an accessor might have a version (possibly an outdated version) of a bucket in a local buffer, with an associated NL mode Bucket lock, BLB, and BDB. To reaccess the bucket, RMS converts the NL mode Bucket lock to EX mode, rereading the value block. RMS compares the new sequence number from the lock value block with the buffer's saved sequence number, stored in the BDB. If the sequence numbers do not match, this buffer contains an outdated copy of the bucket and RMS rereads the bucket from disk. If the accessor subsequently modifies the bucket, it increments the sequence number. When it completes its bucket access, it converts the lock from EX to NL mode, rewriting the value block with the updated sequence number.

RMS maintains a NL mode Bucket lock on a bucket as long as that bucket is in a local or global buffer cache. This preserves the bucket's lock value block and thus its sequence number. One NL mode lock is required per copy of the bucket. Thus, each process that has a copy of a bucket in a local RMS I/O buffer maintains its own NL mode Bucket lock until it reuses that local buffer for a different bucket. For a bucket in a global buffer, however, one copy of the bucket in memory is shared by any interested process on the system. In this case, only one NL mode lock is required per VAXcluster node to preserve the bucket's sequence number.

The first accessor of a bucket in a global buffer converts its Bucket lock to a NL mode system-owned Global Buffer Backing lock (see Section H.7.3.3) when it completes its operation on the bucket. Subsequent accessors merely dequeue their Bucket locks.

An exception to this local conversion to NL mode is the case of a deferred write of modified buckets. For a deferred write, RMS converts the lock to a PW mode lock with an associated blocking AST. When another accessor of the file wants to use the modified bucket, its lock request triggers the execution of the blocking AST procedure, which writes the modified bucket. If no other accessor requests the modified bucket, RMS eventually writes the bucket and dequeues the Bucket lock when cache replacement dictates that the buffer should be reused for another bucket.

H.7.3   Locks Associated with Global Buffers

To minimize I/O operations, RMS can share buffers among multiple accessors of the same file. It maintains these global buffers in system space, within a VMS global section. A file using global buffers has one such global section on each VAXcluster node from which a process accesses the file. When the first process on a VAXcluster node opens a file that uses global buffers, RMS creates the file's global section in that node's memory.

RMS constructs the name of the file's global section by appending the hexadecimal address of the file's FCB to the string "RMS$". Any accessor subsequently opening the file in the same memory space shares the same FCB and thus constructs the same global section name and maps to the existing global section.

Each global buffer global section contains a global buffer header (GBH), a global buffer descriptor (GBD) for each global I/O buffer within the section, and the global buffers themselves. The actual data resides in buckets within the global buffers.

The GBH describes the global section and its locks. It contains the size of the global section, the access count, and the Global Buffer Master lock ID at offset GBH$L_LOCK_ID, among other information.

One GBD exists for each global buffer in the global section. A global buffer's GBD contains the lock ID of the buffer's Global Buffer Backing lock in the field GBD$L_LOCK_ID, the lock sequence number, the offset to the buffer within the global section, and similar information.

RMS maintains a section's GBDs in an interlocked queue ordered by the virtual block number (VBN) of the bucket currently residing in the GBD's associated buffer. The head of the GBD queue is in the GBH, at offset GBH$L_GBD_FLINK.

The Global Buffer Section (GBS) lock serializes access to the global buffer header and thus to the GBD queue and the global buffer pool (see Section H.7.3.2).

RMS deletes a file's global section when the last accessor of the file on a VAXcluster node closes the file.

H.7.3.1 Global Buffer Master Lock

Resource name string	"RMS$" + file ID + device name
Symbol	GBHL_LOCK_ID, IFBL_PAR_LOCK_ID
Mode of acquisition	NL
Scope	UIC-independent
Access mode	Executive
Parent	None
Value block	None
Blocking AST	None
Context	System-owned

RMS creates a Global Buffer Master lock only for a file that uses global buffers. The Global Buffer Master lock is a system-owned NL mode version of the File lock (see Section H.7.1).

When an accessor requests shareable write access to a file, RMS creates a File lock. If the file uses global buffers, RMS converts that File lock to a system-owned NL mode Global Buffer Master lock on the connect of the first record stream. It copies the lock ID of the Global Buffer Master lock to IFB$L_PAR_LOCK_ID, overriding the accessor's File lock as parent of its Bucket locks. RMS then creates a new File lock.

The Global Buffer Master lock's sole purpose is to serve as the parent lock for an accessor's Bucket locks on global buffers. Since a global buffer survives the deletion of processes that use it, the Bucket lock on a global buffer must be backed up with a system-owned lock so that the value block, which maintains the integrity of the bucket, survives. Since a system-owned lock cannot be a sublock of a process-owned lock such as the File lock, a Bucket lock needs a system-owned version of the File lock to act as parent.

RMS dequeues the Global Buffer Master lock when it deletes the global section.

H.7.3.2 Global Buffer Section Lock

Resource name string	"RMS$" + file ID + device name
Symbol	GBSB$L_LOCK_ID

Modes of acquisition	NL, EX
Scope	UIC-independent
Access mode	Executive
Parent	EXE$GL_SYSID_LOCK
Value block	Yes
Blocking AST	Yes
Context	Process-owned

The Global Buffer Section (GBS) lock synchronizes access to a file's global buffer header, the global buffer descriptor queue in the GBH, and thus the global buffer pool. Each VAXcluster node accessing the file has a separate global buffer global section for the file. Therefore, a lock guaranteed to be mastered on the local VAXcluster node is a more efficient way to serialize global section access, so RMS creates the GBS lock as a sublock of EXE$GL_SYSID_LOCK.

The GBS lock resource name string matches that of the file's corresponding File lock, thus uniquely identifying a device and file in a VAXcluster system (see Section H.7.1).

When an accessor connects a record stream to a file that uses global buffers, RMS requests an EX mode GBS lock. The GBS lock remains in EX mode until another accessor sharing the file on the same VAXcluster node requests a GBS lock in EX mode, to search the GBD list, for example.

The request triggers blocking AST notification, and the lock holder converts the initial GBS lock to NL mode, allowing the requestor to acquire its own lock.

Before the original lock holder accesses the global section again, it requests the conversion of its NL mode lock back to EX mode.

Therefore, the accessor that most recently examined the global buffer header or searched the global buffer descriptor queue holds the only granted EX mode lock. Every other accessor sharing the globally buffered file on this VAXcluster node holds a NL mode lock or is waiting for a new or converted EX mode lock.

When an accessor closes the file, RMS dequeues its GBS lock.

RMS creates a global buffer synchronization block (GBSB) in the P1 space of each accessor holding a NL mode or EX mode GBS lock. The GBSB is similar to the SFSB for the File lock. It maintains information about the lock and the associated global section, including the lock ID at GBSB$L_LOCK_ID. The GBSB also contains the lock value block, the resource name copied from the SFSB, and three status bits:

Bit Field Name	*Meaning if Set*
GBSB$V_TAKEN	GBS lock is held in EX mode
GBSB$V_INUSE	GBS lock is in use by a record stream
GBSB$V_WANTED	GBS lock is wanted by another accessor

These status bits describe the state of the GBS lock and are treated like the corresponding status bits in the SFSB (see Section H.7.1).

H.7.3.3 Global Buffer Backing Lock

Resource name string	Bucket virtual block number
Symbol	GBD$L_LOCK_ID
Mode of acquisition	NL
Scope	UIC-independent
Access mode	Executive
Parent	IFB$L_PAR_LOCK_ID
Value block	Yes
Blocking AST	None
Context	System-owned

The Global Buffer Backing lock ensures the integrity of buckets contained in global buffers. To guard the integrity of a bucket, its sequence number must be preserved in the lock value block of a Bucket lock. However, a global buffer can contain a bucket that no longer has any current accessors and therefore would have no Bucket locks. Therefore, a system-owned lock must be used to prevent the loss of the bucket's sequence number.

Before reading a bucket from a file into a buffer, an accessor acquires a process-owned Bucket lock. For each global buffer within the global section, the original accessor that stores a bucket in a global buffer converts its process-owned Bucket lock to a NL mode system-owned Global Buffer Backing lock when it completes its access to the bucket. It saves the lock ID in the buffer's GBD at the offset GBD$L_LOCK_ID.

A subsequent accessor of the bucket in this global buffer acquires its own Bucket lock. When it completes its access, it can safely dequeue its Bucket lock, since a Global Buffer Backing lock already exists for the bucket.

RMS also stores the sequence number of a bucket in a global buffer in the buffer's associated GBD. RMS copies the sequence number from the Bucket lock value block of the first accessor of the bucket and updates it for each subsequent accessor. When each accessor obtains its Bucket lock, RMS compares the sequence number in the Bucket lock value block with the saved sequence number in the GBD. If they do not match, RMS rereads the bucket from disk into the global buffer.

RMS dequeues the Global Buffer Backing lock when cache replacement policy dictates that the global buffer should be reused for another bucket or when the global section is deleted.

Since the Global Buffer Backing lock must be system-owned, and system-owned locks cannot be sublocks of process-owned locks, the Global Buffer Master lock was instituted (see Section H.7.3.1).

H.7.4   **Record Lock**

Resource name string	Record file address
Symbol	RLB$L_LOCK_ID
Modes of acquisition	CR, PR, PW, EX
Scope	UIC-independent
Access mode	Executive
Parent	SFSB$L_LOCK_ID
Value block	None
Blocking AST	None
Context	Process-owned

A Record lock coordinates access to a record in a bucket. It is always process-owned and always a subblock of the File lock. RMS builds the Record lock resource name string from the three-word record file address (RFA), which locates the record within the file. The resource name string consists of RFA4, the last of the three words, followed by two bytes of zeros, followed by RFA0, the first word (see the *VMS Record Management Services Manual*).

If a file is opened in a shareable manner with record locking enabled, the following locking options in the user-specified RAB at field RAB$L_ROP determine the RMS lock mode:

Bit Field State	*Lock Mode*
RAB$V_REA clear and RAB$V_RLK clear	EX
RAB$V_RLK set	PW
RAB$V_REA set and RAB$V_RLK clear	PR
RAB$V_NLK set	CR

- EX mode is the default.
- PW mode locks the record for write access, allowing readers at CR mode but no other writers.
- PR mode locks the record for read access, allowing other readers at CR or PR mode but no writers.
- The RAB$V_NLK option temporarily takes a CR mode lock to verify that the record is not locked against reading (in EX mode). These CR mode locks are never returned to the application.

A record stream associates each of its Record locks with a record lock block (RLB). An RLB contains the resource name, an identifier for the owning stream, and the lock status block, including the lock ID. RLBs are linked to the stream's IRAB at the IRBL_RLB_FLINK/IRBL_RLB_BLINK queue.

Application record deadlocks are possible because of the control that an application has over its record locking, especially when it selects the manual unlocking (RAB$V_ULK) option.

H.8   IMAGE ACTIVATOR AND INSTALL UTILITY LOCK USE

H.8.1   KFE Lock

Resource name string	"INSTALL$KNOWN FILE"
Symbol	EXE$GQ_KFE_LCKNAM
Modes of acquisition	PR, EX
Scope	UIC-independent
Access mode	Executive
Parent	EXE$GL_SYSID_LOCK
Value block	None
Blocking AST	None
Context	Process-owned

Section H.8.2 describes the use of the KFE lock.

H.8.2   Install Lock

Resource name string	"INSTALL$INSLOCK"
Symbol	None
Mode of acquisition	PW
Scope	UIC-independent
Access mode	Executive
Parent	EXE$GL_SYSID_LOCK
Value block	None
Blocking AST	None
Context	Process-owned

The Install Utility manages the known file entry (KFE) list and requires read and write access to it. The image activator system service requires protected read access to the KFE list before opening images. The Install Utility and the image activator coordinate access to the KFE list through the KFE lock and use the Install lock to provide priority access to image activation.

Each VAXcluster node maintains a private KFE list. KFE locks are requested as sublocks of the lock ID stored in EXE$GL_SYSID_LOCK to guarantee that they will be unique to the local node and mastered there. The resource is declared to be systemwide because the activation of images and use of the Install Utility is not restricted to a single UIC group. Multiple processes running from different UIC groups are synchronized.

All code paths in the image activator and the Install Utility that read the KFE list acquire PR mode locks on the KFE resource. In addition, the Install Utility ensures that readers of the KFE list (particularly the image activator) are not blocked too long by multiple writers of the KFE (for example, several INSTALL ADD commands). Code paths that write the KFE must acquire the Install lock in PW mode before acquiring the KFE lock in EX mode. Since only one writer at a time can acquire the Install lock, other writers queue for the Install lock rather than for the KFE lock.

When a writing process completes, it first converts the EX mode lock on the KFE to a PR mode lock. The only possible waiting requests are PR mode requests, and these are granted. The writer next dequeues the Install lock, allowing another writer to acquire it. This new writer requests an EX mode lock on the KFE. The request is granted when the readers complete and release their PR mode locks.

The combination of these two locks guarantees that writers cannot block readers for extended time periods.

H.9   DECNET LOCK USE

In VAXcluster configurations, the network ancillary control process (NET-ACP) uses two categories of locks: locks to implement VAXcluster alias functions and locks to implement network proxy access functions.

H.9.1   VAXcluster Alias Locks

H.9.1.1   Master Registration Lock

Resource name string	"CLU$NETACP_" + alias node address
Symbol	None
Modes of acquisition	NL, CR, PW, EX
Scope	UIC-specific
Access mode	Kernel
Parent	None
Value block	Yes
Blocking AST	Yes
Context	Owned by NETACP process

The NETACP process on each VAXcluster node that participates in the Alias Node service enqueues a lock on a resource whose name contains the alias node address. This lock is called the Master Registration lock (MRL) and is normally held at CR mode. The MRL is used as the parent lock for all other VAXcluster alias locks.

The value block in the MRL contains a quadword bit mask, with a bit set for each VAXcluster node participating in the VAXcluster alias. A new node enqueues the MRL in PW mode, uses the value block to determine the first free alias index number from this bit mask, allocates that index number for its own use, updates the value block, and stores its alias index at NET$GW_CLUSTER_INDEX. The MRL is then converted to a NL mode lock, updating the value block. The new participant next converts the lock to EX mode. This forces delivery of blocking ASTs to the current members, notifying them of the new VAXcluster alias member.

H.9.1.2 **Individual Index Lock**

Resource name string	"IXL_" + alias index number
Symbol	None
Modes of acquisition	NL, EX
Scope	UIC-specific
Access mode	Kernel
Parent	Master Registration lock
Value block	Yes
Blocking AST	None
Context	Owned by NETACP process

Each participant in the VAXcluster alias scheme requires an Individual Index lock (IXL). An IXL is a sublock of the MRL and has a resource name formed from "IXL_" + alias index number. Its value block contains registration data for the participating member, such as DECnet node address, alias maximum links, and routing/nonrouting status. Each new member enqueues an EX mode lock on its own IXL resource name. The member updates the value block with information about itself by lowering the lock to NL mode. Other participating members cycle through a set of lock states to allow each member to read the updated value block.

H.9.1.3 **Individual Departure Lock**

Resource name string	"IDL_" + alias index number
Symbol	None
Modes of acquisition	CR, EX
Scope	UIC-specific
Access mode	Kernel
Parent	Master Registration lock
Value block	None
Blocking AST	None
Context	Owned by NETACP process

Each participating VAXcluster member enqueues an EX mode lock on its own Individual Departure lock (IDL) resource. All other members request a CR mode lock on that resource, with deadlock search disabled. If a CR request is ever granted, the other member knows that the original member that held the EX mode lock is no longer participating.

H.9.1.4 **Individual Link Registration Lock**

Resource name string	"ILR_" + alias index number
Symbol	None
Modes of acquisition	NL, CR, EX
Scope	UIC-specific

Access mode   Kernel
Parent   Master Registration lock
Value block   Yes
Blocking AST   Yes
Context   Owned by NETACP process

An Individual Link Registration (ILR) lock is a sublock of the MRL. Each alias member has an associated resource, of the form "ILR_" + alias index number. A member always holds an ILR lock for itself in NL mode. In addition, a member that is a router holds a CR mode lock for itself and every other member. Each CR mode lock has an associated blocking AST.

An ILR lock is used for flow control, to send XOFF/XON signals to the router (or routers). When a member can accept no more links, it raises its NL mode lock to EX mode. This triggers the blocking AST on each router's CR mode lock for that member. The router converts the CR mode lock to NL immediately. This allows the EX mode lock to be granted on the initiator.

The EX mode lock is lowered back to NL, updating the value block with current and maximum links for this member. The router requests an EX mode lock, which will be granted when the initiating member lowers back to NL. The router updates its tables based on the new value block, lowers to NL to allow another router to obtain the lock, then finally returns to CR mode.

H.9.2   Network Proxy Access Locks

The NETACP process uses standard RMS locks to synchronize access to the proxy file, NETPROXY.DAT. In addition, it uses the following locks to propagate the volatile proxy database changes to other VAXcluster nodes.

H.9.2.1   Modified Proxy Lock

Resource name string   "NET$NETPROXY_MODIFIED"
Symbol   None
Modes of acquisition   PR, PW
Scope   UIC-independent
Access mode   Kernel
Parent   None
Value block   None
Blocking AST   Yes
Context   Owned by NETACP process

This is the main proxy lock, typically granted to all VAXcluster nodes in PR mode with an associated blocking AST. If proxy information is modified on a participating node, the Authorize Utility or the network management listener (NML) requests that NETACP obtain a new lock on this resource in PW mode. This triggers blocking AST delivery to the NETACP process on

1323

all VAXcluster nodes, including the one that queues the PW lock, as notice of proxy modification.

H.9.2.2   Proxy Function Lock

Resource name string	"NET$NETPROXY_FNCT"
Symbol	None
Modes of acquisition	NL, EX
Scope	UIC-independent
Access mode	Kernel
Parent	None
Value block	Yes
Blocking AST	None
Context	Owned by NETACP process

The Proxy Function lock is used to transmit the function to be performed on the NETPROXY.DAT file, for example, Rebuild_Proxy, Add_Proxy, and Delete_Proxy. The function code is transmitted in the value block. Holding this lock in EX mode also serializes NETACP's use of the Proxy Key locks.

H.9.2.3   Proxy Key Locks

Resource name string	"NET$NETPROXY_KEY" + key number
Symbol	None
Modes of acquisition	NL, EX
Scope	UIC-independent
Access mode	Kernel
Parent	None
Value block	Yes
Blocking AST	None
Context	Owned by NETACP process

NETACP uses this key value to determine whether a record with the specified key exists in the NETPROXY.DAT database used by the local node. The value blocks of these four key locks pass the RMS key values desired for the NETPROXY.DAT indexed file.

The four key numbers allow a total of 64 bytes of key information:

- NET$NETPROXY_KEY1 : first 16 bytes of the key
- NET$NETPROXY_KEY2 : second 16 bytes of the key
- NET$NETPROXY_KEY3 : third 16 bytes of the key
- NET$NETPROXY_KEY4 : fourth 16 bytes of the key

H.10   JOB CONTROLLER LOCK USE

The job controller processes running on multiple VAXcluster nodes use a variety of locks to synchronize their activities. Many of these locks coordinate access to records within the queue file. Since the queue file is accessed through RMS, standard RMS locking activity occurs as well (see Section H.7). This, however, is transparent to the job controller.

H.10.1   **Remote Request Lock (or Doorbell Lock)**

Resource name string	"JBC$" + SCSNODE
Symbol	None
Modes of acquisition	NL, EX
Scope	UIC-specific
Access mode	User
Parent	None
Value block	None
Blocking AST	Yes
Context	Owned by job controller process

During queue file initialization, the job controller uses the SCS node name of the system on which it executes to build a resource name. It requests an EX mode lock on that resource, specifying a blocking AST address. This doorbell lock is used by other VAXcluster nodes to determine if the node is available and has completed job controller initialization and to notify the node of an incoming work request. When a job controller receives a user request for a queue managed on another node, it uses that node name to build a resource name and requests an EX mode lock on that resource, specifying the LCK$V_ NOQUEUE flag. If the desired VAXcluster node exists and has performed job controller initialization, it already has an EX mode lock on its own name. The new request fails immediately in this case. If the request completes successfully, the remote node either does not exist or has not performed job controller initialization.

H.10.2   **Queue File Master Lock**

Resource name string	"JBC$" + queue file device name + queue file ID
Symbol	None
Mode of acquisition	EX
Scope	UIC-specific
Access mode	User
Parent	None
Value block	None
Blocking AST	None
Context	Owned by job controller process

During queue file initialization, the job controller requests an EX mode lock on the Queue File Master resource, setting the LCK$V_NODLCKWT flag so deadlock searches are never performed. The lock is granted to the first requestor, which becomes the queue file master. All other requests are placed on the wait queue. If the queue file master ever leaves the VAXcluster system, the next request on the wait queue is granted and a job controller running on another node becomes the new queue file master.

H.10.3   **Queue File Lock**

Resource name string	"JBC$" + queue file device name + queue file ID + "LOCK"
Symbol	None
Modes of acquisition	NL, EX
Scope	UIC-specific
Access mode	User
Parent	None
Value block	Yes
Blocking AST	None
Context	Owned by job controller process

The Queue File lock acts as a transaction-level lock on the queue file. Normally, all VAXcluster nodes hold the lock in NL mode. Before initiating a transaction, the job controller converts the NL mode lock to EX mode, reading the value block. On completion of a transaction, the job controller converts the EX mode lock to NL mode, writing the value block.

The value block of this lock coordinates the cleanup of the queue file when a job controller process or a VAXcluster node exits unexpectedly. It contains the SCS node name of the last node to leave the VAXcluster system or experience job controller failure.

Queue cleanup consists of reinitializing all executor queues that were assigned to the failing node and requeuing or deleting all jobs that were executing on those queues. When a node or job controller process fails, the remaining job controller processes are notified. All try to convert the Queue File lock to EX mode. The first to acquire the Queue File lock in EX mode performs the necessary cleanup, then loads the name of the failed node into the value block and lowers the lock to NL. Each remaining job controller process acquires the lock in turn, discovers that the value block contains the name of the failed node, and merely releases the lock. When the failed node reenters the VAXcluster system, it acquires the Queue File lock in EX mode and checks the lock value block. If it finds its own name in the lock value block, it zeros the first word. This way, if the same node should leave the VAXcluster system again, the other nodes will not mistakenly believe that cleanup has been performed.

H.10.4   **Queue File Initialization Lock**

Resource name string	"JBC$INITIALIZE"
Symbol	None
Mode of acquisition	EX

Scope	UIC-specific
Access mode	User
Parent	None
Value block	None
Blocking AST	None
Context	Owned by job controller process

In response to a command to start its queue management function, the job controller requests an EX mode lock on the Queue File Initialization resource. Holding this lock, the job controller creates and initializes or locates and reconstructs the queue file. It then dequeues the lock.

H.10.5   GETQUI Locks

Resource name string	Record number + byte offset within record
Symbol	None
Modes of acquisition	PR, PW
Scope	UIC-specific
Access mode	User
Parent	Queue File lock
Value block	None
Blocking AST	Yes
Context	Owned by job controller process

The job controller's support routines for the Get Queue Information ($GETQUI) system service maintain a list of descriptors for active queue context information across a user's $GETQUI requests. These descriptors exist as records within the queue file. Each descriptor is associated with a lock and contains the lock ID and reference count. These locks are normally held in PR mode. When information within a descriptor must be modified, the modifying node converts its lock to PW mode. This initiates blocking AST delivery to any processes holding PR locks, causing them to dequeue their locks so the PW lock can be granted.

H.10.6   Master ORB Lock

Resource name string	"ORB$LOCK"
Symbol	None
Mode of acquisition	NL
Scope	UIC-independent
Access mode	User
Parent	None
Value block	None
Blocking AST	None
Context	Owned by job controller process

The Master ORB lock and its sublocks are used to synchronize clusterwide access to an object rights block (ORB) and the protection information it contains.

Each job controller normally maintains a NL mode lock on this resource, requested during queue file initialization. The lock is used as the parent lock for individual job controller ORB locks describing access control lists (ACLs) on queues. The resource tree is also referenced by the Change Access Control List ($CHANGE_ACL) system service.

H.10.7   Job Controller ORB Locks

Resource name string	"ORB$JBC_" + ORB record number
Symbol	None
Mode of acquisition	EX
Scope	UIC-independent
Access mode	User
Parent	ORB Master lock
Value block	None
Blocking AST	None
Context	Owned by job controller process

These sublocks of the Master ORB lock are associated with ORB records in the queue file that describe ACLs on queues.

H.11   SYSGEN LOCK USE

H.11.1   SYSGEN Database Lock

Resource name string	"SYSGEN$_DATABASE"
Symbol	None
Mode of acquisition	EX
Scope	UIC-independent
Access mode	Executive
Parent	EXE$GL_SYSID_LOCK
Value block	None
Blocking AST	None
Context	Process-owned

The SYSGEN commands LOAD, RELOAD, AUTOCONFIGURE, and CONNECT require exclusive access to a system's SYSGEN database. SYSGEN protects its database from concurrent access by SYSGEN executing in multiple processes through an EX mode lock on the systemwide resource "SYSGEN$_DATABASE". SYSGEN uses the lock ID stored in EXE$GL_SYSID_LOCK as the parent lock to restrict the resource scope to the local system.

H.12   **SYSMAN LOCK USE**

H.12.1   **SMISERVER Main Lock**

Resource name string	"SMISERVER$" + SCSNODE
Symbol	None
Mode of acquisition	EX
Scope	UIC-independent
Access mode	Executive
Parent	None
Value block	None
Blocking AST	None
Context	Owned by SMISERVER process

The SMISERVER process uses the Main lock to ensure that only one SMI-SERVER process at a time exists on a system. It requests an EX mode lock on the resource using the LCK$V_NOQUEUE flag. If the request is not granted immediately, another SMISERVER process is already running; the current one is redundant and deletes itself.

When SMISERVER performs a clusterwide Set Time ($SETIME) system service, it synchronizes using the Set Time lock (see Section H.2.2).

H.12.2   **Parameter Lock**

Resource name string	"SYSPARMS_LOCK"
Symbol	None
Modes of acquisition	NL, PR, EX
Scope	UIC-independent
Access mode	Executive
Parent	EXE$GL_SYSID_LOCK
Value block	Yes
Blocking AST	None
Context	Process-owned

SYSMAN uses the Parameter lock to synchronize access to the current and active SYSGEN parameters on a system. It obtains the Parameter lock in PR mode before reading the current or active SYSGEN parameters. When the read completes, it converts the lock to NL mode. SYSMAN enqueues the Parameter lock in EX mode before writing the current or active SYSGEN parameters. When the write completes, it again converts the lock to NL mode. The Parameter lock is dequeued when this SYSMAN session completes.

Index

NOTE: Page numbers for figures, tables, and examples reflect the first references to these units in the text, not their actual placement.

Index

Index

Index

Index

1406

Index

Books from Digital Press

These books may be purchased from technical reference bookstores or by calling 1-800-DIGITAL. For a copy of the latest catalog, contact Digital Press, 12 Crosby Drive, Bedford, Massachusetts 01730 (617-276-1536).

VAX/VMS: Writing Real Programs in DCL

PAUL C. ANAGNOSTOPOULOS

Taking up where the VAX/VMS documentation leaves off, this book describes how to write applications using Digital Command Language as a general purpose programming language. EY-C168E-DP.

X Window System Toolkit

The Complete Programmer's Guide and Specification

PAUL J. ASENTE AND RALPH R. SWICK

Written by the X Toolkit's leading designers and reflecting the MIT X Consortium toolkit standard, this book includes both a programmer's guide with extensive examples and the detailed specification. EY-E757E-DP.

UNIX for VMS Users

PHILIP E. BOURNE

The only book on UNIX for VMS users, this volume is invaluable for those making the transition between the two operating systems. It does not assume too high or low a level of knowledge and uses prior experience as a teaching tool. EY-C177E-DP.

VAX Architecture Reference Manual, Second Edition

EDITED BY RICHARD A. BRUNNER

Covering every VAX instruction addressing mode, instruction, and register, this reference is essential for the computer professional using any VAX from the MicroVAX II to the VAX 9000. EY-F576E-DP.

Software Design Techniques for Large Ada Systems

WILLIAM E. BYRNE

Drawing on the author's practical experience, this book introduces design strategies for controlling the complexity of large computer programs. EY-E761E-DP.

Information Technology Standardization

Theory, Organizations and Processes

CARL F. CARGILL

Explaining the need for and the philosophy behind standards in the telecommunications industry, Cargill covers existing international, national, and regional standards, the organizations and processes that set them, and future developments. EY-C167E-DP.

Digital Guide to Developing International Software

CORPORATE USER PUBLICATIONS GROUP

An approach to simplifying the adaptation of software for local markets, this book introduces the packaging and design guidelines recommended by Digital for products developed for overseas markets. EY-F577E-DP.

The Digital Guide to Software Development

CORPORATE USER PUBLICATIONS GROUP

The first published description of the methodology and tools used by Digital to develop software products, this guide offers an inside look at practices based on Digital's phase-review process. EY-C178E-DP.

Kermit: A File Transfer Protocol

FRANK DA CRUZ

From instructions for basic use to a detailed description of the Kermit protocol, this book demonstrates how to transfer information between diverse computer systems and data communications environments. EY-6705E-DP.

Writing VAX/VMS Applications Using Pascal

THEO DE KLERK

Programmers will appreciate this book's methodology for producing high-quality applications by focusing on the most important aspects of VMS. It provides numerous working program examples and coverage of the VAX calling standard, System Services and Run Time Library routines and their implementations. *Available in May 1991.* EY-F592E-DP.

Using MS-DOS Kermit

Connecting Your PC to the Electronic World

CHRISTINE M. GIANONE

This clearly written book describes how to use Kermit, the popular communications protocol and terminal emulator. It includes a 5.25-inch diskette with MS-DOS Kermit, Version 3. EY-C204E-DP.

RDb/VMS: A Comprehensive Guide

LILIAN HOBBS AND KEN ENGLAND

The authors have drawn on their extensive experience to introduce and discuss the functionality of this relational database product. *Available in May 1991.* EY-H873E-DP.

The User's Directory of Computer Networks

EDITED BY TRACY L. LAQUEY

This comprehensive guide to academic and research networks offers descriptions, user information, maps, site contact names and addresses, host lists and member organizations for more than 50 national and international networks. EY-C200E-DP.

Computer Programming and Architecture

The VAX, Second Edition

HENRY M. LEVY AND RICHARD H. ECKHOUSE, JR.

The authors' unique systems approach uses the VAX to teach assembly language programming and computer architecture. They cover higher-level concepts and other architectures such as RISC and the Intel 80386 for comparison. EY-6740E-DP.

VMS File System Internals

KIRBY MCCOY

This comprehensive study of the VMS file system examines the components, interfaces, and basic synchronization mechanisms needed to store and manage files and information. EY-F575E-DP.

Technical Aspects of Data Communication, Third Edition

JOHN E. MCNAMARA

This standard reference effectively covers the spectrum of data communication technology, from a simple UART asynchronous interface through more intricate system design problems. EY-8262E-DP.

Operating Systems Concepts

A Practical Approach Using VAX/VMS

DAVID DONALD MILLER

Using a hands-on approach, this practical reference illustrates general principles with the VAX/VMS operating system. Numerous diagrams, exercises, and other learning aids make this volume ideal for both professional and classroom use. *Available in May 1991.* EY-F590E-DP.

The VMS User's Guide

JAMES F. PETERS AND PATRICK HOLMAY

Up to date with VMS Version 5.0, this volume provides hands-on experience in customizing a working environment through step-by-step instructions, exercises, and review questions. EY-6739E-DP.

The Matrix

Computer Networks and Conferencing Systems Worldwide

JOHN S. QUARTERMAN

Even its users do not know how far the matrix of society and technology extends. This exhaustive survey of computer networking in the U.S. and worldwide maps the limits today. EY-C176E-DP.

X and Motif Quick Reference Guide

RANDI ROST

Based on the latest versions of the X Window System and OSF/Motif software, this convenient one-volume reference combines all the most pertinent information on Xlib, X Toolkit Intrinsics, and the Motif programming libraries. EY-E758E-DP.

X Window System

The Complete Reference to Xlib, Protocol, ICCCM, XLFD: Second Edition

ROBERT W. SCHEIFLER AND JAMES GETTYS

Written by the major developers of the X Window System and updated to Version 11, Release 4, the four parts of this comprehensive volume conform to the standard specifications produced by the MIT Consortium. EY-E755E-DP.

Common Lisp

The Language: Second Edition

GUY L. STEELE JR.

Reflecting the latest changes to the Common Lisp programming language, this edition of a definitive reference bridges the gap between the new ANSI standards and the language described in the first edition. EY-C187E-DP.

Working with WPS-PLUS

CHARLOTTE TEMPLE AND DOLORES CORDEIRO

A how-to manual for readers with an understanding of word processing, this book offers helpful hints and advice on advanced techniques. EY-C198E-DP.

Digital Technical Journal

This topical quarterly journal is devoted to the technologies used in the design, manufacture, and maintenance of Digital's products. Individual copies may be purchased by calling 1-800-DIGITAL. Subscription information may be obtained from: Digital Technical Journal, Digital Equipment Corporation, 146 Main Street, Maynard, MA 01754-2571. Telephone: (508) 493-2894. FAX: (508) 493-3253. NEARNET: DTJ@CRL.DEC.COM.

Fiber Distributed Data Interface. Vol. 3, No. 2. *Available April 1991.* EY-H876E-DP.

Transaction Processing, Databases, and Fault-tolerant Systems. Vol. 3, No. 1. 1991. EY-F588E-DP.

VAX 9000 System. Vol. 2, No. 4. 1990. EY-E762E-DP.

DECwindows Program. Vol. 2, No. 3. 1990. EY-E756E-DP.

VAX 6000 Model 400 System. Vol. 2, No. 2. 1990. EY-C197E-DP.

Compound Document Architecture. Vol. 2, No. 1. 1990. EY-C196E-DP.

Distributed Systems. Vol. 1, No. 9. 1989. EY-C179E-DP.

Storage Technology. Vol. 1, No. 8. 1989. EY-C166E-DP.

CVAX-based Systems. Vol. 1, No. 7. 1988. EY-6742E-DP.

Software Productivity Tools. Vol. 1, No. 6. 1988. EY-8259E-DP.

VAXcluster Systems. Vol. 1, No. 5. 1987. EY-8258E-DP.

VAX 8800 Family. Vol. 1, No. 4. 1987. EY-6711E-DP.

Networking Products. Vol. 1, No. 3. 1986. EY-6715E-DP.

MicroVAX II System. Vol. 1, No. 2. 1986. EY-3474E-DP.

VAX 8600 Processor. Vol. 1, No. 1. 1985. EY-3435E-DP.